CODE OF CANONS
OF THE EASTERN
CHURCHES

LATIN-ENGLISH EDITION

NEW ENGLISH TRANSLATION

 CANON LAW SOCIETY OF AMERICA

CODEX CANONUM ECCLESIARUM ORIENTALIUM

AUCTORITATE

IOANNIS PAULI PP.II

PROMULGATUS

FONTIUM ANNOTATIONE AUCTUS

LIBRERIA EDITRICE VATICANA

1995

CODE OF CANONS OF THE EASTERN CHURCHES

LATIN-ENGLISH EDITION

NEW ENGLISH TRANSLATION

Prepared under the auspices of the
Canon Law Society of America

CANON LAW SOCIETY OF AMERICA
Washington, DC 20064

CONTENTS

OUTLINE OF THE
CODE OF CANONS OF
THE EASTERN CHURCHES

FOREWORD TO THE TRANSLATION

HISTORY OF THE PROJECT

On 25 October 1990, during the 28th general assembly of the Synod of Bishops, Pope John Paul II referred to the *Codex Iuris Canonici, Pastor Bonus* and the *Codex Canonum Ecclesiarum Orientalium* as a single *corpus iuris canonici* of the Catholic Church. The Canon Law Society of America (CLSA), in publishing the revised English translation of the common law of the Eastern Catholic Churches brings this body of law to the English-speaking world.

It is to the credit of the CLSA Board of Governors that the decision to make an English translation of the Eastern Code was taken contemporaneously with the act of promulgation. In 1992 *Code of Canons of the Eastern Churches-Latin-English Edition* appeared, the first vernacular edition of the Eastern Code.

In 1995, the Pontifical Council for the Interpretation of Legislative Texts published the *Codex Canonum Ecclesiarum Orientalium Auctoritate Ioannes Paulus II Promulgatus Fontium Annotatione Auctus.* The need to correct the imprecisions of the first translation and the additional tools included in the augmented Latin edition motivated the Board of Governors of the CLSA to establish in October 1995, an *ad hoc* committee entrusted with the task of revising the English translation of the *Codex Canonum Ecclesiarum Orientalium.* The members were Chorbishop John D. Faris (chairperson) and Jobe Abbass, O.F.M. Conv. At the discretion of the chairperson, Becket Soule, O.P. and George Nedungatt, S.J. were requested to serve as consultors for the committee.

In August, 1999, the committee submitted the revised text to the Executive Coordinator and the CLSA Board of Governors.

In accord with no. 3 of the norms regarding the translation of the code (27 October 1990), the text was submitted to the National Conference of Catholic Bishops for the opinions of the Eastern Catholic Eparchial Bishops in the United States. In a letter dated 19 September 2000, Sister Sharon Euart, RSM, associate general secretary of the National Conference of Catholic Bishops, informed the CLSA that the text had received the required approval of the Eparchial Bishops.

In addition to a refinement of the translation itself, the new edition contains important elements. *Pastor bonus,* the 1988 apostolic constitution on the Roman Curia and the 1983 norms for the causes of saints.

The sources of law have been included in the text as well as guide ("Access to the Sources") to facilitate access to these sources. Becket Soule, O.P. prepared an extensive analytical index based on Ivan Žužek, S.J.'s *Index Analyticus Codicis Canonum Ecclesiarum Orientalium.* The concordance of the *Codex Canonum Ecclesiarum Orientalium* and the *Codex Iuris Canonici,* from Victor J. Pospishil's *Eastern Catholic Church Law* is also included.

Arthur J. Espelage, O.F.M., the Executive Coordinator of the CLSA, served as the general editor, proofreading the translation and coordinating the inclusion of all the supplementary material.

PRINCIPLES GUIDING THE TRANSLATION

The following principles were followed in the translation of the Latin text:

1. The English translation does not replace the Latin original. The Latin version remains the only official version and has the force of law. The Latin text must be consulted for clarification of meaning and, for that reason, is published in this work along with the English translation.

2. While faithful to the original, the translation intends to be intelligible to the educated English speaker.

3. Terms and phrases are translated consistently throughout unless the context requires a variation.

4. Appropriate grammatical principles are employed to provide a readable text consonant with contemporary usage. Whenever possible the active voice is employed. At times, the lengthy Latin sentences are rendered into brief English sentences.

5. Certain technical terms (e.g., *sui iuris*) are retained in the English translation.

As the Eastern Catholic Churches embark on the third millennium, the Canon Law Society of America hopes that this English translation of their common law will serve as a useful tool in their programs of conciliar renewal.

ABBREVIATIONS

Documents of recent Ecumenical Councils are referred to as used, and accordingly, these abbreviations are not indicated below. The same holds true for the four *motu proprio*, previous legislation for Eastern Catholics, *Crebrae allatae sunt, Sollicitudinem Nostram, Postquam Apostolicis Litteris,* and *Cleri sanctitati;* and likewise the titles of the Churches, the Rites, sees of bishops, metropolitans or patriarchs and, generally speaking, the names of places which occur throughout the footnotes.

a.	annus
aa.	anni
adh.	adhortatio
all.	allocutio
Anc.	Synodus Ancyrana, a. 314
Ant.	Synodus Antiochena, a. 341
ap.	apostolica
Ap.	Apostolicus
Apost.	Canones Sanctorum Apostolorum
App.	Apostolici
Archiep.	Archiepiscopus
art.	articulus
artt.	articuli
auxil.	auxiliaris
Basilic.	*Basilicorum Libri LX* (H.J. Scheltema- D. Holwenda- N. Vander Val), Scripta Universitatis Groninganae, volumina I–VIII, Gravenhage, 1955– Groningen, 1988.
c.	circa
C.	*Codex Iustinianus* (recognovit Paulus Krueger), *Corpus iuris civilis,* volumen secundum, Berolini, 1900, pp. 1–513
C.G.	Congregatio generalis
C.P.	Congregatio particularis
can.	canon
cann.	canones
cap.	caput
capp.	capita
Carth.	Synodus Carthaginensis, a. 419
Chalc.	Concilium Chalcedonense, a. 451
circ. (circul.)	circularis

Collectanea	*Collectanea S. Congregationis de Propaganda Fide seu Decreta Instructiones Rescripta pro Apostolicis Missionibus*, vol. I–II, Romae, 1907 (Reference is made to the number of the document)
Collectio Lacensis	*Acta et Decreta Sacrorum Conciliorum recentiorum, Collectio Lacensis auctoribus presbyteris S.J. e domo B. M-V. Sine Labe Conceptae ad Lacum*, Friburgi Brisgoviae, tomi I–VI, 1870–1872
Cons. pro Publ. Eccl. Neg.	Consilium pro Publicis Ecclesiae Negotiis
const.	constitutio
Consist. secr.	Consistorium secretum
Constantien.	Concilium Constantiense, aa. 1414–1418
Constantinop., a. 394	Synodus Constantinopolitana, a. 394
Constantinop. I	Concilium Constantinopolitanum I, a. 381
Constantinop. IV	Concilium Constantinopolitanum IV, aa. 869–870
CP.	Constantinopolitanus
D.	*Iustiniani Digesta* (recognovit Theodorus Mommsen), *Corpus iuris civilis*, volumen primum, Berolini, 1902, pp. 1–882
damn.	damnatus
decis.	decisio
De Martinis	*Iuris Pontificii de Propaganda Fide pars prima complectens Bullas Brevia Acta S. S. . . . cur ac studio Raphaëlis De Martinis . . . vol. I–VII*, Romae, 1888–1897; *Iuris Pontificii de Propaganda Fide pars secunda complectens Decreta, Instructiones, Encyclicas Litteras etc. ab eadem Congregatione lata . . . cura ac studio Raphaëlis De Martinis . . .* , Romae, 1909 (Reference is made to the number of the document)
decl.	declaratio
decr.	decretum
Del. (Deleg.)	Delegatus
encycl.	encyclica
ep.	epistula
Ep.	Episcopus (Episcopi)
Epp.	Episcopi
Eph.	Concilium Ephesinum, a. 431
Flor.	Concilium Florentinum, aa. 1431–1445
Fonti	Sacra Congregazione "Pro Ecclesia Orientali", Codificazione canonica ori entale, *Fonti*, fasc. I–VIII, X–XV, Romae, 1930–1934. (In fascicule I reference is made to the pages, in others to the number of the document)
Gang.	Synodus Gangrensis, a.c. 340
gen.	generalis
hom.	homilia
Instit.	*Iustiniani Institutiones* (recognovit Paulus Krueger), *Corpus iuris civilis*, volumen primum, Berolini, 1902, pp. 1–56
instr.	instructio
interpr. auth.	interpretatio authentica
introduc.	introductio
Laod.	Synodus Laodicensis, ad finem saeculi IV
Lat. IV	Concilium Lateranense IV, a. 1215

Lat. V	Concilium Lateranense V, aa. 1512–1517
litt.	litterae
Lugd. I	Concilium Lugdunense I, a. 1245
Lugd. II	Concilium Lugdunense II, a. 1274
M.	Magnus
m.p.	motu proprio
Mansi	F. Labeo-J. D. Mansi, *Sacrorum conciliorum nova et amplissima collectio*, tomi I–LIV, Romae, 1759–1927
Metrop.	Metropolita
Migne PG	J.P. Migne, *Patrologiae cursus completus*, series graeco-latina, vol. 1–165, Lutetiae Parisiorum, 1857–1866
Migne PL	J.P. Migne, *Patrologiae cursus completus*, series latina, vol. 1–221, Lutetiae Parisiorum, 1844–1864
Mission.	Missiones
n.	numerus
Neoc.	Synodus Neocaesariensis, aa. 314–319
Nic. I	Concilium Nicaenum I, a. 325
Nic. II	Concilium Nicaenum II, a. 787
Nov.	*Iustiniani Novellae* (recognovit Rudolfus Schoell), *Corpus iuris civilis*, volumen tertium, Berolini, 1899, pp. 1–810
Ochoa	Institutum Iuridicum Claretianum, *Leges Ecclesiae post Codicem Iuris canonici editae:* collegit . . . Xaverius Ochoa . . . , vol. I–VI, Romae, 1966–1987
orat.	Oratio Sancti Theodori Studitae
Patr. (Patriarch.)	Patriarcha
Pitra	I.B. Pitra, *Iuris ecclesiastici Graecorum historia et monumenta*, tomus I, Romae, 1864; tomus II, Romae, 1868
poenae monast.	Poenae monasteriales Sancti Theodori Studitae
Pont. Comm. ad Cod. Can. Auth. Interpr.	Pontificia Commissio ad Codicis Canones Authentice Interpretandos
Pont. Comm. ad Red.	Pontificia Commissio ad Redigendum Codicem Iuris Canonici Orientalis
Pont. Comm. Cod. Iur. Can. Auth. Interpr.	Pontificia Commissio Codici Iuris Canonici Authentice Interpretando
Pont. Comm. Cod. Iur. Can. Orient. Recogn.	Pontificia Commissio Codici Iuris Canonici Orientalis Recognoscendo
Pont. Comm. Decr. Conc. Vat. II Interpr.	Pontificia Commissio Decretis Concilii Vaticani II Interpretandis
Pont. Comm. pro Russia	Pontificia Commissio pro Russia
pr.	principium seu textus initialis documenti
praescr.	praescriptus
prolog.	prologus
prooem.	prooemium

prop.	propositio, propositiones
Protodeut.	Synodus Protodeutera, a. 861
prov.	provincialis, provincia
Quinisext.	Concilium Quinisextum seu Trullanum, a. 691
reg.	regula
regg.	regulae
regulae fus.	Regulae fusius tractatae Sancti Basilii Magni
rescr.	rescriptum
resol.	resolutio
S.	Sanctus
s. (sess.)	sessio
Sacerd.	Sacerdotes
Sard.	Synodus Sardicensis, a. 343–344
S.C.C.	Sacra Congregatio Concilii
S.C. Consist.	Sacra Congregatio Consistorii (Consistorialis)
S.C. de Discip. Sacr.	Sacra Congregatio de Disciplina Sacramentorum
S.C. de Prop. Fide	Sacra Congregatio de Propaganda Fide
S.C. de Prop. Fide (pro Neg. Rit. Orient.)	Sacra Congregatio de Propaganda Fide pro Negotiis Ritus Orientalis
S.C. de Religiosis	Sacra Congregatio de Religiosis
S.C. de Sem. et Stud. Univ.	Sacra Congregatio de Seminariis et Studiorum Universitatibus
S.C. Ep. et Reg.	Sacra Congregatio Episcoporum et Regularium
S.C. Indulg.	Sacra Congregatio Indulgentiarum
S.C. pro Causis Sanctorum	Sacra Congregatio pro Causis Sanctorum
S.C. pro Doctr. Fidei	Sacra Congregatio pro Doctrina Fidei
S.C. pro Eccl. Orient.	Sacra Congregatio pro Ecclesia Orientali (Ecclesiis Orientalibus)
S.C. pro Inst. Cath.	Sacra Congregatio pro Institutione Catholica
S.C.S. Off.	Sacra Congregatio Sancti Officii
Secret. ad Christ. Unit. Fov.	Secretariatus ad Christianorum Unitatem Fovendam
Secret. Status	Secreteria Status
sect.	sectio
serm.	sermones
Sign. Apost.	Supremum Tribunal Signaturae Apostolicae
S. Paenit. Ap.	Sacra Paenitentiaria Apostolica
S. Rom. Rotae Trib.	Sacrae Romanae Rotae Tribunal
S. Soph.	Synodus Sanctae Sophiae, a. 879
Syn.	Synodus
testam.	Testamentum Sancti Theodori Studitae
tit.	titulus
Trid. (Trident.)	Concilium Tridentinum, aa. 1545–1563
Vat. I	Concilium Vaticanum I, aa. 1869–1870
Vat. II	Concilium Vaticanum II, aa. 1962–1965
Vic.	Vicarius

APOSTOLIC CONSTITUTION

SACRI CANONES

JOHN PAUL, BISHOP
Servant of the servants of God
For everlasting memory
To his venerable brethren
The patriarchs, archbishops, bishops
And his beloved sons
The Presbyters,
Deacons and the other Christian Faithful
Of the Eastern Churches

The SACRED CANONS are, according to a summary description given by the seventh ecumenical council of Nicea, those that have been put forth by the divine Apostles, as tradition has it, and by "the six holy and universal synods and local councils" as well as "by our holy Fathers." Hence the Fathers of the same council, which assembled at the See of Nicea in 787 and was presided over by the legates of our predecessor Hadrian I, confirmed in its first canon "the integral and immutable binding force" of the same sacred canons, "rejoicing over them like one who has found rich spoils."

Indeed, that same council, when it affirmed that the authors of the sacred canons were enlightened "by one and the same Spirit" and had established "those things that are beneficial," considered those canons to be a single body of ecclesiastical law, and confirmed it as a "code" for all of the Eastern Churches. The Quinisext Synod had previously done this, assembled in the Trullan chamber of the city of Constantinople in 691, by defining the sphere of these laws more clearly in its second canon.

In the wonderfully great variety of rites, that is, of the liturgical, theological, spiritual, and disciplinary heritage of those Churches that have their origins in the venerable Alexandrian, Antiochene, Armenian, Chaldean and Constantinopolitan traditions, the sacred canons are rightly regarded as a notable constituent of that same heritage, constituting a single, common canonical foundation of Church order. Indeed, scarcely, or at least rarely, is there an Eastern collection of disciplinary norms in which the sacred canons—already numbering more than 500 before the Council of Chalcedon—are not enforced or invoked as the primary laws of the Church established or recognized by an authority that is superior to the same Churches. It was always clear to each of the Churches that any ordering of ecclesiastical discipline would only be firm if grounded in norms deriving from traditions recognized by the supreme authority of the Church or contained in canons promulgated by it, and that rules of particular law had to conform to the higher law in order to be valid, but that they were null if they differed from it.

"It was through fidelity to this sacred heritage of ecclesiastical discipline that the particular appearance of the East was preserved in spite of so many dire sufferings and hardships which the Eastern Churches have endured both in ancient times and recently; and this was of course not without great benefit to souls" (*AAS* 66 [1974] 245). These words of Paul VI of happy memory, uttered in the Sistine Chapel during his address before the first plenary session of the members of the Commission for the Revision of the Code of Eastern Canon Law, recall what was enjoined by the Second Vatican Council concerning "utmost fidelity" in the observance of the said disciplinary heritage by all the Churches. These words also echo the conciliar demand that the Churches "should endeavor to return to the traditions of their forefathers" in case in certain matters "they have improperly deviated owing to the circumstances of the times or persons" (Decr. *Orientalium Ecclesiarum*, n. 6).

It is significant that the Second Vatican Council makes it quite clear that "a scrupulous fidelity to the ancient traditions" together with "prayers, good example, better mutual understanding, collaboration and a brotherly regard for what concerns others and their sensibilities" can contribute most to enable the Eastern Churches in full communion with the Roman Apostolic See to fulfill "their special task of fostering the unity of all Christians, particularly of the Eastern Christians" (Decr. *Orientalium Ecclesiarum*, n. 24) according to the principles of the decree "On Ecumenism."

It should not be forgotten that the Eastern Churches that are not yet in full communion with the Catholic Church are governed by the same and basically single heritage of canonical discipline, namely, the "sacred canons" of the first centuries of the Church.

With regard to the whole question of the ecumenical movement, which has been set in motion by the Holy Spirit for the realization of the perfect unity of the entire Church of Christ, the new Code is not at all an obstacle, but rather a great help. Indeed, this Code protects that fundamental right of the human person, namely, of professing the faith in whatever their rite, drawn frequently from their very mother's womb, which is the rule of all "ecumenism." Nor should we neglect that the Eastern Catholic Churches, discharging the tranquility of order desired by the Second Vatican Council, "are to flourish and fulfill their role entrusted to them with a new apostolic vigor" (Decr. *Orientalium Ecclesiarum,* n. 1). Thus it happens that the canons of the *Code of Canons of the Eastern Churches* must have the same firmness as the laws of the *Code of Canon Law* of the Latin Church, that is, that they remain in force until abrogated or changed by the supreme authority of the Church for just reasons. The most serious of those reasons is the full communion of all the Eastern Churches with the Catholic Church, in addition to being most in accord with the desire of our Savior Jesus Christ himself.

Nevertheless, the heritage of the sacred canons common to all of the Eastern Churches during the passing centuries has coalesced in a wonderful fashion with the special character of each group of the Christian faithful from which the individual churches are formed and has imbued their entire culture, very often in one and the same nation, with the name of Christ and his evangelical message, which belongs to the very heart of these peoples without reproach and worthy of every consideration.

When our predecessor, Leo XIII, declared at the end of the nineteenth century that "the legally approved diversity of Eastern liturgical forms and discipline" is "an ornament for the whole Church and a confirmation of the divine unity of the Catholic faith," he considered that this diversity was that to which "nothing else is possibly more wonderful in illustrating the note of *catholicity* in the Church of God" (Leo XIII, ap. letter *Orientalium dignitas,* 30 Nov. 1894, prooem.). The unanimous voice of the Fathers of the Second Vatican Council proclaims the same thing, that "the diversity of the Churches united together demonstrates in a very clear fashion the catholicity of the undivided Church" (Const. *Lumen Gentium,* 23), and "in no way harms the Church's unity, but rather declares it" (decr. *Orientalium Ecclesiarum,* n. 2).

Keeping all these things in mind, we consider that this Code, which we now promulgate, must be considered to be assessed most of all according to the ancient law of the Eastern Churches. At the same time, we are clearly conscious both of the unity and diversity harmonizing to the same end and coalescing, so that the "vitality of the whole Church never appears to be aging. She stands out even more wondrously as the Bride of Christ, whom the wisdom of the holy Fathers recognized as being foreshadowed in the prophecy of David: *The queen stands at your right hand, arrayed in apparel embroidered in gold . . ."(Ps.* 44; Leo XIII, ap. letter *Orientalium dignitas,* 30 Nov. 1894, prooem.).

From the very beginnings of the codification of the canons of the Eastern Churches, the constant will of the Roman Pontiffs has been to promulgate two Codes: one for the Latin Church, the other for the Eastern Churches. This demonstrates very clearly that they wanted to preserve that which in God's providence had taken place in the Church: that the Church, gathered by the one Spirit breathes, as it were, with the two lungs of East and West, and burns with the love of Christ, having one heart, as it were, with two ventricles.

The firm and unwavering intention of the supreme legislator in the Church is likewise clear regarding the faithful preservation and accurate observance of all of the Eastern rites derived from the above-mentioned five traditions, expressed in the Code again and again with their own norms.

This is also evident in the various forms of the hierarchical constitution of the Eastern Churches: the patriarchal Churches are preeminent among these, in which the patriarchs and synods are sharers in the supreme authority of the Church by canon law. With these forms, delineated in their own title at the opening of the Code, there is immediately evident both the appearance of each and every Eastern Church as it has been sanctioned by canon law and their autonomous status, as well as their full communion with the Roman Pontiff, the successor of Saint Peter, who, presiding over the whole assembly of charity, safeguards legitimate diversity and, at the same time, keeps watch that individuality serves unity rather than harming it (cf. const. *Lumen gentium*, n. 13).

Furthermore, in this area full attention should be given to all those things that this Code entrusts to the particular law of individual Churches *sui iuris*, which are not considered necessary to the common good of all of the Eastern Churches. Our intention regarding these things is that those who enjoy legislative power in each of the Churches should take counsel as soon as possible for particular norms, keeping in mind the traditions of their own rite and the precepts of the Second Vatican Council.

The faithful protection of the rites must clearly be in conformity with the ultimate goal of all the laws of the Church, which is set forth in the economy of the salvation of souls. Therefore, this Code has not accepted anything that has lapsed or was superfluous in previous legislation, or that is not suited to the region or the necessity of the times. But in establishing new laws those things were uppermost in our mind which really responded in the best way to the desired economy of the salvation of souls in the richness of the life of the Eastern Churches, while displaying a coherence and agreement with sound tradition. This was set out, according to the direction of our predecessor Paul VI, at the beginning of the work of revising the Code: "new norms should appear not, as it were, as a foreign body intruded into an ecclesiastical structure, but like a spontaneous blossoming from already existing norms" (*AAS* 66 [1974] 246).

These things become splendidly clear from the Second Vatican Council, since that Council "brought forth from the treasury of tradition what is old and what is new" (ap. const. *Sacrae disciplinae leges, AAS* 75 [1983] Part II, XII), by carrying over into newness of life the tradition from the Apostles, through the Fathers, everywhere integral to the message of the gospel.

The *Code of Canons of the Eastern Churches* should be considered as a new complement to the teaching proposed by the Second Vatican Council. By the publication of this Code, the canonical ordering of the whole Church is thus at length completed, following as it does the *Code of Canon Law* of the Latin Church, promulgated in 1983, and the "Apostolic Constitution on the Roman Curia" of 1988, which is added to both Codes as the primary instrument of the Roman Pontiff for "the communion that binds together, as it were, the whole Church" (ap. const. *Pastor bonus,* n. 2).

But now if we turn our attention to the first steps of the canonical codification of the Eastern Churches, the Code appears as a port, reached after a voyage of more than sixty years. For this is a body of laws in which all the canons of ecclesiastical discipline common to the Eastern Catholic Churches are first collected together in one place and promulgated by the supreme legislator in the Church. This has taken place after the many, great labors of the three commissions instituted by that legislator; the first of these was the "Cardinalatial Commission for Preparatory Studies on Eastern Codification" erected in 1929 by our predecessor Pius XI (*AAS* 21 [1929] 669), under the presidency of Cardinal Pietro Gasparri. The members of this Commission were Cardinals Luigi Sincero, Bonaventura Cerretti and Franz Ehrle, with the assistance of the secretary, Bishop (later Cardinal) Amleto Giovanni Cicognani, an assessor of the "Sacred Congregation for the Eastern Church," as it was then called.

The work of two groups of experts, for the most part taken from the heads of the Eastern Churches, was of great importance, as a matter of fact, to the preparatory studies; this work was brought to completion within six years (cf. *L'Osservatore Romano,* 2 April 1930, p. 1). When the death of Cardinal Pietro Gasparri intervened, it was decided to continue by constituting the "Pontifical Commission for the Codification of the 'Code of Eastern Canon Law.'" This commission was erected on 17 July 1935 to determine, as its title indicated, the text of the canons and to supervise the composition of the "Code of Eastern Canon Law." It should be noted in this regard that the Supreme Pontiff himself, in the *Notice* of the institution of the Commission which appeared in the official commentary *Acta Apostolicae Sedis* (*AAS* 27 [1935] 306–308), determined that the title of the future Code was to be enclosed in quotation marks, to indicate that, although it was the best, it was selected "until a better could be found."

The presidents of the "Commission for the Codification of the 'Code of Eastern Canon Law'" were Cardinal Luigi Sincero, until his death; Cardinal Massimo Massimi; and, after his death, Cardinal Gregory Peter XV Agagianian, the Patriarch of the Armenian Church.

Among the cardinals who were, along with the president, made the first members of the Commission, namely, Eugenio Pacelli, Julio Serafini, and Pietro Fumasoni-Biondi, the name of Cardinal Eugenio Pacelli stands out. Later on, by the great providence of God, he brought to completion, in his great solicitude for the good of the Eastern Churches, almost the whole work of canonical codification as Vicar of Christ and Pastor of the whole Church. For, of the twenty-four titles with which the Code of Eastern Canon Law had been put together in the aforesaid Commission by his will, he promulgated no less than ten, of more urgent importance, by means of four apostolic letters *motu proprio (Crebrae allatae sunt, Sollicitudinem nostram, Postquam apostolicis litteris* and *Cleri sanctitati).* The rest, approved at the same time by the cardinal members of the Commission and for the most part already printed with a pontifical mandate "for promulgation," but, coming at the end of that pontificate and at the same time as John XXIII, his successor in the chair of Saint Peter, called the Second Vatican Council, remained in the archives of the Commission.

However, with the passing of years, until the conclusion of that Commission in the middle of 1972, the college of members was increased by pontifical mandate as several cardinals performed their work with diligence, with other members succeeding those who had died. After the Second Vatican Council was finally concluded, all the patriarchs of the Eastern Catholic Churches were added to the Commission in 1965. But by the beginning of the final year of the Commission for the Codification of the Code of Eastern Canon Law, the college of members consisted of the six heads of the Eastern Churches and the Prefect of the Congregation for the Eastern Churches.

Also, from the very beginning of the Commission for the Codification of the Code of Eastern Canon Law, and for a long time thereafter, Father (later Cardinal) Acacio Coussa, B.A., served as its secretary and labored with great zeal and wisdom. We remember him here with praise, along with the distinguished consultors of the Commission.

The constitution and form of the Pontifical Commission for the Revision of the Code of Eastern Canon Law, established during the middle of 1972, safeguarded its Eastern character, since it was composed from the multiplicity of Churches, with the Eastern patriarchs being elevated in the first place. But the work of the Commission kept in mind its collegial character, for the canons, formulated by groups of expert men chosen from all of the Churches, and worked out gradually, were sent to all the bishops of the Eastern Catholic Churches before all others, so that they might give their opinions in a collegial fashion, insofar as this was possible. Later on, these drafts, revised repeatedly in special study groups according to the wishes of the bishops, after a diligent examination by the members of the Commission and further modified if the case warranted, were accepted by the general consent of votes in a plenary meeting of the members in November 1988.

We must truly recognize that this Code is "the work of the Easterners themselves," according to the wishes of our predecessor Paul VI expressed in his address at the solemn inauguration of the Commission's work (*AAS* 66 [1974] 246). We are deeply grateful to each and every one of those who participated in this work.

Among the first, we thankfully remember the name of the late Cardinal Joseph Parecattil of the Malabar Church, who served with distinction as president of the Commission for the new Code for almost the entire time, except for the last three years. Together with him, we remember in particular the late Archbishop Clement Ignatius Mansourati of the Syrian Church, who served as vice-president of the Commission in the first, particularly difficult years.

It is a pleasure also to mention the living as well: in the first place, our venerable brothers Miroslav Stephan Marusyn, now appointed as archbishop and secretary of the Congregation for the Eastern Churches, and who served for a long time in a distinguished manner as vice-president of the Commission, as well as Bishop Emile Eid, the current vice-president, who brought the work for the most part to a happy conclusion; after these we remember our beloved Ivan Žužek, a priest of the Society of Jesus, who labored with assiduous zeal as secretary of the Commission from the very beginning, and the others who were valuable parts of the Commission, whether as members, the patriarchs, cardinals, archbishops and bishops, or else as consultors and co-operators in the study groups and in other functions. Finally, we recall the observers, invited from the Orthodox Churches for the sake of the desired unity of all the Churches, who were a great assistance by their useful presence and collaboration.

We have great hope that this Code "will be translated happily into the action of daily life" and "will furnish a genuine testimony of reverence and love for ecclesiastical law," as Paul VI of blessed memory had hoped (*AAS* 66 [1974] 247), as well as establishing that same order of tranquillity among the Eastern Churches, so clear in antiquity, that we desired with an ardent spirit for the entire ecclesial society when we promulgated the Code of Canon Law for the Latin Church. This is a matter of order, "which, granting the primacy to love, grace and charism, at the same time facilitates their ordered development both in the life of the ecclesial society and even in the lives of the individuals who belong to it" (*AAS* 75 [1983] Part II, XI).

"Let joy and peace, with justice and obedience, commend" this Code as well, "and let that which is commanded by the head be observed by the members" (*ibid.,* XIII), so that, with everyone's united strength, the mission of the universal Church may increase, and the kingdom of Christ the "Pantokrator" may be more fully established (cf. John Paul II, *Allocution to the Roman Curia,* 28 June 1986, *AAS* 97 [1987] 196).

We beseech the holy ever-Virgin Mary, to whose most tender protection we have repeatedly commended the preparation of this Code, to ask her Son with a mother's plea that this Code may become a vehicle of that love which must be inwardly fastened in the heart of every human creature: this is the love that was so splendidly drawn forth from the heart of Christ after it was pierced by a lance on the cross, according to that outstanding witness, Saint John the Apostle.

Therefore, having called upon the assistance of divine grace, sustained by the authority of the blessed apostles Peter and Paul, with full knowledge and assenting to the requests of the patriarchs, archbishops and bishops of the Eastern Churches, who have cooperated with us in collegial affection, making use of the fullness of the apostolic power with which we are endowed, by means of this our constitution we promulgate the present Code as it has been arranged and revised, to have force from this time forward. We decree and order that it is to have the force of law for all Eastern Catholic Churches from now on, and we entrust it to the hierarchs of those Churches to be kept with care and vigilance.

However, so that everyone to whom this pertains may have a close examination of the prescripts of this Code before they come into effect, we declare and decree that they come into force on the first day of October 1991, on the feast of the Patronage of the Blessed Virgin Mary in many Churches of the East.

Anything else to the contrary whatsoever, even worthy of most special mention, notwithstanding.

We therefore urge all our beloved children to carry out these indicated precepts with a sincere intention and a ready will; you should be certain that the Eastern Churches will have the greatest possible regard for the good of the souls of the Christian faithful with a zealous discipline, that they may flourish more and more, and discharge the function entrusted to them, under the protection of the blessed and glorious Virgin Mary, who is truly called "Theotokos" and shines forth as the exalted Mother of the universal Church.

Given in Rome at Saint Peter's, on 18th day of October, in the year 1990, the thirteenth of our pontificate.

—*Pope John Paul II*

PREFACE TO THE LATIN EDITION

One hundred and fifty years have not yet passed since Pius IX thought of "collecting and publishing the laws of the Church, as he reflected on the fact that new attention should be given to Eastern affairs, rites should be enhanced, customs corrected and discipline restored. Nor did it escape that most wise Pontiff that one must begin with the earliest Greek sources, from which so much later came to the East and ultimately to the North" (Pitra, *Iuris...*, pref.). At the request of the Supreme Pontiff, John Baptist Pitra, OSB, later a cardinal, went in search of the scattered sources of Eastern law. With the assistance of the pope, Pitra collected the results of his investigation, and with the pope's support, he published what he had collected in two volumes under the title *Iuris ecclesiastici graecorum historia et monumenta*.

This Roman Pontiff, after he had examined everything, so that "the deposit of faith may be preserved whole and entire in the East, so that ecclesiastical discipline may proceed in a prosperous manner, and so that the sacred liturgy may shine in all holiness and splendor" (*Acta Pii IX* III, 402–403), constituted a special committee of cardinals, called the "Congregation for the Propagation of the Faith for Affairs of the Eastern Rite," with the apostolic constitution *Romani Pontifices* (6 January 1862). He delineated the scope of business it was to administer, and also wished that this congregation should have a Cardinal *ponens* in a stable manner and by pontifical appointment "to undertake the task of directing carefully those studies necessary for collecting the canons of the Eastern Church and for examining, where necessary, all Eastern books of whatever sort, whether they concern versions of the Bible, catechesis, or discipline" (ibid., 410).

While studies concerning Eastern canonical matters were beginning, some bishops of the Eastern Churches, who had been asked to propose questions for the First Vatican Council, thought that the revision of Eastern canon law should be dealt with by that council. The primary spokesman for these views was Gregory Yussuf, Patriarch of the Melkite Church, who seriously lamented the poverty of canon law suited to his own and each other Eastern rite (Mansi 49, 200), as well as Joseph Papp-Szilagyi, Eastern rite bishop of Oradea Mare, who desired the restoration of many headings of ecclesiastical discipline, describing almost a complete Code (ibid. 49, 198).

The First Vatican Council's preparatory "Commission on Missions and Churches of the Eastern rite," in its sixth session, recognized that the Eastern Churches very much needed a Code of canon law, which would constitute their discipline: that is, a Code of great authority, complete, common to all nations, and suited to the circumstances of the times (ibid. 49, 1012).

But since that Commission abandoned this opinion as their work progressed, invoking instead a disciplinary unity in the whole Church (ibid. 50: 31*, 34*, 45*–46*, 74*–75*), it happened that strong voices were raised in the council hall in favor of safeguarding the discipline of the Easterners.

Among those who spoke in this sense, the Patriarch Joseph Audu, the head of the Chaldean Catholic Church, distinguished himself. In the sixteenth General Congregation of the Council, he actively defended a variety "in those things other than matters of faith," inasmuch as they "are certainly a proof of divine power and omnipotence in the unity of the Catholic Church." On behalf of his patriarchal Church, he asked in the first place that "when the favor is granted, a place and time be assigned" for "a new canon law" to be compiled, corresponding to the ancient canons as well as the wishes of the Council, and that it be submitted for the approval of the Council Fathers (ibid. 50, 515 and 516).

After the First Vatican Council was adjourned before it had completed its work because of the pressure of events, Leo XIII, fully informed about all Eastern matters in many "conferences with the Eastern patriarchs," was pleased to extol with great praises "the variety of Eastern liturgy and discipline, approved by law," which admirably illustrated the mark of catholicity in the Church of God (apostolic letter *Orientalium dignitas*, 30 November 1894, pref.).

Under the wise governance of that pontiff, and since the revision of the canonical discipline of the Eastern Churches was everywhere desired, while at the same time nothing seemed more preferable than that this matter should be undertaken by each individual Church and then submitted to the Apostolic See for approval, many particular synods were assembled. Prominent among these were the Syrian Synod of Sharfet assembled in 1888, the Ruthenian Synod of L'viv held in 1891, the two Romanian Synods of Alba-Julienses which met in 1882 and 1900, and the Synod of Alexandria celebrated by the Copts in 1898. The last of these synods, in which the principal divisions of canonical discipline for each one of the Churches were almost completely revised, was the Synod of the Armenians which St. Pius X ordered to be held at Rome in 1911, so that it might consider "the rights of the patriarchs and bishops, the correct administration of the faithful, the discipline of the clergy, institutes of monks, the needs of missions, the beauty of divine worship, the Sacred Liturgy" (letter *Vobis plane*, 30 August 1911).

The acts and decrees of the above-mentioned synods, if they are compared together with those others published in previous times such as the acts and decrees of the Maronite Synod of Mount Lebanon, held in 1736 and approved *in forma specifica* by Benedict XIV (brief *Singularis Romanorum*, 1 September 1741), as well as the Greek-Melkite Synod of Aïn-Traz celebrated in 1835, almost produce the impression that, at that time, the disciplinary patrimony of all the Eastern Churches, confirmed by the sacred canons of the primitive Church, was being in some fashion obscured, and that as many canonical orderings approved by the supreme authority of the Church would be required as there were Eastern "rites" in the bosom of the Catholic Church. Meanwhile, on the other hand, the "Code of Canon Law" for the Latin Church, begun with such spirit and wise counsel by St. Pius X with the apostolic letter *Arduum sane munus* on 19 March 1904, was being drafted in rapid stages.

In 1917, Benedict XV not only promulgated the *Code of Canon Law* for the Latin Church, "fulfilling the expectation of the whole catholic world" (motu proprio *Cum iuris canonici*, 15 September 1917), but also reflected with great interest on the Eastern Churches, which, as he wrote, "offer in the ancient memory of their times such a bright light of sanctity and teaching, so that even now, after such a great passage of time, they illumine with their luster the rest of the Christian world" (motu proprio *Dei providentis*, 1 May 1917). He instituted the "Sacred Congregation for the Eastern Church" on 1 May 1917, and, as provided in the *Code of Canon Law* promulgated on Pentecost of that year, he provided it "with all of the faculties which the other Congregations have for the Churches of the Latin rite" (can. 257 §2), only with certain exceptions. This was done in order to provide appropriately for the achievement of those objects which could hardly be realized by the individual Eastern Churches, on account of the difficult nature of juridical affairs. Furthermore, in October of that year, he founded in Rome "a special center for higher studies concerning Eastern matters," namely the Pontifical Institute for Eastern Studies, "for the purpose of awakening the Christian East to the hope of its ancient prosperity." He ordered "the canon law of all the Eastern Christian peoples" to be studied and taught in this institute, in addition to other disciplines (*motu proprio Orientis catholici*, 15 October 1917).

Indeed, in the first years of its work, the Sacred Congregation "for the Eastern Church" gave several responses to the Churches in which the canon laws had been sufficiently neglected or which contained many things which were fallen into disuse, obsolete or incomplete, or concerning areas in which, in the light of the recently promulgated *Code of Canon Law,* those Churches felt that they could make progress, while almost laying aside their own tradition. The congregation did this so that new laws might be produced in the synods of the individual Churches, in the manner of former times, and be submitted for the review of the Apostolic See.

The opinion gradually prevailed, however, in all the Churches, that there could be nothing better than the collection into one organic "body of laws" of those laws that were common to all the Eastern Churches or which were considered should be so, compiled under the care of the Apostolic See and promulgated by the Sovereign Pontiff.

Therefore, Pius XI, in an audience granted on 3 August 1927 to the cardinal secretary of the Sacred Congregation for the Eastern Church, Luigi Sincero, after considering the requests of the cardinal members of that Congregation who had assembled a few days earlier in a plenary meeting, thought that a codification of Eastern canon law was not only necessary, but should be counted among the most urgent affairs, and he decreed that he himself would preside over it.

Nevertheless, the codification of the canonical discipline of the Eastern Churches actually has its beginning in 1929.

At the beginning of that year, on 5 January, the Supreme Pontiff ordered a consultation with the heads of the Eastern Churches, especially the patriarchs, "so that they might freely indicate, after gathering their opinions, what they think about this important task, and at the same time express their mind about how, and in what way, the work should be undertaken, especially with regard to the discipline, traditions, necessities and privileges of each rite, so that the codification would be truly useful to the clergy and people of those Churches." Furthermore, on 20 July he ordered the patriarchs and archbishops who preside over each rite to choose a suitable priest, each for his own rite, to assist diligently in this work (*AAS* 21 [1929] 669).

On 27 April, in an audience granted to the cardinal secretary of the Sacred Congregation for the Eastern Church, the Supreme Pontiff constituted for himself a special "Presidential Council" for Eastern codification, which he had doubtless been intending to do since 1927. Its members were Cardinals Pietro Gasparri, Luigi Sincero and Bonaventura Cerretti; a small commission of consultors, consisting of three legal experts, was added to this council.

In that same year, after the responses of the heads of the Eastern Churches concerning the opportuneness of the Eastern codification to be undertaken by the care of the Apostolic See and the manner of proceeding in such an important task had been duly collected and carefully considered, the Presidential Council met in plenary session on 4 July. The Council not only discovered a nearly unanimous sentiment among the Easterners in complete favor of such a project, but also referred to the Supreme Pontiff numerous suggestions regarding this enterprise.

After carefully evaluating these things, the Supreme Pontiff determined the following, in an "Announcement" on 17 July 1935:

1) that historical-canonical studies, which are called *preparatory*, are to be undertaken concerning the laws and customs of each of the Churches by priests whom the bishops are to send to Rome;

2) that drafts of canons, redacted by the above-mentioned delegated priests, are to be sent to the ordinaries for their observations;

3) that the juridical sources of each of the Churches, particularly the canonical ones, are to be researched and published under the direction of experts in the history and science of canon law" (*AAS* 27 [1935] 306-307).

Pius XI, in an audience on 23 November 1929, proposed the "Cardinalatial Commission for Studies Preparatory to the Eastern Codification" for these above-mentioned studies; the announcement of this commission was given in the official commentary *Acta Apostolicae Sedis* on 2 December 1929 (p. 669). The president of this Commission was Cardinal Pietro Gasparri; its members were Cardinals Luigi Sincero, Bonaventura Cerretti and Franz Ehrle. An assessor of the Sacred Congregation for the Eastern Church, Father Amleto Cicognani, later a cardinal, was named the Commission's secretary.

Two groups of experts were added to the commission of cardinals, according to the criteria set forth by the Supreme Pontiff in an audience of 13 July of that year: namely, a college of Eastern delegates to undertake the preparatory work of drafting the Code of Eastern Canon Law as an aid to the members of the commission of cardinal fathers, and a college of consultors "to collect sources for the eastern canonical codification."

Fourteen priests were included in the first college, at the express wish of the Supreme Pontiff chosen "synodally" by the bishops of each of the Eastern Churches, to "represent" truly those bishops and so that the voice of the East might thus fully resound in an Eastern Code from its very beginning. Four religious, very learned in canon law and living in Rome, were added to these priests.

In the other college were included twelve priests who were experts in their knowledge of the sources, well known for their learning. Their task, according to the wishes of the Supreme Pontiff, was so to collect the sources of Eastern canonical discipline that it might not only be of benefit to scholarship, but might also and primarily assist greatly in carrying out the codification of the Eastern canons.

At the request of the Supreme Pontiff in an audience on 7 March 1930, the names of these priests, who worked with great distinction in the preparation of the Eastern codification, were announced publicly in the newspaper *L'Osservatore Romano* on the following 2 April.

Six years of untiring study and intense work by the commission brought the preparatory work on the Eastern codification to an end. Indeed, all of the headings of canonical discipline, in the manner requested unanimously by the delegates of the Eastern Churches, were discussed time and again in 183 meetings, and then appropriately arranged in several *schemata*, which were sent to the bishops of the East, so that they might make their opinions known. The ancient and more recent sources of canonical discipline were selected most diligently by the members of the commission and published in thirteen large volumes by the Sacred Congregation for the Eastern Church; in 1934, they were made available not only to the commission, but also to institutes of higher studies. All this bears witness to the continual care of Pius XI for the Eastern canonical codification; he wished to be fully informed of the work of the commission in twenty four "audiences," and after the preparatory studies were completed, he spared no effort to proceed as quickly as possible to drafting the "Code of Eastern Canon Law," as he wished to refer to the Code being prepared "until a better title may be found" (in an audience of 5 July 1935).

In 1935, during an audience on 7 June, the Supreme Pontiff decided to establish a new commission that would organize the work of preparing the Code, and that would draft the text of the canons after examining carefully the observations of the Eastern bishops on the previous *schemata*. This appeared as an "Notice" in the official commentary *Acta Apostolicae Sedis* on 17 June of that year (*AAS* 27 [1935] 306–306), where, in addition to the name, the composition and competence of the commission was determined. This "Pontifical Commission for the Codification of the "Code of Eastern Canon Law," as it was called, consisted of only four cardinal members at the beginning: Luigi Sincero, who was president, Eugenio Pacelli, who later became Pius XII, Julio Serafini and Pietro Fumasoni-Biondi. For the next thirty-seven years, the duration of the life of the Commission, many cardinals were numbered among the members of this Commission, some succeeding others who had died; when the Second Vatican Council had concluded, all the patriarchs of the Eastern Catholic Churches were included as well.

When Cardinal Luigi Sincero died on 7 February 1936, he was succeeded on the 17th of that month as president of the Commission by Cardinal Massimo Massimi, under whose wise leadership the difficult work of drafting the Code of Eastern Canon Law was nearly brought to completion. Three notable parts of the Code, promulgated by Pius XII before the death of this cardinal, are a testimony to this.

Cardinal Peter XV Agagianian succeeded as president; until the end of 1962, he had been head of the Armenian Catholic Church; he directed the Commission until his death on 6 May 1971.

Father Acacio Coussa, B.A., was named secretary of the Commission, and he fulfilled this office with great fidelity until he was created a cardinal. Then, after the work of drafting the Code of Eastern Canon Law was interrupted by the Second Vatican Council, Father Daniel Faltin, O.F.M.Conv., functioned as "Assistant" until the Commission went out of existence.

As an aid to the cardinal members of the Commission, thirteen experts were appointed as consultors, most of whom were selected from among the priests of the Eastern Churches; their names were announced in a "Notice" in the *Acta Apostolicae Sedis* (27 [1935] 308). The principal function of the college of consultors was to review the observations of the Eastern bishops on the previously drafted *schemata* and to add their own comments for the cardinal members of the Commission. These matters were admirably carried out in seventy-eight sessions, the last of which was held on 3 November 1939.

The Cardinal Fathers, meeting seventy-three times, diligently drafted the Code of Eastern Canon Law, constantly supported by the Supreme Pontiff, who never ceased to follow the whole work of redaction with assiduous care, and who examined by his personal study the individual articles of the canons. He wished that the complete body of the law should be divided into twenty-four titles, in the manner of many eastern collections of the genuine tradition.

In 1943 and 1944, this Corpus, already published in one volume, was submitted to a careful work of "coordination" by the well known experts Acacio Coussa, B.A., Aemilius Herman, S.J., and Arcadius Larraona, C.M.F. Later, when the text of the whole Code had been printed a second time, and it had been revised again and again by the Cardinal Fathers, meeting on nineteen occasions during 1945, it was presented in January, 1948, to the Supreme Pontiff.

With regard to the promulgation, it was felt to be best to proceed in stages. Therefore, at the beginning of 1949, the Supreme Pontiff ordered the printing for promulgation of the canons on the sacrament of matrimony, since they were considered the most urgent, and later, for the administration of justice, the canons on procedure. These comprised titles XIII and XXI in the schema of the future Code.

When this was done, the canons "On the sacrament of matrimony" were promulgated on 22 February 1949, the feast of Saint Peter's Chair at Antioch, with the apostolic letter *motu proprio Crebrae allatae sunt* (*AAS* 41 [1949] 89–119); they were to come into force on the following 2 May.

The canons "On trials" were promulgated by the apostolic letter *motu proprio Sollicitudinem nostram* on the feast of the Epiphany, 6 January 1950 (*AAS* 42 [1950] 5–120); they were to have a *vacatio* of a whole year, coming into force on 6 January of the following year.

On the feast of Saint Cyril of Alexandria, bishop and doctor, the canons "On Religious," "On the Temporal Goods of the Church," and "On the meaning of words" were promulgated by the apostolic letter *motu proprio Postquam Apostolicis Litteris*, 9 February 1952 (*AAS* 44 [1952] 65–150), to come into effect on 21 November of that year, the feast of the Presentation of the Blessed Virgin Mary. The three sections which are contained in this apostolic letter constituted the following titles in the order of the schema of the future Code:

Tit. XIV On monks and other religious
Tit. XIX On the temporal goods of the Church
Tit. XXIV On the meaning of words

Finally, by the apostolic letter *motu proprio Cleri sanctitati*, issued on 2 June 1957 (*AAS* 49 [1957] 433–600), Pius XII, as a sort of saint's day gift, promulgated the canons "On the Eastern Rites" and "On persons," which were to begin to come into force on the feast of the Annunciation of the Blessed Virgin Mary in the following year. These canons belonged to the five titles which follow from the *schema* of the future Code:

Tit. II On the Eastern rites
Tit. III On physical and moral persons
Tit. IV On clerics in general
Tit. V On clerics in particular
Tit. XVII On the laity

Of the 2666 canons which the schema of the future Code of 1945 contained, three-fifths were promulgated. The remaining 1095 canons remained in the archives of the Commission.

When the Second Vatican Council was called by John XXIII, since it was foreseen that the canonical discipline of the whole Church must be revised according to the conclusions and principles of the Council, the redaction of the Code of Eastern Canon Law was, properly speaking, interrupted; nevertheless, other functions of the Commission continued. Of these, the following are worthy of mention: the function of giving authentic interpretations of the parts of the Code which had already been promulgated, and the role of supervising the edition of the *Fontes* of Eastern canon law.

In the middle of 1972, the Supreme Pontiff, Paul VI, instituted the Pontifical Commission for the Revision of the Code of Eastern Canon Law, and determined that the former Commission, which had been erected in 1935 to "redact" the Code, should go out of existence. The announcement of this was published in the newspaper *L'Osservatore Romano* on 16 June 1972.

The form of the new Commission safeguarded its Eastern character. The college of members of the Commission, originally twenty-four in number, but later expanded to thirty-eight, was composed of the patriarchs and the other heads of the Eastern Catholic Churches, with the addition of those cardinals in charge of the dicasteries of the Roman Curia that have competence over Eastern Churches. A college of seventy consultors added to the Commission consisted for the most part of bishops and presbyters of the Eastern Churches, with the addition of some clerics of the Latin rite and lay persons knowledgeable in Eastern canonical discipline.

Nor should it be forgotten that several well known men from those Eastern Churches which are not yet in full communion with the Catholic Church were also invited as observers to collaborate in the work of the revision of the Code.

The task of president of the Commission was entrusted to Cardinal Joseph Parecattil, Archbishop of Ernakulam of the Malabar Church. He fulfilled this office in an outstanding manner until the last day of his life (20 February 1987). With the death of the cardinal president, the office of president of the Commission remained vacant thereafter.

Ignatius Clemens Mansourati, titular bishop of Apamaea of the Syrians was appointed as Vice-President of the Commission; he remained in that position for five years. Miroslav Stephan Marusyn, titular bishop of Cadi of the Ukrainian Church, succeeded him on 15 June 1977, and served as Vice-President until the end of 1982. On 20 December of that year, Emile Eid, titular bishop of Sarepta of the Maronites, was named as Vice-President of the Commission.

Fr. Ivan Žužek, a member of the Society of Jesus, was named the Commission's secretary; he was originally appointed as Pro-Secretary, but became Secretary on 22 October 1977.

The mandate entrusted to the Commission by the Supreme Pontiff was to revise completely, primarily in the light of the decrees of the Second Vatican Council, the whole Code of Eastern Canon Law, both those parts which had already been published, as well as those sections that had not yet been promulgated, although a draft had been brought to completion by the former commission.

The Supreme Pontiff, Paul VI, at the solemn inauguration of the work of the Commission held in the Sistine Chapel on 18 March 1974, firmly established the *Magna Charta* of the whole revision process and illustrated it with eloquent words. The Supreme Pontiff required a twofold concern on the part of the Commission above all else, namely, that the canon law of the Eastern Catholic Churches be revised according to the intention of the Fathers of the Second Vatican Council and according to the authentic Eastern tradition.

Especially solicitous for the salvation of souls, which is the ultimate goal of every ecclesiastical norm, the Supreme Pontiff in that same speech particularly highlighted the salutary and new impulse to restore the Christian life that the Second Vatican Council had desired and promoted for the whole Church. He also ordered that the Code should respond to the needs of modern life and the true conditions of time and place, which are continually and quickly changing. The Code should preserve a coherence and agreement with sound tradition, and at the same time be in keeping with the special task which pertains to the Christian faithful of the Eastern Churches, "the task of promoting the unity of all Christians, particularly of Eastern Christians, according to the principles of the decree . . . On Ecumenism" (*OE* 24).

The plenary session of the members of the Commission, which met from 18–23 March 1974, and in which through the generous will of the Supreme Pontiff all of the consultors of the Commission, as well as some observers from the Eastern non-Catholic Churches participated without a deliberative vote, approved certain principles with a nearly unanimous vote, by which the consultors of the Commission should be guided in various "study groups" in composing the drafts of the canons.

Among these principles, which were published in full in three languages in the acts of the Commission (*Nuntia* 3), the main ones were: 1) keeping in mind the single patrimony of the ancient canons, what has been handed down concerning the single Code for all of the Eastern Churches should also be completely suited to the modern circumstances of life; 2) the character of the Code should be truly Eastern, that is, it should be in conformity with the postulates of the Second Vatican Council in preserving the proper disciplines of the Eastern Churches "for these are guaranteed by ancient tradition, and seem to be better suited to the customs of their faithful and to the good of their souls" (*OE* 5), and therefore the Code must reflect the discipline that is contained in the sacred canons and in the customs common to all of the Eastern Churches; 3) the Code should be completely consonant with the special task entrusted to the Eastern Catholic Churches by the Second Vatican Council of fostering the unity of all Christians, particularly of the East, according to the principles of the Council's decree "On ecumenism;" 4) the Code is to be juridical in nature, as is fitting: therefore, it is to define clearly and safeguard the rights and obligations of individual physical and juridic persons toward one another and toward ecclesiastical society; 5) in the very formulation of laws, the Code should take into account charity and humanity, temperance and moderation, in addition to justice, to foster most of all the salvation of souls with pastoral care, and therefore it should not impose norms to be kept in the strict sense unless this is required by the common good and the general ecclesiastical discipline; 6) the principle of "subsidiarity," as it is called, should be preserved in the Code, so that it should contain only those laws that are considered to be common to all of the Eastern Catholic Churches, in the judgment of the Supreme Pontiff, leaving everything else to the particular law of the individual Churches.

With respect to the systematic ordering of the Code, it should be noted that the Code of Eastern Canon Law, entrusted for revision to the Commission after a renewed study carried out by the two previous Commissions beginning in 1929, was divided not into books, like the Code of the Latin Church, but into twenty-four titles, by the will of the Supreme Pontiffs Pius XI and Pius XII. For Pius XI expressly decreed on 8 February 1937 that the Code should be systematically organized into titles. But Pius XII, who was knowledgeable from his personal work done while part of the Commission before his election as Supreme Pontiff as well as by subsequently following the work of the Commission with careful and constant attention, in an audience on 26 December 1945 (cf. *Nuntia* 26, pp. 82–83) approved the organization of the Code into twenty-four titles in a form that had been unanimously approved and accepted by the cardinal members of the Commission in their plenary session on 20 November of that same year, although the pontiff moved some sections from one title to another.

There was no serious reason to call this systematic arrangement, approved by the popes, into question. Indeed, the study groups of the Commission's consultors, when addressing the issue, endorsed the same arrangement on the basis of several arguments, as well as because it was appropriate to the circumstances of modern life. Therefore, Bishop Miroslav Stephan Marusyn, Vice-President of the Commission, explained this to the 1980 Synod of Bishops. This arrangement was acceptable to the consultative bodies and there were hardly any contrary opinions. The members of the Commission, in a plenary meeting held in November 1988, approved this arrangement as a norm for "the order of proceeding."

The first text of the Code revised by the consultors of the Commission was completed during a period of six years. The consultors, divided into ten study groups, assiduously performed their work, meeting nearly one hundred times in meetings that often lasted fifteen days.

This text, appropriately distributed in eight drafts, was submitted at various times to the Supreme Pontiff to receive his approval before being sent to the consultative bodies, that is, to the entire episcopate of the Eastern Catholic Churches, to the dicasteries of the Roman Curia, to the institutes of higher learning in Rome and to the unions of superiors general of religious. These bodies were asked to express their observations and opinions within six months from the time in which the schemata were sent to them.

The order in which the *schemata* were sent to the consultative bodies was as follows: in June 1980, the "*Schema* of canons on divine worship and particularly the sacraments;" in December 1980, the "*Schema* of canons on monks and other religious as well as on members of other institutes of consecrated life;" in June 1981, the "*Schema* of canons on the evangelization of the peoples, the teaching office of the Church and ecumenism;" in September 1981, the "*Schema* of canons on general norms and on the temporal goods of the Church;" in November 1981, the "*Schema* of canons on clerics and the laity;" in February 1982, the "*Schema* of canons on the protection of rights, or on procedures;" and in October 1984, the "*Schema* of canons on the hierarchical constitution of the Eastern Churches."

Nothing shows the collegial nature of the revision of the Code more than the great mass, the weighty importance and gravity of the observations, supported by arguments, that came to the Commission. The whole episcopate of the Eastern Catholic Churches and the other consultative bodies made an extremely valuable and serious contribution to the work of revising the Code. It should also be observed in this matter that the drafts were published with the intention that everything which had been done by the Commission would be made public, and so that everyone, particularly experts in canon law, could express their opinions and thus contribute to the successful outcome of the Code.

All the observations, without exception, were arranged in an orderly fashion and sent again to special study groups to produce a further revision, taking into account the desires of the consultative bodies. In these groups, the consultors of the Commission and some other men who had particular expertise in the material being treated revised the text of the Code again. The text thus revised again is found published in the journal *Nuntia* in the reports of the acts of the Commission.

The corrected drafts, appropriately revised in a single text of thirty titles, was entrusted to a special study group called the "Coordinating Committee." This group was to ensure the internal coherence and unity of the Code, to avoid ambiguities and discrepancies, to reduce juridical terms to a univocal meaning, insofar as this was possible, to remove elements that were repetitious or out of place, and to provide consistency in orthography and punctuation.

In October 1986, the "*Schema* of the Code of Eastern Canon Law" was printed and offered to the Supreme Pontiff, who ordered, on the seventeenth of that month, the feast of Saint Ignatius of Antioch, that it be sent to the members of the Commission for the examination and judgment.

The observations of the members of the Commission, appropriately arranged, were submitted for the examination of a special study group of consultors, called the "Committee for the examination of observations," which met twice for fifteen days. After carefully considering the observations, this committee was to propose appropriate amendments to the text of the canons, or, in case the text of the canon was to be retained, to explain the reasons which counseled against accepting the observations on the formulated text. The observations, together with the opinions of the group, were collected into one volume and sent to the members of the Commission in April 1988; they were examined and considered by the members of the Commission in a plenary meeting of the Commission held several months later.

Meanwhile, the "Coordinating Committee," which had never stopped working, proposed many emendations to be included in the text of the canons, for the most part of a stylistic nature; other changes, which affected the substance of the canons, the committee decided should be made *ex officio*, so that a complete agreement between the canons would be preserved, and so that, as far as possible, the *lacunae* of the law could be filled in by appropriate norms. All these things, collected together and sent to the members of the Commission in July 1988, were submitted to their examination and judgment.

The plenary assembly of the members of the Commission, convoked at the mandate of the Supreme Pontiff to determine by vote whether the whole text of the revised Code was ready to be sent immediately to the Supreme Pontiff for promulgation at a time and in a manner which seemed best to him, was celebrated in the Bologna Hall of the Apostolic Palace from 3 to 14 November 1988. At this meeting, discussion took place regarding questions that were proposed at the request of at least five members of the Commission. The definitive vote on the draft of the Code, that, at the request of the members of the Commission, took place on each title separately, had this outcome: all the titles were approved by the majority of the members, most of them passing almost unanimously.

The final draft was emended according to the wishes of the members of the Commission and given the title "Code of Canons of the Eastern Churches." Having been produced in ten copies by means called *informatica*, it was delivered to the Supreme Pontiff on 28 January 1989, with the request that it be promulgated.

The Supreme Pontiff himself, however, with the assistance of some experts and after consultation with the Vice-President and Secretary of the Pontifical Commission for the Revision of the Code of Eastern Canon Law, revised this final *schema* of the Code, ordered it to be published, and finally on 1 October 1990 decreed that the new Code should be promulgated on the 18th of that month.

CODE OF CANONS OF THE EASTERN CHURCHES

LATIN-ENGLISH EDITION

NEW ENGLISH TRANSLATION

PRELIMINARY CANONS

CAN. 1 The canons of this Code concern all and only the Eastern Catholic Churches, unless, with regard to relations with the Latin Church, it is expressly established otherwise.

CAN. 2 The canons of the Code, in which the ancient law of the Eastern Churches has been mostly received or adapted, are to be assessed chiefly by that law.

CAN. 3 The Code, although it often refers to the prescripts of liturgical books, does not for the most part determine liturgical matters; therefore, these prescripts are to be diligently observed, unless they are contrary to the canons of the Code.

CAN. 4 The canons of the Code neither abrogate nor derogate from the agreements entered into or approved by the Holy See with nations or other political societies. They therefore continue in force as they have been up to the present, notwithstanding any contrary prescriptions of the Code.

CAN. 5 Acquired rights as well as privileges up to this time granted by the Apostolic See to physical and juridic persons, which are in use and have not been revoked, remain intact unless they are expressly revoked by the canons of this Code.

CAN. 6 With the entry into force of the Code:

1° all common or particular laws contrary to

CAN. 1 Canones huius Codicis omnes et solas Ecclesias orientales catholicas respiciunt, nisi, relationes cum Ecclesia latina quod attinet, aliud expresse statuitur.

CAN. 2 Canones Codicis, in quibus plerumque ius antiquum Ecclesiarum orientalium recipitur vel accommodatur, praecipue ex illo iure aestimandi sunt.

CAN. 3 Codex, etsi saepe ad praescripta librorum liturgicorum se refert, de re liturgica plerumque non decernit; quare haec praescripta sedulo servanda sunt, nisi Codicis canonibus sunt contraria.

CAN. 4 Canones Codicis initas aut approbatas a Sancta Sede conventiones cum nationibus aliisve societatibus politicis non abrogant neque eis derogant; eaedem idcirco perinde ac in praesens vigere pergent contrariis Codicis praescriptis minime obstantibus.

CAN. 5 Iura quaesita itemque privilegia, quae a Sede Apostolica ad haec usque tempora personis physicis vel iuridicis concessa in usu sunt nec revocata, integra manent, nisi Codicis canonibus expresse revocantur.

CAN. 6 Codice vim obtinente:

1° abrogatae sunt omnes leges iuris

1: Sanctiones promulgatoriae in m.p. Pii XII: *Crebrae allatae sunt,* 22 feb. 1949; *Sollicitudinem Nostram,* 6 ian. 1950; *Postquam Apostolicis Litteris,* 9 feb. 1952; *Cleri sanctitati,* 2 iun. 1957.

2: Chalc. can. 1; Quinisext. can. 2; Nic. II, can. 1;

Constantinop. IV, can. 1.

4: BENEDICTUS XV, all. (in Consis. secr.), 21 nov. 1921; Vat. II, decr. *Christus Dominus,* 20; PAULUS VI, m.p. *Ecclesiae sanctae,* 6 aug. 1966, I, 18 §2.

the canons of the Code or which concern matters which are integrally reordered in this Code are abrogated;

2° all customs reprobated by the canons of this Code or which are contrary to them, unless they are centennial or immemorial, are revoked.

communis vel iuris particularis, quae sunt canonibus Codicis contrariae aut quae materiam respiciunt in Codice ex integro ordinatam;

2° revocatae sunt omnes consuetudines, quae canonibus Codicis reprobantur aut quae eis contrariae sunt nec centenariae vel immemorabiles.

TITLE I. THE RIGHTS AND OBLIGATIONS OF ALL THE CHRISTIAN FAITHFUL

TITULUS I. DE CHRISTIFIDELIBUS EORUMQUE OMNIUM IURIBUS ET OBLIGATIONIBUS

CAN. 7 §1. The Christian faithful are those who, incorporated as they are into Christ through baptism, are constituted as the people of God; and so, participating in their own way in the priestly, prophetic and royal function of Christ, they are called, each according to his or her condition, to exercise the mission which God has entrusted to the Church to fulfill in the world.

§2. This Church, constituted and organized in this world as a society, subsists in the Catholic Church, governed by the successor of Peter and the bishops in communion with him.

CAN. 8 In full communion with the Catholic Church on this earth are those baptized persons who are joined with Christ in its visible structure by the bonds of the profession of faith, the sacraments and ecclesiastical governance.

CAN. 9 §1. Catechumens are joined with the Church in a special manner in that, under the influence of the Holy Spirit, they express an explicit desire to be incorporated into the Church; they are, therefore, joined to the Church by that very desire and by the life of faith, hope and charity which they lead; the Church already cherishes them as their own.

CAN. 7 §1. Christifideles sunt, qui per baptismum Christo incorporati in populum Dei sunt constituti atque hac ratione muneris Christi sacerdotalis, prophetici et regalis suo modo participes secundum suam cuiusque condicionem ad missionem exercendam vocantur, quam Deus Ecclesiae in mundo implendam concredidit.

§2. Haec Ecclesia in hoc mundo ut societas constituta et ordinata subsistit in Ecclesia catholica a successore Petri et Episcopis in communione cum eo gubernata.

CAN. 8 In plena communione cum Ecclesia catholica his in terris sunt illi baptizati, qui in eius compage visibili cum Christo iunguntur vinculis professionis fidei, sacramentorum et ecclesiastici regiminis.

CAN. 9 §1. Speciali ratione cum Ecclesia conectuntur catechumeni, qui Spiritu Sancto movente expetunt explicita voluntate, ut eidem incorporentur, ideoque hac ipsa voluntate et vita fidei, spei et caritatis, quam agunt, coniunguntur cum Ecclesia, quae eos iam ut suos fovet.

7 §1: Vat. II, const. *Lumen gentium,* 31 "Nomine," 9 "In omni," 10, 12 "Populus," 13; decr. *Apostolicam actuositatem,* 2.

7 §2: Vat. II, const. *Lumen gentium,* 8 "Haec est;" const. *Gaudium et spes,* 40.

8: Vat. II, const. *Lumen gentium,* 14 "Illi plene;" decr. *Unitatis redintegratio,* 3 "In hac."

9 §1: Vat. II, const. *Lumen gentium,* 14 "Catechumeni;" decr. *Ad gentes,* 14 "Status."

§2. The Church has a special concern for catechumens, invites them to lead the evangelical life and introduces them into participation in the Divine Liturgy, the sacraments and the divine praises, and already grants them various prerogatives which are proper to Christians.

CAN. 10 Deeply attached to the word of God and adhering to the living authentic magisterium of the Church, the Christian faithful are bound to maintain integrally the faith, which was preserved and transmitted at a great price by their forefathers, and to profess it openly as well as to acquire a deeper practical understanding of it and to make it fruitful in works of charity.

CAN. 11 Based on their rebirth in Christ there is truly an equality of dignity and activity among all the Christian faithful. In virtue of this dignity they all cooperate, each according to his or her own condition and function, in the building up of the Body of Christ.

CAN. 12 The Christian faithful are bound by the obligation in the manner of their conduct to maintain always communion with the Church.

§2. They are to fulfill with great diligence their obligations to the universal Church and to their own Church *sui iuris.*

CAN. 13 All the Christian faithful must strive, each according to his or her own condition, to lead a holy life and to promote the growth of the Church and its continual sanctification.

CAN. 14 All the Christian faithful have the

§2. Catechumenorum specialem curam habet Ecclesia, quae, dum eos ad vitam evangelicam ducendam invitat eosque in participationem Divinae Liturgiae, sacramentorum et laudum divinarum introducit, eisdem varias iam largitur praerogativas, quae christianorum sunt propriae.

CAN. 10 Verbo Dei inhaerentes atque vivo Ecclesiae magisterio authentico adhaerentes tenentur christifideles fidem immenso pretio a maioribus custoditam ac transmissam integre servare et aperte profiteri necnon eam et exercendo magis intellegere et in operibus caritatis fructificare.

CAN. 11 Inter christifideles omnes ex eorum quidem in Christo regeneratione viget vera circa dignitatem et actionem aequalitas, qua cuncti secundum suam cuiusque condicionem et munus ad aedificationem Corporis Christi cooperantur.

CAN. 12 §1. Christifideles obligatione tenentur sua cuiusque agendi ratione ad communionem semper servandam cum Ecclesia.

§2. Magna cum diligentia obligationes impleant, quibus tenentur erga universam Ecclesiam et propriam Ecclesiam sui iuris.

CAN. 13 Omnes christifideles secundum suam cuiusque condicionem ad sanctam vitam ducendam atque ad Ecclesiae incrementum eiusque iugem sanctificationem promovendam vires suas conferre debent.

CAN. 14 Omnes christifideles ius et

---

9 §2: Vat. II, const. *Sacrosanctum Concilium*, 64; decr. *Ad gentes*, 14.

10: Vat. II, const. *Lumen gentium*, 11 "Indoles," 12 "Populus;" const. *Dei Verbum*, 10 "Sacra." * Syn. Libanen. Maronitarum, a. 1736, pars I, cap. I, 1.

11: Vat. II, const. *Lumen gentium*, 32 "Unus" et "Si igitur;" const. *Gaudium et spes*, 29, 49 "Haec," 61 "Maior;" Synodus Episcoporum, *Elapso oecumenico*, 22 oct. 1969, I, 2 "Distinctio" et "Par igitur."

12 §1: Vat. II, const. *Lumen gentium*, 11 "Indoles,"

13 "Ad novum" et "Ad hanc;" const. *Gaudium et spes*, 1; Synodus Episcoporum, *Elapso oecumenico*, 22 oct. 1969, I, 2.

12 §2: Vat. II, const. *Lumen gentium*, 30; decr. *Apostolicam actuositatem*, 10.

13: Vat. II, const. *Lumen gentium*, 11 "Tot," 39–42; decr. *Apostolicam actuositatem*, 6.

14: Vat. II, const. *Lumen gentium*, 33 "Omnibus;" decr. *Apostolicam actuositatem*, 3 "Omnibus;" decr. *Ad gentes*, 5, 35, 36 "Ut membra."

right and obligation to work so that the divine message of salvation may more and more reach all people of all times and of all the world.

CAN. 15 §1. The Christian faithful, conscious of their own responsibility, are bound to accept with Christian obedience what the pastors of the Church, who represent Christ, declare as teachers of the faith or determine as leaders of the Church.

§2. The Christian faithful are free to make known their needs, especially their spiritual needs, and their desires to the pastors of the Church.

§3. In keeping with their knowledge, competence and position, they have the right and at times even the duty, to manifest their views on matters regarding the good of the Church to the pastors of the Church and also to other Christian faithful, with due regard for the integrity of faith and morals and respect toward the same pastors, with consideration for the common benefit and the dignity of persons.

CAN. 16 The Christian faithful have the right to receive from the pastors of the Church, assistance out of the spiritual goods of the Church, especially from the word of God and from the sacraments.

CAN. 17 The Christian faithful have the right to worship God according to the prescriptions of their own Church *sui iuris* and to follow their own form of spiritual life in accord with the teaching of the Church.

CAN. 18 The Christian faithful are free to

obligationem habent allaborandi, ut divinum salutis nuntium ad omnes homines omnium temporum ac totius orbis magis magisque perveniat.

CAN. 15 §1. Quae Ecclesiae Pastores Christum repraesentantes tamquam fidei magistri declarant aut tamquam Ecclesiae rectores statuunt, christifideles propriae responsabilitatis conscii christiana oboedientia prosequi tenentur.

§2. Christifidelibus integrum est, ut necessitates suas, praesertim spirituales, suaque optata Ecclesiae Pastoribus patefaciant.

§3. Pro scientia, competentia et praestantia, quibus pollent, ipsis ius est, immo et aliquando obligatio, ut sententiam suam de his, quae ad bonum Ecclesiae pertinent, Ecclesiae Pastoribus manifestent eamque, salva integritate fidei et morum ac reverentia erga eosdem Pastores attentisque utilitate communi et personarum dignitate, ceteris christifidelibus notam faciant.

CAN. 16 Ius est christifidelibus, ut ex spiritualibus Ecclesiae bonis, praesertim ex verbo Dei et sacramentis, adiumenta ab Ecclesiae Pastoribus accipiant.

CAN. 17 Ius est christifidelibus, ut cultum divinum persolvant secundum praescripta propriae Ecclesiae sui iuris utque propriam vitae spiritualis formam sequantur doctrinae quidem Ecclesiae consentaneam.

CAN. 18 Integrum est christifidelibus, ut

15 §1: Vat. II, const. *Lumen gentium,* 37 "Laici," 25 "Inter;" decr. *Presbyterorum ordinis,* 9 "Novi."

15 §2: Vat. II, const. *Lumen gentium,* 37 "Laici;" decr. *Presbyterorum ordinis,* 9 "Presbyteros."

15 §3: Vat. II, const. *Lumen gentium,* 37 "Laici;" decr. *Inter mirifica,* 8; decr. *Apostolicam actuositatem,* 6 "Cum;" decr. *Presbyterorum ordinis,* 9 "Presbyteros;" const. *Gaudium et spes,* 92 "Quod."

16: Vat. II, const. *Lumen gentium,* 37 "Laici;" PIUS XII, m.p. *Cleri sanctitati,* 2 iun. 1957, can. 527.

17: Vat. II, const. *Sacrosanctum Concilium,* 4; decr. *Orientalium Ecclesiarum,* 2–3, 5.

18: PIUS XI, litt. encycl. *Quadragesimo anno,* 15 maii 1931, I ab "Maxima igitur . . . ;" PIUS XII, m.p. *Cleri sanctitati,* 2 iun. 1957, can. 531; IOANNES XXIII, litt. encycl. *Pacem in terris,* 11 apr. 1963, I "Ex eo autem;" Vat. II, decr. *Apostolicam actuositatem,* 18–21; decr. *Presbyterorum ordinis,* 8 "Spiritu;" const. *Gaudium et spes,* 68 "Inter."

found and to direct associations which serve charitable and pious purposes or which promote the Christian vocation in the world and, therefore, to hold meetings to pursue together these purposes.

CAN. 19   Since they participate in the mission of the Church, all the Christian faithful have the right to promote or to support apostolic action on their own initiative in keeping their own state and condition. No initiative, however, may lay claim the name *Catholic* without the consent of the competent ecclesiastical authority.

CAN. 20   Since the Christian faithful are called by baptism to lead a life in harmony with the gospel teaching, they have the right to a Christian education by which they are properly instructed on how to achieve the maturity of the human personality and at the same time to know and live the mystery of salvation.

CAN. 21   Those who are engaged in the sacred sciences have a just freedom of inquiry and of expressing their opinion prudently on matters in which they possess expertise, while observing the submission due to the magisterium of the Church.

CAN. 22   All the Christian faithful have the right to be free from any kind of coercion in choosing a state in life.

CAN. 23   No one is permitted to harm ille-

libere condant atque moderentur consociationes ad fines caritatis vel pietatis aut ad vocationem christianam in mundo fovendam utque conventus habeant ad eosdem fines in communi persequendos.

CAN. 19   Christifideles cuncti, quippe qui Ecclesiae missionem participent, ius habent, ut propriis inceptis apostolicam actionem promoveant vel sustineant secundum suum cuiusque statum et condicionem; nullum tamen inceptum nomen catholicum sibi vindicet, nisi consensus accessit auctoritatis competentis ecclesiasticae.

CAN. 20   Christifideles, quippe qui baptismo ad vitam doctrinae evangelicae congruentem ducendam vocentur, ius habent ad educationem christianam, qua ad maturitatem humanae personae prosequendam atque simul ad mysterium salutis cognoscendum et vivendum rite instruantur.

CAN. 21   Qui in scientias sacras incumbunt, iusta libertate fruuntur inquirendi necnon mentem suam prudenter in eis aperiendi, in quibus peritiam habent, servato debito erga magisterium Ecclesiae obsequio.

CAN. 22   Christifideles omnes ius habent, ut a quacumque coactione sint immunes in statu vitae eligendo.

CAN. 23   Nemini licet bonam famam,

19: Vat. II, decr. *Apostolicam actuositatem,* 24 "Plurima," 25 "Prae;" const. *Lumen gentium,* 37 "Sacri;" decr. *Presbyterorum ordinis,* 9 "Presbyteros."

20: Vat. II, decl. *Gravissimum educationis,* 2.

21: Vat. II, const. *Gaudium et spes,* 59 "Sacra," 62; decl. *Gravissimum educationis,* 10 "Altioris;" IOANNES PAULUS II, const. ap. *Sapientia christiana,* 15 apr. 1979, art. 39.

22: IOANNES XXIII, litt. encycl. *Pacem in terris,* 11 apr. 1963, I "Insuper;" Vat. II, const. *Gaudium et spes,* 26 "Simul," 29 "Sane," 52 "Familia." - BENEDICTUS XIV, instr. *Eo quamvis tempore,* 4 maii 1745, §21; litt. encycl. *Anno vertente,* 19 iun. 1750, §7; S.C. de Prop. Fide, (C.P.), 29 apr. 1754; S.C.S. Off., instr. (ad Ep. Rituum Orient.), a. 1883, tit. VI, art. 3; PIUS XII, m.p.

Crebrae allatae sunt, 2 feb. 1949, can. 78 §1; m.p. *Postquam Apostolicis Litteris,* 9 feb. 1952, can. 74 §1 n. 4; m.p. *Cleri sanctitati,* 2 iun. 1957, can. 158. * Syn. Zamosten. Ruthenorum, a. 1720, tit. III, §8 "Si nullum" et "Cum autem;" Syn. Libanen. Maronitarum, a. 1736, pars II, cap. XI, 8, VIII; pars IV, cap. II, 21, XVII; Syn. prov. Alba-Iulien. et Fagarasien. Rumenorum, a. 1872, tit. V, cap. VIII, I, d); a. 1882, tit. IV, sect. I, cap. II, §5, b); Syn. Sciarfen. Syrorum, a. 1888, cap. V, art. XV, §8, 3; Syn. Alexandrin. Coptorum, a. 1898, sect. II, cap. III, art. VIII, §5, 4, IV; Syn. Armen., a. 1911, 569.

23: Vat. II, const. *Gaudium et spes,* 26 "Simul;" IOANNES XXIII, litt. encycl. *Pacem in terris,* 11 apr. 1963, I "Homo."

gitimately the good reputation which another person enjoys nor violate the right of any person to protect his or her own privacy.

CAN. 24 §1. The Christian faithful can legitimately vindicate and defend the rights which they have in the Church in the competent ecclesiastical forum according to the norm of law.

§2. Further, if they are summoned to a trial by the competent authority, the Christian faithful also have the right to be judged according to the prescripts of the law, to be applied with equity.

§3. The Christian faithful have the right not to be punished with canonical penalties except in accord with the norm of law.

CAN. 25 §1. The Christian faithful are obliged to assist with the needs of the Church, so that the Church has what is necessary for its proper ends, especially what is needed for divine worship, for works of the apostolate and of charity and for the appropriate support of its ministers.

§2. They are also obliged to promote social justice and, mindful of the precept of the Lord, to help the poor from their own resources.

CAN. 26 §1. In exercising their rights, the Christian faithful, both as individuals and gathered in associations, must take account of the common good of the Church, as well as the rights of others and their own duties to others.

§2. Ecclesiastical authority has the competence to regulate, in view of the common good, the exercise of the rights which are proper to the Christian faithful.

qua quis gaudet, illegitime laedere nec ius ullius personae ad propriam intimitatem tuendam violare.

CAN. 24 §1. Christifidelibus competit, ut iura, quae in Ecclesia habent, legitime vindicent atque defendant in foro competenti ecclesiastico ad normam iuris.

§2. Christifidelibus ius quoque est, ut, si ad iudicium ab auctoritate competenti vocantur, iudicentur servatis iuris praescriptis cum aequitate applicandis.

§3. Christifidelibus ius est, ne poenis canonicis nisi ad normam legis puniantur.

CAN. 25 §1. Christifideles obligatione tenentur necessitatibus subveniendi Ecclesiae, ut eidem praesto sint, quae ad fines ei proprios praesertim ad cultum divinum, ad opera apostolatus et caritatis atque ad congruam ministrorum sustentationem necessaria sunt.

§2. Obligatione quoque tenentur iustitiam socialem promovendi necnon ex propriis reditibus pauperibus subveniendi praecepti Domini memores.

CAN. 26 §1. In iuribus suis exercendis christifideles et singuli et in consociationibus adunati rationem habere debent boni communis Ecclesiae necnon iurium aliorum atque suarum erga alios obligationum.

§2. Auctoritati ecclesiasticae competit intuitu boni communis exercitium iurium, quae christifidelibus sunt propria, moderari.

24 §1: Pıus XII, m.p. *Sollicitudinem Nostram*, 6 ian. 1950, can. 161.

25 §1: Vat. II, decr. *Presbyterorum ordinis*, 20 "Servitio," 21; decr. *Ad gentes*, 36; Pıus XII, m.p. *Postquam Apostolicis Litteris*, 9 feb. 1952, can. 233; Paulus VI, adh. ap. *Nobis in animo*, 25 mar. 1974, "Quapropter."

25 §2: Vat. II, decr. *Apostolicam actuositatem*, 8; decl. *Dignitatis humanae*, 1, 6, 14; const. *Gaudium et spes*, 26, 29, 42 "Missio," 65 "Meminerint," 68–69, 72, 75, 88.

TITLE II. CHURCHES *SUI IURIS* AND RITES

TITULUS II. DE ECCLESIIS SUI IURIS ET DE RITIBUS

CAN. 27 A community of the Christian faithful, which is joined together by a hierarchy according to the norm of law and which is expressly or tacitly recognized as *sui iuris* by the supreme authority of the Church, is called in this Code a Church *sui iuris*.

CAN. 28 §1. A rite is a liturgical, theological, spiritual and disciplinary heritage, differentiated by the culture and the circumstances of the history of peoples, which is expressed by each Church *sui iuris* in its own manner of living the faith.

§2. The rites dealt with in this Code, unless it is established otherwise, are those which arose from the Alexandrian, Antiochene, Armenian, Chaldean and Constantinopolitan traditions.

CHAPTER I. Ascription to a Church *Sui Iuris*

CAN. 29 §1. A son or daughter who has not yet completed fourteen years of age is ascribed by virtue of baptism to the Church *sui iuris* to which his or her Catholic father is as-

CAN. 27 Coetus christifidelium hierarchia ad normam iuris iunctus, quem ut sui iuris expresse vel tacite agnoscit suprema Ecclesiae auctoritas, vocatur in hoc Codice Ecclesia sui iuris.

CAN. 28 §1. Ritus est patrimonium liturgicum, theologicum, spirituale et disciplinare cultura ac rerum adiunctis historiae populorum distinctum, quod modo fidei vivendae uniuscuiusque Ecclesiae sui iuris proprio exprimitur.

§2. Ritus, de quibus in Codice agitur, sunt, nisi aliud constat, illi, qui oriuntur ex traditionibus Alexandrina, Antiochena, Armena, Chaldaea et Constantinopolitana.

CAPUT I. De Ascriptione Alicui Ecclesiae Sui Iuris

CAN. 29 §1. Filius, qui decimum quartum aetatis annum nondum explevit, per baptismum ascribitur Ecclesiae sui iuris, cui pater catholicus ascriptus est; si vero sola

27: Pius XII, m.p. *Postquam Apostolicis Litteris*, 9 feb. 1952, can. 303 §1 n. 1; Vat. II, const. *Lumen gentium*, 23 "Cura;" decr. *Orientalium Ecclesiarum*, 2–3; decr. *Unitatis redintegratio*, 16.

28 §1: Vat. II, const. *Lumen gentium*, 23 "Cura;" decr. *Orientalium Ecclesiarum*, 3; decr. *Unitatis redintegratio*, 15 "Ditissimum," 17.

28 §2: Pius XII, m.p. *Postquam Apostolicis Litteris*, 9 feb. 1952, can. 303 §1 n. 1.

29 §1: Pius XII, m.p. *Cleri sanctitati*, 2 iun. 1957,

can. 6 §§1–2. - S.C. de Prop. Fide, instr. (pro Graeco-Melchit.), 15 feb. 1746; Benedictus XIV, const. *Etsi pastoralis*, 26 maii 1742, §II, XI; ep. encycl. *Demandatam*, 24 dec. 1743, §§17–18; const. *Praeclaris*, 18 mar. 1746, ab "Avendo;" S.C. de Prop. Fide, decr. 6 oct. 1863, C), a); ep. (ad Ep. auxil. Strigonien.), 27 apr. 1903, n. 3; Pont. Comm. ad Cod. Can. Auth. Interpr., resp. 16 oct. 1919, 11; S.C. pro Eccl. Orient., decr. 1 mar. 1929, art. 43. * Syn. Armen., a. 1911, 624.

cribed; or if only the mother is Catholic, or if both parents are of the same mind in requesting it, to the Church *sui iuris* of the mother, without prejudice to particular law enacted by the Apostolic See.

§2. If, however, a person who has not yet completed fourteen years of age:

1° is born of an unwed mother, he or she is ascribed to the Church *sui iuris* to which the mother belongs;

2° is born of unknown parents, he or she is ascribed to the Church *sui iuris* to which belong those to whose care he or she has been legitimately entrusted; if, however, it is a case of an adoptive father and mother, §1 should be applied;

3° is born of non-baptized parents, he or she is ascribed to the Church *sui iuris* to which belongs the one who has undertaken his or her education in the Catholic faith.

CAN. 30 Anyone to be baptized who has completed the fourteenth year of age can freely select any Church *sui iuris* in which he or she then is ascribed by virtue of baptism received in that same Church, with due regard for particular law established by the Apostolic See.

CAN. 31 No one is to presume to induce in any way the Christian faithful to transfer to another Church *sui iuris*.

CAN. 32 §1. No one can validly transfer to

mater est catholica aut si ambo parentes concordi voluntate petunt, ascribitur Ecclesiae sui iuris, ad quam mater pertinet, salvo iure particulari a Sede Apostolica statuto.

§2. Si autem filius, qui decimum quartum aetatis annum nondum explevit, est:

1° a matre non nupta natus, ascribitur Ecclesiae sui iuris, ad quam mater pertinet;

2° ignotorum parentum, ascribitur Ecclesiae sui iuris, cui ascripti sunt ii, quorum curae legitime commissus est; si vero de patre et matre adoptantibus agitur, applicetur §1;

3° parentum non baptizatorum, ascribitur Ecclesiae sui iuris, ad quam pertinet ille, qui eius educationem in fide catholica suscepit.

CAN. 30 Quilibet baptizandus, qui decimum quartum aetatis annum explevit, libere potest seligere quamcumque Ecclesiam sui iuris, cui per baptismum in eadem susceptum ascribitur, salvo iure particulari a Sede Apostolica statuto.

CAN. 31 Nemo quemvis christifidelem ad transitum ad aliam Ecclesiam sui iuris ullo modo inducere praesumat.

CAN. 32 §1. Nemo potest sine consen-

---

29 §2, 1°: S.C. pro Eccl. Orient., decr. 24 maii 1930, art. 48.

30: Pius XII, m.p. *Cleri sanctitati,* 2 iun. 1957, can. 12.

31: Pius XII, m.p. *Cleri sanctitati,* 2 iun. 1957, cann. 7 et 1 §3. - S.C. de Prop. Fide, 28 iul. 1626, n. 2, ad II; 21 maii 1627; instr. (pro Graeco-Melchit.), 15 feb. 1746; Benedictus XIV, ep. encycl. *Demandatam,* 24 dec. 1743, §§12, 15; const. *Praeclaris,* 18 mar. 1746; ep. encycl. *Allatae sunt,* 26 iul. 1755, §21; S.C. de Prop. Fide, (C.G.), 10 mar. 1760; decr. 6 oct. 1863, A), c); Leo XIII, litt. ap. *Orientalium,* 30 nov. 1894, I;

Pont. Comm. pro Russia, instr. 26 aug. 1929, I "Item;" Vat. II, decr. *Orientalium Ecclesiarum,* 21 nov. 1964, 4. * Syn. Armen., a. 1911, 617.

32 §1: Pius XII, m.p. *Cleri sanctitati,* 2 iun. 1957, can. 8 §§1–2. - Nicolaus V, const. *Pervenit,* 6 sep. 1448; S.C. de Prop. Fide, 30 nov. 1629; 7 iun. 1639, 7; S.C.S. Off., 3 aug. 1639; S.C. de Prop. Fide, (C. G.), 2 apr. 1669, I; Benedictus XIV, const. *Etsi pastoralis,* 26 maii 1742, §II, XIII–XIV; S.C. de Prop. Fide, instr. (pro Graeco-Melchit.), 15 feb. 1746; Benedictus XIV, const. *Praeclaris,* 18 mar. 1746, ab "Avendo;" ep. encÿcl. *Allatae sunt,* 26 iul. 1755, §§20–21; S.C. de Prop.

another Church *sui iuris* without the consent of the Apostolic See.

§2. In the case of Christian faithful of an eparchy of a certain Church *sui iuris* who petition to transfer to another Church *sui iuris* which has its own eparchy in the same territory, this consent of the Apostolic See is presumed, provided that the eparchial bishops of both eparchies consent to the transfer in writing.

CAN. 33   A wife is free to transfer to the Church of the husband in the celebration of or during the marriage; when the marriage has ended, she can freely return to the original Church *sui iuris*.

CAN. 34   If the parents, or the Catholic spouse in the case of a mixed marriage, transfer to another Church *sui iuris,* children who have not completed fourteen years of age, by the law itself are ascribed to the same Church; if, however, in a marriage between Catholics, only one parent transfers to another Church *sui iuris,* the children transfer only if both parents have given consent. Upon completion of the fourteenth year of age, the children can return to the original Church *sui iuris*.

CAN. 35   Baptized non-Catholics coming

su Sedis Apostolicae ad aliam Ecclesiam sui iuris valide transire.

§2. Si vero agitur de christifideli eparchiae alicuius Ecclesiae sui iuris, qui transire petit ad aliam Ecclesiam sui iuris, quae in eodem territorio propriam eparchiam habet, hic consensus Sedis Apostolicae praesumitur, dummodo Episcopi eparchiales utriusque eparchiae ad transitum scripto consentiant.

CAN. 33   Integrum est mulieri ad Ecclesiam sui iuris viri transire in matrimonio celebrando vel eo durante; matrimonio autem soluto libere potest ad pristinam Ecclesiam sui iuris redire.

CAN. 34   Si ad aliam Ecclesiam sui iuris transeunt parentes vel in matrimonio mixto coniux catholicus, filii infra decimum quartum aetatis annum expletum ipso iure eidem Ecclesiae ascribuntur; si vero in matrimonio inter catholicos unus tantum parentum ad aliam Ecclesiam sui iuris transit, filii transeunt solummodo, si ambo parentes consenserunt; expleto vero decimo quarto aetatis anno filii ad pristinam Ecclesiam sui iuris redire possunt.

CAN. 35   Baptizati acatholici ad plenam

Fide, (C.G.), 8 mar. 1757; (C.G.), 12 mar. 1759; GREGORIUS XVI, ep. encycl. *Inter gravissimas,* 3 feb. 1832, §7; S.C. de Prop. Fide, decr. 20 nov. 1838; litt. 17 sep. 1842; PIUS IX, litt. ap. *Ubi inscrutabili,* 3 iul. 1848, 4; S.C. de Prop. Fide, decr. 6 oct. 1863, A), a), C), d); instr. (ad Del. Ap. Mesopotamiae), 15 iul. 1876; LEO XIII, litt. ap. *Orientalium,* 30 nov. 1894, VII, XI; S.C. de Prop. Fide, decr. 1 maii 1897, 2; ep. (ad Ep. auxil. Strigonien.), 27 apr. 1903, nn. 1, 5; ep. 15 iun. 1912; PIUS X, const. *Tradita ab antiquis,* 14 sep. 1912; S.C. pro Eccl. Orient., decr. 6 dec. 1928; decr. 23 nov. 1940. * Syn. Sciarfen. Syrorum, a. 1888, cap. III, art. IX, 8, 18–20; Syn. Alexandrin. Coptorum, a. 1898, sect. II, cap. I, art. V, XIX; Syn. Armen., a. 1911, 617, 627.

33: PIUS XII, m.p. *Cleri sanctitati,* 2 iun. 1957, can. 9. - CLEMENS VIII, instr. *Sanctissimus,* 31 aug. 1595, §5 "Latina uxor;" S.C.S. Off., decr. 26 nov. 1626; 13 feb. 1669; BENEDICTUS XIV, const. *Etsi pastoralis,* 26 maii 1742, §VIII, VII–X; S.C. de Prop. Fide, (C.G.),

12 mar. 1759, "Cum vero;" (C.G.), decr. 19 maii 1759; (C.G.), 25 iul. 1887, ad 2–4; LEO XIII, litt. ap. *Orientalium,* 30 nov. 1894, VIII; S.C. pro Eccl. Orient., decr. 24 maii 1930, art. 44; Pont. Comm. ad Cod. Can. Auth. Interpr., resp. 29 apr. 1940, I. * Syn. Sciarfen. Syrorum, a. 1888, cap. III, art. IX, 9–10; Syn. Alexandrin. Coptorum, a. 1898, sect. II, cap. I, art. V, XXIII; Syn. Armen., a. 1911, 622.

34: PIUS XII, m.p. *Cleri sanctitati,* 2 iun. 1957, can. 10.

35: Vat. II, decr. *Orientalium Ecclesiarum,* 4; PIUS XII, m.p. *Cleri sanctitati,* 2 iun. 1957, can. 11 §1. - BENEDICTUS XIV, ep. encycl. *Allatae sunt,* 26 iul. 1755, §19; S.C. de Prop. Fide, instr. (ad Del. Ap. Mesopotamiae), 15 iul. 1876; S.C. de Prop. Fide, (C.G.), 1 iun. 1885, ad 2. * Syn. Sciarfen. Syrorum, a. 1888, cap. III, art. IX, 21; Syn. Alexandrin. Coptorum, a. 1898, sect. II, cap. I, art. V, XX; Syn. Armen., a. 1911, 617, 626.

into full communion with the Catholic Church should retain and practice their own rite and should observe it everywhere in the world as much as humanly possible. Thus, they are to be ascribed to the Church *sui iuris* of the same rite with due regard for the right of approaching the Apostolic See in special cases of persons, communities or regions.

CAN. 36 Every transfer to another Church *sui iuris* takes effect at the moment a declaration is made before the local hierarch of the same Church or the proper pastor or a priest delegated by either of them and two witnesses, unless the rescript of the Apostolic See provides otherwise.

CAN. 37 Every ascription to a Church *sui iuris* or transfer to another Church *sui iuris* is to be recorded in the baptismal register of the parish where the baptism was celebrated, even if it is a parish of the Latin Church; if, however, this cannot be done, it is to be recorded in another document by the pastor in the parish archive of the Church *sui iuris* to which the ascription was made.

CAN. 38 Christian faithful of Eastern Churches, even if committed to the care of a hierarch or pastor of another Church *sui iuris*, nevertheless remain ascribed in their own Church *sui iuris*.

CHAPTER II. The Observation of Rites

CAN. 39 The rites of the Eastern Churches, as the patrimony of the whole Church of

communionem cum Ecclesia catholica convenientes proprium ubique terrarum retineant ritum eumque colant et pro viribus observent, proinde ascribantur Ecclesiae sui iuris eiusdem ritus salvo iure adeundi Sedem Apostolicam in casibus specialibus personarum, communitatum vel regionum.

CAN. 36 Omnis transitus ad aliam Ecclesiam sui iuris vim habet a momento declarationis factae coram eiusdem Ecclesiae Hierarcha loci vel parocho proprio aut sacerdote ab alterutro delegato et duobus testibus, nisi rescriptum Sedis Apostolicae aliud fert.

CAN. 37 Omnis ascriptio alicui Ecclesiae sui iuris vel transitus ad aliam Ecclesiam sui iuris in libro baptizatorum paroeciae, etiam, si casus fert, Ecclesiae latinae, ubi baptismus celebratus est, adnotetur; si vero fieri non potest, in alio documento in archivo paroeciali parochi proprii Ecclesiae sui iuris, cui ascriptio facta est, asservando.

CAN. 38 Christifideles Ecclesiarum orientalium, etsi curae Hierarchae vel parochi alterius Ecclesiae sui iuris commissi, tamen propriae Ecclesiae sui iuris permanent ascripti.

CAPUT II. De Ritibus Servandis

CAN. 39 Ritus Ecclesiarum orientalium ut universae Ecclesiae Christi patrimonium,

36: Pius XII, m.p. *Cleri sanctitati,* 2 iun. 1957, can. 13 §1.

37: Pius XII, m.p. *Cleri sanctitati,* 2 iun. 1957, can. 13 §2.

38: Pius XII, m.p. *Cleri sanctitati,* 2 iun. 1957, can. 14; Leo XIII, litt. ap. *Orientalium,* 30 nov. 1894, IX.

39: Vat. II, decr. *Orientalium Ecclesiarum,* 1–2; Pius XII, m.p. *Cleri Sanctitati,* 2 iun. 1957, can. 1 §1. - S. Leo IX, litt. *In terra pax,* 2 sep. 1053, XXIX; Innocentius III, litt. *Inter quatuor,* 2 aug. 1206, "Postulasti

postmodum;" (in Lat. IV), a. 1215, 4 "Licet Graecos;" Innocentius IV, ep. *Cum te de cetero,* 27 aug. 1247; ep. *Sub catholicae,* 6 mar. 1254, prooem.; Nicolaus III, instr. *Istud est memoriale,* 9 oct. 1278, "De ceteris;" Leo X, litt. ap. *Accepimus nuper,* 18 maii 1521; Paulus III, litt. ap. *Dudum,* 23 dec. 1534; Pius IV, const. *Romanus Pontifex,* 16 feb. 1564, §5; Clemens VIII, const. *Magnus Dominus,* 23 dec. 1595, §10; Paulus V, const. *Solet circumspecta,* 10 dec. 1615, §3; Benedictus XIV, ep. encycl. *Demandatam,* 24 dec. 1743, §3; ep. en-

Christ in which shines forth the tradition coming down from the Apostles through the Fathers, and which, in its variety, affirms the divine unity of the Catholic faith, are to be observed and promoted conscientiously.

CAN. 40 §1. Hierarchs who preside over Churches *sui iuris* and all other hierarchs are to care with the greatest diligence for the faithful and accurate observance of their own rite; nor are they to allow changes to be made in it except by reason of its organic progress; they are nonetheless to keep in mind mutual goodwill and the unity of Christians.

§2. Other clerics and members of institutes of consecrated life are bound to observe faithfully their own rite and to acquire always a greater knowledge and more complete practice of it.

§3. Also, the other Christian faithful are to foster the knowledge and appreciation of their own rite and are bound to observe it everywhere unless an exception is provided by the law.

CAN. 41 The Christian faithful of any

in quo elucet ea, quae ab Apostolis per Patres est traditio, et quod fidei catholicae divinam unitatem in varietate affirmat, religiose serventur et promoveantur.

CAN. 40 §1. Hierarchae, qui Ecclesiis sui iuris praesunt, aliique Hierarchae omnes studiosissime curent fidelem custodiam et accuratam observantiam proprii ritus nec in eo mutationes admittant nisi ratione eius organici progressus, prae oculis tamen habentes mutuam benevolentiam et unitatem christianorum.

§2. Ceteri clerici et sodales institutorum vitae consecratae omnes proprium ritum fideliter observare necnon eius in dies maiorem cognitionem perfectioremque usum acquirere tenentur.

§3. Ceteri quoque christifideles proprii ritus cognitionem et aestimationem foveant eumque ubique observare tenentur, nisi iure aliquid excipitur.

CAN. 41 Christifideles cuiusvis Ecclesi-

---

cycl. *Allatae sunt,* 26 iul. 1755, §§3, 6–19, 32; Pius VI, litt. encycl. *Catholicae Communionis,* 24 maii 1787; Pius IX, litt. *In suprema,* 6 ian. 1848, "Idem;" litt. ap. *Ecclesiam Christi,* 26 nov. 1853; all. *In Apostolicae Sedis,* 19 dec. 1853; const. *Romani Pontifices,* 6 ian. 1862; ep. *Non sine gravissimo,* 24 feb. 1870; Leo XIII, litt. ap. *Praeclara,* 20 iun. 1894, 7; litt. ap. *Orientalium,* 30 nov. 1894, prooem. * Syn. Sciarfen. Syrorum, a. 1888, cap. III, art. I; Syn. Leopolien. Ruthenorum, a. 1891, tit. IV, 2; Syn. Alexandrin. Coptorum, a. 1898, sect. II, cap. I, art. 1, 8; Syn. Armen., a. 1911, 613.

40 §1: Pius XII, m.p. *Cleri sanctitati,* 2 iun. 1957, cann. 1 §2, 4. - Paulus V, const. *Fraternitatis tuae,* 9 mar. 1610; S.C. de Prop. Fide, decr. 2 apr. 1669, II; decr. 15 mar. 1729; Benedictus XIII, litt. ap. *Quamquam sollicitudini,* 13 aug. 1729; Benedictus XIV, ep. encycl. *Demandatam,* 24 dec. 1743, §3; S.C. de Prop. Fide, instr. (ad Ep. Latinum Babylonen.), 23 sep. 1783, "Prorsus;" Pius VI, litt. encycl. *Catholicae Communionis,* 24 maii 1787; S.C. de Prop. Fide (pro Neg. Rit. Orient.), decr. 18 aug. 1913, art. 3; decr. 17 aug. 1914, art. 3; S.C. pro Eccl. Orient., decr. 1 mar. 1929, art. 3; decr. 24 maii 1930, art. 3; Vat. II, decr. *Orientalium Ecclesiarum,* 6. * Syn. Libanen. Maroni-

tarum, a. 1736, pars I, cap. III, 5; pars II, cap. I, 2; Syn. Leopolien. Ruthenorum, a. 1891, tit. IX, cap. II, 12; Syn. Alexandrin. Coptorum, a. 1898, sect. II, cap. I, art. I, 9; Syn. prov. Alba-Iulien. et Fagarasien. Rumenorum, a. 1900, tit. II, cap. I, §5; Syn. Armen., a. 1911, 611.

40 §2: Vat. II, decr. *Orientalium Ecclesiarum,* 6; Pius XII, m.p. *Cleri sanctitati,* 2 iun. 1957, can. 2 §1. - S.C. de Prop. Fide, reg. (pro Sacerd. Coptis), 15 mar. 1790, VIII; (C.G.), 11 dec. 1838, 17–19; S.C.S. Off., 14 iun. 1843; S.C. de Prop. Fide, decr. 6 oct. 1863, B), c), C), a); S.C.S. Off., decr. 6 sep. 1865; S.C. de Prop. Fide, (C.G.), 30 apr. 1866, 3. * Syn. Sciarfen. Syrorum, a. 1888, cap. III, art. IX, 1, 2, 6; Syn. Alexandrin. Coptorum, a. 1898, sect. II, cap. I, art. V, XI, XIII; Syn. Armen., a. 1911, 613, 619–620.

40 §3: Vat. II, decr. *Orientalium Ecclesiarum,* 6; Pius XII, m.p. *Cleri sanctitati,* 2 iun. 1957, can. 2 §2. - S.C. de Prop. Fide, instr. (ad Del. Ap. Aegypti), 30 apr. 1862. * Syn. Sciarfen. Syrorum, a. 1888, cap. XII, 4.

41: Vat. II, decr. *Orientalium Ecclesiarum,* 6. - Benedictus XV, m.p. *Orientis catholici,* 15 oct. 1917; Pius XI, litt. encycl. *Rerum orientalium,* 8 sep. 1928.

Church *sui iuris,* even the Latin Church, who by reason of their office, ministry, or function have frequent dealings with the Christian faithful of another Church *sui iuris,* are to have an accurate formation in the knowledge and practice of the rite of the same Church in keeping with the importance of the office, ministry or function they hold.

ae sui iuris, etiam Ecclesiae latinae, qui ratione officii, ministerii vel muneris frequentes cum christifidelibus alterius Ecclesiae sui iuris relationes habent, in cognitione et cultu ritus eiusdem Ecclesiae accurate pro gravitate officii, ministerii vel muneris, quod implent, instituantur

CAN. 42 Just as by the Lord's decision Saint Peter and the other Apostles constitute one college, so in a like manner the Roman Pontiff, the successor of Peter, and the bishops, successors of the apostles, are joined together.

CAN. 42 Sicut statuente Domino sanctus Petrus et ceteri Apostoli unum Collegium constituunt, pari ratione Romanus Pontifex, successor Petri, et Episcopi, successores Apostolorum, inter se coniunguntur.

CHAPTER I. **The Roman Pontiff**

CAPUT I. **De Romano Pontifice**

CAN. 43 The bishop of the Roman Church, in whom continues the office *(munus)*

CAN. 43 Ecclesiae Romanae Episcopus, in quo permanet munus a Domino singulari-

42: Vat. II, const. *Lumen gentium,* 22 "Sicut" et *Nota explicativa praevia* ad const. *Lumen gentium,* n. 1.

43: Vat. II, const. *Lumen gentium,* 20 "Episcopi," 22 "Collegium," 18 "Haec," 23 et *Nota explicativa praevia* ad const. *Lumen gentium,* n. 3; Pius XII, m.p. *Cleri sanctitati,* 2 iun. 1957, can. 162 §§1–2. - S. Soph. can. 1; S. Clemens, litt. *Propter subitas,* a. 90– 99; S. Soter, litt. a. c. 170, "A principio;" S. Victor, litt. a. c. 190, "Nos ergo;" S. Callistus I, decr. a. 217–222; S. Damasus, litt. *Quod vestra caritas,* a. 378/82; decr. *Post has omnes,* a. 382; S. Innocentius I, litt. *In requirendis,* 7 ian. 417; S. Zosimus, litt. *Quamvis Patrum,* 21 mar. 418; S. Bonifacius I, litt. *Inter caeteras,* a. 419; litt. *Retro maioribus,* 11 mar. 422; litt. *Manet beatum,* 11 mar. 422; litt. *Institutio universalis,* 11 mar. 422; S. Coelestinus I, litt. *Tandem malorum,* 15 mar. 432, " . . . Elaborate;" S. Xystus III, litt. *Si ecclesiastici corporis,* 17 sep. 433, "Haec sanctitatem;" S. Leo M., litt. *Omnis admonitio,* 12 ian. 444; litt. *Quantum dilectioni,* 21 iun. 445; litt. *Credebamus post,* [6] ian. 446; litt. *Quanta fraternitati,* a. 446; S. Simplicius, litt. *Cuperem quidem,* 10 ian. 476, "Haec, venerabilis;" S. Felix III, litt. *Postquam sanctae,* mar. 483; litt. *Olim nobis,* 5 oct. 484; litt. *Multa sunt,* a. 490; S. Gelasius, litt. *Quod plena cupimus,* 1 mar. 492; litt. *Famuli vestrae,* a. 494; litt. *Ex epistola,* a. 492–496, "Sed quolibet;" litt. *Valde mirati sumus,* 5 feb. 496; S. Anastasius II, litt. *Exordium pontificatus,* a. 496; S. Ioannes II, litt. *Inter claras,* 25 mar. 534; S. Gregorius M., litt. *Piis-*

simus atque, iun. 595; litt. *Suavissima mihi,* nov. 597; S. Agatho, litt. *Consideranti mihi,* mar. 680; litt. *Omnium bonorum,* mar. 680; Hadrianus I, litt. *Pastoralibus curis,* 26 mar. 785, "Porro post;" litt. *Deus qui dixit,* 26 oct. 785; S. Nicolaus I, litt. *Principatum divinae,* 25 sep. 860; litt. *Si serenissimi,* 18 mar. 862; litt. *Postquam beato,* 18 mar. 862; litt. *. . . et divinorum,* a. 863; litt. *Proposueramus quidem,* a. 865, ab ". . . Verumtamen;" litt. *Dici non potest,* 13 nov. 866; Iohannes VIII, litt. *Si ergo,* a. 873–875; litt. *Ad hanc quippe,* 16 apr. 878; litt. *Inter claras sapientiae,* 16 aug. 879, "Nunc itaque;" Stephanus V, litt. *Cum Deo propitio,* a. 885; litt. *Vestrae serenitatis,* a. 885; litt. *Quia te zelo,* a. 885; Iohannes X, litt. *Cum religio,* a. 925; S. Leo IX, litt. *In terra pax,* 2 sep. 1053, XXXII; litt. *Congratulamur vehementer,* a. 1052/53, "Quod ipse;" litt. *Quantas gratias,* a. 1054; S. Gregorius VII, litt. *Summae sedis specula,* 6 iun. 1080; Hadrianus IV, litt. *Ex quo,* a. 1154/1159, "Traditum est;" litt. *Inter omnia,* 13 iun. 1157; Alexander III, litt. *Apostolica sedes,* 27 sep. 1177; Coelestinus III, litt. *Fundavit Deus,* 20 feb. 1196; Innocentius III, litt. *Reprobata quondam,* 1–15 aug. 1198; litt. *Apostolicae Sedis auctoritas,* 8 ian. 1199; litt. *Apostolicae Sedis primatus,* 12 nov. 1199; litt. *Multae nobis,* 13 nov. 1199; litt. *Ex eo te radicatum,* 23 nov. 1199; litt. *Is Ecclesiam,* 24 nov. 1199; litt. *Non processit,* 1 iun. 1202; litt. *Licet apostolica sedes,* maii 1205; litt. *Licet hactenus,* 7 oct. 1207; litt. *Inconsutilis,* 30 aug. 1213; litt. *Licet olim,* 31 aug. 1213; Gregorius IX, ep. *Quia Christi,* 18 iul. 1231; Professio fidei (in Lugd. II) a

given by the Lord uniquely to Peter, the first of the Apostles, and to be transmitted to his successors, is the head of the college of bishops, the Vicar of Christ and pastor of the entire Church on earth. By virtue of his office *(munus)* he possesses supreme, full, immediate and universal ordinary power in the Church which he is always able to exercise freely.

CAN. 44 §1. The Roman Pontiff obtains supreme and full power in the Church by his acceptance of legitimate election together with episcopal ordination. Therefore, a person elected to the supreme pontificate who is marked with episcopal character obtains this power from the moment of acceptance. If the person elected lacks episcopal character, however, he is to be ordained a bishop immediately.

§2. If it happens that the Roman Pontiff resigns his office *(munus)*, it is required for validity that the resignation is made freely and properly manifested, but not that it is accepted by anyone.

CAN. 45 §1. By virtue of his office *(munus)*,

ter Petro, primo Apostolorum, concessum et successoribus eius transmittendum, Collegii Episcoporum est caput, Vicarius Christi atque universae Ecclesiae his in terris Pastor, qui ideo vi muneris sui suprema, plena, immediata et universali in Ecclesia gaudet potestate ordinaria, quam semper libere exercere potest.

CAN. 44 §1. Supremam et plenam in Ecclesia potestatem Romanus Pontifex obtinet legitima electione ab ipso acceptata una cum ordinatione episcopali; quare eandem potestatem obtinet a momento acceptationis electus ad summum pontificatum, qui episcopali charactere insignitus est; si vero charactere episcopali electus caret, statim ordinetur Episcopus.

§2. Si contingit, ut Romanus Pontifex muneri suo renuntiet, ad validitatem requiritur, ut renuntiatio libere fiat et rite manifestetur, non vero, ut a quopiam acceptetur.

CAN. 45 §1. Romanus Pontifex vi sui

Michaele Palaeologo Gregorio X oblata, a. 1274; BONIFACIUS VIII, bulla, *Unam Sanctam*, 18 nov. 1302; IOHANNES XXII, ep. *Salvator noster*, 29 apr. 1319; BENEDICTUS XII, a. 1341, prop. 90, Armenorum, damn.; EUGENIUS IV (in Flor.), const. *Laetentur coeli*, 6 iul. 1439, "Item;" PIUS IV, const. *Iniunctum nobis*, 13 nov. 1564, Professio fidei Trident., §1; GREGORIUS XIII, const *Sanctissimus*, a. 1575, Professio fidei Graecis praescr., §5; BENEDICTUS XIV, const. *Etsi pastoralis*, 26 maii 1742, §I, VI; ep. *Nuper ad nos*, 16 mar. 1743; Professio fidei Maronitis praescr., §5; S.C. de Prop. Fide, litt. encycl. (ad Patriarchas Orientis), 6 iun. 1803; PIUS IX, ep. encycl. *Amantissimus*, 8 apr. 1862, 1; litt. ap. *Reversurus*, 12 iul. 1867; ep. encycl. *Quartus supra*, 6 ian. 1873, 6; Vat. I, sess. IV, cap. III, *De vi et ratione primatus Romani pontificis*; LEO XIII, ep. encycl. *Satis cognitum*, 29 iun. 1896; S.C. de Prop. Fide, instr. 31 iul. 1902, I, i); S. PIUS X, litt. encycl. *Pascendi*, 8 sep. 1907; PIUS XI, litt. encycl. *Ecclesiam Dei*, 12 nov. 1923; litt. encycl. *Mortalium animos*, 6 ian. 1928; Vat. II, decr. *Orientalium Ecclesiarum*, 3; decr. *Unitatis redintegratio*, 2 "Ad hanc;" decr. *Christus Dominus*, 2 "In hac."

44 §1: PAULUS VI, const. ap. *Romano Pontifici eligendo*, 1 oct. 1975, 88; PIUS XII, m.p. *Cleri sanctitati*, 2 iun. 1957, can. 163. - PIUS X, litt. encycl. *Pascendi*, 8 sep. 1907; PIUS XII, const. ap. *Vacantis Apostolicae Sedis*, 8 dec. 1945, 101; IOANNES XXIII, m.p. *Summi Pontificis electio*, 5 sep. 1962, XIX.

44 §2: PIUS XII, m.p. *Cleri sanctitati*, 2 iun. 1957, can. 165.

45 §1: Vat. II, decr. *Christus Dominus*, 2, 8; PIUS XII, m.p. *Cleri sanctitati*, 2 iun. 1957, can. 162 §2. - GREGORIUS XIII, const. *Sanctissimus*, a. 1575, Professio fidei Graecis praescr., §5; BENEDICTUS XIV, const. *Etsi pastoralis*, 26 maii 1742, §I, VI; ep. *Nuper ad nos*, 16 mar. 1743, Professio fidei Maronitis praescr., §5; PIUS IX, litt. ap. *Reversurus*, 12 iul. 1867; Vat. I, sess. IV, cap. III, *De vi et ratione primatus Romani pontificis*; LEO XIII, ep. encycl. *Satis cognitum*, 29 iun. 1896; PIUS XI, litt. encycl. *Mortalium animos*, 6 ian. 1928, "Iamvero;" PIUS XI, litt. encycl. *Ad salutem*, 20 apr. 1930, "Alte;" litt. encycl. *Lux veritatis*, 25 dec. 1931, I; PIUS XII, litt. encycl. *Mystici Corporis*, 29 iun. 1943, "Non est" - "Itaque" et "Quoniam vero;" litt.

the Roman Pontiff not only possesses power over the entire Church but also obtains the primacy of ordinary power over all the eparchies and their groupings. Moreover, this primacy strengthens and protects the proper, ordinary and immediate power which bishops possess in the eparchy entrusted to their care.

§2. In fulfilling the office *(munus)* of the supreme pastor of the entire Church, the Roman Pontiff is always united in communion with the other bishops and with the entire Church. He nevertheless has the right, according to the needs of the Church, to determine the manner, whether personal or collegial, of exercising this office *(munus)*.

§3. No appeal or recourse is permitted against a sentence or decree of the Roman Pontiff.

CAN. 46 §1. Bishops assist the Roman Pontiff in exercising his office *(munus)*. They are able to render him cooperative assistance in various ways, among which is the synod of bishops. To assist him there are also cardinals, the Roman curia, pontifical legates and other persons and various institutions according to the needs of the times; all these persons and institutions fulfill the function entrusted to them in his name and by his authority for the good of all the Churches, according to the norms established by the Roman Pontiff himself.

muneris non modo in universam Ecclesiam potestate gaudet, sed et super omnes eparchias earumque coetus potestatis ordinariae obtinet principatum, quo quidem simul roboratur atque vindicatur potestas propria, ordinaria et immediata, quam in eparchiam suae curae commissam Episcopi habent.

§2. Romanus Pontifex in munere supremi universae Ecclesiae Pastoris explendo communione cum ceteris Episcopis immo et universa Ecclesia semper est coniunctus; ipsi ius tamen est determinare secundum necessitates Ecclesiae modum sive personalem sive collegialem huius muneris exercendi.

§3. Contra sententiam vel decretum Romani Pontificis non datur appellatio neque recursus.

CAN. 46 §1. In eius munere exercendo Romano Pontifici praesto sunt Episcopi, qui eidem cooperatricem operam dare possunt variis rationibus, inter quas est Synodus Episcoporum; auxilio praeterea ei sunt Patres Cardinales, Curia Romana, Legati pontificii necnon aliae personae itemque varia secundum necessitates temporum instituta; quae personae omnes et instituta nomine et auctoritate eiusdem munus sibi commissum explent in bonum omnium Ecclesiarum secundum normas ab ipso Romano Pontifice statutas.

---

encycl. *Sempiternus rex*, 8 sep. 1951, "Iuvat hic;" Vat. II, const. *Lumen gentium*, 13, 18, 22, 27; decr. *Orientalium Ecclesiarum*, 3.

45 §2: Vat. II, *Nota explicativa praevia* ad const. *Lumen gentium*, nn. 3–4; const. *Lumen gentium* 13, 18, 22–23, 27; decr. *Ad gentes*, 22 "Ad hoc;" Pius XII, litt. encycl. *Mystici Corporis*, 29 iun. 1943, "Non est" - "Ac praeterea;" litt. encycl. *Fidei donum*, 21 apr. 1957, II "Procul dubio."

45 §3: Pius XII, m.p. *Cleri sanctitati*, 2 iun. 1957, can. 173 §2. - S. Zosimus, litt. *Quamvis Patrum*, 21 mar. 418; S. Bonifacius I, litt. *Retro maioribus*, 11

mar. 422; S. Leo IX, litt. *In terra pax*, 2 sep. 1053, XXXII; Pius II, const. *Exsecrabilis*, 18 ian. 1459, §2; Iulius II, const. *Suscepti regiminis*, 1 iul. 1509, §1; Vat. I, sess. IV, cap. III, *De vi et ratione primatus Romani pontificis*, "Et quoniam."

46 §1: Vat. II, decr. *Christus Dominus*, 9–10; Pius XII, m.p. *Cleri sanctitati*, 2 iun. 1957, cann. 175–215; Paulus VI, m.p. *Apostolica sollicitudo*, 15 sep. 1965; m.p. *Pro comperto sane*, 6 aug. 1967; const. ap. *Regimini Ecclesiae universae*, 15 aug. 1967; m.p. *Sollicitudo omnium Ecclesiarum*, 24 iun. 1969; Ioannes Paulus II, const. ap. *Pastor Bonus*, 28 iun. 1988.

§2. The participation of patriarchs and of all the other hierarchs who preside over Churches *sui iuris* in the synod of bishops is regulated by special norms established by the Roman Pontiff himself.

CAN. 47   When the Roman see is vacant or entirely impeded, nothing is to be altered in the governance of the entire Church; the special laws issued for these circumstances, however, are to be observed.

CAN. 48   In this Code the term "Apostolic See" or "Holy See" applies not only to the Roman Pontiff but also, unless it is otherwise specified by the law or is clear from the nature of the matter, to the dicasteries and other institutions of the Roman curia.

§2. Patriarcharum ceterorumque Hierarcharum, qui Ecclesiis sui iuris praesunt, participatio in Synodo Episcoporum regitur normis specialibus ab ipso Romano Pontifice statutis.

CAN. 47   Sede Romana vacante aut prorsus impedita nihil innovetur in universae Ecclesiae regimine; serventur autem leges speciales pro eisdem adiunctis latae.

CAN. 48   Nomine Sedis Apostolicae vel Sanctae Sedis in hoc Codice veniunt non solum Romanus Pontifex, sed etiam, nisi aliter iure cavetur vel ex natura rei constat, Dicasteria aliaque Curiae Romanae instituta.

CHAPTER II.   The College of Bishops

CAN. 49   The college of bishops, whose head is the Roman Pontiff and whose members are bishops by virtue of sacramental ordination and hierarchical communion with the head of the college and its members, and in which the apostolic body continues in an unbroken manner, together with its head and never without this head, is also the subject of supreme and full power over the entire Church.

CAN. 50   §1. The college of bishops exer-

CAPUT II.   **De Collegio Episcoporum**

CAN. 49   Collegium Episcoporum, cuius caput est Romanus Pontifex cuiusque membra sunt Episcopi vi sacramentalis ordinationis et hierarchica communione cum Collegii capite et membris et in quo corpus apostolicum continuo perseverat, una cum capite suo et numquam sine hoc capite subiectum quoque supremae et plenae potestatis in universam Ecclesiam exsistit.

CAN. 50   §1. Potestatem in universam

---

46 §2: Secret. Status, *Ordo Synodi Episcoporum celebrandae,* 8 dec. 1966; Cons. pro Publ. Eccl. Neg., *Ordo Synodi Episcoporum celebrandae recognitus et auctus,* 24 iun. 1969, art. 5, §1, n. 1, a; §2, n. 1, a; §3, n. 1.

47: PIUS XII, m.p. *Cleri sanctitati,* 2 iun. 1957, can. 187; PIUS XII, const. ap. *Vacantis Apostolicae Sedis,* 8 dec. 1945, 1–28; IOANNES XXIII, m.p. *Summi Pontificis electio,* 5 sep. 1962, prooem.; PAULUS VI, const. ap. *Regimini Ecclesiae universae,* 15 aug. 1967, prooem. "Eadem;" const. ap. *Romano Pontifici eligendo,* 1 oct. 1975, 1–26; IOANNES PAULUS II, const. ap. *Pastor Bonus,* 28 iun. 1988, art. 6.

49: Vat. II, const. *Lumen gentium,* 22, 20, 23 et *Nota explicativa praevia* ad const. *Lumen gentium,* n.

2; decr. *Christus Dominus,* 4; decr. *Ad gentes,* 38 "Episcopi omnes." - Trid., sess. XXIII, *De ordine,* cap. 4, can. 8; Vat. I, sess. IV, cap. III, *De vi et ratione primatus Romani pontificis;* LEO XIII, ep. encycl. *Satis cognitum,* 29 ian. 1896, 25–30; PIUS XI, litt. encycl. *Ecclesiam Dei,* 12 nov. 1923, initio et "Itaque;" Synodus Episcoporum, *Elapso Oecumenico,* 22 oct. 1969, II–III.

50 §1: Vat. II, const. *Lumen gentium,* 22 "Collegium," 25 "Licet;" decr. *Christus Dominus,* 4; PIUS XII, m.p. *Cleri sanctitati,* 2 iun. 1957, can. 173 §1. - S. COELESTINUS I, litt. *Spiritus Sancti,* 8 maii 431; EUGENIUS IV (in Flor.), const. *Exsultate Deo,* 22 nov. 1439, §8.

cises power over the entire Church in a solemn manner in an ecumenical council.

§2. The college of bishops exercises this same power through the united action of the bishops dispersed in the world, which the Roman Pontiff has publicly declared or freely accepted as such so that it becomes a true collegial act.

§3. It is for the Roman Pontiff, according to the needs of the Church, to select and promote the ways by which the college of bishops can collegially exercise its function regarding the entire Church.

CAN. 51 §1. It is for the Roman Pontiff alone to convoke an ecumenical council, to preside over it personally or through others, to transfer, suspend or dissolve a council, and to confirm its decrees.

§2. It is for the Roman Pontiff to determine the matters to be treated in an ecumenical council and to establish the order to be observed in the same council. To the questions proposed by the Roman Pontiff, the fathers of the ecumenical council can add others which are to be approved by the Roman Pontiff.

CAN. 52 §1. All the bishops and only the bishops who are members of the college of bishops have the right and obligation to take part in an ecumenical council with a deliberative vote.

§2. Moreover, some others who are not bish-

Ecclesiam Collegium Episcoporum sollemni modo exercet in Concilio Oecumenico.

§2. Eandem potestatem Collegium Episcoporum exercet per unitam Episcoporum in mundo dispersorum actionem, quae ut talis a Romano Pontifice est indicta aut libere recepta ita, ut verus actus collegialis efficiatur.

§3. Romani Pontificis est secundum necessitates Ecclesiae seligere et promovere modos, quibus Collegium Episcoporum munus suum in universam Ecclesiam collegialiter exercet.

CAN. 51 §1. Solius Romani Pontificis est Concilium Oecumenicum convocare, eidem per se vel per alios praeesse, item Concilium transferre, suspendere vel dissolvere eiusque decreta confirmare.

§2. Eiusdem Romani Pontificis est res in Concilio Oecumenico tractandas determinare atque ordinem in eodem Concilio servandum constituere; propositis a Romano Pontifice quaestionibus Patres Concilii Oecumenici alias addere possunt ab eodem Romano Pontifice approbandas.

CAN. 52 §1. Ius et obligatio est omnibus et solis Episcopis, qui membra sunt Collegii Episcoporum, ut Concilio Oecumenico cum suffragio deliberativo intersint.

§2. Ad Concilium Oecumenicum insuper

---

50 §2: Vat. II, const. *Lumen gentium,* 22 "Collegium;" decr. *Christus Dominus,* 4 "Eadem."

50 §3: Vat. II, *Nota explicativa praevia* ad const. *Lumen gentium,* n. 3; const. *Lumen gentium,* 22.

51 §1: Vat. II, const. *Lumen gentium,* 22 "Collegium;" Pius XII, m.p. *Cleri sanctitati,* 2 iun. 1957, cann. 167, 172. - S. Damasus, litt. *Confidimus,* a. 372; S. Leo M., litt. *Quam vigilanter,* 21 mar. 453; S. Gelasius, litt. *Valde mirati sumus,* 5 feb. 496, "Quibus convenienter;" S. Nicolaus I, litt. *Postquam beato,* 18 mar. 862, "Quod dicitis;" litt. *Proposueramus quidem,* a. 865, ". . . Quamvis dixeritis;" Leo XIII, ep. encycl. *Satis cognitum,* 29 iun. 1896, 30.

51 §2: Pius XII, m.p. *Cleri sanctitati,* 2 iun. 1957,

cann. 167 §2, 171; Ioannes XXIII, const. ap. *Humanae salutis,* 25 dec. 1961, "Priusquam;" m.p. *Appropinquante Concilio,* 6 aug. 1962; all. 11 oct. 1962; Vat. II, const. *Lumen gentium,* 22 et *Nota explicativa praevia* ad const. *Lumen gentium,* n. 3.

52 §1: Pius XII, m.p. *Cleri sanctitati,* 2 iun. 1957, can. 168 §1 n. 2 et §2; Ioannes XXIII, const. ap. *Humanae salutis,* 25 dec. 1961, "Volumus."

52 §2: Pius XII, m.p. *Cleri sanctitati,* 2 iun. 1957, can. 168 §1 nn. 3–4 et §§2–3; Ioannes XXIII, const. *Humanae salutis,* 25 dec. 1961, "Volumus;" m.p. *Appropinquante Concilio,* 6 aug. 1962 et *Ordo Concilii Oecumenici celebrandi,* art. 1.

ops can be called to an ecumenical council by the supreme authority of the Church, to whom it belongs to determine their roles in the council.

CAN. 53   If the Apostolic See becomes vacant during the celebration of an ecumenical council, this council is interrupted by virtue of the law itself until the new Roman Pontiff orders the ecumenical council to be continued or dissolves it.

CAN. 54   §1. The decrees of an ecumenical council do not have obligatory force unless they are approved by the Roman Pontiff together with the council fathers, confirmed by him and promulgated at his order.

§2. To have obligatory force, decrees that the college of bishops issues when it places a truly collegial action in another way initiated or freely accepted by the Roman Pontiff need the same confirmation and promulgation.

aliquot, qui episcopali dignitate non sunt insigniti, vocari possunt a suprema Ecclesiae auctoritate, cuius est eorum partes in Concilio determinare.

CAN. 53 Si contingit, ut Sedes Apostolica durante Concilii Oecumenici celebratione vacet, ipso iure hoc intermittitur, donec novus Romanus Pontifex Concilium Oecumenicum continuari iusserit aut dissolverit.

CAN. 54 §1. Concilii Oecumenici decreta vim obligandi non habent, nisi una cum Concilii Patribus a Romano Pontifice approbata ab eodem sunt confirmata et eiusdem iussu promulgata.

§2. Hac confirmatione et promulgatione, vim obligandi ut habeant, etiam egent decreta, quae fert Collegium Episcoporum, cum actionem proprie collegialem ponit secundum alium a Romano Pontifice indictum vel libere receptum modum.

53: Pius XII, m.p. *Cleri sanctitati*, 2 iun. 1957, can. 174.

54 §1: Vat. II, const. *Lumen gentium*, 22 "Collegium;" Formula approbationis, confirmationis et promulgationis in Concilio Vaticano II adhibita;

Pius XII, m.p. *Cleri sanctitati*, 2 iun. 1957, cann. 167 §2, 172.

54 §2: Vat. II, const. *Lumen gentium*, 22 et *Nota explicativa praevia* ad const. *Lumen gentium*, n. 4.

CAN. 55 According to the most ancient tradition of the Church, already recognized by the first ecumenical councils, the patriarchal institution has flourished in the Church. Therefore, special honor is to be accorded to the patriarchs of the Eastern Churches, who each presides over his respective patriarchal Church as its father and head.

CAN. 56 A patriarch is a bishop who has power over all the bishops including metropolitans and other Christian faithful of the Church over which he presides, according to the norm of law approved by the supreme authority of the Church.

CAN. 57 §1. The erection, restoration, modification and suppression of patriarchal Churches are reserved to the supreme authority of the Church.

CAN. 55 Secundum antiquissimam Ecclesiae traditionem iam a primis Conciliis Oecumenicis agnitam viget in Ecclesia institutio patriarchalis; quare singulari honore prosequendi sunt Ecclesiarum orientalium Patriarchae, qui suae quisque Ecclesiae patriarchali tamquam pater et caput praesunt.

CAN. 56 Patriarcha est Episcopus, cui competit potestas in omnes Episcopos non exceptis Metropolitis ceterosque christifideles Ecclesiae, cui praeest, ad normam iuris a suprema Ecclesiae auctoritate approbati.

CAN. 57 §1. Erectio, restitutio, immutatio et suppressio Ecclesiarum patriarchalium supremae Ecclesiae auctoritati reservatur.

55: Vat. II, decr. *Orientalium Ecclesiarum*, 7, 9; const. *Lumen gentium*, 23 "Cura Evangelium;" Pius XII, m.p. *Cleri sanctitati*, 2 iun. 1957, can. 216 §1. - Nic. I, can. 6; Constantinop. I, cann. 2–3; Chalc. cann. 9, 28; Innocentius I, litt. *Et onus et honor*, a. c. 415; Constantinop. IV, cann. 17, 21; Innocentius III, litt. *Solitae benignitatis*, a. 1201/2, "Circa illum;" litt. *Quod die*, 1 iun. 1202, "Nos igitur;" litt. *Evangelica docente*, 21 ian. 1205, "Et ego videns;" litt. *Inter quatuor*, 2 aug. 1206; litt. *Scriptum est*, 18 aug. 1212; Lat. IV, cann. 5, 30; Flor., Decr. pro Graecis, 6 iul. 1439; Pius VII, litt. ap. *Simul ac spectabilium*, 8 iul. 1815; Leo XIII, m.p. *Auspicia rerum*, 19 mar. 1896, "Huiusce." * Syn. Libanen. Maronitarum, a. 1736, pars III, cap. VI, 1; Syn. Bekorkien. Maronitarum, a. 1856, sess. IV "In quanto;" Syn. Sciarfen. Syrorum, a. 1888, cap. V, art. XIII, §3, 3; cap. VII, art. III, 6 "His;" Syn. Alexandrin. Coptorum, a. 1898, sect. II, cap. III, art. VII, §4, XVI; sect.

III, cap. I, art. III; Syn. Armen., a. 1911, 154–155.

56: Vat. II, decr. *Orientalium Ecclesiarum*, 7 "Nomine vero;" Pius XII, m.p. *Cleri sanctitati*, 2 iun. 1957, can. 216 §2 n. 1. - Nic. I, can. 6; Constantinop. I, can. 2; Constantinop. IV, cann. 17, 21; Innocentius III, litt. *Quia divinae*, 4 ian. 1215, "Quae omnia;" Leo XIII, litt. ap. *Orientalium*, 30 nov. 1894, XIII. * Syn. Mar Isaaci Chaldaeorum, a. 410, can. 12; Syn. Sciarfen. Syrorum, a. 1888, cap. VIII, art. II "Post;" Syn. Armen., a. 1911, 182.

57 §1: Pius XII, m.p. *Cleri sanctitati*, 2 iun. 1957, can. 159. - Carth. cann. 17, 55; S. Innocentius I, litt. *Et onus et honor*, a. c. 415, "Nam quod;" S. Nicolaus I, litt. *Ad consulta vestra*, 13 nov. 866, LXXIII; Innocentius III, litt. *Rex regum*, 25 feb. 1204; Leo XII, const. ap. *Petrus Apostolorum princeps*, 15 aug. 1824; Leo XIII, litt. ap. *Christi Domini*, 26 nov. 1895, ab "Itaque."

§2. Only the supreme authority of the Church can modify the title that has been legitimately recognized or granted to each patriarchal Church.

§3. A patriarchal Church must have a permanent see for the residence of the patriarch inside its own territory, if possible in a principal city, from which the patriarch takes his title. This see cannot be transferred except for a most grave reason and with the consent of the synod of bishops of the patriarchal Church and having obtained the assent of the Roman Pontiff.

CAN. 58 Patriarchs of Eastern Churches precede all bishops of any degree everywhere in the world, with due regard for special norms of precedence established by the Roman Pontiff.

CAN. 59 §1. Patriarchs of Eastern Churches, even if some are later to others in time, are all equal by reason of patriarchal dignity with due regard for the precedence of honor among them.

§2. The order of precedence among the ancient patriarchal sees of the Eastern Churches is that in the first place comes the see of Constan-

§2. Titulum unicuique Ecclesiae patriarchali legitime agnitum vel concessum tantum suprema Ecclesiae auctoritas immutare potest.

§3. Ecclesia patriarchalis intra fines proprii territorii habere debet fixam sedem residentiae Patriarchae in civitate principe, ex qua Patriarcha titulum desumit, si fieri potest, constitutam; haec sedes transferri non potest nisi gravissima de causa, de consensu Synodi Episcoporum Ecclesiae patriarchalis et habito Romani Pontificis assensu.

CAN. 58 Patriarchae Ecclesiarum orientalium ubique terrarum praecedunt omnes Episcopos cuiuscumque gradus salvis normis specialibus de praecedentia a Romano Pontifice statutis.

CAN. 59 §1. Patriarchae Ecclesiarum orientalium, etsi alii aliis tempore posteriores, omnes aequales sunt ratione dignitatis patriarchalis salva inter se honoris praecedentia.

§2. Ordo praecedentiae inter antiquas Sedes patriarchales Ecclesiarum orientalium est, ut primo loco veniat Sedes Constanti-

---

57 §2: Pius XII, m.p. *Cleri sanctitati,* 2 iun. 1957, can. 217 §1. - S.C. de Prop. Fide, (C.P.), 28 ian. 1636.

57 §3: Pius XII, m.p. *Cleri sanctitati,* 2 iun. 1957, can. 218. - Benedictus XIV, litt. ap. *Quoniam, ven. frater,* 6 mar. 1754; S.C. de Prop. Fide, decr. 18 aug. 1816; Pius VII, breve, *In communi,* 1 nov. 1816, §4; S.C. de Prop. Fide, (C.G.), decr. 15 mar. 1819, 14; Gregorius XVI, litt. ap. *Non sine,* 24 dec. 1831. * Syn. Libanen. Maronitarum, a. 1736, pars. III, cap. VI, 5; Syn. Bekorkien. Maronitarum, a. 1790, s. 9; Syn. Sciarfen. Syrorum, a. 1888, cap. VII, art. III, 6 "Patriarchae."

58: Pius XII, m.p. *Cleri sanctitati,* 2 iun. 1957, cann. 185 §1 n. 21 et 215 §2; Pont. Comm. ad Red. Cod. Iur. Can. Orient., interpr. auth. 23 iun. 1958; Paulus VI, m.p. *Purpuratorum Patrum,* 11 feb. 1965, V; m.p. *Sollicitudo omnium Ecclesiarum,* 24 iun. 1969, XII, 4.

59 §1: Vat. II, decr. *Orientalium Ecclesiarum,* 8.

59 §2: Pius XII, m.p. *Cleri sanctitati,* 2 iun. 1957, can. 219 §1 n. 1. - Nic. I, cann. 6–7; Constantinop. I, can. 3; Chalc. can. 28; Carth. prooem. "Et cum recitaret;" S. Leo M., litt. *Quantum dilectioni tuae placet,* 11 iun. 453; S. Nicolaus I, litt. *Ad consulta vestra,* 13 nov. 866, XCII–XCIII; Constantinop. IV, can. 21; S. Leo IX, litt. *Congratulamur vehementer,* a. 1052/3, "Pro cuius;" Innocentius III, litt. *Praerogativa dilectionis,* 30 mar. 1205; litt. *Cum unigenitus,* 25 apr. 1205; litt. *Divisis aliis,* 15 maii 1205, "Vocavit enim;" litt. *Licet apostolica sedes,* maii 1205; litt. *Inter quatuor,* 24 nov. 1205; litt. *Inter quatuor,* 2 aug. 1206; litt. *Scriptum est,* 18 aug. 1212; litt. *Licet secundum,* 22 aug. 1212; Eugenius IV (in Flor.), const. *Laetentur coeli,* 6 iul. 1439, "Renovantes;" S.C. de Prop. Fide, litt. 15 iun. 1867; litt. 9 iul. 1894. * Syn. Sciarfen. Syrorum, a. 1888, cap. VII, art. III, 6.

tinople, after that Alexandria, then Antioch and then Jerusalem.

§3. Among the other patriarchs of the Eastern Churches, precedence is ordered according to the antiquity of the patriarchal see.

§4. Among the patriarchs of the Eastern Churches who have one and the same title but who preside over different patriarchal Churches, the one who was first promoted to the patriarchal dignity has precedence.

CAN. 60 §1. The patriarch, in churches that are designated for the Christian faithful of the Church over which he presides and in liturgical celebrations of the same Church, precedes other patriarchs, even if they are higher in virtue of title of the see or senior according to promotion.

§2. A patriarch who actually possesses patriarchal power precedes those who retain the title of a patriarchal see that they once held.

CAN. 61 A patriarch can have a procurator at the Apostolic See appointed personally by him with the prior assent of the Roman Pontiff.

CAN. 62 A patriarch who has resigned from his office retains his title and honors especially during liturgical celebrations and has the right that a dignified residence be assigned to him with his consent and that he be provided with resources drawn from the goods of the patriarchal Church, with which he can provide for a dignified support corresponding to his title, with due regard for the norm on precedence in can. 60, §2.

nopolitana, post eam Alexandrina, deinde Antiochena et denique Hierosolymitana.

§3. Inter ceteros Patriarchas Ecclesiarum orientalium praecedentia ordinatur secundum antiquitatem Sedis patriarchalis.

§4. Inter Patriarchas Ecclesiarum orientalium, qui unius eiusdemque sunt tituli, diversis tamen Ecclesiis patriarchalibus praesunt, praecedentiam obtinet, qui prius promotus est ad dignitatem patriarchalem.

CAN. 60 §1. Patriarcha in ecclesiis, quae christifidelibus Ecclesiae, cui praeest, destinatae sunt, et in celebrationibus liturgicis eiusdem Ecclesiae praecedit ceteros Patriarchas, etsi sunt Sedis titulo potiores vel promotione seniores.

§2. Patriarcha, qui actu potestatem patriarchalem obtinet, praecedit illos, qui titulum Sedis patriarchalis olim habitae adhuc servant.

CAN. 61 Patriarcha procuratorem apud Sedem Apostolicam habere potest a se de assensu praevio Romani Pontificis nominatum.

CAN. 62 Patriarcha, qui suo officio renuntiavit, suum titulum et honores in celebrationibus liturgicis praesertim servat itemque ius habet, ut sibi digna sedes habitationis de suo consensu assignetur atque media ex bonis Ecclesiae patriarchalis praebeantur, quibus suae sustentationi proprio titulo congruae provideatur firmo circa praecedentiam can. 60, §2.

---

59 §3: Pius XII, m.p. *Cleri sanctitati,* 2 iun. 1957, can. 219 §2.

59 §4: Pius XII, m.p. *Cleri sanctitati,* 2 iun. 1957, can. 219 §1 n. 2. - S.C. de Prop. Fide, litt. 15 iun. 1867.

60 §1: Pius XII, m.p. *Cleri sanctitati,* 2 iun. 1957, can. 219 §3 nn. 1–2.

60 §2: Pius XII, m.p. *Cleri sanctitati,* 2 iun. 1957, can. 219 §3 n. 2.

61: Pius XII, m.p. *Cleri sanctitati,* 2 iun. 1957, can. 220. - Clemens XI, litt. ap. *Singularis argumentum,* 21 maii 1712; S.C. de Prop. Fide, (C.G.), 17 feb. 1772, ad 1–2.

CHAPTER I. The Election of Patriarchs

CAN. 63 A patriarch is canonically elected in the synod of bishops of the patriarchal Church.

CAN. 64 The requirements for one to be considered suitable for the patriarchal dignity are to be specified by particular law, always with due regard for those that are prescribed in can. 180.

CAN. 65 §1. The synod of bishops of the patriarchal Church must be convened in the patriarchal residence or in another place designated by the administrator of the patriarchal Church with the consent of the permanent synod.

§2. The synod of bishops of the patriarchal Church must be convened within one month of the vacancy of the patriarchal see without prejudice to the particular law establishing a longer term, not, however, beyond two months.

CAN. 66 §1. In the election of the patriarch all and only the members of the synod of bishops of the patriarchal Church have an active vote.

§2. It is forbidden for anyone other than the

CAPUT I. **De Electione Patriarcharum**

CAN. 63 Patriarcha canonice eligitur in Synodo Episcoporum Ecclesiae patriarchalis.

CAN. 64 Iure particulari recenseantur ea, quae requiruntur, ut quis ad patriarchalem dignitatem idoneus habeatur, salvis semper eis, quae in can. 180 praescribuntur

CAN. 65 §1. Synodus Episcoporum Ecclesiae patriarchalis coadunari debet in patriarchali residentia aut in alio loco ab Administratore Ecclesiae patriarchalis de consensu Synodi permanentis designando.

§2. Synodi Episcoporum Ecclesiae patriarchalis coadunatio fieri debet intra mensem a Sedis patriarchalis vacatione computandum firmo iure particulari longius tempus, non autem ultra bimestre, statuente.

CAN. 66 §1. In electione Patriarchae voce activa fruuntur omnia et sola Synodi Episcoporum Ecclesiae patriarchalis membra.

§2. Vetitum est quemlibet alium praeter

63: Pius XII, m.p. *Cleri sanctitati*, 2 iun. 1957, can. 221. - S. Nicolaus I, litt. *Ad consulta vestra*, 13 nov. 866, LXXII; Constantinop. IV, can. 22; Clemens XIII, litt. *Succrescente zizania*, 1 aug. 1760; Pius IX, ep. encycl. *Quartus supra*, 6 ian. 1873, 25. * Syn. Libanen. Maronitarum, a. 1736, pars III, cap. VI, 7–8; Syn. Sciarfen. Syrorum, a. 1888, cap. VIII, art. II; Syn. Alexandrin. Coptorum, a. 1898, sect. III, cap. II, art. II; Syn Armen., a. 1911, 164–181.

64: Pius XII, m.p. *Cleri sanctitati*, 2 iun. 1957, can. 231. - Constantinop. IV, can. 5; Ioannes VIII, litt. *Experientia tuae prudentiae*, 16 aug. 879, "Et cum;" litt. *Inter claras sapientiae*, (16 aug.) 879, "Eo tamen."* Syn. Libanen. Maronitarum, a. 1736, pars III, cap. VI, 7, X; Syn. Sciarfen. Syrorum, a. 1888, cap. VIII, art. II; Syn. Alexandrin. Coptorum, a. 1898, sect. III, cap. II, art. II, 5; Syn Armen., a. 1911, 172–173.

65 §1: Pius XII, m.p. *Cleri sanctitati*, 2 iun. 1957, can. 222. * Syn. Libanen. Maronitarum, a. 1736, pars

III, cap. VI, 7, III; Syn. Sciarfen. Syrorum, a. 1888, cap. VIII, art. II "Patriarchae."

65 §2: Pius XII, m.p. *Cleri sanctitati*, 2 iun. 1957, can. 223. * Syn. Libanen. Maronitarum, a. 1736, pars III, cap. VI, 7, V.

66 §1: Pius XII, m.p. *Cleri sanctitati*, 2 iun. 1957, can. 224 §1. - S.C. de Prop. Fide, litt. (ad Patriarcham Syr.), 28 ian. 1792; Pius IX, litt. ap. *Reversurus*, 12 iul. 1867, 15; litt. ap. *Cum ecclesiastica*, 31 aug. 1869, I; ep. encycl. *Quartus supra*, 6 ian. 1873, 27. * Syn. Libanen. Maronitarum, a. 1736, pars III, cap. VI, 7, IV; Syn. Sciarfen. Syrorum, a. 1888, cap. VIII, art. II "Patriarchae;" Syn. Alexandrin. Coptorum, a. 1898, sect. III, cap. II, art. II, 3; Syn. Armen., a. 1911, 170.

66 §2: Pius XII, m.p. *Cleri sanctitati*, 2 iun. 1957, can. 224 §2. - Pius IX, litt. ap. *Reversurus*, 12 iul. 1867, 15. * Syn. Libanen. Maronitarum, a. 1736, pars III, cap. VI, 8.

members of the synod of bishops of the patriarchal Church to be present in the hall at the election of the patriarch, except those clerics who are employed as scrutineers or secretary of the synod, according to the norms of can. 71, §1.

§3. No one is allowed either before or during the synod of bishops of the patriarchal Church to interfere in any manner with the election of the patriarch.

CAN. 67   In the election of the patriarch cann. 947–957 must be observed, any contrary custom being reprobated unless it is provided otherwise by common law.

CAN. 68   §1. All bishops legitimately convoked are bound by a grave obligation to take part in the election.

§2. If a bishop considers himself to be prevented by a just impediment, he is to present his reasons in writing to the synod of bishops of the patriarchal Church. It is for the bishops present in the designated place at the beginning of the sessions of the synod to decide the legitimacy of the impediment.

CAN. 69   Once the convocation has been made canonically, if, after subtracting those prevented by a legitimate impediment, two-thirds of the bishops obliged to attend the synod of bishops of the patriarchal Church are present in the designated place, the synod is to be declared canonical and can proceed with the election.

CAN. 70   Unless particular law has estab-

Synodi Episcoporum Ecclesiae patriarchalis membra electioni Patriarchae in aula interesse eis clericis exceptis, qui ad normam can. 71, §1 ut scrutatores vel actuarius Synodi assumuntur.

§3. Nemini licet ullo modo sive ante Synodum Episcoporum Ecclesiae patriarchalis sive ea durante electioni Patriarchae se immiscere.

CAN. 67   In electione Patriarchae servari debent cann. 947–957 reprobata contraria consuetudine, nisi aliud iure communi statutum est.

CAN. 68   §1. Omnes Episcopi legitime convocati gravi obligatione tenentur, ut intersint electioni.

§2. Si quis Episcopus iusto impedimento se detineri existimat, scripto suas rationes aperiat Synodo Episcoporum Ecclesiae patriarchalis; de legitimitate impedimenti decidere est Episcoporum, qui in loco designato initio sessionum Synodi praesentes sunt.

CAN. 69   Convocatione canonice facta, si duae ex tribus partibus Episcoporum, qui tenentur Synodo Episcoporum Ecclesiae patriarchalis interesse, demptis eis, qui legitimo sunt impedimento detenti, in loco designato praesentes sunt, Synodus canonica declaretur et ad electionem procedi potest.

CAN. 70   Nisi ius particulare aliud statu-

66 §3: Pius XII, m.p. *Cleri sanctitati,* 2 iun. 1957, can. 224, §3. - Constantinop. IV, can. 22; S.C. de Prop. Fide, litt. (ad Patriarcham Syr.), 28 ian. 1792; Pius IX, litt. ap. *Reversurus,* 12 iul. 1867, 15; litt. ap. *Cum ecclesiastica,* 31 aug. 1869, I; ep. encycl. *Quartus supra,* 6 ian. 1873, 25–27. * Syn. Libanen. Maronitarum, a. 1736, pars III, cap. VI, 8.

67: Pius XII, m.p. *Cleri sanctitati,* 2 iun. 1957, cann. 226 §2, 229 §1. * Syn. Libanen. Maronitarum, a. 1736, pars III, cap. VI, 7, VIII, XI et XV; Syn. Sciarfen. Syrorum, a. 1888, cap. VIII, art. II; Syn. Alexandrin. Coptorum, a. 1898, sect. III, cap. II, art. II, 2;

Syn. Armen., a. 1911, 173.

68 §1: Pius XII, m.p. *Cleri sanctitati,* 2 iun. 1957, can. 225 §1. * Syn. Armen., a. 1911, 169.

68 §2: Pius XII, m.p. *Cleri sanctitati,* 2 iun. 1957, can. 225 §2.

69: Pius XII, m.p. *Cleri sanctitati,* 2 iun. 1957, can. 226 §1. * Syn. Libanen. Maronitarum, a. 1736, pars III, cap. VI, 7, VII.

70: Pius XII, m.p. *Cleri sanctitati,* 2 iun. 1957, can. 227. * Syn. Libanen. Maronitarum, a. 1736, pars III, cap. VI, 7, VI.

lished otherwise, the one who is elected from among those present in the first session is to preside over the synod of bishops of the patriarchal Church for the election of the patriarch; in the meantime, the presidency is reserved to the administrator of the patriarchal Church.

CAN. 71 §1. The positions of scrutineers and secretary can also be filled by priests and deacons according to the norm of particular law.

§2. All who are present at the synod are bound to the serious obligation of observing secrecy concerning those matters that directly or indirectly concern the balloting.

CAN. 72 §1. The one who has obtained two-thirds of the votes is elected, unless it is provided in particular law that after an appropriate number of ballotings, at least three, an absolute majority of the votes suffice and that the election be brought to an end according the norms of can. 183, §§3–4.

§2. If the election is not brought to completion within fifteen days from the opening of the synod of bishops of the patriarchal Church, the matter devolves to the Roman Pontiff.

CAN. 73 If the one who is elected is at least a legitimately proclaimed bishop, his election must immediately be intimated to him by the president, or if the president has been elected, by the bishop who is senior by episcopal ordination according to the accepted formula and formality of the patriarchal Church in the name of the entire synod of bishops of the patriarchal Church. If, however, the one who has been elected is not a bishop or has not yet been legit-

it, Synodo Episcoporum Ecclesiae patriarchalis de eligendo Patriarcha praeest, qui inter praesentes in prima sessione electus est; interim praesidentia Administratori Ecclesiae patriarchalis reservatur.

CAN. 71 §1. Scrutatores et actuarius ad normam iuris particularis assumi possunt etiam inter presbyteros et diaconos.

§2. Circa ea, quae scrutinia directe vel indirecte respiciunt, omnes, qui Synodo intersunt, gravi obligatione tenentur servandi secretum.

CAN. 72 §1. Is electus est, qui duas ex tribus partibus suffragiorum rettulit, nisi iure particulari statuitur, ut post congruum numerum scrutiniorum, saltem trium, sufficiat pars absolute maior suffragiorum et ad normam can. 183, §§3 et 4 electio perficiatur.

§2. Si electio intra quindecim dies ab inita Synodo Episcoporum Ecclesiae patriarchalis computandos non peragitur, res ad Romanum Pontificem devolvitur.

CAN. 73 Electio, si electus est saltem Episcopus legitime proclamatus, statim a praeside vel, si praeses est electus, ab Episcopo ordinatione episcopali seniore totius Synodi Episcoporum Ecclesiae patriarchalis nomine formula modoque in propria Ecclesia patriarchali receptis intimanda est electo; si vero electus nondum est Episcopus legitime proclamatus, secreto servato ab omnibus, qui quomodolibet electionis exitum

71 §1: Pius XII, m.p. *Cleri sanctitati,* 2 iun. 1957, can. 228 §1 n. 2. * Syn. Libanen. Maronitarum, a. 1736, pars III, cap. VI, 7, IV, XII, XVI; Syn. Armen., a. 1911, 173.

71 §2: Pius XII, m.p. *Cleri sanctitati,* 2 iun. 1957, can. 239. * Syn. Alexandrin. Coptorum, a. 1898, sect. III, cap. II, art. II, 11.

72 §1: Pius XII, m.p. *Cleri sanctitati,* 2 iun. 1957, can. 230 §§1–2. * Syn. Libanen. Maronitarum, a. 1736,

pars III, cap. VI, 7, XVII; Syn. Sciarfen. Syrorum, a. 1888, cap. VIII, art. II "Suffragiorum;" Syn. Armen., a. 1911, 172.

72 §2: Pius XII, m.p. *Cleri sanctitati,* 2 iun. 1957, can. 232. * Syn. Armen., a. 1911, 173.

73: Pius XII, m.p. *Cleri sanctitati,* 2 iun. 1957, cann. 233, 235 §3 nn. 1–2. * Syn. Libanen. Maronitarum, a. 1736, pars III, cap. VI, 7, XX–XXI; Syn. Armen., a. 1911, 175.

imately proclaimed bishop, observing secrecy on the part of all who in any way know the results of the election even toward the one elected, the synod of bishops of the patriarchal Church is suspended. The intimation is to be done if all the canonical requirements for the episcopal proclamation have been carried out.

CAN. 74 Within two days of useful time after being intimated, the one who has been elected must indicate whether he accepts the election. If he does not accept or does not respond within two days, he loses all the rights he acquired by the election.

CAN. 75 If the one who is elected accepted and is an ordained bishop, the synod of bishops of the patriarchal Church proceeds according to the prescriptions of the liturgical books with his proclamation and enthronement as patriarch; if the one who is elected is not yet an ordained bishop, the enthronement cannot be performed validly before the one who is elected receives episcopal ordination.

CAN. 76 §1. The synod of bishops of the patriarchal Church is to inform as soon as possible the Roman Pontiff by means of a synodal letter that the election and enthronement were canonically carried out and also of the profession of faith and promise to exercise his office faithfully made by the new patriarch in the presence of the synod according to the approved formulas. Synodal letters about the election are to be sent also to the patriarchs of the other Eastern Churches.

noverunt, etiam erga electum, Synodus Episcoporum Ecclesiae patriarchalis suspenditur et intimatio fiat, si omnia canonibus ad proclamationem episcopalem requisita peracta sunt.

CAN. 74 Electus intra biduum utile ab intimatione computandum manifestare debet, num electionem acceptet; si vero non acceptat aut si intra biduum non respondet, omne ius ex electione quaesitum amittit.

CAN. 75 Si electus acceptavit et est Episcopus ordinatus, Synodus Episcoporum Ecclesiae patriarchalis procedat secundum praescripta librorum liturgicorum ad eius ut Patriarchae proclamationem et inthronizationem; si vero electus nondum est Episcopus ordinatus, inthronizatio valide fieri non potest, antequam electus ordinationem episcopalem suscepit.

CAN. 76 §1. Synodus Episcoporum Ecclesiae patriarchalis per synodicas litteras Romanum Pontificem quam primum certiorem faciat de electione et de inthronizatione canonice peractis atque de professione fidei deque promissione fideliter officium suum implendi a novo Patriarcha coram Synodo secundum probatas formulas emissis; synodicae litterae de electione peracta mittantur quoque ad Patriarchas aliarum Ecclesiarum orientalium.

74: Pius XII, m.p. *Cleri sanctitati*, 2 iun. 1957, can. 234.

75: Pius XII, m.p. *Cleri sanctitati*, 2 iun. 1957, can. 235. - Clemens XI, const. ap. *Cum nos,* 21 mar. 1706; S.C. de Prop. Fide, decr. 15 mar. 1729; Pius IX, litt. ap. *Reversurus,* 12 iul. 1867, 16; litt. ap. *Cum ecclesiastica,* 31 aug. 1869, II; litt. encycl. *Quartus supra,* 6 ian. 1873, 33–34; S.C. de Prop. Fide, 30 oct. 1894. * Syn.

Libanen. Maronitarum, a. 1736, pars II, cap. XIV, 47; pars III, cap. VI, 7, XX; Syn. Sciarfen. Syrorum, a. 1888, cap. VIII, art. II ab "Si electus;" Syn. Armen., a. 1911, 175, 180–181.

76 §1: Pius XII, m.p. *Cleri sanctitati,* 2 iun. 1957, cann. 236 §2, 235 §3 n. 1 et §4. - Clemens XI, const. ap. *Cum nos,* 21 mar. 1706.

§2. The new patriarch must request as soon as possible ecclesiastical communion from the Roman Pontiff by means of a letter signed in his own hand.

CAN. 77 §1. The patriarch, though canonically elected, validly exercises his office only after his enthronement, by which he obtains his office with the full effects of law.

§2. The patriarch is not to convoke the synod of bishops of the patriarchal Church nor to ordain bishops before he receives ecclesiastical communion from the Roman Pontiff.

CHAPTER II. The Rights and Obligations of Patriarchs

CAN. 78 §1. The power that the patriarch possesses, according to the norm of the canons and legitimate customs, over bishops and other Christian faithful of the Church over which he presides is ordinary and proper, but personal; therefore, the patriarch cannot constitute a vicar for the entire patriarchal Church nor can he delegate his power to someone for all cases.

§2. The power of the patriarch is exercised

§2. Novus Patriarcha per litteras manu propria subscriptas quam primum expostulare debet a Romano Pontifice ecclesiasticam communionem.

CAN. 77 §1. Patriarcha canonice electus valide exercet suum officium tantummodo ab inthronizatione, qua pleno iure officium obtinet.

§2. Patriarcha, antequam communionem ecclesiasticam a Romano Pontifice accepit, ne Synodum Episcoporum Ecclesiae patriarchalis convocet neque Episcopos ordinet.

CAPUT II. De Iuribus et Obligationibus Patriarcharum

CAN. 78 §1. Potestas, quae Patriarchae ad normam canonum et legitimarum consuetudinum in Episcopos ceterosque christifideles Ecclesiae, cui praeest, competit, est ordinaria et propria, sed ita personalis, ut non possit Vicarium pro tota Ecclesia patriarchali constituere aut potestatem suam alicui ad universitatem casuum delegare.

§2. Potestas Patriarchae exerceri valide

---

76 §2: Pius XII, m.p. *Cleri sanctitati*, 2 iun. 1957, can. 236 §1. - S. Leo IV, litt. *Vidimus animi*, a. 853; S. Nicolaus I, litt. *Ad consulta vestra*, a. 866, LXXIII; Innocentius III, litt. *Quia nobis*, 27 nov. 1202, "Nos ergo;" litt. *Apostolica sedes*, 27 nov. 1202, "Petisti vero;" litt. *Receptis litteris*, 10 sep. 1203, "Nos autem;" litt. *Rex regum*, 25 feb. 1204, "Cum igitur;" litt. *Licet ex eo*, 25 feb. 1204; Pius IV, const. ap. *Venerabilem*, 1 sep. 1562; S.C. de Prop. Fide, (C.P.), 28 ian. 1636, 2–3; Clemens XI, litt. ap. *Divinae bonitatis*, 20 iun. 1715, §3; Benedictus XIV, litt. ap. *Dum nobiscum*, 29 feb. 1744, §1; all. *Ecce iam*, a. 1754, "Libentissime;" Clemens XIII, litt. ap. *Delatis ad nos*, 1 aug. 1760, §5; S.C. de Prop. Fide, litt. (ad Vic. Sedis patriarch. Syrorum), 25 sep. 1802; (C.G.), 1 dec. 1837; Pius IX, litt. ap. *Reversurus*, 12 iul. 1867, 16; litt. ap. *Cum ecclesiastica*, 31 aug. 1869, II; ep. encycl. *Quartus supra*, 6 ian. 1873, 33–34. * Syn. Libanen. Maronitarum, a. 1736, pars III, cap. VI, 7, XXII; Syn. Sciarfen. Syrorum, a. 1888, cap. VII, art. III, 6, 1; cap. VIII, art. II "Post;"

Syn. Alexandrin. Coptorum, a. 1898, sect. III, cap. II, art. II, 9, 13; Syn. Armen., a. 1911, 177, 201.

77 §1: Pius XII, m.p. *Cleri sanctitati*, 2 iun. 1957, can. 238 §1. * Syn. Sciarfen. Syrorum, a. 1888, cap. VIII, art. II "Post;" Syn. Armen., a. 1911, 180.

77 §2: Pius XII, m.p. *Cleri sanctitati*, 2 iun. 1957, can. 238 §3. - Innocentius III, const. ap. *Quia divinae*, 4 ian. 1215; S.C. de Prop. Fide, (C.G.), 1 dec. 1837; Pius IX, litt. ap. *Reversurus*, 12 iul. 1867, 17; litt. ap. *Cum ecclesiastica*, 31 aug. 1869, III; S.C. de Prop. Fide, litt. 30 oct. 1894. * Syn. Libanen. Maronitarum, a. 1736, pars III, cap. VI, 7, XXII; Syn. Armen., a. 1911, 225.

78 §1: Pius XII, m.p. *Cleri sanctitati*, 2 iun. 1957, cann. 240 §1, 241. - Nic. I, can. 6; Constantinop. I, can. 2; S.C. de Prop. Fide, (C.G.), 17 feb. 1772; (C.G.), 15 sep. 1777. * Syn. Sciarfen. Syrorum, a. 1888, cap. VII, art. III; Syn. Alexandrin. Coptorum, a. 1898, sect. III, cap. I, art. III; Syn. Armen., a. 1911, 182.

78 §2: Vat. II, decr. *Orientalium Ecclesiarum*, 9 "Haec;" decr. *Christus Dominus*, 23, 3; Pius XII, m.p.

validly only within the territorial boundaries of the patriarchal Church unless the nature of the matter or the common or particular law approved by the Roman Pontiff establishes otherwise.

CAN. 79   The patriarch represents the patriarchal Church in all its juridic affairs.

CAN. 80   It is for the patriarch:

1° to exercise the rights and to fulfill the obligations of a metropolitan in all places where provinces have not been erected;

2° to supply for the negligence of metropolitans according to the norm of law;

3° during the vacancy of a metropolitan see to exercise the rights and to fulfill the obligations of a metropolitan in the entire province;

4° to warn a metropolitan who has not appointed a finance officer according to can. 262, §1; if the warning has been to no avail, to appoint personally the finance officer.

CAN. 81   The acts of the Roman Pontiff regarding the patriarchal Church are to be made known through the patriarch to the eparchial bishops or others concerned, unless in some case the Apostolic See has taken measures directly.

CAN. 82   §1. By his own right the patriarch can:

potest intra fines territorii Ecclesiae patriarchalis tantum, nisi aliter ex natura rei aut iure communi vel particulari a Romano Pontifice approbato constat.

CAN. 79   In omnibus negotiis iuridicis Ecclesiae patriarchalis Patriarcha eiusdem personam gerit.

CAN. 80   Patriarchae est:

1° Metropolitae iura exercere et obligationes implere in omnibus locis, ubi provinciae erectae non sunt;

2° neglegentiam Metropolitarum ad normam iuris supplere;

3° sede metropolitana vacante Metropolitae iura exercere et obligationes implere in tota provincia;

4° Metropolitam, qui oeconomum ad normam can. 262, §1 non nominavit, monere; monitione in cassum facta oeconomum per se ipsum nominare.

CAN. 81   Romani Pontificis acta ad Ecclesiam patriarchalem pertinentia Episcopis eparchialibus aliisve, ad quos pertinent, per Patriarcham nota fiant, nisi Sedes Apostolica in casu directe providit.

CAN. 82   §1. Patriarcha proprio iure potest:

Cleri sanctitati, 2 iun. 1957, cann. 240 §2, 216 §2 n. 2, 260 §1 n. 2 d); S.C. pro Eccl. Orient., decl. 25 mar. 1970; IOANNES PAULUS II, litt. (ad Archiep. Maiorem Ucrainorum), 5 feb. 1980; decisio de qua in litt. (ad Vice-Praesidem Pont. Comm. Cod. Iur. Can. Orient. Recogn.), 10 nov. 1988. - Apost. can. 34; Nic. I, can. 6; Constantinop. I, can. 2; Eph. can. 8; Chalc. can. 28; Constantinop. IV, can. 23. * Syn. Sciarfen. Syrorum, a. 1888, cap. VII, art. III, 6, 19).

80 1°: PIUS XII, m.p. *Cleri sanctitati*, 2 iun. 1957, can. 242. * Syn. Libanen. Maronitarum, a. 1736, pars III, cap. IV, 14; Syn. Armen., a. 1911, 184.

80 2°: PIUS XII, m.p. *Cleri sanctitati*, 2 iun. 1957, can. 258 n. 2.

80 3°: PIUS XII, m.p. *Cleri sanctitati*, 2 iun. 1957, can. 258 n. 3.

80 4°: PIUS XII, m.p. *Cleri sanctitati*, 2 iun. 1957, can. 280 §2. - Nic. II, can. 11.

81: PIUS XII, m.p. *Cleri sanctitati*, 2 iun. 1957, can. 244 §1. - S.C. de Prop. Fide, instr. (ad Patr. et Epp. Ritus Graeco-Melchit.), 29 maii 1789, n. 18. * Syn. Libanen. Maronitarum, a. 1736, pars I, cap. I, 10; Syn. Sciarfen. Syrorum, a. 1888, cap. VII, art. II, II; Syn. Alexandrin. Coptorum, a. 1898, sect. III, cap. I, art. II, 5, II.

82 §1: PIUS XII, m.p. *Cleri sanctitati*, 2 iun. 1957, can. 245 §1. - S. GENNADIUS CP., ep. ad Martyrium Ep. Antiochenum. * Syn. Sciarfen. Syrorum, a. 1888, cap. VII, art. III, 6, 5); Syn. Alexandrin. Coptorum, a. 1898, sect. III, cap. I, art. III, IV, 5); Syn. Armen., a. 1911, 185.

1° within the scope of his competence, issue decrees that determine more precisely the methods to be observed in applying the law or urge the observance of laws;

2° direct instructions to the Christian faithful of the entire Church over which he presides in order to explain sound doctrine, foster piety, correct abuses, and approve and recommend practices that foster the spiritual welfare of the Christian faithful;

3° issue encyclical letters to the entire Church over which he presides concerning questions regarding his own Church and rite.

§2. The patriarch can issue orders to bishops and other clerics as well as members of institutes of consecrated life of the entire Church over which he presides to have his decrees, instructions, and encyclical letters read and displayed publicly in their churches or houses.

§3. The patriarch will not fail to hear the permanent synod, the synod of bishops of the patriarchal Church, or even the patriarchal assembly in matters that concern the entire Church over which he presides or more serious affairs.

CAN. 83 §1. With due regard for the right and obligation of the eparchial bishop of canonically visiting his own eparchy, the patriarch has the right and obligation to conduct a pastoral visitation of the same eparchy at those times established by particular law.

§2. For serious reasons and with the consent of the permanent synod, the patriarch can visit

1° decreta ferre intra ambitum suae competentiae, quibus pressius determinantur modi in lege applicanda servandi aut legum observantia urgetur;

2° instructiones ad christifideles totius Ecclesiae, cui praeest, dirigere ad sanam doctrinam exponendam, pietatem fovendam, abusus corrigendos et exercitia, quae spirituale christifidelium bonum foveant, approbanda et commendanda;

3° litteras encyclicas toti Ecclesiae, cui praeest, dare circa quaestiones propriam Ecclesiam et ritum respicientes.

§2. Patriarcha Episcopis ceterisque clericis necnon sodalibus institutorum vitae consecratae totius Ecclesiae, cui praeest, praecipere potest, ut sua decreta, instructiones atque litterae encyclicae in propriis ecclesiis vel domibus publice legantur et exponantur.

§3. Patriarcha in omnibus, quae totam Ecclesiam, cui praeest, vel graviora negotia respiciunt, ne omittat audire Synodum permanentem vel Synodum Episcoporum Ecclesiae patriarchalis vel etiam conventum patriarchalem.

CAN. 83 §1. Salvo iure et obligatione Episcopi eparchialis canonice visitandi propriam eparchiam Patriarcha ius et obligationem habet in eadem eparchia visitationem pastoralem peragendi temporibus iure particulari statutis.

§2. Patriarcha potest gravi de causa et de consensu Synodi permanentis aliquam

---

82 §2: Pius XII, m.p. *Cleri sanctitati,* 2 iun. 1957, can. 245 §2.

82 §3: Apost. can. 34.

83 §1: Pius XII, m.p. *Cleri sanctitati,* 2 iun. 1957, can. 246 §1. - Benedictus XIV, const. *Apostolica praedecessorum,* 14 feb. 1742. * Syn. Libanen. Maronitarum, a. 1736, pars III, cap. VI, 2, 11; Syn. Sciar-

fen. Syrorum, a. 1888, cap. VII, art. III, 6, 17); Syn. Alexandrin. Coptorum, a. 1898, sect. III, cap. I, art. III, IV, 6); Syn. Armen., a. 1911, 195, 200, n. 4.

83 §2: Pius XII, m.p. *Cleri sanctitati,* 2 iun. 1957, can. 246 §§2–3. - Constantinop. IV, can. 19; S.C. de Prop. Fide, (C.G.), 17 feb. 1772, 7.

a church, city, or eparchy either personally or through another bishop; during this visitation he can do all those things the eparchial bishop can do during a canonical visitation.

CAN. 84 §1. The patriarch is to take the greatest care that both he and the eparchial bishops of the Church over which he presides, after consultation with the patriarchs and eparchial bishops of the other Churches *sui iuris* who exercise their power in the same territory especially in the assemblies foreseen by law, promote a unity of action among themselves and with all the other Christian faithful of any Church *sui iuris,* and, through concerted efforts, sustain common works that intend to promote more expeditiously the good of religion, to protect more effectively ecclesiastical discipline, and also to foster more harmoniously the unity of all Christians.

§2. The patriarch is also to encourage frequent meetings among the hierarchs and all the other Christian faithful as he, in his discretion, deems beneficial to summon to discuss pastoral matters and other affairs that concern the entire Church over which he presides or a certain province or region.

CAN. 85 §1. For a serious reason the patriarch can, with the consent of the synod of bishops of the patriarchal Church and having consulted the Apostolic See, erect provinces and eparchies, modify their boundaries, unite, divide, and suppress them, and modify their hierarchical status and transfer eparchial sees.

ecclesiam, civitatem, eparchiam per se aut per alium Episcopum visitare et tempore huius visitationis omnia, quae in visitatione canonica Episcopo eparchiali competunt, peragere.

CAN. 84 §1. Maxime curet Patriarcha, ut sive ipse sive Episcopi eparchiales Ecclesiae, cui praeest, collatis consiliis, praesertim in conventibus iure praevisis, cum Patriarchis ac Episcopis eparchialibus aliarum Ecclesiarum sui iuris, qui in eodem territorio potestatem suam exercent, unitatem actionis inter se ceterosque christifideles cuiuscumque Ecclesiae sui iuris promoveant et viribus unitis communia adiuvent opera ad bonum religionis expeditius promovendum, ad disciplinam ecclesiasticam efficacius tuendam necnon ad omnium christianorum unitatem concorditer fovendam.

§2. Foveat quoque Patriarcha frequentes collationes inter Hierarchas ceterosque christifideles, quos pro sua prudentia convocandos censet, de rebus pastoralibus aliisque negotiis, quae aut totam Ecclesiam, cui praeest, aut aliquam provinciam vel regionem respiciunt.

CAN. 85 §1. Patriarcha gravi de causa, de consensu Synodi Episcoporum Ecclesiae patriarchalis et consulta Sede Apostolica potest provincias et eparchias erigere, aliter circumscribere, unire, dividere, supprimere earumque gradum hierarchicum immutare et sedem eparchialem transferre.

---

84 §1: Vat. II, decr. *Orientalium Ecclesiarum,* 4; decr. *Christus Dominus,* 38, 6); Pius XII, m.p. *Cleri sanctitati,* 2 iun. 1957, can. 4.

84 §2: Pius XII, m.p. *Cleri sanctitati,* 2 iun. 1957, can. 247. * Syn. Armen., a. 1911, 235.

85 §1: Vat. II, decr. *Orientalium Ecclesiarum,* 9

"Haec;" Pius XII, m.p. *Cleri sanctitati,* 2 iun. 1957, can. 248 §1 n. 1. - Sard. can. 1; Carth. cann. 56, 98, 118; S.C. de Prop. Fide, decr. 20 iul. 1760; instr. (ad Patr. et Epp. Ritus Graeco-Melchit.), 29 maii 1789, n. 7; 18 sep. 1843, dub. 2. * Syn. Libanen. Maronitarum, a. 1736, pars III, cap. IV, 21; Syn. Armen., a. 1911, 189.

§2. The patriarch, with the consent of the synod of bishops of the patriarchal Church, is competent:

1° to give to an eparchial bishop a coadjutor bishop or auxiliary bishop, observing cann. 181, §1 and 182–187 and 212;

2° for a grave reason, to transfer a metropolitan, eparchial bishop or titular bishop to another metropolitan, eparchial or titular see; if any of these refuse, the synod of bishops of the patriarchal Church is to resolve the matter or defer it to the Roman Pontiff.

§3. The patriarch, with the consent of the permanent synod, can erect, modify and suppress exarchies.

§4. The patriarch is to inform the Apostolic See of these decisions as soon as possible.

CAN. 86   §1. The patriarch is competent:

1° to give to a metropolitan or bishop a patriarchal letter of canonical provision;

2° to ordain metropolitans either personally or, if impeded, through other bishops, and, if particular law so provides, also to ordain all bishops;

3° to enthrone a metropolitan after episcopal ordination.

§2. Patriarchae de consensu Synodi Episcoporum Ecclesiae patriarchalis competit:

1° Episcopo eparchiali Episcopum coadiutorem vel Episcopum auxiliarem dare servatis cann. 181, §1, 182–187 et 212;

2° gravi de causa Metropolitam vel Episcopum eparchialem aut titularem ad aliam sedem metropolitanam, eparchialem vel titularem transferre; si quis renuit, Synodus Episcoporum Ecclesiae patriarchalis rem dirimat vel ad Romanum Pontificem deferat.

§3. Patriarcha de consensu Synodi permanentis potest exarchias erigere, immutare et supprimere.

§4. De his decisionibus Patriarcha quam primum Sedem Apostolicam certiorem faciat.

CAN. 86   §1. Patriarchae competit:

1° Metropolitae vel Episcopo litteras patriarchales de provisione canonica dare;

2° ordinare Metropolitas per se vel, si impeditus est, per alios Episcopos necnon, si ius particulare ita fert, ordinare etiam omnes Episcopos;

3° Metropolitam post ordinationem episcopalem inthronizare.

---

85 §2, 1°: Pius XII, m.p. *Cleri sanctitati,* 2 iun. 1957, can. 248 §1 n. 4. - S.C. de Prop. Fide, (C.P.), 28 aug. 1643, n. 4. * Syn. Libanen. Maronitarum, a. 1736, pars III, cap. IV, 35; cap. VI, 2, 7; Syn. Armen., a. 1911, 193.

85 §2, 2°: Pius XII, m.p. *Cleri sanctitati,* 2 iun. 1957, can. 248 §1 n. 2. - Apost. can. 14; Benedictus XIV, const. *Apostolica praedecessorum,* 14 feb. 1742. * Syn. Libanen. Maronitarum, a. 1736, pars III, cap. IV, 22; cap. VI, 2, 7; Syn. Sciarfen. Syrorum, a. 1888, cap. VII, art. III, 6, 12); Syn. Armen., a. 1911, 192.

85 §3: Pius XII, m.p. *Cleri sanctitati,* 2 iun. 1957, can. 248 §2.

85 §4: Pius XII, m.p. *Cleri sanctitati,* 2 iun. 1957, can. 248 §3.

86 §1, 1°: Pius XII, m.p. *Cleri sanctitati,* 2 iun. 1957, can. 256 §1 n. 2. - Iulius III, const. ap. *Cum nos*

nuper, 28 apr. 1553, "Nec non;" Leo XIII, litt. ap. *Ex officio supremi,* 1 oct. 1894. * Syn. Armen., a. 1911, 242.

86 §1, 2°: Pius XII, m.p. *Cleri sanctitati,* 2 iun. 1957, can. 256 §1 n. 1. - Constantinop. IV, can. 17; Innocentius I, litt. *Et onus et honor,* a. c. 415; Iulius III, const. ap. *Cum nos nuper,* 28 apr. 1553, "Nec non;" Benedictus XIV, const. *Apostolica praedecessorum,* 14 feb. 1742; Leo XIII, litt. ap. *Ex officio supremi,* 1 oct. 1894. * Syn. Sisen. Armenorum, a. 1342; Syn. Libanen. Maronitarum, a. 1736, pars III, cap. IV, 15, 17; cap. VI, 2, 6; Syn. Sciarfen. Syrorum, a. 1888, cap. VIII, art. IV, 2 "Patriarcha;" cap. V, art. XIII, §10, 6; cap. VII, art. III, 6, 7); Syn. Alexandrin. Coptorum, a. 1898, sect. III, cap. I, art. III, 2, IV, 2); cap. II, art. IV, 11; Syn. Armen., a. 1911, 183, n. 2 et 244.

86 §1, 3°: Pius XII, m.p. *Cleri sanctitati,* 2 iun. 1957, can. 256 §1 n. 3.

§2. By virtue of the law itself, the faculty is given to the patriarch to ordain and enthrone metropolitans and other bishops of the Church over which he presides who have been appointed by the Roman Pontiff outside the territorial boundaries of that Church, unless in a special case it is expressly established otherwise.

§3. Episcopal ordination and enthronement must take place within the time limits determined by law; the patriarchal letter of canonical provision is to be issued within ten days of the proclamation of the election; the Apostolic See is to be informed as soon as possible of the episcopal ordination and enthronement.

CAN. 87   The patriarch can see that certain bishops, though not more than three, are elected for the patriarchal curia by the synod of bishops of the patriarchal Church according to the norms of cann. 181, §1 and 182–187 as long as provision is made for their support; he confers on them an office with a residence in the patriarchal curia and can also ordain them after having fulfilled all the requirements for the episcopal proclamation.

CAN. 88   §1. The bishops of the patriarchal Church must show honor and respect *(obsequium)* to the patriarch and must render due obedience to him; the patriarch shall show to these bishops due reverence and treat them with fraternal charity.

§2. The patriarch is to seek to resolve controversies that perhaps might arise among the

§2. Ipso iure Patriarchae facultas datur Metropolitas ceterosque Episcopos Ecclesiae, cui praeest, a Romano Pontifice extra fines territorii eiusdem Ecclesiae constitutos ordinandi et inthronizandi, nisi aliud in casu speciali expresse statuitur.

§3. Ordinatio episcopalis et inthronizatio fieri debent intra terminos iure statutos, litterae patriarchales vero de provisione canonica intra decem dies post electionis proclamationem dandae sunt; de ordinatione episcopali et de inthronizatione Sedes Apostolica quam primum certior fiat.

CAN. 87   Patriarcha potest curare, ut in Synodo Episcoporum Ecclesiae patriarchalis ad normam cann. 181, §1 et 182–187 eligantur, dummodo congruae eorum sustentationi provisum sit, aliquot Episcopi curiae patriarchalis, non tamen ultra tres, quibus officium cum residentia in curia patriarchali conferat, eosque potest peractis omnibus ad proclamationem episcopalem requisitis ordinare.

CAN. 88   §1. Episcopi Ecclesiae patriarchalis Patriarchae honorem et obsequium exhibeant debitamque oboedientiam praestent; Patriarcha vero eosdem Episcopos, qua par est reverentia, prosequatur et fraterna caritate complectatur.

§2. Patriarcha curet, ut controversiae, quae inter Episcopos forte oriuntur, compo-

---

86 §3: Pius XII, m.p. *Cleri sanctitati*, 2 iun. 1957, can. 256 §2.

87: Pius XII, m.p. *Cleri sanctitati*, 2 iun. 1957, can. 257. - S.C. de Prop. Fide, instr. (ad Patr. et Epp. Ritus Graeco-Melchit.), 29 maii 1789, n. 7. * Syn. Libanen. Maronitarum, a. 1736, pars III, cap. IV, 20; cap. VI, 6; Syn. Bekorkien. Maronitarum, a. 1790, s. 1; Syn. Sciarfen. Syrorum, a. 1888, cap. V, art. XIII, §10, 5; cap. X; Syn. Armen., a. 1911, 191.

88 §1: Pius XII, m.p. *Cleri sanctitati*, 2 iun. 1957, can. 259 §1. - Chalc. can. 30; Constantinop. IV, can. 17; Leo XIII, ep. *Omnibus compertum est*, 21 iul. 1900, I–II. * Syn. Armen., a. 1911, 198, 236.

88 §2: Pius XII, m.p. *Cleri sanctitati*, 2 iun. 1957, can. 259 §2. - Leo XIII, ep. *Omnibus compertum est*, 21 iul. 1900, II. * Syn. Libanen. Maronitarum, a. 1736, pars III, cap. VI, 2, 9.

bishops with due regard for the right of deferring them to the Roman Pontiff at any time.

CAN. 89 §1. It is the right and obligation of the patriarch to exercise vigilance according to the norm of law over all clerics; if it appears that one of them merits punishment, he is to warn the hierarch to whom the cleric is immediately subject and, if the warning is in vain, he himself is to take action against the cleric according to the norm of law.

§2. The patriarch can commit a function of conducting affairs that regard the entire patriarchal Church to any cleric, after having consulted with his eparchial bishop or, in the case of a member of a religious institute or a society of the common life in the manner of religious, his major superior, unless particular law of the patriarchal Church requires the consent of the same; he can also subject the cleric immediately to himself while exercising this function.

§3. The patriarch can confer on any cleric a dignity recognized in his own patriarchal Church with due regard for can. 430, provided he has the written consent of the eparchial bishop to whom the cleric is subject or, in the case of a member of a religious institute or of a society of common life in the manner of religious, of his major superior.

CAN. 90 The patriarch can for a serious

nantur firmo iure eas quolibet tempore ad Romanum Pontificem deferendi.

CAN. 89 §1. Patriarchae ius et obligatio est omnibus clericis ad normam iuris vigilandi; si quis poenam mereri videtur, Hierarcham, cui clericus immediate subditus est, moneat et monitione in cassum facta in clericum ipse ad normam iuris procedat.

§2. Munus expediendi negotia, quae totam Ecclesiam patriarchalem respiciunt, Patriarcha committere potest clerico cuilibet consulto eius Episcopo eparchiali vel, si de sodali instituti religiosi vel societatis vitae communis ad instar religiosorum agitur, eius Superiore maiore, nisi ius particulare Ecclesiae patriarchalis eorundem consensum requirit; hunc clericum potest etiam munere durante sibi immediate subdere.

§3. Patriarcha conferre potest dignitatem in propria Ecclesia patriarchali receptam cuilibet clerico firmo can. 430, dummodo accedat consensus scripto datus Episcopi eparchialis, cui clericus subditus est, vel, si de sodali instituti religiosi vel societatis vitae communis ad instar religiosorum agitur, eius Superioris maioris.

CAN. 90 Patriarcha gravi de causa

89 §1: Pius XII, m.p. *Cleri sanctitati,* 2 iun. 1957, can. 260 §1 n. 1. * Syn. Sciarfen. Syrorum, a. 1888, cap. VII, art. III, 6, 14).

89 §2: Pius XII, m.p. *Cleri sanctitati,* 2 iun. 1957, can. 260 §1 n. 2 a). - S.C. de Prop. Fide, (C.G.), 17 feb. 1772, 1–2; instr. (ad Deleg. Ap. apud Maronit.), 28 iun. 1788; (C.G.), 24 sep. 1816. * Syn. Bekorkien. Maronitarum, a 1790, s. 12; Syn. Sciarfen. Syrorum, a. 1888, cap. V, art. XIII; §3, 1, VII; Syn. Armen., a. 1911, 197.

89 §3: Pius XII, m.p. *Cleri sanctitati,* 2 iun. 1957, cann. 41 §1 n. 1, 42 §1. - S.C. pro Eccl. Orient., 10 ian. 1929; resp. 11 iun. 1940. * Syn. Libanen. Maronitarum,

a. 1736, pars II, cap. XIV, 43–45 et 48; pars III, cap. II, 7; cap. III, 3, II–III, et 4; pars IV, cap. I, 15; Syn. Sciarfen. Syrorum, a. 1888, cap. V, art. XIII, §1, 8; §§7 et 9; cap. VI, art. VIII, 6; cap. XI, art. II; Syn. Alexandrin. Coptorum, a. 1898, sect. II, cap. III, art. VII, §1, 7; §6, 3, IX; sect. III, cap. IV, art. III; Syn. Armen., a. 1911, 301–314, 360–366.

90: Pius XII, m.p. *Cleri sanctitati,* 2 iun. 1957, can. 263 §1; m.p. *Postquam Apostolicis Litteris,* 9 feb. 1952, can. 164 §2 n. 1. * Syn. Libanen. Maronitarum, a. 1736, pars III, cap. VI, 2, 16; pars IV, cap. II, 2; Syn. Armen., a. 1911, 197.

reason and after having consulted with the eparchial bishop and with the consent of the permanent synod, exempt a place or, in the very act of its erection, a juridic person not belonging to a religious institute from the power of the eparchial bishop and subject it immediately to himself with respect to the administration of temporal goods and also with respect to persons attached to the same place or juridic person in all matters regarding their function or office.

CAN. 91   The patriarch must be commemorated in the Divine Liturgy and in the divine praises after the Roman Pontiff by all the bishops and other clerics according to the prescriptions of the liturgical books.

CAN. 92   §1. The patriarch is to manifest hierarchical communion with the Roman Pontiff, Successor of Saint Peter, through the fidelity, reverence and obedience that are due to the supreme pastor of the entire Church.

§2. The patriarch must commemorate the Roman Pontiff as a sign of full communion with him in the Divine Liturgy and divine praises according to the prescriptions of the liturgical books; the patriarch is also to see that this is done faithfully by all the bishops and other clerics of the Church over which he presides.

§3. The patriarch is to have frequent dealings

potest consulto Episcopo eparchiali atque de consensu Synodi permanentis locum vel personam iuridicam, quae non ad institutum religiosum pertinet, in ipso actu erectionis a potestate Episcopi eparchialis eximere sibique immediate subicere, quod attinet ad administrationem bonorum temporalium necnon ad personas eidem loco vel personae iuridicae addictas in eis omnibus, quae ad earum munus vel officium spectant.

CAN. 91   Patriarcha commemorari debet in Divina Liturgia et in laudibus divinis post Romanum Pontificem ab omnibus Episcopis ceterisque clericis secundum praescripta librorum liturgicorum.

CAN. 92   §1. Patriarcha manifestet communionem hierarchicam cum Romano Pontifice, sancti Petri successore, per fidelitatem, venerationem et oboedientiam, quae debentur supremo universae Ecclesiae Pastori.

§2. Patriarcha commemorationem Romani Pontificis in signum plenae communionis cum eo in Divina Liturgia et in laudibus divinis secundum praescripta librorum liturgicorum debet facere et curare, ut ab omnibus Episcopis ceterisque clericis Ecclesiae, cui praeest, fideliter fiat.

§3. Patriarchae cum Romano Pontifice

91: Pius XII, m.p. *Cleri sanctitati,* 2 iun. 1957, can. 272. - Protodeut. can. 15; Constantinop. IV, can. 10; Benedictus XIV, ep. encycl. *Ex quo,* 1 mar. 1756, §§9, 18–23; S.C. de Prop. Fide, instr. 31 iul. 1902, 13, e). * Syn. Libanen. Maronitarum, a. 1736, pars III, cap. VI, 2, 17; 3 pars IV, cap. II, 8; Syn. Sciarfen. Syrorum, a. 1888, cap. VII, art. III, 6, 2); Syn. Alexandrin. Coptorum, a. 1898, sect. III, cap. I, art. III, 2, IV, 1); Syn. Armen., a. 1911, 638, b).

92 §1: Pius XII, m.p. *Cleri sanctitati,* 2 iun. 1957, can. 273 n. 1. - Innocentius III, litt. *Apostolicae sedis,* 12 nov. 1199, "Gaudemus autem;" litt. *Multae nobis,* 13 nov. 1199, "Gaudemus autem." * Syn. Libanen. Maronitarum, a. 1736, pars III, cap. VI, 7, XXII.

92 §2: Pius XII, m.p. *Cleri sanctitati,* 2 iun. 1957, cann. 166, 274. - Callixtus III, const. *Reddituri de commisso,* 3 sep. 1457, §1; Benedictus XIV, ep. ency-

cl. *Ex quo,* 1 mar. 1756, §§9–17; S.C. de Prop. Fide, litt. 4 iul. 1833, II; litt. 29 maii 1838; instr. 31 iul. 1902, 13, e). * Syn. Libanen. Maronitarum, a. 1736, pars I, cap. I, 12, 4; pars III, cap. VI, 3; Syn. Sciarfen. Syrorum, a. 1888, cap. VII, art. II, I; Syn. Alexandrin. Coptorum, a. 1898, sect. III, cap. I, art. II, 5, I; Syn. Armen., a. 1911, 153, 638, b).

92 §3: Pius XII, m.p. *Cleri sanctitati,* 2 iun. 1957, cann. 273 n. 2, 275. - Gregorius XIII, const. ap. *Romani Pontificis,* 18 sep. 1579, in fine; Clemens XI, litt. ap. *Singularis argumentum,* 21 maii 1712; Pius IX, litt. ap. *Cum ecclesiastica,* 31 aug. 1869, V. * Syn. Libanen. Maronitarum, a. 1736, pars III, cap. VI, 9; Syn. Sciarfen. Syrorum, a. 1888, cap. VII, art. II, III; Syn. Alexandrin. Coptorum, a. 1898, sect. III, cap. I, art. II, 5, III; Syn. Armen., a. 1911, 152, 200, n. 1.

with the Roman Pontiff. He is to submit to him a report concerning the state of the Church over which he presides according to the special norms regarding the matter. Within a year of his election and afterwards several times during the tenure of his office, he is to visit Rome to venerate the tombs of the apostles Peter and Paul and to present himself to the successor of Saint Peter in primacy over the entire Church.

CAN. 93 The patriarch is to reside in his see and is not to be absent from it except for a canonical reason.

CAN. 94 The patriarch must celebrate the Divine Liturgy for the people of the entire Church over which he presides on feast days established by particular law.

CAN. 95 §1. The obligations of eparchial bishops that are mentioned in can. 196, also bind the patriarch, with due regard for the obligations of individual bishops.

§2. The patriarch is to see that the eparchial bishops faithfully fulfill their pastoral function and that they reside in the eparchy that they govern; he should enkindle their zeal; if they gravely transgress in a certain matter, after having consulted with the permanent synod unless there is danger in delay, the patriarch is to warn them; if the warning does not result in the desired effect, he is to defer the matter to the Roman Pontiff.

CAN. 96 With regard to prayers and pious exercises, provided that they are consonant with his own rite, the patriarch can do the same as the local hierarch in the entire Church over which he presides.

frequens sit consuetudo ac secundum normas specialiter statutas ei relationem de statu Ecclesiae, cui praeest, exhibeat necnon intra annum a sua electione, deinde pluries durante munere visitationem ad Urbem peragat sanctorum Apostolorum Petri et Pauli limina veneraturus atque sancti Petri successori in primatu super universam Ecclesiam se sistat.

CAN. 93 Patriarcha resideat in sede suae residentiae, a qua ne absit nisi canonica ex causa.

CAN. 94 Divinam Liturgiam pro populo totius Ecclesiae, cui praeest, Patriarcha celebrare debet diebus festis iure particulari statutis.

CAN. 95 §1. Episcoporum eparchialium obligationes, de quibus in can. 196, tenent etiam Patriarcham firmis de cetero singulorum Episcoporum obligationibus.

§2. Patriarcha curet, ut Episcopi eparchiales muneri pastorali fideliter satisfaciant et in eparchia, quam regunt, resideant; eorum zelum excitet; si in aliqua re graviter offenderunt, eos consulta, nisi periculum in mora est, Synodo permanenti monere ne omittat et, si monitiones optatum effectum non sortiuntur, rem ad Romanum Pontificem deferat.

CAN. 96 Circa orationes et pietatis exercitia, dummodo proprio ritui consonent, Patriarcha in tota Ecclesia, cui praeest, eadem potest ac Hierarchae loci.

93: Pius XII, m.p. *Cleri sanctitati*, 2 iun. 1957, can. 276. - Constantinop. IV, can. 19. * Syn. Libanen. Maronitarum, a. 1736, pars II, cap. XIV, 14.

94: Pius XII, m.p. *Cleri sanctitati*, 2 iun. 1957, can. 277.

95 §1: Pius XII, m.p. *Cleri sanctitati*, 2 iun. 1957, can. 278 §1. - Constantinop. IV, can. 16 "Si vero."

95 §2: Pius XII, m.p. *Cleri sanctitati*, 2 iun. 1957,

can. 278 §2. * Syn. Libanen. Maronitarum, a. 1736, pars III, cap. VI, 2, 11; Syn. Sciarfen. Syrorum, a. 1888, cap. VII, art. III, 6, 9)–10), 12), 14); Syn. Alexandrin. Coptorum, a. 1898, sect. III, cap. I, art. III, 2, IV, 4); Syn. Armen., a. 1911, 195.

96: Pius XII, m.p. *Cleri sanctitati*, 2 iun. 1957, can. 279 §1. * Syn. Armen., a. 1911, 824–829.

CAN. 97 The patriarch must diligently exercise vigilance over the proper administration of all ecclesiastical property, with due regard for the primary obligation of the individual eparchial bishops as mentioned in can. 1022, §1.

CAN. 98 The patriarch, with the consent of the synod of bishops of the patriarchal Church and the prior assent of the Roman Pontiff, can enter into agreements with a civil authority that are not contrary to the law established by the Apostolic See; the patriarch cannot put these same agreements into effect without having obtained the approval of the Roman Pontiff.

CAN. 99 §1. The patriarch is to see that in the regions where personal statutes are in force that they are observed by everyone.

§2. If in the same place several patriarchs exercise power that has been recognized or conceded in the personal statutes, it is expedient that in matters of greater importance that they act after consulting one another.

CAN. 100 The patriarch can reserve to himself matters that concern several eparchies and affect the civil authorities; he cannot, however, make a decision in these same matters without consulting the eparchial bishops concerned and without the consent of the permanent synod. If, however, the matter is urgent and time is too short to convene the bishops who are members of the permanent synod, they may be substituted for, in this case, by the bishops of the patriarchal curia, if there are any, otherwise, by the two eparchial bishops who are senior according to episcopal ordination.

CAN. 97 Patriarcha diligenter vigilare debet rectae administrationi omnium bonorum ecclesiasticorum firma primaria singulorum Episcoporum eparchialium obligatione, de qua in can. 1022, §1.

CAN. 98 Patriarcha de consensu Synodi Episcoporum Ecclesiae patriarchalis et praevio assensu Romani Pontificis conventiones iuri a Sede Apostolica statuto non contrarias cum auctoritate civili inire potest; easdem autem conventiones Patriarcha ad effectum ducere non potest nisi obtenta Romani Pontificis approbatione.

CAN. 99 §1. Patriarcha curet, ut Statuta personalia in regionibus, in quibus vigent, ab omnibus serventur.

§2. Si plures Patriarchae eodem in loco potestate in Statutis personalibus agnita vel concessa utuntur, expedit, ut in negotiis maioris momenti collatis consiliis agant.

CAN. 100 Negotia, quae plures eparchias respiciunt et auctoritatem civilem tangunt, Patriarcha ad se advocare potest; statuere autem de eisdem non potest nisi consultis Episcopis eparchialibus, quorum interest, et de consensu Synodi permanentis; si vero res urget nec suppetit tempus ad coadunandos Episcopos Synodi permanentis membra, horum vices in casu gerunt Episcopi curiae patriarchalis, si habentur, secus vero duo Episcopi eparchiales ordinatione episcopali seniores.

97: Pius XII, m.p. *Cleri sanctitati,* 2 iun. 1957, can. 280 §1.

98: Pius XII, m.p. *Cleri sanctitati,* 2 iun. 1957, can. 281.

99 §1: Pius XII, m.p. *Cleri sanctitati,* 2 iun. 1957, can. 271 §1. * Syn. Alexandrin. Coptorum, a. 1898,

sect. III, cap. VI, tit. I, 4; tit. IV. art. I, 1, c); tit. V, art. XI, 2–6.

99 §2: Pius XII, m.p. *Cleri sanctitati,* 2 iun. 1957, can. 271 §2.

100: Pius XII, m.p. *Cleri sanctitati,* 2 iun. 1957, can. 259 §4.

CAN. 101 In his own eparchy, in stauropegial monasteries and other places where neither an eparchy nor an exarchy has been erected, the patriarch has the same rights and obligations as an eparchial bishop.

CHAPTER III. The Synod of Bishops of a Patriarchal Church

CAN. 102 §1. All and solely ordained bishops of the patriarchal Church wherever they are constituted, excluding those mentioned in can. 953, §1 or those who are punished by canonical penalties mentioned in cann. 1433 and 1434, must be convoked to the synod of bishops of the patriarchal Church.

§2. With regard to eparchial bishops constituted outside the territorial boundaries of the patriarchal Church and titular bishops, particular law can restrict their deliberative vote, remaining intact the canons concerning the election of the patriarch, bishops and candidates for office mentioned in can. 149.

§3. To expedite certain matters, according to the norm of particular law or with the consent of the permanent synod, others can be invited by the patriarch, especially hierarchs who are not bishops and experts to give their opinions to the bishops gathered in the synod with due regard for can. 66, §2.

CAN. 101 Patriarcha in propria eparchia, in monasteriis stauropegiacis itemque in locis, ubi nec eparchia nec exarchia erecta est, eadem iura et obligationes habet ac Episcopus eparchialis.

CAPUT III. De Synodo Episcoporum Ecclesiae Patriarchalis

CAN. 102 §1. Ad Synodum Episcoporum Ecclesiae patriarchalis vocari debent omnes et soli Episcopi ordinati eiusdem Ecclesiae ubicumque constituti exclusis eis, de quibus in can. 953, §1, vel eis, qui poenis canonicis, de quibus in cann. 1433 et 1434, puniti sunt.

§2. Quod attinet ad Episcopos eparchiales extra fines territorii Ecclesiae patriarchalis constitutos et ad Episcopos titulares, ius particulare eorum suffragium deliberativum coartare potest firmis vero canonibus de electione Patriarchae, Episcoporum et candidatorum ad officia, de quibus in can. 149.

§3. Pro certis negotiis expediendis a Patriarcha ad normam iuris particularis vel de consensu Synodi permanentis alii invitari possunt praesertim Hierarchae non Episcopi ac periti ad suas opiniones Episcopis in Synodo congregatis manifestandas firmo can. 66, §2.

101: Pius XII, m.p. *Cleri sanctitati,* 2 iun. 1957, can. 282. * Syn. Libanen. Maronitarum, a. 1736, pars III, cap. VI, 5.

102 §1: Ant. can. 12; Constantinop. I, can. 6; Carth. cann. 18, 76, 85–86, 95; Basilius M., can. 47; Constantinop. IV, can. 17; Compositiones ex solis episcopis Synodorum Ancyranae, Neocaesariensis, Gangrensis, Antiochenae, Laodicensis, Sardicensis, Carthaginensis; Pius XII, m.p. *Cleri sanctitati,* 2 iun. 1957, cann. 224 §1, 340 §1, 341 §1; S.C. pro Eccl. Orient., decl. 25 mar. 1970, 1. - S. Victor, litt. a. c. 190,

"Poteram autem;" S. Leo M., litt. *Omnium quidem,* 13 ian. 444; Pius IX, litt. ap. *Reversurus,* 12 iul. 1867, 15; const. *Cum ecclesiastica,* 31 aug. 1869; ep. encycl. *Quartus supra,* 6 ian. 1873, 27; S.C. de Prop. Fide, litt. (ad Patriarcham Syr.), 28 ian. 1792. * Syn. Libanen. Maronitarum, a. 1736, pars III, cap. VI, 7, IX; Syn. Sciarfen. Syrorum, a. 1888, cap. VII, art. III, 6, 16); cap. IX, art. IV; Syn. Alexandrin. Coptorum, a. 1898, sect. III, cap. I, art. III, 2, IV, 10); cap. V, 3, I–IV; Syn. Armen., a. 1911, 170, 183, n. 3, 226.

CAN. 103   It is for the patriarch to convoke the synod of bishops of the patriarchal Church and to preside over it.

CAN. 104   §1. All bishops legitimately convoked to the synod of bishops of the patriarchal Church are bound by a serious obligation to attend it, except those who have already resigned from office.

§2. If a bishop considers himself to be prevented by a just impediment, he is to present his reasons in writing to the synod of bishops of the patriarchal Church. It is for the bishops present in the designated place at the beginning of the sessions of the synod to decide the legitimacy of the impediment.

CAN. 105   No member of the synod of bishops of the patriarchal Church can send to the synod a proxy in his place, nor does anyone have several votes.

CAN. 106   §1. The synod of bishops of the patriarchal Church must be convoked whenever:

1° business is to be transacted that pertains to the exclusive competence of the synod of bishops of the patriarchal Church, or for the execution of which the consent of the synod is required;

2° the patriarch, with the consent of the permanent synod, considers it necessary;

CAN. 103 Patriarchae est Synodum Episcoporum Ecclesiae patriarchalis convocare eique praeesse.

CAN. 104 §1. Omnes Episcopi ad Synodum Episcoporum Ecclesiae patriarchalis legitime vocati gravi obligatione tenentur, ut eidem Synodo intersint eis exceptis, qui officio suo iam renuntiaverunt.

§2. Si quis Episcopus iusto impedimento se detineri existimat, scripto suas rationes aperiat Synodo Episcoporum Ecclesiae patriarchalis; de legitimitate impedimenti decidere est Episcoporum, qui in loco designato initio sessionum Synodi praesentes sunt.

CAN. 105 Pro Synodo Episcoporum Ecclesiae patriarchalis nemo ex eiusdem Synodi membris procuratorem sui loco mittere potest nec quisquam plura suffragia habet.

CAN. 106 §1. Synodus Episcoporum Ecclesiae patriarchalis convocari debet, quoties:

1° expedienda sunt negotia, quae ad exclusivam competentiam Synodi Episcoporum Ecclesiae patriarchalis pertinent aut pro quibus peragendis consensus eiusdem Synodi requiritur;

2° Patriarcha de consensu Synodi permanentis id necessarium iudicat;

103: Pius XII, m.p. *Cleri sanctitati,* 2 iun. 1957, can. 340 §1; S.C. pro Eccl. Orient., decl. 25 mar. 1970, 2. - Ant. cann. 19–20; Carth. can. 76; Constantinop. IV, can. 17. * Syn. Sciarfen. Syrorum, a. 1888, cap. VII, art. III, 6, 16); cap. IX, art. IV, 6; Syn. Alexandrin. Coptorum, a. 1898, sect. III, cap. I, art. III, 2, IV, 10); cap. V, 3, I; Syn. Armen., a. 1911, 183, n. 3, 200, n. 5, 225.

104 §1: Pius XII, m.p. *Cleri sanctitati,* 2 iun. 1957, cann. 225 §1, 345 §1 n. 2. - Laod. can. 40; Sard. can. 6; Carth. can. 76; Chalc. can. 19; Quinisext. can. 8. * Syn. Sciarfen. Syrorum, a. 1888, cap. VIII, art. II "Ad hanc;" Syn. Alexandrin. Coptorum, a. 1898, sect. III, cap. II, art. II, 2; Syn. Armen., a. 1911, 227.

104 §2: Pius XII, m.p. *Cleri sanctitati,* 2 iun. 1957,

cann. 225 §2, 345 §1 n. 2. - Laod. can. 40; Chalc. can. 19; Carth. can. 76; Quinisext. can. 8. * Syn. Sciarfen. Syrorum, a. 1888, cap. VIII, art. II "Ad hanc;" Syn. Alexandrin. Coptorum, a. 1898, sect. III, cap. II, art. II, 2; Syn. Armen., a. 1911, 227.

105: Pius XII, m.p. *Cleri sanctitati,* 2 iun. 1957, cann. 226 §2, 252 §2 n. 1, 345 §1 n. 2 et §2. * Syn. Libanen. Maronitarum, a. 1736, pars III, cap. VI, 7, VIII, XI; Syn. Sciarfen. Syrorum, a. 1888, cap. VIII, art. II "Ad hanc;" Syn. Alexandrin. Coptorum, a. 1898, sect. III, cap. II, art. II, 2; Syn. Armen., a. 1911, 227–228.

106 §1: Pius XII, m.p. *Cleri sanctitati,* 2 iun. 1957, can. 344. - Carth. cann. 19, 95; Constantinop. IV, can. 17; Urbanus VIII, const. *Sacrosanctum apostolatus,* 12 mar. 1625; S.C. de Prop. Fide, instr. 9 aug. 1760, n. IV.

3° at least one-third of the members request it for a given matter, with due regard always for the rights of patriarchs, bishops and other persons established by common law.

§2. Moreover the synod of bishops of the patriarchal Church must be convoked at fixed times, even annually, if particular law so establishes it.

CAN. 107 §1. Unless particular law requires a higher quorum, and with due regard for cann. 69, 149 and 183, §1, any session of the synod of bishops of the patriarchal Church is canonical and any given balloting is valid if a majority of the bishops who are obliged to attend it, is present.

§2. With due regard for cann. 72, 149 and 183, §§3–4, the synod of bishops of the patriarchal Church is free to establish norms to determine how many votes and ballotings are required for the synodal decisions to acquire the force of law; otherwise, can. 924 must be observed.

CAN. 108 §1. It is for the patriarch to open the synod of bishops of the patriarchal Church and, with the consent of the same synod, to transfer, prorogue, suspend and dissolve it.

§2. After having heard the members of the synod of bishops of the patriarchal Church, it is also for the patriarch to prepare the agenda as well as to submit it for the approval of the synod at the opening session.

§3. During the synod of bishops of the patriarchal Church, individual bishops can add oth-

3° tertia saltem pars membrorum pro dato negotio id postulat salvis semper iuribus Patriarcharum, Episcoporum aliarumque personarum iure communi statutis.

§2. Synodus Episcoporum Ecclesiae patriarchalis praeterea convocari debet, si ius particulare ita fert, statis temporibus, etiam quotannis.

CAN. 107 §1. Nisi ius particulare maiorem praesentiam exigit et firmis cann. 69, 149 et 183, §1, quaelibet sessio Synodi Episcoporum Ecclesiae patriarchalis canonica atque singulum scrutinium validum est, si maior pars Episcoporum, qui tenentur eidem Synodo interesse, praesens est.

§2. Firmis cann. 72, 149 et 183, §§3 et 4 integrum est Synodo Episcoporum Ecclesiae patriarchalis latis normis statuere, quot suffragia et scrutinia requirantur, ut decisiones synodales vim iuris obtineant; secus servari debet can. 924.

CAN. 108 §1. Patriarchae est Synodum Episcoporum Ecclesiae patriarchalis aperire necnon de eiusdem Synodi consensu transferre, prorogare, suspendere et dissolvere.

§2. Patriarchae quoque est praeauditis Synodi Episcoporum Ecclesiae patriarchalis membris ordinem servandum in quaestionibus examinandis praeparare atque approbationi Synodi initio sessionum subicere.

§3. Synodo Episcoporum Ecclesiae patriarchalis durante singuli Episcopi propositis

106 §2: Pius XII, m.p. *Cleri sanctitati,* 2 iun. 1957, can. 344. - Apost. can. 37; Nic. I, can. 5; Ant. can. 20; Chalc. can. 19; Carth. cann. 21, 55; Quinisext. can. 8; Nic. II, can. 6; Constantinop. IV, can. 17. * Syn. Mar Isaaci Chaldaeorum, a. 410, can. 6; Syn. Libanen. Maronitarum, a. 1736, pars III, cap. IV, 29; cap. VI, 2, 12; Syn. Sciarfen. Syrorum, a. 1888, cap. IX, art. IV, 6; Syn. Alexandrin. Coptorum, a. 1898, sect. III, cap. V, XIV; Syn. Armen., a. 1911, 200, 5, 224.

107 §1: Pius XII, m.p. *Cleri sanctitati,* 2 iun. 1957, can. 346. - Ant. can. 19.

108 §1: Pius XII, m.p. *Cleri sanctitati,* 2 iun. 1957, can. 347 §2.

108 §2: Pius XII, m.p. *Cleri sanctitati,* 2 iun. 1957, can. 347 §1 n. 1. * Syn. Armen., a. 1911, 232.

108 §3: Pius XII, m.p. *Cleri sanctitati,* 2 iun. 1957, can. 347 §1 n. 2.

er items to those proposed if at least one-third of the members taking part in the synod consents.

CAN. 109   After the opening of the synod of bishops of the patriarchal Church, none of the bishops is permitted to absent himself from the sessions of the synod unless it is for a just reason approved by the synod.

CAN. 110   §1. The synod of bishops of the patriarchal Church is exclusively competent to make laws for the entire patriarchal Church that obtain force according to the norm of can. 150, §§2 and 3.

§2. The synod of bishops of the patriarchal Church is a tribunal according to the norm of can. 1062.

§3. The synod of bishops of the patriarchal Church conducts the election of the patriarch, of bishops and of candidates for offices mentioned in can. 149.

§4. The synod of bishops of the patriarchal Church is not competent for administrative acts unless, for certain acts, the patriarch determines otherwise or common law reserves some acts to the synod, with due regard for the canons that require the consent of the synod of bishops of the patriarchal Church.

CAN. 111   §1. The synod of bishops of the patriarchal Church establishes the manner and time of promulgation of laws and the publication of decisions.

§2. Likewise, the synod of bishops of the pa-

quaestionibus possunt alias addere, si saltem tertia pars membrorum, quae Synodo intersunt, consentit.

CAN. 109   Synodo Episcoporum Ecclesiae patriarchalis incohata nemini Episcoporum licet discedere a Synodi sessionibus nisi iusta de causa a Synodo approbata.

CAN. 110   §1. Synodo Episcoporum Ecclesiae patriarchalis exclusive competit leges ferre pro tota Ecclesia patriarchali, quae vim obtinent ad normam can. 150, §§2 et 3.

§2. Synodus Episcoporum Ecclesiae patriarchalis est tribunal ad normam can. 1062.

§3. Synodus Episcoporum Ecclesiae patriarchalis electionem Patriarchae, Episcoporum et candidatorum ad officia, de quibus in can. 149, peragit.

§4. Actus administrativi Synodo Episcoporum Ecclesiae patriarchalis non competunt, nisi pro certis actibus Patriarcha aliud statuit aut iure communi actus aliqui eidem Synodo reservantur et firmis canonibus, qui consensum Synodi Episcoporum Ecclesiae patriarchalis requirunt.

CAN. 111   §1. Synodus Episcoporum Ecclesiae patriarchalis designat modum et tempus promulgationis legum et publicationis decisionum.

§2. Item de secreto servando circa acta

109: Pius XII, m.p. *Cleri sanctitati,* 2 iun. 1957, can. 348.

110 §1: Pius XII, m.p. *Cleri sanctitati,* 2 iun. 1957, can. 243 §1. - Chalc. can. 1; Carth. prooem. et can. 1; Quinisext. can. 2; Nic. II, can. 1. * Syn. Libanen. Maronitarum, a. 1736, pars III, cap. VI, 2, 13.

110 §2: Ant. cann. 4, 12, 14–15; Constantinop. I, can. 6; Sard. cann. 3, 5; Carth. cann. 18–19, 28, 53, 94–95, 100, 125, 127; Protodeut. cann. 13, 15.

111 §1: Pius XII, m.p. *Cleri sanctitati,* 2 iun. 1957, can. 350 §1. - S. Nicolaus I, litt. *Postquam beato,* 18

mar. 862, "Quod dicitis;" S.C. de Prop. Fide, decr. 27 maii 1715; Benedictus XIII, litt. ap. *Apostolatus officium,* 19 iul. 1724; Benedictus XIV, litt. ap. *Singularis Romanorum,* 1 sep. 1741; S.C. de Prop. Fide, (C.G.), 23 maii 1837; litt. 29 maii 1838, "Premesse;" decr. 28 aug. 1841; Pius IX, const. ap. *Commissum humilitati,* 12 iul. 1867, "Quocirca;" Leo XIII, ep. *Litteris datis,* 15 iul. 1901.

111 §2: Pius XII, m.p. *Cleri Sanctitati,* 2 iun. 1957, can. 350 §1. - S. Gregorius M., litt. *Suscepti regiminis,* mense maio a. 599, "Praeterea."

triarchal Church must decide about the observance of secrecy regarding the acts and matters dealt with, without prejudice to the obligation of observing secrecy in cases established by common law.

§3. Acts regarding laws and decisions are to be sent to the Roman Pontiff as soon as possible; certain acts, or even all of them, are to be communicated to the patriarchs of the other Eastern Churches according to the judgment of the synod.

CAN. 112 §1. The promulgation of laws and the publication of decisions of the synod of bishops of the patriarchal Church is the competence of the patriarch.

§2. Until the forthcoming synod, the authentic interpretation of laws of the synod of bishops of the patriarchal Church is the competence of the patriarch, after having consulted with the permanent synod.

CAN. 113 The synod of bishops of the patriarchal Church is to draw up its statutes in which are provided a secretary of the synod, preparatory commissions, the order of procedure as well as other means that they consider effective for the attainment of its goals.

CHAPTER IV. **The Patriarchal Curia**

CAN. 114 §1. The patriarch must have at his see a patriarchal curia, distinct from the curia of the eparchy of the patriarch, which comprises the permanent synod, the bishops of the patriarchal curia, the ordinary tribunal of the pa-

et negotia tractata Synodo Episcoporum Ecclesiae patriarchalis est decidendum salva obligatione secretum servandi in casibus iure communi statutis.

§3. Acta de legibus ac decisionibus quam primum Romano Pontifici mittantur; certa acta vel etiam omnia cum ceteris Ecclesiarum orientalium Patriarchis de iudicio eiusdem Synodi communicentur.

CAN. 112 §1. Patriarchae competit promulgatio legum et publicatio decisionum Synodi Episcoporum Ecclesiae patriarchalis.

§2. Interpretatio authentica legum Synodi Episcoporum Ecclesiae patriarchalis usque ad futuram Synodum Patriarchae consulta Synodo permanenti competit.

CAN. 113 Synodus Episcoporum Ecclesiae patriarchalis sua conficiat statuta, in quibus provideatur de secretaria Synodi, de commissionibus praeparatoriis, de ordine procedendi necnon de aliis mediis, quae fini consequendo efficacius consulant.

CAPUT IV. **De Curia Patriarchali**

CAN. 114 §1. Patriarcha penes suam Sedem habere debet curiam patriarchalem a curia eparchiae Patriarchae distinctam, quae constat ex Synodo permanenti, Episcopis curiae patriarchalis, tribunali ordinario Ecclesi-

111 §3: Pius XII, m.p. *Cleri sanctitati*, 2 iun. 1957, can. 350 §1. - S. Nicolaus I, litt. *Proposueramus quidem*, a. 865, ". . . Quamvis dixeritis." * Syn. Alexandrin. Coptorum, a. 1898, sect. III, cap. V, XII; Syn. Armen., a. 1911, 234, 1000.

112 §1: Pius XII, m.p. *Cleri sanctitati*, 2 iun. 1957, can. 243 §2. * Syn. Armen., a. 1911, 234.

112 §2: Pius XII, m.p. *Cleri sanctitati*, 2 iun. 1957, can. 243 §3. * Syn. Libanen. Maronitarum, a. 1736, pars IV, cap. VII, 8; Syn. Armen., a. 1911, 234, 1006.

114 §1: Pius XII, m.p. *Cleri sanctitati*, 2 iun. 1957, cann. 286 §§1 et 3, 287 §§1–2. - Constantinop. IV, can. 26; S.C. de Prop. Fide, 25 ian. 1830, dub. 10. *Syn. Libanen. Maronitarum, a. 1736, pars III, cap. VI, 6.

triarchal Church, the patriarchal finance officer, the patriarchal chancellor, the liturgical commission as well as other commissions which by law are attached to the patriarchal curia.

§2. Persons belonging to the patriarchal curia can be selected by the patriarch from the clerics of the entire Church over which he presides, having consulted their eparchial bishop or, if it is a case of a member of a religious institute or society of the common life in the manner of religious, their major superior.

§3. The offices of either curia of the patriarch, inasmuch as it is possible, are not to be accumulated in the same persons.

CAN. 115   §1. The permanent synod is composed of the patriarch and four bishops designated for a five-year term.

§2. Three of these bishops are elected by the synod of bishops of the patriarchal Church; among these as least two must be eparchial bishops; one is appointed by the patriarch.

§3. At the same time and in the same manner, insofar as it is possible, four bishops are designated, who, according to the order determined by the synod of bishops of the patriarchal Church, substitute one after another for the impeded members of the permanent synod.

CAN. 116   §1. It is for the patriarch to convoke the permanent synod and to preside over it.

§2. If the patriarch is impeded from participating in the permanent synod, its sessions are presided over by the bishop who is senior by episcopal ordination after the number of members has been restored to five according to the norm of can. 115, §3.

ae patriarchalis, oeconomo patriarchali, cancellario patriarchali, commissione de re liturgica necnon aliis commissionibus, quae iure curiae patriarchali adiunguntur.

§2. Personae ad curiam patriarchalem pertinentes a Patriarcha ex clericis totius Ecclesiae, cui praeest, seligi possunt consulto eorum Episcopo eparchiali vel, si de sodalibus instituti religiosi vel societatis vitae communis ad instar religiosorum agitur, eorum Superiore maiore.

§3. Officia utriusque curiae Patriarchae, quatenus fieri potest, in eisdem personis ne cumulentur.

CAN. 115   §1. Synodus permanens constat ex Patriarcha et quattuor Episcopis ad quinquennium designatis.

§2. Horum Episcoporum tres a Synodo Episcoporum Ecclesiae patriarchalis eliguntur, inter quos saltem duo ex Episcopis eparchialibus esse debent, unus vero a Patriarcha nominatur.

§3. Eodem tempore ac modo designentur quattuor, quatenus fieri potest, Episcopi, qui ex ordine a Synodo Episcoporum Ecclesiae patriarchalis determinato Synodi permanentis membra impedita alternatim substituant.

CAN. 116   §1. Patriarchae est Synodum permanentem convocare eique praeesse.

§2. Si Patriarcha impeditur, ne Synodo permanenti intersit, Synodi sessionibus praeest Episcopus ordinatione episcopali senior inter Synodi membra redintegrato quinario numero ad normam can. 115, §3.

114 §2: PIUS XII, m.p. *Cleri sanctitati,* 2 iun. 1957, can. 286 §2.

114 §3: PIUS XII, m.p. *Cleri sanctitati,* 2 iun. 1957, can. 286 §1.

115 §1: PIUS XII, m.p. *Cleri sanctitati,* 2 iun. 1957, can. 289 §1.

115 §2: PIUS XII, m.p. *Cleri sanctitati,* 2 iun. 1957,

can. 289 §2 et §3 n. 1.

115 §3: PIUS XII, m.p. *Cleri sanctitati,* 2 iun. 1957, can. 289 §3 n. 2.

116 §1: PIUS XII, m.p. *Cleri sanctitati,* 2 iun. 1957, can. 289 §1.

116 §2: PIUS XII, m.p. *Cleri sanctitati,* 2 iun. 1957, can. 290 §1.

§3. If the permanent synod must decide a matter that affects the person of a certain bishop who is a member of the same synod or affects his eparchy or office, he must be heard, but in the synod another bishop substitutes for him according to the norm of can. 115, §3.

CAN. 117   The president and all the other members of the synod who participated in the synod must sign the acts of the synod.

CAN. 118   Voting in the permanent synod must be secret in matters relating to persons; in all other cases if at least one of the members has expressly requested it.

CAN. 119   If a certain matter belonging to the competence of the permanent synod is to be decided while the synod of bishops of the patriarchal Church is being held, the decision on this matter is reserved to the permanent synod unless the patriarch with the consent of the permanent synod judges it opportune to commit the decision to the synod of bishops of the patriarchal Church.

CAN. 120   The permanent synod must be convoked at fixed times, at least twice a year, and whenever the patriarch considers it opportune, as well as whenever decisions are to be made about matters for which common law requires the consent or counsel of the same synod.

CAN. 121   If in the judgment of the synod of bishops of the patriarchal Church, the permanent synod cannot be constituted for a serious reason, the Apostolic See is to be informed; the synod of bishops of the patriarchal Church is to elect two bishops, one of whom must be from the eparchial bishops, who with the patri-

§3. Si Synodus permanens definire debet negotium, quod personam alicuius Episcopi, qui membrum eiusdem Synodi est, vel eius eparchiam aut officium tangit, hic quidem audiendus est, sed in Synodo ei substituatur alius Episcopus ad normam can. 115, §3.

CAN. 117   Praeses et omnia alia membra Synodi permanentis, quae Synodo interfuerunt, actis Synodi subscribere debent.

CAN. 118   Suffragia in Synodo permanenti debent esse secreta, si de personis agitur; in ceteris vero casibus, si saltem unum ex membris id expresse petivit.

CAN. 119   Si quod negotium ad Synodi permanentis competentiam pertinens definiendum est, dum locum habet Synodus Episcoporum Ecclesiae patriarchalis, decisio de hoc negotio Synodo permanenti reservatur, nisi Patriarcha de consensu Synodi permanentis decisionem Synodo Episcoporum Ecclesiae patriarchalis committere opportunum iudicat.

CAN. 120   Synodus permanens convocari debet statis temporibus, saltem bis in anno, et, quoties Patriarcha id opportunum censet, et, quoties expedienda sunt negotia, ad quae ius commune requirit consensum vel consilium eiusdem Synodi.

CAN. 121   Si gravi de causa de iudicio Synodi Episcoporum Ecclesiae patriarchalis Synodus permanens constitui non potest, Sedes Apostolica certior fiat et Synodus Episcoporum Ecclesiae patriarchalis eligat duos Episcopos, quorum unus ex Episcopis eparchialibus esse debet, qui cum Patriarcha

116 §3: Pius XII, m.p. *Cleri sanctitati,* 2 iun. 1957, can. 290 §3.

117: Pius XII, m.p. *Cleri sanctitati,* 2 iun. 1957, can. 291 §1.

118: Pius XII, m.p. *Cleri sanctitati,* 2 iun. 1957, can. 292.

119: Pius XII, m.p. *Cleri sanctitati,* 2 iun. 1957, can. 294.

120: Pius XII, m.p. *Cleri sanctitati,* 2 iun. 1957, can. 295.

121: Pius XII, m.p. *Cleri sanctitati,* 2 iun. 1957, cann. 296–297.

arch act in lieu of the permanent synod for as long as the reason lasts.

CAN. 122 §1. For the administration of the goods of the patriarchal Church, the patriarch, with the consent of the permanent synod, is to appoint a patriarchal finance officer, distinct from the finance officer of the eparchy of the patriarch. The patriarchal finance officer should be one of the Christian faithful who is an expert in economic matters and outstanding for honesty. Anyone who is related to the patriarch up to the fourth degree of consanguinity or affinity inclusively is excluded from being validly appointed.

§2. The patriarchal finance officer is appointed for a term determined by particular law. During this period he or she cannot be removed by the patriarch without the consent of the synod of bishops of the patriarchal Church or, if there is danger in delay, of the permanent synod.

§3. The patriarchal finance officer must submit annually to the permanent synod a written report of the past year of administration as well as the budget of revenue and expenditures for the coming year; the finance officer is to submit an administration report whenever it is requested by the permanent synod.

§4. The synod of bishops of the patriarchal Church can ask from the patriarchal finance officer an administration report and budget of income and expenditures and subject them to its examination.

CAN. 123 §1. In the patriarchal curia there is to be appointed by the patriarch a presbyter or deacon above all reproach, who as patriarchal chancellor presides over the patriarchal

causa perdurante Synodi permanentis vices gerunt.

CAN. 122 §1. Pro administratione bonorum Ecclesiae patriarchalis Patriarcha de consensu Synodi permanentis nominet oeconomum patriarchalem ab oeconomo eparchiae Patriarchae distinctum, qui sit christifidelis in re oeconomica peritus et probitate praestans excluso vero ad validitatem eo, qui cum Patriarcha consanguinitate vel affinitate usque ad quartum gradum inclusive coniunctus est.

§2. Oeconomus patriarchalis nominatur ad tempus iure particulari determinatum; munere durante a Patriarcha amoveri non potest nisi de consensu Synodi Episcoporum Ecclesiae patriarchalis aut, si periculum in mora est, Synodi permanentis.

§3. Oeconomus patriarchalis rationem administrationis exeuntis anni necnon praevisionem accepti et expensi anni incipientis Synodo permanenti quotannis scripto reddere debet; ratio administrationis reddenda est etiam, quoties a Synodo permanenti petitur.

§4. Synodus Episcoporum Ecclesiae patriarchalis potest rationem administrationis necnon praevisionem accepti et expensi ab oeconomo patriarchali exquirere et proprio examini subicere.

CAN. 123 §1. In curia patriarchali nominetur a Patriarcha presbyter vel diaconus omni exceptione maior, qui ut cancellarius patriarchalis cancellariae patriarchali

---

122 §1: Pius XII, m.p. *Postquam Apostolicis Litteris,* 9 feb. 1952, can. 259 §1 et §2 nn. 2–3; m.p. *Cleri sanctitati,* 2 iun. 1957, can. 299 §1 et §2 nn. 2–3. - Chalc. can. 26; Nic. II, can. 11; Theophilus Alexandrin., can. 10; S.C. de Prop. Fide, 1 mar. 1869, dub. 2.
122 §2: Pius XII, m.p. *Postquam Apostolicis Litteris,* 9 feb. 1952, can. 259 §2 n. 3; m.p. *Cleri sanctitati,*

2 iun. 1957, can. 299 §2 n. 3.
122 §3: Pius XII, m.p. *Postquam Apostolicis Litteris,* 9 feb. 1952, can. 259 §3; m.p. *Cleri sanctitati,* 2 iun. 1957, can. 299 §3. - S.C. de Prop. Fide, 1 mar. 1869, dub. 2.
123 §1: Pius XII, m.p. *Cleri sanctitati,* 2 iun. 1957, can. 300.

chancery and the archives of the patriarchal curia, assisted, if the case warrants it, by a vice chancellor, appointed by the patriarch.

§2. In addition to the chancellor and the vice chancellor, who are notaries *ex officio,* the patriarch can appoint other notaries for the entire Church over which he presides, for all of whom cann. 253–254 are to be applied; he can also freely remove these notaries from office.

§3. Concerning the archives of the patriarchal curia, cann. 256–260 are to be observed.

CAN. 124 The liturgical commission, which every patriarchal Church must have, and other commissions prescribed for the Churches *sui iuris,* are erected by the patriarch and are made up of persons appointed by the patriarch; they also are governed by norms established by him, unless the law provides otherwise.

CAN. 125 The expenses of the patriarchal curia are paid from the goods that the patriarch can use for this purpose; if these are not sufficient, the individual eparchies shall share in paying the expenses according to a formula determined by the synod of bishops of the patriarchal Church.

CHAPTER V. **The Vacant or Impeded Patriarchal See**

CAN. 126 §1. The patriarchal see becomes vacant at the death or resignation of the patriarch.

et archivo curiae patriarchalis praeest a vices gerente, si casus fert, a Patriarcha nominato adiutus.

§2. Praeter cancellarium eiusque vices gerentem, qui ex officio suo notarii sunt, Patriarcha alios quoque notarios pro tota Ecclesia, cui praeest, nominare potest, quibus omnibus cann. 253 et 254 applicentur; quos notarios etiam libere ab officio amovere potest.

§3. Circa archivum curiae patriarchalis serventur cann. 256–260.

CAN. 124 Commissio liturgica, quae in omni Ecclesia patriarchali haberi debet, ceteraeque commissiones pro Ecclesiis sui iuris praescriptae a Patriarcha eriguntur, ex personis a Patriarcha nominatis constituuntur necnon normis ab ipso statutis reguntur, nisi aliter iure cavetur.

CAN. 125 Expensae curiae patriarchalis solvantur ex bonis, quibus Patriarcha ad hunc finem uti potest; si haec non sufficiunt, singulae eparchiae pro mensura a Synodo Episcoporum Ecclesiae patriarchalis determinanda ad expensas solvendas concurrant.

CAPUT V. **De Sede Patriarchali Vacante vel Impedita**

CAN. 126 §1. Sedes patriarchalis vacat morte aut renuntiatione Patriarchae.

123 §2: Pius XII, m.p. *Cleri sanctitati,* 2 iun. 1957, can. 301.

123 §3: Pius XII, m.p. *Cleri sanctitati,* 2 iun. 1957, can. 304. - Carth. can. 86.

124: Pius XII, m.p. *Cleri sanctitati,* 2 iun. 1957, can. 302. * Syn. Libanen. Maronitarum, a. 1736, pars I, cap. III, 5; pars III, cap. VI, 2, 22; Syn. Sciarfen. Syrorum, a. 1888, cap. III, art. III, 7, 3); Syn. Alexandrin. Coptorum, a. 1898, sect. II, cap. I, art. I, 9; Syn. Armen., a. 1911, 614.

125: Pius XII, m.p. *Cleri sanctitati,* 2 iun. 1957, can. 305.

126 §1: Pius XII, m.p. *Cleri sanctitati,* 2 iun. 1957, cann. 306, 468 §1. - S.C. de Prop. Fide, decl. 30 ian. 1696; Clemens XIII, litt. ap. *Quam cara semper,* 1 aug. 1760, §2. * Syn. Libanen. Maronitarum, a. 1736, pars III, cap. VI, 7; Syn. Sciarfen. Syrorum, a. 1888, cap. VIII, art. I; Syn. Alexandrin. Coptorum, a. 1898, sect. III, cap. II, art. I; Syn. Armen., a. 1911, 168, 201.

§2. The synod of bishops of the patriarchal Church is competent to accept the resignation of the patriarch, having consulted with the Roman Pontiff, unless the patriarch approaches the Roman Pontiff directly.

CAN. 127   Unless particular law determines otherwise, during a vacancy of the patriarchal see, the administrator of the patriarchal Church is the senior bishop according to episcopal ordination among the bishops of the patriarchal curia or, if there are not any, among the bishops who are members of the permanent synod.

CAN. 128   It is for the administrator of the patriarchal Church:

1° to inform immediately the Roman Pontiff and all the bishops of the patriarchal Church of the vacancy of the patriarchal see;

2° to execute accurately and to see that others execute the special norms prescribed by common or particular law, or by an instruction of the Roman Pontiff, if one is given, for the various circumstances that occur during the vacancy of the patriarchal see;

3° to convoke the bishops to the synod of bishops of the patriarchal Church for the election of a patriarch and to prepare all other things necessary for the synod.

CAN. 129   The administrator of the patriarchal Church in the eparchy of the patriarch, in stauropegial monasteries and in those places where neither an eparchy nor an exarchy is erected, has the same rights and obligations as the administrator of a vacant eparchy.

CAN. 130   §1. To the administrator of the patriarchal Church passes the ordinary power of the patriarch, except in all those matters that

§2. Ad acceptationem renuntiationis Patriarchae competens est Synodus Episcoporum Ecclesiae patriarchalis consulto Romano Pontifice, nisi Patriarcha Romanum Pontificem directe adiit.

CAN. 127   Nisi ius particulare aliud fert, Sede patriarchali vacante Administrator Ecclesiae patriarchalis est Episcopus ordinatione episcopali senior inter Episcopos curiae patriarchalis vel, si desunt, inter Episcopos, qui membra sunt Synodi permanentis.

CAN. 128   Administratoris Ecclesiae patriarchalis est;

1° notitiam de Sedis patriarchalis vacatione statim cum Romano Pontifice necnon cum omnibus Episcopis Ecclesiae patriarchalis communicare;

2° normas speciales, quas pro diversis adiunctis, in quibus Sedis patriarchalis vacatio locum habuit, ius commune vel particulare aut Romani Pontificis instructio, si qua datur, praescribit, accurate exsequi vel curare, ut alii eas exsequantur;

3° Episcopos ad Synodum Episcoporum Ecclesiae patriarchalis de eligendo Patriarcha convocare et cetera omnia ad eandem Synodum necessaria disponere.

CAN. 129   Administrator Ecclesiae patriarchalis in eparchia Patriarchae, in monasteriis stauropegiacis itemque in locis, ubi nec eparchia nec exarchia erecta est, eadem iura et obligationes habet ac Administrator eparchiae vacantis.

CAN. 130   §1. Ad Administratorem Ecclesiae patriarchalis transit potestas ordinaria Patriarchae eis omnibus exclusis, quae

---

127: Pius XII, m.p. *Cleri sanctitati,* 2 iun. 1957, can. 307. - Pius IX, litt. ap. *Reversurus,* 12 iul. 1867, 14.

128: Pius XII, m.p. *Cleri sanctitati,* 2 iun. 1957, can. 308.

129: Pius XII, m.p. *Cleri sanctitati,* 2 iun. 1957, can. 309.

130 §1: Pius XII, m.p. *Cleri sanctitati,* 2 iun. 1957, cann. 310 §1 n. 1, 311 §1.

cannot be performed without the consent of the synod of bishops of the patriarchal Church.

§2. The administrator of a patriarchal Church cannot remove from office the protosyncellus or the syncellus of the eparchy of the patriarch nor innovate anything during the vacancy patriarchal see.

§3. The administrator of a patriarchal Church, even though he lacks the prerogatives of a patriarch, precedes all bishops of the same Church, not however in the synod of bishops of the patriarchal Church to elect the patriarch.

CAN. 131 The administrator of a patriarchal Church must account for his administration to the new patriarch as soon as possible.

CAN. 132 §1. When, for whatever reason, a patriarchal see is so impeded that the patriarch cannot communicate even by letter with the eparchial bishops of the Church over which he presides, according to the norms of can. 130, the governance of the patriarchal Church rests with the eparchial bishop within the territorial boundaries of the same Church who is the senior according to ordination and is not himself impeded, unless the patriarch designated another bishop or, in case of extreme necessity, even a presbyter.

§2. When a patriarch is impeded so that he cannot communicate even by letter with the Christian faithful of his eparchy, the governance of his eparchy rests with the protosyncellus; if the latter is also impeded, it rests with the one designated by the patriarch or with the one who governs the patriarchal Church in the interim.

agi non possunt nisi de consensu Synodi Episcoporum Ecclesiae patriarchalis.

§2. Administrator Ecclesiae patriarchalis non potest Protosyncellum vel Syncellos eparchiae Patriarchae ab officio amovere nec Sede patriarchali vacante quicquam innovare.

§3. Etsi praerogativis Patriarchae caret, Administrator Ecclesiae patriarchalis praecedit omnes Episcopos eiusdem Ecclesiae, non autem in Synodo Episcoporum Ecclesiae patriarchalis de eligendo Patriarcha.

CAN. 131 Administrator Ecclesiae patriarchalis rationem suae administrationis novo Patriarchae quam primum reddere debet.

CAN. 132 §1. Sede patriarchali quacumque de causa ita impedita, ut Patriarcha ne per litteras quidem cum Episcopis eparchialibus Ecclesiae, cui praeest, communicare possit, regimen Ecclesiae patriarchalis est ad normam can. 130 penes Episcopum eparchialem intra fines territorii eiusdem Ecclesiae ordinatione episcopali seniorem, qui ipse impeditus non est, nisi Patriarcha alium Episcopum vel in casu extremae necessitatis etiam presbyterum designavit.

§2. Patriarcha ita impedito, ut ne per litteras quidem cum christifidelibus propriae eparchiae communicare possit, regimen eiusdem eparchiae est penes Protosyncellum; si vero et ipse impeditus est, penes illum, quem designavit Patriarcha vel is, qui Ecclesiam patriarchalem interim regit.

130 §2: Pius XII, m.p. *Cleri sanctitati,* 2 iun. 1957, cann. 311 §2, 310 §2.

130 §3: Pius XII, m.p. *Cleri sanctitati,* 2 iun. 1957, can. 312.

131: Pius XII, m.p. *Cleri sanctitati,* 2 iun. 1957, can. 313.

132 §1: Pius XII, m.p. *Cleri sanctitati,* 2 iun. 1957, cann. 314 §1 nn. 1–2, 467.

132 §2: Pius XII, m.p. *Cleri sanctitati,* 2 iun. 1957, cann. 314 §1 n. 1, 467.

§3. The one who takes up the interim governance is to inform the Roman Pontiff as soon as possible of the impeded patriarchal see and of the assumption of governance.

§3. Qui regimen interim suscepit, Romanum Pontificem quam primum de Sede patriarchali impedita et de assumpto regimine certiorem faciat.

CHAPTER VI. Metropolitans of the Patriarchal Church

CAPUT VI. De Metropolitis Ecclesiae Patriarchalis

CAN. 133 §1. A metropolitan who presides over a province within the territorial boundaries of the patriarchal Church in the eparchies of this province, besides what is granted to him by the common law is:

1° to ordain and enthrone bishops of the province within the time determined by law with due regard for can. 86, §1, n. 2;

2° to convoke the metropolitan synod at the times fixed by the synod of bishops of the patriarchal Church; to prepare in a timely manner items to be discussed in it, to preside at the synod, to transfer, prorogue, suspend or dissolve it;

3° to erect the metropolitan tribunal;

4° to exercise vigilance so that the faith and ecclesiastical discipline are accurately observed;

5° to conduct a canonical visitation, if the eparchial bishop neglected to do so;

6° to appoint or confirm a person who has

CAN. 133 §1. Metropolitae, qui alicui provinciae intra fines territorii Ecclesiae patriarchalis praeest, in eparchiis huius provinciae praeter alia, quae iure communi ei tribuuntur, est;

1° Episcopos provinciae intra tempus iure determinatum ordinare et inthronizare firmo can. 86, §1, n. 2;

2° Synodum metropolitanam temporibus a Synodo Episcoporum Ecclesiae patriarchalis statutis convocare, quaestiones in ea tractandas opportune instruere, Synodo praeesse, eam transferre, prorogare, suspendere et dissolvere;

3° tribunal metropolitanum erigere;

4° vigilare, ut fides et disciplina ecclesiastica accurate serventur;

5° visitationem canonicam peragere, si eam Episcopus eparchialis neglexit;

6° eum, qui legitime ad officium proposi-

---

132 §3: Pius XII, m.p. *Cleri sanctitati,* 2 iun. 1957, can. 314 §3.

133 §1: Pius XII, m.p. *Cleri sanctitati,* 2 iun. 1957, can. 319. - Apost. can. 34; Nic. I, cann. 4, 6–7; Ant. can. 9; Constantinop. I, can. 2; Eph. cann. 1, 8; Chalc. can. 12; Sard. cann. 6, 9; Carth. cann. 17–18, 28, 76. * Syn. Sciarfen. Syrorum, a. 1888, cap. VII, art. IV; Syn. Alexandrin. Coptorum, a. 1898, sect. III, cap. I, art. IV.

133 §1, 1°: Pius XII, m.p. *Cleri sanctitati,* 2 iun. 1957, can. 319 n. 1. - Nic. I, can. 4; Ant. can. 20; Chalc. can. 25; Carth. cann. 18, 20; S. Xystus III, litt. *Si quantum humanis,* 8 iul. 435; S. Leo M., litt. *Omnium quidem,* 13 ian. 444. * Syn. Libanen. Maronitarum, a. 1736, pars III, cap. IV, 17.

133 §1, 2°: Apost. can. 37; Nic. I, can. 5; Ant. cann. 15–20; Chalc. can. 19; Carth. cann. 18, 72; Quinisext. can. 8; Nic. II, can. 6; Constantinop. IV, can. 17 "Consueverunt."

133 §1, 3°: Apost. can. 74; Ant. cann. 12, 14–15, 25; Constantinop. I, can. 6; Eph. can. 1; Sard. cann. 3, 14; Carth. cann. 18–19, 28, 50, 87, 100, 120, 122, 125; Constantinop. IV, can. 26.

133 §1, 4°: Pius XII, m.p. *Cleri sanctitati,* 2 iun. 1957, can. 319 n. 2. - Ant. can. 9.

133 §1, 5°: Pius XII, m.p. *Cleri sanctitati,* 2 iun. 1957, can. 319 n. 4. - Carth. 56; Constantinop. IV, can. 19.

133 §1, 6°: Pius XII, m.p. *Cleri sanctitati,* 2 iun. 1957, can. 319 n. 3. - Nic. II, can. 11.

been legitimately proposed for or elected to an office, if the eparchial bishop, though not prevented by a just impediment, has failed to do so within the time established by law; also, to appoint the eparchial finance officer if the eparchial bishop, though warned, has neglected to make the appointment.

§2. The metropolitan represents the province in all juridic matters of the same.

CAN. 134 §1. The dignity of the metropolitan is always attached to a determined eparchial see.

§2. A metropolitan in his own eparchy has the same rights and obligations as an eparchial bishop.

CAN. 135 The metropolitan is to be commemorated by all bishops and other clerics in the Divine Liturgy and the divine praises according to the prescriptions of the liturgical books.

CAN. 136 A metropolitan who presides over a province precedes everywhere a titular metropolitan.

CAN. 137 The synod of bishops of the patriarchal Church is to define in greater detail the rights and obligations of metropolitans and of the metropolitan synods according to the legitimate customs of its own patriarchal Church and also the circumstances of time and place.

CAN. 138 The rights and obligations of a metropolitan constituted outside the territorial boundaries of the patriarchal Church are the

tus vel electus est, nominare vel confirmare, si Episcopus eparchialis intra tempus iure statutum iusto impedimento non detentus id facere omisit, itemque oeconomum eparchialem nominare, si Episcopus eparchialis monitus eum nominare neglexit.

§2. In omnibus negotiis iuridicis provinciae Metropolita eiusdem personam gerit.

CAN. 134 §1. Metropolitae dignitas semper coniuncta est cum sede eparchiali determinata.

§2. Metropolita in propria eparchia eadem iura et obligationes habet ac Episcopus eparchialis in sua.

CAN. 135 Metropolita commemorandus est ab omnibus Episcopis ceterisque clericis in Divina Liturgia et in laudibus divinis secundum praescripta librorum liturgicorum.

CAN. 136 Metropolita, qui praeest provinciae, praecedit ubique Metropolitam titularem.

CAN. 137 Synodus Episcoporum Ecclesiae patriarchalis pressius determinet iura et obligationes Metropolitarum et Synodorum metropolitanarum secundum legitimas consuetudines propriae Ecclesiae patriarchalis necnon temporum et locorum adiuncta.

CAN. 138 Iura et obligationes Metropolitae extra fines territorii Ecclesiae patriarchalis constituti eadem sunt ac in can. 133,

---

134 §1: Pius XII, m.p. *Cleri sanctitati*, 2 iun. 1957, can. 315. - Apost. 34; Ant. can. 9; Constantinop. IV, can. 17. * Syn. Mar Isaaci Chaldaeorum, a. 410, can. 18.

134 §2: Pius XII, m.p. *Cleri sanctitati*, 2 iun. 1957, can. 318.

135: Pius XII, m.p. *Cleri sanctitati*, 2 iun. 1957, can. 317. - Constantinop. IV, can. 10; Protodeut. cann. 13–14; Benedictus XIV, ep. encycl. *Ex quo*, 1 mar. 1756, §22.

136: Pius XII, m.p. *Cleri sanctitati*, 2 iun. 1957, can. 339 §1. - Chalc. can. 12. * Syn. Armen., a. 1911, 229.

137: Pius XII, m.p. *Cleri sanctitati*, 2 iun. 1957, can. 316. * Syn. Sciarfen. Syrorum, a. 1888, cap. VII, art. IV; Syn. Alexandrin. Coptorum, a. 1898, sect. III, cap. I, art. IV.

138: Pius XII, m.p. *Cleri sanctitati*, 2 iun. 1957, can. 320 §1 nn. 1–5 et §2 nn. 1–2.

same as those prescribed in can. 133, §1, nn. 2–6 and §2 as well as in cann. 135, 136, 160, 1084, §3; concerning other rights and obligations, the metropolitan is to observe the special norms set forth by the synod of bishops of the patriarchal Church and approved by the Apostolic See or established by this same See.

CAN. 139   The eparchial bishop who exercises his power outside the territorial boundaries of the patriarchal Church and does not belong to a province, should designate a certain metropolitan, having consulted with the patriarch and with the approval of the Apostolic See; to this metropolitan belong the rights and obligations mentioned in can. 133, §1, nn. 3–6.

CHAPTER VII. **The Patriarchal Assembly**

CAN. 140   The patriarchal assembly is a consultative group of the entire Church presided over by the patriarch. It assists the patriarch and the synod of bishops of the patriarchal Church in dealing with matters of major importance especially in order to harmonize the forms and methods of the apostolate as well as ecclesiastical discipline, adapting them to the current circumstances of the time and to the common good of the respective Church, but also taking into account the entire territory where several Churches *sui iuris* coexist.

CAN. 141   The patriarchal assembly is to be convoked at least every five years and whenever the patriarch with the consent of the permanent synod or the synod of bishops of the patriarchal Church considers it to be useful.

CAN. 142   §1. It is for the patriarch to convoke and to preside over the patriarchal assembly and also to transfer, prorogue, suspend and

§1, nn. 2–6 et §2 necnon in cann. 135, 136, 160 et 1084, §3 praescribuntur; circa cetera iura et obligationes Metropolita servat normas speciales a Synodo Episcoporum Ecclesiae patriarchalis propositas et a Sede Apostolica approbatas vel ab ipsa hac Sede statutas.

CAN. 139   Episcopus eparchialis, qui extra fines territorii propriae Ecclesiae patriarchalis potestatem suam exercet et ad nullam provinciam pertinet, aliquem Metropolitam consulto Patriarcha et cum approbatione Sedis Apostolicae designet; huic Metropolitae competunt iura et obligationes, de quibus in can. 133, §1, nn. 3–6.

CAPUT VII. **De Conventu Patriarchali**

CAN. 140   Conventus patriarchalis est coetus consultivus totius Ecclesiae, cui Patriarcha praeest, qui Patriarchae atque Synodo Episcoporum Ecclesiae patriarchalis adiutricem operam praestat in negotiis maioris momenti gerendis praesertim ad apostolatus formas ac rationes necnon disciplinam ecclesiasticam cum occurrentibus aetatis adiunctis atque bono communi propriae Ecclesiae, ratione etiam habita boni communis totius territorii, ubi plures Ecclesiae sui iuris exstant, apte componendas.

CAN. 141   Conventus patriarchalis convocari debet quinto saltem quoque anno et de consensu Synodi permanentis aut Synodi Episcoporum Ecclesiae patriarchalis, quoties Patriarchae id utile videtur.

CAN. 142   §1. Patriarchae est conventum patriarchalem convocare, eidem praeesse atque eum transferre, prorogare,

---

139: Pius XII, m.p. *Cleri sanctitati,* 2 iun. 1957, can. 323.

dissolve it. The patriarch is to appoint a vice-president, who presides over the assembly in the absence of the patriarch.

§2. If the patriarchal see becomes vacant, the patriarchal assembly is suspended by virtue of the law itself until the new patriarch makes a decision on the matter.

CAN. 143   §1. To the patriarchal assembly are to be convoked:

1° eparchial bishops and other local hierarchs;

2° titular bishops;

3° presidents of monastic confederations, superiors general of institutes of consecrated life and superiors of monasteries *sui iuris;*

4° rectors of Catholic universities and of ecclesiastical universities as well as deans of faculties of theology and canon law, that are located within the territorial boundaries of the Church in which the assembly is held;

5° rectors of major seminaries;

6° from each eparchy at least one of the presbyters, especially pastors, ascribed to the same eparchy, one of the religious or members of societies of common life according to the manner of religious, as well as two lay persons, unless the statutes determine a greater number, all of whom are designated in a manner determined by the eparchial bishop and indeed, if it is a case of a member of a religious institute or a member of a society of the common life according to the manner of religious, with the consent of the competent superior.

§2. All who are to be convoked to the patriarchal assembly must attend it unless they are detained by a just impediment, of which they are obliged to inform the patriarch; however, eparchial bishops can send a proxy.

suspendere et dissolvere; vice-praesidem, qui in absentia Patriarchae conventui praeest, ipse Patriarcha nominet.

§2. Sede patriarchali vacante conventus patriarchalis suspenditur ipso iure, donec novus Patriarcha de re decreverit.

CAN. 143   §1. Ad conventum patriarchalem convocandi sunt:

1° Episcopi eparchiales ceterique Hierarchae loci;

2° Episcopi titulares;

3° Praesides confoederationum monasticarum, Superiores generales institutorum vitae consecratae atque Superiores monasteriorum sui iuris;

4° rectores catholicarum studiorum universitatum et ecclesiasticarum studiorum universitatum necnon decani facultatum theologiae et iuris canonici, quae intra fines territorii Ecclesiae, cuius conventus tenetur, sedem habent;

5° rectores seminariorum maiorum;

6° ex unaquaque eparchia saltem unus ex presbyteris eidem eparchiae ascriptis praesertim parochis, unus ex religiosis vel sodalibus societatum vitae communis ad instar religiosorum necnon duo laici, nisi statuta maiorem numerum determinant, qui omnes modo ab Episcopo eparchiali determinato designantur et quidem, si de sodalibus instituti religiosi vel societatis vitae communis ad instar religiosorum agitur, de consensu Superioris competentis.

§2. Omnes, qui ad conventum patriarchalem convocandi sunt, eidem interesse debent, nisi iusto detinentur impedimento, de quo Patriarcham certiorem facere tenentur; Episcopi eparchiales vero procuratorem sui loco mittere possunt.

§3. Persons of another Church *sui iuris* can be invited to the patriarchal assembly and can take part in it according to the norm of the statutes.

§4. To the patriarchal assembly can also be invited some observers from other Churches or non-Catholic ecclesial communities.

CAN. 144 §1. With due regard for the right of any of the Christian faithful to propose topics to the hierarchs, it is only for the patriarch or the synod of bishops of the patriarchal Church to determine the subjects to be treated in the patriarchal assembly.

§2. It is for the patriarch to see to it that by means of appropriate commissions and consultations, all the questions are properly studied and sent to the members of the assembly at an opportune time.

CAN. 145 The patriarchal assembly is to have its statutes approved by the synod of bishops of the patriarchal Church which should contain the norms necessary for attaining the purpose of the assembly.

CHAPTER VIII. The Territory of a Patriarchal Church and the Power of the Patriarch and Synods Outside this Territory

CAN. 146 §1. The territory of the Church over which the patriarch presides extends over those regions in which the rite proper to that Church is observed and the patriarch has a legitimately acquired right to erect provinces, eparchies, and exarchies.

§2. If any doubt concerning the territorial boundaries of the patriarchal Church arises or if it is a question of the modification of boundaries, it is for the synod of bishops of the patriarchal Church to investigate the matter. After

§3. Personae alterius Ecclesiae sui iuris ad conventum patriarchalem invitari et in eo partem habere possunt ad normam statutorum.

§4. Ad conventum patriarchalem etiam invitari possunt aliquot observatores ex Ecclesiis vel Communitatibus ecclesialibus acatholicis.

CAN. 144 §1. Firmo iure cuiuslibet christifidelis quaestiones Hierarchis indicandi solius Patriarchae vel Synodi Episcoporum Ecclesiae patriarchalis est argumenta in conventu patriarchali tractanda determinare.

§2. Patriarchae est per opportunas praevias commissiones et consultationes curare, ut omnes quaestiones apte instruantur atque tempore opportuno ad conventus membra mittantur.

CAN. 145 Conventus patriarchalis sua habeat statuta a Synodo Episcoporum Ecclesiae patriarchalis approbata, in quibus normae ad finem conventus obtinendum necessariae contineantur.

CAPUT VIII. **De Territorio Ecclesiae Patriarchalis atque de Potestate Patriarchae et Synodorum extra Hoc Territorium.**

CAN. 146 §1. Territorium Ecclesiae, cui Patriarcha praeest, ad illas regiones extenditur, in quibus ritus eidem Ecclesiae proprius servatur et Patriarcha ius legitime acquisitum habet provincias, eparchias necnon exarchias erigendi.

§2. Si quod dubium de finibus territorii Ecclesiae patriarchalis exoritur aut si de immutatione finium agitur, Synodi Episcoporum Ecclesiae patriarchalis est rem investigare audita superiore auctoritate administrativa

hearing the superior administrative authority of each Church *sui iuris* concerned, and after discussing the matter in the synod, it is up to the same synod to present a properly documented petition for the resolution of the doubt or for the modification of the boundaries to the Roman Pontiff. It is for the Roman Pontiff alone to resolve the doubt authentically or to decree a modification of the boundaries.

CAN. 147 Within the territorial boundaries of the patriarchal Church, the power of the patriarch and the synods is exercised not only over all Christian faithful who are ascribed to that Church, but also over others who do not have a local hierarch of their own Church *sui iuris* constituted in the same territory and, even if they remain ascribed in their own Church, are committed to the care of local hierarchs of that patriarchal Church with due regard for can. 916, §5.

CAN. 148 §1. It is the right and the obligation of the patriarch to seek appropriate information concerning the Christian faithful who reside outside the territorial boundaries of the Church over which he presides, even through a visitor sent by himself with the assent of the Apostolic See.

§2. The visitor, before he begins his function, is to go to the eparchial bishop of those faithful and present his letter of appointment.

§3. When the visitation is completed, the visitor is to send a report to the patriarch, who, after discussing the matter in the synod of bishops of the patriarchal Church, can propose suitable measures to the Apostolic See, in view of providing everywhere in the world for the protection and enhancement of the spiritual good of

uniuscuiusque Ecclesiae sui iuris, cuius interest, necnon re in eadem Synodo discussa petitionem apte instructam de dubio solvendo vel de finibus immutandis Romano Pontifici porrigere, cuius solius est dubium authentice dirimere vel decretum de immutatione finium ferre.

CAN. 147 Intra fines territorii Ecclesiae patriarchalis potestas Patriarchae ac Synodorum exercetur non tantum in omnes christifideles eidem Ecclesiae ascriptos, sed etiam in ceteros, qui Hierarcham loci propriae Ecclesiae sui iuris in eodem territorio constitutum non habent quique, etsi propriae Ecclesiae permanent ascripti, curae Hierarcharum loci eiusdem Ecclesiae patriarchalis committuntur firmo can. 916, §5.

CAN. 148 §1. Patriarchae ius et obligatio est circa christifideles, qui extra fines territorii Ecclesiae, cui praeest, commorantur, opportunas informationes exquirendi etiam per Visitatorem a se de assensu Sedis Apostolicae missum.

§2. Visitator, antequam suum munus init, Episcopum eparchialem horum christifidelium adeat eique nominationis litteras exhibeat.

§3. Visitatione peracta visitator ad Patriarcham relationem mittat, qui re in Synodo Episcoporum Ecclesiae patriarchalis discussa Sedi Apostolicae opportuna media proponere potest, ut ubique terrarum tuitioni atque incremento boni spiritualis christifidelium Ecclesiae, cui praeest, etiam per erec-

---

148 §1: Pius XII, m.p. *Cleri sanctitati,* 2 iun. 1957, can. 262 §1.

148 §2: Pius XII, m.p. *Cleri sanctitati,* 2 iun. 1957, can. 262 §2.

the Christian faithful of the Church over which he presides, even through the erection of parishes and exarchies or eparchies of their own.

CAN. 149 To fill the office of eparchial bishop, coadjutor bishop or auxiliary bishop outside the territorial boundaries of the patriarchal Church, the synod of bishops of the patriarchal Church elects, according to the norms of the canons on the election of bishops, at least three candidates and proposes them through the patriarch to the Roman Pontiff for appointment. Secrecy is to be observed, even toward the candidates, by all who in any way know the results of the election.

CAN. 150 §1. Bishops constituted outside the territorial boundaries of the patriarchal Church have all the synodal rights and obligations of the other bishops of the same Church with due regard for can. 102, §2.

§2. Laws enacted by the synod of bishops of the patriarchal Church and promulgated by the patriarch, have the force of law everywhere in the world if they are liturgical laws. However, if they are disciplinary laws or in the case of other decisions of the synod, they have the force of law within the territorial boundaries of the patriarchal Church.

§3. Eparchial bishops constituted outside the territorial boundaries of the patriarchal Church, who desire to do so, can attribute the force of law to disciplinary laws and other decisions of the synod in their own eparchies, provided they do not exceed their competence; if, however, these laws or decisions are approved by the Apostolic See, they have the force of law everywhere in the world.

tionem paroeciarum ac exarchiarum vel eparchiarum propriarum provideatur.

CAN. 149 Candidatos, saltem tres, ad officium Episcopi eparchialis, Episcopi coadiutoris vel Episcopi auxiliaris extra fines territorii Ecclesiae patriarchalis implendum Synodus Episcoporum Ecclesiae patriarchalis ad normam canonum de electionibus Episcoporum eligit et per Patriarcham Romano Pontifici ad nominationem proponit secreto servato ab omnibus, qui quomodolibet electionis exitum noverunt, etiam erga candidatos.

CAN. 150 §1. Episcopi extra fines territorii Ecclesiae patriarchalis constituti habent omnia iura et obligationes synodalia ceterorum Episcoporum eiusdem Ecclesiae firmo can. 102, §2.

§2. Leges a Synodo Episcoporum Ecclesiae patriarchalis latae et a Patriarcha promulgatae, si leges liturgicae sunt ubique terrarum vigent; si vero leges disciplinares sunt vel si de ceteris decisionibus Synodi agitur, vim iuris habent intra fines territorii Ecclesiae patriarchalis.

§3. Velint Episcopi eparchiales extra fines territorii Ecclesiae patriarchalis constituti legibus disciplinaribus ceterisque decisionibus synodalibus, quae eorum competentiam non excedunt, in propriis eparchiis vim iuris tribuere; si vero hae leges vel decisiones a Sede Apostolica approbatae sunt, ubique terrarum vim iuris habent.

149: S.C. pro Eccl. Orient., decl. 25 mar. 1970, 3.   150 §1: S.C. pro Eccl. Orient., decl. 25 mar. 1970, 1.

TITLE V. MAJOR ARCHIEPISCOPAL CHURCHES

TITULUS V. DE ECCLESIIS ARCHIEPISCOPALIBUS MAIORIBUS

CAN. 151 A major archbishop is the metropolitan of a see determined or recognized by the supreme authority of the Church, who presides over an entire Eastern Church *sui iuris* that is not distinguished with the patriarchal title.

CAN. 152 What is stated in common law concerning patriarchal Churches or patriarchs is understood to be applicable to major archiepiscopal Churches or major archbishops, unless the common law expressly provides otherwise or it is evident from the nature of the matter.

CAN. 153 §1. A major archbishop is elected according to the norm of cann. 63–74.

§2. After the election has been accepted by the person elected, the synod of bishops of the major archiepiscopal Church must inform the Roman Pontiff with a synodal letter about the canonical conduct of the election; the person who has been elected must, in a letter signed in his own hand, petition the confirmation of his election by the Roman Pontiff.

§3. After the confirmation has been obtained,

CAN. 151 Archiepiscopus maior est Metropolita Sedis determinatae vel agnitae a suprema Ecclesiae auctoritate, qui toti cuidam Ecclesiae orientali sui iuris titulo patriarchali non insignitae praeest.

CAN. 152 Quae in iure communi de Ecclesiis patriarchalibus vel de Patriarchis dicuntur, de Ecclesiis archiepiscopalibus maioribus vel de Archiepiscopis maioribus valere intelleguntur, nisi aliter iure communi expresse cavetur vel ex natura rei constat.

CAN. 153 §1. Archiepiscopus maior ad normam cann. 63–74 eligitur.

§2. Post acceptationem electi Synodus Episcoporum Ecclesiae archiepiscopalis maioris per litteras synodicas Romanum Pontificem certiorem facere debet de electione canonice peracta; ipse vero electus per litteras manu propria subscriptas expostulare debet a Romano Pontifice suae electionis confirmationem.

§3. Obtenta confirmatione electus coram

151: Vat. II, decr. *Orientalium Ecclesiarum,* 10; Pius XII, m.p. *Cleri sanctitati,* 2 iun. 1957, cann. 324, 335; m.p. *Sollicitudinem Nostram,* can. 20 §3. - Eph. can. 8; Carth. can. 17; Quinisext. can. 39; Clemens VIII, const. *Decet Romanum Pontificem,* 23 feb. 1596; Pius VII, litt. ap. *In universalis Ecclesiae,* 22 feb. 1807.

152: Vat. II, decr. *Orientalium Ecclesiarum,* 10; Pius XII, m.p. *Sollicitudinem Nostram,* 6 ian. 1950, can. 20 §1; m.p. *Cleri sanctitati,* 2 iun. 1957, cann. 327–331. * Syn. prov. Alba-Iulien. et Fagarasien. Rumenorum, a. 1872, tit. II, cap. III; a. 1900, tit. II, cap.

II, §1; Syn. Leopolien. Ruthenorum, a. 1891, tit. VII, cap. II, 4.

153 §1: Pius XII, m.p. *Cleri sanctitati,* 2 iun. 1957, can. 325 §§1–2. - Quinisext. can. 39.

153 §3: Innocentius III, litt. *Rex regum,* 25 feb. 1204; litt. *Ad honorem Dei,* a. 1204; litt. *Ego . . .,* a. 1204; litt. *Cum omnes,* a. 1204; Innocentius IV, const. ap. *Novit ille,* 20 dec. 1251; Clemens VIII, const. *Decet Romanum Pontificem,* 23 feb. 1596, "Verum;" S.C. de Prop. Fide, 9 iun. 1642.

the person elected must, in the presence of the synod of bishops of the major archiepiscopal Church, make a profession of faith and promise to fulfill his office faithfully; afterwards his proclamation and enthronement are to take place. If, however, the one who is elected is not yet an ordained bishop, the enthronement cannot be done validly before he receives episcopal ordination.

§4. If, however the confirmation is denied, a new election is to be conducted within the time fixed by the Roman Pontiff.

CAN. 154 Major archbishops have the precedence of honor immediately after patriarchs according to the order in which the Church they preside over was erected as a major archiepiscopal Church.

Synodo Episcoporum Ecclesiae archiepiscopalis maioris emittere debet professionem fidei et promissionem fideliter officium suum implendi, deinde procedatur ad eius proclamationem et inthronizationem; si vero electus nondum est Episcopus ordinatus, inthronizatio valide fieri non potest, antequam electus ordinationem episcopalem suscepit.

§4. Si vero confirmatio denegatur, nova electio fiat intra tempus a Romano Pontifice statutum.

CAN. 154 Honoris praecedentiam immediate post Patriarchas Archiepiscopi maiores obtinent secundum ordinem erectionis Ecclesiae, cui praesunt, in Ecclesiam archiepiscopalem maiorem.

TITLE VI. METROPOLITAN CHURCHES AND OTHER CHURCHES *SUI IURIS*

CHAPTER I. **Metropolitan Churches** *Sui Iuris*

CAN. 155 §1. A metropolitan Church *sui iuris* is presided over by a metropolitan of a determined see who has been appointed by the Roman Pontiff and is assisted by a council of hierarchs in accord with the norm of law.

§2. It is solely for the supreme authority of the Church to erect, modify, and suppress metropolitan Churches *sui iuris* as well as to define their territorial boundaries.

CAN. 156 §1. Within three months of his episcopal ordination or, if already an ordained bishop, from his enthronement, the metropolitan is bound by the obligation to request from the Roman Pontiff the pallium, a symbol of metropolitan power and of the full communion of the metropolitan Church *sui iuris* with the Roman Pontiff.

§2. Prior to the imposition of the pallium, the metropolitan cannot convoke the council of hierarchs nor ordain bishops.

CAN. 157 §1. The power that a metropoli-

CAPUT I. **De Ecclesiis** **Metropolitanis Sui Iuris**

CAN. 155 §1. Ecclesiae metropolitanae sui iuris praeest Metropolita sedis determinatae a Romano Pontifice nominatus et a Consilio Hierarcharum ad normam iuris adiutus.

§2. Solius supremae Ecclesiae auctoritatis est Ecclesias metropolitanas sui iuris erigere, immutare et supprimere earumque territorium certis finibus circumscribere.

CAN. 156 §1. Intra tres menses ab ordinatione episcopali vel, si iam Episcopus ordinatus est, ab inthronizatione computandos Metropolita obligatione tenetur a Romano Pontifice petendi pallium, quod est signum suae potestatis metropolitanae atque plenae communionis Ecclesiae metropolitanae sui iuris cum Romano Pontifice.

§2. Ante pallii impositionem Metropolita non potest Consilium Hierarcharum convocare et Episcopos ordinare.

CAN. 157 §1. Potestas, quae Metropo-

---

155 §2: Pius XII, m.p. *Postquam Apostolicis Litteris,* 9 feb. 1952, can. 303 §1 n. 1; m.p. *Cleri sanctitati,* 2 iun. 1957, can. 159. - Innocentius III, litt. *Rex regum,* 25 feb. 1204.

156 §1: Pius XII, m.p. *Cleri sanctitati,* 2 iun. 1957,

can. 321 §1. - Carth. can. 17; Constantinop. IV, can. 27. * Syn. prov. Alba-Iulien. et Fagarasien. Rumenorum, a. 1872, tit. II, cap. III, 7.

156 §2: Pius XII, m.p. *Cleri sanctitati,* 2 iun. 1957, can. 321 §2.

tan possesses in accord with the norm of law over the bishops and other Christian faithful of the metropolitan Church over which he presides, is ordinary and proper, but it is personal so that he cannot constitute a vicar for the entire metropolitan Church *sui iuris* nor delegate his power to someone for all cases.

§2. The power of the metropolitan and the council of hierarchs is exercised validly only within the territorial boundaries of the metropolitan Church *sui iuris.*

§3. The metropolitan represents the metropolitan Church *sui iuris* in all its juridic affairs.

CAN. 158 §1. The see of the metropolitan Church *sui iuris* is in the principal city from which the metropolitan, who presides in that Church, takes his title.

§2. The metropolitan, in the eparchy entrusted to him, has the same rights and obligations as an eparchial bishop.

CAN. 159 In the metropolitan Church *sui iuris* over which he presides, besides that which is accorded to him by common law or particular law established by the Roman Pontiff, the metropolitan is competent:

1° to ordain and enthrone bishops of the same Church within the time determined by law;

2° to convoke the council of hierarchs in ac-

litae ad normam iuris in Episcopos ceterosque christifideles Ecclesiae metropolitanae, cui praeest, competit, est ordinaria et propria, sed ita personalis, ut ipse non possit Vicarium pro tota Ecclesia metropolitana sui iuris constituere aut potestatem suam alicui ad universitatem casuum delegare.

§2. Potestas Metropolitae et Consilii Hierarcharum valide exercetur solummodo intra fines territorii Ecclesiae metropolitanae sui iuris.

§3. In omnibus negotiis iuridicis Ecclesiae metropolitanae sui iuris Metropolita eiusdem personam gerit.

CAN. 158 §1. Ecclesiae metropolitanae sui iuris sedes est in civitate principe, a qua Metropolita, qui eidem Ecclesiae praeest, titulum desumit.

§2. Metropolita in eparchia sibi concredita eadem iura et obligationes habet ac Episcopus eparchialis in sua.

CAN. 159 In Ecclesia metropolitana sui iuris, cui praeest, Metropolitae praeter ea, quae iure communi vel iure particulari a Romano Pontifice statuto ei tribuuntur, competit:

1° Episcopos eiusdem Ecclesiae intra tempus iure determinatum ordinare et inthronizare;

2° Consilium Hierarcharum ad normam

---

157 §2: Apost. cann. 14, 34–35; Nic. I, can. 6; Ant. cann. 13, 22; Constantinop. I, can. 2; Eph. can. 8; Chalc. can. 28; Constantinop. IV, can. 23.

158 §2: Pius XII, m.p. *Cleri sanctitati,* 2 iun. 1957, can. 318.

159: Pius XII, m.p. *Cleri sanctitati,* 2 iun. 1957, can. 320. - Nic. I, can. 7; Chalc. can. 12.

159, 1°: Pius XII, m.p. *Cleri sanctitati,* 2 iun. 1957, cann. 320 n. 4, 319 n. 1. - Nic. I, cann. 4, 6; Eph. can. 8; Chalc. can. 25; Sard. can 6; Carth. cann. 18–19, 89; S. Xystus III, litt. *Si quantum humanis,* 8 iul. 435; S. Leo M., litt. *Omnium quidem,* 13 ian. 444. * Syn.

prov. Alba-Iulien. et Fagarasien. Rumenorum, a. 1872, tit. II, cap. III, 3).

159, 2°: Pius XII, m.p. *Cleri sanctitati,* 2 iun. 1957, can. 340 §2. - Apost. can. 37; Nic. I, can. 5; Ant. cann. 16–20; Laod. can. 40; Chalc. can. 19; Carth. cann. 18, 76; Quinisext. can. 8; Nic. II, can. 6; Constantinop. IV, can. 17 "Consueverunt." * Syn. prov. Cobrin. Ruthenorum, a. 1626, XIII; Syn. prov. Alba-Iulien. et Fagarasien. Rumenorum, a. 1872, tit. II, cap. III, 3); tit. III, cap. III "Synodorum;" Syn. Leopolien. Ruthenorum, a. 1891, tit. XIV, 3.

cord with the norm of law, to prepare an agenda of the questions to be treated in it, to preside, transfer, prorogue, suspend or dissolve it;

3° to erect the metropolitan tribunal;
4° to exercise vigilance so that the faith and ecclesiastical discipline are accurately observed;
5° to conduct a canonical visitation if the eparchial bishop has neglected to do so;

6° to appoint an administrator of an eparchy in the case mentioned in can. 221, n. 4;
7° to appoint or confirm a person who has been legitimately proposed for or elected to an office if the eparchial bishop, though not prevented by a just impediment, has failed to do so within the time fixed by law; also, to appoint the eparchial finance officer if the eparchial bishop, though warned, has neglected to make the appointment.

8° to communicate the acts of the Roman Pontiff to the eparchial bishops and others concerned, unless the Apostolic See has directly provided for it, and see to the faithful execution of the prescriptions contained in these acts.

CAN. 160 In extraordinary matters or those entailing special difficulty, the eparchial bishops are not to fail to hear the metropolitan nor the metropolitan the eparchial bishops.

iuris convocare, quaestiones in eodem tractandas opportune instruere, eidem praeesse atque id transferre, prorogare, suspendere et dissolvere;

3° tribunal metropolitanum erigere;
4° vigilare, ut fides et disciplina ecclesiastica accurate serventur;
5° visitationem canonicam in eparchiis peragere, si eam Episcopus eparchialis neglexit;

6° nominare Administratorem eparchiae in casu, de quo in can. 221, n. 4;
7° eum, qui legitime ad officium propositus vel electus est, nominare vel confirmare, si Episcopus eparchialis intra tempus iure statutum iusto impedimento non detentus id facere omisit, itemque oeconomum eparchialem nominare, si Episcopus eparchialis monitus eum nominare neglexit;

8° Romani Pontificis acta cum Episcopis eparchialibus aliisque, ad quos pertinent, communicare, nisi Sedes Apostolica directe providit, et praescriptorum, quae in his actis continentur, fidelem exsecutionem curare.

CAN. 160 In negotiis extraordinariis vel specialem difficultatem secum ferentibus Episcopi eparchiales Metropolitam et Metropolita Episcopos eparchiales audire ne omittant.

159, 3°: Apost. can. 74; Ant. cann. 12, 14–15, 25; Constantinop. I, can. 6; Eph. can. 1; Sard. cann. 3, 14; Carth. cann. 19, 28, 87, 100, 120, 125; Constantinop. IV, can. 26.
159, 4°: Pius XII, m.p. *Cleri sanctitati,* 2 iun. 1957, can. 320 n. 2. - Ant. can. 9. * Syn. Zamosten. Ruthenorum, a. 1720, tit. V; Syn. prov. Alba-Iulien. et Fagarasien. Rumenorum, a. 1872, tit. II, cap. III, 6).
159, 5°: Pius XII, m.p. *Cleri sanctitati,* 2 iun. 1957, can. 320 n. 3. - Constantinop. IV, can. 19. * Syn. prov. Alba-Iulien. et Fagarasien. Rumenorum, a. 1872, tit. II, cap. III, 6).

159, 6°: Pius XII, m.p. *Cleri sanctitati,* 2 iun. 1957, can. 470 §2.
159, 7°: Pius XII, m.p. *Cleri sanctitati,* 2 iun. 1957, can. 320 §1 n. 4. - Nic. II, can. 11.
159, 8°: Pius XII, m.p. *Cleri sanctitati,* 2 iun. 1957, can. 320 §2 n. 1.
160: Pius XII, m.p. *Cleri sanctitati,* 2 iun. 1957, cann. 259 §3, 320 §2 n. 2. - Apost. can. 34; Ant. cann. 9, 11. * Syn. prov. Alba-Iulien. et Fagarasien. Rumenorum, a. 1872, tit. II, cap. II, 2); a. 1900, tit. II, cap. II, §1.

CAN. 161 The metropolitan is to be commemorated after the Roman Pontiff by all the bishops and other clerics in the Divine Liturgy and in the divine praises, according to the prescriptions of the liturgical books.

CAN. 162 The metropolitan should commemorate the Roman Pontiff in the Divine Liturgy and in the divine praises as a sign of full communion with him, according to the prescriptions of the liturgical books; he should also see to it that this is done faithfully by all the bishops and the other clerics of the Church over which he presides.

CAN. 163 The metropolitan is to have frequent dealings with the Roman Pontiff. The visit he has to make every five years according to the norm of can. 208, §2, is to be made, as far as possible, together with all the bishops of the metropolitan Church over which he presides.

CAN. 164 §1. All and only the ordained bishops of the metropolitan Church *sui iuris,* wherever they are constituted, must be called to the council of hierarchs, except those mentioned in can. 953, §1 or those who have been punished with the canonical penalties mentioned in cann. 1433 and 1434. Bishops of another Church *sui iuris* can be invited as guests only if the majority of the members of the council of hierarchs agrees.

§2. Eparchial bishops and coadjutor bishops have a deliberative vote in the council of hier-

CAN. 161 Metropolita commemorandus est post Romanum Pontificem ab omnibus Episcopis ceterisque clericis in Divina Liturgia et in laudibus divinis secundum praescripta librorum liturgicorum.

CAN. 162 Metropolita commemorationem Romani Pontificis in signum plenae communionis cum eo in Divina Liturgia et in laudibus divinis secundum praescripta librorum liturgicorum debet facere et curare, ut ab omnibus Episcopis ceterisque clericis Ecclesiae metropolitanae, cui praeest, fideliter fiat

CAN. 163 Metropolitae cum Romano Pontifice frequens sit consuetudo; visitatio vero, quam singulis quinquenniis ad normam can. 208, §2 peragere debet, quatenus fieri potest, una cum omnibus Episcopis Ecclesiae metropolitanae, cui praeest, fiat.

CAN. 164 §1. Ad Consilium Hierarcharum vocari debent omnes et soli Episcopi ordinati eiusdem Ecclesiae metropolitanae sui iuris ubicumque constituti exclusis eis, de quibus in can. 953, §1, vel eis, qui poenis canonicis, de quibus in cann. 1433 et 1434, puniti sunt; Episcopi alterius Ecclesiae sui iuris nonnisi ut hospites invitari possunt, si maiori parti membrorum Consilii Hierarcharum id placet.

§2. Suffragium deliberativum in Consilio Hierarcharum habent Episcopi eparchiales et

161: Pius XII, m.p. *Cleri sanctitati,* 2 iun. 1957, can. 317. - Constantinop. IV, can. 10; Protodeut. cann. 14–15; Benedictus XIV, ep. encycl. *Ex quo,* 1 mar. 1756, §22. * Syn. prov. Alba-Iulien. et Fagarasien. Rumenorum, a. 1872, tit. II, cap. III, 1); Syn. Leopolien. Ruthenorum, a. 1891, tit. VII, cap. II, 4.

162: Pius XII, m.p. *Cleri sanctitati,* 2 iun. 1957, cann. 166, 330 §1. - Callixtus III, const. *Reddituri de commisso,* 3 sep. 1457, §1; Benedictus XIV, ep. encycl. *Ex quo,* 1 mar. 1756, §§9–17; S.C. de Prop. Fide, litt. 4 iul. 1833, n. II; litt. 29 maii 1838; instr. 31 iul. 1902,

13, e). * Syn. Zamosten. Ruthenorum, a. 1720, tit. I "Eadem;" Syn. prov. Alba-Iulien. et Fagarasien. Rumenorum, a. 1872, tit. II, cap. II "Et quoniam."

164 §1: Vat. II, decr. *Orientalium Ecclesiarum,* 23; Pius XII, m.p. *Cleri sanctitati,* 2 iun. 1957, cann. 340 §2, 342–343. - Apost. can. 34; Clemens XIII, litt. ap. *In summo apostolatus,* 15 iun. 1765; S.C. de Prop. Fide, litt. (ad Ep. Magno Varadinen. Rumen.), 23 sep. 1871, n. 2. * Syn. prov. Alba-Iulien. et Fagarasien. Rumenorum, a. 1872, tit. II, cap. III, 3); tit. III, cap. III; Syn. Leopolien. Ruthenorum, a. 1891, tit. XIV, 1–2.

archs; the other bishops of the metropolitan Church *sui iuris* can have this vote if this is expressly established in particular law.

CAN. 165 §1. All bishops legitimately called to the council of hierarchs are bound by a grave obligation to attend it, except those who have already resigned from office.

§2. If a bishop considers himself to be prevented by a just impediment, he is to present his reasons in writing to the council of hierarchs. It is for the bishops who have a deliberative vote and who are present in the designated place at the beginning of the sessions of the council are to decide on the legitimacy of the impediment.

§3. No member of the council of hierarchs can send a proxy nor does anyone have more than one vote.

§4. After the council of hierarchs has begun, it is not permitted for any of those who must attend it to absent himself except for a just reason approved by the president of the council.

CAN. 166 §1. Unless particular law requires a higher quorum, any session of the council of hierarchs is canonical and any given balloting is valid if a majority of the bishops who are obliged to attend is present.

§2. The council of hierarchs decides matters by an absolute majority of those who have a deliberative vote and who are present.

CAN. 167 §1. With due regard for the

Episcopi coadiutores; ceteri vero Episcopi Ecclesiae metropolitanae sui iuris hoc suffragium habere possunt, si hoc in iure particulari expresse statuitur.

CAN. 165 §1. Omnes Episcopi ad Consilium Hierarcharum legitime vocati gravi obligatione tenentur, ut eidem Consilio intersint eis exceptis, qui officio suo iam renuntiaverunt.

§2. Si quis Episcopus iusto impedimento se detineri existimat, scripto suas rationes aperiat Consilio Hierarcharum; de legitimitate impedimenti decidere est Episcoporum, qui suffragium deliberativum habent et in loco designato initio sessionum Consilii praesentes sunt.

§3. Nemo ex Consilii Hierarcharum membris procuratorem sui loco mittere potest nec quisquam plura suffragia habet.

§4. Consilio Hierarcharum incohato nemini eorum, qui interesse debent, licet discedere nisi iusta de causa a Consilii praeside approbata.

CAN. 166 §1. Nisi ius particulare maiorem praesentiam exigit, quaelibet Consilii Hierarcharum sessio canonica atque singulum scrutinium validum est, si maior pars Episcoporum, qui tenentur Consilio Hierarcharum interesse, praesens est.

§2. Consilium Hierarcharum negotia decidit ad partem absolute maiorem suffragiorum eorum, qui suffragium deliberativum habent et praesentes sunt.

CAN. 167 §1. Firmis canonibus, in

---

165 §1: Pius XII, m.p. *Cleri sanctitati,* 2 iun. 1957, can. 341 §1. - Laod. can. 40; Chalc. can. 19; Sard. can. 6; Carth. can. 76; Quinisext. can. 8; Constantinop. IV, can. 17. * Syn. prov. Alba-Iulien. et Fagarasien. Rumenorum, a. 1872, tit. II, cap. III, 3); tit. III, cap. III "Membra."

165 §2: Pius XII, m.p. *Cleri sanctitati,* 2 iun. 1957, can. 345 §1 n. 2.

165 §3: Pius XII, m.p. *Cleri sanctitati,* 2 iun. 1957, can. 345.

165 §4: Pius XII, m.p. *Cleri sanctitati,* 2 iun. 1957, can. 348. * Syn. prov. Alba-Iulien. et Fagarasien. Rumenorum, a. 1872, tit. III, cap. III "Membra."

166 §1: Pius XII, m.p. *Cleri sanctitati,* 2 iun. 1957, can. 346.

canons in which the power of the council of hierarchs to enact laws and norms is expressly treated, this council can also enact them in cases in which common law remits the matter to the particular law of a Church *sui iuris.*

§2. The metropolitan is to inform the Apostolic See as soon as possible of the laws and norms enacted by the council of hierarchs. Laws and norms cannot be validly promulgated before the metropolitan has written notification from the Apostolic See of the reception of the acts of the council. The metropolitan is also to inform the Apostolic See of other acts of the council of hierarchs.

§3. The metropolitan is to see to it that the laws of the council of hierarchs are promulgated and its decisions published.

§4. Without prejudice to the canons that deal expressly with the administrative acts of the metropolitan who presides in a metropolitan Church *sui iuris,* it is for him also to perform those administrative acts which are committed by common law to the superior administrative authority of a Church *sui iuris,* however, with the consent of the council of hierarchs

CAN. 168 Concerning the appointment of the metropolitan and bishops, the council of hierarchs is to compile for each case a list of at least three of the more suitable candidates and to send it to the Apostolic See, observing secrecy even toward the candidates. In order to compile the list, the members of the council of hierarchs, if they consider it opportune, can inquire of some presbyters or other Christian faithful who are outstanding in wisdom for their opinion about the needs of the Church and the special qualities of the candidate for the episcopate.

quibus expresse de potestate Consilii Hierarcharum leges et normas ferendi agitur, hoc Consilium eas ferre potest etiam in eis casibus, in quibus ius commune rem remittit ad ius particulare Ecclesiae sui iuris.

§2. De legibus et normis a Consilio Hierarcharum latis Metropolita Sedem Apostolicam quam primum certiorem faciat nec leges ac normae valide promulgari possunt, antequam Metropolita notitiam a Sede Apostolica scripto datam habuit de Consilii actorum receptione; etiam de ceteris in Consilio Hierarcharum gestis Metropolita Sedem Apostolicam certiorem faciat.

§3. Metropolitae est curare promulgationem legum et publicationem decisionum Consilii Hierarcharum.

§4. Firmis canonibus, in quibus expresse de actibus administrativis Metropolitae, qui Ecclesiae metropolitanae sui iuris praeest, agitur, eius est etiam illos actus administrativos ponere, qui iure communi superiori auctoritati administrativae Ecclesiae sui iuris committuntur, de consensu tamen Consilii Hierarcharum.

CAN. 168 Ad Metropolitae et Episcoporum nominationem quod attinet, Consilium Hierarcharum pro unoquoque casu elenchum componat trium saltem candidatorum magis idoneorum eundemque Sedi Apostolicae secreto servato, etiam erga candidatos, mittat; quem elenchum ut componant, membra Consilii Hierarcharum, si id expedire iudicant, de necessitatibus Ecclesiae et de dotibus specialibus candidati ad episcopatum sententiam aliquorum presbyterorum vel aliorum christifidelium sapientia praestantium exquirere possunt.

167 §2: Pius XII, m.p. *Cleri Sanctitati,* 2 iun. 1957, can. 350 §1. * Syn. Zamosten. Ruthenorum, a. 1720, tit. V; Syn. prov. Alba-Iulien. et Fagarasien. Rumenorum, a. 1872, tit. III, cap. III "Obiecta."

CAN. 169 The council of hierarchs is to see that the pastoral needs of the Christian faithful are provided for; in these matters it can determine what seems opportune to promote the growth of faith, to foster common pastoral action, to regulate the morals, to observe their own rite and ecclesiastical discipline.

CAN. 170 The council of hierarchs is to convene at least once a year and whenever required by special circumstances or business is to be transacted that is reserved to this council by common law, or for the execution of which the consent of this council is needed.

CAN. 171 The council of hierarchs is to draw up its statutes, to be transmitted to the Apostolic See, which provide for a secretary of the council, preparatory commissions, the order of procedure as well as other means which are conducive to attain effectively its purpose.

CAN. 172 In the metropolitan Church *sui iuris,* an assembly is be held in accord with the norms of cann. 140-145 and is to be convoked at least every five years; what is said in these canons regarding the patriarch applies to the metropolitan.

CAN. 173 §1. During the vacancy of the metropolitan see in a metropolitan Church *sui iuris:*

1° the administrator of the metropolitan

CAN. 169 Consilium Hierarcharum curet, ut necessitatibus pastoralibus christifidelium provideatur, atque de eis potest statuere, quae ad fidei incrementum provehendum, ad actionem pastoralem communem fovendam, ad moderandos mores, ad proprium ritum necnon ad disciplinam ecclesiasticam communem servandam opportuna esse videntur.

CAN. 170 Consilium Hierarcharum locum habeat semel saltem in anno et, quoties id postulant specialia adiuncta aut expedienda sunt negotia iure communi huic Consilio reservata vel pro quibus peragendis consensus eiusdem Consilii requiritur.

CAN. 171 Consilium Hierarcharum sua conficiat statuta Sedi Apostolicae transmittenda, in quibus provideatur de secretaria Consilii, de commissionibus praeparatoriis, de ordine procedendi necnon de aliis mediis, quae fini consequendo efficacius consulant.

CAN. 172 In Ecclesia metropolitana sui iuris conventus ad normam cann. 140–145 habeatur et quinto saltem quoque anno convocetur; quae ibidem de Patriarcha dicuntur, Metropolitae competunt.

CAN. 173 §1. Sede metropolitana in Ecclesiis metropolitanis sui iuris vacante:

1° Administrator Ecclesiae metropoli-

169: Pius XII, m.p. *Cleri sanctitati,* 2 iun. 1957, can. 349. - Apost. can. 37; Nic. I, can. 5; Constantinop. I, can. 2; Ant. can. 20; Laod. can. 40; Carth. can. 95; Chalc. cann. 17, 19; Nic. II, can. 6; Quinisext. cann. 8, 25; Constantinop. IV, can. 26; S. Basilius M., can. 47; S. C. de Prop. Fide, (C.P.), instr. (ad Poloniae Nuntium), 31 maii 1629; (C.P.), 7 iun. 1638; litt. (ad Ep. Fagarasien. et Alba-Iulien.), 12 iul. 1867, n. 1; Leo XIII, ep. *Litteris datis,* 15 iun. 1901. * Syn. Zamosten. Ruthenorum, a. 1720, tit. IV; Syn. prov.

Alba-Iulien. et Fagarasien. Rumenorum, a. 1872, tit. III, cap. III "Praecipua."

170: Pius XII, m.p. *Cleri sanctitati,* 2 iun. 1957, can. 344. - Apost. can. 37; Nic. I, can. 5; Ant. can. 20; Chalc. can. 19; Carth. can. 18; Quinisext. can. 8; Nic. II, can. 6; Constantinop. IV, can. 17; Urbanus VIII, const. *Sacrosanctum apostolatus,* 12 mar. 1625; S.C. de Prop. Fide, instr. 9 aug. 1760, n. IV. * Syn. prov. Alba-Iulien. et Fagarasien. Rumenorum, a. 1872, tit. III, cap. III.

Church *sui iuris* is the eparchial bishop of the same Church who is senior by episcopal ordination; he is to inform the Roman Pontiff as soon as possible of the vacancy of the metropolitan see;

2° to the administrator of a metropolitan Church *sui iuris* passes the ordinary power of the metropolitan in all matters, excluding those which cannot be executed without the consent of the council of hierarchs;

3° during the vacancy of the metropolitan see, no innovation is to be made.

§2. In these Churches when a metropolitan see is impeded, what has been established for an impeded patriarchal see in can. 132, §1 is to be observed; what is said there about the patriarch applies to the metropolitan.

§3. Concerning the vacant or impeded see of the eparchy of the metropolitan cann. 221–233 are to be observed.

CHAPTER II. Other Churches *Sui Iuris*

CAN. 174 A Church *sui iuris,* that is neither patriarchal, major archiepiscopal nor metropolitan is entrusted to a hierarch who presides over it according to the norm of common law and the particular law established by the Roman Pontiff.

CAN. 175 These Churches depend immediately on the Apostolic See. The rights and obligations mentioned in can. 159, nn. 3–8 are exercised by a hierarch delegated by the Apostolic See.

CAN. 176 If common law relegates something to particular law or to the higher administrative authority of a Church *sui iuris,* the competent authority in these Churches is the hierarch who presides over it in accordance with the norm of law; however, he needs the consent of the Apostolic See, unless it is expressly stated otherwise.

tanae sui iuris est Episcopus eparchialis eiusdem Ecclesiae ordinatione episcopali senior, qui quam primum Romanum Pontificem de sedis metropolitanae vacatione certiorem faciat;

2° ad Administratorem Ecclesiae metropolitanae sui iuris transit potestas ordinaria Metropolitae eis omnibus exclusis, quae agi non possunt nisi de consensu Consilii Hierarcharum;

3° sede metropolitana vacante nihil innovetur.

§2. Sede metropolitana in his Ecclesiis impedita serventur ea, quae de Sede patriarchali impedita in can. 132, §1 statuta sunt; quae ibidem de Patriarcha dicuntur, Metropolitae competunt.

§3. Circa sedem vacantem vel impeditam eparchiae Metropolitae serventur cann. 221–233.

CAPUT II. De Ceteris Ecclesiis Sui Iuris

CAN. 174 Ecclesia sui iuris, quae neque est patriarchalis nec archiepiscopalis maior nec metropolitana, concreditur Hierarchae, qui ei praeest ad normam iuris communis et iuris particularis a Romano Pontifice statuti.

CAN. 175 Hae Ecclesiae immediate a Sede Apostolica dependent; iura et obligationes vero, de quibus in can. 159, nn. 3–8, Hierarcha a Sede Apostolica delegatus exercet.

CAN. 176 Si ius commune aliquid remittit ad ius particulare aut ad superiorem auctoritatem administrativam Ecclesiae sui iuris, auctoritas competens in his Ecclesiis est Hierarcha, qui ei ad normam iuris praeest, de consensu Sedis Apostolicae, nisi aliud expresse statuitur.

TITLE VII. EPARCHIES AND BISHOPS

EPARCHIIS ET
DE EPISCOPIS

CHAPTER I. **Bishops**

CAPUT I. **De Episcopis**

CAN. 177 §1. An eparchy is a portion of the people of God that is entrusted to a bishop to shepherd, with the cooperation of the presbyters, in such a way that, adhering to its pastor and gathered by him through the gospel and the Eucharist in the Holy Spirit, it constitutes a particular Church in which the one, holy, catholic and apostolic Church of Christ truly exists and is operative.

§2. In the erection, modification, and suppression of eparchies within the territorial boundaries of the patriarchal Church, can. 85, §1 is to be observed; in other cases for the erection, modification and suppression of eparchies, only the Apostolic See is competent.

CAN. 178 The eparchial bishop, to whom the eparchy has been entrusted to shepherd in his own name, governs it as the vicar and legate of Christ; the power which he exercises personally in the name of Christ, is proper, ordinary, and immediate, although by the supreme au-

CAN. 177 §1. Eparchia est populi Dei portio, quae Episcopo cum cooperatione presbyterii pascenda concreditur ita, ut Pastori suo adhaerens et ab eo per Evangelium et Eucharistiam in Spiritu Sancto congregata Ecclesiam particularem constituat, in qua vere inest et operatur una, sancta, catholica et apostolica Christi Ecclesia.

§2. In erectione, immutatione et suppressione eparchiarum intra fines territorii Ecclesiae patriarchalis servandus est can. 85, §1; in ceteris casibus eparchiarum erectio, immutatio et suppressio competit soli Sedi Apostolicae.

CAN. 178 Episcopus eparchialis, cui scilicet eparchia nomine proprio pascenda concredita est, eam ut vicarius et legatus Christi regit; potestas, qua ipse nomine Christi personaliter fungitur, est propria, ordinaria et immediata, etsi a suprema Ecclesiae

177 §1: Vat. II, decr. *Christus Dominus,* 11 "Dioecesis;" const. *Lumen gentium,* 25 "Inter," 26 "Episcopus," 28 "Presbyteri;" const. *Sacrosanctum Concilium,* 41; decr. *Presbyterorum ordinis,* 4 "Populus."

177 §2: Pius XII, m.p. *Cleri sanctitati,* 2 iun. 1957, cann. 159, 248 §1 n. 1. - S. Innocentius I, litt. *Et onus et honor,* a. c. 415, "Nam quod sciscitaris;" Chalc. can. 12; Carth. cann. 17, 55; S. Nicolaus I, litt. *Ad consulta vestra,* 13 nov. 866, "A quo autem;" Leo XII, const. ap. *Petrus Apostolorum princeps,* 15 aug. 1824; Leo XIII, litt. ap. *Christi Domini,* a. 1895. Vat. II, decr.

Orientalium Ecclesiarum, 9 "Haec."

178: Vat. II, const. *Lumen gentium,* 27; decr. *Christus Dominus,* 8, a), 11; Pius XII, m.p. *Cleri sanctitati,* 2 iun. 1957, cann. 392 §1, 397 §1. - Apost. cann. 34, 39; Ant. can. 9; Trid., sess. XXIII, *De ordine,* cap. 4, can. 8; Vat. I, sess. IV, cap. III, *De vi et ratione primatus Romani pontificis;* Leo XIII, ep. encycl. *Satis cognitum,* 29 iun. 1896 "Si Petri. * Syn. Mar Isaaci Chaldaeorum, a. 410, can. 18; Syn. Sciarfen. Syrorum, a. 1888, cap. IX, art. V, 1.

thority of the Church its exercise is ultimately regulated and can be circumscribed within certain limits in view of the benefit of the Church or of the Christian faithful.

CAN. 179 Bishops to whom no eparchy has been entrusted for governance in their own name, no matter what other function they exercise or have exercised in the name of the Church, are called titular bishops.

ART. I. *The Election of Bishops*

CAN. 180 In order for a person to be considered suitable for the episcopate, he must:

1° be outstanding in solid faith, good morals, piety, zeal for souls and prudence;

2° have a good reputation;

3° not be bound by a marriage bond;

4° be at least thirty-five years old;

5° be constituted in the order of presbyter for at least five years;

6° hold a doctorate or licentiate or at least have expertise in some sacred science.

CAN. 181 §1. Within the territorial bound-

auctoritate exercitium eiusdem potestatis ultimatim regitur et certis limitibus intuitu utilitatis Ecclesiae vel christifidelium circumscribi potest.

CAN. 179 Episcopi, quibus eparchia nomine proprio regenda concredita non est, quodcumque aliud munus in Ecclesia exercent vel exercuerunt, Episcopi titulares vocantur.

ART. I. *De Electione Episcoporum*

CAN. 180 Ut quis idoneus ad episcopatum habeatur, requiritur, ut sit:

1° firma fide, bonis moribus, pietate, animarum zelo et prudentia praestans;

2° bona existimatione gaudens;

3° vinculo matrimonii non ligatus;

4° annos natus saltem triginta quinque;

5° a quinquennio saltem in ordine presbyteratus constitutus;

6° in aliqua scientia sacra doctor vel licentiatus vel saltem peritus.

CAN. 181 §1. Episcopi intra fines terri-

180: Pius XII, m.p. *Cleri sanctitati,* 2 iun. 1957, can. 394 §§1–2. - Nic. II, can. 2; S. Leo M., litt. *Quanta fraternitati,* a. 446, "In civitatibus;" S.C. de Prop. Fide, instr. 31 iul. 1902, 8. * Syn. Mar Isaaci Chaldaeorum, a. 410, can. 1; Syn. Sisen. Armenorum, a. 1246, can. 1; Syn. Zamosten. Ruthenorum, a. 1720, tit. VI; Syn. Libanen. Maronitarum, a. 1736, pars III, cap. IV, 3, 16; Syn. Sciarfen. Syrorum, a. 1888, cap. V, art. XIII, §10, 4; Syn. Leopolien. Ruthenorum, a. 1891, tit. VII, cap. III, 2.

180, 1°: Pius XII, m.p. *Cleri sanctitati,* 2 iun. 1957, can. 394 §1 n. 5. - Laod. can. 12; Sard. can. 2; Carth. can. 50; S. Hormisdas, litt. *De laboribus tui,* 3 dec. 519. * Syn. Alexandrin. Coptorum, a. 1898, sect. III, cap. II, art. IV, 6; Syn. Armen., a. 1911, 247.

180, 3°: Pius XII, m.p. *Cleri sanctitati,* 2 iun. 1957, can. 394 §1 n. 2. - Apost. can. 40; Quinisext. cann. 12, 48; S. Leo M., litt. *Quanta fraternitati,* a. 446, "Nam cum;" S.C. de Prop. Fide, decis. 22 sep. 1862. * Syn. prov. Alba-Iulien. et Fagarasien. Rumenorum, a. 1872, tit. V, cap. VII, I, g); Syn. Sciarfen. Syrorum, a.

1888, cap. VI, art. VII, 1; Syn. Alexandrin. Coptorum, a. 1898, sect. II, cap. III, art. VII, §5, II.

180, 4°: Pius XII, m.p. *Cleri sanctitati,* 2 iun. 1957, can. 394 §1 n. 3. * Syn. Sciarfen. Syrorum, a. 1888, cap. V, art. XIII, §10, 4.

180, 5°: Pius XII, m.p. *Cleri sanctitati,* 2 iun. 1957, can. 394 §1 n. 4. - Apost. can. 80; Laod. can. 12; Sard. can. 10; Constantinop. IV, can. 5; Pius IX, all. *Cum ex hac vita,* 12 iul. 1867, "Cum autem." * Syn. Sciarfen. Syrorum, a. 1888, cap. V, art. XIII, §10, 4.

180, 6°: Pius XII, m.p. *Cleri sanctitati,* 2 iun. 1957, can. 394 §1 n. 6.

181 §1: Pius XII, m.p. *Cleri sanctitati,* 2 iun. 1957, can. 251. - Nic. I, cann. 4, 6; Eph. can. 8; Ant. cann. 16, 19, 23; Laod. can. 12; Carth. cann. 50, 78; Nic. II, can. 3; S. Iulius, litt. *Legi litteras,* a. 341, "At nunc ignoro;" Constantinop. IV, can. 22; Innocentius IV, ep. *Iustis petentium,* 8 aug. 1243; Iulius III, const. ap. *Cum nos nuper,* 28 apr. 1553, "Nec non;" Benedictus XIV, const. *Apostolica praedecessorum,* 14 feb. 1742, §11; all. *Neminem vestrum,* 12 maii 1754, "Illud;" S.C.

aries of the patriarchal Church, bishops are designated to a vacant eparchial see or to discharge another function by canonical election in accord with the norms of cann. 947–957, unless otherwise provided by common law.

§2. The Roman Pontiff without prejudice to cann. 149 and 168 appoints other bishops.

CAN. 182 §1. Only members of the synod of bishops of the patriarchal Church can propose candidates suitable for the episcopate. In accord with the norm of particular law, they are to collect the information and documents that are necessary to demonstrate the suitability of the candidates. In doing so, they may, if they consider it opportune, hear secretly and individually some presbyters or also other Christian faithful outstanding in prudence and Christian life.

§2. The bishops are to inform the patriarch of their findings in a timely manner before the convocation of the synod of bishops of the patriarchal Church. The patriarch is to send this dossier, adding, if the case so suggests, further information of his own, to all the members of the synod.

§3. Unless particular law approved by the Roman Pontiff determines otherwise, the synod of bishops of the patriarchal Church is to examine the names of the candidates and draw up by secret ballot a list of the candidates. This list

torii Ecclesiae patriarchalis ad sedem eparchialem vacantem vel aliud munus implendum designantur electione canonica ad normam cann. 947–957, nisi aliter iure communi cavetur.

§2. Ceteri Episcopi a Romano Pontifice nominantur firmis cann. 149 et 168.

CAN. 182 §1. Candidatos ad episcopatum idoneos sola Synodi Episcoporum Ecclesiae patriarchalis membra proponere possunt, quorum est etiam ad normam iuris particularis informationes et documenta, quae necessaria sunt, ut candidatorum idoneitas comprobetur, colligere auditis, si opportunum ducunt, secreto et singillatim aliquibus presbyteris vel etiam aliis christifidelibus prudentia et vita christiana praestantibus.

§2. Episcopi de informationibus Patriarcham tempore opportuno ante Synodi Episcoporum Ecclesiae patriarchalis convocationem certiorem faciant; Patriarcha vero propriis, si casus fert, additis informationibus rem ad omnia Synodi membra mittat.

§3. Nisi ius particulare a Romano Pontifice approbatum aliud fert, Synodus Episcoporum Ecclesiae patriarchalis nomina candidatorum examinet et secreto scrutinio elenchum candidatorum componat, qui per

---

de Prop. Fide, decr. 20 iul. 1760, ad 7; CLEMENS XIII, litt. ap. *Libentissime occasionem,* 1 aug. 1760; S.C. de Prop. Fide, instr. (ad Patr. et Epp. Ritus Graeco-Melchit.), 29 maii 1789, nn. 7–8; PIUS VII, litt. ap. *Ubi primum,* 3 iun. 1816, §3; breve (ad Patr. et Epp. Melchit.), *Tristis quidem,* 3 iun. 1816, §4; GREGORIUS XVI, 24 dec. 1831; PIUS IX, litt. ap. *Reversurus,* 12 iul. 1867, 20–21; all. *Cum ex hac vita,* 12 iul. 1867, "Cum autem;" const. *Cum ecclesiastica,* 31 aug. 1869, VI; ep. encycl. *Quartus supra,* 6 ian. 1873, 25–32. * Syn. Mar Isaaci Chaldaeorum, a. 410, cann. 1, 20; Syn. Libanen. Maronitarum, a. 1736, pars III, cap. IV, 15, 35; Syn.

Sciarfen. Syrorum, a. 1888, cap. VIII, art. IV; Syn. Alexandrin. Coptorum, a. 1898, sect. III, cap. II, art. IV; Syn. Armen., a. 1911, 190, 239.

181 §2: PIUS XII, m.p. *Cleri sanctitati,* 2 iun. 1957, can. 392 §2.

182 §2: PIUS XII, m.p. *Cleri sanctitati,* 2 iun. 1957, can. 252 §1 nn. 1–2. - PIUS IX, ep. encycl. *Quartus supra,* 6 ian. 1873, 26–27. * Syn. Libanen. Maronitarum, a. 1736, pars III, cap. IV, 15–16; Syn. Armen., a. 1911, 239.

182 §3: PIUS XII, m.p. *Cleri sanctitati,* 2 iun. 1957, cann. 254 §1, 252 §2 n. 2.

is to be transmitted through the patriarch to the Apostolic See to obtain the assent of the Roman Pontiff.

§4. Once the assent of the Roman Pontiff has been given for the individual candidates, it is valid until it is explicitly revoked, in which case the name of the candidate is to be removed from the list.

CAN. 183 §1. Once the convocation has been done canonically, if, after subtracting those prevented by a legitimate impediment, two-thirds of the bishops obliged to attend the synod of bishops of the patriarchal Church are present in the designated place, the synod is to be declared canonical and the election can proceed.

§2. The bishops are freely to elect the one whom before all others they consider before the Lord to be worthy and suitable.

§3. For an election an absolute majority of the votes of those present is required; after three inconclusive ballotings, in the fourth balloting votes are cast only between those two candidates who received the greater number of votes in the third balloting.

§4. If in the third or fourth balloting, because of a tie vote, it is not clear who the candidate is for the new balloting or who has been elected, the tie is resolved in favor of the one who is senior according to presbyteral ordination. If no one precedes the others by presbyteral ordination, the one who is senior by age.

CAN. 184 §1. If the one elected is on the list of candidates to which the Roman Pontiff has

Patriarcham ad Sedem Apostolicam mittatur ad assensum Romani Pontificis obtinendum.

§4. Assensus Romani Pontificis semel praestitus pro singulis candidatis valet, donec explicite revocatus erit, quo in casu nomen candidati ex elencho expungendum est.

CAN. 183 §1. Convocatione canonice facta, si duae ex tribus partibus Episcoporum, qui tenentur Synodo Episcoporum Ecclesiae patriarchalis interesse, demptis eis, qui legitimo sunt impedimento detenti, in loco designato praesentes sunt, Synodus canonica declaretur et ad electionem procedi potest.

§2. Episcopi, quem prae ceteris dignum et idoneum coram Domino censent, libere eligant.

§3. Ad electionem requiritur pars absolute maior suffragiorum eorum, qui praesentes sunt; post tria inefficacia scrutinia suffragia feruntur in quarto scrutinio super eis duobus tantummodo candidatis, qui in tertio scrutinio maiorem partem suffragiorum receperunt.

§4. Si in tertio aut quarto scrutinio ob paritatem suffragiorum non constat, quis sit candidatus pro novo scrutinio vel quis electus sit, paritas dirimatur in favorem eius, qui est ordinatione presbyterali senior; si nemo ordinatione presbyterali alios praecedit, qui est aetate senior.

CAN. 184 §1. Si electus est ex recensitis in elencho candidatorum, ad quem Ro-

---

182 §4: Pius XII, m.p. *Cleri sanctitati,* 2 iun. 1957, can. 254 §2 n. 2.

183 §2: Pius XII, m.p. *Cleri sanctitati,* 2 iun. 1957, can. 252 §2 n. 2.

183 §3: Pius XII, m.p. *Cleri sanctitati,* 2 iun. 1957,

can. 252 §2 n. 3. - Nic. I, can. 6; Ant. can. 19. * Syn. Armen., a. 1911, 241.

184 §1: Pius XII, m.p. *Cleri sanctitati,* 2 iun. 1957, can. 254 §2 n. 1.

already given assent, he is to be intimated secretly of his election by the patriarch.

§2. If the one elected accepts the election, the patriarch is to inform immediately the Apostolic See of the acceptance of the election and of the day of proclamation.

CAN. 185 §1. If the one elected is not on the list of candidates, in order to obtain the assent of the Roman Pontiff, the patriarch is to inform immediately the Apostolic See that the election took place. Secrecy, even toward the one elected, is to be observed by all who in any way know the results of the election, until notification of the assent reaches the patriarch.

§2. When the assent of the Roman Pontiff has been obtained, the patriarch is to intimate the election secretly to the one elected and act in accord with the norm of can. 184, §2.

CAN. 186 §1. If the synod of bishops of the patriarchal Church cannot be convened, the patriarch, after consulting the Apostolic See, is to seek the votes of the bishops by letter. In this case, the patriarch must employ for the validity of the act the services of two bishops as scrutineers, who are to be designated in accord with the norm of particular law, or, lacking this, by the patriarch with the consent of the permanent synod.

§2. The scrutineers, observing secrecy, open the letters of the bishops, count the votes and along with the patriarch sign a written report about the conduct of the balloting.

§3. If in this single balloting one of the candidates obtains an absolute majority of the votes

manus Pontifex assensum iam praestitit, peracta electio a Patriarcha sub secreto intimanda est electo.

§2. Si electus electionem acceptavit, Patriarcha de acceptatione electionis atque de die proclamationis statim Sedem Apostolicam certiorem faciat.

CAN. 185 §1. Si electus non est ex recensitis in elencho candidatorum, statim Patriarcha Sedem Apostolicam de peracta electione certiorem faciat ad obtinendum Romani Pontificis assensum secreto servato ab omnibus, qui quomodolibet electionis exitum noverunt, etiam erga electum, donec de assensu notitia ad Patriarcham pervenerit.

§2. Obtento assensu Romani Pontificis Patriarcha sub secreto electionem intimet electo et ad normam can. 184, §2 agat.

CAN. 186 §1. Si Synodus Episcoporum Ecclesiae patriarchalis congregari non potest, Patriarcha consulta Sede Apostolica suffragia Episcoporum per litteras exquirat; quo in casu Patriarcha ad validitatem actus uti debet opera duorum Episcoporum scrutatorum, qui designandi sunt ad normam iuris particularis vel, si deest, a Patriarcha de consensu Synodi permanentis.

§2. Scrutatores secreto servato litteras Episcoporum aperiant, suffragia numerent et relationi scripto datae de peracto scrutinio una cum Patriarcha subscribant.

§3. Si quis ex candidatis in hoc unico scrutinio partem absolute maiorem suffragio-

184 §2: Pius XII, m.p. *Cleri sanctitati,* 2 iun. 1957, can. 254 §2 n. 2.

185 §1: Pius XII, m.p. *Cleri sanctitati,* 2 iun. 1957, can. 253 §§1–2. - Pius IX, all. *Cum ex hac vita,* 12 iul. 1867, "Cum autem;" const. *Cum ecclesiastica,* 31 aug. 1869, VI. * Syn. Sciarfen. Syrorum, a. 1888, cap. VIII, art. IV, "Obtenta;" Syn. Alexandrin. Coptorum, a.

1898, sect. III, cap. II, art. IV, 10; Syn. Armen., a. 1911, 242.

186 §1: Pius XII, m.p. *Cleri sanctitati,* 2 iun. 1957, can. 255 §§1–2. - Nic. I, can. 4; Ant. can. 19; Carth. can. 13. * Syn. Armen., a. 1911, 240.

186 §2: Pius XII, m.p. *Cleri sanctitati,* 2 iun. 1957, can. 255 §§1–2.

of the members of the synod, he is to be held elected; and the patriarch is to proceed in accord with the norms of cann. 184 and 185. Otherwise, the patriarch is to defer the matter to the Apostolic See.

CAN. 187 §1. For promoting anyone to the episcopate, a canonical provision is necessary with which he is constituted the eparchial bishop of a particular eparchy or a particular function in the Church is committed to him.

§2. Before episcopal ordination the candidate is to make the profession of faith and promise of obedience to the Roman Pontiff and, in patriarchal Churches, also a promise of obedience to the patriarch in those matters in which he is subject to the patriarch in accord with the norm of law.

CAN. 188 §1. Unless prevented by a legitimate impediment, a person who is to be promoted to the episcopate must receive episcopal ordination within three months from the day of proclamation in the case of election or from the reception of the apostolic letter in the case of an appointment.

§2. The eparchial bishop must take canonical possession of the eparchy within four months from the day of episcopal election or appointment.

CAN. 189 §1. The eparchial bishop takes canonical possession of the eparchy by the legitimately conducted enthronement itself, during which the apostolic or patriarchal letter of canonical provision is publicly read.

rum Synodi membrorum obtinuit, electus habeatur et Patriarcha ad normam can. 184 vel 185 procedat; secus Patriarcha rem ad Sedem Apostolicam deferat.

CAN. 187 §1. Cuilibet ad episcopatum promovendo necessaria est provisio canonica, qua Episcopus eparchialis determinatae eparchiae constituitur vel aliud determinatum munus ei in Ecclesia committitur.

§2. Candidatus ante ordinationem episcopalem emittat professionem fidei necnon promissionem oboedientiae erga Romanum Pontificem et in Ecclesiis patriarchalibus etiam promissionem oboedientiae erga Patriarcham in eis, in quibus Patriarchae ad normam iuris subiectus est.

CAN. 188 §1. Nisi legitimo impedimento detinetur, promovendus ad episcopatum debet intra tres menses a die proclamationis, si de electo agitur, vel a receptis apostolicis litteris, si de nominato agitur, computandos ordinationem episcopalem suscipere.

§2. Episcopus eparchialis intra quattuor menses a sua electione vel nominatione computandos debet possessionem canonicam eparchiae capere.

CAN. 189 §1. Possessionem canonicam eparchiae capit Episcopus eparchialis ipsa inthronizatione legitime peracta, in qua publice litterae apostolicae vel patriarchales de provisione canonica leguntur.

187 §1: Pius XII, m.p. *Cleri sanctitati,* 2 iun. 1957, can. 395 §1. - Innocentius IV, const. ap. *Iustis petentium,* 8 aug. 1243.

187 §2: Pius XII, m.p. *Cleri sanctitati,* 2 iun. 1957, can. 395 §2. * Syn. Sciarfen. Syrorum, a. 1888, cap. V, art. XIII, §3, 1, II; Syn. Alexandrin. Coptorum, a. 1898, sect. II, cap. III, art. VII, §4, II; sect. III, cap. II, art. II, 13; Syn. Armen., a. 1911, 245.

188 §1: Pius XII, m.p. *Cleri sanctitati,* 2 iun. 1957,

can. 396 §1. - Apost. can. 36; Ant. cann. 17–18; Chalc. can. 25; Quinisext. can. 37. * Syn. Libanen. Maronitarum, a. 1736, pars III, cap. IV, 17; Syn. Sciarfen. Syrorum, a. 1888, cap. IX, art. II, 5.

188 §2: Pius XII, m.p. *Cleri sanctitati,* 2 iun. 1957, can. 396 §1.

189 §1: Pius XII, m.p. *Cleri sanctitati,* 2 iun. 1957, can. 397 §3.

§2. A document is to be drawn up about the conduct of the enthronement; it is to be signed by the eparchial bishop along with the chancellor of the curia and at least two witnesses and is to be kept in the archives of the eparchial curia.

§3. Before the enthronement the bishop may not involve himself in the governance of the eparchy in virtue of any title, either personally or through others. If he had some office in the eparchy, he can retain and exercise it.

ART. II. *The Rights and Obligations of Eparchial Bishops*

CAN. 190 The eparchial bishop represents the eparchy in all its juridic affairs.

CAN. 191 §1. The eparchial bishop governs the eparchy entrusted to him with legislative, executive and judicial power.

§2. The eparchial bishop personally exercises legislative power; he exercises executive power either personally or through a protosyncellus or syncellus; he exercises judicial power either personally or through a judicial vicar and judges.

CAN. 192 §1. In the exercise of his pastoral function, the eparchial bishop is to show that he is concerned for all the Christian faithful who are committed to his care, regardless of age, condition, nation or Church *sui iuris,* both those who live within the territory of his

§2. De peracta inthronizatione documentum conficiatur ab ipso Episcopo eparchiali una cum cancellario et saltem duobus testibus subscribendum et in archivo curiae eparchialis asservandum.

§3. Ante inthronizationem Episcopus in regimen eparchiae neque per se neque per alios nec ullo titulo se ingerat; si vero aliquod officium in eparchia habet, illud retinere et exercere potest.

ART. II. *De Iuribus et Obligationibus Episcoporum Eparchialium*

CAN. 190 In omnibus negotiis iuridicis eparchiae Episcopus eparchialis eiusdem personam gerit.

CAN. 191 §1. Episcopi eparchialis est eparchiam sibi concreditam cum potestate legislativa, exsecutiva et iudiciali regere.

§2. Potestatem legislativam exercet Episcopus eparchialis ipse per se; potestatem exsecutivam exercet sive per se sive per Protosyncellum vel Syncellos; potestatem iudicialem sive per se sive per Vicarium iudicialem et iudices.

CAN. 192 §1. In exercendo suo munere pastorali Episcopus eparchialis sollicitum se praebeat erga omnes christifideles, qui eius curae committuntur, cuiusvis sunt aetatis, condicionis, nationis vel Ecclesiae sui iuris tum in territorio eparchiae habitantes tum in

189 §2: Pius XII, m.p. *Cleri sanctitati,* 2 iun. 1957, can. 397 §3.

189 §3: Pius XII, m.p. *Cleri sanctitati,* 2 iun. 1957, can. 397 §2.

190: Pius XII, m.p. *Cleri sanctitati,* 2 iun. 1957, can. 398.

191 §1: Pius XII, m.p. *Cleri sanctitati,* 2 iun. 1957, can. 399 §1. - Apost. can. 39; Ant. can. 9; Trid., sess. VI, *Decr. de resid. episcoporum . . .,* cap. 3; sess. XIII, *De ref.,* can. 1; Vat. II, const. *Lumen gentium,* 27. * Syn. Libanen. Maronitarum, a. 1736, pars III, cap. IV,

19; Syn. Sciarfen. Syrorum, a. 1888, cap. IX, art. V.

191 §2: Pius XII, m.p. *Sollicitudinem Nostram,* 6 ian. 1950, cann. 37 §1, 40 §1; m.p. *Cleri sanctitati,* 2 iun. 1957, cann. 428, 432 §1, 434; Vat. II, decr. *Christus Dominus,* 27 "Eminens;" Commissio Centralis Coordinandis post Concilium Laboribus et Concilii Decretis Interpretandis, resp. 10 iun. 1966; Paulus VI, m.p. *Ecclesiae sanctae,* 6 aug. 1966, I, 14 §2.

192 §1: Vat. II, decr. *Christus Dominus,* 11 "Ad suum," 16 "In exercendo" et "Fidelium," 18 "Peculiaris."

eparchy and those who are staying in it temporarily; he is to extend his apostolic spirit also to those who cannot sufficiently avail themselves of ordinary pastoral care due to their condition in life as well as to those who are far from the practice of their religion.

§2. The eparchial bishop is to see in a special way that all Christian faithful committed to his care foster unity among Christians according to principles approved by the Church.

§3. The eparchial bishop is to consider the non-baptized as being committed to him in the Lord and see that the love of Christ shines upon them from the witness of the Christian faithful living in ecclesiastical communion.

§4. The eparchial bishop is to have special concern for presbyters; he is to listen to them as his helpers and advisers; safeguard their rights and ensure that they fulfill the obligations proper to their state. He is to see that the means and institutions they need to foster their spiritual and intellectual life are available to them.

§5. The eparchial bishop is to see that provisions are made in accord with the norm of law for the clerics and, if they are married, for their families, in the matter of suitable means of livelihood, of adequate insurance and social security as well as health assistance.

CAN. 193 §1. The eparchial bishop to whose care the Christian faithful of another Church *sui iuris* have been committed is bound by the serious obligation of providing everything so that these Christian faithful retain the rite of their respective Church, cherish and ob-

eodem ad tempus versantes, animum intendens apostolicum ad eos etiam, qui ob vitae suae condicionem ordinaria cura pastorali non satis frui possunt, necnon ad eos, qui a religionis praxi defecerunt.

§2. Speciali modo curet Episcopus eparchialis, ut omnes christifideles suae curae commissi unitatem inter christianos foveant secundum principia ab Ecclesia approbata.

§3. Episcopus eparchialis commendatos sibi in Domino habeat non baptizatos et curet, ut et eis ex testimonio christifidelium in communione ecclesiastica viventium eluceat caritas Christi.

§4. Episcopus eparchialis speciali sollicitudine prosequatur presbyteros, quos tamquam adiutores et consiliarios audiat, eorum iura tueatur et curet, ut obligationes suo statui proprias impleant eisdemque praesto sint media et institutiones, quibus ad vitam spiritualem et intellectualem fovendam egent.

§5. Curet Episcopus eparchialis, ut clericorum eorumque familiae, si coniugati sunt, congruae sustentationi atque congruenti praecaventiae et securitati sociali necnon assistentiae sanitariae ad normam iuris provideatur.

CAN. 193 §1. Episcopus eparchialis, cuius curae christifideles alterius Ecclesiae sui iuris commissi sunt, gravi obligatione tenetur omnia providendi, ut hi christifideles propriae Ecclesiae ritum retineant eumque colant ac pro viribus observent et cum auc-

192 §2: Vat. II, decr. *Christus Dominus,* 16 "Fratres."

192 §3: Vat. II, decr. *Christus Dominus,* 16 "Fratres," 11 "Ad suum."

192 §4: Vat. II, const. *Lumen gentium,* 28 "Pres-

byteri;" decr. *Christus Dominus,* 16 "Sacerdotes" et "Solliciti."

192 §5: Vat. II, decr. *Presbyterorum ordinis,* 20–21.

193 §1: Vat. II, decr. *Orientalium Ecclesiarum,* 4, 6; Pius XII, m.p. *Cleri sanctitati,* 2 iun. 1957, can. 14.

serve it as far as possible. He is also to ensure that they foster relations with the superior authority of their Church.

§2. The eparchial bishop is to provide for the spiritual needs of these Christian faithful, if it is possible, by means of presbyters or pastors of the same Church *sui iuris* as the Christian faithful or even through a syncellus constituted for the care of these Christian faithful.

§3. Eparchial bishops who appoint such presbyters, pastors or syncelli for the care of the Christian faithful of patriarchal Churches are to draw up a plan in consultation with the respective patriarchs. If these agree, they are to act on their own authority and inform the Apostolic See as soon as possible; should the patriarchs disagree for whatever reason, the matter is to be referred to the Apostolic See.

CAN. 194 The eparchial bishop can confer dignities upon clerics subject to them, others excluded, in accord with the norm of the particular law of their own Church *sui iuris.*

CAN. 195 The eparchial bishop is to foster to the greatest extent possible vocations to the priesthood, diaconate and monastic life as well as to other institutes of consecrated life and to the missions.

CAN. 196 §1. The eparchial bishop is bound to present and explain to the Christian

toritate superiore eiusdem Ecclesiae relationes foveant.

§2. Spiritualibus necessitatibus horum christifidelium Episcopus eparchialis provideat, si fieri potest, per presbyteros vel parochos eiusdem Ecclesiae sui iuris ac christifideles aut etiam per Syncellum ad curam horum christifidelium constitutum.

§3. Episcopi eparchiales, qui huiusmodi presbyteros, parochos vel Syncellos ad curam christifidelium Ecclesiarum patriarchalium constituunt, rationes cum Patriarchis, quorum interest, ineant et illis consentientibus propria auctoritate agant certiore quam primum facta Sede Apostolica; si vero Patriarchae quacumque de causa dissentiunt, res ad Sedem Apostolicam deferatur.

CAN. 194 Episcopus eparchialis dignitates clericis sibi subditis ceteris exclusis conferre potest ad normam tamen iuris particularis propriae Ecclesiae sui iuris.

CAN. 195 Vocationes sacerdotales, diaconales, monachorum ceterorumque sodalium institutorum vitae consecratae ac missionales quam maxime Episcopus eparchialis foveat.

CAN. 196 §1. Veritates fidei credendas et moribus applicandas Episcopus

193 §2: Vat. II, decr. *Christus Dominus,* 23, 3) "Hunc."

194: Pius XII, m.p. *Cleri sanctitati,* 2 iun. 1957, can. 41 §1 n. 2 et §3, can. 42. - S.C. pro Eccl. Orient., 10 ian. 1929; resp. 11 iun. 1940. * Syn. Libanen. Maronitarum, a. 1736, pars III, cap. II, 7; Syn. Sciarfen. Syrorum, a. 1888, cap. V, art. XIII, §1, 8; §§7, 9 ; cap. VI, art. VIII, 6; cap. XI, art. II; Syn. Alexandrin. Coptorum, a. 1898, sect. II, cap. III, secunda pars, art. VII, §1, 7; §6, 3, IX; sect. III, cap. IV, art. III; Syn. Armen., a. 1911, 301–314, 360–366, 724.

195: Vat. II, decr. *Christus Dominus,* 15 "Qua;" const. *Lumen gentium,* 27 "Episcopus;" decr. *Optatam totius,* 2 "Episcoporum;" decr. *Ad gentes* 20 ab "Ut hoc."

196 §1: Vat. II, const. *Lumen Gentium,* 25 "Inter;" decr. *Christus Dominus,* 13–14; Pius XII, m.p. *Cleri sanctitati,* 2 iun. 1957, can. 400 §1. - S. Basilius M., can. 1; Quinisext. can. 19; S. Leo M., litt. *Laetificaverunt me,* 10 mar. 454; Trid., sess. V, *Decr. secundum,* 9; sess. XXV, *Decr. de purgatorio; De invocatione, veneratione et reliquiis sanctorum, et sacris imaginibus;* S.C.S. Off., 13 mar. 1625, §5; S.C. de Prop. Fide, decr. 13 apr. 1807, I, III, XV; Gregorius XVI, ep. encycl. *Inter gravissimas,* 3 feb. 1832, §8; S. Pius X, litt. encycl. *Pascendi,* 8 sep. 1907, 3–4; Paulus VI, adh. ap. *Quinque iam anni,* 8 dec. 1970, I "Concilium." * Syn. Sciarfen. Syrorum, a. 1888; cap. IX, art. I, 10 et 12; cap. XIX, art. II "Circa;" Syn. Alexandrin. Coptorum, a. 1898, sect. III, cap. III, art. I, I, 3.

faithful the truths of the faith that are to be believed and applied to moral issues; he is himself to preach frequently. He is also to ensure that the prescriptions of the law concerning the ministry of the word of God be carefully observed, especially those about the homily and catechetical formation, so that the whole of Christian doctrine is handed on to all.

§2. The eparchial bishop is to safeguard firmly the integrity and unity of faith.

CAN. 197 Mindful of the obligation by which he is bound to give an example of holiness in charity, humility and simplicity of life, the eparchial bishop is by all means to promote the holiness of the Christian faithful according to the vocation of each. Since he is the principal dispenser of the mysteries of God, he is to strive that the Christian faithful committed to his care grow in grace through the celebration of the sacraments and especially by participation in the Divine Eucharist and that they know the paschal mystery in depth and live it so that they become one Body in the unity of the love of Christ.

CAN. 198 The eparchial bishop is to celebrate the Divine Liturgy frequently for the people of the eparchy entrusted to him; he must celebrate on the days prescribed by the particular law of his own Church *sui iuris.*

CAN. 199 §1. As the moderator, promoter and guardian of the entire liturgical life in the eparchy entrusted to him, the eparchial bishop must be vigilant that it be fostered to the greatest extent possible and be ordered according to

eparchialis christifidelibus proponere et illustrare tenetur per se ipse frequenter praedicans; curet etiam, ut praescripta iuris de verbi Dei ministerio, de homilia praesertim et institutione catechetica sedulo serventur ita, ut universa doctrina christiana omnibus tradatur.

§2. Integritatem et unitatem fidei Episcopus eparchialis firmiter tueatur.

CAN. 197 Episcopus eparchialis, cum memor sit se obligatione teneri exemplum sanctitatis praebendi in caritate, humilitate et vitae simplicitate, omni ope promovere studeat sanctitatem christifidelium secundum suam cuiusque vocationem atque, cum sit praecipuus mysteriorum Dei dispensator, annitatur, ut christifideles suae curae commissi sacramentorum celebratione et praesertim Divinae Eucharistiae participatione in gratia crescant atque paschale mysterium penitus cognoscant et vivant ita, ut unum efficiant Corpus in unitate caritatis Christi.

CAN. 198 Divinam Liturgiam pro populo eparchiae sibi concreditae Episcopus eparchialis frequenter celebret; diebus vero iure particulari propriae Ecclesiae sui iuris praescriptis celebrare debet.

CAN. 199 §1. Episcopus eparchialis utpote totius vitae liturgicae in eparchia sibi concredita moderator, promotor atque custos vigilet, ut illa quam maxime foveatur atque secundum praescripta necnon legiti-

---

196 §2: Vat. II, const. *Lumen gentium,* 23 "Collegialis;" PAULUS VI, adh. ap. *Quinque iam anni,* 8 dec. 1970, I "Est quidem."

197: Vat. II, decr. *Christus Dominus,* 15; const. *Lumen gentium,* 41 "Gregis."

198: PIUS XII, m.p. *Cleri sanctitati,* 2 iun. 1957, can. 404. - Trid., sess. XXIII, *De ref.,* can. 1; S.C. de Prop. Fide, 23 mar. 1863, 1; LEO XIII, litt. ap. *In suprema,* 10 iun. 1882; S.C. de Prop. Fide, (C.G.), litt. en-

cycl. (ad Delegatos App. pro Orient.), 8 nov. 1882; litt. (ad Metrop. Alba-Iulien. et Fagarasien.), 30 iun. 1885. * Syn. Libanen. Maronitarum, a. 1736, pars III, cap. IV, 19; Syn. Sciarfen. Syrorum, a. 1888, cap. IX, art. I, 15; Syn. Leopolien. Ruthenorum, a. 1891, tit. IV, cap. II, 1; Syn. Alexandrin. Coptorum, a. 1898, sect. III, cap. III, art. I, II, 1; Syn. Armen., a. 1911, 252.

199 §1: Vat. II, decr. *Christus Dominus,* 15; const. *Lumen gentium,* 26 "Omnis."

the prescriptions and legitimate customs of his own Church *sui iuris.*

§2. The eparchial bishop is to see that in his own cathedral at least part of the divine praises are celebrated, even daily, according to the legitimate customs of his own Church *sui iuris;* also, that in all parishes, to the extent that this is possible, the divine praises are celebrated on Sundays, feast days, principal solemnities and their vigils.

§3. The eparchial bishop is to preside frequently at the divine praises in the cathedral or other Church, especially on holy days of obligation and on other solemnities in which a sizeable part of the people participate.

CAN. 200 It is for the eparchial bishop to celebrate sacred functions in the entire eparchy which he must conduct solemnly according to the prescriptions of the liturgical books and vested in all pontifical insignia; he may not do this outside the boundaries of his own eparchy without the consent of the eparchial bishop, either expressly given or at least reasonably presumed.

CAN. 201 §1. Since he is obliged to safeguard the unity of the entire Church, the eparchial bishop is to promote the common discipline of the Church as well as to urge the observance of all ecclesiastical laws and legitimate customs.

§2. The eparchial bishop is to be vigilant lest abuses creep into ecclesiastical discipline, espe-

mas consuetudines propriae Ecclesiae sui iuris ordinetur.

§2. Curet Episcopus eparchialis, ut in propria ecclesia cathedrali celebretur saltem pars laudum divinarum, etiam cottidie, secundum legitimas consuetudines propriae Ecclesiae sui iuris; item, ut in qualibet paroecia pro viribus diebus dominicis et festis atque praecipuis sollemnitatibus earumque vigiliis laudes divinae celebrentur.

§3. Episcopus eparchialis frequenter praesit laudibus divinis in ecclesia cathedrali aliave ecclesia praesertim diebus festis de praecepto aliisque sollemnitatibus, in quibus partem habet notabilis populi pars.

CAN. 200 Episcopi eparchialis est in tota eparchia functiones sacras celebrare, quae secundum praescripta librorum liturgicorum ab ipso omnibus insignibus pontificalibus induto sollemniter perficiendae sunt, non vero extra fines propriae eparchiae sine expresso vel saltem rationabiliter praesumpto Episcopi eparchialis consensu.

CAN. 201 §1. Universae Ecclesiae unitatem cum tueri debeat, Episcopus eparchialis disciplinam ecclesiasticam communem promovere necnon observantiam omnium legum ecclesiasticarum atque legitimarum consuetudinum urgere tenetur.

§2. Vigilet Episcopus eparchialis, ne abusus in disciplinam ecclesiasticam irrepant

199 §2: Pius XII, m.p. *Cleri sanctitati,* 2 iun. 1957, can. 401. - Laod. can. 18; S.C. de Prop. Fide, litt. 4 iul. 1833, X. * Syn. Libanen. Maronitarum, a. 1736, pars III, cap. IV, 2 in fine; Syn. Leopolien. Ruthenorum, a. 1891, tit. IV, cap. III, 3.

199 §3: Vat. II, const. *Sacrosanctum Concilium,* 41. * Syn. Sciarfen. Syrorum, a. 1888, cap. III, art. VI, 15.

200: Pius XII, m.p. *Cleri sanctitati,* 2 iun. 1957, can. 402 §1. - S.C. de Prop. Fide, ep. et instr. (ad Ep. Enonensem), a. 1784, §1. * Syn. Libanen. Maronitarum, a. 1736, pars III, cap. IV, 24.

201 §1: Vat. II, const. *Lumen gentium,* 23 "Collegialis;" Pius XII, m.p. *Cleri sanctitati,* 2 iun. 1957, can.

400 §2.

201 §2: Pius XII, m.p. *Cleri sanctitati,* 2 iun. 1957, can. 400 §3. - Trid., sess. XIV, *De ref.,* prooem.; sess. XXV, *Decr. de purgatorio; De invocatione, veneratione et reliquiis sanctorum, et sacris imaginibus;* S. Leo M., *Laetificaverunt me,* 10 mar. 454; Gregorius XVI, ep. encycl. *Inter gravissimas,* 3 feb. 1832, §8; S.C.S. Off. 13 mar. 1625, 5; decr. 5 aug. 1745. * Syn. Zamosten. Ruthenorum, a. 1720, tit. VI; Syn. Libanen. Maronitarum, a. 1736, pars II, cap. XIV, 51; pars III, cap. I, 14; Syn. Sciarfen. Syrorum, a. 1888, cap. V, art. V, §10, V; Syn. Alexandrin. Coptorum, a. 1898, sect. III, cap. III, art. I, I, 3 et II, 3; Syn. Armen., a. 1911, 249.

cially concerning the ministry of the word of God, the celebration of the sacraments and sacramentals, the worship of God and the cult of the saints, as well as the execution of pious wills.

CAN. 202 The eparchial bishops of several Churches *sui iuris* exercising power in the same territory are to ensure that through the exchange of views in periodic meetings, they foster unity of action and, by combined resources, help advance common works more readily to promote of the good of religion and more effectively safeguard ecclesiastical discipline.

CAN. 203 §1. The eparchial bishop is to foster various forms of the apostolate in the eparchy and see that all of the works of the apostolate in the entire eparchy or in its particular districts are coordinated under his direction, with due regard for the character of each apostolate.

§2. The eparchial bishop is to be solicitous regarding the obligation that the Christian faithful have to exercise some apostolate, each one according to his or her condition and aptitude, and he is to exhort them to participate in and support the various works of the apostolate according to the needs of place and time.

§3. The eparchial bishop is to promote associations of the Christian faithful that directly or indirectly pursue a spiritual end by establishing, approving, praising, or commending them if it is beneficial, in accord with the norm of the law.

CAN. 204 §1. The eparchial bishop is

praesertim circa verbi Dei ministerium, celebrationem sacramentorum et sacramentalium, cultum Dei et Sanctorum, exsecutionem piarum voluntatum.

CAN. 202 Episcopi eparchiales plurium Ecclesiarum sui iuris in eodem territorio potestatem suam exercentes curent, ut collatis consiliis in periodicis conventibus unitatem actionis foveant et viribus unitis communia adiuvent opera ad bonum religionis expeditius promovendum et ad disciplinam ecclesiasticam efficacius tuendam.

CAN. 203 §1. Varias apostolatus formas in eparchia foveat Episcopus eparchialis atque curet, ut in tota eparchia vel in eiusdem particularibus districtibus omnia opera apostolatus servata uniuscuiusque propria indole sub suo moderamine coordinentur.

§2. Urgeat Episcopus eparchialis obligationem, qua tenentur christifideles ad apostolatum pro sua quisque condicione et aptitudine exercendum, atque eos adhortetur, ut varia opera apostolatus secundum necessitates loci et temporis participent et adiuvent.

§3. Consociationes christifidelium, quae finem spiritualem directe aut indirecte persequuntur, Episcopus eparchialis promoveat eas, si id expedit, erigendo, approbando, laudando vel commendando ad normam iuris.

CAN. 204 §1. Episcopus eparchialis,

202: Vat. II, decr. *Orientalium Ecclesiarum,* 4.

203 §1: Vat. II, decr. *Christus Dominus,* 17 "Variae."

203 §2: Vat. II, decr. *Christus Dominus,* 17 "Sedulo."

203 §3: Vat. II, decr. *Christus Dominus,* 17 "Sedulo."

204 §1: Pius XII, m.p. *Cleri sanctitati,* 2 iun. 1957, can. 403 §1. - Ant. can. 21; Sard. can. 3; Carth. can. 71; Constantinop. IV, can. 19; Trid., sess. VI, *Decr. de resid. episcoporum . . .,* cap. 1; sess. XXIII, *De ref.,* can.

1; S. Paulus V, litt. ap. *Erga Maronitarum,* 21 oct. 1619; S.C. de Prop. Fide, 22 mar. 1625, n. 13; decr. 13 apr. 1807, V; Benedictus XIV, litt. ap. *Quoniam ven. frater,* 6 mar. 1754; Pius IX, all. *Cum ex hac vita,* 12 iul. 1867, "Cum autem." * Syn. Zamosten. Ruthenorum, a. 1720, tit. VI "Quam;" Syn. Libanen. Maronitarum, a. 1736, pars II, cap. XIV, 14; pars III, cap. IV, 19; Syn. Bekorkien. Maronitarum, a. 1790, s. 6; Syn. Sciarfen. Syrorum, a. 1888, cap. IX, art. II; Syn. Alexandrin. Coptorum, a. 1898, sect. III, cap. III, art. II; Syn. Armen., a. 1911, 261.

bound by the obligation of residing in his own eparchy, even if he has a coadjutor or auxiliary bishop.

§2. Apart from such obligations that legitimately require his absence from his eparchy, the bishop may each year be absent for a just cause for not longer than one continuous or interrupted month, provided precautions are taken that the eparchy not suffer any harm from his absence.

§3. On days of more solemn feasts, established by particular law according to the tradition of his own Church *sui iuris,* the eparchial bishop is not to be absent from his eparchy, except for some grave cause.

§4. If an eparchial bishop exercising his power within the territorial boundaries of the patriarchal Church has been illegitimately absent for more than six months from the eparchy entrusted to him, the patriarch is immediately to defer the matter to the Roman Pontiff. In other cases this is to be done by the metropolitan or, if the metropolitan himself has been illegitimately absent, the eparchial bishop senior in episcopal ordination and subject to that same metropolitan.

CAN. 205 §1. The eparchial bishop is bound by the obligation of canonically visiting his eparchy either entirely or in part every year so that at least every five years he will have visited the entire eparchy either personally or, if he

etsi Episcopum coadiutorem vel Episcopum auxiliarem habet, obligatione tenetur in eparchia propria residendi.

§2. Praeterquam causa obligationum, quae legitime absentiam a propria eparchia requirunt, Episcopus eparchialis ab eparchia iusta de causa quotannis abesse potest non ultra mensem continuum aut intermissum, dummodo cautum sit, ne ex ipsius absentia eparchia quicquam detrimenti capiat.

§3. Diebus vero praecipuarum sollemnitatum iure particulari secundum traditionem propriae Ecclesiae sui iuris statutarum Episcopus eparchialis a propria eparchia ne absit nisi gravi de causa.

§4. Si Episcopus eparchialis intra fines territorii Ecclesiae patriarchalis potestatem suam exercens ultra sex menses ab eparchia sibi concredita illegitime afuit, Patriarcha rem ad Romanum Pontificem statim deferat; in ceteris casibus hoc faciat Metropolita, vel, si ipse Metropolita illegitime afuit, Episcopus eparchialis ordinatione episcopali senior eidem Metropolitae subiectus.

CAN. 205 §1. Tenetur Episcopus eparchialis obligatione eparchiam vel ex toto vel ex parte quotannis canonice visitandi ita, ut singulis saltem quinquenniis totam eparchiam ipse per se vel, si legitime est im-

204 §2: Pius XII, m.p. *Cleri Sanctitati,* 2 iun. 1957, can. 403 §2. - Sard. cann. 3, 11; Constantinop. IV, can. 19. * Syn. Libanen. Maronitarum, a. 1736, pars II, cap. XIV, 14; pars III, cap. IV, 19; Syn Armen., a. 1911, 261.

204 §3: Pius XII, m.p. *Cleri Sanctitati,* 2 iun. 1957, can. 403 §3. * Syn. Zamosten. Ruthenorum, a. 1720, tit. VI "Quam;" Syn. Sciarfen. Syrorum, a. 1888, cap. IX, art. II; Syn. Alexandrin. Coptorum, a. 1898, sect. III, cap. III, art. II; Syn Armen., a. 1911, 261.

204 §4: Pius XII, m.p. *Cleri Sanctitati,* 2 iun. 1957, can. 403 §4. - Protodeut. can. 16. * Syn. prov. Alba-Iulien. et Fagarasien. Rumenorum, a. 1872, tit. II, cap.

III, 5; Syn. Sciarfen. Syrorum, a. 1888, cap. VII, art. III, 6, 10).

205 §1: Pius XII, m.p. *Cleri sanctitati,* 2 iun. 1957, can. 409 §1. - S.C. de Prop. Fide, (C.G.), 8 iul. 1774, 2. * Syn. Zamosten. Ruthenorum, a. 1720, tit. VI "Tam;" Syn. Libanen. Maronitarum, a. 1736, pars III, cap. IV, 28; Syn. Ain-Trazen. Graeco-Melchitarum, a. 1835, can. 21; Syn. Sciarfen. Syrorum, a. 1888, cap. IX, art. III; Syn. Leopolien. Ruthenorum, a. 1891, tit. VII, cap. III, 2, 2; Syn. Alexandrin. Coptorum, a. 1898, sect. III, cap. III, art. III; Syn. Armen., a. 1911, 253.

is legitimately impeded, by means of the coadjutor bishop, an auxiliary bishop, the protosyncellus or syncellus, or some other presbyter.

§2. Persons, Catholic institutions, sacred things and places within the boundaries of the eparchy are subject to the canonical visitation of the eparchial bishop.

§3. The eparchial bishop can visit members of religious institutes as well as those of societies of common life in the manner of the religious who are of pontifical or patriarchal right and their houses only in the cases expressed in law.

CAN. 206 §1. The eparchial bishop exercising his authority in the territorial boundaries of the patriarchal Church is obliged to submit a report every five years to the patriarch on the state of the eparchy entrusted to him, in the manner determined by the synod of bishops of the patriarchal Church. The bishop is to send a copy of the report to the Apostolic See as soon as possible.

§2. Other eparchial bishops must make the same report to the Apostolic See every five years, and, if it is a case of bishops of a patriarchal Church or metropolitan Church *sui iuris,* they are to send a copy of the report to the patriarch or metropolitan as soon as possible.

CAN. 207 An eparchial bishop of any Church *sui iuris,* even of the Latin Church, is to inform the Apostolic See on the occasion of the

peditus, per Episcopum coadiutorem aut per Episcopum auxiliarem aut per Protosyncellum vel Syncellum aut per alium presbyterum canonice visitet.

§2. Visitationi canonicae Episcopi eparchialis obnoxiae sunt personae, instituta catholica, res et loca sacra, quae intra fines eparchiae sunt.

§3. Sodales institutorum religiosorum necnon societatum vitae communis ad instar religiosorum iuris pontificii vel patriarchalis eorumque domus Episcopus eparchialis visitare potest tantum in casibus iure expressis.

CAN. 206 §1. Episcopus eparchialis intra fines territorii Ecclesiae patriarchalis potestatem suam exercens tenetur singulis quinquenniis relationem Patriarchae facere circa statum eparchiae sibi concreditae secundum modum a Synodo Episcoporum Ecclesiae patriarchalis statutum; exemplar relationis Episcopus quam primum ad Sedem Apostolicam mittat.

§2. Ceteri Episcopi eparchiales singulis quinquenniis eandem relationem Sedi Apostolicae facere debent et, si de Episcopis alicuius Ecclesiae patriarchalis vel Ecclesiae metropolitanae sui iuris agitur, exemplar relationis Patriarchae vel Metropolitae quam primum mittant.

CAN. 207 Episcopus eparchialis cuiuscumque Ecclesiae sui iuris, etiam Ecclesiae latinae, Sedem Apostolicam certiorem faciat

205 §2: Pius XII, m.p. *Cleri sanctitati,* 2 iun. 1957, can. 410 §1. * Syn. Zamosten. Ruthenorum, a. 1720, tit. VI "Nulla;" Syn. Libanen. Maronitarum, a. 1736, pars III, cap. IV, 28; Syn. Sciarfen. Syrorum, a. 1888, cap. IX, art. III; Syn. Alexandrin. Coptorum, a. 1898, sect. III, cap. III, art. III; Syn. Armen., a. 1911, 254.

205 §3: Pius XII, m.p. *Cleri sanctitati,* 2 iun. 1957, can. 410 §2.

206 §1: Pius XII, m.p. *Cleri sanctitati,* 2 iun. 1957, can. 405 §2. * Syn. Armen., a. 1911, 258.

206 §2: Pius XII, m.p. *Cleri sanctitati,* 2 iun. 1957, can. 405 §1; Ioannes Paulus II, const. ap. *Pastor bonus,* 18 iun. 1988, art. 32. - Pius IX, ep. encycl. *Amantissimus,* 8 apr. 1862, 4. * Syn. prov. Alba-Iulien. et Fagarasien. Rumenorum, a. 1872, tit. II, cap. IV, 3) "Item;" Syn. Alexandrin. Coptorum, a. 1898, sect. III, cap. I, art. II, III; Syn. Armen., a. 1911, 259.

207: Pius XII, m.p. *Cleri sanctitati,* 2 iun. 1957, can. 406.

quinquennial report, about the state and needs of the Christian faithful who, even if they are ascribed in another Church *sui iuris,* are committed to his care.

CAN. 208 §1. An eparchial bishop exercising authority within the territorial boundaries of the patriarchal Church, within five years of his enthronement, is to make a visit to Rome along with the patriarch, insofar as this can be done, so that he may venerate the tombs of blessed apostles Peter and Paul and present himself to the successor of Saint Peter in primacy over the entire Church.

§2. Other eparchial bishops are to visit Rome personally every five years or, if legitimately impeded, through another; if it is a case of bishops of a patriarchal Church, it is desirable that at least at some time that the visit be made with the patriarch.

CAN. 209 §1. The eparchial bishop must commemorate the Roman Pontiff before all others as a sign of full communion with him in the Divine Liturgy and the divine praises according to the prescriptions of the liturgical books and to see that it is done faithfully by the other clerics of the eparchy.

§2. The eparchial bishop must be commemorated by all the clerics in the Divine Liturgy

occasione relationis quinquennalis de statu et necessitatibus christifidelium, qui, etsi alii Ecclesiae sui iuris ascripti, eius curae commissi sunt.

CAN. 208 §1. Episcopus eparchialis intra fines territorii Ecclesiae patriarchalis potestatem suam exercens intra quinquennium a sua inthronizatione computandum visitationem ad Urbem peragat, si fieri potest una cum Patriarcha, sanctorum Apostolorum Petri et Pauli limina veneraturus atque sancti Petri successori in primatu super universam Ecclesiam se sistat.

§2. Ceteri Episcopi eparchiales singulis quinquenniis per se vel, si legitime sunt impediti, per alium visitationem ad Urbem peragere debent; si vero de Episcopis alicuius Ecclesiae patriarchalis agitur, optandum est, ut visitatio saltem aliquoties una cum Patriarcha fiat.

CAN. 209 §1. Commemorationem Romani Pontificis ante omnes in signum plenae communionis cum eo in Divina Liturgia et in laudibus divinis secundum praescripta librorum liturgicorum Episcopus eparchialis facere debet et curare, ut a ceteris clericis eparchiae fideliter fiat.

§2. Episcopus eparchialis commemorandus est ab omnibus clericis in Divina Liturgia

208 §2: Pius XII, m.p. *Cleri sanctitati,* 2 iun. 1957, cann. 405 §3, 407–408; Ioannes Paulus II, const. ap. *Pastor bonus,* 18 iun. 1988, artt. 28–32 cum Adnexo I. - S.C. de Prop. Fide, 12 nov. 1696, n. 7, ad I. * Syn. Alexandrin. Coptorum, a. 1898, sect. III, cap. I, art. II, III; Syn. Armen., a. 1911, 259.

209 §1: Pius XII, m.p. *Cleri sanctitati,* 2 iun. 1957, can. 166. - Callixtus III, const. *Reddituri de commisso,* 3 sep. 1457, §1; Benedictus XIV, ep. encycl. *Ex quo,* 1 mar. 1756, §§9–17; S.C. de Prop. Fide, litt. 4 iul. 1833, II; litt. 29 maii 1838; instr. 31 iul. 1902, 13, e). * Syn. Zamosten. Ruthenorum, a. 1720, tit. I; Syn. Libanen. Maronitarum, a. 1736, pars I, cap. I, 12, 4; pars III, cap.

VI, 3; Syn. prov. Alba-Iulien. et Fagarasien. Rumenorum, a. 1872, tit. II, cap. II, c) "Et quoniam;" Syn. Sciarfen. Syrorum, a. 1888, cap. VII, art. II, 5, 1; Syn. Alexandrin. Coptorum, a. 1898, sect. III, cap. I, art. II, 5, I; Syn. Armen., a. 1911, 153, 638, b).

209 §2: Pius XII, m.p. *Cleri sanctitati,* 2 iun. 1957, can. 413. - Protodeut. can. 13; Benedictus XIV, ep. encycl. *Ex quo,* 1 mar. 1756, §§18–23. * Syn. prov. Alba-Iulien. et Fagarasien. Rumenorum, a. 1872, tit. II, cap. IV, 3) "Episcopi;" Syn. Sciarfen. Syrorum, a. 1888, cap. IX, art. VI, 2; Syn. Alexandrin. Coptorum, a. 1898, sect. III, cap. III, art. IV, 2, II; Syn. Armen., a. 1911, 638, b).

and the divine praises according to the prescriptions of the liturgical books.

CAN. 210 §1. An eparchial bishop who has completed his seventy-fifth year of age or who, due to ill health or to some other grave reason, has become less able to fulfill his office, is requested to present his resignation from office.

§2. This resignation from office by the eparchial bishop is to be presented to the patriarch in the case of an eparchial bishop exercising authority within the territorial boundaries of the patriarchal Church; in other cases, it is presented to the Roman Pontiff; further, if the bishop belongs to a patriarchal Church, the patriarch is to be notified as soon as possible.

§3. To accept this resignation the patriarch needs the consent of the permanent synod, unless a request for resignation was made previously by the synod of bishops of the patriarchal Church.

CAN. 211 §1. An eparchial bishop, whose resignation from office was accepted, obtains the title of eparchial bishop emeritus of the eparchy he governed. He can retain a residence in the eparchy itself unless in certain cases due to special circumstances it is provided otherwise by the Apostolic See or, if it is an eparchy within the territorial boundaries of the patriarchal Church, by the patriarch with the consent of the synod of bishops of the patriarchal Church.

§2. The synod of bishops of the patriarch Church or council of hierarchs must see that provision is made for the suitable and dignified support of the bishop emeritus, with due regard for the primary obligation which rests with the eparchy he served.

et in laudibus divinis secundum praescripta librorum liturgicorum.

CAN. 210 §1. Episcopus eparchialis, qui septuagesimum quintum annum aetatis explevit aut ob infirmam valetudinem aliave gravi de causa officio suo implendo minus aptus evasit, rogatur, ut renuntiationem ab officio exhibeat.

§2. Renuntiatio ab officio Episcopi eparchialis exhibenda est Patriarchae, si de Episcopo eparchiali intra fines territorii Ecclesiae patriarchalis potestatem suam exercente agitur; in ceteris casibus renuntiatio Romano Pontifici exhibenda est et praeterea, si Episcopus ad Ecclesiam patriarchalem pertinet, Patriarchae quam primum notificanda.

§3. Ad acceptationem renuntiationis Patriarcha indiget consensu Synodi permanentis, nisi praecessit invitatio ad renuntiandum a Synodo Episcoporum Ecclesiae patriarchalis facta.

CAN. 211 §1. Episcopus eparchialis, cuius renuntiatio ab officio acceptata est, titulum Episcopi emeriti eparchiae, quam rexit, obtinet atque sedem habitationis in ipsa eparchia servare potest, nisi certis in casibus ob specialia adiuncta a Sede Apostolica vel, si de eparchia intra fines territorii Ecclesiae patriarchalis sita agitur, a Patriarcha de consensu Synodi Episcoporum Ecclesiae patriarchalis aliter providetur.

§2. Synodus Episcoporum Ecclesiae patriarchalis vel Consilium Hierarcharum curare debet, ut congruae et dignae Episcopi emeriti sustentationi provideatur, attenta quidem primaria obligatione, qua tenetur eparchia, cui inservivit.

210 §1: Vat. II, decr. *Christus Dominus,* 21; PAULUS VI, m.p. *Ecclesiae sanctae,* 6 aug. 1966, I, 11.
211 §1: Vat. II, decr. *Christus Dominus,* 21; PAULUS VI, m.p. *Ecclesiae sanctae,* 6 aug. 1966, I, 11.
211 §2: Vat. II, decr. *Christus Dominus,* 21; PAULUS VI, m.p. *Ecclesiae sanctae,* 6 aug. 1966, I, 11.

ART. III. *Coadjutor Bishops and Auxiliary Bishops*

ART. III. *De Episcopis Coadiutoribus et de Episcopis Auxiliaribus*

CAN. 212 §1. If the pastoral needs of the eparchy suggest it, one or several auxiliary bishops are to be appointed at the request of the eparchial bishop.

§2. In more serious circumstances, even of a personal nature, a coadjutor bishop can be appointed *ex officio* with the right of succession and endowed with special powers.

CAN. 213 §1. In addition to the rights and obligations established in common law, a coadjutor bishop also has those that are determined in the letter of canonical provision.

§2. The rights and obligations of a coadjutor bishop appointed by the patriarch are determined by the patriarch himself after consultation with the permanent synod; however, if it is the case of a coadjutor bishop who is to be endowed with all the rights and obligations of an eparchial bishop, the consent of the synod of bishops of the patriarchal Church is required.

§3. The rights and obligations of auxiliary bishops are those established by common law.

CAN. 214 §1. In order to take canonical possession of office, the coadjutor bishop and the auxiliary bishop must show the letter of canonical provision to the eparchial bishop.

§2. The coadjutor bishop must also show the letter of canonical provision to the college of eparchial consultors.

§3. If the eparchial bishop is completely im-

CAN. 212 §1. Si necessitates pastorales eparchiae id suadent, unus vel plures Episcopi auxiliares petente Episcopo eparchiali constituantur.

§2. Gravioribus in adiunctis, etiam indolis personalis, constitui potest ex officio Episcopus coadiutor cum iure successionis specialibus potestatibus praeditus.

CAN. 213 §1. Episcopus coadiutor praeter iura et obligationes, quae iure communi statuuntur, etiam ea habet, quae in litteris de provisione canonica determinantur.

§2. Iura et obligationes Episcopi coadiutoris a Patriarcha constituti determinat ipse Patriarcha consulta Synodo permanenti; si vero de Episcopo coadiutore omnibus iuribus et obligationibus Episcopi eparchialis instruendo agitur, requiritur consensus Synodi Episcoporum Ecclesiae patriarchalis.

§3. Iura et obligationes Episcopi auxiliaris ea sunt, quae iure communi statuuntur.

CAN. 214 §1. Episcopus coadiutor et Episcopus auxiliaris, ut sui officii possessionem canonicam capiant, debent litteras de provisione canonica Episcopo eparchiali ostendere.

§2. Episcopus coadiutor debet praeterea litteras de provisione canonica ostendere collegio consultorum eparchialium.

§3. Si vero Episcopus eparchialis plene

---

212 §1: Vat. II, decr. *Christus Dominus,* 25, 26 "Bono;" PAULUS VI, m.p. *Ecclesiae sanctae,* 6 aug. 1966, I, 13 §1; PIUS XII, m.p. *Cleri sanctitati,* 2 iun. 1957, cann. 417, 248 §1 n. 4, 327 §1.

212 §2: Vat. II, decr. *Christus Dominus,* 25; PIUS XII, m.p. *Cleri sanctitati,* 2 iun. 1957, cann. 417, 248 §1 n. 4, 327 §1.

213 §1: PIUS XII, m.p. *Cleri sanctitati,* 2 iun. 1957, can. 418 §1 n. 1; Vat. II, decr. *Christus Dominus,* 25 .

213 §2: PIUS XII, m.p. *Cleri sanctitati,* 2 iun. 1957, can. 418 §1 n. 2.

214 §1: PIUS XII, m.p. *Cleri sanctitati,* 2 iun. 1957, can. 419 §1.

214 §2: PIUS XII, m.p. *Cleri sanctitati,* 2 iun. 1957, can. 419 §2.

214 §3: PIUS XII, m.p. *Cleri sanctitati,* 2 iun. 1957, can. 419 §3.

peded, it is sufficient that the coadjutor bishop and the auxiliary bishop show the letter of canonical provision to the college of eparchial consultors.

§4. The chancellor of the curia must be present when the letter of canonical provision is presented and is to make a record of the fact.

CAN. 215 §1. The coadjutor bishop takes the place of the eparchial bishop when he is absent or impeded. He must be appointed protosyncellus and the eparchial bishop is to commit to him, in preference to others, those things which by law require a special mandate.

§2. The eparchial bishop, without prejudice for §1, is to appoint the auxiliary bishop as protosyncellus. If, however, there are several, he is to appoint one of them protosyncellus and the others syncelli.

§3. The eparchial bishop, in assessing matters of great importance, especially those of a pastoral nature, is to consult the auxiliary bishop in preference to others.

§4. The coadjutor bishop and the auxiliary bishop, inasmuch as they are called to share in the concerns of the eparchial bishop, are to exercise their office so that in all matters they act in unanimous agreement with him.

CAN. 216 §1. The coadjutor bishop and the auxiliary bishop who are not legitimately prevented by a just impediment must, whenever requested by the eparchial bishop, carry out those functions that it is the duty of the eparchial bishop to perform.

§2. The eparchial bishop is not to commit habitually to others those episcopal rights and

est impeditus, sufficit, ut Episcopus coadiutor et Episcopus auxiliaris litteras de provisione canonica ostendant collegio consultorum eparchialium.

§4. Ostensioni litterarum de provisione canonica adesse debet cancellarius, qui rem in acta referat.

CAN. 215 §1. Episcopus coadiutor vices gerit Episcopi eparchialis absentis vel impediti; nominari debet Protosyncellus et ei prae aliis Episcopus eparchialis committat ea, quae ex iure mandatum speciale requirunt.

§2. Episcopus eparchialis firma §1 nominet Episcopum auxiliarem Protosyncellum; si tamen plures sunt, unum ex eis nominet Protosyncellum, alios vero Syncellos.

§3. Episcopus eparchialis in perpendendis causis maioris momenti praesertim indolis pastoralis Episcopos auxiliares prae ceteris consulat.

§4. Episcopus coadiutor et Episcopus auxiliaris eo, quod in partem sollicitudinis Episcopi eparchialis vocati sunt, ita officium suum exerceant, ut in omnibus negotiis unanima consensione cum ipso agant.

CAN. 216 §1. Episcopus coadiutor et Episcopus auxiliaris iusto impedimento non detenti debent, quoties sunt ab Episcopo eparchiali requisiti, functiones obire, quas Episcopus eparchialis ipse peragere deberet.

§2. Quae episcopalia iura et functiones Episcopus coadiutor et Episcopus auxiliaris

214 §4: Pius XII, m.p. *Cleri sanctitati,* 2 iun. 1957, can. 419 §2.

215 §1: Pius XII, m.p. *Cleri sanctitati,* 2 iun. 1957, can. 418 §§2–4.

215 §2: Vat. II, decr. *Christus Dominus,* 26 "Quodsi;" Paulus VI, m.p. *Ecclesiae sanctae,* 6 aug. 1966, I, 13 §2.

215 §3: Vat. II, decr. *Christus Dominus,* 26 "Quodsi."

215 §4: Vat. II, decr. *Christus Dominus,* 25 "Iamvero."

216 §1: Pius XII, m.p. *Cleri sanctitati,* 2 iun. 1957, can. 418 §4.

216 §2: Pius XII, m.p. *Cleri sanctitati,* 2 iun. 1957, can. 418 §3.

functions that the coadjutor bishop and the auxiliary bishop can and are willing to exercise.

CAN. 217 The coadjutor bishop and the auxiliary bishop are bound by the obligation of residing in the eparchy. They are not to be away from it for longer than a brief period except to fulfill some function outside the eparchy or are on vacation, which are not to extend more than a month.

CAN. 218 Regarding resignation from office by the coadjutor bishop or the auxiliary bishop, cann. 210 and 211, §2 are to be applied. These bishops are given the title of emeritus of the office they previously carried out.

ART. IV. *The Vacant or Impeded Eparchial See*

CAN. 219 The eparchial see becomes vacant by the death, resignation, transfer or privation of office of the eparchial bishop.

CAN. 220 Concerning vacant sees within the territorial boundaries of the patriarchal Church, in addition to cann. 225–232 and without prejudice to cann. 222 and 223, the following norms are to be observed:

1° the patriarch is to inform the Apostolic See as soon as possible of the vacancy of the eparchial see;

2° until the appointment of an administrator of the eparchy, the ordinary power of the eparchial bishop transfers to the patriarch, unless otherwise provided by the particular law of the patriarchal Church or by the Roman Pontiff;

possunt et volunt exercere, Episcopus eparchialis habitualiter aliis ne committat.

CAN. 217 Episcopus coadiutor et Episcopus auxiliaris obligatione tenentur residendi in eparchia, a qua praeterquam ratione alicuius muneris extra eparchiam implendi aut feriarum causa, quae ultra mensem ne protrahantur, ne discedant nisi ad breve tempus.

CAN. 218 Ad renuntiationem ab officio Episcopi coadiutoris vel Episcopi auxiliaris quod attinet, applicentur cann. 210 et 211, §2; his Episcopis tribuitur emeriti titulus officii, quod antea expleverunt.

ART. IV. *De Sede Eparchiali Vacante vel Impedita*

CAN. 219 Sedes eparchialis vacat Episcopi eparchialis morte, renuntiatione, translatione ac privatione.

CAN. 220 Circa sedes eparchiales vacantes intra fines territorii Ecclesiae patriarchalis sitas praeter cann. 225–232 et firmis cann. 222 et 223 haec servanda sunt:

1° Patriarcha de sedis eparchialis vacatione quam primum certiorem faciat Sedem Apostolicam;

2° usque ad nominationem Administratoris eparchiae potestas ordinaria Episcopi eparchialis transit ad Patriarcham, nisi aliter iure particulari Ecclesiae patriarchalis vel a Romano Pontifice provisum est;

217: Pius XII, m.p. *Cleri sanctitati,* 2 iun. 1957, can. 420.

218: Vat. II, decr. *Christus Dominus,* 21; Paulus VI, m.p. *Ecclesiae sanctae,* 6 aug. 1966, I, 11.

219: Pius XII, m.p. *Cleri sanctitati,* 2 iun. 1957, can. 468 §1. * Syn. Sciarfen. Syrorum, a. 1888, cap. VIII, art. III; Syn. Alexandrin. Coptorum, a. 1898, sect. III, cap. II, art. III.

220, 1°: Pius XII, m.p. *Cleri sanctitati,* 2 iun. 1957, can. 249 §1 n. 1.

220, 2°: Pius XII, m.p. *Cleri sanctitati,* 2 iun. 1957, cann. 469, 473 §1, 475. * Syn. Sciarfen. Syrorum, a. 1888, cap. VIII, art. III; Syn. Alexandrin. Coptorum, a. 1898, sect. III, cap. II, art. III, 1; Syn. Armen., a. 1911, 298.

3° it is for the patriarch to appoint an administrator of the eparchy within a month of useful time from the reception of notice of the vacancy of the eparchial see, after consulting the bishops of the patriarchal curia, if there are any, otherwise after consulting the permanent synod. If the month elapses without this being done, the appointment of the administrator devolves to the Apostolic See;

4° the administrator of the eparchy, after making the profession of faith in the presence of the patriarch obtains his power, but is not to exercise it without taking canonical possession of the office by presenting his letter of appointment to the college of eparchial consultors;

5° the patriarch is to ensure that a worthy and suitable eparchial bishop be assigned to the vacant eparchial see as soon as possible, but not beyond the deadline established by common law.

CAN. 221 Excepting the vacant eparchial sees mentioned in can. 220, in other cases of a vacancy of the eparchial see, in addition to cann. 225–232 and without prejudice to cann. 222 and 223, the following norms are to be observed:

1° the metropolitan, or otherwise he who presides over the college of eparchial consultors in accord with the norm of can. 271, §5, is to inform the Apostolic See as soon as possible of the vacancy of the eparchial see and, in case of an eparchy of a patriarchal Church, also the patriarch;

2° unless otherwise provided by the Apostol-

3° Patriarchae est nominare Administratorem eparchiae intra mensem utilem ab accepta notitia de sedis eparchialis vacatione computandum consultis Episcopis curiae patriarchalis, si habentur, secus consulta Synodo permanenti; elapso inutiliter mense, Administratoris nominatio ad Sedem Apostolicam devolvitur;

4° Administrator eparchiae emissa coram Patriarcha professione fidei potestatem obtinet non exercendam tamen nisi capta possessione canonica officii, quae fit ostendendo litteras eius nominationis collegio consultorum eparchialium;

5° Patriarchae est curare, ut sedi eparchiali vacanti quam primum nec ultra terminos iure communi statutos dignus idoneusque Episcopus eparchialis detur.

CAN. 221 Exceptis sedibus eparchialibus vacantibus, de quibus in can. 220, in ceteris casibus sede eparchiali vacante praeter cann. 225–232 et firmis cann. 222 et 223 haec servanda sunt:

1° Metropolita, secus ille, qui ad normam can. 271, §5 collegio consultorum eparchialium praeest, Sedem Apostolicam et, si de eparchia Ecclesiae patriarchalis agitur, etiam Patriarcham quam primum de sedis eparchialis vacatione certiorem faciat;

2° regimen eparchiae, nisi a Sede Apos-

220, 3°:Pius XII, m.p. *Cleri sanctitati,* 2 iun. 1957, can. 249 §1 n. 4. * Syn. Alexandrin. Coptorum, a. 1898, sect. III, cap. I, art. III, IV, 3); cap. II, art. III, 1.

220, 4°: Pius XII, m.p. *Cleri sanctitati,* 2 iun. 1957, can. 476 §1.

220, 5°: Pius XII, m.p. *Cleri sanctitati,* 2 iun. 1957, can. 249 §3. - Chalc. can. 25; S. Paulus V, litt. ap. *Erga Maronitarum,* 21 oct. 1619. * Syn. Libanen. Maronitarum, a. 1736, pars III, cap. IV, 17; Syn. Sciarfen.

Syrorum, a. 1888, cap. VIII, art. IV, 1; Syn. Alexandrin. Coptorum, a. 1898, sect. III, cap. II, art. IV.

221, 1°: Pius XII, m.p. *Cleri sanctitati,* 2 iun. 1957, can. 470 §4.

221, 2°: Vat. II, decr. *Christus Dominus,* 26 "Nisi;" Paulus VI, m.p. *Ecclesiae sanctae,* 6 aug. 1966, I, 13 §3; Pius XII, m.p. *Cleri sanctitati,* 2 iun. 1957, cann. 473, 434.

ic See, until the appointment of an administrator, the governance of the eparchy transfers to the auxiliary bishop; if there are several auxiliary bishops, to the senior by episcopal ordination; if there is no auxiliary bishop, to the college of eparchial consultors. The aforementioned govern the eparchy in the interim with that authority that common law accords to a protosyncellus.

3° the college of eparchial consultors must elect an administrator of the eparchy within eight days from the reception of the notification of the vacancy of the eparchial see; for the validity of the election, an absolute majority of the votes of the members of the college is required;

4° if within eight days the administrator of the eparchy has not been elected or if the one elected lacks the qualities required in can. 227, §2 for the validity of the election, the appointment of the administrator of the eparchy devolves to the metropolitan or, if there is no metropolitan or he is impeded, to the Apostolic See;

5° the administrator of an eparchy once legitimately elected or appointed obtains immediately his power and does not need any confirmation; he is to inform the Apostolic See as soon as possible of his election or of his appointment by the metropolitan and, if he belongs to a patriarchal Church, also the patriarch.

CAN. 222 Upon the vacancy of the eparchial see, the coadjutor bishop, provided that he has already taken canonical possession of his office, becomes by the law itself, the administrator of the eparchy until his enthronement as eparchial bishop.

tolica aliter provisum est, usque ad constitutionem Administratoris eparchiae transit ad Episcopum auxiliarem vel, si plures sunt, ad Episcopum auxiliarem ordinatione episcopali seniorem vel, si Episcopus auxiliaris non habetur, ad collegium consultorum eparchialium; praedicti eparchiam interim regunt potestate, quam ius commune Protosyncello agnoscit;

3° collegium consultorum eparchialium intra octo dies ab accepta notitia de sedis eparchialis vacatione computandos debet Administratorem eparchiae eligere, sed ad validitatem electionis requiritur pars absolute maior suffragiorum membrorum eiusdem collegii;

4° si intra octo dies Administrator eparchiae electus non est vel si electus condicionibus in can. 227, §2 ad validitatem electionis requisitis caret, nominatio Administratoris eparchiae devolvitur ad Metropolitam vel, si hic deest vel est impeditus, ad Sedem Apostolicam;

5° Administrator eparchiae legitime electus vel nominatus statim potestatem obtinet neque indiget ulla confirmatione; de sua electione vel ex parte Metropolitae nominatione quam primum Sedem Apostolicam certiorem faciat et, si ad Ecclesiam patriarchalem pertinet, etiam Patriarcham.

CAN. 222 Episcopus coadiutor, dummodo officii sui possessionem canonicam iam ceperit, sede eparchiali vacante ipso iure evadit Administrator eparchiae, donec ut Episcopus eparchialis inthronizatus erit.

221, 3°: Pius XII, m.p. *Cleri sanctitati*, 2 iun. 1957, can. 470 §1. * Syn. Leopolien. Ruthenorum, a. 1891, tit. VII, cap. II, 5.

221, 4°: Pius XII, m.p. *Cleri sanctitati*, 2 iun. 1957, can. 470 §2.

221, 5°: Pius XII, m.p. *Cleri sanctitati*, 2 iun. 1957, cann. 476 §2, 470 §4.

222: Pius XII, m.p. *Cleri sanctitati*, 2 iun. 1957, can. 421 §1.

CAN. 223 In the case of a transfer to another eparchial see, the eparchial bishop must take canonical possession of the new eparchy within two months from the notification of the transfer. In the interim, in the former eparchy;

1° he has the rights and obligations of the administrator of the eparchy;

2° he retains the honorific privileges of eparchial bishops;

3° he continues to receive the entire income of the previous office.

CAN. 224 §1. Upon the vacancy of the eparchial see, the protosyncellus and the syncelli immediately cease from office unless they are:

1° ordained bishops;

2° constituted in the eparchy of the patriarch;

3° constituted in an eparchy located within the territorial boundaries of the patriarchal Church, until the administrator of the eparchy takes canonical possession of his office.

§2. Actions legitimately taken by the protosyncellus and syncelli who cease from office immediately at the vacancy of the eparchial see have force until they receive certain notice of the vacancy of the eparchial see.

§3. During the vacancy of the eparchial see, the auxiliary bishop retains the power, to be exercised under the authority of the administrator, which are granted to him by law and that he had as protosyncellus or syncellus when the see

CAN. 223 In casu translationis ad aliam sedem eparchialem Episcopus intra duos menses ab intimatione translationis computandos debet possessionem canonicam novae eparchiae capere; interim vero in priore eparchia:

1° Administratoris eparchiae iura et obligationes habet;

2° privilegia honorifica Episcoporum eparchialium conservat;

3° reditus prioris officii integros percipit.

CAN. 224 §1. Protosyncellus et Syncelli sede eparchiali vacante statim ab officio cessant, nisi sunt:

1° Episcopi ordinati;

2° in eparchia Patriarchae constituti;

3° in eparchia intra fines territorii Ecclesiae patriarchalis sita constituti, donec Administrator eparchiae possessionem canonicam sui officii ceperit.

§2. Quae a Protosyncello et Syncellis, qui sede eparchiali vacante statim ab officio cessant, legitime gesta sunt, donec certam notitiam de sedis eparchialis vacatione acceperint, vim habent.

§3. Episcopus auxiliaris sede eparchiali vacante retinet potestates a iure quidem collatas et sub auctoritate Administratoris eparchiae exercendas, quas sede eparchiali plena ut Protosyncellus vel Syncellus

223: Pius XII, m.p. *Cleri sanctitati,* 2 iun. 1957, can. 468 §3. * Syn. Sciarfen. Syrorum, a. 1888, cap. VIII, art. IV "Episcopus."

224 §1: Pius XII, m.p. *Cleri sanctitati,* 2 iun. 1957, can. 437 §1.

224 §1, 1°: Paulus VI, m.p. *Ecclesiae sanctae,* 6 aug. 1966, I, 14 §5.

224 §1, 2°: Pius XII, m.p. *Cleri sanctitati,* 2 iun. 1957, can. 437 §2.

224 §1, 3°: Pius XII, m.p. *Cleri sanctitati,* 2 iun. 1957, can. 469. * Syn. Sciarfen. Syrorum, a. 1888, cap. VIII, art. III "Cum;" Syn. Armen., a. 1911, 298.

224 §2: Pius XII, m.p. *Cleri sanctitati,* 2 iun. 1957, can. 468 §2.

224 §3: Paulus VI, m.p. *Ecclesiae sanctae,* 6 aug. 1966, I, 14 §5; Pius XII, m.p. *Cleri sanctitati,* 2 iun. 1957, can. 421 §2.

was occupied, unless it is established otherwise by the Apostolic See or by the particular law of his patriarchal Church.

CAN. 225 §1. Only one administrator of the eparchy is elected or appointed; any contrary custom being reprobated.

§2. If the eparchial finance officer becomes administrator of the eparchy, the finance council elects another interim eparchial finance officer.

CAN. 226 In constituting the administrator of an eparchy neither the patriarch nor the college of eparchial consultors can retain for themselves any part of the power, nor determine a time limit for holding the office nor preordain any other restrictions.

CAN. 227 §1. The administrator of an eparchy should be a person who is outstanding in integrity, piety, sound doctrine and prudence.

§2. To be elected or appointed validly to the office of administrator of the eparchy, one should be a bishop or a presbyter who is not bound by the bond of matrimony, who has completed thirty five years of age and who has not already been elected, proposed, appointed or transferred to the same vacant see. If these conditions have been neglected, the acts of the one elected or appointed as administrator of the eparchy are null by the law itself.

CAN. 228 §1. During the vacancy of the see no innovation is to be made.

§2. Those who have the interim governance of the eparchy are forbidden to do anything that

habebat, nisi aliud a Sede Apostolica vel iure particulari propriae Ecclesiae patriarchalis statuitur.

CAN. 225 §1. Unus tantum eligitur vel nominatur Administrator eparchiae reprobata contraria consuetudine.

§2. Si oeconomus eparchialis fit Administrator eparchiae, alium oeconomum eparchialem consilium a rebus oeconomicis interim eligat.

CAN. 226 In Administratore eparchiae constituendo nullam sibi potestatis partem nec Patriarcha nec collegium consultorum eparchialium retinere potest nec gerendo officio tempus determinare aliasve restrictiones praestituere.

CAN. 227 §1. Administrator eparchiae sit integritate, pietate, sana doctrina et prudentia praestans.

§2. Valide ad officium Administratoris eparchiae eligi vel nominari tantum potest Episcopus aut presbyter, qui vinculo matrimonii non est ligatus, tricesimum quintum aetatis annum explevit et ad eandem sedem eparchialem vacantem non est iam electus, nominatus vel translatus; si hae condiciones posthabitae sunt, actus illius, qui Administrator eparchiae electus vel nominatus est, ipso iure nulli sunt.

CAN. 228 §1. Sede eparchiali vacante nihil innovetur.

§2. Illi, qui interim eparchiae regimen curant, vetantur quidpiam agere, quod vel

---

225 §2: Pius XII, m.p. *Cleri sanctitati*, 2 iun. 1957, can. 475.

226: Pius XII, m.p. *Cleri sanctitati*, 2 iun. 1957, can. 475.

227 §1: Pius XII, m.p. *Cleri sanctitati*, 2 iun. 1957, can. 472 §2.

227 §2: Pius XII, m.p. *Cleri sanctitati*, 2 iun. 1957, can. 472 §§1, 3.

228 §1: Pius XII, m.p. *Cleri sanctitati*, 2 iun. 1957, can. 474 §1. - Ancyr. can. 15. * Syn. Zamosten. Ruthenorum, a. 1720, tit. VI "Ut etiam;" Syn. Alexandrin. Coptorum, a. 1898, sect. III, cap. II, art. III, 3.

228 §2: Pius XII, m.p. *Cleri sanctitati*, 2 iun. 1957, can. 474 §2. * Syn. Zamosten. Ruthenorum, a. 1720, tit. VI "Ut etiam;" Syn. Sciarfen. Syrorum, a. 1888, cap. VIII, art. III, 2–3; Syn. Armen., a. 1911, 299.

could be prejudicial to the eparchy or to the rights of the bishop. They as well as others are specifically forbidden to remove, destroy or alter any documents of the eparchial curia either personally or through another.

CAN. 229 The administrator of the eparchy has the same rights and obligations as the eparchial bishop, unless the law provides otherwise or it is evident from the nature of the matter.

CAN. 230 Unless otherwise legitimately provided:

1° the administrator of the eparchy has the right to a just remuneration, which is to be established by particular law or is determined by legitimate custom and which must be drawn from the goods of the eparchy;

2° the other emoluments due to the eparchial bishop during the vacancy of the eparchial see are to be reserved to the future eparchial bishop for the needs of the eparchy, observing the prescriptions of the particular law that determine the manner in which the emoluments must be spent.

CAN. 231 §1. The resignation of the administrator of an eparchy is to be made to the patriarch if he designated the administrator, otherwise to the college of eparchial consultors, in which case it is not necessary that the resignation be accepted for it to be valid.

§2. The removal of an administrator of an eparchy within the territorial boundaries of the patriarchal Church is the competency of the patriarch with the consent of the permanent synod; otherwise, it is reserved to the Apostolic See.

eparchiae vel episcopalibus iuribus praeiudicium afferre potest; speciatim prohibentur ipsi ac omnes alii, ne sive per se sive per alium documenta curiae eparchialis subtrahant, destruant vel mutent.

CAN. 229 Administrator eparchiae eadem iura et obligationes habet ac Episcopus eparchialis, nisi aliter iure cavetur vel ex natura rei constat.

CAN. 230 Nisi aliter est legitime provisum:

1° Administrator eparchiae ius habet ad iustam remunerationem lege iuris particularis statuendam vel legitima consuetudine determinatam, quae desumi debet ex bonis eparchiae;

2° cetera emolumenta ad Episcopum eparchialem spectantia, dum sedes eparchialis vacat, futuro Episcopo eparchiali pro necessitatibus eparchiae reserventur servatis praescriptis iuris particularis, quae modum, quo emolumenta erogari debent, determinant.

CAN. 231 §1. Renuntiatio Administratoris eparchiae exhibenda est Patriarchae, si ipse Administratorem designavit, secus collegio consultorum eparchialium, quo in casu eam acceptari, ut valeat, necesse non est.

§2. Amotio Administratoris eparchiae intra fines territorii Ecclesiae patriarchalis pertinet ad Patriarcham de consensu Synodi permanentis; secus vero Sedi Apostolicae reservatur.

229: Pius XII, m.p. *Cleri sanctitati,* 2 iun. 1957, cann. 473, 478. * Syn. Sciarfen. Syrorum, a. 1888, cap. VIII, art. III; Syn. Alexandrin. Coptorum, a. 1898, sect. III, cap. II, art. III, 1; Syn. Armen., a. 1911, 298.

230, 1°: Pius XII, m.p. *Cleri sanctitati,* 2 iun. 1957, can. 479 n. 1. * Syn. Sciarfen. Syrorum, a. 1888, cap. VIII, art. III.

230, 2°: Pius XII, m.p. *Cleri sanctitati,* 2 iun. 1957, can. 472 n. 2. - Chalc. can. 25. * Syn. Zamosten. Ruthenorum, a. 1720, tit. VI "Ut etiam."

231 §1: Pius XII, m.p. *Cleri sanctitati,* 2 iun. 1957, can. 480 §1. * Syn. Sciarfen. Syrorum, a. 1888, cap. VIII, art. III.

§3. After the death, resignation or removal of the administrator of the eparchy, a new one is to be constituted by the same authority and in the same manner as prescribed for the previous one.

§4. The administrator of an eparchy ceases from his office once the new eparchial bishop has taken canonical possession of the eparchy. The new eparchial bishop can require an account of his administration.

CAN. 232 §1. The eparchial finance officer, during the vacancy of the eparchial see, is to discharge his office under the authority of the administrator of the eparchy. The administration of the ecclesiastical goods which on account of the vacancy of the eparchial see do not have an administrator devolves upon him, unless the patriarch or the college of eparchial consultors has provided otherwise.

§2. For the resignation or removal of the eparchial finance officer during the vacancy of the see, can. 231, §§1 and 2 is to be observed.

§3. When the right of the eparchial finance officer comes to an end in whatever manner, within the territorial boundaries of the patriarchal Church the election or appointment of a new finance officer pertains to the patriarch after having consulted the bishops of the patriarchal curia, if there are any, otherwise, having consulted the permanent synod. In other cases, the finance officer is elected by the college of eparchial consultors.

§4. The eparchial finance officer must give an

§3. Post mortem, renuntiationem vel amotionem Administratoris eparchiae novus constituatur ab eadem auctoritate et eodem modo ac pro priore praescriptum est.

§4. Administrator eparchiae cessat ab officio capta a novo Episcopo eparchiali possessione canonica eparchiae; novus Episcopus eparchialis rationem administrationis ab eo exigere potest.

CAN. 232 §1. Oeconomus eparchialis sede eparchiali vacante officium suum impleat sub auctoritate Administratoris eparchiae; ad oeconomum eparchialem devolvitur administratio bonorum ecclesiasticorum, quae ob sedis eparchialis vacationem administratorem non habent, nisi Patriarcha aut collegium consultorum eparchialium aliter providerunt.

§2. Ad renuntiationem vel amotionem oeconomi eparchialis sede eparchiali vacante quod attinet, servandus est can. 231, §§1 et 2.

§3. Resoluto quovis modo iure oeconomi eparchialis intra fines territorii Ecclesiae patriarchalis novi oeconomi electio vel nominatio pertinet ad Patriarcham consultis Episcopis curiae patriarchalis, si habentur, secus consulta Synodo permanenti; in ceteris casibus oeconomus eligitur a collegio consultorum eparchialium.

§4. Oeconomus eparchialis novo Epi-

231 §3: Pius XII, m.p. *Cleri sanctitati,* 2 iun. 1957, can. 480 §1. * Syn. Sciarfen. Syrorum, a. 1888, cap. VIII, art. III.

231 §4: Pius XII, m.p. *Cleri sanctitati,* 2 iun. 1957, cann. 480 §2, 482. * Syn. Zamosten. Ruthenorum, a. 1720, tit. V; Syn. Sciarfen. Syrorum, a. 1888, cap. VIII, art. III; Syn. Alexandrin. Coptorum, a. 1898, sect. III, cap. II, art. III, 4; Syn. Armen., a. 1911, 322.

232 §1: Pius XII, m.p. *Cleri sanctitati,* 2 iun. 1957, can. 481 §1. * Syn. Libanen. Maronitarum, a. 1736, pars III, cap. IV, 27; Syn. Leopolien. Ruthenorum, a. 1891, tit. VII, cap. II, 5.

232 §2: Pius XII, m.p. *Cleri sanctitati,* 2 iun. 1957, can. 481 §§2, 4.

232 §3: Pius XII, m.p. *Cleri sanctitati,* 2 iun. 1957, can. 481 §3.

232 §4: Pius XII, m.p. *Cleri sanctitati,* 2 iun. 1957, can. 481 §5.

account of his administration to the new eparchial bishop; once he has done this, he ceases in office unless he is confirmed in his office by the bishop.

CAN. 233 §1. When the eparchial see is so impeded by the imprisonment, banishment, exile or incapacity of the eparchial bishop, that he is unable to communicate even by letter with the Christian faithful committed to him, the governance of the eparchy is the responsibility of the coadjutor bishop, unless otherwise provided by the patriarch with the consent of the permanent synod, in eparchies located within the territorial boundaries of the Church over which he presides, or by the Apostolic See. If there is no coadjutor bishop, or if he is impeded, it is the responsibility of the protosyncellus or syncellus or another suitable priest designated by the eparchial bishop. This priest has, by virtue of the law itself, the rights and obligations of a protosyncellus. At a suitable time the eparchial bishop can designate several to succeed one another in office.

§2. If there are none of the aforesaid or they are impeded from assuming the governance of the eparchy, it is for the college of eparchial consultors to elect a priest who is to govern the eparchy.

§3. The person who undertakes the governance of an eparchy within the territorial boundaries of the patriarchal Church is to inform the patriarch as soon as possible that the eparchial see is impeded and of his assumption of office. In other cases the person is to inform the Apostolic See and, if he belongs to a patriarchal Church, also the patriarch.

scopo eparchiali rationem reddere debet suae administrationis, qua reddita, nisi ab eodem in officio suo confirmatur, ab officio cessat.

CAN. 233 §1. Sede eparchiali per Episcopi eparchialis captivitatem, relegationem, exilium aut inhabilitatem ita impedita, ut ne per litteras quidem cum christifidelibus sibi commissis communicare ipse possit, regimen eparchiae est penes Episcopum coadiutorem, nisi aliter providit Patriarcha de consensu Synodi permanentis in eparchiis sitis intra fines territorii Ecclesiae, cui praeest, aut Sedes Apostolica; si vero Episcopus coadiutor deest aut impeditus est, penes Protosyncellum, Syncellum vel alium idoneum sacerdotem ab Episcopo eparchiali designatum, cui ipso iure competunt iura et obligationes Protosyncelli; potest vero Episcopus eparchialis tempore opportuno plures designare, qui sibi invicem in officio succedunt.

§2. Si iidem desunt aut impediti sunt, ne eparchiae regimen assumant, collegii consultorum eparchialium est sacerdotem eligere, qui eparchiam regat.

§3. Qui eparchiam intra fines territorii Ecclesiae patriarchalis regendam suscepit, quam primum Patriarcham certiorem faciat de sede eparchiali impedita et de assumpto officio; in ceteris casibus certiorem faciat Sedem Apostolicam et, si ad Ecclesiam patriarchalem pertinet, etiam Patriarcham.

---

233 §1: Pius XII, m.p. *Cleri sanctitati*, 2 iun. 1957, can. 467 §1.

233 §2: Pius XII, m.p. *Cleri sanctitati*, 2 iun. 1957,

can. 467 §2 n. 1.

233 §3: Pius XII, m.p. *Cleri sanctitati*, 2 iun. 1957, can. 467 §3.

ART. V. *Apostolic Administrators*

CAN. 234 §1. Sometimes for grave and special reasons the Roman Pontiff commits the governance of an eparchy, whether the eparchial see is occupied or vacant, to an apostolic administrator.

§2. The rights, obligations and privileges of the apostolic administrator are drawn from his letter of appointment.

CHAPTER II. Organs Assisting the Eparchial Bishop in the Governance of the Eparchy

ART. I. *The Eparchial Assembly*

CAN. 235 The eparchial assembly assists the eparchial bishop in matters that regard the special needs of the eparchy or its benefits.

CAN. 236 The eparchial assembly is to be convoked whenever, in the judgment of the eparchial bishop and after consultation with the presbyteral council, the circumstances recommend it.

CAN. 237 §1. It is for the eparchial bishop to convoke the eparchial assembly, to preside over it personally or through another, to transfer, prorogue, suspend, or dissolve it.

§2. If the eparchial see becomes vacant, the eparchial assembly is by virtue of the law itself suspended until the new eparchial bishop decides on the matter.

ART. V. *De Administratoribus Apostolicis*

CAN. 234 §1. Eparchiae regimen sede eparchiali sive plena sive vacante aliquando Romanus Pontifex gravibus et specialibus de causis Administratori apostolico committit.

§2. Iura, obligationes et privilegia Administratoris apostolici desumuntur ex litteris suae nominationis.

CAPUT II. **De Organis Episcopum Eparchialem in Regimine Eparchiae Adiuvantibus**

ART. I. *De Conventu Eparchiali*

CAN. 235 Conventus eparchialis adiutricem praestat operam Episcopo eparchiali in eis, quae ad speciales necessitates vel utilitatem eparchiae referuntur.

CAN. 236 Conventus eparchialis convocetur, quoties iudicio Episcopi eparchialis et consulto consilio presbyterali adiuncta id suadent.

CAN. 237 §1. Episcopi eparchialis est conventum eparchialem convocare, eidem per se vel per alium praeesse, eum transferre, prorogare, suspendere et dissolvere.

§2. Sede eparchiali vacante conventus eparchialis suspenditur ipso iure, donec novus Episcopus eparchialis de re decreverit.

---

234 §1: Pius XII, m.p. *Cleri sanctitati,* 2 iun. 1957, can. 352.

234 §2: Pius XII, m.p. *Cleri sanctitati,* 2 iun. 1957, cann. 353–361.

235: Pius XII, m.p. *Cleri sanctitati,* 2 iun. 1957, can. 422 §1. * Syn. Libanen. Maronitarum, a. 1736, pars III, cap. IV, 29; Syn. Zamosten. Ruthenorum, a. 1720, tit. VI "Praeter;" Syn. prov. Alba-Iulien. et Fa-garasien. Rumenorum, a. 1872, tit. III, cap. IV; Syn. Sciarfen. Syrorum, a. 1888, cap. IX, art. I, 4; art. IV, 7; Syn. Leopolien. Ruthenorum, a. 1891, tit. XIV; Syn. Armen., a. 1911, tit. II, cap. VII.

236: Pius XII, m.p. *Cleri sanctitati,* 2 iun. 1957, can. 422 §1.

237 §1: Pius XII, m.p. *Cleri sanctitati,* 2 iun. 1957, can. 423 §§1–2.

CAN. 238 §1. The following should be convoked to the eparchial assembly and they must attend it:

1° the coadjutor bishop and the auxiliary bishops;

2° the protosyncellus, syncelli, judicial vicar and the eparchial finance officer;

3° the eparchial consultors;

4° the rector of the eparchial major seminary;

5° the protopresbyters;

6° at least one pastor from each district, to be elected by all of those who have actually the care of souls there, with the protopresbyter presiding over the election; another presbyter is also to be elected to substitute for him if he is impeded;

7° the members of the presbyteral council and some delegates of the pastoral council, if it exists, elected by the same council in accord with the manner and number established by particular law;

8° some deacons elected in accord with the norms of particular law;

9° superiors of monasteries *sui iuris* and some superiors of other institutes of consecrated life which have a house in the eparchy, elected in accord with the manner and number established by particular law;

10° lay persons elected by the pastoral council, if it exists, or elected in some other manner determined by the eparchial bishop so that the number of lay persons does not exceed one-third of the members of the eparchial assembly.

CAN. 238 §1. Ad conventum eparchialem convocandi sunt eumque adire debent:

1° Episcopus coadiutor et Episcopi auxiliares;

2° Protosyncellus, Syncelli, Vicarius iudicialis ac oeconomus eparchialis;

3° consultores eparchiales;

4° rector seminarii eparchialis maioris;

5° protopresbyteri;

6° unus saltem parochus ex unoquoque districtu eligendus ab omnibus, qui ibi actu curam animarum habent, protopresbytero electioni praesidente; item eligendus est alius presbyter, qui eodem impedito eius locum teneat;

7° membra consilii presbyteralis atque aliquot delegati consilii pastoralis, si exstat, ab eodem consilio eligendi modo et numero iure particulari statutis;

8° aliquot diaconi ad normam iuris particularis electi;

9° Superiores monasteriorum sui iuris atque aliquot Superiores ceterorum institutorum vitae consecratae, quae in eparchia domum habent, eligendi modo et numero iure particulari statutis;

10° laici electi a consilio pastorali, si exstat, secus modo ab Episcopo eparchiali determinato ita, ut numerus laicorum tertiam partem membrorum conventus eparchialis non superet.

238 §1: * Syn. Zamosten. Ruthenorum, a. 1720, tit. VI "Caeterum."

238 §1, 2°: Pius XII, m.p. *Cleri sanctitati,* 2 iun. 1957, can. 424 §1 n. 1.

238 §1, 3°: Pius XII, m.p. *Cleri sanctitati,* 2 iun. 1957, can. 424 §1 n. 2.

238 §1, 4°: Pius XII, m.p. *Cleri sanctitati,* 2 iun. 1957, can. 424 §1 n. 3.

238 §1, 5°: Pius XII, m.p. *Cleri sanctitati,* 2 iun. 1957, can. 424 §1 n. 4. * Syn. prov. Alba-Iulien. et Fagarasien. Rumenorum, a. 1872, tit. II, cap. VIII, II, 6).

238 §1, 6°: Pius XII, m.p. *Cleri sanctitati,* 2 iun. 1957, can. 424 §1 n. 6. * Syn. prov. Alba-Iulien. et Fagarasien. Rumenorum, a. 1872, tit. II, cap. IX, 7).

238 §1, 8°: Pius XII, m.p. *Cleri sanctitati,* 2 iun. 1957, can. 424 §1 n. 8.

238 §1, 9°: Pius XII, m.p. *Cleri sanctitati,* 2 iun. 1957, can. 424 §1 n. 7.

238 §1, 10°: Pius XII, m.p. *Cleri sanctitati,* 2 iun. 1957, can. 424 §1.

§2. The eparchial bishop, if he judges it opportune, can invite to the eparchial assembly others also, not excluding persons of other Churches *sui iuris,* to all of whom he can even grant the right to vote.

§3. Some observers from non-Catholic Churches or ecclesial communities can also be invited to the eparchial assembly.

CAN. 239 Those who must attend the eparchial assembly cannot send a proxy to attend the eparchial assembly in their place, even if they are legitimately prevented by an impediment, but they are to inform the eparchial bishop of the impediment.

CAN. 240 §1. Without prejudice to the right of any of the Christian faithful to suggest the subjects to be dealt with at the eparchial assembly, it is solely for the eparchial bishop to determine the topics to be dealt with in this assembly.

§2. The eparchial bishop is to appoint in a timely manner one or several commissions to prepare the topics to be dealt with in the assembly.

§3. The eparchial bishop is also to see that all who have been convoked to the assembly are given in a timely manner the program of topics to be treated.

§4. All the subjects proposed to the eparchial assembly are to be submitted to free discussion during its sessions.

CAN. 241 The eparchial bishop is the sole

§2. Episcopus eparchialis, si opportunum iudicat, potest ad conventum eparchialem invitare alios quoque non exclusis personis aliarum Ecclesiarum sui iuris, quibus omnibus etiam ius suffragium ferendi concedere potest.

§3. Ad conventum eparchialem etiam invitari possunt aliquot observatores ex Ecclesiis vel Communitatibus ecclesialibus acatholicis.

CAN. 239 Ii, qui conventum eparchialem adire debent, non possunt, etsi legitimo impedimento detenti sunt, mittere procuratorem, qui eorum nomine conventui eparchiali intersit, sed Episcopum eparchialem de impedimento certiorem faciant.

CAN. 240 §1. Firmo iure cuiuslibet christifidelis quaestiones in conventu eparchiali tractandas indicandi solius Episcopi eparchialis est argumenta in hoc conventu tractanda statuere.

§2. Episcopus eparchialis tempore opportuno unam vel plures constituat commissiones, quarum est argumenta in conventu eparchiali tractanda apparare.

§3. Curet etiam Episcopus eparchialis , ut tempore opportuno omnibus, qui convocati sunt, argumentorum tractandorum schema tradatur.

§4. Propositae quaestiones omnes liberae disceptationi in sessionibus conventus eparchialis subiciantur.

CAN. 241 Solus est in conventu

238 §2: Pius XII, m.p. *Cleri sanctitati,* 2 iun. 1957, can. 424 §2.

239: Pius XII, m.p. *Cleri sanctitati,* 2 iun. 1957, can. 425 §1.

240 §2: Pius XII, m.p. *Cleri sanctitati,* 2 iun. 1957, can. 426 §1.

240 §3: Pius XII, m.p. *Cleri sanctitati,* 2 iun. 1957,

can. 426 §2.

240 §4: Pius XII, m.p. *Cleri sanctitati,* 2 iun. 1957, can. 427.

241: Pius XII, m.p. *Cleri sanctitati,* 2 iun. 1957, can. 428; Vat. II, const. *Lumen gentium,* 27 "Episcopi;" decr. *Christus Dominus,* 8, a). * Syn. Sciarfen. Syrorum, a. 1888, cap. IX, art. V, 2 "Potestas autem."

legislator in the eparchial assembly; the others have only a consultative vote; he alone signs whatever decisions have been taken in the eparchial assembly. If they are promulgated in the same assembly, they begin to oblige immediately, unless expressly provided otherwise.

CAN. 242 The eparchial bishop is to communicate the text of the laws, declarations and decrees that have been issued at the eparchial assembly to the authority determined by the particular law of his Church *sui iuris.*

ART. II. *The Eparchial Curia*

CAN. 243 §1. The eparchial bishop must have at his see an eparchial curia, which assists him in the governance of the eparchy entrusted to him.

§2. To the eparchial curia belong the protosyncellus, syncelli, judicial vicar, eparchial finance officer and the finance council, chancellor, eparchial judges, promoter of justice and defender of the bond, notaries and other persons included by the eparchial bishop to discharge properly the offices of the eparchial curia.

§3. For the needs or the benefit of the eparchy, the eparchial bishop can also set up other offices in the eparchial curia.

CAN. 244 §1. The appointment and removal from office of those who exercise an office in the eparchial curia belongs to the eparchial bishop.

§2. All who are admitted to an office in the eparchial curia must:

eparchiali legislator Episcopus eparchialis ceteris tantum suffragium consultivum habentibus; solus subscribit decisionibus quibuscumque, quae in conventu eparchiali factae sunt; quae, si in eodem conventu promulgantur, statim obligare incipiunt, nisi aliter expresse cavetur.

CAN. 242 Textum legum, declarationum et decretorum, quae in conventu eparchiali data sunt, Episcopus eparchialis communicet cum auctoritate, quam ius particulare propriae Ecclesiae sui iuris determinavit.

ART. II. *De Curia Eparchiali*

CAN. 243 §1. Episcopus eparchialis penes suam sedem habere debet curiam eparchialem, quae ipsum iuvat in regimine eparchiae sibi commissae.

§2. Ad curiam eparchialem pertinent Protosyncellus, Syncelli, Vicarius iudicialis, oeconomus eparchialis et consilium a rebus oeconomicis, cancellarius, iudices eparchiales, promotor iustitiae et defensor vinculi, notarii et aliae personae, quae ad curiae eparchialis officia recte implenda ab Episcopo eparchiali assumuntur.

§3. Episcopus eparchialis necessitatibus vel utilitate eparchiae exigentibus alia quoque officia in curia eparchiali constituere potest.

CAN. 244 §1. Nominatio et amotio ab officio eorum, qui officia in curia eparchiali exercent, spectat ad Episcopum eparchialem.

§2. Omnes, qui ad officia in curia eparchiali admittuntur, debent:

---

243 §1: Vat. II, decr. *Christus Dominus,* 27 "Curia;" Pius XII, m.p. *Cleri sanctitati,* 2 iun. 1957, can. 429 §1. * Syn. Armen., a. 1911, 315–327.
243 §2: Pius XII, m.p. *Cleri sanctitati,* 2 iun. 1957, can. 429 §2; Vat. II, decr. *Christus Dominus,* 27 "Emi-

nens."
243 §3: Pius XII, m.p. *Cleri sanctitati,* 2 iun. 1957, can. 429 §3.
244 §1: Pius XII, m.p. *Cleri sanctitati,* 2 iun. 1957, cann. 94 §1, 430 §1.

1° make a promise to carry out the office faithfully in the manner determined by the law or by the eparchial bishop;

2° observe secrecy within the limits and according to the manner determined by the law or by the eparchial bishop.

1° The Protosyncellus and the Syncelli

CAN. 245 In each eparchy a protosyncellus is to be appointed who, endowed with ordinary vicarious power in accord with the norm of common law, assists the eparchial bishop in governing the whole eparchy.

CAN. 246 As often as the good governance of the eparchy requires it, one or several syncelli can be appointed, who have by virtue of the law itself the same authority as that which is attributed by common law to the protosyncellus but limited to a given section of the eparchy, or to certain kinds of affairs or for the Christian faithful ascribed to another Church *sui iuris* or for a certain group of persons.

CAN. 247 §1. The protosyncellus and the syncelli are freely appointed by the eparchial bishop and can freely be removed by him, without prejudice to can. 215, §§ 1 and 2.

§2. The protosyncellus and the syncelli are to be celibate presbyters, unless the particular law of their Church *sui iuris* has established otherwise; if possible, they should be from the clerics ascribed to the eparchy; they are to be not less

1° promissionem emittere de officio fideliter implendo secundum modum iure aut ab Episcopo eparchiali determinatum;

2° secretum servare intra limites et secundum modum iure aut ab Episcopo eparchiali determinatos.

1° De Protosyncello et de Syncellis

CAN. 245 In unaquaque eparchia constituendus est Protosyncellus, qui potestate ordinaria vicaria ad normam iuris communis praeditus Episcopum eparchialem in totius eparchiae regimine adiuvet.

CAN. 246 Quoties rectum eparchiae regimen id requirit, constitui possunt unus aut plures Syncelli, qui nempe ipso iure in determinata eparchiae parte aut in certo negotiorum genere aut circa christifideles alii Ecclesiae sui iuris ascriptos certive personarum coetus eandem habet potestatem ac ius commune Protosyncello tribuit.

CAN. 247 §1. Protosyncellus et Syncelli libere ab Episcopo eparchiali nominantur et ab eo libere amoveri possunt firmo can. 215, §§1 et 2.

§2. Protosyncellus et Syncellus sint sacerdotes caelibes, nisi ius particulare propriae Ecclesiae sui iuris aliud statuit, quatenus fieri potest ex clericis eparchiae ascriptis, annos nati non minus triginta, in aliqua scientia

---

244 §2, 1°: Pius XII, m.p. *Cleri sanctitati,* 2 iun. 1957, can. 430 §1 n. 1.

244 §2, 2°: Pius XII, m.p. *Cleri sanctitati,* 2 iun. 1957, can. 430 §2 n. 3.

245: Vat. II, decr. *Christus Dominus,* 27 "Eminens;" Pius XII, m.p. *Cleri sanctitati,* 2 iun. 1957, can. 432 §2. - S.C. de Prop. Fide, 29 dec. 1812. * Syn. Zamosten. Ruthenorum, a. 1720, tit. VII; Syn. Libanen. Maronitarum, a. 1736, pars III, cap. III, 3; Syn. prov. Alba-Iulien. et Fagarasien. Rumenorum, a. 1872, tit. II, cap. VI; Syn. Sciarfen. Syrorum, a. 1888,

cap. XI, art. I; Syn. Alexandrin. Coptorum, a. 1898, sect. III, cap. IV, art. I; Syn. Armen., a. 1911, 272, 274, 294–300.

246: Vat. II, decr. *Christus Dominus,* 23, 3) "Hunc," 27 "Eminens;" Paulus VI, m.p. *Ecclesiae sanctae,* 6 aug. 1966, I, 14 §§1–2.

247 §1: Pius XII, m.p. *Cleri sanctitati,* 2 iun. 1957, can. 432 §2; Paulus VI, m.p. *Ecclesiae sanctae,* 6 aug. 1966, I, 14 §§2, 5.

247 §2: Pius XII, m.p. *Cleri sanctitati,* 2 iun. 1957, can. 433 §1.

than thirty years of age, have a doctorate, licentiate or expertise in some sacred science; be commendable for sound doctrine, uprightness, prudence and practical experience.

§3. The office of protosyncellus or syncellus is not to be conferred on the blood relatives of the eparchial bishop up to the fourth degree inclusively.

§4. The eparchial bishop can also take the protosyncellus or syncelli from another eparchy, or from another Church *sui iuris,* however, with the consent of their eparchial bishop.

CAN. 248 §1. Unless it is expressly provided otherwise by common law, the protosyncellus throughout the whole eparchy and the syncelli within the limits of the office conferred on them have the same executive power of governance as the eparchial bishop, excepting those things that the eparchial bishop has reserved to himself or to others or that by law require his own special mandate, so that if this mandate is not obtained, the act for which the mandate is required is null.

§2. Within the scope of their competence the protosyncellus and the syncelli have also those habitual faculties that the Apostolic See has granted to the eparchial bishop and can also execute the rescripts of the Apostolic See or of the patriarch, unless it has been expressly provided otherwise or unless the execution was entrusted to the bishop because of personal considerations.

CAN. 249 The protosyncellus and the syncelli must give a report to the eparchial bishop concerning the more important matters, which are to be handled or have been handled. They are never to act against his intention and mind.

sacra doctores vel licentiati vel saltem periti, sana doctrina, probitate, prudentia ac rerum gerendarum experientia commendati.

§3. Protosyncelli vel Syncelli officium ne conferatur Episcopi eparchialis consanguineis usque ad quartum gradum inclusive.

§4. Episcopus eparchialis potest Protosyncellum et Syncellos etiam ex alia eparchia vel ex alia Ecclesia sui iuris assumere de consensu tamen eorum Episcopi eparchialis.

CAN. 248 §1. Nisi aliter iure communi expresse cavetur, Protosyncello in tota eparchia, Syncellis vero intra ambitum officii sibi collati eadem competit potestas regiminis exsecutiva ac Episcopo eparchiali eis exceptis, quae Episcopus eparchialis sibi vel aliis reservavit aut quae ex iure requirunt ipsius mandatum speciale, quo non obtento actus, ad quem huiusmodi mandatum requiritur, est nullus.

§2. Protosyncello et Syncellis intra ambitum eorum competentiae competunt etiam facultates habituales a Sede Apostolica Episcopo eparchiali concessae necnon rescriptorum Sedis Apostolicae vel Patriarchae exsecutio, nisi aliter expresse cautum est aut electa est industria personae Episcopi eparchialis.

CAN. 249 Protosyncellus et Syncelli de praecipuis negotiis et gerendis et gestis Episcopo eparchiali referre debent nec umquam contra eius voluntatem et mentem agant.

247 §3: Pius XII, m.p. *Cleri sanctitati,* 2 iun. 1957, can. 433 §2.

247 §4: Pius XII, m.p. *Cleri sanctitati,* 2 iun. 1957, can. 433 §3.

248 §1: Pius XII, m.p. *Cleri sanctitati,* 2 iun. 1957, can. 434 §1; Paulus VI, m.p. *Ecclesiae sanctae,* 6 aug. 1966, I, 14 §2.

248 §2: Pius XII, m.p. *Cleri sanctitati,* 2 iun. 1957, can. 434 §2; Paulus VI, m.p. *Ecclesiae sanctae,* 6 aug. 1966, I, 14 §2.

249: Paulus VI, m.p. *Ecclesiae sanctae,* 6 aug. 1966, I, 14, §3; Pius XII, m.p. *Cleri sanctitati,* 2 iun. 1957, can. 435 §§1–2.

CAN. 250 The protosyncellus and the syncelli who are presbyters have the privileges and insignia of the dignity next to that of the bishop during their function *(durante munere).*

CAN. 251 §1. The protosyncellus and the syncelli cease from office with the expiration of the determined period, by resignation accepted by the eparchial bishop, or by removal.

§2. During the vacancy of the eparchial see, can. 224 is to be observed concerning the protosyncellus and the syncelli.

§3. With the suspension of the office of the eparchial bishop, the power of the protosyncellus and the syncelli is suspended, unless they are ordained bishops.

2° The Chancellor, Other Notaries and the Archives of the Eparchial Curia

CAN. 252 §1. In the eparchial curia, a chancellor is to be appointed who is to be a presbyter or deacon. His principal obligation, unless established otherwise by particular law, is to see that the acts of the curia are drawn up and dispatched, and that they are conserved in the archives of the eparchial curia.

§2. If it is deemed necessary, the chancellor may be given an assistant, who is to be called vice-chancellor.

§3. The chancellor as well as the vice-chancellor are by virtue of the law itself notaries of the eparchial curia.

CAN. 253 §1. Besides the chancellor, other notaries may be appointed whose signature au-

CAN. 250 Protosyncelli et Syncelli presbyteri durante munere habent privilegia et insignia primae post episcopalem dignitatis.

CAN. 251 §1. Protosyncellus et Syncelli ab officio cessant elapso tempore determinato, renuntiatione ab Episcopo eparchiali acceptata vel amotione.

§2. Sede eparchiali vacante circa Protosyncellum et Syncellos servetur can. 224.

§3. Suspenso officio Episcopi eparchialis suspenditur potestas Protosyncelli et Syncellorum, nisi Episcopi ordinati sunt.

2° De Cancellario Aliisque Notariis et de Archivo Curiae Eparchialis

CAN. 252 §1. In curia eparchiali constituatur cancellarius, qui sit presbyter vel diaconus, cuius praecipua obligatio, nisi aliud iure particulari statuitur, est curare, ut acta curiae redigantur et expediantur atque in archivo curiae eparchialis asserventur.

§2. Si necesse videtur, cancellario dari potest adiutor, cui nomen sit vice-cancellarii.

§3. Cancellarius necnon vice-cancellarius sunt ipso iure notarii curiae eparchialis.

CAN. 253 §1. Praeter cancellarium constitui possunt alii notarii, quorum subscriptio

250: Pius XII, m.p. *Cleri sanctitati,* 2 iun. 1957, can. 436 §2. * Syn. Alexandrin. Coptorum, a. 1898, sect. II, cap. III, art. VII, §6, 3, IX.

251 §1: Pius XII, m.p. *Cleri sanctitati,* 2 iun. 1957, can. 437 §1; Paulus VI, m.p. *Ecclesiae sanctae,* 6 aug. 1966, I, 14 §5.

251 §3: Pius XII, m.p. *Cleri sanctitati,* 2 iun. 1957, can. 437 §1; Paulus VI, m.p. *Ecclesiae sanctae,* 6 aug. 1966, I, 14 §4.

252 §1: Pius XII, m.p. *Cleri sanctitati,* 2 iun. 1957, can. 439 §1. * Syn. Zamosten. Ruthenorum, a. 1720, tit. VIII; Syn. Armen., a. 1911, 317–319.

252 §2: Pius XII, m.p. *Cleri sanctitati,* 2 iun. 1957, can. 439 §2.

252 §3: Pius XII, m.p. *Cleri sanctitati,* 2 iun. 1957, can. 439 §3.

253 §1: Pius XII, m.p. *Cleri sanctitati,* 2 iun. 1957, can. 440 §§1–2.

thenticates public documents whether in respect to all acts, or for judicial acts alone, or only for acts of a certain issue or business.

§2. Notaries are to be of unblemished reputation and above all suspicion. In cases that could involve the reputation of a cleric the notary must be a priest.

CAN. 254 It is for the notary to:

1° write the acts and documents concerning decrees, arrangements, obligations or other matters that require their intervention;

2° put faithfully into writing what has taken place and to sign the respective acts noting the place, the day, the month and the year;

3° furnish acts or documents, while observing all that must be observed, to those who legitimately request them, and declare copies made of them to conform to the original.

CAN. 255 The chancellor and other notaries can be freely removed from office by the eparchial bishop, but not by the eparchial administrator except with the consent of the college of eparchial consultors.

CAN. 256 §1. The eparchial bishop is to set up in a safe place the archive of the eparchial curia in which documents pertaining to affairs of the eparchy are to be preserved.

§2. With all diligence and care, an inventory is to be drawn up of the documents that are preserved in the archive of the eparchial curia with a brief synopsis of each of the documents.

CAN. 257 §1. The archive of the eparchial curia is to be locked and the key kept by the eparchial bishop and the chancellor; no one is

publicam fidem facit et quidem sive ad quaelibet acta sive ad acta iudicialia dumtaxat sive ad acta certae causae aut negotii tantum.

§2. Notarii debent esse integrae famae et omni suspicione maiores; in causis, quibus fama clerici in discrimen vocari potest, notarius debet esse sacerdos.

CAN. 254 Notariorum est:

1° conscribere acta et documenta circa decreta, dispositiones, obligationes vel alia, quae eorum operam requirunt;

2° scripto fideliter redigere ea, quae geruntur, et actis de his rebus cum indicatione loci, diei, mensis et anni subscribere;

3° acta vel documenta legitime petenti servatis servandis exhibere et eorum exemplaria cum originali conformia declarare.

CAN. 255 Cancellarius aliique notarii libere ab officio amoveri possunt ab Episcopo eparchiali, non autem ab Administratore eparchiae nisi de consensu collegii consultorum eparchialium.

CAN. 256 §1. Episcopus eparchialis in loco tuto archivum curiae eparchialis constituat, in quo documenta, quae ad negotia eparchiae spectant, asserventur.

§2. Omni diligentia ac sollicitudine conficiatur inventarium documentorum, quae in archivo curiae eparchialis asservantur, cum brevi eorum synopsi.

CAN. 257 §1. Archivum curiae eparchialis clausum sit oportet eiusque clavem habeant Episcopus eparchialis et

253 §2: Pius XII, m.p. *Cleri sanctitati,* 2 iun. 1957, can. 440 §§3–4.

254: Pius XII, m.p. *Cleri sanctitati,* 2 iun. 1957, can. 441 §1.

255: Pius XII, m.p. *Cleri sanctitati,* 2 iun. 1957, can. 440 §5.

256 §1: Pius XII, m.p. *Cleri sanctitati,* 2 iun. 1957,

can. 442 §1.

256 §2: Pius XII, m.p. *Cleri sanctitati,* 2 iun. 1957, can. 442 §2.

257 §1: Pius XII, m.p. *Cleri sanctitati,* 2 iun. 1957, can. 444 §§1–2. * Syn. Libanen. Maronitarum, a. 1736, pars III, cap. V, 10; Syn. Armen., a. 1911, 320.

permitted to enter it without the permission of the eparchial bishop alone or the protosyncellus along with the chancellor.

§2. Interested parties have the right to receive, personally or by proxy, an authentic copy of documents that are of their nature public and that concern their own personal status.

CAN. 258 It is not permitted to remove documents from the archive of the eparchial curia except for a brief time and with the permission either of the eparchial bishop alone or the protosyncellus along with the chancellor.

CAN. 259 §1. There is also to be a secret archive in the eparchial curia or at least a secret safe in the archive of the eparchial curia, which is securely closed and locked and which cannot be removed from the place; in it documents to be kept under secrecy are to be kept.

§2. Each year, the procedural acts for inflicting penalties in matters of morals are to be destroyed whenever the guilty parties have died, or ten years have passed from the end of the case. A brief summary of the facts and the text of the definitive sentence or decree are to be retained.

CAN. 260 §1. Only the eparchial bishop should have the key to the secret archives or the secret safe.

§2. When the eparchial see is vacant, the secret archive or secret safe is not to be opened except in a case of true necessity and then by the eparchial administrator himself.

§3. Documents are not to be removed from the secret archive or secret safe.

cancellarius; nemini licet in illud ingredi sine licentia aut solius Episcopi eparchialis aut Protosyncelli simul et cancellarii.

§2. Ius est eis, quorum interest, ut documentorum, quae natura sua sunt publica quaeque ad statum suae personae pertinent, exemplar authenticum per se vel per procuratorem recipiant.

CAN. 258 Ex archivo curiae eparchialis non licet efferre documenta nisi ad breve tempus tantum atque de licentia aut solius Episcopi eparchialis aut Protosyncelli simul et cancellarii.

CAN. 259 §1. Sit in curia eparchiali etiam archivum secretum aut saltem in archivo curiae eparchialis armarium secretum omnino clausum et obseratum, quod de loco amoveri non potest, in quo documenta secreto servanda asserventur.

§2. Singulis annis destruantur acta procedurarum in poenis irrogandis in materia morum, quarum rei vita cesserunt aut quae a decennio terminatae sunt, retento facti brevi summario et textu sententiae definitivae vel decreti.

CAN. 260 §1. Archivi secreti vel armarii secreti clavem habeat solus Episcopus eparchialis.

§2. Sede eparchiali vacante archivum secretum vel armarium secretum ne aperiantur nisi in casu verae necessitatis ab ipso Administratore eparchiae.

§3. Ex archivo secreto vel armario secreto documenta ne efferantur.

257 §2: Pius XII, m.p. *Cleri sanctitati,* 2 iun. 1957, can. 451.

258: Pius XII, m.p. *Cleri sanctitati,* 2 iun. 1957, can. 445 §1. * Syn. Libanen. Maronitarum, a. 1736, pars III, cap. V, 10; Syn. Armen., a. 1911, 320.

259 §1: Pius XII, m.p. *Cleri sanctitati,* 2 iun. 1957, can. 446 §1.

259 §2: Pius XII, m.p. *Cleri sanctitati,* 2 iun. 1957, can. 446 §1.

260 §1: Pius XII, m.p. *Cleri sanctitati,* 2 iun. 1957, can. 446 §3.

260 §2: Pius XII, m.p. *Cleri sanctitati,* 2 iun. 1957, can. 449 §1.

260 §3: Pius XII, m.p. *Cleri sanctitati,* 2 iun. 1957, can. 449 §1.

CAN. 261 §1. The eparchial bishop is to ensure that the acts and documents of the archive of the cathedral, of the parochial and other Churches situated within the territorial boundaries of the eparchy are carefully kept and that two copies are made of the inventory of the acts and documents. One of these is to be kept in the Church's own archive and the other in the archive of the eparchial curia.

§2. For the inspection or removal of the acts and documents of these archives, norms established by the eparchial bishop are to be observed.

3° The Eparchial Finance Officer and Finance Council

CAN. 262 §1. After consulting the college of eparchial consultors and the finance council, the eparchial bishop is to appoint an eparchial finance officer, who is to be a member of the Christian faithful, expert in financial matters and outstanding for honesty.

§2. The eparchial finance officer is appointed for a term determined by particular law; he or she is not to be removed during the term of office except for a serious reason, to be assessed by the eparchial bishop after consulting the college of eparchial consultors and the finance council.

§3. Under the power of the eparchial bishop, who is to determine in greater detail the rights and relationships of the eparchial finance officer to the finance council, the eparchial finance officer is to administer the temporal goods of

CAN. 261 §1. Curet Episcopus eparchialis, ut etiam acta et documenta archivorum ecclesiarum cathedralium, paroecialium aliarumque intra fines territorii eparchiae exstantium diligenter asserventur atque actorum et documentorum inventarii duo exemplaria conficiantur, quorum alterum in proprio archivo, alterum in archivo curiae eparchialis asserventur.

§2. Ut acta et documenta ad haec archiva pertinentia inspiciantur aut efferantur, serventur normae ab Episcopo eparchiali statutae.

3° De Oeconomo Eparchiali et de Consilio a Rebus Oeconomicis

CAN. 262 §1. Episcopus eparchialis consultis collegio consultorum eparchialium atque consilio a rebus oeconomicis nominet oeconomum eparchialem, qui sit christifidelis in re oeconomica peritus et probitate praestans.

§2. Oeconomus eparchialis nominatur ad tempus iure particulari determinatum; munere durante ne amoveatur nisi gravi de causa ab Episcopo eparchiali aestimanda consultis collegio consultorum eparchialium atque consilio a rebus oeconomicis.

§3. Oeconomi eparchialis est sub Episcopi eparchialis potestate, qui eius iura ac relationes ad consilium a rebus oeconomicis pressius determinet, bona temporalia eparchiae administrare, administrationi

261 §1: Pius XII, m.p. *Cleri sanctitati*, 2 iun. 1957, can. 450 §1. * Syn. Libanen. Maronitarum, a. 1736, pars III, cap. III, 2, V.

261 §2: Pius XII, m.p. *Cleri sanctitati*, 2 iun. 1957, can. 451 §2.

262 §1: Pius XII, m.p. *Postquam Apostolicis Litteris*, 9 feb. 1952, can. 262 §§1 et 2 n. 1; m.p. *Cleri sanctitati*, 2 iun. 1957, can. 438 §§1 et 2 n. 1. - Chalc. can. 26; Nic. II, can. 11; Theophilus Alexandrin., can. 10.

* Syn. Mar Isaaci Chaldaeorum, a. 410, can. 15; Syn. Libanen. Maronitarum, a. 1736, pars III, cap. II, 8; cap. IV, 27; Syn. prov. Alba-Iulien. et Fagarasien. Rumenorum, a. 1882, tit. II, sect. IV, cap. I; Syn. Sciarfen. Syrorum, a. 1888, cap. XIII, art. VII.

262 §3: Pius XII, m.p. *Postquam Apostolicis Litteris*, 9 feb. 1952, can. 262 §3; m.p. *Cleri sanctitati*, 2 iun. 1957, can. 437 §3.

the eparchy, to oversee the administration of ecclesiastical goods throughout the eparchy, to provide for their preservation, safety and increase, to supply for the negligence of local administrators and to administer the goods that lack an administrator designated by the law.

§4. The eparchial finance officer must give an report of his or her administration to the eparchial bishop every year and as often as it is requested by the same bishop; the eparchial bishop is to examine the report submitted by the eparchial finance officer through the finance council.

§5. With regard to the obligations of the eparchial finance officer during the vacancy of the eparchial see, can. 232 is to be observed.

CAN. 263 §1. The eparchial bishop is to erect a finance council consisting of a president, who is the eparchial bishop himself, and of some suitable persons who are expert, if possible, also in civil law. These persons are to be appointed by the eparchial bishop after consulting the college of eparchial consultors, unless this is already provided for in some other equivalent manner by the particular law of his Church *sui iuris,* always ensuring that those who have been elected or appointed by others need the confirmation of the eparchial bishop.

§2. The eparchial finance officer is by virtue of the law itself a member of the finance council.

§3. Those who are related to the eparchial bishop up to the fourth degree inclusive of consanguinity or affinity are excluded from membership on the finance council.

§4. The eparchial bishop, in the more im-

bonorum ecclesiasticorum in tota eparchia vigilare, eorum conservationi, tutelae et incremento providere, administratorum localium neglegentiam supplere et bona ecclesiastica, quae administratore iure designato carent, per se administrare.

§4. Oeconomus eparchialis rationem administrationis Episcopo eparchiali quotannis et, quoties ab ipso Episcopo petitur, reddere debet; Episcopus eparchialis vero per consilium a rebus oeconomicis rationes ab oeconomo eparchiali exhibitas examinet.

§5. Circa obligationes oeconomi eparchialis sede eparchiali vacante servandus est can. 232.

CAN. 263 §1. Episcopus eparchialis consilium a rebus oeconomicis erigat, quod constet ex praeside, qui est ipse Episcopus eparchialis, et aliquot personis idoneis etiam iuris civilis, si fieri potest, peritis ab Episcopo eparchiali consulto collegio consultorum eparchialium nominandis, nisi iure particulari propriae Ecclesiae sui iuris iam alio aequivalenti modo provisum est, firmo semper, ut ab aliis electi vel nominati indigeant confirmatione Episcopi eparchialis.

§2. Oeconomus eparchialis ipso iure est membrum consilii a rebus oeconomicis.

§3. A consilio a rebus oeconomicis excluduntur ii, qui cum Episcopo eparchiali usque ad quartum gradum inclusive consanguinitatis vel affinitatis coniuncti sunt.

§4. Episcopus eparchialis in actibus

---

262 §4: Pius XII, m.p. *Postquam Apostolicis Litteris,* 9 feb. 1952, can. 262 §4; m.p. *Cleri sanctitati,* 2 iun. 1957, can. 438 §4.

263 §1: Pius XII, m.p. *Postquam Apostolicis Litteris,* 9 feb. 1952, can. 263 §1. - Ant. can. 25; Carth. can. 33.

263 §2: Pius XII, m.p. *Postquam Apostolicis Litteris,* 9 feb. 1952, can. 263 §3.

263 §3: Pius XII, m.p. *Postquam Apostolicis Litteris,* 9 feb. 1952, can. 263 §2.

263 §4: Pius XII, m.p. *Postquam Apostolicis Litteris,* 9 feb. 1952, can. 263 §4.

portant acts concerning financial matters, is not to fail to hear the finance council. The members of this council have only a consultative vote, unless their consent is required by common law in cases specifically mentioned or by the founding document.

§5. Besides the other functions committed to it by common law, it is for the finance council to prepare every year the budget for the coming year in the governance of the whole eparchy as well as to approve the report of receipts and expenses of the past year.

ART. III. *The Presbyteral Council and College of Eparchial Consultors*

CAN. 264 A presbyteral council must be established in the eparchy, that is a body of priests representing the presbyterate, and which, in accord with the norm of the law, assists the eparchial bishop by its advice in those things that regard the needs of pastoral activity and the good of the eparchy.

CAN. 265 The presbyteral council is to have its own statutes approved by the eparchial bishop, without prejudice to the norms of common law and the particular law of the respective Church *sui iuris*.

CAN. 266 The following norms are to be observed in constituting the presbyteral council:

1° an appropriate portion of the members are to be elected by the priests themselves in accord with the norm of the particular law of the respective Church *sui iuris;*

maioris momenti rem oeconomicam respicientibus consilium a rebus oeconomicis audire ne praetermittat; huius autem membra tantum suffragium consultivum habent, nisi iure communi in casibus specialiter expressis vel ex documento fundationis eorum consensus exigitur.

§5. Praeter alia munera ipsi iure communi commissa consilii a rebus oeconomicis est quotannis rationem apparare quaestuum et erogationum, quae pro toto eparchiae regimine anno venturo praevidentur, necnon anno exeunte rationem accepti et expensi approbare.

ART. III. *De Consilio Presbyterali et de Collegio Consultorum Eparchialium*

CAN. 264 In eparchia constitui debet consilium presbyterale, scilicet coetus sacerdotum presbyterium repraesentans, qui Episcopum eparchialem suo consilio ad normam iuris adiuvet in eis, quae ad necessitates operis pastoralis et bonum eparchiae spectant.

CAN. 265 Consilium presbyterale habeat propria statuta ab Episcopo eparchiali approbata firmis normis iuris communis et iuris particularis propriae Ecclesiae sui iuris.

CAN. 266 Circa constitutionem consilii presbyteralis haec serventur:

1° congrua pars membrorum ad normam iuris particularis propriae Ecclesiae sui iuris eligatur a sacerdotibus ipsis;

264: Paulus VI, m.p. *Ecclesiae sanctae,* 6 aug. 1966, I, 15 §§1, 3; Vat. II, decr. *Presbyterorum ordinis,* 7 "Presbyteri omnes;" const. *Lumen gentium,* 28 "Presbyteri;" decr. *Christus Dominus,* 27 "Inter," 28

"Necessitudines."

265: Paulus VI, m.p. *Ecclesiae sanctae,* 6 aug. 1966, I, 15 §1.

2° some priests, in accord with the norm of the statutes, must be *ex officio* members, that is belong to the council in virtue of the offices they hold;

3° the eparchial bishop is free to appoint some members.

CAN. 267 §1. In electing the members of the presbyteral council, the following have active and passive voice:

1° all presbyters ascribed in the eparchy;

2° other priests who have domicile or quasi-domicile in the eparchy and at the same time exercise some function for the good of the eparchy.

§2. To the extent provided in the statutes, active and passive voice can also be conferred upon other priests who have domicile or quasi-domicile in the eparchy.

CAN. 268 The manner of electing members to the presbyteral council is to be determined by the statutes so that, insofar as it is possible, the priests of the presbyterate are represented, taking into account especially the different ministries and the various districts of the eparchy.

CAN. 269 §1. It is for the eparchial bishop to convoke the presbyteral council, to preside over it and to determine its agenda or to receive proposals from the members.

§2. The eparchial bishop is to hear the presbyteral council in matters of greater importance and he must consult it in cases expressly determined by common law; however, he needs its consent only in cases expressly determined by common law, without prejudice to the right of the patriarch regarding matters of the eparchy

2° aliquot sacerdotes ad normam statutorum esse debent membra nata, qui scilicet ratione officii sibi demandati ad consilium pertinent;

3° Episcopo eparchiali integrum est aliquot membra libere nominare.

CAN. 267 §1. In elegendis membris consilii presbyteralis vocem activam et passivam habent:

1° omnes presbyteri eparchiae ascripti;

2° ceteri sacerdotes, qui in eparchia domicilium vel quasi-domicilium habent et simul in eiusdem eparchiae bonum aliquod munus exercent.

§2. Quatenus in statutis providetur, vox activa et passiva conferri potest etiam aliis sacerdotibus, qui domicilium vel quasi-domicilium in eparchia habent.

CAN. 268 Modus eligendi membra consilii presbyteralis a statutis determinandus est ita, ut, quatenus fieri potest, sacerdotes presbyterii repraesententur ratione habita praesertim diversorum ministeriorum variorumque eparchiae districtuum.

CAN. 269 §1. Episcopi eparchialis est consilium presbyterale convocare, eidem praeesse atque quaestiones in eodem tractandas determinare aut a membris propositas accipere.

§2. Episcopus eparchialis consilium presbyterale audiat in negotiis maioris momenti et in casibus iure communi expressis consulere debet; eius autem consensu eget solummodo in casibus iure communi expresse determinatis firmo iure Patriarchae circa negotia eparchiae, quam ipse regit, con-

---

267 §1, 2°: PAULUS VI, m.p. *Ecclesiae sanctae,* 6 aug. 1966, I, 15 §2.
269 §2: PAULUS VI, m.p. *Ecclesiae sanctae,* 6 aug.

1966, I, 15 §§1, 3; Vat. II, decr. *Presbyterorum ordinis,* 7 "Presbyteri omnes."

he governs to have only to consult the presbyteral council even in these cases.

§3. The presbyteral council can never act without the eparchial bishop, who alone has the responsibility to make public those things that have been done in the council.

CAN. 270 §1. The members of the presbyteral council are to be designated for a term determined in the statutes so that the whole council or some part of it is renewed within a five-year period.

§2. When the eparchial see is vacant the presbyteral council ceases and its functions are fulfilled by the college of eparchial consultors; within a year from taking canonical possession of the eparchy, the eparchial bishop must establish a new presbyteral council.

§3. If the presbyteral council is no longer fulfilling the function committed to it for the good of the eparchy or is gravely abusing it, the eparchial bishop can dissolve it after consulting with the metropolitan or, if it is a question of the metropolitan see itself, after consulting the eparchial bishop senior in episcopal ordination, who is subject to the same metropolitan; but he must establish a new presbyteral council within a year.

CAN. 271 §1. The eparchial bishop must establish a college of eparchial consultors that is competent in those functions determined by law.

§2. The college of eparchial consultors is to be constituted for a five-year period but upon the expiration of the term, they continue in the exercise of their functions until a new college is established.

silium presbyterale etiam in his casibus nonnisi consulendi.

§3. Consilium presbyterale numquam agere potest sine Episcopo eparchiali, ad quem solum etiam cura spectat ea divulgandi, quae in ipso consilio gesta sunt.

CAN. 270 §1. Membra consilii presbyteralis designentur ad tempus in statutis determinandum ita tamen, ut integrum consilium vel aliqua eius pars intra quinquennium renovetur.

§2. Sede eparchiali vacante consilium presbyterale cessat eiusque munera implentur a collegio consultorum eparchialium; intra annum a capta possessione canonica eparchiae computandum Episcopus eparchialis debet novum consilium presbyterale constituere.

§3. Si consilium presbyterale munus sibi in bonum eparchiae commissum non implet aut eodem graviter abutitur, Episcopus eparchialis consulto Metropolita aut, si de ipsa sede metropolitana agitur, consulto Episcopo eparchiali ordinatione episcopali seniore eidem Metropolitae subiecto illud dissolvere potest, sed intra annum novum consilium presbyterale constituere debet.

CAN. 271 §1. Episcopus eparchialis constituere debet collegium consultorum eparchialium, cui competunt munera iure determinata.

§2. Collegium consultorum eparchialium ad quinquennium constituitur, quo tamen elapso munera sua propria exercere pergit, donec novum collegium constitutum erit.

---

270 §2: Paulus VI, m.p. *Ecclesiae sanctae,* 6 aug. 1966, I, 15 §4.

271 §1: Pius XII, m.p. *Cleri sanctitati,* 2 iun. 1957, can. 458 §1.

271 §2: Pius XII, m.p. *Cleri sanctitati,* 2 iun. 1957, can. 462 §§1–2.

§3. The members of the college of eparchial consultors must be not less than six nor more than twelve in number; if, for any reason whatever, within the determined five-year period there are fewer than the minimum number of members of the college, the eparchial bishop is to restore the college by appointment of new members, otherwise the college cannot act validly.

§4. The members of the college of eparchial consultors are freely appointed by the eparchial bishop from those who, at the time of their appointment, are members of the presbyteral council.

§5. The eparchial bishop presides over the college of eparchial consultors; when the eparchial see is vacant or impeded, it is presided over by the one who in the interim holds the place of the eparchial bishop or, if none has been designated, by the priest of the same college who is senior by sacred ordination.

§6. Whenever the law establishes that the eparchial bishop needs the consent of the college of eparchial consultors, it is sufficient for the patriarch, in the matters of the eparchy that he himself governs, that he consult this college.

ART. IV. *The Pastoral Council*

CAN. 272 In the eparchy, if pastoral circumstances recommend it, a pastoral council is to be established which, under the authority of the eparchial bishop, is competent to investigate, assess and propose practical conclusions

§3. Membra collegii consultorum eparchialium debent esse numero non minus quam sex nec plus quam duodecim; si quacumque de causa intra determinatum quinquennium numerus minimus membrorum collegii iam non habetur, Episcopus eparchialis quam primum collegium nominatione novi membri integret, secus collegium valide agere non potest.

§4. Membra collegii consultorum eparchialium libere nominantur ab Episcopo eparchiali ex eis, qui tempore nominationis sunt membra consilii presbyteralis.

§5. Collegio consultorum eparchialium praeest Episcopus eparchialis; sede eparchiali vacante vel impedita is, qui interim Episcopi eparchialis locum tenet aut, si constitutus non est, sacerdos in eodem collegio sacra ordinatione senior.

§6. Quoties ius statuit Episcopum eparchialem indigere consensu collegii consultorum eparchialium, Patriarcha in negotiis eparchiae, quam ipse regit, sufficit, ut hoc collegium consulat.

ART. IV. *De Consilio Pastorali*

CAN. 272 In eparchia, si adiuncta pastoralia id suadent, constituatur consilium pastorale, cuius est sub auctoritate Episcopi eparchialis ea, quae ad opera pastoralia in eparchia spectant, investigare, perpendere

---

271 §3: Pius XII, m.p. *Cleri sanctitati,* 2 iun. 1957, cann. 461 §1, 462 §3; Pont. Comm. Cod. Iur. Can. Auth. Interpr., resp. 11 iul. 1984, III, b).

271 §4: Pius XII, m.p. *Cleri sanctitati,* 2 iun. 1957, can. 460; Pont. Comm. Cod. Iur. Can. Auth. Interpr., resp. 11 iul. 1984, III, a).

271 §5: Pius XII, m.p. *Cleri sanctitati,* 2 iun. 1957,

can. 462 §§4–5.

271 §6: Pius XII, m.p. *Cleri sanctitati,* 2 iun. 1957, can. 459 §2.

272: Vat. II, decr. *Christus Dominus,* 27 "Valde;" decr. *Ad gentes,* 30; Paulus VI, m.p. *Ecclesiae sanctae,* 6 aug. 1966, I, 16 §1.

about those things that regard pastoral activity in the eparchy.

CAN. 273 §1. The pastoral council, which is only a consultative body, consists of clerics, religious or members of societies of common life in the manner of religious, and especially, of lay persons designated in a manner determined by the eparchial bishop.

§2. The pastoral council is to be so established that, insofar as possible, it represents the Christian faithful of the eparchy with regard to the types of persons, associations and other endeavors.

§3. Along with these Christian faithful, if it is opportune, the eparchial bishop can also invite others to the pastoral council, even if they are of another Church *sui iuris*.

§4. No one is to be designated to the pastoral council except those Christian faithful who are outstanding in firm faith, good morals and prudence.

CAN. 274 §1. The pastoral council is constituted for a term according to the prescriptions of the statutes issued by the eparchial bishop.

§2. During the vacancy of the eparchial see the pastoral council ceases.

CAN. 275 It is for the eparchial bishop alone to convoke the pastoral council according to the needs of the apostolate, to preside over it and to publish the matters dealt with in it.

ART. V. *Protopresbyters*

CAN. 276 §1. The protopresbyter is a presbyter who is placed in charge of a district consisting of several parishes to discharge there in

CAN. 273 §1. Consilium pastorale, quod coetus consultivus tantum est, constat ex clericis, ex religiosis vel sodalibus societatum vitae communis ad instar religiosorum et praesertim ex laicis designatis modo ab Episcopo eparchiali determinato.

§2. Consilium pastorale ita constituatur, ut, quatenus fieri potest, christifideles eparchiae ratione habita diversorum generum personarum, consociationum et aliorum inceptorum repraesententur.

§3. Una cum his christifidelibus Episcopus eparchialis potest alios quoque, etiam alterius Ecclesiae sui iuris, pro opportunitate ad consilium pastorale invitare.

§4. Ad consilium pastorale ne designentur nisi christifideles certa fide, bonis moribus et prudentia praestantes.

CAN. 274 §1. Consilium pastorale constituitur ad tempus secundum praescripta statutorum, quae ab Episcopo eparchiali dantur.

§2. Sede eparchiali vacante consilium pastorale cessat.

CAN. 275 Ad solum Episcopum eparchialem pertinet consilium pastorale secundum necessitates apostolatus convocare, eidem praeesse et ea, quae in eodem tractata sunt, publicare.

ART. V. *De Protopresbyteris*

CAN. 276 §1. Protopresbyter est presbyter, qui districtui ex pluribus paroeciis constanti praeficitur, ut ibidem nomine

273 §1: Vat. II, decr. *Christus Dominus,* 27 "Valde;" PAULUS VI, m.p. *Ecclesiae sanctae,* 6 aug. 1966, I, 16 §§2–3.

274 §1: PAULUS VI, m.p. *Ecclesiae sanctae,* 6 aug. 1966, I, 16 §2.

275: PAULUS VI, m.p. *Ecclesiae sanctae,* 6 aug. 1966, I, 16 §2.

276 §1: PIUS XII, m.p. *Cleri sanctitati,* 2 iun. 1957, can. 483; PAULUS VI, m.p. *Ecclesiae sanctae,* 6 aug. 1966, I, 19 §1; Vat. II, decr. *Christus Dominus,* 30, 1).

the name of the eparchial bishop the functions determined by law.

§2. It belongs to the eparchial bishop, after consulting the presbyteral council, to establish, change and suppress such districts according to the needs of pastoral action.

CAN. 277 §1. The office of protopresbyter, without prejudice to the particular law of the respective Church *sui iuris,* must not be joined in a stable manner to the office of the pastor of any particular parish. The eparchial bishop, if he considers it opportune, having heard the pastors and parochial vicars of the district in question, is to appoint as protopresbyter a presbyter who is outstanding in doctrine and apostolic initiative especially among the pastors.

§2. The protopresbyter is appointed for a term determined by particular law.

§3. For a just reason, the eparchial bishop can remove the protopresbyter from office.

CAN. 278 §1. Besides the powers and faculties conferred on him by particular law, the protopresbyter has the right and obligation:

1° to promote and coordinate common pastoral activity;

2° to see that clerics lead a life befitting their

Episcopi eparchialis munera iure determinata expleat.

§2. Huiusmodi districtus erigere, immutare et supprimere secundum necessitates actionis pastoralis pertinet ad Episcopum eparchialem consulto consilio presbyterali.

CAN. 277 §1. Ad protopresbyteri officium, quod salvo iure particulari propriae Ecclesiae sui iuris cum officio parochi certae paroeciae stabiliter coniungi non debet, Episcopus eparchialis nominet auditis, si opportunum ducit, parochis et vicariis paroecialibus districtus, de quo agitur, presbyterum doctrina et apostolica alacritate praestantem praesertim inter parochos.

§2. Protopresbyter nominatur ad tempus iure particulari determinatum.

§3. Episcopus eparchialis protopresbyterum iusta de causa ab officio amovere potest.

CAN. 278 §1. Protopresbytero praeter potestates et facultates a iure particulari ei collatas ius et obligatio est:

1° actionem pastoralem communem promovendi et coordinandi;

2° prospiciendi, ut clerici vitam ducant

- Laod. can. 57. * Syn. Zamosten. Ruthenorum, a. 1720, tit. IX; Syn. Libanen. Maronitarum, a. 1736, pars III, cap. III, 3, I–II; Syn. prov. Alba-Iulien. et Fagarasien. Rumenorum, a. 1872, tit. II, capp. 7–8; Syn. Leopolien. Ruthenorum, a. 1891, tit. VII, cap. V; Syn. Sciarfen. Syrorum, a. 1888, cap. V, art. XIII, §9, 1; cap. XI, art. II, 2; Syn. Alexandrin. Coptorum, a. 1898, sect. III, cap. IV, art. II; Syn. Armen., a. 1911, 273, 301–314.

276 §2: Pius XII, m.p. *Cleri sanctitati,* 2 iun. 1957, can. 161 §§1–2; Paulus VI, m.p. *Ecclesiae sanctae,* 6 aug. 1966, I, 19 §2.

277 §1: Pius XII, m.p. *Cleri sanctitati,* 2 iun. 1957, can. 484 §1; Paulus VI, m.p. *Ecclesiae sanctae,* 6 aug. 1966, I, 19 §1.

277 §2: Paulus VI, m.p. *Ecclesiae sanctae,* 6 aug. 1966, I, 19 §2.

277 §3: Pius XII, m.p. *Cleri sanctitati,* 2 iun. 1957, can. 484 §2; Paulus VI, m.p. *Ecclesiae sanctae,* 6 aug. 1966, I, 19 §2.

278 §1: Pius XII, m.p. *Cleri sanctitati,* 2 iun. 1957, can. 485 §1.

278 §1, 1°: Paulus VI, m.p. *Ecclesiae sanctae,* 6 aug. 1966, I, 19 §1.

278 §1, 2°: Pius XII, m.p. *Cleri sanctitati,* 2 iun. 1957, can. 485 §1 n. 1. * Syn. Zamosten. Ruthenorum, a. 1720, tit. 3, §1 "Licebit;" tit. X "Et quia;" tit. XV "Ut autem;" Syn. Libanen. Maronitarum, a. 1736, pars III, cap. III, 4, VI; Syn. prov. Alba-Iulien. et Fagarasien. Rumenorum, a. 1872, tit. VII, cap. I "Demum;" a. 1900, tit. III, cap. III "Protopopae;" Syn. Leopolien. Ruthenorum, a. 1891, tit. II, cap. II; tit. IV, cap. VIII, 15; tit. VII, cap. VI, 6.

state and discharge their obligations diligently;

3° to see that the Divine Liturgy and the divine praises are celebrated according to the prescriptions of the liturgical books; that the decor and neatness of the Churches and sacred furnishings are carefully maintained especially in the celebration of the Divine Liturgy and the custody of the Divine Eucharist; that the parish registers are correctly entered and safely kept; that ecclesiastical goods are carefully administered; finally, that the rectory is looked after with due care.

§2. In the district entrusted to him the protopresbyter is to:

1° arrange that the clerics attend meetings that the local hierarch judges suitable for the promotion of the sacred sciences and pastoral matters;

2° take care that spiritual resources are available to the clerics; he is to have the utmost solicitude for those who are in acutely difficult circumstances or are beset with problems.

§3. The protopresbyter is to take care that when pastors and, if they are married, their families, are known to be seriously ill, they do not lack spiritual and material assistance and that the funeral of the departed is worthily celebrated. He is also to take steps that during their sickness or at their death, books, documents, sacred furnishings and other things that pertain to the Church are not lost or removed.

§4. The protopresbyter is bound by the obligation to visit the parishes in accord with the arrangements made by the eparchial bishop.

proprio statui congruam atque suis obligationibus diligenter satisfaciant;

3° providendi, ut Divina Liturgia et laudes divinae secundum praescripta librorum liturgicorum celebrentur, ut decor et nitor ecclesiarum sacraeque supellectilis praesertim in celebratione Divinae Liturgiae et custodia Divinae Eucharistiae accurate serventur, ut recte conscribantur et asserventur libri paroeciales, ut bona ecclesiastica sedulo administrentur, denique, ut domus paroecialis debita diligentia curetur.

§2. In districtu sibi concredito protopresbyter:

1° operam det, ut clerici frequentent collationes, quas Hierarcha loci opportunas iudicat ad scientias sacras et res pastorales promovendas;

2° curet, ut clericis subsidia spiritualia praesto sint, itemque maxime sollicitus sit de eis, qui in difficilioribus versantur circumstantiis aut problematibus anguntur.

§3. Curet protopresbyter, ne parochi, quos graviter aegrotantes novit, eorumque familia, si coniugati sunt, spiritualibus et materialibus auxiliis careant atque ut eorum, qui decesserunt, funera digne celebrentur; provideat quoque, ne occasione aegrotationis vel mortis depereant aut asportentur libri, documenta, sacra supellex aliaque, quae ad Ecclesiam pertinent.

§4. Protopresbyter obligatione tenetur secundum determinationem ab Episcopo eparchiali factam paroecias visitandi.

278 §1, 3°: Pius XII, m.p. *Cleri sanctitati,* 2 iun. 1957, can. 485 §1 nn. 1–4. * Syn. Zamosten. Ruthenorum, a. 1720, tit. III, §4 "Quoniam;" Syn. prov. Alba-Iulien. et Fagarasien. Rumenorum, a. 1900, tit. III, cap. I, 2 et 13, d); cap. II, 7.

278 §2, 1°: Pius XII, m.p. *Cleri sanctitati,* 2 iun. 1957, can. 486 §1.

278 §3: Pius XII, m.p. *Cleri sanctitati,* 2 iun. 1957, can. 485 §3.

278 §4: Pius XII, m.p. *Cleri sanctitati,* 2 iun. 1957, can. 485 §2. * Syn. Libanen. Maronitarum, a. 1736, pars III, cap. III, 4, VI; Syn. Leopolien. Ruthenorum, a. 1891, tit. VII, cap. III, 2, 2.

CHAPTER III. **Parishes, Pastors and Parochial Vicars**

CAN. 279 A parish is a definite community of the Christian faithful established on a stable basis in the eparchy, whose pastoral care is committed to a pastor.

CAN. 280 §1. As a rule, a parish is to be territorial, that is, it is to embrace all the Christian faithful of a certain territory. If, however, in the judgment of the eparchial bishop it is advisable, after consulting the presbyteral council, personal parishes are to be erected, by reason of nationality, of language, of ascription of the Christian faithful to another Church *sui iuris* or indeed of some other clearly distinguishing factor.

§2. It is for the eparchial bishop to erect, modify and suppress parishes, after consulting the presbyteral council.

§3. A legitimately erected parish is by virtue of the law itself a juridic person.

CAN. 281 §1. A pastor is a presbyter to whom the care of souls in a given parish is committed as to its own shepherd; he is the foremost collaborator of the eparchial bishop in the parish under the authority of the same eparchial bishop.

CAPUT III. **De Paroeciis, de Parochis et de Vicariis Paroecialibus**

CAN. 279 Paroecia est certa communitas christifidelium in eparchia stabiliter constituta, cuius cura pastoralis committitur parocho.

CAN. 280 §1. Paroecia regulariter sit territorialis, quae scilicet omnes complectatur christifideles certi territorii; si vero de iudicio Episcopi eparchialis consulto consilio presbyterali id expedit, erigantur paroeciae personales ratione nationis, linguae, ascriptionis christifidelium alii Ecclesiae sui iuris immo vel alia definita ratione determinatae.

§2. Paroecias erigere, immutare et supprimere est Episcopi eparchialis consulto consilio presbyterali.

§3. Paroecia legitime erecta ipso iure persona iuridica est.

CAN. 281 §1. Parochus est presbyter, cui ut praecipuo cooperatori Episcopi eparchialis tamquam pastori proprio cura animarum committitur in determinata paroecia sub auctoritate eiusdem Episcopi eparchialis.

279: Pius XII, m.p. *Cleri sanctitati,* 2 iun. 1957, cann. 160 §§1–3, 489 §1; Vat. II, decr. *Sacrosanctum Concilium,* 42; decr. *Christus Dominus,* 30 "Praecipua;" decr. *Apostolicam actuositatem,* 10 "Paroecia" et "Colant;" decr. *Ad gentes,* 37 "Cum." - S.C. de Prop. Fide, instr. (ad Patr. et Epp. Ritus Graeco-Melchit.), 29 maii 1789, n. 14. * Syn. Zamosten. Ruthenorum, a. 1720, tit. X "Quamquam;" Syn. Libanen. Maronitarum, a. 1736, pars III, cap. III, 2, III; Syn. prov. Alba-Iulien. et Fagarasien. Rumenorum, a. 1872, tit. II, cap. IX; Syn. Sciarfen. Syrorum, a. 1888, cap. XI, art. III, 2; cap. XII, 1; Syn. Alexandrin. Coptorum, a. 1898, sect. III, cap. IV, art. IV, §1, I; Syn. Armen., a. 1911, 328.

280 §1: Pius XII, m.p. *Cleri sanctitati,* 2 iun. 1957, can. 160 §§1–2, 4; Vat. II, decr. *Christus Dominus,* 23,

3) "Hunc;" decr. *Orientalium Ecclesiarum,* 4; Paulus VI, m.p. *Ecclesiae sanctae,* 6 aug. 1966, I, 21, §1. - Innocentius III (in Lat. IV), a. 1215, cap. IX "Quoniam in plerisque." * Syn. Sciarfen. Syrorum, a. 1888, cap. XII, 5; Syn. Alexandrin. Coptorum, a. 1898, sect. III, cap. IV, art. IV, §1, II.

280 §2: Paulus VI, m.p. *Ecclesiae sanctae,* 6 aug. 1966, I, 21 §3; Vat. II, decr. *Christus Dominus,* 32; Pont. Comm. Decr. Conc. Vat. II Interpr., resp. 3 iul 1969; Pius XII, m.p. *Cleri sanctitati,* 2 iun. 1957, can. 160 §1.

281 §1: Vat. II, decr. *Christus Dominus,* 30 "Praecipua;" Pius XII, m.p. *Cleri sanctitati,* 2 iun. 1957, cann. 160 §1, 489 §1. * Syn. Libanen. Maronitarum, a. 1736, pars III, cap. III, 2, I; Syn. Leopolien. Ruthenorum, a. 1891, tit. VII, cap. VI, I.

§2. A juridic person cannot validly be a pastor.

CAN. 282 §1. The eparchial bishop, but not the administrator of an eparchy, after consulting the presbyteral council, and with the consent of the major superior of a religious institute or society of common life in the manner of religious, can erect a parish in the Church of the same institute or society with due regard for can. 480.

§2. This erection must be made by means of a written agreement made between the eparchial bishop and the major superior of the religious institute or society of common life in the manner of religious and is to establish precisely the parochial ministry to be fulfilled, the persons to be attached to the parish, the financial arrangements, the rights and obligations of the members of the same institute or society in that Church and those of the pastor.

CAN. 283 The eparchial bishop is not to remove from the pastor, except for a grave reason, the partial or total care of certain groups of persons, buildings and places that are in the territory of the parish and are not exempt by law.

CAN. 284 §1. The right of appointing pastors belongs solely to the eparchial bishop, who freely appoints them.

§2. To entrust a parish to a member of a religious institute or society of common life in the

§2. Persona iuridica valide parochus esse non potest.

CAN. 282 §1. Episcopus eparchialis, non vero Administrator eparchiae, potest consulto consilio presbyterali ac de consensu Superioris maioris instituti religiosi vel societatis vitae communis ad instar religiosorum paroeciam erigere in ecclesia eiusdem instituti vel societatis firmo can. 480.

§2. Haec erectio fieri debet mediante conventione scripto data inter Episcopum eparchialem et Superiorem maiorem instituti religiosi vel societatis vitae communis ad instar religiosorum, qua accurate statuantur, quae ad ministerium paroeciale implendum, ad personas paroeciae addicendas, ad res oeconomicas spectent, ac quaenam sint iura et obligationes sodalium eiusdem instituti vel societatis in illa ecclesia et quaenam parochi.

CAN. 283 Episcopus eparchialis certos coetus personarum, aedificia et loca, quae in paroeciae territorio sunt et iure non exempta, a parochi cura ex toto aut ex parte ne subducat nisi gravi de causa.

CAN. 284 §1. Ius nominandi parochos competit soli Episcopo eparchiali, qui eos libere nominat.

§2. Ad paroeciam vero sodali instituti religiosi vel societatis vitae communis ad instar

281 §2: Pius XII, m.p. *Cleri sanctitati,* 2 iun. 1957, can. 490 §1 n. 2.

282 §1: Paulus VI, m.p. *Ecclesiae sanctae,* 6 aug. 1966, I, 33 §1; Pius XII, m.p. *Cleri sanctitati,* 2 iun. 1957, can. 490 §1.

282 §2: Paulus VI, m.p. *Ecclesiae sanctae,* 6 aug. 1966, I, 33 §1; Pius XII, m.p. *Cleri sanctitati,* 2 iun. 1957, cann. 490–492.

283: Pius XII, m.p. *Cleri sanctitati,* 2 iun. 1957, can. 505 §2.

284 §1: Pius XII, m.p. *Cleri sanctitati,* 2 iun. 1957, can. 496 §1; Vat. II, decr. *Christus Dominus,* 28 "Omnes."

284 §2: Pius XII, m.p. *Cleri sanctitati,* 2 iun. 1957, cann. 496 §1, 497; m.p. *Postquam Apostolicis Litteris,* 9 feb. 1952, cann. 155–156, 180; Paulus VI, m.p. *Ecclesiae sanctae,* 6 aug. 1966, I, 30 §2, 33. - Benedictus XIV, litt. ap. *Super familiam,* 30 mar. 1756, §7. * Syn. Armen., a. 1911, 773–774.

manner of religious, the major superior proposes for appointment a suitable priest of his institute or society to the eparchial bishop, with due regard for agreements entered into with the eparchial bishop or other authority determined by the particular law of the respective Church *sui iuris.*

§3. The pastor is permanent in his office, therefore he is not to be appointed for a determined period of time unless:

1° it concerns a member of a religious institute or society of common life in the manner of religious;

2° a candidate agrees to this in writing;

3° it concerns a special case, in which case the consent of the college of eparchial consultors is required;

4° the particular law of his Church *sui iuris* permits it.

CAN. 285 §1. In order for a presbyter to be named pastor it is necessary that he be of good morals, sound doctrine, zealous for souls, endowed with prudence and the other virtues and qualities required by law in order to fulfill the parochial ministry in a praiseworthy manner.

§2. If the presbyter is married, good morals are required in his wife and his children who live with him.

§3. After he has weighed all the circumstances, the eparchial bishop is to confer a vacant parish on the one whom he judges suitable

religiosorum concredendam Superior maior presbyterum idoneum sui instituti vel societatis Episcopo eparchiali ad nominationem proponit salvis conventionibus initis cum Episcopo eparchiali vel alia auctoritate a iure particulari propriae Ecclesiae sui iuris determinata.

§3. Parochus in suo officio stabilis est, quare ad tempus determinatum ne nominetur nisi:

1° agitur de sodali instituti religiosi vel societatis vitae communis ad instar religiosorum;

2° candidatus ad hoc scripto consensit;

3° agitur de casu speciali, quo in casu requiritur consensus collegii consultorum eparchialium;

4° ius particulare propriae Ecclesiae sui iuris id permittit.

CAN. 285 §1. Ut presbyter parochus nominari possit, oportet sit bonis moribus, sana doctrina, animarum zelo, prudentia ceterisque virtutibus et dotibus praeditus, quae ad ministerium paroeciale cum laude implendum iure requiruntur.

§2. Si presbyter matrimonio est iunctus, boni mores et in uxore et in filiis suis secum degentibus requiruntur.

§3. Paroeciam vacantem Episcopus eparchialis conferat illi, quem omnibus perpensis adiunctis aestimat idoneum omni per-

---

284 §3: Vat. II, decr. *Christus Dominus,* 31 "Praeterea;" Pius XII, m.p. *Cleri sanctitati,* 2 iun. 1957, can. 494 §1. - S.C. pro Eccl. Orient., decr. 1 mar. 1929, art. 15; decr. 24 maii 1930, art. 18. * Syn. prov. Alba-Iulien. et Fagarasien. Rumenorum, a. 1872, tit. II, cap. IX, 6); Syn. Sciarfen. Syrorum, a. 1888, cap. XI, art. III, 5, X; Syn. Armen., a. 1911, 359.

284 §3, 1°: Pius XII, m.p. *Cleri sanctitati,* 2 iun. 1957, can. 494 §5; m.p. *Postquam Apostolicis Litteris,* 9 feb. 1952, can. 180 §2; Paulus VI, m.p. *Ecclesiae*

sanctae, 6 aug. 1966, I, 32. - S.C. de Prop. Fide, (C.G.), 13 maii 1839.

285 §1: Pius XII, m.p. *Cleri sanctitati,* 2 iun. 1957, can. 493; Vat. II, decr. *Christus Dominus,* 31 "In iudicio."

285 §3: Pius XII, m.p. *Cleri sanctitati,* 2 iun. 1957, can. 500 §§1–3; Paulus VI, m.p. *Ecclesiae sanctae,* 6 aug. 1966, I, 19 §2. * Syn. prov. Alba-Iulien. et Fagarasien. Rumenorum, a. 1872, tit. IV, cap. IV; Syn. Armen., a. 1911, 262.

without any partiality; in order to make a judgment concerning a person's suitability he is to listen to the protopresbyter, conduct appropriate inquiries and, if he considers it opportune, also listen to other Christian faithful, especially clerics.

CAN. 286 When the eparchial see is vacant or impeded, the administrator of the eparchy or another who governs the eparchy in the interim, is competent:

1° to name as pastor a presbyter proposed by a major superior in accord with the norm of can. 284, §2;

2° to appoint a pastor from other presbyters if the eparchial see has been vacant or impeded for at least one year.

CAN. 287 §1. A pastor is to have the parochial care of only one parish; however, the care of several neighboring parishes can be entrusted to the same pastor due to a dearth of presbyters or for other circumstances.

§2. In the same parish there is to be only one pastor; however, if the particular law of the Church *sui iuris* allows it, a parish may be entrusted to several presbyters; the same particular law is to determine precisely the rights and obligations of the moderator, who directs the common action and reports on it to the eparchial bishop, and what are those of the other presbyters.

CAN. 288 The pastor acquires the care of souls by canonical provision; however, he is not allowed to exercise his office unless he has taken canonical possession of the parish in accord with the norm of particular law.

sonarum acceptione remota; ut iudicium de idoneitate ferat, audiat protopresbyterum aptasque investigationes peragat auditis, si opportunum ducit, etiam aliis christifidelibus praesertim clericis.

CAN. 286 Sede eparchiali vacante aut impedita ad Administratorem eparchiae aliumve, qui eparchiam interim regit, pertinet;

1° parochum nominare presbyterum a Superiore maiore ad normam can. 284, §2 propositum;

2° parochum ex aliis presbyteris nominare, si sedes eparchialis unum saltem annum vacavit aut impedita est.

CAN. 287 §1. Parochus unius paroeciae tantum curam paroecialem habeat; ob penuriam tamen presbyterorum aut alia adiuncta plurium vicinarum paroeciarum cura eidem parocho concredi potest.

§2. In eadem paroecia unus tantum habeatur parochus; si vero ius particulare propriae Ecclesiae sui iuris permittit, ut paroecia pluribus presbyteris committatur, idem ius particulare accurate determinet, quaenam sint iura et obligationes moderatoris, qui actionem communem dirigat atque de eadem Episcopo eparchiali respondeat, et quaenam ceterorum presbyterorum.

CAN. 288 Parochus a provisione canonica obtinet curam animarum, quam tamen eidem exercere non licet nisi capta ad normam iuris particularis possessione canonica paroeciae.

286: Pius XII, m.p. *Cleri sanctitati,* 2 iun. 1957, can. 496 §2 nn. 2–3.

287 §1: Pius XII, m.p. *Cleri sanctitati,* 2 iun. 1957, can. 501 §1. * Syn. Zamosten. Ruthenorum, a. 1720, tit. III §7 "Quia;" Syn. Libanen. Maronitarum, a. 1736, pars III, cap. III, 2, III; Syn. Sciarfen. Syrorum,

a. 1888, cap. XI, art. III, 4.

287 §2: Pius XII, m.p. *Cleri sanctitati,* 2 iun. 1957, can. 501 §2 n. 1. * Syn. Libanen. Maronitarum, a. 1736, pars II, cap. XIV, 32; Syn. Sciarfen. Syrorum, a. 1888, cap. XI, art. III, 5 "Si in eadem."

CAN. 289 §1. In carrying out the teaching function, the pastor is bound by the obligation of preaching the word of God to all the Christian faithful so that, rooted in faith, hope and charity, they may grow in Christ and that the Christian community may render such witness of love as the Lord commended. The pastor is also to lead the Christian faithful to the full knowledge of the mystery of salvation by a catechetical formation that is adapted to the age of each one. To impart this formation he is to seek not only the assistance of members of religious institutes or societies of common life in the manner of religious, but also the cooperation of lay persons.

§2. In discharging the sanctifying function, the pastor is to take care that the celebration of the Divine Liturgy is the center and culmination of the whole life of the Christian community. He is to strive to ensure that the Christian faithful are nourished with spiritual food through devout and frequent reception of the sacraments and through conscious and active participation in the divine praises. He is also to be aware of the great role the sacrament of penance has in fostering Christian life; therefore, he is to make himself readily available to administer this sacrament, calling upon, if necessary, also other priests who are versed in various languages.

§3. In fulfilling the governing function, the pastor is to ensure first of all that he knows his flock. Being a servant for all the sheep, he is to

CAN. 289 §1. In exsequendo munere docendi parochus obligatione tenetur verbum Dei praedicandi omnibus christifidelibus, ut hi in fide, spe et caritate radicati in Christo crescant et communitas christiana illud testimonium caritatis reddat, quod Dominus commendavit; itemque institutione catechetica christifideles ad plenam mysterii salutis cognitionem ducendi unicuique aetati accommodatam; ad hanc institutionem tradendam non solum sodalium institutorum religiosorum vel societatum vitae communis ad instar religiosorum auxilium quaerat, sed etiam laicorum cooperationem.

§2. In perficiendo munere sanctificandi curet parochus, ut celebratio Divinae Liturgiae centrum sit et culmen totius vitae communitatis christianae; itemque allaboret, ut christifideles spirituali pabulo pascantur per devotam et frequentem sacramentorum susceptionem atque per consciam et actuosam in laudibus divinis participationem; meminerit etiam parochus quam maxime sacramentum paenitentiae ad vitam christianam fovendam conferre; quare facilem se praebeat ad hoc sacramentum ministrandum vocatis ad hoc, si opus est, aliis etiam sacerdotibus, qui varias linguas callent.

§3. In adimplendo munere regendi imprimis curet parochus, ut proprium gregem cognoscat; cum autem omnium ovium sit

289 §1: Vat. II, decr. *Christus Dominus,* 30, 2) "In exsequendo;" Pius XII, m.p. *Cleri sanctitati,* 2 iun. 1957, cann. 508 §1 et 510. * Syn. Libanen. Maronitarum, a. 1736, pars III, cap. III, 2, XI; Syn. Sciarfen. Syrorum, a. 1888, cap. XIX, art. II.

289 §2: Vat. II, decr. *Christus Dominus,* 30, 2) "In perficiendo;" Pius XII, m.p. *Cleri sanctitati,* 2 iun. 1957, can. 508 §1. * Syn. Zamosten. Ruthenorum, a. 1720, tit. III, pr.; Syn. Libanen. Maronitarum, a. 1736, pars III, cap. III, 2, I, IX–X; Syn. Ain-Trazen. Graeco-Melchitarum, a. 1835, can. 5, 5; Syn. Leopolien.

Ruthenorum, a. 1891, tit. VII, cap. VI, 3.

289 §3: Vat. II, decr. *Christus Dominus,* 30, 2) "In officio;" Pius XII, m.p. *Cleri sanctitati,* 2 iun. 1957, cann. 508 §1, 509. * Syn. Zamosten. Ruthenorum, a. 1720, tit. III, §6 "Et quia;" Syn. Libanen. Maronitarum, a. 1736, pars II, cap. I, 4; cap. VIII, 12; cap. IX, 1; Syn. Ain-Trazen. Graeco-Melchitarum, a. 1835, can. 22; Syn. Sciarfen. Syrorum, a. 1888, cap. V, art. IX; Syn. Leopolien. Ruthenorum, a. 1891, tit. VII, cap. VI, 5; Syn. Alexandrin. Coptorum, a. 1898, sect. II, cap. III, art. VI, X.

foster the growth of Christian life both in individual members of the Christian faithful and in their associations, especially those directed to apostolate, and in the entire parish community. He is to visit the homes and schools in keeping with his pastoral function; be eager to provide for the needs of adolescents and youths; seek out with paternal love the poor and the sick. Finally, he is to have a special care for workers and is to take measures so that the Christian faithful offer assistance in the works of the apostolate.

CAN. 290 §1. The pastor represents the parish in all its juridic affairs.

§2. Sacred functions of greater importance, such as the celebration of the sacraments of Christian initiation, the blessing of marriages, without prejudice to can. 302, §2, the ecclesiastical funeral rites, belong to the pastor; therefore, parochial vicars are not allowed to carry them out except by the permission, at least presumed, of the pastor himself.

CAN. 291 All offerings, except those mentioned in cann. 715–717, that are received on the occasion of performing some pastoral function by the pastor and the other clerics attached to the parish, are to be put into the parish fund unless, with respect of voluntary offerings, there is a clear contrary intention on the donor's part. It is the competence of the eparchial bishop, after consulting the presbyteral council, to establish regulations concerning the destination of these offerings and to provide for the remuner-

minister, vitae christianae incrementum foveat tum in singulis christifidelibus tum in consociationibus praesertim apostolatui addictis tum in tota communitate paroeciali; domos igitur et scholas visitet, prout munus pastorale id exigit; adulescentibus et iuvenibus studiose prospiciat; pauperes et infirmos paterna caritate prosequatur; specialem denique curam de opificibus habeat atque allaboret, ut christifideles operibus apostolatus auxilium praestent.

CAN. 290 §1. In omnibus negotiis iuridicis paroeciae parochus eiusdem personam gerit.

§2. Functiones sacrae maioris momenti, ut sunt celebratio sacramentorum initiationis christianae, benedictio matrimoniorum firmo can. 302, §2, exsequiae ecclesiasticae ad parochum spectant ita, ut vicariis paroecialibus eas perficere non liceat nisi de licentia saltem praesumpta ipsius parochi.

CAN. 291 Oblationes omnes eis exceptis, de quibus in cann. 715–717, quae occasione perfuncti muneris pastoralis a parocho ceterisque clericis paroeciae addictis recipiuntur, ad massam paroecialem deferri debent, nisi de contraria offerentis voluntate constat circa oblationes plene voluntarias; Episcopo eparchiali consulto consilio presbyterali competit statuere praescripta, quibus destinationi harum oblationum necnon iustae remunerationi parochi ceterorumque

290 §2: Pius XII, m.p. *Cleri sanctitati*, 2 iun. 1957, can. 503. - S.C. de Prop. Fide, decr. 6 oct. 1863, E), c). * Syn. Ain-Trazen. Graeco-Melchitarum, a. 1835, can. 5, prooem. et 1; Syn. prov. Alba-Iulien. et Fagarasien. Rumenorum, a. 1872, tit. II, cap. IX, 1)–2); Syn. Alexandrin. Coptorum, a. 1898, sect. III, cap. V, art. IV, §1, VII.

291: Pius XII, m.p. *Cleri sanctitati*, 2 iun. 1957,

can. 504. - S.C. de Prop. Fide, instr. (ad Del. Ap. Aegypti), 30 apr. 1862, *Il 4 dubbio*; decr. 6 oct. 1863, E), e). * Syn. Libanen. Maronitarum, a. 1736, pars II, cap. I, 7; Syn. Sciarfen. Syrorum, a. 1888, cap. V, art. I, 9; Syn. Leopolien. Ruthenorum, a. 1891, tit. IX, cap. II, 5; Syn. Alexandrin. Coptorum, a. 1898, sect. II, cap. III, art. I, 12, VIII; sect. III, cap. IV, art. IV, §1, VII, 6.

ation of the pastor and the other parish clerics in accord with the norm of can. 390.

CAN. 292 §1. The pastor is bound by the obligation of residing in the rectory near the parish Church. However the local hierarch, for a just cause, can permit him to reside elsewhere so long as the parochial ministry suffers no harm from it.

§2. Unless there is a grave reason to the contrary, the pastor may each year be absent from his parish for a period not exceeding one month, continual or otherwise. The days that the pastor spends on his annual spiritual retreat are not counted in this vacation period. If the pastor wishes to be absent from the parish for more than a week, he is obliged to inform his local hierarch about this.

§3. It is for the eparchial bishop to establish norms by which, during the absence of the pastor, the care of the parish is provided for by a priest having the required powers and faculties.

CAN. 293 The pastor is to be mindful of his duty to set, with his daily behavior and solicitude, a good example of a truly priestly and pastoral ministry, to the baptized and non-baptized, to Catholics and non-Catholics; of his duty to give witness of truth and life to all; and, as a good shepherd, to seek out also those who, though baptized in the Catholic Church, have distanced themselves from the reception of the sacraments or have even abandoned the faith.

paroeciae clericorum ad normam can. 390 provideatur.

CAN. 292 §1. Parochus obligatione tenetur residendi in domo paroeciali prope ecclesiam paroecialem; potest tamen Hierarcha loci iusta de causa permittere, ut alibi commoretur, dummodo ministerium paroeciale nihil inde detrimenti capiat.

§2. Nisi gravis obstat ratio, parocho feriarum gratia licet quotannis a paroecia abesse non ultra mensem continuum aut intermissum; quod in tempus feriarum dies non computantur, quibus semel in anno parochus recessui spirituali vacat; parochus autem, si ultra hebdomadam a paroecia abesse vult, tenetur de hoc proprium Hierarcham loci certiorem facere.

§3. Episcopi eparchialis est normas statuere, quibus prospiciatur, ut parochi absentia durante curae paroeciae provideatur per sacerdotem debitis potestatibus et facultatibus praeditum.

CAN. 293 Memor sit parochus se debere sua cottidiana conversatione et sollicitudine baptizatis et non baptizatis, catholicis et acatholicis, exemplum ministerii vere sacerdotalis et pastoralis exhibere omnibusque testimonium veritatis et vitae reddere et ut bonus pastor illos quoque quaerere, qui baptizati quidem in Ecclesia catholica a susceptione sacramentorum se abstinent vel immo a fide defecerunt.

292 §1: Pius XII, m.p. *Cleri sanctitati,* 2 iun. 1957, can. 506 §1. * Syn. Zamosten. Ruthenorum, a. 1720, tit. III "Itaque;" Syn. Libanen. Maronitarum, a. 1736, pars II, cap. XIV, 15; pars III, cap. III, 2, II; Syn. Ain-Trazen. Graeco-Melchitarum, a. 1835, can. 14; Syn. Sciarfen. Syrorum, a. 1888, cap. V, art. I, 9: Syn. Leopolien. Ruthenorum, a. 1891, tit. VII, cap. VI, 6.

292 §2: Pius XII, m.p. *Cleri sanctitati,* 2 iun. 1957, can. 506 §§2–3, 5. * Syn. Libanen. Maronitarum, a.

1736, pars II, cap. XIV, 15; pars III, cap. III, 2, II.

292 §3: Pius XII, m.p. *Cleri sanctitati,* 2 iun. 1957, can. 506 §§4–5. * Syn. Libanen. Maronitarum, a. 1736, pars II, cap. XIV, 15; pars III, cap. III, 2, II; Syn. Ain-Trazen. Graeco-Melchitarum, a. 1835, can. 14; Syn. Leopolien. Ruthenorum, a. 1891, tit. VII, cap. VI, 6.

293: Vat. II, const. *Lumen gentium,* 28 "Fidelium."

CAN. 294 The pastor is frequently to celebrate the Divine Liturgy for the people of the parish entrusted to him but is bound to celebrate it for them on the days prescribed by the particular law of his Church *sui iuris.*

CAN. 295 In the parish there are to be appropriate councils dealing with pastoral and financial matters, in accord with the norms of the particular law of its own Church *sui iuris.*

CAN. 296 §1. In the parish there are to be parish registers, namely, of the baptized, of marriages, of the deceased and others in accord with the norms of the particular law of the respective Church *sui iuris* or, lacking these, those laid down by the eparchial bishop. The pastor, with respect to these same norms, is to see that the parish registers are filled in and preserved properly.

§2. In the register of baptisms, a note is to be made of the ascription of the baptized persons to a determined Church *sui iuris* in accord with the norm of can. 37, of the administration of chrismation with holy myron as well as what pertains to the canonical status of the Christian faithful by reason of marriage, with due regard for can. 840, §3, of adoption, of sacred orders or of perpetual profession in a religious institute. These annotations are always to be reported on the baptismal certificate.

CAN. 294 Divinam Liturgiam pro populo paroeciae sibi concreditae parochus frequenter celebret, diebus vero iure particulari propriae Ecclesiae sui iuris praescriptis celebrare tenetur.

CAN. 295 In paroecia habeantur ad normam iuris particularis propriae Ecclesiae sui iuris opportuna consilia ad res pastorales et oeconomicas tractandas.

CAN. 296 §1. In paroecia habeantur libri paroeciales, liber scilicet baptizatorum, matrimoniorum, defunctorum aliique secundum normas iuris particularis propriae Ecclesiae sui iuris aut, si hae desunt, ab ipso Episcopo eparchiali statutas; prospiciat parochus, ut libri paroeciales servatis eisdem normis recte conscribantur atque asserventur.

§2. In libro baptizatorum adnotentur quoque ascriptio baptizati determinatae Ecclesiae sui iuris ad normam can. 37, ministratio chrismationis sancti myri necnon, quae ad christifidelium pertinent statum canonicum ratione matrimonii salvo quidem can. 840, §3, ratione adoptionis itemque ratione ordinis sacri vel professionis perpetuae in instituto religioso; hae adnotationes in testimonium baptismi semper referantur.

294: Pius XII, m.p. *Cleri sanctitati,* 2 iun. 1957, can. 507 §§1–4. - Syn. Trid., sess. XXIII, de ref., c. 1; S.C. de Prop. Fide (ad Patriarcham Chaldaeorum Timotheum Hindi), 5 apr. 1760; 16 aug. 1784, dub. 31; (C.G.), 23 mar. 1863, 1; litt. encycl. (ad Deleg. Ap. pro Oriente), 8 nov. 1882, I; Leo XIII, litt. ap. *In suprema,* 10 iun. 1882. * Syn. prov. Alba-Iulien. et Fagarasien. Rumenorum, a. 1872, tit. V, cap. IV "Quoad S. Liturgiae;" a. 1900, tit. III, cap. I, 12; Syn. Leopolien. Ruthenorum, a. 1891, tit. IV, cap. II, 1; tit. VII, cap. VI, 2.

295: Vat. II, decr. *Apostolicam actuositatem,* 26; decr. *Presbyterorum ordinis,* 17 "Bona."

296 §1: Pius XII, m.p. *Cleri sanctitati,* 2 iun. 1957, can. 511 §1. - Benedictus XIV, const. *Apostolica praedecessorum,* 14 feb. 1742; S.C. de Prop. Fide, reg. (pro Sacerd. Coptis), 15 mar. 1790, XII; decr. 6 oct. 1863, C), a). * Syn. Sergii Patriarchae Maronit., 18 sep. 1596, cann. I, XIV; Syn. Zamosten. Ruthenorum, a. 1720, tit. III, §1 "Denique;" Syn. Libanen. Maronitarum, a. 1736, pars II, cap. XI, 5; cap. XII, 20; pars III, cap. III, 2, V; Syn. Sciarfen. Syrorum, a. 1888, cap. V, art. XI, 6; art. XV, §1, 1, X; Syn. Leopolien. Ruthenorum, a. 1891, tit. VII, cap. VI, 7; Syn. Alexandrin. Coptorum, a. 1898, sect. II, cap. III, art. VI, *De Coemeterio,* VI; art. VIII, §2, 7, VI; sect. III, cap. IV, art. IV, §2, III.

296 §2: Pius XII, m.p. *Cleri sanctitati,* 2 iun. 1957, can. 511 §2. * Syn. Zamosten. Ruthenorum, a. 1720, tit. III, §1 "Si acciderit."

§3. Certificates issued about the canonical status of the Christian faithful and all documents that can have juridical importance are to be signed by the pastor himself or his delegate and secured with the parish seal.

§4. In the parish there is to be an archive in which the parish registers are to be kept along with the letters of hierarchs and other documents that may be necessary or useful to preserve. All these are to be inspected by the eparchial bishop or his delegate on the occasion of the canonical visitation or at some other suitable time. The pastor is to take care that they do not come into unauthorized hands.

§5. Older parish registers are also to be preserved diligently in accord with the norm of particular law.

CAN. 297 §1. The pastor ceases from office by resignation accepted by the eparchial bishop, expiration of a determined term, removal or transfer.

§2. When a pastor has completed his seventy-fifth year of age, he is requested to submit his resignation from office to the eparchial bishop, who, after considering all the circumstances of person and place, is to decide whether to accept or defer the resignation; the eparchial bishop, taking into account the norms of particular law of his own Church *sui iuris,* is to provide for the suitable support and residence of the resigned pastor.

CAN. 298 If the parish becomes vacant or the pastor is impeded by any cause whatever from exercising his pastoral function in the parish, the eparchial bishop is to appoint as

§3. Testimonia, quae de statu canonico christifidelium dantur, et omnia documenta, quae momentum habere possunt iuridicum ab ipso parocho eiusve delegato subscribantur et sigillo paroeciali muniantur.

§4. In paroecia habeatur archivum, in quo libri paroeciales asserventur una cum Hierarcharum epistulis aliisque documentis necessitatis vel utilitatis causa servandis; quae omnia ab Episcopo eparchiali eiusve delegato visitationis canonicae vel alio tempore opportuno inspicienda parochus caveat, ne ad extraneorum manus perveniant.

§5. Libri paroeciales antiquiores quoque asserventur ad normam iuris particularis.

CAN. 297 §1. Parochus ab officio cessat renuntiatione ab Episcopo eparchiali acceptata, elapso tempore determinato, amotione vel translatione.

§2. Parochus expleto septuagesimo quinto aetatis anno rogatur, ut renuntiationem ab officio exhibeat Episcopo eparchiali, qui omnibus personae et loci inspectis adiunctis de eadem acceptanda aut differenda decernat; renuntiantis congruae sustentationi et habitationi ab Episcopo eparchiali providendum est attentis normis iuris particularis propriae Ecclesiae sui iuris.

CAN. 298 Si vacat paroecia aut parochus quacumque de causa a munere pastorali in paroecia exercendo impeditur, Episcopus eparchialis quam primum aliquem

---

296 §3: Pius XII, m.p. *Cleri sanctitati,* 2 iun. 1957, can. 511 §5.

296 §4: Pius XII, m.p. *Cleri sanctitati,* 2 iun. 1957, can. 511 §5.

297 §1: Vat. II, decr. *Christus Dominus,* 31; Paulus VI, m.p. *Ecclesiae sanctae,* 6 aug. 1966, I, 20.

297 §2: Vat. II, decr. *Christus Dominus,* 31 "Parochi;" Paulus VI, m.p. *Ecclesiae sanctae,* 6 aug. 1966, I, 20 §3.

298: Pius XII, m.p. *Cleri sanctitati,* 2 iun. 1957, can. 513 n. 1.

soon as possible a priest as parochial adminis-trator.

CAN. 299 §1. The parochial administrator has the same rights and obligations as the pas-tor, unless the eparchial bishop determines otherwise.

§2. The parochial administrator may not do anything that can prejudice the rights of the pastor or do harm to the parish property.

§3. After he has discharged his function, the parochial administrator is to give an account to the pastor.

CAN. 300 §1. When the parish is vacant or when the pastor is absolutely impeded from ex-ercising his pastoral function, before the ap-pointment of a parochial administrator, the pa-rochial vicar assumes the interim care of the parish; if there are several parochial vicars, the one who is the senior by presbyteral ordination; if there are no vicars, by the nearest pastor. The eparchial bishop is to determine at the appro-priate time which parish is to be considered nearest to each parish.

§2. The one who assumes the interim gover-nance of a parish is immediately to inform the eparchial bishop.

CAN. 301 §1. If it is necessary or opportune for the necessary pastoral care of a parish, there can be one or more parochial vicars to support the pastor; these must be presbyters.

sacerdotem nominet administratorem paroe-ciae.

CAN. 299 §1. Administrator paroeciae eadem iura et obligationes habet ac parochus, nisi ab Episcopo eparchiali aliud statuitur.

§2. Administratori paroeciae nihil agere licet, quod praeiudicium afferre potest iuribus parochi aut damno esse potest bonis paroecialibus.

§3. Administrator paroeciae expleto munere parocho rationem reddat.

CAN. 300 §1. Paroecia vacante itemque parocho a munere pastorali ex-ercendo penitus impedito ante administra-toris paroeciae nominationem curam paroe-ciae interim assumat vicarius paroecialis et quidem, si plures sunt, eorum ordinatione presbyterali senior aut, si vicarii desunt, parochus vicinior; Episcopus eparchialis autem tempestive determinet, quaenam cuique paroecia vicinior habenda sit.

§2. Qui paroeciae regimen interim as-sumpsit, Episcopum eparchialem de re sta-tim certiorem faciat.

CAN. 301 §1. Si ad curam pastoralem paroeciae debite implendam necesse aut op-portunum est, parocho adiungi possunt unus vel plures vicarii paroeciales, qui debent esse presbyteri.

299 §1: Pius XII, m.p. *Cleri sanctitati,* 2 iun. 1957, can. 514 §1. * Syn. Leopolien. Ruthenorum, a. 1891, tit. VII, cap. VII, 1.

299 §2: Pius XII, m.p. *Cleri sanctitati,* 2 iun. 1957, can. 514 §1. * Syn. Leopolien. Ruthenorum, a. 1891, tit. VII, cap. VII, 1.

299 §3: Pius XII, m.p. *Cleri sanctitati,* 2 iun. 1957, can. 514 §2.

300 §1: Pius XII, m.p. *Cleri sanctitati,* 2 iun. 1957, can. 513 n. 2. * Syn. prov. Alba-Iulien. et Fagarasien. Rumenorum, a. 1872, tit. II, cap. VIII, II, 5); Syn. Ar-

men., a. 1911, 352.

300 §2: Pius XII, m.p. *Cleri sanctitati,* 2 iun. 1957, can. 513 n. 3.

301 §1: Pius XII, m.p. *Cleri sanctitati,* 2 iun. 1957, cann. 516 §1 n. 1, 517 §1. - Benedictus XIV, const. *Etsi pastoralis,* 26 maii 1742, §V, IX. * Syn. Zamosten. Ruthenorum, a. 1720, tit. III, §7 "Quia;" Syn. prov. Alba-Iulien. et Fagarasien. Rumenorum, a. 1872, tit. II, cap. IX, 7) "Necessitate;" Syn. Armen., a. 1911, 347; 353.

§2. A parochial vicar can be appointed either for the whole parish or for a specified part of the parish.

§3. The eparchial bishop freely appoints the parochial vicar after hearing the pastor, unless he decides it more prudent to do otherwise. If it is a question of a member of a religious institute or society of common life in the manner of religious, can. 284, §2 is to be observed.

CAN. 302 §1. The rights and obligations of the parochial vicar are to be drawn from common law and from particular law as well as from the letter of the eparchial bishop; they are to be exercised under the authority of the pastor. But, unless expressly provided otherwise and with the exception of the obligation mentioned in can. 294, the parochial vicar by virtue of his office must help the pastor in the entire parochial ministry and, if need should arise, to substitute for the pastor.

§2. The parochial vicar does not have the faculty of blessing marriages by virtue of his office. However, this faculty, even the general faculty, can be conferred upon him by the local hierarch or, within the boundaries of the parish, by the pastor. If it has been conferred upon him, the parochial vicar can confer it in turn upon other priests in individual cases.

§3. The parochial vicar, as a cooperator of the pastor, is to make himself readily available for active work in the day to day pastoral function. Between the pastor and the parochial vicar the relationship is to be fraternal; mutual love and reverence are to prevail always; they are to assist

§2. Vicarius paroecialis constitui potest sive pro tota paroecia sive pro determinata paroeciae parte.

§3. Vicarium paroecialem libere nominat Episcopus eparchialis audito, nisi aliter prudenter iudicat, parocho et, si de sodali instituti religiosi vel societatis vitae communis ad instar religiosorum agitur, servato can. 284, §2.

CAN. 302 §1. Vicarii paroecialis iura et obligationes ex iure communi et particulari necnon ex litteris Episcopi eparchialis desumantur et sub auctoritate parochi exercenda sunt; sed, nisi aliter expresse cavetur et excepta obligatione, de qua in can. 294, vicarius paroecialis debet ratione officii parochum adiuvare in toto ministerio paroeciali et, si res fert, parochi vicem supplere.

§2. Ratione autem officii vicarius paroecialis facultate matrimonia benedicendi praeditus non est; hanc tamen facultatem, etiam generalem, ei conferre potest praeter Hierarcham loci etiam parochus intra fines paroeciae; quam facultatem, si ipsi collata est, vicarius paroecialis aliis quoque sacerdotibus singulis in casibus conferre potest.

§3. Vicarius paroecialis tamquam parochi cooperator praestantem et actuosam operam cottidie impendat in munere pastorali; inter parochum et vicarium paroecialem fraterna habeatur conversatio, mutua caritas et reverentia semper vigeat iidemque consiliis, auxilio et exemplo se invicem adiu-

301 §2: Pius XII, m.p. *Cleri sanctitati,* 2 iun. 1957, can. 517 §2. * Syn. Armen., a. 1911, 353.

301 §3: Pius XII, m.p. *Cleri sanctitati,* 2 iun. 1957, can. 517 §§3–4. * Syn. Zamosten. Ruthenorum, a. 1720, tit. III, §7 "Quia;" Syn. prov. Alba-Iulien. et Fagarasien. Rumenorum, a. 1872, tit. II, cap. IX, 7 "Parochus."

302 §1: Pius XII, m.p. *Cleri sanctitati,* 2 iun. 1957,

can. 517 §6. * Syn. prov. Alba-Iulien. et Fagarasien. Rumenorum, a. 1872, tit. II, cap. IX, 7) "Necessitate;" Syn. Leopolien. Ruthenorum, a. 1891, tit. VII, cap. VII, 2–8; Syn. Armen., a. 1911, 353.

302 §2: Pius XII, m.p. *Cleri sanctitati,* 2 iun. 1957, can. 517 §6.

302 §3: Vat. II, decr. *Christus Dominus,* 30, 3); const. *Lumen gentium,* 28 "Vi communis."

each other with advice, support and example in order to provide parochial care with unanimity of mind and joint endeavor.

§4. The parochial vicar is bound by the obligation of residing in the parish according to the prescriptions of the eparchial bishop or legitimate custom; the parochial vicar has the same rights to vacation as the pastor.

CAN. 303 The parochial vicar can be removed by the eparchial bishop for a just cause; however, if the parochial vicar is a member of a religious institute or society of common life in the manner of religious, can. 1391, §2 is to be observed.

CHAPTER IV. Rectors of Churches

CAN. 304 The rector of a church is a presbyter to whom is entrusted the care of a church that is neither a parochial Church nor is connected with a house of an institute of consecrated life.

CAN. 305 §1. The rector of a church is appointed by the eparchial bishop, without prejudice to the right of the major superior of a religious institute or society of common life in the manner of religious to propose a suitable presbyter of his institute or society for the appointment.

§2. Even if the Church belongs to some clerical institute of consecrated life of pontifical or patriarchal law, it is the competence of the eparchial bishop to appoint the rector of a church proposed by the superior.

vent curae paroeciali concordi voluntate communique studio providentes.

§4. Vicarius paroecialis obligatione tenetur in paroecia residendi secundum praescripta Episcopi eparchialis vel legitimas consuetudines; circa tempus feriarum vero vicarius paroecialis idem ius habet ac parochus.

CAN. 303 Vicarius paroecialis potest ab Episcopo eparchiali amoveri iusta de causa; si vero vicarius paroecialis est sodalis instituti religiosi vel societatis vitae communis ad instar religiosorum, servetur can. 1391, §2.

CAPUT IV. **De Rectoribus Ecclesiarum**

CAN. 304 Rector ecclesiae est presbyter, cui cura demandatur alicuius ecclesiae, quae nec paroecialis est nec adnexa domui instituti vitae consecratae.

CAN. 305 §1. Rector ecclesiae nominatur ab Episcopo eparchiali salvo iure Superioris maioris instituti religiosi vel societatis vitae communis ad instar religiosorum presbyterum idoneum sui instituti vel societatis ad nominationem proponendi.

§2. Etsi ecclesia pertinet ad aliquod institutum vitae consecratae clericale iuris pontificii vel patriarchalis, Episcopo eparchiali competit rectorem ecclesiae a Superiore propositum nominare.

302 §4: Pius XII, m.p. *Cleri sanctitati,* 2 iun. 1957, can. 517 §5. * Syn. Armen., a. 1911, 356.

303: Pius XII, m.p. *Cleri sanctitati,* 2 iun. 1957, cann. 518 §1, 494 §5; Paulus VI, m.p. *Ecclesiae sanctae,* 6 aug. 1966, I, 32.

304: Pius XII, m.p. *Cleri sanctitati,* 2 iun. 1957,

can. 519 §1.

305 §1: Pius XII, m.p. *Cleri sanctitati,* 2 iun. 1957, can. 520 §1.

305 §2: Pius XII, m.p. *Cleri sanctitati,* 2 iun. 1957, can. 520 §2.

§3. If the Church is attached to a seminary or other college which is directed by presbyters, the rector of the seminary or college is at the same time the rector of the Church, unless the eparchial bishop has determined otherwise.

CAN. 306 §1. It is not permitted for the rector of a church in the Church committed to him to perform parochial functions, except with the consent of or, if necessary, delegation from the pastor, with due regard for can. 336, §2.

§2. The rector of the Church can celebrate the Divine Liturgy and the divine praises there with due regard for the legitimate statutes of foundation and as long as, in the judgment of the local hierarch, they are in no way prejudicial to the parochial ministry.

CAN. 307 If he thinks it advisable, the local hierarch can order the rector of a church to celebrate specific sacred functions, even parochial ones, in the Church entrusted to him, and to make the Church available to certain groups of the Christian faithful.

CAN. 308 Without the permission of the rector of the Church or higher authority, at least presumed, no one is allowed to celebrate the Divine Liturgy or the divine praises, administer the sacraments or perform other sacred functions in the Church; but this permission must be given or denied in accord with the norm of the law.

CAN. 309 Under the authority of the local hierarch and with due regard for the legitimate statutes and acquired rights, the rector of the Church must see that the Divine Liturgy, sacraments and the divine praises are celebrated in

§3. Si ecclesia coniuncta est cum seminario aliove collegio, quod a presbyteris regitur, rector seminarii vel collegii est simul rector ecclesiae, nisi aliud Episcopus eparchialis statuit.

CAN. 306 §1. In ecclesia sibi commissa rectori ecclesiae functiones paroeciales peragere non licet nisi consentiente aut, si res fert, delegante parocho et firmo can. 336, §2.

§2. Rector ecclesiae potest ibidem Divinam Liturgiam et laudes divinas celebrare salvis legitimis fundationis statutis atque, dummodo haec de iudicio Hierarchae loci nullo modo ministerio paroeciali praeiudicium afferant.

CAN. 307 Hierarcha loci, si id opportunum censet, potest rectori ecclesiae praecipere, ut determinatas in ecclesia sibi commissa celebret functiones sacras, etiam paroeciales, necnon ut ecclesia pateat certis christifidelium coetibus.

CAN. 308 Sine rectoris ecclesiae vel auctoritatis superioris licentia saltem praesumpta nemini licet in ecclesia Divinam Liturgiam vel laudes divinas celebrare, sacramenta ministrare aliasve functiones sacras peragere; haec vero licentia dari vel denegari debet ad normam iuris.

CAN. 309 Rector ecclesiae sub auctoritate Hierarchae loci servatisque legitimis statutis et iuribus quaesitis debet curare, ut Divina Liturgia, sacramenta et laudes divinae secundum praescripta librorum liturgicorum

305 §3: Pius XII, m.p. *Cleri sanctitati,* 2 iun. 1957, can. 520 §3.

306 §1: Pius XII, m.p. *Cleri sanctitati,* 2 iun. 1957, can. 521.

306 §2:Pius XII, m.p. *Cleri sanctitati,* 2 iun. 1957, can. 522.

307: Pius XII, m.p. *Cleri sanctitati,* 2 iun. 1957, can. 523 n. 1.

308: Pius XII, m.p. *Cleri sanctitati,* 2 iun. 1957, can. 524.

309: Pius XII, m.p. *Cleri sanctitati,* 2 iun. 1957, can. 525 §1.

the Church according to the prescriptions of the liturgical books and of the law; that obligations are faithfully fulfilled; that the ecclesiastical property is carefully administered; that provision is made for the maintenance and the adornment of the sacred furnishings and buildings. He must also ensure that nothing whatever is done that is in any way unbecoming to the holiness of the place and to the reverence due to the house of God.

CAN. 310 The eparchial bishop can remove the rector of a church for a just cause. If the rector of the Church is a member of a religious institute or society of common life in the manner of religious, can. 1391, §2 is to be observed.

et iuris in ecclesia celebrentur, onera fideliter impleantur, bona ecclesiastica diligenter administrentur, sacrae supellectilis atque aedium sacrarum conservationi et decori provideatur nec quidpiam fiat, quod sanctitati loci ac reverentiae domui Dei debitae quoquo modo non congruat.

CAN. 310 Rectorem ecclesiae Episcopus eparchialis amovere potest iusta de causa; si vero rector ecclesiae est sodalis instituti religiosi vel societatis vitae communis ad instar religiosorum, servetur can. 1391, §2.

310: Pius XII, m.p. *Cleri sanctitati,* 2 iun. 1957, can. 526.

TITLE VIII. EXARCHIES AND EXARCHS

CAN. 311 §1. An exarchy is a portion of the people God which, because of special circumstances, is not erected as an eparchy, and which being delimited territorially or on some other criterion, is entrusted to an exarch to shepherd.

§2. In the erection, modification, and suppression of an exarchy located within the territorial boundaries of the patriarchal Church, can. 85, §3 is to be observed. For the erection, modification, and suppression of other exarchies, only the Apostolic See is competent.

CAN. 312 The exarch governs the exarchy either in the name of the one who appointed him or in his own name. This must be established in the erection or modification of the exarchy.

CAN. 313 What is said in the law concerning eparchies or eparchial bishops applies also to exarchies or exarchs, unless it is expressly provided otherwise in the law or is evident from the nature of the matter.

CAN. 314 §1. Within the territorial boundaries of the patriarchal Church, the exarch is appointed by the patriarch with the consent of the permanent synod and without prejudice to

CAN. 311 §1. Exarchia est populi Dei portio, quae ob specialia adiuncta ut eparchia non est erecta quaeque territorialiter vel alia ratione circumscripta Exarcho pascenda concreditur.

§2. In erectione, immutatione et suppressione exarchiae, quae intra fines territorii Ecclesiae patriarchalis sita est, servandus est can. 85, §3; erectio, immutatio et suppressio ceterarum exarchiarum soli Sedi Apostolicae competit.

CAN. 312 Exarchus exarchiam regit aut nomine illius, a quo nominatus est, aut nomine proprio; de qua re in erectione vel immutatione exarchiae constare debet.

CAN. 313 Quae in iure de eparchiis vel de Episcopis eparchialibus dicuntur, valent etiam de exarchiis vel de Exarchis, nisi aliter iure expresse cavetur vel ex natura rei constat.

CAN. 314 §1. Intra fines territorii Ecclesiae patriarchalis Exarchus nominatur a Patriarcha de consensu Synodi permanentis et firmis cann. 181–188, si de Exarcho agitur,

---

311 §1: Pius XII, m.p. *Cleri sanctitati,* 2 iun. 1957, cann. 366 §1, 388 §1. * Syn. Sciarfen. Syrorum, a. 1888, cap. V, art. XIII, §9, 3, 6); Syn. Armen., a. 1911, 196.

311 §2: Pius XII, m.p. *Cleri sanctitati,* 2 iun. 1957, cann. 159, 248 §2, 328, 362 §1.

312: Pius XII, m.p. *Cleri sanctitati,* 2 iun. 1957,

cann. 362, 363 §1, 366 §1, 388 §1.

313: Pius XII, m.p. *Cleri sanctitati,* 2 iun. 1957, cann. 367 §1, 391, 363 §2.

314 §1: Pius XII, m.p. *Cleri sanctitati,* 2 iun. 1957, cann. 363 §1, 366 §2, 388 §2. - S.C. pro Eccl. Orient., decr. 1 mar. 1929, art. 1; decr. 24 maii 1930, art. 1.

cann. 181–188 if the exarch is one who is to be ordained bishop. In other cases, for the appointment of the exarch only the Apostolic See is competent.

§2. An exarch appointed by the patriarch cannot be removed from office except with the consent of the synod of bishops of the patriarchal Church.

§3. The exarch takes canonical possession of the exarchy entrusted to him by presenting the decree of appointment to him who is governing the exarchy in the interim.

CAN. 315 §1. An exarch constituted outside the territorial boundaries of the patriarchal Church can ask the patriarch for suitable presbyters to undertake the pastoral care of the Christian faithful. The patriarch is to satisfy this request, as far as possible.

§2. Presbyters sent to the exarchy by the patriarch, either for a determined or indeterminate time, are considered attached to the exarchy and are subject in all things to the power of the exarch.

CAN. 316 Recourse against the decrees of an exarch who governs an exarchy in the name of the Roman Pontiff or the patriarch is made respectively to the Apostolic See or the patriarch. Recourse against decrees of an exarch who governs an exarchy in his own name is made in accord with the ordinary norm of the law.

CAN. 317 Exarchs are bound by the oblig-

qui Episcopus ordinandus est; in ceteris casibus nominatio Exarchi competit soli Sedi Apostolicae.

§2. Exarchus a Patriarcha nominatus ab officio amoveri non potest nisi de consensu Synodi Episcoporum Ecclesiae patriarchalis.

§3. Exarchus possessionem canonicam exarchiae sibi concreditae capit decretum nominationis ostendens ei, qui interim exarchiam regit.

CAN. 315 §1. Exarchus extra fines territorii Ecclesiae patriarchalis constitutus a Patriarcha presbyteros idoneos expetere potest, qui curam pastoralem christifidelium in exarchia suscipiant; Patriarcha autem, quatenus fieri potest, petitioni Exarchi satisfaciat.

§2. Presbyteri a Patriarcha ad tempus determinatum aut indeterminatum in exarchiam missi exarchiae addicti habentur et in omnibus subsunt potestati Exarchi.

CAN. 316 A decretis Exarchi, qui nomine Romani Pontificis vel Patriarchae exarchiam regit, recursus fit respective ad Sedem Apostolicam vel Patriarcham; a decretis Exarchi, qui nomine proprio exarchiam regit, recursus fit ad ordinariam normam iuris.

CAN. 317 Exarchus obligatione tenetur

314 §2: Pius XII, m.p. *Cleri sanctitati,* 2 iun. 1957, can. 388 §2.

314 §3: Pius XII, m.p. *Cleri sanctitati,* 2 iun. 1957, cann. 366 §3, 389.

315 §1: Pius XII, m.p. *Cleri sanctitati,* 2 iun. 1957, can. 369 §1.

315 §2: Pius XII, m.p. *Cleri sanctitati,* 2 iun. 1957, can. 369 §2.

316: Pius XII, m.p. *Cleri sanctitati,* 2 iun. 1957, cann. 372, 391.

317: Pius XII, m.p. *Cleri sanctitati,* 2 iun. 1957, can. 375. - S.C. de Prop. Fide (pro Neg. Rit. Orient.), decr. 18 aug. 1913, art. 9; decr. 17 aug. 1914, art. 8; S.C. pro Eccl. Orient., decr. 1 mar. 1929, art. 9; decr. 24 maii 1930, art. 9.

ation of visiting the tombs of the holy Apostles Peter and Paul according to the norm can. 208, except exarchs who govern an exarchy entrusted to them in the name of the patriarch.

CAN. 318 §1. Exarchs appointed by the patriarch must send a written report every five years to the patriarch about the spiritual and temporal state of the exarchy.

§2. An exarch appointed by the Roman Pontiff must present the same report to the Apostolic See every five years and, if he belongs to a patriarchal Church, he must also send a copy of the report to the patriarch as soon as possible.

CAN. 319 §1. The exarch is bound by the laws concerning the eparchial assembly, the eparchial curia, the presbyteral council, the college of eparchial consultors and the pastoral council, but they may be equitably adapted to the peculiar nature of places and persons, in the judgment of the authority who erected or modified the exarchy.

§2. If the college of consultors cannot be constituted according to the norm of can. 271, §3, the exarch is to constitute a group of not less than three presbyters noted for their prudence and chosen, if possible, from among the members of the presbyteral council, if it exists. He must seek the consent or advice of this committee whenever the law states that the eparchial bishop needs the consent or advice of the college of eparchial consultors in order to act.

CAN. 320 §1. The government of an exarchy that is vacant or impeded transfers to the

sanctorum Apostolorum Petri et Pauli limina visitandi ad normam can. 208 exceptis Exarchis, qui nomine Patriarchae exarchiam sibi concreditam regunt.

CAN. 318 §1. Exarchus a Patriarcha nominatus debet quinto quoque anno relationem scripto datam ad Patriarcham de statu spirituali et temporali exarchiae mittere.

§2. Exarchus a Romano Pontifice nominatus eandem relationem Sedi Apostolicae singulis quinquenniis debet facere et, si ad Ecclesiam patriarchalem pertinet, etiam Patriarchae exemplar relationis quam primum mittere.

CAN. 319 §1. Legibus de conventu eparchiali, de curia eparchiali, de consilio presbyterali, de collegio consultorum eparchialium et de consilio pastorali Exarchus tenetur locorum et personarum ratione iudicio auctoritatis, quae exarchiam erexit vel immutavit, aeque accommodatis.

§2. Si collegium consultorum ad normam can. 271, §3 constitui non potest, Exarchus constituat coetum ex prudentioribus presbyteris non minus quam tribus, quatenus fieri potest inter membra consilii presbyteralis, si hoc exstat, selectis, cuius consensum vel consilium exquirere debet, quoties ius statuit Episcopum eparchialem ad agendum indigere consensu vel consilio collegii consultorum eparchialium.

CAN. 320 §1. Exarchiae vacantis vel impeditae regimen transit ad Protosyncellum

---

318 §1: Pius XII, m.p. *Cleri sanctitati,* 2 iun. 1957, can. 390.

318 §2: Pius XII, m.p. *Cleri sanctitati,* 2 iun. 1957, can. 376. - S.C. de Prop. Fide (pro Neg. Rit. Orient.), decr. 18 aug. 1913, art. 9; S.C. pro Eccl. Orient., decr. 1 mar. 1929, art. 9; decr. 24 maii 1930, art. 9.

319 §1: Pius XII, m.p. *Cleri sanctitati,* 2 iun. 1957, cann. 377–379, 380 §2, 391.

319 §2: Pius XII, m.p. *Cleri sanctitati,* 2 iun. 1957, cann. 377, 391.

320 §1: Pius XII, m.p. *Cleri sanctitati,* 2 iun. 1957, cann. 365, 384.

protosyncellus or, if there is none, to the pastor who is senior by presbyteral ordination.

§2. He to whom falls the interim governance of the exarchy must as soon as possible inform the authority that is competent to appoint the exarch, so that he may provide for it. Meanwhile he can use all the powers and faculties, whether ordinary or delegated that the exarch had, unless they were committed to the latter because of personal considerations.

CAN. 321 §1. While in office, an exarch who is not an ordained bishop has the privileges and insignia of the first dignity after the episcopal dignity.

§2. As to whether these privileges and insignia are to be retained or not after the expiration of his function, particular law is to be observed.

aut, si deest, ad parochum ordinatione presbyterali seniorem.

§2. Ille, ad quem exarchiae regimen interim devenit, quam primum debet certiorem facere auctoritatem, cuius est Exarchum nominare, ut provideat; interim vero uti potest omnibus potestatibus et facultatibus sive ordinariis sive delegatis, quas Exarchus habuit, nisi eidem commissae sunt industria personae Exarchi.

CAN. 321 §1. Exarchus, qui Episcopus ordinatus non est, habet durante munere privilegia et insignia primae post episcopalem dignitatis.

§2. In his privilegiis et insignibus retinendis vel minus expleto munere servetur ius particulare.

---

320 §2: Pius XII, m.p. *Cleri sanctitati,* 2 iun. 1957, can. 385.

321 §1: Pius XII, m.p. *Cleri sanctitati,* 2 iun. 1957, cann. 387 §1, 391.

TITLE IX. ASSEMBLIES OF HIERARCHS OF SEVERAL CHURCHES *SUI IURIS*

TITULUS IX. DE CONVENTIBUS HIERARCHARUM PLURIUM ECCLESIARUM SUI IURIS

CAN. 322 §1. Where it seems advisable in the judgment of the Apostolic See, periodic assemblies are to be held of patriarchs, metropolitans of metropolitan Churches *sui iuris,* eparchial bishops, and, if the statutes so state, other local hierarchs of various Churches *sui iuris,* even of the Latin Church, exercising their authority in the same nation or region. These assemblies are to be convoked at regular intervals by the patriarch or another authority designated by the Apostolic See. The purpose of these meetings is that, by sharing the insights of wisdom born of experience and by the exchange of views, the pooling of their resources is achieved for the common good of the Churches, so that unity of action is fostered, common works are facilitated, the good of religion is more readily promoted and ecclesiastical discipline is preserved more effectively.

§2. The decisions of this assembly do not have juridically binding force unless they deal with matters that cannot be prejudicial to the rite of each Church *sui iuris* or to the power of the patriarchs, of synods, of metropolitans and of the councils of hierarchs; further, they have to have been passed at least by two-thirds of the

CAN. 322 §1. Ubi id de iudicio Sedis Apostolicae opportunum videtur, Patriarchae, Metropolitae Ecclesiarum metropolitanarum sui iuris, Episcopi eparchiales et, si statuta ita ferunt, etiam ceteri Hierarchae loci plurium Ecclesiarum sui iuris, etiam Ecclesiae latinae, in eadem natione vel regione potestatem suam exercentes ad periodicos conventus statis temporibus convocandi sunt a Patriarcha aliave auctoritate a Sede Apostolica designata, ut communicatis prudentiae et experientiae luminibus et collatis consiliis sancta fiat ad commune Ecclesiarum bonum virium conspiratio, qua unitas actionis foveatur, communia opera iuventur, bonum religionis expeditius promoveatur atque disciplina ecclesiastica efficacius servetur.

§2. Decisiones huius conventus vim iuridice obligandi non habent, nisi de eis agitur, quae nulli possunt esse praeiudicio ritui uniuscuiusque Ecclesiae sui iuris vel potestati Patriarcharum, Synodorum, Metropolitarum atque Consiliorum Hierarcharum atque simul saltem per duas ex tribus par-

---

322 §1: Vat. II, decr. *Christus Dominus,* 37, 38, 6); decr. *Orientalium Ecclesiarum,* 4.

members having a deliberative vote and approved by the Apostolic See.

§3. A decision, even if passed by a unanimous vote, which in any way whatever exceeds the competence of this assembly, is devoid of all force until it is approved by the Roman Pontiff himself.

§4. Every assembly of hierarchs of several Churches *sui iuris* is to draw up its own statutes in which, as far as possible, the participation of the hierarchs of those Churches that are not yet in full communion with the Catholic Church is also to be fostered. The statutes, to have force, must be approved by the Apostolic See.

tibus suffragiorum membrorum suffragium deliberativum habentium latae necnon a Sede Apostolica approbatae sunt.

§3. Decisio, etsi unanimo suffragio facta, quae quomodocumque competentiam huius conventus excedit, omni vi caret, donec ab ipso Romano Pontifice approbata erit.

§4. Unusquisque conventus Hierarcharum plurium Ecclesiarum sui iuris sua conficiat statuta, in quibus foveatur, quatenus fieri potest, etiam participatio Hierarcharum Ecclesiarum, quae nondum sunt in plena communione cum Ecclesia catholica; statuta, ut valeant, a Sede Apostolica approbari debent.

CAN. 323 §1. Clerics, who are also called sacred ministers, are Christian faithful who, chosen by the competent ecclesiastical authority, by means of a gift of the Holy Spirit received in sacred ordination, are deputed to be ministers of the Church, participating in the mission and power of Christ the Pastor.

§2. By reason of sacred ordination, by divine institution clerics are distinguished from the other Christian faithful.

CAN. 324 Clerics, joined among themselves in hierarchical communion and constituted in various degrees, participate in various ways in the one divinely instituted ecclesiastical ministry.

CAN. 325 By reason of sacred ordination clerics are distinguished as bishops, presbyters and deacons.

CAN. 326 Clerics are constituted in the degrees of orders by sacred ordination itself; but they cannot exercise their power except in accord with the norm of law.

CAN. 327 If besides bishops, presbyters or

CAN. 323 §1. Clerici, qui etiam ministri sacri vocantur, sunt christifideles, qui ab auctoritate competenti ecclesiastica electi per donum Spiritus Sancti in sacra ordinatione receptum deputantur, ut in Christi Pastoris missione et potestate partem habentes Ecclesiae sint ministri.

§2. Ratione sacrae ordinationis clerici ex divina institutione a ceteris christifidelibus distinguuntur.

CAN. 324 Clerici inter se communione hierarchica iuncti et in variis gradibus constituti unum ministerium ecclesiasticum divinitus institutum diversimode participant.

CAN. 325 Clerici ratione sacrae ordinationis distinguuntur in Episcopos, presbyteros et diaconos.

CAN. 326 Clerici in gradibus ordinis ipsa sacra ordinatione constituuntur; potestatem autem exercere non possunt nisi ad normam iuris.

CAN. 327 Si praeter Episcopos, pres-

323 §1: Pius XII, m.p. *Cleri sanctitati*, 2 iun. 1957, can. 38 §1 n. 1; Vat. II, decr. *Presbyterorum ordinis*, 2 "Idem," 7 "Presbyteri omnes," 12 "Sacramenta;" const. *Lumen gentium*, 10 "Sacerdotium," 29 "In gradu."

323 §2: Vat. II, const. *Lumen gentium*, 32 "Si igitur," 10 "Sacerdotium," 20, 31 "Nomine;" Pius XII, m.p. *Cleri sanctitati*, 2 iun. 1957, can. 38 §1 n. 2. - S. Clemens I, ep. *Ecclesia Dei*, a. c. 96, "Cum igitur;" Trid., sess. XXIII, *De ordine*, cap. 4, can. 4.

324: Vat. II, const. *Lumen gentium*, 28 "Christus" et "Presbyteri," 29 "In gradu;" decr. *Presbyterorum ordinis*, 2 "Officium," 7 "Presbyteri omnes."

325: Pius XII, m.p. *Cleri sanctitati*, 2 iun. 1957, can. 38 §3; Vat. II, const. *Lumen gentium*, 28 "Christus." - S. Clemens I, ep. *Ecclesia Dei*, a. c. 96, "Apos-

toli nobis;" Trid., sess. XXIII, *De ordine*, cap. 4, cann. 2, 6–7.

326: Pius XII, m.p. *Cleri sanctitati*, 2 iun. 1957, can. 39; Vat. II, const. *Lumen gentium*, 22 "Sicut," 29 "In gradu;" decr. *Presbyterorum ordinis*, 2 "Officium," 8 "Presbyteri." - Nic. II, can. 14; S. Tarasius CP., ep. ad Epp. Siciliae; Trid., sess. XXIII, *De ordine*, cap. 4, can. 7.

327: Pius XII, m.p. *Cleri sanctitati*, 2 iun. 1957, can. 40. * Syn. Zamosten. Ruthenorum, a. 1720, tit. III, §7 "Quoniam;" Syn. Libanen. Maronitarum, a. 1736, pars III, cap. II, 1; Syn. prov. Alba-Iulien. et Fagarasien. Rumenorum, a. 1872, tit. V, cap. 7 "Ordinum;" Syn. Sciarfen. Syrorum, a. 1888, cap. V, art. XIII, §1, 5; Syn. Alexandrin. Coptorum, a. 1898, sect. II, cap. III, art. VII, §1, 5; Syn Armen., a. 1911, 515–519.

deacons, other ministers also, constituted in minor orders and generally called minor clerics, are admitted or instituted for the service of the people of God or to exercise functions of the sacred liturgy, they are governed only by the particular law of the proper Church *sui iuris*.

byteros vel diaconos alii etiam ministri in ordine minore constituti et generatim clerici minores vocati ad populi Dei servitium vel ad functiones sacrae liturgiae exercendas admittuntur vel instituuntur, iidem reguntur tantum iure particulari propriae Ecclesiae sui iuris.

CHAPTER I. The Formation of Clerics

CAN. 328 It is the proper right and obligation of the Church to form clerics and its other ministers; this obligation is fulfilled in a particular way and most directly in the erection and governance of seminaries.

CAN. 329 §1. The task of fostering vocations, especially to the sacred ministries, belongs to the whole Christian community, which, given its co-responsibility, must be solicitous for the needs of ministry of the entire Church:

1° parents, teachers and other primary educators of Christian life are to take care that families and schools are so animated by the spirit of the gospel that boys and young men can freely hear and respond willingly to the Lord who calls them by means of the Holy Spirit;

2° clerics, especially pastors, are to strive to discern and foster vocations both in adolescents and in others, even of a more advanced age;

3° it is especially for the eparchial bishop, joining forces with other hierarchs, to stir up his flock in promoting vocations and coordinating initiatives.

§2. Particular law is to provide that either re-

CAPUT I. De Institutione Clericorum

CAN. 328 Ecclesiae proprium ius et obligatio est clericos aliosque suos ministros instituendi; quae obligatio singulariter et impensius exercetur seminariis erigendis et regendis.

CAN. 329 §1. Opus fovendarum vocationum praesertim ad ministeria sacra ad totam communitatem christianam pertinet, quae pro sua corresponsabilitate sollicita sit oportet de necessitatibus ministerii universae Ecclesiae:

1° curent parentes, magistri aliique vitae christianae primi educatores, ut familiis et scholis spiritu evangelico animatis pueri et iuvenes Dominum per Spiritum Sanctum vocantem libere auscultare eique libenter respondere possint;

2° clerici, imprimis parochi, studeant vocationes sive in adulescentibus sive in aliis, etiam provectioris aetatis, dignoscere atque fovere;

3° Episcopi eparchialis praecipue est coniunctis viribus cum aliis Hierarchis in vocationibus provehendis gregem suum excitare inceptaque coordinare.

§2. Iure particulari provideatur, ut opera

328: Pius IX, *Syllabus errorum*, a. 1864, prop. 45–46; Vat. II, decr. *Optatam totius*, prooem., 1; S.C. de Sem. et Stud. Univ., ep. 14 maii 1965; Ioannes Paulus II, ep. *Magnus dies*, 8 apr. 1979, "Eadem."
329 §1: Vat. II, decr. *Optatam totius*, 2; decr. *Presbyterorum ordinis*, 11 "Pastor."
329 §1, 1°: Vat. II, decr. *Optatam totius*, 2 "Foven-

darum;" decr. *Apostolicam actuositatem*, 11 "Cum."
329 §1, 2°: Vat. II, decr. *Optatam totius*, 2 "Fovendarum;" decr. *Presbyterorum ordinis*, 11 "Pastor."
329 §1, 3°: Vat. II, decr. *Optatam totius*, 2 "Episcoporum;" decr. *Christus Dominus*, 15 "Quae."
329 §2: Vat. II, decr. *Optatam totius*, 2 "Opus;" decr. *Presbyterorum ordinis*, 11 "Ipsis."

gional or, in so far as is possible, eparchial projects for promoting vocations are instituted in
all Churches; these projects must be open to the
needs of the entire Church, especially missionary needs.

CAN. 330 §1. It is for the synod of bishops
of the patriarchal Church or council of hierarchs to issue a program of formation of clerics,
in which the common law must be set forth in
a more detailed manner for seminaries located
within the territorial boundaries of its own
Church. In other cases it is for the eparchial
bishop to develop this type of program for his
own eparchy, without prejudice to can. 150, §3.
It is also up to the same authorities to modify
this program.

§2. The formation program can, by common
agreement, be common to an entire region or
nation or even with other Churches *sui iuris,*
provided care is taken that it is not detrimental
to the specific character of the rites.

§3. Faithfully observing common law and
taking into account the tradition of its own
Church *sui iuris,* the formation program of clerics is to include, in addition to others, more
specific norms regarding the personal, spiritual, doctrinal and pastoral formation of students
as well as individual disciplines to be taught and
the curriculum of courses and examinations.

ART. I. *The Erection and Governance
of Seminaries*

CAN. 331 §1. In the minor seminary, those
who seem to show signs of a vocation to the sacred ministry are especially to be educated, so
that they can more easily and clearly discern it

ad vocationes provehendas sive regionalia
sive, quatenus fieri potest, eparchialia in omnibus Ecclesiis instituantur, quae aperta sint
oportet ad universae Ecclesiae necessitates,
praecipue missionales.

CAN. 330 §1. Synodi Episcoporum Ecclesiae patriarchalis vel Consilii Hierarcharum est edere rationem institutionis clericorum, qua ius commune pressius explicandum est pro seminariis intra fines territorii
propriae Ecclesiae sitis; in ceteris casibus
vero Episcopi eparchialis est conficere huius
generis rationem eparchiae suae propriam
firmo can. 150, §3; istarum auctoritatum est
rationem etiam immutare.

§2. Ratio institutionis clericorum potest
esse, conventionibus etiam initis, communis
toti regioni vel nationi vel immo aliis Ecclesiis sui iuris cauto, ne quid indoles rituum
detrimenti capiat.

§3. Ratio institutionis clericorum, iure
communi fideliter servato et prae oculis
habita traditione propriae Ecclesiae sui iuris,
comprehendat praeter alia normas magis
speciales circa formationem personalem,
spiritualem, doctrinalem et pastoralem alumnorum necnon circa singulas disciplinas
tradendas atque ordinationem cursuum et
examinum.

ART. I. *De Seminariis Erigendis
et Regendis*

CAN. 331 §1. In seminario minore instituuntur imprimis ii, qui indicia vocationis ad
ministeria sacra exhibere videntur, ut facilius
et clarius eam sibi dignoscere deditoque ani-

---

330 §1: Vat. II, decr. *Optatam totius,* 1.

331 §1: Vat. II, decr. *Optatam totius,* 3; Pius XII,
adh. ap. *Menti Nostrae,* 23 sep. 1950, III "Animad-
vertendum;" S.C. pro Inst. Cath., *Ratio fundamen-*

talis institutionis sacerdotalis, 6 ian. 1970, 11, 13, 18. *
Syn. Leopolien. Ruthenorum, a. 1891, tit. VIII, cap. I,
1–3; Syn. Armen., a. 1911, 701–702.

themselves and cultivate it with dedication; in accord with the norm of particular law, others also can be educated who, even though they do not seem to be called to the clerical state, can be educated to fulfill certain ministries or apostolic works. Other institutes which, according to their statutes, serve the same purposes, even if they differ in name, are equivalent to a minor seminary.

§2. In the major seminary the vocation of those who by certain signs are already considered suitable to assume the sacred ministries permanently is more intensely cultivated, proven and confirmed.

CAN. 332 §1. A minor seminary should be erected in each eparchy if the good of the Church requires it and the personnel and financial resources permit it.

§2. A major seminary must be erected that serves either one very large eparchy or, if not a whole Church *sui iuris,* at least, by agreement, several eparchies of the same Church *sui iuris,* or even of different Churches *sui iuris* that have an eparchy in the same region or nation so that, whether by the appropriate number of students or the number of properly qualified moderators and teachers, as well as by sufficient material resources, and the best combined efforts, formation is provided for which nothing is left wanting.

CAN. 333 Even if it is preferable that a seminary, especially minor seminaries, be re-

mo excolere possint; ad normam iuris particularis institui etiam possunt ii, qui, etsi ad statum clericalem vocati non videntur, ad quaedam ministeria vel opera apostolatus implenda formari possunt. Alia vero instituta, quae ex propriis statutis eisdem finibus inserviunt, etsi nomine differunt, seminario minore aequiparantur.

§2. In seminario maiore plenius excolitur, probatur atque confirmatur vocatio eorum, qui certis signis idonei iam aestimantur ad ministeria sacra stabiliter suscipienda.

CAN. 332 §1. Seminarium minus erigatur in unaquaque eparchia, si id postulat bonum Ecclesiae et vires opesque sinunt.

§2. Erigendum est seminarium maius, quod inserviat aut uni amplissimae eparchiae aut, si non toti Ecclesiae sui iuris, saltem conventionibus initis pluribus eparchiis eiusdem Ecclesiae sui iuris, immo et diversarum Ecclesiarum sui iuris, quae in eadem regione vel natione eparchiam habent, ita, ut tum congruo alumnorum numero tum ea, qua par est, moderatorum ac magistrorum probe paratorum copia necnon subsidiis sufficientibus optimisque viribus coniunctis institutioni provideatur, cui nihil desideratur.

CAN. 333 Etsi optandum est, ut alumnis unius Ecclesiae sui iuris seminarium,

---

331 §2: Vat. II, decr. *Optatam totius,* 4; S.C. pro Inst. Cath., *Ratio fundamentalis institutionis sacerdotalis,* 6 ian. 1970, 20.

332 §1: * Syn. Leopolien. Ruthenorum, a. 1891, tit. VIII, cap. I, 1.

332 §2: Vat. II, decr. *Optatam totius,* 4, 7; S.C. pro Inst. Cath., *Ratio fundamentalis institutionis sacerdotalis,* 6 ian. 1970, 21; S.C. pro Eccl. Orient., decr. 1 mar. 1929, art. 11; decr. 24 maii 1930, artt. 11–13. * Syn. Zamosten. Ruthenorum, a. 1720, tit. XV; Syn. Liba-

nen. Maronitarum, a. 1736, pars IV, cap. VI, 2, II; Syn. Ain-Trazen. Graeco-Melchitarum, a. 1835, can. 20; Syn. prov. Alba-Iulien. et Fagarasien. Rumenorum, a. 1872, tit. IX, cap. I; Syn. Sciarfen. Syrorum, a. 1888, cap. XIX, art. 1; Syn. Alexandrin. Coptorum, a. 1898, sect. II, cap. III, art. VII, §2, 5; Syn. Leopolien. Ruthenorum, a. 1891, tit. VIII, cap. II, 1–3.

333: * Syn. Libanen. Maronitarum, a. 1736, pars IV, VI, 6, VIII.

served to students of one Church *sui iuris,* on account of special circumstances, students of another Church *sui iuris* can be admitted into the same seminary.

CAN. 334 §1. A seminary is erected by the eparchial bishop for his own eparchy; a seminary common to different eparchies is erected by the eparchial bishops of the same eparchies or by a higher authority, however, with the consent of the council of hierarchs if it is the case of a metropolitan of a metropolitan Church *sui iuris* or with the consent of the synod of bishops of the patriarchal Church if it is a patriarch.

§2. Eparchial bishops, for whose subjects a common seminary was erected, cannot validly erect another seminary without the consent of the authority that erected the common seminary, or, if it concerns a seminary erected by the eparchial bishops themselves, without the unanimous consent of the parties of the agreement or without the consent of the higher authority.

CAN. 335 §1. A legitimately erected seminary is by the law itself a juridic person.

§2. In all juridical matters the rector of the seminary represents it, unless particular law or the statutes of the seminary establish otherwise.

CAN. 336 §1. A seminary common to different eparchies is subject to the hierarch designated by those who erected the seminary.

§2. The seminary is exempt from parochial governance. The rector of the seminary or his delegate fulfills the office of pastor for those who are in the seminary, except for matrimonial matters and with due regard for can. 734.

CAN. 337 §1. A seminary should have its

praecipue minus, reservetur, ob speciales circumstantias in idem seminarium alumni etiam aliarum Ecclesiarum sui iuris admitti possunt.

CAN. 334 §1. Seminarium pro propria eparchia erigitur ab Episcopo eparchiali; seminarium pluribus eparchiis commune ab Episcopis eparchialibus earundem eparchiarum vel ab auctoritate superiore, tamen de consensu Consilii Hierarcharum, si de Metropolita Ecclesiae metropolitanae sui iuris agitur, aut de consensu Synodi Episcoporum Ecclesiae patriarchalis, si de Patriarcha.

§2. Episcopi eparchiales, pro quorum subditis seminarium commune erectum est, non possunt aliud seminarium valide erigere sine consensu auctoritatis, quae seminarium commune erexit, aut, si de seminario ab ipsis Episcopis eparchialibus erecto agitur, sine unanimi consensu partium convenientium vel sine consensu auctoritatis superioris.

CAN. 335 §1. Seminarium legitime erectum ipso iure persona iuridica est.

§2. In omnibus negotiis iuridicis rector seminarii eiusdem personam gerit, nisi ius particulare vel statuta seminarii aliud statuunt.

CAN. 336 §1. Seminarium pluribus eparchiis commune subiectum est Hierarchae designato ab eis, qui seminarium erexerunt.

§2. Exemptum a regimine paroeciali seminarium est; pro omnibus, qui in seminario sunt, parochi officium, excepta materia matrimoniali et firmo can. 734, impleat rector seminarii eiusve delegatus.

CAN. 337 §1. Seminarium propria

334 §1: Vat. II, decr. *Optatam totius,* 7.

own statutes, in which are determined first of all the specific purpose of the seminary and the competence of the authorities. Furthermore, the statutes are to establish the manner of appointment or election, term in office, rights and obligations and the just remuneration of the moderators, officials, teachers and counselors as well as methods by which they and even the students participate in the concerns of the rector especially in the observance of the seminary discipline.

§2. The seminary should also have its own directory in which the norms of the program of formation of clerics are applied to the special circumstances of the seminary and in which the most important points of seminary discipline, with due regard for the statutes, concerning the formation of students as well as the daily routine and ordering of the entire seminary, are defined in greater detail.

§3. The statutes of the seminary need the approval of the authority that erected the seminary and that is also competent, in case of necessity, to modify them. Regarding the directory, these prerogatives pertain to the authority determined in the statutes.

CAN. 338   §1. In every seminary there is to be a rector, and if the case warrants, a finance officer and other moderators and officials.

§2. In accord with the norm of the statutes, overall governance of the seminary is the responsibility of the rector. It is for him to enforce the observance of the statutes and the seminary directory by every one, to coordinate the works

statuta habeat, in quibus determinentur imprimis finis specialis seminarii et competentia auctoritatum; statuantur praeterea modus nominationis vel electionis, duratio in officio, iura et obligationes atque iusta remuneratio moderatorum, officialium et magistrorum ac consiliorum necnon rationes, quibus ipsi immo et alumni curam rectoris in disciplina seminarii praesertim servanda participent.

§2. Seminarium habeat quoque proprium directorium, quo normae rationis institutionis clericorum adiunctis specialibus accommodatae in effectum ducantur necnon pressius determinentur potiora disciplinae seminarii capita, quae firmis statutis ad institutionem alumnorum ac vitam cottidianam totiusque seminarii ordinem spectant.

§3. Statuta seminarii approbatione indigent auctoritatis, quae seminarium erexit cuique etiam competit, si casus fert, ea mutare; haec circa directorium spectant ad auctoritatem in statutis determinatam.

CAN. 338   §1. In quolibet seminario habeantur rector et, si casus fert, oeconomus aliique moderatores et officiales.

§2. Rectoris est ad normam statutorum moderamen generale seminarii curare, statutis et directorio seminarii ab omnibus observandis instare, opera aliorum moderatorum et officialium coordinare totiusque

---

337 §2: S.C. pro Inst. Cath., *Ratio fundamentalis institutionis sacerdotalis,* 6 ian. 1970, 25.

337 §3: S.C. pro Inst. Cath., *Ratio fundamentalis institutionis sacerdotalis,* 6 ian. 1970, 25.

338 §1: S.C. pro Inst. Cath., *Ratio fundamentalis institutionis sacerdotalis,* 6 ian. 1970, 27–28; Vat. II, decr. *Optatam totius,* 5. * Syn. prov. Alba-Iulien. et

Fagarasien. Rumenorum, a. 1872, tit. IX, cap. I; Syn. Sciarfen. Syrorum, a. 1888, cap. XIX, art. I "Committi;" Syn. Leopolien. Ruthenorum, a. 1891, tit. VIII, cap. II, 3–8; Syn. Armen., a. 1911, 707–708.

338 §2: S.C. pro Inst. Cath., *Ratio fundamentalis institutionis sacerdotalis,* 6 ian. 1970, 29.

of other moderators and officials, and to foster the unity and collaboration of the whole seminary.

CAN. 339 §1. There is also to be at least one spiritual father, distinct from the rector; the students can also freely go to any other presbyter approved by the rector for their spiritual direction.

§2. Besides the ordinary confessors, other confessors are to be designated or invited, keeping intact the right of the students to go to any confessor, even outside the seminary, without prejudice to the discipline of the seminary.

§3. In making judgments about persons it is not permitted to ask for the opinion of confessors or spiritual fathers.

CAN. 340 §1. If courses for teaching the disciplines are set up in the seminary itself, there must be an adequate number of teachers properly selected and truly expert in their own science and, in major seminaries, possessing appropriate academic degrees.

§2. The teachers should update regularly their professional preparation. Cooperating harmoniously among themselves and with the moderators of the seminary, they are to serve the goal of an integrated formation of the future ministers of the Church, while aiming at the unity of faith and of formation among the varieties of disciplines.

§3. Teachers of the sacred sciences, following the footsteps of the holy fathers and particular-

seminarii unitatem ac collaborationem fovere.

CAN. 339 §1. Assit quoque saltem unus pater spiritualis a rectore distinctus, praeter quem alumni quemlibet alium presbyterum a rectore ad eorundem directionem spiritualem approbatum libere petere possunt.

§2. Praeter confessarios ordinarios alii quoque confessarii sint designati vel invitati integro alumnorum iure quemlibet confessarium, etiam extra seminarium, salva disciplina seminarii petendi.

§3. In iudicandis personis non licet confessariorum vel patrum spiritualium votum exquirere.

CAN. 340 §1. Si cursus tradendarum disciplinarum in ipso seminario instituuntur, assit congruus numerus magistrorum apte selectorum in sua quisque scientia vere peritorum, in seminario maiore quidem congruis gradibus academicis ornatorum.

§2. Praeparatione propria constanter ad diem perducta magistri conferant inter se et cum seminarii moderatoribus concorditer cooperantes ad integram futurorum Ecclesiae ministrorum institutionem, inter varietates disciplinarum unitati fidei ac formationi intenti.

§3. Magistri scientiarum sacrarum vestigia sanctorum Patrum ac ab Ecclesia col-

339 §1: S.C. pro Inst. Cath., *Ratio fundamentalis institutionis sacerdotalis,* 6 ian. 1970, 27, 55. * Syn. Monast. SS. Salvatoris, Melchitarum, a. 1811, 2, pars II, cap. V, reg. I; Syn. prov. Alba-Iulien. et Fagarasien. Rumenorum, a. 1872, tit. IX, cap. I; Syn. Sciarfen. Syrorum, a. 1888, cap. XIX, art. I "Committi;" Syn. Leopolien. Ruthenorum, a. 1891, tit. VIII, cap. II, 4; Syn. Armen., a. 1911, 708.

339 §2: S.C. pro Inst. Cath., *Ratio fundamentalis institutionis sacerdotalis,* 6 ian. 1970, 55.

339 §3: Pius XI, litt. encycl. *Ad catholici sacerdotii,* 20 dec. 1935, III "Neque."

340 §1: Vat. II, decr. *Optatam totius,* 5 "Cum;" S.C. pro Inst. Cath., *Ratio fundamentalis institutionis sacerdotalis,* 6 ian. 1970, 32–34. * Syn. prov. Alba-Iulien. et Fagarasien. Rumenorum, a. 1872, tit. IX, cap. I; Syn. Leopolien. Ruthenorum, a. 1891, tit. VIII, cap. II, 6; Syn. Armen., a. 1911, 709.

340 §2: S.C. pro Inst. Cath., *Ratio fundamentalis institutionis sacerdotalis,* 6 ian. 1970, 36, 38, 90.

ly the doctors of the East highly praised by the Church, are to strive to illustrate doctrine from the magnificent treasure handed down by them.

CAN. 341 §1. It is for the authority that erected the seminary to take care to provide for the expenses of the seminary even by taxes and offerings mentioned in cann. 1012 and 1014.

§2. Religious houses are also subject to the seminary tax unless their only support comes from alms or they actually have a study center mentioned in cann. 471, §2 and 536, §2.

laudatorum Doctorum praesertim Orientis secuti ex praeclaro thesauro ab eisdem tradito doctrinam illustrare nitantur.

CAN. 341 §1. Auctoritatis, quae seminarium erexit, est curare, ut provideatur seminarii expensis etiam per tributa vel oblationes, de quibus in cann. 1012 et 1014.

§2. Tributo pro seminario obnoxiae sunt etiam domus religiosorum, nisi solis eleemosynis sustentantur aut in eis sedes studiorum, de qua in cann. 471, §2 et 536, §2, actu habetur.

ART. II. *Formation for Ministry*

CAN. 342 §1. Only those students are to be admitted into the seminary who, from documents required by the norms of the statutes, are found to be qualified.

§2. No one is to be received unless it is certainly established that he has received the sacraments of baptism and chrismation with holy myron.

§3. Those who previously were students in another seminary or in some religious institute or society of common life in the manner of religious are not to be admitted before having obtained the testimony of the rector or the superior, especially regarding the reason for dismissal or departure.

CAN. 343 Students, even if admitted into a seminary of another Church *sui iuris* or into a common seminary for several Churches *sui iuris,* are to be formed in their own rite; any contrary custom being reprobated.

CAN. 344 §1. Adolescents and young men living in a minor seminary are to have appro-

ART. II. *De Institutione ad Ministeria*

CAN. 342 §1. Ii tantum in seminarium admittantur alumni, qui probantur ex documentis ad normam statutorum requisitis habiles esse.

§2. Nemo recipiatur, nisi certo constat de susceptis sacramentis baptismi et chrismationis sancti myri.

§3. Qui antea in alio seminario vel in aliquo instituto religioso vel societate viate communis ad instar religiosorum alumni fuerunt, ne admittantur nisi obtento testimonio rectoris aut Superioris praesertim de causa dimissionis vel discessus.

CAN. 343 Alumni, etsi in seminarium alterius Ecclesiae sui iuris vel plurium Ecclesiarum sui iuris commune admissi, proprio ritu instituantur reprobata contraria consuetudine.

CAN. 344 §1. Adulescentes et iuvenes in seminario minore degentes congruentem

342 §1: Vat. II, decr. *Optatam totius,* 6; S.C.S. Off., monitum, 15 iul. 1961, 4; S.C. pro Inst. Cath., *Ratio fundamentalis institutionis sacerdotalis,* 6 ian. 1970, 11, 39.

344 §1: Vat. II, decr. *Optatam totius,* 3; S.C. pro Inst. Cath., *Ratio fundamentalis institutionis sacerdotalis,* 6 ian. 1970, 12–13.

priate relationships with their families and peers which they need for sound psychological, particularly emotional, development; however, they are carefully to avoid all things that, according to sound psychological and pedagogical norms, can diminish in any way the free choice of a state of life.

§2. Students, assisted by suitable spiritual direction, are to be trained in making personal and responsible decisions in the light of the gospel and for cultivating continually the various gifts of their talents, not omitting any appropriate virtues of human nature.

§3. The curriculum of a minor seminary is to include those studies required in each nation for beginning higher studies, and in so far as the program of studies permits, also those that are especially useful for undertaking the sacred ministry. Care is generally to be taken that students obtain a civil degree, so that their studies can be pursued somewhere else as well, if such happens to be their choice.

§4. Students more advanced in age are to be formed either in a seminary or a special institute, taking into account each one's earlier formation.

CAN. 345 The formation of students is to be completed in the major seminary, supplementing those things which, perhaps, in individual cases, were lacking in their formation in the minor seminary, by integrating the spiritual, intellectual and pastoral formation so that they may be effective ministers of Christ in the midst of the Church, light and salt for the contemporary world.

servent consuetudinem cum propriis familiis et coaetaneis, qua indigent ad sanam evolutionem psychologicam, praesertim affectivam; sedulo autem vitentur omnia, quae secundum sanas psychologiae et paedagogiae normas liberam electionem status quocumque modo minuere possunt.

§2. Apta directione spirituali adiuti assuescant alumni ad decisiones personales et responsabiles in luce Evangelii faciendas et ad suas varias ingenii dotes iugiter excolendas non praetermissis ullis virtutibus humanae naturae congruentibus.

§3. Curriculum studiorum seminarii minoris comprehendat ea, quae in unaquaque natione ad studia superiora incohanda requiruntur et, quatenus ratio studiorum permittit, etiam ea, quae praesertim ad ministeria sacra suscipienda utilia sunt; communiter curetur, ut alumni civilem studiorum titulum consequantur et perinde studia etiam alibi prosequi possint, si ad id eligendum perventum est.

§4. Alumni provectioris aetatis instituantur sive in seminario sive in instituto speciali ratione habita etiam praecedentis uniuscuiusque formationis.

CAN. 345 Institutio alumnorum in seminario maiore perficiatur suppletis eis, quae forte in singulis casibus institutioni seminario minori propriae defuerunt, formatione spirituali, intellectuali et pastorali inter se integrantibus ita, ut efficiantur ministri Christi in medio Ecclesiae, lux et sal mundi huius temporis.

344 §2: S.C. pro Inst. Cath., *Ratio fundamentalis institutionis sacerdotalis,* 6 ian. 1970, 14.

344 §3: S.C. pro Inst. Cath., *Ratio fundamentalis institutionis sacerdotalis,* 6 ian. 1970, 16, 67.

344 §4: Vat. II, decr. *Optatam totius,* 3 "Pari;" S.C. pro Inst. Cath., *Ratio fundamentalis institutionis sacerdotalis,* 6 ian. 1970, 19.

345: Vat. II, decr. *Optatam totius,* 4, 13.

CAN. 346 §1. Those aspiring to the sacred ministry are to be formed in such a way that they learn to cultivate in the Holy Spirit an intimate familiarity with Christ and to seek God in all things so that, impelled by the love of Christ the Pastor, they become solicitous to gain all people for the kingdom of God by the gift of their very lives.

§2. Day by day let them draw strength, especially from the word of God and the sacraments, for their spiritual life and strength for their work of apostolate:

1° through watchful and constant meditation on the word of God and by means of a faithful explanation of it according to the Fathers, let the students acquire the habit of configuring their lives ever more to the life of Christ; and, fortified in faith, hope and charity, let them train to live according to the pattern of the gospel;

2° let them participate assiduously in the Divine Liturgy in such a way that it may be the source and summit of the life of the seminary, as it is for all Christian life;

3° let them learn to celebrate constantly the divine praises according to their own rite and draw nourishment from it for their spiritual life;

4° having great regard for spiritual direction, let them learn how to examine their conscience rightly, and let them receive the sacrament of penance frequently;

5° let them venerate with filial piety Holy

CAN. 346 §1. Aspirantes ad ministeria sacra formentur, ut in Spiritu Sancto consortium familiare cum Christo colant et in omnibus Deum quaerant ita, ut Christi Pastoris caritate impulsi omnes homines dono suae ipsorum vitae regno Dei lucrifacere solliciti fiant.

§2. Ex verbo Dei et sacramentis imprimis vim pro sua vita spirituali et apostolico labore robur in dies hauriant:

1° verbi Dei vigili atque constanti meditatione et secundum Patres fideli illustratione assuescant alumni ad suam vitam magis vitae Christi configurandam et in fide, spe et caritate firmati se exerceant ad vivendum secundum formam Evangelii;

2° participent assidue Divinae Liturgiae, quae appareat et seminarii vitae, sicut est totius vitae christianae, fons et culmen;

3° laudes divinas iugiter celebrare secundum proprium ritum addiscant et ex eis vitam spiritualem alant;

4° directione spirituali magni habita addiscant conscientiam suam recte discutere et sacramentum paenitentiae frequenter suscipiant;

5° Sanctam Mariam semper Virginem,

---

346 §1: Vat. II, decr. *Optatam totius,* 8 "Institutio;" S.C. pro Inst. Cath., *Ratio fundamentalis institutionis sacerdotalis,* 6 ian. 1970, 44.

346 §2, 1°: Vat. II, decr. *Optatam totius,* 8 "Institutio." * Syn. Leopolien. Ruthenorum, a. 1891, tit. VIII, cap. II, 15.

346 §2, 2°: Vat. II, const. *Lumen gentium,* 11 "Indoles;" decr. *Optatam totius,* 8 "Institutio;" S.C. pro Inst. Cath., *Ratio fundamentalis institutionis sacerdotalis,* 6 ian. 1970, 52. * Syn. Sciarfen. Syrorum, a. 1888, cap. XIX, art. I "Horae;" Syn. Leopolien. Ruthenorum, a. 1891, tit. VIII, cap. II, 15.

346 §2, 3°: Vat. II, decr. *Optatam totius,* 8 "Institutio;" S.C. pro Inst. Cath., *Ratio fundamentalis institutionis sacerdotalis,* 6 ian. 1970, 53.

346 §2, 4°: S.C. pro Inst. Cath., *Ratio fundamentalis institutionis sacerdotalis,* 6 ian. 1970, 45, 55. * Syn. prov. Alba-Iulien. et Fagarasien. Rumenorum, a. 1872, tit. IX, cap. I "Ac in;" Monast. SS. Salvatoris, Melchitarum, a. 1811, 2, pars II, cap. V, reg. I.

346 §2, 5°: Vat. II, decr. *Optatam totius,* 8 "Institutio;" S.C. pro Inst. Cath., *Ratio fundamentalis institutionis sacerdotalis,* 6 ian. 1970, 54, e). * Syn. Leopolien. Ruthenorum, a. 1891, tit. VIII, cap. II, 15.

Mary, the ever virgin Mother of God, whom Christ has made Mother of all;

6° exercises of piety are to be cultivated that are helpful to the spirit of prayer and make for the strengthening and defense of an apostolic vocation, especially those exercises that are commended by the venerable tradition of their own Church *sui iuris;* likewise recommended are spiritual retreats, instruction concerning the sacred ministry, and exhortation about spiritual life;

7° the students are to be educated to have the sense of the Church and of its service as well as in the virtue of obedience and in fraternal co-operation;

8° they are to be helped also in cultivating all those other virtues that have great relevance to their vocation, such as discernment of spirits, chastity, fortitude; let them also esteem and cultivate those virtues that are most valued by people and commend the minister of Christ, among which are sincerity, a keen concern for justice, a spirit of poverty, fidelity to one's promises, good manners, modesty in conversation joined with charity.

§3. The disciplinary norms of the seminary are to be applied having regard for the maturity of the students so that, while they learn by degrees to direct themselves, they become accustomed to using their freedom wisely and acting voluntarily and diligently.

CAN. 347 Doctrinal instruction should be

Dei Matrem, quam Christus omnium hominum Matrem constituit, filiali pietate prosequantur;

6° foveantur quoque pietatis exercitia, quae ad spiritum orationis vocationisque apostolicae robur ac munimen conducunt, ea imprimis, quae a veneranda traditione propriae Ecclesiae sui iuris commendata sunt; utcumque suadetur recessus spiritualis et instructio de ministeriis sacris, exhortatio in via spiritus;

7° ad sensum Ecclesiae et servitii eius educantur alumni necnon ad virtutem oboedientiae et ad sociam cum fratribus cooperationem;

8° ad ceteras quoque virtutes, quae ad vocationem suam maxime conferunt, excolendas adiuventur sicut discretio spirituum, castitas, animi fortitudo; illas quoque virtutes aestiment atque excolant, quae inter homines pluris fiunt et Christi ministrum commendant, quarum sunt animi sinceritas, assidua iustitiae cura, spiritus paupertatis, in promissis servata fides, in agendo urbanitas, in colloquendo modestia cum caritate coniuncta.

§3. Disciplinares seminarii normae secundum alumnorum maturitatem ita applicentur, ut alumni, dum gradatim sibi moderari addiscunt, libertate sapienter uti, sponte et diligenter agere assuescant.

CAN. 347 Institutio doctrinalis eo ten-

346 §2, 6°: Vat. II, decr. *Optatam totius,* 8 "Enixe;" S.C. pro Inst. Cath., *Ratio fundamentalis institutionis sacerdotalis,* 6 ian. 1970, 54 "Quae," 56. * Syn. Sciarfen. Syrorum, a. 1888, cap. XIX, art. I "Horae;" Syn. Leopolien. Ruthenorum, a. 1891, tit. VIII, cap. II, 15.

346 §2, 7°: S.C. pro Inst. Cath., *Ratio fundamentalis institutionis sacerdotalis,* 6 ian. 1970, 47; Vat. II,

decr. *Optatam totius,* 9; decr. *Presbyterorum ordinis,* 8 "Presbyteri," 15.

346 §2, 8°: Vat. II, decr. *Optatam totius,* 11 "Christianae;" S.C. pro Inst. Cath. *Ratio fundamentalis institutionis sacerdotalis,* 6 ian. 1970, 50–51.

346 §3: Vat. II, decr. *Optatam totius,* 11 "Vitae."

347: S.C. pro Inst. Cath., *Ratio fundamentalis institutionis sacerdotalis,* 6 ian. 1970, 59.

taught so that the students, endowed with the general culture of the surroundings and times and investigating the undertakings and accomplishments of the human spirit, may acquire broad and solid doctrine in the sacred sciences, so that educated with a fuller understanding of the faith and strengthened in the light of Christ the Teacher, they may be able more effectively to illuminate the people of their time and to serve truth.

CAN. 348 §1. For those who are destined for the priesthood, the studies of the major seminary, with due regard for can. 345, are to comprise courses in philosophy and theology, which can be pursued either successively or conjointly. These studies are to encompass at least six complete years in such a way that two full years are devoted to the philosophical disciplines and four full years to theological studies.

§2. The philosophical-theological course should begin with an introduction into the mystery of Christ and the economy of salvation, taking into consideration the order or hierarchy of the truths of Catholic doctrine, and should not be concluded without showing the relationship between all the disciplines and their coherent composition.

CAN. 349 §1. Philosophical instruction must aim to complete a formation in the human sciences; therefore, having taken into account the wisdom both of the ancient and the recent ages, of the whole human family and especially of their own culture, the perennially valid philosophical patrimony is to be sought to be known.

dat, ut alumni cultura generali loci et temporis callentes ingeniique humani conata et peracta scrutantes amplam atque solidam doctrinam in scientiis sacris acquirant ita, ut fidei pleniore intellectu eruditi et firmati Christi Magistri luce homines sui temporis efficacius illuminare ac veritati inservire possint.

CAN. 348 §1. Pro eis, qui ad sacerdotium destinantur, studia seminarii maioris firmo can. 345 complectantur cursus philosophicos et theologicos, qui aut successive aut coniuncte peragi possunt; eadem studia completum saltem sexennium comprehendant ita quidem, ut tempus philosophicis disciplinis dedicatum integrum biennium, tempus vero studiis theologicis integrum quadriennium adaequet.

§2. Cursus philosophico-theologici initium sumant introductione in mysterium Christi et oeconomiam salutis nec concludantur, quin ostendatur ratione habita ordinis seu hierarchiae veritatum doctrinae catholicae omnium disciplinarum inter se relatio atque cohaerens compositio.

CAN. 349 §1. Philosophica institutio eo tendat, ut formationem in scientiis humanis perficiat; quare, ratione habita sapientiae tum antiquae tum recentis aetatis sive universae familiae humanae sive praesertim propriae culturae, quaeratur imprimis patrimonium philosophicum perenniter validum.

---

348 §1: S.C. pro Inst. Cath., *Ratio fundamentalis institutionis sacerdotalis,* 6 ian. 1970, 61, b)–c). * Syn. Armen., a. 1911, 711.

348 §2: Vat. II, decr. *Optatam totius,* 14; decr. *Unitatis redintegratio,* 11 "Insuper;" S.C. pro Inst.

Cath., *Ratio fundamentalis institutionis sacerdotalis,* 6 ian. 1970, 62, 90.

349 §1: Vat. II, decr. *Optatam totius,* 15 "Philosophicae;" S.C. pro Inst. Cath., *Ratio fundamentalis institutionis sacerdotalis,* 6 ian. 1970, 71.

§2. Historical and systematic courses are to be taught in such a way that students can easily discern truth and falsehood with a sharp intellectual discretion, can properly pursue theological investigations with a mind open to God who speaks, and be made better prepared for carrying out the ministry by a dialogue with the intellectuals of today.

CAN. 350 §1. Theological disciplines are to be taught in the light of faith in such a way that students deeply penetrate Catholic doctrine drawn from divine revelation and express it in their own culture so that it may be nourishment for their own spiritual life and a very useful instrument for more effectively exercising the ministry.

§2. It is necessary that Sacred Scripture be like the soul of all of theology, and must influence all sacred disciplines; therefore in addition to exegesis, an accurate methodology, the principal chapters of the economy of salvation as well as the principal themes of biblical theology are to be taught.

§3. Liturgy is to be taught, taking into account its special importance inasmuch as it is a necessary source of doctrine and of a truly Christian spirit.

§4. As long as the unity that Christ wished for His Church has not been fully realized, ecumenism is to be one of the necessary dimensions every theological discipline.

CAN. 351 Teachers of the sacred sciences,

§2. Cursus historici et systematici ita tradantur, ut alumni discretione intellectuali acuta vera et falsa facilius secernere possint et mente Deo loquenti aperta investigationes theologicas rite prosequi possint et aptiores fiant ad ministeria obeunda colloquio inito cum excultis quoque hominibus huius temporis.

CAN. 350 §1. Disciplinae theologicae in lumine fidei ita tradantur, ut alumni doctrinam catholicam ex divina Revelatione haustam profunde penetrent atque in sua cultura exprimant ita, ut sit et alimentum propriae vitae spiritualis et ad ministerium efficacius obeundum perutile instrumentum.

§2. Universae theologiae veluti anima sit oportet Sacra Scriptura, quae omnes disciplinas sacras informare debet; unde doceantur praeter exegeseos accuratam methodum capita oeconomiae salutis principalia necnon potiora themata theologiae biblicae.

§3. Liturgia edoceatur ratione habita eius specialis momenti utpote necessarius fons doctrinae et spiritus vere christiani.

§4. Donec unitas, quam Christus Ecclesiae suae vult, non plene in actum deducatur, oecumenismus sit una ex necessariis rationibus cuiuscumque disciplinae theologicae.

CAN. 351 Magistri scientiarum

349 §2: Vat. II, decr. *Optatam totius,* 15 "Philosophicae;" S.C. pro Inst. Cath., *Ratio fundamentalis institutionis sacerdotalis,* 6 ian. 1970, 70, 72.

350 §1: Vat. II, decr. *Optatam totius,* 16 "Disciplinae;" S.C. pro Inst. Cath., *Ratio fundamentalis institutionis sacerdotalis,* 6 ian. 1970, 76.

350 §2: Vat. II, decr. *Optatam totius,* 16 "Sacrae" et "Theologia;" S.C. pro Inst. Cath., *Ratio fundamentalis institutionis sacerdotalis,* 6 ian. 1970, 78.

- Pius XII, litt. encycl. *Divino afflante Spiritu,* 30 sep. 1943, II "Neminem."

350 §3: Vat. II, decr. *Optatam totius,* 16 "Item;" S.C. pro Inst. Cath., *Ratio fundamentalis institutionis sacerdotalis,* 6 ian. 1970, 79.

350 §4: Secret. ad Christ. Unit. Fov., *Directorium* II, 16 apr. 1970, 71.

351: S.C. pro Inst. Cath., *Ratio fundamentalis institutionis sacerdotalis,* 6 ian. 1970, 86–87.

since they teach with a mandate from the ecclesiastical authority, are faithfully to teach the doctrine proposed by it, and are to submit *(obsequuantur)* humbly in all things to the constant magisterium and supervision of the Church.

CAN. 352 §1. Pastoral formation is to be adapted according to the conditions of place and time, to the aptitude of the students whether celibate or married, and to the needs of the ministry for which they are preparing themselves.

§2. Students are to be instructed especially in the catechetical and homiletic arts, liturgical celebration, parochial administration, dialogue of evangelization with non-believers or non-Christians, or with the less fervent Christian faithful, the social apostolate and the instruments of social communication, not neglecting auxiliary disciplines such as psychology and pastoral sociology.

§3. Even though students are preparing themselves for the ministry in their own Church *sui iuris*, they are to be formed in a truly universal spirit by which they are internally prepared to respond in the service of souls everywhere in the world. Therefore, they are to be instructed about the needs of the entire Church and especially about the apostolate of ecumenism and evangelization.

CAN. 353 In accord with the norm of particular law, there are to be exercises and experiences that reinforce pastoral formation, in areas

sacrarum, cum de mandato auctoritatis ecclesiasticae doceant, doctrinam ab ipsa propositam fideliter tradant et in omnibus magisterio constanti ac moderationi Ecclesiae humiliter obsequantur.

CAN. 352 §1. Formatio pastoralis aptanda est ad loci et temporis condiciones, ad dotes alumnorum sive caelibum sive coniugatorum et ad necessitates ministeriorum, ad quae se praeparant.

§2. Instituantur alumni imprimis in arte catechetica et homiletica, celebratione liturgica, administratione paroeciae, dialogo evangelizationis cum non credentibus vel non christianis vel christifidelibus minus fervidis, apostolatu sociali et instrumentorum communicationis socialis non posthabitis disciplinis auxiliaribus sicut psychologia et sociologia pastoralis.

§3. Etsi se praeparant alumni ad ministeria in propria Ecclesia sui iuris obeunda, ad spiritum vere universalem formentur, quo ubique terrarum in servitium animarum occurrere animo parati sint; edoceantur ideo de universae Ecclesiae necessitatibus et praesertim de apostolatu oecumenismi et evangelizationis.

CAN. 353 Habeantur ad normam iuris particularis exercitationes et probationes ad formationem praecipue pastoralem firman-

---

352 §1: S.C. pro Inst. Cath., *Ratio fundamentalis institutionis sacerdotalis,* 6 ian. 1970, 94, 79 "Theologia pastoralis;" Vat. II, decr. *Optatam totius,* 19.

352 §2: Vat. II, decr. *Optatam totius,* 19–20; S.C. pro Inst. Cath. *Ratio fundamentalis institutionis sacerdotalis,* 6 ian. 1970, 80, 94–96.

352 §3: Vat. II, decr. *Optatam totius,* 9, 20; decr. *Christus Dominus,* 6 "Quare;" decr. *Ad gentes,* 39

"Professores;" decr. *Presbyterorum ordinis,* 10 "Donum;" Pius XI, litt. encycl. *Rerum Orientalium,* 8 sep. 1928, "Quare;" S.C. de Sem. et Stud. Univ., litt. 28 aug. 1929; S.C. pro Inst. Cath., *Ratio fundamentalis institutionis sacerdotalis,* 6 ian. 1970, 80 "Sic."

353: Vat. II, decr. *Optatam totius,* 21; S.C. pro Inst. Cath., *Ratio fundamentalis institutionis sacerdotalis,* 6 ian. 1970, 42, 97–99.

such as social or charitable service, catechetical instruction, but especially in the pastoral internship during philosophical-theological formation, and in the diaconal internship before presbyteral ordination.

CAN. 354 The formation of deacons not destined for the priesthood is to be adapted specifically from the norms given above so that the curriculum of studies extends at least three years, keeping in mind the traditions of their own Church *sui iuris* concerning the service *(diaconia)* of the liturgy, the word and charity.

CAN. 355 Candidates for ordination are to be properly taught the obligations of clerics and led to accept and fulfill them magnanimously.

CAN. 356 §1. The rector is to send a report regarding the progress of the formation of the students each year to their respective eparchial bishop or, as the case may be, to their major superior; with regard to the status of the seminary, to those who erected it.

§2. The eparchial bishop or major superior is to visit the seminary frequently to look after the formation of his students, especially in the case of those who are to be promoted to sacred orders.

CHAPTER II. The Ascription of Clerics to an Eparchy

CAN. 357 §1. Every cleric must be ascribed as a cleric either to an eparchy, an exarchy, a religious institute or a society of common life in the manner of religious or to an institute or association that has obtained the right to ascribe

dam conferentes, sicut servitium sociale vel caritativum, institutio catechetica, praesertim vero tirocinium pastorale decursu formationis philosophico-theologicae et tirocinium diaconale ante ordinationem presbyteralem.

CAN. 354 Institutio diaconis ad sacerdotium non destinatis propria ex normis supra datis aptetur ita, ut curriculum studiorum saltem per triennium protrahatur prae oculis habitis propriae Ecclesiae sui iuris traditionibus de diaconia liturgiae, verbi et caritatis.

CAN. 355 Ordinandi debite edoceantur de obligationibus clericorum atque ad eas magno animo suscipiendas et implendas educentur.

CAN. 356 §1. Rector seminarii singulis annis relationem de profectu formationis alumnorum mittat ad eorundem Episcopum eparchialem aut, si casus fert, Superiorem maiorem; de statu autem seminarii ad eos, qui seminarium erexerunt.

§2. Episcopus eparchialis vel Superior maior suorum alumnorum formationi consulturi frequenter seminarium visitent, praesertim si agitur de promovendis ad ordines sacros.

CAPUT II. De Ascriptione Clericorum Alicui Eparchiae

CAN. 357 §1. Quilibet clericus debet esse ut clericus ascriptus aut alicui eparchiae aut exarchiae aut instituto religioso aut societati vitae communis ad instar religiosorum aut instituto vel consociationi, quae ius cleri-

355: Vat. II, decr. *Optatam totius,* 9 "De oneribus," 10; decr. *Presbyterorum ordinis,* 16; Paulus VI, litt. encycl. *Sacerdotalis caelibatus,* 24 iun. 1967, 69.

357 §1: Pius XII, m.p. *Cleri sanctitati,* 2 iun. 1957, can. 44. - Chalc. can. 6; Vat. II, decr. *Presbyterorum*

ordinis, 10 "Normae." * Syn. Libanen. Maronitarum, a. 1736, pars II, cap. XIV, 12; Syn. Sciarfen. Syrorum, a. 1888, cap. V, art. XIII, §3, 1, VI; cap. XI, art. III, 3; Syn. Alexandrin. Coptorum, a. 1898, sect. II, cap. III, art. VII, §4, V.

clerics either from the Apostolic See or, within the territorial boundaries of the Church over which he presides, from the patriarch with the consent of the permanent synod.

§2. What is established concerning the ascription of clerics to an eparchy and their dismissal from it, is also applicable, with due adaptations, to the other juridic persons mentioned above and also, if the particular law so states, to the patriarchal Church itself, unless the law has expressly provided otherwise.

CAN. 358 Through diaconal ordination, one is ascribed as a cleric to the eparchy for whose service he is ordained, unless in accord with the norm of particular law of his own Church *sui iuris*, he has already been ascribed to the same eparchy.

CAN. 359 For a cleric already ascribed to an eparchy to transfer validly to another eparchy, he must obtain from his eparchial bishop a dimissorial letter signed by the same and also a letter of ascription signed by the eparchial bishop of the eparchy in which he wishes to be ascribed.

CAN. 360 §1. Retaining his ascription, a cleric may move to another eparchy for a specified time, which is renewable more than once by means of a written agreement between both eparchial bishops in which the rights and obligations of the cleric or of the parties are determined.

§2. Five years after a legitimate move, a cleric is ascribed by virtue of the law itself in the

cos sibi ascribendi adepta sunt a Sede Apostolica vel intra fines territorii Ecclesiae, cui praeest, a Patriarcha de consensu Synodi permanentis.

§2. Quod de clericorum alicui eparchiae ascriptione et de dimissione ab ea statuitur, valet congrua congruis referendo etiam de aliis supra dictis personis iuridicis necnon iure particulari ita ferente de ipsa Ecclesia patriarchali, nisi aliter iure expresse cautum est.

CAN. 358 Per ordinationem diaconalem aliquis ut clericus ascribitur eparchiae, pro cuius servitio ordinatur, nisi ad normam iuris particularis propriae Ecclesiae sui iuris eidem eparchiae iam ascriptus est.

CAN. 359 Ut clericus alicui eparchiae iam ascriptus ad aliam eparchiam valide transire possit, a suo Episcopo eparchiali obtinere debet litteras dimissionis ab eodem subscriptas et pariter ab Episcopo eparchiali eparchiae, cui ascribi desiderat, litteras ascriptionis ab eodem subscriptas.

CAN. 360 §1. Transmigratio clerici in aliam eparchiam retenta ascriptione fit ad tempus determinatum, etiam pluries renovandum, per conventionem scripto factam inter utrosque Episcopos eparchiales, qua iura et obligationes clerici vel partium stabiliantur.

§2. Quinquennio elapso post legitimam transmigrationem clericus ipso iure eparchi-

---

357 §2: Pius XII, m.p. *Cleri sanctitati*, 2 iun. 1957, can. 52.

358: Pius XII, m.p. *Cleri sanctitati*, 2 iun. 1957, can. 45.

359: Pius XII, m.p. *Cleri sanctitati*, 2 iun. 1957, can. 47. - Nic. cann. 15–16; Chalc. cann. 5, 10, 20; Carth. cann. 54, 90; Quinisext. can. 17; Nic. II, cann. 10, 15; S. Leo M., litt. *Grato animo*, 6 ian. 446; litt. *Quanta fraternitati*, a. 446, "Alienum clericum." *

Syn. Libanen. Maronitarum, a. 1736, pars II, cap. XIV, 16–17; pars III, cap. IV, 24; Syn. Sciarfen. Syrorum, a. 1888, cap. IX, art. I, 16; cap. XI, art. III, 5, X; Syn. Armen., a. 1911, 541.

360 §1: Paulus VI, m.p. *Ecclesiae sanctae*, 6 aug. 1966, I, 3 §5.

360 §2: Paulus VI, m.p. *Ecclesiae sanctae*, 6 aug. 1966, I, 3 §5.

host eparchy, if, after his desire was manifested in writing to both eparchial bishops, it was not objected to by either of them in writing within four months.

CAN. 361 A cleric who is solicitous about the universal Church, chiefly for the sake of evangelization, is not to be denied a transfer or move to another eparchy suffering from a severe shortage of clerics, so long as he is prepared and suitable for carrying out the ministry there, unless there is a true need in his own eparchy or Church *sui iuris*.

CAN. 362 §1. For a just reason a cleric can be recalled from the other eparchy by his own eparchial bishop or returned by the hosting eparchial bishop, observing the agreements made as well as equity.

§2. One legitimately returning to his own eparchy from another does so without prejudice to and having preserved all of the rights that he would have had if he had exercised the sacred ministry there.

CAN. 363 The following cannot validly ascribe a cleric to an eparchy, dismiss him from it, or grant permission to the cleric to move outside of it:

1° the administrator of the patriarchal Church, without the consent of the permanent synod; the patriarchal exarch and the administrator of an eparchy without the consent of the patriarch;

2° in other cases, the administrator of an eparchy, unless the eparchial see has been vacant for a year, and then only with the consent of the college of eparchial consultors.

ae hospiti ascribitur, si huic voluntati eius utrique Episcopo eparchiali scripto manifestatae neuter intra quattuor menses scripto contradixit.

CAN. 361 Clerico praesertim evangelizationis causa universae Ecclesiae sollicito transitus vel transmigratio in aliam eparchiam gravi clericorum penuria laborantem, dummodo sit ad ministeria ibi peragenda paratus atque aptus, ne denegetur nisi ob veram necessitatem propriae eparchiae vel Ecclesiae sui iuris.

CAN. 362 §1. Iusta de causa clericus ex transmigratione revocari potest a proprio Episcopo eparchiali vel remitti ab Episcopo eparchiali hospite conventionibus initis necnon aequitate servatis.

§2. Ex transmigratione in propriam eparchiam legitime redeunti salva et tecta sint omnia iura, quae haberet, si in ea sacro ministerio addictus esset.

CAN. 363 Clericum eparchiae ascribere vel ab ea dimittere vel licentiam transmigrandi clerico concedere valide non possunt:

1° Administrator Ecclesiae patriarchalis sine consensu Synodi permanentis; Exarchus patriarchalis et Administrator eparchiae sine consensu Patriarchae;

2° in ceteris casibus Administrator eparchiae nisi post annum a sedis eparchialis vacatione et de consensu collegii consultorum eparchialium.

361: Paulus VI, m.p. *Ecclesiae sanctae,* 6 aug. 1966, I, 3 §2; Vat. II, decr. *Christus Dominus,* 6 "Quare;" decr. *Presbyterorum ordinis,* 10 "Donum."

362 §2: Paulus VI, m.p. *Ecclesiae sanctae,* 6 aug. 1966, I, 3 §4.

363, 1°: Pius XII, m.p. *Cleri sanctitati,* 2 iun. 1957, can. 48 n. 2.

363, 2°: Pius XII, m.p. *Cleri sanctitati,* 2 iun. 1957, can. 48 n. 3.

CAN. 364 The ascription of a cleric to some eparchy does not cease except by valid ascription to another eparchy or by loss of the clerical state.

CAN. 365 §1. For a licit transfer or move to another eparchy, just causes such as the advantage of the Church or the good of the cleric himself are required; however, permission is not to be denied except for serious reasons.

§2. If the particular law of the Church *sui iuris* so prescribes, it is also required for the licit transfer to an eparchy of another Church *sui iuris* that the eparchial bishop releasing the cleric obtain the consent of the authority determined by the same particular law.

CAN. 366 §1. The eparchial bishop is not to ascribe an extern cleric to his eparchy unless:

1° the needs or advantage of the eparchy require it;

2° he is convinced that the cleric has the aptitude to carry out the ministry, especially if the cleric came from another Church *sui iuris;*

3° he is convinced by a legitimate document that the cleric has obtained legitimate dismissal from his eparchy; and he has obtained from the dismissing eparchial bishop, secretly if appropriate, suitable testimonials concerning the background and morals of the cleric;

4° the cleric has declared in writing that he is devoting himself to service of the new eparchy in accord with the norm of law.

§2. The eparchial bishop is to inform the previous eparchial bishop about the completed ascription of the cleric into his eparchy as soon as possible.

CAN. 364 Ascriptio clerici alicui eparchiae non cessat nisi alteri eparchiae valida ascriptione vel amissione status clericalis.

CAN. 365 §1. Ad licitum transitum vel transmigrationem requiruntur iustae causae, quales sunt Ecclesiae utilitas vel bonum ipsius clerici; licentia autem ne denegetur nisi exstantibus gravibus causis.

§2. Iure particulari Ecclesiae sui iuris ita ferente ad licitum transitum ad eparchiam alterius Ecclesiae sui iuris requiritur etiam, ut Episcopus eparchialis clericum dimittens consensum auctoritatis ab eodem iure particulari determinatae obtineat.

CAN. 366 §1. Episcopus eparchialis suae eparchiae alienum clericum ne ascribat, nisi:

1° necessitates vel utilitas eparchiae id exigunt;

2° sibi constat de aptitudine clerici ad ministeria peragenda, praesertim si clericus ab alia Ecclesia sui iuris pervenit;

3° sibi ex legitimo documento constat de legitima dimissione ex eparchia et habet ab Episcopo eparchiali dimittente opportuna testimonia de curriculo vitae et moribus clerici, etiam, si opus est, sub secreto.

4° clericus scripto declaravit se novae eparchiae servitio devovere ad normam iuris.

§2. Episcopus eparchialis de peracta suae eparchiae ascriptione clerici priorem Episcopum eparchialem quam primum certiorem faciat.

364: Pius XII, m.p. *Cleri sanctitati*, 2 iun. 1957, can. 50.

365 §1: Pius XII, m.p. *Cleri sanctitati*, 2 iun. 1957, can. 50; Paulus VI, m.p. *Ecclesiae sanctae*, 6 aug.

1966, I, 3 §2; Vat. II, decr. *Presbyterorum ordinis*, 10; decr. *Christus Dominus*, 6. - Carth. can. 55.

366 §1: Pius XII, m.p. *Cleri sanctitati*, 2 iun. 1957, can. 51.

CHAPTER III. The Rights and Obligations of Clerics

CAN. 367 Clerics have as their first obligation to announce the Kingdom of God to all and to make manifest the love of God toward all humanity in the ministry of the word and sacraments and even in their whole lives, so that all, loving one another and loving God above all things, may be built up and increase in the Body of Christ which is the Church.

CAN. 368 Clerics are bound in a special manner to the perfection which Christ proposes to his disciples, since they are consecrated to God in a new way by sacred ordination, so that they may become more suitable instruments of Christ, the Eternal Priest, in the service of the people of God, and at the same time be exemplary models to the flock.

CAN. 369 §1. Clerics are to devote themselves daily to the reading and meditation of the word of God, so that having become faithful and attentive hearers of Christ, they can be true ministers of preaching. They are to be assiduous in prayer, in liturgical celebrations and especially in their devotion to the mystery of the Eucharist. They are daily to examine their con-

CAPUT III. De Iuribus et Obligationibus Clericorum

CAN. 367 Clerici primam habent obligationem Regnum Dei omnibus annuntiandi et amorem Dei erga homines in ministerio verbi et sacramentorum, immo et tota vita repraesentandi ita, ut omnes invicem et super omnia Deum diligentes in Corpus Christi, quod est Ecclesia, aedificentur atque crescant.

CAN. 368 Ad perfectionem, quam Christus suis discipulis proponit, speciali ratione tenentur clerici, cum Deo sacra ordinatione novo modo sint consecrati, ut Christi aeterni Sacerdotis in servitium populi Dei aptiora instrumenta efficiantur et simul sint gregi forma exemplaris.

CAN. 369 §1. Clerici in lectionem et meditationem verbi Dei cottidie incumbant ita, ut Christi auditores fideles atque attenti facti evadant veraces ministri praedicationis; in oratione, in celebrationibus liturgicis et praesertim in devotione erga mysterium Eucharistiae assidui sint; conscientiam suam cottidie discutiant et sacramentum paeniten-

---

367: Vat. II, decr. *Presbyterorum ordinis,* 4 "Populus;" Synodus Episcoporum, *Ultimis temporibus,* 30 nov. 1971, Descriptio Status Rerum, 6 "Sic mundus."

368: Vat. II, decr. *Presbyterorum ordinis,* 12 "Sacramento," 13 "Sanctitatem;" const. *Lumen gentium,* 28 "Christus," 41 "Gregis" et "Presbyteri;" Pius XII, m.p. *Cleri sanctitati,* 2 iun. 1957, can. 60. - S. Basilius M., can. 93; S. Tarasius CP., ep. ad Epp. Siciliae; Trid., sess. XIV, *De ref.,* prooem.; sess. XXII, *De ref.,* can. 1; S.C. de Prop. Fide, reg. (pro Sacerd. Coptis), 15 mar. 1790, XX; Pius IX, ep. encycl. *Amantissimus,* 8 apr. 1862, 5; Pius XI, litt. encycl. *Ad catholici sacerdotii fastigium,* 20 dec. 1935, II "Quamobrem." * Syn. Zamosten. Ruthenorum, a. 1720, tit. IV; Syn. Libanen. Maronitarum, a. 1736, pars III, cap. I, 14; Syn. Sciarfen. Syrorum, a. 1888, cap. VI, art. II; art. V, 3; Syn. Leopolien. Ruthenorum, a. 1891, tit. IX,

cap. II, 1; Syn. Armen., a. 1911, 714.

369 §1: Pius XII, m.p. *Cleri sanctitati,* 2 iun. 1957, can. 61; Vat. II, const. *Dei Verbum,* 25 "Quapropter;" decr. *Presbyterorum ordinis,* 12–14, 18; const. *Lumen gentium,* 41 "Presbyteri;" Synodus Episcoporum, *Ultimis temporibus,* 30 nov. 1971, Pars Altera, I, 3. - Benedictus XIV, const. *Etsi pastoralis,* 26 maii 1742, §VI, I; S.C. de Prop. Fide, decr. 13 apr. 1807, XIV. * Syn. Zamosten. Ruthenorum, a. 1720, tit. III, §5 "Ipsi;" Syn. prov. Alba-Iulien. et Fagarasien. Rumenorum, a. 1872, tit. VII, cap. II; Syn. Sciarfen. Syrorum, a. 1888, cap. VI, art. V, 2; Syn. Leopolien. Ruthenorum, a. 1891, tit. VII, cap. VI, 8; tit. IX, cap. II, 16–18; cap. III, 4; Syn. Alexandrin. Coptorum, a. 1898, sect. II, cap. III, art. VII, §6, 1, I; Syn. Armen., a. 1911, 474.

sciences and frequently receive the sacrament of penance. They are to honor Holy Mary, the ever Virgin Mother of God, and implore from her the grace of conforming themselves to her Son. They are to carry out the other pious exercises of their own Church *sui iuris.*

§2. They are to attach great importance to spiritual direction and to take time for spiritual retreats at the times established according to the prescriptions of the particular law.

CAN. 370 Clerics are bound by a special obligation to show reverence and obedience to the Roman Pontiff, the patriarch and the eparchial bishop.

CAN. 371 §1. Clerics have the right to obtain from their eparchial bishop, after the requirements of law have been satisfied, a certain office, ministry or function to be exercised in the service of the Church.

§2. Clerics must accept and faithfully carry out every office, ministry, or function committed to them by the competent authority whenever, in the judgment of this same authority, the needs of the Church require it.

§3. In order to be able exercise a civil profession, the permission of their own hierarch is required.

CAN. 372 §1. After completing the formation that is required for sacred orders, clerics are

tiae frequenter suscipiant; Sanctam Mariam semper Virginem, Dei Matrem colant et ab ea gratiam se conformandi eius Filio implorent aliaque propriae Ecclesiae sui iuris exercitia pietatis peragant.

§2. Directionem spiritualem magni faciant et statutis temporibus secundum iuris particularis praescripta recessibus spiritualibus vacent.

CAN. 370 Clerici speciali obligatione tenentur Romano Pontifici, Patriarchae et Episcopo eparchiali reverentiam et oboedientiam exhibendi.

CAN. 371 §1. Ius habent clerici obtinendi a proprio Episcopo eparchiali praemissis iure requisitis aliquod officium, ministerium vel munus in servitium Ecclesiae exercendum.

§2. Suscipiendum est clericis ac fideliter implendum omne officium, ministerium vel munus ab auctoritate competenti eis commissum, quandocumque id de eiusdem auctoritatis iudicio necessitates Ecclesiae exigunt.

§3. Ut vero professionem civilem exercere possint, requiritur licentia proprii Hierarchae.

CAN. 372 §1. Institutione, quae ad ordines sacros requiritur, peracta in scientias

---

369 §2: Pius XII, m.p. *Cleri sanctitati,* 2 iun. 1957, can. 62. - Pius XI, litt. encycl. *Ad catholici sacerdotii fastigium,* 20 dec. 1935, IV; Vat. II, decr. *Christus Dominus,* 16 "Solliciti;" decr. *Presbyterorum ordinis,* 18 "Ad suum." * Syn. Libanen. Maronitarum, a. 1736, pars III, cap. I, 16; Syn. prov. Alba-Iulien. et Fagarasien. Rumenorum, a. 1872, tit. VII, cap. II; Syn. Sciarfen. Syrorum, a. 1888, cap. VI, art. V, 1; cap. IX, art. I, 5; Syn. Leopolien. Ruthenorum, a. 1891, tit. IX, cap. II, 18; Syn. Alexandrin. Coptorum, a. 1898, sect. II, cap. III, art. VII, §6, 1, I.

370: Pius XII, m.p. *Cleri sanctitati,* 2 iun. 1957, can. 63; Vat. II, decr. *Presbyterorum ordinis,* 7 "Pres-

byteri autem." - Apost. cann. 31, 39, 55; Ant. can. 5; Laod. can. 56; Chalc. can. 8; Carth. can. 31. * Syn. Libanen. Maronitarum, a. 1736, pars III, cap. III, 1; Syn. Leopolien. Ruthenorum, a. 1891, tit. IX, cap. II, 10.

371 §2: Pius XII, m.p. *Cleri sanctitati,* 2 iun. 1957, can. 64. - S.C. pro Eccl. Orient., decr. 15 maii 1929, 20. * Syn. Armen., a. 1911, 734.

372 §1: Pius XII, m.p. *Cleri sanctitati,* 2 iun. 1957, can. 65 §1; Vat. II, decr. *Optatam totius,* 22; decr. *Presbyterorum ordinis,* 19 "Presbyteri." - Pius XI, litt. encycl. *Ad catholici sacerdotii fastigium,* 20 dec. 1935, II ab "Verumtamen;" S.C. pro Eccl. Orient., decr. 27

not to stop devoting attention to the sacred sciences. Indeed they are to strive to acquire a more profound and updated knowledge and use of them through formative courses approved by their own hierarch.

§2. They are to attend conferences that the hierarch has judged suitable for promoting the sacred sciences and pastoral affairs.

§3. Further, they are not to neglect to acquire for themselves as much knowledge of profane sciences, especially those sciences connected more intimately with the sacred sciences, which cultured persons ought to have.

CAN. 373 Clerical celibacy chosen for the sake of the kingdom of heaven and highly suited to the priesthood is to be greatly esteemed everywhere, according to the tradition of the entire Church; likewise, the state of married clerics, sanctioned in the practice of primitive Church and in the Eastern Churches through the ages, is to be held in honor.

CAN. 374 Clerics, celibate as well as mar-

sacras incumbere ne desinant clerici, immo profundiorem et ad diem accommodatam earundem cognitionem et usum acquirere satagant per cursus formativos a proprio Hierarcha approbatos.

§2. Frequentent quoque collationes, quas Hierarcha opportunas iudicavit ad scientias sacras et res pastorales promovendas.

§3. Scientiarum profanarum quoque, earum praesertim, quae cum scientiis sacris artius cohaereant, talem sibi copiam comparare ne neglegant, qualem excultos homines habere decet.

CAN. 373 Caelibatus clericorum propter regnum coelorum delectus et sacerdotio tam congruus ubique permagni faciendus est, prout fert universae Ecclesiae traditio; item status clericorum matrimonio iunctorum praxi Ecclesiae primaevae et Ecclesiarum orientalium per saecula sancitus in honore habendus est.

CAN. 374 Clerici caelibes et coniugati

ian. 1940. n. 13. * Syn. Libanen. Maronitarum, a. 1736, pars III, cap. I, 13; Syn. prov. Alba-Iulien. et Fagarasien. Rumenorum, a. 1872, tit. VII, cap. I; Syn. Sciarfen. Syrorum, a. 1888, cap. VI, art. VI; Syn. Leopolien. Ruthenorum, a. 1891, tit. IX, cap. III, 1–3, 7; Syn. Alexandrin. Coptorum, a. 1898, sect. II, cap. III, art. VII, §6, 1, III.

372 §2: Pius XII, m.p. *Cleri sanctitati,* 2 iun. 1957, can. 67 §§1–3; Vat. II, decr. *Christus Dominus,* 16 "Solliciti;" Paulus VI, m.p. *Ecclesiae sanctae,* 6 aug. 1966, 7 "Curent." * Syn. Sergii Patriarchae Maronitarum, 18 sep. 1596, can. V; Syn. Libanen. Maronitarum, a. 1736, pars I, cap. II, 6; Syn. prov. Alba-Iulien. et Fagarasien. Rumenorum, a. 1872, tit. VII, cap. II, b) "Eo;" Syn. Sciarfen. Syrorum, a. 1888, cap. 1888, cap. VI, art. VI, 3; Syn. Leopolien. Ruthenorum, a. 1891, tit. IX, cap. III, 9; Syn. Armen., a. 1911, 297.

372 §3: Pius XII, m.p. *Cleri sanctitati,* 2 iun. 1957, can. 65 §3; Vat. II, decr. *Presbyterorum ordinis,* 19 "Cum."

373: Pius XII, m.p. *Cleri sanctitati,* 2 iun. 1957, cann. 68, 71; Vat. II, decr. *Orientalium Ecclesiarum,* 17; decr. *Presbyterorum ordinis,* 16; Synodus Episcoporum, *Ultimis temporibus,* 30 nov. 1971, Pars Altera,

I, 4, c); Ioannes Paulus II, ep. *Novo incipiente,* 8 apr. 1979, 8. - Apost. can. 5; Carth. can. 3; Quinisext. cann. 3, 6, 13, 30; S. Cyrillus Alexandrin., can. 4; S. Nicephorus CP., can. 156; Innocentius III, litt. *Cum olim,* 5 sep. 1203; Benedictus XIV, ep. encycl. *Allatae sunt,* 26 iul. 1755, §22; S.C. de Prop. fide, litt. 4 iul. 1833, IX; instr. (ad Archiep. Fagarasien. et Alba-Iulien.), 15 mar. 1858; Pius XI, litt. encycl. *Ad catholici sacerdotii fastigium,* 20 dec. 1935, II, ab "Praeclarissimum." * Syn. Iosephi Patriarchae Maronitarum, 3 nov. 1596, can. II; Syn. Diamper. Syro-Malabarensium, a. 1599, CLXXIII–CLXXV; Syn. Libanen. Maronitarum, a. 1736, pars II, cap. XIV, 35; Syn. Monast. SS. Salvatoris, Melchitarum, a. 1811, 2, pars II, cap. I, reg. VI; pars III, cap. I, regg. III–IV, VI; Syn. prov. Alba-Iulien. et Fagarasien. Rumenorum, a. 1872, tit. VII, capp. III–IV; Syn. Sciarfen. Syrorum, a. 1888, cap. V, art. XIII, §5, 3; cap. VI, art. VII, 1–2; Syn. Armen., a. 1911, 737.

374: Pius XII, m.p. *Cleri sanctitati,* 2 iun. 1957, cann. 73–74. - Nic. I, can. 3; Quinisext. can. 5; Nic. II, can. 18; S. Basilius M., cann. 69, 88; S.C. de Prop. Fide, instr. (ad Archiep. Fagarasien. et Alba-Iulien. Graeci Ritus), 24 mar. 1858. * Rabbula, cann. 27, 29;

ried, should shine forth with the splendor of chastity; it is for particular law to establish suitable means to attain this end.

CAN. 375 Married clerics are to offer an outstanding example to other Christian faithful in conducting family life and in educating children.

CAN. 376 The praiseworthy common life among celibate clerics is to be fostered, insofar as possible, so that they may be mutually helped in cultivating the spiritual and intellectual life and may be able to collaborate more effectively in the ministry.

CAN. 377 All clerics must celebrate the divine praises according to the particular law of their own Church *sui iuris.*

CAN. 378 In accord with the norm of particular law, clerics are to celebrate the Divine Liturgy frequently, especially on Sundays and holy days of obligation; indeed daily celebration is strongly encouraged.

CAN. 379 Clerics, united by the bond of charity with their fellow brothers of whatever Church *sui iuris,* are to cooperate for the same purpose, namely, for the building up of the Body of Christ. Consequently, whatever their

castitatis decore elucere debent; iuris particularis est statuere opportuna media ad hunc finem assequendum adhibenda.

CAN. 375 In vita familiari ducenda atque filiis educandis clerici coniugati ceteris christifidelibus praeclarum exemplum praebeant.

CAN. 376 Vita communis inter clericos caelibes laudanda, quatenus fieri potest, foveatur, ut ipsi in vita spirituali et intellectuali colenda mutuo adiuventur et aptius in ministerio cooperari possint.

CAN. 377 Omnes clerici laudes divinas celebrare debent secundum ius particulare propriae Ecclesiae sui iuris.

CAN. 378 Divinam Liturgiam clerici frequenter ad normam iuris particularis celebrent praesertim diebus dominicis et festis de praecepto; immo enixe commendatur celebratio cottidiana.

CAN. 379 Clerici confratribus cuiuslibet Ecclesiae sui iuris vinculo caritatis uniti ad unum omnes conspirent, ad aedificationem nempe Corporis Christi, et proinde, cuiuscumque sunt condicionis, etsi diversis officiis

Syn. Zamosten. Ruthenorum, a. 1720, tit. X "A suspecta;" Syn. Libanen. Maronitarum, a. 1736, pars III, cap. I, 15; Syn. Ain-Trazen. Graeco-Melchitarum, a. 1835, can. 12; Syn. Sciarfen. Syrorum, a. 1888, cap. VI, art. III, 1–3; art. VII, 4; Syn. Leopolien. Ruthenorum, a. 1891, tit. IX, cap. II, 7–8; Syn. Alexandrin. Coptorum, a. 1898, sect. II, cap. III, art. VII, §6, 1, II.

375: Carth. cann. 15 "Et ut," 35.

376: Pius XII, m.p. *Cleri sanctitati,* 2 iun. 1957, can. 75; Vat. II, decr. *Presbyterorum ordinis,* 8 "Spiritu."

377: Pius XII, m.p. *Cleri sanctitati,* 2 iun. 1957, can. 76; Vat. II, decr. *Orientalium Ecclesiarum,* 22. - Laod. can. 18; Innocentius IV, ep. *Sub catholicae,* 6 mar. 1254, "Sacerdotes;" Benedictus XIV, const. *Etsi pastoralis,* 26 maii 1742, §VII, V; instr. *Eo quamvis tempore,* 4 maii 1745, §§42–45. * Syn. Mar Isaaci Chaldaeorum, a. 410, can. 15; Rabbula, can. 52; S. Nerses Glaien. Armenorum, a. 1166; Syn. Diamper.

Syro-Malabarensium, a. 1599, CLXIII–CLXV; Syn. Libanen. Maronitarum, a. 1736, pars II, cap. XIV, 34; pars III, cap. I, 13; Syn. prov. Alba-Iulien. et Fagarasien. Rumenorum, a. 1872, tit. VII, cap. II "Eo;" Syn. Sciarfen. Syrorum, a. 1888, cap. III, art. VI; cap. VI, art. IV; Syn. Leopolien. Ruthenorum, a. 1891, tit. IV, cap. III; Syn. Alexandrin. Coptorum, a. 1898, sect. II, cap. II, art. I; Syn. Armen., a. 1911, 740.

378: Vat. II, decr. *Presbyterorum ordinis,* 13 "Ut Sacrorum," 18 "Unionem;" decr. *Orientalium Ecclesiarum,* 15; Synodus Episcoporum, *Ultimis temporibus,* 30 nov. 1971, Pars Altera, I, 3 "Exemplo." - S. Basilius M., can. 94; Syn. Trid., sess. XXIII, *De ref.,* can. 14; S.C. de Prop. Fide, instr. 31 iul. 1902, 6. * Syn. Libanen. Maronitarum, a. 1736, pars III, cap. I, 13; Syn. Leopolien. Ruthenorum, a. 1891, tit. IX, cap. II, 16; Syn. Armen., a. 1911, 449, 739.

379: Vat. II, decr. *Presbyterorum ordinis,* 8 "Presbyteri."

condition, and though holding different offices, they are to cooperate among themselves and help one another.

CAN. 380 All clerics are to be solicitous in promoting vocations to the sacred ministry and for pursuing a life in institutes of consecrated life, not only by preaching, catechesis and other opportune means, but especially by the witness of life and ministry.

CAN. 381 §1. Clerics, enkindled with apostolic zeal, are to be an example to all in works of charity and hospitality especially toward the sick, the afflicted, the persecuted, the exiled and the refugees.

§2. Clerics, unless prevented by a just impediment, are bound by the obligation to provide assistance out of the spiritual goods of the Church, especially the word of God and the sacraments, to the Christian faithful, if they request it in an opportune manner, are properly disposed, and are not prohibited by law from receiving the sacraments.

§3. Clerics are to recognize and promote the dignity of lay persons and the specific role they have in the mission of the Church, especially by acknowledging the manifold charisms of lay persons and by directing their competence and experience for the good of the Church, especially in ways foreseen by the law.

CAN. 382 Clerics are to abstain completely from all those things unbecoming to their

fungentes, inter se cooperentur seque invicem adiuvent.

CAN. 380 Sollicitudinem habeant clerici omnes vocationes ad ministeria sacra et ad vitam in institutis vitae consecratae ducendam promovendi non solum praedicatione, catechesi aliisve opportunis mediis, sed imprimis vitae ac ministerii testimonio.

CAN. 381 §1. Zelo apostolico ardentes clerici omnibus exemplo sint in beneficentia et hospitalitate praesertim erga aegrotantes, afflictos, persecutionem patientes, exiliatos et profugos.

§2. Obligatione tenentur clerici, nisi iusto impedimento sunt detenti, suppeditandi ex spiritualibus Ecclesiae bonis verbi Dei praesertim et sacramentorum adiumenta christifidelibus, qui opportune petunt, rite sunt dispositi nec iure a sacramentis suscipiendis prohibentur.

§3. Clerici laicorum dignitatem atque propriam partem, quam in missione Ecclesiae habent, agnoscant et promoveant praesertim charismata laicorum multiformia probantes necnon competentiam et experientiam eorum in bonum Ecclesiae vertentes speciatim modis iure praevisis.

CAN. 382 Abstineant prorsus clerici ab eis omnibus, quae statum eorum secundum

380: Vat. II, decr. *Presbyterorum ordinis,* 11.

381 §1: Vat. II, decr. *Presbyterorum ordinis,* 8 "Spiritu."

381 §2: Vat. II, const. *Lumen gentium,* 37 "Laici;" const. *Sacrosanctum Concilium,* 19; decr. *Presbyterorum ordinis,* 5 "Deus," 9 "Presbyteros."

381 §3: Vat. II, decr. *Presbyterorum ordinis,* 9 "Presbyteros;" decr. *Apostolicam actuo-sitatem,* 25 "Prae oculis."

382: Pius XII, m.p. *Cleri sanctitati,* 2 iun. 1957, cann. 79–80 §1, 81. - Apost. cann. 42–43, 54; Laod. cann. 24, 27, 54–55; Carth. cann. 16, 40; Quinisext.

cann. 9, 24, 50–51; Nic. II, can. 22; S. TARASIUS CP., ep. ad Epp. Siciliae; S.C.S. Off., decr. 26 mar. 1942. * Syn. Mar Isaaci Chaldaeorum, a. 410, can. 8; Rabbula, cann. 47, 50; Syn. Zamosten. Ruthenorum, a. 1720, tit. X; Syn. Libanen. Maronitarum, a. 1736, pars III, cap. I, 5–12; Syn. prov. Alba-Iulien. et Fagarasien. Rumenorum, a. 1872, tit. VII, cap. II, b); cap. VI; Syn. Sciarfen. Syrorum, a. 1888, cap. VI, art. III; Syn. Leopolien. Ruthenorum, a. 1891, tit. IX, cap. II, 3–4; Syn. Alexandrin. Coptorum, a. 1898, sect. II, cap. III, art. VII, §6, 2. ▲ C. 1, 4, 34.

state, in accord with the norms defined in detail by particular law, and also are to avoid those things that are alien to it.

CAN. 383 Even though it is appropriate that clerics have civil and political rights no different than other citizens, nevertheless:

1° they are forbidden to assume public offices that entail a participation in the exercise of civil power;

2° since military service is less appropriate for those in the clerical state, clerics are not to take it up voluntarily except with permission of their hierarch;

3° they are to avail themselves of exemptions granted in their favor by civil laws, agreements or customs from exercising public functions and offices alien to the clerical state as well as military service.

CAN. 384 §1. As ministers of reconciliation of all in the love of Christ, clerics are to be attentive to foster peace, unity and harmony based on justice among all people.

§2. Clerics are not to have an active role in political parties nor in the direction of labor unions unless, in the judgment of the eparchial bishop or, if particular law so states, of the patriarch or of another authority, the need to protect the rights of the Church or to promote the common good requires it.

normas iure particulari pressius determinatas dedecent, et etiam evitent ea, quae ab eo aliena sunt.

CAN. 383 Clerici, etsi non secus ac ceteri cives iura civilia et politica aequo iure habeant oportet, tamen:

1° officia publica, quae participationem in exercitio potestatis civilis secumferunt, assumere vetantur;

2° cum servitium militare statui clericali minus congruat, illud ne capessant voluntarii nisi de sui Hierarchae licentia;

3° utantur exceptionibus, quas ab exercendis muneribus et officiis publicis a statu clericali alienis necnon servitio militari in eorum favorem concedunt leges civiles aut conventiones vel consuetudines.

CAN. 384 §1. Ministri reconciliationis omnium in Christi caritate satagant clerici pacem, unitatem et concordiam iustitia innixam inter homines fovere.

§2. In factionibus politicis atque in moderandis consociationibus syndicalibus activam partem ne habeant, nisi iudicio Episcopi eparchialis vel iure particulari ita ferente Patriarchae aut alterius auctoritatis iura Ecclesiae tuenda aut bonum commune promovendum id requirunt.

383, 1°: Pius XII, m.p. *Cleri sanctitati,* 2 iun. 1957, cann. 56, 80 §§2–4; Synodus Episcoporum, *Ultimis temporibus,* 30 nov. 1971, Pars Altera, I, 2, b). - Apost. cann. 6, 81; Chalc. cann. 3, 7; Carth. can. 16; Nic. II, can. 10; Protodeut. can. 11; Constantinop. IV, can. 24; S. Tarasius CP., ep. ad Epp. Siciliae. * Rabbula, can. 51; Syn. Zamosten. Ruthenorum, a. 1720, tit. X "Mercaturae;" Syn. Libanen. Maronitarum, a. 1736, pars III, cap. I, 9–10; Syn. Ain-Trazen. Graeco-Melchitarum, a. 1835, can. 16; Syn. prov. Alba-Iulien. et Fagarasien. Rumenorum, a. 1872, tit. VII, cap. II, b); Syn. Sciarfen. Syrorum, a. 1888, cap. VI, art. III; Syn. Leopolien. Ruthenorum, a. 1891, tit. IX, cap. II, IV. ▲ C. 1, 3, 2 et 6; Nov. 123, 6, pr.

383, 2°: Pius XII, m.p. *Cleri sanctitati,* 2 iun. 1957, cann 82 §1, 56. - Apost. can. 83, Chalc. can. 7. * Syn. Diamper. Syro-Malabarensium, a. 1599, CLXXIII; Syn. Alexandrin. Coptorum, a. 1898, sect. II, cap. III, art. VII, §7, III. ▲ C. 1, 3, 2 et 6, Nov. 123, 6, pr.

383, 3°: Pius XII, m.p. *Cleri sanctitati,* 2 iun. 1957, cann. 56, 58.

384 §1: Synodus Episcoporum, *Ultimis temporibus,* 30 nov. 1971, Pars Altera, I, 1, d) "Presbyteri;" 2, b) "Presbyteri;" *Convenientes,* 30 nov. 1971, II "Ecclesia accepit;" Vat. II, const. *Gaudium et spes,* 92 "Quod;" decr. *Presbyterorum ordinis,* 6 "Munus."

384 §2: Synodus Episcoporum, *Ultimis temporibus,* 30 nov. 1971, Pars Altera, I, 2, b) "Assumptio."

CAN. 385 §1. Clerics, imbued with the spirit of poverty of Christ, are to strive to lead a simple life and thus to be witnesses to the heavenly goods before the world; using spiritual discretion let them put their temporal goods to correct use; and from the goods they acquire on the occasion of the exercise of an ecclesiastical office, ministry, or function, let them first provide for their own suitable support and for the fulfillment of their obligations and then devote and share the rest in works of the apostolate or of charity.

§2. Clerics are forbidden to exercise by themselves or through another any commerce or business affairs whether for their own benefit or for that of another, except with permission of the authority defined by particular law of their own Church *sui iuris* or by the Apostolic See.

§3. A cleric is forbidden to post bond, even from his own goods, unless he has consulted his own eparchial bishop or, as the case may be, his major superior.

CAN. 386 §1. Clerics, even if they do not have a residential office, nevertheless are not to leave their eparchy for a notable period of time determined by particular law without the permission, at least presumed, of their local hierarch.

§2. A cleric who is residing outside his own

CAN. 385 §1. Spiritu paupertatis Christi imbuti clerici studeant simplicitate vitae supernorum bonorum coram mundo testes esse et bona temporalia discretione spirituali recto usui destinent; bona autem, quae occasione exercitii officii, ministerii vel muneris ecclesiastici sibi comparant, provisa ex eis sua congrua sustentatione et obligationum proprii status impletione, operibus apostolatus vel caritatis impertiant atque communicent.

§2. Prohibentur clerici per se vel per alios negotiationem aut mercaturam exercere sive in propriam sive in aliorum utilitatem nisi de licentia auctoritatis iure particulari propriae Ecclesiae sui iuris determinatae aut Sedis Apostolicae.

§3. A fideiubendo, etiam de bonis propriis, clericus prohibetur nisi consulto proprio Episcopo eparchiali vel, si casus fert, Superiore maiore.

CAN. 386 §1. Clerici, etsi officium residentiale non habent, a sua tamen eparchia per notabile tempus iure particulari determinandum sine licentia saltem praesumpta Hierarchae loci proprii ne discedant.

§2. Clericus, qui extra propriam eparchi-

---

385 §1: Vat. II, decr. *Presbyterorum ordinis*, 17.

385 §2: Pius XII, m.p. *Cleri sanctitati*, 2 iun. 1957, can. 83. - Apost. can. 44; Nic. I, can. 17; Laod. can. 4; Chalc. can. 3; Carth. cann. 5, 16; Quinisext. can. 9; Nic. II, can. 15; S. Nicephorus CP., can. 167. * Syn. Diamper. Syro-Malabarensium, a. 1599, CLXXI–CLXXII; Syn. Zamosten. Ruthenorum, a. 1720, tit. X "Mercaturae;" Syn. Libanen. Maronitarum, a. 1736, pars III, cap. I, 9; Syn. Ain-Trazen. Graeco-Melchitarum, a. 1835, can. 13; Syn. prov. Alba-Iulien. et Fagarasien. Rumenorum, a. 1872, tit. VII, cap. II, b); Syn. Sciarfen. Syrorum, a. 1888, cap. VI, art. III, 14; Syn. Leopolien. Ruthenorum, a. 1891, tit. IX, cap. II, 4; Syn. Alexandrin. Coptorum, a. 1898, sect. II, cap.

III, art. VII, §6, 2, IX.

385 §3: Pius XII, m.p. *Cleri sanctitati*, 2 iun. 1957, can. 78. - Apost. can. 20; S. Tarasius CP., ep. ad Epp. Siciliae. * Rabbula, can. 66; Syn. Libanen. Maronitarum, a. 1736, pars III, cap. I, 10; Syn. prov. Alba-Iulien. et Fagarasien. Rumenorum, a. 1872, tit. VII, cap. II, b).

386 §1; Pius XII, m.p. *Cleri sanctitati*, 2 iun. 1957, can. 84. - Apost. can. 15; Nic. I, can. 16; Ant. can. 3; Laod. can. 42; Sard. can. 16; Quinisext. cann. 17–18; Nic. II, can. 10.

386 §2: Pius XII, m.p. *Cleri sanctitati*, 2 iun. 1957, can. 87.

eparchy is subject to the eparchial bishop in those matters that regard the obligations of his state of life. If he foresees that he will live there for a lengthy time, he is to inform the local hierarch without delay.

CAN. 387 With regard to the attire of clerics, particular law is to be observed.

CAN. 388 Clerics cannot make use of rights and insignia attached to dignities conferred on them outside the place in which the authority who conferred the dignity exercises his power or who granted consent in writing to the conferral of the same dignity without exception, unless they are accompanying the authority who granted the dignity or are representing him or have obtained the consent of the local hierarch.

CAN. 389 Clerics are to strive to avoid any controversies; if however controversies arose among them, they are to be referred to the forum of the Church; this should also be done, if possible, also in the case of controversies between clerics and other Christian faithful.

CAN. 390 §1. Clerics have the right to suitable support and to receive a just remuneration for carrying out the office or function committed to them; in the case of married clerics, remuneration must be adequate for the support of their families, unless this has been otherwise sufficiently provided.

am commoratur, Episcopo eparchiali loci in eis, quae eiusdem clerici status obligationes respiciunt, subditus est; si ibi per tempus non breve commoraturus est, Hierarcham loci sine mora certiorem faciat.

CAN. 387 Quod ad vestis habitum clericorum spectat, ius particulare servetur.

CAN. 388 Clerici iuribus et insignibus, quae adnexa sunt dignitatibus sibi collatis, uti non possunt extra loca, ubi suam potestatem exercet auctoritas, quae dignitatem concessit vel ad eiusdem dignitatis concessionem nihil excipiens scripto consensit, aut nisi auctoritatem, quae dignitatem concessit, comitantur vel eiusdem personam gerunt aut nisi consensum Hierarchae loci obtinuerunt.

CAN. 389 Clerici quaslibet contentiones evitare studeant; si tamen quaedam contentio exsurrexit inter eos, ad forum Ecclesiae deferatur et hoc, si fieri potest, etiam fiat, si de contentionibus inter clericos et alios christifideles agitur.

CAN. 390 §1. Clerici ius habent ad congruam sustentationem et ideo pro implendo eis commisso officio vel munere iustam remunerationem percipiendi, quae, si agitur de clericis coniugatis, consulere debet etiam eorum familiae sustentandae, nisi aliter iam sufficienter provisum est.

387: Pius XII, m.p. *Cleri sanctitati,* 2 iun. 1957, can. 77 §1. - Quinisext. can. 27; Nic. II, can. 16. * Syn. Diamper. Syro-Malabarensium, a. 1599, CLXX; Syn. Zamosten. Ruthenorum, a. 1720, tit. X "Praeterea;" Syn. Libanen. Maronitarum, a. 1736, pars III, cap. I, 2–3; Syn. Ain-Trazen. Graeco-Melchitarum, a. 1835, can. 11; Syn. prov. Alba-Iulien. et Fagarasien. Rumenorum, a. 1872, tit. VII, cap. VII; Syn. Sciarfen. Syrorum, a. 1888, cap. VI, art. VIII; Syn. Leopolien. Ruthenorum, a. 1891, tit. IX, cap. II, 3; Syn. Alexandrin. Coptorum, a. 1898, sect. II, cap. III, art. VII, §6, 1, IV et 3 "Praeterea," IX.

388: Pius XII, m.p. *Cleri sanctitati,* 2 iun. 1957, cann. 41–42; S.C. de Prop. Fide (pro Neg. Rit. Orient.), ep. circ. 1 ian. 1912, "Persaepe;" S.C. pro Eccl. Orient., 10 ian. 1929.

389: Pius XII, m.p. *Cleri sanctitati,* 2 iun. 1957, can. 55. - Ant. can. 12; Chalc. can. 9; Carth. cann. 15, 104; S.C.S. Off., (Mission. Arcipelagi), 3 aug. 1639, ad 2. * Syn. Libanen. Maronitarum, a. 1736, pars III, cap. I, 18; Syn. Sciarfen. Syrorum, a. 1888, cap. VI, art. I, 4; Syn. Alexandrin. Coptorum, a. 1898, sect. II, cap. III, art. VII, §7, II. ▲ C. 1, 4, 13; Nov. 83, praef.

390 §1: Vat. II, decr. *Presbyterorum ordinis,* 20; Paulus VI, m.p. *Ecclesiae sanctae,* 6 aug. 1966, I, 8 "Curent;" Synodus Episcoporum, *Ultimis temporibus,* 30 nov. 1971, Pars Altera, II, 4 "Remuneratio." - Apost. can. 59.

§2. They also have the right that there be provided for themselves as well as for their families, if they are married, suitable pension funds, social security as well as health benefits. In order for this right to be put into practice effectively, clerics are obliged on their part to contribute to the fund mentioned in can. 1021, §2 in accord with the norm of particular law.

CAN. 391 Clerics are free, without prejudice to can. 578, §3, to associate with others for the purpose of pursuing ends suitable to the clerical state; it pertains to the eparchial bishop to judge authentically concerning this suitabi-lity.

CAN. 392 Clerics are entitled to annual vacations for a proper period of time to be determined by the particular law.

CAN. 393 Clerics, whatever their condition, are to have in their heart a solicitude for all the Churches, and therefore manifest a disposition to be of service wherever there is an urgent need and especially to exercise, with the permission or encouragement of their own eparchial bishop or superior, their ministry in the missions or in regions suffering from a shortage of clerics.

CHAPTER IV. The Loss of the Clerical State

CAN. 394 Sacred ordination, once validly received, never becomes null. A cleric however loses the clerical state:

1° by a judicial sentence or an administrative decree that declares the invalidity of the sacred ordination;

§2. Item ius habent, ut sui suaeque familiae, si coniugati sunt, congruenti praecaventiae et securitati sociali necnon assistentiae sanitariae provideatur; ut hoc ius ad effectum deduci possit, obligatione tenentur clerici instituto, de quo in can. 1021, §2, ad normam iuris particularis pro sua parte conferre.

CAN. 391 Integrum est clericis firmo can. 578, §3 se cum aliis consociare ad fines consequendos statui clericali congruentes; competit autem Episcopo eparchiali de hac congruentia authentice iudicare.

CAN. 392 Ius clericorum est ad debitum quotannis feriarum tempus iure particulari determinandum.

CAN. 393 Clericis, cuiuscumque sunt condicionis, cordi sit sollicitudo omnium Ecclesiarum et ideo se ad inserviendum, ubicumque urget necessitas, promptos exhibeant et praesertim permittente vel exhortante proprio Episcopo eparchiali vel Superiore ad suum ministerium in missionibus vel regionibus clericorum penuria laborantibus exercendum.

CAPUT IV. De Amissione Status Clericalis

CAN. 394 Sacra ordinatio semel valide suscepta numquam irrita fit; clericus tamen statum clericalem amittit:

1° sententia iudiciali aut decreto administrativo, quo invaliditas sacrae ordinationis declaratur;

390 §2: Pius XII, m.p. *Cleri sanctitati,* 2 iun. 1957, can. 59; Vat. II, decr. *Presbyterorum ordinis,* 21; Paulus VI, m.p. *Ecclesiae sanctae,* 6 aug. 1966, I, 8; Synodus Episcoporum, *Ultimis temporibus,* 30 nov. 1971, Pars Altera, II, 4 "Remuneratio."
391: Vat. II, decr. *Presbyterorum ordinis,* 8 "Spiritu."

392: Vat. II, decr. *Presbyterorum ordinis,* 20.
393: Vat. II, decr. *Presbyterorum ordinis,* 10 "Donum;" decr. *Christus Dominus,* 6 "Episcopi."
394: Pius XII, m.p. *Cleri sanctitati,* 2 iun. 1957, can. 155 §1.

2° by the penalty of deposition legitimately imposed;

3° by a rescript of the Apostolic See or of the patriarch, in accord with the norm of can. 397; this rescript cannot be granted licitly by the patriarch and is not granted by the Apostolic See to deacons without serious cause nor to presbyters without most serious cause.

CAN. 395 A cleric who loses the clerical state in accord with the norm of law, loses with it the rights proper to the clerical state and is no longer bound by any obligations of the clerical state without prejudice, however, to can. 396; he is forbidden to exercise the power of orders, without prejudice to cann. 725 and 735, §2; he is deprived of all offices, ministries, functions and any delegated power by the law itself.

CAN. 396 Except for the case in which the invalidity of sacred ordination has been declared, loss of the clerical state does not carry with it a dispensation from the obligation of celibacy, which is granted only by the Roman Pontiff.

CAN. 397 The patriarch, with the consent of the synod of bishops of the patriarchal Church or, if there is danger in delay, of the permanent synod, can grant the removal of the clerical state to clerics having domicile or quasi-domicile within the territorial boundaries of his own patriarchal Church and who are not bound by the obligation of clerical celibacy or, if bound, are not petitioning a dispensation

2° poena depositionis legitime irrogata;

3° rescripto Sedis Apostolicae vel ad normam can. 397 Patriarchae; hoc vero rescriptum diaconis sine gravibus, presbyteris vero sine gravissimis causis a Patriarcha licite concedi non potest nec a Sede Apostolica conceditur.

CAN. 395 Clericus, qui statum clericalem ad normam iuris amittit, cum eo amittit iura statui clericali propria nec ullis iam tenetur obligationibus status clericalis firmo tamen can. 396; potestatem ordinis exercere prohibetur salvis cann. 725 et 735, §2; ipso iure privatur omnibus officiis, ministeriis, muneribus et qualibet potestate delegata.

CAN. 396 Praeter casus, in quibus invaliditas sacrae ordinationis declarata est, amissio status clericalis non secumfert dispensationem ab obligatione caelibatus, quae a solo Romano Pontifice conceditur.

CAN. 397 Patriarcha de consensu Synodi Episcoporum Ecclesiae patriarchalis vel, si periculum in mora est, Synodi permanentis, amissionem status clericalis concedere potest clericis intra fines territorii propriae Ecclesiae patriarchalis domicilium vel quasi-domicilium habentibus, qui obligatione caelibatus non tenentur aut, si tenentur, dispensationem ab hac obligatione non petunt; in

394, 3°: PAULUS VI, litt. encycl. *Sacerdotalis caelibatus,* 24 iun. 1967, 84–88; S.C. pro Doctr. Fidei, *Normae,* 13 ian. 1971, I–V; litt. circ. 13 ian. 1971; decl. 26 iun. 1972, I–IV; IOANNES PAULUS II, ep. *Novo incipiente,* 8 apr. 1979, 9; S.C. pro Doctr. Fidei, litt. *De modo procedendi,* 14 oct. 1980; *Normae procedurales,* 14 oct. 1980.

395: PIUS XII, m.p. *Cleri sanctitati,* 2 iun. 1957,

can. 157; S.C. pro Doctr. Fidei, *Normae,* 13 ian. 1971, V–VII.

396: PIUS XII, m.p. *Cleri sanctitati,* 2 iun. 1957, can. 157 §2; PAULUS VI, m.p. *De Episcoporum muneribus,* IX, 1; S.C. pro Doctr. Fidei, decl. 26 iun. 1972, III; IOANNES PAULUS II, ep. *Novo incipiente,* 8 apr. 1979, 9; S.C. pro Doctr. Fidei, litt. *De modo procedendi,* 14 oct. 1980, 4–6; *Normae procedurales,* 14 oct. 1980, art. 8.

from this obligation; in other cases the matter is deferred to the Apostolic See.

CAN. 398   One who has lost the clerical state by a rescript of the Apostolic See can be readmitted among the clerics only by the Apostolic See; but one who obtained removal from the clerical state from the patriarch can be readmitted among the clerics also by the patriarch.

ceteris casibus res ad Sedem Apostolicam deferatur.

CAN. 398   Qui rescripto Sedis Apostolicae statum clericalem amisit, inter clericos a sola Sede Apostolica denuo admitti potest; qui vero a Patriarcha amissionem status clericalis obtinuit, etiam a Patriarcha inter clericos denuo admitti potest.

398: Pius XII, m.p. *Cleri sanctitati,* 2 iun. 1957, cann. 156 §2, 260 §1 n. 2 c).

CAN. 399 The designation of "lay persons" is applied in this Code to the Christian faithful whose proper and specific quality is secularity and who, living in the world, participate in the mission of the Church, but are not in sacred orders nor ascribed in the religious state.

CAN. 400 Lay persons, in addition to those obligations and rights that are common to all the Christian faithful and those that are determined in other canons, have the same rights and obligations that are listed in the canons of this title.

CAN. 401 It is for lay persons, according to their own vocation, in the first place to seek the kingdom of God; they do this by dealing with and regulating temporal matters in conformity with God. Therefore in their private, family, and politico-social life it is for them to be witnesses to Christ and manifest him to others, to defend just legislation in society, and radiating faith, hope and charity, to act like leaven for the sanctification of the world.

CAN. 402 Lay persons have the right to have recognized that freedom in the affairs of the earthly city that belongs to all citizens. In exercising this freedom, however, they are to take care that their actions are imbued with the spirit of the gospel and are to take into account the doctrine set forth by the magisterium of the Church; but they are to avoid proposing their own judgment as the doctrine of the Church in questions which are open to various opinions.

CAN. 399 Nomine laicorum in hoc Codice intelleguntur christifideles, quibus indoles saecularis propria ac specialis est quique in saeculo viventes missionem Ecclesiae participant neque in ordine sacro constituti neque statui religioso ascripti sunt.

CAN. 400 Laici praeter ea iura et obligationes, quae cunctis christifidelibus sunt communia et ea, quae in aliis canonibus statuuntur, eadem iura et obligationes habent ac in canonibus huius tituli recensentur.

CAN. 401 Laicorum imprimis est ex vocatione propria res temporales gerendo et secundum Deum ordinando Regnum Dei quaerere ideoque in vita privata, familiari et politico-sociali testes Christo esse ac ipsum aliis manifestare, leges iustas in societate propugnare atque fide, spe et caritate fulgentes fermenti instar ad mundi sanctificationem conferre.

CAN. 402 Ius est laicis, ut ipsis agnoscatur ea in rebus civitatis terrenae libertas, quae omnibus civibus competit; eadem tamen libertate utentes curent, ut suae actiones spiritu evangelico imbuantur, et ad doctrinam attendant ab Ecclesiae magisterio propositam caventes tamen, ne in quaestionibus opinabilibus propriam sententiam ut doctrinam Ecclesiae proponant.

399: Vat. II, const. *Lumen gentium,* 31; decr. *Apostolicam actuositatem,* 2.

401: Vat. II, const. *Lumen gentium,* 31 "Laicis;" *Gaudium et spes,* 43 "Laicis;" Pius XII, m.p. *Cleri*

sanctitati, 2 iun. 1957, can. 528.

402: Vat. II, const. *Lumen gentium,* 37 "Sacri;" const. *Gaudium et spes,* 43; decr. *Presbyterorum ordinis,* 9 "Presbyteros."

CAN. 403 §1. With due regard for the right and obligation to observe everywhere their own rite, lay persons have the right to participate actively in the liturgical celebrations of any Church *sui iuris* whatsoever, according to the prescripts of the liturgical books.

§2. If the necessity of the Church or genuine advantage so recommend, and when sacred ministers are lacking, certain functions of the sacred ministers may be committed to lay persons, in accord with the norm of law.

CAN. 404 §1. In addition to catechetical instruction, which should be received from infancy, lay persons have the right and obligation to acquire an understanding, appropriate to the capacity and condition of each one's natural ability, of the doctrine revealed by Christ and taught by the authentic magisterium of the Church, so that they may be able not only to live according to that doctrine, but also to make it known, and, if need be, to defend it.

§2. Lay persons also have the right to acquire a fuller understanding of the sacred sciences that are taught in ecclesiastical universities or faculties or in institutes of religious studies by attending classes and pursuing academic degrees.

§3. Likewise, observing the prescripts as to required suitability, lay persons are qualified to receive a mandate from the competent ecclesiastical authority to teach the sacred sciences.

CAN. 403 §1. Firmo iure et obligatione proprium ritum ubique servandi laici ius habent actuose in celebrationibus liturgicis cuiuscumque Ecclesiae sui iuris participandi secundum praescripta librorum liturgicorum.

§2. Si Ecclesiae necessitates vel vera utilitas id suadent et ministri sacri desunt, possunt laicis quaedam ministrorum sacrorum functiones committi ad normam iuris.

CAN. 404 §1. Praeter institutionem catecheticam inde ab infantia habendam laici ius et obligationem habent acquirendi cognitionem uniuscuiusque ingenii dotibus et condicioni aptatam doctrinae a Christo revelatae et a magisterio authentico Ecclesiae traditae non solum, ut secundum eiusdem doctrinam vivere valeant, sed etiam, ut ipsi eam enuntiare atque, si opus est, defendere possint.

§2. Ius quoque habent acquirendi pleniorem illam cognitionem in scientiis sacris, quae in ecclesiasticis studiorum universitatibus vel facultatibus aut in institutis scientiarum religiosarum traduntur, ibidem lectiones frequentando et gradus academicos consequendo.

§3. Item servatis praescriptis circa idoneitatem requisitam statutis habiles sunt ad mandatum docendi disciplinas sacras ab auctoritate competenti ecclesiastica recipiendum.

403 §1: Vat. II, const. *Sacrosanctum Concilium,* 14.

403 §2: Vat. II, const. *Lumen gentium,* 35 "Proinde;" decr. *Apostolicam actuositatem,* 24 "Potest."

404 §1: Vat. II, const. *Lumen gentium,* 35 "Proinde;" decl. *Dignitatis humanae,* 14; decr. *Apostolicam actuositatem,* 29; decr. *Ad gentes,* 26 "Quare," 41.

404 §2: IOANNES PAULUS II, const. ap. *Sapientia christiana,* 15 apr. 1979, art. 31; Vat. II, const. *Gaudium et spes,* 62 "Qui;" decl. *Gravissimum educationis,* 10 "In universitatibus."

404 §3: IOANNES PAULUS II, const. ap. *Sapientia christiana,* 15 apr. 1979, art. 27; Vat. II, decr. *Ad gentes,* 41.

CAN. 405 Lay persons should study zealously their liturgical, spiritual, theological and disciplinary patrimony, so that mutual goodwill, esteem and unity of action between the lay members of different Churches *sui iuris* is fostered, and so that the variety of rites does not harm the common good of the society in which they live, but rather may daily contribute to that same good.

CAN. 406 Lay persons, aware of the obligation mentioned in can. 14, should know that this obligation is more pressing in those circumstances in which people can hear the gospel and know Christ only through them.

CAN. 407 Lay persons who live in the married state in accord with their own vocation are bound by a special obligation to work for the building up of the people of God through their marriage and their family.

CAN. 408 §1. Lay persons who excel in the necessary knowledge, experience and integrity, are qualified to be heard as experts or consultors by ecclesiastical authorities, whether individually or as members of various councils and assemblies, whether parochial, eparchial or patriarchal.

§2. Besides those ecclesiastical functions to which lay persons are by common law admitted, they may be admitted by a competent authority to other functions, except those that require sacred orders or that are expressly forbidden to lay persons by the particular law of their own Church *sui iuris*.

CAN. 405 Patrimonio liturgico, theologico, spirituali et disciplinari etiam laici sedulo studeant ita tamen, ut mutua benevolentia ac aestimatio atque unitas actionis inter laicos diversarum Ecclesiarum sui iuris foveantur nec varietas rituum noceat bono communi societatis, in qua vivunt, sed potius ad idem bonum in dies magis conducat.

CAN. 406 Laici memores obligationis, de qua in can. 14, sciant illam eo magis urgere in eis adiunctis, in quibus nonnisi per ipsos Evangelium audire et Christum cognoscere homines possunt.

CAN. 407 Laici, qui in statu coniugali vivunt, secundum propriam vocationem speciali obligatione tenentur per matrimonium et familiam ad aedificationem populi Dei allaborandi.

CAN. 408 §1. Habiles sunt laici debita scientia, experientia et honestate praestantes, ut tamquam periti aut consultores ab auctoritatibus ecclesiasticis audiantur sive singuli sive ut membra variorum consiliorum et conventuum, ut paroecialium, eparchialium, patriarchalium.

§2. Praeterquam ad munera ecclesiastica, ad quae laici iure communi admittuntur, ipsi ab auctoritate competenti ad alia quoque munera assumi possunt eis exceptis, quae ordinem sacrum requirunt vel quae iure particulari propriae Ecclesiae sui iuris laicis expresse vetantur.

405: Vat. II, decr. *Orientalium Ecclesiarum,* 4, 6.

406: Vat. II, const. *Lumen gentium,* 33 "Apostolatus;" decr. *Ad gentes,* 21 "Praecipuum;" decr. *Apostolicam actuositatem,* 10 "Utpote," 17.

407: Vat. II, decr. *Apostolicam actuositatem,* 11; const. *Gaudium et spes,* 52 "Christifideles."

408 §1: Vat. II, const. *Lumen gentium,* 33 "Praeter," 37 "Sacri;" decr. *Christus Dominus,* 10

"Denique," 27 "Valde;" decr. *Apostolicam actuositatem,* 20, b), 26; decr. *Ad gentes,* 30; decr. *Presbyterorum ordinis,* 17 "Bona."

408 §2: Vat. II, const. *Lumen gentium,* 33 "Praeter," 37 "Sacri;" decr. *Christus Dominus,* 27; decr. *Apostolicam actuositatem,* 24 "Potest;" decr. *Ad gentes,* 17.

§3. Lay persons are fully subject to ecclesiastical authority with respect to the exercise of ecclesiastical functions.

CAN. 409 §1. Lay persons who are appointed permanently or temporarily to some special service of the Church are obliged to acquire the appropriate training required to fulfill their function duly; they are obliged to discharge this function conscientiously, diligently and with dedication.

§2. They have the right to a just remuneration suited to their condition by which they can, with due regard for the prescripts of civil law, provide decently for their own needs and those of their family. They likewise have the right for suitable insurance, social security and health care to be provided for themselves and their family.

§3. Circa muneris ecclesiastici exercitium laici plene subduntur auctoritati ecclesiasticae.

CAN. 409 §1. Laici, qui permanenter aut ad tempus speciali Ecclesiae servitio addicuntur, obligatione tenentur, ut aptam acquirant formationem ad munus suum debite implendum requisitam utque hoc munus conscie, impense et diligenter impleant.

§2. Ipsi ius habent ad iustam remunerationem suae condicioni aptatam, qua decenter, servatis quoque iuris civilis praescriptis, necessitatibus propriis ac familiae providere possint; itemque ius habent, ut sui suaeque familiae congruenti praecaventiae et securitati sociali necnon assistentiae sanitariae provideatur.

408 §3: Vat. II, decr. *Apostolicam actuositatem,* 20, d).

409 §2: Vat. II, decr. *Apostolicam actuositatem,* 22 "Pastores;" decr. *Ad gentes,* 17 "Multiplicentur."

TITLE XII. MONKS AND OTHER RELIGIOUS AS WELL AS MEMBERS OF OTHER INSTITUTES OF CONSECRATED LIFE

TITULUS XII. DE MONACHIS CETERISQUE RELIGIOSIS ET DE SODALIBUS ALIORUM INSTITUTORUM VITAE CONSECRATAE

CHAPTER I. Monks and Other Religious

CAPUT I. De Monachis Ceterisque Religiois

ART. I. *General Canons*

ART. I. *Canones Generales*

CAN. 410 The religious state is a stable manner of living in common in an institute approved by the Church, by which the Christian faithful, more closely following Christ, Teacher and Exemplar of Holiness, under the influence of the Holy Spirit, are consecrated by a new and special title through the public vows of obedience, chastity and poverty, observed in accord with the norm of the statutes under a legitimate superior, renounce the world and totally dedicate themselves to the attainment of perfect charity in the service of the Kingdom of God for the building up of the Church and the salvation of the world as a sign of the foretelling of heavenly glory.

CAN. 410 Status religiosus est stabilis in communi vivendi modus in aliquo instituto ab Ecclesia approbato, quo christifideles Christum, Magistrum et Exemplum Sanctitatis, sub actione Spiritus Sancti pressius sequentes novo ac speciali titulo consecrantur per vota publica oboedientiae, castitatis et paupertatis sub legitimo Superiore ad normam statutorum servanda, saeculo renuntiant ac totaliter se devovent caritatis perfectioni assequendae in servitium Regni Dei pro Ecclesiae aedificatione et mundi salute utpote signa coelestem gloriam praenuntiantia.

CAN. 411 The religious state must be fostered and promoted by all.

CAN. 411 Status religiosus ab omnibus fovendus et promovendus est.

410: Pius XII, m.p. *Postquam Apostolicis Litteris,* 9 feb. 1952, can. 1; Vat. II, const. *Lumen gentium,* 43–44; decr. *Perfectae caritatis,* 1, 2, a) et e), 5, 12, 25; Paulus VI, adh. ap. *Evangelica testificatio,* 29 iun. 1971, 7. - S. Basilius M., regulae fus., 7, 41; S. Theodorus Studita, ep. I, 10; ep. II, 104, 128, 159, 164–165; serm. 11–12, 19, 35, 60, 82, 87, 89, 95, 104, 110; orat. 11, cap. II; testam. "confiteor;" iambi, 25.

411: Pius XII, m.p. *Postquam Apostolicis Litteris,* 9 feb. 1952, can. 2; Vat. II, const. *Lumen gentium,* 44 "Cum," 46 "Idcirco." - Chalc. can. 4.

1° Dependence of Religious on the Eparchial Bishop, the Patriarch and the Apostolic See

1° De Dependentia Religiosorum ab Episcopo Eparchiali, a Patriarcha, a Sede Apostolica

CAN. 412 §1. All religious are subject to the Roman Pontiff as their highest superior, whom they are also bound by the obligation to obey by virtue of the vow of obedience.

§2. In order better to provide for the good of institutes and the needs of the apostolate, the Roman Pontiff, by reason of his primacy in the entire Church and with a view to common advantage, can exempt institutes of consecrated life from the governance of the eparchial bishop and subject them to himself alone or to another ecclesiastical authority.

CAN. 413 Unless the law provides otherwise, religious institutes are subject with respect to internal governance and religious discipline directly and exclusively to the Apostolic See if they are of pontifical right; if they are of patriarchal or eparchial right, they are directly subject to the patriarch or eparchial bishop, with due regard for can. 418, §2.

CAN. 414 §1. In what pertains to monasteries and congregations of eparchial right, it is for the eparchial bishop:

1° to approve the typica of monasteries and the statutes of congregations as well as changes introduced into them in accord with the norm of law except those that a higher authority has approved;

CAN. 412 §1. Religiosi omnes subduntur Romano Pontifici ut suo supremo Superiori, cui obligatione parendi tenentur etiam vi voti oboedientiae.

§2. Quo melius institutorum bono atque apostolatus necessitatibus provideatur, Romanus Pontifex ratione sui primatus in universam Ecclesiam intuitu utilitatis communis instituta vitae consecratae ab Episcopi eparchialis regimine eximere potest sibique soli vel alii auctoritati ecclesiasticae subicere.

CAN. 413 Ad regimen internum et disciplinam religiosam quod attinet, instituta religiosa, nisi aliter iure cavetur, si sunt iuris pontificii, immediate et exclusive Sedi Apostolicae subiecta sunt; si vero sunt iuris patriarchalis vel eparchialis, immediate subiecta sunt Patriarchae vel Episcopo eparchiali firmo can. 418, §2.

CAN. 414 §1. Ad monasteria et congregationes iuris eparchialis quod attinet, Episcopo eparchiali competit:

1° typica monasteriorum et statuta congregationum atque immutationes in ea ad normam iuris introductas approbare salvis eis, quae ab auctoritate superiore approbata sunt;

412 §1: Pius XII, m.p. *Postquam Apostolicis Litteris,* 9 feb. 1952, can. 23.

412 §2: Vat. II, const. *Lumen gentium,* 45 "Quo;" decr. *Christus Dominus,* 35, 3); Pius XII, m.p. *Postquam Apostolicis Litteris,* 9 feb. 1952, can. 312 §2 n. 4. - Callistus III, const. *Urget nos,* 20 apr. 1457, §3; Leo XIII, litt. ap. *Singulare praesidium,* 12 maii 1882, "Cum susceptum."

413: Pius XII, m.p. *Postquam Apostolicis Litteris,* 9 feb. 1952, cann. 312 §2 nn. 1–3, 313 §2 n. 2; Vat. II, const. *Lumen gentium,* 45 "Quo;" decr. *Christus Dominus,* 35, 3).

414 §1: Pius XII, m.p. *Postquam Apostolicis Litteris,* 9 feb. 1952, can. 24 §1. - Chalc. cann. 4, 8; Benedictus XIV, ep. encycl. *Demandatam,* 24 dec. 1743, §20; S.C. de Prop. Fide, decr. 15 mar. 1819, 3; decr. 22 feb. 1877, 1. * Syn. Libanen. Maronitarum, a. 1736, pars IV, cap. II, 2; cap. III, 3; Syn. prov. Alba-Iulien. et Fagarasien. Rumenorum, a. 1872, tit. VIII, cap. II; Syn. Armen., a. 1911, 758.

414 §1, 1°: Pius XII, m.p. *Postquam Apostolicis Litteris,* 9 feb. 1952, can. 18 §3.

2° to give dispensations from the same typica or statutes, which exceed the power of the religious superiors and which are legitimately requested from him, in single cases and on individual occasions;

3° to visit monasteries, even dependent ones, as well as the individual houses of congregations in his territory, whenever he conducts a canonical visitation there or whenever truly special reasons in his judgment suggest it;

§2. These rights belong to the patriarch with respect to orders and congregations of patriarchal right that have their principal house within the territorial boundaries of the Church; otherwise the same rights with respect to all orders, as well as to monasteries and congregations that are not of eparchial right, belong solely to the Apostolic See .

§3. If a congregation of eparchial right has expanded to other eparchies, nothing in the statutes themselves can be changed validly except with the consent of the eparchial bishop of the eparchy in which the principal house is located, after having consulted, however, the eparchial bishops in whose eparchies the other houses are located.

CAN. 415 §1. All religious are subject to the power of the local hierarch in matters that pertain to the public celebration of divine worship, to the preaching of the word of God to the people, to the religious and moral education of the Christian faithful, especially of children, to cat-

2° dispensationes ab eisdem typicis vel statutis, quae potestatem Superiorum religiosorum excedunt et ab ipso legitime petuntur, singulis in casibus et per modum actus dare;

3° visitare monasteria, etiam dependentia, necnon singulas domos congregationum in suo territorio, quoties visitationem canonicam ibi peragit aut quoties rationes vere speciales eius iudicio id suadent.

§2. Haec iura Patriarchae competunt circa ordines et congregationes iuris patriarchalis, quae intra fines territorii Ecclesiae, cui praeest, domum principem habent; secus eadem iura circa ordines omnes necnon circa monasteria et congregationes, quae non sunt iuris eparchialis, competunt soli Sedi Apostolicae.

§3. Si congregatio iuris eparchialis ad alias eparchias propagatur, nihil in ipsis statutis valide mutari potest nisi de consensu Episcopi eparchialis eparchiae, in qua sita est domus princeps, consultis tamen Episcopis eparchialibus, in quorum eparchiis ceterae domus sitae sunt.

CAN. 415 §1. Religiosi omnes subsunt potestati Hierarchae loci in eis, quae spectant ad publicam celebrationem cultus divini, ad verbi Dei praedicationem populo tradendam, ad christifidelium praesertim puerorum religiosam et moralem educationem, ad insti-

---

414 §1, 2°: PIUS XII, m.p. *Postquam Apostolicis Litteris*, 9 feb. 1952, can. 26 §3.

414 §1, 3°: PIUS XII, m.p. *Postquam Apostolicis Litteris*, 9 feb. 1952, can. 44 §1; m.p. *Cleri sanctitati*, 2 iun. 1957, can. 410 §1. * Syn. Zamosten. Ruthenorum, a. 1720, tit. VI "Monasteria;" Syn. Libanen. Maronitarum, a. 1736, pars III, cap. III, 4, VI; Syn. Sciarfen. Syrorum, a. 1888, cap. IX, art. III, 4; Syn. Armen., a. 1911, 758, 776.

414 §2: PIUS XII, m.p. *Postquam Apostolicis Litteris*, 9 feb. 1952, cann. 18 §§1–2, 42. * Syn. Libanen. Maronitarum, a. 1736, pars IV, cap. II, 9.

414 §3: PIUS XII, m.p. *Postquam Apostolicis Litteris*, 9 feb. 1952, can. 18 §3.

415 §1: Vat. II, decr. *Christus Dominus*, 35, 4); PAULUS VI, m.p. *Ecclesiae sanctae*, 6 aug. 1966, I, 25 §1.

echetical and liturgical instruction, to the decorum of the clerical state, as well as to various works that regard the apostolate.

§2. It is the right and obligation of the eparchial bishop to visit the individual monasteries and houses of orders and congregations with regard to these matters whenever he conducts a canonical visitation there or whenever in his judgment grave causes suggest it.

§3. The eparchial bishop can entrust apostolic works or functions proper to the eparchy to religious only with the consent of the competent superiors, with due regard for common law and observance of the religious discipline of the institutes, their own character and specific purpose.

§4. Religious who have committed a delict outside their house and have not been punished by their own superior, having been warned by the local hierarch, can be punished by that hierarch even if they have legitimately left the house and returned to it.

CAN. 416 Patriarchs as well as local hierarchs are to promote meetings with superiors of religious at fixed times and whenever it appears opportune, in order that the apostolic works that the members exercise be carried out cooperatively and harmoniously.

CAN. 417 If abuses have crept into the

tutionem catecheticam et liturgicam, ad status clericalis decorem necnon ad varia opera in eis, quae apostolatum respiciunt.

§2. Episcopo eparchiali ius et obligatio est singula monasteria atque domos ordinum et congregationum in eius territorio sita visitare his in rebus, quoties visitationem canonicam ibi peragit aut quoties graves causae eius iudicio id suadent.

§3. Episcopus eparchialis nonnisi de consensu Superiorum competentium potest religiosis opera apostolatus vel munera eparchiae propria committere firmo iure communi ac servata institutorum disciplina religiosa, indole propria atque fine specifico.

§4. Religiosi, qui extra domum delictum commiserunt nec a proprio Superiore ab Hierarcha loci praemonito puniuntur, ab hoc puniri possunt, etsi domo legitime exierunt et domum reversi sunt.

CAN. 416 Patriarchae necnon Hierarchae loci conventus promoveant cum Superioribus religiosorum, statis temporibus et quoties id opportunum videtur, ut pro operibus apostolatus, quae a sodalibus exercentur, collatis consiliis concorditer procedant.

CAN. 417 Si in domus institutorum iuris

415 §2: Pius XII, m.p. *Postquam Apostolicis Litteris,* 9 feb. 1952, can. 44 §2 n. 2; Paulus VI, m.p. *Ecclesiae sanctae,* 6 aug. 1966, I, 38 et 39 §2. * Syn. Zamosten. Ruthenorum, a. 1720, tit. VI; Syn. Libanen. Maronitarum, a. 1736, pars III, cap. III, 4, VI; pars IV, cap. II, 9; cap. III, 19; Syn. Sciarfen. Syrorum, a. 1888, cap. IX, art. III, 4; Syn. Armen., a. 1911, 758, 776.

415 §3: Pius XII, m.p. *Postquam Apostolicis Litteris,* 9 feb. 1952, can. 181 §1; Vat. II, decr. *Christus Dominus,* 35, 1–2; Paulus VI, m.p. *Ecclesiae sanctae,* 6 aug. 1966, I, 31. - Benedictus XIV, litt. ap. *Super*

familiam, 30 mar. 1756, §7. * Syn. Libanen. Maronitarum, a. 1736, pars IV, cap. II, 7; Syn. Gusten. Maronitarum, a. 1768, can. 1; Syn. prov. Alba-Iulien. et Fagarasien. Rumenorum, a. 1872, tit. VIII, cap. II "Episcopus;" Syn. Armen., a. 1911, 771–772.

415 §4: Pius XII, m.p. *Postquam Apostolicis Litteris,* 9 feb. 1952, can. 165 §2. * Syn. Libanen. Maronitarum, a. 1736, pars IV, cap. II, 9.

417: Pius XII, m.p. *Postquam Apostolicis Litteris,* 9 feb. 1952, can. 166 §1. * Syn. Libanen. Maronitarum, a. 1736, pars IV, cap. II, 9.

houses of institutes of patriarchal or pontifical right or their Churches and the superior, having been warned by the local hierarch, has failed to take care of it, the same local hierarch is bound by obligation to defer the matter immediately to the authority to which the institute itself is immediately subject.

patriarchalis vel pontificii eorumve ecclesias abusus irrepserunt et Superior ab Hierarcha loci monitus prospicere neglexit, idem Hierarcha loci obligatione tenetur rem statim deferendi ad auctoritatem, cui institutum ipsum immediate subiectum est.

2° Superiors and Members of Religious Institutes

2° De Superioribus et de Sodalibus Institutorum Religiosorum

CAN. 418 §1. Major superiors are: the president of a monastic confederation, the superior of a monastery *sui iuris,* the superior general of an order or congregation, the provincial superior, their vicars and others who have power like that of provincials, and also those who, in the absence of the above-mentioned persons, in the interim legitimately succeed them in office.

CAN. 418 §1. Superiores maiores sunt Praeses confoederationis monasticae, Superior monasterii sui iuris, Superior generalis ordinis vel congregationis, Superior provincialis, eorundem vicarii aliique ad instar provincialium potestatem habentes itemque ii, qui, si praedicti desunt, interim legitime succedunt in officium.

§2. Under the designation "superior of monks and other religious" does not come either the local hierarch or the patriarch, with due regard for the canons that assign to the patriarch or local hierarch power over them.

§2. Nomine Superioris monachorum ceterorumque religiosorum non venit Hierarcha loci nec Patriarcha firmis canonibus, qui Patriarchae vel Hierarchae loci potestatem in ipsos tribuunt.

CAN. 419 §1. The president of a monastic federation, the superior of a non-confederated monastery *sui iuris,* and the superior general of an order or congregation, must send a report on the state of the institutes over which they preside to the authority to which they are immediately subject at least every five years, according to the formula established by the same authority.

CAN. 419 §1. Praeses confoederationis monasticae, Superior monasterii sui iuris non confoederati et Superior generalis ordinis vel congregationis relationem de statu institutorum, quibus praesunt, quinto saltem quoque anno ad auctoritatem, cui immediate subditi sunt, mittere debent secundum formulam ab eadem auctoritate statutam.

§2. Superiors of institutes of eparchial or patriarchal right are to send a copy of the report also to the Apostolic See.

§2. Superiores institutorum iuris eparchialis vel patriarchalis exemplar relationis etiam Sedi Apostolicae mittant.

CAN. 420 §1. Major superiors, whom the typicon of a monastery or the statutes of an or-

CAN. 420 §1. Superiores maiores, quos ad munus visitatoris typicum monasterii aut

---

418 §1: Pius XII, m.p. *Postquam Apostolicis Litteris,* 9 feb. 1952, can. 312 §5 n. 1.

418 §2: Pius XII, m.p. *Postquam Apostolicis Litteris,* 9 feb. 1952, can. 312 §5 n. 2.

419 §1: Pius XII, m.p. *Postquam Apostolicis Litteris,* 9 feb. 1952, cann. 39 §1, 40.

420 §1: Pius XII, m.p. *Postquam Apostolicis Litteris,* 9 feb. 1952, can. 41.

der or congregation designate for the function of visitator, are to visit at the time determined in them all the houses subject to them personally or through others if they are legitimately impeded.

§2. Members are to act with trust toward a visitator, to whose legitimate questioning they are bound to respond truthfully in charity. Moreover, it is not permitted for anyone in any way to divert members from this obligation or otherwise to impede the purpose of the visitation.

§3. The local hierarch must visit all religious houses if the major superior, to whom the visitation belongs by law, has not visited them for a period of five years and, having been warned by the local hierarch, has failed to visit them.

CAN. 421 Superiors are bound by the grave obligation to take care that the members entrusted to them arrange their life in accord with their own typicon or statutes; superiors are to help the members by example and encouragement in attaining the purpose of the religious state; they are to meet the personal needs of the members appropriately, solicitously to care for and visit the sick, to correct the restless, to console the faint of heart, and to be patient toward all.

CAN. 422 §1. Superiors are to have a permanent council established in accord with the norm of the typicon or statutes, whose assistance they are to use in exercising their office; in cases prescribed by law, they are bound to obtain its consent or counsel in accord with the norm of can. 934.

statuta ordinis vel congregationis designant, temporibus in eisdem determinatis omnes domos sibi subiectas visitent per se vel per alios, si sunt legitime impediti.

§2. Sodales cum visitatore fiducialiter agant, cui legitime interroganti respondere tenentur secundum veritatem in caritate; nemini vero licet quoquo modo sodales ab hac obligatione avertere aut visitationis finem aliter impedire.

§3. Hierarcha loci debet omnes domos religiosas visitare, si Superior maior, cui visitatio iure competit, intra quinque annos eas non visitavit et monitus ab Hierarcha loci eas visitare neglexit.

CAN. 421 Superiores gravi obligatione tenentur curandi, ut sodales sibi commissi vitam secundum typicum vel statuta propria componant; Superiores sodales exemplo et hortatione iuvent in fine status religiosi assequendo, eorum necessitatibus personalibus convenienter subveniant, infirmos sedulo curent ac visitent, corripiant inquietos, consolentur pusillanimes, patientes sint erga omnes.

CAN. 422 §1. Superiores permanens habeant consilium ad normam typici vel statutorum constitutum, cuius opera in officio exercendo utantur; in casibus iure praescriptis eius consensum aut consilium ad normam can. 934 exquirere tenentur.

420 §2: Pius XII, m.p. *Postquam Apostolicis Litteris,* 9 feb. 1952, can. 45 §1.

420 §3: Pius XII, m.p. *Postquam Apostolicis Litteris,* 9 feb. 1952, can. 44 §3.

421: Pius XII, m.p. *Postquam Apostolicis Litteris,* 9 feb. 1952, can. 37; Vat. II, decr. *Perfectae caritatis,* 14 "Superiores." - S. Basilius M., regulae fus., 25; S. Pa-

chomius, reg. 159; S. Theodorus Studita, ep. II, 43, 97–98, 133; ep. 80; sermo 84; iambi, 6.

422 §1: Pius XII, m.p. *Postquam Apostolicis Litteris,* 9 feb. 1952, can. 48 §1. - S. Basilius M., regulae fus., 48; S. Theodorus Studita, sermo 117; Vat. II, decr. *Perfectae caritatis,* 14 "Superiores."

§2. Particular law is to establish whether in houses of less than six members there must be a council.

CAN. 423   A monastery, monastic federation, order and congregation and their provinces and legitimately erected houses are by the law itself juridic persons. However, the typicon or statutes can exclude or restrict their capacity to acquire, possess, administer, and alienate temporal goods.

CAN. 424   In the typicon or statutes, norms are to be established concerning the use and administration of goods in order to foster, express and protect their own poverty.

CAN. 425   The temporal goods of religious institutes are governed by cann. 1007–1054, unless the common law provides otherwise or it is evident from the nature of the matter.

CAN. 426   Each and every religious, whether superiors or subjects, must not only faithfully and integrally observe the vows that they have professed, but also arrange their lives according to the typicon or statutes, having faithfully observed the mind and designs of the founder, and thereby strive for the perfection of their state.

CAN. 427   Each and every religious is bound by the obligation that the common law

§2. Iure particulari statuatur, utrum in domibus, in quibus minus quam sex sodales degunt, consilium haberi debeat necne.

CAN. 423   Monasterium, confoederatio monastica, ordo et congregatio eorumque provinciae et domus legitime erecta ipso iure sunt personae iuridicae; capacitatem vero eorum acquirendi, possidendi, administrandi et alienandi bona temporalia typicum vel statuta excludere aut coartare possunt.

CAN. 424   In typico vel statutis normae statuantur de usu et administratione bonorum ad propriam paupertatem fovendam, exprimendam et tuendam.

CAN. 425   Bona temporalia institutorum religiosorum reguntur cann. 1007–1054, nisi aliter iure communi cavetur vel ex natura rei constat.

CAN. 426   Omnes et singuli religiosi, Superiores aeque ac subditi, debent non solum, quae emiserunt vota, fideliter integreque servare, sed etiam secundum typicum vel statuta mente et propositis fundatoris fideliter servatis vitam componere atque ita ad perfectionem sui status contendere.

CAN. 427   Omnes et singuli religiosi tenentur obligationibus, quae clericis iure

---

422 §2: Pius XII, m.p. *Postquam Apostolicis Litteris,* 9 feb. 1952, cann. 48 §1, 312 §3 n. 2.

423: Pius XII, m.p. *Postquam Apostolicis Litteris,* 9 feb. 1952, can. 63 §§1–2; Paulus VI, m.p. *Ecclesiae sanctae,* 6 aug. 1966, II, 24. * Syn. Libanen. Maronitarum, a. 1736, pars IV, cap. II, 21, VIII.

424: Vat. II, decr. *Perfectae caritatis,* 13; Paulus VI, m.p. *Ecclesiae sanctae,* 6 aug. 1966, II, 23.

425: Pius XII, m.p. *Postquam Apostolicis Litteris,* 9 feb. 1952, cann. 64–66; S.C. pro Eccl. Orient., decr. 27 iun. 1972, 9. - S. Theodorus Studita, ep. I, 10, in fine. * Syn. Libanen. Maronitarum, a. 1736, pars IV, cap. II, 3.

426: Pius XII, m.p. *Postquam Apostolicis Litteris,* 9 feb. 1952, can. 136; Vat. II, const. *Lumen gentium,*

45; decr. *Perfectae caritatis,* 2, b); Paulus VI, m.p. *Ecclesiae sanctae,* 6 aug. 1966, II, 16 §3. - S. Basilius M., regulae fus., 5, 8, 24, 35, 37–38, 41, 43, 48; S. Pachomius, regg. 3, 6, 8, 10, 30, 58, 62, 64, 84, 99, 123, 144, 157–158, 184; S. Theodorus Studita, ep. II, 43, 159, 164, 180; serm. 17, 104; S. Athanasius Athonita, diatyposis, "Ἀταφυλαχθῆναι." * Syn. Libanen. Maronitarum, a. 1736, pars IV, cap. II, 21, VI.

427: Pius XII, m.p. *Postquam Apostolicis Litteris,* 9 feb. 1952, can. 135. - Laod. can. 24; Chalc. cann. 3–4, 7; Nic. II, can. 22; S. Theodorus Studita, ep. I, 27. * Syn. Libanen. Maronitarum, a. 1736, pars IV, cap. II, 13; Syn. Ain-Trazen. Graeco-Melchitarum, a. 1835, can. 13; Syn. Sciarfen. Syrorum, a. 1888, cap. VI, art. III, 5, 8–9, 11, 14–15.

prescribes for clerics, unless the law provides otherwise or it is evident from the nature of the matter.

CAN. 428 A member in perpetual vows is ascribed to a religious institute as a cleric by diaconal ordination or, in the case of a cleric already ascribed to an eparchy, by perpetual profession.

CAN. 429 Letters of religious sent to their superiors and also to the local hierarch, patriarch, legate of the Roman Pontiff and the Apostolic See, as well as letters that they themselves receive from them, are not subject to any inspection.

CAN. 430 It is not permitted to confer on religious merely honorific titles of dignities or offices, unless the typicon or statutes permit this, with due regard for the titles of the offices of major superior that the religious have already exercised.

CAN. 431 §1. Without the written consent of his or her major superior, a religious cannot be promoted after first profession to a dignity or office outside the institute, except those that the synod of bishops confers through a completed election and with due regard for can. 89, §2; after having fulfilled the function, the religious must return to the monastery, order or congregation.

§2. A religious who becomes patriarch, bishop or exarch:

1° remains bound by the vows and the other

communi praescribuntur, nisi aliter iure cavetur vel ex natura rei constat.

CAN. 428 Instituto religioso sodalis a votis perpetuis ut clericus ascribitur ordinatione diaconali vel in casu clerici alicui eparchiae iam ascripti professione perpetua.

CAN. 429 Litterae religiosorum ad Superiores eorum necnon ad Hierarcham loci, Patriarcham, Legatum Romani Pontificis et Sedem Apostolicam missae itemque litterae, quas ipsi ab eisdem recipiunt, nulli inspectioni obnoxiae sunt.

CAN. 430 Non licet titulos mere honorificos dignitatum vel officiorum religiosis conferre, nisi agitur typico vel statutis id permittentibus de titulis officiorum Superiorum maiorum, quae religiosi iam exercuerunt.

CAN. 431 §1. Religiosus sine consensu scripto dato proprii Superioris maioris non potest inde a prima professione ad dignitatem vel officium extra proprium institutum promoveri eis exceptis, quae per electionem a Synodo Episcoporum Ecclesiae patriarchalis peractam conferuntur, et firmo can. 89, §2; expleto munere ad monasterium, ordinem vel congregationem redire debet.

§2. Religiosus, qui fit Patriarcha, Episcopus vel Exarchus:

1° manet votis ligatus ceterisque suae

428: Pius XII, m.p. *Cleri sanctitati,* 2 iun. 1957, can. 46 §§1–2; Pius XII, m.p. *Postquam Apostolicis Litteris,* 9 feb. 1952, can. 121.

429: Pius XII, m.p. *Postquam Apostolicis Litteris,* 9 feb. 1952, can. 158.

430: Pius XII, m.p. *Postquam Apostolicis Litteris,* 9 feb. 1952, can. 47 §1. * Syn. Libanen. Maronitarum, a. 1736, pars III, cap. III, 4, V.

431 §1: Pius XII, m.p. *Postquam Apostolicis Lit-*

teris, 9 feb. 1952, can. 175. - Clemens VIII, instr. *Sanctissimus,* 31 aug. 1595, §6 "Numquam;" Benedictus XIII, litt. ap. *Cum, sicut,* 16 dec. 1728, §§1–2. * Syn. Libanen. Maronitarum, a. 1736, pars IV, cap. II, 7; Syn. prov. Alba-Iulien. et Fagarasien. Rumenorum, a. 1872, tit. VIII, cap. II "Episcopus;" Syn. Armen., a. 1911, 771–772.

431 §2, 1°: Pius XII, m.p. *Postquam Apostolicis Litteris,* 9 feb. 1952, can. 176. - Constantinop. IV, can. 27.

obligations of his profession, except those that he himself prudently judges cannot be reconciled with his dignity. He lacks active and passive voice in his own monastery, order or congregation, is exempt from the power of the superiors, and in virtue of the vow of obedience remains subject only to the Roman Pontiff;

2° after having fulfilled the function, however, the religious who returns to the monastery, order or congregation, with due regard for cann. 62 and 211 for other matters, can have active and passive voice if the typicon or statutes permit it.

§3. A religious who becomes patriarch, bishop or exarch:

1° if he has lost the capacity to acquire the ownership of goods through profession, he has the use, revenue, and administration of the goods that have accrued to him. A patriarch, eparchial bishop or exarch, however, acquires property on behalf of the patriarchal Church, the eparchy, or exarchy; others on behalf of the monastery or order;

2° if he has not lost the ownership of goods through profession, he recovers the use, revenue and administration of the goods that he had; those things that accrue to him afterwards, he fully acquires for himself.

3° in either case, he must dispose of goods according to the intention of the donors when they do not accrue to him personally.

CAN. 432 A dependent monastery, a house or province of a religious institute of any Church *sui iuris,* also of the Latin Church, that with the consent of the Apostolic See is ascribed to an-

professionis obligationibus adhuc tenetur eis exceptis, quae cum sua dignitate ipse prudenter iudicat componi non posse; voce activa et passiva in proprio monasterio, ordine vel congregatione caret; a potestate Superiorum eximitur et vi voti oboedientiae soli Romano Pontifici manet obnoxius;

2° expleto munere vero, qui ad monasterium, ordinem vel congregationem firmis de cetero cann. 62 et 211 redit, vocem activam et passivam habere potest, si typicum vel statuta id permittunt.

§3. Religiosus, qui fit Patriarcha, Episcopus vel Exarchus:

1° si per professionem capacitatem acquirendi dominii bonorum amisit, bonorum, quae ipsi obveniunt, habet usum, usumfructum et administrationem; proprietatem vero Patriarcha, Episcopus eparchialis, Exarchus acquirit Ecclesiae patriarchali, eparchiae, exarchiae; ceteri monasterio vel ordini;

2° si per professionem dominium bonorum non amisit, bonorum, quae habebat, recuperat usum, usumfructum et administrationem; quae postea ipsi obveniunt, sibi plene acquirit;

3° in utroque casu de bonis, quae ipsi obveniunt non intuitu personae, debet disponere secundum offerentium voluntatem.

CAN. 432 Monasterium dependens, domus vel provincia instituti religiosi cuiusvis Ecclesiae sui iuris, etiam Ecclesiae latinae, quod de consensu Sedis Apostolicae alii Ec-

431 §2, 2°: Pius XII, m.p. *Postquam Apostolicis Litteris,* 9 feb. 1952, can. 178; S.C. pro Eccl. Orient., decr. 27 iun. 1972, 22.

431 §3: Pius XII, m.p. *Postquam Apostolicis Litteris,* 9 feb. 1952, can. 177. - S.C. de Prop. Fide, 5 iul.

1631, n. 17. * Syn. Libanen. Maronitarum, a. 1736, pars III, cap. IV, 27, III; Syn. Armen., a. 1911, 918, n. 4.

432: Pius XII, m.p. *Postquam Apostolicis Litteris,* 9 feb. 1952, can. 5.

other Church *sui iuris,* must observe the law of this latter Church, except for the prescripts of the typicon or statutes that regard the internal governance of the same institute or for the privileges granted by the Apostolic See.

clesiae sui iuris ascribitur, ius huius Ecclesiae servare debet salvis praescriptis typici vel statutorum, quae internum regimen eiusdem instituti respiciunt, et privilegiis a Sede Apostolica concessis.

ART. II. *Monasteries*

ART. II. *De Monasteriis*

CAN. 433 §1. A monastery is a religious house in which the members strive for evangelical perfection by the observance of the rules and traditions of monastic life.

§2. A monastery *sui iuris* is one that does not depend on another one and is governed by its own typicon approved by competent authority.

CAN. 433 §1. Monasterium dicitur domus religiosa, in qua sodales ad evangelicam perfectionem tendunt servatis regulis et traditionibus vitae monasticae.

§2. Monasterium sui iuris est illud, quod ab alio monasterio non dependet et regitur proprio typico ab auctoritate competenti approbato.

CAN. 434 A monastery is of pontifical right if the Apostolic See has erected it or recognized it as such by its decree; of patriarchal right, if it is a stauropegial one; of eparchial right, if it has been erected by a bishop, but has not obtained a decree of recognition from the Apostolic See.

CAN. 434 Monasterium est iuris pontificii, si a Sede Apostolica erectum aut per eiusdem decretum ut tale agnitum est; iuris patriarchalis, si est stauropegiacum; iuris eparchialis, si ab Episcopo erectum, decretum agnitionis Sedis Apostolicae consecutum non est.

1° Erection and Suppression of Monasteries

1° De Erectione et Suppressione Monasteriorum

CAN. 435 §1. It is for the eparchial bishop to erect a monastery *sui iuris,* after having consulted the patriarch within the territorial boundaries of the patriarchal Church, or the Apostolic See in other cases.

§2. The erection of a stauropegial monastery is reserved to the patriarch.

CAN. 435 §1. Episcopi eparchialis est erigere monasterium sui iuris consulto intra fines territorii Ecclesiae patriarchalis Patriarcha aut in ceteris casibus consulta Sede Apostolica.

§2. Patriarchae reservatur erectio monasterii stauropegiaci.

---

433 §1: Pius XII, m.p. *Postquam Apostolicis Litteris,* 9 feb. 1952, cann. 8 §1 n. 1, 313 §3; Vat. II, decr. *Perfectae caritatis,* 9 "Fideliter."

433 §2: Pius XII, m.p. *Postquam Apostolicis Litteris,* 9 feb. 1952, can. 313 §2 n. 2 b).

434: Pius XII, m.p. *Postquam Apostolicis Litteris,* 9 feb. 1952, cann. 312 §2 nn. 1–3, 313 §2 n. 2.

435 §1: Pius XII, m.p. *Postquam Apostolicis Lit-*

teris, 9 feb. 1952, can. 8 §1 n. 1. - Chalc. can. 4; Protodeut. can. 1. * Syn. Zamosten. Ruthenorum, a. 1720, tit. XI "Praeterea;" Syn. Libanen. Maronitarum, a. 1736, pars IV, cap. II, 1 et 7; cap. III, 1; Syn. prov. Alba-Iulien. et Fagarasien. Rumenorum, a. 1872, tit. VIII, cap. II "Quoad."

435 §2: Pius XII, m.p. *Postquam Apostolicis Litteris,* 9 feb. 1952, cann. 8 §2, 313 §2 n. 2 a).

CAN. 436 §1. Any monastery *sui iuris* can have dependent monasteries. Some of these are filial if, by reason of the very act of erection or the decree issued according to the typicon, they can aspire to the status of monastery *sui iuris;* however, others are subsidiary.

§2. For the valid erection of a dependent monastery, the written consent is required of the authority to which the monastery *sui iuris* is subject and of the eparchial bishop of the place where this monastery is being erected.

CAN. 437 §1. The permission to erect a monastery, even a dependent one, entails the right to have a church and to perform sacred ministries as well as exercise pious works that are proper to the monastery in accord with the norm of the typicon, without prejudice to the clauses legitimately attached.

§2. Written permission of the eparchial bishop is required for any monastery to build and open schools, guest houses or similar buildings distinct from the monastery.

§3. In order to convert a monastery to other uses, the same formalities are required as for erecting it, unless it concerns a change that refers only to internal governance and religious discipline.

CAN. 438 §1. It is for the patriarch to suppress, within the territorial boundaries of the Church over which he presides, a monastery *sui iuris* or a filial one of eparchial right or a stauropegial one, for a grave cause, with the consent of the permanent synod and at the request of,

CAN. 436 §1. Quodvis monasterium sui iuris monasteria dependentia habere potest, quorum alia sunt filialia, si ex ipso actu erectionis vel ex decreto secundum typicum lato ad condicionem monasterii sui iuris tendere possunt, alia vero sunt subsidiaria.

§2. Ad valide erigendum monasterium dependens requiritur consensus scripto datus auctoritatis, cui monasterium sui iuris subiectum est, et Episcopi eparchialis loci, ubi hoc monasterium erigitur.

CAN. 437 §1. Licentia erigendi monasterium, etiam dependens, secumfert ius habendi ecclesiam et ministeria sacra peragendi itemque pia opera, quae monasterii ad normam typici sunt propria, exercendi salvis clausulis legitime appositis.

§2. Ut aedificentur et aperiantur schola, hospitium vel similis aedes separata a monasterio, requiritur pro quovis monasterio consensus scripto datus Episcopi eparchialis.

§3. Ut monasterium in alios usus convertatur, eadem sollemnia requiruntur ac ad erigendum illud, nisi agitur de conversione, quae ad internum regimen et disciplinam religiosam dumtaxat refertur.

CAN. 438 §1. Patriarchae est supprimere intra fines territorii Ecclesiae, cui praeest, monasterium sui iuris vel filiale iuris eparchialis vel stauropegiacum gravi de causa, de consensu Synodi permanentis et rogante vel consulto Episcopo eparchiali, si

436 §1: Pius XII, m.p. *Postquam Apostolicis Litteris,* 9 feb. 1952, can. 313 §2 n. 2 b).

436 §2: Pius XII, m.p. *Postquam Apostolicis Litteris,* 9 feb. 1952, can. 8 §1 n. 2.

437 §1: Pius XII, m.p. *Postquam Apostolicis Litteris,* 9 feb. 1952, can. 9 §1. * Syn. Libanen. Maronitarum, a. 1736, pars IV, cap. I, 8.

437 §2: Pius XII, m.p. *Postquam Apostolicis Litteris,* 9 feb. 1952, can. 9 §2 n. 1. * Syn. Armen., a. 1911, 777.

437 §3: Pius XII, m.p. *Postquam Apostolicis Litteris,* 9 feb. 1952, can. 9 §3. * Syn. Armen., a. 1911, 777.

438 §1: Pius XII, m.p. *Postquam Apostolicis Litteris,* 9 feb. 1952, can. 10 §1.

or after having consulted, the eparchial bishop if the monastery is of eparchial right, and after having consulted the superior of the monastery and the president of the confederation, if the monastery is confederated, without prejudice to suspensive recourse to the Roman Pontiff.

§2. Other monasteries *sui iuris* or filial monasteries can be suppressed only by the Apostolic See.

§3. A subsidiary monastery can be suppressed by a decree issued by the superior of the monastery on which it depends, in accord with the norm of the typicon and with the consent of the eparchial bishop.

§4. The goods of the suppressed monastery *sui iuris* go to the confederation if it was confederated; otherwise, to the eparchy or, if it was stauropegial, to the patriarchal Church. However, the goods of a suppressed dependent monastery go to the monastery *sui iuris*. Regarding the goods of a suppressed monastery of pontifical right, however, it is reserved for the Apostolic See to decide, without prejudice in every case to the intention of the donors.

CAN. 439 §1. Several monasteries *sui iuris* of the same eparchy and subject to the same eparchial bishop can enter into a confederation with the written consent of that eparchial bishop, whose competence it also is to approve the statutes of the confederation.

§2. A confederation of several monasteries *sui iuris* of different eparchies or of stauropegial monasteries located within the territorial boundaries of the patriarchal Church can be entered into after having consulted the eparchial

monasterium est iuris eparchialis, et consulto Superiore monasterii et Praeside confoederationis, si monasterium est confoederatum, salvo recursu in suspensivo ad Romanum Pontificem.

§2. Cetera monasteria sui iuris vel filialia sola Sedes Apostolica supprimere potest.

§3. Monasterium subsidiarium supprimi potest decreto dato a Superiore monasterii, a quo dependet, ad normam typici et de consensu Episcopi eparchialis.

§4. Bona monasterii sui iuris suppressi cedunt confoederationi, si fuit confoederatum; secus eparchiae vel, si fuit stauropegiacum, Ecclesiae patriarchali; bona autem monasterii dependentis suppressi cedunt monasterio sui iuris; de bonis vero suppressi monasterii iuris pontificii Sedi Apostolicae reservatur statuere salva omni in casu offerentium voluntate.

CAN. 439 §1. Plura eiusdem eparchiae monasteria sui iuris Episcopo eparchiali subiecta confoederationem inire possunt de consensu scripto dato eiusdem Episcopi eparchialis, cuius est etiam confoederationis statuta approbare.

§2. Confoederatio inter plura monasteria sui iuris diversarum eparchiarum vel stauropegiaca intra fines territorii Ecclesiae patriarchalis sita iniri potest consultis Episcopis eparchialibus, quorum interest, et de consen-

438 §2: Pius XII, m.p. *Postquam Apostolicis Litteris,* 9 feb. 1952, can. 10 §2.

438 §3: Pius XII, m.p. *Postquam Apostolicis Litteris,* 9 feb. 1952, can. 10 §3.

438 §4: Pius XII, m.p. *Postquam Apostolicis Litteris,* 9 feb. 1952, can. 10 §4.

439 §1: Pius XII, m.p. *Postquam Apostolicis Litteris,* 9 feb. 1952, can. 11. - S. Basilius M., regulae fus., 35. * Syn. Zamosten. Ruthenorum, a. 1720, tit. XI "Cum experientia;" Syn. Libanen. Maronitarum, a. 1736, pars IV, cap. III, 2.

bishops who have an interest and with the consent of the patriarch, to whom the approval of the confederation's statutes is reserved.

§3. In other cases, the Apostolic See is to be approached regarding forming a confederation.

CAN. 440 §1. The aggregation of a non-confederated monastery *sui iuris* to, and the separation of a confederated monastery from, a confederation is reserved to the same authority mentioned in can. 439.

§2. A confederation, however, within the territorial boundaries of the patriarchal Church can be suppressed only by the patriarch with the consent of the synod of bishops of the patriarchal Church, after having consulted the eparchial bishops who have an interest and the president of the confederation, without prejudice to suspensive recourse to the Roman Pontiff. The suppression of other confederations is reserved to the Apostolic See.

§3. It is reserved to the authority that suppressed the confederation to make decisions regarding the goods that belong to the suppressed confederation, without prejudice to the intention of the donors; in such case, the patriarch needs the consent of the permanent synod.

2° The Superiors, Synaxes, and Finance Officers of Monasteries

CAN. 441 §1. In monasteries, superiors, and synaxes have that power which is determined by common law and the typicon.

§2. Superiors in monasteries *sui iuris* have the power of governance insofar as it is ex-

su Patriarchae, cui reservatur quoque confoederationis statuta approbare.

§3. In ceteris casibus de confoederatione ineunda Sedes Apostolica adeatur.

CAN. 440 §1. Monasterii sui iuris non confoederati aggregatio et confoederati a confoederatione separatio eidem auctoritati reservatur, de qua in can. 439.

§2. Confoederatio autem intra fines territorii Ecclesiae patriarchalis supprimi non potest nisi a Patriarcha de consensu Synodi Episcoporum Ecclesiae patriarchalis, consultis Episcopis eparchialibus, quorum interest, ac Praeside confoederationis salvo recursu in suspensivo ad Romanum Pontificem; ceterarum confoederationum suppressio reservatur Sedi Apostolicae.

§3. De bonis, quae ad ipsam confoederationem suppressam pertinent, statuere reservatur auctoritati, quae confoederationem suppressit, salva offerentium voluntate; Patriarcha hoc in casu indiget consensu Synodi permanentis.

2° De Monasteriorum Superioribus, Synaxibus et Oeconomis

CAN. 441 §1. In monasteriis Superiores et Synaxes eam potestatem habent, quae iure communi et typico determinatur.

§2. Superiores in monasteriis sui iuris habent potestatem regiminis, quatenus ipsis

---

440 §1: Pius XII, m.p. *Postquam Apostolicis Litteris,* 9 feb. 1952, can. 12 §1.

440 §2: Pius XII, m.p. *Postquam Apostolicis Litteris,* 9 feb. 1952, can. 12 §2.

440 §3: Pius XII, m.p. *Postquam Apostolicis Litteris,* 9 feb. 1952, can. 12 §3.

441 §1: Pius XII, m.p. *Postquam Apostolicis Litteris,* 9 feb. 1952, can. 26 §1 et §2 n. 2. - S. Theodorus Studita, ep. I, 10; S. Athanasius Athonita, diatyposis, "Μετὰ."

441 §2: Pius XII, m.p. *Postquam Apostolicis Litteris,* 9 feb. 1952, can. 26 §2.

pressly granted to them by law or by the authority to which they are subject, with due regard for can. 979.

§3. The power of the president of a monastic confederation, beyond those things determined by common law, must be determined in the statutes of the same confederation.

CAN. 442 With due regard for the typicon of the monastery *sui iuris* requiring more, for a person to be qualified to receive the office of superior, it is required that the person have made perpetual profession, be professed at least ten years, and be at least forty years old.

CAN. 443 §1. The superior of a monastery *sui iuris* is elected at the synaxis, convened in accord with the norms of the typicon and having observed cann. 947–960, without prejudice to the right of the eparchial bishop to preside at the synaxis of election personally or through another.

§2. At the synaxis of election of the superior of a confederated monastery *sui iuris,* however, the president of the same confederation presides at the election personally or through another.

CAN. 444 §1. The office of superior of a monastery *sui iuris* is conferred for an indeterminate time, unless the typicon determines otherwise.

§2. Unless the typicon prescribes otherwise,

a iure vel ab auctoritate, cui subditi sunt, expresse conceditur, firmo can. 979.

§3. Potestas Praesidis confoederationis monasticae praeter ea, quae iure communi determinata sunt, in statutis eiusdem confoederationis determinanda est.

CAN. 442 Firmo monasterii sui iuris typico, quod potiora exigit, ut quis habilis sit ad officium Superioris monasterii sui iuris suscipiendum, requiritur, ut professionem perpetuam emiserit, per decem saltem annos professus sit et annos quadraginta expleverit.

CAN. 443 §1. Superior monasterii sui iuris eligitur in Synaxi ad normas typici coadunata et servatis cann. 947–960, salvo iure Episcopi eparchialis ut Synaxi electionis per se vel per alium praesit.

§2. In electione vero Superioris monasterii sui iuris confoederati Synaxi electionis praeest per se vel per alium Praeses eiusdem confoederationis.

CAN. 444 §1. Officium Superioris monasterii sui iuris confertur ad tempus indeterminatum, nisi aliud fert typicum.

§2. Nisi typicum aliud praescribit, Supe-

441 §3: Pius XII, m.p. *Postquam Apostolicis Litteris,* 9 feb. 1952, can. 28.

442: Pius XII, m.p. *Postquam Apostolicis Litteris,* 9 feb. 1952, can. 31 nn. 2–5. - S. Basilius M., regulae fus., 35, 43. * Syn. Libanen. Maronitarum, a. 1736, pars IV, cap. III, 10.

443 §1: Pius XII, m.p. *Postquam Apostolicis Litteris,* 9 feb. 1952, cann. 34 §1 et §3 nn. 1–2, 35 §1. - S. Theodorus Studita, ep. II, 126 "Hortamur," 146; S. Athanasius Athonita, typicum, "Ταυτα;" Clemens XIII, litt. ap. *Ex iniuncto,* 10 ian. 1759, §1. * Syn.

Zamosten. Ruthenorum, a. 1720, tit. XII "Electiones;" Syn. Libanen. Maronitarum, a. 1736, pars IV, cap. III, 11; Syn. Leopolien. Ruthenorum, a. 1891, tit. X, 5.

443 §2: Pius XII, m.p. *Postquam Apostolicis Litteris,* 9 feb. 1952, can. 34 §2.

444 §1: Pius XII, m.p. *Postquam Apostolicis Litteris,* 9 feb. 1952, can. 32 §1. * Syn. Libanen. Maronitarum, a. 1736, pars IV, cap. III, 12.

444 §2: Pius XII, m.p. *Postquam Apostolicis Litteris,* 9 feb. 1952, can. 32 §3 n. 1.

superiors of dependent monasteries are constituted by the superior of the monastery *sui iuris* for a time determined in the typicon itself, with the consent of the council if the monastery is filial, but after having consulted the same council if it is subsidiary.

§3. However, superiors who have completed the seventy-fifth year of age or who have become unfit to fulfill their office because of failing health or another grave cause, are to present a resignation from office to the synaxis; it is for the synaxis to accept it.

CAN. 445   The members of the synaxis of election are seriously to strive to elect those whom they know before the Lord to be truly worthy and suitable for the office of superior, avoiding any abuse, especially that of procuring votes for themselves or for others.

CAN. 446   The superior is to reside in his or her own monastery and is not to be absent from it except in accord with the norm of the typicon.

CAN. 447   §1. For the administration of the temporal goods in a monastery, there is to be a finance officer, who is to perform his or her office under the direction of the superior.

§2. The superior of a monastery *sui iuris* is not to carry out the office of finance officer of the same monastery; the office of finance officer of a dependent monastery, however, even if it is better that it be distinguished from the office of superior, can nevertheless be joined with it, if necessity demands it.

riores monasteriorum dependentium constituuntur ad tempus in ipso typico determinatum a Superiore monasterii sui iuris de consensu sui consilii, si monasterium est filiale, consulto vero eodem consilio, si est subsidiarium.

§3. Superiores vero, qui septuagesimum quintum aetatis annum expleverunt vel qui ob infirmam valetudinem aliave gravi de causa officio suo implendo minus apti evaserunt, renuntiationem ab officio Synaxi, cuius est eam acceptare, exhibeant.

CAN. 445   Sodales Synaxis electionis eos eligere satagant, quos in Domino vere dignos et idoneos ad officium Superioris agnoscunt, se abstinentes a quovis abusu et praesertim a suffragiorum procuratione tam pro se ipsis quam pro aliis.

CAN. 446   In proprio monasterio Superior resideat neque ab eodem discedat nisi ad normam typici.

CAN. 447   §1. Pro administratione bonorum temporalium sit in monasterio oeconomus, qui officio suo fungatur sub moderamine Superioris.

§2. Superior monasterii sui iuris officium oeconomi eiusdem monasterii simul ne gerat; officium vero oeconomi monasterii dependentis, etsi melius ab officio Superioris distinguitur, componi tamen cum eo potest, si necessitas id exigit.

445: Pius XII, m.p. *Postquam Apostolicis Litteris,* 9 feb. 1952, cann. 34 §1, 35 §2.

446: Pius XII, m.p. *Postquam Apostolicis Litteris,* 9 feb. 1952, can. 36. - S. Theodorus Studita, ep. I, 10; sermo 92.

447 §1: Pius XII, m.p. *Postquam Apostolicis Litteris,* 9 feb. 1952, can. 48 §2. - Nic. II, can. 11; S. Basilius M., regulae fus., 34; S. Theodorus Studita, ser-

mo 48; ep. I, 10 in fine; ep. 96; iambi, 7; S. Athanasius Athonita, typicum, "Εἰσηγητέον" ("Τὸ χρυσίον"). * Syn. Libanen. Maronitarum, a. 1736, pars IV, cap. II, 4 et 21, VII; cap. III, 3–4.

447 §2: Pius XII, m.p. *Postquam Apostolicis Litteris,* 9 feb. 1952, can. 48 §4. * Syn. Libanen. Maronitarum, a. 1736, pars IV, cap. III, 3–4.

§3. The superior of the monastery *sui iuris* appoints the finance officer with the consent of his or her council, unless the typicon determines otherwise.

§3. Oeconomus nominatur a Superiore monasterii sui iuris de consensu sui consilii, nisi typicum aliud fert.

3° Admission to a Monastery Sui Iuris and the Novitiate

3° De Admissione in Monasterium Sui Iuris et de Novitiatu

CAN. 448 For one to be admitted into a monastery *sui iuris,* it is required that the person be moved by the right intention, be suitable for leading the monastic life, and not be prevented by any impediment established by law.

CAN. 448 Ut quis in monasterium sui iuris admittatur, requiritur, ut recta intentione moveatur, ad vitam monasticam ducendam sit idoneus nec ullo detineatur impedimento iure statuto.

CAN. 449 Before being admitted to the novitiate, a candidate must live in the monastery under the special care of an experienced member for a period of time determined in the typicon.

CAN. 449 Candidatus, antequam ad novitiatum admittitur, per temporis spatium in typico determinatum in monasterio degere debet sub speciali cura probati sodalis.

CAN. 450 With due regard for the prescripts of the typicon that require more, the following cannot be admitted validly to the novitiate:

CAN. 450 Firmis praescriptis typici, quae potiora exigunt, ad novitiatum valide admitti non possunt:

1° non-Catholics;

1° acatholici;

2° those who have been punished with canonical penalties, except those mentioned in can. 1426;

2° qui poena canonica puniti sunt exceptis poenis, de quibus in can. 1426, §1;

3° those threatened by a grave penalty on account of a delict for which they have been legitimately accused;

3° ii, quibus imminet gravis poena ob delictum, de quo legitime accusati sunt;

447 §3: Pius XII, m.p. *Postquam Apostolicis Litteris,* 9 feb. 1952, can. 48 §5. - S. Athanasius Athonita, typicum, "Ἐ'ισηγητέον" ("Τὸ χρυσίον"). * Syn. Libanen. Maronitarum, a. 1736, pars IV, cap. II, 4 et 21, VII.

448: Pius XII, m.p. *Postquam Apostolicis Litteris,* 9 feb. 1952, cann. 70, 84 §2 n. 1. - S. Basilius M., can. 18; Quinisext. cann. 40, 43; S.C. pro Eccl. Orient., decr. 27 ian. 1940, I, n. 3; decr. 27 iun. 1972, 15; Vat. II, decr. *Perfectae caritatis,* 12 in fine.

449: Pius XII, m.p. *Postquam Apostolicis Litteris,* 9 feb. 1952, cann. 71–73. - S. Basilius M., can. 18; regulae fus., 10, 15; S. Pachomius, reg. 49; S. Theodorus Studita, ep. II, 165 "Secunda;" hypotyposis, 24; S.

Athanasius Athonita, hypotyposis, "Χρῆγινώσκειν, ὠζότε;" S.C. pro Eccl. Orient., decr. 27 iun. 1972, 5.

450: Pius XII, m.p. *Postquam Apostolicis Litteris,* 9 feb. 1952, can. 74 §1. - Chalc. can. 4; S. Basilius M., regulae fus., 15; S.C. de Prop. Fide, litt. (ad Rectores . . .), 29 dec. 1668.

450, 1°: Pius XII, m.p. *Postquam Apostolicis Litteris,* 9 feb. 1952, can. 70. - S.C. de Prop. Fide, 18 iun. 1844, dub. 11. * Syn. Libanen. Maronitarum, a. 1736, pars I, cap. I, 3.

450, 2°: Pius XII, m.p. *Postquam Apostolicis Litteris,* 9 feb. 1952, can. 74 §1 nn. 1–2.

450, 3°: Pius XII, m.p. *Postquam Apostolicis Litteris,* 9 feb. 1952, can. 74 §1 n. 2.

4° those who have not yet completed eighteen years of age, unless it concerns a monastery that has temporary profession, in which case seventeen years of age is sufficient;

5° those who enter the monastery induced by force, grave fear, or fraud or those whom a superior, induced in the same way, has received;

6° spouses during a marriage;

7° those who are bound by the bond of religious profession or by another sacred bond in an institute of consecrated life, unless it is a question of legitimate transfer.

CAN. 451 No one can be admitted licitly to the novitiate of a monastery of another Church *sui iuris* without the permission of the Apostolic See, unless it concerns a candidate who is destined for a dependent monastery, mentioned in can. 432, of his or her own Church.

CAN. 452 §1. Clerics ascribed to an eparchy cannot be admitted licitly to the novitiate without consulting their own eparchial bishop, nor can they be admitted licitly if the eparchial bishop objects to it because their departure will result in grave harm to souls that cannot by any means be prevented otherwise, or if it concerns those who are destined to sacred orders in a monastery but are prevented by some impediment established by law.

§2. Likewise, parents whose assistance is nec-

4° qui duodevicesimum aetatis annum nondum expleverunt, nisi agitur de monasterio, in quo habetur professio temporaria, quo in casu sufficit aetas septemdecim annorum;

5° qui monasterium ingrediuntur vi, metu gravi aut dolo inducti vel ii, quos Superior eodem modo inductus recipit;

6° coniuges durante matrimonio;

7° qui ligantur vinculo professionis religiosae vel alio sacro vinculo in instituto vitae consecratae, nisi de legitimo transitu agitur.

CAN. 451 Nemo licite ad novitiatum monasterii alterius Ecclesiae sui iuris admitti potest sine licentia Sedis Apostolicae, nisi de candidato agitur, qui destinatus est monasterio dependenti, de quo in can. 432, propriae Ecclesiae.

CAN. 452 §1. Clerici eparchiae ascripti ad novitiatum licite admitti non possunt nisi consulto proprio Episcopo eparchiali; nec licite admitti possunt, si Episcopus eparchialis contradicit ex eo, quod eorum discessus in grave animarum detrimentum cedit, quod aliter vitari minime potest, aut si de iis agitur, qui ad ordines sacros in monasterio destinati aliquo impedimento iure statuto detinentur.

§2. Item licite in monasterium admitti

450, 4°: Pius XII, m.p. *Postquam Apostolicis Litteris,* 9 feb. 1952, cann. 74 §1 n. 3, 88 §1 n. 1, 107. - Carth. can. 126; Quinisext. can. 40; S. Basilius M., can. 18 in fine; regulae fus., 15; S. Theodorus Studita, ep. II, 165. * Syn. Zamosten. Ruthenorum, a. 1720, tit. XI "Novitii;" tit. XII "Puella;" Syn. Libanen. Maronitarum, a. 1736, pars IV, cap. II, 21, XIV; cap. III, 6.

450, 5°: Pius XII, m.p. *Postquam Apostolicis Litteris,* 9 feb. 1952, can. 74 §1 n. 4. * Syn. Libanen. Maronitarum, a. 1736, pars IV, cap. II, 21, XVII.

450, 6°: Pius XII, m.p. *Postquam Apostolicis Litteris,* 9 feb. 1952, can. 74 §1 n. 5. - S. Basilius M., regulae fus., 12; Quinisext. can. 48; S. Theodorus Studita, ep. II, 51.

450, 7°: Pius XII, m.p. *Postquam Apostolicis Litteris,* 9 feb. 1952, can. 74 §1 n. 6.

451: Pius XII, m.p. *Postquam Apostolicis Litteris,* 9 feb. 1952, can. 74 §2 n. 6. - Leo XIII, litt. ap. *Singulare praesidium,* 12 maii 1882, "Quo tutius;" S.C. de Prop. Fide, (C.G.), 1 iun. 1885, ad I; S.C. de Prop. Fide (pro Neg. Rit. Orient.), ep. 15 iun. 1912. * Syn. Alexandrin. Coptorum, a. 1898, sect. II, cap. I, art. V, XVI.

452 §1: Pius XII, m.p. *Postquam Apostolicis Litteris,* 9 feb. 1952, can. 74 §2 nn. 1, 5.

452 §2: Pius XII, m.p. *Postquam Apostolicis Litteris,* 9 feb. 1952, can. 74 §2 n. 4.

essary in raising and educating their children cannot be licitly admitted to a monastery, nor can children who must support a father or mother, a grandfather or grandmother who are in grave need, unless the monastery has provided otherwise for this.

CAN. 453 §1. It is for the superior of a monastery *sui iuris* to admit to the novitiate, after having consulted his or her council.

§2. The suitability and full freedom of a candidate in choosing the monastic state must be evident to the superior himself or herself, after having used appropriate means.

§3. Regarding the documents to be presented by the candidates and the various proofs to be gathered of their good conduct and suitability, the prescripts of the typicon are observed.

CAN. 454 Norms are to be determined in the typicon concerning the dowry, if required, to be offered by the candidates and administered under the special supervision of the local hierarch, as well as regarding the restitution of the entire dowry, without the income already accrued, to one who is leaving the monastery for whatever reason.

CAN. 455 The novitiate begins with the reception of the monastic habit or in another manner prescribed in the typicon.

CAN. 456 §1. A monastery *sui iuris* can have its own novices who are to be initiated into monastic life in the same monastery under the direction of a suitable member.

non possunt parentes, quorum opera est ad filios alendos et educandos necessaria, aut filii, qui patri vel matri, avo vel aviae in gravi necessitate constitutis subvenire debent, nisi monasterium aliter de re providit.

CAN. 453 §1. Superioris monasterii sui iuris est admittere ad novitiatum consulto suo consilio.

§2. Ipsi Superiori constare debet opportunis mediis adhibitis de idoneitate atque de plena libertate candidati in statu monastico eligendo.

§3. Circa documenta a candidatis praestanda necnon circa diversa testimonia de eorum bonis moribus et idoneitate colligenda serventur praescripta typici.

CAN. 454 In typico determinandae sunt normae circa dotem, si requiritur, a candidatis praestandam et sub speciali vigilantia Hierarchae loci administrandam necnon de integra dote sine fructibus iam maturis quavis de causa a monasterio discedenti restituenda.

CAN. 455 Novitiatus incipit a susceptione habitus monastici vel alio modo in typico praescripto.

CAN. 456 §1. Monasterium sui iuris habere potest proprios novitios, qui in eodem monasterio sub ductu idonei sodalis vitae monasticae initiantur.

453 §1: Pius XII, m.p. *Postquam Apostolicis Litteris,* 9 feb. 1952, can. 75. * Syn. Libanen. Maronitarum, a. 1736, pars IV, cap. III, 6.

453 §2: Pius XII, m.p. *Postquam Apostolicis Litteris,* 9 feb. 1952, can. 84 §2. - S. Basilius M., can. 18 in fine.

453 §3: Pius XII, m.p. *Postquam Apostolicis Litteris,* 9 feb. 1952, cann. 76–78. - S. Basilius M., regulae fus., 10; Leo XIII, litt. ap. *Orientalium,* 30 nov. 1894, X; S.C. de Prop. Fide (pro Neg. Rit. Orient.),

ep. 15 iun. 1912.

454: Pius XII, m.p. *Postquam Apostolicis Litteris,* 9 feb. 1952, cann. 79–83. - Nic. II, can. 19. * Syn. Zamosten. Ruthenorum, a. 1720, tit. XI "Praeterea;" tit. XII "Dos" et "Si qua;" Syn. Libanen. Maronitarum, a. 1736, pars IV, cap. III, 7.

455: Pius XII, m.p. *Postquam Apostolicis Litteris,* 9 feb. 1952, can. 85.

456 §1: Pius XII, m.p. *Postquam Apostolicis Litteris,* 9 feb. 1952, can. 86 §1.

§2. The novitiate, for validity, must be made in the monastery *sui iuris* itself or, by a decision of the superior, after having consulted his or her council, in another monastery *sui iuris* of the same confederation.

§3. However, if a monastery *sui iuris*, either confederated or non-confederated, cannot satisfy the prescripts regarding the formation of novices, the superior is bound by obligation to send the novices to another monastery in which the same prescripts are to be observed conscientiously.

CAN. 457 §1. The novitiate, for validity, must be made for three full and continuous years; however, in monasteries in which temporary profession precedes perpetual profession, a novitiate of one year is sufficient.

§2. In every year of the novitiate, an absence of less than three months, either continuous or interrupted, does not affect the validity of the novitiate, but the unfinished time must be made up if it exceeds fifteen days.

§3. The novitiate is not to be extended beyond three years, with due regard for can. 461, §2.

CAN. 458 §1. For the formation of the novices, a member is to be placed in charge as director according to norm of the typicon. This member is to be distinguished for prudence, charity, piety, knowledge and observance of monastic life, and professed for at least ten years.

§2. The rights and obligations of this director, especially in matters regarding the formation of the novices as well as relations with the

§2. Novitiatus, ut validus sit, peragi debet in ipso monasterio sui iuris aut Superioris decisione consulto eius consilio in alio monasterio sui iuris eiusdem confoederationis.

§3. Si vero aliquod monasterium sui iuris sive confoederatum sive non confoederatum praescripta de institutione novitiorum implere non potest, Superior tenetur obligatione novitios mittendi in aliud monasterium, in quo eadem praescripta religiose servantur.

CAN. 457 §1. Novitiatus, ut validus sit, per triennium integrum et continuum peragi debet; in monasteriis vero, in quibus professio temporaria praemittitur professioni perpetuae, sufficit unus annus novitiatus.

§2. In unoquoque anno novitiatus absentia tribus mensibus sive continuis sive intermissis brevior validitatem non afficit, sed tempus deficiens, si quindecim dies superat, suppleri debet.

§3. Novitiatus ultra triennium ne extendatur firmo can. 461, §2.

CAN. 458 §1. Novitiorum institutioni praeficiendus est ut magister ad normam typici sodalis prudentia, caritate, pietate, scientia et vitae monasticae observantia praestans, decem saltem annos professus.

§2. Iura et obligationes huius magistri in eis praesertim, quae ad modum institutionis novitiorum necnon ad relationes ad Synaxim

456 §2: Pius XII, m.p. *Postquam Apostolicis Litteris,* 9 feb. 1952, cann. 86 §2, 88 §1 n. 4.

456 §3: Pius XII, m.p. *Postquam Apostolicis Litteris,* 9 feb. 1952, can. 86 §§2–5.

457 §1: Pius XII, m.p. *Postquam Apostolicis Litteris,* 9 feb. 1952, can. 88 §1 n. 2. - Protodeut. can. 5.

457 §2: Pius XII, m.p. *Postquam Apostolicis Lit-*

teris, 9 feb. 1952, can. 89 §§1–2.

458 §1: Pius XII, m.p. *Postquam Apostolicis Litteris,* 9 feb. 1952, can. 92 §1. * Syn. Zamosten. Ruthenorum, a. 1720, tit. XII "Puella."

458 §2: Pius XII, m.p. *Postquam Apostolicis Litteris,* 9 feb. 1952, cann. 92 §3–97.

synaxis and the superior of the monastery, are to be determined in the typicon.

CAN. 459 §1. During the novitiate, the novices are to strive continuously so that, under the guidance of the director, their hearts are formed by the study of the typicon, by pious meditations and assiduous prayer, by thoroughly learning what pertains to the vows and the virtues, and by suitable exercises to root out vices, to curb passions and to acquire virtues.

§2. During the novitiate, novices are not to be assigned to works outside the monastery, nor are they to devote time to the study of literature, science or the arts.

CAN. 460 A novice cannot validly renounce his or her goods in any manner or burden the same with obligations, with due regard for can. 467, §1.

CAN. 461 §1. A novice can freely leave the monastery or be dismissed for a just cause by the superior or the synaxis in accord with the typicon.

§2. At the end of the novitiate, if judged suitable, a novice is to be admitted to profession; otherwise the novice is to be dismissed. If there is a doubt about the suitability of a novice, the time of novitiate can be extended in accord with the norm of the typicon, but not beyond one year.

4° Consecration or Monastic Profession

CAN. 462 §1. The monastic state is definitively assumed by perpetual profession, which

et Superiorem monasterii spectant, determinentur in typico.

CAN. 459 §1. Tempore novitiatus iugiter incumbendum est, ut sub ductu magistri informetur novitii animus studio typici, piis meditationibus assiduaque prece, eis perdiscendis, quae ad vota et ad virtutes pertinent, exercitationibus opportunis ad vitia extirpanda, ad compescendos animi motus, ad virtutes acquirendas.

§2. Tempore novitiatus ne destinentur novitii operibus exterioribus monasterii nec dedita opera studiis vacent litterarum, scientiarum aut artium.

CAN. 460 Novitius non potest valide suis bonis quovis modo renuntiare aut eadem obligare firmo can. 467, §1.

CAN. 461 §1. Novitius potest monasterium sui iuris libere deserere aut a Superiore vel a Synaxi secundum typicum iusta de causa dimitti.

§2. Exacto novitiatu, si iudicatur idoneus, novitius ad professionem admittatur, secus dimittatur; si vero dubium superest de eius idoneitate, potest novitiatus tempus ad normam typici prorogari, non tamen ultra annum.

4° De Consecratione seu Professione Monastica

CAN. 462 §1. Status monasticus definitive assumitur professione perpetua, in qua

459 §1: Pius XII, m.p. *Postquam Apostolicis Litteris,* 9 feb. 1952, can. 98 §1. - S. Pachomius, regg. 139–140.

459 §2: Pius XII, m.p. *Postquam Apostolicis Litteris,* 9 feb. 1952, can. 98 §3.

460: Pius XII, m.p. *Postquam Apostolicis Litteris,* 9 feb. 1952, can. 102. * Syn. Libanen. Maronitarum, a. 1736, pars IV, cap. II, 21, XV.

461 §1: Pius XII, m.p. *Postquam Apostolicis Litteris,* 9 feb. 1952, can. 105 §1. - S. Theodorus Studita, ep. II, 165 "Secunda." * Syn. Zamosten. Ruthenorum, a. 1720, tit. XI "Novitii."

461 §2: Pius XII, m.p. *Postquam Apostolicis Litteris,* 9 feb. 1952, can. 105 §2. * Syn. Libanen. Maronitarum, a. 1736, pars IV, cap. II, 21, XV.

462 §1: Protodeut. can. 6.

includes the three perpetual vows of obedience, chastity and poverty.

§2. In making profession, the prescripts of the typicon and liturgical books are to be observed.

CAN. 463 The typicon of the monastery is to be observed in what pertains to the different degrees of monastic profession, without prejudice to the juridic force of the profession according to common law.

CAN. 464 For the validity of perpetual monastic profession, it is required that:

1° the novitiate has been validly completed;

2° the novice be admitted to profession by the superior of his or her own monastery with the consent of the council and that the profession be received by that superior personally or through another;

3° the profession be expressed, and made and received without force, grave fear or fraud;

4° the other requirements in the typicon for the validity of the profession be fulfilled.

CAN. 465 What is prescribed by common law regarding temporary profession is also valid for monasteries in which this profession, in accord with the typicon, is made in advance of perpetual profession.

CAN. 466 Perpetual monastic profession renders acts that are contrary to the vows invalid if the acts can be nullified.

CAN. 467 §1. A candidate for perpetual

comprehenduntur tria vota perpetua oboedientiae, castitatis et paupertatis.

§2. In emittenda professione serventur praescripta typici et librorum liturgicorum.

CAN. 463 Quod attinet ad diversos professionis monasticae gradus, standum est typico monasterii salva vi iuridica professionis secundum ius commune.

CAN. 464 Ad validitatem professionis monasticae perpetuae requiritur, ut:

1° novitiatus valide peractus sit;

2° novitius admittatur ad professionem a Superiore proprii monasterii sui iuris de consensu sui consilii necnon recipiatur professio ab eodem Superiore per se vel per alium;

3° professio sit expressa nec vi, metu gravi aut dolo emissa vel recepta;

4° cetera ad validitatem professionis in typico requisita impleantur.

CAN. 465 Ea, quae iure communi de professione temporaria praescribuntur, valent etiam de monasteriis, in quibus talis professio secundum typicum professioni perpetuae praemittitur.

CAN. 466 Professio monastica perpetua actus votis contrarios reddit invalidos, si actus irriti fieri possunt.

CAN. 467 §1. Candidatus ad profes-

462 §2: PIUS XII, m.p. *Postquam Apostolicis Litteris,* 9 feb. 1952, can. 112 §1.

463: PIUS XII, m.p. *Postquam Apostolicis Litteris,* 9 feb. 1952, can. 109.

464: PIUS XII, m.p. *Postquam Apostolicis Litteris,* 9 feb. 1952, can. 106 §1. - Carth. can. 126; S. THEODORUS STUDITA, ep. 293.

464, 2°: Carth. can. 6; Protodeut. can. 2.

464, 3°: S. NICOLAUS I, litt. *Ad consulta vestra,* 13

nov. 866, LXXXVII.

466: PIUS XII, m.p. *Postquam Apostolicis Litteris,* 9 feb. 1952, can. 115.

467 §1: PIUS XII, m.p. *Postquam Apostolicis Litteris,* 9 feb. 1952, can. 117 §1. - Protodeut. can. 6; S. BASILIUS M., regulae fus., 9. * Syn. Zamosten. Ruthenorum, a. 1720, tit. XI "Novitii;" Syn. Libanen. Maronitarum, a. 1736, pars IV, cap. II, 21, XV.

monastic profession must, within sixty days before profession, renounce in favor of whomever the candidate wishes all goods that he or she has on the condition that the profession subsequently takes place; a renunciation made before this time is by the law itself null.

§2. Once profession has been made, all necessary steps are to be taken at once so that the renunciation also becomes effective in civil law.

CAN. 468 §1. Any temporal goods by whatever title that accrue to the member after perpetual profession are acquired for the monastery.

§2. The monastery must be responsible for the debts and obligations that the member has contracted with the permission of the superior; if the member contracted the debts without the permission of the superior, however, the member himself or herself must be responsible.

§3. It remains firm, however, that against one who has profited from the contract entered into, an action can always be brought.

CAN. 469 Having made perpetual profession, the member loses by the law itself whatever offices he or she may have, and his or her own eparchy, and is aggregated to the monastery with the full effects of the law.

CAN. 470 A written record of the perpetual profession that has been made, signed by the member himself or herself and by the one who received the profession, even by delegation, is to be kept in the archive of the monastery. The su-

sionem monasticam perpetuam debet intra sexaginta dies ante professionem omnibus bonis, quae actu habet, cui mavult, sub condicione secuturae professionis renuntiare; renuntiatio ante hoc tempus facta ipso iure nulla est.

§2. Emissa professione ea omnia statim fiant, quae necessaria sunt, ut renuntiatio etiam iure civili effectum consequatur.

CAN. 468 §1. Quaecumque bona temporalia quovis titulo sodali post professionem perpetuam obveniunt, a monasterio acquiruntur.

§2. De debitis et obligationibus, quae sodalis post professionem perpetuam contraxit de licentia Superioris, respondere debet monasterium; si vero sine licentia Superioris debita contraxit, ipse sodalis respondere debet.

§3. Firmum tamen est contra eum, in cuius rem aliquid ex inito contractu versum est, semper posse actionem institui.

CAN. 469 Sodalis emissa professione perpetua amittit ipso iure quaelibet officia, si quae habet, et propriam eparchiam atque pleno iure monasterio aggregatur.

CAN. 470 Documentum emissae professionis perpetuae ab ipso sodali et ab eo, qui professionem etiam ex delegatione recepit, subscriptum asservetur in archivo monasterii; Superior proprii monasterii sui

---

467 §2: Pius XII, m.p. *Postquam Apostolicis Litteris,* 9 feb. 1952, can. 117 §2.

468 §1: Pius XII, m.p. *Postquam Apostolicis Litteris,* 9 feb. 1952, can. 118. * Syn. Libanen. Maronitarum, a. 1736, pars IV, cap. II, 21, VII.

468 §2: Pius XII, m.p. *Postquam Apostolicis Litteris,* 9 feb. 1952, can. 68 §§2–3.

468 §3: Pius XII, m.p. *Postquam Apostolicis Lit-*

teris, 9 feb. 1952, can. 68 §5.

469: Pius XII, m.p. *Postquam Apostolicis Litteris,* 9 feb. 1952, cann. 120–121. - S. Nicephorus CP., can. 157.

470: Pius XII, m.p. *Postquam Apostolicis Litteris,* 9 feb. 1952, can. 112 §3. - S. Basilius M., regulae fus., 15. * Syn. Zamosten. Ruthenorum, a. 1720, tit. XII, "Puella."

perior of the monastery *sui iuris* must notify the pastor, with whom the baptism of the member was registered, about the profession as soon as possible.

iuris debet de eadem quam primum certiorem facere parochum, apud quem baptismus sodalis adnotatus est.

5° Formation of Members and Monastic Discipline

5° De Institutione Sodalium et de Disciplina Monastica

CAN. 471 §1. The manner of formation of members is to be determined in the typicon in such a way that they are continually motivated to pursue more fully a life of holiness and also that their natural abilities are developed through the study of sacred doctrine and the acquisition of human culture according to the needs of the times, and that they thereby become more prepared for the exercise of the arts and works that are legitimately undertaken by the monastery.

CAN. 471 §1. Modus institutionis sodalium in typico ita determinetur, ut ad vitam sanctitatis plenius assequendam permanenter excitentur necnon ut ipsorum ingenii dotes evolvantur studio sacrae doctrinae et acquisitione humanae culturae pro temporum necessitatibus et sic aptiores evadant in exercitio artium atque operum, quae a monasterio legitime assumuntur.

§2. In addition, the formation of monks destined for sacred orders must be done in accord with the formation program for clerics, mentioned in can. 330, in the monastery itself, if it has a place of studies set up according to can. 340, §1, or under the guidance of an approved moderator in another seminary or institute of higher studies approved by ecclesiastical authority.

§2. Institutio monachorum, qui ad ordines sacros destinantur, praeterea fieri debet secundum rationem institutionis clericorum, de qua in can. 330, in ipso monasterio, si sedem studiorum ad normam can. 340, §1 instructam habet, aut sub ductu probati moderatoris in alio seminario vel instituto studiorum superiorum ab auctoritate ecclesiastica approbato.

CAN. 472 The superior of a monastery *sui iuris* can give dimissorial letters for sacred ordination to his members in perpetual vows in accord with the norm of the typicon. These letters must be sent to the eparchial bishop of the place where the monastery, even a dependent one, is located or, if it concerns a stauropegial monastery, to the bishop designated by the patriarch.

CAN. 472 Superior monasterii sui iuris ad normam typici dare potest suis sodalibus a votis perpetuis litteras dimissorias ad sacram ordinationem; hae litterae mittendae sunt Episcopo eparchiali loci, ubi monasterium, etiam dependens, situm est vel, si de monasterio stauropegiaco agitur, Episcopo a Patriarcha designato.

---

471 §1: Vat. II, decr. *Perfectae caritatis*, 18; PAULUS VI, m.p. *Ecclesiae sanctae*, 6 aug. 1966, II, 16 §1, 33, 38.

471 §2: PIUS XII, m.p. *Postquam Apostolicis Litteris*, 9 feb. 1952, cann. 123–127.

472: PIUS XII, m.p. *Postquam Apostolicis Litteris*, 9 feb. 1952, cann. 131–132. - INNOCENTIUS III, litt. *Re-*

gularem vitam, a. 1198, "Sane novalium." * Syn. Zamosten. Ruthenorum, a. 1720, tit. III, §7 "In propria;" Syn. Libanen. Maronitarum, a. 1736, pars II, cap. 14, 10; pars IV, cap. II, 8; Syn. Armen., a. 1911, 763.

CAN. 473 §1. In individual monasteries, the divine praises are to be celebrated daily in accord with the norm of the typicon and legitimate customs. Likewise, the Divine Liturgy is to be celebrated on all days except those that are excluded by the prescripts of the liturgical books.

§2. The superiors of monasteries are to take care that all members, in accord with the norm of the typicon:

1° participate daily in the divine praises and Divine Liturgy whenever they are celebrated if they are not legitimately impeded; take time for contemplation of divine realities, and diligently apply themselves to other pious exercises;

2° can freely and frequently approach spiritual fathers and confessors;

3° make a spiritual retreat for several days every year.

CAN. 474 §1. The members of monasteries are to receive the sacrament of penance frequently in accord with the norm of the typicon.

§2. Without prejudice to the typicon, which suggests confession be made to certain confessors, all members of a monastery can receive the sacrament of penance from any priest endowed with the faculty of administering this sacrament, with due regard for monastic discipline.

CAN. 475 §1. In individual monasteries,

CAN. 473 §1. In singulis monasteriis laudes divinae cottidie celebrentur ad normam typici et legitimarum consuetudinum; item omnibus diebus celebretur Divina Liturgia eis exceptis, qui praescriptis librorum liturgicorum excipiuntur.

§2. Curent Superiores monasteriorum, ut omnes sodales ad normam typici:

1° legitime non impediti cottidie laudibus divinis atque Divinae Liturgiae, quoties celebratur, participent, contemplationi rerum divinarum vacent et in alia pietatis exercitia sedulo incumbant;

2° libere ac frequenter ad patres spirituales et confessarios accedere possint;

3° quotannis per aliquot dies recessui spirituali vacent.

CAN. 474 §1. Sodales monasteriorum frequenter ad normam typici sacramentum paenitentiae suscipiant.

§2. Firmo typico, quod confessionem suadet apud determinatos confessarios, omnes sodales monasterii sacramentum paenitentiae suscipere possunt a quocumque sacerdote facultate hoc sacramentum ministrandi praedito firma disciplina monastica.

CAN. 475 §1. In singulis monasteriis

473 §1: Pius XII, m.p. *Postquam Apostolicis Litteris,* 9 feb. 1952, can. 157 §§1, 4. - S. Basilius M., regulae fus., 37; S. Pachomius, regg. 9, 11, 141; S. Theodorus Studita, sermo 99; poenae monast., 1–8; Rabbula, can. 15; Vat. II, decr. *Perfectae caritatis,* 6. * Syn. Libanen. Maronitarum, a. 1736, pars IV, cap. II, 7 et 21, XII; cap. III, 15; Syn. Leopolien. Ruthenorum, a. 1891, tit. IV, cap. III, 3.

473 §2, 1°: Pius XII, m.p. *Postquam Apostolicis Litteris,* 9 feb. 1952, can. 138 §1 n. 2 et §2. - S. Basilius M., can. 94; S. Theodorus Studita, ep. I, 57; poenae monast., 1–10, 62; S.C.C., decr. 20 dec. 1905, 7; Vat. II, decr. *Perfectae caritatis,* 6. * Syn. Libanen. Maronitarum, a. 1736, pars II, cap. XII, 16.

473 §2, 2°: Pius XII, m.p. *Postquam Apostolicis Litteris,* 9 feb. 1952, can. 138 §1 n. 3; Vat. II, decr. *Perfectae caritatis,* 14 "Superiores."

473 §2, 3°: Pius XII, m.p. *Postquam Apostolicis Litteris,* 9 feb. 1952, can. 138 §2 n. 1.

474 §1: Pius XII, m.p. *Postquam Apostolicis Litteris,* 9 feb. 1952, can. 138 §1 n. 3; S.C. pro Eccl. Orient., decr. 27 iun. 1972, 6.

474 §2: Pius XII, m.p. *Postquam Apostolicis Litteris,* 9 feb. 1952, cann. 51, 52 §2, 53 §3, 54; Vat. II, decr. *Perfectae caritatis,* 14 "Superiores."

475 §1: Pius XII, m.p. *Postquam Apostolicis Litteris,* 9 feb. 1952, cann. 50 §1, 52–53, 57, 59. - Benedictus XIV, ep. encycl. *Demandatam,* 24 dec. 1743,

according to the number of members, several spiritual fathers and confessors are to be designated by the superior of the monastery, in the case of presbyter-monks of the same monastery who are endowed with the faculty of administering the sacrament of penance; otherwise, however, by the local hierarch, after having heard the superior of the monastery *sui iuris,* who, beforehand, must consult the community involved.

§2. For monasteries in which there are no presbyter-monks, the local hierarch is to designate in the same manner a priest, who regularly is to celebrate the Divine Liturgy and preach the word of God in the monastery, with due regard for can. 612, §2.

CAN. 476 Members of a monastery, whether inside or outside the monastery, are to wear the monastic habit prescribed by their own typicon.

CAN. 477 §1. Cloister is to be observed in monasteries in the manner prescribed in the typicon, without prejudice to the right of the superior to admit, on individual occasions and for a grave reason, into parts subject to cloister persons of the opposite sex besides those who can enter the cloister according to the typicon.

§2. The parts of the monastery subject to cloister are to be clearly indicated.

plures pro sodalium numero patres spirituales et confessarii designentur ab ipso Superiore monasterii, si de presbyteris-monachis eiusdem monasterii agitur, qui facultate sacramentum paenitentiae ministrandi praediti sunt, secus vero ab Hierarcha loci audito Superiore monasterii sui iuris, qui praevie communitatem, cuius interest, consulere debet.

§2. Pro monasteriis, in quibus presbyteri-monachi non sunt, Hierarcha loci eodem modo designet sacerdotem, cuius est regulariter in monasterio Divinam Liturgiam celebrare et verbum Dei praedicare firmo can. 612, §2.

CAN. 476 Sodales monasterii tam intra quam extra monasterium habitum monasticum a proprio typico praescriptum induant.

CAN. 477 §1. In monasterio servetur clausura modo in typico praescripto, salvo iure Superioris per modum actus et gravi de causa in partes clausurae obnoxias admittendi personas alterius sexus praeter illas, quae secundum typicum clausuram ingredi possunt.

§2. Partes monasterii clausurae obnoxiae manifesto indicentur.

§24; S.C. de Prop. Fide, (C.G.), decr. 15 mar. 1819, 3; (C.G.), 11 dec. 1838, ad 9; S.C.S. Off., 5 iul. 1899; S.C. pro Eccl. Orient., decr. 27 iun. 1972, 7. * Syn. Zamosten. Ruthenorum, a. 1720, tit. XII "Confessarii;" Syn. Libanen. Maronitarum, a. 1736, pars IV, cap. III, 3, 14.

475 §2: Pius XII, m.p. *Postquam Apostolicis Litteris,* 9 feb. 1952, can. 61.

476: Pius XII, m.p. *Postquam Apostolicis Litteris,* 9 feb. 1952, can. 139; Vat. II, decr. *Perfectae caritatis,* 17; Paulus VI, m.p. *Ecclesiae sanctae,* 6 aug. 1966, I, 25 §2 d). -S. Basilius M., regulae fus., 22; S. Theodorus Studita, ep. II, 52, 137. * Syn. Libanen. Maronitarum, a. 1736, pars IV, cap. II, 21, I; Syn. Ain-

Trazen. Graeco-Melchitarum, a. 1835, can. 17.

477 §1: Pius XII, m.p. *Postquam Apostolicis Litteris,* 9 feb. 1952, can. 140 §1; Vat. II, decr. *Perfectae caritatis,* 7, 16; Paulus VI, m.p. *Ecclesiae sanctae,* 6 aug. 1966, II, 30–32. - Quinisext. cann. 41, 46–47; Nic. II, cann. 18, 20, 22; S. Nicephorus CP., cann. 51, 104; S. Pachomius, regg. 52–57; S. Theodorus Studita, ep. I, 10; S. Sabba, typicum; Rabbula, cann. 1–2, 12–14. * Syn. Zamosten. Ruthenorum, a. 1720, tit. XI "Faeminis;" tit. XII "Quia;" Syn. Libanen. Maronitarum, a. 1736, pars IV, cap. II, 14–16, 21, X; cap. III, 18.

477 §2: Pius XII, m.p. *Postquam Apostolicis Litteris,* 9 feb. 1952, can. 140 §3 n. 1.

§3. It is for the superior of a monastery *sui iuris*, with the consent of the council and after having notified the eparchial bishop, to prescribe precisely the boundaries of the cloister or to change them for a just cause.

CAN. 478 The superior of a monastery *sui iuris* can permit members to live outside the monastery for a time determined in the typicon. However, for an absence which exceeds one year, unless it is for the purpose of studies or ill health, the permission of the authority to which the monastery is subject is required.

CAN. 479 If, in the judgment of the local hierarch, the assistance of monasteries is necessary in the instruction of the people, all superiors who are requested by the same hierarch must give the people such instruction, personally or through others, in their own churches.

CAN. 480 A parish cannot be erected in the church of a monastery, nor can monks be appointed pastors, without the consent of the patriarch within the territorial boundaries of the Church over which he presides or, in other cases, of the Apostolic See.

6° Hermits

CAN. 481 A hermit is a member of a monastery *sui iuris* who devotes himself or herself entirely to heavenly contemplation and is separated totally from people and the world.

CAN. 482 In order to undertake the eremi-

§3. Clausurae fines accurate praescribere aut iusta de causa mutare est Superioris monasterii sui iuris de consensu sui consilii atque certiore facto Episcopo eparchiali.

CAN. 478 Superior monasterii potest permittere, ut sodales extra monasterium degant ad tempus in typico determinatum; ad absentiam vero, quae unum annum excedit, nisi causa studiorum vel infirmitatis intercedit, requiritur licentia auctoritatis, cui monasterium subiectum est.

CAN. 479 Si de iudicio Hierarchae loci auxilium monasteriorum ad institutionem catecheticam populi necessarium est, omnes Superiores ab eodem Hierarcha requisiti debent per se vel per alios illam populo tradere in propriis ecclesiis.

CAN. 480 In ecclesia monasterii paroecia erigi non potest nec monachi parochi nominari possunt sine consensu Patriarchae intra fines territorii Ecclesiae, cui praeest, aut in ceteris casibus Sedis Apostolicae.

6° De Eremitis

CAN. 481 Eremita est sodalis monasterii sui iuris, qui in coelestium contemplatione se totum collocat et ab hominibus mundoque ex toto segregatur.

CAN. 482 Ad vitam eremiticam legitime

477 §3: Pius XII, m.p. *Postquam Apostolicis Litteris,* 9 feb. 1952, can. 140 §3 n. 2.

478: Pius XII, m.p. *Postquam Apostolicis Litteris,* 9 feb. 1952, cann. 145, 152–153. - Quinisext. cann. 41, 46; S. Pachomius, regg. 53–56; S.C. de Prop. Fide, decr. 20 aug. 1853; Secret. Status, rescr. 6 nov. 1964, 15. * Syn. Libanen. Maronitarum, a. 1736, pars IV, cap. III, 18; Syn. Ain-Trazen. Graeco-Melchitarum, a. 1835, can. 14.

479: Pius XII, m.p. *Postquam Apostolicis Litteris,* 9 feb. 1952, can. 154 §§1, 3; Paulus VI, m.p. *Ecclesiae*

sanctae, 6 aug. 1966, I, 36 §2. - S.C. de Prop. Fide, instr. 8 dec. 1845; decr. 25 apr. 1850, 3.

481: Pius XII, m.p. *Postquam Apostolicis Litteris,* 9 feb. 1952, can. 313 §4. - Quinisext. can. 41; S. Theodorus Studita, orat. 12. * Syn. Libanen. Maronitarum, a. 1736, pars IV, cap. II, 21, XX, XXII.

482: Quinisext. can. 42; S. Sabba, typicum; S. Athanasius Athonita, typicum ""Ἐκ δὴ τούτων" et "Εἰ δὲ και;". * Syn. Libanen. Maronitarum, a. 1736, pars IV, cap. II, 21, XX.

tical life legitimately, it is necessary that a member has obtained the permission of the superior of the monastery *sui iuris* to which the member belongs, with the consent of the council, and has lived in the monastery at least six years from the day of perpetual profession.

CAN. 483   The place where a hermit lives is to be designated by the superior of the monastery and separated in a special manner from the world and other parts of the monastery; but, if the place is found outside the monastery's property, the written consent of the eparchial bishop is also required.

CAN. 484   The hermit depends on the superior of the monastery and is obliged by the canons on monks and the typicon of the monastery insofar as they can be reconciled with the eremitical life.

CAN. 485   The superior of the monastery *sui iuris* can, with the consent of the council, impose an end to the eremitical life for a just cause, even against the hermit's will.

7° The Stauropegial Monastery

CAN. 486   §1. The patriarch can, for a grave cause, having consulted the eparchial bishop and with the consent of the permanent synod, grant to a monastery *sui iuris* the status of a stauropegial monastery in the very act of erection.

§2. The stauropegial monastery is directly subject to the patriarch in such a way that only he himself has the same rights and obligations as an eparchial bishop with respect to the mon-

aggrediendam requiritur, ut sodalis licentiam Superioris monasterii sui iuris, ad quod pertinet, de consensu eius consilii obtinuerit et saltem sex annos a die perpetuae professionis computandos vitam in monasterio peregerit.

CAN. 483   Locus, ubi eremita vivit, sit a Superiore monasterii designatus atque speciali modo a saeculo et a ceteris partibus monasterii segregatus; si vero locus extra saepta monasterii invenitur, requiritur insuper consensus scripto datus Episcopi eparchialis.

CAN. 484   Eremita a Superiore monasterii dependet atque canonibus de monachis et typico monasterii obligatur, quatenus cum vita eremitica componi possunt.

CAN. 485   Superior monasterii sui iuris potest de consensu sui consilii imponere finem vitae eremiticae iusta de causa, etiam invito eremita.

7° De Monasterio Stauropegiaco

CAN. 486   §1. Patriarcha gravi de causa, consulto Episcopo eparchiali atque de consensu Synodi permanentis potest in ipso actu erectionis monasterio sui iuris statum monasterii stauropegiaci concedere.

§2. Monasterium stauropegiacum Patriarchae immediate subiectum est ita, ut ipse solus eadem iura et obligationes habet ac Episcopus eparchialis circa monasterium, so-

---

483: * Syn. Libanen. Maronitarum, a. 1736, pars IV, cap. II, 21, XX.

484: Pius XII, m.p. *Postquam Apostolicis Litteris,* 9 feb. 1952, can. 4. - Quinisext. can. 42. * Syn. Libanen. Maronitarum, a. 1736, pars IV, cap. II, 1 et 21, XX.

486 §1: Pius XII, m.p. *Postquam Apostolicis Litteris,* 9 feb. 1952, can. 164 §2 n. 1; m.p. *Cleri sanctitati,*

2 iun. 1957, can. 263 §1. * Syn. Libanen. Maronitarum, a. 1736, pars III, cap. VI, 2, 16; pars IV, cap. II, 2.

486 §2: Pius XII, m.p. *Postquam Apostolicis Litteris,* 9 feb. 1952, can. 164 §1 et §2 nn. 2–3; m.p. *Cleri sanctitati,* 2 iun. 1957, can. 263 §§2–3. * Syn. Libanen. Maronitarum, a. 1736, pars III, cap. VI, 2, 16; pars IV, cap. II, 2; Syn. Armen., a. 1911, 197.

astery, the members ascribed to it, as well as the persons who live day and night in the monastery. Other persons, however, connected with the monastery are subject immediately and exclusively to the patriarch only in those matters that regard their functions or offices.

dales eidem ascriptos necnon personas, quae diu noctuque in monasterio degunt; ceterae vero personae monasterio addictae immediate et exclusive Patriarchae subduntur in eis solummodo, quae ad eorum munus vel officium spectant.

8° Transfer to Another Monastery

8° De Transitu ad Aliud Monasterium

CAN. 487 §1. A member cannot transfer from one monastery *sui iuris* to another of the same confederation without the written consent of the president of the confederation.

§2. For a transfer from a non-confederated monastery to another monastery subject to the same authority, the consent of the same authority is required; if, however, the monastery to which the transfer is made is subject to another authority, the consent of this authority is also required.

§3. The patriarch, the eparchial bishop and the president of the confederation cannot give this consent without having consulted the superior of the monastery *sui iuris* from which the transfer is made.

§4. For the validity of the transfer to a monastery of another Church *sui iuris* the consent of the Apostolic See is also required.

§5. The transfer occurs by admission granted by the superior of the new monastery *sui iuris* with the consent of the synaxis.

CAN. 488 §1. The one who transfers to another monastery *sui iuris* of the same confedera-

CAN. 487 §1. Sodalis non potest transire a monasterio sui iuris ad aliud eiusdem confoederationis sine consensu scripto dato Praesidis confoederationis.

§2. Ad transitum a monasterio non confoederato ad aliud monasterium eidem auctoritati subiectum requiritur consensus eiusdem auctoritatis; si vero monasterium, ad quod transitus fit, alii auctoritati subiectum est, requiritur etiam consensus huius auctoritatis.

§3. Patriarcha, Episcopus eparchialis et Praeses confoederationis hunc consensum dare non possunt nisi consulto Superiore monasterii sui iuris, a quo transitus fit.

§4. Ad validitatem transitus ad monasterium alterius Ecclesiae sui iuris requiritur insuper consensus Sedis Apostolicae.

§5. Transitus fit admissione a Superiore novi monasterii sui iuris de consensu Synaxis concessa.

CAN. 488 1. Transiens ad aliud monasterium sui iuris eiusdem confoederationis nec

---

487 §1: Pius XII, m.p. *Postquam Apostolicis Litteris,* 9 feb. 1952, can. 182 §1. - Protodeut. can. 4.

487 §2: Pius XII, m.p. *Postquam Apostolicis Litteris,* 9 feb. 1952, can. 182 §§2–3. - Nic. II, can. 21; S. Theodorus Studita, ep. II, 196; Honorius III, ep. *Religiosam vitam eligentibus,* 25 oct. 1216; ep. *Religiosam vitam . . . infringat,* 29 ian. 1218. * Syn. Libanen. Maronitarum, a. 1736, pars IV, cap. II, 10 et 12, V.

487 §3: Pius XII, m.p. *Postquam Apostolicis Lit-*

teris, 9 feb. 1952, can. 182 §§2–3.

487 §4: Pius XII, m.p. *Postquam Apostolicis Litteris,* 9 feb. 1952, cann. 74 §2 n. 6, 182 §1.

487 §5: Pius XII, m.p. *Postquam Apostolicis Litteris,* 9 feb. 1952, can. 183 §2 n. 2.

488 §1: Pius XII, m.p. *Postquam Apostolicis Litteris,* 9 feb. 195, cann. 183 §2 n. 1, 185 n. 1. * Syn. Libanen. Maronitarum, a. 1736, pars IV, cap. II, 21, XVI.

tion does not go through the novitiate nor make a new profession and, from the day of the transfer, loses the rights and is released from the obligations toward the former monastery and assumes the rights and obligations of the second and, if he is a cleric, is also ascribed to it as a cleric.

§2. The one who transfers from one monastery *sui iuris* to another monastery *sui iuris* that does not belong to any confederation or belongs to a different one shall observe the prescripts of the typicon of the monastery to which the transfer is made, regarding the obligation to go through novitiate and make profession. If there is no provision for it in the typicon, however, the person neither goes through novitiate nor makes a new profession, but the effects of the transfer take place from the day on which the transfer occurs, unless the superior of the monastery requires the person to go through some probationary period, not longer than a year, in the new monastery. When the probationary period has passed, he or she either is to be ascribed permanently to the new monastery by the superior with the consent of the council or synaxis, in accord with the norm of the typicon, or is to return to the original monastery.

§3. In a transfer from a monastery *sui iuris* to an order or congregation, cann. 544 and 545 are to be observed with the necessary adaptations.

§4. The monastery *sui iuris* from which the member transfers is to keep the goods that have been already acquired by it because of the member. With respect to the dowry, it belongs to the monastery to which the transfer is made, from the day of transfer, without the revenues that have already accrued.

novitiatum peragit nec novam professionem emittit et a die transitus amittit iura et solvitur ab obligationibus prioris monasterii, alterius iura et obligationes suscipit et, si clericus est, eidem etiam ut clericus ascribitur.

§2. Transiens a monasterio sui iuris ad aliud monasterium sui iuris ad nullam vel ad diversam confoederationem pertinens servet praescripta typici monasterii, ad quod fit transitus, circa obligationem peragendi novitiatum et emittendi professionem; si vero in typico de re non cavetur, nec novitiatum peragit nec novam professionem emittit, sed effectus transitus locum habent a die, quo transitus fit, nisi Superior monasterii ab eo exigit, ut aliquod tempus non ultra annum experimenti causa in monasterio transigat; transacto experimenti tempore aut a Superiore de consensu sui consilii vel Synaxis ad normam typici stabiliter novo monasterio ascribatur aut ad pristinum monasterium redeat.

§3. In transitu a monasterio sui iuris ad ordinem vel congregationem serventur congrua congruis referendo cann. 544 et 545.

§4. Monasterium sui iuris, a quo sodalis discedit, bona servat, quae ipsius sodalis ratione iam ei quaesita sunt; quod spectat ad dotem, ea debetur sine fructibus iam maturis a die transitus monasterio, ad quod transitus fit.

---

488 §2: Pius XII, m.p. *Postquam Apostolicis Litteris,* 9 feb. 1952, can. 183 §2 n. 2.

488 §4: Pius XII, m.p. *Postquam Apostolicis Litteris,* 9 feb. 1952, can. 185 n. 2.

9° Exclaustration and Separation from the Monastery

9° De Exclaustratione et de Discessu a Monasterio

CAN. 489 §1. The indult of exclaustration can be granted only to a member of a monastery *sui iuris* who is in perpetual vows. When the member himself or herself petitions, the indult can be granted by the authority to whom the monastery is subject, after having heard the superior of the monastery *sui iuris* along with the council.

CAN. 489 §1. Indultum exclaustrationis a monasterio sui iuris nonnisi sodali a votis perpetuis concedere potest ad petitionem ipsius sodalis auctoritas, cui monasterium subiectum est, audito Superiore monasterii sui iuris una cum suo consilio.

§2. The eparchial bishop can grant this indult only for up to three years.

§2. Episcopus eparchialis hoc indultum nonnisi ad triennium concedere potest.

CAN. 490 Exclaustration can be imposed at the request of the superior of the monastery *sui iuris* with the consent of the council by the authority to which the monastery is subject for a grave cause, with equity and charity observed.

CAN. 490 Petente Superiore monasterii sui iuris de consensu sui consilii exclaustratio imponi potest ab auctoritate, cui monasterium subiectum est, gravi de causa servata aequitate et caritate.

CAN. 491 The exclaustrated member remains bound by the vows and the other obligations of monastic profession that can be reconciled with his or her state; the member must put off the monastic habit; during the time of the exclaustration he or she lacks active and passive voice and is subject to the eparchial bishop of the place where he or she resides, in place of the superior of his or her own monastery also in virtue of the vow of obedience.

CAN. 491 Sodalis exclaustratus manet votis ligatus atque ceteris obligationibus professionis monasticae, quae cum suo statu componi possunt, adhuc tenetur; habitum monasticum debet deponere; perdurante tempore exclaustrationis caret voce activa et passiva; Episcopo eparchiali loci, ubi commoratur, loco Superioris proprii monasterii subditus est etiam vi voti oboedientiae.

CAN. 492 §1. The member in perpetual vows shall not request the indult to leave the monastery and return to secular life except for the most grave causes, considered before the Lord. The religious is to present a petition to the superior of the monastery *sui iuris,* who is to send it, along with a personal opinion and the opinion of the council to the Apostolic See.

CAN. 492 §1. Sodalis a votis perpetuis indultum discedendi a monasterio et redeundi ad vitam saecularem ne petat nisi gravissimis de causis coram Domino perpensis; petitionem suam deferat Superiori monasterii sui iuris, qui eam una cum voto suo suique consilii ad Sedem Apostolicam mittat.

§2. An indult of this type is reserved to the Apostolic See.

§2. Huiusmodi indultum Sedi Apostolicae reservatur.

489 §1: Pius XII, m.p. *Postquam Apostolicis Litteris,* 9 feb. 1952, can. 188. - S.C.S. Off. (Novae Aureliae), 2 aug. 1876.

491: Pius XII, m.p. *Postquam Apostolicis Litteris,* 9 feb. 1952, can. 189.

492 §2: Pius XII, m.p. *Postquam Apostolicis Litteris,* 9 feb. 1952, can. 190 §1.

CAN. 493   §1. The indult to leave the monastery and return to secular life granted legitimately and intimated to the member, unless it has been rejected by the member in the act of intimation, entails by the law itself the dispensation from the vows and from all obligations arising from profession, but not from the ones that are attached to a sacred order if he is in sacred orders.

§2. If a member who left the monastery and returned to secular life is again received into the monastery, he or she is to go through the novitiate and make profession again as if he or she had never been in religious life.

CAN. 494   §1. If a monk who is in perpetual vows and sacred orders has obtained the indult to leave the monastery and return to the world, he cannot exercise sacred orders until he has found a benevolent eparchial bishop to receive him.

§2. The eparchial bishop can receive him either absolutely or on an experimental basis for five years. In the first case, the monk is to be ascribed to the eparchy by the law itself; in the other case, it is after the completion of five years, unless he has been expressly dismissed beforehand.

CAN. 495   A member who, after making profession, has left the monastery illegitimately must return to the monastery without delay. The superiors must solicitously seek out the member and, if he or she returns moved by sincere penance, receive the member back; otherwise, in accord with the norm of law the member is to be punished or even dismissed.

CAN. 493   §1. Indultum discedendi a monasterio et redeundi ad vitam saecularem legitime concessum et sodali intimatum, nisi in actu intimationis ab ipso sodali reiectum est, ipso iure secumfert dispensationem a votis necnon ab omnibus obligationibus ex professione ortis, non vero ab illis ordini sacro adnexis, si sodalis in ordine sacro constitutus est.

§2. Si sodalis, qui a monasterio discessit et ad vitam saecularem rediit, in monasterium rursus recipitur, novitiatum ac professionem instaurat, perinde ac si numquam vitae religiosae addictus esset.

CAN. 494   §1. Monachus a votis perpetuis et in ordine sacro constitutus, si indultum discedendi a monasterio et redeundi ad saeculum obtinuit, non potest ordines sacros exercere, donec Episcopum eparchialem benevolum receptorem invenerit.

§2. Episcopus eparchialis eum recipere potest sive absolute sive experimenti causa ad quinquennium; in primo casu monachus est ipso iure eparchiae ascriptus, in altero vero exacto quinquennio, nisi antea expresse dimissus est.

CAN. 495   Sodalis, qui post emissam professionem monasterium illegitime deseruit, debet sine mora ad monasterium redire; Superiores debent eum sollicite requirere et, si vera paenitentia motus redit, suscipere; secus vero ad normam iuris puniatur vel etiam dimittatur.

493 §1: Pius XII, m.p. *Postquam Apostolicis Litteris,* 9 feb. 1952, can. 191 §1.

493 §2: Pius XII, m.p. *Postquam Apostolicis Litteris,* 9 feb. 1952, can. 191 §2; S.C. pro Eccl. Orient., decr. 27 iun. 1972, 13.

494 §1: Pius XII, m.p. *Postquam Apostolicis Litteris,* 9 feb. 1952, can. 192 §2.

494 §2: Pius XII, m.p. *Postquam Apostolicis Litteris,* 9 feb. 1952, can. 192 §3.

495: Pius XII, m.p. *Postquam Apostolicis Litteris,* 9 feb. 1952, cann. 195–196. - Protodeut. cann. 3–4; S. Theodorus Studita, ep. I, 8–9, 14, 20; ep. II, 164 "De renuntiatione." * Syn. Libanen. Maronitarum, a. 1736, pars IV, cap. II, 12, II; cap. III, 21.

CAN. 496 §1. One who during temporary profession wishes for a grave cause to leave the monastery and return to secular life is to present a petition to his or her superior of the monastery *sui iuris.*

§2. The superior is to send this petition, along with a personal opinion and the opinion of the council, to the eparchial bishop whose competence it is in this case, even for a monastery of pontifical right, to grant the indult to leave the monastery and return to secular life, unless particular law reserves this to the patriarch for monasteries located within the territorial boundaries of the patriarchal Church.

10° Dismissal of Monks

CAN. 497 §1. A member must be held dismissed from a monastery by the law itself, who:

1° has publicly rejected the Catholic faith;

2° has celebrated marriage or attempted it, even only civilly.

§2. In these cases, after the proofs have been collected, the superior of the monastery *sui iuris,* having consulted the council, is to issue a declaration of the fact so that the dismissal is established juridically, and, as soon as possible, the superior is to notify the authority to which the monastery is immediately subject about the matter.

CAN. 498 §1. After divesting himself or herself of the monastic habit, a member who is the cause of imminent and most grave external scandal or harm to the monastery can be expelled immediately by the superior of the monastery *sui iuris* with the consent of the council,

CAN. 496 §1. Qui perdurante professione temporaria gravi de causa a monasterio discedere et ad vitam saecularem redire vult, petitionem suam Superiori monasterii sui iuris deferat.

§2. Superior hanc petitionem una cum voto suo suique consilii ad Episcopum eparchialem mittat, cuius est, etsi de monasteriis iuris pontificii agitur, hoc in casu indultum discedendi a monasterio et ad vitam saecularem redeundi concedere, nisi ius particulare id pro monasteriis intra fines territorii Ecclesiae patriarchalis sitis Patriarchae reservat.

10° De Dimissione Monachorum

CAN. 497 §1. Ipso iure dimissus a monasterio habendus est sodalis qui:

1° fidem catholicam publice abiecit;

2° matrimonium celebravit vel etiam civiliter tantum attentavit.

§2. His in casibus Superior monasterii sui iuris consulto suo consilio sine mora collectis probationibus declarationem facti emittat, ut iuridice constet de dimissione, atque quam primum de re auctoritatem, cui monasterium immediate subiectum est, certiorem faciat.

CAN. 498 §1. Sodalis, qui causa est imminentis et gravissimi sive exterioris scandali sive erga monasterium damni, a Superiore monasterii sui iuris de consensu eius consilii statim ex monasterio eici potest habitu monastico statim deposito.

---

496 §2: Pius XII, m.p. *Postquam Apostolicis Litteris,* 9 feb. 1952, can. 190 §2.

497 §1: Pius XII, m.p. *Postquam Apostolicis Litteris,* 9 feb. 1952, can. 197 §1 nn. 1, 3.

497 §1, 2°: * Syn. Libanen. Maronitarum, a. 1736, pars IV, cap. II, 11.

497 §2: Pius XII, m.p. *Postquam Apostolicis Litteris,* 9 feb. 1952, can. 197 §2.

498 §1: Pius XII, m.p. *Postquam Apostolicis Litteris,* 9 feb. 1952, can. 198 §1 n. 1. - Nic. II, can. 19.

§2. The superior of the monastery *sui iuris,* if the case warrants, is to take care that the dismissal process progresses in accord with the norm of law or defer the matter to the authority to which the monastery is subject.

§3. A member expelled from the monastery, who has been constituted in a sacred order, is forbidden to exercise the order unless the authority to which the monastery is subject decides otherwise.

CAN. 499 A member can be dismissed during temporary profession by the superior of the monastery *sui iuris* with the consent of the council according to can. 552, §§2 and 3, but, for validity, the dismissal must be confirmed by the eparchial bishop, or by the patriarch if particular law so establishes for monasteries situated within the territorial boundaries of the patriarchal Church.

CAN. 500 §1. To dismiss a member in perpetual vows, with due regard for can. 497, the president of a monastic confederation or the superior of a non-confederated monastery *sui iuris* is competent, each of them with the consent of the council, which in this case must consist of at least five members for validity, including the presiding superior, in such a way that, if the number of ordinary councillors is insufficient or they are absent, others are to be called according to the typicon or the statutes of the confederation; the voting, however, must be done secretly.

§2. In addition to other conditions that may be established in the typicon, to decide validly on dismissal it is required that:

§2. Superior monasterii sui iuris, si casus fert, curet, ut processus dimissionis ad normam iuris promoveatur, aut rem auctoritati, cui monasterium subiectum est, deferat.

§3. Sodalis ex monasterio eiectus, qui in ordine sacro constitutus est, ab exercitio ordinis sacri prohibetur, nisi auctoritas, cui monasterium subiectum est, aliter decernit.

CAN. 499 Perdurante professione temporaria sodalis dimitti potest a Superiore monasterii sui iuris de consensu eius consilii secundum can. 552, §§2 et 3, sed dimissio, ut valeat, confirmari debet ab Episcopo eparchiali vel, si ius particulare ita fert pro monasteriis intra fines territorii Ecclesiae patriarchalis sitis, a Patriarcha.

CAN. 500 §1. Ad dimittendum sodalem a votis perpetuis firmo can. 497 competens est Praeses confoederationis monasticae vel Superior monasterii sui iuris non confoederati, uterque de consensu sui consilii, quod in casu simul cum Superiore praeside ex quinque saltem membris ad validitatem constare debet ita, ut, si desunt vel absunt ordinarii consiliarii, alii ad normam typici vel statutorum confoederationis advocentur; suffragatio autem secreto fieri debet.

§2. Ad dimissionem valide decernendam praeter alias condiciones in typico forte statutas requiritur, ut:

498 §2: Pius XII, m.p. *Postquam Apostolicis Litteris,* 9 feb. 1952, can. 198 §3. * Syn. Armen., a. 1911, 768.

499: Pius XII, m.p. *Postquam Apostolicis Litteris,* 9 feb. 1952, can. 199 §1 n. 1, §2 nn. 1–2.

500 §1: Pius XII, m.p. *Postquam Apostolicis Litteris,* 9 feb. 1952, can. 204. - S. Theodorus Studita,

ep. II, 196.

500 §2: Pius XII, m.p. *Postquam Apostolicis Litteris,* 9 feb. 1952, cann. 202–219. * Syn. Ain-Trazen. Graeco-Melchitarum, a. 1835, can. 18; Syn. Libanen. Maronitarum, a. 1736, pars IV, cap. II, 12, I; Syn. Armen., a. 1911, 768.

1° the causes for dismissal be grave, culpable and juridically proven along with a lack of reform;

2° the dismissal was preceded, unless the nature of the cause for dismissal precludes it, by two warnings with the formal threat of dismissal, that were in vain;

3° the causes were clearly indicated in writing to the member, giving the member, after each warning, full opportunity for self-defense;

4° the useful time established in the typicon has elapsed since the last warning.

§3. The written responses of the member are attached to the acts, which are to be submitted to those persons mentioned in §1.

§4. The decree of dismissal cannot be executed unless it is approved by the authority to which the monastery is subject.

CAN. 501 §1. The decree of dismissal is to be intimated as soon as possible to the member concerned.

§2. However, the member can, within fifteen days, either make recourse with suspensive effect against the decree of dismissal or, unless the decree of dismissal has been confirmed by the Apostolic See, request that the case be handled judicially.

§3. The Apostolic See or the patriarch, if it concerns a member who has domicile within the territorial boundaries of the patriarchal Church, deals with the recourse against the decree of dismissal.

1° causae dimissionis sint graves, culpabiles et iuridice comprobatae una cum defectu emendationis;

2° dimissioni praecesserint, nisi natura causae dimissionis id excludit, duae monitiones cum formali comminatione dimissionis, quae in cassum cesserunt;

3° causae dimissionis sodali scripto manifestatae sint data ei post singulas monitiones plena opportunitate se defendendi;

4° tempus utile in typico statutum ab ultima monitione elapsum sit.

§3. Responsiones sodalis scripto datae alligantur actis, quae eis, de quibus in §1, submittenda sunt.

§4. Decretum dimissionis exsecutioni mandari non potest, nisi est ab auctoritate, cui monasterium subiectum est, approbatum.

CAN. 501 §1. Decretum dimissionis quam primum sodali, cuius interest, intimetur.

§2. Sodalis vero potest adversus decretum dimissionis intra quindecim dies cum effectu suspensivo sive recursum interponere sive, nisi decretum dimissionis a Sede Apostolica confirmatum est, postulare, ut causa via iudiciali tractetur.

§3. De recursu adversus decretum dimissionis videt Sedes Apostolica vel, si de sodali agitur, qui domicilium intra fines territorii Ecclesiae patriarchalis habet, Patriarcha.

500 §2, 1°: Pius XII, m.p. *Postquam Apostolicis Litteris,* 9 feb. 1952, cann. 199 §3 nn. 1–2, 208 nn. 1 et 3, 209. - S. Basilius M., regulae fus., 28; S. Nicephorus CP., can. 137.

500 §2, 2°: Pius XII, m.p. *Postquam Apostolicis Litteris,* 9 feb. 1952, cann. 199 §3 n. 2, 212–214.

500 §2, 3°: Pius XII, m.p. *Postquam Apostolicis Litteris,* 9 feb. 1952, cann. 199 §4 n. 3, 203 §3.

500 §2, 4°: Pius XII, m.p. *Postquam Apostolicis Litteris,* 9 feb. 1952, can. 212.

500 §3: Pius XII, m.p. *Postquam Apostolicis Litteris,* 9 feb. 1952, can. 199 §3 n. 3.

500 §4: Pius XII, m.p. *Postquam Apostolicis Litteris,* 9 feb. 1952, cann. 205 §§2–4, 218. * Syn. Ain-Trazen. Graeco-Melchitarum, a. 1835, can. 18; Syn. Libanen. Maronitarum, a. 1736, pars IV, cap. II, 12, I; Syn. Armen., a. 1911, 768.

501 §2: Pius XII, m.p. *Postquam Apostolicis Litteris,* 9 feb. 1952, can. 199 §3 n. 4.

501 §3: Pius XII, m.p. *Postquam Apostolicis Litteris,* 9 feb. 1952, cann. 215–216.

§4. If the case is to be handled judicially, it is to be dealt with by the tribunal of the authority immediately superior to the one that has confirmed the decree of dismissal. However, the superior who has issued the decree of dismissal is to hand over the acts assembled in the matter to the same tribunal; it is to proceed according to the canons regarding a penal trial, with no appeal.

CAN. 502 By legitimate dismissal, excluding the dismissal mentioned in can. 497, all bonds as well as obligations arising from monastic profession cease by the law itself, and, if the member has been constituted in a sacred order, can. 494 must be observed.

CAN. 503 §1. One who leaves a monastery legitimately or has been dismissed from it legitimately can request nothing from the monastery for any work done in it.

§2. Nevertheless, the institute is to observe equity and charity toward a member who is separated from it.

ART. III. *Orders and Congregations*

CAN. 504 §1. An order is a society erected by a competent ecclesiastical authority, in which the members, although they are not monks, make a profession that is equivalent to monastic profession.

§2. A congregation is a society erected by a competent ecclesiastical authority, in which the members make profession with the three public vows of obedience, chastity and poverty, which, however, are not equivalent to monastic

§4. Si vero causa via iudiciali tractanda est, de ea videt tribunal auctoritatis immediate superioris ei, qui decretum dimissionis confirmavit; Superior vero, qui decretum dimissionis tulit, acta in re collecta tradat eidem tribunali et procedatur secundum canones de iudicio poenali appellatione remota.

CAN. 502 Legitima dimissione, ea exclusa, de qua in can. 497, ipso iure cessant omnia vincula necnon obligationes ex professione monastica orta et, si sodalis in ordine sacro constitutus est, servari debet can. 494.

CAN. 503 §1. Qui a monasterio legitime discedit vel ab eo legitime dimissus est, nihil ab eo repetere potest ob quamlibet operam in eo praestitam.

§2. Monasterium tamen aequitatem et caritatem servet erga sodalem, qui ab eo separatur.

ART. III. *De Ordinibus et Congregationibus*

CAN. 504 §1. Ordo est societas ab auctoritate competenti ecclesiastica erecta, in qua sodales, etsi non sunt monachi, professionem emittunt, quae professioni monasticae aequiparatur.

§2. Congregatio est societas ab auctoritate competenti ecclesiastica erecta, in qua sodales professionem emittunt cum tribus votis publicis oboedientiae, castitatis et paupertatis, quae tamen professioni monasticae

502: Pius XII, m.p. *Postquam Apostolicis Litteris,* 9 feb. 1952, cann. 200, 192 §§1 et 3, 223 §2.

503 §1: Pius XII, m.p. *Postquam Apostolicis Litteris,* 9 feb. 1952, can. 194 §1.

503 §2: Pius XII, m.p. *Postquam Apostolicis Litteris,* 9 feb. 1952, can. 222 §1 n. 5.

504 §1: Pius XII, m.p. *Postquam Apostolicis Litteris,* 9 feb. 1952, can. 314 §1.

504 §2: Pius XII, m.p. *Postquam Apostolicis Litteris,* 9 feb. 1952, can. 314 §2.

profession, but have their own force in accord with the norm of law.

CAN. 505 §1. An order is of pontifical right if the Apostolic See erected it or recognized it as such by its decree; an order is of patriarchal right if, having been erected by a patriarch, it has not obtained the decree of recognition of the Apostolic See.

§2. A congregation is:

1° of pontifical right, if the Apostolic See erected it or recognized it as such by its decree;

2° of patriarchal right, if a patriarch has erected it or recognized it as such by his decree, and it has not obtained a decree of recognition of the Apostolic See;

3° of eparchial right, having been erected by an eparchial bishop, it has not obtained a decree of recognition of the Apostolic See or a patriarch.

§3. An order or congregation is clerical if, by reason of the purpose or intention set forth by the founder or by virtue of legitimate custom, it is under the direction of presbyters, assumes ministries proper to sacred orders, and is recognized as such by ecclesiastical authority.

1° Erection and Suppression of an Order, Congregation, Province, House

CAN. 506 §1. An eparchial bishop can erect only congregations, but he is not to erect them without having consulted the Apostolic See and, in addition, within the territorial boundaries of the patriarchal Church, without having consulted the patriarch.

non aequiparatur, sed propriam vim habet ad normam iuris.

CAN. 505 §1. Ordo est iuris pontificii, si a Sede Apostolica erectus aut per eiusdem decretum ut talis agnitus est; iuris patriarchalis vero, si a Patriarcha erectus decretum agnitionis Sedis Apostolicae consecutus non est.

§2. Congregatio est:

1° iuris pontificii, si a Sede Apostolica erecta aut per eiusdem decretum ut talis agnita est;

2° iuris patriarchalis, si a Patriarcha erecta aut per eiusdem decretum ut talis agnita est nec decretum agnitionis Sedis Apostolicae consecuta est;

3° iuris eparchialis, si ab Episcopo eparchiali erecta decretum agnitionis Sedis Apostolicae vel Patriarchae consecuta non est.

§3. Ordo vel congregatio est clericalis, si ratione finis seu propositi a fundatore intenti vel vi legitimae consuetudinis sub moderamine est presbyterorum, ministeria ordini sacro propri assumit et ut talis ab auctoritate ecclesiastica agnoscitur.

1° De Erectione et de Suppressione Ordinis, Congregationis, Provinciae, Domus

CAN. 506 §1. Episcopus eparchialis erigere potest tantum congregationes; sed eas ne erigat nisi consulta Sede Apostolica et insuper intra fines territorii Ecclesiae patriarchalis nisi consulto Patriarcha.

505 §1: PIUS XII, m.p. *Postquam Apostolicis Litteris,* 9 feb. 1952, can. 312 §2.

505 §2: PIUS XII, m.p. *Postquam Apostolicis Litteris,* 9 feb. 1952, can. 312 §2.

505 §3: PIUS XII, m.p. *Postquam Apostolicis Litteris,* 9 feb. 1952, can. 314 §3.

506 §1: PIUS XII, m.p. *Postquam Apostolicis Litteris,* 9 feb. 1952, can. 13 §1 n. 1.

§2. A patriarch can erect orders and congregations with the consent of the permanent synod and after having consulted the Apostolic See.

§3. A congregation of eparchial right which, within the territorial boundaries of the patriarchal Church, has expanded to several eparchies of the same territory, can become of patriarchal right by a decree of the patriarch, after having consulted those who have an interest and with the consent of the permanent synod.

CAN. 507 §1. A legitimately erected order, also of patriarchal right, even if it consists of only one house, cannot be suppressed except by the Apostolic See, to which it is also reserved to decide regarding the goods of the suppressed order, without prejudice to the intention of the donors.

§2. A legitimately erected congregation of patriarchal or eparchial right, even if it consists of only one house, can be suppressed, besides by the Apostolic See, by the patriarch within the territorial boundaries of the Church over which he presides, after having consulted those concerned and with the consent of the permanent synod as well as the Apostolic See.

CAN. 508 §1. A province indicates a part of the same order or congregation consisting of several houses, which a major superior governs directly.

§2. To divide an order or congregation into provinces, to join provinces, redefine their boundaries, or suppress and erect new ones, pertains to the authority determined by the statutes of the order or congregation.

§2. Patriarcha erigere potest ordines et congregationes de consensu Synodi permanentis atque Sede Apostolica consulta.

§3. Intra fines territorii Ecclesiae patriarchalis congregatio iuris eparchialis, quae in plures eparchias eiusdem territorii diffusa est, fieri potest iuris patriarchalis decreto Patriarchae consultis eis, quorum interest, et de consensu Synodi permanentis.

CAN. 507 §1. Ordo, etiam iuris patriarchalis, legitime erectus, etsi ex una tantum domo constat, supprimi non potest nisi a Sede Apostolica, cui etiam reservatur de bonis suppressi ordinis statuere salva offerentium voluntate.

§2. Congregationem iuris patriarchalis vel eparchialis legitime erectam, etsi ex una tantum domo constat, supprimere potest praeter Sedem Apostolicam Patriarcha intra fines territorii Ecclesiae, cui praeest, consultis eis, quorum interest, et de consensu Synodi permanentis necnon Sedis Apostolicae.

CAN. 508 §1. Provincia indicat partem eiusdem ordinis vel congregationis ex pluribus domibus constantem, quam Superior maior immediate regit.

§2. Ordinem vel congregationem in provincias dividere, provincias coniungere, aliter circumscribere vel supprimere novasque erigere, pertinet ad auctoritatem a statutis ordinis vel congregationis determinatam.

506 §2: Pius XII, m.p. *Postquam Apostolicis Litteris,* 9 feb. 1952, can. 13 §1 n. 2.

506 §3: Pius XII, m.p. *Postquam Apostolicis Litteris,* 9 feb. 1952, can. 13 §2.

507 §1: Pius XII, m.p. *Postquam Apostolicis Litteris,* 9 feb. 1952, can. 14 §1.

507 §2: Pius XII, m.p. *Postquam Apostolicis Litteris,* 9 feb. 1952, can. 14 §2.

508 §1: Pius XII, m.p. *Postquam Apostolicis Litteris,* 9 feb. 1952, can. 314 §4.

508 §2: Pius XII, m.p. *Postquam Apostolicis Litteris,* 9 feb. 1952, can. 15 §1; S.C. pro Eccl. Orient., decr. 27 iun. 1972, 1.

§3. Decisions regarding the goods of the suppressed province, without prejudice to justice and the intention of the donors, unless the statutes provide otherwise, pertains to the general synaxis or, in urgent need, the superior general with the consent of the council.

CAN. 509 §1. An order or congregation cannot validly erect a house without the written consent of the eparchial bishop. If it is a question of erecting the first house of an order or congregation of patriarchal right in some eparchy, the consent of the patriarch is required within the territorial boundaries of the patriarchal Church or, in other cases, the Apostolic See.

§2. That which is stated in can. 437 is also valid regarding houses of orders and congregations.

CAN. 510 A house of an order or congregation cannot be suppressed validly except after having consulted the eparchial bishop. The suppression of the only house of an order or congregation, however, is reserved to the same authority that is competent, according to can. 507, to suppress that same order or congregation.

§3. De bonis suppressae provinciae statuere salva iustitia et offerentium voluntate spectat, nisi statuta aliter cavent, ad Synaxim generalem vel urgente necessitate ad Superiorem generalem de consensu sui consilii.

CAN. 509 §1. Ordo vel congregatio domum valide erigere non potest nisi de consensu scripto dato Episcopi eparchialis; si agitur de erigenda prima domo ordinis vel congregationis iuris patriarchalis in aliqua eparchia, requiritur intra fines territorii Ecclesiae patriarchalis consensus Patriarchae vel in ceteris casibus Sedis Apostolicae.

§2. Quae dicuntur in can. 437, valent etiam de domibus ordinum et congregationum.

CAN. 510 Domus ordinis vel congregationis valide supprimi non potest nisi consulto Episcopo eparchiali; suppressio vero unicae domus ordinis vel congregationis eidem auctoritati reservatur, cuius est secundum can. 507 ipsum ordinem vel congregationem supprimere.

2° Superiors, Synaxes and Finance Officers in Orders and Congregations

CAN. 511 §1. The superiors and synaxes in orders and congregations have that power that is determined by common law and the statutes.

§2. In clerical orders and congregations of

2° De Superioribus, de Synaxibus et de Oeconomis in Ordinibus et Congregationibus

CAN. 511 §1. In ordinibus et congregationibus Superiores et Synaxes eam potestatem habent, quae iure communi et statutis determinatur.

§2. In ordinibus et congregationibus cle-

---

508 §3: Pius XII, m.p. *Postquam Apostolicis Litteris,* 9 feb. 1952, can. 15 §2.

509 §1: Pius XII, m.p. *Postquam Apostolicis Litteris,* 9 feb. 1952, can. 17; S.C. pro Eccl. Orient., decr. 27 iun. 1972, 2.

509 §2: Pius XII, m.p. *Postquam Apostolicis Litteris,* 9 feb. 1952, can. 10 §3.

510: Pius XII, m.p. *Postquam Apostolicis Litteris,* 9 feb. 1952, cann. 20 §§1–4, 14 §2.

511 §1: Pius XII, m.p. *Postquam Apostolicis Litteris,* 9 feb. 1952, can. 26 §1 et §2 n. 2.

511 §2: Pius XII, m.p. *Postquam Apostolicis Litteris,* 9 feb. 1952, can. 26 §2 n. 1.

pontifical or patriarchal right, however, superiors and synaxes have, in addition, the power of governance for the external and internal forum in accord with the norm of the statutes.

CAN. 512 §1. The general synaxis, which is the highest authority in accord with the norm of the statutes, is to be composed in such a way that, representing the entire order or congregation, it becomes a true sign of its unity in charity.

§2. Not only provinces and houses, but also every member can freely send his or her wishes to the general synaxis in the manner determined in the statutes.

CAN. 513 §1. In order for members to be appointed or elected validly to the office of superior, a suitable time is required after perpetual profession, to be determined by the statutes, which, if it concerns major superiors, must be at least ten years from first profession.

§2. If it concerns a superior general, in addition, it is required for validity that he or she be at least thirty-five years old.

CAN. 514 §1. Superiors are to be constituted for a determined and appropriate period of time, unless the statutes establish otherwise for the superior general.

§2. Nevertheless, before the determined time has elapsed, they can be removed from office or transferred to another for reasons and according to the manner determined by the statutes.

§3. The statutes are to provide suitable norms so that the members are not superiors for too long without interruption.

ricalibus iuris pontificii vel patriarchalis autem Superiores et Synaxes insuper habent potestatem regiminis pro foro externo et interno ad normam statutorum.

CAN. 512 §1. Synaxis generalis, quae superior auctoritas ad normam statutorum est, efformetur ita, ut totum ordinem vel congregationem repraesentans verum signum eiusdem unitatis in caritate fiat.

§2. Non solum provinciae et domus, sed etiam omnis sodalis optata sua modo in statutis determinato Synaxi generali libere mittere potest.

CAN. 513 §1. Ut sodales ad officium Superioris valide nominentur aut eligantur, requiritur congruum tempus post professionem perpetuam a statutis determinandum, quod, si de Superioribus maioribus agitur, debet esse saltem decennium a prima professione computandum.

§2. Si de Superiore generali agitur, praeterea ad validitatem requiritur, ut annos triginta quinque expleverit.

CAN. 514 §1. Superiores ad tempus determinatum et conveniens temporis spatium constituantur, nisi pro Superiore generali aliud ferunt statuta.

§2. Possunt tamen antequam tempus determinatum elapsum est ab officio amoveri vel ad aliud transferri ob causas et secundum modum a statutis determinata.

§3. In statutis aptis normis provideatur, ne sodales diutius sine intermissione Superiores sint.

512 §1: Vat. II, decr. *Perfectae caritatis,* 14 "Capitula;" PAULUS VI, m.p. *Ecclesiae sanctae,* 6 aug. 1966, II, 1, 18.

513 §1: S.C. pro Eccl. Orient., decr. 27 iun. 1972, 3; PIUS XII, m.p. *Postquam Apostolicis Litteris,* 9 feb. 1952, can. 31 nn. 2–4. - * Syn. Libanen. Maronitarum, a. 1736, pars IV, cap. III, 10.

513 §2: S.C. pro Eccl. Orient., decr. 27 iun. 1972, 3; PIUS XII, m.p. *Postquam Apostolicis Litteris,* 9 feb. 1952, can. 31 n. 5.

514 §1: PIUS XII, m.p. *Postquam Apostolicis Litteris,* 9 feb. 1952, can. 32 §§2–3. * Syn. Libanen. Maronitarum, a. 1736, pars IV, cap. III, 12.

CAN. 515 §1. The superior general is designated by election in accord with the norm of the statutes.

§2. Other superiors are to be designated in accord with the norm of the statutes, but in such a way that, if they are elected, they need the confirmation of a competent major superior; if, however, they are appointed, a suitable consultation is to precede.

§3. In elections, cann. 947–960 as well as can. 445 are to be observed carefully.

CAN. 516 §1. There are to be finance officers in orders and congregations for the administration of temporal goods: a general finance officer who administers the goods of the entire order or congregation, a provincial finance officer for the province, a local finance officer for the individual houses; all of these are to exercise their office under the direction of the superior.

§2. A major superior cannot fulfill the office of general finance officer and provincial finance officer. However, the office of local finance officer, even if it is better that it be distinguished from the office of superior, can nevertheless be combined with it, if necessity demands it.

§3. If the statutes are silent on the manner of designating finance officers, the major superior is to appoint them, with the consent of his or her council.

CAN. 515 §1. Superior generalis electione designetur ad normam statutorum.

§2. Ceteri Superiores ad normam statutorum designentur, ita tamen, ut, si eliguntur, confirmatione Superioris maioris competentis indigeant; si vero nominantur, apta consultatio praecedat.

§3. In electionibus sedulo serventur cann. 947–960 necnon can. 445.

CAN. 516 §1. Sint pro administratione bonorum temporalium in ordinibus et congregationibus oeconomi: oeconomus generalis, qui bona totius ordinis vel congregationis administret, oeconomus provincialis, qui provinciae, oeconomus localis, qui singularum domorum; qui omnes officio suo fungantur sub moderamine Superioris.

§2. Oeconomi generalis et oeconomi provincialis officium implere Superior maior ipse non potest; officium vero oeconomi localis, etsi melius ab officio Superioris distinguitur, componi tamen cum eo potest, si necessitas id exigit.

§3. Si de modo oeconomos designandi statuta silent, ii a Superiore maiore de consensu sui consilii nominentur.

515 §1: Pius XII, m.p. *Postquam Apostolicis Litteris,* 9 feb. 1952, cann. 34–35 §§1–2. - S. Basilius M., regulae fus., 43; S. Theodorus Studita, ep. II, 126, 130, 146; Clemens XIII, litt. ap. *Ex iniuncto,* 10 ian. 1759. * Syn. Zamosten. Ruthenorum, a. 1720, tit. XII "Electiones;" Syn. Libanen. Maronitarum, a. 1736, pars IV, cap. II, 4 et 21, XIII.

516 §1: Pius XII, m.p. *Postquam Apostolicis Litteris,* 9 feb. 1952, can. 48 §2. - S. Basilius M., regulae fus., 34; Nic. II, can. 11; S. Theodorus Studita, sermo 48; ep. I, 10 in fine; ep. 36, 96; iambi, 7; S. Athanasius

Athonita, typicum, "Εἰσηγητέον" ("Τὸ χρυσίον"). * Syn. Libanen. Maronitarum, a. 1736, pars IV, cap. II, 4; cap. III, 4.

516 §2: Pius XII, m.p. *Postquam Apostolicis Litteris,* 9 feb. 1952, can. 48 §3. * Syn. Libanen. Maronitarum, a. 1736, pars IV, cap. III, 4.

516 §3: Pius XII, m.p. *Postquam Apostolicis Litteris,* 9 feb. 1952, can. 48 §5. - S. Athanasius Athonita, typicum, "Εἰσηγητέον" ("Τὸ χρυσίον"). * Syn. Libanen. Maronitarum, a. 1736, pars IV, cap. II, 4.

3° Admission to Orders and Congregations and the Novitiate

3° De Admissione in Ordines et Congregationes et de Novitiatu

CAN. 517 §1. The required age for valid admission to the novitiate of an order or congregation is seventeen years old. Regarding other requirements for valid admission to the novitiate, cann. 448, 450, 452, and 454 are to be observed.

§2. No one can be admitted licitly to the novitiate of a religious institute of another Church *sui iuris* without the permission of the Apostolic See, unless it concerns a candidate destined for a province or house, mentioned in can. 432, of his or her own Church.

CAN. 518 Before being admitted to the novitiate, a candidate is to be suitably prepared under the special care of an experienced member for the time and according to the manner determined by the statutes.

CAN. 519 The right to admit candidates to the novitiate belongs to major superiors in accord with the norm of the statutes and having observed can. 453, §§2 and 3.

CAN. 520 The novitiate begins in the manner prescribed by the statutes.

CAN. 521 The erection, transfer and suppression of the location of the novitiate is done through a decree of the superior general with the consent of his or her council.

CAN. 522 §1. The novitiate, to be valid, must be made in the house in which the novitiate is located. In special cases and as an exception, by a grant of the superior general with the

CAN. 517 §1. Aetas ad validam admissionem in novitiatum ordinis vel congregationis requisita est decimus septimus annus expletus; circa cetera requisita ad admissionem in novitiatum serventur cann. 448, 450, 452 et 454.

§2. Ad novitiatum instituti religiosi alterius Ecclesiae sui iuris nemo licite admitti potest sine licentia Sedis Apostolicae, nisi de candidato agitur, qui destinatus est provinciae vel domui, de qua in can. 432, propriae Ecclesiae.

CAN. 518 Antequam candidatus ad novitiatum admittitur, sit congruenter praeparatus sub speciali cura probati sodalis per tempus et secundum modum a statutis determinatum.

CAN. 519 Ius admittendi candidatos ad novitiatum pertinet ad Superiores maiores ad normam statutorum servato can. 453, §§2 et 3.

CAN. 520 Novitiatus incipit modo a statutis praescripto.

CAN. 521 Sedis novitiatus erectio, translatio et suppressio fit per decretum Superioris generalis de consensu eius consilii.

CAN. 522 §1. Novitiatus ut validus sit, peragi debet in domo, in qua est sedes novitiatus; in casibus specialibus et ad modum exceptionis ex concessione Superioris gene-

517 §1: Pius XII, m.p. *Postquam Apostolicis Litteris,* 9 feb. 1952, can. 88 §1 n. 1.

517 §2: Pius XII, m.p. *Postquam Apostolicis Litteris,* 9 feb. 1952, can. 74 §2 n. 6.

518: Pius XII, m.p. *Postquam Apostolicis Litteris,* 9 feb. 1952, can. 71 §1; S.C. pro Eccl. Orient., decr. 27 iun. 1972, 5.

519: Pius XII, m.p. *Postquam Apostolicis Litteris,* 9 feb. 1952, can. 75.

520: Pius XII, m.p. *Postquam Apostolicis Litteris,* 9 feb. 1952, can. 85.

521: Pius XII, m.p. *Postquam Apostolicis Litteris,* 9 feb. 1952, can. 87 §1; S.C. pro Eccl. Orient., decr. 27 iun. 1972, 10, a)–b).

522 §1: Pius XII, m.p. *Postquam Apostolicis Litteris,* 9 feb. 1952, can. 88 §1 n. 4; Secret. Status, rescr. 6 nov. 1964, 18; S.C. pro Eccl. Orient., decr. 27 iun. 1972, 10, c).

consent of his or her council, the novitiate can be made in another house of the same order or congregation under the direction of some experienced member who substitutes for the director of novices.

§2. A major superior can permit a group of novices to reside for a certain period of time in another house of their own order or congregation designated by him or her.

CAN. 523 §1. To be valid, a novitiate must include one full and continuous year. However, an absence of less than three months, either continuous or interrupted, does not affect validity but, if the unfinished time exceeds fifteen days, it must be made up even though it had been dedicated to apostolic exercises to complete the formation of the novices.

§2. If a longer time for the novitiate is prescribed in the statutes, it is not required for the validity of profession.

CAN. 524 §1. A director is to be appointed for the formation of the novices according to norm of the statutes; the director is to be a member at least ten years professed, outstanding in prudence, charity, piety, knowledge, and the observance of the religious state and, in a clerical order or congregation, constituted in the order of the presbyterate.

§2. If necessary, the director is to be given assistants who are subject to the director in everything regarding the direction of the novitiate and the formation of the novices.

§3. It is for the director alone to provide for the formation of the novices; the direction of

ralis de consensu eius consilii novitiatus peragi potest in alia eiusdem ordinis vel congregationis domo sub moderamine alicuius probati sodalis, qui vices magistri novitiorum gerit.

§2. Superior maior permittere potest, ut novitiorum coetus per certum temporis spatium in alia proprii ordinis vel congregationis domo a se designata commoretur.

CAN. 523 §1. Ad validitatem novitiatus requiritur, ut annum integrum et continuum complectatur; absentia vero tribus mensibus sive continuis sive intermissis brevior validitatem non afficit, sed tempus deficiens, si quindecim dies superat, suppleri debet, etsi exercitationibus apostolicis ad novitiorum institutionem perficiendam deditum erat.

§2. Si longius tempus novitiatus in statutis praescribitur, illud non requiritur, ut valeat professio.

CAN. 524 §1. Novitiorum institutioni praeficiendus est ut magister ad normam statutorum sodalis prudentia, caritate, pietate, scientia et status religiosi observantia praestans, decem saltem annos professus et, si de ordine vel congregatione clericali agitur, in ordine presbyteratus constitutus.

§2. Magistro, si opus est, cooperatores dentur, qui in omnibus ei subsint circa moderamen novitiatus et institutionem novitiorum.

§3. Solius magistri est consulere novitiorum institutioni et ad ipsum solum novitiatus

522 §2: S.C. pro Eccl. Orient., decr. 27 iun. 1972, 10, c)–d).

523 §1: Pius XII, m.p. *Postquam Apostolicis Litteris*, 9 feb. 1952, can. 88 §1 n. 3; S.C. pro Eccl. Orient., decr. 27 iun. 1972, n. 11, a)–d).

523 §2: Pius XII, m.p. *Postquam Apostolicis Litteris*, 9 feb. 1952, can. 88 §2.

524 §1: Pius XII, m.p. *Postquam Apostolicis Lit-*

teris, 9 feb. 1952, can. 92 §1; S.C. pro Eccl. Orient., decr. 27 iun. 1972, 3. * Syn. Zamosten. Ruthenorum, a. 1720, tit. XII "Puella."

524 §2: Pius XII, m.p. *Postquam Apostolicis Litteris*, 9 feb. 1952, can. 92 §2.

524 §3: Pius XII, m.p. *Postquam Apostolicis Litteris*, 9 feb. 1952, can. 94 §1.

the novitiate belongs to that director alone in such a way that no one is allowed to interfere in these matters under any pretext whatsoever, except those superiors to which it is permitted by the statutes, and visitators. With regard to the religious discipline of the entire house, however, the director, in the same way as the novices, is subject to the superior.

§4. The novice is subject to the power of the director and the superiors and is obliged to obey them.

CAN. 525 §1. Those things prescribed in cann. 459–461 are also valid in orders and congregations.

§2. Before making temporary profession, novices must cede to whom they wish, for the entire time in which they are bound by the same profession, the administration of the goods they actually have and those that may accrue to them later, and they must dispose freely of their use and revenue.

moderamen spectat ita, ut nemini liceat his se quovis praetextu immiscere exceptis illis Superioribus, quibus id a statutis permittitur, ac visitatoribus; ad disciplinam religiosam vero totius domus quod attinet, magister, quemadmodum et novitii, Superiori subditus est.

§4. Novitius potestati magistri ac Superiorum subest eisque oboedire tenetur.

CAN. 525 §1. Ea, quae praescribuntur in cann. 459–461, valent etiam de ordinibus et congregationibus.

§2. Antequam professionem temporariam emittit, novitius debet ad totum tempus, quo eadem professione ligatus est, bonorum suorum, quae actu habet et quae ipsi forte postea supervenient, administrationem cedere, cui mavult, et de eorundem usu et usufructu libere disponere.

4° Profession in Orders and Congregations

CAN. 526 §1. Temporary profession, with the three vows of obedience, chastity and poverty, is to be made for the time determined in the statutes.

§2. This profession can be renewed several times in accord with the norm of the statutes but in such a manner that, all together, the time is never less than three years nor longer than six years.

CAN. 527 For the validity of the temporary profession, it is required that:

4° De professione in Ordinibus et Congregationibus

CAN. 526 §1. Professio temporaria cum tribus votis oboedientiae, castitatis et paupertatis emittatur ad tempus in statutis determinatum.

§2. Haec professio ad normam statutorum pluries renovari potest ita tamen, ut complexive numquam ad tempus, quod triennio brevius vel sexennio longius est, extendatur.

CAN. 527 Ad validitatem professionis temporariae requiritur, ut:

524 §4: Pius XII, m.p. *Postquam Apostolicis Litteris,* 9 feb. 1952, can. 94 §2.
525 §2: Pius XII, m.p. *Postquam Apostolicis Litteris,* 9 feb. 1952, can. 103 §1.
526 §1: Pius XII, m.p. *Postquam Apostolicis Litteris,* 9 feb. 1952, can. 110 §1. - Leo XIII, litt. ap. *Sin-*

gulare praesidium, 12 maii 1882, "Post;" S.C. de Prop. Fide, decr. 3 maii 1902.
526 §2: Pius XII, m.p. *Postquam Apostolicis Litteris,* 9 feb. 1952, can. 110 §2; S.C. pro Eccl. Orient., decr. 27 iun. 1972, 12.

1° the novitiate has been validly completed;

2° the novice be admitted to profession by the competent superior according to the statutes with the consent of his or her council, and the profession is to be received by the same superior personally or through another;

3° the profession be expressed, and not made or received by force, grave fear or fraud;

4° the other requirements in the statutes for the validity of the profession are fulfilled.

CAN. 528   A member in temporary vows is bound to observe the statutes by the same obligation as a member in perpetual vows; the member lacks active and passive voice, unless the statutes expressly provide otherwise.

CAN. 529   §1. Temporary profession renders acts contrary to the vows illicit, but not invalid.

§2. This profession does not deprive the member of ownership of his or her goods nor of the capacity to acquire other goods. However, the member is not permitted gratuitously to give up ownership of his or her goods through an act *inter vivos.*

§3. Nevertheless, whatever a member in temporary vows acquires through his or her effort or in consideration of the order or congregation, the member acquires for the order or institute itself; unless the contrary is legitimately proven, the member is presumed to acquire in consideration of the order or congregation.

§4. The member in temporary vows can change the cession or disposition mentioned in can. 525, §2, not by his or her own decision, but with the consent of the major superior, provid-

1° novitiatus valide peractus sit;

2° novitius admittatur ad professionem a Superiore competenti secundum statuta de consensu sui consilii necnon recipiatur professio ab eodem Superiore per se vel per alium;

3° professio sit expressa nec vi, metu gravi aut dolo emissa vel recepta;

4° cetera ad validitatem professionis in statutis requisita impleantur.

CAN. 528   Sodalis a votis temporariis eadem obligatione ac sodalis a votis perpetuis tenetur observandi statuta; voce activa et passiva caret, nisi aliter in statutis expresse cavetur.

CAN. 529   §1. Professio temporaria actus votis contrarios reddit illicitos, sed non invalidos.

§2. Haec professio non aufert sodali proprietatem bonorum suorum neque capacitatem alia bona acquirendi; sodali tamen non licet per actum inter vivos dominium bonorum suorum titulo gratioso abdicare.

§3. Quidquid autem sodalis a votis temporariis industria sua aut intuitu ordinis vel congregationis acquirit, ipsi ordini vel congregationi acquirit; nisi contrarium legitime probatur, sodalis praesumitur acquirere intuitu ordinis vel congregationis.

§4. Cessionem vel dispositionem, de quibus in can. 525, §2, sodalis a votis temporariis mutare potest non quidem proprio arbitrio, sed de Superioris maioris consensu,

528: Pius XII, m.p. *Postquam Apostolicis Litteris,* 9 feb. 1952, can. 114, nn. 2–3. - S.C. de Prop. Fide, 4 mar. 1895, dub. 4–5.

529 §1: Pius XII, m.p. *Postquam Apostolicis Litteris,* 9 feb. 1952, can. 115.

529 §2: Pius XII, m.p. *Postquam Apostolicis Litteris,* 9 feb. 1952, cann. 116 §1, 119 n. 1.

529 §3: Pius XII, m.p. *Postquam Apostolicis Litteris,* 9 feb. 1952, can. 116 §2. - S. Theodorus Studita, quotidianae monachorum poenae, 7; S.C. de Prop. Fide, instr. (ad Monachos Maronit. Libanen.), 4 feb. 1895.

529 §4: Pius XII, m.p. *Postquam Apostolicis Litteris,* 9 feb. 1952, can. 116 §3.

ed that the change, at least regarding a significant part of the goods, is not made in favor of the order or congregation. The cession and disposition of this type, however, cease to have force upon departure from the order or congregation.

§5. If the member in temporary vows has contracted debts and obligations, that member must be responsible, unless he or she, with the permission of the superior, has transacted business of the order or congregation.

§6. Once temporary profession has been made, any offices whatsoever of the professed become vacant by the law itself.

CAN. 530 In congregations, at least before perpetual profession, a member is to make a will, which is to be valid also in civil law.

CAN. 531 By perpetual profession, a member definitively assumes the religious state, loses his or her own eparchy, and is fully aggregated to the order or congregation.

CAN. 532 For the validity of perpetual profession, in addition to the requirements mentioned in can. 464, it is required that it be preceded by temporary profession, in accord with the norm of can. 526.

CAN. 533 In orders, perpetual profession is equivalent to perpetual monastic profession; thus cann. 466–468 are valid regarding it.

CAN. 534 In congregations:
1° the canonical effects of perpetual profes-

dummodo mutatio saltem de notabili bonorum parte ne fiat in favorem ordinis vel congregationis; per discessum autem ab ordine vel congregatione eiusmodi cessio ac dispositio habere vim desinit.

§5. Si sodalis a votis temporariis debita et obligationes contraxit, ipse respondere debet, nisi de Superioris licentia negotium ordinis vel congregationis gessit.

§6. Emissa professione temporaria ipso iure vacant quaelibet professi officia.

CAN. 530 In congregationibus sodalis saltem ante professionem perpetuam testamentum, quod etiam in iure civili validum sit, libere condat.

CAN. 531 Per professionem perpetuam sodalis statum religiosum definitive assumit, propriam eparchiam amittit ac ordini vel congregationi pleno iure aggregatur.

CAN. 532 Ad validitatem professionis perpetuae praeter requisita, de quibus in can. 464, requiritur, ut praecesserit professio temporaria ad normam can. 526.

CAN. 533 In ordinibus professio perpetua professioni perpetuae monasticae aequiparatur, proinde valent de ea cann. 466–468.

CAN. 534 In congregationibus:
1° effectus canonici professionis perpe-

529 §5: Pius XII, m.p. *Postquam Apostolicis Litteris,* 9 feb. 1952, can. 68 §§2–3.

529 §6: Pius XII, m.p. *Postquam Apostolicis Litteris,* 9 feb. 1952, can. 120. - S. Nicephorus CP., can. 157.

530: Pius XII, m.p. *Postquam Apostolicis Litteris,* 9 feb. 1952, can. 103 §3; S.C. pro Eccl. Orient., decr. 27 iun. 1972, 16.

531: Pius XII, m.p. *Postquam Apostolicis Litteris,* 9 feb. 1952, can. 121.

532: Pius XII, m.p. *Postquam Apostolicis Litteris,* 9 feb. 1952, can. 106 §2.

533: Pius XII, m.p. *Postquam Apostolicis Litteris,* 9 feb. 1952, can. 314 §1.

534, 1°: Pius XII, m.p. *Postquam Apostolicis Litteris,* 9 feb. 1952, can. 115.

sion remain the same as those determined in can. 529 for temporary profession unless the common law provides otherwise;

2° the major superior, with the consent of his or her council, can concede to a member in perpetual vows who requests it permission to cede his or her goods, with due regard for the norms of prudence;

3° It is for the general synaxis to introduce into the statutes, if it seems opportune, the obligatory renunciation by a member of his or her patrimony, acquired or to be acquired; this cannot be done, however, before perpetual profession.

CAN. 535 §1. In making any profession whatever, the prescripts of the statutes are to be observed.

§2. A written record of the profession that has been made, signed by the member himself or herself and by the one who received the profession, even by delegation, is to be kept in the archive of the order or congregation. The major superior must notify as soon as possible the pastor where the baptism of the member was registered, about the profession.

5° Formation of Members and Religious Discipline in Orders and Congregations

CAN. 536 §1. The manner of formation of members, having observed can. 471, §1, is determined in the statutes.

§2. In addition, the formation of members destined for sacred orders must be done in ac-

tuae iidem manent ac in can. 529 de professione temporaria determinantur, nisi aliter iure communi cavetur;

2° Superior maior de consensu sui consilii potest sodali a votis perpetuis id petenti licentiam bona sua cedendi salvis normis prudentiae concedere;

3° Synaxis generalis est in statuta introducere, si opportunum videtur, renuntiationem obligatoriam patrimonii a sodali acquisiti vel acquirendi, quae tamen ante professionem perpetuam fieri non potest.

CAN. 535 §1. In emittenda quavis professione serventur praescripta statutorum.

§2. Documentum emissae professionis ab ipso sodali et ab eo, qui professionem, etiam ex delegatione, recepit, subscriptum asservetur in archivo ordinis vel congregationis; si de professione perpetua agitur, Superior maior debet de eadem quam primum certiorem facere parochum, apud quem sodalis baptismus adnotatus est.

5° De Institutione Sodalium et de Disciplina Religiosa in Ordinibus et Congregationibus

CAN. 536 §1. Modus institutionis sodalium servato can. 471, §1 determinatur in statutis.

§2. Institutio sodalium, qui ad ordines sacros destinantur, praeterea fieri debet se-

534, 2°: Secret. Status, rescr. 6 nov. 1964, 16; S.C. pro Eccl. Orient., decr. 27 iun. 1972, 18.

534, 3°: Vat. II, decr. *Perfectae caritatis*, 13 "Congregationes;" PAULUS VI, m.p. *Ecclesiae sanctae*, 6 aug. 1966, II, 24.

535 §1: PIUS XII, m.p. *Postquam Apostolicis Lit-*

teris, 9 feb. 1952, can. 112 §1.

535 §2: PIUS XII, m.p. *Postquam Apostolicis Litteris*, 9 feb. 1952, can. 112 §3.

536 §2: PIUS XII, m.p. *Postquam Apostolicis Litteris*, 9 feb. 1952, cann. 124–126; S.C. pro Eccl. Orient., decr. 27 ian. 1940, n. 4.

cord with the formation program for clerics, mentioned in can. 330, in a place of studies of the order or congregation approved by the general synaxis or the major superiors in accord with the norm of the statutes. However, if their own place of studies in accord with can. 340, §1, cannot be had, the members must be instructed under the guidance of an experienced moderator in another seminary or institute of higher studies approved by ecclesiastical authority.

CAN. 537 §1. Major superiors can give dimissorial letters for sacred ordination to members in perpetual vows.

§2. The bishop, to whom the superior must send the dimissorial letters, is the eparchial bishop of the place where the candidate for ordination has a domicile; to another bishop, instead, if the eparchial bishop has given permission, or is of a different Church *sui iuris* than that of the candidate, or is absent or, finally, if the eparchial see is vacant and the one who governs it is not an ordained bishop. In individual cases, it is necessary that these matters be established for the ordaining bishop by an authentic document of the eparchial curia.

CAN. 538 §1. In individual houses of orders and congregations, the divine praises are to be celebrated in accord with the norm of the statutes and legitimate customs.

§2. The superiors are to see that all members fulfill in accord with the norm of the statutes what is prescribed in can. 473, §2.

§3. Members of orders and congregations are

cundum rationem institutionis clericorum, de qua in can. 330, in sede studiorum ordinis vel congregationis a Synaxi generali vel a Superioribus maioribus ad normam statutorum approbata; si vero sedes studiorum propria ad normam can. 340, §1 haberi non potest, sodales institui debent sub ductu probati moderatoris in alio seminario vel instituto studiorum superiorum ab auctoritate ecclesiastica approbato.

CAN. 537 §1. Superiores maiores ad normam statutorum dare possunt litteras dimissorias ad sacram ordinationem sodalibus a votis perpetuis.

§2. Episcopus, ad quem Superior litteras dimissorias mittere debet, est Episcopus eparchialis loci, ubi ordinandus domicilium habet; ad alium Episcopum vero, si Episcopus eparchialis licentiam dedit aut est alterius Ecclesiae sui iuris ac ordinandus aut est absens aut denique, si sedes eparchialis vacat et eam regit, qui Episcopus ordinatus non est; de quibus necesse est Episcopo ordinanti in singulis casibus constet authentico curiae eparchialis documento.

CAN. 538 §1. In singulis domibus ordinum et congregationum laudes divinae celebrentur ad normam statutorum et legitimarum consuetudinum.

§2. Curent Superiores, ut omnes sodales ad normam statutorum ea, quae in can. 473, §2 praescribuntur, impleant.

§3. Sodales ordinum et congregationum

537 §1: Pius XII, m.p. *Postquam Apostolicis Litteris*, 9 feb. 1952, can. 131; Secret. Status, rescr. 6 nov. 1964, 11. * Syn. Zamosten. Ruthenorum, a. 1720, tit. III, §7 "In propria;" Syn. Libanen. Maronitarum, a. 1736, pars II, cap. XIV, 10.

537 §2: Pius XII, m.p. *Postquam Apostolicis Litteris*, 9 feb. 1952, can. 132. * Syn. Zamosten. Rutheno-

rum, a. 1720, tit. III, §7 "In propria;" Syn. Libanen. Maronitarum, a. 1736, pars II, cap. XIV, 10; Syn. Bekorkien. Maronitarum, a. 1790, s. 9.

538 §1: Pius XII, m.p. *Postquam Apostolicis Litteris*, 9 feb. 1952, can. 157 §2. - S. Basilius M., regulae fus., 37.

to receive the sacrament of penance frequently and are to observe can. 474, §2.

CAN. 539 §1. Superiors are to see that suitable confessors are available to the members.

§2. Confessors in clerical orders and congregations of pontifical or patriarchal right are to be designated by the major superior in accord with the norm of the statutes; in other cases, however, by the local hierarch, after having heard the superior who must consult the interested community beforehand.

CAN. 540 Regarding the habit of the members, the prescripts of the statutes and, outside their own houses, also the norms of the eparchial bishop must be followed.

CAN. 541 The norms regarding cloister are to be determined in the statutes of the individual orders and congregations in accord with their own character, with due regard for the right of superiors, even local, to permit otherwise in individual instances and for a just cause.

CAN. 542 Superiors are to see that members designated by them especially in the eparchy where they live, if requested by the local hierarch or pastor to provide help for the needs of the Christian faithful, willingly offer assistance, whether inside or outside their own churches, without prejudice to the character of their institute and religious discipline.

CAN. 543 A member of an order or congregation, who is a pastor, is still bound by the

sacramentum paenitentiae frequenter suscipiant et servetur can. 474, §2.

CAN. 539 §1. Superiores curent, ut sodalibus idonei confessarii praesto sint.

§2. Confessarii in ordinibus et congregationibus clericalibus iuris pontificii vel patriarchalis a Superiore maiore ad normam statutorum designentur; in ceteris casibus vero ab Hierarcha loci audito Superiore, qui praevie communitatem, cuius interest, consulere debet.

CAN. 540 Ad habitum sodalium quod spectat, standum est praescriptis statutorum et extra proprias domus etiam normis Episcopi eparchialis.

CAN. 541 Normae circa clausuram in statutis singulorum ordinum et congregationum secundum propriam indolem determinentur firmo iure Superiorum, etiam localium, per modum actus et iusta de causa aliud permittendi.

CAN. 542 Curent Superiores, ut sodales a se designati praesertim in eparchia, in qua degunt, si ab Hierarcha loci vel parocho eorum auxilium requiritur ad consulendum necessitatibus christifidelium, illud intra et extra proprias ecclesias salvis instituti indole et disciplina religiosa libenter praestent.

CAN. 543 Sodalis ordinis vel congregationis, qui parochus est, manet votis ligatus

---

539 §1: Pius XII, m.p. *Postquam Apostolicis Litteris,* 9 feb. 1952, can. 138 §1 n. 3.

539 §2: Pius XII, m.p. *Postquam Apostolicis Litteris,* 9 feb. 1952, cann. 50 §1, 53, 56–57, 59.

540: Pius XII, m.p. *Postquam Apostolicis Litteris,* 9 feb. 1952, can. 139; Vat. II, decr. *Perfectae caritatis,* 17; Paulus VI, m.p. *Ecclesiae sanctae,* 6 aug. 1966, I, 25, d).

541: Pius XII, m.p. *Postquam Apostolicis Litteris,* 9 feb. 1952, cann. 150–153; Vat. II, decr. *Perfectae ca-*

ritatis, 16; S.C. pro Eccl. Orient., decr. 27 iun. 1972, 19–20.

542: Pius XII, m.p. *Postquam Apostolicis Litteris,* 9 feb. 1952, can. 154 §§1, 3; Paulus VI, m.p. *Ecclesiae sanctae,* 6 aug. 1966, I, 36 §2. - Chalc. can. 4; S.C. de Prop. Fide, instr. 8 dec. 1845; decr. 25 apr. 1850, 3.

543: Pius XII, m.p. *Postquam Apostolicis Litteris,* 9 feb. 1952, cann. 179–180, 155. - Benedictus XIV, litt. ap. *Super familiam,* 30 mar. 1756, §7. * Syn. Armen., a. 1911, 778, 918, n. 3.

vows and the other obligations of his profession as well as of the statutes insofar as the observance of these obligations can be compatible with the duties of his office. He is subject to the superiors in what pertains to religious discipline but, in those matters that regard the office of pastor, he has the same rights and obligations as other pastors and is subject in the same manner to the eparchial bishop.

atque ceteris suae professionis obligationibus necnon statutis adhuc tenetur, quatenus horum observantia cum sui officii obligationibus consistere potest; ad disciplinam religiosam quod attinet, subest Superiori, in eis vero, quae ad officium parochi spectant, eadem iura et obligationes habet ac ceteri parochi eodemque modo Episcopo eparchiali subest.

6° Transfer to Another Order or Congregation or to a Monastery Sui Iuris

6° De Transitu ad Alium Ordinem vel Congregationem aut ad Monasterium Sui Iuris

CAN. 544 §1. Within the territorial boundaries of the patriarchal Church, a member can transfer validly to another religious institute with the written consent of the patriarch and with the consent of his or her own superior general and the superior general of the order or congregation to which he or she wishes to transfer, or, if it concerns transfer to a monastery, of the superior of the monastery *sui iuris;* for the granting of their consent, the superiors need the prior consent of their council or, if it concerns a monastery, of the synaxis.

CAN. 544 §1. Intra fines territorii Ecclesiae patriarchalis sodalis ad aliud institutum religiosum valide transire potest de consensu scripto dato Patriarchae et de consensu proprii Superioris generalis et Superioris generalis ordinis vel congregationis, ad quem transire vult, aut, si de transitu ad monasterium agitur, Superioris monasterii sui iuris; ad hunc consensum praestandum Superiores indigent praevio consensu sui consilii vel, si de monasterio agitur, Synaxis.

§2. A member can validly transfer from a congregation of eparchial right to another religious institute of eparchial right with the written consent of the eparchial bishop of the place where the principal house of the religious institute is located, to which transfer is made, after having consulted the superior general of the congregation from which transfer is made, and with the consent of the superior general of the congregation or the superior of the monastery *sui iuris* to which transfer is made. For the granting of this consent, the superiors need the prior consent of their council or, if it concerns a monastery, of the synaxis.

§2. Sodalis valide transire potest a congregatione iuris eparchialis ad aliud institutum religiosum iuris eparchialis de consensu scripto dato Episcopi eparchialis loci, ubi est domus princeps instituti religiosi, ad quod fit transitus, consulto Superiore generali congregationis, a qua fit transitus, et consentiente Superiore generali congregationis aut Superiore monasterii sui iuris, ad quod fit transitus; ad hunc consensum praestandum Superiores indigent praevio consensu sui consilii vel, si de monasterio agitur, Synaxis.

544 §1: Pius XII, m.p. *Postquam Apostolicis Litteris,* 9 feb. 1952, can. 182 §2.

544 §2: Pius XII, m.p. *Postquam Apostolicis Litteris,* 9 feb. 1952, can. 182 §3.

§3. In other cases the member cannot validly transfer to another religious institute without the consent of the Apostolic See.

§4. The consent of the Apostolic See is required for the validity of a transfer to a religious institute of another Church *sui iuris.*

CAN. 545 §1. The one who transfers must go through the entire novitiate, unless the superior general or the superior of the monastery *sui iuris,* each of them with the consent of their council, on account of special circumstances, reduces the time of the novitiate, but not less than six months. During the novitiate, while the vows remain in force, the rights and particular obligations that the member had in the previous order or congregation are suspended, and the member is subject to the superiors and director of novices of the new religious institute also by virtue of the vow of obedience.

§2. After having completed the novitiate, one who is already professed in perpetual vows, publicly makes perpetual profession according to the prescripts of the statutes of the new religious institute. By this profession, the member is fully aggregated to the new institute and, if he is a cleric, he is also ascribed to it as a cleric. But one who is still professed in temporary vows, is to make a temporary profession in the same manner for at least three years, unless the member went through the entire three years of novitiate in the monastery *sui iuris* to which he or she transferred.

§3. If a member does not make the profession in the new religious institute, the member must return to the original institute, unless in the interim the time of profession has lapsed.

§3. Ceteris in casibus sodalis non potest ad aliud institutum religiosum valide transire nisi de consensu Sedis Apostolicae.

§4. Ad validitatem transitus ad institutum religiosum alterius Ecclesiae sui iuris requiritur consensus Sedis Apostolicae.

CAN. 545 §1. Transiens novitiatum ex toto peragere debet, nisi Superior generalis vel Superior monasterii sui iuris, uterque de consensu sui consilii, tempus novitiatus ob specialia adiuncta reducit, sed non infra sex menses; novitiatu durante manentibus votis iura et obligationes particulares, quae sodalis in priore ordine vel congregatione habuit, suspensa sunt et ipse Superioribus et magistro novitiorum novi instituti religiosi subest etiam vi voti oboedientiae.

§2. Post peractum novitiatum transiens, qui iam professus a votis perpetuis est, publice professionem perpetuam emittat secundum praescripta statutorum novi institutui religiosi, qua professionae novo instituto plene aggregatur et, si clericus est, ei etiam ut clericus ascribitur; qui vero adhuc professus a votis temporariis est, eodem modo professionem temporariam emittat saltem per triennium duraturam, nisi totum triennium novitiatus in monasterio sui iuris, ad quod transit, peregit.

§3. Si in novo instituto religioso sodalis professionem non emittit, ad pristinum redire debet, nisi interim tempus professionis elapsum est.

544 §3: Pius XII, m.p. *Postquam Apostolicis Litteris,* 9 feb. 1952, can. 182 §1.

544 §4: Pius XII, m.p. *Postquam Apostolicis Litteris,* 9 feb. 1952, cann. 74 §2 n. 6, 182 §1.

545 §1: Pius XII, m.p. *Postquam Apostolicis Litteris,* 9 feb. 1952, can. 183 §1 n. 1.

545 §2: Pius XII, m.p. *Postquam Apostolicis Litteris,* 9 feb. 1952, cann. 184–185.

545 §3: Pius XII, m.p. *Postquam Apostolicis Litteris,* 9 feb. 1952, cann. 183 §1 n. 2, 184.

§4. Regarding goods and dowry, can. 488, §4 is to be observed.

§4. Circa bona et dotem servetur can. 488, §4.

7° Exclaustration and Leaving the Order or Congregation

7° De Exclaustratione et de Discessu ab Ordine vel Congregatione

CAN. 546 §1. One professed in temporary vows can freely leave the religious institute when the time of profession has elapsed.

CAN. 546 §1. Professus a votis temporariis elapso professionis tempore libere potest institutum religiosum derelinquere.

§2. One who, while still in temporary vows, requests for a grave cause to leave the order or congregation, can obtain from the superior general with the consent of his or her council the indult to leave the order or congregation definitively and return to secular life, with the effects mentioned in can. 493; in congregations of eparchial right, the indult, to be valid, must be confirmed by the eparchial bishop of the place where the principal house of the same congregation is located.

§2. Qui perdurantibus votis temporariis gravi de causa petit, ut ordinem vel congregationem derelinquat, a Superiore generali de consensu eius consilii consequi potest indultum definitive ab ordine vel congregatione discedendi et ad vitam saecularem redeundi cum effectibus, de quibus in can. 493; in congregationibus iuris eparchialis indultum ut valeat confirmari debet ab Episcopo eparchiali loci, ubi est domus princeps eiusdem congregationis.

CAN. 547 §1. The major superior, for a just cause and having consulted the council, can exclude a member in temporary vows from renewing his or her vows or from making perpetual profession.

CAN. 547 §1. Superior maior iusta de causa consulto suo consilio sodalem a votis temporariis a renovandis eisdem votis vel ab emittenda professione perpetua excludere potest.

§2. Physical or psychic illness, even contracted after profession, which in the judgment of experts renders the member in temporary vows unsuited to lead the life of the religious institute, constitutes a cause for not admitting the member to renew temporary profession or to make perpetual profession, unless the illness was contracted through the negligence of the institute or through work performed in the institute.

§2. Infirmitas physica vel psychica, etiam post professionem temporariam contracta, quae de iudicio peritorum sodalem a votis temporariis reddit ineptum ad vitam in instituto religioso ducendam, causam constituit eum non admittendi ad professionem temporariam renovandam vel ad professionem perpetuam emittendam, nisi ob neglegentiam instituti vel ob laborem in instituto peractum infirmitas contracta est.

545 §4: Pius XII, m.p. *Postquam Apostolicis Litteris,* 9 feb. 1952, can. 185 n. 2.
    546 §1: Pius XII, m.p. *Postquam Apostolicis Litteris,* 9 feb. 1952, can. 187.
    546 §2: Pius XII, m.p. *Postquam Apostolicis Litteris,* 9 feb. 1952, cann. 190 §2, 191 §1; Secret. Status,
rescr. 6 nov. 1964, 14.
    547 §1: Pius XII, m.p. *Postquam Apostolicis Litteris,* 9 feb. 1952, cann. 187, 111 §1.
    547 §2: Pius XII, m.p. *Postquam Apostolicis Litteris,* 9 feb. 1952, can. 187.

§3. If, however, a member becomes insane during the period of temporary vows, even though unable to make a new profession, the member cannot be dismissed from the institute.

CAN. 548 §1. An indult of exclaustration can be conceded by the authority to which the order or congregation is subject, having heard the superior general along with his or her council; the imposition of exclaustration is made by the same authority, at the petition of the superior general with the consent of his or her council.

§2. In other respects, cann. 489–491 are to be observed regarding exclaustration.

CAN. 549 §1. A member in perpetual vows is not to request an indult to leave an order or congregation and to return to secular life except for the most grave causes. The religious is to present his or her petition to the superior general, who is to send it, along with a personal opinion and the opinion of his or her council to the competent authority.

§2. An indult of this type in orders is reserved to the Apostolic See; but in congregations, in addition to the Apostolic See, it can also be granted by:

1° the patriarch with respect to all members who have a domicile within the territorial boundaries of the Church over which he presides, after having consulted, if it concerns a congregation of eparchial right, the eparchial bishop;

2° the eparchial bishop of the eparchy in which the member has a domicile, if it concerns a congregation of eparchial right.

§3. An indult to leave an order or congregation has the same canonical effects as established in can. 493; with regard to a member who

§3. Si vero sodalis perdurantibus votis temporariis amens evasit, etsi novam professionem emittere non potest, ab instituto tamen dimitti non potest.

CAN. 548 §1. Indultum exclaustrationis concedi potest ab auctoritate, cui ordo vel congregatio subiectus est, audito Superiore generali una cum suo consilio; impositio vero exclaustrationis ab eadem auctoritate fit petente Superiore generali de consensu sui consilii.

§2. De cetero circa exclaustrationem serventur cann. 489–491.

CAN. 549 §1. Sodalis a votis perpetuis indultum discedendi ab ordine vel congregatione et ad vitam saecularem redeundi ne petat nisi gravissimis de causis; petitionem suam deferat Superiori generali, qui eam una cum voto suo suique consilii ad auctoritatem competentem mittat.

§2. Huiusmodi indultum in ordinibus Sedi Apostolicae reservatur; in congregationibus vero praeter Sedem Apostolicam id concedere potest etiam:

1° Patriarcha omnibus sodalibus, qui domicilium intra fines territorii Ecclesiae, cui praeest, habent, consulto, si de congregationibus iuris eparchialis agitur, Episcopo eparchiali;

2° Episcopus eparchialis eparchiae, in qua sodalis domicilium habet, si agitur de congregatione iuris eparchialis.

§3. Indultum discedendi ab ordine vel congregatione eosdem effectus canonicos habet ac in can. 493 statuuntur; de sodali

---

548 §1: Pius XII, m.p. *Postquam Apostolicis Litteris,* 9 feb. 1952, can. 188. - S.C.S. Off., (Novae Aureliae), 2 aug. 1876.

549 §2: Pius XII, m.p. *Postquam Apostolicis Litteris,* 9 feb. 1952, can. 190.

has been constituted in a sacred order, however, can. 494 is also applicable.

CAN. 550 A member who is absent illegitimately from a house of his or her own order or congregation with the intention of withdrawing from the power of the superiors, is to be sought out solicitously by the same superiors. If, however, within the time prescribed by the statutes the member does not return, he or she is to be punished in accord with the norm of law or even dismissed.

8° Dismissal from an Order or Congregation

CAN. 551 What is prescribed in cann. 497 and 498 concerning dismissal or expulsion is applicable also for members of orders or congregations. However, the competent authority is the major superior, having consulted his or her council or, if it concerns expulsion, with the consent of the same council. If there is danger in delay and there is not enough time to approach the major superior, even the local superior, with the consent of his or her council, can expel a member, notifying the major superior immediately.

CAN. 552 §1. A member in temporary vows can be dismissed by the superior general with the consent of his or her council, unless the statutes reserve the dismissal to the eparchial bishop or another authority to which the order or congregation is subject.

§2. In deciding about the dismissal, in addition to other conditions that may be prescribed by the statutes, the following must be observed:

1° the causes for dismissal must be grave, and

---

vero, qui in ordine sacro constitutus est, valet praeterea can. 494.

CAN. 550 Sodalis, qui ex domo proprii ordinis vel congregationis illegitime abest cum animo se subducendi a potestate Superiorum, sollicite ab eisdem Superioribus quaeratur; si vero intra tempus a statutis praescriptum non redit, ad normam iuris puniatur vel etiam dimittatur.

8° De Dimissione ab Ordine vel Congregatione

CAN. 551 Quae de dimissione vel de eiectione in cann. 497 et 498 praescribuntur, valent etiam de sodalibus ordinum vel congregationum; auctoritas competens vero est Superior maior consulto suo consilio aut, si de eiectione agitur, de consensu eiusdem consilii; si periculum est in mora nec tempus suppetit adeundi Superiorem maiorem, etiam Superior localis de consensu sui consilii et statim certiore facto Superiore maiore sodalem eicere potest.

CAN. 552 §1. Sodalis a votis temporariis dimitti potest a Superiore generali de consensu sui consilii, nisi in statutis dimissio reservatur Episcopo eparchiali vel alii auctoritati, cui ordo vel congregatio subiectus est.

§2. Ad dimissionem decernendam praeter alias condiciones a statutis forte praescriptas serventur:

1° causae dimissionis debent esse

550: Pius XII, m.p. *Postquam Apostolicis Litteris,* 9 feb. 1952, can. 195.

551: Pius XII, m.p. *Postquam Apostolicis Litteris,* 9 feb. 1952, cann. 197–198.

552 §1: Pius XII, m.p. *Postquam Apostolicis Lit-*

teris, 9 feb. 1952, can. 199 §1 nn. 2–3 et §2; S.C. pro Eccl. Orient., decr. 27 iun. 1972, 21.

552 §2, 1°: Pius XII, m.p. *Postquam Apostolicis Litteris,* 9 feb. 1952, can. 199 §3 n. 1.

on the part of the member also external and imputable;

2° the lack of a religious spirit, which can be of scandal to others, is a sufficient cause for dismissal if a repeated warning, along with salutary penance, have been in vain;

3° the dismissing authority must have come to know the reasons with certainty, although it is not necessary that they be formally proven. Yet, they must always be made known to the member, granting the member full opportunity of self-defense, and the member's responses are to be faithfully submitted to the dismissing authority.

§3. A recourse against the decree of dismissal has suspensive effect.

CAN. 553   The dismissal of a member in perpetual vows is within the competence of the superior general; in other respects, cann. 500–503 are to be observed.

CHAPTER II. Societies of Common Life according to the Manner of Religious

CAN. 554   §1. An institute in which the members profess the evangelical counsels by some sacred bond but not by religious vows, and imitate the manner of life of the religious state, under the governance of superiors according to the statutes, is a society of common life according to the manner of religious.

§2. This society is of pontifical right, patriarchal right or eparchial right according to the norm of can. 505, §2, but it is clerical in accord with the norm of can. 505, §3; it depends upon

graves et ex parte sodalis etiam externae et culpabiles;

2° defectus spiritus religiosi, qui aliis scandalo esse potest, est sufficiens dimissionis causa, si repetita monitio una cum salutari paenitentia in cassum cessit;

3° auctoritati dimittenti causae dimissionis certo innotescere debent, etsi necesse non est, ut eaedem formaliter comprobentur; sed sodali semper manifestari debent data ei plena opportunitate se defendendi, eiusque responsiones auctoritati dimittenti fideliter subiciantur.

§3. Recursus contra decretum dimissionis effectum suspensivum habet.

CAN. 553   Ad dimittendum sodalem a votis perpetuis competens est Superior generalis; de cetero observandi sunt cann. 500–503.

CAPUT II. De Societatibus Vitae Communis ad Instar Religiosorum

CAN. 554   §1. Institutum, in quo sodales consilia evangelica aliquo sacro vinculo, non vero votis religiosis profitentur atque vivendi rationem status religiosi imitantur sub regimine Superiorum secundum statuta, est societas vitae communis ad instar religiosorum.

§2. Haec societas est iuris pontificii, iuris patriarchalis vel eparchialis ad normam can. 505, §2; est vero clericalis ad normam can. 505, §3; dependet ab auctoritate ecclesiasti-

---

552 §2, 2°: Pius XII, m.p. *Postquam Apostolicis Litteris*, 9 feb. 1952, can. 199 §3 n. 2.

552 §2, 3°: Pius XII, m.p. *Postquam Apostolicis Litteris*, 9 feb. 1952, can. 199 §3 n. 3.

552 §3: Pius XII, m.p. *Postquam Apostolicis Litteris*, 9 feb. 1952, can. 199 §3 n. 4.

553: Pius XII, m.p. *Postquam Apostolicis Litteris*, 9 feb. 1952, can. 203 §2.

554 §1: Pius XII, m.p. *Postquam Apostolicis Litteris*, 9 feb. 1952, can. 224 §1.

554 §2: Pius XII, m.p. *Postquam Apostolicis Litteris*, 9 feb. 1952, can. 224 §2.

ecclesiastical authority as congregations do in accord with the norm of cann. 413–415, 419, 420, §3 and, without prejudice to particular law established by the Apostolic See, can. 418, §2.

§3. Members of these societies, in what pertains to canonical effects, are equivalent to religious unless the law provides otherwise or it is evident from the nature of the matter.

CAN. 555   All members of these societies are subject to the Roman Pontiff as their supreme superior, whom they are bound by obligation to obey also in virtue of the bond of obedience.

CAN. 556   Regarding the erection and suppression of a society and its provinces and houses, the same norms are applicable as those established for congregations in cann. 506–510 .

CAN. 557   Governance is to be determined by the statutes of the society but, in all matters, the norms that have been established for congregations in cann. 422 and 511–515 are to be applied, unless the nature of the matter prevents it.

CAN. 558   §1. A society and its legitimately erected provinces and houses are, by the law itself, juridic persons in accord with the norm of can. 423.

§2. The administration of goods is governed by cann. 424, 425, and 516.

§3. Whatever members acquire in consideration of the society is acquired for the society; members retain, acquire and administer other goods according to the statutes.

CAN. 559   §1. In admitting candidates into

ca ut congregationes ad normam cann. 413–415, 419, 420, §3 et, salvo iure particulari a Sede Apostolica statuto, can. 418, §2.

§3. Sodales harum societatum, ad effectus canonicos quod attinet, religiosis aequiparantur, nisi aliter iure cavetur vel ex natura rei constat.

CAN. 555   Sodales omnes harum societatum subduntur Romano Pontifici ut suo supremo Superiori, cui parendi obligatione tenentur etiam vi sacri vinculi oboedientiae.

CAN. 556   Circa erectionem et suppressionem societatis eiusque provinciarum vel domorum eadem valent ac quae de congregationibus in cann. 506–510 statuta sunt.

CAN. 557   Regimen determinatur statutis societatis, sed in omnibus applicentur, nisi rei natura obstat, quae de congregationibus in cann. 422 et 511–515 statuta sunt.

CAN. 558   §1. Societas eiusque provinciae et domus legitime erectae ipso iure sunt personae iuridicae ad normam can 423.

§2. Administratio bonorum regitur cann. 424, 425 et 516.

§3. Quidquid sodalibus obvenit intuitu societatis, societati acquiritur; cetera bona sodales secundum statuta retinent, acquirunt ac administrant.

CAN. 559   §1. In admittendis candidatis

---

554 §3: Pius XII, m.p. *Postquam Apostolicis Litteris,* 9 feb. 1952, can. 229 §1.

555: Pius XII, m.p. *Postquam Apostolicis Litteris,* 9 feb. 1952, can. 23.

556: Pius XII, m.p. *Postquam Apostolicis Litteris,* 9 feb. 1952, can. 225.

557: Pius XII, m.p. *Postquam Apostolicis Litteris,* 9 feb. 1952, can. 226. - S.C. de Religiosis, decr. 5 aug. 1913.

558 §1: Pius XII, m.p. *Postquam Apostolicis Litteris,* 9 feb. 1952, can. 227 §1.

558 §2: Pius XII, m.p. *Postquam Apostolicis Litteris,* 9 feb. 1952, can. 227 §2.

558 §3: Pius XII, m.p. *Postquam Apostolicis Litteris,* 9 feb. 1952, can. 227 §3.

559 §1: Pius XII, m.p. *Postquam Apostolicis Litteris,* 9 feb. 1952, can. 228 §1.

the society, the statutes are to be observed, without prejudice to cann. 450 and 451.

§2. Regarding the formation of members the statutes are likewise to be observed but, regarding the formation of those destined for sacred orders, in addition, the canons on the formation of clerics are to be observed.

CAN. 560 §1. The major superior of a society can give his perpetually coopted members dismissorial letters for sacred ordination in accord with the norm of the statutes; these letters must be sent to the bishop mentioned in can. 537, §2.

§2. A permanently coopted member is ascribed in the society as a cleric by diaconal ordination or, in the case of a cleric already ascribed to some eparchy, by perpetual cooptation.

CAN. 561   Members of a society are bound by the obligation that common law prescribes for clerics, unless the law provides otherwise or it is evident from the nature of the matter, with due regard for the rights and obligations determined in the statutes.

CAN. 562 §1. With respect to transfer to another society of common life according to the manner of religious or to a religious institute, consent is required of the superior general of the society from which the transfer is made and, if it involves a transfer to a society or institute of another Church *sui iuris,* also the consent of the Apostolic See.

§2. A member who transfers to a religious institute must go through the entire novitiate and is equivalent to the other novices of the same institute; regarding profession, the statutes of the new institute must be followed.

in societatem serventur statuta salvis cann. 450 et 451.

§2. Circa institutionem sodalium item serventur statuta; in instituendis vero illis, qui ad ordines sacros destinantur, serventur praeterea canones de institutione clericorum.

CAN. 560 §1. Superior maior societatis ad normam statutorum dare potest suis sodalibus perpetuo cooptatis litteras dimissorias ad sacram ordinationem; hae litterae mittendae sunt Episcopo, de quo in can. 537, §2.

§2. Sodalis perpetuo cooptatus ut clericus societati ascribitur ordinatione diaconali vel in casu clerici alicui eparchiae iam ascripti perpetua cooptatione.

CAN. 561   Sodales societatis tenentur obligationibus, quae clericis iure communi praescribuntur, nisi aliter iure cavetur vel ex natura rei constat, firmis iuribus et obligationibus in statutis determinatis.

CAN. 562 §1. Circa transitum ad aliam societatem vitae communis ad instar religiosorum vel institutum religiosum requiritur consensus Superioris generalis societatis, a qua transitus fit, et, si de transitu ad societatem vel institutum alterius Ecclesiae sui iuris agitur, etiam consensus Sedis Apostolicae.

§2. Sodalis, qui transit ad institutum religiosum, integrum novitiatum peragere debet et ceteris novitiis eiusdem instituti aequiparatur; circa professionem standum est statutis novi instituti.

559 §2: Pius XII, m.p. *Postquam Apostolicis Litteris,* 9 feb. 1952, can. 228 §2.
560 §1: Pius XII, m.p. *Postquam Apostolicis Litteris,* 9 feb. 1952, can. 228 §3.

561: Pius XII, m.p. *Postquam Apostolicis Litteris,* 9 feb. 1952, can. 229 §1.
562 §1: Pius XII, m.p. *Postquam Apostolicis Litteris,* 9 feb. 1952, can. 231.

§3. With due regard for cann. 497 and 498, to dismiss a perpetually coopted member the superior general is competent, having observed in other respects cann. 500–503; a temporarily coopted member, however, is dismissed in accord with the norm of can. 552.

§4. The statutes are to determine the authority who is competent to dissolve the sacred bond.

CHAPTER III. Secular Institutes

CAN. 563 §1. A secular institute is a society in which the members:

1° strive to dedicate themselves totally to God through profession of the three evangelical counsels according to the statutes, strengthened by a certain sacred bond recognized by the Church;

2° exercise apostolic activity like leaven in the world and from the world in such a way that all things are imbued with the spirit of the gospel for the strengthening and growth of the Body of Christ;

3° do not imitate the manner of life of religious, but live a life of communion among themselves according to their own statutes;

4° clerics or lay persons remain everyone in their state in what pertains to all canonical effects.

§2. Secular institutes are of pontifical right, patriarchal right or eparchial right in accord with the norm of can. 505, §2.

CAN. 564 Members of secular institutes are subject to the Roman Pontiff as their supreme superior, whom they are bound by obligation to obey also by virtue of the sacred bond of obedience.

CAN. 565 A member of a secular institute

§3. Firmis cann. 497 et 498 ad dimittendum sodalem perpetuo cooptatum competens est Superior generalis servatis de cetero cann. 500–503; sodalis temporarie cooptatus vero dimittitur ad normam can. 552.

§4. In statutis societatis determinetur auctoritas, cuius est sacrum vinculum solvere.

CAPUT III. **De Institutis Saecularibus**

CAN. 563 §1. Institutum saeculare est societas, in qua sodales:

1° ad seipsos Deo totos dedicandum per professionem trium consiliorum evangelicorum secundum statuta aliquo sacro vinculo ab Ecclesia recognito firmatam tendunt;

2° actuositatem apostolicam ad instar fermenti in saeculo et ex saeculo exercent ita, ut omnia ad robur et incrementum Corporis Christi spiritu evangelico imbuantur;

3° vivendi rationem religiosorum non imitantur, sed vitam communionis inter se secundum propria statuta agunt;

4° clerici vel laici, ad omnes effectus canonicos quod attinet, in suo quisque statu manent.

§2. Instituta saecularia sunt iuris pontificii, iuris patriarchalis vel iuris eparchialis ad normam can. 505, §2.

CAN. 564 Sodales institutorum saecularium subduntur Romano Pontifici ut suo supremo Superiori, cui parendi obligatione tenentur etiam vi sacri vinculi oboedientiae.

CAN. 565 Sodalis instituti saecularis

562 §3: Pius XII, m.p. *Postquam Apostolicis Litteris,* 9 feb. 1952, can. 231.

563 §1: Vat. II, decr. *Perfectae caritatis,* 11.

is ascribed through diaconal ordination as a cleric in the eparchy for whose service he has been ordained, unless he is ascribed to the same institute by virtue of a concession of the Apostolic See or, if it concerns a secular institute of patriarchal right, of the patriarch.

CAN. 566 Regarding erection and suppression of secular institutes, their statutes, as well as their dependence on ecclesiastical authority, the norms established for congregations in cann. 414, 506, 507, §2, 509 and 510 are to be observed.

CAN. 567 §1. Secular institutes and their legitimately erected provinces and houses are, by the law itself, juridic persons in accord with the norm of can. 423.

§2. The administration of goods is governed by cann. 424 and 425.

CAN. 568 §1. In admitting candidates, the statutes are to be observed with due regard for can. 450.

§2. A perpetually coopted member of a secular institute is dismissed by a decree issued in accord with the norm of the statutes; this decree cannot be executed unless it is approved by the eparchial bishop or by the competent higher authority. It is for the same eparchial bishop or authority also to dissolve the sacred bond.

CAN. 569 It is for the particular law of each Church *sui iuris* to establish more detailed norms regarding secular institutes.

CHAPTER IV. **Other Forms of Consecrated Life and Societies of Apostolic Life**

CAN. 570 By means of particular law, other kinds of ascetics who imitate eremitical life, whether they belong to an institute of conse-

per ordinationem diaconalem ut clericus ascribitur eparchiae, pro cuius servitio ordinatus est, nisi vi concessionis Sedis Apostolicae vel, si de instituto saeculari iuris patriarchalis agitur, Patriarchae eidem instituto ascribitur.

CAN. 566 Circa erectionem et suppressionem institutorum saecularium, eorum statuta necnon dependentiam ab auctoritate ecclesiastica serventur, quae de congregationibus in cann. 414, 506, 507, §2, 509 et 510 statuta sunt.

CAN. 567 §1. Instituta saecularia eorumque provinciae et domus legitime erectae ipso iure sunt personae iuridicae ad normam can. 423.

§2. Administratio bonorum regitur cann. 424 et 425.

CAN. 568 §1. In admittendis candidatis serventur statuta firmo can. 450.

§2. Sodalis instituto saeculari perpetuo cooptatus dimittitur decreto ad normam statutorum dato, quod exsecutioni mandari non potest, nisi est ab Episcopo eparchiali vel ab auctoritate superiore competenti approbatum; eiusdem Episcopi eparchialis vel auctoritatis est etiam sacrum vinculum solvere.

CAN. 569 Iuris particularis uniuscuiusque Ecclesiae sui iuris est pressius de institutis saecularibus statuere.

CAPUT IV. **De Aliis Formis Vitae Consecratae atque de Societatibus Vitae Apostolicae**

CAN. 570 Iure particulari aliae species constitui possunt ascetarum, qui vitam eremiticam imitantur, sive ad instituta vitae

---

570: Vat. II, const. *Lumen gentium*, 41 "In variis."
- S. BASILIUS M., can. 18.

crated life or not, can be constituted. Consecrated virgins and widows living apart in the world, having publicly professed chastity, can also be established.

CAN. 571 The approval of new forms of consecrated life is reserved solely to the Apostolic See. The patriarch and eparchial bishops, however, are to strive to discern new gifts of consecrated life entrusted to the Church by the Holy Spirit and are to assist promoters in order that they better express their proposals; they are to protect them by appropriate statutes.

CAN. 572 Societies of apostolic life, whose members, without religious vows, pursue the apostolic goal proper to the society and, leading a life in common as brothers and sisters according to their own manner of life, striving for the perfection of charity through the observance of their constitutions, and that resemble institutes of the consecrated life, are governed only by the particular law of their own Church *sui iuris* or established by the Apostolic See.

consecratae pertinent sive non; item virgines et viduae consecratae seorsum in saeculo castitatem professione publica profitentes constitui possunt.

CAN. 571 Novas formas vitae consecratae approbare soli Sedi Apostolicae reservatur; Patriarchae autem atque Episcopi eparchiales nova vitae consecratae dona a Spiritu Sancto Ecclesiae concredita discernere satagant et promotores adiuvent, quo meius proposita exprimant et aptis statutis protegant.

CAN. 572 Societates vitae apostolicae, quarum sodales sine votis religiosis finem apostolicum societatis proprium prosequuntur et, vitam fraternam in communi ducentes secundum propriam vitae rationem, per observantiam constitutionum ad perfectionem caritatis tendunt, quaeque institutis vitae consecratae accedunt, reguntur tantum iure particulari propriae Ecclesiae sui iuris vel a Sede apostolica statuto.

571: Vat. II, const. *Lumen gentium,* 45 "Cum;" decr. *Perfectae caritatis,* 1; decr. *Ad gentes,* 18.

TITLE XIII. ASSOCIATIONS OF THE CHRISTIAN FAITHFUL

TITULUS XIII. DE CHRISTIFIDELIUM CONSOCIATIONIBUS

CAN. 573 §1. Associations that are erected by competent ecclesiastical authority or approved by a decree of the same authority, are juridic persons in the Church and are called *public associations.*

§2. Other associations, even if praised or recommended by ecclesiastical authority, are called *private associations;* these associations are not recognized in the Church, unless their statutes are reviewed by competent authority; regarding the others, they are regulated only by particular law, with due regard for can. 577.

CAN. 574 Without prejudice in any case for can. 18, it is for to the competent ecclesiastical authority alone to erect associations of the Christian faithful which set out to teach Christian doctrine in the name of the Church or to promote public worship or which aim at other ends whose pursuit by their nature is reserved to the same ecclesiastical authority.

CAN. 575 §1. The authority competent to erect or approve associations of the Christian faithful is, for associations and their confederations:

1° the eparchial bishop for eparchial associations, but not the administrator of the eparchy,

CAN. 573 §1. Consociationes ab auctoritate competenti ecclesiastica erectae vel ab ipsa per decretum approbatae sunt personae iuridicae in Ecclesia et vocantur consociationes publicae.

§2. Ceterae consociationes, etsi ab auctoritate ecclesiastica laudantur vel commendantur, consociationes privatae vocantur; hae consociationes in Ecclesia non agnoscuntur, nisi earum statuta ab auctoritate competenti recognoscuntur, de cetero vero reguntur tantummodo iure particulari firmo can. 577.

CAN. 574 Salvo de cetero can. 18 solius auctoritatis ecclesiasticae competentis est erigere christifidelium consociationes, quae sibi proponunt doctrinam christianam nomine Ecclesiae tradere aut cultum publicum promovere vel quae alios intendunt fines, quorum prosecutio natura sua eidem auctoritati ecclesiasticae reservatur.

CAN. 575 §1. Auctoritas competens ad erigendas vel approbandas christifidelium consociationes est pro consociationibus et earundem confoederationibus:

1° eparchialibus Episcopus eparchialis, non vero Administrator eparchiae, eis tamen

---

573 §1: Pius XII, m.p. *Cleri sanctitati,* 2 iun. 1957, cann. 530, 532 §1.

573 §2: Pius XII, m.p. *Cleri sanctitati,* 2 iun. 1957, can. 530; Vat. II, decr. *Apostolicam actuositatem,* 24.

574: Vat. II, decr. *Apostolicam actuositatem,* 24

"Quaedam;" Pius XII, m.p. *Cleri sanctitati,* 2 iun. 1957, can. 531.

575 §1: Pius XII, m.p. *Cleri sanctitati,* 2 iun. 1957, can. 533 §1.

excepting those associations whose erection has been reserved to others by apostolic or patriarchal privilege;

2° the patriarch after consultation with his permanent synod, or the metropolitan after consultation with the two eparchial bishops senior in episcopal ordination, for associations open to all the Christian faithful of any patriarchal or metropolitan Church *sui iuris* and that have their headquarters within the territorial boundaries of the same Church;

3° the Apostolic See for other types.

§2. For the erection of a branch of any non-eparchial association, the written consent of the eparchial bishop is required; however, the consent given by an eparchial bishop for the erection of a house of a religious institute also allows for the erection, in the same house or a church attached to it, of an association proper to the institute.

CAN. 576 §1. Every association is to have its own statutes, in which the association's name, purpose, headquarters, governance, and conditions required for membership are determined. Further, the statutes are to determine policies in accordance with the rite of the association's Church *sui iuris* and the needs of time and place or usefulness.

§2. The statutes and their modification require the approval of the ecclesiastical authority that erected or approved the association.

CAN. 577 §1. Any association is subject to the vigilance of the ecclesiastical authority that erected or approved it; this authority is to see that the integrity of faith and morals is maintained in it, and to watch lest abuses creep into ecclesiastical discipline.

consociationibus exceptis, quarum erectio ex privilegio apostolico vel patriarchali aliis reservata est;

2° quae omnibus christifidelibus alicuius Ecclesiae patriarchalis vel metropolitanae sui iuris patent quaeque sedem principem intra fines territorii eiusdem Ecclesiae habent, Patriarcha consulta Synodo permanenti vel Metropolita consultis duobus Episcopis eparchialibus ordinatione episcopali senioribus;

3° alterius speciei Sedes Apostolica.

§2. Ad erectionem sectionis cuiuscumque consociationis non eparchialis requiritur consensus scripto datus Episcopi eparchialis; consensus tamen ab Episcopo eparchiali praestitus pro erectione domus instituti religiosi valet etiam ad erigendam in eadem domo vel ecclesia ei adnexa consociationem, quae illius instituti est propria.

CAN. 576 §1. Omnis consociatio sua habeat statuta, quibus determinantur consociationis nomen, finis, sedes, regimen et condiciones requisitae ad ascriptionem; praeterea in statutis determinantur agendi rationes attentis ritu propriae Ecclesiae sui iuris, necessitatibus loci et temporis vel utilitate.

§2. Statuta eorumque immutatio approbatione indigent auctoritatis ecclesiasticae, quae consociationem erexit vel approbavit.

CAN. 577 §1. Quaelibet consociatio subest vigilantiae auctoritatis ecclesiasticae, quae eam erexit vel approbavit; huius auctoritatis est curare, ut in eadem integritas fidei et morum servetur, et vigilare, ne in disciplinam ecclesiasticam abusus irrepant.

---

575 §2: Pius XII, m.p. *Cleri sanctitati,* 2 iun. 1957, can. 533 §2.

576 §1: Pius XII, m.p. *Cleri sanctitati,* 2 iun. 1957, cann. 535, 536 §1.

576 §2: Pius XII, m.p. *Cleri sanctitati,* 2 iun. 1957, can. 536.

§2. It is for the eparchial bishop to be vigilant of all associations exercising activity in his territory, and if the case warrants, to notify the authority that has erected or approved them, and further, if the action of the association causes serious harm to ecclesiastical doctrine or discipline, or is a scandal to the Christian faithful, to apply appropriate remedies in the meantime.

CAN. 578 §1. The reception of members is to be done in accord with the norm of common law and the statutes of the association.

§2. The same person can be a member of several associations.

§3. Members of religious institutes can enroll in associations, according to the norm of the typicon or statutes, with the consent of their superior.

CAN. 579 No association of the Christian faithful can ascribe its members as clerics without a special concession of the Apostolic See, or, if it is an association mentioned can. 575, §1, n. 2, by the patriarch, with the consent of the permanent synod.

CAN. 580 One who has publicly rejected the Catholic faith, or has publicly abandoned communion with the Catholic Church, or has been punished with major excommunication, cannot validly be received into associations; but if he or she has already been legitimately ascribed, he or she should be declared by the local hierarch to be dismissed by the law itself.

CAN. 581 No one who has legitimately become a member of an association may be dismissed from it except for a just reason in accord

§2. Episcopi eparchialis est vigilare omnibus consociationibus in suo territorio activitatem exercentibus et, si casus fert, auctoritatem, quae consociationem erexit vel approbavit, certiorem facere et insuper, si actio consociationis in grave damnum cedit doctrinae vel disciplinae ecclesiasticae aut scandalo est christifidelibus, remedia opportuna interim adhibere.

CAN. 578 §1. Membrorum receptio fiat ad normam iuris communis ac statutorum consociationis.

§2. Eadem persona ascribi potest pluribus consociationibus.

§3. Sodales institutorum religiosorum possunt consociationibus ad normam typici vel statutorum de consensu sui Superioris nomen dare.

CAN. 579 Nulla consociatio christifidelium propria membra ut clericos sibi ascribere potest nisi ex speciali concessione a Sede Apostolica vel, si de consociatione, de qua in can. 575, §1, n. 2, agitur, a Patriarcha de consensu Synodi permanentis data.

CAN. 580 Qui fidem catholicam publice abiecit vel a communione cum Ecclesia catholica publice defecit vel excommunicatione maiore irretitus est, valide in consociationes recipi non potest; si vero iam legitime ascriptus est, ab Hierarcha loci ipso iure dimissus declaretur.

CAN. 581 Nemo legitime ascriptus a consociatione dimittatur nisi iusta de causa ad normam iuris communis et statutorum.

577 §2: Pius XII, m.p. *Cleri sanctitati*, 2 iun. 1957, can. 538 §1; Paulus VI, m.p. *Ecclesiae sanctae*, 6 aug. 1966, I, 35.

578 §1: Pius XII, m.p. *Cleri sanctitati*, 2 iun. 1957, cann. 540, 542 §1.

578 §2: Pius XII, m.p. *Cleri sanctitati*, 2 iun. 1957, can. 541 §2.

578 §3: Pius XII, m.p. *Cleri sanctitati*, 2 iun. 1957, can. 541 §4.

580: Pius XII, m.p. *Cleri sanctitati*, 2 iun. 1957, cann. 541 §1 n. 1, 544 §2.

581: Pius XII, m.p. *Cleri sanctitati*, 2 iun. 1957, can. 544 §1.

with the norms of common law and of the statutes.

CAN. 582 A legitimately erected and approved association administers temporal goods according to the norms of the cann. 1007–1054 and its own statutes, under the vigilance of the authority that erected or approved it, to whom the association must render an account of its administration each year.

CAN. 583 §1. Associations erected or approved by the Apostolic See can be suppressed only by the Apostolic See.

§2. Other associations can be suppressed not only by the Apostolic See but, without prejudice to can. 927 §2, and with due regard for the right of recourse with suspensive effect according to the norm of law:

1° by the patriarch with the consent of his permanent synod; or by the metropolitan who presides in a metropolitan Church *sui iuris*, with the consent of the two senior eparchial bishops according to episcopal ordination;

2° by an eparchial bishop if the associations were erected or approved by him.

CAN. 582 Consociatio legitime erecta vel approbata bona temporalia ad normam cann. 1007–1054 et statutorum administrat sub vigilantia auctoritatis, quae eam erexit vel approbavit, cui quotannis administrationis rationem reddere debet.

CAN. 583 §1. Consociationes a Sede Apostolica erectae vel approbatae nonnisi ab eadem supprimi possunt.

§2. Ceterae consociationes, firmo can. 927, §2 et salvo iure recursus in suspensivo ad normam iuris, praeterquam a Sede Apostolica supprimi possunt:

1° a Patriarcha de consensu Synodi permanentis vel a Metropolita, qui Ecclesiae metropolitanae sui iuris praeest, de consensu duorum Episcoporum eparchialium ordinatione episcopali seniorum;

2° ab Episcopo eparchiali, si ab eo erectae vel approbatae sunt.

582: Pius XII, m.p. *Cleri sanctitati*, 2 iun. 1957, can. 539 §1; m.p. *Postquam Apostolicis Litteris*, 9 feb. 1952, can. 273.

583 §1: Pius XII, m.p. *Cleri sanctitati*, 2 iun. 1957, can. 547 §2.

583 §2: Pius XII, m.p. *Cleri sanctitati*, 2 iun. 1957, can. 547.

TITLE XIV. EVANGELIZATION OF PEOPLES

CAN. 584 §1. Obeying the mandate of Christ to evangelize all peoples, and moved by the grace and charity of the Holy Spirit, the Church recognizes herself to be totally missionary.

§2. The evangelization of the peoples should be so done that, preserving the integrity of faith and morals, the gospel can be expressed in the culture of each individual people; namely, in catechetics, in their own liturgical rites, in sacred art, in particular law, and, in short, in the whole ecclesial life.

CAN. 585 §1. It is for each Church *sui iuris* continually to take care that, through suitably prepared preachers sent by a competent authority in accord with the norms of the common law, the gospel is preached in the whole world under the guidance of the Roman Pontiff.

§2. There should be a commission in the synod of bishops or the council of hierarchs to foster a more effective cooperation among all the eparchies in the missionary activity of the Church.

§3. In the individual eparchies a priest is to

CAN. 584 §1. Christi mandato omnes gentes evangelizandi obsequens et Spiritus Sancti gratia caritateque mota Ecclesia se totam missionariam agnoscit.

§2. Evangelizatio gentium ita fiat, ut servata integritate fidei et morum Evangelium se in cultura singulorum populorum exprimere possit, in catechesi scilicet, in ritibus propriis liturgicis, in arte sacra, in iure particulari ac demum in tota vita ecclesiali.

CAN. 585 §1. Singularum Ecclesiarum sui iuris est iugiter curare, ut per praecones apte praeparatos et ab auctoritate competenti ad normam iuris communis missos Evangelium praedicetur in universum mundum sub moderamine Romani Pontificis.

§2. Synodo Episcoporum Ecclesiae patriarchalis vel Consilio Hierarcharum assit commissio ad omnium eparchiarum efficaciorem collaborationem provehendam in activitate Ecclesiae missionali.

§3. In singulis eparchiis sacerdos de-

---

584 §1: Vat. II, decr. *Ad gentes,* 35, 2 "Ecclesia," 6 "Hoc munus;" const. *Lumen gentium,* 17, 20 "Missio," 23 "Cura;" decl. *Dignitatis humanae,* 13 "In societate;" PAULUS VI, m.p. *Ecclesiae sanctae,* 6 aug. 1966, III "Cum" et 1; adh. ap. *Evangelii nuntiandi,* 8 dec. 1975, 59.

584 §2: Vat. II, decr. *Ad gentes,* 9, 19 "Opus" et "In huiusmodi;" PAULUS VI, m.p. *Ecclesiae sanctae,* 6 aug. 1966, III, 18; adh. ap. *Evangelii nuntiandi,* 8 dec. 1975, 20 "Evangelium," 63; Synodus Episcoporum,

nuntius, 28 oct. 1977, pars I, 5.

585 §1: Vat. II, decr. *Orientalium Ecclesiarum,* 3; const. *Lumen gentium,* 23 "Cura;" decr. *Ad gentes,* 6 "Hoc munus," 29 "Cura," 38 "Episcopi;" PAULUS VI, adh. ap. *Evangelii nuntiandi,* 8 dec. 1975, 68 "En verae."

585 §2: PAULUS VI, m.p. *Ecclesiae sanctae,* 6 aug. 1966, III, 9; Vat. II, decr. *Ad gentes,* 38.

585 §3: PAULUS VI, m.p. *Ecclesiae sanctae,* 6 aug. 1966, III, 4; Vat. II, decr. *Ad gentes,* 38.

be designated to promote undertakings in an effective way on behalf of the missions.

§4. The Christian faithful are to promote among themselves and others an understanding and love for the missions, to pray for them, to inspire vocations and support them generously with their own offerings.

CAN. 586 It is strictly forbidden to coerce, to induce through improper practices or to allure anyone to join the Church; however, all the Christian faithful are to take care that the right to religious freedom is maintained, lest anyone be hindered from embracing the Church by unjust harassment.

CAN. 587 §1. Persons who desire to join the Church are to be admitted with liturgical ceremonies to the catechumenate, which is not a mere presentation of teachings and precepts, but a formation in the whole Christian life and a suitably extended apprenticeship.

§2. Persons who are ascribed in the catechumenate have the right to be admitted to the liturgy of the word and other liturgical celebrations not reserved to the Christian faithful.

§3. It is for particular law to enact norms to regulate the catechumenate, determining what is to be done by the catechumens and what prerogatives are recognized as theirs.

CAN. 588 Catechumens are free to be ascribed to any Church *sui iuris*, in accord with the norm of can. 30; however, care should be taken lest anything should be recommended

signetur ad incepta pro missionibus efficaciter promovenda.

§4. Christifideles cognitionem et amorem missionum in se ipsis et in aliis foveant, pro illis orent atque vocationes excitent illasque suis subsidiis liberaliter sustineant.

CAN. 586 Severe prohibetur, ne quis ad Ecclesiam amplectendam cogatur vel artibus importunis inducatur aut alliciatur; omnes vero christifideles curent, ut vindicetur ius ad libertatem religiosam, ne quis iniquis vexationibus ab Ecclesia deterreatur.

CAN. 587 §1. Qui se Ecclesiae coniungere volunt, caerimoniis liturgicis admittantur ad catechumenatum, qui non sit mera dogmatum praeceptorumque expositio, sed totius vitae christianae institutio et tirocinium debite protractum.

§2. Qui catechumenatui ascripti sunt, ius habent, ut admittantur ad liturgiam verbi aliasque celebrationes liturgicas christifidelibus non reservatas.

§3. Iuris particularis est normas ferre, quibus catechumenatus ordinetur determinando, quaenam a catechumenis sint praestanda et quaenam eis agnoscantur praerogativae.

CAN. 588 Integrum est catechumenis ascribi cuivis Ecclesiae sui iuris ad normam can. 30; caveatur tamen, ne quid ipsis suadeatur, quod obstare possit eorundem

585 §4: Vat. II, const. *Lumen gentium*, 23 "Cura;" decr. *Ad gentes*, 36, 38–39, 41; decr. *Perfectae caritatis*, 20; Paulus VI, m.p. *Ecclesiae sanctae*, 6 aug. 1966, III, 3.

586: Vat. II, decr. *Ad gentes*, 13 "Ecclesia," 12; decl. *Dignitatis humanae*, 2 "Haec," 4, 10 "Caput;" Paulus VI, adh. ap. *Evangelii nuntiandi*, 8 dec. 1975, 80 "Vitium."

587 §1: Vat. II, decr. *Ad gentes*, 14 "Qui." - Nic. I, can. 14; Constantinop. I, can. 7; Quinisext. can. 95.

587 §2: Vat. II, decr. *Ad gentes*, 14 "Qui." - Nic. I, can. 14; Constantinop. I, can. 7; Quinisext. can. 95; Neoc. can. 5; Laod. can. 19; Theophilus Alexandrinus, can. 8.

588: Pius XII, m.p. *Cleri sanctitati*, 2 iun. 1957, can. 12.

that might prevent their ascription in the Church *sui iuris* more appropriate to their culture.

CAN. 589 Missionaries, either native or non-native, are to be qualified in the necessary skills and ability; they are to be suitably formed in missiology and missionary spirituality, as well as instructed in the history and culture of the peoples to be evangelized.

CAN. 590 In missionary activity attention must be paid that young Churches reach maturity as soon as possible and become fully established so that, under the guidance of their own hierarchy, they can provide for themselves, and undertake and continue the work of evangelization.

CAN. 591 Missionaries are to be diligent in ensuring that:

1° vocations to the sacred ministries are prudently promoted among neophytes so that the young Churches may flourish with native clerics as soon as possible;

2° catechists should be so formed that, as valid cooperators of the sacred ministers, they may be able to discharge their task in the work of evangelization and in liturgical service in the best possible way. Provision is to be made by particular law for the just remuneration of the catechists.

CAN. 592 §1. In mission territories suitable forms of lay apostolate are to be fostered with special care; institutes of consecrated life are to be promoted, taking into account the particular qualities and character of the different peoples; schools and other such institutions of

ascriptioni Ecclesiae, quae eorum culturae magis consentanea est.

CAN. 589 Missionarii sive exteri sive autochthoni sint congruis dotibus et ingenio idonei; sint apte instituti in missiologia et in spiritualitate missionaria necnon instructi in historia et cultura populorum, qui evangelizandi sunt.

CAN. 590 In activitate missionali curandum est, ut novellae Ecclesiae quam primum maturitatem consequantur atque plene constituantur ita, ut sub ductu propriae hierarchiae sibi providere et opus evangelizandi assumere atque continuare possint.

CAN. 591 Missionarii sedulo curent, ut:

1° vocationes ad ministeria sacra inter neophytos prudenter promoveantur ita, ut novellae Ecclesiae quam primum autochthonis clericis floreant;

2° catechistae ita instituantur, ut tamquam validi cooperatores ministrorum sacrorum munus suum in evangelizatione necnon in actione liturgica quam optime exsequi possint; iure particulari provideatur, ut catechistae iustam remunerationem habeant.

CAN. 592 §1. Speciali cura in territoriis missionum aptae formae apostolatus laicorum foveantur; instituta vitae consecratae, ratione habita singulorum populorum ingenii et indolis, promoveantur; scholae et alia huiusmodi educationis christianae et pro-

589: Vat. II, decr. *Ad gentes,* 16, 23, 25–26.
590: Vat. II, const. *Lumen gentium,* 17; decr. *Ad gentes,* 6, 15, 16 "Gaudio," 18–20.
591, 1°: Vat. II, decr. *Ad gentes,* 15 "Iamvero," 16

"Quae."
591, 2°: Vat. II, decr. *Ad gentes,* 17, 26 "Fratres."
592 §1: Vat. II, decr. *Ad gentes,* 15, 18–19.

Christian education and cultural progress are to be established as needed.

§2. Moreover, dialogue and cooperation with non-Christians are to be fostered earnestly and prudently.

CAN. 593   §1. As all the presbyters of whatever condition working in a mission territory form one presbyterate, they are to cooperate zealously in the work of evangelization.

§2. They are to cooperate readily, in accordance with can. 908, with other Christian missionaries, so that they can render united witness to Christ the Lord.

CAN. 594   Mission territories are those recognized as such by the Apostolic See.

gressus culturalis instituta, ut opus est, constituantur.

§2. Item dialogus et cooperatio cum non-christianis sedulo et prudenter foveantur.

CAN. 593   §1. Omnes presbyteri cuiuscumque condicionis in territoriis missionum operam praestantes utpote unum presbyterium efformantes ardenter in evangelizatione cooperentur.

§2. Ipsi cum ceteris missionariis christianis, ut unum pro Christo Domino testimonium reddant, libenter collaborent ad normam can. 908.

CAN. 594   Territoria missionum sunt, quae Sedes Apostolica ut talia agnovit.

592 §2: Vat. II, decr. *Ad gentes,* 11–12, 15.

593 §1: Vat. II, decr. *Ad gentes,* 20 "Presbyteri."

TITLE XV. THE
ECCLESIASTICAL
MAGISTERIUM

TITULUS XV. DE
MAGISTERIO
ECCLESIASTICO

CHAPTER I. The Teaching Function of the Church in General

CAPUT I. De Ecclesiae Munere Docendi in Genere

CAN. 595 § 1. Christ the Lord has entrusted to the Church the deposit of faith so that, with the assistance of the Holy Spirit, it may conscientiously guard the revealed truth, profoundly investigate it and faithfully proclaim and expound it; hence, the Church has the innate right, independent of any human power, and obligation to preach the gospel to all people.

§2. It belongs to the Church always and everywhere to announce moral principles, even those pertaining to the social order, and to

CAN. 595 §1. Ecclesiae, cui Christus Dominus depositum fidei concredidit, ut Spiritu Sancto assistente veritatem revelatam sancte custodiret, penitus perscrutaretur, fideliter annuntiaret atque exponeret, ius nativum a qualibet humana potestate independens et obligatio est omnibus hominibus Evangelium praedicandi.

§2. Ecclesiae competit semper et ubique principia moralia, etiam ad ordinem socialem spectantia, annuntiare necnon iudicium ferre

---

595 §1: Vat. II, const. *Dei Verbum,* 10 "Munus;" decr. *Inter mirifica,* 3; const. *Lumen gentium,* 24–25; decr. *Christus Dominus,* 19; decl. *Dignitatis humanae,* 13; Vat. I, sess. III, cap. II, *De revelatione;* cap. III, *De fide;* cap. IV, *De fide et ratione;* sess. IV, cap. IV, *De Romani pontificis infallibili magisterio.* - INNOCENTIUS III, ep. *Eius exemplo,* 18 dec. 1208, Professio fidei Waldensibus praescr.; CLEMENS VI, ep. *Super quibusdam,* 29 sep. 1351; EUGENIUS IV (in Flor.), const. *Cantate Domino,* 4 feb. 1441, §15; PIUS IV, const. *Iniunctum nobis,* 13 nov. 1564, Professio fidei Trident.; GREGORIUS XIII, const. *Sanctissimus,* a. 1575, Professio fidei Graecis praescr.; BENEDICTUS XIV, ep. *Nuper ad Nos,* 16 mar. 1743, Professio fidei Maronitis praescr.; PIUS VI, const. *Auctorem fidei,* 28 aug. 1794, prop. 1, 85, Synodi Pistorien., damn.; PIUS VIII, litt. ap. *Litteris altero,* 25 mar. 1830; GREGORIUS XVI, ep. encycl. *Summo iugiter,* 27 maii 1832; ep. encycl. *Mirari vos,* 15 aug. 1832; ep. encycl. *Commissum divinitus,* 17 maii 1835; PIUS IX, ep. encycl. *Qui pluribus,* 9 nov. 1846; all. *Ubi primum,* 17 dec. 1847; ep. encycl. *Nostis et Nobiscum,* 5 dec. 1849; litt. ap. *Multiplices inter,* 10 iun. 1851; all. *Singulari quadam,* 9 dec. 1854; ep. encycl. *Singulari quidem,* 17 mar. 1856; all. *Iamdudum cernimus,* 18 mar. 1861; all. *Maxima quidem,* 9 iun. 1862; ep. ency-

cl. *Quanto conficiamur moerore,* 10 aug. 1863; ep. *Tuas libenter,* 21 dec. 1863; ep. *Quum non sine,* 14 iul. 1864; Syllabus errorum, a. 1864, prop. 15–18, 21; S.C.S. Off., litt. 8 nov. 1865; PIUS IX, ep. *Inter gravissimas,* 28 oct. 1870; ep. encycl. *Vix dum a Nobis,* 7 mar. 1874; LEO XIII, ep. encycl. *Immortale Dei,* 1 nov. 1885; ep. *Officio sanctissimo,* 22 dec. 1887; ep. *Sicut acceptum,* 29 apr. 1889; litt. encycl. *Sapientiae,* 10 ian. 1890; lit. encycl. *Providentissimus Deus,* 18 nov. 1893; ep. encycl. *Satis cognitum,* 29 iun. 1896; ep. *Testem,* 22 ian. 1899; S.C.S. Off., decr. 4 iul. 1907, prop. 2–6, 22, 31, 59–62, damn.; PIUS XII, litt. encycl. *Mystici Corporis,* 29 iun. 1943; IOANNES XXIII, all. *Gaudet Mater Ecclesia,* 11 oct. 1962; PAULUS VI, hom. 7 dec. 1965; adh. ap. *Quinque iam anni,* 8 dec. 1970; Synodus Episcoporum, decl. 25 oct. 1974, 4; PAULUS VI, adh. ap. *Evangelii nuntiandi,* 8 dec. 1975, 6–15; IOANNES PAULUS II, litt. encycl. *Redemptor hominis,* 4 mar. 1979, 19.

595 §2: Vat. II, decr. *Christus Dominus,* 12; decl. *Dignitatis humanae,* 15; const. *Gaudium et spes,* 76 "Res," 89 "Ecclesia;" IOANNES XXIII, litt. encycl. *Pacem in terris,* 11 apr. 1963, V "Has;" PAULUS VI, litt. encycl. *Humanae vitae,* 25 iul. 1968, 4; Synodus Episcoporum, 30 nov. 1971, II *De iustitia in mundo,* III.

make judgments about any human matter whatever in so far as this is required by the dignity and the fundamental rights of the human person or the salvation of souls.

CAN. 596 The function of teaching in the name of the Church belongs only to bishops; nevertheless, that function is shared, in accord with the norm of law, both by those who have been made collaborators of the bishops through sacred orders and by those who, though not in sacred orders, have received the mandate to teach.

CAN. 597 §1. The Roman Pontiff, in virtue of his office *(munus)*, enjoys infallible teaching authority if, as supreme pastor and teacher of all the Christian faithful whose duty it is to confirm his fellow believers in the faith, he proclaims by a definitive act that a doctrine of faith or morals is to be held.

§2. The college of bishops also possesses infallible teaching authority if the bishops, assembled in an ecumenical council, exercise their teaching authority, and, as teachers and judges of faith and morals for the entire Church, declare that a doctrine of faith or morals must be held definitively; or when, dispersed throughout the world but preserving the bond of communion among themselves and with the successor of Peter, and teaching authentically together with the Roman Pontiff matters of faith and morals, they agree that a particular position is to be held as definitive.

§3. No doctrine is understood to be infallibly defined unless it is clearly established as such.

CAN. 598 §1. A person must believe with divine and Catholic faith all those things con-

de quibuslibet rebus humanis, quatenus dignitas personae humanae eiusque iura fundamentalia aut salus animarum id exigunt.

CAN. 596 In nomine Ecclesiae docendi munus solis Episcopis competit; in eodem tamen munere partem habent ad normam iuris sive ii, qui Episcoporum per ordinem sacrum effecti sunt cooperatores, sive ii, qui in ordine sacro non constituti mandatum docendi receperunt.

CAN. 597 §1. Infallibilitate in magisterio vi muneris sui gaudet Romanus Pontifex, si ut supremus omnium christifidelium Pastor et Doctor, cuius est fratres suos in fide confirmare, doctrinam de fide vel de moribus tenendam definitivo actu proclamat.

§2. Infallibilitate in magisterio pollet quoque Collegium Episcoporum, si magisterium exercent Episcopi in Concilio Oecumenico coadunati, qui ut fidei et morum doctores et iudices pro universa Ecclesia doctrinam de fide vel de moribus ut definitive tenendam declarant, aut si per orbem dispersi communionis nexum inter se et cum sancti Petri successore servantes una cum eodem Romano Pontifice authentice res fidei vel morum docentes in unam sententiam tamquam definitive tenendam conveniunt.

§3. Infallibiliter definita nulla intelligitur doctrina, nisi id manifesto constat.

CAN. 598 §1. Fide divina et catholica ea omnia credenda sunt, quae verbo Dei

---

596: Vat. II, const. *Lumen gentium,* 25 "Inter;" const. *Dei Verbum,* 10.

597 §1: Vat. II, const. *Lumen gentium,* 25 "Haec;" Vat. I, sess. IV, const. *Pastor aeternus,* cap. 4.

597 §2: Vat. II, const. *Lumen gentium,* 25 "Licet." 598: Vat. II, const. *Lumen gentium,* 25; const. *Dei Verbum,* 5, 10; Trid., sess. IV; Vat. I, sess. III, cap. II, *De revelatione;* cap. III, *De fide;* cap. IV, *De fide et ra-*

tione; De revelatione, can. 4; *De fide,* can. 6; *De fide et ratione,* can. 3; sess. IV, cap. IV, *De Romani pontificis infallibili magisterio.* - S. INNOCENTIUS I, ep. *Consulenti tibi,* 20 feb. 405, c. 7; Nic. II, actio VIII, *De imaginibus, humanitate Christi, traditione;* BENEDICTUS XII, const. *Benedictus Deus,* 29 ian. 1336; CLEMENS VI, ep. *Super quibusdam,* 29 sep. 1351; MARTINUS V (in Constantien.), const. *Inter cunctas,* 22 feb.

tained in the word of God written or handed down, that is, in the one deposit of faith entrusted to the Church, and at the same time proposed as divinely revealed either by the solemn magisterium of the Church or by its ordinary and universal magisterium that is manifested by the common adherence of the Christian faithful under the leadership of the sacred magisterium; therefore, all are bound to avoid any doctrines whatsoever contrary to them.

§2. Furthermore, each and every thing set forth definitively by the magisterium of the Church regarding teaching on faith and morals must be firmly accepted and held; namely, those things required for the holy keeping and faithful exposition of the deposit of faith; therefore, anyone who rejects propositions that are to be held definitively sets himself against the teaching of the Catholic Church.

CAN. 599   Although not an assent of faith, a religious submission of intellect and will must be given to a doctrine on faith and morals that the Roman Pontiff or the college of bishops enunciate when they exercise the authentic magisterium even if they do not intend to pro-

scripto vel tradito, uno scilicet deposito fidei Ecclesiae commisso, continentur et simul ut divinitus revelata proponuntur sive ab Ecclesiae magisterio sollemni sive ab eius magisterio ordinario et universali, quod quidem communi adhaesione christifidelium sub ductu sacri magisterii manifestatur; tenentur igitur omnes christifideles quascumque devitare doctrinas eisdem contrarias.

§2. Firmiter etiam amplectenda ac retinenda sunt omnia et singula quae circa doctrinam de fide vel moribus ab Ecclesiae magisterio definitive proponunter, scilicet quae ad idem fidei depositum sancte custodiendum et fideliter exponendum requiruntur, ideoque doctrinae Ecclesiae catholicae adversatur qui easdem propositiones definitive tenendas recusat.*

CAN. 599   Non quidem fidei assensus, religiosum tamen intellectus et voluntatis obsequium praestandum est doctrinae de fide et de moribus, quam sive Romanus Pontifex sive Collegium Episcoporum enuntiant, cum magisterium authenticum exercent, etsi de-

---

1418, art. 6 de quo errorum Wicleff et Husz suspecti interrogandi; Eugenius IV (in Flor.), const. *Cantate Domino,* 4 feb. 1441, §6; Leo X, const. *Exsurge Domine,* 15 iun. 1520, errores 27, 29–30, Martini Luther, damn.; Pius IV, const. *Iniunctum nobis,* 13 nov. 1564, Professio fidei Trident.; Gregorius XIII, const. *Sanctissimus,* a. 1575, Professio fidei Graecis praescr.; Innocentius XI, breve, 11 apr. 1682, art. 4, Cleri Gallicani, reiectus; Alexander VIII, const. *Inter multiplices,* 4 aug. 1690, §2; S.C.S. Off., decr. 7 dec. 1690, prop. 29–30, damn.; Benedictus XIV, ep. *Nuper ad Nos,* 16 mar. 1743, Professio fidei Maronitis praescr.; Pius VI, const. *Auctorem fidei,* 28 aug. 1794, prop. 6, Synodi Pistorien., damn.; Pius IX, litt. ap. *Multiplices inter,* 10 iun. 1851; ep. *Tuas libenter,* 21 dec. 1863; Syllabus errorum, a. 1864, prop. 21; S.C.S. Off., litt. 8 nov. 1865; Pius IX, ep. *Inter gravissimas,* 28 oct. 1870; all. *Ordinem Vestrum,* 27 oct. 1871; Leo XIII, litt. encycl. *Libertas,* 20 iun. 1888; ep. *Sicut acceptum,* 29 apr. 1889; litt. encycl. *Sapientiae,* 10 ian. 1890; litt. en-

cycl. *Providentissimus Deus,* 18 nov. 1893; ep. encycl. *Satis cognitum,* 29 iun. 1896; ep. encycl. *Caritatis studium,* 25 iul. 1898; ep. *Testem,* 22 ian 1899; S.C. de Prop. Fide, instr. 31 iul. 1902, I, k); Leo XIII, litt. ap. *Vigilantiae,* 30 oct. 1902; S.C.S. Off., decr. 4 iul. 1907, prop. 2–7, 21–24, 26–27, 31, 61, damn.; Pius X, litt. encycl. *Pascendi,* 8 sep. 1907; Pius XII, const. ap. *Munificentissimus Deus,* 1 nov. 1950; S.C. pro Doctr. Fidei, ep. 24 iul. 1966; Synodus Episcoporum, decl. 28 oct. 1967; S.C. pro Doctr. Fidei, decl. 24 iun. 1973, 2–5.

*598 §2: Joannes Paulus PP. II, Ap. litt. m.p. *Ad tuendam fidem,* 18 maii 1998, *Acta Apostolicae Sedis* 90 (1998) 460. — Trans.

599: Vat. II, const. *Lumen gentium,* 25; notificatio *Quaesitum est,* 15 nov. 1965. - Pius XII, litt. encycl. *Humani generis,* 12 aug. 1950, "Neque putandum;" S.C. pro Doctr. Fidei, ep. 24 iul. 1966; Synodus Episcoporum, decl. 28 oct. 1967, II; S.C. pro Doctr. Fidei, decl. 24 iun. 1973, 2–5.

claim it by a definitive act; therefore the Christian faithful are to take care to avoid those things that do not agree with it.

CAN. 600 Bishops who are in communion with the head and members of the college, whether teaching individually, or gathered together in synods or in particular councils, even if not infallible in their teaching, are authentic instructors and teachers of the faith for the Christian faithful entrusted to their care. The Christian faithful are bound to adhere with religious submission of intellect to the authentic magisterium of their bishops.

CAN. 601 Each Church has the grave task, which is to be carried out in the first place by the patriarchs and the bishops in a manner adapted to each generation and culture, of answering the perennial questions concerning the meaning of life and to provide for Christian solutions to the more pressing problems, having examined the signs of the times in the light of the gospel, so that the light of Christ might shine more brightly everywhere, illuminating all people.

CAN. 602 In pastoral care not only the principles of sacred sciences, but also the contributions of other sciences are to be recognized and utilized, so that the Christian faithful may be led to a more conscious and reflective life of faith.

CAN. 603 Literature and the arts, given their unique power to express and communicate the sense of faith, are to be promoted, recognizing due freedom and cultural diversity.

finitivo actu eandem proclamare non intendunt; christifideles ergo curent, ut devitent, quae cum eadem non congruunt.

CAN. 600 Episcopi, qui sunt in communione cum Collegii capite et membris, sive singuli sive in Synodis aut in Conciliis particularibus congregati, etsi infallibilitate in docendo non pollent, christifidelium suae curae commissorum authentici sunt fidei doctores et magistri; cui magisterio authentico suorum Episcoporum christifideles religioso animi obsequio adhaerere tenentur.

CAN. 601 Singulis Ecclesiis onus incumbit imprimis a Patriarchis et Episcopis exercendum modo unicuique generationi et culturae accommodato ad perennes hominum interrogationes de sensu vitae respondendi necnon christianae solutioni problematum urgentiorum sub luce Evangelii signa temporum perscrutando consulendi ita, ut clarescat ubique magis lux Christi illuminans omnes homines.

CAN. 602 In cura pastorali non tantum principia scientiarum sacrarum, sed etiam inventa aliarum scientiarum agnoscantur et ita adhibeantur, ut christifideles ad magis consciam et reflexam vitam fidei ducantur.

CAN. 603 Litterarum artiumque cultus pro earum vi ad sensum fidei singulari efficacia exprimendum et communicandum agnitis iusta libertate et diversitate culturali provehatur.

600: Vat. II, const. *Lumen gentium*, 25. - Pius VI, const. *Auctorem fidei*, 28 aug. 1794, prop. 6, Synodi Pistorien., damn.; GREGORIUS XVI, ep. encycl. *Mirari vos*, 15 aug. 1832; Pius IX, ep. *Tuas libenter*, 21 dec. 1863; Leo XIII, ep. *Est sane molestum*, 17 dec. 1888; Pius X, litt. encycl. *Acerbo nimis*, 15 apr. 1905; Pius XII, all. 31 maii 1954; S.C. pro Doctr. Fidei, ep. 24 iul. 1966; Synodus Episcoporum, decl. 28 oct. 1967, II.

601: Vat. II, const. *Gaudium et Spes*, 4 "Ad tale," 46.

602: Vat. II, const. *Gaudium et Spes*, 62.

603: Vat. II, const. *Gaudium et Spes*, 62 "Suo" et "Exinde."

CAN. 604 It is above all for the pastors of the Church to be diligent in ensuring that amidst the varieties of doctrinal enunciations in the various Churches, the same sense of faith is preserved and promoted, so that the integrity and unity of faith suffer no harm, but rather that the catholicity of the Church is brought into a better light through legitimate diversity.

CAN. 605 It pertains to the bishops, especially as they are assembled in synods or councils, but in a unique way to the Apostolic See, to promote authoritatively, to guard and to defend conscientiously the integrity and unity of faith and good morals, even, when there is need, reprobating opinions that are contrary to them, or warning about those things that can endanger them.

CAN. 606 §1. It is for theologians, given their profound understanding of the mystery of salvation and their expertise in the sacred and related sciences as well as in current questions, to explain and defend the faith of the Church and to pave the way for doctrinal progress, while faithfully submitting to the authentic magisterium of the Church and at the same time availing themselves of proper freedom.

§2. In the research and expression of theological truths, it is for them to be solicitous to edify the community of faith and also to cooperate with the bishops resourcefully in the discharge of their teaching function.

§3. Those engaged in theological disciplines in seminaries, universities and faculties are to

CAN. 604 Ecclesiae Pastorum imprimis est sedulo curare, ut inter varietates enuntiationum doctrinae in variis Ecclesiis idem sensus fidei servetur atque promoveatur ita, ut integritas et unitas fidei damnum non patiatur, immo catholicitas Ecclesiae per legitimam diversitatem in meliorem lucem ponatur.

CAN. 605 Ad Episcopos praesertim in Synodis vel Consiliis coadunatos, singulariter vero ad Sedem Apostolicam pertinet integritatem et unitatem fidei bonosque mores auctoritative promovere, custodire et religiose defendere, etiam reprobando, quatenus opus est, sententias, quae eisdem contrariae sunt, vel monendo de eis, quae eadem in discrimen ponere possunt.

CAN. 606 §1. Theologorum est pro sua mysterii salutis profundiore intellegentia et scientiarum sacrarum affiniumque necnon novarum quaestionum peritia fideliter magisterio Ecclesiae authentico obsequentes simulque ea, qua par est, libertate utentes fidem Ecclesiae illustrare et defendere progressuique doctrinali consulere.

§2. In veritatibus theologicis investigandis et exprimendis eorum est communitatis fidei aedificandae sollicitos esse atque cum Episcopis in eorum munere docendi sollerter cooperari.

§3. Qui in theologicas disciplinas praesertim in seminariis, studiorum universitati-

604: Vat. II, const. *Lumen gentium,* 18, 25 "Inter;" decr. *Orientalium Ecclesiarum,* 2; decr. *Unitatis redintegratio,* 4 "Quae," 17; PAULUS VI, all. 29 sep. 1963, "Unitatis redintegratio. . .;" all. 14 sep. 1964, "Vos denique;" all. 1 oct. 1966, "Veritati autem."

605: Vat. II, const. *Lumen gentium,* 18, 23 "Collegialis," 25 "Inter;" decr. *Christus Dominus,* 13; PAULUS

VI, adh. ap. *Quinque iam anni,* 8 dec. 1970.

606 §1: Vat. II, const. *Gaudium et Spes,* 44 "Praeteritorum," 62; const. *Dei Verbum,* 23; PAULUS VI, all. 4 dec. 1963 "Huius generis;" all. 1 oct. 1966.

606 §2: PAULUS VI, all. 1 oct. 1966, "Animadversionum prima."

606 §3: Vat. II, const. *Gaudium et spes,* 62 "Qui."

seek to cooperate with those well-versed in other fields of learning by the sharing of views and resources.

bus et facultatibus incumbunt, cum hominibus, qui in aliis scientiis excellunt, collatis consiliis atque viribus cooperari studeant.

CHAPTER II. The Ministry of the Word of God

CAPUT II. De Verbi Dei Ministerio

CAN. 607 The ministry of the word of God, namely preaching, catechesis and every form of Christian instruction, among which the liturgical homily should hold an eminent place, is to be beneficially nourished by Sacred Scripture and based on sacred tradition; the celebration of the word of God is to be opportunely fostered.

CAN. 608 Bishops, priests and deacons, each one according to the grade of his sacred order, exercise in the first place the function of the ministry of the word of God, to be exercised in accord with the norm of law. Other Christian faithful, too, are to take part in it readily, according to each one's aptitude and state of life, and after receiving a mandate.

CAN. 607 Verbi Dei ministerium, praedicatio nempe, catechesis omnisque instructio christiana, inter quae homilia liturgica eximium locum habeat oportet, Sacra Scriptura salubriter nutriatur atque sacra traditione innitatur; celebratio verbi Dei vero opportune foveatur.

CAN. 608 Episcopi, presbyteri et diaconi pro suo cuiusque ordinis sacri gradu primi munus verbi Dei ministerii habent ad normam iuris exercendum; ceteri vero christifideles pro sua cuiusque idoneitate, statu vitae et mandato accepto libenter hoc ministerium participent.

ART. I. *The Preaching of the Word of God*

ART. I. *De Verbi Dei Praedicatione*

CAN. 609 The eparchial bishop is competent to regulate the preaching of the word of God in his territory, with due regard for the common law.

CAN. 610 §1. Bishops have the right to preach the word of God everywhere, unless the eparchial bishop in a special case expressly forbids it.

CAN. 609 Verbi Dei praedicationem moderari in suo territorio competit Episcopo eparchiali firmo iure communi.

CAN. 610 §1. Episcopis ius est verbum Dei ubique terrarum praedicare, nisi Episcopus eparchialis in casu speciali expresse renuit.

607: Vat. II, const. *Dei Verbum,* 24. - Quinisext. can. 19.

608: Vat. II, const. *Lumen gentium,* 28 "Christus," 29, 33, 35; decr. *Christus Dominus,* 12, 13 "Doctrinam;" decr. *Presbyterorum ordinis,* 4; decr. *Apostolicam actuositatem,* 3 "Omnibus," 10 "Utpote," 20, d), 24, 31, a); decr. *Ad gentes,* 41; PAULUS VI, adh. ap. *Quinque iam anni,* 8 dec. 1970, I "Concilium;" adh.

ap. *Evangelii nuntiandi,* 8 dec. 1975, 66–70.

609: Vat. II, const. *Lumen gentium,* 27; decr. *Christus Dominus,* 13 "Varia." - Quinisext. cann. 19–20.

610 §1: PAULUS VI, m.p. *Pastorale munus,* 30 nov. 1963, II, 1; PIUS XII, m.p. *Cleri sanctitati,* cann. 185 §1, 416.

§2. Priests have the faculty to preach where they are legitimately sent or invited.

§3. Deacons also have the same faculty unless particular law establishes otherwise.

§4. In extraordinary circumstances, especially to supply for the scarcity of clerics, the eparchial bishop can also give a mandate to preach to other Christian faithful, even in church, with due regard for can. 614 §4.

CAN. 611 By virtue of office, all to whom the care of souls has been committed have the faculty to preach; they can also invite to preach to those committed to their care any presbyter or, with due regard for can. 610 §3, any deacon, unless these are legitimately prohibited.

CAN. 612 §1. In clerical religious institutes or societies of common life according to the manner of religious of pontifical or patriarchal right, it is the responsibility of the major superiors to regulate preaching.

§2. All superiors, even local ones, of whatever institute of consecrated life, can invite to preach to their own members any presbyter or, with due regard for can. 610, §3, any deacon, unless these are legitimately prohibited.

CAN. 613 Against a decree of a hierarch forbidding someone to preach there is recourse *in devolutivo* only, which must be resolved without delay.

CAN. 614 §1. The homily, by which during the course of the liturgical year the mysteries of faith and the norms of Christian living are expounded from Sacred Scripture, is strongly recommended as part of the liturgy itself.

§2. Pastors and rectors of churches have the

§2. Presbyteri facultate praediti sunt praedicandi ibi, quo legitime mittuntur vel invitantur.

§3. Eadem facultate praedicandi praediti sunt etiam diaconi, nisi ius particulare aliud statuit.

§4. In extraordinariis adiunctis maxime ad supplendam penuriam clericorum ceteris quoque christifidelibus dari potest ab Episcopo eparchiali mandatum praedicandi etiam in ecclesia firmo can. 614, §4.

CAN. 611 Vi officii facultate praedicandi praediti sunt omnes, quibus cura animarum commissa est, qui etiam invitare possunt ad praedicandum suae curae commissis quemlibet presbyterum vel firmo can. 610, §3 diaconum, nisi legitime prohibiti sunt.

CAN. 612 §1. In institutis religiosis vel societatibus vitae communis ad instar religiosorum clericalibus iuris pontificii vel patriarchalis praedicationem moderari pertinet ad Superiores maiores.

§2. Invitare vero ad praedicandum propriis sodalibus quemlibet presbyterum vel firmo can. 610, §3 diaconum, nisi legitime prohibiti sunt, possunt omnes Superiores, etiam locales, cuiuslibet instituti vitae consecratae.

CAN. 613 Contra decretum Hierarchae, quo quis prohibetur praedicare, datur recursus in devolutivo tantum, qui sine mora definiendus est.

CAN. 614 §1. Homilia, qua per anni liturgici cursum ex Sacra Scriptura mysteria fidei et normae vitae christianae exponuntur, ut pars ipsius liturgiae valde commendatur.

§2. Parochis et rectoribus ecclesiarum

---

610 §2: Vat. II, decr. *Presbyterorum ordinis*, 4.
614 §1: Vat. II, const. *Sacrosanctum Concilium*, 35, 2), 52; const. *Dei Verbum*, 24; decr. *Presbyterorum or-* dinis, 4.
614 §2: Vat. II, const. *Sacrosanctum Concilium*, 52. - Quinisext. can. 19; Trid., sess. V, *Decretum se-*

obligation to take care that a homily is preached during the Divine Liturgy at least on Sundays and holy days of obligation; it is not to be omitted except for a grave cause.

§3. It is not permitted for a pastor to have another habitually discharge his obligation of preaching to the people committed to his pastoral care except for a just cause approved by the local hierarch.

§4. The homily is reserved to a priest or, according to norm of particular law, also to a deacon.

CAN. 615 Eparchial bishops are to issue norms so that special series of sacred preaching are held at suitable times for the spiritual renewal of the Christian people.

CAN. 616 §1. The preachers of the word of God should leave aside words of human wisdom and abstruse themes and preach to the Christian faithful the entire mystery of Christ, who is the way, the truth and the life; let them show that earthly things and human institutions are also ordered, according to the plan of God the Creator, to the salvation of humanity, and that they can therefore make no small contribution to building up of the Body of Christ.

§2. Let them teach also the doctrine of the

incumbit obligatio curandi, ut saltem diebus dominicis et festis de praecepto intra Divinam Liturgiam homilia habeatur, quae ne omittatur nisi gravi de causa.

§3. Parocho non licet obligationem populo eius curae pastorali commisso praedicandi per alium habitualiter persolvere nisi iusta de causa ab Hierarcha loci approbata.

§4. Homilia sacerdoti aut, ad normam iuris particularis, etiam diacono reservatur.

CAN. 615 Episcopi eparchiales normis datis curent, ut opportunis temporibus ad populi christiani renovationem spiritualem specialis series sacrae praedicationis habeatur.

CAN. 616 §1. Verbi Dei praedicatores sepositis humanae sapientiae verbis abstrusisque argumentis christifidelibus praedicent integrum mysterium Christi, qui est via et veritas et vita; ostendant res terrestres et instituta humana secundum Dei Creatoris consilium ad hominum salutem quoque ordinari et ideo ad aedificationem Corporis Christi non parum conferre posse.

§2. Edoceant ideo etiam doctrinam Ec-

---

cundum, 9–11; sess. XXII, *De missae sacrificio*, cap. 8; sess. XXIV, *De ref.*, can. 7; INNOCENTIUS XIII, const. *Apostolici ministerii*, 23 maii 1723, §11; BENEDICTUS XIII, const. *In Supremo*, 23 sep. 1724, §§9, 28; const. *Pastoralis officii*, 27 mar. 1726, §3; BENEDICTUS XIV, ep. encycl. *Ubi primum*, 3 dec. 1740, §3; ep. encycl. *Etsi minime*, 7 feb. 1742, §5; const. *Ad militantis*, 30 mar. 1742, §8; const. *Firmandis*, 6 nov. 1744, §9; litt. encycl. *Cum religiosis*, 26 iun. 1754, §4; PIUS X, litt. encycl. *Acerbo nimis*, 15 apr. 1905, 16, VI. * Syn. Sciarfen. Syrorum, a. 1888, cap. XI, art. III, 5, III; Syn. Alexandrin. Coptorum, a. 1898, sect. III, cap. IV, art. IV, §2, V; Syn. Leopolien. Ruthenorum, a. 1891, tit. VII, cap. VI, 2; Syn. Armen., a. 1911, 813.

614 §3: Trid., sess. XXIV, *De ref.*, can. 4; INNOCENTIUS XIV, const. *Apostolici ministerii*, 23 maii 1723, §11; BENEDICTUS XIII, const. *In supremo*, 23 sep.

1724, §§9, 28; const. *Pastoralis officii*, 27 mar. 1726, §3.

614 §4: Pont. Comm. Decr. Conc. Vat. II Interpr., resp. 11 ian. 1971, I. - Quinisext. can. 64.

615: Trid., sess. XXIV, *De ref.*, can. 4.

616 §1: Vat. II, decr. *Christus Dominus*, 12. - Trid., sess. XXIV, *De ref.*, can. 7; sess. XXV, *De purgatorio*; LEO X (in Lat. V), const. *Supernae Maiestatis*, 19 dec. 1516; BENEDICTUS XIV, ep. encycl. *Etsi minime*, 7 feb. 1742, §5; PIUS IX, ep. encycl. *Qui pluribus*, 9 nov. 1846, 6; S.C.S. Off., instr. 10 maii 1884, 5; PIUS X, litt. encycl. *Acerbo nimis*, 15 apr. 1905, 13; m.p. *Sacrorum antistitum*, 1 sep. 1910, nn. 2–3, 5; BENEDICTUS XV, litt. encycl. *Humani generis*, 15 iun. 1917, 11–12.

616 §2: Vat. II, decr. *Christus Dominus*, 12 "Ostendant;" const. *Gaudium et spes*, 41; PAULUS VI, adh. ap. *Evangelii nuntiandi*, 8 dec. 1975, 29.

Church about the dignity of the human person and fundamental human rights, about family life, social and civil life, the meaning of justice to be pursued in economic life and work, which can contribute to the building of peace on earth and bring about the development of peoples.

ART. II. *Catechetical Formation*

CAN. 617 Each Church *sui iuris,* and particularly their bishops, have a grave obligation to provide for catechesis, by which faith matures and the disciple of Christ is formed through a deeper and more systematic understanding of the teaching of Christ and through closer union, day by day, to the person of Christ.

CAN. 618 Before all others it is parents who have the obligation to form their children, by word and example, in faith and Christian living; those who take the place of parents and sponsors are bound by an equal obligation.

CAN. 619 Besides the Christian family, the parish itself and every ecclesial community must ensure the catechetical formation of their members and their integration in the same community, by assuring those conditions in

clesiae de dignitate personae humanae eiusque iuribus fundamentalibus, de vita familiari, de consortio civili et sociali necnon de sensu iustitiae in vita oeconomica et laboris persequendo, qui confert ad pacem in terris construendam et ad progressum populorum consequendum.

ART. II. *De Institutione Catechetica*

CAN. 617 Singularum Ecclesiarum sui iuris praesertim vero earum Episcoporum est gravis obligatio catecheseos tradendae, qua fides ad maturitatem adducatur et formetur Christi discipulus per cognitionem profundiorem et magis ordinatam doctrinae Christi et per adhaesionem in dies artiorem ipsius Personae.

CAN. 618 Parentes primi obligatione tenentur verbo et exemplo filios in fide et vitae christianae praxi efformandi; pari obligatione tenentur ii, qui parentum locum tenent, atque patrini.

CAN. 619 Praeter familiam christianam ipsa paroecia atque quaevis communitas ecclesialis curare debent membrorum suorum institutionem catecheticam atque eorum integrationem in ipsam communitatem illas

617: IOANNES PAULUS II, litt. *Catechesi tradendae,* 16 oct. 1979, 19, 62–63; Vat. II, decr. *Christus Dominus,* 14; decl. *Gravissimum educationis,* 4; PAULUS VI, adh. ap. *Evangelii nuntiandi,* 8 dec. 1975, 44; Synodus Episcoporum, nuntius, 28 oct. 1977, 7; IOANNES PAULUS II, litt. encycl. *Redemptor hominis,* 4 mar. 1979, 19 "Haec." - BENEDICTUS XIV, ep. encycl. *Etsi minime,* 7 feb. 1742, §§2, 5; S.C. de Prop. Fide, (C.G.), 28 nov. 1785; PIUS X, litt. encycl. *Acerbo nimis,* 15 apr. 1905, 12–13; PIUS XI, m.p. *Orbem catholicum,* 29 iun. 1923. * Syn. Leopolien. Ruthenorum, a. 1891, tit. I, cap. VIII, 1; Syn. Armen., a. 1911, 804–805.

618: Vat. II, decl. *Gravissimum educationis,* 3, 6 "Parentes," 7 "Parentibus," 8 "Meminerint;" const. *Lumen gentium,* 11 "Qui vero," 35 "Quo;" decr. *Apostolicam actuositatem,* 11 "Coniuges," 30 "Formatio" et "Parentum;" const. *Gaudium et spes,* 48 "Unde;"

PAULUS VI, adh. ap. *Evangelii nuntiandi,* 8 dec. 1975, 71; IOANNES PAULUS II, litt. encycl. *Redemptor hominis,* 4 mar. 1979, 19 "Praeterea;" adh. ap. *Catechesi tradendae,* 16 oct. 1979, 68.

619: IOANNES PAULUS II, adh. ap. *Catechesi tradendae,* 16 oct. 1979, 24 "Communitatis," 67; Vat. II, decr. *Christus Dominus,* 30, 2) "In exsequendo," 35, 4); PAULUS VI, adh. ap. *Evangelii nuntiandi,* 8 dec. 1975, 68–71. * Syn. Zamosten. Ruthenorum, a. 1720, tit. II; Syn. Libanen. Maronitarum, a. 1736, pars I, cap. II; Syn. Gusten. Maronitarum, a. 1768, can. 19; Syn. Bekorkien. Maronitarum, a. 1790, s. 11; Syn. Sciarfen. Syrorum, a. 1888, cap. XI, art. II, 1; art. III, 2; Syn. Leopolien. Ruthenorum, a. 1891, tit. I, cap. VIII; Syn. Alexandrin. Coptorum, a. 1898, sect. III, cap. IV, art. IV, §2, V; Syn. Armen., a. 1911, 806–809.

which they can live most fully what they have learned.

CAN. 620 Associations and movements and groups of the Christian faithful, having as their goal piety, the apostolate, or charitable works and assistance, are to ensure the religious formation of their members under the guidance of the local hierarch.

CAN. 621 §1. The synod of bishops of the patriarchal Church or the council of hierarchs is competent within the territorial boundaries of their own Church to enact norms on catechetical formation, suitably arranged in a catechetical directory, observing what has been prescribed by the supreme authority of the Church.

§2. In this catechetical directory the special character of the Eastern Churches is to be taken into account, so that the biblical and liturgical dimensions as well as the traditions of the respective Church *sui iuris* in patrology, hagiography, and even iconography are highlighted in imparting catechesis.

§3. The synod of bishops of the patriarchal Church or the council of hierarchs is to see to it that catechisms adapted to the various groups of the Christian faithful are prepared along with aids and resources and that the different catechetical initiatives are promoted and are coordinated among themselves.

CAN. 622 §1. In each Church *sui iuris* there is to be a catechetical commission, which can be established together with the other Churches *sui iuris* for the same territory or socio-cultural region.

§2. This catechetical commission is to avail itself of a catechetical center, which is to be of

praebendo condiciones, in quibus ea, quae didicerunt, quam plenissime vivere possunt.

CAN. 620 Consociationes et motus et circuli christifidelium, sive ad fines pietatis et apostolatum sive ad opera caritatis et adiumenti intendunt, formationem religiosam membrorum suorum curent sub ductu Hierarchae loci.

CAN. 621 §1. Synodo Episcoporum Ecclesiae patriarchalis vel Consilio Hierarcharum competit intra fines territorii propriae Ecclesiae normas de institutione catechetica in directorium catecheticum apte componendas ferre servatis eis, quae a suprema Ecclesiae auctoritate praescripta sunt.

§2. In directorio catechetico ratio habeatur indolis specialis Ecclesiarum orientalium ita, ut momentum biblicum et liturgicum necnon traditiones propriae Ecclesiae sui iuris in patrologia, hagiographia et ipsa iconographia in catechesi tradenda eluceant.

§3. Synodi Episcoporum Ecclesiae patriarchalis vel Consilii Hierarcharum est curare, ut catechismi ad varios coetus christifidelium accommodati simul cum subsidiis ac instrumentis provideantur necnon varia incepta catechetica provehantur atque inter se componantur.

CAN. 622 §1. In quavis Ecclesia sui iuris assit commissio de re catechetica, quae etiam cum aliis Ecclesiis sui iuris pro eodem territorio vel regione socio-culturali constitui potest.

§2. Commissioni de re catechetica praesto sit etiam centrum catecheticum,

---

620: IOANNES PAULUS II, adh. ap. *Catechesi tradendae,* 16 oct. 1979, 24 "Communitatis," 70.

621 §1: Vat. II, decr. *Christus Dominus,* 44 "Conficiantur," 13–14, 36, 38, 6); decr. *Ad gentes,* 31;

IOANNES PAULUS II, adh. ap. *Catechesi tradendae,* 16 oct. 1979, 50, 63.

621 §2: Quinisext. can. 19.

service to the same Churches in accomplishing their catechetical tasks in a coordinated and more efficacious way and to assure the formation, including ongoing formation, of catechists.

CAN. 623 §1. It is for the eparchial bishop to promote, direct, and regulate catechetical formation in his eparchy with the utmost solicitude.

§2. For this purpose the services of an eparchial catechetical center are to be available in the eparchial curia.

CAN. 624 §1. The pastor should, adhering to the norms established by the competent authority, make the utmost effort to give catechesis to all persons entrusted to his pastoral care, whatever their age or condition.

§2. Presbyters and deacons attached to a parish are bound to render their assistance to the pastor; members of religious institutes, however, are to assist in accordance with cann. 479 and 542.

§3. Other Christian faithful, properly formed, are to be ready to offer their help in giving catechesis.

CAN. 625 Catechesis should be ecumeni-

cuius est subsidio esse eisdem Ecclesiis ad incepta catechetica coordinate et efficacius persolvenda atque inservire catechistarum formationi etiam permanenti.

CAN. 623 §1. Episcopi eparchialis est institutionem catecheticam in sua eparchia summa cum sollicitudine provehere, dirigere atque moderari.

§2. Ad quem finem assit curiae eparchiali centrum catecheticum eparchiale.

CAN. 624 §1. Parochus summam operam dare debet attentis normis ab auctoritate competenti statutis ad catechesim tradendam omnibus suae curae pastorali commissis, cuiuscumque sunt aetatis vel condicionis.

§2. Parochis adiutricem operam praestare tenentur presbyteri et diaconi paroeciae addicti; sodales autem institutorum religiosorum ad normam cann. 479 et 542.

§3. Alii christifideles rite formati libenter suam adiutricem operam catechesi tradendae conferant.

CAN. 625 Rationem oecumenicam

---

623 §1: Vat. II, const. *Lumen gentium,* 25 "Inter," 27; decr. *Christus Dominus,* 2 "Episcopi," 13–14, 35, 4); IOANNES PAULUS II, adh. ap. *Catechesi tradendae,* 16 oct. 1979, 63.

624 §1: Vat. II, decr. *Christus Dominus,* 30, 2); IOANNES PAULUS II, adh. ap. *Catechesi tradendae,* 16 oct. 1979, 67 "Ut paucis." - Trid., sess. XXIV, *De ref.,* cann. 4, 7; INNOCENTIUS XIII, const. *Apostolici ministerii,* 23 maii 1723, §11; BENEDICTUS XIII, const. *In Supremo,* 23 sep. 1724, §§9, 28; BENEDICTUS XIV, ep. encycl. *Ubi primum,* 3 dec. 1740, §3; ep. encycl. *Etsi minime,* 7 feb. 1742, §5; const. *Firmandis,* 6 nov. 1744, §9; S.C. de Prop. Fide, (C.G.), 21 sep. 1840, ad 2; PIUS X, litt. encycl. *Acerbo nimis,* 15 apr. 1905, 11–12. * Syn. Zamosten. Ruthenorum., a. 1720, tit. II; Syn. Libanen. Maronitarum, a. 1736, pars I, cap. II; Syn. Sciarfen.

Syrorum, a. 1888, cap. XI, art. III, 5, III, 2; Syn. Leopolien. Ruthenorum, a. 1891, tit. VII, caput VI, 2; Syn. Alexandrin. Coptorum, a. 1898, sect. III, cap. IV, art. IV, §2, V; Syn. Armen., a. 1911, 804–807.

624 §2: Vat. II, decr. *Christus Dominus,* 30, 2), 35; const. *Lumen gentium,* 28–29; PAULUS VI, adh. ap. *Evangelii nuntiandi,* 8 dec. 1975, 68–69; IOANNES PAULUS II, adh. ap. *Catechesi tradendae,* 16 oct. 1979, 64–65. - PIUS XI, m.p. *Orbem Catholicum,* 29 iun. 1923, "Illud." * Syn. Armen., a. 1911, 805–810.

624 §3: Vat. II, decr. *Christus Dominus,* 30, 2); PAULUS VI, adh. ap. *Evangelii nuntiandi,* 8 dec. 1975, 70; IOANNES PAULUS II, adh. ap. *Catechesi tradendae,* 16 oct. 1979, 66.

625: IOANNES PAULUS II, adh. ap. *Catechesi tradendae,* 16 oct. 1979, 32, 33 "Talis."

cal in orientation and present the correct image of other Churches and ecclesial communities; above all care is to be taken that the proper perspective of Catholic catechesis is safeguarded.

CAN. 626 All who are engaged in catechesis should remember that they represent the Church and that they have been sent to communicate the revealed word of God, not their own; they are therefore to present the entire doctrine of the Church, adapted, however, to those they are catechizing and responsive to the demands of their culture.

CHAPTER III. **Catholic Education**

CAN. 627 §1. Care for the education of children belongs primarily to their parents or to those who take their place. Therefore it is for them to educate their children in the context of a Christian family illumined by faith and animated by mutual love, especially in piety toward God and love of neighbor.

§2. To the extent that it is beyond their own resources to provide for the overall education of their children, it is also up to them to entrust others with a share of their educational task and to choose those means of education that are necessary or useful.

§3. It is necessary that parents have just freedom in the choice of the means of education, with due regard for can. 633; therefore, the Christian faithful are to see that this right is recognized by the civil society and even fostered by suitable assistance in accord with the requirements of justice.

habeat oportet catechesis rectam imaginem aliarum Ecclesiarum atque Communitatum ecclesialium praebendo; curandum tamen omnino est, ut in tuto ponatur recta ratio catecheseos catholicae.

CAN. 626 Meminerint omnes, qui catechesi tradendae inserviunt, se Ecclesiae partes gerere et ad verbum Dei revelatum, non proprium communicandum missos esse; proinde doctrinam Ecclesiae integram modo catechizandis quidem accommodato eorumque culturae exigentiis respondenti proponant.

CAPUT III. **De Educatione Catholica**

CAN. 627 §1. Cura filios educandi imprimis spectat ad parentes vel ad eorum locum tenentes; quare eorundem est in familiae christianae ambitu fide illuminato atque amore mutuo animato filios educare praesertim ad pietatem erga Deum et dilectionem proximi.

§2. Si propriae vires transcenduntur, ut consulatur integrae filiorum educationi, parentum quoque est aliis partem muneris educationis concredere necnon eligere instrumenta educationis necessaria vel utilia.

§3. Parentes in instrumentis educationis eligendis iustam libertatem habeant oportet firmo can. 633; quare operam dent christifideles, ut hoc ius a societate civili agnoscatur et secundum exigentias iustitiae congruis etiam subsidiis foveatur.

626: IOANNES PAULUS II, adh. ap. *Catechesi tradendae,* 16 oct. 1979, 22, 30–31, 52–53.

627 §1: Vat. II, decl. *Gravissimum educationis,* 3, 6.

627 §2: Vat. II, decl. *Gravissimum educationis,* 6, 7 "Parentibus."

627 §3: Vat. II, decl. *Gravissimum educationis,* 6–7.

CAN. 628 §1. The Church, since it has generated new creatures through baptism, is to care for their Catholic education together with parents.

§2. All those to whom the care of souls has been committed must help parents in educating their children, make them aware of their rights and obligations, and provide for the religious education especially of young people.

CAN. 629 All educators are to see to the formation of the whole human person in such a way that young people, having cultivated their physical, intellectual, and moral talents harmoniously, and being well versed in the Christian virtues, may be disposed to knowing and loving God more perfectly, to evaluating human and moral values with right conscience and embracing them in true freedom, and, having developed a sense of justice and social responsibility, to pursuing loving fellowship with others.

CAN. 630 §1. The Christian faithful are to work generously so that the appropriate benefits of education and instruction can be extended to all people everywhere, with special concern for the less fortunate.

§2. All the Christian faithful should support the initiatives of the Church in promoting education, especially in erecting, directing and supporting schools.

ART. 1. *Schools, Especially Catholic Schools*

CAN. 631 §1. Among the various means of education, the Catholic school is to be fostered with special care and should be the focus of the

CAN. 628 §1. Ecclesiae, cum novas creaturas per baptismum generaverit, est simul cum parentibus earundem educationem catholicam curare.

§2. Omnes, quibus cura animarum commissa est, debent auxilio esse parentibus ad filios educandos, eosdem proprii iuris et obligationis conscios reddere et educationi religiosae praesertim iuventutis providere.

CAN. 629 Curent omnes educatores, ut attendatur integrae personae humanae formationi ita, ut dotibus physicis, intellectualibus et moralibus harmonice excultis iuvenes virtutibus christianis instructi conformentur ad Deum perfectius cognoscendum et diligendum, ad valores humanos et morales recta conscientia aestimandos et vera libertate amplectendos et simul exculto sensu iustitiae et responsabilitatis socialis ad fraternum cum aliis consortium prosequendum.

CAN. 630 §1. Magno animo operam dent christifideles, ut congrua educationis et instructionis beneficia ad omnes homines ubique terrarum citius extendi possint speciali cura habita illorum, qui sunt tenuioris fortunae.

§2. Faveant omnes christifideles inceptis Ecclesiae ad educationem provehendam aptis, praecipue ad scholas erigendas, dirigendas et sustinendas.

ART. 1. *De Scholis Praesertim Catholicis*

CAN. 631 §1. Inter varia instrumenta educationis speciali cura fovenda est schola catholica, in quam convergat oportet sollici-

---

628 §1: Vat. II, decl. *Gravissimum educationis,* introd. in fine, 2, 3 "Singulari," 4.

628 §2: Vat. II, decl. *Gravissimum educationis,* 2.

629: Vat. II, decl. *Gravissimum educationis,* 1–3.

630 §1: Vat. II, decl. *Gravissimum educationis,* 1 "Similiter."

630 §2: Vat. II, decl. *Gravissimum educationis,* 9 "Sancta."

631 §1: Vat. II, decl. *Gravissimum educationis,* 5.

concern of parents, teachers, and the ecclesial community.

§2. It is the right of the Church to establish and supervise schools of any type or level.

CAN. 632 A school is not juridically considered "Catholic" unless it was established as such by the eparchial bishop or a higher ecclesiastical authority or has been recognized as such by them.

CAN. 633 §1. The eparchial bishop is competent to judge any school whatever and to decide whether it fulfills the requirements of Christian education or not; for a grave cause, he is also competent to forbid the Christian faithful from attending a particular school.

§2. Parents should send their children to Catholic schools, all other things being equal.

CAN. 634 §1. The Catholic school has a particular obligation to create an atmosphere animated by the gospel spirit of freedom and love in the scholastic community, to assist adolescents in the development of their own personality in such a way that at one and the same time they grow in accord with that new creature that they have become through baptism; further, it should so orient the whole of human culture to the message of salvation that the understanding which the students gradually acquire of the world, of life and of humankind may be illumined by faith.

§2. It is for a Catholic school to adapt these matters to its particular circumstances, under the supervision of the competent ecclesiastical authority, if the majority of its pupils are non-Catholics.

§3. It is for a Catholic school, no less than

tudo parentum, magistrorum necnon communitatis ecclesialis.

§2. Ecclesiae ius est scholas cuiusvis generis et gradus erigendi ac moderandi.

CAN. 632 Schola in iure non reputatur catholica, nisi ut talis erecta est ab Episcopo eparchiali vel ab auctoritate superiore ecclesiastica aut ab eisdem ut talis agnita.

CAN. 633 §1. Episcopo eparchiali competit de scholis quibuslibet iudicare et decernere, utrum exigentiis educationis christianae respondeant necne; item eidem competit gravi de causa frequentiam alicuius scholae christifidelibus prohibere.

§2. Parentes filios in scholas catholicas ceteris paribus mittendos curent.

CAN. 634 §1. Scholae catholicae est obligatio propria communitatis scholaris ambitum spiritu evangelico libertatis et caritatis animatum creare, adulescentes adiuvare, ut in propria persona evolvenda una simul crescant secundum novam creaturam, quae per baptismum effecti sunt, atque universam culturam humanam ad nuntium salutis ordinare ita, ut cognitio, quam alumni de mundo, vita et homine gradatim acquirunt, fide illuminetur.

§2. Haec adiunctis propriis accommodare moderante auctoritate competenti ecclesiastica est ipsius scholae catholicae, si maiore ex parte ab alumnis acatholicis frequentatur.

§3. Scholae catholicae est non minus

---

631 §2: Vat. II, decl. *Gravissimum educationis,* 8 "Schola."

632: Vat. II, decr. *Apostolicam actuositatem,* 24 "Plurima."

633 §2: Vat. II, decl. *Gravissimum educationis,* 8 in fine.

634 §1: Vat. II, decl. *Gravissimum educationis,* 8 "Ecclesiae."

634 §2: Vat. II, decl. *Gravissimum educationis,* 9.

634 §3: Vat. II, decl. *Gravissimum educationis,* 8 "Ecclesiae."

other schools, to pursue cultural goals as well as the human and social formation of the young.

CAN. 635   The eparchial bishop is to see to it that Catholic schools are established especially in those places where other schools are lacking or are inadequate; professional and technical schools are also to be established as required, especially by particular circumstances of place and time.

CAN. 636   §1. Catechetical formation in any school whatever is subject to the authority and vigilance of the eparchial bishop.

§2. It is also for the eparchial bishop to appoint or approve teachers of Catholic religion as well as to remove them or demand their removal, if necessary, for reasons of faith or morals.

CAN. 637   In schools in which Catholic instruction is lacking or, in the judgment of the eparchial bishop, is deficient, there is a need to provide true Catholic formation for all Catholic students.

CAN. 638   §1. The eparchial bishop has the right of canonical visitation for all Catholic schools in his eparchy, except those schools reserved to students of institutes of consecrated life of pontifical or patriarchal right, without prejudice in each case to the autonomy of those institutes of consecrated life in the supervision of their schools.

§2. Where there are several eparchial bishops, the right of canonical visitation belongs to the one who founded or approved the school, unless it is stipulated otherwise in the statutes of foundation or in a special agreement made by the same bishops.

quam aliarum scholarum fines culturales et humanam socialemque iuvenum formationem prosequi.

CAN. 635   Episcopi eparchialis praecipue est curare, ut habeantur scholae catholicae, praesertim ubi aliae scholae desunt vel adaequatae non sunt, etiam scholae professionales et technicae, quatenus pro loci et temporis adiunctis speciali ratione requiruntur.

CAN. 636   §1. Institutio catechetica in scholis quibuslibet Episcopi eparchialis auctoritati et vigilantiae subiecta est.

§2. Episcopi eparchialis quoque est nominare aut approbare magistros religionis catholicae eosque, si ratio fidei vel morum id requirit, amovere vel exigere, ut amoveantur.

CAN. 637   In scholis, in quibus institutio catholica deest vel ad iudicium Episcopi eparchialis non sufficit, supplenda est vera formatio catholica omnium alumnorum catholicorum.

CAN. 638   §1. Episcopo eparchiali competit ius canonice visitandi omnes scholas catholicas in eius eparchia exsistentes exceptis scholis, quae exclusive patent propriis alumnis instituti vitae consecratae iuris pontificii vel patriarchalis, et salva omni in casu institutorum vitae consecratae autonomia circa proprias scholas moderandas.

§2. Ubi sunt plures Episcopi eparchiales, ius canonice visitandi competit illi, qui scholam fundavit vel approbavit, nisi aliter in statutis fundationis aut conventione speciali inter eosdem inita cavetur.

635: Vat. II, decl. *Gravissimum educationis,* 9 "Ceterum."

636 §1: Trid., sess. XXV, *De ref.,* cap. 2; Vat. II, decr. *Christus Dominus,* 35, 4); PAULUS VI, m.p. *Ec-*

clesiae sanctae, 6 aug. 1966, I, 39.

638 §1: Trid., sess. XXII, *De ref.,* can. 8; Vat. II, decr. *Christus Dominus,* 35, 4); PAULUS VI, m.p. *Ecclesiae sanctae,* 6 aug. 1966, I, 39.

CAN. 639 Teachers, inasmuch as they have the principal responsibility that a Catholic school concretely achieve its purpose and its initiatives, should be outstanding in doctrine and exemplary in the witness of their lives; they are to collaborate primarily with the parents, but also with other schools.

CAN. 639 Magistri, cum maxime sint auctores, ut schola catholica sua proposita et incepta ad rem deducere possit, debent esse doctrina praestantes atque vitae testimonio exemplares et sociam imprimis cum parentibus, sed et cum aliis scholis praestent operam.

ART. II. *Catholic Universities*

ART. II. *De Catholicis Studiorum Universitatibus*

CAN. 640 §1. The Catholic university aims at bringing the Christian viewpoint to bear on the program to promote the whole range of higher culture in a public, stable and universal manner; therefore it provides higher education in research, reflection and teaching, in which the various areas of human understanding are illumined by the light of the gospel.

CAN. 640 §1. Catholica studiorum universitas hunc finem prosequitur, ut publica, stabilis atque universalis praesentia efficiatur mentis christianae in totius culturae altioris promovendae studio; ideo constituit investigationis, reflexionis et instructionis superioris ordinis institutionem, in qua Evangelii luce multifaria cognitio humana illustretur.

§2. Other institutes of higher education or autonomous Catholic faculties having the same purpose are equivalent to Catholic universities; however ecclesiastical universities and faculties, dealt with in cann. 646–650, are not.

§2. Alia instituta studiorum superiorum vel facultates catholicae autonomae, quae eundem finem prosequuntur, catholicae studiorum universitati aequiparantur, non autem ecclesiasticae studiorum universitates et facultates, de quibus in cann. 646–650.

CAN. 641 In Catholic universities each field of study is to be cultivated according to its own principles, its own method, and its own freedom of scientific inquiry, so that as time goes on a deeper understanding of these disciplines may be acquired, and by paying careful attention to contemporary problems and research, the convergence of faith and reason in the one truth may be seen more clearly, and that persons outstanding in doctrine may be formed

CAN. 641 In catholicis studiorum universitatibus singulae disciplinae propriis principiis, propria methodo atque propria inquisitionis scientificae libertate ita excolantur, ut profundior in dies earum disciplinarum intellegentia obtineatur et, novis progredientis aetatis quaestionibus ac investigationibus accuratissime consideratis, altius perspiciatur, quomodo fides et ratio in unum verum conspirent, atque formentur homines doctri-

---

639: Vat. II, decl. *Gravissimum educationis,* 8 "Meminerint;" decr. *Apostolicam actuositatem,* 30 "Scholarum."

640 §1: Vat. II, decl. *Gravissimum educationis,* 10 "Altioris;" IOANNES PAULUS II, const. ap. *Sapientia christiana,* 15 apr. 1979, Prooemium, II.

640 §2: IOANNES PAULUS II, const. ap. *Sapientia christiana,* 15 apr. 1979, artt. 86–87.

641: Vat. II, decl. *Gravissimum educationis,* 10 "Altioris;" IOANNES PAULUS II, const. ap. *Sapientia christiana,* 15 apr. 1979, Prooemium, II "Quare."

who are ready to fill the more responsible positions in society and to bear witness to their faith in the world.

CAN. 642 §1. A Catholic university is an institute of higher studies that is erected as such or is approved either by the higher administrative authority of a Church *sui iuris* after previous consultation with the Apostolic See, or by the Apostolic See itself; such erection or approval must be established by means of a public document.

§2. Within the territorial boundaries of the patriarchal Church this higher authority is the patriarch with the consent of the synod of bishops of the patriarchal Church.

CAN. 643 In Catholic universities in which there is no faculty of theology, at least courses in theology are to be given adapted to the students of the various faculties.

CAN. 644 Those who teach subjects regarding faith and morals in Catholic universities must possess a mandate of the ecclesiastical authority designated by those mentioned in can. 642; the same authority can withdraw this mandate for a grave cause, especially if the teachers lack scientific or pedagogical suitability, experience, or integrity of doctrine.

CAN. 645 It is the responsibility of hierarchs, after due consultation, to provide Catholic residences and university centers for other universities, where carefully chosen and prepared Christian faithful can offer spiritual and intellectual help to young university students on a permanent basis.

na vere praestantes ad graviora officia in societate obeunda parati atque fidei in mundo testes.

CAN. 642 §1. Catholica studiorum universitas est institutum studiorum superiorum, quod ut talis erectum aut approbatum est sive a superiore auctoritate administrativa Ecclesiae sui iuris praevie consulta Sede Apostolica sive ab ipsa Sede Apostolica; de quo constare debet publico documento.

§2. Intra fines territorii Ecclesiae patriarchalis haec superior auctoritas est Patriarcha de consensu Synodi Episcoporum Ecclesiae patriarchalis.

CAN. 643 In catholicis studiorum universitatibus, in quibus nulla facultas theologiae exstat, saltem cursus theologici studentibus variarum facultatum accommodati tradantur.

CAN. 644 Qui disciplinas ad fidem et mores spectantes docent in catholicis studiorum universitatibus, muniti esse debent mandato auctoritatis ecclesiasticae designatae ab eis, de quibus in can. 642; eadem auctoritas hoc mandatum gravi de causa auferre potest praesertim si deficiunt idoneitas scientifica vel paedagogica, probitas vel doctrinae integritas.

CAN. 645 Hierarcharum est collatis consiliis providere, ut etiam apud alias universitates convictus et centra universitaria catholica habeantur, in quibus christifideles accurate selecti et praeparati iuventuti universitariae spirituale et intellectuale adiutorium permanens praebeant.

642 §1: Vat. II, decr. *Apostolicam actuositatem,* 24 "Plurima."

643: Vat. II, decl. *Gravissimum educationis,* 10 "In universitatibus."

644: Ioannes Paulus II, const. ap. *Sapientia christiana,* 15 apr. 1979, art. 27.

645: Vat. II, decl. *Gravissimum educationis,* 10 "Quandoquidem."

ART. III. *Ecclesiastical Universities and Faculties*

ART. III. *De Ecclesiasticis Studiorum Universitatibus et Facultatibus*

CAN. 646 Hierarchs above all are constantly to promote ecclesiastical universities and faculties, that is, those which deal especially with Christian revelation and the sciences connected with it and so are closely linked with the Church's function of evangelization.

CAN. 646 Assidue provehendae sunt imprimis ab Hierarchis ecclesiasticae studiorum universitates et facultates, eae nempe, quae de divina Revelatione et de scientiis cum ea conexis praesertim agunt ac propterea cum evangelizandi munere Ecclesiae artius coniunguntur.

CAN. 647 The goal of ecclesiastical universities and faculties is:

1° to inquire more deeply and scientifically into divine revelation and related matters, to analyze and to structure systematically the truths of divine revelation, to study contemporary problems in its light, and to present these matters to the people of today in a way that is suited to their culture.

2° to give higher education to students of various disciplines according to Catholic doctrine and to prepare them properly for various apostolates or ministries or for teaching the same disciplines, and to promote ongoing formation.

CAN. 647 Ecclesiasticae studiorum universitatis vel facultatis finis est:

1° divinam Revelationem et ea, quae cum eadem coniuncta sunt, profundius et scientifice investigare, divinae Revelationis veritates systematice enucleare ac ordinare, novas progredientis aetatis quaestiones in eius luce considerare et coaevis hominibus ratione propriae culturae accommodata exhibere;

2° studentes in variis disciplinis secundum doctrinam catholicam altius instituere eosque ad diversa opera apostolatus, ministerii vel magisterii in eisdem disciplinis congrue praeparare atque formationem continuam promovere.

CAN. 648 Ecclesiastical universities and faculties are those, having been canonically erected or approved by the competent ecclesiastical authority, that cultivate and teach the sacred sciences and related subjects and have the right to confer academic degrees with canonical effects.

CAN. 648 Ecclesiasticae studiorum universitates et facultates sunt, quae ab auctoritate competenti ecclesiastica canonice erectae vel approbatae scientias sacras et scientias cum eisdem conexas excolunt et tradunt et auctae sunt iure conferendi gradus academicos, qui effectus canonicos habent.

CAN. 649 The erection or approval of ecclesiastical universities or faculties is done either by the Apostolic See or by the higher adminis-

CAN. 649 Erectio vel approbatio ecclesiasticarum studiorum universitatum vel facultatum fit a Sede Apostolica aut a superi-

646: IOANNES PAULUS II, const. ap. *Sapientia christiana,* 15 apr. 1979, Prooemium, III; art. 4.

647: IOANNES PAULUS II, const. ap. *Sapientia christiana,* 15 apr. 1979, art. 3, §§1–2.

648: IOANNES PAULUS II, const. ap. *Sapientia*

christiana, 15 apr. 1979, artt. 2, 6, 9, §1; S.C. pro Inst. Cath., *Ordinationes,* 29 apr. 1979, art. 1.

649: IOANNES PAULUS II, const. ap. *Sapientia christiana,* 15 apr. 1979, art. 5.

trative authority referred to in can. 642 together with the Apostolic See.

CAN. 650 Regarding the statutes of the ecclesiastical universities and faculties, especially with regard to the governance, administration, the appointment of teachers and their leaving office, program of studies, and conferral of academic degrees, the norms given by the Apostolic See are to be followed.

CHAPTER IV. Instruments of Social Communication and Specifically Books

CAN. 651 §1. In order to fulfill its function of announcing the gospel throughout the world, the Church is bound to make use of appropriate means. Therefore, it is necessary to vindicate everywhere the right to the use of the means of social communication and specifically to the freedom of the press.

§2. All the Christian faithful for their part are to collaborate in this great mission of the Church, and support and foster the initiatives of this apostolate. Moreover, those especially who are experts in the production and the transmission of communications should solicitously offer their help to the pastoral activity of the bishops and earnestly endeavor that the use of the media be imbued with the spirit of Christ.

CAN. 652 §1. Eparchial bishops are to see that, particularly with the help of institutes of social communication, the Christian faithful are taught to use the media critically and advantageously; they are to foster cooperation among such institutes; they are to provide for the training of experts; and finally, they are to promote

ore auctoritate administrativa, de qua in can. 642, una cum Sede Apostolica.

CAN. 650 Circa statuta ecclesiasticae studiorum universitatis vel facultatis, praesertim quod attinet ad regimen, administrationem, docentium nominationem vel cessationem ab officio, rationem studiorum et graduum academicorum collationem, servandae sunt normae a Sede Apostolica latae.

CAPUT IV. **De Instrumentis Communicationis Socialis et in Specie de Libris**

CAN. 651 §1. Ad Evangelium ubique terrarum annuntiandi munus obeundum Ecclesia aptis mediis uti tenetur et ideo ius instrumenta communicationis socialis adhibendi et in specie scripta libere typis edendi ei ubique vindicetur oportet.

§2. Omnes christifideles pro sua parte in tanta missione Ecclesiae collaborent inceptaque huius apostolatus sustineant ac foveant; insuper ii praesertim, qui in communicationibus efficiendis et transmittendis periti sunt, actioni pastorali Episcoporum adiutricem operam sollicite praestent atque omni studio satagant, ut eorundem instrumentorum usus spiritu Christi imbuatur.

CAN. 652 §1. Episcopi eparchiales curent, ut auxilio praesertim institutorum de instrumentis communicationis socialis christifideles edoceantur de critico et proficuo usu eorundem instrumentorum; inter varia haec instituta cooperationem foveant; peritorum formationi provideant; denique, quod magis

---

650: IOANNES PAULUS II, const. ap. *Sapientia christiana,* 15 apr. 1979, art. 7; S.C. pro Inst. Cath., *Ordinationes,* 29 apr. 1979.

651 §1: Vat. II, decr. *Inter mirifica,* 3.
651 §2: Vat. II, decr. *Inter mirifica,* 13, 16–17.
652 §1: Vat. II, decr. *Inter mirifica,* 3, 15.

good initiatives, in the first place by praising and blessing good books, a policy that can be more effective than the censure and condemnation of evil.

§2. To safeguard the integrity of faith and morals, the eparchial bishop, the synod of bishops of the patriarchal Church, the council of hierarchs, and the Apostolic See are competent to forbid the Christian faithful to use or to pass on to others instruments of social communication, to the extent that these are detrimental to that same integrity.

CAN. 653 It is for the particular law to establish more detailed norms about the use of radio, cinema, television and the like dealing with Catholic doctrine or morals.

CAN. 654 The norms of common law on books apply also to any other writings or messages whatever reproduced by any technical means and intended for public distribution.

CAN. 655 §1. It is necessary for the Christian faithful to have full access to the Sacred Scripture. Therefore, under the care of the eparchial bishops, suitable and correct translations, furnished with sufficient explanations, are to be prepared where they are lacking, even in collaboration with other Christians, insofar as this can be done properly and usefully.

§2. All the Christian faithful, especially the pastors of souls, should be concerned to spread copies of the Sacred Scripture, furnished with suitable notes, appropriate for the use of non-Christians as well.

§3. For liturgical and catechetical purposes,

quam mala castigando et condemnando effici potest, incepta bona promoveant laudando et benedicendo imprimis bonos libros.

§2. Ad integritatem fidei et morum tuendam Episcopo eparchiali, Synodo Episcoporum Ecclesiae patriarchalis, Consilio Hierarcharum atque Sedi Apostolicae competit prohibere, ne christifideles instrumentis communicationis socialis, quatenus eidem integritati detrimento sunt, utantur vel ea cum aliis communicent.

CAN. 653 Iuris particularis est normas pressius statuere de usu radiophonico, cinematographico, televisifico et eiusmodi in tractandis eis, quae ad doctrinam catholicam aut mores referunt.

CAN. 654 Normae iuris communis de libris valent etiam de quibuslibet aliis scriptis aut sermonibus per inventa technica quomodolibet reproductis et divulgationi publicae destinatis.

CAN. 655 §1. Christifidelibus aditus ad Sacram Scripturam late pateat oportet; proinde aptae et rectae versiones sufficientibus explicationibus instructae, ubi desunt, conficiantur cura Episcoporum eparchialium, immo, quatenus id convenienter et utiliter fieri potest, communi cum aliis christianis opera.

§2. Omnibus christifidelibus, praesertim pastoribus animarum curae sit diffundere exemplaria Sacrae Scripturae aptis instructa adnotationibus ad usum etiam non-christianorum accommodatis.

§3. Ad usum liturgicum vel catecheticum

---

652 §2: S.C. pro. Doctr. Fidei, decr. 19 mar. 1975, "Ut vero;" notificatio, 14 iun. 1966; decr. 15 nov. 1966; Vat. II, decr. *Inter mirifica,* 3.

654: S.C. pro Doctr. Fidei, decr. 19 mar. 1975, art. 1, 2.

655 §1: Vat. II, const. *Dei Verbum,* 22; S.C. pro Doctr. Fidei, decr. 19 mar. 1975, art. 2, 2.

655 §2: Vat. II, const. *Dei Verbum,* 25 "Insuper."

655 §3: S.C. pro Doctr. Fidei, decr. *Ecclesiae Pastorum,* 19 mar. 1975, art. 2, 1.

only those editions of the Sacred Scripture that have received ecclesiastical approval are to be used; other editions must have at least ecclesiastical permission.

CAN. 656 §1. In liturgical celebrations, only books that have received ecclesiastical approval are to be used.

§2. Books of prayers or devotions, intended for the public or private use of the Christian faithful, require ecclesiastical permission.

CAN. 657 §1. The approval of liturgical texts, after prior review of the Apostolic See, is reserved in patriarchal Churches to the patriarch with the consent of the synod of bishops of the patriarchal Church, in metropolitan Churches *sui iuris* to the metropolitan with the consent of the council of hierarchs; in other Churches this right rests exclusively with the Apostolic See, and, within the limits set by it, to bishops and to their legitimately constituted assemblies.

§2. The same authorities are also competent to approve the translations of these books intended for liturgical use, after sending a report to the Apostolic See in the case of patriarchal Churches and metropolitan Churches *sui iuris*.

§3. To reprint liturgical books or their translations into another language, or even parts thereof, if intended for liturgical use, it is required and sufficient to establish their correspondence with an approved edition by the attestation of the local hierarch referred to in can. 662, § 1.

§4. In making changes in liturgical texts, attention is to be paid to can. 40, §1.

CAN. 658 §1. Catechisms and other writ-

eae tantum editiones Sacrae Scripturae adhibeantur, quae approbatione ecclesiastica praeditae sunt; ceterae editiones saltem licentia ecclesiastica munitae esse debent.

CAN. 656 §1. In celebrationibus liturgicis adhibeantur tantum libri approbatione ecclesiastica praediti.

§2. Libri precum vel devotionum ad usum publicum vel privatum christifidelium destinati indigent licentia ecclesiastica.

CAN. 657 §1. Textuum liturgicorum approbatio praevia Sedis Apostolicae recognitione reservatur in Ecclesiis patriarchalibus Patriarchae de consensu Synodi Episcoporum Ecclesiae patriarchalis; in Ecclesiis metropolitanis sui iuris Metropolitae de consensu Consilii Hierarcharum; in ceteris Ecclesiis hoc ius est solius Sedis Apostolicae atque intra limites ab eadem statutos Episcoporum eorumque coetuum legitime constitutorum.

§2. Eisdem auctoritatibus quoque competit ius approbandi versiones eorundem librorum ad usum liturgicum destinatas facta relatione, si de Ecclesiis patriarchalibus vel metropolitanis sui iuris agitur, ad Sedem Apostolicam.

§3. Ad iterum edendos libros liturgicos vel eorum in aliam linguam versiones ad usum liturgicum destinatas vel eorum partes requiritur et sufficit, ut constet de concordantia cum editione approbata ex attestatione Hierarchae loci, de quo in can. 662, §1.

§4. In mutationibus textuum liturgicorum attendatur can. 40, §1.

CAN. 658 §1. Catechismi necnon alia

---

656 §2: S.C. pro Doctr. Fidei, decr. *Ecclesiae Pastorum*, 19 mar. 1975, art. 3, 3.

657 §1: Pius XII, m.p. *Cleri sanctitati*, 2 iun. 1957, can. 279 §2; S.C. pro Doctr. Fidei, decr. 19 mar. 1975,

art. 3, 1; Vat. II, const. *Sacrosanctum Concilium*, 22, 40.

658 §1: S.C. pro Doctr. Fidei, decr. 19 mar. 1975, art. 4, 1.

ings intended for catechetical instruction in schools of whatever kind and grade, and their translations, require ecclesiastical approval.

§2. The same norm is to be applied also to other books dealing with faith and morals, if they are used as textbooks for catechetical instruction.

CAN. 659　It is recommended that any writings whatever that explain the faith or morals of the Church have at least ecclesiastical permission, without prejudice to the prescripts of institutes of consecrated life, which require more.

CAN. 660　Unless there is a just and reasonable cause, the Christian faithful may not write anything in newspapers, magazines or periodicals that are wont to attack openly the Catholic religion or good morals; clerics and members of religious institutes, moreover, need the permission of those referred to in can. 662.

CAN. 661　§1. Ecclesiastical permission, expressed only with the word *imprimatur,* means that the work is free from errors regarding Catholic faith and morals.

§2. Approval granted by competent authority shows that the text is accepted by the Church or that the work is in accord with the authentic doctrine of the Church.

§3. If a work in addition is praised or blessed by the eparchial bishop or a higher authority, this means that it expresses well the authentic doctrine of the Church and therefore is to be recommended.

CAN. 662　§1. Ecclesiastical approval or permission to publish books can be granted, unless expressly stated otherwise in the law, either by the local hierarch of the author or of the

scripta ad institutionem catecheticam in scholis cuiusque generis et gradus destinata eorumve versiones approbatione ecclesiastica egent.

§2. Eadem norma applicanda est ad alios quoque libros de fide aut moribus tractantes, si adhibentur ut textus, quo institutio catechetica nitatur.

CAN. 659　Commendatur, ut scripta quaelibet, quae fidem catholicam aut mores illustrant, saltem licentia ecclesiastica munita sint, salvis praescriptis institutorum vitae consecratae, quae plus exigunt.

CAN. 660　In diariis, foliis aut libellis periodicis, qui religionem catholicam aut bonos mores manifesto impetere solent, ne quid scribant christifideles nisi iusta et rationabili de causa; clerici autem et sodales institutorum religiosorum insuper nonnisi de licentia eorum, de quibus in can. 662.

CAN. 661　§1. Licentia ecclesiastica cum solo verbo imprimatur expressa significat opus ab erroribus circa fidem catholicam et mores esse immune.

§2. Approbatio vero ab auctoritate competenti concessa ostendit textum ab Ecclesia acceptum aut opus doctrinae authenticae Ecclesiae consonum esse.

§3. Si opus insuper ab Episcopo eparchiali vel ab auctoritate superiore laudatum vel benedictum est, hoc significat illud doctrinam authenticam Ecclesiae bene exprimere ideoque commendandum esse.

CAN. 662　§1. Approbatio vel licentia ecclesiastica ad libros edendos, nisi aliud iure expresse statuitur, concedi potest sive ab Hierarcha loci proprio auctoris sive ab Hi-

658 §2: S.C. pro Doctr. Fidei, decr. 19 mar. 1975, art. 4, 2.

659: S.C. pro Doctr. Fidei, decr. 19 mar. 1975, art. 4, 3 et art. 5, 1; resp. 25 iun. 1980, II.

660: S.C. pro Doctr. Fidei, decr. 19 mar. 1975, art. 5, 2.

662 §1: S.C. pro Doctr. Fidei, decr. 19 mar. 1975, art. 1, 1.

place of publication, or finally by a higher authority having executive power of governance over these persons or places.

§2. Members of religious institutes, in order to publish writings dealing with religious and moral topics, also need the permission of their major superior in accord with the norm of the typicon or statutes.

CAN. 663 §1. Permission to publish a work or its approval, praise, or blessing applies only to the original text, but not to new editions or translations.

§2. In case of editions of the Sacred Scripture or other books requiring ecclesiastical approval in accord with the norm of law, approval legitimately granted by one hierarch is not enough for its use in another eparchy, but the explicit consent of the hierarch of that eparchy is required.

CAN. 664 §1. The local hierarch can entrust the judgment of books to censors selected from the list drawn up by the synod of bishops of the patriarchal Church or the council of hierarchs, or to others, according to his prudence; furthermore, a special commission of censors may be set up for the local hierarch, the synod of bishops of the patriarchal Church, or the council of hierarchs to consult.

§2. The censors selected are to be outstanding for their learning, right doctrine and prudence; in carrying out their office they are to give their judgment without any partiality but

erarcha loci, ubi publici iuris fiunt, sive denique ab auctoritate superiore, quae in personas vel locos potestatem regiminis exsecutivam exercet.

§2. Sodales institutorum religiosorum, ut scripta quaestiones de fide catholica aut moribus tractantia edere possint, licentia quoque egent sui Superioris maioris ad normam typici vel statutorum.

CAN. 663 §1. Licentia aliquod opus edendi aut alicuius operis approbatio, laudatio vel benedictio valet pro textu originali, non autem pro novis editionibus vel versionibus.

§2. Si agitur de editionibus Sacrae Scripturae vel aliis libris, qui approbatione ecclesiastica ad normam iuris indigent, approbatio ab uno Hierarcha loci legitime concessa non sufficit, ut iidem in alia eparchia adhiberi possint, sed requiritur explicitus consensus Hierarchae loci eiusdem eparchiae.

CAN. 664 §1. Iudicium de libris committi potest ab Hierarcha loci censoribus ex elencho a Synodo Episcoporum Ecclesiae patriarchalis vel Consilio Hierarcharum confecto aut pro eius prudentia aliis personis, quibus confidit; denique constitui potest commissio specialis censorum, quam Hierarcha loci, Synodus Episcoporum Ecclesiae patriarchalis vel Consilium Hierarcharum consulere possunt.

§2. Censores eligantur scientia, recta doctrina et prudentia praestantes et in suo obeundo officio omni personarum acceptione seposita iudicium ferant secundum

---

662 §2: Leo XIII, const. *Officiorum ac munerum,* 25 ian. 1897, 36; Pius X, m.p. *Sacrorum Antistitum,* 1 sep. 1910, IV in fine.

663 §1: Leo XIII, const. *Officiorum ac munerum,* 25 ian. 1897, 44.

664 §1: S.C. pro Doctr. Fidei, decr. 19 mar. 1975, art. 6, 1. - Leo XIII, const. *Officiorum ac munerum,* 25

ian. 1897, 38; Pius X, m.p. *Sacrorum Antistitum,* 1 sep. 1910, IV.

664 §2: S.C. pro Doctr. Fidei, decr. 19 mar. 1975, art. 6, 2. - Leo XIII, const. *Officiorum ac munerum,* 25 ian. 1897, 39; Pius X, m.p. *Sacrorum Antistitum,* 1 sep. 1910, IV.

in accordance with Catholic doctrine as proposed by the Church's authentic magisterium.

§3. The censors must give their opinion in writing; if it is favorable, the hierarch may grant permission or approval, according to his discretion, expressly in his own name; otherwise he must inform the author of the reasons for the refusal.

CAN. 665 §1. Pastors and rectors of churches are to be careful that in their Churches icons or images that are not in keeping with genuine sacred art, or books that are not in harmony with the Christian religion or morals, are not displayed, sold or distributed.

§2. Likewise, pastors and rectors of churches and directors of Catholic schools have to take care that shows of whatever type conducted under their sponsorship are selected with a sense of Christian discretion.

§3. All the Christian faithful should be careful not to bring spiritual harm upon themselves or others by buying, selling, reading, or passing on to others those things mentioned in §1.

CAN. 666 §1. The intellectual work of an author is under the protection of the law, whether as the expression of the author's personality or as the source of patrimonial rights.

§2. The texts of laws and the official acts of whatever ecclesiastical authority and their authentic collections are under the protection of law; therefore they may not be republished without obtaining the permission of the same or a higher authority, and observing the conditions laid down by it.

§3. More detailed norms about this matter may be issued in the particular law of each Church *sui iuris*, in accordance with the civil laws concerning the rights of authors.

doctrinam catholicam, sicut a magisterio authentico Ecclesiae proponitur.

§3. Censores opinionem scripto dare debent; quae si favet, Hierarcha pro suo prudenti iudicio licentiam aut approbationem concedat expresso suo nomine; secus rationes denegationis cum operis auctore communicet.

CAN. 665 §1. Caveant parochi et rectores ecclesiarum, ne in suis ecclesiis icones vel imagines ab arte sacra germana alienae aut libri religioni christianae vel moribus minus consonantes exponantur, vendantur aut distribuantur.

§2. Item parochorum et rectorum ecclesiarum necnon moderatorum scholarum catholicarum est curare, ut spectacula cuiusvis speciei sub eorum patrocinio volvenda sensu discretionis christianae seligantur.

§3. Caveant christifideles omnes, ne ea, de quibus in §1, emendo, vendendo, legendo vel cum aliis communicando sibi aliisve damnum spirituale inferant.

CAN. 666 §1. Opus intellectuale auctoris sub tutela iuris est sive, quatenus manifestat personalitatem illius, sive, quatenus fons est iurium patrimonialium.

§2. Sub tutela iuris sunt textus legum et actorum officialium cuiuscumque auctoritatis ecclesiasticae atque eorum collectiones authenticae; ideoque ea iterum edere non licet nisi impetrata eiusdem vel auctoritatis superioris licentia et servatis condicionibus ab eadem praescriptis.

§3. Iure particulari uniuscuiusque Ecclesiae sui iuris normae magis determinatae de hac re ferantur servatis praescriptis iuris civilis circa iura auctoris.

664 §3: S.C. pro Doctr. Fidei, decr. 19 mar. 1975, art. 6, 3. - Pius X, m.p. *Sacrorum Antistitum*, 1 sep. 1910, IV.

665 §1: S.C. pro Doctr. Fidei, decr. 19 mar. 1975, art. 4, 4.

TITLE XVI. DIVINE WORSHIP AND ESPECIALLY THE SACRAMENTS

TITULUS XVI. DE CULTU DIVINO ET PRAESERTIM DE SACRAMENTIS

CAN. 667 Through the sacraments, which the Church is bound to dispense in order to communicate the mysteries of Christ under visible signs, our Lord Jesus Christ sanctifies people by the power of the Holy Spirit, so that they may become in a unique way true worshipers of God the Father and be inserted into Christ and the Church, His Body; therefore, all the Christian faithful, but especially the sacred ministers, are to observe diligently the prescripts of the Church in the conscientious celebration and reception of the sacraments.

CAN. 668 §1. Divine worship, if carried out in the name of the Church by persons legitimately appointed for this and through acts approved by the ecclesiastical authority, is called public; otherwise, it is called private.

§2. For the regulation of divine public worship the competent authority is the one mentioned in can. 657, with due regard for can. 199, §1; no other person can add to, remove, or modify that which was established by this authority.

CAN. 669 Since the sacraments are the same for the entire Church and belong to the

CAN. 667 Per sacramenta, quae Ecclesia dispensare tenetur, ut sub signo visibili mysteria Christi communicet, Dominus noster Iesus Christus homines in virtute Spiritus Sancti sanctificat, ut singulari modo Dei Patris veri adoratores fiant, eosque sibi ipsi et Ecclesiae, suo Corpori, inserit; quare christifideles omnes, praesertim vero ministri sacri, eisdem sacramentis religiose celebrandis et suscipiendis praescripta Ecclesiae diligenter servent.

CAN. 668 §1. Cultus divinus, si defertur nomine Ecclesiae a personis legitime ad hoc deputatis et per actus ab auctoritate ecclesiastica approbatos, dicitur publicus; secus privatus.

§2. Ad cultus divini publici ordinationem auctoritas competens ea est, de qua in can. 657, firmo can. 199, §1; nemo alius quidquam ab hac auctoritate statutis addat, ab eis demat aut eadem mutet.

CAN. 669 Cum sacramenta eadem sint pro universa Ecclesia et ad divinum deposi-

---

667: Eugenius IV (in Flor.), const. *Exsultate Deo*, 22 nov. 1439, §9; Trid., sess. VII, *Canones de sacramentis in genere;* Iohannes XXII, ep. *Salvator noster*, 29 apr. 1319, "Tenet;" Benedictus XII, a. 1341, prop. 42, Armenorum, damn.; Pius IV, const. *Iniunctum nobis*, 13 nov. 1564, Professio fidei Trident.; Gregorius XIII, const. *Sanctissimus*, a. 1575, Professio fidei Graecis praescr., §9; Benedictus XIV, ep. *Nuper ad*

Nos, 16 mar. 1743, Professio fidei Maronitis praescr., §5; Pius XII, litt. encycl. *Mediator Dei*, 20 nov. 1947, I "Ecclesia" et "Utique;" Vat. II, const. *Sacrosanctum Concilium*, 6–7, 14, 26–28, 59; const. *Lumen gentium*, 7 "In corpore;" Synodus Episcoporum, *Ultimis temporibus*, 30 nov. 1971, Pars Altera, I, d).

668 §2: Vat. II, const. *Sacrosanctum Concilium*, 22 §3.

divine deposit, it is for the supreme authority of the Church alone to approve or define those things required for their validity.

CAN. 670 §1. Catholic Christian faithful can for a just reason attend the liturgical worship of other Christians and take part in the same, observing those things established by the eparchial bishop or by a higher authority by reason of the degree of communion with the Catholic Church.

§2. If non-Catholic Christians lack a place in which divine worship can be celebrated with dignity, the eparchial bishop can grant the use of a Catholic building or cemetery or church in accord with the norm of particular law of his own Church *sui iuris.*

CAN. 671 §1. Catholic ministers licitly administer the sacraments only to the Catholic Christian faithful, who, likewise, licitly receive the sacraments only from Catholic ministers.

§2. If, however, necessity requires it or genuine spiritual advantage suggests it and provided that the danger of error or indifferentism is avoided, it is licit for the Catholic Christian faithful, for whom it is physically or morally impossible to approach a Catholic minister, to receive the sacraments of penance, the Eucharist and anointing of the sick from non-Catholic ministers, in whose churches these sacraments are valid.

§3. Likewise Catholic ministers licitly administer the sacraments of penance, the Eucharist and anointing of the sick to Christian faithful of Eastern Churches who do not have full communion with the Catholic Church if

tum pertineant, solius supremae Ecclesiae auctoritatis est approbare vel definire, quae ad eorum validitatem sunt requisita.

CAN. 670 §1. Christifideles catholici iusta de causa adesse possunt cultui divino aliorum christianorum et in eo partem habere servatis eis, quae habita ratione gradus communionis cum Ecclesia catholica ab Episcopo eparchiali aut ab auctoritate superiore statuta sunt.

§2. Si christianis acatholicis desunt loca, in quibus cultum divinum digne celebrent, Episcopus eparchialis usum aedificii catholici vel coemeterii vel ecclesiae concedere potest ad normam iuris particularis propriae Ecclesiae sui iuris.

CAN. 671 §1. Ministri catholici sacramenta licite solis christifidelibus catholicis ministrant, qui pariter eadem a solis ministris catholicis licite suscipiunt.

§2. Si vero necessitas id postulat aut vera spiritualis utilitas id suadet et dummodo periculum vitetur erroris vel indifferentismi, licet christifidelibus catholicis, quibus physice aut moraliter impossibile est accedere ad ministrum catholicum, sacramenta paenitentiae, Eucharistiae et unctionis infirmorum suscipere a ministris acatholicis, in quorum Ecclesiis valida exsistunt praedicta sacramenta.

§3. Item ministri catholici licite sacramenta paenitentiae, Eucharistiae et unctionis infirmorum ministrant christifidelibus Ecclesiarum orientalium, quae plenam communionem cum Ecclesia catholica non habent,

670 §1: Vat. II, decr. *Orientalium Ecclesiarum,* 26, 28; decr. *Unitatis redintegratio,* 8; Secret. ad Christ. Unit. Fov., *Directorium* I, 14 maii 1967, 50–51, 59.

670 §2: Secret. ad Christ. Unit. Fov., *Directorium* I, 14 maii 1967, 52, 61.

671 §1: Vat. II, decr. *Orientalium Ecclesiarum,* 26; decr. *Unitatis redintegratio,* 8.

671 §2: Vat. II, decr. *Orientalium Ecclesiarum,* 27;

Secret. ad Christ. Unit. Fov., *Directorium* I, 14 maii 1967, 42–44; *Déclaration,* 7 ian. 1970, 3, 6 "Le catholique."

671 §3: Vat. II, decr. *Orientalium Ecclesiarum,* 27; decr. *Unitatis redintegratio,* 15 "Cum;" Secret. ad Christ. Unit. Fov., *Directorium* I, 14 maii 1967, 39, 46; *Déclaration,* 7 ian. 1970, 3, 6; instr. 1 iun. 1972, 5; *Communicatio,* 17 oct. 1973, 8.

they ask for them on their own and are properly disposed. This holds also for the Christian faithful of other Churches, who according to the judgment of the Apostolic See, are in the same condition as the Eastern Churches as far as the sacraments are concerned.

§4. If there is a danger of death or another matter of serious necessity in the judgment of the eparchial bishop, the synod of bishops of the patriarchal Church or the council of hierarchs, Catholic ministers licitly administer the same sacraments also to other Christians not having full communion with the Catholic Church, who cannot approach the ministers of their own ecclesial communities and who request them on their own, provided they manifest a faith consonant with that of the Catholic Church concerning these sacraments and are rightly disposed.

§5. For the cases in §§2, 3 and 4, norms of particular law are to be enacted only after consultation with at least the local competent authority of the non-Catholic Church or ecclesial community concerned.

CAN. 672 §1. The sacraments of baptism, chrismation with holy myron and sacred ordination cannot be repeated.

§2. If a prudent doubt exists as to whether they have been truly or validly celebrated, and

si sua sponte id petunt et rite sunt dispositi; quod etiam valet circa christifideles aliarum Ecclesiarum, quae iudicio Sedis Apostolicae, ad sacramenta quod attinet, in pari condicione ac praedictae Ecclesiae orientales versantur.

§4. Si vero adest periculum mortis aut de iudicio Episcopi eparchialis aut Synodi Episcoporum Ecclesiae patriarchalis vel Consilii Hierarcharum alia urget gravis necessitas, ministri catholici licite eadem sacramenta ministrant ceteris quoque christianis plenam communionem cum Ecclesia catholica non habentibus, qui ad ministrum propriae Communitatis ecclesialis accedere non possunt atque sua sponte id petunt, dummodo circa eadem sacramenta fidem manifestent fidei Ecclesiae catholicae consentaneam et rite sint dispositi.

§5. Pro casibus, de quibus in §§2, 3 et 4, normae iuris particularis ne ferantur nisi post consultationem cum auctoritate competenti saltem locali Ecclesiae vel Communitatis ecclesialis acatholicae, cuius interest.

CAN. 672 §1. Sacramenta baptismi, chrismationis sancti myri et sacrae ordinationis iterari non possunt.

§2. Si vero prudens dubium exsistit, num re vera aut num valide celebrata sint, dubio

---

671 §4: Secret. ad Christ. Unit. Fov., *Directorium* I, 14 maii 1967, 55; instr. 1 iun. 1972, 6; *Communicatio,* 17 oct. 1973, 6.

671 §5: Secret. ad Christ. Unit. Fov., *Directorium* I, 14 maii 1967, 42; *Déclaration,* 7 ian. 1970, 5; *Communicatio,* 17 oct. 1973, 8, b).

672 §1: EUGENIUS IV (in Flor.), const. *Exsultate Deo,* 22 nov. 1439, §9; Trid., sess. VII, *Canones de sacramentis in genere.* can. 9; *De baptismo,* cann. 11, 13; sess. XXIII, *De ordine,* cap. 4, can. 4; Apost. cann. 47, 68; Carth. can. 48; Quinisext. can. 95; S. BASILIUS M., cann. 1, 47; TIMOTHEUS ALEXANDRIN., can. 19; S. Stephanus, litt. a. 258; S. NICOLAUS I, litt. *Ad consulta vestra,* 13 nov. 866, XV; Professio fidei (in Lugd. II) a Michaele Palaeologo Gregorio X oblata, a. 1274; IOHANNES XXII, ep. *Salvator noster,* 29 apr. 1319 "Sed;"

PIUS IV, const. *Iniunctum nobis,* 13 nov. 1564, Professio fidei Trident., §1; GREGORIUS XIII, const. *Sanctissimus,* a. 1575, Professio fidei Graecis praescr., §9; BENEDICTUS XIV, ep. *Nuper ad Nos,* 16 mar. 1743, Professio fidei Maronitis praescr., §5; ep. encycl. *Ex quo,* 1 mar. 1756, §55. * Syn. Zamosten. Ruthenorum, a. 1720, tit. III, §2 "Sacramentum."

672 §2: Quinisext. can. 84; S. BASILIUS M., cann. 1, 47; TIMOTHEUS ALEXANDRIN., can. 19; Clemens VIII, instr. *Sanctissimus,* 31 aug. 1595, §§1, 4 "Si Episcopus;" BENEDICTUS XIV, const. *Etsi pastoralis,* 26 maii 1742, §III, II–III; ep. encycl. *Demandatam,* 24 dec. 1743, §14; S.C.S. Off., (Jerosolym.), 14 ian. 1885; S.C. de Prop. Fide, instr. 31 iul. 1902, 3; Secret. ad Christ. Unit. Fov., *Directorium* I, 14 maii 1967, 15. * Syn. Ain-Trazen. Graeco-Melchitarum, a. 1835, can. 2.

the doubt remains after a serious investigation, they are to be administered conditionally.

CAN. 673　The celebration of the sacraments, above all the Divine Liturgy, as an action of the Church, inasmuch as it is possible, should be done with active participation of the Christian faithful.

CAN. 674　§1. In celebrating the sacraments, that which is contained in the liturgical books is to be observed accurately.

§2. The minister should celebrate the sacraments according to the liturgical prescripts of his own Church *sui iuris,* unless the law establishes otherwise or he himself has obtained a special faculty from the Apostolic See.

CHAPTER I. Baptism

CAN. 675　§1. In baptism a person through washing with natural water with the invocation

quidem post seriam investigationem permanente sub condicione ministrentur.

CAN. 673　Celebratio sacramentorum, imprimis Divinae Liturgiae, utpote actio Ecclesiae, quatenus fieri potest, cum actuosa participatione christifidelium fiat.

CAN. 674　§1. In sacramentis celebrandis accurate serventur ea, quae in libris liturgicis continentur.

§2. Minister sacramenta celebret secundum praescripta liturgica propriae Ecclesiae sui iuris, nisi aliud iure statuitur vel ipse specialem facultatem a Sede Apostolica obtinuit.

CAPUT I. De Baptismo

CAN. 675　§1. In baptismo homo per lavacrum aquae naturalis cum invocatione

---

673: Vat. II, const. *Sacrosanctum Concilium,* 14, 26–27, 48.

674 §1: Trid., sess. VII, *Canones de sacramentis in genere,* can. 13; Pius IV, const. *Iniunctum Nobis,* 13 nov. 1564, Professio fidei Trident., §1; Pius V, const. *Providentia,* 20 aug. 1566, §1; Gregorius XIII, const. *Sanctissimus,* a. 1575, Professio fidei Graecis praescr., §10; Benedictus XIV, const. *Etsi pastoralis,* 26 maii 1742, §IX, I; ep. encycl. *Demandatam,* 24 dec. 1743, §11; ep. encycl. *Allatae sunt,* 26 iul. 1755, §34; S.C. de Prop. Fide, litt. 4 iul. 1833; (C.G.), 30 apr. 1866, ad 2; Pius X, const. *Tradita ab antiquis,* 14 sep. 1912, I. * Syn. Zamosten. Ruthenorum, a. 1720, tit. III, introd. "Laudabilis;" Syn. Libanen. Maronitarum, a. 1736, pars II, cap. I, 2; cap. XIII, 7; pars IV, cap. V, 1; Syn. Ain-Trazen. Graeco-Melchitarum, a. 1835, cann. 2, 8; Syn. prov. Alba-Iulien. et Fagarasien. Rumenorum, a. 1872, tit. V, cap. I "Quapropter;" Syn. Sciarfen. Syrorum, a. 1888, cap. III, art. IX, 1–2; cap. V, art. I, 7; art. III, 3, VI; Syn. Leopolien. Ruthenorum, a. 1891, tit. IV, cap. I, 10; Syn. Alexandrin. Coptorum, a. 1898, sect. II, cap. III, art. I, 12, I; art. II, 7, VIII; art. IV, secunda pars, I, III; Syn. Armen., a. 1911, 441, 613, 619.

674 §2: Pius XII, m.p. *Cleri sanctitati,* 2 iun. 1957, can. 2 §1. - S.C.S. Off., 14 iun. 1843; decr. 6 sep. 1865; S.C. de Prop. Fide, reg. (pro Sacerd. Coptis), 15 mar. 1790, VIII; (C.G.), 11 dec. 1838, ad 17–19; decr. 6 oct.

1863, C), a); (C.G.), 30 apr. 1966, ad 3. * Syn. Sciarfen. Syrorum, a. 1888, cap. III, art. IX, 6; Syn. Alexandrin. Coptorum, a. 1898, sect. II, cap. I, art. V, XI et XIII; Syn. Armen., a. 1911, 620.

675 §1: Eugenius IV (in Flor.), const. *Exsultate Deo,* 22 nov. 1439, §10; (in Flor.), const. *Cantate Domino,* 4 feb. 1441, §13; Trid., sess. V, *De peccato originali,* 3–4; sess. VI, *De iustificatione,* capp. 4, 7; sess. VII, *Canones de sacramentis in genere,* can. 1; *De baptismo,* cann. 2, 5; sess. XIV, *De poenitentia,* cann. 1–2. - Apost. cann. 49–50; Carth. can. 110; Innocentius IV, ep. *Sub catholicae,* 6 mar. 1254, §3, 3; Benedictus XII, a. 1341, prop. 58, Armenorum, damn.; S.C. de Prop. Fide, (C.P.), 12 maii 1630; (C.P.), 13 feb. 1631; (C.P.), 27 mar. 1631; (C.P.), 4 iul. 1633; S.C.S. Off., 8 sep. 1633; 14 iun. 1741, ab "Inoltre;" Benedictus XIV, const. *Etsi pastoralis,* 26 maii 1742, §II, II, V; ep. *Nuper ad Nos,* 16 mar. 1743, Professio fidei Maronitis praescr., §5; S.C.S. Off., instr. (ad Vic. Ap. Abissiniae), 2 maii 1858; Vat. II, const. *Lumen gentium,* 11 "Indoles," 40; decr. *Ad gentes,* 14 "Deinde." * Syn. Diamper. Syro-Malabarensium a. 1599, LXXII–LXXIII; Syn. Zamosten. Ruthenorum, a. 1720, tit. III, §1 "Persuasum;" Syn. Libanen. Maronitarum, a. 1736, pars II, cap. II, 1–2, 4; Syn. prov. Alba-Iulien. et Fagarasien. Rumenorum, a. 1872, tit. V, cap. II; Syn. Sciarfen. Syrorum, a. 1888, cap. V, art. II, 3,

of the name of God the Father, Son and Holy Spirit, is freed from sin, reborn to new life, puts on Christ and is incorporated in the Church which is His Body.

§2. Only by the actual reception of baptism is a person made capable for the other sacraments.

CAN. 676 In a case of urgent necessity, baptism can be licitly administered by doing only those things that are necessary for validity.

CAN. 677 §1. Baptism is administered ordinarily by a priest; but, without prejudice to particular law, the proper pastor of the person to be baptized, or another priest with the permission of the same pastor or the local hierarch, is competent for its administration. This permission is legitimately presumed for a serious cause.

§2. In case of necessity, however, baptism can be administered by a deacon or, in his absence or if he is impeded, by another cleric, a member of an institute of consecrated life, or by any other member of the Christian faithful; even by the mother or father if another person is not available who knows how to baptize.

CAN. 678 §1. In the territory of another it is not licit for anyone to administer baptism

nominis Dei Patris et Filii et Spiritus Sancti a peccato liberatur, ad vitam novam regeneratur, Christum induit et Ecclesiae, quae eius Corpus est, incorporatur.

§2. Tantummodo baptismo in re suscepto homo fit capax ceterorum sacramentorum.

CAN. 676 In casu necessitatis urgentis ministrari licet baptismum ea tantum ponendo, quae sunt ad validitatem necessaria.

CAN. 677 §1. Baptismus ministratur ordinarie a sacerdote; sed eius ministratio competit salvo iure particulari parocho proprio baptizandi aliive sacerdoti de eiusdem parochi vel Hierarchae loci licentia, quae gravi de causa legitime praesumitur.

§2. In casu autem necessitatis baptismum ministrare licet diacono aut eo absente vel impedito alii clerico, sodali instituti vitae consecratae vel cuilibet alii christifideli; patri vero vel matri, si alius, qui baptizandi modum novit, praesto non est.

CAN. 678 §1. In alieno territorio nemini licet sine debita licentia baptismum minis-

---

XI; Syn. Leopolien. Ruthenorum, a. 1891, tit. II, cap. I, 1, c); Syn. ALEXANDRIN. Coptorum, a. 1898, sect. II, cap. III, art. II, 7, IX; Syn. Armen. a. 1911, 376–377.

676: * Syn. Libanen. Maronitarum, a. 1736, pars II, cap. II, 6; Syn. Ain-Trazen. Graeco-Melchitarum, a. 1835, can. 1, 5; Syn. Sciarfen. Syrorum, a. 1888, cap. V, art. II, 3, XIII; Syn. Leopolien. Ruthenorum, a. 1891, tit. II, cap. I, 2; Syn. Alexandrin. Coptorum, a. 1898, sect. II, cap. III, art. II, 7, XX.

677 §1: EUGENIUS IV (in Flor.), const. *Exsultate Deo*, 22 nov. 1439, §10; Vat. II, const. *Lumen gentium*, 26 "Ita," 28 "Fidelium;" decr. *Presbyterorum ordinis*, 5 "Deus." * Syn. Zamosten. Ruthenorum, a. 1720, tit. III, §1 "Parochi;" Syn. Libanen. Maronitarum, a. 1736, pars II, cap. II, 3; pars III, cap. III, 2, X; Syn.

Sciarfen. Syrorum, a. 1888, cap. V, art. II, 3, V et XII; Syn. Alexandrin. Coptorum, a. 1898, sect. II, cap. III, art. II, 7, XVIII.

677 §2: S. NICEPHORUS CP., cann. 19, 200; S. NICOLAUS I, litt. *Ad consulta vestra*, 13 nov. 866, XV–XVI, CIV; EUGENIUS IV (in Flor.), const. *Exsultate Deo*, 22 nov. 1439, §10; (in Flor.), const. *Cantate Domino*, 4 feb. 1441, §13; BENEDICTUS XIV, ep. *Nuper ad Nos*, 16 mar. 1743, Professio fidei Maronitis praescr., §5; S.C. de Prop. Fide, instr. 31 iul. 1902, 3. * Syn. Libanen. Maronitarum, a. 1736, pars II, cap. II, 3 et 5; Syn. Sciarfen. Syrorum, a. 1888, cap. V, art. II, 3, XIII; Syn. Alexandrin. Coptorum, a. 1898, sect. II, cap. III, art. II, 7, XIX.

without the required permission; this permission cannot be denied by a pastor of a different Church *sui iuris* to a priest of the Church *sui iuris* in which the person to be baptized is to be ascribed.

§2. In places where there are not a few Christian faithful lacking a pastor of the Church *sui iuris* in which they are ascribed, the eparchial bishop should designate a presbyter of that Church, if it is possible, who should administer baptism.

CAN. 679 Any person not yet baptized and only such a person is capable of receiving baptism.

CAN. 680 An aborted fetus, if it is alive and if it can be done, should be baptized.

CAN. 681 §1. For an infant to be licitly baptized it is required that:

1° there is a founded hope that the infant will be educated in the Catholic Church, with due regard for §5;

2° the parents, or at least one of them, or the person who legitimately takes their place, consent.

§2. Abandoned infants and foundlings, unless their baptism is certainly established, are to be baptized.

§3. Those who lack the use of reason from infancy are to be baptized as infants.

§4. Infants whether of Catholic or even of non-Catholic parents who are in such a critical situation that it can be prudently foreseen that they will die before they reach the use of reason, are licitly baptized.

trare; haec vero licentia a parocho diversae Ecclesiae sui iuris denegari non potest sacerdoti Ecclesiae sui iuris, cui baptizandus ascribendus est.

§2. In locis, ubi non pauci degunt christifideles parochum Ecclesiae sui iuris, cui ascripti sunt, non habentes, Episcopus eparchialis presbyterum eiusdem Ecclesiae designet, si fieri potest, qui baptismum ministret.

CAN. 679 Baptismi suscipiendi capax est omnis et solus homo nondum baptizatus.

CAN. 680 Foetus abortivus, si vivit et si id fieri potest, baptizetur.

CAN. 681 §1. Ut infans licite baptizetur, oportet:

1° spes habeatur fundata eum in fide Ecclesiae catholicae educatum iri firma §5;

2° parentes, saltem eorum unus, aut is, qui legitime eorundem locum tenet, consentiant.

§2. Infans expositus et inventus, nisi de eiusdem baptismo certe constat, baptizetur.

§3. Rationis usu ab infantia destituti baptizandi sunt ut infantes.

§4. Infans sive parentum catholicorum sive etiam acatholicorum, qui in eo versatur vitae discrimine, ut prudenter praevideatur moriturus, antequam usum rationis attingit, licite baptizatur.

679: Trid., sess. V, *De peccato originali,* 3–4; sess. VII, *De baptismo,* cann. 12–13. - Carth. can. 110; TIMOTHEUS ALEXANDRIN., can. 4; INNOCENTIUS III, ep. *Eius exemplo,* 18 dec. 1208; BENEDICTUS XIV, ep. *Postremo mense,* 28 feb. 1747, 21; S.C. pro Doctr. Fidei, instr. 20 oct. 1980, 4–10.

681 §1, 1°: S.C. pro Doctr. Fidei, instr. 20 oct. 1980, 14–15, 22.

681 §1, 2°: BENEDICTUS XIV, ep. *Postremo mense,* 28 feb. 1747, 4–6, 14–17, 19–21.

681 §2: Carth. can. 72; Quinisext. can. 84; BENEDICTUS XIV, ep. *Postremo mense,* 28 feb. 1747, 8–11.

681 §4: BENEDICTUS XIV, ep. *Postremo mense,* 28 feb. 1747, 8, 23; S.C. pro Doctr. Fidei, instr. 20 oct. 1980, 15.

§5. Infants of non-Catholic Christians are licitly baptized if their parents or at least one of them or the person who legitimately takes their place request it and if it is physically or morally impossible for them to approach their own minister.

CAN. 682 §1. For a person who is no longer an infant to be baptized, it is required that he or she manifest a desire to receive baptism and be sufficiently instructed in the truths of the faith and be proven in the Christian life; he or she is to be exhorted to have sorrow for personal sins.

§2. A person who is no longer an infant and who is in danger of death can be baptized if he or she has an understanding of the principal truths of the faith and in any way manifests the intention of receiving baptism.

CAN. 683 Baptism must be celebrated according the liturgical prescripts of the Church *sui iuris* in which in accord with the norm of law the person to be baptized is to be ascribed.

CAN. 684 §1. According to the most ancient tradition of the Churches the person who is to be baptized should have at least one sponsor.

§2. In fulfilling the function of a sponsor, the sponsor is to assist at the Christian initiation of a person who is no longer an infant, or to present the infant to be baptized and to help the

§5. Infans christianorum acatholicorum licite baptizatur, si parentes aut unus saltem eorum aut is, qui legitime eorundem locum tenet, id petunt et si eis physice aut moraliter impossibile est accedere ad ministrum proprium.

CAN. 682 §1. Ut infantia egressus baptizari possit, requiritur, ut voluntatem suam baptismum suscipiendi manifestet, sufficienter in veritatibus fidei sit instructus et in vita christiana probatus; admoneatur etiam, ut de peccatis suis doleat.

§2. Infantia egressus, qui in periculo mortis versatur, baptizari potest, si quam de praecipuis veritatibus fidei habet cognitionem et quovis modo intentionem suam baptismum suscipiendi manifestavit.

CAN. 683 Baptismus celebrari debet secundum praescripta liturgica Ecclesiae sui iuris, cui ad normam iuris baptizandus ascribendus est.

CAN. 684 §1. Ex vetustissimo Ecclesiarum more baptizandus unum saltem habeat patrinum.

§2. Patrini ex suscepto munere est baptizando, qui infantia egressus est, in initiatione christiana astare vel baptizandum infantem praesentare atque operam dare, ut baptiza-

682 §1: Laod. cann. 46–47; Quinisext. can. 78; S. NICEPHORUS CP., can. 190; Trid., sess. VI, *De iustificatione,* cap. 6; BENEDICTUS XIV, ep. *Postremo mense,* 28 feb. 1747, 18, 32–51.

682 §2: Laod. can. 47; S. CYRILLUS ALEXANDRIN., can. 5; S. NICEPHORUS CP., can. 6.

683: CLEMENS VIII, instr. *Sanctissimus,* 31 aug. 1595, §5 "Proles sequatur;" BENEDICTUS XIV, const. *Etsi pastoralis,* 26 maii 1742, §II, VIII–X; ep. encycl. *Demandatam,* 24 dec. 1743, §§17–18; S.C. de Prop. Fide, decr. 6 oct. 1863, D), c), d), e). * Syn. Sciarfen. Syrorum, a. 1888, cap. III, art. IX, 12; Syn. Alexandrin. Coptorum, a. 1898, sect. II, cap. I, art. V, XXV; Syn.

Armen., a. 1911, 623.

684 §1: S. NICOLAUS I, litt. *Ad consulta vestra,* 13 nov. 866, XVIII; S.C. de Prop. Fide, reg. (pro Sacerd. Coptis), 15 mar. 1790, XI. * Syn. Diamper. Syro-Malabarensium, a. 1599, LXXXVII; Syn. Zamosten. Ruthenorum, a. 1720, tit. III, §1 "Unum;" Syn. Ain-Trazen. Graeco-Melchitarum, a. 1835, can. 1, 4; Syn. Sciarfen. Syrorum, a. 1888, cap. V, art. II, 3, XV; Syn. Alexandrin. Coptorum, a. 1898, sect. II, cap. III, art. II, 7, XXIII.

684 §2: * Syn. Zamosten. Ruthenorum, a. 1720, tit. III, §1 "Unum;" Syn. Leopolien. Ruthenorum, a. 1891, tit. II, cap. I, 3.

baptized person lead a Christian life in harmony with baptism and fulfill faithfully the obligations connected with it.

CAN. 685 §1. For a person to fulfill validly the role of a sponsor it is necessary that he or she:

1° be initiated with the three sacraments of baptism, chrismation with holy myron and the Eucharist;

2° belong to the Catholic Church, with due regard for §3;

3° have the intention of carrying out the responsibility of sponsor;

4° be designated by the person to be baptized or the parents or guardians, or, if there are not any, by the minister;

5° not be a father, mother or spouse of the person to be baptized;

6° not be bound by excommunication, even a minor one, suspension, deposition or deprived of the right of acting in the function of a sponsor.

§2. To assume licitly the role of sponsor, it is further required that the sponsor should be of the age required by particular law and lead a life in harmony with the faith and the function to be undertaken.

§3. For a just cause, it is permitted to admit the Christian faithful of another Eastern non-Catholic Church to the function of a sponsor, but always at the same time with a Catholic sponsor.

tus vitam christianam baptismo congruam ducat et obligationes cum eo cohaerentes fideliter impleat.

CAN. 685 §1. Ut quis patrini munere valide fungatur, requiritur, ut:

1° sit tribus sacramentis baptismi, chrismationis sancti myri et Eucharistiae initiatus;

2° ad Ecclesiam catholicam pertineat firma §3;

3° intentionem id munus gerendi habeat;

4° sit ab ipso baptizando aut eius parentibus vel tutoribus aut, si desunt, a ministro designatus;

5° non sit pater aut mater aut coniux baptizandi;

6° non sit poena excommunicationis, etiam minoris, suspensionis, depositionis vel privationis iuris patrini munus gerendi punitus.

§2. Ut quis patrini munere licite fungatur, insuper requiritur, ut aetatem iure particulari requisitam habeat atque vitam ducat fidei et muneri suscipiendo congruam.

§3. Iusta de causa licet admittere christifidelem alicuius Ecclesiae orientalis acatholicae ad munus patrini, sed semper simul cum patrino catholico.

685 §1: S. THEODORUS STUDITA, ep. II, 219, interr. XIV; S.C.S. Off., 14 oct. 1676, ad 1; 5 nov. 1676; (Mission. Aegypti), 9 dec. 1745; (Smyrn.), 30 iun. et 7 iul. 1864, ad 4. * Syn. Libanen. Maronitarum, a. 1736, pars II, cap. II, 11; Syn. prov. Alba-Iulien. et Fagarasien. Rumenorum, a. 1872, tit. V, cap. II, 4; Syn. Sciarfen. Syrorum, a. 1888, cap. V, art. II, 3, XV; Syn. Alexandrin. Coptorum, a. 1898, sect. II, cap. III, art. II, 7, XXIV–XXVI; Syn. Armen., a. 1911, 389.

685 §2: S.C. de Prop. Fide, reg. (pro Sacerd. Coptis), 15 mar. 1790, XI; S. Paenit. Ap., 10 dec. 1860, ad 19. * Syn. Libanen. Maronitarum, a. 1736, pars I, cap. II, 5; pars II, cap. II, 11; Syn. prov. Alba-Iulien. et Fagarasien. Rumenorum, a. 1872, tit. V, cap. II, 4); Syn. Sciarfen. Syrorum, a. 1888, cap. V, art. II, 3, XV; Syn. Alexandrin. Coptorum, a. 1898, sect. II, cap. III, art. II, 7, XXIV–XXVI; Syn. Armen., a. 1911, 389.

685 §3: Secret. ad Christ. Unit. Fov., *Directorium* I, 14 maii 1967, 48.

CAN. 686 §1. Parents are bound by the obligation that the infant be baptized as soon as possible according to legitimate custom.

§2. The pastor is to see to it that the parents of the infant to be baptized and the future sponsors are instructed about the meaning of this sacrament and the obligations connected with it and that they are suitably prepared for the celebration of the sacrament.

CAN. 687 §1. Outside of a case of necessity, baptism is to be celebrated in a parish church with due regard for legitimate customs.

§2. Baptism can be administered in private homes according to the prescripts of particular law or with the permission of the local hierarch.

CAN. 688 The person who administers the baptism is to see to it that, unless there is a sponsor, there be at least one witness, by whom the celebration of the baptism can be proven.

CAN. 689 §1. The pastor of the place where the baptism is celebrated must record carefully and without delay in the baptismal register, the names of those baptized, making

CAN. 686 §1. Parentes obligatione tenentur, ut infans quam primum secundum legitimam consuetudinem baptizetur.

§2. Curet parochus, ut infantis baptizandi parentes itemque, qui munus patrini sunt suscepturi, de significatione huius sacramenti deque obligationibus cum eo cohaerentibus congrue edoceantur et ad celebrationem sacramenti apte praeparentur.

CAN. 687 §1. Baptismus extra casum necessitatis in ecclesia paroeciali celebrandus est salvis legitimis consuetudinibus.

§2. In domibus autem privatis baptismus ministrari potest ad normam iuris particularis vel de Hierarchae loci licentia.

CAN. 688 Qui baptismum ministrat, curet, ut, nisi adest patrinus, habeatur saltem testis, a quo celebratio baptismi probari potest.

CAN. 689 §1. Parochus loci, ubi baptismus celebratur, debet nomina baptizatorum mentione facta de ministro, parentibus ac patrinis necnon, si assunt, testibus, de

---

686 §1: Eugenius IV (in Flor.), const. *Cantate Domino*, 4 feb. 1441, §13; Trid., sess. VII, *De baptismo*, cann. 12–13; S.C. de Prop. Fide, instr. 31 iul. 1902, 3; S.C.S. Off., monitum, 18 feb. 1958; S.C. pro Doctr. Fidei, instr. 20 oct. 1980, 7. * Syn. Sergii Patriarchae Maronitarum, 18 sep. 1596, can. 1; Syn. Diamper. Syro-Malabarensium, a. 1599, LXXVI; Syn. Libanen. Maronitarum, a. 1736, pars II, cap. II, 7; Syn. Gusten. Maronitarum, a. 1768, can. 23; Syn. Ain-Trazen. Graeco-Melchitarum, a. 1835, can. 1, 1; Syn. Sciarfen. Syrorum, a. 1888, cap. V, art. II, 3, III; Syn. Leopolien. Ruthenorum, a. 1891, tit. II, cap. I, 1, a); Syn. Alexandrin. Coptorum, a. 1898, sect. II, cap. III, art. II, 7, III.

686 §2: S.C. pro Doctr. Fidei, instr. 20 oct. 1980, 28, 30.

687 §1: Quinisext. can. 59. * S. Macarius Hierosolymitan., can. 2; Nerses Astaraken., can. 14; Syn. Zamosten. Ruthenorum, a. 1720, tit. III, §1 "Quamquam;" Syn. Libanen. Maronitarum, a. 1736, pars II, cap. II, 9; Syn. Gusten. Maronitarum, a. 1768, can. 23; Syn. Ain-Trazen. Graeco-Melchitarum, a.

1835, can. 1, 2 et 6; Syn. Sciarfen. Syrorum, a. 1888, cap. V, art. II, 3, I; Syn. Leopolien. Ruthenorum, a. 1891, tit. II, cap. I, 1, b); Syn. Alexandrin. Coptorum, a. 1898, sect. II, cap. III, art. II, 7, I; Syn. Armen., a. 1911, 385.

687 §2: * Syn. Zamosten. Ruthenorum, a. 1720, tit. III, §1 "Quamquam;" Syn. Leopolien. Ruthenorum, a. 1891, tit. II, cap. I, 1, b).

688: Benedictus XIV, ep. *Postremo mense*, 28 feb. 1747, 31, 55; S.C. de Prop. Fide, instr. (ad Vic. Ap. Indiar. Orient.), 8 sep. 1869, 43.

689 §1: Trid., sess. XXIV, *De ref. matrim.*, cap. 2; Benedictus XIV, const. *Firmandis*, 6 nov. 1744, §9; S.C.S. Off., (Mission. Aegypti), 9 dec. 1745, "Officium;" S.C. de Prop. Fide, instr. (ad Vic. Ap. Indiar. Orient.), 8 sep. 1869, 21. * Syn. Zamosten. Ruthenorum, a. 1720, tit. III, §1 "Denique;" Syn. Libanen. Maronitarum, a. 1736, pars II, cap. II, 13; Syn. Ain-Trazen. Graeco-Melchitarum, a. 1835, can. 1, 3; Syn. Sciarfen. Syrorum, a. 1888, cap. V, art. II, 3, XXI.

mention also of the minister, the parents, the sponsors, and also the witnesses, if there are any, the place and date of the baptism. The place of birth and the Church *sui iuris* in which the baptized persons are ascribed are also to be indicated.

§2. If it is a case of a child born of an unwed mother, the name of the mother is to be indicated if her maternity is publicly established or if she requests it on her own in writing or before two witnesses; likewise the name of the father is to be indicated if his paternity is proven with some public document or by his own declaration made before the pastor and two witnesses; in other cases the name of the baptized is to be recorded with no indication made of the name of the father or parents.

§3. If it is a case of an adopted child, the names of the adoptive parents are recorded, and at least if it is done in the civil records of the region, the names of the natural parents, in accord with the norms of §§1 and 2 and attentive to particular law.

CAN. 690 If the baptism was administered neither by the pastor nor in his presence, the minister must notify the local pastor.

CAN. 691 To prove a baptism, if it is not prejudicial to anyone, it suffices to have the declaration of one witness who is above suspicion or even the declaration of the baptized person founded on solid arguments, especially if the person received baptism when no longer an infant.

loco ac die baptismi, in librum baptizatorum sedulo et sine mora referre, simul indicatis loco nativitatis necnon Ecclesia sui iuris, cui baptizati ascribuntur.

§2. Si de filio agitur ex matre non nupta nato, nomen matris inserendum est, si publice de eius maternitate constat aut mater sua sponte scripto vel coram duobus testibus id petit; item nomen patris inserendum est, si eius paternitas probatur aliquo documento publico aut ipsius declaratione coram parocho et duobus testibus facta; in ceteris casibus inscribatur nomen baptizati nulla indicatione de patris aut parentum nomine facta.

§3. Si de filio adoptivo agitur, inscribantur nomina adoptantium necnon, saltem si ita fit in actu civili regionis, parentum naturalium ad normam §§1 et 2 attento iure particulari.

CAN. 690 Si baptismus nec a parocho nec eo praesente ministratus est, minister de re certiorem facere debet parochum loci.

CAN. 691 Ad baptismum probandum, si nemini fit praeiudicium, sufficit declaratio unius testis omni exceptione maioris aut declaratio ipsius baptizati argumentis indubiis fundata, praesertim si ipse infantia egressus baptismum suscepit.

690: S.C. de Prop. Fide, decr. 6 oct. 1863, C), a).
691: Carth. can. 75; Quinisext. can. 84; S.C.S. Off.,
5 ian. 1724; BENEDICTUS XIV, ep. *Postremo mense,* 28

feb. 1747, 31, 55; S.C. de Prop. Fide, instr. (ad Vic. Ap. Indiar. Orient.), 8 sep. 1869, 43, 2.

CHAPTER II. Chrismation with Holy Myron

CAN. 692 It is necessary for those who have been baptized to be chrismated with holy myron, so that signed with the seal of the gift of the Holy Spirit they may become more suitable witnesses and co-builders of the Kingdom of Christ.

CAN. 693 Holy myron, which is made from the oil of olives or other plants and from aromatics, is confected only by a bishop, without prejudice to particular law which reserves this power to the patriarch.

CAN. 694 According to the tradition of the Eastern Churches, chrismation with holy myron is administered by a presbyter either in conjunction with baptism or separately.

CAPUT II. De Chrismatione Sancti Myri

CAN. 692 Oportet eos, qui baptizati sunt, sancto myro chrismari, ut sigillo doni Spiritus Sancti signati aptiores testes atque coaedificatores Regni Christi efficiantur.

CAN. 693 Sanctum myrum, quod ex oleo olivarum aut aliarum plantarum et ex aromatibus constat, a solo Episcopo conficitur salvo iure particulari, secundum quod haec potestas Patriarchae reservatur.

CAN. 694 Ex Ecclesiarum orientalium traditione chrismatio sancti myri sive coniunctim cum baptismo sive separatim ministratur a presbytero.

692: Laod. can. 48; Constantinop. I, can. 7; Eu-GENIUS IV (in Flor.), const. *Exsultate Deo,* 22 nov. 1439, §§9–10; Trid., sess. VII, *Canones de sacramentis in genere,* can. 1; *De confirmatione,* cann. 1–2; Vat. II, const. *Lumen gentium,* 11 "Indoles;" decr. *Ad gentes,* 36 "Ut membra;" decr. *Presbyterorum ordinis,* 5 "Deus;" PAULUS VI, const. ap. *Divinae consortium naturae,* 15 aug. 1971. * Syn. Zamosten. Ruthenorum, a. 1720, tit. III, §2; Syn. Libanen. Maronitarum, a. 1736, pars II, cap. III, 2; Syn. prov. Alba-Iulien. et Fagarasien. Rumenorum, a. 1872, tit. V, cap. III.

693: Carth. can. 6; Vat. II, decr. *Orientalium Ecclesiarum,* 13; const. *Lumen gentium,* 26 "Ita;" PIUS XII, m.p. *Cleri sanctitati,* 2 iun. 1957, can. 285 §2. - GREGORIUS VII, litt. *Summae Sedis,* 6 iun. 1080, "Quorundam;" INNOCENTIUS III, const. ap. *Quia divinae,* 4 ian. 1215, "Nam cum olim;" INNOCENTIUS IV, ep. *Sub catholice,* 6 mar. 1254, §3, 5; EUGENIUS IV (in Flor.), const. *Exsultate Deo,* 22 nov. 1439, §11; LEO X, const. ap. *Cunctarum,* 1 aug. 1515; Trid., sess. VII, *De confirmatione,* can. 3; sess. XXIII, *De ordine,* cann. 4, 7; CLEMENS VIII, instr. *Sanctissimus,* 31 aug. 1595, §3 "Non sunt cogendi;" BENEDICTUS XIV. *Etsi pastoralis,* 26 mar. 1742, §III, I et §IV; instr. *Eo quamvis tempore,* 4 maii 1745, §8; ep. encycl. *Ex quo,* 1 mar. 1756, §§49–58. * Syn. Sisen. Armenorum, a. 1342, "Item . . . quod verum chrisma;" Syn. Sergii Patriarchae Maronitarum, 18 sep. 1596, 9; Syn. Diamper. Syro-Malabarensium, a. 1599, CCVII; Syn. Zamosten. Ruthenorum, a. 1720, tit. III, §2 "Sacrum;"

Syn. Libanen. Maronitarum, a. 1736, pars II, cap. II, 12; cap. III, 3, 6; Syn. prov. Alba-Iulien. et Fagarasien. Rumenorum, a. 1872, tit. V, cap. III; Syn. Sciarfen. Syrorum, a. 1888, cap. V, art. III, IV–VI, X; Syn. Leopolien. Ruthenorum, a. 1891, tit. II, cap. II; Syn. Alexandrin. Coptorum, a. 1898, sect. II, cap. I, art. V, XII; cap. III, art. III, XI–XX; Syn. Armen., a. 1911, 395, 404.

694: Vat. II, decr. *Orientalium Ecclesiarum,* 13–14. - INNOCENTIUS IV, ep. *Sub catholice,* 6 mar. 1254, §3, 4; Professio fidei (in Lugd. II) a Michaele Palaeologo Gregorio X oblata, a. 1274; EUGENIUS IV (in Flor.), const. *Exsultate Deo,* 22 nov. 1439, §11; CLEMENS VIII, instr. *Sanctissimus,* 31 aug. 1595, initio; BENEDICTUS XIV, const. *Etsi pastoralis,* 26 maii 1742, §II, I–II et §III, I, IV; ep. encycl. *Demandatam,* 24 dec. 1743, §14; instr. *Eo quamvis tempore,* 4 maii 1745, §§6–9; ep. encycl. *Anno vertente,* 19 iun. 1750, §5; ep. encycl. *Allatae sunt,* 26 iul. 1755, ab §22; S.C. de Prop. Fide, reg. (pro Sacerd. Coptis), 15 mar. 1790, XIV. * Syn. Sisen. Armenorum, a. 1342 "Item . . . utriusque Armeniae;" Syn. Zamosten. Ruthenorum, a. 1720, tit. III, §2; Syn. Libanen. Maronitarum, a. 1736, pars II, cap. II, 15; cap. III, 2, 8; Syn. Ain-Trazen. Graeco-Melchitarum, a. 1835, can. 2; Syn. prov. Alba-Iulien. et Fagarasien. Rumenorum, a. 1872, tit. V, cap. III; Syn. Sciarfen. Syrorum, a. 1888, cap. V, art. III, 4, I; art. XIII, §8, 5; Syn. Alexandrin. Coptorum, a. 1898, sect. II, cap. III, art. III, 4; Syn. Armen., a. 1911, 392.

CAN. 695 §1. Chrismation with holy myron must be administered in conjunction with baptism, except in a case of true necessity, in which case, however, care is to be taken to have it administered as soon as possible.

§2. If the celebration of chrismation with holy myron is not done together with baptism, the minister is obliged to notify the local pastor where the baptism was administered.

CAN. 696 §1. All presbyters of the Eastern Churches can validly administer this sacrament either along with baptism or separately to all the Christian faithful of any Church *sui iuris,* including the Latin Church.

§2. The Christian faithful of Eastern Churches validly receive this sacrament even from presbyters of the Latin Church, according to the faculties they have.

§3. Any presbyter licitly administers this sacrament only to the Christian faithful of his own Church *sui iuris;* but when it is a case of the Christian faithful of other Churches *sui iuris,* he acts licitly if they are his subjects, or those whom he licitly baptizes in virtue of another title, or those who are in danger of death, and always with due regard for the agreements entered between Churches *sui iuris* in this matter.

CAN. 697 The sacramental initiation in

CAN. 695 §1. Chrismatio sancti myri ministrari debet coniunctim cum baptismo, salvo casu verae necessitatis, in quo tamen curandum est, ut quam primum ministretur.

§2. Si celebratio chrismationis sancti myri non fit simul cum baptismo, minister tenetur de ea certiorem facere parochum loci, ubi baptismus ministratus est.

CAN. 696 §1. Omnes presbyteri Ecclesiarum orientalium chrismationem sancti myri sive coniunctim cum baptismo sive separatim valide ministrare possunt omnibus christifidelibus cuiusque Ecclesiae sui iuris, etiam Ecclesiae latinae.

§2. Christifideles Ecclesiarum orientalium chrismationem sancti myri valide suscipere possunt etiam a presbyteris Ecclesiae latinae secundum facultates, quibus praediti sunt.

§3. Quivis presbyter solis christifidelibus propriae Ecclesiae sui iuris chrismationem sancti myri licite ministrat; quod vero ad christifideles aliarum Ecclesiarum sui iuris attinet, hoc licite fit, si agitur de propriis subditis, de eis, quos ex alio titulo legitime baptizat, vel de eis, qui in periculo mortis versantur, et salvis semper conventionibus hac in re inter Ecclesias sui iuris initis.

CAN. 697 Initiatio sacramentalis in

695 §1: Laod. can. 48; BENEDICTUS XII, a. 1341, prop. 58 et 64, Armenorum, damn.; S.C.S. Off., instr. (ad Ep. Scepusien.), a. 1782; litt. 16 mar. 1872; 2 apr. 1879; (Ierosolym.), 14 ian. 1885; 22 apr. 1896; S.C. de Prop. Fide, instr. 31 iul. 1902, 4. * Syn. Diamper. Syro-Malabarensium, a. 1599, XCIV; Syn. Libanen. Maronitarum, a. 1736, pars II, cap. III, 7; Syn. Ain-Trazen. Graeco-Melchitarum, a. 1835, can. 2; Syn. Sciarfen. Syrorum, a. 1888, cap. V, art. III, 4, I; Syn. Alexandrin. Coptorum, a. 1898, sect. II, cap. III, art. III, 5, I.

696 §1: Vat. II, decr. *Orientalium Ecclesiarum,* 14;

S.C.S. Off., 22 apr. 1896; S.C. pro Eccl. Orient., decr. 1 maii 1948.

696 §3: S.C.S. Off., instr. (ad Ep. Scepusien.), a. 1782; S.C. de Prop. Fide, reg. (pro Sacerd. Coptis), 15 mar. 1790, XIII; decr. 6 oct. 1863, C), a); (C.G.), 5 iul. 1886; S.C. pro Eccl. Orient., decr. 1 maii 1948. * Syn. Alexandrin. Coptorum, a. 1898, sect. II, cap. I, art. V, XIII; Syn. Zamosten. Ruthenorum, a. 1720, tit. III, §1 "Si acciderit;" Syn. Armen., a. 1911, 398.

697: Trid., sess. XXI, *De communione,* cap. 4, can. 4; S.C. de Prop. Fide, 5 apr. 1729, ad 3; BENEDICTUS XIV, const. *Etsi pastoralis,* 26 maii 1742, §II, VII; en-

the mystery of salvation is completed with the reception of the Divine Eucharist; therefore after baptism and chrismation with holy myron, the Divine Eucharist is to be administered as soon as possible in accord with the norms of the particular law of each Church *sui iuris*.

mysterium salutis susceptione Divinae Eucharistiae perficitur, ideoque Divina Eucharistia post baptismum et chrismationem sancti myri christifideli ministretur quam primum secundum normam iuris particularis propriae Ecclesiae sui iuris.

CHAPTER III. Divine Eucharist

CAPUT III. **De Divina Eucharistia**

CAN. 698 What the Lord Jesus himself did at the Last Supper is perpetuated in the Divine Liturgy by the power of the Holy Spirit through the ministry of the priest who acts in the person of Christ at the oblation of the Church. The Lord Jesus gave to his disciples his Body, which was to be offered for us on the cross, and his Blood, which was to be poured out for us, thus instituting the true and mystical sacrifice. In this, the bloody sacrifice of the cross is commemorated with thanksgiving, is actuated and shared by the Church through oblation and through communion, in order to signify and perfect the unity of the people of God and to edify the Body of Christ, namely the Church.

CAN. 698 In Divina Liturgia per ministerium sacerdotis in persona Christi super oblationem Ecclesiae agentis perpetuatur virtute Spiritus Sancti, quod ipse fecit in novissima Cena Dominus Jesus, qui discipulis dedit Corpus Suum in Cruce pro nobis offerendum Sanguinemque Suum pro nobis effundendum, verum mysticumque instaurans sacrificium, quo cruentum illud Crucis sacrificium cum gratiarum actione commemoratur, actuatur et ab Ecclesia participatur tum oblatione tum communione ad significandam et perficiendam unitatem populi Dei in aedificationem Corporis Sui, quod est Ecclesia.

cycl. *Allatae sunt,* 26 iul. 1755, §24. * Syn. Sisen. Armenorum, a. 1342, "Item . . . fit baptizatus verus;" Syn. Sergii Patriarchae Maronitarum, a. 1596, can. 7; Syn. Zamosten. Ruthenorum, a. 1720, tit. III, §3 "Etsi;" Syn. Libanen. Maronitarum, a. 1736, pars II, cap. II, 12; cap. XII, 13; Syn. prov. Alba-Iulien. et Fagarasien. Rumenorum, a. 1872, tit. V, cap. IV "Subiectum;" Syn. Sciarfen. Syrorum, a. 1888, cap. V, art. IV, §5, 2, III; Syn. Alexandrin. Coptorum, a. 1898, sect. II, cap. III, art. IV, prima pars, VI, II–III; Syn. Armen., a. 1911, 391, 422–423, 637, d).

698: S. IOANNES CHRYSOSTOMUS, *De proditione Judae,* hom. I, 6 et hom. II, 6; *De sacerdotio,* lib. 3, 4 et lib. 6, 4; Professio fidei (in Lugd. II) a Michaele Palaeologo Gregorio X oblata, a. 1274; EUGENIUS IV (in Flor.), const. *Exsultate Deo,* 22 nov. 1439, §12; Trid., sess. XIII, *De Eucharistia,* capp. 1–5, cann. 1–3, 8; sess. XXI, *De communione,* cap. 3, can. 3; sess. XXII, *De sacrificio missae,* capp. 1–2, cann. 1–4; PIUS IV, const. *Iniunctum nobis,* 13 nov. 1564, Professio fidei Trident.; GREGORIUS XIII, const. *Sanctissimus,* a. 1575, Professio fidei Graecis praescr., §§12–13; BENEDICTUS XIV, const. *Etsi pastoralis,* 26 maii 1742, §VI, XV; ep. *Nuper ad Nos,* 16 mar. 1743, Professio fidei Maronitis praescr., §5; Vat. II, const. *Sacrosanctum Concilium,* 10, 47; const. *Lumen gentium,* 3, 11 "Indoles," 17, 28 "Christus," 50 "Nobilissime;" decr. *Presbyterorum ordinis,* 5, 13 "Ut Sacrorum;" decr. *Ad gentes,* 39 "Presbyteri;" PAULUS VI, ep. ap. *Investigabiles divitias Christi,* 6 feb. 1965, "Quoniam;" IOANNES PAULUS II, lit. encycl. *Redemptor hominis,* 4 mar. 1979, 20; ep. ap. 2 ian. 1980, III ab "Eucharistiam." * Syn. Libanen. Maronitarum, a. 1736, pars II, cap. XII, 1–6; Syn. prov. Alba-Iulien. et Fagarasien. Rumenorum, a. 1872, tit. V, cap. IV; Syn Armen., a. 1911, 433.

CAN. 699 §1. Only bishops and presbyters have the power to celebrate the Divine Liturgy.

§2. Along with bishops and presbyters, deacons have a very close share in the celebration of the Divine Liturgy and have a ministry proper to them according to the prescripts of the liturgical books.

§3. The other Christian faithful, by virtue of their baptism and chrismation with holy myron, take part in the celebration of the Divine Liturgy in the manner determined by the liturgical books or particular law and participate actively in the sacrifice of Christ; they do so more fully if they receive the Body and Blood of Christ from the same sacrifice.

CAN. 700 §1. With regard to the manner of celebrating the Divine Liturgy, whether it should be done individually or in concelebration, attention should be given above all to the pastoral needs of the Christian faithful.

§2. If it is possible, presbyters are to celebrate the Divine Liturgy together with a bishop presiding or with another presbyter, since thus the unity of the priesthood and of the sacrifice will be properly manifested. Each priest, however, has a complete right to celebrate the Divine Liturgy individually, not, however, simultaneously with a concelebration taking place in the same Church.

CAN. 699 §1. Potestatem celebrandi Divinam Liturgiam habent soli Episcopi et presbyteri.

§2. Diaconi cum Episcopis et presbyteris proprio ministerio secundum praescripta librorum liturgicorum in celebratione Divinae Liturgiae artiorem partem habent.

§3. Ceteri christifideles virtute baptismi atque chrismationis sancti myri in celebrationem Divinae Liturgiae concurrentes modo in libris liturgicis vel iure particulari determinato in Sacrificio Christi actuose participant et quidem plenius, si ex eodem Sacrificio Corpus et Sanguinem Domini sumunt.

CAN. 700 §1. Quod ad modum Divinam Liturgiam celebrandi spectat, utrum singillatim an in concelebratione facienda sit, prae oculis habeantur imprimis pastorales christifidelium necessitates.

§2. Si tamen fieri potest, Divinam Liturgiam presbyteri una cum Episcopo praeside aut cum alio presbytero celebrent, cum ita opportune unitas sacerdotii ac sacrificii manifestetur; integrum tamen manet ius uniuscuiusque sacerdotis Divinam Liturgiam singillatim celebrandi, non autem eodem tempore, quo in eadem ecclesia concelebratio habetur.

699 §1: Nic. I, can. 18; S. Basilius M., can. 93; Eugenius IV (in Flor.), const. *Exsultate Deo,* 22 nov. 1439, §12; (in Flor.), const. *Cantate Domino,* 4 feb. 1441, §25; Trid., sess. XXII, *De sacrificio missae,* cap. 1, can. 2; sess. XXIII, *De ordine,* can. 1; Benedictus XIV, ep. encycl. *Ex quo,* 1 mar. 1756, §§41–42; Vat. II, const. *Lumen gentium,* 10 "Sacerdotium," 26 "Episcopus," 28 "Christus."

699 §2: Vat. II, const. *Lumen gentium,* 29. - Nic. I, can. 18; Anc. can. 2; Quinisext. can. 7; Timotheus Alexandrin., cann. 22, 24.

699 §3: Vat. II, const. *Lumen gentium,* 10; const. *Sacrosanctum Concilium,* 14, 26, 33, 48; decr. *Presbyterorum ordinis,* 5 "Est ergo;" decr. *Orientalium Ec-* clesiarum, 15.

700 §2: Benedictus XIV, ep. encycl. *Demandatam,* 24 dec. 1743, §9; const. *Praeclaris,* 18 mar. 1746, "Non credette;" ep. encycl. *Allatae sunt,* 26 iul. 1755, §38; S.C.S. Off., dubium, 23 maii 1957. * Syn. Libanen. Maronitarum, a. 1736, pars II, cap. XIII, 18; Syn. Ain-Trazen. Graeco-Melchitarum, a. 1835, can. 8, 5; Syn. Sciarfen. Syrorum, a. 1888, cap. V, art. V, §7, 3, III; Syn. Leopolien. Ruthenorum, a. 1891, tit. IV, cap. I, 11; Syn. Alexandrin. Coptorum, a. 1898, sect. II, cap. III, art. IV, secunda pars, I, 2, VIII; Syn. prov. Alba-Iulien. et Fagarasien. Rumenorum, a. 1900, tit. III, cap. I, 8.

CAN. 701 For a just cause and with the permission of the eparchial bishop, bishops and presbyters of different churches *sui iuris* can concelebrate, especially to foster love and to manifest the unity of the Churches. All follow the prescripts of the liturgical books of the principal celebrant, avoiding any liturgical syncretism whatever, and preferably with all wearing the liturgical vestments and insignia of their own Church *sui iuris*.

CAN. 702 Catholic priests are forbidden to concelebrate the Divine Liturgy with non-Catholic priests or ministers.

CAN. 703 §1. A priest who is a stranger is not to be admitted to the celebration of the Divine Liturgy, unless he shows the rector of the church a letter of recommendation from his own hierarch, or the rector is satisfied in some other way about his propriety.

§2. The eparchial bishop is free to make more specific norms concerning this matter that are to be observed by all priests, even those who are exempt in any way.

CAN. 704 The Divine Liturgy can be praiseworthily celebrated on any day except those that are excluded according to the prescripts of the liturgical books of the Church *sui iuris* in which the priest is ascribed.

CAN. 705 §1. A Catholic priest can cele-

CAN. 701 Concelebratio inter Episcopos et presbyteros diversarum Ecclesiarum sui iuris iusta de causa praesertim caritatem fovendi atque unionem inter Ecclesias manifestandi gratia de Episcopi eparchialis licentia fieri potest omnibus praescripta librorum liturgicorum primi celebrantis sequentibus, remoto quolibet syncretismo liturgico et retentis optabiliter vestibus liturgicis et insignibus propriae Ecclesiae sui iuris.

CAN. 702 Sacerdotes catholici vetiti sunt una cum sacerdotibus vel ministris acatholicis Divinam Liturgiam concelebrare.

CAN. 703 §1. Sacerdos extraneus ad celebrandam Divinam Liturgiam non admittatur, nisi rectori ecclesiae litteras commendatitias sui Hierarchae exhibet aut alio modo ipsi rectori de eius probitate satis constat.

§2. Integrum est Episcopo eparchiali hac de re normas magis determinatas ferre ab omnibus sacerdotibus, etiam quomodocumque exemptis, servandas.

CAN. 704 Divina Liturgia omnibus diebus laudabiliter celebrari potest exceptis eis, qui secundum praescripta librorum liturgicorum Ecclesiae sui iuris, cui sacerdos ascriptus est, excluduntur.

CAN. 705 §1. Sacerdos catholicus Di-

702: Secret. ad Christ. Unit. Fov., *Déclaration*, 7 ian. 1970, 10.

703 §1: Apost. can. 33; Laod. can. 41; Chalc. can. 13; S.C. de Prop. Fide, 5 iul. 1631; S.C. pro Eccl. Orient., monitum, 20 iul. 1937. * Syn. Zamosten. Ruthenorum, a. 1720, tit. III, §4 "Perniciosissimum;" Syn. Libanen. Maronitarum, a. 1736, pars II, cap. XIII, 12, II et 14; pars III, cap. IV, 24; Syn. Ain-Trazen. Graeco-Melchitarum, a. 1835, can. 14; Syn. prov. Alba-Iulien. et Fagarasien. Rumenorum, a. 1872, tit. II, cap. IX, 1); Syn. Sciarfen. Syrorum, a. 1888, cap. V, art. V, §2, VII; cap. XI, art. III, 5, V "Inter;" Syn. Alexandrin. Coptorum, a. 1898, sect. II, cap. III, art. IV, secunda pars, IV, XIII; Syn. Armen., a. 1911, 342, 444, 764.

704: Vat. II, decr. *Presbyterorum ordinis*, 13 "Ut." - Laod. cann. 49, 51; Quinisext. can. 52; Trid., sess. XXIII, *De ref.*, can. 14; S.C. de Prop. Fide, (C.P.), 31 mar. 1729; BENEDICTUS XIV, ep. encycl. *Demandatam*, 24 dec. 1743, §8; S.C. de Prop. Fide, instr. 31 iul. 1902, 6. * Syn. Libanen. Maronitarum, a. 1736, pars III, cap. I, 13; Syn. Ain-Trazen. Graeco-Melchitarum, a. 1835, can. 3; Syn. Leopolien. Ruthenorum, a. 1891, tit. IV, cap. I, 1–4; Syn. Alexandrin. Coptorum, a. 1898, sect. II, cap. III, art. IV, secunda pars, IV, IX; Syn. prov. Alba-Iulien. et Fagarasien. Rumenorum, a. 1900, tit. III, cap. I, 5; Syn. Armen., a. 1911, 449–450, 739.

705 §1: Laod. can. 58; S. CYRILLUS ALEXANDRIN., can. 8; S. NICEPHORUS CP., cann. 95, 97–98; EUGE-

brate the Divine Liturgy on the altar of any Catholic Church.

§2. In order for a priest to be able to celebrate the Divine Liturgy in a non-Catholic Church, he needs the permission of the local hierarch.

CAN. 706 The sacred gifts offered in the Divine Liturgy are pure wheat bread recently made, so that there is no danger of corruption, and uncorrupt natural grape wine.

CAN. 707 §1. The particular law of each Church *sui iuris* must establish accurately

vinam Liturgiam celebrare potest super altare cuiusvis ecclesiae catholicae.

§2. Ut sacerdos Divinam Liturgiam in ecclesia acatholicorum celebrare possit, licentia eget Hierarchae loci.

CAN. 706 In Divina Liturgia sacra dona, quae offeruntur, sunt panis mere triticeus recenter confectus ita, ut nullum sit periculum corruptionis, et vinum naturale de genimine vitis non corruptum.

CAN. 707 §1. Circa panis eucharistici confectionem, preces a sacerdotibus ante

---

NIUS IV (in Flor.), bulla, *Benedictus sit Deus,* 7 aug. 1445, "Item . . . presules;" CLEMENS VIII, instr. *Sanctissimus,* 31 aug. 1595, §2 "Si Graeci velint;" S.C. de Prop. Fide, (C.P.), 31 dec. 1745, art. IV, n. 3; BENEDICTUS XIV, ep. encycl. *Allatae sunt,* 26 iul. 1755, §§35–36; S.C. de Prop. Fide, reg. (pro Sacerd. Coptis), 15 mar. 1790, X; 16 aug. 1831; GREGORIUS XVI, ep. encycl. *Inter gravissimas,* 3 feb. 1832, §§6–7; S.C. de Prop. Fide, decr. 6 oct. 1863, B). * Syn. Zamosten. Ruthenorum, a. 1720, tit. III "Cum;" Syn. Libanen. Maronitarum, a. 1736, pars II, cap. XIII, 12, III et 15; Syn. Sciarfen. Syrorum, a. 1888, cap. V, art. V, §2, I–II; Syn. Alexandrin. Coptorum, a. 1898, sect. II, cap. III, art. IV, secunda pars, IV, I; Syn. prov. Alba-Iulien. et Fagarasien. Rumenorum, a. 1872, tit. V, cap. IV "Locus;" Syn. Armen., a. 1911, 440, 652.

705 §2: Secret. pro Christ. Unit. Fov., *Directorium* I, 14 maii 1967, 36, b), 52. - S. NICEPHORUS CP., cann. 36–37; S.C. de Prop. Fide, (C.P.), 7 maii 1631, ad 2; decr. 24 sep. 1632; instr. 12 mar. 1809; S.C.S. Off., (Archiep. Antibaren.), 1 dec. 1757.

706: Apost. can. 3; Carth. can. 37; Quinisext. cann. 28, 32; GREGORIUS VII, litt. *Summae sedis specula,* 6 iun. 1080, "Quorumdam;" IOHANNES XXII, ep. *Exsultavit cor nostrum,* 28 mar. 1318; ep. *Salvator noster,* 29 apr. 1319; EUGENIUS IV (in Flor.), const. *Exsultate Deo,* 22 nov. 1439, §12; (in Flor.), const. *Cantate Domino,* 4 feb. 1441, §25; GREGORIUS XIII, const. *Sanctissimus,* a. 1575, Professio fidei Graecis praescr., §3; S.C. de Prop. Fide, (C.G.), 30 ian. 1635; Trid., sess. XXII, *De sacrificio missae,* capp. 1, 7, can. 9; BENEDICTUS XIV, ep. *Nuper ad Nos,* 16 mar. 1743, Professio fidei Maronitis praescr., §5; ep. encycl. *Allatae sunt,* 26 iul. 1755, §§6, 22; S.C.S. Off., 7 aug. 1704, ad 2; S.C. de Prop. Fide, litt. 4 iul. 1833, III. * Syn. Alexandrin. Coptorum, a. 1898, sect. II, cap. III, art. IV, prima pars, IV, I.

707 §1: *De confectione panis eucharistici:* GREGORIUS VII, litt. *Summae sedis specula,* 6 iun. 1080, "De

reliquo;" GREGORIUS IX, ep. *Cum iuxta testimonium veritatis,* 18 maii 1233, "Verumtamen;" Professio fidei (in Lugd. II) a Michaele Palaeologo Gregorio X oblata, a. 1274; EUGENIUS IV (in Flor.), const. *Laetentur coeli,* 6 iul. 1439, §4; LEO X, litt. ap. *Accepimus nuper,* 18 maii 1521; PAULUS III, litt. ap. *Dudum,* 23 dec. 1534; GREGORIUS XIII, const. *Sanctissimus,* a. 1575, Professio fidei Graecis praescr., §3; PAULUS V, litt. ap. *Plane repleta,* 1 ian. 1606; BENEDICTUS XIV, const. *Etsi pastoralis,* 26 maii 1742, §I, II, §VI, X; ep. *Nuper ad Nos,* 16 mar. 1743, Professio fidei Maronitis praescr., §5; ep. encycl. *Allatae sunt,* 26 iul. 1755, §§22–23, 34; PIUS X, const. *Tradita ab antiquis,* 14 sep. 1912, 2; S.C. de Prop. Fide, 23 iun. 1633, n. 2; decr. 20 nov. 1838; instr. 31 iul. 1902, 1, e). * Syn. Zamosten. Ruthenorum, a. 1720, tit. III, §§3, 4 "Tametsi;" Syn. Libanen. Maronitarum, a. 1736, pars II, cap. XII, 7; Syn. Sciarfen. Syrorum, a. 1888, cap. V, art. IV, §4, 1, IV, VII–VIII; Syn. Alexandrin. Coptorum, a. 1898, sect. II, cap. III, art. IV, prima pars, IV, 4; Syn. Armen., a. 1911, 436.

De praecibus praeparatoriis: * Syn. Leopolien. Ruthenorum, a. 1891, tit. IV, cap. I, 9; tit. IX, cap. II, 16; Syn. Armen., a. 1911, 442.

De ieiunio eucharistico: PIUS XII, const. *Christus Dominus,* 6 ian. 1953; m.p. *Sacram Communionem,* 19 mar. 1957, 2–4; S.C.S. Off., litt. 22 mar. 1923; decl. 16 nov. 1923; instr. 6 ian. 1953. - Carth. can. 41; Quinisext. can. 29; TIMOTHEUS ALEXANDRIN., can. 16; S. NICEPHORUS CP., can. 34; S. NICOLAUS I, litt. *Ad consulta vestra,* 13 nov. 866, LXV. * S. ISAAC M., can. 28; Nerses Astaraken., can. 22; Syn. Diamper. Syro-Malabarensium, a. 1599, CI; Syn. Zamosten. Ruthenorum, a. 1720, tit. III, §4 "In honorem;" Syn. Libanen. Maronitarum, a. 1736, pars II, cap. XII, 17; Syn. Sciarfen. Syrorum, a. 1888, cap. V, art. V, §2, VIII; Syn. Leopolien. Ruthenorum, a. 1891, tit. IV, cap. I, 7; Syn. Alexandrin. Coptorum, a. 1898, sect. II, cap. III, art. IV, prima pars, VI, IX, V; Syn. Armen., a. 1911, 419.

norms regarding the preparation of the eucharistic bread, the prayers to be recited by the priests before the Divine Liturgy, the observance of the eucharistic fast, the liturgical vestments, the time and place of the celebration and other similar matters.

§2. Without causing astonishment to the Christian faithful, it is permitted to use the liturgical vestments and bread of another Church *sui iuris*, if the liturgical vestments and bread of one's own Church *sui iuris* are not available.

CAN. 708 The local hierarchs and the pastors are to ensure that the Christian faithful are very carefully instructed regarding the obligation of receiving the Divine Eucharist in danger of death and also at those times that are established by praiseworthy tradition or the particular law of the respective Church *sui iuris*, especially at Easter time, when Christ the Lord bequeathed the eucharistic mysteries.

CAN. 709 §1. The priest distributes the Di-

celebrationem Divinae Liturgiae persolvendas, ieiunium eucharisticum servandum, vestes liturgicas, tempus et locum celebrationis et huiusmodi iure particulari uniuscuiusque Ecclesiae sui iuris normae accurate statui debent.

§2. Remota christifidelium admiratione licet uti vestibus liturgicis et pane alterius Ecclesiae sui iuris, si vestes liturgicae et panis propriae Ecclesiae sui iuris praesto non sunt.

CAN. 708 Curent Hierarchae loci ac parochi, ut omni diligentia christifideles instruantur de obligatione Divinam Eucharistiam suscipiendi in periculo mortis necnon temporibus a laudabilissima traditione vel iure particulari propriae Ecclesiae sui iuris statutis, praesertim vero tempore Paschali, in quo Christus Dominus eucharistica mysteria tradidit.

CAN. 709 §1. Divinam Eucharistiam

De vestibus liturgicis: * Syn. Libanen. Maronitarum, a. 1736, pars II, cap. XIII, 8 "Sacra;" Syn. Sciarfen. Syrorum, a. 1888, cap. V, art. V, §3; Syn. Leopolien. Ruthenorum, a. 1891, tit. IV, cap. I, 7; Syn. Alexandrin. Coptorum, a. 1898, sect. II, cap. III, art. IV, secunda pars, II.
De tempore celebrationis: INNOCENTIUS IV, ep. *Sub catholicae,* 6 mar. 1254, §3, 9; S.C. de Prop. Fide, instr. 31 iul. 1902, 6; PIUS XII, const. *Christus Dominus,* 6 ian. 1953, VI; S.C.S. Off., decr. 31 maii 1953; PIUS XII, m.p. *Sacram Communionem,* 19 mar. 1957, 1. * Syn. Zamosten. Ruthenorum, a. 1720, tit. III, §4 "Illud;" Syn. Libanen. Maronitarum, a. 1736, pars II, cap. XIII, 16; Syn. Sciarfen. Syrorum, a. 1888, cap. V, art. V, §2, VIII; Syn. Leopolien. Ruthenorum, a. 1891, tit. IV, cap. I, 13–15; Syn. Alexandrin. Coptorum, a. 1898, sect. II, cap. III, art. IV, secunda pars, IV, VIII; Syn. prov. Alba-Iulien. et Fagarasien. Rumenorum, a. 1900, tit. III, cap. I, 7; Syn. Armen., a. 1911, 439.
708: Nic. I, can. 13; S. GREGORIUS NYSSEN., cann. 2, 5, (b); S. CYRILLUS ALEXANDRIN., can. 5; S. NICEPHORUS CP., cann. 34, 183; INNOCENTIUS III, litt. *Quia divinae,* 4 ian. 1215, "Nam cum olim" et "Statuimus;" LEO X, const. ap. *Cunctarum,* 1 aug. 1515; Trid., sess. XIII, *De Eucharistia,* can. 9; S.C.S. Off., 12

dec. 1821; S.C. de Prop. Fide, instr. (ad Del. Ap. Aegypti), 30 apr. 1862, ad 2; (C.G.), 11 dec. 1838, ad 23; litt. encycl. 26 feb. 1896; instr. 31 iul. 1902, 6; PIUS X, const. *Tradita ab antiquis,* 14 sep. 1912, IV–V; S.C. pro Eccl. Orient., decl. 14 apr. 1924; resol. 26 ian. 1925. * Syn. Diamper. Syro-Malabarensium, a. 1599, XCIX, CII; Syn. Zamosten. Ruthenorum, a. 1720, tit. III, §5 "Quia;" Syn. Libanen. Maronitarum, a. 1736, pars II, cap. IV, 8; cap. XII, 14, 18–19; pars III, cap. III, 2, X–XI; Syn. prov. Alba-Iulien. et Fagarasien. Rumenorum, a. 1872, tit. V, cap. IV "Synodus;" Syn. Sciarfen. Syrorum, a. 1888, cap. III, art. IX, 14; cap. V, art. IV, §5, 2, IV; Syn. Leopolien. Ruthenorum, a. 1891, tit. II, cap. III, 7–8; Syn. Alexandrin. Coptorum, a. 1898, sect. II, cap. III, art. IV, prima pars, VI, IX; Syn. Armen., a. 1911, 341, 415–416, 423.
709 §1: Nic. I, can. 18; Quinisext. can. 58; Trid., sess. XIII, *De Eucharistia,* cap. 8; sess. XXIII, *De ordine,* cap. 1; S.C. de Prop. Fide, instr. 31 iul. 1902, 6. * Syn. Libanen. Maronitarum, a. 1736, pars II, cap. XII, 11; pars III, cap. II, 4; Syn. Sciarfen. Syrorum, a. 1888, cap. V, art. IV, §4, 4; cap. V, art. XIII, §5, 4, 2); Syn. Alexandrin. Coptorum, a. 1898, sect. II, cap. III, art. IV, prima pars, VII, 2 et 3, VI; Syn. Armen., a. 1911, 410.

vine Eucharist or, if the particular law of his Church *sui iuris* provides for it, also the deacon.

§2. The synod of bishops of the patriarchal Church or the council of hierarchs is free to establish suitable norms according to which other Christian faithful, too, may distribute the Divine Eucharist.

CAN. 710 Regarding the participation of infants in the Divine Eucharist after baptism and chrismation with holy myron, suitable precautions are to be taken and the prescripts of the liturgical books of the respective Church *sui iuris* are to be observed.

CAN. 711 A person who is conscious of serious sin is not to celebrate the Divine Liturgy nor receive the Divine Eucharist unless a serious reason is present and there is no opportunity to receive the sacrament of penance; in this case the person should make an act of perfect contrition, including the intention of confessing as soon as possible.

CAN. 712 Those who are publicly unworthy are forbidden to receive the Divine Eucharist.

distribuit sacerdos vel iure particulari propriae Ecclesiae sui iuris ita ferente etiam diaconus.

§2. Integrum est Synodo Episcoporum Ecclesiae patriarchalis vel Consilio Hierarcharum opportunas normas statuere, secundum quas etiam alii christifideles Divinam Eucharistiam distribuere possunt.

CAN. 710 Circa infantium in Divina Eucharistia participationem post baptismum et chrismationem sancti myri serventur opportunis adhibitis cautelis praescripta librorum liturgicorum propriae Ecclesiae sui iuris.

CAN. 711 Qui peccati gravis sibi conscius est, Divinam Liturgiam ne celebret neque Divinam Eucharistiam suscipiat, nisi adest gravis ratio et deest opportunitas sacramentum paenitentiae suscipiendi; quo in casu elicere debet actum perfectae contritionis, qui includit propositum quam primum ad hoc sacramentum accedendi.

CAN. 712 Arcendi sunt a susceptione Divinae Eucharistiae publice indigni.

710: Leo X, litt. ap. *Accepimus nuper,* 18 maii 1521; Paulus III, litt. ap. *Dudum,* 23 dec. 1534; Trid., sess. XXI, *De communione,* cap. 4, can. 4; Gregorius XIII, const. ap. *Benedictus Deus,* 14 feb. 1577; Benedictus XIV, const. *Etsi pastoralis,* 26 maii 1742, §II, VII; ep. encycl. *Allatae sunt,* 26 iul. 1755, §24; S.C. de Prop. Fide, 5 apr. 1729; S.C.S. Off., 14 iun. 1741. * Syn. Sisen. Armenorum, a. 1342, "Item . . . fit baptizatus verus;" Syn. Sergii Patriarchae Maronitarum, a. 1596, can. 7; Syn. Zamosten. Ruthenorum, a. 1720, tit. III, §3 "Etsi;" Syn. Libanen. Maronitarum, a. 1736, pars II, cap. XII, 13; Syn. prov. Alba-Iulien. et Fagarasien. Rumenorum, a. 1872, tit. V, cap. 4 "Subiectum;" Syn. Sciarfen. Syrorum, a. 1888, cap. V, art. II, 3, XIX; art. IV, §5, 2, III; Syn. Alexandrin. Coptorum, a. 1898, sect. II, cap. III, art. IV, prima pars, VI, II–III; Syn. Armen., a. 1911, 391, 422–423, 637, d).

711: Trid., sess. XIII, *De Eucharistia,* cap. 7, can. 11; S. Nicephorus CP., can. 10; Benedictus XIV,

const. *Etsi pastoralis,* 26 maii 1742, §VI, I; S.C.S. Off., decr. 18 mar. 1666, prop. 38–39 damn.; S.C.C., decr. 20 dec. 1905, 3. * Syn. Diamper. Syro-Malabarensium, a. 1599, C, CV; Syn. Libanen. Maronitarum, a. 1736, pars II, cap. XII, 16; Syn. prov. Alba-Iulien. et Fagarasien. Rumenorum, a. 1872, tit. V, cap. IV "Subiectum;" Syn. Sciarfen. Syrorum, a. 1888, cap. V, art. IV, §5, 2, V; Syn. Alexandrin. Coptorum, a. 1898, sect. II, cap. III, art. IV, prima pars, IV, IX, I.

712: S. Basilius M., cann. 23–24; Timotheus Alexandrin., can. 25; S. Paenit. Ap., 10 dec. 1860, ad 20; S.C.S. Off., decr. 1 iul. 1949, ad 3. * Syn. Diamper. Syro-Malabarensium, a. 1599, C; Syn. Zamosten. Ruthenorum, a. 1720, tit. III, §3 "Ne alicuius;" Syn. Libanen. Maronitarum, a. 1736, pars II, cap. XII, 12; Syn. Sciarfen. Syrorum, a. 1888, cap. V, art. IV, §5, 2, I–II; Syn. Alexandrin. Coptorum, a. 1898, sect. III, cap. III, art. IV, prima pars, VI, IX, II; Syn Armen., a. 1911, 418, 426.

CAN. 713 §1. The Divine Eucharist is to be distributed in the celebration of the Divine Liturgy unless a just cause suggests otherwise.

§2. Concerning the preparation for participation in the Divine Eucharist through fast, prayers and other works, the Christian faithful are to observe faithfully the norms of the Church *sui iuris* in which they are ascribed, not only within the territorial boundaries of the same Church, but, inasmuch as it is possible, everywhere.

CAN. 714 §1. In churches where there is public divine worship and at least several times a month the Divine Liturgy is celebrated, the Divine Eucharist is to be reserved, especially for the sick, observing faithfully the prescripts of the liturgical books of the respective Church *sui iuris,* and is to be adored with the greatest reverence by the Christian faithful.

§2. The reservation of the Divine Eucharist is under the vigilance and regulation of the local hierarch.

CAN. 715 §1. It is permitted for priests to

CAN. 713 §1. Divina Eucharistia distribuenda est in celebratione Divinae Liturgiae, nisi iusta causa aliud suadet.

§2. Circa praeparationem participationis Divinae Eucharistiae per ieiunium, preces aliaque opera christifideles fideliter normas Ecclesiae sui iuris, cui ascripti sunt, servent non solum intra fines territorii eiusdem Ecclesiae, sed, quatenus fieri potest, ubique terrarum.

CAN. 714 §1. In ecclesiis, ubi cultus divinus publicus et saltem aliquoties in mense Divina Liturgia celebratur, Divina Eucharistia custodiatur praesertim pro infirmis, praescriptis librorum liturgicorum propriae Ecclesiae sui iuris fideliter servatis, atque summa reverentia a christifidelibus adoretur.

§2. Custodia Divinae Eucharistiae subest vigilantiae ac moderamini Hierarchae loci.

CAN. 715 §1. Sacerdotibus licet obla-

713 §2: TIMOTHEUS ALEXANDRIN., can. 16; S. NICOLAUS I, litt. *Ad consulta vestra,* 13 nov. 866, LXV; S. NICEPHORUS CP., can. 34; S. ISAAC M., can. 29; Nerses Astaraken., can. 22. * Syn. Diamper. Syro-Malabarensium, a. 1599, CI; Syn. prov. Alba-Iulien. et Fagarasien. Rumenorum, a. 1872, tit. V, cap. IV "Synodus;" Syn. Sciarfen. Syrorum, a. 1888, cap. V, art. IV, §5, 2, VI; Syn. Alexandrin. Coptorum, a. 1898, sect. II, cap. III, art. IV, prima pars, VI, IX, V–VI; Syn. Armen., a. 1911, 419.

714 §1: S. BASILIUS M., cann. 93–94; TIMOTHEUS ALEXANDRIN., can. 24; Trid., sess. XIII, *De Eucharistia,* capp. 5–6, cann. 6–7; BENEDICTUS XIV, const. *Etsi pastoralis,* 26 maii 1742, §VI, IV–V, VII; const. *Praeclaris,* 18 mar. 1746, "Perché poi;" S.C. de Prop. Fide, litt. (ad Patr. Cyrillum Melkit.), 7 maii 1746. * Syn. Diamper. Syro-Malabarensium, a. 1599, XCVII–XCVIII; Syn. Zamosten. Ruthenorum, a. 1720, tit. III, §3 "Statuit," §4 "Quoniam;" Syn. Libanen. Maronitarum, a. 1736, pars II, cap. XII, 4, 23–24; Syn. prov. Alba-Iulien. et Fagarasien. Rumenorum, a. 1872, tit. V, cap. IV "In asservanda;" Syn. Sciarfen.

Syrorum, a. 1888, cap. V, art. IV, §7; Syn. Alexandrin. Coptorum, a. 1898, sect. II, cap. III, prima pars, VIII; Syn. Armen., a. 1911, 412–413.

715 §1: BENEDICTUS XIV, ep. encycl. *Demandatam,* 24 dec. 1743, §10; const. *Praeclaris,* 18 mar. 1746, "Non credette;" S.C. de Prop. Fide, decr. 13 apr. 1807, XVI; litt. encycl. (ad Epp. Orient.), 20 ian. 1893; S.C.C., decr. 11 maii 1904; litt. 22 maii 1907; S.C. de Prop. Fide, 15 iul. 1908; S.C. pro Eccl. Orient., 1 feb. 1933, 8; PAULUS VI, m.p. *Firma in traditione,* 13 iun. 1974. * Syn. Diamper. Syro-Malabarensium, a. 1599, CXXXIV; Syn. Zamosten. Ruthenorum, a. 1720, tit. III, §4 "Denique;" Syn. Libanen. Maronitarum, a. 1736, pars II, cap. XIII, 13; Syn. Bekorkien. Maronitarum, a. 1790, s. 11; Syn. prov. Alba-Iulien. et Fagarasien. Rumenorum, a. 1872, tit. V, cap. IV "Quodpiam;" Syn. Sciarfen. Syrorum, a. 1888, cap. V, art. V, §10; Syn. Leopolien. Ruthenorum, a. 1891, tit. IV, cap. II; Syn. Alexandrin. Coptorum, a. 1898, sect. II, cap. III, art. IV, secunda pars, V; Syn. Armen., a. 1911, 445–446.

receive the offerings that the Christian faithful, following a custom approved by the Church, give for celebrating the Divine Liturgy for their intentions.

§2. It is also permitted, if it is thus established by legitimate custom, to receive offerings for the Liturgy of the Pre-Sanctified and for commemorations in the Divine Liturgy.

CAN. 716 Without prejudice to can. 1013, it is earnestly recommended that eparchial bishops introduce, to the extent possible, the practice whereby on the occasion of the Divine Liturgy only those offerings are received that the Christian faithful make of their own accord. Even without any offering, individual priests are to celebrate readily the Divine Liturgy for the intentions of the Christian faithful, especially of the poor.

CAN. 717 If they accept offerings for the Divine Liturgy from the Christian faithful of another Church *sui iuris,* priests are bound by the grave obligation of observing the norms of that Church regarding those offerings, unless it is established otherwise by the donor.

CHAPTER IV. **Sacrament of Penance**

CAN. 718 In the sacrament of penance the Christian faithful who, having committed sins after baptism, led by the Holy Spirit, turn to God in their hearts and, moved by sorrow for

tiones recipere, quas christifideles secundum probatum Ecclesiae morem pro celebratione Divinae Liturgiae ad proprias intentiones ipsis offerunt.

§2. Licet etiam, si ita fert legitima consuetudo, oblationes recipere pro Liturgia Praesanctificatorum et pro commemorationibus in Divina Liturgia.

CAN. 716 Firmo can. 1013 enixe commendatur, ut Episcopi eparchiales, quatenus fieri potest, praxim introducant, secundum quam solum eae oblationes occasione Divinae Liturgiae recipiantur, quas christifideles sua sponte offerunt; singuli vero sacerdotes libenter etiam sine ulla oblatione Divinam Liturgiam ad intentionem christifidelium praecipue egentium celebrent.

CAN. 717 Sacerdotes, si oblationes ad Divinam Liturgiam celebrandam a christifidelibus alterius Ecclesiae sui iuris accipiunt, gravi obligatione tenentur de his oblationibus servandi normas illius Ecclesiae, nisi aliud constat ex parte offerentis.

CAPUT IV. **De Sacramento Paenitentiae**

CAN. 718 In sacramento paenitentiae christifideles, qui, peccatis post baptismum commissis, ad Deum a Spiritu Sancto ducti corde convertuntur et dolore de peccatis

715 §2: Syn. Ain-Trazen. Graeco–Melchitarum, a. 1835, can. 3; Syn. Leopolien. Ruthenorum, a. 1891, tit. IV, cap. II, 3; Syn. prov. Alba-Iulien. et Fagarasien. Rumenorum, a. 1900, tit. III, cap. I, 5.

718: Vat. II, const. *Lumen gentium,* 11 "Qui vero," 28 "Christus;" decr. *Christus Dominus,* 30, 2) "In perficiendo;" decr. *Presbyterorum ordinis,* 5 "Deus." - Quinisext. can. 102; Professio fidei (in Lugd. II) a Michaele Palaeologo Gregorio X oblata, a. 1274; BENEDICTUS XII, a. 1341, prop. 48, 51–52, Armeno-

rum, damn.; EUGENIUS IV (in Flor.), const. *Exsultate Deo,* 22 nov. 1439, §13; Trid., sess. VI, *De iustificatione,* cap. 14, can. 29; sess. VII, *Canones de sacramentis in genere,* can. 1; sess. XIV, *De poenitentia;* S.C. pro Doctr. Fidei, *Normae pastorales,* 16 iun. 1972, initio. * Syn. Diamper. Syro-Malabarensium, a. 1599, CXXXV; Syn. Zamosten. Ruthenorum, a. 1720, tit. III, §5; Syn. Libanen. Maronitarum, a. 1736, pars II, cap. IV, 1–2; Syn. prov. Alba-Iulien. et Fagarasien. Rumenorum, a. 1872, tit. V, cap. V; Syn. Armen., a. 1911, 454–457.

their sins, resolve to lead a new life. Through the ministry of the priest, to whom they make confession and from whom they accept a fitting penance, they obtain forgiveness from God and at the same time are reconciled with the Church, which they have wounded through sin. Thus this sacrament contributes greatly to the fostering of Christian life and disposes the Christian faithful for the reception of the Divine Eucharist.

CAN. 719 Anyone who is aware of serious sin is to receive the sacrament of penance as soon as possible; it is strongly recommended to all the Christian faithful that they receive this sacrament frequently especially during the times of fasts and penance observed in their own Church *sui iuris.*

CAN. 720 §1. Individual and integral confession and absolution constitute the sole ordinary means by which a member of the Christian faithful who is conscious of grave sin is reconciled with God and the Church. Physical or moral impossibility alone excuses from such confession, in which case reconciliation can be effected by other means also.

§2. General absolution without prior individual confession cannot be imparted to several penitents together unless:

1° there is imminent danger of death, and there is no time for the priest or priests to administer the sacrament of penance to the individual penitents;

moti propositum novae vitae ineunt, per ministerium sacerdotis, facta ipsi confessione et dignae satisfactionis acceptatione, veniam a Deo obtinent simulque cum Ecclesia, quam peccando vulneraverunt, reconciliantur; quo modo hoc sacramentum quam maxime ad vitam christianam fovendam confert et ad Divinam Eucharistiam suscipiendam disponit.

CAN. 719 Qui gravis peccati sibi conscius est, quam primum fieri potest, sacramentum paenitentiae suscipiat; omnibus vero christifidelibus enixe commendatur, ut frequenter et praesertim temporibus ieiunii et paenitentiae in propria Ecclesia sui iuris servandis hoc sacramentum suscipiant.

CAN. 720 §1. Individualis et integra confessio atque absolutio solum constituunt modum ordinarium, quo christifidelis peccati gravis sibi conscius cum Deo et Ecclesia reconciliatur; sola impossibilitas physica vel moralis ab huiusmodi confessione excusat, quo in casu aliis quoque modis reconciliatio haberi potest.

§2. Absolutio pluribus simul paenitentibus sine praevia individuali confessione generali modo impertiri non potest, nisi:

1° imminet periculum mortis et tempus non suppetit sacerdoti vel sacerdotibus ad ministrandum sacramentum paenitentiae singulis paenitentibus;

719: TIMOTHEUS ALEXANDRIN., can. 18; INNOCENTIUS III, litt. *Quia divinae,* 4 ian. 1215, "Nam cum olim;" LEO X, const. ap. *Cunctarum,* 1 aug. 1515; S.C. pro Doctr. Fidei, *Normae pastorales,* 16 iun. 1972, VII. * Syn. Diamper. Syro-Malabarensium, a. 1599, CXXXVII; Syn. Zamosten. Ruthenorum, a. 1720, tit. III, §5 "Quia;" Syn. Libanen. Maronitarum, a. 1736, pars II, cap. IV, 8; Syn. Ain-Trazen. Graeco-Melchitarum, a. 1835, can. 4, 5; Syn. Sciarfen. Syrorum, a. 1888, cap. V, art. VI, 5, VII; Syn. Leopolien. Ruthenorum, a. 1891, tit. II, cap. IV, 2; Syn. Alexandrin. Coptorum, a. 1898, sect. II, cap. III, art. IV, prima pars, VI, VI; art. V, 13, VII; Syn. Armen., a. 1911, 472.

720 §1: S.C. pro Doctr. Fidei, *Normae Pastorales,* 16 iun. 1972, I.

720 §2, 1°: S. Paenit. Ap., *Facultates,* 30 aug. 1939, 2–3; S.C. Consist., *Index facultatum,* 8 dec. 1939, 14, b; S. Paenit. Ap., instr. 25 mar. 1944, I; S.C. pro Doctr. Fidei, *Normae Pastorales,* 16 iun. 1972, II.

2° there is a grave necessity, that is, if, considering the number of penitents, there is not a supply of priests present to administer the sacrament of penance to individual penitents within a reasonable time so that, through no fault of their own, they would be forced to forego the sacramental grace or the reception of the Divine Eucharist for a long time. The necessity is not considered sufficient when it is not possible for confessors to be available merely because of a large gathering of penitents such as can happen on some great feast day or pilgrimage.

§3. The eparchial bishop is competent to decide whether such grave necessity exists. He can, after having held consultation with patriarchs and eparchial bishops of other Churches *sui iuris* who exercise their power in the same territory, determine the cases of such necessity even through general prescripts.

CAN. 721 §1. For the Christian faithful to benefit from a general sacramental absolution given to a number of people, they have not only to be properly disposed but at the same time personally be resolved to confess in due time each of the grave sins that they cannot for the moment so confess.

§2. The Christian faithful are to be instructed to the extent that it is possible about these requirements and, furthermore, are to be exhorted even in danger of death to make an act of contrition personally.

CAN. 722 §1. Only a priest is the minister of the sacrament of penance.

2° est gravis necessitas, videlicet si attento paenitentium numero sacerdotum copia praesto non est ad ministrandum singulis paenitentibus sacramentum paenitentiae intra congruum tempus ita, ut sine propria culpa gratia sacramentali aut susceptione Divinae Eucharistiae diu carere cogantur; necessitas vero non censetur sufficiens, cum confessarii praesto esse non possunt ratione solius magni concursus paenitentium, qualis haberi potest in magna aliqua sollemnitate aut peregrinatione.

§3. Decernere, num detur talis gravis necessitas, competit Episcopo eparchiali, qui collatis consiliis cum Patriarchis et Episcopis eparchialibus aliarum Ecclesiarum sui iuris in eodem territorio potestatem suam exercentibus casus talis necessitatis etiam generalibus praescriptis determinare potest.

CAN. 721 §1. Ut christifidelis sacramentali absolutione una simul pluribus data frui possit, requiritur non solum, ut sit rite dispositus, sed etiam ut simul sibi proponat singillatim debito tempore confiteri peccata gravia, quae in praesens ita confiteri non potest.

§2. Christifideles, quatenus fieri potest, de his requisitis edoceantur et praeterea, etiam in casu periculi mortis, exhortentur, ut actum contritionis unusquisque eliciat.

CAN. 722 §1. Sacramentum paenitentiae a solo sacerdote ministratur.

---

720 §2, 2°: S.C. pro Doctr. Fidei, *Normae pastorales*, 16 iun. 1972, III; resp. 20 ian. 1978; S. Paenit. Ap., resp. 10 dec. 1940; instr., 25 mar. 1944, II; IOANNES PAULUS II, all. 30 ian. 1981, "Nel rinnovare."

720 §3: S.C. pro Doctr. Fidei, *Normae Pastorales*, 16 iun. 1972, V.

721 §1: S.C. pro Doctr. Fidei, *Normae pastorales*, 16 iun. 1972, VII; S. Paenit. Ap., *Facultates*, 30 aug. 1939, 2; resp. 10 dec. 1940; instr. 25 mar. 1944, IV.

721 §2: S. Paenit. Ap., instr. 25 mar. 1944, V; S.C. pro Doctr. Fidei, *Normae Pastorales*, 16 iun. 1972, VIII.

722 §1: EUGENIUS IV (in Flor.), const. *Exsultate Deo*, 22 nov. 1439, §13; Trid., sess. VI, *De iustificatione*, cap. 14; sess. XIV, *De poenitentia*, capp. 1–2, 5–7, 9, can. 10; sess. XXIII, *De ordine*, cap. 1; Vat. II, decr. *Presbyterorum ordinis*, 5 "Deus."

§2. All bishops can by virtue of the law itself administer the sacrament of penance anywhere, unless with regard to liceity, the eparchial bishop expressly denies this in a special case.

§3. However, for presbyters to act validly, they must also have the faculty to administer the sacrament of penance; this faculty is conferred either by the law itself or by a special grant made by competent authority.

§4. Presbyters who have the faculty to administer the sacrament of penance by virtue of their office or by virtue of a concession of the local hierarch of the eparchy in which they are ascribed or in which they have domicile, can validly administer the sacrament of penance anywhere to any of the Christian faithful, unless a certain local hierarch in a special case expressly denies it. They use these faculties licitly, observing the norms established by the eparchial bishop and also with at least the presumed permission of the rector of the church or, in the case of a house of an institute of consecrated life, of the superior.

CAN. 723 §1. In virtue of his office and

§2. Episcopi omnes ubique terrarum sacramentum paenitentiae ipso iure ministrare possunt, nisi, ad liceitatem quod spectat, Episcopus eparchialis in casu speciali expresse renuit.

§3. Presbyteri vero ut valide agant, debent praeterea esse praediti facultate sacramentum paenitentiae ministrandi, quae facultas confertur sive ipso iure sive speciali collatione ab auctoritate competenti facta.

§4. Presbyteri, qui facultate sacramentum paenitentiae ministrandi praediti sunt vi officii vel vi collationis Hierarchae loci eparchiae, cui ascripti sunt aut in qua domicilium habent, sacramentum paenitentiae valide ministrare possunt ubique terrarum quibuslibet christifidelibus, nisi quis Hierarcha loci in casu speciali expresse renuit; eadem facultate licite utuntur servatis normis ab Episcopo eparchiali latis necnon de licentia saltem praesumpta rectoris ecclesiae vel, si de domo instituti vitae consecratae agitur, Superioris.

CAN. 723 §1. Vi officii pro sua quisque

722 §2: PAULUS VI, m.p. *Pastorale munus,* 30 nov. 1963, II, 2.

722 §3: EUGENIUS IV (in Flor.), const. *Exsultate Deo,* 22 nov. 1439, §13; Trid., sess. XXIII, *De ref.,* can. 15. - GREGORIUS XV, const. *Inscrutabili,* 5 feb. 1622, §1; BENEDICTUS XIV, const. *Etsi pastoralis,* 26 maii 1742, §V, V–VII; PIUS VI, const. *Auctorem Fidei,* 28 aug. 1794, prop. 37, Synodi Pistorien., damn. * Syn. Diamper. Syro-Malabarensium, a. 1599, CXLV; Syn. Zamosten. Ruthenorum, a. 1720, tit. III, §5 "Qui;" Syn. Libanen. Maronitarum, a. 1736, pars II, cap. IV, 4–7; pars III, cap. III, 1; Syn. Ain-Trazen. Graeco-Melchitarum, a. 1835, can. 4, 2; Syn. prov. Alba-Iulien. et Fagarasien. Rumenorum, a. 1872, tit. V, cap. V "Minister;" Syn. Sciarfen. Syrorum, a. 1888, cap. V, art. VI, 4; Syn. Leopolien. Ruthenorum, a. 1891, tit. II, cap. IV, 4; Syn. Alexandrin. Coptorum, a. 1898, sect. II, cap. III, art. V, 12; Syn. Armen., a. 1911, 463–464.

722 §4: Vat. II, decr. *Orientalium Ecclesiarum,* 16.

- CLEMENS VIII, instr. *Sanctissimus,* 31 aug. 1595, §3; S.C. de Prop. Fide, 1 iun. 1626, n. 6; BENEDICTUS XIV, const. *Etsi pastoralis,* 26 maii 1742, §V, V–VI; S.C.S. Off., 15 maii 1766; S.C. de Prop. Fide, instr. (ad Patr. et Epp. Ritus Graeco-Melchit.), 29 maii 1789, n. 2; instr. (ad Archiep. Aleppen.), 2 iun. 1835; (C.G.), 11 dec. 1838, a); 31 mar. 1843; instr. (ad Del. Ap. Aegypti), 30 apr. 1862, n. 2; decr. 6 oct. 1863, C), b), E), b); S.C. de Prop. Fide (pro Neg. Ritus Orient.), decr. 18 aug. 1913, art. 28; decr. 17 aug. 1914, art. 22; decr. 27 mar. 1916, 9; S.C. pro Eccl. Orient., decr. 1 mar. 1929, art. 31; decr. 24 maii 1930, art. 36. * Syn. Sciarfen. Syrorum, a. 1888, cap. III, art. IX, 14; Syn. Alexandrin. Coptorum, a. 1898, sect. II, cap. I, art. V, 13, VII; Syn. Armen., a. 1911, 625.

723 §1: Trid., sess. XXIII, *De ref.,* can. 15; BENEDICTUS XIV, const. *Etsi pastoralis,* 26 maii 1742, §V, VII. * Syn. Sciarfen. Syrorum, a. 1888, cap. V, art. VI, 5, VIII.

within the limits of his jurisdiction, besides the local hierarch, the pastor too and any other who takes the place of the pastor, has the faculty to administer the sacrament of penance.

§2. In virtue of his office, every superior of a religious institute or of a society of common life in the manner of religious of pontifical or patriarchal right, if he is a priest, has the faculty to administer the sacrament of penance to the members of his own institute and also to those who reside in his house day and night.

CAN. 724 §1. Only the local hierarch is competent to confer on any presbyter by a special concession the faculty of administering the sacrament of penance to any of the Christian faithful.

§2. The superior of an institute of consecrated life, provided he has executive power of governance, can confer the faculty mentioned in can. 723, §2 on any presbyter in accord with the norms of the typicon or statutes.

CAN. 725 Any priest can validly and licitly absolve from any sins any penitents who are in danger of death, even if another priest is present who has the faculty to administer the sacrament of penance.

CAN. 726 §1. The faculty to administer the sacrament of penance may not be revoked except for a grave cause.

§2. If the faculty to administer the sacrament of penance, granted by the hierarch mentioned in can. 722, §4 is revoked, the presbyter loses it everywhere; if it is revoked by another compe-

dicione facultate sacramentum paenitentiae ministrandi praeditus est praeter Hierarcham loci etiam parochus aliusque, qui loco parochi est.

§2. Vi officii facultate sacramentum paenitentiae ministrandi praeditus est etiam omnis Superior instituti religiosi vel societatis vitae communis ad instar religiosorum iuris pontificii vel patriarchalis, si sacerdos est, erga sodales proprii instituti necnon erga illos, qui diu noctuque in eius domo degunt.

CAN. 724 §1. Soli Hierarchae loci competit facultatem sacramentum paenitentiae quibuslibet christifidelibus ministrandi speciali collatione conferre presbyteris quibuscumque.

§2. Superior instituti vitae consecratae, dummodo potestate regiminis exsecutiva praeditus sit, facultatem, de qua in can. 723, §2, conferre potest ad normam typici vel statutorum cuilibet presbytero.

CAN. 725 Omnis sacerdos quoslibet paenitentes in periculo mortis versantes valide et licite absolvere potest a quibusvis peccatis, etsi praesens est alius sacerdos facultate sacramentum paenitentiae ministrandi praeditus.

CAN. 726 §1. Facultas sacramentum paenitentiae ministrandi ne revocetur nisi gravi de causa.

§2. Revocata facultate sacramentum paenitentiae ministrandi collata ab Hierarcha, de quo in can. 722, §4, presbyter eandem amittit ubique terrarum; revocata autem

---

724 §1: Trid., sess. XXII, *De ref.*, can. 15. * Syn. Diamper. Syro-Malabarensium, a. 1599, CXLV; Syn. Zamosten. Ruthenorum, a. 1720, tit. III, §5 "Qui;" Syn. Libanen. Maronitarum, a. 1736, pars III, cap. III, 1; pars IV, cap. II, 8; Syn. Bekorkien. Maronitarum, a. 1790, s. 9; Syn. Ain-Trazen. Graeco-Melchitarum,

a. 1835, can. 4, 2; Syn. Sciarfen. Syrorum, a. 1888, cap. V, art. VI, 5, VIII; Syn. Armen., a. 1911, 760.
725: Neoc. can. 2; Carth. can. 7; Trid., sess. XIV, *De poenitentia,* cap. 7; S.C.S. Off., (C.G.), 28 aug. 1669, ad 4; (Smyrnen.), 30 iun. et 7 iul. 1864, ad 6.

tent authority, the presbyter loses it only within the jurisdiction of the one who revokes it.

§3. Apart from revocation, the faculty mentioned in can. 722, §4 ceases by the loss of office, ascription to an eparchy, or domicile.

CAN. 727 In some cases, in order to provide for the salvation of souls it may be appropriate to restrict the faculty to absolve from sins and reserve it to a determined authority; this, however, cannot be done without the consent of the synod of bishops of the patriarchal Church, or the council of hierarchs, or the Apostolic See.

CAN. 728 §1. Absolution from the following sins is reserved to the Apostolic See:

1° direct violation of the sacramental seal;

2° absolution of an accomplice in a sin against chastity.

§2. It is reserved to the eparchial bishop to absolve from the sin of procuring a completed abortion.

CAN. 729 Any reservation of the absolution from sin lacks all force:

1° if a sick person who cannot leave the house makes a confession, or a spouse confesses in order to celebrate marriage;

2° if, in the prudent judgment of the confessor, the faculty cannot be requested from the competent authority without grave inconvenience to the penitent or without danger of violation of the sacramental seal;

3° outside the territorial boundaries in which the authority who makes the reservation exercises power.

ab alia auctoritate competenti eandem amittit in dicione revocantis tantum.

§3. Praeterquam revocatione facultas sacramentum paenitentiae ministrandi, de qua in can. 722, §4, cessat amissione officii, ascriptionis eparchiae vel domicilii.

CAN. 727 In nonnullis casibus ad salutem animarum providendam opportunum esse potest facultatem a peccatis absolvendi limitare atque determinatae auctoritati reservare; hoc tamen fieri non potest nisi de consensu Synodi Episcoporum Ecclesiae patriarchalis vel Consilii Hierarcharum vel Sedis Apostolicae.

CAN. 728 §1. Sedi Apostolicae reservatur absolvere a sequentibus peccatis:

1° directae violationis sigilli sacramentalis;

2° absolutionis complicis in peccato contra castitatem.

§2. Episcopo eparchiali vero reservatur absolvere a peccato procurationis abortus effectu secuto.

CAN. 729 Quaevis reservatio absolutionis a peccato omni vi caret:

1° si confessionem peragit aegrotus, qui domo egredi non potest, vel sponsus matrimonii celebrandi causa;

2° si de prudenti iudicio confessarii absolvendi facultas ab auctoritate competenti peti non potest sine gravi paenitentis incommodo vel sine periculo violationis sigilli sacramentalis;

3° extra fines territorii, in quo auctoritas reservans potestatem exercet.

727: Trid., sess. XIV, *De poenitentia,* cap. 7, can. 11; Leo XIII, litt. ap. *Orientalium,* 30 nov. 1894, VI; S.C.S. Off., instr. 13 iul. 1916. * Syn. Diamper. Syro-Malabarensium, a. 1599, CXLVI–CXLVII; Syn. Zamosten. Ruthenorum, a. 1720, tit. III, §5 "Denique;" Syn. Libanen. Maronitarum, a. 1736, pars II, cap. V; Syn. Sciarfen. Syrorum, a. 1888, cap. V, art. VII; cap. VII, art. III, 6, 15); Syn. Alexandrin. Coptorum, a. 1898, sect. II, cap. III, art. V, *De peccatis reservatis*; Syn. Armen., a. 1911, 477–481.

CAN. 730 Absolution of an accomplice in a sin against chastity is invalid except in danger of death.

CAN. 731 One who confesses a false denunciation of an innocent confessor to the ecclesiastical authority of the crime of solicitation to sin against chastity is not to be absolved unless that person first retracts formally the denunciation and is prepared to repair damages if there are any.

CAN. 732 §1. The confessor is to offer an appropriate cure for the illness by imposing appropriate works of penance in keeping with the quality, seriousness and number of the sins, and considering the condition of the penitent as well as his or her disposition for conversion.

§2. The priest is to remember that he is placed by God as a minister of divine justice and mercy; as a spiritual father he should also offer appropriate counsel so that the penitent might progress in his or her vocation to sanctity.

CAN. 733 §1. The sacramental seal is inviolable; therefore, the confessor must diligently refrain either by word, sign or any other manner from betraying the penitent for any cause.

§2. The obligation of observing secrecy also

CAN. 730 Absolutio complicis in peccato contra castitatem invalida est praeterquam in periculo mortis.

CAN. 731 Qui confitetur se falso confessarium innocentem apud auctoritatem ecclesiasticam denuntiavisse de delicto sollicitationis ad peccatum contra castitatem, ne absolvatur, nisi antea falsam denuntiationem formaliter retractavit et paratus est damna, si quae habentur, reparare.

CAN. 732 §1. Pro qualitate, gravitate et numero peccatorum, habita ratione paenitentis condicionis necnon eiusdem ad conversionem dispositionis, confessarius convenientem morbo afferat medicinam opportuna opera paenitentiae imponens.

§2. Meminerit sacerdos se divinae iustitiae et misericordiae ministrum a Deo constitutum esse; tamquam pater spiritualis etiam opportuna consilia praebeat, ut quis progredi possit in sua vocatione ad sanctitatem.

CAN. 733 §1. Sacramentale sigillum inviolabile est; quare caveat diligenter confessarius, ne verbo aut signo aut alio quovis modo et quavis de causa prodat aliquatenus paenitentem.

§2. Obligatione secretum servandi

730: BENEDICTUS XIV, const. *Apostolici muneris,* 8 feb. 1745; PIUS IX, const. *Apostolicae Sedis,* 12 oct. 1869, §I, 10. * Syn. Armen., a. 1911, 475.

731: BENEDICTUS XIV, const. *Sacramentum Poenitentiae,* 1 iun. 1741, §3; const. *Etsi pastoralis,* 26 maii 1742, §IX, V; const. *Apostolici muneris,* 8 feb. 1745, §2; S.C. de Prop. Fide, litt. encycl. 6 aug. 1885, 2. * Syn. Armen., a. 1911, 476.

732 §1: Quinisext. can. 102; S. NICEPHORUS CP., cap. 9; EUGENIUS IV (in Flor.), const. *Exsultate Deo,* 22 nov. 1439, §13; Trid., sess. XIV, *De poenitentia,* capp. 3, 5, 8–9, cann. 4, 12–15; BENEDICTUS XIV, const. *Etsi pastoralis,* 26 maii 1742, §V, I; ep. encycl. *Ex quo,* 1 mar. 1756, §48. * Syn. Zamosten. Ruthenorum, a. 1720, tit. III, §5 "Quia;" Syn. Libanen. Maronitarum, a. 1736, pars II, cap. IV, 10; Syn. prov.

Alba-Iulien. et Fagarasien. Rumenorum, a. 1872, tit. V, cap. V, 3; Syn. Alexandrin. Coptorum, a. 1898, sect. II, cap. III, art. V, 13, XI; Syn Armen., a. 1911, 459–461.

732 §2: Apost. can. 52; Quinisext. can. 102; S. NICEPHORUS CP., cap. 9; Trid., sess. XIV, *De poenitentia,* cap. 8.

733 §1: S. NICEPHORUS CP., can. 222; S.C. de Prop. Fide, decr. 13 apr. 1807, XVII. * Syn. Zamosten. Ruthenorum, a. 1720, tit. III, §5 "Si quis;" Syn. Libanen. Maronitarum, a. 1736, pars II, cap. IV, 15; Syn. prov. Alba-Iulien. et Fagarasien. Rumenorum, a. 1872, tit. V, cap. V, 3 "Quum;" Syn. Alexandrin. Coptorum, a. 1898, sect. II, cap. III, art. V, 13, XII; Syn Armen., a. 1911, 470.

733 §2: S.C. de Prop. Fide, (C.G.), 6 sep. 1630.

binds an interpreter if one is present, and also all others to whom knowledge of the sins from confession comes in any way.

CAN. 734 §1. A confessor is absolutely prohibited the use of the knowledge acquired from confession when it might harm the penitent, even if every danger of revelation is excluded.

§2. One who is placed in authority can in no way use for external governance knowledge about sins that he has received in confession at any time.

§3. Directors of institutes of education ordinarily do not administer the sacrament of penance to their students.

CAN. 735 §1. Everyone to whom the care of souls is committed is bound in virtue of this function by a grave obligation to provide for the administration of the sacrament of penance to the Christian faithful committed to him, who opportunely ask for it; these are also to be given the opportunity to make individual confession on days and at times arranged to accommodate them.

§2. In case of urgent necessity, any priest who has the faculty of administering the sacrament of penance, but in danger of death any other priest as well, must administer this sacrament.

CAN. 736 §1. The proper place for the celebration of the sacrament of penance is a church, without prejudice to particular law.

tenentur quoque interpres, si datur, necnon omnes alii, ad quos ex confessione notitia peccatorum quoquo modo pervenit.

CAN. 734 §1. Omnino confessario prohibetur scientiae ex confessione acquisitae usus cum paenitentis gravamine, etiam quovis revelationis periculo excluso.

§2. Qui in auctoritate est constitutus, notitia, quam de peccatis in confessione quovis tempore excepta habet, ad externum regimen nullo modo uti debet.

§3. Moderatores instituti educationis sacramentum paenitentiae suis alumnis ordinarie ne ministrent.

CAN. 735 §1. Omnis, cui cura animarum vi muneris est demandata, gravi tenetur obligatione providendi, ut sacramentum paenitentiae ministretur christifidelibus sibi commissis, qui opportune id petunt, eisdemque occasio praebeatur accedendi ad confessionem individualem diebus ac horis in eorum commodum statutis.

§2. Urgente necessitate omnis sacerdos, qui facultate sacramentum paenitentiae ministrandi praeditus est, in periculo mortis vero etiam quilibet alius sacerdos, hoc sacramentum ministrare debet.

CAN. 736 §1. Locus proprius sacramentum paenitentiae celebrandi est ecclesia salvo iure particulari.

734 §1: S.C.S. Off., decr. 18 nov. 1682; instr. 15 iun. 1915.

734 §2: CLEMENS VIII, decr. *Sanctissimus*, 26 maii 1593, §4.

735 §1: Vat. II, decr. *Christus Dominus*, 30, 2) "In perficiendo;" decr. *Presbyterorum ordinis*, 13 "Ut sacrorum;" S.C. pro Doctr. Fidei, *Normae Pastorales*, 16 iun. 1972, IV, IX, XII. - S. NICEPHORUS CP., can. 9; S.C. de Prop. Fide, reg. (pro Sacerd. Coptis), 15

mar. 1790, V.

736 §1: GREGORIUS XVI, ep. encycl. *Inter gravissimas*, 3 feb. 1832, §7. * Syn. Libanen. Maronitarum, a. 1736, pars II, cap. IV, 10; Syn. Ain-Trazen. Graeco-Melchitarum, a. 1835, can. 4, 1; Syn. Leopolien. Ruthenorum, a. 1891, tit. II, cap. IV, 5; Syn. Sciarfen. Syrorum, a. 1888, cap. V, art. VI, 5, IV; Syn. Alexandrin. Coptorum, a. 1898, sect. II, cap. III, art. V, 13, IV; Syn. Armen., a. 1911, 465.

§2. Because of sickness or another just cause, this sacrament can be celebrated also outside its proper place.

CHAPTER V. **Anointing of the Sick**

CAN. 737 §1. By the sacramental anointing of the sick performed with prayer by a priest, the Christian faithful who are gravely ill and sincerely contrite receive grace, by which, strengthened by the hope of eternal reward and freed from sins, they are disposed to amend their life and are helped to overcome their sickness or to suffer it patiently.

§2. In those Churches in which there is the custom for several priests together to administer the sacrament of the anointing of the sick, care should be taken to preserve this custom as much as possible.

CAN. 738 The Christian faithful are to receive the anointing of the sick gladly whenever they are gravely ill; pastors of souls and the relatives of the sick are to see to it that the sick find relief in this sacrament at an opportune time.

§2. Ob infirmitatem vel alia iusta de causa hoc sacramentum celebrari potest etiam extra locum proprium.

CAPUT V. **De Unctione Infirmorum**

CAN. 737 §1. Sacramentali unctione infirmorum a sacerdote cum oratione peracta christifideles morbo gravi affecti cordeque contriti gratiam percipiunt, qua spe aeterni praemii roborati et a peccatis soluti ad emendationem vitae disponuntur et ad infirmitatem superandam patienterve sufferendam adiuvantur.

§2. In Ecclesiis, in quibus mos est, ut sacramentum unctionis infirmorum a pluribus sacerdotibus simul ministretur, curandum est, ut, quatenus fieri potest, hic mos servetur.

CAN. 738 Christifideles unctionem infirmorum libenter suscipiant, quandocumque graviter aegrotant; curent autem pastores animarum et infirmorum propinqui, ut tempore opportuno hoc sacramento infirmi subleventur.

---

736 §2: S.C. de Prop. Fide, decr. 13 apr. 1807, XIII; decr. 22 sep. 1838, "Denique;" decr. 18 feb. 1851. * Syn. Sciarfen. Syrorum, a. 1888, cap. V, art. VI, 5, V–VI; Syn. Alexandrin. Coptorum, a. 1898, sect. II, cap. III, art. V, 13, VI; Syn. Armen., a. 1911, 466.

736 §1: Professio fidei (in Lugd. II) a Michaele Palaeologo Gregorio X oblata, a. 1274; EUGENIUS IV (in Flor.), const. *Exsultate Deo,* 22 nov. 1439, §14; Trid., sess. XIV, *De extrema unctione,* cap. 1, cann. 1–3; BENEDICTUS XIV, const. *Etsi pastoralis,* 26 maii 1742, §V, II–III; ep. encycl. *Ex quo,* 1 mar. 1756, §§44–48; Vat. II, const. *Sacrosanctum Concilium,* 73; const. *Lumen gentium,* 5 "Qui vero;" decr. *Presbyterorum ordinis,* 5 "Deus;" PAULUS VI, const. ap. *Sacram unctionem infirmorum,* 30 nov. 1972. * Syn. Diamper. Syro-Malabarensium, a. 1599, CLIII–CLIV; Syn. Zamosten. Ruthenorum, a. 1720, tit. III, §6 "Sacra;" Syn. Libanen. Maronitarum, a. 1736, pars II, cap. VIII, 1; Syn. Ain-Trazen. Graeco-Melchitarum, a. 1835, can. 5; Syn. prov. Alba-Iulien. et Fagarasien.

Rumenorum, a. 1872, tit. V, cap. VI "Extrema;" Syn. Sciarfen. Syrorum, a. 1888, cap. V, art. VIII, 1–2; Syn. Leopolien. Ruthenorum, a. 1891, tit. II, cap. V; Syn. Alexandrin. Coptorum, a. 1898, sect. II, cap. III, art. VI, 1–2; Syn. Armen., a. 1911, 493–494.

737 §2: * Syn. Zamosten. Ruthenorum, a. 1720, tit. III, §6 "Quamquam;" Syn. Libanen. Maronitarum, a. 1736, pars II, cap. VIII, 8; Syn. Ain-Trazen. Graeco-Melchitarum, a. 1835, can. 5, 2; Syn. prov. Alba-Iulien. et Fagarasien. Rumenorum, a. 1872, tit. V, cap. VI "Quod;" Syn. Sciarfen. Syrorum, a. 1888, cap. V, art. VIII, 3; Syn. Alexandrin. Coptorum, a. 1898, sect. II, cap. III, art. VI, 7, I; Syn. Armen., a. 1911, 500.

738: INNOCENTIUS IV, ep. *Sub catholicae,* 6 mar. 1254, §3, 6; EUGENIUS IV (in Flor.), const. *Exsultate Deo,* 22 nov. 1439, §14; Trid., sess. XIV, *De extrema unctione,* capp. 1–3; BENEDICTUS XIV, const. *Etsi pastoralis,* 26 maii 1742, §V, II; ep. encycl. *Ex quo,* 1 mar. 1756, §§46–47; S.C. de Prop. Fide, instr. 31 iul. 1902, 7.

CAN. 739 §1. All priests, and only priests, validly administer the anointing of the sick.

§2. The administration of the anointing of the sick belongs to the pastor, the parochial vicar and to all other priests as regards those committed to their care in virtue of their office. Any priest, however, can, and in case of necessity even must, licitly administer this sacrament with at least the presumed permission of those mentioned.

CAN. 740 The Christian faithful who are gravely ill and are unconscious or have lost the use of reason, are presumed to want to have this sacrament administered to them in danger of death, or even at another time according to the discretion of the priest.

CAN. 741 The oil for use in the sacrament of the anointing the sick is to be blessed, and, indeed, unless the particular law of his Church *sui iuris* warrants otherwise, by the priest who administers the sacrament himself.

CAN. 742 The anointings are to be carefully performed in the words, order and manner prescribed in the liturgical books; in case of necessity, however, a single anointing with the proper formula is sufficient.

CAN. 739 §1. Unctionem infirmorum valide ministrant omnes et soli sacerdotes.

§2. Unctionem infirmorum ministrare pertinet ad parochum, vicarium paroecialem atque omnes alios sacerdotes circa illos, quorum cura eis ex officio commissa est; de licentia saltem praesumpta praedictorum quilibet sacerdos hoc sacramentum licite ministrare potest, in casu necessitatis vero etiam debet.

CAN. 740 Christifideles graviter aegrotantes, qui sensus vel usum rationis amiserunt, praesumuntur velle sibi hoc sacramentum ministrari in periculo mortis vel etiam ad iudicium sacerdotis alio tempore.

CAN. 741 Oleum in sacramento unctionis infirmorum adhibendum debet esse benedictum et quidem, nisi aliud fert ius particulare propriae Ecclesiae sui iuris, ab ipso sacerdote, qui sacramentum ministrat.

CAN. 742 Unctiones verbis, ordine et modo praescriptis in libris liturgicis accurate peragantur; in casu tamen necessitatis sufficit una unctio cum propria formula.

---

739 §1: EUGENIUS IV (in Flor.), const. *Exsultate Deo,* 22 nov. 1439, §14; Trid., sess. XIV, *De extrema unctione,* capp. 1–3, can. 4; BENEDICTUS XIV, const. *Etsi pastoralis,* 26 maii 1742, §V, III; ep. encycl. *Ex quo,* 1 mar. 1756, §§45–46. * Syn. Zamosten. Ruthenorum, a. 1720, tit. III, §6 "Porro;" Syn. Libanen. Maronitarum, a. 1736, pars II, cap. VIII, 7; Syn. Alexandrin. Coptorum, a. 1898, sect. II, cap. III, art. VI, 7; Syn. Armen., a. 1911, 495, 499.

739 §2: S.C. de Prop. Fide, litt. 11 oct. 1780; decr. 6 oct. 1863, C), d). * Syn. Libanen. Maronitarum, a. 1736, pars II, cap. VIII, 7; pars III, cap. III, 2, X; Syn Armen., a. 1911, 502–503.

741: EUGENIUS IV (in Flor.), const. *Exsultate Deo,* 22 nov. 1439, §14; CLEMENS VIII, instr. *Sanctissimus,* 31 aug. 1595, §3; BENEDICTUS XIV, ep. encycl. *Ex quo,* 1 mar. 1756, §§46–47. * Syn. Duinen. Armenorum, a. 719, can. 11; Syn. Diamper. Syro-Malabarensium, a. 1599, CLIV–CLVI; Syn. Zamosten. Ruthenorum, a. 1720, tit. III, §6 "Eius;" Syn. Libanen. Maronitarum,

a. 1736, pars II, cap. VIII, 2–4; Syn. Ain-Trazen. Graeco-Melchitarum, a. 1835, can. 5, 2 et 4; Syn. prov. Alba-Iulien. et Fagarasien. Rumenorum, a. 1872, tit. V, cap. VI "Materia;" Syn. Sciarfen. Syrorum, a. 1888, cap. V, art. VIII, 5, I; Syn. Leopolien. Ruthenorum, a. 1891, tit. II, cap. V, 4; Syn. Alexandrin. Coptorum, a. 1898, sect. II, cap. III, art. VI, 4; Syn. Armen., a. 1911, 496.

742: EUGENIUS IV (in Flor.), const. *Exsultate Deo,* 22 nov. 1439, §14; Trid., sess. XIV, *De extrema unctione,* cap. 1. * Syn. Diamper. Syro-Malabarensium, a. 1599, CLIV; Syn. Zamosten. Ruthenorum, a. 1720, tit. III, §6 "Porro;" Syn. Libanen. Maronitarum, a. 1736, pars II, cap. VIII, 5–6; Syn. prov. Alba-Iulien. et Fagarasien. Rumenorum, a. 1872, tit. V, cap. VII "Forma;" Syn. Sciarfen. Syrorum, a. 1888, cap. V, art. VIII, 3; Syn. Leopolien. Ruthenorum, a. 1891, tit. II, cap. V, 3; Syn. Alexandrin. Coptorum, a. 1898, sect. II, cap. III, art. VI, 7, II–III; Syn Armen., a. 1911, 497–498.

CHAPTER VI. Sacred Ordination

CAN. 743 Through sacramental ordination performed by the bishop, sacred ministers are constituted by the working of the power of the Holy Spirit; they are endowed with and share in varying degrees in the task and power entrusted by Christ the Lord to his apostles to announce the gospel, to shepherd and sanctify the people of God.

ART. I. *The Minister of Sacred Ordination*

CAN. 744 Only a bishop validly administers sacred ordination by the imposition of hands and by the prayers prescribed by the Church.

CAN. 745 Episcopal ordination is reserved in accord with the norm of law to the Roman Pontiff, patriarch or metropolitan, so that no other bishop is permitted to ordain anyone a bishop unless it is previously established that there is a legitimate mandate.

CAN. 746 §1. A bishop should be ordained by three bishops, except in case of extreme necessity.

§2. If bishops of the same Church *sui iuris* as the first ordaining bishop cannot be present, the second and the third bishop can be of another Church *sui iuris*.

CAPUT VI. De Sacra Ordinatione

CAN. 743 Per sacramentalem ordinationem ab Episcopo peractam Spiritus Sancti operante virtute ministri sacri constituuntur, qui munere et potestate a Christo Domino Apostolis suis concreditis adaugentur et in variis gradibus fruuntur Evangelium annuntiandi, populum Dei pascendi et sanctificandi.

ART. I. De Sacre Ordinationis Ministro

CAN. 744 Solus Episcopus sacram ordinationem valide ministrat manuum impositione et oratione ab Ecclesia praescripta.

CAN. 745 Ordinatio episcopalis reservatur ad normam iuris Romano Pontifici, Patriarchae vel Metropolitae ita, ut nulli Episcopo liceat quemquam ordinare Episcopum, nisi antea constat de legitimo mandato.

CAN. 746 §1. Episcopus ordinetur ab Episcopis tribus excepto casu extremae necessitatis.

§2. Episcopus secundus et tertius, si adesse non possunt Episcopi eiusdem Ecclesiae sui iuris ac primus Episcopus ordinans, possunt esse alterius Ecclesiae sui iuris.

743: Trid., sess. XXIII, *De ordine*; Vat. II, const. *Lumen gentium*, 10 "Sacerdotium," 11 "Qui vero," 20 "Missio;" decr. *Presbyterorum ordinis*, 2 "Idem," 5 "Deus," 12.

744: Apost. can. 2; Anc. can. 13; Ant. cann. 9–10; Chalc. cann. 25, 28; S. BASILIUS M., can. 1 "Οἱ δὲ κααῦροὶ;" EUGENIUS IV (in Flor.), const. *Exsultate Deo*, 22 nov. 1439, §15; Trid., sess. XXIII, *De ordine*, cap. 4, can. 7; Vat. II, const. *Lumen gentium*, 21 "Ad tanta," 28 "Christus;" decr. *Presbyterorum ordinis*, 5 "Deus." * Syn. Diamper. Syro-Malabarensium, a. 1599, CLVII; Syn. Zamosten. Ruthenorum, a. 1720, tit. III, §7 "Porro;" Syn. Libanen. Maronitarum, a. 1736, pars II, cap. XIV, 6; Syn. prov. Alba-Iulien. et

Fagarasien. Rumenorum, a. 1872, tit. V, cap. VII "Minister;" Syn. Sciarfen. Syrorum, a. 1888, cap. V, art. XIII, §1, II; Syn. Alexandrin. Coptorum, a. 1898, cap. III, art. VII, §1, 8 "In collatione."

745: PIUS XII, m.p. *Cleri sanctitati*, 2 iun. 1957, cann. 242, 256 §1 n. 1, 319 n. 1, 320 §1 n. 4, 326 §1 n. 2; Vat. II, decr. *Christus Dominus*, 20; PAULUS VI, m.p. *Ecclesiae Sanctae*, 6 aug. 1966, I, 10.

746 §1: Apost. can. 1; Carth. cann. 13, 49; Constantinop., a. 394, can. 1 "Nectarius;" S.C.S. Off., 13 mar. 1669, 2; S.C. de Prop. Fide, 18 aug. 1845, dub. 7. * Syn. Mar Isaaci Chaldaeorum, a. 410, cann. 1, 11.

746 §2: PAULUS V, litt. ap. *In supremo*, 10 dec. 1615.

CAN. 747 A candidate to the diaconate or presbyterate should be ordained by his own eparchial bishop or by another bishop with legitimate dimissorial letters.

CAN. 748 §1. The proper eparchial bishop in the matter of the sacred ordination of one who is to be ascribed to a certain eparchy, is the bishop of the eparchy in which the candidate has domicile, or of the eparchy for whose service the candidate has declared in writing that he wishes to devote himself; in the matter of the sacred ordination of one who is already ascribed to an eparchy, it is the bishop of that eparchy.

§2. An eparchial bishop cannot ordain a candidate subject to him who is ascribed to another Church *sui iuris* without the permission of the Apostolic See; if, however, it is a case of a candidate who is ascribed to a patriarchal Church and has a domicile or quasi-domicile within the territorial boundaries of the same Church, the patriarch can also grant this permission.

CAN. 749 A bishop is prohibited from celebrating sacred ordination in another eparchy without the permission of the eparchial bishop, unless the particular law of a patriarchal Church, with regard to the patriarch, establishes otherwise.

CAN. 747 Candidatus ad diaconatum vel presbyteratum a proprio Episcopo eparchiali ordinetur aut ab alio Episcopo cum legitimis litteris dimissoriis.

CAN. 748 §1. Episcopus eparchialis proprius, quod attinet ad sacram ordinationem eius, qui alicui eparchiae ascribatur, est Episcopus eparchiae, in qua candidatus habet domicilium, aut eparchiae, pro cuius servitio candidatus se devovere velle scripto declaravit; quod attinet ad sacram ordinationem eius, qui alicui eparchiae iam est ascriptus, est Episcopus illius eparchiae.

§2. Candidatum sibi subditum alii Ecclesiae sui iuris ascriptum Episcopus eparchialis ordinare non potest nisi de licentia Sedis Apostolicae; si vero de candidato agitur, qui Ecclesiae patriarchali ascriptus est et intra fines territorii eiusdem Ecclesiae domicilium vel quasi-domicilium habet, hanc licentiam etiam Patriarcha concedere potest.

CAN. 749 In aliena eparchia Episcopus prohibetur sacram ordinationem celebrare sine licentia Episcopi eparchialis, nisi ius particulare Ecclesiae patriarchalis, ad Patriarcham quod attinet, aliud statuit.

747: Nic. I, can. 16; Anc. can. 13; Ant. cann. 9–10; Sard. cann. 14*, 15; Carth. can. 54; S. BASILIUS M., can. 89; INNOCENTIUS III, litt. *Ad translationem,* a. 1200; CLEMENS VIII, instr. *Sanctissimus,* 31 aug. 1595, §4; BENEDICTUS XIV, const. *Etsi pastoralis,* 26 maii 1742, §VII, VIII–IX. * Syn. Zamosten. Ruthenorum, a. 1720, tit. III, §7 "In propria;" Syn. Libanen. Maronitarum, a. 1736, pars II, cap. XIV, 8; pars III, cap. IV, 24; Syn. Sciarfen. Syrorum, a. 1888, cap. V, art. XIII, §3, 3; Syn. Alexandrin. Coptorum, a. 1898, sect. II, cap. III, art. VII, §4, XIII; Syn. Armen., a. 1911, 530–531, 541–542.

748 §1: * Syn. Zamosten. Ruthenorum, a. 1720, tit. III, §7 "In propria;" Syn. Libanen. Maronitarum, a. 1736, pars II, cap. XIV, 9; pars III, cap. IV, 24; pars IV, cap. II, 8; Syn. Sciarfen. Syrorum, a. 1888, cap. V, art. XIII, §3, 3; Syn. Alexandrin. Coptorum, a. 1898,

sect. II, cap. III, art. VII, §4, XV; Syn. Armen., a. 1911, 541.

748 §2: Ant. can. 9; COELESTINUS III, litt. *Cum secundum,* a. 1191/8; LEO X, litt. ap. *Accepimus nuper,* 18 maii 1521; PAULUS III, litt. ap. *Dudum,* 23 dec. 1534; CLEMENS VIII, instr. *Sanctissimus,* 31 aug. 1595, §7; BENEDICTUS XIV, const. *Etsi pastoralis,* 26 maii 1742, §VII, I, XVI, XX, XXIV et §IX, XIII. * Syn. Libanen. Maronitarum, a. 1736, pars II, cap. XIV, 33, 50; Syn. Armen., a. 1911, 531.

749: Apost. can. 35; Ant. cann. 13, 22; Constantinop. I, can. 2; S.C.C., 17 aug. 1641, ad 1. * Syn. Zamosten. Ruthenorum, a. 1720, tit. III, §7 "Porro;" Syn. Libanen. Maronitarum, a. 1736, pars II, cap. XIV, 7; Syn. Sciarfen. Syrorum, a. 1888, cap. V, art. XIII, §3, 3; Syn. Alexandrin. Coptorum, a. 1898, sect. II, cap. III, art. VII, §4, XI, XIII.

CAN. 750 §1. With due regard for cann. 472, 537, and 560, § 1, the following can grant dimissorial letters:

1° one's own eparchial bishop;

2° the administrator of a patriarchal Church and also, with the consent of college of eparchial consultors, the administrator of an eparchy.

§2. The administrator of a patriarchal Church is not to grant dimissorial letters to those who were rejected by the patriarch, nor the administrator of eparchy to those who were rejected by the eparchial bishop.

CAN. 751 Dimissorial letters are not to be granted unless all the testimonials required by law have been obtained.

CAN. 752 Dimissorial letters can be sent from the proper eparchial bishop to any bishop of the same Church *sui iuris;* not, however, to a bishop of a church different than that of the candidate, without the permission of those mentioned in can. 748, §2.

CAN. 753 Dimissorial letters can be limited by restrictions or revoked by the one who granted them or by his successor, but once they have been granted, they do not cease to be operative when the authority of the one granting them ceases.

ART. II. *The Subject of Sacred Ordination*

CAN. 754 Only a baptized man is able to receive sacred ordination validly.

CAN. 755 The eparchial bishop and the major superior can only for a very grave cause,

CAN. 750 §1. Litteras dimissorias firmis cann. 472, 537 et 560, §1 dare possunt:

1° Episcopus eparchialis proprius;

2° Administrator Ecclesiae patriarchalis atque de consensu collegii consultorum eparchialium Administrator eparchiae.

§2. Administrator Ecclesiae patriarchalis litteras dimissorias ne concedat eis, qui a Patriarcha reiecti sunt, nec Administrator eparchiae eis, qui ab Episcopo eparchiali reiecti sunt.

CAN. 751 Litterae dimissoriae ne concedantur nisi habitis antea omnibus testimoniis, quae iure exiguntur.

CAN. 752 Litterae dimissoriae mitti possunt ab Episcopo eparchiali proprio ad quemlibet eiusdem Ecclesiae sui iuris Episcopum, non autem ad Episcopum alterius Ecclesiae ac ordinandus, nisi de licentia eorum, de quibus in can. 748, §2.

CAN. 753 Litterae dimissoriae ab ipso concedente aut ab eius successore limitibus circumscribi aut revocari possunt, sed semel concessae non exstinguuntur resoluto iure concedentis.

ART. II. *De Sacrae Ordinationis Subiecto*

CAN. 754 Sacram ordinationem valide suscipere potest solus vir baptizatus.

CAN. 755 Episcopus eparchialis et Superior maior nonnisi gravissima de causa,

750 §1, 2°: * Syn. Alexandrin. Coptorum, a. 1898, sect. III, cap. II, art. III, 2.

752: CLEMENS VIII, instr. *Sanctissimus,* 31 aug. 1595, §7; BENEDICTUS XIV, const. *Etsi pastoralis,* 26 maii 1742, §VII, I, XVII, XXII–XXV et §IX, XIII. * Syn. Alexandrin. Coptorum, a. 1898, sect. II, cap. III, art. VII, §4, XII–XIII; Syn. Armen., a. 1911, 531.

754: Nic. I, can. 19; S. LEO M., litt. *Omnis admonitio,* 12 ian. 444; Vat. II, decr. *Presbyterorum ordinis,* 2 "Officium;" S.C. pro Doctr. Fidei, decl. 15 oct. 1976; IOANNES PAULUS II, ep. ap. *Mulieris dignitatem,* 15 aug. 1988, 26. * Syn. Ain-Trazen. Graeco-Melchitarum, a. 1835, can. 6.

even if it is an occult one, forbid a deacon who is subject to him and who is destined for the presbyterate from being advanced to the presbyterate, with due regard for recourse in accord with the norm of law.

CAN. 756 It is not permitted to compel anyone in any way for any reason whatever to receive sacred orders or to turn away from receiving orders anyone who is suitable in accord with the norm of law.

CAN. 757 He who refuses to receive a higher sacred order cannot be forbidden the exercise of the sacred order he has received unless he is hindered by a canonical impediment or there is some other serious obstacle in the judgment of the eparchial bishop or the major superior.

1° Requirements for Candidates for Sacred Ordination

CAN. 758 §1. For a person to be ordained licitly the following are required:

1° reception of chrismation with holy myron;

2° conduct and physical and psychic qualities consistent with the reception of the sacred order;

3° the age prescribed by law;

4° due knowledge;

etsi occulta, diacono sibi subdito ad presbyteratum destinato ascensum ad ipsum presbyteratum prohibere possunt salvo iure recursus ad normam iuris.

CAN. 756 Non licet aliquem quovis modo qualibet de causa ad ordines sacros suscipiendos cogere vel ad normam iuris idoneum ab eisdem suscipiendis avertere.

CAN. 757 Is, qui superiorem ordinem sacrum suscipere recusat, non potest prohiberi a suscepti ordinis sacri exercitio, nisi impedimento canonico detinetur aliave gravis de iudicio Episcopi eparchialis vel Superioris maioris obest causa.

1° De Requisitis in Candidatis ad Sacram Ordinationem

CAN. 758 §1. Ut quis licite ordinari possit, requiruntur:

1° chrismationis sancti myri susceptio;

2° mores atque qualitates physicae et psychicae ordini sacro suscipiendo congruentes;

3° aetas iure praescripta;

4° debita scientia;

756: BENEDICTUS XIV, instr. *Eo quamvis tempore,* 4 maii 1745, §21; ep. encycl. *Anno vertente,* 19 iun. 1750, §7; S.C. de Prop. Fide, (C.P.), 29 apr. 1754, "Frater;" PIUS XII, m.p. *Cleri sanctitati,* 2 iun. 1957, can. 158; Vat. II, decr. *Optatam totius,* 6.

758 §1: CLEMENS VIII, instr. *Sanctissimus,* 31 aug. 1595, §4; S.C.S. Off., (Ierosolym.), 14 ian. 1885. * Syn. Diamper. Syro-Malabarensium, a. 1599, CLIX; Syn. Zamosten. Ruthenorum, a. 1720, tit. III, §7 "Si vero;" Syn. Libanen. Maronitarum, a. 1736, pars II, cap. XIV, 27–29; Syn. Ain-Trazen. Graeco-Melchitarum, a. 1835, can. 6; Syn. prov. Alba-Iulien. et Fagarasien. Rumenorum, a. 1872, tit. V, cap. VII, I; Syn. Sciarfen. Syrorum, a. 1888, cap. V, art. XIII, §2; Syn. Alexandrin. Coptorum, a. 1898, sect. II, cap. III, art. VII, §2;

Syn. Armen., a. 1911, 525–529.

758 §1, 2°: Apost. can. 78; Nic. I, cann. 2, 9, 19; Carth. can. 57; S. BASILIUS M., can. 69; S. TARASIUS CP., ep. ad Epp. Siciliae; S. NICEPHORUS CP., cann. 21, 92.

758 §1, 4°: * S. NERSES GLAIEN., Armenorum, ep. past., a. 1166, cap. V "Nemo e vobis propter;" Syn. Diamper. Syro-Malabarensium, a. 1599, CLXXXII; Syn. Zamosten. Ruthenorum, a. 1720, tit. III, §7 "Post;" Syn. Libanen. Maronitarum, a. 1736, pars II, cap. XIV, 30; Syn. prov. Alba-Iulien. et Fagarasien. Rumenorum, a. 1872, tit. V, cap. VII, I, a); Syn. Sciarfen. Syrorum, a. 1888, cap. V, art. XIII, §2, 4; Syn. Alexandrin. Coptorum, a. 1898, sect. II, cap. III, art. VII, §2, III; Syn. Armen., a. 1911, 525.

5° reception of lower orders in accord with the norm of the particular law of each Church *sui iuris;*

6° observance of the interstices prescribed by particular law.

§2. It is furthermore required that the candidate not be impeded in accord with the norm of can. 762.

§3. The particular law of each Church *sui iuris* or special norms established by the Apostolic See are to be followed in admitting married men to sacred orders.

CAN. 759 §1. The age prescribed for the diaconate is twenty-three years completed, for the presbyterate twenty-four years completed, with due regard for particular law of a Church *sui iuris* requiring a higher age.

§2. Dispensation beyond a year from the age required by common law is reserved to the patriarch in the case of a candidate who has a domicile or quasi-domicile within the territorial boundaries of the patriarchal Church; otherwise, to the Apostolic See.

CAN. 760 §1. It is permissible to ordain a deacon only after he has successfully completed the fourth year of a curriculum of philo-

5° ordinum inferiorum susceptio ad normam iuris particularis propriae Ecclesiae sui iuris;

6° interstitiorum iure particulari praescriptorum observatio.

§2. Requiritur praeterea, ne candidatus impeditus sit ad normam can. 762.

§3. Circa coniugatos ad ordines sacros admittendos servetur ius particulare propriae Ecclesiae sui iuris vel normae speciales a Sede Apostolica statutae.

CAN. 759 §1. Aetas praescripta ad diaconatum est vicesimus tertius annus expletus, ad presbyteratum vicesimus quartus expletus firmo iure particulari propriae Ecclesiae sui iuris provectiorem aetatem exigente.

§2. Dispensatio ultra annum ab aetate iure communi praescripta reservatur Patriarchae, si de candidato agitur, qui domicilium vel quasi-domicilium intra fines territorii Ecclesiae patriarchalis habet; secus Sedi Apostolicae.

CAN. 760 §1. Diaconum ordinare licet tantum post feliciter expletum quartum curriculi studiorum philosophico-theologicorum

758 §1, 5°: Protodeut. can. 17; Constantinop. IV, can. 5.

758 §3: Pius XII, m.p. *Cleri sanctitati,* 2 iun. 1957, can. 71. - Apost. can. 5; Carth. can. 4; Quinisext. cann. 3, 6, 13, 30; S. Cyrillus Alexandrin., can. 4, (a); S. Nicephorus CP., can. 156; Innocentius III, litt. *Cum olim,* 5 sep. 1203; Benedictus XIV, ep. encycl. *Allatae sunt,* 26 iul. 1755, §22; S.C. de Prop. Fide, litt. 4 iul. 1833, IX; litt. encycl. 1 oct. 1890; litt. 12 apr. 1894; decr. 1 maii 1897; Pius X, litt. ap. *Ea semper,* 14 iun. 1907, artt. X–XII; S.C. de Prop. Fide, decr. 18 aug. 1913, artt. 10–11; S.C. pro Eccl. Orient., decr. 1 mar. 1929, art. 12; decr. 23 dec. 1929, 6; decr. 24 maii 1930, art. 15; Pius XI, litt. encycl. *Ad Catholici Sacerdotii,* 20 dec. 1935, II "Praeclarissimum;" Paulus VI, litt. ap. *Episcopalis potestatis,* 2 maii 1967, VIII, 1–2. * Syn. Iosephi Patriarchae Maronitarum, 3 nov. 1596, can. II; Syn. Diamper. Syro-Malabarensium, a. 1599, CLXXIV–CLXVI; Syn. Libanen. Maronitarum, a.

1736, pars II, cap. XIV, 35; Syn. Monast. SS. Salvatoris, Melchitarum, a. 1811, pars II, cap. I, reg. VI; pars III, cap. I, regg. III–IV, VI; Syn. prov. Alba-Iulien. et Fagarasien. Rumenorum, a. 1872, tit. VII, cap. IV; Syn. Sciarfen. Syrorum, a. 1888, cap. V, art. XIII, §5, 3; cap. VI, art. VII; Syn. Alexandrin. Coptorum, a. 1898, sect. II, cap. III, art. VII, §5, I, III–IV; Syn. Armen., a. 1911, 737.

759 §1: Neoc. can. 11; Carth. can. 16; Quinisext. can. 14; S. Nicephorus CP., can. 21; Benedictus XIV, const. *Etsi pastoralis,* 26 maii 1742, §VII, XIX; instr. *Eo quamvis tempore,* 4 maii 1745, §§18–23. * Syn. Mar Isaaci Chaldaeorum, a. 410, can. 16; Syn. Diamper. Syro-Malabarensium, a. 1599, CLIX; Syn. Zamosten. Ruthenorum, a. 1720, tit. III, §7 "Cum;" Syn. Libanen. Maronitarum, a. 1736, pars II, cap. XIV, 26; Syn Armen., a. 1911, 526–527.

760 §1: Vat. II, decr. *Optatam totius,* 12. * Syn. Armen., a. 1911, 525.

sophical-theological studies, unless the synod of bishops of the patriarchal Church or the council of hierarchs determines otherwise.

§2. In the case of a candidate who is not destined for the priesthood, it is permissible to ordain him a deacon only after he has successfully completed the third year of studies mentioned in can. 354; but if it happens that he is later admitted to the priesthood, he must first complete his theological studies in the appropriate manner.

CAN. 761 For a candidate for the order of diaconate or presbyterate to be licitly ordained, he must submit to his own eparchial bishop or major superior a declaration signed in his own hand, in which he attests that he will, of his own accord and freely, receive the sacred order and accept the obligations attached to it and that he will devote himself perpetually to the ecclesiastical ministry, requesting at the same time to be admitted to receive the sacred order.

2° Impediments from Receiving or Exercising Sacred Orders

CAN. 762 §1. The following are impeded from receiving sacred orders:

1° a person who labors under some form of insanity or other psychic illness because of which, after consultation with experts, he is judged incapable of rightly carrying out the ministry;

2° a person who has committed the delict of apostasy, heresy or schism;

annum, nisi Synodus Episcoporum Ecclesiae patriarchalis vel Consilium Hierarcharum aliud statuit.

§2. Si vero de candidato ad sacerdotium non destinato agitur, eum diaconum ordinare licet tantum post feliciter expletum tertium annum studiorum, de quibus in can. 354; si vero forte in posterum ad sacerdotium admittitur, antea studia theologica opportune complere debet.

CAN. 761 Candidatus ad ordinem diaconatus vel presbyteratus, ut licite ordinetur, Episcopo eparchiali proprio aut Superiori maiori declarationem tradere debet manu propria subscriptam, qua testificatur se sua sponte ac libere ordinem sacrum et obligationes eidem ordini adnexas suscepturum atque se ministerio ecclesiastico perpetuo mancipaturum esse, simul petens, ut ad ordinem sacrum suscipiendum admittatur.

2° De Impedimentis Suscipiendi vel Exercendi Ordines Sacros

CAN. 762 §1. A suscipiendis ordinibus sacris est impeditus:

1° qui aliqua forma laborat amentiae aliusve infirmitatis psychicae, qua consultis peritis inhabilis iudicatur ad ministerium rite implendum;

2° qui delictum apostasiae, haereseos aut schismatis commisit;

---

760 §2: S. Leo M., litt. *Omnium quidem,* 13 ian. 444; * Syn. Mar Isaaci Chaldaeorum, a. 410, can. 16; Syn. Zamosten. Ruthenorum, a. 1720, tit. III, §7 "Cum;" Syn. Armen., a. 1911, 263.

762 §1: * Syn. Zamosten. Ruthenorum, a. 1720, tit. III, §7 "Noverint;" Syn. Libanen. Maronitarum, a. 1736, pars II, cap. VI, 6–7; cap. XIV, 6, 19; Syn. prov. Alba-Iulien. et Fagarasien. Rumenorum, a. 1872, tit.

V, cap. VII, I–II; Syn. Sciarfen. Syrorum, a. 1888, cap. V, art. XIV; Syn. Alexandrin. Coptorum, a. 1898, sect. II, cap. III, art. VII, §3; Syn. Armen., a. 1911, 533–537.

762 §1, 2°: Apost. can. 62; Nic. I, can. 10; S. Petrus Alexandrin., can. 10; Theophilus Alexandrin., can. 7; Innocentius I, litt. *Magna me gratulatio,* 13 dec. 414, "Si quis vero."

3° a person who has attempted marriage, even only a civil one, either while he was impeded from entering marriage due to an existing matrimonial bond, sacred orders or a public perpetual vow of chastity, or with a woman bound by a valid marriage or by the same type of vow;

4° a person who has committed voluntary homicide or who has procured a completed abortion, and all persons who positively cooperated in either;

5° a person who has seriously and maliciously mutilated himself or another person, or a person who has attempted suicide;

6° a person who has performed an act of orders that has been reserved to those who are in the order of episcopacy or presbyterate while the person either lacked that order or had been forbidden its exercise by a canonical penalty;

7° a person who holds an office or position of administration that is forbidden to clerics, for which he must render an account, until he becomes free by relinquishing the office and position of administration and has rendered an account of it;

8° a neophyte, unless he has been sufficiently proven in the judgment of the hierarch.

§2. The acts that are mentioned in §1, nn. 2–6 do not produce impediments unless they were serious and external sins perpetrated after baptism.

CAN. 763 The following are impeded from exercising sacred orders:

1° a person who illegitimately received sacred orders while under an impediment from receiving sacred orders;

3° qui matrimonium, etiam civile tantum, attentavit, sive ipse vinculo matrimoniali aut ordine sacro aut voto publico perpetuo castitatis a matrimonio celebrando impeditus, sive cum muliere matrimonio valido coniuncta aut eodem voto ligata;

4° qui voluntarium homicidium perpetravit aut abortum procuravit effectu secuto omnesque positive cooperantes;

5° qui se ipsum vel alium graviter et dolose mutilavit vel sibi vitam adimere tentavit;

6° qui actum ordinis posuit in ordine episcopatus vel presbyteratus constitutis reservatum vel eodem carens vel ab eiusdem exercitio aliqua poena canonica prohibitus;

7° qui officium vel administrationem gerit clericis vetitam, cuius rationem reddere debet, donec deposito officio et administratione atque rationibus redditis liber factus erit;

8° neophytus, nisi iudicio Hierarchae sufficienter probatus est.

§2. Actus, ex quibus impedimenta, de quibus in §1, nn. 2–6 oriri possunt, illa non pariunt, nisi fuerunt peccata gravia et externa post baptismum perpetrata.

CAN. 763 Ab exercendis ordinibus sacris est impeditus:

1° qui impedimento ordines sacros suscipiendi, dum afficiebatur, illegitime ordines sacros suscepit;

762 §1, 3°: Apost. can. 61; Neoc. can. 1; THEOPHILUS ALEXANDRIN., can. 3.

762 §1, 4°: S. GREGORIUS Nyss., can. 5, (α),

762 §1, 5°: Apost. cann. 22–23; Nic. I, can. 1.

762 §1, 6°: Apost. cann. 12, 28; Nic. I, can. 16; Ant. can. 4; Carth. can. 29; CLEMENS VIII, instr. *Sanctis-*

simus, 31 aug. 1595, §4 "Graeci sine litteris;" BENEDICTUS XIV, const. *Etsi pastoralis,* 26 maii 1742, §VII, IX; S.C. de Prop. Fide, decr. 13 apr. 1807, VIII.

762 §1, 8°: Apost. can. 80; Nic. I, can. 2; Laod. can. 3; Constantinop. IV, can. 5; S. NICEPHORUS CP., can. 21.

2° a person who committed a crime or an act that is mentioned in can. 762, §1, nn. 2–6;

3° a person who is afflicted with insanity or with another psychic illness that is mentioned in can. 762, §1, n. 1, until the hierarch, after consultation with an expert, permits the exercise of that sacred order.

CAN. 764 Impediments for receiving or exercising sacred orders cannot be established by particular law; a custom introducing a new impediment or contrary to an impediment established by common law is reprobated.

CAN. 765 Ignorance of impediments does not exempt from them.

CAN. 766 Impediments are multiplied when they arise from different causes, not however by the repetition of the same cause, unless it is a case of the impediment arising from voluntary homicide or from the procurement of a completed abortion.

CAN. 767 §1. The eparchial bishop or the hierarch of an institute of consecrated life can dispense his subjects from the impediments of receiving or exercising sacred orders except in the following cases:

1° if the fact on which the impediment is based has been brought to the judicial forum;

2° from the impediments mentioned in can. 762, §1, nn. 2–4.

§2. Dispensation from these impediments is reserved to the patriarch for candidates or clerics who have a domicile or quasi-domicile within the territorial boundaries of the Church over which he presides; otherwise, it is reserved to the Apostolic See.

§3. A confessor has the same powers of dispensing in the more urgent occult cases, in which the competent authority cannot be

2° qui delicta vel actus commisit, de quibus in can. 762, §1, nn. 2–6;

3° qui amentia aliave infirmitate psychica, de qua in can. 762, §1, n. 1, afficitur, donec Hierarcha consulto perito eiusdem ordinis sacri exercitium permiserit.

CAN. 764 Impedimenta suscipiendi vel exercendi ordines sacros iure particulari statui non possunt; consuetudo vero novum impedimentum inducens aut impedimento iure communi statuto contraria reprobatur.

CAN. 765 Ignorantia impedimentorum ab eisdem non eximit.

CAN. 766 Impedimenta multiplicantur ex diversis suis causis, non autem ex repetita eadem causa, nisi agitur de impedimento ex homicidio voluntario aut ex procurato abortu effectu secuto.

CAN. 767 §1. Episcopus eparchialis vel Hierarcha instituti vitae consecratae potest sibi subditos dispensare ab impedimentis suscipiendi vel 4exercendi ordines sacros sequentibus exceptis:

1° si factum, quo impedimentum innititur, ad forum iudiciale deductum est;

2° ab impedimentis, de quibus in can. 762, §1, nn. 2–4.

§2. Dispensatio ab his impedimentis reservatur Patriarchae circa candidatos vel clericos, qui domicilium vel quasi-domicilium intra fines territorii Ecclesiae, cui praeest, habent; secus Sedi Apostolicae.

§3. Eadem potestas dispensandi competit cuilibet confessario in casibus occultis urgentioribus, in quibus auctoritas compe-

---

767 §2: Pius XII, *Cleri sanctitati*, 2 iun. 1957, can. 265, n. 1. * Syn. Libanen. Maronitarum, a. 1736, pars II, cap. VI, 11; pars III, cap. IV, 30; Syn. Sciarfen. Syrorum, a. 1888, cap. V, art. XIV, §1, 3; Syn. Alexandrin. Coptorum, a. 1898, sect. III, cap. III, art. I, III, 3; Syn. Armen., a. 1911, 537.

reached and there is a danger of grave harm or infamy, but only to ensure that the penitents can licitly exercise the sacred orders already received, with due regard for the responsibility of approaching that authority as soon as possible.

CAN. 768 §1. In the petition for obtaining a dispensation, all the impediments are to be indicated; a general dispensation, however, is valid also for those impediments that were omitted in good faith, except those referred to in can. 762, §1, n. 4, or those taken to the judicial forum, not however for those omitted in bad faith.

§2. If it is a case of an impediment arising from voluntary homicide or from the procurement of an abortion, the number of delicts must also be mentioned for the dispensation to be valid.

§3. A general dispensation from impediments to receive sacred orders is valid for all orders.

ART. III. *Those Things That Must Precede Sacred Ordination*

CAN. 769 §1. The authority who admits a candidate to sacred ordination should obtain:

1° the declaration referred to in can. 761, as well as a certificate of the last sacred ordination or, in the case of the first sacred ordination, a certificate of baptism and chrismation with holy myron;

2° if the candidate is married, a certificate of marriage and the written consent of his wife;

tens adiri non potest et periculum imminet gravis damni vel infamiae, sed ad hoc dumtaxat, ut paenitentes ordines sacros iam susceptos exercere licite possint firmo onere adeundi quam primum eandem auctoritatem.

CAN. 768 §1. In precibus ad obtinendam dispensationem omnia impedimenta indicanda sunt; dispensatio generalis vero valet etiam pro impedimentis bona fide reticitis eis exceptis, de quibus in can. 762, §1, n. 4, aliisve ad forum iudiciale deductis, non autem pro reticitis mala fide.

§2. Si agitur de impedimento ex voluntario homicidio aut ex procurato abortu, etiam numerus delictorum ad validitatem dispensationis exprimendus est.

§3. Dispensatio generalis ab impedimentis suscipiendi ordines sacros valet pro omnibus ordinibus.

ART. III. *De Eis, Quae Sacrae Ordinationi Praemitti Debent*

CAN. 769 §1. Auctoritas, quae candidatum ad sacram ordinationem admittit, obtineat:

1° declarationem, de qua in can. 761, necnon testimonium ultimae sacrae ordinationis aut, si de prima sacra ordinatione agitur, etiam testimonium baptismi et chrismationis sancti myri;

2° si candidatus est matrimonio iunctus, testimonium matrimonii et consensum uxoris scripto datum;

769 §1: Nic. II, can. 2; S. BASILIUS M., can. 89; THEOPHILUS ALEXANDRIN., can. 7; S. CYRILLUS ALEXANDRIN., can. 4, (a); S. CORNELIUS, litt. *Ut autem scias,* a. 251, "Agendum;" S.C. pro Eccl. Orient., decr. 27 ian. 1940, nn. 7–12; S.C.S. Off., monitum, 15 iul. 1961, 4); Vat. II, decr. *Optatam totius,* 6, 12; PAULUS VI, litt. encycl. *Sacerdotalis coelibatus,* 24 iun. 1967, 63, 71; S.C. pro Inst. Cath., *Ratio funda-* *mentalis institutionis sacerdotalis,* 6 ian. 1970, 39–42. * Syn. Zamosten. Ruthenorum, a. 1720, tit. III, §7 "Cum" - "Ut autem;" Syn. Libanen. Maronitarum, a. 1736, pars II, cap. XIV, 10–11, 20; Syn. Bekorkien. Maronitarum, a. 1790, s. 6; Syn. Ain-Trazen. Graeco-Melchitarum, a. 1835, can. 6; Syn. Sciarfen. Syrorum, a. 1888, cap. V, art. XIII, §2, 3.

3° a certificate of completed studies;

4° a testimonial letter regarding the good conduct of the candidate from the rector of the seminary or from the superior of the institute of consecrated life or from the presbyter to whom the candidate was entrusted outside the seminary;

5° the testimonial letter referred to in can. 771, §3;

6° testimonial letters, if it is considered expedient, of other eparchial bishops or of superiors of institutes of consecrated life, where the candidate resided for some time, concerning the qualities of the candidate and his freedom from all canonical impediments.

§2. These documents are to be kept in the archive of the same authority.

CAN. 770 The ordaining bishop presented with legitimate dimissorial letters stating that the candidate is suited to receive the sacred order, can abide by this attestation, but is not bound to do so. If indeed in conscience he considers the candidate unsuitable, he is not to ordain him.

CAN. 771 §1. The names of the candidates for promotion to sacred orders are to be made known publicly in the parish church of each candidate in accord with the norm of particular law.

§2. All the Christian faithful are bound by the obligation to disclose any impediments they know to the eparchial bishop or to the pastor before the sacred ordination.

§3. The eparchial bishop shall charge the pastor who gives public notice and, if it seems expedient, also another presbyter, to inquire diligently about the life and conduct of the candi-

3° testimonium de peractis studiis;

4° testimoniales litteras rectoris seminarii vel Superioris instituti vitae consecratae aut presbyteri, cui candidatus extra seminarium commendatus est, de bonis moribus eiusdem candidati;

5° testimoniales litteras, de quibus in can. 771, §3;

6° testimoniales litteras, si id expedire iudicat, aliorum Episcoporum eparchialium vel Superiorum institutorum vitae consecratae, ubi candidatus per aliquod tempus commoratus est, de candidati qualitatibus deque eius libertate ab omni impedimento canonico.

§2. Haec documenta asserventur in archivo eiusdem auctoritatis.

CAN. 770 Episcopus ordinans cum legitimis litteris dimissoriis, quibus asseritur candidatum ad ordinem sacrum suscipiendum idoneum esse, potest huic attestationi acquiescere, sed non tenetur; si vero pro sua conscientia censet candidatum non esse idoneum, eum ne ordinet.

CAN. 771 §1. Nomina candidatorum ad ordines sacros promovendorum publice nota fiant in ecclesia paroeciali uniuscuiusque candidati ad normam iuris particularis.

§2. Omnes christifideles obligatione tenentur impedimenta, si qua noverunt, Episcopo eparchiali vel parocho ante sacram ordinationem revelandi.

§3. Parocho, qui publicationem peragit, et etiam alii presbytero, si id expedire videtur, Episcopus eparchialis committat, ut de candidatorum vita et moribus a personis fide

---

771 §1: THEOPHILUS ALEXANDRIN., can. 7. * Syn. Zamosten. Ruthenorum, a. 1720, tit. III, §7 "Illi;" Syn. Libanen. Maronitarum, a. 1736, pars II, cap. XIV, 27; Syn. Armen., a. 1911, 538–539.

771 §2: THEOPHILUS ALEXANDRIN., can. 7.
771 §3: * Syn. Zamosten. Ruthenorum, a. 1720, tit. III, §7 "Illi."

dates from trustworthy persons and to send testimonial letters to the eparchial curia concerning that inquiry and notice.

§4. The eparchial bishop should not omit to make other investigations, even private, if he judges it opportune.

CAN. 772 Every candidate for promotion to sacred ordination must make a spiritual retreat as determined by particular law.

ART. IV. *Time, Place, Registration and Certification of Sacred Ordination*

CAN. 773 Sacred ordinations should be celebrated with the greatest number of Christian faithful possible in a church on a Sunday or feast day, unless a just cause suggests otherwise.

CAN. 774 §1. After the celebration of sacred ordination, the names of each of those ordained, of the ordaining bishop, the place and date of the sacred ordination are to be recorded in a special book to be kept in the archive of the eparchial curia.

§2. The ordaining bishop is to give an authentic certificate of the reception of ordination to each of the ordained. Those who were ordained with dimissorial letters by a bishop should submit the certificate to their own eparchial bishop or major superior so that the sacred ordination can be recorded in a special register that is to be kept in the archive.

CAN. 775 The eparchial bishop or the major superior is to send a notification of the or-

dignis diligenter exquirat et testimoniales litteras illam investigationem et publicationem referentes ad curiam eparchialem mittat.

§4. Episcopus eparchialis alias investigationes, etiam privatas, si opportunum ducit, facere ne omittat.

CAN. 772 Omnis candidatus ad sacram ordinationem promovendus recessui spirituali vacet modo iure particulari determinato.

ART. IV. *De Sacrae Ordinationis Tempore, Loco, Adnotatione et Testimonio*

CAN. 773 Sacrae ordinationes cum christifidelium quam maxima frequentia celebrentur in ecclesia die dominico vel festo, nisi iusta causa aliud suadet.

CAN. 774 §1. Celebrata sacra ordinatione nomina singulorum ordinatorum ac Episcopi ordinantis, locus et dies sacrae ordinationis adnotentur in speciali libro in archivo curiae eparchialis asservando.

§2. Singulis ordinatis det Episcopus ordinans authenticum sacrae ordinationis susceptae testimonium; qui, si ab Episcopo cum litteris dimissoriis ordinati sunt, illud proprio Episcopo eparchiali vel Superiori maiori exhibeant pro sacrae ordinationis adnotatione in speciali libro in archivo asservando.

CAN. 775 Episcopus eparchialis aut Superior maior notitiam sacrae ordinationis

---

772: * Syn. Zamosten. Ruthenorum, a. 1720, tit. III, §7 "Ut autem;" Syn. Libanen. Maronitarum, a. 1736, pars II, cap. XIV, 30; Syn. Gusten. Maronitarum, a. 1768, can. 11; Syn. Sciarfen. Syrorum, a. 1888, cap. V, art. XIII, §2, 6; Syn. Leopolien. Ruthenorum, a. 1891, tit. II, cap. VI, 3; Syn. Armen., a. 1911, 526.

773: * Syn. Libanen. Maronitarum, a. 1736, pars II, cap. XIV, 18; Syn. Sciarfen. Syrorum, a. 1888, cap.

V, art. XIII, §3, 2; Syn. Alexandrin. Coptorum, a. 1898, sect. II, cap. III, art. VII, §4, VIII, X, XII; Syn. Armen., a. 1911, 543.

774 §1: * Syn. Zamosten. Ruthenorum, a. 1720, tit. III, §7 "Illud;" Syn. Libanen. Maronitarum, a. 1736, pars II, cap. XIV, 36; Syn. Sciarfen. Syrorum, a. 1888, cap. V, art. XIII, §3, 4; Syn. Alexandrin. Coptorum, a. 1898, sect. II, cap. III, art. VII, §4, XVII.

dination of each deacon to the pastor of the parish where the baptism of the ordained was registered.

uniuscuiusque diaconi mittat ad parochum apud quem ordinati baptismus adnotatus est.

CHAPTER VII. Marriage

CAN. 776 §1. By the marriage covenant, founded by the Creator and ordered by His laws, a man and a woman by irrevocable personal consent establish between themselves a partnership of the whole of life; this covenant is by its very nature ordered to the good of the spouses and to the procreation and education of children.

§2. By Christ's institution, a valid marriage between baptized persons is by that very fact a sacrament in which the spouses are united by God after the pattern of Christ's indefectible union with the Church, and are, as it were, consecrated and strengthened by sacramental grace.

§3. The essential properties of marriage are unity and indissolubility, which in the marriage between baptized persons they acquire a special firmness by reason of the sacrament.

CAPUT VII. De Matrimonio

CAN. 776 §1. Matrimoniale foedus a Creatore conditum eiusque legibus instructum, quo vir et mulier irrevocabili consensu personali totius vitae consortium inter se constituunt, indole sua naturali ad bonum coniugum ac ad filiorum generationem ed educationem ordinatur.

§2. Ex Christi institutione matrimonium validum inter baptizatos eo ipso est sacramentum, quo coniuges ad imaginem indefectibilis unionis Christi cum Ecclesia a Deo uniuntur gratiaque sacramentali veluti consecrantur et roborantur.

§3. Essentiales matrimonii proprietates sunt unitas et indissolubilitas, quae in matrimonio inter baptizatos specialem obtinent firmitatem ratione sacramenti.

---

776 §1: Vat. II, const. *Gaudium et spes,* 48; decr. *Apostolicam actuositatem,* 11; Pius XII, m.p. *Crebrae allatae sunt,* 22 feb. 1949, can. 2 §1. - Eugenius IV (in Flor.), const. *Exsultate Deo,* 22 nov. 1439, §16; S.C. de Prop. Fide, instr. (ad Ep. Graeco-Rumen.), a. 1858; Leo XIII, ep. encycl. *Arcanum,* 10 feb. 1880; Pius XI, litt. encycl. *Casti connubii,* 31 dec. 1930; S.C.S. Off., decr. 1 apr. 1944; Pius XII, all. 29 oct. 1951, IV; Paulus VI, litt. encycl. *Humanae vitae,* 25 iul. 1968, 8; all. 9 feb. 1976.

776 §2: Vat. II, const. *Lumen gentium,* 11 "Tandem coniuges," 41 "Coniuges autem;" const. *Gaudium et spes,* 48 "Christus Dominus;" Pius XII, m.p. *Crebrae allatae sunt,* 22 feb. 1949, can. 1 §§1–2. - Professio fidei (in Lugd. II) a Michaele Palaeologo Gregorio X oblata, a. 1274; Eugenius IV (in Flor.), const. *Exsultate Deo,* 22 nov. 1439, §16; Trid., sess. VII, *Canones de sacramentis in genere,* can. 1; sess. XXIV, *De matrimonio,* prooem. et can. 1; S.C. de Prop. Fide, instr. (ad Ep. Graeco- Rumen.), a. 1858; Leo XIII, ep.

encycl. *Arcanum,* 10 feb. 1880; Pius XI, litt. encycl. *Casti connubii,* 31 dec. 1930, I "Et quoniam."

776 §3; Pius XII, m.p. *Crebrae allatae sunt,* 22 feb. 1949, can. 2 §2; Vat. II, const. *Gaudium et spes,* 48 "Quae intima." - S. Gregorius M., litt. *Magnas omnipotenti,* a. 601; Professio fidei (in Lugd. II) a Michaele Palaeologo Gregorio X oblata, a. 1274; Benedictus XII, a. 1341, prop. 102, Armenorum, damn.; Eugenius IV (in Flor.), const. *Exsultate Deo,* 22 nov. 1439, §16; Trid., sess. XXIV, *De matrimonio,* can. 2; *De ref. matrimonii,* capp. 1, 7; Clemens VIII, instr. *Sanctissimus,* 31 aug. 1595, §5; Benedictus XIV, const. *Etsi pastoralis,* 26 maii 1742, §VIII, II; Benedictus XIV, ep. *Nuper ad Nos,* 16 mar. 1743, Professio fidei Maronitis praescr., §5; S.C. de Prop. Fide, instr. (ad Ep. Graeco-Rumen.), a. 1858; Leo XIII, ep. encycl. *Arcanum,* 10 feb. 1880; S.C.S. Off., instr. (ad Ep. Rituum Orient.), a. 1883; Pius XI, litt. encycl. *Casti connubii,* 31 dec. 1930, I; Paulus VI, litt. encycl. *Humanae vitae,* 25 iul. 1968, 25.

CAN. 777 Out of marriage arise equal rights and obligations between the spouses regarding what pertains to the partnership of conjugal life.

CAN. 778 All persons can enter into marriage who are not prohibited by law.

CAN. 779 Marriage enjoys the favor of the law; consequently, in doubt, the validity of a marriage is to be upheld until the contrary is proven.

CAN. 780 §1. Even if only one party is Catholic, the marriage of Catholics is governed not only by divine law but also by canon law, without prejudice to the competence of civil authority concerning the merely civil effects of marriage.

§2. Marriage between a Catholic and a baptized non-Catholic is governed, with due regard for divine law, also by:

1° the law proper to the Church or ecclesial community to which the non-Catholic belongs, if that community has its own matrimonial law;

2° the law to which the non-Catholic is subject, if the ecclesial community to which the person belongs has no matrimonial law of its own.

CAN. 781 If sometimes the Church must pronounce a judgment about the validity of a marriage between baptized non-Catholics:

1° regarding the law to which the parties were subject at the time of their wedding, can. 780, §2 is to be observed;

CAN. 777 Ex matrimonio oriuntur inter coniuges aequa iura et obligationes circa ea, quae ad consortium vitae coniugalis pertinent.

CAN. 778 Omnes possunt matrimonium inire, qui iure non prohibentur.

CAN. 779 Matrimonium gaudet favore iuris; quare in dubio standum est pro validitate matrimonii, donec contrarium probetur.

CAN. 780 §1. Matrimonium catholicorum, etsi una tantum pars est catholica, regitur iure non solum divino, sed etiam canonico salva competentia auctoritatis civilis circa effectus mere civiles matrimonii.

§2. Matrimonium inter partem catholicam et partem baptizatam acatholicam salvo iure divino regitur etiam:

1° iure proprio Ecclesiae vel Communitatis ecclesialis, ad quam pars acatholica pertinet, si haec Communitas ius matrimoniale proprium habet;

2° iure, quo pars acatholica tenetur, si Communitas ecclesialis, ad quam pertinet, iure matrimoniali proprio caret.

CAN. 781 Si quando Ecclesia iudicare debet de validitate matrimonii acatholicorum baptizatorum:

1° quod attinet ad ius, quo partes tempore celebrationis matrimonii tenebantur, servetur can. 780, §2;

777: Pius XII, m.p. *Crebrae allatae sunt,* 22 feb. 1949, can. 100; Paulus VI, litt. encycl. *Humanae vitae,* 25 iul. 1968, 2, 10; Ioannes Paulus II, litt. ap. *Familiaris consortio,* 22 nov. 1981, 22 "Ad mulierem."

778: Pius XII, m.p. *Crebrae allatae sunt,* 22 feb. 1949, can. 25; S.C.S. Off., resp. 27 ian. 1949; resp. 22 dec. 1949; Ioannes XXIII, litt. encycl. *Pacem in terris,* 11 apr. 1963, I "Insuper hominibus." - Professio fidei (in Lugd. II) a Michaele Palaeologo Gregorio X oblata, a. 1274.

779: Pius XII, m.p. *Crebrae allatae sunt,* 22 feb. 1949, can. 3. - S.C.S. Off., 18 mar. 1903, ad 2; Pius XII, all. 3 oct. 1941.

780 §1: Pius XII, m.p. *Crebrae allatae sunt,* 22 feb. 1949, can. 5. - Pius VI, const. *Auctorem fidei,* 28 aug. 1794, prop. 58, Synodi Pistorien., damn.; Leo XIII, ep. encycl. *Arcanum,* 10 feb. 1880; Pius XI, litt. encycl. *Casti connubii,* 31 dec. 1930, III "Quid" - "Itaque."

780 §2, 1°: Vat. II, decr. *Unitatis redintegratio,* 16; decl. *Dignitatis humanae,* 4 "His igitur."

2° regarding the form of marriage celebration, the Church recognizes any form prescribed or admitted by the law to which the parties were subject at the time of their wedding, provided that the consent was expressed publicly and, if at least one of the parties is a baptized member of an Eastern non-Catholic Church, the marriage was celebrated with a sacred rite.

CAN. 782 §1. The engagement, which according to the ancient tradition of the Eastern Churches laudably precedes marriage, is governed by the particular law of the respective Church *sui iuris*.

§2. The promise of marriage is no ground for an action to obtain the celebration of marriage; nevertheless, there is action for the reparation of damages, if reparation is due.

ART. I. *Pastoral Care and Those Things That Must Precede the Celebration of Marriage*

CAN. 783 §1. Pastors of souls are obliged to see to it that the Christian faithful are prepared for the matrimonial state:

1° by preaching and catechesis suited to young people and adults, by which the Christian faithful are instructed concerning the meaning of Christian marriage, the mutual obligations of spouses, and the primary right and obligation of parents to care, according to

2° quod attinet ad formam celebrationis matrimonii, Ecclesia agnoscit quamlibet formam iure praescriptam vel admissam, cui partes tempore celebrationis matrimonii subiectae erant, dummodo consensus expressus sit forma publica et, si una saltem pars est christifidelis alicuius Ecclesiae orientalis acatholicae, matrimonium ritu sacro celebratum sit.

CAN. 782 §1. Sponsalia, quae laudabiliter matrimonio praemittuntur ex antiquissima Ecclesiarum orientalium traditione, reguntur iure particulari propriae Ecclesiae sui iuris.

§2. Ex matrimonii promissione non datur actio ad petendam matrimonii celebrationem; datur tamen ad reparationem damnorum, si qua debetur.

ART. I. *De Cura Pastorali et de Eis, Quae Matrimonii Celebrationi Praemitti Debent*

CAN. 783 §1. Pastores animarum obligatione tenentur curandi, ut christifideles ad statum matrimonialem praeparentur:

1° praedicatione et catechesi iuvenibus et adultis aptata, quibus christifideles instituantur de significatione matrimonii christiani, de obligationibus coniugum inter se necnon de iure primario et obligatione, quae parentes habent, filiorum educationem physicam,

---

782 §1: Pius XII, m.p. *Crebrae allatae sunt,* 22 feb. 1949, can. 6 §§1–2. * Syn. Libanen. Maronitarum, a. 1736, pars II, cap. XI, 3; Syn. Ain-Trazen. Graeco-Melchitarum, a. 1835, can. 7, 1–2; Syn. prov. Alba-Iulien. et Fagarasien. Rumenorum, a. 1872, tit. V, cap. VIII, II, 1); a. 1882, tit. IV, sect. I, §20; Syn. Sciarfen. Syrorum, a. 1888, cap. V, art. XV §§1–2; Syn. Alexandrin. Coptorum, a. 1898, sect. II, cap. III, art. VIII, §1; Syn. Armen., a. 1911, 547, 553, 577.

782 §2: Pius XII, m.p. *Crebrae allatae sunt,* 22 feb. 1949, can. 6 §3. * Syn. Libanen. Maronitarum, a. 1736, pars II, cap. XI, 9, III; Syn. Sciarfen. Syrorum, a. 1888, cap. V, art. XV, §7, 3; Syn. Alexandrin. Coptorum, a. 1898, sect. II, cap. III, art. VIII, §5, 3, III.

783 §1, 1°: Pius XII, m.p. *Crebrae allatae sunt,* 22 feb. 1949, cann. 8, 102; Vat. II, const. *Gaudium et spes,* 47, 52; Ioannes Paulus II, litt. ap. *Familiaris consortio,* 22 nov. 1981, 66.

their abilities, for the physical, religious, moral, social and cultural education of their children;

2° by personal instruction of the couple by which they are prepared for their new state.

§2. It is strongly recommended to Catholic couples to receive the Divine Eucharist at the celebration of marriage.

§3. After the celebration of marriage, pastors of souls should assist the couple so that by faithfully observing and safeguarding their marriage covenant they may day by day achieve a holier and fuller family life.

CAN. 784 In the particular law of each Church *sui iuris,* after consultation with the eparchial bishops of other Churches *sui iuris* exercising their power in the same territory, norms are to be established concerning the examination of the couple and other means for inquiries that are to be carried out before the marriage, especially those that concern baptism and the freedom to marry, which are to be diligently observed so that the celebration of the marriage can proceed.

CAN. 785 §1. Pastors of souls are obliged

religiosam, moralem, socialem et culturalem pro viribus curandi;

2° instructione sponsorum personali ad matrimonium, qua sponsi ad novum statum disponantur.

§2. Enixe commendatur sponsis catholicis, ut in matrimonio celebrando Divinam Eucharistiam suscipiant.

§3. Celebrato vero matrimonio pastores animarum auxilium coniugibus praebeant, ut matrimoniale foedus fideliter servantes atque tuentes ad sanctiorem in dies plenioremque in familia vitam ducendam perveniant.

CAN. 784 Iure particulari uniuscuiusque Ecclesiae sui iuris, collatis consiliis cum Episcopis eparchialibus aliarum Ecclesiarum sui iuris in eodem territorio potestatem suam exercentibus, statuantur normae de examine sponsorum et de aliis mediis ad investigationes, praecipue quod ad baptismum et ad statum liberum spectat, quae ante matrimonium peragendae sunt, quibus diligenter observatis procedi potest ad matrimonii celebrationem.

CAN. 785 §1. Pastores animarum obli-

783 §1, 2°: Pius XII, m.p. *Crebrae allatae sunt,* 22 feb. 1949, can. 23; Vat. II, const. *Gaudium et spes,* 52; Pius XI, litt. encycl. *Casti connubii,* 31 dec. 1930, III; Ioannes Paulus II, litt. ap. *Familiaris consortio,* 22 nov. 1981, 66 "Praeparatio proxima." * Syn. Zamosten. Ruthenorum, a. 1720, tit. III, §8 "Si nullum;" Syn. Libanen. Maronitarum, a. 1736, pars II, cap. XI, 2; Syn. Sciarfen. Syrorum, a. 1888, cap. V, art. XV, §12, V; Syn. Alexandrin. Coptorum, a. 1898, sect. II, cap. III, art. VIII, §2, 7, V.

783 §2: * Syn. Diamper. Syro-Malabarensium, a. 1599, CLXXXVIII; Syn. Zamosten. Ruthenorum, a. 1720, tit. III, §8 "Accessuri;" Syn. Libanen. Maronitarum, a. 1736, pars II, cap. XI, 2; Syn. Sciarfen. Syrorum, a. 1888, cap. V, art. XV, §12, I et V; Syn. Leopolien. Ruthenorum, a. 1891, tit. II, cap. VII, 5; Syn. Alexandrin. Coptorum, a. 1898, sect. II, cap. III, art. VIII, §2, 7, II.

783 §3: Vat. II, const. *Lumen gentium,* 41 "Coniuges;" const. *Gaudium et spes,* 52 "Sacerdotum."

784: Pius XII, m.p. *Crebrae allatae sunt,* 22 feb. 1949, cann. 10–16, 18, 20. - S.C. de Prop. Fide, reg. (pro Sacerd. Coptis), 15 mar. 1790, XV; decr. 6 oct. 1863, D), a); S.C.S. Off., instr. (ad Ep. Orient.), 22 aug. 1890. * Syn. Sergii Patriarchae Maronitarum, 18 sep. 1596, can. XIV; Syn. Diamper. Syro-Malabarensium, a. 1599, CLXXXVI; Syn. Zamosten. Ruthenorum, a. 1720, tit. III, §8; Syn. Libanen. Maronitarum, a. 1736, pars II, cap. III, 12; cap. XI, 27; Syn. Ain-Trazen. Graeco-Melchitarum, a. 1835, can. 7, 3 et 8; Syn. Sciarfen. Syrorum, a. 1888, cap. V, art. XV, §12, VI–VII; Syn. Alexandrin. Coptorum, a. 1898, sect. II, cap. III, art. VIII, §2, 7, V; Syn. prov. Alba-Iulien. et Fagarasien. Rumenorum, a. 1872, tit. V, cap. VIII, II, 3; cap. IX; a. 1882, tit. IV, sect. I, §§27–30, 42.

785 §1: Pius XII, m.p. *Crebrae allatae sunt,* 22 feb. 1949, can. 9 §1. * Syn. Zamosten. Ruthenorum, a. 1720, tit. III, §8; Syn. prov. Alba-Iulien. et Fagarasien. Rumenorum, a. 1872, tit. V, cap. VIII "Curent;" Syn. Sciarfen. Syrorum, a. 1888, cap. V, art. XV, §12, VI.

according to the needs of time and place to prevent by suitable means every danger of an invalid or illicit celebration of marriage, and thus, before the marriage is celebrated, it must be established that nothing stands in the way of its valid and licit celebration.

§2. In danger of death, if other means of proof cannot be obtained and there are no contrary indications, the affirmation of the spouses is sufficient, even under oath if the case warrants it, that they have been baptized and that they are not hindered by any impediment.

CAN. 786 All the Christian faithful are obliged to reveal any impediments of which they are aware to the pastor or the local hierarch before the celebration of the marriage.

CAN. 787 The pastor who has made the investigation is immediately to notify the pastor who is to bless the marriage of the results of this investigation by means of an authentic document.

CAN. 788 If after a diligent investigation there persists any doubt concerning the existence of an impediment, the pastor is to defer the matter to the local hierarch.

CAN. 789 Although the marriage can be entered validly with regard to other matters, the priest, beyond the other cases defined by law, is not to bless without the permission of the local hierarch:

1° the marriage of transients;

2° a marriage that cannot be recognized or entered into in accord with the norms of civil law;

gatione tenentur pro necessitatibus locorum et temporum omnia pericula a matrimonio invalide ac illicite celebrando remediis opportunis arcendi; ideo, antequam matrimonium celebratur, constare debet nihil eius validae ac licitae celebrationi obstare.

§2. In periculo mortis, si aliae probationes haberi non possunt, sufficit, nisi contraria assunt indicia, affirmatio sponsorum, si casus fert, etiam iurata, se baptizatos esse et nullo detineri impedimento.

CAN. 786 Omnes christifideles obligatione tenentur impedimenta, si qua noverunt, parocho aut Hierarchae loci ante matrimonii celebrationem revelandi.

CAN. 787 Parochus, qui investigationes peregit, de harum exitu statim per authenticum documentum certiorem faciat parochum, cuius est matrimonium benedicere.

CAN. 788 Si quod dubium post accuratas investigationes adhuc superest de exsistentia impedimenti, parochus rem ad Hierarcham loci deferat.

CAN. 789 Etsi matrimonium de cetero valide celebrari potest, sacerdos praeter alios casus iure determinatos sine licentia Hierarchae loci ne benedicat:

1° matrimonium vagorum;

2° matrimonium, quod ad normam iuris civilis agnosci vel iniri non potest;

---

785 §2: Pius XII, m.p. *Crebrae allatae sunt,* 22 feb. 1949, can. 9 §2. - S.C. de Prop. Fide, ep. (ad Ep. Nicopolitan.), 25 ian. 1817.

786: Pius XII, m.p. *Crebrae allatae sunt,* 22 feb. 1949, can. 17.

787: Pius XII, m.p. *Crebrae allatae sunt,* 22 feb. 1949, can. 19.

788: Pius XII, m.p. *Crebrae allatae sunt,* 22 feb.

1949, can. 21 §1 n. 3. - S.C. de Prop. Fide, reg. (pro Sacerd. Coptis), 15 mar. 1790, XV; S.C.S. Off., instr. (ad Deleg. Ap. Aegypti), 13 ian. 1869; (Constantinop.), 2 apr. 1873.

789, 1°: Pius XII, m.p. *Crebrae allatae sunt,* 22 feb. 1949, can. 22. * Syn. Zamosten. Ruthenorum, a. 1720, tit. III, §8 "Eo vero;" Syn. Sciarfen. Syrorum, a. 1888, cap. V, art. XV, §12, VIII.

3° the marriage of a person who is bound by natural obligations toward a third party or toward children arising from a prior union with that party;

4° the marriage of a minor child of a family whose parents are unaware of or opposed to the marriage;

5° the marriage of one who is forbidden by an ecclesiastical sentence to enter into a new marriage unless the person fulfills certain conditions;

6° the marriage of a person who has publicly rejected the Catholic faith, even if that person did not become a member of a non-Catholic Church or ecclesial communion; the local hierarch in this case will not grant permission unless the norms of can. 814 are observed, making any necessary adaptations.

3° matrimonium eius, qui obligationibus naturalibus tenetur erga tertiam partem filiosve ex praecedenti unione cum illa parte ortos;

4° matrimonium filii familias minoris insciis aut invitis parentibus;

5° matrimonium eius, qui sententia ecclesiastica vetatur transire ad novum matrimonium, nisi quasdam condiciones implet;

6° matrimonium eius, qui publice fidem catholicam abiecit, etsi ad Ecclesiam vel Communitatem ecclesialem acatholicam non transiit; Hierarcha loci vero hoc in casu licentiam ne concedat nisi servato can. 814 congrua congruis referendo.

ART. 11. *Diriment Impediments in General*

ART. 11. *De Impedimentis Dirimentibus in Genere*

CAN. 790 §1. A diriment impediment renders a person unqualified to celebrate marriage validly.

§2. An impediment, even if only one of the parties has it, still renders the marriage invalid.

CAN. 790 §1. Impedimentum dirimens personam inhabilem reddit ad matrimonium valide celebrandum.

§2. Impedimentum, etsi ex alterutra tantum parte se habet, matrimonium tamen reddit invalidum.

CAN. 791 An impediment that can be proven in the external forum is considered to be a public one; otherwise it is occult.

CAN. 791 Publicum censetur impedimentum, quod probari in foro externo potest; secus est occultum.

CAN. 792 Diriment impediments are not to be established by the particular law of a Church *sui iuris* except for a most grave cause,

CAN. 792 Iure particulari Ecclesiae sui iuris impedimenta dirimentia ne statuantur nisi gravissima de causa, collatis consiliis

---

789, 4°: Pius XII, m.p. *Crebrae allatae sunt,* 22 feb. 1949, can. 24. - S. Basilius M., cann. 38, 40, 42. * Syn. Libanen. Maronitarum, a. 1736, pars II, cap. XI, 19; Syn. Ain-Trazen. Graeco-Melchitarum, a. 1835, cann. 7, 9; Syn. prov. Alba-Iulien. et Fagarasien. Rumenorum, a. 1882, tit. IV, sect. I, §33; Syn. Sciarfen. Syrorum, a. 1888, cap. V, art. XV, §3, 8; Syn. Alexandrin. Coptorum, a. 1898, sect. II, cap. III, art. VIII, §2, 7, I.

790 §1: Pius XII, m.p. *Crebrae allatae sunt,* 22 feb. 1949, can. 26 §2.

790 §2: Benedictus XIV, ep. *Singulari,* 9 feb. 1749, §8.

791: Pius XII, m.p. *Crebrae allatae sunt,* 22 feb. 1949, can. 27.

792: Pius XII, m.p. *Crebrae allatae sunt,* 22 feb. 1949, can. 28 §2.

after having consulted with eparchial bishops of other Churches *sui iuris* who have an interest, and after consultation with the Apostolic See; however, no lower authority can establish new diriment impediments.

CAN. 793   A custom that introduces a new impediment or is contrary to existing impediments is reprobated.

CAN. 794   §1. The local hierarch can prohibit the marriage of the Christian faithful subject to him wherever they are and also of other Christian faithful of his own Church *sui iuris* actually present within the territorial boundaries of his eparchy in a special case, but only for a time, for a grave cause and as long as that cause exists.

§2. If the local hierarch is one who exercises his power within the territorial boundaries of the patriarchal Church, the patriarch can add an invalidating clause to the prohibition; in other cases only the Apostolic See can do so.

CAN. 795   §1. The local hierarch can dispense the Christian faithful subject to him wherever they are as well as other Christian faithful ascribed to another Church *sui iuris* actually present within the territorial boundaries of his eparchy from impediments of ecclesiastical law except those that follow:

1° sacred orders;

cum Episcopis eparchialibus aliarum Ecclesiarum sui iuris, quorum interest, et consulta Sede Apostolica; nulla auctoritas inferior autem nova impedimenta dirimentia statuere potest.

CAN. 793   Consuetudo novum impedimentum inducens aut impedimentis exsistentibus contraria reprobatur.

CAN. 794   §1. Hierarcha loci christifidelibus sibi subditis ubicumque commorantibus necnon ceteris christifidelibus propriae Ecclesiae sui iuris intra fines territorii eparchiae actu degentibus vetare potest matrimonium in casu speciali, sed ad tempus tantum, gravi de causa eaque perdurante.

§2. Si de Hierarcha loci agitur, qui intra fines territorii Ecclesiae patriarchalis potestatem suam exercet, Patriarcha tali vetito clausulam dirimentem addere potest; ceteris in casibus vero sola Sedes Apostolica.

CAN. 795   §1. Hierarcha loci christifideles sibi subditos ubicumque commorantes necnon ceteros christifideles propriae Ecclesiae sui iuris ascriptos et intra fines territorii eparchiae actu degentes dispensare potest ab impedimentis iuris ecclesiastici sequentibus exceptis:

1° ordinis sacri;

793: Pius XII, m.p. *Crebrae allatae sunt,* 22 feb. 1949, can. 30.

794 §1: Pius XII, m.p. *Crebrae allatae sunt,* 22 feb. 1949, can. 29 §1. * Syn. prov. Alba-Iulien. et Fagarasien. Rumenorum, a. 1882, tit. IV, sect. I, §32; Syn. Sciarfen. Syrorum, a. 1888, cap. V, art. XV, §7, 6; Syn. Armen., a. 1911, 577, n. 2.

794 §2: Pius XII, m.p. *Crebrae allatae sunt,* 22 feb. 1949, can. 29 §2. - S.C. de Prop. Fide, (C.P.), 22 ian. 1629.

795 §1: Pius XII, m.p. *Crebrae allatae sunt,* 22 feb. 1949, can. 32 §1; Vat. II, decr. *Christus Dominus,* 8, b); Paulus VI, m.p. *Pastorale munus,* 30 nov. 1963, I, 19; litt. ap. *Episcopalis potestatis,* 2 maii 1967, VIII, 6–10;

Pont. Comm. ad Red. Cod. Iur. Can. Orient., interpr. auth. 3 maii 1953, ad can. 32 §5. * Syn. Diamper. Syro-Malabarensium, a. 1599, CLXXXIX–CXCI; Syn. Libanen. Maronitarum, a. 1736, pars II, cap. XI, 12–16; pars III, cap. IV, 30; Syn. Ain-Trazen. Graeco-Melchitarum, a. 1835, can. 7, 2; Syn. prov. Alba-Iulien. et Fagarasien. Rumenorum, a. 1872, tit. V, cap. VIII, II, 5), e); a. 1882, tit. IV, sect. I, cap. IV; Syn. Sciarfen. Syrorum, a. 1888, cap. V, art. XV, §§9, 11; Syn. Leopolien. Ruthenorum, a. 1891, tit. II, cap. VII, 1; Syn. Alexandrin. Coptorum, a. 1898, sect. II, cap. III, art. VIII, §5, 4; sect. III, cap. III, art. IV, 1, II; Syn. Armen., a. 1911, 578.

2° public perpetual vows of chastity in a religious institute, unless it is a case of congregations of eparchial right;

3° conjugicide.

§2. Dispensation from these impediments is reserved to the Apostolic See; however, the patriarch can dispense from the impediment of conjugicide as well as of the one of a public perpetual vow of chastity made in congregations of any juridical condition.

§3. A dispensation is never given from the impediment of consanguinity in the direct line or in the second degree of the collateral line.

CAN. 796 §1. In danger of death, the local hierarch can dispense the Christian faithful subject to him wherever they are and other Christian faithful actually present within the territorial boundaries of his eparchy from the form of the celebration of marriage prescribed by law and from each and every impediment of ecclesiastical law, whether public or occult, except the impediment of the sacred order of priesthood.

§2. In the same situation and only for those cases in which the local hierarch cannot be reached, the following have the same power: the pastor; another priest endowed with the faculty of blessing the marriage and the Catholic priest referred to in can 832, §2; the confessor, if it is a question of an occult impediment for the internal forum, whether within or outside the act of sacramental confession.

§3. The local hierarch is not considered to be

2° voti publici perpetui castitatis in instituto religioso emissi, nisi agitur de congregationibus iuris eparchialis;

3° coniugicidii.

§2. Dispensatio ab his impedimentis reservatur Sedi Apostolicae; Patriarcha vero dispensare potest ab impedimentis coniugicidii et voti publici perpetui castitatis in congregationibus cuiusvis condicionis iuridicae emissi.

§3. Numquam datur dispensatio ab impedimento consanguinitatis in linea recta aut in secundo gradu lineae collateralis.

CAN. 796 §1. Urgente periculo mortis Hierarcha loci christifideles sibi subditos ubicumque commorantes necnon ceteros christifideles intra fines territorii eparchiae actu degentes dispensare potest a forma celebrationis matrimonii iure praescripta et ab omnibus et singulis impedimentis iuris ecclesiastici sive publicis sive occultis excepto impedimento ordinis sacri sacerdotii.

§2. In eisdem rerum adiunctis et solum in casibus, in quibus ne Hierarcha loci quidem adiri potest, eandem potestatem dispensandi habent parochus, alius sacerdos facultate matrimonium benedicendi praeditus et sacerdos catholicus, de quo in can. 832, §2; confessarius vero eandem potestatem habet, si agitur de impedimento occulto, pro foro interno sive intra sive extra actum sacramentalis confessionis.

§3. Hierarcha loci censetur adiri non

---

795 §3: Pius XII, m.p. *Crebrae allatae sunt*, 22 feb. 1949, can. 66 §3.

796 §1: Pius XII, m.p. *Crebrae allatae sunt*, 22 feb. 1949, can. 33; Paulus VI, m.p. *Pastorale munus*, 30 nov. 1963, I, 20. * Syn. Sciarfen. Syrorum, a. 1888, cap. V, art. XV, §9, 1; Syn. Alexandrin. Coptorum, a. 1898, sect. II, cap. III, art. VIII, §6, 5; Syn. Armen., a. 1911, 579.

796 §2: Pius XII, m.p. *Crebrae allatae sunt*, 22 feb. 1949, can. 34 §1. * Syn. Sciarfen. Syrorum, a. 1888, cap. V, art. XV, §9, 1; Syn. Alexandrin. Coptorum, a. 1898, sect. II, cap. III, art. VIII, §6, 5; Syn. Armen., a. 1911, 578.

796 §3: Pius XII, m.p. *Crebrae allatae sunt*, 22 feb. 1949, can. 34 §2.

accessible if he can be contacted only by means other than letter or personal access.

CAN. 797 §1. If an impediment is discovered after everything is prepared for the celebration of marriage and the marriage cannot be delayed without probable danger of grave harm until a dispensation is obtained from the competent authority, the power of dispensing from all impediments except those referred to in can. 795, §1, nn. 1 and 2 is held by the local hierarch and, provided the case is occult, all persons referred to in can. 796, §2, observing all the conditions prescribed in the canon.

§2. This power is also operative for the convalidation of a marriage if there is the same danger in delay and there is not sufficient time to have recourse to the competent authority.

CAN. 798 The priests referred to in cann. 796, §2 and 797, §1 are to inform immediately the local hierarch of a dispensation or convalidation granted for the external forum and it is to be recorded in the marriage register.

CAN. 799 Unless there is a contrary determination in a rescript of the Apostolic See or of the patriarch or local hierarch within the limits of their competency, a dispensation from an occult impediment granted in the internal non-sacramental forum is to be recorded in the secret archive of the eparchial curia; no other dispensation for the external forum is necessary, even if the occult impediment should become public later.

posse, si tantum alio modo quam per epistulam vel personalem accessum id fieri potest.

CAN. 797 §1. Si impedimentum detegitur, dum iam omnia parata sunt ad matrimonium celebrandum nec matrimonium sine probabili gravis mali periculo deferri potest, donec ab auctoritate competenti dispensatio obtenta erit, potestatem dispensandi ab omnibus impedimentis, eis exceptis, de quibus in can. 795, §1, nn. 1 et 2, habent Hierarcha loci et, dummodo casus sit occultus, omnes, de quibus in can. 796, §2, servatis condicionibus ibidem praescriptis.

§2. Haec potestas valet etiam ad matrimonium convalidandum, si idem periculum est in mora nec tempus suppetit adeundi auctoritatem competentem.

CAN. 798 Sacerdotes, de quibus in cann. 796, §2 et 797, §1, de concessa dispensatione vel convalidatione pro foro externo Hierarcham loci statim certiorem faciant eaque adnotetur in libro matrimoniorum.

CAN. 799 Nisi aliud fert rescriptum Sedis Apostolicae aut intra limites eorum competentiae Patriarchae vel Hierarchae loci, dispensatio in foro interno non sacramentali concessa ab impedimento occulto adnotetur in archivo secreto curiae eparchialis nec alia dispensatio pro foro externo est necessaria, etsi postea occultum impedimentum publicum evasit.

797 §1: Pius XII, m.p. *Crebrae allatae sunt,* 22 feb. 1949, can. 35 §§1, 3. * Syn. Sciarfen. Syrorum, a. 1888, cap. V, art. XV, §9, 1; Syn. Alexandrin. Coptorum, a. 1898, sect. II, cap. III, art. VIII, §6, 6; Syn. Armen., a. 1911, 578.

797 §2: Pius XII, m.p. *Crebrae allatae sunt,* 22 feb. 1949, can. 35 §2. - S.C.S. Off., litt. encycl. 20 feb. 1888;

6 iul. 1898, ad 3.

798: Pius XII, m.p. *Crebrae allatae sunt,* 22 feb. 1949, can. 36.

799: Pius XII, m.p. *Crebrae allatae sunt,* 22 feb. 1949, can. 37. * Syn. prov. Alba-Iulien. et Fagarasien. Rumenorum, a. 1882, tit. IV, sect. I, §44.

ART. III. *Impediments Specifically*

ART. III. *De Impedimentis in Specie*

CAN. 800 §1. A man before he has completed his sixteenth year of age and a woman before she has completed her fourteenth year of age, cannot validly celebrate marriage.

§2. It is within the power of the particular law of any Church *sui iuris* to establish a higher age for the licit celebration of marriage.

CAN. 801 §1. By its very nature, marriage is invalidated by antecedent and perpetual impotence to have sexual intercourse, whether on the part of the man or the woman, whether absolute or relative.

§2. If the impediment of impotence is doubtful, either by reason of doubt of law or doubt of fact, marriage is neither to be impeded nor is it to be declared null as long as the doubt exists.

§3. Sterility neither prohibits nor invalidates marriage, with due regard for can. 821.

CAN. 802 §1. A person who is held by the bond of a prior marriage invalidly attempts marriage.

§2. Even if the first marriage is invalid or dis-

CAN. 800 §1. Vir ante decimum sextum aetatis annum expletum, mulier ante decimum quartum aetatis annum expletum matrimonium valide celebrare non possunt.

§2. Integrum est iuri particulari Ecclesiae sui iuris aetatis annum superiorem ad licitam matrimonii celebrationem statuere.

CAN. 801 §1. Impotentia coeundi antecedens et perpetua sive ex parte viri sive ex parte mulieris sive absoluta sive relativa matrimonium ex ipsa eius natura dirimit.

§2. Si impedimentum impotentiae dubium est sive dubio iuris sive dubio facti, matrimonium non est impediendum nec stante dubio nullum declarandum.

§3. Sterilitas matrimonium nec prohibet nec dirimit firmo can. 821.

CAN. 802 §1. Invalide matrimonium attentat, qui vinculo tenetur prioris matrimonii.

§2. Etsi prius matrimonium invalidum

---

800 §1: Pius XII, m.p. *Crebrae allatae sunt,* 22 feb. 1949, can. 57 §1. - S.C. de Prop. Fide, instr. 31 iul. 1902, 9. * S. Nerses Glaien. Armenorum, ep. past., a. 1166, cap. V "Nemo e sacerdotibus coronam;" Syn. Sergii Patriarchae Maronitarum, 18 sep. 1596, can. XIII; Syn. Diamper. Syro-Malabarensium, a. 1599, CXCIII; Syn. Zamosten. Ruthenorum, a. 1720, tit. III, §8 "Caeterum;" Syn. Libanen. Maronitarum, a. 1736, pars II, cap. XI, 9, VI; Syn. Ain-Trazen. Graeco-Melchitarum, a. 1835, can. 7, 4; Syn. prov. Alba-Iulien. et Fagarasien. Rumenorum, a. 1872, tit. V, cap. VIII, I, a); a. 1882, tit. IV, sect. I, §4, c); Syn. Sciarfen. Syrorum, a. 1888, cap. V, art. XV, §8, 5; Syn. Alexandrin. Coptorum, a. 1898, sect. II, cap. III, art. VIII, §5, 4, V; Syn. Armen., a. 1911, 571, n. 1; ▲ Instit. 1, 10, pr.; D. 23, 2, 4; C. 5, 60, 3; Basilic. 28, 4, 3.

801 §1: Pius XII, m.p. *Crebrae allatae sunt,* 22 feb. 1949, can. 58 §1. - Sixtus V, ep. *Cum frequenter,* 27 iun. 1587; S.C.S. Off., instr. (ad Ep. Rituum Orient.), 1883, tit. VI, art. 5; S.C. pro Doctr. Fidei, decr. 13 maii 1977.

801 §2: Pius XII, m.p. *Crebrae allatae sunt,* 22 feb. 1949, can. 58 §2. - S.C.S. Off., resp. 16 feb. 1935; resp. 28 sep. 1957; resp. 28 ian. 1964; resp. 25 mar. 1964.

801 §3: Pius XII, m.p. *Crebrae allatae sunt,* 22 feb. 1949, can. 58 §3.

802 §1: Pius XII, m.p. *Crebrae allatae sunt,* 22 feb. 1949, can. 59 §1. - Apost. can. 48; Carth. can. 102; Quinisext. can. 87; S. Basilius M., cann. 9, 46, 48, 77; Timotheus Alexandrin., can. 15; Syn. Trid., sess. XXIV, *De matrimonio,* can. 7; Eugenius IV (in Flor.), const. *Exsultate Deo,* 22 nov. 1439, §16; Benedictus XIV, ep. *Nuper ad Nos,* 16 mar. 1743, Professio fidei Maronitis praescr., §5; S.C. de Prop. Fide, instr. (ad Vic. Ap. Constantinop.), 1 oct. 1785; instr. (ad Ep. Graeco-Rumen.), a. 1858; Leo XIII, ep. encycl. *Arcanum,* 10 feb. 1880; S.C.S. Off., instr. (ad Ep. Rituum Orient.), a. 1883, tit. VI, art. 4; S.C. de Prop. Fide, instr. 31 iul. 1902, 9. * Syn. Zamosten. Ruthenorum, a. 1720, tit. III, §8 "Parochus."

802 §2: Pius XII, m.p. *Crebrae allatae sunt,* 22 feb. 1949, can. 59 §2. - S. Basilius M., cann. 31, 36;

solved for any cause, it is not permitted to celebrate another marriage before the invalidity or dissolution of the first is legitimately and certainly established.

CAN. 803 §1. Marriage with a non-baptized person cannot validly be celebrated.

§2. If at the time of the celebration of marriage the party was commonly held to be baptized or his or her baptism was doubtful, the validity of the marriage is to be presumed, in accord with the norm of can. 779, until it is proven with certainty that one party was baptized and the other was not.

§3. Concerning the conditions for dispensing, can. 814 is to be applied.

CAN. 804 Persons who are in sacred orders invalidly attempt marriage.

CAN. 805 Persons who are bound by a public perpetual vow of chastity in a religious institute invalidly attempt marriage.

CAN. 806 Marriage cannot be celebrated validly with a person who has been abducted, or at least detained, with a view to marriage, un-

aut solutum est qualibet ex causa, non licet aliud matrimonium celebrare, antequam de prioris invaliditate aut solutione legitime et certo constat.

CAN. 803 §1. Matrimonium cum non baptizatis valide celebrari non potest.

§2. Si pars tempore celebrati matrimonii tamquam baptizata communiter habebatur aut eius baptismus erat dubius, praesumenda est ad normam can. 779 validitas matrimonii, donec certo probetur alteram partem baptizatam esse, alteram vero non baptizatam.

§3. Circa condiciones dispensandi applicetur can. 814.

CAN. 804 Invalide matrimonium attentat, qui in ordine sacro est constitutus.

CAN. 805 Invalide matrimonium attentat, qui votum publicum perpetuum castitatis in instituto religioso emisit.

CAN. 806 Cum persona abducta vel saltem retenta intuitu matrimonii cum ea celebrandi matrimonium valide celebrari non

---

LUCIUS III, litt. *Dominus ac Redemptor*, a. 1181/5; S.C.S. Off., instr. (ad Del. Ap. Aegypti), 13 ian. 1861; instr. (ad Ep. Orient.), 22 aug. 1890, 11.

803 §1: PIUS XII, m.p. *Crebrae allatae sunt*, 22 feb. 1949, can. 60 §1; - Chalc. can. 14; Quinisext. can. 72; S.C.S. Off., instr. (ad omnes Ep. Ritus Orient.), 12 dec. 1888, 1; * Syn. Partaven. Armenorum, a. 771, can. 11; Syn. Libanen. Maronitarum, a. 1736, pars II, cap. XI, 8, VII et 17; Syn. Ain-Trazen. Graeco-Melchitarum, a. 1835, can. 7, 1; Syn. prov. Alba-Iulien. et Fagarasien. Rumenorum, a. 1872, tit. V, cap. VIII, I, i); a. 1882. tit. IV, sect. I, §10; Syn. Sciarfen. Syrorum, a. 1888, cap. V, art. XV, §8, 14; Syn. Alexandrin. Coptorum, a. 1898, sect. II, cap. III, art. VIII, §5, 4, XIII; Syn. Armen., a. 1911, 571, n. 10.

803 §2: PIUS XII, m.p. *Crebrae allatae sunt,* 22 feb. 1949, can. 60 §2.

803 §3: PIUS XII, m.p. *Crebrae allatae sunt,* 22 feb. 1949, can. 61.

804: PIUS XII, m.p. *Crebrae allatae sunt,* 22 feb. 1949, can. 62. - Quinisext. cann. 3, 6, 26; S. BASILIUS M., can. 27; TIMOTHEUS ALEXANDRIN., cann. 27–28;

S.C. de Prop. Fide, (C.P.), 18 sep. 1629; S.C.S. Off., decr. 3 iun. 1635, ad 1–2; 5 aug. 1650, ad 1; 29 ian. 1660; mandatum, 5 maii 1660; (C.G.), 28 aug. 1669, 1; BENEDICTUS XIV, const. *Etsi pastoralis,* 26 maii 1742, §VII, XXVII; instr. *Eo quamvis tempore,* 4 maii 1745, §§39–40; S.C. de Prop. Fide, litt. (ad Vic. gen. Fagarasien.), 5 feb. 1746; litt. (ad Metrop. Alba-Iulien. et Fagarasien.), 31 maii 1892. * Syn. Libanen. Maronitarum, a. 1736, pars II, cap. XI, 8, IX; cap. XIV, 35; pars III, cap. II, 3; Syn. prov. Alba-Iulien. et Fagarasien. Rumenorum, a. 1872, tit. VII, cap. V; a. 1882, tit. IV, sect. I, §11; Syn. Sciarfen. Syrorum, a. 1888, cap. V, art. XV, §8, 8; Syn. Alexandrin. Coptorum, a. 1898, sect. II, cap. III, art. VIII, §5, 4, XI; Syn. Armen., a. 1911, 571, n. 4.

805: PIUS XII, m.p. *Crebrae allatae sunt,* 22 feb. 1949, can. 63. - Chalc. can. 16; Quinisext. can. 44; S.C.S. Off., instr. (ad Ep. Rituum Orient.), a. 1883, tit. VI, art. 5 *"Adnotatio specialis."*

806: PIUS XII, m.p. *Crebrae allatae sunt,* 22 feb. 1949, can. 64. - S. BASILIUS M., cann. 22, 30.

less such a person has first been separated from the one responsible for the abduction or detention, and having been set in a safe and free place then freely chooses marriage.

CAN. 807 §1. A person who, with the intention of celebrating marriage with a certain person, brings about the death of that person's spouse or his or her own spouse, invalidly attempts this marriage.

§2. They also invalidly attempt marriage between themselves who have brought about the death of a spouse through mutual physical or moral cooperation.

CAN. 808 §1. In the direct line of consanguinity marriage is invalid between all ancestors and descendants.

§2. In a collateral line of consanguinity, marriage is invalid up to and including the fourth degree.

§3. Marriage is never to be permitted if there is a doubt whether the parties are related by consanguinity in any degree of the direct line or in the second degree of the collateral line.

§4. The impediment of consanguinity is not multiplied.

CAN. 809 §1. Affinity invalidates a mar-

potest, nisi postea illa ab abducente vel retinente separata et in loco tuto ac libero constituta matrimonium sua sponte eligit.

CAN. 807 §1. Qui intuitu matrimonii cum certa persona celebrandi eius coniugi vel proprio coniugi mortem intulit, invalide hoc matrimonium attentat.

§2. Invalide quoque matrimonium inter se attentant, qui mutua opera physica vel morali mortem coniugi intulerunt.

CAN. 808 §1. In linea recta consanguinitatis matrimonium invalidum est inter omnes ascendentes et descendentes.

§2. In linea collaterali invalidum est usque ad quartum gradum inclusive.

§3. Numquam matrimonium permittatur, si quod subest dubium, num partes sint consanguineae in aliquo gradu lineae rectae aut in secundo gradu lineae collateralis.

§4. Impedimentum consanguinitatis non multiplicatur.

CAN. 809 §1. Affinitas matrimonium

807 §1: Pius XII, m.p. *Crebrae allatae sunt,* 22 feb. 1949, can. 65 nn. 2–3. * Syn. Zamosten. Ruthenorum, a. 1720, tit. III, §8 "Caeterum;" Syn. Libanen. Maronitarum, a. 1736, pars II, cap. XI, 8, VI; Syn. prov. Alba-Iulien. et Fagarasien. Rumenorum, a. 1872, tit. V, cap. VIII, I, k); a. 1882, tit. IV, sect. I, §13; Syn. Sciarfen. Syrorum, a. 1888, cap. V, art. XV, §8, 16; Syn. Alexandrin. Coptorum, a. 1898, sect. II, cap. III, art. VIII, §5, 4, XV; Syn. Armen., a. 1911, 571, n. 11.

807 §2: Pius XII, m.p. *Crebrae allatae sunt,* 22 feb. 1949, can. 65 n. 3. * Syn. prov. Alba-Iulien. et Fagarasien. Rumenorum, a. 1882, tit. IV, sect. I, §13.

808 §1: Pius XII, m.p. *Crebrae allatae sunt,* 22 feb. 1949, can. 66 §§1–2. - S. Nicolaus I, litt. *Ad consulta vestra,* a. 866, XXXIX; Clemens VIII, breve, *Christi fidelium,* 17 aug. 1599; S.C.S. Off., instr. (Ad Ep. Rituum Orient.), a. 1883, tit. VI, art. I. * Syn. Diamper. Syro-Malabarensium, a. 1599, CLXXXIX; Syn. Zamosten. Ruthenorum, a. 1720, tit. III, §8 "Caeterum;" Syn. Libanen. Maronitarum, a. 1736,

pars II, cap. XI, 8, IV; Syn. Ain-Trazen. Graeco-Melchitarum, a. 1835, can. 7, 2; Syn. prov. Alba-Iulien. et Fagarasien. Rumenorum, a. 1872, tit. V, cap. VIII, I, l), α); a. 1882, tit. IV, sect. I, §14; Syn. Sciarfen. Syrorum, a. 1888, cap. V, art. XV, §8, 10; Syn. Alexandrin. Coptorum, a. 1898, sect. II, cap. III, art. VIII, §5, 4, VIII; Syn. Armen., a. 1911, 571, n. 5.

808 §2: Pius XII, m.p. *Crebrae allatae sunt,* 22 feb. 1949, can. 66 §2. - Quinisext. can. 54; Timotheus Alexandrin., can. 11. * Syn. Sahapivan. Armenorum, aa. 446–447, can. 13; Syn. Sisen. Armenorum, a. 1342, "Responsio: Secundum antiquam consuetudinem."

808 §3: Pius XII, m.p. *Crebrae allatae sunt,* 22 feb. 1949, can. 66 §3.

808 §4: Pius XII, m.p. *Crebrae allatae sunt,* 22 feb. 1949, can. 66 §2.

809 §1: Pius XII, m.p. *Crebrae allatae sunt,* 22 feb. 1949, can. 67 §1. - Neoc. can. 2; Quinisext. can. 54; S. Basilius M., cann. 23, 76, 78, 87; Timotheus Alexandrin., can. 11; Theophilus Alexandrin.,

riage in the direct line in any degree whatsoever; in the collateral line, in the second degree.

§2. The impediment of affinity is not multiplied.

CAN. 810 §1. The impediment of public propriety arises:

1° from an invalid marriage after which the couple have lived together;

2° from notorious or public concubinage;

3° from the cohabitation of a couple who are bound to the form of marriage celebration prescribed by law but have attempted marriage before a civil official or a non-Catholic minister.

§2. This impediment invalidates marriage in the first degree of the direct line between a man and the blood relatives of the woman and between a woman and the blood relatives of the man.

CAN. 811 §1. From baptism there arises a spiritual relationship between a sponsor and the

dirimit in quolibet gradu lineae rectae et in secundo gradu lineae collateralis.

§2. Impedimentum affinitatis non multiplicatur.

CAN. 810 §1. Impedimentum publicae honestatis oritur.

1° ex matrimonio invalido post instauratam vitam communem;

2° ex notorio vel publico concubinatu;

3° ex instauratione vitae communis eorum, qui ad formam celebrationis matrimonii iure praescriptam astricti matrimonium attentaverunt coram officiali civili aut ministro acatholico.

§2. Hoc impedimentum matrimonium dirimit in primo gradu lineae rectae inter virum et consanguineas mulieris itemque inter mulierem et viri consanguineos.

CAN. 811 §1. Ex baptismo oritur inter patrinum et baptizatum eiusque parentes

can. 5; S. NICEPHORUS CP., can. 81; CLEMENS VIII, breve, *Christi fidelium,* 17 aug. 1599; S.C.S. Off., instr. (ad Ep. Rituum Orient.), a. 1883, tit. VI, art. I. * Syn. Diamper. Syro-Malabarensium, a. 1599, CLXXXIX; Syn. Zamosten. Ruthenorum, a. 1720, tit. III, §8 "Caeterum;" Syn. Libanen. Maronitarum, a. 1736, pars II, cap. XI, 8, V; Syn. Ain-Trazen. Graeco-Melchitarum, a. 1835, can. 7, 2; Syn. prov. Alba-Iulien. et Fagarasien. Rumenorum, a. 1872, tit. V, cap. VIII, I, m); a. 1882, tit. IV, sect. I, §17; Syn. Sciarfen. Syrorum, a. 1888, cap. V, art. XV, §8, 12; Syn. Alexandrin. Coptorum, a. 1898, sect. II, cap. III, art. VIII, §5, 4, IX; Syn. Armen., a. 1911, 571, n. 6.

809 §2: PIUS XII, m.p. *Crebrae allatae sunt,* 22 feb. 1949, can. 67 §2.

810 §1: PIUS XII, m.p. *Crebrae allatae sunt,* 22 feb. 1949, can. 69. - CLEMENS VIII, breve, *Christi fidelium,* 17 aug. 1599; S.C.S. Off., instr. (ad Ep. Rituum Orient.), a. 1883, tit. VI, art. 2. * Syn. Zamosten. Ruthenorum, a. 1720, tit. III, §8 "Caeterum;" Syn. Libanen. Maronitarum, a. 1736, pars II, cap. XI, 8, XI; Syn. prov. Alba-Iulien. et Fagarasien. Rumenorum, a. 1872, tit. V, cap. VIII, I, n); a. 1882, tit. IV, sect. I, §18; Syn. Sciarfen. Syrorum, a. 1888, cap. V, art. XV, §8, 13; Syn. Alexandrin. Coptorum, a. 1898, sect. III, cap. III, art. VIII, §5, 4, XII; Syn. Armen., a. 1911, 571,

n. 7.

810 §2: PIUS XII, m.p. *Crebrae allatae sunt,* 22 feb. 1949, can. 69.

811 §1: PIUS XII, m.p. *Crebrae allatae sunt,* 22 feb. 1949, can. 70 §§1 et 2 n. 1. - Quinisext. can. 53; S. NICEPHORUS CP., cann. 124, 185; S. NICOLAUS I, litt. *Ad consulta vestra,* 13 nov. 866, II; CLEMENS VIII, breve, *Christi fidelium,* 17 aug. 1599; BENEDICTUS XIV, const. *Etsi pastoralis,* 26 maii 1742, §VIII, VI; S.C. de Prop. Fide, reg. (pro Sacerd. Coptis), 15 mar. 1790, XI; S.C.S. Off., instr. (ad Ep. Rituum Orient.), a. 1883, tit. VI, art. I; litt. (Leopol. Ruthen.), 29 apr. 1894; S.C. de Prop. Fide, (C.G.), litt. (ad Archiep. Fagarasien.), 25 iun. 1897. * Syn. Diamper. Syro-Malabarensium, a. 1599, CXCI; Syn. Zamosten. Ruthenorum, a. 1720, tit. III, §1 "Unum;" Syn. Libanen. Maronitarum, a. 1736, pars II, cap. II, 10; pars III, cap. XI, 8, IV "Cognatio Spiritualis;" Syn. Ain-Trazen. Graeco-Melchitarum, a. 1835, can. 1, 4; Syn. prov. Alba-Iulien. et Fagarasien. Rumenorum, a. 1872, tit. V, cap. VIII, I, l), β); a. 1882, tit. IV, sect. I, §15; Syn. Sciarfen. Syrorum, a. 1888, cap. V, art. II, 3, XXII; art. XV, §8, 11; Syn. Alexandrin. Coptorum, a. 1898, sect. II, cap. III, art. II, XXVII; sect. II, cap. III, art. VIII, §5, 4, VIII; Syn. Armen., a. 1911, 571, n. 9.

baptized person and the parents of the same that invalidates marriage.

§2. If a baptism is repeated under condition, a spiritual relationship does not arise, unless the same sponsor was employed for the second ceremony.

CAN. 812 Those who are legally related by reason of adoption cannot validly marry each other if their relationship is in the direct line or in the second degree of the collateral line.

cognatio spiritualis, quae matrimonium dirimit.

§2. Si iteratur baptismus sub condicione, cognatio spiritualis non oritur, nisi iterum idem patrinus adhibitus est.

CAN. 812 Matrimonium inter se valide celebrare non possunt, qui cognatione legali ex adoptione orta in linea recta aut in secundo gradu lineae collateralis coniuncti sunt.

ART. IV. *Mixed Marriages*

CAN. 813 Marriage between two baptized persons, one of whom is Catholic and the of other whom is non-Catholic, is prohibited without the prior permission of the competent authority.

CAN. 814 For a just cause the local hierarch can grant permission; however, he is not to grant it unless the following conditions are fulfilled:

1° the Catholic party declares that he or she is prepared to remove dangers of falling away

ART. IV. *De Matrimoniis Mixtis*

CAN. 813 Matrimonium inter duas personas baptizatas, quarum altera est catholica, altera vero acatholica, sine praevia auctoritatis competentis licentia prohibitum est.

CAN. 814 Licentiam iusta de causa concedere potest Hierarcha loci; eam vero ne concedat nisi impletis condicionibus, quae sequuntur:

1° pars catholica declaret se paratam esse pericula a fide deficiendi removere atque

811 §2: PIUS XII, m.p. *Crebrae allatae sunt,* 22 feb. 1949, can. 70 §2 n. 2.

812: PIUS XII, m.p. *Crebrae allatae sunt,* can. 71. * Syn. Libanen. Maronitarum, a. 1736, pars II, cap. XI, 8, IV "Cognatio Legalis;" Syn. Ain-Trazen. Graeco-Melchitarum, a. 1835, can. 7, 2; Syn. prov. Alba-Iulien. et Fagarasien. Rumenorum, a. 1872, tit. V, cap. VIII, I, l), γ); a. 1882, tit. IV, sect. I, §16; Syn. Sciarfen. Syrorum, a. 1888, cap. V, art. XV, §8, 11; Syn. Alexandrin. Coptorum, a. 1898, sect. II, cap. III, art. VIII, §5, 4, VIII; Syn. Armen., a. 1911, 571, n. 8; ▲ Instit. 1, 10, 1–3.

813: PIUS XII, m.p. *Crebrae allatae sunt,* 22 feb. 1949, can. 50. - Laod. cann. 10, 31; Chalc. can. 14; Carth. can. 21; Quinisext. can. 72; S.C. de Prop. Fide, instr. (ad Ep. Graeco-Rumen.), a. 1858; S.C.S. Off., instr. (ad Archiep. Corcyren.), 3 ian. 1871, 3; LEO XIII, ep. encycl. *Arcanum,* 10 feb. 1880; S.C.S. Off., instr. (ad omnes Ep. Ritus Orientalis), 12 dec. 1888, 1–4. * Syn. Libanen. Maronitarum, a. 1736, pars II, cap. XI, 8, VII; Syn. Ain-Trazen. Graeco-Melchitarum, a.

1835, can. 7, 1; Syn. prov. Alba-Iulien. et Fagarasien. Rumenorum, a. 1872, tit. V, cap. IX; a. 1882, tit. IV, sect. I, §31; Syn. Sciarfen. Syrorum, a. 1888, cap. V, art. XV, §7, 5; Syn. Leopolien. Ruthenorum, a. 1891, tit. II, cap. VII, 4; Syn. Alexandrin. Coptorum, a. 1898, sect. II, cap. III, art. VIII, §5, 3, IV; Syn. Armen., a. 1911, 577, n. 5.

814: PIUS XII, m.p. *Crebrae allatae sunt,* 22 feb. 1949, can. 51. - S.C. de Prop. Fide, instr. (ad Ep. Graeco-Rumen.), a. 1858; S.C.S. Off., instr. (ad Archiep. Corcyren.), 3 ian. 1871, 3; instr. (ad omnes Ep. Ritus Orient.), 12 dec. 1888, 4–5; 10 feb. 1892; decr. 14 iun. 1932; decr. 16 ian. 1942. * Syn. Libanen. Maronitarum, a. 1736, pars II, cap. XI, 17; Syn. prov. Alba-Iulien. et Fagarasien. Rumenorum, a. 1872, tit. V, cap. IX; a. 1882, tit. IV, sect. I, §31; Syn. Sciarfen. Syrorum, a. 1888, cap. V, art. XV, §7, 5; Syn. Leopolien. Ruthenorum, a. 1891, tit. II, cap. VII, 4; Syn. Alexandrin. Coptorum, a. 1898, sect. II, cap. III, art. VIII, §5, 3, IV "Si propter."

from the faith and makes a sincere promise to do all in his or her power to have all the children baptized and educated in the Catholic Church;

2° the other party is to be informed in good time of these promises that the Catholic party has to make, so that it is clear that the other party is truly aware of the promise and obligation of the Catholic party;

3° both parties are to be instructed on the essential ends and properties of marriage, which are not to be excluded by either spouse.

CAN. 815 The particular law of each Church *sui iuris* is to specify the manner in which these declarations and promises, which are always required, are to be made, and to determine how they can be established in the external forum and how the non-Catholic party is to be informed of them.

CAN. 816 Local hierarchs and other pastors of souls are to see that the Catholic spouse and the children born of a mixed marriage are not without the spiritual help needed to fulfill their obligations of conscience; they are also to assist the spouses to foster the unity of partnership in their conjugal and family life.

ART. V. *Matrimonial Consent*

CAN. 817 §1. Matrimonial consent is an act of the will by which a man and woman, through an irrevocable covenant, mutually give and accept each other in order to establish marriage.

§2. No human power can replace this matrimonial consent.

sinceram promissionem praestet se omnia pro viribus facturam esse, ut omnes filii in Ecclesia catholica baptizentur et educentur;

2° de his promissionibus a parte catholica faciendis altera pars tempestive certior fiat ita, ut constet ipsam vere consciam esse promissionis et obligationis partis catholicae;

3° ambae partes edoceantur de finibus et proprietatibus essentialibus matrimonii a neutro sponso excludendis.

CAN. 815 Iure particulari uniuscuiusque Ecclesiae sui iuris statuatur modus, quo hae declarationes et promissiones, quae semper requiruntur, faciendae sint, et modus determinetur, quo de eisdem et in foro externo constet et pars acatholica certior fiat.

CAN. 816 Hierarchae loci aliique pastores animarum curent, ne coniugi catholico et filiis ex matrimonio mixto natis auxilium spirituale desit ad eorum obligationes conscientiae implendas, atque coniuges adiuvent ad consortii vitae coniugalis et familiaris unitatem fovendam.

ART. V. *De Consensu Matrimoniali*

CAN. 817 §1. Consensus matrimonialis est actus voluntatis, quo vir et mulier foedere irrevocabili se mutuo tradunt et accipiunt ad constituendum matrimonium.

§2. Consensus matrimonialis nulla humana potestate suppleri potest.

817 §1: Pius XII, m.p. *Crebrae allatae sunt,* 22 feb. 1949, can. 72 §2; Vat. II, const. *Gaudium et spes,* 48; Paulus VI, litt. encycl. *Humanae vitae,* 25 iul. 1968, 8. - Eugenius IV (in Flor.), const. *Exsultate Deo,* 22 nov. 1439, §16; S.C. de Prop. Fide, instr. (ad Vic. Ap. Constantinop.), 1 oct. 1785.

817 §2: Pius XII, m.p. *Crebrae allatae sunt,* 22 feb. 1949, can. 72 §1. - Benedictus XIII, a. 1341, prop. 100, Armenorum, damn.; Pius XI, litt. encycl. *Casti connubii,* 31 dec. 1930, "At, quamquam;" Paulus VI, all. 9 feb. 1976. * Syn. Zamosten. Ruthenorum, a. 1720, tit. III, §8 "Cum autem liber." ▲ D. 23, 2, 2.

CAN. 818 They are incapable of celebrating marriage:

1° who lack the sufficient use of reason;

2° who suffer from grave lack of discretion of judgment concerning essential matrimonial rights and obligations mutually handed over and accepted;

3° who cannot assume the essential obligations of matrimony due to causes of a psychic nature.

CAN. 819 In order to have matrimonial consent, it is necessary that the couple be at least not ignorant of the fact that marriage is a permanent partnership between a man and a woman, ordered to the procreation of children through some sexual cooperation.

CAN. 820 §1. Error about a person renders a marriage invalid.

§2. Error about a quality of a person, even if it occasions the marriage, does not render the marriage invalid, unless this quality was directly and principally intended.

CAN. 821 A person who celebrates marriage deceived by fraud perpetrated to secure consent, concerning some quality of the other party that of its very nature can seriously disturb the partnership of conjugal life, celebrates it invalidly.

CAN. 822 Error concerning the unity, indissolubility or sacramental dignity of matrimony does not vitiate matrimonial consent so long as it does not determine the will.

CAN. 823 The knowledge or opinion of

CAN. 818 Sunt incapaces matrimonii celebrandi:

1° qui sufficienti usu rationis carent;

2° qui laborant gravi defectu discretionis iudicii circa iura et obligationes matrimoniales essentiales mutuo tradenda et acceptanda;

3° qui ob causas naturae psychicae obligationes matrimonii essentiales assumere non possunt.

CAN. 819 Ut consensus matrimonialis haberi possit, necesse est, ut matrimonium celebrantes saltem non ignorent matrimonium esse consortium permanens inter virum et mulierem ordinatum ad filios cooperatione aliqua sexuali procreandos.

CAN. 820 §1. Error in persona invalidum reddit matrimonium.

§2. Error in qualitate personae, etsi dat causam matrimonio, matrimonium non dirimit, nisi haec qualitas directe et principaliter intenditur.

CAN. 821 Qui matrimonium celebrat deceptus dolo ad obtinendum consensum patrato circa aliquam alterius partis qualitatem, quae sua natura consortium vitae coniugalis graviter perturbare potest, invalide celebrat.

CAN. 822 Error circa matrimonii unitatem vel indissolubilitatem aut sacramentalem dignitatem, dummodo non determinet voluntatem, non vitiat consensum matrimonialem.

CAN. 823 Scientia aut opinio nullitatis

818, 3°: Ioannes Paulus II, all. 5 feb. 1987; all. 25 ian. 1988.

819: Pius XII, m.p. *Crebrae allatae sunt,* 22 feb. 1949, can. 73 §1.

820 §1: Pius XII, m.p. *Crebrae allatae sunt,* 22 feb. 1949, can. 74 §1.

820 §2: Pius XII, m.p. *Crebrae allatae sunt,* 22 feb. 1949, can. 74 §2. - S. Basilius M., cann. 40, 42. * Syn. Libanen. Maronitarum, a. 1736, pars II, cap. XI,

8, II; Syn. Sciarfen. Syrorum, a. 1888, cap. V, art. XV, §8, 2 et 4; Syn. Alexandrin. Coptorum, a. 1898, sect. II, cap. III, art. VIII, §5, 4, II; Syn. Armen., a. 1911, 568.

822: Pius XII, m.p. *Crebrae allatae sunt,* 22 feb. 1949, can. 75. - S.C. de Prop. Fide, instr. (ad Vic. Ap. Constantinop.), 1 oct. 1785.

823: Pius XII, m.p. *Crebrae allatae sunt,* 22 feb. 1949, can. 76. - S.C. de Prop. Fide, instr. (ad Vic. Ap. Constantinop.), 1 oct. 1785.

the nullity of a marriage does not necessarily exclude matrimonial consent.

CAN. 824 §1. The internal consent of the mind is presumed to conform to the words or signs used in the celebration of the marriage.

§2. But if either or both parties through a positive act of the will should exclude marriage itself, or any essential element of marriage or an essential property, the marriage is invalidly celebrated.

CAN. 825 A marriage is invalid that is celebrated by reason of force or grave fear imposed from without, even if not purposely, from which the person has no other escape than by choosing marriage.

CAN. 826 Marriage based on a condition cannot be validly celebrated.

CAN. 827 Even if a marriage was celebrated invalidly by reason of an impediment or defect of form prescribed by law for celebrating marriage, the consent once given is presumed to persist until it is established that it has been revoked.

ART. VI. *The Form for the Celebration of Marriage*

CAN. 828 §1. Only those marriages are valid that are celebrated with a sacred rite, in the presence of the local hierarch, local pastor, or a

matrimonii consensum matrimonialem non necessario excludit.

CAN. 824 §1. Internus animi consensus praesumitur conformis verbis vel signis in celebrando matrimonio adhibitis.

§2. Sed si alterutra vel utraque pars positivo voluntatis actu excludit matrimonium ipsum vel matrimonii essentiale aliquod elementum vel essentialem aliquam proprietatem, invalide matrimonium celebrat.

CAN. 825 Invalidum est matrimonium celebratum ob vim vel metum gravem ab extrinseco etiam inconsulto incussum, a quo ut quis se liberet, eligere cogatur matrimonium.

CAN. 826 Matrimonium sub condicione valide celebrari non potest.

CAN. 827 Etsi matrimonium invalide ratione impedimenti vel defectus formae celebrationis matrimonii iure praescriptae celebratum est, consensus praestitus praesumitur perseverare, donec de eius revocatione constiterit.

ART. VI. *De Forma Celebrationis Matrimonii*

CAN. 828 §1. Ea tantum matrimonia valida sunt, quae celebrantur ritu sacro coram Hierarcha loci vel parocho loci vel

824 §1: Pius XII, m.p. *Crebrae allatae sunt,* 22 feb. 1949, can. 77 §1. - S.C. de Prop. Fide, instr. (Ad Vic. Ap. Constantinop.), 1 oct. 1785.

824 §2: Pius XII, m.p. *Crebrae allatae sunt,* 22 feb. 1949, can. 77 §2. - S.C. de Prop. Fide, instr. (ad Vic. Ap. Constantinop.), 1 oct. 1785.

825: Pius XII, m.p. *Crebrae allatae sunt,* 22 feb. 1949, can. 78 §1. - S.C.S. Off., instr. (ad Ep. Rituum Orient.), a. 1883, tit. VI, art. 3. * Syn. Zamosten. Ruthenorum, a. 1720, tit. III, §8 "Cum autem liber;" Syn. Libanen. Maronitarum, a. 1736, pars II, cap. XI, 8, VIII; Syn. prov. Alba-Iulien. et Fagarasien. Rumenorum, a. 1872, tit. V, cap. VIII, I, d); a. 1882, tit. IV, sect. I, §5, b); Syn. Sciarfen. Syrorum, a. 1888, cap. V, art. XV, §8, 3; Syn. Alexandrin. Coptorum, a. 1898,

sect. II, cap. III, art. VIII, §5, 4, IV; Syn. Armen., a. 1911, 569.

826: Pius XII, m.p. *Crebrae allatae sunt,* 22 feb. 1949, can. 83. * Syn. prov. Alba-Iulien. et Fagarasien. Rumenorum, a. 1882, tit. IV, sect. I, §5, d); Syn. Sciarfen. Syrorum, a. 1888, cap. V, art. XV, §3, 6; Syn. Armen., a. 1911, 564–567.

827: Pius XII, m.p. *Crebrae allatae sunt,* 22 feb. 1949, can. 84.

828 §1: Pius XII, m.p. *Crebrae allatae sunt,* 22 feb. 1949, can. 85 §1. - S. Nicephorus CP., cann. 90, 199; S. Nicolaus I, litt. *Ad consulta vestra,* 13 nov. 866, III; S.C. de Prop. Fide, instr. (ad Vic. Ap. Constantinop.), 1 oct. 1785; litt. (ad Ep. Nicopolitan.), 11 ian. 1817; S.C. de Prop. Fide (pro Neg. Rit. Orient.), decr.

priest who has been given the faculty of blessing the marriage by either of them, and at least two witnesses, according, however to the prescripts of the following canons, without prejudice to the exceptions referred to in cann. 832 and 834, §2.

§2. The very intervention of a priest who assists and blesses is regarded as a sacred rite for the present purpose.

CAN. 829 §1. From the day of taking canonical possession of office and as long as they legitimately hold office, everywhere within the boundaries of their territory, local hierarchs and local pastors validly bless the marriage of parties whether they are subjects or non-subjects, provided that at least one of the parties is ascribed in his Church *sui iuris*.

§2. A personal hierarch and a personal pastor, by virtue of their office, validly bless marriages within the limits of their jurisdiction only of those of whom at least one party is their subject.

§3. By the law itself, the patriarch is endowed with the faculty personally to bless marriages everywhere, as long as at least one of the parties is ascribed to the Church over which he presides, observing the other requirements of law.

CAN. 830 §1. As long as they legitimately hold office, the local hierarch and the local pastor can give the faculty to bless a determined

sacerdote, cui ab alterutro collata est facultas matrimonium benedicendi, et duobus saltem testibus secundum tamen praescripta canonum, qui sequuntur, et salvis exceptionibus, de quibus in cann. 832 et 834, §2.

§2. Sacer hic censetur ritus ipso interventu sacerdotis assistentis et benedicentis.

CAN. 829 §1. Hierarcha loci et parochus loci capta possessione canonica officii, dum legitime officio funguntur, intra fines sui territorii ubique valide benedicunt matrimonium, sive sponsi sunt subditi sive, dummodo alterutra saltem pars sit ascripta propriae Ecclesiae sui iuris, non subditi.

§2. Hierarcha et parochus personalis vi officii matrimonium solummodo eorum, quorum saltem alteruter sibi subditus est, intra fines suae dicionis valide benedicunt.

§3. Patriarcha ipso iure facultate praeditus est servatis aliis de iure servandis matrimonia per se ipsum benedicendi ubique terrarum, dummodo alterutra saltem pars ascripta sit Ecclesiae, cui praeest.

CAN. 830 §1. Hierarcha loci et parochus loci, dum legitime officio funguntur, possunt sacerdotibus cuiusvis Ecclesiae sui

---

18 aug. 1913, art. 36; decr. 17 aug. 1914, art. 30; decr. 27 mar. 1916, 17; S.C. pro Eccl. Orient., decr. 1 mar. 1929, art. 39; decr. 24 maii 1930, art. 45; Pont. Comm. ad Red. Cod. Iur. Can. Orient., interpr. auth. 8 ian. 1953, I; interpr. auth. 3 maii 1953, ad can. 85 §2. * Syn. Sergii Patriarchae Maronitarum, 18 sep. 1596, can. XIV; Syn. Diamper. Syro-Malabarensium, a. 1599, CLXXXV; Syn. Zamosten. Ruthenorum, a. 1720, tit. III, §8; Syn. Libanen. Maronitarum, a. 1736, pars II, cap. XI, 8, XII et 28; pars III, cap. III, 2, X; Syn. prov. Alba-Iulien. et Fagarasien. Rumenorum, a. 1882, tit. IV, sect. I, §§23–25; Syn. Sciarfen. Syrorum, a. 1888, cap. V, art. XV, §12; Syn. Alexandrin. Coptorum, a.

1898, sect. II, cap. III, art. VIII, §5, 4, XVI; Syn. Armen., a. 1911, 575.

828 §2: Pius XII, m.p. *Crebrae allatae sunt,* 22 feb. 1949, can. 85 §2.

829 §1: Pius XII, m.p. *Crebrae allatae sunt,* 22 feb. 1949, can. 86 §§1–2. - Pont. Comm. ad Red. Cod. Iur. Can. Orient., interpr. auth. 8 iul. 1952; interpr. auth. 3 maii 1953, ad can. 86 §1 n. 2. * Syn. Leopolien. Ruthenorum, a. 1891, tit. II, cap. VII, 3.

829 §2: Pius XII, const. ap. *Exsul Familia,* 1 aug. 1952, 35–36 et 39.

830 §1: Pius XII, m.p. *Crebrae allatae sunt,* 22 feb. 1949, can. 87 §1 n. 1.

marriage within their own territorial boundaries to priests of any Church *sui iuris,* even the Latin Church.

§2. However, only the local hierarch can give a general faculty for blessing marriages with due regard for can. 302, §2.

§3. In order that the conferral of the faculty for blessing a marriage be valid, it must be expressly given to specified priests; further, if the faculty is general, it must be given in writing.

CAN. 831 §1. The local hierarch or local pastor licitly blesses a marriage:

1° after he has established the domicile, quasi-domicile, or month-long residence, or, if it is a case of a transient, the actual residence of either party in the place of the marriage;

2° if, when these conditions are lacking, he has the permission of the hierarch or pastor of the domicile or quasi-domicile of either of the parties, unless a just cause excuses;

3° also, in a place exclusively of another Church *sui iuris,* unless the hierarch who exercises power in that place expressly refuses.

§2. The marriage is to be celebrated before the pastor of the groom, unless particular law determines otherwise or a just cause excuses.

CAN. 832 §1. If the priest who is compe-

iuris, etiam Ecclesiae latinae, facultatem conferre, intra fines sui territorii determinatum matrimonium benedicendi.

§2. Facultatem generalem vero matrimonia benedicendi conferre potest solus Hierarcha loci firmo can. 302, §2.

§3. Collatio facultatis matrimonia benedicendi, ut valida sit, determinatis sacerdotibus expresse immo, si de facultate generali agitur, scripto conferri debet.

CAN. 831 §1. Hierarcha loci vel parochus loci matrimonium licite benedicunt:

1° postquam sibi constitit de domicilio vel quasi-domicilio vel menstrua commoratione aut, si de vago agitur, actuali commoratione alterutrius sponsi in loco matrimonii;

2° habita, si hae condiciones desunt, licentia Hierarchae vel parochi domicilii vel quasi-domicilii alterutrius partis, nisi iusta causa excusat;

3° in loco quoque exclusivo alterius Ecclesiae sui iuris, nisi Hierarcha, qui in hoc loco potestatem suam exercet, expresse renuit.

§2. Matrimonium coram sponsi parocho celebretur, nisi vel ius particulare aliud fert vel iusta causa excusat.

CAN. 832 §1. Si haberi vel adiri non

---

830 §2: Pius XII, m.p. *Crebrae allatae sunt,* 22 feb. 1949, can. 87 §1 n. 2.

830 §3: Pius XII, m.p. *Crebrae allatae sunt,* 22 feb. 1949, can. 87 §1 n. 1.

831 §1, 1°: Pius XII, m.p. *Crebrae allatae sunt,* 22 feb. 1949, can. 88 §1 n. 2. * Syn. Libanen. Maronitarum, a. 1736, pars II, cap. XI, 28.

831 §1, 2°: Pius XII, m.p. *Crebrae allatae sunt,* 22 feb. 1949, can. 88 §1 n. 3.

831 §1, 3°: Pont. Comm. ad Red. Cod. Iur. Can. Orient., interpr. auth. 8 iul. 1952.

831 §2: Pius XII, m.p. *Crebrae allatae sunt,* 22 feb. 1949, can. 88 §3. - Benedictus XIV, const. *Etsi pastoralis,* 26 maii 1742, §VIII, XI–XII; S.C. de Prop.

Fide, decr. 6 oct. 1863, C), c), D), b); S.C. de Prop. Fide (pro Neg. Rit. Orient.), decr. 18 aug. 1913, art. 37; decr. 17 aug. 1914, art. 30; decr. 27 mar. 1916, 17; S.C. pro Eccl. Orient., decr. 1 mar. 1929, art. 39; decr. 24 maii 1930, art. 45; decr. 23 nov. 1940, art. 39; Pont. Comm. ad Red. Cod. Iur. Can. Orient., interpr. auth. 3 maii 1953, ad can. 88 §3. * Syn. Libanen. Maronitarum, a. 1736, pars II, cap. XI, 28; Syn. Sciarfen. Syrorum, a. 1888, cap. III, art. IX, 11; Syn. Alexandrin. Coptorum, a. 1898, sect. II, cap. I, art. V, XXIV; Syn. Armen., a. 1911, 622.

832 §1: Pius XII, m.p. *Crebrae allatae sunt,* 22 feb. 1949, can. 89.

tent in accord with the norm of law cannot be present or be approached without grave inconvenience, those who intend to celebrate a true marriage can validly and licitly celebrate it in the presence of witnesses only:

1° in danger of death;

2° apart from the danger of death, provided it is prudently foreseen that this state of affairs will continue for a month.

§2. In either case, if another priest is at hand, he is to be called upon, if it is possible, to bless the marriage, without prejudice to the validity of the marriage celebrated in the presence of only the witnesses; in such cases even a non-Catholic priest may be called.

§3. If the marriage was celebrated in the presence only of witnesses, the spouses shall not neglect to receive the nuptial blessing from a priest as soon as possible.

CAN. 833 §1. The local hierarch can give to any Catholic priest the faculty of blessing the marriage of the Christian faithful of an Eastern non-Catholic Church if those faithful cannot approach a priest of their own Church without great difficulty and if they voluntarily ask for the blessing as long as nothing stands in the way of a valid and licit celebration.

§2. If possible, before blessing the marriage, the Catholic priest is to notify the competent authority of those Christian faithful about the matter.

CAN. 834 §1. The form for the celebration of marriage by law is to be observed if at least one of the parties celebrating the marriage was baptized in the Catholic Church or was received into it.

§2. If, however, a Catholic party ascribed to

potest sine gravi incommodo sacerdos ad normam iuris competens, celebrare intendentes verum matrimonium illud valide ac licite coram solis testibus celebrare possunt:

1° in periculo mortis;

2° extra periculum mortis, dummodo prudenter praevideatur earum rerum condicionem esse per mensem duraturam.

§2. In utroque casu, si praesto est alius sacerdos, ille, si fieri potest, vocetur, ut matrimonium benedicat salva matrimonii validitate coram solis testibus; eisdem in casibus etiam sacerdos acatholicus vocari potest.

§3. Si matrimonium celebratum est coram solis testibus, coniuges a sacerdote quam primum benedictionem matrimonii suscipere ne neglegant.

CAN. 833 §1. Hierarcha loci cuilibet sacerdoti catholico facultatem conferre potest matrimonium christifidelium alicuius Ecclesiae orientalis acatholicae, qui sacerdotem propriae Ecclesiae sine gravi incommodo adire non possunt, benedicendi, si sua sponte id petunt et dummodo nihil validae vel licitae celebrationi matrimonii obstet.

§2. Sacerdos catholicus, si fieri potest, antequam matrimonium benedicit, auctoritatem competentem illorum christifidelium de hac re certiorem faciat.

CAN. 834 §1. Forma celebrationis matrimonii iure praescripta servanda est, si saltem alterutra pars matrimonium celebrantium in Ecclesia catholica baptizata vel in eandem recepta est.

§2. Si vero pars catholica alicui Ecclesi-

---

832 §2: Pius XII, m.p. *Crebrae allatae sunt,* 22 feb. 1949, can. 89 n. 2.

834 §1: Pius XII, m.p. *Crebrae allatae sunt,* 22 feb.

1949, can. 90 §1.

834 §2: Vat. II, decr. *Orientalium Ecclesiarum,* 18; S.C. pro Eccl. Orient., decr. 22 feb. 1967.

an Eastern Church celebrates a marriage with one who belongs to an Eastern non-Catholic Church, the form for the celebration of marriage prescribed by law is to be observed only for liceity; for validity, however, the blessing of a priest is required, while observing the other requirements of law.

CAN. 835 Dispensation from the form for the celebration of marriage required by law is reserved to the Apostolic See or the patriarch, who will not grant it except for a most grave cause.

CAN. 836 Apart from a case of necessity, in the celebration of marriage the prescripts of the liturgical books and the legitimate customs are to be observed.

CAN. 837 §1. For the valid celebration of marriage, it is necessary for the parties to be present together and express mutually their marriage consent.

§2. Marriage cannot be validly celebrated by proxy unless the particular law of the respective Church *sui iuris* establishes otherwise, in which case it must provide the conditions under which such a marriage can be celebrated.

CAN. 838 §1. Marriage is to be celebrated

ae orientali sui iuris ascripta matrimonium celebrat cum parte, quae ad Ecclesiam orientalem acatholicam pertinet, forma celebrationis matrimonii iure praescripta servanda est tantum ad liceitatem; ad validitatem autem requiritur benedictio sacerdotis servatis aliis de iure servandis.

CAN. 835 Dispensatio a forma celebrationis matrimonii iure praescripta reservatur Sedi Apostolicae vel Patriarchae, qui eam ne concedat nisi gravissima de causa.

CAN. 836 Extra casum necessitatis in matrimonii celebratione serventur praescripta librorum liturgicorum et legitimae consuetudines.

CAN. 837 §1. Ad matrimonium valide celebrandum necesse est, ut partes sint praesentes una simul et consensum matrimonialem mutuo exprimant.

§2. Matrimonium per procuratorem valide celebrari non potest, nisi iure particulari propriae Ecclesiae sui iuris aliud statuitur, quo in casu etiam de condicionibus, sub quibus tale matrimonium celebrari potest, providendum est.

CAN. 838 §1. Matrimonium celebretur

836: PIUS XII, m.p. *Crebrae allatae sunt,* 22 feb. 1949, can. 91. - S. NICEPHORUS CP., can. 90. * Syn. Duinen. Armenorum, a. 719, can. 15; Syn. Diamper. Syro-Malabarensium, a. 1599, CLXXXV; Syn. Zamosten. Ruthenorum, a. 1720, tit. III, §8 "Quoniam;" Syn. Libanen. Maronitarum, a. 1736, pars III, cap. III, 2, X; Syn. Leopolien. Ruthenorum, a. 1891, tit. II, cap. VII, 6; Syn. Sciarfen. Syrorum, a. 1888, cap. V, art. XV, §12, IV; Syn. Alexandrin. Coptorum, a. 1898, sect. II, cap. III, art. VIII, §2, III; Syn. Armen., a. 1911, 576.

837 §1: PIUS XII, m.p. *Crebrae allatae sunt,* 22 feb. 1949, can. 79 §§1-2. - EUGENIUS IV (in Flor.), const. *Exsultate Deo,* 22 nov. 1439, §16. * Syn. Zamosten. Ruthenorum, a. 1720, tit. III, §8 "Si nullum;" Syn. Libanen. Maronitarum, a. 1736, pars II, cap. XI, 27;

Syn. Ain-Trazen. Graeco-Melchitarum, a. 1835, can. 7, 3; Syn. prov. Alba-Iulien. et Fagarasien. Rumenorum, a. 1872, tit. V, cap. VIII "Causa;" Syn. Sciarfen. Syrorum, a. 1888, cap. V, art. XV, §3, 4; Syn. Alexandrin. Coptorum, a. 1898, sect. II, cap. III, art. VIII, §2, IV; Syn. Armen., a. 1911, 563.

837 §2: PIUS XII, m.p. *Crebrae allatae sunt,* 22 feb. 1949, cann. 80-82. * Syn. Libanen. Maronitarum, a. 1736, pars II, cap. XI, 29; Syn. Sciarfen. Syrorum, a. 1888, cap. V, art. XV, §3, 7; Syn. Armen., a. 1911, 563.

838 §1: PIUS XII, m.p. *Crebrae allatae sunt,* 22 feb. 1949, can. 98. * Syn. Zamosten. Ruthenorum, a. 1720, tit. III, §8 "Si nullum;" Syn. Libanen. Maronitarum, a. 1736, pars II, cap. XI, 26; Syn. Sciarfen. Syrorum, a. 1888, cap. V, art. XV, §12, V.

in a parish church, or with the permission of the local hierarch or the local pastor, in another sacred place; however, it cannot be celebrated in other places without the permission of the local hierarch.

§2. Concerning the time of the celebration of marriage, the norms established by the particular law of the respective Church *sui iuris* are to be observed.

CAN. 839 Before or after the canonical celebration of marriage, it is forbidden to have another religious celebration of the same marriage to furnish or renew consent; likewise, a religious celebration is forbidden in which both the Catholic priest and non-Catholic minister ask for the consent of the parties.

CAN. 840 §1. Permission for a secret marriage can be granted by the local hierarch for a grave and urgent cause and also includes the grave obligation of observing secrecy on the part of the local hierarch, the pastor, the priest who was granted the faculty of blessing the marriage, witnesses, and the one spouse if the other does not consent to revealing it.

§2. The obligation of observing secrecy ceases on the part of the local hierarch if grave scandal or grave harm to the sanctity of marriage is threatened by the observance of secrecy.

§3. A marriage that is secretly celebrated is to be recorded only in the special register that is to be kept in the secret archive of the eparchial curia unless a very grave cause prevents it.

in ecclesia paroeciali aut de licentia Hierarchae loci vel parochi loci in alio loco sacro; in aliis autem locis celebrari non potest nisi de licentia Hierarchae loci.

§2. Circa tempus celebrationis matrimonii servandae sunt normae iure particulari propriae Ecclesiae sui iuris statutae.

CAN. 839 Vetita est ante vel post canonicam celebrationem alia eiusdem matrimonii celebratio religiosa ad matrimonialem consensum praestandum vel renovandum; item vetita est celebratio religiosa, in qua et sacerdos catholicus et minister acatholicus partium consensum exquirunt.

CAN. 840 §1. Permissio matrimonii secreti ab Hierarcha loci gravi et urgenti de causa concedi potest et secumfert gravem obligationem secretum servandi ex parte Hierarchae loci, parochi, sacerdotis facultate matrimonium benedicendi praediti, testium et alterius coniugis, altero non consentiente divulgationi.

§2. Obligatio secretum servandi ex parte Hierarchae loci cessat, si grave scandalum aut gravis erga matrimonii sanctitatem iniuria ex secreti observantia imminet.

§3. Matrimonium secreto celebratum in speciali tantummodo libro in archivo secreto curiae eparchialis asservando adnotetur, nisi gravissima causa obstat.

---

838 §2: Pius XII, m.p. *Crebrae allatae sunt,* 22 feb. 1949, can. 97 §§1–2. - Laod. can. 52; S. Nicolaus I, litt. *Ad consulta vestra,* 13 nov. 866, XLVIII; S.C. de Prop. Fide, decr. 6 oct. 1863, C), c). * Syn. Duinen. Armenorum, a. 719, can. 5; Syn. Diamper. Syro-Malabarensium, a. 1599, CXCII; Syn. Libanen. Maronitarum, a. 1736, pars II, cap. XI, 9, II; Syn. prov. Alba-Iulien. et Fagarasien. Rumenorum, a. 1872, tit. V, cap. VIII, II, 4; a. 1882, tit. IV, sect. I, §22; Syn. Sciarfen. Syrorum, a. 1888, cap. V, art. XV, §7, 2; Syn. Alexandrin. Coptorum, a. 1898, sect. II, cap. III, art. VIII, §5,

3, V; Syn. Armen., a. 1911, 577, n. 1.

839: Pius XII, m.p. *Crebrae allatae sunt,* 22 feb. 1949, can. 53 §§1–2. - S.C.S. Off., instr. (ad omnes Ep. Ritus Orient.), 12 dec. 1888, 7–8; resp. 9 feb. 1965.

840 §1: Pius XII, m.p. *Crebrae allatae sunt,* 22 feb. 1949, cann. 93–94.

840 §2: Pius XII, m.p. *Crebrae allatae sunt,* 22 feb. 1949, can. 95.

840 §3: Pius XII, m.p. *Crebrae allatae sunt,* 22 feb. 1949, can. 96. * Syn. Sciarfen. Syrorum, a. 1888, cap. V, art. XV, §12, IX.

CAN. 841 §1. As soon as possible after the celebration of marriage, the pastor of the place where it was celebrated or the one who acts in his place, even if neither blessed the marriage, is to record in the marriage register the names of the couple, of the priest who blessed the marriage, of the witnesses, the place and date of the celebration of the marriage and, if the case warrants, the dispensation from form or from impediments along with who granted it and what the impediment was and its degree, the faculty granted to bless the marriage, and other details in the manner prescribed by the respective eparchial bishop.

§2. Furthermore, the local pastor is to record in the baptismal register that the spouse celebrated marriage in his parish on a certain day. If the spouse was baptized elsewhere, the local pastor is to send an attestation of marriage himself or through the eparchial curia to the pastor of the place where the spouse's baptism was recorded. He is not to be satisfied until he receives notification that the information has been entered in the baptismal register.

§3. If the marriage was celebrated in accord with the norm of can. 832, the priest, if he blessed it, or the witnesses and the spouses, must see to it that the celebration of the marriage is entered in the prescribed books as soon as possible.

CAN. 842 If a marriage is convalidated for the external forum, or is declared null or is legitimately dissolved other than by death, the pastor of the place of the marriage celebration must be notified, so that an entry may be made in the marriage and baptismal registers.

CAN. 841 §1. Celebrato matrimonio parochus loci celebrationis vel is, qui eius vices gerit, etsi neuter matrimonium benedixit, quam primum adnotet in libro matrimoniorum nomina coniugum, sacerdotis benedicentis ac testium, locum et diem celebrati matrimonii, dispensationem, si casus fert, a forma celebrationis matrimonii vel ab impedimentis eiusque auctorem una cum impedimento eiusque gradu, facultatem matrimonium benedicendi collatam atque alia secundum modum a proprio Episcopo eparchiali praescriptum.

§2. Praeterea parochus loci in libro baptizatorum adnotet coniugem tali die in sua paroecia matrimonium celebravisse; si vero coniux alibi baptizatus est, parochus loci testimonium matrimonii mittat per se vel per curiam eparchialem ad parochum, apud quem coniugis baptismus adnotatus est, nec acquiescat, donec notitiam de adnotatione matrimonii in libro baptizatorum receperit.

§3. Si matrimonium ad normam can. 832 celebratum est, sacerdos, si illud benedixit, secus testes et coniuges curare debent, ut celebratio matrimonii in praescriptis libris quam primum adnotetur.

CAN. 842 Si matrimonium vel convalidatur pro foro externo vel nullum declaratur vel legitime praeterquam morte solvitur, parochus loci celebrationis matrimonii certior fieri debet, ut adnotatio in libris matrimoniorum et baptizatorum fiat.

---

841 §1: Pius XII, m.p. *Crebrae allatae sunt,* 22 feb. 1949, can. 92 §1. * Syn. Zamosten. Ruthenorum, a. 1720, tit. III, §8 "Tandem;" Syn. Libanen. Maronitarum, a. 1736, pars II, cap. XI, 30; Syn. prov. Alba- Iulien. et Fagarasien. Rumenorum, a. 1882, tit. IV, sect. I, §37; Syn. Sciarfen. Syrorum, a. 1888, cap. V, art. XV, §12, IX; Syn. Alexandrin. Coptorum, a. 1898, sect. II, cap. III, art. VIII, §2, 7, VI.

ART. VII. *Convalidation of Marriage*

1° *Simple Convalidation*

CAN. 843 §1. To convalidate a marriage that is invalid due to a diriment impediment, it is required that the impediment cease or that it be dispensed and that at least the party who is aware of the impediment renew consent.

§2. This renewal of consent is required for the validity of the convalidation, even if both parties furnished consent at the beginning and have not revoked it later.

CAN. 844 The renewal of consent must be a new act of the will concerning a marriage that the party renewing consent knows or thinks was invalid from the beginning.

CAN. 845 §1. If the impediment is a public one, the consent is to be renewed by both parties according to the form for the celebration of marriage required by law.

§2. If the impediment is occult, it suffices that the consent be renewed privately and in secret by the party who is aware of the impediment, provided the other party perseveres in the consent already given; or by both parties when each of them knows about the impediment.

CAN. 846 §1. A marriage that is invalid due to a defect of consent is convalidated when the party who has not consented now gives consent, provided the consent given by the other party perseveres.

§2. If the defect of consent cannot be proven,

ART. VII. *De Matrimonii Convalidatione*

1° *De convalidatione simplici*

CAN. 843 §1. Ad convalidandum matrimonium invalidum ob impedimentum dirimens requiritur, ut cesset impedimentum vel ab eodem dispensetur et consensum renovet saltem pars impedimenti conscia.

§2. Haec renovatio requiritur ad validitatem convalidationis, etsi initio utraque pars consensum praestitit nec postea revocavit.

CAN. 844 Renovatio consensus debet esse novus voluntatis actus in matrimonium, quod pars renovans scit aut opinatur ab initio invalidum fuisse.

CAN. 845 §1. Si impedimentum est publicum, consensus ab utraque parte renovandus est forma celebrationis matrimonii iure praescripta.

§2. Si impedimentum est occultum, satis est, ut consensus renovetur privatim et secreto; a parte quidem impedienti conscia, dummodo altera in consensu praestito perseveret, aut ab utraque parte, si impedimentum est utrique parti notum.

CAN. 846 §1. Matrimonium invalidum ob defectum consensus convalidatur, si pars, quae non consensit, iam consentit, dummodo consensus ab altera parte praestitus perseveret.

§2. Si defectus consensus probari non

843 §1: PIUS XII, m.p. *Crebrae allatae sunt,* 22 feb. 1949, can. 122. * Syn. prov. Alba-Iulien. et Fagarasien. Rumenorum, a. 1882, tit. IV, sect. I, §46; Syn. Sciarfen. Syrorum, a. 1888, cap. V, art. XV, §10; Syn. Alexandrin. Coptorum, a. 1898, sect. II, cap. III, pars II, art. VIII, §7.

844: PIUS XII, m.p. *Crebrae allatae sunt,* 22 feb. 1949, can. 123.

845 §1: PIUS XII, m.p. *Crebrae allatae sunt,* 22 feb. 1949, can. 124 §1.

845 §2: PIUS XII, m.p. *Crebrae allatae sunt,* 22 feb. 1949, can. 124 §§2–3.

846 §1: PIUS XII, m.p. *Crebrae allatae sunt,* 22 feb. 1949, can. 125 §1.

846 §2: PIUS XII, m.p. *Crebrae allatae sunt,* 22 feb. 1949, can. 125 §2.

it suffices that the party who did not consent gives consent privately and in secret.

§3. If the defect of consent can be proven, it is necessary that the consent be given according to the form for the celebration of marriage prescribed by law.

CAN. 847 If a marriage that is invalid because of a defect of the form of marriage celebration prescribed by law is to become valid, it must be celebrated anew in this form.

2° Radical Sanation

CAN. 848 §1. The radical sanation of an invalid marriage is its convalidation without the renewal of consent, granted by competent authority and including a dispensation from an impediment, if there was one, and from the form for the celebration of marriage prescribed by law, if it was not observed, as well as the retroactivity into the past of canonical effects.

§2. The convalidation occurs at the moment the favor is granted; it is understood to be retroactive, however, to the moment the marriage was celebrated unless something else is expressly stated in the concession.

CAN. 849 §1. A radical sanation of the marriage can be granted validly even when either or both of the parties are unaware of it.

§2. A radical sanation is not to be granted except for a grave cause and unless it is probable that the parties intend to persevere in the partnership of conjugal life.

CAN. 850 §1. An invalid marriage can be

potest, satis est, ut pars, quae non consensit, privatim et secreto consensum praestet.

§3. Si defectus consensus probari potest, necesse est, ut consensus renovetur forma celebrationis matrimonii iure praescripta.

CAN. 847 Matrimonium invalidum ob defectum formae celebrationis matrimonii iure praescriptae, ut validum fiat, denuo hac forma celebrari debet.

2° De Sanatione in Radice

CAN. 848 §1. Matrimonii invalidi sanatio in radice est eiusdem sine renovatione consensus convalidatio ab auctoritate competenti concessa secumferens dispensationem ab impedimento, si adest, atque a forma celebrationis matrimonii iure praescripta, si servata non est, necnon retrotractionem effectuum canonicorum ad praeteritum.

§2. Convalidatio fit a momento concessionis gratiae; retrotractio vero intelligitur facta ad momentum celebrationis matrimonii, nisi aliter in concessione expresse cavetur.

CAN. 849 §1. Sanatio matrimonii in radice valide concedi potest etiam alterutra vel utraque parte inscia.

§2. Sanatio in radice ne concedatur nisi gravi de causa et nisi probabile est partes in consortio vitae coniugalis perseverare velle.

CAN. 850 §1. Matrimonium invalidum

---

846 §3: Pius XII, m.p. *Crebrae allatae sunt,* 22 feb. 1949, can. 125 §3.

847: Pius XII, m.p. *Crebrae allatae sunt,* 22 feb. 1949, can. 126.

848 §1: Pius XII, m.p. *Crebrae allatae sunt,* 22 feb. 1949, can. 127 §1. * Syn. Sciarfen. Syrorum, a. 1888, cap. V, art. XV, §10, 5; Syn. Alexandrin. Coptorum,

a. 1898, sect. II, cap. III, art. VIII, §7, 5.

848 §2: Pius XII, m.p. *Crebrae allatae sunt,* 22 feb. 1949, can. 127 §2.

849 §1: Pius XII, m.p. *Crebrae allatae sunt,* 22 feb. 1949, can. 127 §3.

850 §1: Pius XII, m.p. *Crebrae allatae sunt,* 22 feb. 1949, can. 128 §1.

sanated provided the consent of each party continues to exist.

§2. A marriage that is invalid due to an impediment of divine law cannot be sanated validly until after the impediment has ceased to exist.

CAN. 851 §1. If consent is lacking in both or either of the parties, a marriage cannot be radically sanated, whether the consent was lacking from the beginning or was given in the beginning but afterwards revoked.

§2. If, however, consent was indeed lacking in the beginning but afterwards was given, a sanation can be granted from the moment the consent was given.

CAN. 852 A patriarch and an eparchial bishop can grant a radical sanation in individual cases, if the validity of the marriage is hindered by a defect of the form for the celebration of marriage prescribed by law or by some impediment from which he can dispense; also in cases prescribed by law if the conditions mentioned in can. 814 are fulfilled. In other cases, and if it is a question of impediments of divine law that have now ceased, a radical sanation can be granted only by the Apostolic See.

ART. VIII. *The Separation of the Spouses*

1° Dissolution of the Bond

CAN. 853 The sacramental bond of marriage, once the marriage has been consummat-

sanari potest, dummodo consensus utriusque partis perseveret.

§2. Matrimonium invalidum ob impedimentum iuris divini valide sanari non potest, nisi postquam impedimentum cessavit.

CAN. 851 §1. Si in utraque vel alterutra parte deest consensus, matrimonium non potest valide sanari in radice, sive consensus ab initio defuit, sive ab initio praestitus postea revocatus est.

§2. Si vero consensus ab initio quidem defuit, sed postea praestitus est, sanatio concedi potest a momento praestiti consensus.

CAN. 852 Patriarcha et Episcopus eparchialis concedere possunt sanationem in radice in singulis casibus, si validitati matrimonii obstat defectus formae celebrationis matrimonii iure praescriptae vel aliquod impedimentum, a quo ipsi dispensare possunt, et in casibus iure praescriptis, si impletae sunt condiciones, de quibus in can. 814; in ceteris casibus et si de impedimento iuris divini agitur, quod iam cessavit, sanatio in radice concedi potest a sola Sede Apostolica.

ART. VIII. *De Separatione Coniugum*

1° De Dissolutione Vinculi

CAN. 853 Matrimonii vinculum sacramentale matrimonio consummato nulla hu-

850 §2: PIUS XII, m.p. *Crebrae allatae sunt*, 22 feb. 1949, can. 128 §2; PAULUS VI, m.p. *Episcopalis potestatis*, 2 maii 1967, VIII, 13, b).

851 §1: PIUS XII, m.p. *Crebrae allatae sunt*, 22 feb. 1949, can. 129 §1.

851 §2: PIUS XII, m.p. *Crebrae allatae sunt*, 22 feb. 1949, can. 129 §2.

852: PIUS XII, m.p. *Crebrae allatae sunt*, 22 feb. 1949, can. 130 §2; PAULUS VI, m.p. *Pastorale munus*, 30 nov. 1963, I, 21–22; m.p. *Episcopalis potestatis*, 2 maii 1967, VIII, 13, a), c).

853: PIUS XII, m.p. *Crebrae allatae sunt*, 22 feb. 1949, can. 107; Vat. II, const. *Gaudium et spes*, 48 "Intima." - BENEDICTUS XII, a. 1341, prop. 102, Armenorum, damn.; CLEMENS VIII, instr. *Sanctissimus*, 31 aug. 1595, §5 "Matrimonia;" S.C. de Prop. Fide, instr. (ad Ep. Graeco-Rumen.), a. 1858; LEO XIII, ep. encycl. *Arcanum*, 10 feb. 1880; S.C.S. Off., instr. (ad Ep. Rituum Orient.), a. 1883, tit. V, art. 4; PIUS XI, litt. encycl. *Casti connubii*, 31 dec. 1930; PIUS XII, all. 6 oct. 1946, II.

ed, cannot be dissolved by any human power or by any cause other than death.

CAN. 854 §1. In virtue of the pauline privilege, a marriage entered into by two non-baptized persons is dissolved by the law itself in favor of the faith of the party who received baptism, if a new marriage is celebrated by the latter, provided the non-baptized party departs.

§2. The non-baptized party is considered to depart, if he or she is unwilling to cohabit peacefully with the baptized party without offence to the Creator, unless the baptized party has, after the reception of baptism, given the other party just cause for departure.

CAN. 855 §1. In order for the baptized party to celebrate another marriage validly, the non-baptized party must be interrogated as to whether:

1° he or she wants to receive baptism;

2° he or she at least wishes to cohabit with the baptized party in peace without insult to the Creator.

§2. This interrogation must be conducted after baptism, but the local hierarch for a grave cause can permit the interrogation to be conducted before the baptism or even dispense with the interrogation either before or after the baptism, if by means of at least a summary and extra-judicial process, it is established that it cannot be done or that it would be useless.

CAN. 856 §1. Ordinarily the interrogation is made by the authority of the local hierarch of the converted party; if the other party requests time for responding, the same hierarch is to

mana potestate nullaque causa praeterquam morte dissolvi potest.

CAN. 854 §1. Matrimonium initum a duobus non baptizatis solvitur ex privilegio paulino in favorem fidei partis, quae baptismum suscepit, ipso iure, si novum matrimonium ab eadem parte celebratur, dummodo pars non baptizata discedat.

§2. Discedere censetur pars non baptizata, si non vult pacifice cohabitare cum parte baptizata sine contumelia Creatoris, nisi haec post baptismum susceptum iustam illi dedit discedendi causam.

CAN. 855 §1. Ut pars baptizata novum matrimonium valide celebret, pars non baptizata interpellari debet, num:

1° velit et ipsa baptismum suscipere;

2° saltem velit cum parte baptizata pacifice cohabitare sine contumelia Creatoris.

§2. Haec interpellatio post baptismum fieri debet; sed Hierarcha loci gravi de causa potest permittere, ut interpellatio ante baptismum fiat, immo potest ab interpellatione dispensare sive ante sive post baptismum, si modo procedendi saltem summario et extraiudiciali constat eam fieri non posse aut fore inutilem.

CAN. 856 §1. Interpellatio fit regulariter de auctoritate Hierarchae loci partis conversae, a quo concedendum est alteri coniugi spatium temporis ad respondendum, si id

854 §1: Pius XII, m.p. *Crebrae allatae sunt,* 22 feb. 1949, can. 109. - Benedictus XIV, ep. *Postremo mense,* 28 feb. 1747, §58.

854 §2: Pius XII, m.p. *Crebrae allatae sunt,* 22 feb. 1949, cann. 110, 112–113. - Quinisext. can. 72.

855 §1: Pius XII, m.p. *Crebrae allatae sunt,* 22 feb. 1949, can. 110 §1. - Quinisext. can. 72.

855 §2: Pius XII, m.p. *Crebrae allatae sunt,* 22 feb. 1949, can. 110 §2; Paulus VI, m.p. *Pastorale munus,* 30 nov. 1963, I, 23.

856 §1: Pius XII, m.p. *Crebrae allatae sunt,* 22 feb. 1949, can. 111 §1.

grant it with the warning that after the period elapsed without any answer, the person's silence is considered to be a negative response.

§2. An interrogation can also be done privately by the converted party and is indeed licit, if the form prescribed above cannot be observed.

§3. In either case, there must be legitimate proof in the external forum of the interrogation having been done and of its outcome.

CAN. 857 The baptized party has the right of celebrating a new marriage with a Catholic party if:

1° the other party responds negatively to the interrogation;

2° the interrogation is legitimately omitted;

3° the non-baptized party, either already interrogated or not, at first persevering in peaceful cohabitation but later departed without just cause, in which case, however, an interrogation is to be done in accord with the norms of cann. 855 and 856.

CAN. 858 The local hierarch for a serious cause can permit the baptized party who uses the pauline privilege to celebrate marriage with a non-Catholic party, whether baptized or non-baptized; in this case, the prescripts of the canons on mixed marriages must also be observed.

CAN. 859 §1. If a non-baptized man having simultaneously several non-baptized wives receives baptism in the Catholic Church and if it is difficult for him to remain with the first of them, he can keep any one of the rest and dismiss all others. The same applies to a non-bap-

petivit, eo tamen monito, ut hoc spatio temporis inutiliter elapso eius silentium pro responsione negativa habeatur.

§2. Interpellatio etiam privatim facta ab ipsa parte conversa valet, immo est licita, si forma superius praescripta servari non potest.

§3. In utroque casu de interpellatione facta deque eiusdem exitu in foro externo legitime constare debet.

CAN. 857 Pars baptizata ius habet novum matrimonium celebrandi cum parte catholica, si:

1° altera pars negative interpellationi respondit;

2° interpellatio legitime omissa est;

3° pars non baptizata, sive iam interpellata sive non, antea perseverans in pacifica cohabitatione postea sine iusta causa discessit; quo in casu vero interpellatio ad normam cann. 855 et 856 praemittenda est.

CAN. 858 Hierarcha loci tamen gravi de causa concedere potest, ut pars baptizata, utens privilegio paulino, celebret matrimonium cum parte acatholica sive baptizata sive non baptizata servatis etiam praescriptis canonum de matrimoniis mixtis.

CAN. 859 §1. Non baptizatus, qui plures uxores non baptizatas simul habet, suscepto in Ecclesia catholica baptismo, si ei durum est cum earum prima permanere, unam ex illis ceteris dimissis retinere potest; idem valet de muliere non baptizata,

856 §2: Pius XII, m.p. *Crebrae allatae sunt,* 22 feb. 1949, can. 111 §2.

856 §3: Pius XII, m.p. *Crebrae allatae sunt,* 22 feb. 1949, can. 111 §2.

857: Pius XII, m.p. *Crebrae allatae sunt,* 22 feb. 1949, cann. 112–113.

857, 1°: Pius XII, m.p. *Crebrae allatae sunt,* 22 feb.

1949, can. 112. - Quinisext. can. 72.

858: Paulus VI, m.p. *Pastorale munus,* 30 nov. 1963, I, 20.

859 §1: Pius XII, m.p. *Crebrae allatae sunt,* 22 feb. 1949, can. 114; Paulus III, const. *Altitudo,* 1 iun. 1537; Pius V, const. *Romani Pontificis,* 2 aug. 1571; S.C.S. Off., resp. 30 iun. 1937.

tized woman who has simultaneously several non-baptized husbands.

§2. In this case the marriage is to be celebrated according to the form prescribed by law while observing the other requirements of law.

§3. The local hierarch, after considering the moral, social, and economic conditions of the place and of the persons, is to take care that sufficient provision is made for the needs of those who are dismissed in accord with the norms of justice, charity, and equity.

CAN. 860 A non-baptized person who, having received baptism in the Catholic Church, cannot reestablish cohabitation with a non-baptized spouse due to captivity or persecution, can licitly celebrate another marriage, even if the other party has received baptism in the meantime, with due regard for can. 853.

CAN. 861 In a doubtful matter the privilege of the faith enjoys the favor of the law.

CAN. 862 A non-consummated marriage can be dissolved by the Roman Pontiff for a just cause, at the request of both or either of the parties, even if the other is unwilling.

2º Separation while the Bond Endures

CAN. 863 §1. It is earnestly recommended that a spouse, motivated by charity and solicitous for the good of the family, should not refuse to pardon an adulterous partner and not

quae plures maritos non baptizatos simul habet.

§2. In hoc casu matrimonium forma celebrationis matrimonii iure praescripta celebrandum est servatis etiam aliis de iure servandis.

§3. Hierarcha loci condicione morali, sociali, oeconomica locorum et personarum prae oculis habita curet, ut eorum, qui dimissi sunt, necessitatibus satis provisum sit secundum normas iustitiae, caritatis et aequitatis.

CAN. 860 Non baptizato, qui suscepto in Ecclesia catholica baptismo cum coniuge non baptizato ratione captivitatis vel persecutionis cohabitationem restaurare non potest, aliud matrimonium celebrare licet, etsi altera pars baptismum interea suscepit, firmo can. 853.

CAN. 861 In re dubia privilegium fidei gaudet favore iuris.

CAN. 862 Matrimonium non consummatum solvi potest iusta de causa a Romano Pontifice utraque parte rogante vel alterutra, etsi altera est invita.

2º De Separatione Manente Vinculo

CAN. 863 §1. Enixe commendatur, ut coniux caritate motus et boni familiae sollicitus veniam non abnuat comparti adulterae atque consortium vitae coniugalis non dis-

859 §2: S.C.S. Off., resp. 30 iun. 1937.

860: Pius XII, m.p. *Crebrae allatae sunt,* 22 feb. 1949, can. 114. - Gregorius XIII, const. *Populis,* 25 ian. 1585.

861: Pius XII, m.p. *Crebrae allatae sunt,* 22 feb. 1949, can. 116; S.C.S. Off., decr. 10 iun. 1937.

862: Pius XII, m.p. *Crebrae allatae sunt,* 22 feb. 1949, can. 108. - Trid., sess. XXIV, *De matrimonio,* can. 6; S.C. de Prop. Fide, instr. (ad Ep. Graeco-Rumen.), a. 1858.

863 §1: Pius XII, m.p. *Crebrae allatae sunt,* 22 feb. 1949, can. 118 §1. - S. Basilius M., can. 9; S. Nicolaus I, litt. *Ad consulta vestra,* 13 nov. 866, XCVI; Eugenius IV (in Flor.), const. *Exsultate Deo,* 22 nov. 1439, §16; Trid., sess. XXIV, *De matrimonio,* can. 7; Benedictus XIV, ep. *Nuper ad Nos,* 16 mar. 1743, Professio fidei Maronitis praescr., §5; S.C. de Prop. Fide, instr. (ad Ep. Graeco-Rumen.), a. 1858; Pius IX, ep. *Verbis exprimere,* 15 aug. 1859; S.C. de Prop. Fide, instr. 31 iul. 1902, 1, f).

break off the partnership of conjugal life; however, if a spouse has not expressly or tacitly condoned the other's fault, he or she has the right to sever the partnership of conjugal life, provided he or she has not consented to the adultery, nor given cause to it, nor also committed adultery.

§2. Tacit condonation occurs if the innocent spouse, after becoming aware of the adultery, has willingly engaged in a relationship of marital affection with the other spouse. Tacit condonation is presumed, however, if the innocent spouse has maintained the partnership of conjugal life for six months without taking the matter to the ecclesiastical or the civil authority.

§3. The innocent spouse who has voluntarily severed the partnership of conjugal life must within six months file a suit for separation before the competent ecclesiastical authority. After having examined all the circumstances, the said authority is to consider whether the innocent spouse can be brought to condone the fault and not prolong the separation permanently.

CAN. 864 §1. If either of the spouses has rendered common life dangerous or unduly hard for the other spouse or the children, this provides the other spouse with a legitimate cause to leave either by a decree of the local hierarch or, if there is danger in delay, even on his or her own authority.

§2. The particular law of the Churches *sui iuris* can determine other reasons in keeping with the customs of the people and circumstances of the place.

§3. In all cases once the cause for the separation has ceased, the partnership of conjugal life

rumpat; si vero eiusdem culpam expresse aut tacite non condonavit, ius ei est solvendi consortium vitae coniugalis, nisi in adulterium consensit aut eidem causam dedit vel ipse quoque adulterium commisit.

§2. Tacita condonatio habetur, si coniux innocens, postquam de adulterio certior factus est, sua sponte cum altero coniuge maritali affectu conversatus est; praesumitur vero, si per sex menses consortium vitae coniugalis servavit neque auctoritatem ecclesiasticam vel civilem de re adiit.

§3. Si coniux innocens sua sponte consortium vitae coniugalis solvit, debet intra sex menses causam separationis deferre ad auctoritatem competentem, quae omnibus inspectis adiunctis perpendat, num coniux innocens adduci possit, ut culpam condonet et separationem non protrahat.

CAN. 864 §1. Si alteruter coniugum vitam communem coniugi vel filiis periculosam aut nimis duram reddit, alteri legitimam praebet causam discedendi decreto Hierarchae loci et etiam propria auctoritate, si periculum est in mora.

§2. Iure particulari Ecclesiae sui iuris aliae causae pro moribus populorum et locorum circumstantiis statui possunt.

§3. In omnibus casibus causa separationis cessante consortium vitae coniugalis

863 §2: Pius XII, m.p. *Crebrae allatae sunt,* 22 feb. 1949, can. 118 §2.

863 §3: Pius XII, m.p. *Crebrae allatae sunt,* 22 feb. 1949, can. 119.

864 §1: Pius XII, m.p. *Crebrae allatae sunt,* 22 feb. 1949, can. 120 §1 n. 1. - Benedictus XIV, ep. *Nuper ad Nos,* 16 mar. 1743, Professio fidei Maronitis praescr., §5.

864 §3: Pius XII, m.p. *Crebrae allatae sunt,* 22 feb. 1949, can. 120 §1 n. 2.

is to be restored, unless it has been provided otherwise by the competent authority.

CAN. 865   When the separation of spouses is effected, provision is always opportunely to be made for the due support and education of the children.

CAN. 866   The innocent spouse may laudably readmit the other spouse to the partnership of conjugal life, in which case he or she renounces the right to separation.

CHAPTER VIII. Sacramentals, Sacred Times and Places, Veneration of the Saints, a Vow and an Oath

ART. I. *Sacramentals*

CAN. 867   §1. Sacramentals are sacred signs that by a certain imitation of the sacraments signify the effects, especially spiritual ones, which are obtained through the prayers of the Church. Through the sacramentals people are disposed to receive the principal effect of the sacraments and the various circumstances of life are sanctified.

§2. Regarding sacramentals, the norms of the particular law of the respective Church *sui iuris* are to be observed.

ART. II. *Sacred Places*

CAN. 868   Sacred places, which are destined for divine worship, cannot be erected without the permission of the eparchial bishop, unless it is expressly established otherwise by common law.

restaurandum est, nisi ab auctoritate competenti aliud statuitur.

CAN. 865   Facta separatione coniugum opportune semper cavendum est de debita filiorum sustentatione et educatione.

CAN. 866   Coniux innocens laudabiliter alterum coniugem ad consortium vitae coniugalis rursus admittere potest, quo in casu iuri separationis renuntiat.

CAPUT VIII. **De Sacramentalibus, de Locis et de Temporibus Sacris, de Cultu Sanctorum, de Voto et de Iureiurando**

ART. I. *De Sacramentalibus*

CAN. 867   §1. Per sacramentalia, quae sacra sunt signa, quibus ad aliquam sacramentorum imitationem effectus praesertim spirituales significantur et ex Ecclesiae impetratione obtinentur, homines ad praecipuum sacramentorum effectum suscipiendum disponuntur et varia vitae adiuncta sanctificantur.

§2. Circa sacramentalia serventur normae iuris particularis propriae Ecclesiae sui iuris.

ART. II. *De Locis Sacris*

CAN. 868   Loca sacra, quae ad cultum divinum destinantur, nonnisi de licentia Episcopi eparchialis erigi possunt, nisi aliud iure communi expresse statuitur.

865: Pius XII, m.p. *Crebrae allatae sunt*, 22 feb. 1949, can. 121.

866: Pius XII, m.p. *Crebrae allatae sunt*, 22 feb. 1949, can. 119.

867 §1: Vat. II, const. *Sacrosanctum Concilium*, 60. - Nic. II, actio VII, *Definitio de sacris imaginibus*.

867 §2: * Syn. Diamper. Syro-Malabarensium, a.

1599, CCXVII, CCXXIII; Syn. Libanen. Maronitarum, a. 1736, pars II, cap. VIII, 9; pars III, cap. II, 6, I; cap. III, 2, X; pars IV, cap. II, 5 et 11; Syn. prov. Alba-Iulien. et Fagarasien. Rumenorum, a. 1900, tit. III, cap. II, 13; Syn. Sciarfen. Syrorum, a. 1888, cap. III, art. VIII; Syn. Leopolien. Ruthenorum, a. 1891, tit. III; Syn. Armen., a. 1911, 586–593.

1° Churches

CAN. 869 A church is a building exclusively dedicated for divine worship by consecration or blessing.

CAN. 870 No building destined to be a church is to be built without the express consent of the eparchial bishop given in writing, unless otherwise established by common law.

CAN. 871 §1. Cathedral churches and, if possible, parish churches, churches of monasteries and churches attached to religious houses, should be dedicated by consecration.

§2. Consecration is reserved to the eparchial bishop, who can confer the faculty of consecrating to another bishop; after the consecration or blessing has been performed, a document is to be drawn up for preservation in the archive of the eparchial curia.

CAN. 872 §1. Anything that is not in harmony with the sanctity of the place is forbidden in a church.

§2. All those involved are to take care that such cleanliness is maintained in a church as befits the house of God, and that secure means are taken to protect the sacred and precious objects.

CAN. 873 §1. If a church cannot at all be used any longer for divine worship and there is

1° De Ecclesiis

CAN. 869 Ecclesia est aedes exclusive cultui divino dedicata consecratione vel benedictione.

CAN. 870 Nulla aedes ad ecclesiam destinata aedificetur sine expresso Episcopi eparchialis consensu scripto dato, nisi aliter iure communi cavetur.

CAN. 871 §1. Consecratione dedicentur ecclesiae cathedrales et, si fieri potest, ecclesiae paroeciales, ecclesiae monasteriorum et ecclesiae domui religiosae adnexae.

§2. Consecratio reservatur Episcopo eparchiali, qui potest alii Episcopo facultatem ecclesiam consecrandi conferre; de peracta consecratione vel benedictione ecclesiae redigatur documentum in archivo curiae eparchialis asservandum.

CAN. 872 §1. Arcendum est ab ecclesiis, quidquid a loci sanctitate absonum est.

§2. Curent omnes, ad quos pertinet, ut in ecclesiis illa munditia servetur, quae domum Dei decet, mediaque securitatis adhibeantur ad res sacras et pretiosas tuendas.

CAN. 873 §1. Si qua ecclesia nullo modo amplius ad cultum divinum adhiberi

---

869: Quinisext. cann. 31, 59, 74, 76; S. CYRILLUS ALEXANDRIN., can. 8; Protodeut. can. 12; LEO X (in Lat. V), const. *Dum intra,* 19 dec. 1516, §12; Trid., sess. XXII, *De observandis et evitandis in celebratione missae,* "Deinde." * Syn. Sciarfen. Syrorum, a. 1888, cap. III, art. V, 1; Syn. Alexandrin. Coptorum, a. 1898, sect. II, cap. I, art. IV, 1 et 13; Syn. Armen., a. 1911, 652, 661–662.

870: Chalc. can. 4; Nic. II, cann. 10, 17. * Syn. Libanen. Maronitarum, a. 1736, pars IV, cap. I, 1; Syn. Armen., a. 1911, 651–652, 660.

872 §1: Quinisext. cann. 74, 76; Trid., sess. XXII, *De observandis et evitandis in celebratione missae,* "Deinde;" PIUS V, const. *Cum primus,* 1 apr. 1566, §4;

URBANUS VIII, const. *Cum Ecclesiae,* 30 ian. 1642; BENEDICTUS XIV, const. *Ad militantis,* 30 mar. 1742, §6; ep. encycl. *Annus qui,* 19 feb. 1749, §1; PIUS VI, encycl. *Inscrutabile,* 25 dec. 1775, §5; S.C. de Prop. Fide, decr. 13 apr. 1807, III–IV; S.C. Consist., decr. *Maxima cura,* 20 aug. 1910, can. 1, 9; decr. 10 dec. 1912; PIUS XII, litt. encycl. *Mediator Dei,* 20 nov. 1947, IV "Cupimus;" Vat. II, const. *Sacrosanctum Concilium,* 122, 124. * Syn. Diamper. Syro-Malabarensium, a. 1599, CCXXVIII– CCXXXI; Syn. Armen., a. 1911, 655, 658.

872 §2: Vat. II, decr. *Presbyterorum ordinis,* 5 "Domus."

873 §1: Quinisext. can. 49; Trid., sess. XXI, *De ref.,* can. 7.

no possibility of restoring it, it can be reduced by the eparchial bishop to profane but not sordid use.

§2. If other grave reasons suggest that a certain church is no longer to be used for divine worship, the eparchial bishop can reduce it to profane but not sordid use, provided that the good of souls suffers no harm thereby. Before doing so he must consult the presbyteral council and have the consent of those who legitimately claim rights over the Church.

2° Cemeteries and Ecclesiastical Funerals

CAN. 874 §1. The Catholic Church has the right to possess its own cemeteries.

§2. Where possible, the Church is to have its own cemeteries, or at least an area in public cemeteries reserved for the deceased Christian faithful; both are to be blessed. If this cannot be done, the grave is to be blessed on the occasion of the funeral.

§3. Any contrary custom being reprobated, the dead are not to be buried in churches except in the case of one who was a patriarch, bishop or exarch,.

§4. Parishes, monasteries and other religious institutes can have their own cemeteries.

CAN. 875 Ecclesiastical funerals, with which the Church prays for spiritual assistance for the

potest et possibilitas non datur eam reficiendi, ab Episcopo eparchiali in usum profanum non sordidum redigi potest.

§2. Si aliae graves causae suadent, ut aliqua ecclesia ad cultum divinum amplius non adhibeatur, Episcopus eparchialis eam in usum profanum non sordidum redigere potest consulto consilio presbyterali, de consensu eorum, qui iura in eandem sibi legitime vindicant, et dummodo salus animarum nihil inde detrimenti capiat.

2° De Coemeteriis et de Exsequiis Ecclesiasticis

CAN. 874 §1. Ius est Ecclesiae catholicae possidendi propria coemeteria.

§2. Coemeteria Ecclesiae propria, ubi fieri potest, habeantur vel saltem spatia in coemeteriis civilibus christifidelibus defunctis destinata alterutra benedicenda; si vero haec obtineri non possunt, occasione exsequiarum tumulus benedicetur.

§3. In ecclesiis defuncti ne sepeliantur reprobata contraria consuetudine, nisi de eis agitur, qui Patriarchae, Episcopi vel Exarchi fuerunt.

§4. Paroeciae, monasteria ceteraque instituta religiosa propria coemeteria habere possunt.

CAN. 875 Exsequiis ecclesiasticis, quibus Ecclesia defunctis spiritualem opem

874 §2: Laod. can. 9; Leo X (in Lat. V), const. *Dum intra,* 19 dec. 1516, §12; Benedictus XIV, ep. encycl. *Inter omnigenas,* 2 feb. 1744, §5; S.C.S. Off., 13 apr. 1853; 3 aug. 1897. * Syn. Libanen. Maronitarum, a. 1736, pars II, cap. X, 7–11; Syn. prov. Alba-Iulien. et Fagarasien. Rumenorum, a. 1872, tit. VI, cap. XI; Syn. Sciarfen. Syrorum, a. 1888, cap. V, art. XI; Syn. Leopolien. Ruthenorum, a. 1891, tit. XII, cap. II; Syn. Alexandrin. Coptorum, a. 1898, sect. II, cap. III, art. VI, *De Coemeterio;* Syn. Armen., a. 1911, 663–668, 673.

874 §3: * Syn. Libanen. Maronitarum, a. 1736,

pars II, cap. X, 7–11; Syn. Sciarfen. Syrorum, a. 1888, cap. V, art. X, 5, 11; Syn. Alexandrin. Coptorum, a. 1898, sect. II, cap. III, art. VI, *De Coemeterio,* V.

875: * Syn. Libanen. Maronitarum, a. 1736, pars II, cap. X, 1–2; Syn. prov. Alba-Iulien. et Fagarasien. Rumenorum, a. 1872, tit. VI, cap. XI; Syn. Sciarfen. Syrorum, a. 1888, cap. V, art. X; Syn. Leopolien. Ruthenorum, a. 1891, tit. XII, cap. I, §I; Syn. Alexandrin. Coptorum, a. 1898, sect. II, cap. III, art. VI, *De Exequiis et Sepultura;* Syn. Armen., a. 1911, 665, 670–672, 674.

dead, honors their bodies, and at the same time brings the solace of hope to the living, must be given to all the deceased Christian faithful and catechumens, unless they have been deprived of it by law.

CAN. 876 §1. Baptized non-Catholics can be accorded an ecclesiastical funeral according to the prudent judgment of the local hierarch, unless there is proof about their contrary wish and provided their own minister is not available.

§2. Children, whose parents had intended to baptize them, and others who had seemed to be in some way close to the Church, but who died before they received baptism, can be given an ecclesiastical funeral according to the prudent judgment of the local hierarch.

§3. Those who had opted for the cremation of their own body are to be granted an ecclesiastical funeral unless there is proof that their choice was motivated by reasons opposed to Christian life; but the funeral is to be so celebrated that it is clear that the Church prefers burial of bodies to cremation and that scandal is avoided.

CAN. 877 An ecclesiastical funeral is to be denied to sinners to whom this cannot be granted without public scandal to the Christian faithful, unless before death they had given some signs of repentance.

CAN. 878 §1. All personal favoritism is to be avoided in the celebration of ecclesiastical funerals.

§2. With due regard for can. 1013, it is strong-

impetrat, eorum corpora honorat simulque vivis spei solacium affert, omnes christifideles et catechumeni defuncti donari debent, nisi eisdem iure privati sunt.

CAN. 876 §1. Concedi possunt exsequiae ecclesiasticae acatholicis baptizatis de prudenti Hierarchae loci iudicio, nisi constat de contraria eorum voluntate et dummodo minister proprius haberi non possit.

§2. Parvuli, quos parentes baptizare intendebant, aliique, qui aliquo modo Ecclesiae propinqui videbantur, sed antequam baptismum susceperunt, decesserunt, exsequiis ecclesiasticis item de prudenti Hierarchae loci iudicio donari possunt.

§3. Illis, qui proprii cadaveris cremationem elegerunt, nisi constat eos id fecisse rationibus ductos vitae christianae adversis, concedendae sunt exsequiae ecclesiasticae eo tamen modo celebratae, ut non lateat Ecclesiam corporum sepulturam cremationi anteponere utque scandalum vitetur.

CAN. 877 Exsequiis ecclesiasticis privandi sunt, nisi ante mortem aliqua dederunt paenitentiae signa, peccatores, quibus eaedem non sine publico christifidelium scandalo concedi possunt.

CAN. 878 §1. In exsequiarum ecclesiasticarum celebratione omnis personarum acceptio vitetur.

§2. Firmo can. 1013 enixe commendatur,

---

876 §1: Secret. ad Christ. Unit. Fov., *Directorium* I, 14 maii 1967, 52, 59–60; S.C. pro Doctr. Fidei, decr. 11 iun. 1976.

876 §3: S.C.S. Off., instr. 5 iul. 1963.

877: S.C. pro Doctr. Fidei, decr. 20 sep. 1973. - Lat. II, can. 13; Trid., sess. XXV, *De ref.*, cap. 19. * Syn. Libanen. Maronitarum, a. 1736, pars II, cap. X, 12;

Syn. prov. Alba-Iulien. et Fagarasien. Rumenorum, a. 1872, tit. VI, cap. XI "Cum sepulturae denegatio;" Syn. Sciarfen. Syrorum, a. 1888, cap. V, art. XI, 7; Syn. Leopolien. Ruthenorum, a. 1891, tit. XII, cap. II, 1–2; Syn. Alexandrin. Coptorum, a. 1898, sect. II, cap. III, art. VI, *De Coemeterio*, VII; Syn. Armen., a. 1911, 672.

ly recommended that eparchial bishops introduce the practice, insofar as this is possible, of receiving only those offerings that the Christian faithful offer voluntarily on the occasion of an ecclesiastical funeral.

CAN. 879 After the burial, an entry is to be made in the register of the dead, in accord with the norm of particular law.

ART. III. *Feast Days and Days of Penance*

CAN. 880 §1. The supreme authority of the Church alone is to establish, transfer or suppress feast days and days of penance that are common to all of the Eastern Churches, with due regard for §3.

§2. The competence to constitute, transfer or suppress feast days and days of penance for individual Churches *sui iuris* belongs also to the authority in those Churches that is competent to establish particular law. It may do so, however, only after taking into account the other Churches *sui iuris* and without prejudice to can. 40, §1.

§3. Feast days of obligation common to all the Eastern Churches, besides Sundays, are the Nativity of Our Lord Jesus Christ, the Epiphany, the Ascension, the Dormition of Holy Mary the Mother of God and the Holy Apostles

ut Episcopi eparchiales, quatenus fieri potest, praxim introducant, secundum quam occasione exsequiarum ecclesiasticarum solum eae oblationes recipiantur, quas christifideles sua sponte offerunt.

CAN. 879 Expleta tumulatione adnotatio in libro defunctorum fiat ad normam iuris particularis.

ART. III. *De Diebus Festis et Paenitentiae*

CAN. 880 §1. Dies festos et paenitentiae omnibus Ecclesiis orientalibus communes constituere, transferre aut supprimere solius est supremae Ecclesiae auctoritatis firma §3.

§2. Dies festos et paenitentiae singulis Ecclesiis sui iuris proprios constituere, transferre aut supprimere competit etiam auctoritati, cuius est ius particulare earundem Ecclesiarum statuere, debita tamen habita ratione aliarum Ecclesiarum sui iuris et firmo can. 40, §1.

§3. Dies festi de praecepto omnibus Ecclesiis orientalibus communes, praeter dies dominicos, sunt dies Nativitatis Domini Nostri Iesu Christi, Epiphaniae, Ascensionis, Dormitionis Sanctae Dei Genitricis Mariae ac

880 §1: Vat. II, decr. *Orientalium Ecclesiarum*, 19; S.C. pro Eccl. Orient., decr. 28 ian. 1949. - LEO M., litt. *Quod saepissime*, 15 apr. 454, "Petitionem autem;" INNOCENTIUS III, const. *Quia divinae*, 4 ian. 1215; S.C. de Prop. Fide, (C.P.), 7 maii 1631; PIUS VI, litt. ap. *Assueto paterne*, 8 apr. 1775.

880 §2: Vat. II, decr. *Orientalium Ecclesiarum*, 19; PIUS XII, m.p. *Cleri sanctitati*, 2 iun. 1957, can. 264. - S.C. de Prop. Fide, (C.G.), 7 feb. 1624; 1 iun. 1626, n. 7; 30 ian. 1635, "Proposta ultima;" 28 iun. 1635; S.C.S. Off., 4 apr. 1658, n. 5; S.C. de Prop. Fide, 4 feb. 1665, n. 28, §5; 4 feb. 1676, n. 31, ad 3; BENEDICTUS XIV, litt. ap. *Demandatam*, 24 dec. 1743, §§5–6; const. *Praeclaris*, 18 mar. 1746 "La Santità" - "Tali cose;" S.C. de Prop. Fide, 8 aug. 1774; PIUS VI, litt. *Assueto pa-*

terne, 8 apr. 1775, §3; S.C. de Prop. Fide, (C.P.), 29 sep. 1781; 25 ian. 1830; 13 maii 1844, dub. 2, b); 18 iun. 1844, dub. 7. * Syn. Sergii Patriarchae Maronitarum, 18 sep. 1596, can. XVII; Syn. Diamper. Syro-Malabarensium, a. 1599, CCVIII–CCXVI; Syn. Zamosten. Ruthenorum, a. 1720, tit. XVI; Syn. Libanen. Maronitarum, a. 1736, pars I, cap. IV; pars III, cap. VI, 2, 21; Syn. Ain-Trazen. Graeco-Melchitarum, a. 1835, can. 10; Syn. prov. Alba-Iulien. et Fagarasien. Rumenorum, a. 1872, tit. VI, cap. VIII; Syn. Sciarfen. Syrorum, a. 1888, cap. IV; Syn. Leopolien. Ruthenorum, a. 1891, tit. IV, cap. IV, I–II; tit. XI; Syn. Alexandrin. Coptorum, a. 1898, sect. II, cap. II, artt. II–III; Syn. Armen., a. 1911, 676–700.

Peter and Paul, without prejudice to the particular law of a Church *sui iuris* approved by the Apostolic See by which certain feast days of obligation are suppressed or transferred to a Sunday.

CAN. 881 §1. The Christian faithful are bound by the obligation to participate on Sundays and feast days in the Divine Liturgy, or according to the prescripts or legitimate custom of their own Church *sui iuris,* in the celebration of the divine praises.

§2. In order for the Christian faithful to fulfill this obligation more easily, the useful time runs from the evening of the vigil until the end of the Sunday or feast day.

§3. The Christian faithful are strongly recommended to receive the Divine Eucharist on these days and indeed more frequently, even daily.

§4. The Christian faithful should abstain from those work or business matters that impede the worship to be rendered to God, the joy that is proper to the Lord's day, or the proper relaxation of mind and body.

CAN. 882 On the days of penance the Christian faithful are obliged to observe fast or

dies Sanctorum Apostolorum Petri et Pauli, salvo iure particulari Ecclesiae sui iuris a Sede Apostolica approbato, quo quidam dies festi de praecepto supprimuntur vel ad diem dominicum transferuntur.

CAN. 881 §1. Christifideles obligatione tenentur diebus dominicis et festis de praecepto Divinam Liturgiam participandi aut secundum praescripta vel legitimam consuetudinem propriae Ecclesiae sui iuris celebrationem laudum divinarum.

§2. Quo facilius christifideles hanc obligationem implere possint, statuitur tempus utile decurrere inde a vesperis vigiliae usque ad finem diei dominici vel festi de praecepto.

§3. Enixe commendatur christifidelibus, ut his diebus immo frequentius vel etiam cottidie Divinam Eucharistiam suscipiant.

§4. Abstineant christifideles his diebus ab illis operibus et negotiis, quae cultum Deo reddendum, laetitiam diei Domini propriam aut debitam mentis ac corporis relaxationem impediunt.

CAN. 882 Diebus paenitentiae christifideles obligatione tenentur ieiunium

---

881 §1: Vat. II, decr. *Orientalium Ecclesiarum,* 19; const. *Sacrosanctum Concilium,* 106. -Laod. can. 29; Quinisext. can. 80; S. NICOLAUS I, litt. *Ad consulta vestra,* 13 nov. 866, IX; S.C. de Prop. Fide, (C.G.), 11 dec. 1838, ad 14; instr. (ad Del. Ap. Aegypti), 30 apr. 1862 "Circa;" instr. 31 iul. 1902, 10; S.C. de Prop. Fide (pro Neg. Rit. Orient.), decr. 18 aug. 1913, art. 33; decr. 17 aug. 1914, art. 27; decr. 27 mar. 1916, 14; S.C. pro Eccl. Orient., decr. 1 mar. 1929, art. 36; decr. 24 maii 1930, art. 42. * Syn. Duinen. Armenorum., a. 719, can. 31; Syn. Diamper. Syro-Malabarensium, a. 1599, CXXXI–CXXXII; Syn. Libanen. Maronitarum, a. 1736, pars II, cap. XIII, 12, VI; Syn. prov. Alba-Iulien. et Fagarasien. Rumenorum, a. 1872, tit. VI, cap. II "Quamobrem;" Syn. Sciarfen. Syrorum, a. 1888, cap. IV, art. II, 1; Syn. Leopolien. Ruthenorum, a. 1891, tit. IV, cap. I, 13; Syn. Alexandrin. Coptorum, a. 1898, sect. II, cap. II, art. III, 4; Syn. Armen., a. 1911, 683.

881 §2: Vat. II, decr. *Orientalium Ecclesiarum,* 15.
881 §3: Vat. II, decr. *Orientalium Ecclesiarum,* 15;

IOANNES PAULUS II, ep. ap. 2 ian. 1980, III "Inde." - Apost. can. 9; Ant. can. 2; S. BASILIUS M., can. 94; TIMOTHEUS ALEXANDRIN., can. 3; Trid., sess. XIII, *De Eucharistia,* cap. 8; sess. XXII, *De sacrificio missae,* cap. 6; S.C.C., decr. 20 dec. 1905, 6. * Syn. Libanen. Maronitarum, a. 1736, pars II, cap. XII, 15; cap. XIII, 9; Syn. Sciarfen. Syrorum, a. 1888, cap. V, art. IV, §5, 2, IV.

881 §4: Vat. II, const. *Sacrosanctum Concilium,* 106. - S. NICOLAUS I, litt. *Ad Consulta vestra,* 13 nov. 866, X–XII, XXIV, XXVI. * Syn. Ain-Trazen. Graeco-Melchitarum, a. 1835, can. 10; Syn. prov. Alba-Iulien. et Fagarasien. Rumenorum, a. 1872, tit. VI, cap. II "Porro."

882: Apost. can. 69; Gang. cann. 18–19; Laod. can. 50; Quinisext. cann. 29, 56, 89; S. DIONYSIUS ALEXANDRIN., can. 1; S. PETRUS ALEXANDRIN., can. 15; TIMOTHEUS ALEXANDRIN., cann. 8, 10, 18, 23; THEOPHILUS ALEXANDRIN., can. 1; S. NICEPHORUS CP., cann. 1–3, 43–44, 68, 71, 75; S. NICOLAUS I, litt. *Ad consulta ves-*

abstinence in the manner established by the particular law of their Church *sui iuris*.

CAN. 883 §1. As regards feast days and days of penance, the Christian faithful who are outside the territorial boundaries of their own Church *sui iuris* can adapt themselves fully to the norms in force where they are staying.

§2. In families in which the spouses are ascribed to different Churches *sui iuris*, it is permitted to observe the norms of one or the other Church *sui iuris* in the matter of feast days and days of penance.

ART. IV. *Veneration of the Saints, of Sacred Images and Relics*

CAN. 884 To foster the sanctification of the people of God, the Church recommends to the special and filial veneration of the Christian faithful the Holy ever-Virgin Mary, the Mother

vel abstinentiam servandi modo iure particulari propriae Ecclesiae sui iuris statuto.

CAN. 883 §1. Christifideles extra fines territorii propriae Ecclesiae sui iuris versantes circa dies festos et paenitentiae ad normas in loco, ubi degunt, vigentes se plene conformare possunt.

§2. In familiis, in quibus coniuges diversis Ecclesiis sui iuris ascripti sunt, circa dies festos et paenitentiae praescripta unius vel alterius Ecclesiae sui iuris observare licet.

ART. IV. *De Cultu Sanctorum, Sacrarum Iconum vel Imaginum et Reliquiarum*

CAN. 884 Ad sanctificationem populi Dei fovendam Ecclesia speciali et filiali christifidelium venerationi commendat Sanctam Mariam semper Virginem, Dei Matrem,

---

tra, 13 nov. 866, LX; INNOCENTIUS IV, ep. *Sub catholicae*, 6 mar. 1254, "De ieiunio;" CLEMENS VIII, instr. *Sanctissimus*, 31 aug. 1595, §6; S.C. de Prop. Fide, (C.P.), 31 mar. 1729; BENEDICTUS XIV, ep. encycl. *Demandatam*, 24 dec. 1743, §§5–6; S.C. de Prop. Fide, litt. (ad Patr. Melkit. Cyrillum), 7 maii 1746; litt. 4 iul. 1833, XI. * Nerses Astaraken., can. 28; Syn. Sisen. Armenorum, aa. 1204, 1246, 1307, 1342; Syn. Diamper. Syro-Malabarensium, a. 1599, CCX–CCXII; Syn. Zamosten. Ruthenorum, a. 1720, tit. XVI "Sicut;" Syn. Libanen. Maronitarum, a. 1736, pars I, cap. IV; Syn. Ain-Trazen. Graeco-Melchitarum, a. 1835, can. 23; Syn. prov. Alba-Iulien. et Fagarasien. Rumenorum, a. 1872, tit. VI, cap. VIII; Syn. Sciarfen. Syrorum, a. 1888, cap. IV, art. I; Syn. Leopolien. Ruthenorum, a. 1891, tit. XI; Syn. Alexandrin. Coptorum, a. 1898, sect. II, cap. II, art. II; Syn. Armen., a. 1911, 689–700.

883 §1: Vat. II, decr. *Orientalium Ecclesiarum*, 21. - CLEMENS VIII, instr. *Sanctissimus*, 31 aug. 1595, §6 "Graeci existentes;" S.C.S. Off., 7 iun. 1673, ad 1 et 3; 13 mar. 1727, ad 1; S.C. de Prop. Fide (pro Neg. Rit. Orient.), decr. 18 aug. 1913, art. 33; decr. 14 aug. 1914, art. 27; decr. 27 mar. 1916, 14; S.C. pro Eccl. Orient., decr. 1 mar. 1929, art. 36; decr. 24 maii 1930, art. 41.

883 §2: Vat. II, decr. *Orientalium Ecclesiarum*, 21. - S.C. de Prop. Fide, (C.P.), 12 mar. 1635; S.C.S. Off., 13 mar. 1727, ad 2–3; S.C. de Prop. Fide, 25 ian. 1830; (C.P.), 28 dec. 1842; PIUS IX, litt. ap. *Plura sapienter*,

11 iun. 1847, §5; S.C. de Prop. Fide, decr. 6 oct. 1863, D), c); (C.G.), 25 iul. 1887, ad 1. * Syn. Sciarfen. Syrorum, a. 1888, cap. III, art. IX, 9; Syn. Alexandrin. Coptorum, a. 1898, sect. II, cap. I, art. V, XXIII; Syn. Armen., a. 1911, 622.

884: Vat. II, const. *Lumen gentium*, 50–69; const. *Sacrosanctum Concilium*, 103–104, 111. - Symbolum Nicaeno-Constantinopolitanum; Eph. antecedentia, cap. XXVI, XI; actio I "Multi sane;" Chalc. actio V, Symbolum; Constantinop. II, collatio octava, VI; Trid., sess. XXV, *De invocatione, veneratione et reliquiis Sanctorum, et sacris imaginibus*; PIUS IV, const. *Iniunctum nobis*, 13 nov. 1564, Professio fidei Trident.; BENEDICTUS XIV, ep. *Nuper ad Nos*, 16 mar. 1743, Professio fidei Maronitis praescr., §5; PIUS IX, bulla, *Ineffabilis Deus*, 8 dec. 1854; PIUS XII, litt. encycl. *Mediator Dei*, 20 nov. 1947, III "Etenim" - "Sanctos;" const. ap. *Munificentissimus Deus*, 1 nov. 1950; litt. encycl. *Fulgens corona*, 8 sep. 1953; litt. encycl. *Ad Caeli Reginam*, 11 oct. 1954; PAULUS VI, litt. encycl. *Mense maii*, 29 apr. 1965; litt. encycl. *Christi Matri*, 15 sep. 1965; adh. ap. *Signum magnum*, 13 maii 1967; adh. ap. *Marialis cultus*, 2 feb. 1974, I–II. * Syn. Diamper. Syro-Malabarensium, a. 1599, XXIII; Syn. Libanen. Maronitarum, a. 1736, pars I, cap. V, 1–2; Syn. Sciarfen. Syrorum, a. 1888, cap. I, art. VI; Syn. Alexandrin. Coptorum, a. 1898, sect. I, cap. II, art. IV; Syn. Armen., a. 1911, 87–90.

of God, whom Christ made Mother of all. The Church also promotes the true and authentic cult of the other saints, by whose example the Christian faithful are edified and through whose intercession they are sustained.

CAN. 885 It is permissible to venerate with public worship only those servants of God who have been inscribed among the saints or the blessed by authority of the Church.

CAN. 886 The practice of exposing sacred icons or images in churches for the veneration of the Christian faithful is to continue in the manner and order to be determined by the particular law of the respective Church *sui iuris.*

CAN. 887 §1. Sacred icons or precious images, that is, those that are outstanding due to antiquity or art, that are exposed in churches for the veneration of the Christian faithful, cannot be transferred to another church or alienated without the written consent given by the hierarch who exercises authority over that same Church, with due regard for cann. 1034–1041.

§2. Sacred icons or precious images are also not to be restored without the written consent given by the same hierarch, who is to consult experts before he grants it.

CAN. 888 §1. It is not permitted to sell sacred relics.

§2. Well-known relics, icons or images that are held in great veneration by the people in a

quam Christus hominum omnium Matrem constituit, atque verum et authenticum promovet cultum aliorum Sanctorum, quorum quidem exemplo christifideles aedificantur et intercessione sustentantur.

CAN. 885 Cultu publico eos tantum servos Dei venerari licet, qui auctoritate Ecclesiae inter Sanctos vel Beatos relati sunt.

CAN. 886 Firma maneat praxis in ecclesiis sacras icones vel imagines venerationi christifidelium proponendi modo et ordine iure particulari propriae Ecclesiae sui iuris statuendis.

CAN. 887 §1. Sacrae icones vel imagines pretiosae, id est vetustate aut arte praestantes in ecclesiis venerationi christifidelium expositae, in aliam ecclesiam transferri vel alienari non possunt nisi de consensu scripto dato Hierarchae, qui in eandem ecclesiam potestatem suam exercet, firmis cann. 1034–1041.

§2. Sacrae icones vel imagines pretiosae etiam ne restaurentur nisi de consensu scripto dato eiusdem Hierarchae, qui, antequam eum concedit, peritos consulat.

CAN. 888 §1. Sacras reliquias vendere non licet.

§2. Insignes reliquiae, icones vel imagines, quae in aliqua ecclesia magna populi

885: S.C.S. Off., decr. 13 mar. 1625; S.C. de Prop. Fide, (C.P.), 7 mar. 1631 "Ad quintum;" (C.P.), 30 ian. 1635, "Proposita quaestione 4;" URBANUS VIII, const. *Coelestis Hierusalem,* 5 iul. 1634, §§1–2; BENEDICTUS XIV, ep. *Iampridem,* 28 feb. 1747, 6–7; const. *Quamvis iusto,* 30 apr. 1749, §12; ep. *Beatus Andreas,* 22 feb. 1755, §21. * Syn. Zamosten. Ruthenorum, a. 1720, tit. XVII; Syn. Libanen. Maronitarum, a. 1736, pars I, cap. V, 8.

886: Vat. II, const. *Sacrosanctum Concilium,* 125, 111. - Nic. II, actio VII, *Definitio de sacris imaginibus;* Trid., sess. XXV, *De invocatione, veneratione et reliquiis Sanctorum et sacris imaginibus;* PIUS IV, const. *Iniunctum Nobis,* 13 nov. 1564, Professio fidei

Trident.; GREGORIUS XIII, const. *Sanctissimus,* a. 1575, Professio fidei Graecis praescr., §15; INNOCENTIUS XI, const. *Coelestis Pastor,* 20 nov. 1687, prop. 18, Michaelis de Molina, damn.; BENEDICTUS XIV, ep. *Nuper ad Nos,* 16 mar. 1743, Professio fidei Maronitis praescr., §5; PIUS VI, const. *Auctorem fidei,* 28 aug. 1794, prop. 70–71, Synodi Pistorien., damn.; S.C.S. Off., instr. 30 iun. 1952. * Syn. Diamper. Syro-Malabarensium, a. 1599, XXXI; Syn. Libanen. Maronitarum, a. 1736, pars I, cap. V, 3–7 et 9; Syn. Sciarfen. Syrorum, a. 1888, cap. I, art. V.

888 §2: Nic. II, can. 7; Trid., sess. XXV, *De invocatione, veneratione et reliquiis Sanctorum et sacris imaginibus;* PIUS IV, const. *Iniunctum nobis,* 13 nov.

certain church cannot in any manner be validly alienated nor perpetually transferred to another Church without the consent of the Apostolic See or the patriarch, who can give it only with the consent of the permanent synod, with due regard for can. 1037.

§3. Regarding the restoration of these icons or images, can. 887, §2 is to be observed.

ART. V. *A Vow and an Oath*

CAN. 889 §1. A vow is a deliberate and free promise made to God concerning a possible and better good; the virtue of religion requires that it be fulfilled.

§2. All who have an appropriate use of reason are capable of making a vow, unless they are prohibited by law.

§3. A vow made as a result of grave and unjust fear or fraud is null by the law itself.

§4. A vow is public if it is accepted in the name of the Church by a legitimate ecclesiastical superior; otherwise, it is private.

CAN. 890 By its nature a vow obliges no one except the one who made it.

CAN. 891 A vow ceases when the time appointed for the fulfillment of the obligation has passed, when there is a substantial change in the matter promised or when the condition on which the vow depends or the purpose for which it was made no longer exists; it also ceases through dispensation or commutation.

CAN. 892 One who has power over the matter of a vow can suspend the obligation of the vow for as long as its fulfillment brings disadvantage to that person.

CAN. 893 §1. The following persons can

veneratione honorantur, non possunt valide quoquo modo alienari neque in aliam ecclesiam perpetuo transferri nisi de consensu Sedis Apostolicae vel Patriarchae, qui eum dare non potest nisi de consensu Synodi permanentis firmo can. 1037.

§3. Circa restaurationem harum iconum vel imaginum servetur can. 887, §2.

ART. V. *De Voto et de Iureiurando*

CAN. 889 §1. Votum, promissio scilicet deliberata ac libera Deo facta de bono possibili et meliore, ex virtute religionis impleri debet.

§2. Voti sunt capaces omnes congruentem usum rationis habentes, nisi iure prohibentur.

§3. Votum ex metu gravi et iniuste incusso vel ex dolo emissum ipso iure nullum est.

§4. Votum est publicum, si nomine Ecclesiae a legitimo Superiore ecclesiastico acceptatur; secus est privatum.

CAN. 890 Votum neminem obligat ratione sui nisi emittentem.

CAN. 891 Cessat votum elapso tempore ad finiendam obligationem apposito, mutatione substantiali materiae promissae, deficiente condicione, de qua votum pendet, aut eiusdem causa finali, dispensatione, commutatione.

CAN. 892 Qui potestatem in voti materiam habet, potest voti obligationem tamdiu suspendere, quamdiu voti impletio sibi praeiudicium affert.

CAN. 893 §1. A votis privatis iusta de

1564, Professio fidei Trident.; S.C. Indulg., 17 nov. 1676. * Syn. Diamper. Syro-Malabarensium, a. 1599, XXX; Syn. Zamosten. Ruthenorum, a. 1720, tit. XVII; Syn. Libanen. Maronitarum, a. 1736, pars I, cap. V, 1, 9–11.

889 §2: Trid., sess. VII, *De baptismo,* can. 9.

889 §4: Pius XII, m.p. *Postquam Apostolicis Litteris,* 9 feb. 1952, can. 311 n. 1. - S.C. de Prop. Fide, (C.P.), 4 iul. 1634, "Proposita;" Vat. II, const. *Lumen gentium,* 44 "Per vota."

891: Benedictus XIV, ep. encycl. *Inter praeteritos,* 3 dec. 1749, §§45–47.

dispense from a private vow for a just cause provided the dispensation does not injure the acquired rights of others:

1° for his subjects, any hierarch, pastor, and the local superior of an institute of consecrated life who has the power of governance;

2° for the other Christian faithful of his own Church *sui iuris,* the local hierarch, provided they actually reside within the territorial boundaries of his eparchy, and also a local pastor within the territorial boundaries of his own parish;

3° for those who reside day and night in a house of an institute of consecrated life, the local superior who has the power of governance, and the major superior.

§2. This dispensation can be granted by any confessor under the same condition, but only for the internal forum,

CAN. 894 Vows made before monastic or religious profession are suspended while the person who made the vow remains in the monastery, order or congregation.

CAN. 895 An oath is the invocation of the divine Name as witness to the truth. It can be made before the Church only in cases determined by law; otherwise it produces no canonical effect.

causa dispensare potest, dummodo dispensatio ne laedat iura aliis quaesita:

1° sibi subditos omnis Hierarcha, parochus et Superior localis instituti vitae consecratae, qui potestatem regiminis habet;

2° ceteros christifideles propriae Ecclesiae sui iuris Hierarcha loci, dummodo intra fines territorii eparchiae actu degant; itemque parochus loci intra fines territorii propriae paroeciae;

3° eos, qui diu noctuque in domo instituti vitae consecratae degunt, Superior localis, qui potestatem regiminis habet, eiusque Superior maior.

§2. Haec dispensatio sub eadem condicione, sed pro foro interno tantum concedi potest a quolibet confessario.

CAN. 894 Vota ante professionem religiosam emissa suspenduntur, dum vovens in monasterio, ordine vel congregatione permanet.

CAN. 895 Iusiurandum, id est invocatio Nominis divini in testem veritatis, coram Ecclesia praestari potest tantummodo in casibus iure statutis; secus nullum parit effectum canonicum.

895: S. BASILIUS M., cann. 10, 17, 29; INNOCENTIUS III, litt. ap. *Rex Regum* (ad Primatem Bulgarorum), 25 feb. 1204; ep. *Eius exemplo,* 18 dec. 1208, Professio fidei Waldensibus praescr.; IOANNES XXI, litt. encycl. *Gloriosam Ecclesiam,* 23 ian. 1318, §§18–19; MARTINUS V (in Constantien.), const. *Inter cunctas,* 22 feb. 1418, art. 43, Ioannis Wicleff, damn.; artt. 12–14 de quibus errorum Wicleff et Hus suspecti interrogandi; GREGORIUS XII, const. *Inter Apostolicas,* 5 sep. 1584; S.C.S. Off., decr. 4 mar. 1679, prop. 24–28 damn.; INNOCENTIUS XII, const. *Ecclesiae catholicae,* 22 sep. 1695, §§1–2; CLEMENS XI, const. *Unigenitus,* 8 sep. 1713, prop. 101, Paschasii Quesnel, damn.; const. *Pastoralis officii,* 28 aug. 1718, §4; CLEMENS XIII, litt. *Delatis ad nos,* 1 aug. 1760, §5; litt. *Romani Pontificis* (ad Patr. Graeco-Melkitarum), 9 iul. 1764, §4; S.C. de Prop. Fide, (C.G.), 26 aug. 1793, ad 4; PIUS VI, const. *Auctorem fidei,* 28 aug. 1794, prop. 75, Synodi Pistorien., damn.; PIUS VII, litt. *Ubi primum* (ad Archiep. Alep.

electum), 3 iun. 1816, §2; LEO XII, const. *Quo graviora,* 13 mar. 1825, §14; litt. *Apostolatus officium* (ad Patr. Graeco-Melchitarum), 4 iul. 1828; PIUS IX, litt. *Supremi Apostolatus,* 22 mar. 1869, §4; PIUS XII, m.p. *Sollicitudinem Nostram,* 6 ian. 1950, cann. 136–137, 138 §3, 265 §3, 266, 268, 289–291, 320–321, 352–360, 559; m.p. *Postquam Apostolicis Litteris,* 9 feb. 1952, cann. 263 §5, 267 n. 1; m.p. *Cleri sanctitati,* 2 iun. 1957, cann. 113 §1, 179, 236 §2, 255 §1, 395 §2, 430 §2 n. 1, 461 §2. * Syn. Zamosten. Ruthenorum, a. 1720, tit. VI "Ut etiam;" Syn. Libanen. Maronitarum, a. 1736, pars IV, cap. I, 12; Syn. Ain-Trazen. Graeco-Melchitarum, a. 1835, can. 20; Syn. prov. Alba-Iulien. et Fagarasien. Rumenorum, a. 1882, tit. V, §§48, 90; Syn. Sciarfen. Syrorum, a. 1888, cap. V, art. XIII, §10, 4 "His;" cap. VIII, art. II "Decet" Syn. Alexandrin. Coptorum, a. 1898, sect. III, cap. II, art. II, 11 et 13; cap. V, 3, VI; cap. VI, tit. II, 6–7; tit. V, art. IV, 1, 26–27, 31–33, 35; tit. VI, art. III, 1–2; Syn. Armen., a. 1911, 201, 245, 317, 332.

TITULUS XVII. DE

BAPTIZATIS ACATHOLICIS

AD PLENAM

COMMUNIONEM CUM

ECCLESIA CATHOLICA

CONVENIENTIBUS

TITLE XVII. BAPTIZED NON-CATHOLICS COMING INTO FULL COMMUNION WITH THE CATHOLIC CHURCH

CAN. 896 For those who have been baptized in non-Catholic Churches or ecclesial communities and who ask of their own accord to enter into full communion with the Catholic Church, whether as individuals or as groups, no burden is to be imposed beyond what is necessary.

CAN. 897 A member of the Christian faithful of an Eastern non-Catholic Church is to be received into the Catholic Church with only the profession of the Catholic faith, after a doctrinal and spiritual preparation that is suited to that person's condition.

CAN. 898 §1. Besides the Roman Pontiff, the patriarch with the consent of the synod of bishops of the patriarchal Church, or the metropolitan of a metropolitan Church *sui iuris* with the consent of the council of hierarchs, can receive a bishop of an Eastern non-Catholic Church into the Catholic Church.

§2. The right of receiving anyone else into the Catholic Church pertains to the hierarch of the place, or if the particular law so warrants, also to the patriarch.

CAN. 896 Eis, qui in Ecclesiis vel Communitatibus ecclesialibus acatholicis baptizati sunt et ad plenam communionem cum Ecclesia catholica convenire sua sponte petunt, sive agitur de singulis sive de coetibus, nihil ultra imponatur oneris quam ea, quae necessaria sunt.

CAN. 897 Christifidelis alicuius Ecclesiae orientalis acatholicae in Ecclesiam catholicam recipiendus est cum sola professione fidei catholicae, praemissa praeparatione doctrinali et spirituali pro sua cuiusque condicione.

CAN. 898 §1. Episcopum alicuius Ecclesiae orientalis acatholicae in Ecclesiam catholicam recipere potest praeter Romanum Pontificem etiam Patriarcha de consensu Synodi Episcoporum Ecclesiae patriarchalis vel Metropolita Ecclesiae metropolitanae sui iuris de consensu Consilii Hierarcharum.

§2. Ius recipiendi in Ecclesiam catholicam quemlibet alium spectat ad Hierarcham loci vel, si ita fert ius particulare, etiam ad Patriarcham.

896: Act. 15, 18; Vat. II, decr. *Unitatis redintegratio*, 18.
897: Vat. II, decr. *Orientalium Ecclesiarum*, 25.

898 §2: Pont. Comm. pro Russia, instr. 26 aug. 1929.

§3. The right of receiving individual lay persons into the Catholic Church belongs also to the pastor, unless this is prohibited by particular law.

CAN. 899 A cleric of an Eastern non-Catholic Church entering into full communion with the Catholic Church can exercise his sacred order in accord with the norms established by the competent authority; a bishop, however, cannot validly exercise the power of governance except with the assent of the Roman Pontiff, head of the college of bishops.

CAN. 900 §1. A person who has not yet completed his or her fourteenth year is not to be received, if the parents are opposed to it.

§2. If grave inconveniences are foreseen either to the Church or to the person from receiving such a person, the reception is to be deferred, unless there is imminent danger of death.

CAN. 901 If non-Catholics, who do not belong to an Eastern Church, are received into the Catholic Church, the norms given above are to be observed with the necessary adaptations, provided they have been validly baptized.

§3. Ius recipiendi in Ecclesiam catholicam singulos laicos spectat quoque ad parochum, nisi iure particulari prohibetur.

CAN. 899 Clericus alicuius Ecclesiae orientalis acatholicae ad plenam communionem cum Ecclesia catholica conveniens potest proprium ordinem sacrum exercere secundum normas ab auctoritate competenti statutas; Episcopus autem potestatem regiminis valide exercere non potest nisi de assensu Romani Pontificis, Collegii Episcoporum capitis.

CAN. 900 §1. Qui decimum quartum aetatis annum nondum explevit, ne recipiatur renitentibus parentibus.

§2. Si ex eiusdem receptione gravia praevidentur incommoda vel Ecclesiae vel ipso, receptio differatur, nisi periculum mortis imminet.

CAN. 901 Si acatholici, qui non ad aliquam Ecclesiam orientalem pertinent, in Ecclesiam catholicam recipiuntur, servandae sunt normae supra datae congrua congruis referendo, dummodo sint valide baptizati.

899: Vat. II, decr. *Orientalium Ecclesiarum*, 25; *Nota explicativa praevia* ad const. *Lumen gentium*, n. 2.

TITLE XVIII. ECUMENISM OR FOSTERING THE UNITY OF CHRISTIANS

TITULUS XVIII. DE OECUMENISMO SEU DE CHRISTIANORUM UNITATE FOVENDA

CAN. 902 Since solicitude for the restoration of the unity of all Christians belongs to the entire Church, all the Christian faithful, but especially the Church's pastors, should pray and work for that fullness of unity desired by the Lord, resourcefully taking part in the ecumenical activities set in motion by the grace of the Holy Spirit.

CAN. 903 The Eastern Catholic Churches have a special function of fostering unity among all Eastern Churches, first of all through prayers, by the example of life, by conscientious fidelity to the ancient traditions of the Eastern Churches, by better knowledge of each other, by working together, and by fraternal respect for the feelings of others and their history.

CAN. 904 §1. Ecumenical initiatives are to be promoted in every Church *sui iuris* through special norms of particular law, while the Roman Apostolic See functions as the moderator of the movement for the entire Church.

§2. For this purpose, there should be in each Church *sui iuris* a commission of experts on ecumenism, that is to be set up, if circumstances

CAN. 902 Cum sollicitudo cunctorum christianorum unitatis instaurandae ad totam Ecclesiam spectet, omnes christifideles, praesertim vero Ecclesiae Pastores, debent pro ea a Domino optata Ecclesiae unitatis plenitudine orare et allaborare sollerter participando operi oecumenico Spiritus Sancti gratia suscitato.

CAN. 903 Ad Ecclesias orientales catholicas speciale pertinet munus unitatem inter omnes Ecclesias orientales fovendi precibus imprimis, vitae exemplo, religiosa erga antiquas traditiones Ecclesiarum orientalium fidelitate, mutua et meliore cognitione, collaboratione ac fraterna rerum animorumque aestimatione.

CAN. 904 §1. Incepta motus oecumenici in unaquaque Ecclesia sui iuris sedulo provehantur normis specialibus iuris particularis moderante eundem motum Sede Apostolica Romana pro universa Ecclesia.

§2. Ad hunc finem habeatur in unaquaque Ecclesia sui iuris commissio peritorum de re oecumenica constituenda, si rerum

---

902: Vat. II, decr. *Unitatis redintegratio,* 5, 1, 4 "Cum," 8 "Sollemne," 24; const. *Lumen gentium,* 13 "Ad hanc," 15; decr. *Orientalium Ecclesiarum,* 30 "Interim;" Secret. ad Christ. Unit. Fov., *Directorium* I, 14 maii 1967, 1–2; *Directorium* II, 16 apr. 1970, Prooem. - Leo XIII, m.p. *Optatissime,* 19 mar. 1895.

903: Vat. II, decr. *Orientalium Ecclesiarum,* 24;

decr. *Unitatis redintegratio,* 17 "Haec." - Leo XIII, litt. ap. *Orientalium,* 30 nov. 1894, "Iam."

904 §1: Secret. ad Christ. Unit. Fov., *Directorium* I, 14 maii 1967, 2; *Directorium* II, 16 apr. 1970, Prooem. "Ecclesiae Pastoribus."

904 §2: Secret. ad Christ. Unit. Fov., *Directorium* I, 14 maii 1967, 7.

so suggest, in consultation with the patriarchs and eparchial bishops of other Churches *sui iuris* who exercise their power in the same territory.

§3. A council for the promotion of ecumenical movement is to be available to the eparchial bishops either for each of the eparchies or, if it seems preferable, for several eparchies. In eparchies that cannot have a council of their own, there is to be at least one of the Christian faithful appointed by the eparchial bishop with the special function of promoting this movement.

CAN. 905 In carrying out ecumenical work especially through sincere and frank dialogue and with initiatives undertaken together with other Christians, due prudence must be observed, avoiding the dangers of false irenicism, indifferentism as well as immoderate zeal.

CAN. 906 In order that the Christian faithful may acquire a clearer knowledge of what is truly taught and handed down by the Catholic Church and by the other Churches or ecclesial communities, they are to be applied especially by preachers of the word, by those in charge of the media of social communication, and by all who are engaged as teachers or as directors in Catholic schools and especially in institutes of higher studies.

CAN. 907 Directors of schools, hospitals and other similar Catholic institutions are to see to it that other Christians who attend these institutions or stay there have the facilities to obtain spiritual assistance and to receive the sacraments from their own ministers.

adiuncta id suadent, collatis consiliis cum Patriarchis et Episcopis eparchialibus aliarum Ecclesiarum sui iuris, qui in eodem territorio potestatem suam exercent.

§3. Item Episcopis eparchialibus assit vel pro unaquaque eparchia vel, si visum est, pro pluribus eparchiis consilium de motu oecumenico provehendo; in eis autem eparchiis, quae proprium consilium habere non possunt, unus saltem assit christifidelis ab Episcopo eparchiali nominatus cum speciali munere hunc motum provehendi.

CAN. 905 In opere oecumenico persolvendo praesertim aperto ac fidenti dialogo et inceptis cum aliis christianis communibus servanda est debita prudentia evitatis periculis falsi irenismi, indifferentismi necnon zeli immoderati.

CAN. 906 Quo clarius innotescat christifidelibus, quid reapse doceatur et tradatur ab Ecclesia catholica et ab aliis Ecclesiis vel Communitatibus ecclesialibus, diligenter operam dent praesertim praedicatores verbi Dei, ii, qui instrumenta communicationis socialis moderantur, atque omnes, qui vires impendunt sive ut magistri sive ut moderatores in scholis catholicis, praesertim autem in institutis studiorum superiorum.

CAN. 907 Curent moderatores scholarum, nosocomiorum ceterorumque similium institutorum catholicorum, ut alii christiani ea frequentantes vel ibi degentes a propriis ministris adiumentum spirituale consequi et sacramenta suscipere possint.

904 §3: Secret. ad Christ. Unit. Fov., *Directorium* I, 14 maii 1967, 3.

905: Secret. ad Christ. Unit. Fov., *Directorium* I, 14 maii 1967, 2; Vat. II, decr. *Orientalium Ecclesiarum,* 26; decr. *Unitatis redintegratio,* 4 "Quae omnia," 8 "Attamen."

906: Vat. II, decr. *Unitatis redintegratio,* 9–10; Secret. ad Christ. Unit. Fov., *Directorium* II, 16 apr. 1970, 2; IOANNES PAULUS II, adh. ap. *Cathechesi tradendae,* 16 oct. 1979, 32.

907: Secret. ad Christ. Unit. Fov., *Directorium* I, 14 maii 1967, 53–54, 62–63.

CAN. 908 It is desirable that the Catholic faithful, while observing the norms on *communicatio in sacris,* undertake any project in which they can cooperate with other Christians, not only by themselves but together: for example, charitable works and works of social justice, the defense of the dignity and the fundamental rights of the human person, promotion of peace, days of commemoration for one's country, national holidays.

CAN. 908 Optandum est, ut christifideles catholici servatis normis de communicatione in sacris quodvis negotium, in quo cum aliis christianis cooperari possunt, non seorsum, sed coniunctim persolvant, cuiusmodi sunt opera caritatis ac socialis iustitiae, defensio dignitatis personae humanae eiusque iurium fundamentalium, promotio pacis, dies commemorationis pro patria, festa nationalia.

908: Secret. ad Christ. Unit. Fov., *Directorium* I, 14 maii 1967, 33; decr. *Unitatis redintegratio,* 12.

TITLE XIX. PERSONS AND JURIDIC ACTS

TITULUS XIX. DE PERSONIS ET DE ACTIBUS IURIDICIS

CHAPTER I. **Persons**

ART. I. *Physical Persons*

CAN. 909 §1. A person who has completed the eighteenth year of age has reached majority; below this age, a person is a minor.

§2. A minor before the completion of the seventh year is called an infant and is considered not responsible for himself or herself *(non sui compos)*. With the completion of the seventh year, however, a minor is presumed to have the use of reason.

§3. Whoever habitually lacks the use of reason is considered not responsible for oneself *(non sui compos)* and is equated with infants.

CAN. 910 §1. A person who has reached majority has the full exercise of his or her rights.

§2. A minor, in the exercise of his or her rights, is subject to the power of parents or guardians except in those matters in which minors are exempted from their authority by divine law or canon law. Regarding the appointment of guardians, the prescripts of civil law are to be observed unless canon law or the particular law of his or her Church *sui iuris* provides otherwise and with due regard for the right of the eparchial bishop, if necessary, personally to appoint guardians.

CAPUT I. **De Personis**

ART. I. *De personis physicis*

CAN. 909 §1. Persona, quae duodevicesimum aetatis annum explevit, maior est; infra hanc aetatem minor.

§2. Minor ante plenum septennium dicitur infans et censetur non sui compos; expleto autem septennio usum rationis habere praesumitur.

§3. Quicumque usu rationis habitu caret, censetur non sui compos et infantibus assimilatur.

CAN. 910 §1. Persona maior plenum habet suorum iurium exercitium.

§2. Persona minor in exercitio suorum iurium potestati parentum vel tutorum subest eis exceptis, in quibus minores iure divino vel canonico ab eorum potestate exempti sunt; ad constitutionem tutorum quod attinet, serventur praescripta iuris civilis, nisi aliter iure communi vel iure particulari propriae Ecclesiae sui iuris cavetur et firmo iure Episcopi eparchialis tutores, si opus est, per se ipsum constituendi.

909 §1: Pius XII, m.p. *Cleri sanctitati,* 2 iun. 1957, can. 17 §1. ▲ D. 4, 4, 1; 23, 1, 14; C. 6, 30, 18, pr.

909 §2: Pius XII, m.p. *Cleri sanctitati,* 2 iun. 1957, can. 17 §3 n. 1. ▲ Instit. 3, 19, 10.

909 §3: Pius XII, m.p. *Cleri sanctitati,* 2 iun. 1957, can. 17 §3 n. 2. ▲ Instit. 3, 19, 10; D. 44, 7, 1, (12–13).

910 §1: Pius XII, m.p. *Cleri sanctitati,* 2 iun. 1957, can. 18.

910 §2: Pius XII, m.p. *Cleri sanctitati,* 2 iun. 1957, can. 18. ▲ Instit. 3, 19, 8–10; D. 44, 7, 43; C. 6, 30, 18.

CAN. 911 A person is said to be a traveler *(peregrinus)* in an eparchy different from that in which the person has a domicile or quasi-domicile; a person is said to be a transient *(vagus)*, however, if the person does not have a domicile or quasi-domicile anywhere.

CAN. 912 §1. Domicile is acquired by residence within the territory of a certain parish or at least of an eparchy, which either is joined with the intention of remaining there permanently unless called away or has in fact been protracted for five complete years.

§2. Quasi-domicile is acquired by residence within the territory of a certain parish or at least of an eparchy, which either is joined with the intention of remaining there for at least three months unless called away or has in fact been protracted for three complete months.

CAN. 913 Members of religious institutes as well as societies of common life according to the manner of religious acquire a domicile in the place in the house to which they are ascribed is located; they acquire a quasi-domicile in the place where their residence has been protracted for at least three months.

CAN. 914 Spouses are to have a common domicile or quasi-domicile; for a just cause, however, each can have their own domicile or quasi-domicile.

CAN. 915 §1. A minor necessarily retains the domicile and quasi-domicile of the one to whose power the minor is subject. A minor who is no longer an infant can also acquire a quasi-domicile of one's own; a minor who is legitimately emancipated in accord with the norm of

CAN. 911 Persona dicitur peregrinus in eparchia diversa ab illa, in qua domicilium vel quasi-domicilium habet; dicitur vero vagus, si nullibi domicilium vel quasi-domicilium habet.

CAN. 912 §1. Domicilium acquiritur ea in territorio alicuius paroeciae aut saltem eparchiae commoratione, quae aut coniuncta est cum animo ibi perpetuo manendi, si nihil inde avocat, aut ad quinquennium completum reapse est protracta.

§2. Quasi-domicilium acquiritur ea in territorio alicuius paroeciae aut saltem eparchiae commoratione, quae aut coniuncta est cum animo ibi manendi saltem per tres menses, si nihil inde avocat, aut ad tres menses completos reapse est protracta.

CAN. 913 Sodales institutorum religiosorum necnon societatum vitae communis ad instar religiosorum domicilium acquirunt in loco, ubi sita est domus, cui ascribuntur; quasi-domicilium in loco, ubi eorum commoratio ad tres saltem menses est protracta.

CAN. 914 Coniuges commune habeant domicilium vel quasi-domicilium; iusta de causa vero uterque habere potest proprium domicilium vel quasi-domicilium.

CAN. 915 §1. Minor necessario retinet domicilium et quasi-domicilium illius, cuius potestati subditus est; infantia egressus potest etiam quasi-domicilium proprium acquirere atque legitime ad normam iuris civilis emancipatus etiam proprium domicilium.

911: Pius XII, m.p. *Postquam Apostolicis Litteris,* 9 feb. 1952, can. 304. ▲ D. 50, 16, 239, (2–3); C. 10, 40 (39), 1 et 3–5 et 7.

912 §1: Pius XII, m.p. *Cleri sanctitati,* 2 iun. 1957, can. 20 §1. * Syn. Libanen. Maronitarum, a. 1736, pars II, cap. XIV, 9. ▲ D. 47, 10, 5, (2); 50, 1, 17, (13); 50, 16, 203; C. 10, 40 (39), 2 et 7, (1).

912 §2: Pius XII, m.p. *Cleri sanctitati,* 2 iun. 1957, can. 20 §2.

914: Pius XII, m.p. *Cleri sanctitati,* 2 iun. 1957, can. 21 §1. ▲ D. 5, 1, 65; 50, 1, 32; C. 12, 1, 13; Basilic. 7, 5, 64.

915 §1: Pius XII, m.p. *Cleri sanctitati,* 2 iun. 1957, can. 21 §2. ▲ D. 50, 1, 3–4.

civil law can also acquire a domicile of one's own.

§2. Whoever for some other reason than minority has been placed legitimately under guardianship or curatorship has the domicile and quasi-domicile of the guardian or curator.

CAN. 916 §1. Through both domicile and quasi-domicile, each person acquires his or her own local hierarch and pastor of the Church *sui iuris* to which he or she is ascribed, unless common law provides otherwise.

§2. The proper pastor of one who has only an eparchial domicile or quasi-domicile is the pastor of the place where the person is actually residing.

§3. The proper local hierarch and pastor of a transient is the pastor of his or her church and the local hierarch where the transient is actually residing.

§4. If there is no pastor for the Christian faithful of a certain Church *sui iuris,* the eparchial bishop for those same faithful is to designate the pastor of another Church *sui iuris,* who is to assume their care as their proper pastor, with the consent, however, of the eparchial bishop of the pastor to be designated.

§5. In places where not even an exarchy has

§2. Quicumque alia ratione quam minoritate in tutelam vel curatelam legitime traditus est, domicilium et quasi-domicilium habet tutoris vel curatoris.

CAN. 916 §1. Et per domicilium et per quasi-domicilium suum quisque proprium Hierarcham loci et parochum Ecclesiae sui iuris, cui ascriptus est, sortitur, nisi aliter iure communi cavetur.

§2. Parochus proprius illius, qui non habet nisi eparchiale domicilium vel quasi-domicilium, est parochus loci, ubi actu commoratur.

§3. Proprius vagi Hierarcha loci et parochus est eius Ecclesiae parochus et Hierarcha loci, ubi vagus actu commoratur.

§4. Si deest parochus pro christifidelibus alicuius Ecclesiae sui iuris, eorundem Episcopus eparchialis designet parochum alterius Ecclesiae sui iuris, qui eorum curam tamquam parochus proprius suscipiat, de consensu vero Episcopi eparchialis parochi designandi.

§5. In locis, ubi ne exarchia quidem pro

915 §2: Pius XII, m.p. *Cleri sanctitati,* 2 iun. 1957, can. 21 §3.

916 §1: Pius XII, m.p. *Cleri sanctitati,* 2 iun. 1957, can. 22 §1. - Lat. IV, can. 9.

916 §2: Pius XII, m.p. *Cleri sanctitati,* 2 iun. 1957, can. 22 §5.

916 §3: Pius XII, m.p. *Cleri sanctitati,* 2 iun. 1957, can. 22 §4.

916 §4: Pius XII, m.p. *Cleri sanctitati,* 2 iun. 1957, can. 22 §2. - S.C. de Prop. Fide, litt. 11 oct. 1780; instr. (ad. Ep. Latin. Babylonen.), 23 sep. 1783, "Prorsus" et "Si vero;" (C.G.), 29 mar. 1824; (C.G.), 11 dec. 1838, 15–16; Pius IX, all. *Probe noscitis,* 3 iul. 1848; S.C. de Prop. Fide, instr. (ad Del. Ap. Aegypti), 30 apr. 1862, "Il 4 dubbio;" (C.G.), 1 iun. 1885, ad 4; (C.G.), 25 iul. 1887, ad 4 "A quonam;" Leo XIII, litt. ap. *Orientali-*

um, 30 nov. 1894, II; S.C. de Prop. Fide, litt. encycl. 26 feb. 1896; decr. 1 maii 1897; S.C. de Prop. Fide (pro Neg. Rit. Orient.), decr. 18 aug. 1913, artt. 22–23; decr. 17 aug. 1914, art. 18; S.C. pro Eccl. Orient., decr. 1 mar. 1929, art. 19; decr. 24 maii 1930, artt. 21–22. * Syn. Libanen. Maronitarum, a. 1736, pars II, cap. I, 5; Syn. Sciarfen. Syrorum, a. 1888, cap. III, art. IX, 17; Syn. Alexandrin. Coptorum, a. 1898, sect. II, cap. I, art. V, IX; Syn. Armen., a. 1911, 621, 627.

916 §5: Pius XII, m.p. *Cleri sanctitati,* 2 iun. 1957, can. 22 §3. - Pius IV, const. *Romanus Pontifex,* 16 feb. 1564, §2; Pius IX, litt. *Ubi inscrutabili,* 3 iul. 1848, §3; Leo XIII, litt. ap. *Orientalium,* 30 nov. 1894, IX; S.C. de Prop. Fide, litt. (ad Ep. Strigonien.), 1 oct. 1907. * Syn. Alexandrin. Coptorum, a. 1898, sect. II, cap. I, art. V, X; Syn. Armen., a. 1911, 621

been erected for the Christian faithful of a certain Church *sui iuris,* the local hierarch of another Church *sui iuris,* even the Latin Church, is to be considered as the proper hierarch of these faithful, with due regard for can. 101. If, however, there are several local hierarchs, that one whom the Apostolic See has designated is to be considered as their proper hierarch or, if it concerns the Christian faithful of a certain patriarchal Church, the one whom the patriarch has designated with the assent of the Apostolic See.

CAN. 917 Domicile and quasi-domicile are lost by departure from a place with the intention of not returning, without prejudice to cann. 913 and 915.

CAN. 918 Consanguinity is computed through lines and degrees:

1° In the direct line, there are as many degrees as there are persons, not counting the common ancestor;

2° In the collateral line, there are as many degrees as there are persons in both lines, not counting the common ancestor.

CAN. 919 §1. Affinity arises from a valid marriage and exists between one spouse and the blood relatives of the other.

§2. A blood relative of either one of the spouses is related by affinity to the other spouse by the same line and by the same degree.

christifidelibus alicuius Ecclesiae sui iuris erecta est, tamquam proprius eorundem christifidelium Hierarcha habendus est Hierarcha loci alterius Ecclesiae sui iuris, etiam Ecclesiae latinae, firmo can. 101; si vero plures sunt, ille habendus est tamquam proprius, quem designavit Sedes Apostolica vel, si de christifidelibus alicuius Ecclesiae patriarchalis agitur, Patriarcha de assensu Sedis Apostolicae.

CAN. 917 Domicilium et quasi-domicilium amittitur discessu a loco cum animo non revertendi salvis cann. 913 et 915.

CAN. 918 Consanguinitas computatur per lineas et gradus:

1° in linea recta tot sunt gradus, quot personae stipite dempto;

2° in linea collaterali tot sunt gradus, quot personae in utroque tractu stipite dempto.

CAN. 919 §1. Affinitas oritur ex matrimonio valido ac viget inter alterutrum coniugem et consanguineos alterius.

§2. Qua linea et quo gradu aliquis alterutrius coniugis est consanguineus, alterius est affinis.

917: Pius XII, m.p. *Cleri sanctitati,* 2 iun. 1957, can. 23. ▲ D. 50, 1, 29.

918: Pius XII, m.p. *Cleri sanctitati,* 2 iun. 1957, can. 24 §§1–3. * Syn. Libanen. Maronitarum, a. 1736, pars II, cap. XI, 8, IV; Syn. prov. Alba-Iulien. et Fagarasien. Rumenorum, a. 1872, tit. V, cap. VIII, I, l); Syn Sciarfen. Syrorum, a. 1888, cap. V, art. XV, §8, 10; Syn. Alexandrin. Coptorum, a. 1898, sect. II, art. VIII, §5, VIII; Syn. Armen., a. 1911, 571, n. 5. ▲ Instit. 3, 6, pr.-7; D. 38, 10, 1 et 10, (9–11).

919 §1: Pius XII, m.p. *Cleri sanctitati,* 2 iun. 1957, can. 25 §1 nn. 1–2. * Syn. Libanen. Maronitarum, a. 1736, pars II, cap. XI, 8, V; Syn. prov. Alba-Iulien. et Fagarasien. Rumenorum, a. 1872, tit. V, cap. VIII, I, m); a. 1882, tit. IV, sect. I, §17; Syn. Sciarfen. Syrorum, a. 1888, cap. V, art. XV, §8, 12; Syn. Alexandrin. Coptorum, a. 1898, sect. II, art. VIII, §5, IX; Syn. Armen., a. 1911, 571, n. 6. ▲ D. 38, 10, 4, (3 et 8) et 6–8 et 10, pr.

919 §2: Pius XII, m.p. *Cleri sanctitati,* 2 iun. 1957, can. 25 §1 n. 3.

ART. II. *Juridic Persons*

CAN. 920 Besides physical persons, there are also in the Church juridic persons, either aggregates of persons or aggregates of things, that is, subjects in canon law of obligations and rights that correspond to their nature.

CAN. 921 §1. Juridic persons are constituted for a purpose that is in keeping with the mission of the Church either by the very prescript of law or by special concession of competent authority given through a decree.

§2. Churches *sui iuris,* provinces, eparchies, exarchies, as well as other institutes expressly established as such in common law are by the law itself juridic persons.

§3. The competent authority is not to confer juridic personality except on those aggregates of persons or of things that pursue a truly useful purpose and, all things considered, have the means that are foreseen to be sufficient to achieve their designated purpose.

CAN. 922 §1. Every juridic person, erected by a special concession of the competent ecclesiastical authority must have its own statutes, approved by the authority that is competent to erect it as a juridic person.

§2. With due regard for common law, the statutes, to be approved, must provide more detailed provisions about the following:

1° the specific purpose of the juridic person;

2° the nature of the juridic person;

3° who is competent for the guidance of the juridic person and how is it to be exercised;

4° who is to represent the juridic person in the ecclesiastical and civil forum;

ART. II. *De Personis Iuridicis*

CAN. 920 In Ecclesia praeter personas physicas sunt etiam personae iuridicae, sive sunt universitates personarum sive universitates rerum, subiecta scilicet in iure canonico iurium et obligationum, quae earum indoli congruunt.

CAN. 921 §1. Personae iuridicae constituuntur in finem missioni Ecclesiae congruentem aut ex ipso iuris praescripto aut ex speciali concessione auctoritatis competentis ecclesiasticae per decretum data.

§2. Ipso iure personae iuridicae sunt Ecclesiae sui iuris, provinciae, eparchiae, exarchiae, necnon alia instituta, de quibus hoc in iure communi expresse statuitur.

§3. Auctoritas competens personalitatem iuridicam ne conferat nisi eis universitatibus personarum aut rerum, quae finem specificum reapse utilem persequuntur et omnibus perpensis media habent, quae sufficere praevidentur ad finem praestitutum assequendum.

CAN. 922 §1. Quaelibet persona iuridica ex speciali concessione auctoritatis competentis ecclesiasticae erecta habere debet propria statuta ab auctoritate, quae ad eandem personam iuridicam erigendam competens est, approbata.

§2. Firmo iure communi in statutis, ut approbari possint, de sequentibus pressius providendum est:

1° de fine specifico personae iuridicae;

2° de natura personae iuridicae;

3° cui competat moderatio personae iuridicae et quomodo exercenda sit;

4° quis in foro ecclesiastico et civili personam iuridicam repraesentet;

920: Pius XII, m.p. *Cleri sanctitati,* 2 iun. 1957, can. 27. ▲ D. 3, 4, 1, pr.; 47, 22, 3.

5° who is competent to dispose of the goods of the juridic person and who should be the executor in the case of the extinction of the juridic person, its division into several juridic persons, its merger with other juridic persons, always having observed the intentions of the donors as well as acquired rights.

§3. Before its statutes are approved, a juridic person cannot transact business validly.

CAN. 923 An aggregate of persons cannot be erected as a juridic person unless it consists of at least three physical persons.

CAN. 924 With regard to collegial acts, unless the law has expressly provided otherwise:

1° when the majority of those who must be convoked are present, that which is approved by the absolute majority of those present has the force of law; if the votes were equal, however, the one presiding is to break the tie by his or her vote;

2° if the acquired rights of individuals are affected, the consent of each of them is required;

3° regarding elections, can. 956 is to be observed.

CAN. 925 If even one member of the juridic person survives and it nevertheless does not cease to exist according to the statutes, that member has the exercise of all the rights of the same juridic person.

CAN. 926 §1. Unless the law has provided otherwise, the goods and rights of juridic persons that lack members must be conserved, administered or exercised through the care of that authority that is competent, in the case of extinction, to decide on these matters. In accord

5° cui competat de bonis personae iuridicae disponere et quisnam sit exsecutor in casu exstinctionis personae iuridicae, divisionis in plures personas iuridicas vel coniunctionis cum aliis personis iuridicis, servatis semper offerentium voluntatibus necnon iuribus quaesitis.

§3. Antequam statuta approbata sunt, persona iuridica valide agere non potest.

CAN. 923 Universitas personarum in personam iuridicam erigi non potest nisi saltem ex tribus personis physicis constat.

CAN. 924 Ad actus collegiales quod attinet, nisi aliud iure expresse statutum est:

1° id vim habet iuris, quod praesente quidem maiore parte eorum, qui convocari debent, placuit parti absolute maiori eorum, qui sunt praesentes; si vero suffragia aequalia fuerunt, praeses suo suffragio paritatem dirimat;

2° si vero iura quaesita singulorum tanguntur, consensus uniuscuiusque eorum requiritur;

3° circa electiones servetur can. 956.

CAN. 925 Si vel unum membrum personae iuridicae superest et tamen ea secundum statuta esse non desiit, exercitium omnium iurium eiusdem personae iuridicae illi membro competit.

CAN. 926 §1. Nisi aliter iure cautum est, bona et iura personae iuridicae, quae membris caret, illius auctoritatis cura conservari, administrari vel exerceri debent, cui in casu exstinctionis de eisdem statuere competit; haec auctoritas debet ad normam iuris

923: Pius XII, m.p. *Cleri sanctitati,* 2 iun. 1957, can. 28 §2. ▲ D. 50, 16, 85.

924: Pius XII, m.p. *Cleri sanctitati,* 2 iun. 1957, can. 29 §1. - S.C. de Prop. Fide, instr. (ad Patr. et Epp. Graeco-Melkitas), 29 maii 1789, n. 19. * Syn. Armen.,

a. 1911, 233. ▲ D. 3, 4, 3–4; 50, 1, 19; 50, 17, 160.

925: Pius XII, m.p. *Cleri sanctitati,* 2 iun. 1957, can. 30 §2. ▲ D. 3, 4, 7, (2); Basilic. 8, 2, 107.

926 §1: Pius XII, m.p. *Cleri sanctitati,* 2 iun. 1957, can. 31 §1 n. 1.

with the norm of law, this authority must provide for the faithful satisfaction of the liabilities that burden those goods as well as take care that the intention of the founders or donors is meticulously observed.

§2. Without prejudice to the norms of law, the ascription of members of this juridic person can and, according to the case, must be done by that authority that has the immediate care of that juridic person; the same is to be observed if the members who remain are incapable by law of carrying out the ascription.

§3. The appointment of administrators of an aggregate of things devolves upon the immediately higher authority, if it cannot be done in accord with the norm of law; the same authority has the duty of administration in accord with the norm of §1, until he has appointed a suitable administrator.

CAN. 927 §1. A juridic person is perpetual by its nature; nevertheless, it is extinguished if it is suppressed by competent authority or if, in fact, it has ceased to exist for a hundred years.

§2. A juridic person can be suppressed only for a grave cause, after having consulted its moderators and observed what the statutes prescribe in the case of suppression.

CAN. 928 Except for cases mentioned by common law:

1° it is for the patriarch, having consulted the permanent synod, to suppress juridic persons erected or approved by him; however, with the consent of the synod of bishops of the patriarchal Church, the patriarch can suppress any juridic person except those that the Apostolic See has erected or approved;

fideli impletioni providere onerum, quae illa bona gravant, necnon curare, ut fundatorum vel oblatorum voluntas adamussim servetur.

§2. Ascriptio membrorum huius personae iuridicae salvis normis iuris ab illa auctoritate fieri potest et secundum casus debet, cui eiusdem personae immediata cura competit; idem servetur, si membra, quae remanent, ascriptionis peragendae iure incapacia sunt.

§3. Nominatio administratorum universitatis rerum, si ad normam iuris fieri non potest, ad auctoritatem immediate superiorem devolvitur; eidem auctoritati onus incumbit administrationis ad normam §1, donec idoneum administratorem nominaverit.

CAN. 927 §1. Persona iuridica natura sua perpetua est; tamen exstinguitur, si ab auctoritate competenti supprimitur vel si facto per centum annorum spatium esse desiit.

§2. Persona iuridica supprimi potest nonnisi gravi de causa consultis eiusdem moderatoribus et servatis, quae in statutis de casu suppressionis praescribuntur.

CAN. 928 Salvis casibus iure communi expressis:

1° Patriarchae est consulta Synodo permanenti supprimere personas iuridicas ab ipso erectas vel approbatas; de consensu vero Synodi Episcoporum Ecclesiae patriarchalis Patriarcha quamvis personam iuridicam supprimere potest illis exceptis, quae a Sede Apostolica erectae vel approbatae sunt;

926 §2: Pius XII, m.p. *Cleri sanctitati*, 2 iun. 1957, can. 31 §1 n. 2.

926 §3: Pius XII, m.p. *Cleri sanctitati*, 2 iun. 1957, can. 31 §2.

927 §1: Pius XII, m.p. *Cleri sanctitati*, 2 iun. 1957, can. 30 §1. ▲ C. 1, 3, 55 (57), (3).

2° it is for the eparchial bishop, having consulted the college of eparchial consultors, to suppress those juridic persons he personally erected, unless a higher authority has approved them;

3° in other cases, an authority that erects juridic persons cannot suppress them validly without the consent of a higher authority.

CAN. 929 When the territory of a juridic person is divided in such a way that either a part of it is united with another juridic person or that a distinct juridic person is erected from the separated part, the authority competent to make the division must divide, in accord with justice and equity, the common goods that had been destined for the advantage of the entire territory and the debts that had been contracted on behalf of the entire territory, without prejudice to all and individual obligations as well as the intentions of pious founders or donors, legitimately acquired rights, and the statutes that govern the juridical person.

CAN. 930 On the extinction of a juridic person, its goods go to the juridic person immediately superior, always without prejudice to the intentions of the founders and donors, acquired rights and the statutes that were governing the extinct juridic person.

CHAPTER II. **Juridic Acts**

CAN. 931 §1. For the validity of a juridic act, it is required that the act be placed by a qualified and competent person and include those things that essentially constitute the act itself as well as the formalities and requirements imposed by law for the validity of the act.

2° Episcopi eparchialis est consulto collegio consultorum eparchialium illas personas iuridicas supprimere, quas ipse erexit, nisi ab auctoritate superiore approbatae sunt;

3° in ceteris casibus, qui personas iuridicas erigit, eas supprimere valide non potest, nisi consensus auctoritatis superioris accedit.

CAN. 929 Diviso territorio personae iuridicae ita, ut vel illius pars alii personae iuridicae uniatur vel distincta persona iuridica pro parte dismembrata erigatur, etiam bona communia, quae in commodum totius territorii erant destinata, et debita, quae pro toto territorio contracta erant, ab auctoritate, cui divisio competit, ex bono et aequo dividi debent salvis omnibus et singulis obligationibus itemque salvis piorum fundatorum vel oblatorum voluntatibus, iuribus quaesitis ac statutis, quibus persona iuridica regitur.

CAN. 930 Exstincta persona iuridica eius bona fiunt personae iuridicae immediate superioris salvis semper fundatorum vel oblatorum voluntatibus, iuribus quaesitis ac statutis, quibus exstincta persona iuridica regebatur.

CAPUT II. **De Actibus Iuridicis**

CAN. 931 §1. Ad validitatem actus iuridici requiritur, ut a persona habili et competenti sit positus atque in eodem assint, quae actum ipsum essentialiter constituunt, necnon sollemnia et requisita iure ad validitatem actus imposita.

929: Pius XII, m.p. *Postquam Apostolicis Litteris,* 9 feb. 1952, can. 237. * Syn. Sciarfen. Syrorum, a. 1888, cap. XII, 9.

930: Pius XII, m.p. *Postquam Apostolicis Litteris,* 9 feb. 1952, can. 238.

931 §1: Pius XII, m.p. *Sollicitudinem Nostram,* 6 ian. 1950, can. 200 §1. ▲ C. 1, 14, 5.

§2. A juridic act placed in accord with the norm of law with respect to its external elements is presumed valid.

CAN. 932 §1. A juridic act placed out of force inflicted on a person from without, which the person was not able to resist in any way, is considered as null.

§2. A juridic act placed out of some other force, grave fear, unjustly inflicted, or out of fraud is valid unless the law provides otherwise. It can be rescinded, however, through the sentence of a judge, either on the petition of the injured party or of the party's successors in law or *ex officio*.

CAN. 933 A juridic act placed out of ignorance or out of error concerning something that constitutes its substance or that amounts to a condition *sine qua non* is null. Otherwise it is valid unless the law makes other provision. An act placed out of ignorance or error, however, can give rise to a rescissory action in accord with the norm of law.

CAN. 934 §1. If it is established by law that to place a juridical act an authority needs the consent or counsel of some group of persons, the group must be convoked in accord with the norm of can. 948, unless, when it concerns seeking counsel only, particular law provides otherwise for cases stated by that law. For such a juridic act to be valid, however, it is required that the consent of an absolute majority of those present be obtained or that the counsel of all be sought, with due regard for §2, n.3.

§2. If it is established by law that to place a juridic act an authority needs the consent or counsel of certain persons as individuals:

§2. Actus iuridicus circa sua elementa externa ad normam iuris positus praesumitur validus.

CAN. 932 §1. Actus iuridicus positus ex vi ab extrinseco personae illata, cui ipsa nequaquam resistere potuit, pro nullo habetur.

§2. Actus iuridicus positus ex alia vi vel metu gravi et iniuste incusso aut ex dolo valet, nisi aliter iure cavetur; sed potest a iudice per sententiam rescindi sive ad petitionem partis laesae eiusve in iure successorum sive ex officio.

CAN. 933 Actus iuridicus positus ex ignorantia aut ex errore, qui versatur circa id, quod eius substantiam constituit, aut qui recidit in condicionem sine qua non, nullus est; secus valet, nisi aliter iure cavetur, sed actus iuridicus ex ignorantia aut ex errore positus locum dare potest actioni rescissoriae ad normam iuris.

CAN. 934 §1. Si iure statuitur ad actum iuridicum ponendum auctoritatem indigere consensu aut consilio alicuius personarum coetus, convocari debet coetus ad normam can. 948, nisi aliter iure particulari cavetur pro casibus ab eodem iure statutis, in quibus de consilio tantum exquirendo agitur; ut autem actus iuridicus valeat requritur, ut obtineatur consensus partis absolute maioris eorum, qui sunt praesentes, aut omnium exquiratur consilium, firma §2, n. 3.

§2. Si iure statuitur ad actum iuridicum ponendum auctoritatem indigere consensu aut consilio aliquarum personarum, ut singularum:

---

932 §1: Pius XII, m.p. *Cleri sanctitati*, 2 iun. 1957, can. 32 §1. ▲ D. 4, 2, 1; C. 2, 4, 13; Basilic. 10, 2, 1 et 3–4.

932 §2: Pius XII, m.p. *Cleri sanctitati*, 2 iun. 1957, can. 38, §1. ▲ D. 4, 2, 5–7 et 9, (pr. et 1) et 21, (1); Basilic. 10, 2, 3–4 et 9.

933: Pius XII, m.p. *Cleri sanctitati*, 2 iun. 1957, can. 33. ▲ D. 50, 17, 116, (2); C. 3, 32, 18.

934 §1: Pius XII, m.p. *Cleri sanctitati*, 2 iun. 1957, can. 35 §1 n. 3.

1° if consent is required, the juridic act of an authority who does not seek the consent of those persons or who acts contrary to the opinion of all or any of them is invalid;

2° if counsel is required, the juridic act of an authority who does not consult those persons is invalid;

3° although in no way obliged to accept their opinion, even if unanimous, an authority is nonetheless not to act contrary to that opinion, especially if unanimous, without a reason that is overriding in the authority's judgment.

§3. An authority that needs consent or counsel must provide those whose consent or counsel is required with the necessary information and ensure in every way their free expression of opinion.

§4. All those whose consent or counsel is required are obliged to offer their opinion sincerely and to observe secrecy; moreover, the authority can insist upon this obligation.

CAN. 935 Whoever illegitimately inflicts damage upon someone by a juridic act or by any other act placed by fraud or negligence is obliged to repair the damage inflicted.

1° si consensus exigitur, invalidus est actus iuridicus auctoritatis consensum earum personarum non exquirentis aut contra earum vel alicuius votum agentis;

2° si consilium exigitur, invalidus est actus iuridicus auctoritatis easdem personas non consulentis;

3° auctoritas, quamvis nulla obligatione teneatur accedendi ad earundem consilium, etsi concors, tamen sine praevalenti ratione, suo iudicio aestimanda, ab earundem consilio praesertim concordi ne discedat.

§3. Illis, quorum consensus aut consilium requiritur, auctoritas, quae consensu vel consilio indiget, informationes necessarias praebere et eorum liberam mentis manifestationem omni modo tueri debet.

§4. Omnes, quorum consensus aut consilium requiritur, obligatione tenentur sententiam suam sincere proferendi atque secretum servandi, quae quidem obligatio ab auctoritate urgeri potest.

CAN. 935 Quicumque illegitime actu iuridico immo quovis alio actu dolo vel culpa posito alii damnum infert, obligatione tenetur damnum illatum reparandi.

934 §2, 1°: Pius XII, m.p. *Cleri sanctitati,* 2 iun. 1957, can. 35 §1 n. 1.

934 §2, 2°: Pius XII, m.p. *Cleri sanctitati,* 2 iun. 1957, can. 35 §1 n. 2.

934 §2, 3°: Pius XII, m.p. *Cleri sanctitati,* 2 iun. 1957, can. 35 §1 n. 2.

934 §4: Pius XII, m.p. *Cleri sanctitati,* 2 iun. 1957, can. 35 §4.

935: Pius XII, m.p. *Cleri sanctitati,* 2 iun. 1957, can. 34.

CAN. 936 §1. An office in the Church is any function constituted in a stable manner by the Lord himself or by competent authority to be exercised for a spiritual purpose.

§2. The rights and obligations proper to individual offices are determined by the law by which the office is constituted or by the decree of the competent authority.

§3. The canonical provision of offices is also the competence of the authority to whom it belongs to erect, change, and suppress them unless the law expressly provides otherwise or it is evident from the nature of the matter.

CAN. 937 §1. One who erects an office must see that the means required for its fulfillment are available and that just remuneration of those who carry out the office is provided.

§2. The particular law of each Church *sui iuris* is to determine in greater detail how these prescripts are to be put into effect, unless provision has already been made for certain matters by common law.

CHAPTER I. Canonical Provision of Offices

CAN. 938 An office cannot be acquired validly without canonical provision.

CAN. 939 Canonical provision of an office is made:

CAN. 936 §1. In Ecclesia officium est quodlibet munus ab ipso Domino vel ab auctoritate competenti stabiliter constitutum in finem spiritualem exercendum.

§2. Iura et obligationes singulis officiis propria determinantur eo iure, quo officium constituitur, vel decreto auctoritatis competentis.

§3. Auctoritatis, cuius est officium constituere, est etiam illud immutare, supprimere et de eius provisione canonica providere, nisi aliter iure expresse cavetur vel ex natura rei constat.

CAN. 937 §1. Qui officium erigit, curare debet, ut praesto sint media ad eiusdem implementum necessaria utque prospiciatur iustae remunerationi eorum, qui officio funguntur.

§2. Iure particulari uniuscuiusque Ecclesiae sui iuris pressius determinetur modus, quo haec praescripta ad effectum deducantur, nisi de quibusdam iure communi iam provisum est.

CAPUT I. **De Provisione Canonica Officiorum**

CAN. 938 Officium sine provisione canonica valide obtineri non potest.

CAN. 939 Provisio canonica officii fit:

---

936 §3: Vat. II, decr. *Presbyterorum ordinis,* 20 "Officio;" Pius XII, m.p. *Postquam Apostolicis Litteris,* 9 feb. 1952, can. 305 §1.

938: Pius XII, m.p. *Cleri sanctitati,* 2 iun. 1957,

can. 88 §1. - Constantinop. IV, can. 12.

939: Pius XII, m.p. *Cleri sanctitati,* 2 iun. 1957, can. 89.

1° through free conferral made by a competent authority;

2° if election preceded it, through its confirmation or, if the election does not need confirmation, through acceptance of the one elected;

3° if postulation preceded it, through its admission.

CAN. 940 §1. To be promoted to an office, a person must be suitable, that is, endowed with those qualities required by law.

§2. When the person promoted to the office lacks the required qualities, the provision is null only if the law has so provided; otherwise, it is valid but can be rescinded by decree of competent authority, having observed equity.

CAN. 941 Canonical provision, for which no time limit has been prescribed by law, is never to be deferred beyond six months of useful time computed from the receipt of the news of the vacancy of the office.

CAN. 942 Two or more offices, which together cannot appropriately be fulfilled at the same time by the same person, are not to be conferred upon one person unless there is a true necessity.

CAN. 943 §1. The provision of an office that by law is not vacant is null by the law itself, and is not validated by subsequent vacancy of the office.

§2. However, if it concerns an office that by law is conferred for a determined time the canonical provision can be made within six months before this time has passed; it takes effect on the day of the vacancy of the office.

1° per liberam collationem ab auctoritate competenti factam;

2° si praecessit electio, per eius confirmationem vel, si electio non eget confirmatione, per electi acceptationem;

3° si praecessit postulatio, per eius admissionem.

CAN. 940 §1. Ut quis ad officium promoveatur, debet esse idoneus, scilicet eis qualitatibus praeditus, quae iure requiruntur.

§2. Quoties provisus caret qualitatibus requisitis, provisio est nulla solummodo, si ita iure cautum est; secus est valida, sed rescindi potest per decretum auctoritatis competentis aequitate servata.

CAN. 941 Provisio canonica, cui nullus terminus est iure praescriptus, numquam differatur ultra sex menses utiles ab accepta notitia de officii vacatione computandos.

CAN. 942 Nemini conferantur duo vel plura officia, quae una simul ab eodem congrue impleri non possunt, nisi adest vera necessitas.

CAN. 943 §1. Provisio officii, quod de iure non vacat, ipso iure nulla est nec subsequenti officii vacatione convalidatur.

§2. Si vero agitur de officio, quod de iure ad tempus determinatum confertur, provisio canonica intra sex menses, antequam hoc tempus elapsum est, fieri potest et effectum habet a die officii vacationis.

---

940 §1: Pius XII, m.p. *Cleri sanctitati,* 2 iun. 1957, can. 95 §1.

940 §2: Pius XII, m.p. *Cleri sanctitati,* 2 iun. 1957, can. 95 §3.

941: Pius XII, m.p. *Cleri sanctitati,* 2 iun. 1957,

can. 97.

942: Pius XII, m.p. *Cleri sanctitati,* 2 iun. 1957, can. 98 §§1–2. - Chalc. can. 10; Nic. II, can. 15.

943 §1: Pius XII, m.p. *Cleri sanctitati,* 2 iun. 1957, can. 91 §1.

§3. A promise of an office, no matter by whom it is made, has no canonical effect.

CAN. 944 An office vacant by law, which may be possessed illegitimately by someone, can be conferred provided that in accord with the norm of law it has been declared that the possession is not canonical and mention of this declaration is made in the letter of conferral.

CAN. 945 A person who confers an office substituting for another who is negligent or impeded acquires no power thereafter over the person upon whom the office was conferred, but the juridic condition of that person is the same as if canonical provision had been made according to the ordinary norm of law.

CAN. 946 Provision of an office made because of grave fear, unjustly inflicted, fraud, substantial error or simony is null by the law itself.

ART. I. *Election*

CAN. 947 §1. Unless the law has provided otherwise, if a group has the right of election to office, the election is never to be delayed beyond three months of useful time computed from the receipt of the notice of vacancy of the office. If this time limit has passed without result, the competent authority that has the right of confirming the election or the right of providing for the office successively is to make provision freely for the vacant office.

§2. The competent authority can make provision freely for the vacant office even if the group lost its right to vote in another way.

§3. Promissio alicuius officii, a quocumque est facta, nullum effectum canonicum habet.

CAN. 944 Officium de iure vacans, quod forte ab aliquo illegitime possidetur, conferri potest, dummodo ad normam iuris declaratum sit eam possessionem non esse canonicam et de hac declaratione mentio fiat in litteris collationis.

CAN. 945 Qui, alium neglegentem vel impeditum supplens, officium confert, nullam inde potestatem acquirit in personam, cui collatum est, sed huius condicio iuridica eadem est, ac si provisio canonica ad ordinariam normam iuris facta esset.

CAN. 946 Officii provisio facta ex metu gravi iniuste incusso, dolo, errore substantiali vel simoniace ipso iure nulla est.

ART. I. *De Electione*

CAN. 947 §1. Si cui coetui est ius eligendi ad officium, electio, nisi aliter iure cautum est, numquam differatur ultra trimestre utile ab accepta notitia de officii vacatione computandum; quo termino inutiliter elapso auctoritas competens, cui ius confirmandi electionem vel ius providendi successive competit, officio vacanti libere provideat.

§2. Auctoritas competens officio vacanti libere providere potest etiam si coetus ius eligendi alio modo amisit.

---

943 §3: Pius XII, m.p. *Cleri sanctitati,* 2 iun. 1957, can. 91 §2.

944: Pius XII, m.p. *Cleri sanctitati,* 2 iun. 1957, can. 92.

945: Pius XII, m.p. *Cleri sanctitati,* 2 iun. 1957, can. 100.

946: Pius XII, m.p. *Cleri sanctitati,* 2 iun. 1957, can. 93.

947 §1: Pius XII, m.p. *Cleri sanctitati,* 2 iun. 1957, can. 103.

947 §2: Pius XII, m.p. *Cleri sanctitati,* 2 iun. 1957, can. 120.

CAN. 948 §1. Without prejudice to particular law, the person presiding is to convoke the group of electors at a place and time that is convenient for them; the notice of convocation, however, if it must be personal, is valid if it is given in the place of domicile or quasi-domicile or in the place of residence.

§2. If anyone of those to be convoked was overlooked and for that reason was absent, the election is valid but, at the petition of the same person and when the oversight and absence have been proven, the election must be rescinded by the competent authority, even after confirmation, provided that it is evident, in accord with the norm of law, that a recourse had been lodged at least within three days computed from the receipt of notice of the election.

§3. However, if more than a third of the electors were overlooked, the election is null by the law itself, unless all those overlooked, in fact, took part.

CAN. 949 §1. When the notice of the convocation has been given canonically, those present at the place and on the day stated in the notice have the right to vote. Voting validly by letter or proxy is by law excluded, unless the law provides otherwise.

§2. If one of the electors is present in the house where the election occurs but cannot be present at the election due to ill health, his or her written vote is to be sought by the tellers.

CAN. 950 Even if a person has the right to vote in his or her own name under several titles, the person can vote only once.

CAN. 948 §1. Salvo iure particulari coetus praeses electores convocet loco ac tempore ipsis convenienti; convocatio, si personalis esse debet, valet, si fit vel in loco domicilii aut quasi-domicilii vel in loco commorationis.

§2. Si quis ex vocandis neglectus et ideo absens est, electio valet, sed ad eius petitionem debet probata praeteritione et absentia ab auctoritate competenti rescindi etiam post confirmationem, dummodo ad normam iuris constet recursum saltem intra triduum ab accepta notitia de electione computandum interpositum esse.

§3. Si vero plures quam tertia pars electorum neglecti sunt, electio est ipso iure nulla, nisi omnes neglecti reapse interfuerunt.

CAN. 949 §1. Convocatione canonice facta ius suffragium ferendi pertinet ad eos, qui praesentes sunt loco et die in convocatione statutis excluso iure valide ferendi suffragia per epistulam vel procuratorem, nisi aliter iure cavetur.

§2. Si quis ex electoribus praesens in domo est, in qua fit electio, sed electioni ob infirmam valetudinem interesse non potest, suffragium eius scriptum a scrutatoribus exquiratur.

CAN. 950 Etsi quis plures ob titulos ius suffragium nomine proprio ferendi habet, non potest nisi unum ferre.

948 §1: Pius XII, m.p. *Cleri sanctitati,* 2 iun. 1957, can. 104 §1.
948 §2: Pius XII, m.p. *Cleri sanctitati,* 2 iun. 1957, can. 104 §2.
948 §3: Pius XII, m.p. *Cleri sanctitati,* 2 iun. 1957, can. 104 §§3–4.

949 §1: Pius XII, m.p. *Cleri sanctitati,* 2 iun. 1957, can. 105.
949 §2: Pius XII, m.p. *Cleri sanctitati,* 2 iun. 1957, can. 110.
950: Pius XII, m.p. *Cleri sanctitati,* 2 iun. 1957, can. 106.

CAN. 951 No one who does not belong to the group can be admitted to vote; otherwise, the election is null by the law itself.

CAN. 952 If the freedom in an election has been impeded in any way, the election is null by the law itself.

CAN. 953 §1. The following are unqualified to vote:

1° a person incapable of a human act;

2° a person who lacks active voice;

3° a person who has publicly rejected the Catholic faith or has publicly defected from the Catholic Church.

§2. If one of the above is admitted, the person's vote is null, but the election is valid unless it is evident that, with that vote subtracted, the one elected did not receive the required number of votes.

CAN. 954 §1. A vote is null, unless it is:

1° free; therefore, a vote is null if the elector has been coerced directly or indirectly by grave fear or fraud to vote for a certain person or different persons separately;

2° secret, certain, absolute, determined, any contrary custom being reprobated.

§2. Conditions attached to a vote before the election are to be considered as not having been added.

CAN. 955 §1. Before an election begins, at least two tellers are to be designated from the membership of the group.

§2. The tellers are to gather the votes, to ex-

CAN. 951 Nemo coetui extraneus admitti potest ad suffragium ferendum; secus electio ipso iure nulla est.

CAN. 952 Si libertas in electione quoquo modo impedita est, electio ipso iure nulla est.

CAN. 953 §1. Inhabilis est suffragium ferendi:

1° incapax actus humani;

2° carens voce activa;

3° qui fidem catholicam publice abiecit vel a communione cum Ecclesia catholica publice defecit.

§2. Si quis ex praedictis admittitur, eius suffragium est nullum, sed electio valet, nisi constat eo dempto electum non rettulisse requisitum numerum suffragiorum.

CAN. 954 §1. Suffragium est nullum, nisi est:

1° liberum, et ideo nullum est suffragium, si elector metu gravi aut dolo directe vel indirecte adactus est ad eligendam certam personam aut plures disiunctim;

2° secretum, certum, absolutum, determinatum reprobata contraria consuetudine.

§2. Condiciones ante electionem suffragio appositae tamquam non adiectae habentur.

CAN. 955 §1. Antequam incipit electio, designentur ex gremio coetus duo saltem scrutatores.

§2. Scrutatores suffragia colligant et

951: Pius XII, m.p. *Cleri sanctitati,* 2 iun. 1957, can. 107.

952: Pius XII, m.p. *Cleri sanctitati,* 2 iun. 1957, can. 108. - Apost. can. 30; Laod. can. 13; Nic. II, can. 3; Constantinop. IV, cann. 12, 22.

953 §1: Pius XII, m.p. *Cleri sanctitati,* 2 iun. 1957, can. 109 §1 nn. 1 et 4–5.

953 §2: Pius XII, m.p. *Cleri sanctitati,* 2 iun. 1957, can. 109 §2.

954 §1: Pius XII, m.p. *Cleri sanctitati,* 2 iun. 1957, can. 111 §1.

954 §2: Pius XII, m.p. *Cleri sanctitati,* 2 iun. 1957, can. 111 §2.

955 §1: Pius XII, m.p. *Cleri sanctitati,* 2 iun. 1957, can. 113 §1.

955 §2: Pius XII, m.p. *Cleri sanctitati,* 2 iun. 1957, can. 113 §2.

amine in the presence of the one presiding over the election whether the number of ballots corresponds to the number of electors, to count the votes themselves, and to announce openly how many votes each person has received.

§3. If the number of votes does not equal the number of electors, the voting is without effect.

§4. The ballots are to be destroyed immediately after each vote count has been completed or, if several vote counts are held in the same session, after the session.

§5. The secretary is to transcribe accurately all the acts of an election and, after they have been read in the presence of the electors, they are to be signed at least by the secretary, the one presiding, and the tellers and be preserved in the archive of the group.

CAN. 956 §1. In elections, unless common law provides otherwise, when the majority of those who must be convoked are present, that which is approved by the absolute majority of those present or, after two indecisive ballots, by a relative majority on the third ballot, has the force of law. If, however, the votes are equal after the third ballot, the one who is senior in age is considered elected, unless it concerns elections among only clerics or religious, in which cases the one is considered elected who is senior by sacred ordination, or, among religious, the one who is senior by first profession.

§2. It is for the one presiding at the election to announce the person who has been elected.

CAN. 957 §1. An election must be intimated immediately to the person elected in writing or in some other legitimate manner.

coram praeside electionis inspiciant, an schedularum numerus respondeat numero electorum, suffragia ipsa scrutentur palamque faciant, quot quisque rettulerit.

§3. Si numerus suffragiorum non aequatur numero eligentium, nihil est actum.

§4. Schedulae statim peracto unoquoque scrutinio vel post sessionem, si in eadem sessione habentur plura scrutinia, destruantur.

§5. Omnia electionis acta ab eo, qui actuarii munere fungitur, accurate describantur et, postquam coram electoribus perlecta sunt, saltem ab eodem actuario, praeside ac scrutatoribus subscribantur atque in archivo coetus asserventur.

CAN. 956 §1. In electionibus, nisi aliter iure communi cavetur, id vim iuris habet, quod praesente quidem maiore parte eorum, qui convocari debent, placuit parti absolute maiori eorum, qui sunt praesentes, aut post duo inefficacia scrutinia parti relative maiori in tertio scrutinio; si vero suffragia aequalia fuerunt post tertium scrutinium, electus habeatur aetate senior, nisi agitur de electionibus inter solos clericos vel religiosos, quibus in casibus electus habeatur sacra ordinatione senior vel inter religiosos prima professione senior.

§2. Praesidis electionis est electum proclamare.

CAN. 957 §1. Electio scripto vel alio legitimo modo statim intimanda est electo.

955 §3: Pius XII, m.p. *Cleri sanctitati*, 2 iun. 1957, can. 113 §3.

955 §4: Pius XII, m.p. *Cleri sanctitati*, 2 iun. 1957, can. 113 §4.

955 §5: Pius XII, m.p. *Cleri sanctitati*, 2 iun. 1957, can. 113 §5.

956 §1: Pius XII, m.p. *Cleri sanctitati*, 2 iun. 1957, can. 29 §1 n. 1. - S.C. de Prop. Fide, instr. (ad Patr. et Epp. Graeco-Melkitas), 29 maii 1789, n. 19. ▲ D. 3, 4, 3–4; 50, 1, 19; 50, 17, 160.

956 §2: Pius XII, m.p. *Cleri sanctitati*, 2 iun. 1957, can. 116.

957 §1: Pius XII, m.p. *Cleri sanctitati*, 2 iun. 1957, can. 117 §1. * Syn. Armen., a. 1911, 242.

§2. The person elected must indicate clearly to the one presiding over the group whether or not he or she accepts the election within eight useful days computed from receiving intimation; otherwise the election has no effect.

§3. If the one elected does not accept, the person loses every right arising from the election nor is the election validated by a subsequent acceptance, but the person can be elected again. The group must proceed to a new election within a month computed from notification of non-acceptance of the election.

CAN. 958 Unless the law provides otherwise, the person elected, by accepting election, acquires the office in full right immediately, if the election does not need confirmation; otherwise the person acquires only the right to seek confirmation of the election.

CAN. 959 §1. If the election requires confirmation, the person elected must personally or through another seek confirmation from the competent authority not beyond eight days computed from the day of acceptance of the election; otherwise the person is deprived of any right arising from the election, unless it is proved that the person was prevented from seeking confirmation by a just impediment.

§2. Before receiving confirmation, the person elected is not permitted to become involved in the administration of the office; acts that may be placed by the person are null.

CAN. 960 §1. The competent authority cannot deny confirmation if the person elected has been found suitable and the election was conducted in accord with the norm of law.

§2. Electus debet intra octiduum utile a recepta intimatione computandum manifestare praesidi coetus, utrum electionem acceptet necne; secus electio effectum non habet.

§3. Si electus non acceptat, omne ius ex electione ortum amittit nec electio subsequenti acceptatione convalidatur; rursus autem eligi potest; coetus intra mensem a cognita notitia de electione non acceptata computandum ad novam electionem procedere debet.

CAN. 958 Electus acceptatione electionis, si confirmatione non eget, officium pleno iure statim obtinet, nisi aliter iure cavetur; secus non acquirit nisi ius ad exigendam confirmationem electionis.

CAN. 959 §1. Electus, si electio confirmatione indiget, debet non ultra octo dies a die acceptatae electionis computandos confirmationem ab auctoritate competenti petere per se vel per alium; secus omni iure ex electione orto privatur, nisi probat se a petenda confirmatione iusto impedimento fuisse detentum.

§2. Ante acceptam confirmationem electo non licet se immiscere administrationi officii et actus ab eo forte positi nulli sunt.

CAN. 960 §1. Auctoritati competenti, si electum repperit idoneum et electio ad normam iuris peracta est, confirmationem denegare non licet.

957 §2: Pius XII, m.p. *Cleri sanctitati*, 2 iun. 1957, can. 117 §2.

957 §3: Pius XII, m.p. *Cleri sanctitati*, 2 iun. 1957, can. 118 §1.

958: Pius XII, m.p. *Cleri sanctitati*, 2 iun. 1957, can. 118 §2.

959 §1: Pius XII, m.p. *Cleri sanctitati*, 2 iun. 1957, can. 119 §1. * Syn. Armen., a. 1911, 243.

959 §2: Pius XII, m.p. *Cleri sanctitati*, 2 iun. 1957, can. 118 §3.

960 §1: Pius XII, m.p. *Cleri sanctitati*, 2 iun. 1957, can. 119 §2.

§2. Once confirmation has been received, the person elected acquires the office in full right, unless the law provides otherwise.

ART. II. *Postulation*

CAN. 961 If a canonical impediment that can be dispensed prevents the election of a person whom the electors believe to be more suitable and whom they prefer, by their votes they can postulate that person from the competent authority, unless the law provides otherwise.

CAN. 962 At least two-thirds of the votes are required for a postulation to have force; otherwise, the election is to proceed as if nothing has been done.

CAN. 963 §1. The group must send the postulation as soon as possible, not beyond eight days, to the competent authority to whom confirmation of the election belongs. If this authority does not have the power to dispense from the impediment and wishes to admit the postulation, it must obtain a dispensation from the competent authority. If confirmation is not required, a postulation must be sent to the authority competent to grant the dispensation.

§2. If a postulation has not been sent within the prescribed time, it is null by the law itself, and the group loses the right of electing for that occasion unless it is proved that sending the postulation had been prevented by a just impediment.

§3. The person postulated acquires no right of postulation; the competent authority is not obliged to admit the postulation.

§2. Recepta confirmatione electus pleno iure officium obtinet, nisi aliter iure cavetur.

ART. II. *De Postulatione*

CAN. 961 Electores, si electioni illius, quem aptiorem putant ac praeferunt, impedimentum canonicum obest, a quo dispensari potest, suis suffragiis eum possunt, nisi aliter iure cavetur, ab auctoritate competenti postulare.

CAN. 962 Ut postulatio vim habeat, saltem duae ex tribus partibus suffragiorum requiruntur; secus ad electionem procedatur, ac si nihil actum sit.

CAN. 963 §1. Coetus postulationem quam primum nec ultra octo dies mittere debet ad auctoritatem competentem, ad quam pertinet electionem confirmare; quae auctoritas, si potestatem ab impedimento dispensandi non habet et postulationem admittere vult, dispensationem ab auctoritate competenti obtinere debet; si non requiritur confirmatio, postulatio mitti debet ad auctoritatem competentem ad dispensationem concedendam.

§2. Si intra praescriptum tempus postulatio missa non est, ipso iure nulla est et coetus pro ea vice ius eligendi amittit, nisi probat se a mittenda postulatione iusto impedimento detentum fuisse.

§3. Postulato nullum ius acquiritur ex postulatione; quam admittendi auctoritas competens obligatione non tenetur.

960 §2: Pius XII, m.p. *Cleri sanctitati,* 2 iun. 1957, can. 119 §4.
961: Pius XII, m.p. *Cleri sanctitati,* 2 iun. 1957, can. 121 §1.
962: Pius XII, m.p. *Cleri sanctitati,* 2 iun. 1957, can. 122 §2.

963 §1: Pius XII, m.p. *Cleri sanctitati,* 2 iun. 1957, can. 123 §1.
963 §2: Pius XII, m.p. *Cleri sanctitati,* 2 iun. 1957, can. 123 §2.
963 §3: Pius XII, m.p. *Cleri sanctitati,* 2 iun. 1957, can. 123 §3.

§4. Electors cannot revoke a postulation sent to a competent authority.

CAN. 964 §1. If a postulation has not been admitted by the competent authority, the right of electing reverts to the group.

§2. However, admission of the postulation is to be intimated immediately to the one postulated and can. 957, §§2 and 3 are to be observed.

§3. A person who accepts a postulation that has been admitted acquires the office in full right immediately.

CHAPTER II. Loss of Office

CAN. 965 §1. In addition to other cases prescribed by law, an office is lost by the lapse of a determined time, by reaching the age determined by law, by resignation, by transfer, by removal, and by privation.

§2. An office is not lost by the expiration in any way of the authority of the one who conferred it, unless the law provides otherwise.

§3. Loss of an office by the lapse of a determined time or by the reaching the age determined by law takes effect only from the moment when the competent authority has intimated it in writing.

§4. The title of *emeritus* can be conferred upon a person who loses an office because of reaching the age determined by law or because of resignation.

CAN. 966 Loss of an office that has taken effect is to be made known as soon as possible

§4. Postulationem ad auctoritatem competentem missam electores revocare non possunt.

CAN. 964 §1. Non admissa ab auctoritate competenti postulatione ius eligendi ad coetum redit.

§2. Admissio vero postulationis statim intimetur postulato et servetur can. 957, §§2 et 3.

§3. Qui admissam postulationem acceptat, pleno iure statim officium obtinet.

CAPUT II. De Amissione Officii

CAN. 965 §1. Amittitur officium praeter alios casus iure praescriptos elapso tempore determinato, expleta aetate iure definita, renuntiatione, translatione, amotione necnon privatione.

§2. Resoluto quovis modo iure auctoritatis, a qua est collatum, officium non amittitur, nisi aliter iure cavetur.

§3. Elapso tempore determinato vel expleta aetate iure definita amissio officii effectum habet tantum a momento, quo ab auctoritate competenti scripto intimata est.

§4. Ei, qui ob expletam aetatem iure definitam aut renuntiationem officium amittit, titulus emeriti conferri potest.

CAN. 966 Amissio officii, quae effectum sortita est, quam primum omnibus nota fiat,

963 §4: Pius XII, m.p. *Cleri sanctitati,* 2 iun. 1957, can. 123 §4.

964 §1: Pius XII, m.p. *Cleri sanctitati,* 2 iun. 1957, can. 124 §1.

964 §2: Pius XII, m.p. *Cleri sanctitati,* 2 iun. 1957, can. 124 §2.

964 §3: Pius XII, m.p. *Cleri sanctitati,* 2 iun. 1957,

can. 124 §2.

965 §1: Pius XII, m.p. *Cleri sanctitati,* 2 iun. 1957, can. 125 §1.

965 §2: Pius XII, m.p. *Cleri sanctitati,* 2 iun. 1957, can. 125 §2.

966: Pius XII, m.p. *Cleri sanctitati,* 2 iun. 1957, can. 133 §2.

to all those who have some right over the canonical provision of the office.

quibus aliquod ius in provisione canonica officii competit.

ART. I. *Resignation*

ART. I. *De Renuntiatione*

CAN. 967 A person who is responsible for himself or herself *(sui compos)* can resign from an office for a just cause.

CAN. 967 Qui sui compos est, potest officio iusta de causa renuntiare.

CAN. 968 A resignation made out of grave fear that is inflicted unjustly or out of fraud, substantial error, or simony is null by the law itself.

CAN. 968 Renuntiatio facta ex metu gravi et iniuste incusso, dolo, errore substantiali aut simoniace ipso iure nulla est.

CAN. 969 To be valid, a resignation must be made in writing or in the presence of two witnesses, to the authority to whom it pertains to make canonical provision of the office in question; unless acceptance is needed, it takes effect immediately.

CAN. 969 Renuntiatio, ut valeat, scripto vel coram duobus testibus auctoritati fieri debet, cui provisio canonica officii, de quo agitur, competit; nisi acceptatione eget, statim effectum sortitur.

CAN. 970 §1. A resignation that needs acceptance takes effect after acceptance of the resignation has been intimated to the person resigning; if, however, acceptance of the resignation has not been intimated to the person resigning within three months, the resignation lacks all force.

CAN. 970 §1. Renuntiatio, quae acceptatione eget, effectum sortitur, postquam renuntianti acceptatio renuntiationis intimata est; si vero intra tres menses renuntianti acceptatio renuntiationis intimata non est, renuntiatio omni vi caret.

§2. A resignation can be revoked by the one resigning only before its acceptance has been intimated.

§2. Renuntiatio nonnisi antequam eius acceptatio intimata est, a renuntiante revocari potest.

§3. The authority is not to accept a resignation that is not based on a just and proportionate cause.

§3. Auctoritas renuntiationem iusta et proportionata causa non innixam ne acceptet.

CAN. 971 One who has resigned an office can obtain the same office by some other title.

CAN. 971 Ille, qui officio renuntiavit, idem officium alio ex titulo consequi potest.

967: Pius XII, m.p. *Cleri sanctitati,* 2 iun. 1957, can. 126.

968: Pius XII, m.p. *Cleri sanctitati,* 2 iun. 1957, can. 127.

969: Pius XII, m.p. *Cleri sanctitati,* 2 iun. 1957, cann. 128–129, 133 §1.

970 §1: Pius XII, m.p. *Cleri sanctitati,* 2 iun. 1957,

cann. 132 §2, 131 §2.

970 §2: Pius XII, m.p. *Cleri sanctitati,* 2 iun. 1957, cann. 133 §1, 131 §2.

970 §3: Pius XII, m.p. *Cleri sanctitati,* 2 iun. 1957, can. 131 §1.

971: Pius XII, m.p. *Cleri sanctitati,* 2 iun. 1957, can. 133 §1.

ART. II. *Transfer*

CAN. 972 §1. A transfer can be made only by a person who has the right of providing for the office that is lost as well as for the office that is conferred.

§2. If a transfer is made when the officeholder is unwilling, a grave cause is required and the manner of proceeding prescribed by law is to be observed, without prejudice to the norms concerning members of religious institutes or societies of common life according to the manner of religious and always with due regard for the right of proposing contrary arguments.

§3. To take effect, a transfer must be intimated in writing.

CAN. 973 §1. In the case of a transfer, the prior office becomes vacant by taking canonical possession of the other office, unless the law provides otherwise or competent authority has prescribed otherwise.

§2. The person transferred receives the remuneration assigned to the prior office until the person has taken canonical possession of the other office.

ART. III. *Removal*

CAN. 974 §1. A person is removed from office either by a decree issued legitimately by competent authority, without prejudice to rights possibly acquired by contract, or by the law itself in accord with the norm of can. 976.

§2. To take effect, the decree of removal must be intimated in writing.

CAN. 975 §1. Unless the law provides

ART. II. *De Translatione*

CAN. 972 §1. Translatio ab eo tantum fieri potest, qui ius habet providendi officio, quod amittitur, et simul officio, quod confertur.

§2. Si translatio fit invito eo, qui officium detinet, requiritur gravis causa et servetur modus procedendi iure praescriptus salvis normis circa sodales instituti religiosi vel societatis vitae communis ad instar religiosorum et firmo semper iure rationes contrarias exponendi.

§3. Translatio ut effectum sortiatur, scripto intimanda est.

CAN. 973 §1. In casu translationis prius officium vacat capta possessione canonica alterius officii, nisi aliter iure cautum aut ab auctoritate competenti praescriptum est.

§2. Remunerationem cum priore officio conexam translatus percipit, donec alterius possessionem canonicam ceperit.

ART. III. *De Amotione*

CAN. 974 §1. Ab officio aliquis amovetur sive decreto ab auctoritate competenti legitime lato servatis quidem iuribus forte ex contractu quaesitis sive ipso iure ad normam can. 976.

§2. Decretum amotionis ut effectum sortiatur, scripto intimandum est.

CAN. 975 §1. Nisi aliter iure cavetur,

---

972 §1: Pius XII, m.p. *Cleri sanctitati*, 2 iun. 1957, can. 135 §1. - Nic. II, can. 10.

972 §2: Pius XII, m.p. *Cleri sanctitati*, 2 iun. 1957, can. 135 §2.

973 §1: Pius XII, m.p. *Cleri sanctitati*, 2 iun. 1957, can. 136 §1.

973 §2: Pius XII, m.p. *Cleri sanctitati*, 2 iun. 1957,

can. 136 §2.

974 §1: Pius XII, m.p. *Cleri sanctitati*, 2 iun. 1957, can. 134 §1.

974 §2: Pius XII, m.p. *Cleri sanctitati*, 2 iun. 1957, can. 134 §3.

975 §1: Pius XII, m.p. *Cleri sanctitati*, 2 iun. 1957, can. 134 §1.

otherwise, a person cannot be removed from an office conferred for an indeterminate time except for a grave cause and having observed the manner prescribed by law. The same is valid for the removal of a person from an office conferred for a determined time before this time has elapsed.

§2. A person upon whom an office is conferred at the prudent discretion of a competent authority according to the prescripts of the law can, upon the judgment of the same authority, be removed from that office for a cause considered just, with equity observed.

CAN. 976 §1. The following are removed from an office by the law itself:

1° a person who has lost the clerical state;

2° a person who has publicly rejected the Catholic faith or publicly defected from communion with the Catholic Church;

3° a cleric who has attempted marriage, even if only civilly.

§2. The removal mentioned in §1, nn. 2 and 3 can be enforced only if it is established by a declaration of a competent authority.

CAN. 977 If a person is removed not by the law itself, but by a decree of competent authority from an office that provides the person's support, the same authority is to take care that support is provided for a suitable time, unless other provision is made.

ART. IV. *Privation*

CAN. 978 Privation of office can only be inflicted as a penalty for a delict.

ab officio quod confertur ad tempus indeterminatum non potest aliquis amoveri nisi gravi de causa et servato modo iure praescripto; idem valet, ut quis ab officio, quod ad tempus determinatum confertur, amoveri possit, antequam hoc tempus elapsum est.

§2. Ab officio, quod secundum iuris praescripta alicui confertur ad prudentem discretionem auctoritatis competentis, potest aliquis iusta de causa de iudicio eiusdem auctoritatis aestimanda amoveri aequitate servata.

CAN. 976 §1. Ipso iure ab officio amovetur:

1° qui statum clericalem amisit;

2° qui fidem catholicam publice abiecit vel a communione cum Ecclesia catholica publice defecit;

3° clericus, qui matrimonium, etsi civile tantum, attentavit.

§2. Amotio, de qua in §1, nn. 2 et 3, urgeri tantum potest, si de eadem auctoritatis competentis declaratione constat.

CAN. 977 Si quis non quidem ipso iure, sed per decretum auctoritatis competentis amovetur ab officio, quo eiusdem subsistentiae providetur, eadem auctoritas curet, ut ipsius subsistentiae per congruum tempus prospiciatur, nisi aliter provisum est.

ART. IV. *De Privatione*

CAN. 978 Privatio officii nonnisi in poenam delicti infligi potest.

975 §2: Pius XII, m.p. *Cleri sanctitati*, 2 iun. 1957, can. 134 §2.

976 §1: Pius XII, m.p. *Cleri sanctitati*, 2 iun. 1957, can. 130 nn. 4–5.

TITLE XXI. THE POWER OF GOVERNANCE

TITULUS XXI. DE POTESTATE REGIMINIS

TITULUS XXI. DE POTESTATE REGIMINIS

CAN. 979 §1. Those who have been constituted in a sacred order are qualified, in accord with the norm of law, for the power of governance, which exists in the Church by divine institution.

§2. Other members of the Christian faithful can cooperate in the exercise of the power of governance in accord with the norm of law.

CAN. 980 §1. The power of governance is either in the external forum or in the internal forum, whether sacramental or non-sacramental.

§2. If the power of governance is exercised for the internal forum alone, the effects that its exercise are meant to have for the external forum are not recognized there, except insofar as the law establishes it in determined cases.

CAN. 981 §1. The ordinary power of governance is that which is joined to a certain office by the law itself; delegated, that which is granted to a person but not by means of an office.

§2. The ordinary power of governance can be either proper or vicarious.

CAN. 982 §1. Habitual faculties are regulated by the prescripts for delegated power.

§2. Nevertheless, unless the grant has ex-

CAN. 979 §1. Potestatis regiminis, quae ex divina institutione est in Ecclesia, ad normam iuris habiles sunt, qui in ordine sacro sunt constituti.

§2. In exercitio potestatis regiminis ceteri christifideles ad normam iuris cooperari possunt.

CAN. 980 §1. Potestas regiminis alia est fori externi, alia fori interni sive sacramentalis sive non sacramentalis.

§2. Si potestas regiminis exercetur pro solo foro interno, effectus, quos eius exercitium natum est habere pro foro externo, in hoc foro non recognoscuntur, nisi quatenus id determinatis pro casibus iure statuitur.

CAN. 981 §1. Potestas regiminis ordinaria ea est, quae ipso iure alicui officio adnectitur; delegata, quae ipsi personae non mediante officio conceditur.

§2. Potestas regiminis ordinaria potest esse sive propria sive vicaria.

CAN. 982 §1. Facultates habituales reguntur praescriptis de potestate delegata.

§2. Facultas habitualis vero Hierarchae

979 §1: Pius XII, m.p. *Cleri sanctitati,* 2 iun. 1957, can. 138. - Pius VI, const. *Auctorem fidei,* 28 aug. 1794, prop. 2, Synodi Pistorien., damn.

979 §2: Vat. II, const. *Lumen gentium,* 33 "Praeter;" decr. *Apostolicam actuositatem,* 24 "Quaedam;" Paulus VI, litt. ap. *Cum matrimonialium,* 8 sep. 1973, artt. V–VI; Secret. Status, facultas data Sign. Apost., 1 oct. 1974.

980 §1: Pius XII, m.p. *Cleri sanctitati,* 2 iun. 1957,

can. 138.

980 §2: Pius XII, m.p. *Cleri sanctitati,* 2 iun. 1957, can. 143 §1.

981 §1: Pius XII, m.p. *Cleri sanctitati,* 2 iun. 1957, can. 139 §1. - S.C. de Prop. Fide, litt. encycl. (ad Deleg. Ap. pro Orient.), 8 nov. 1882.

981 §2: Pius XII, m.p. *Cleri sanctitati,* 2 iun. 1957, can. 139 §2.

pressly provided otherwise or the hierarch was chosen for personal qualifications, a habitual faculty granted to a hierarch is not withdrawn when the authority of the hierarch to whom it was granted expires, but the faculty transfers to any hierarch who succeeds him in governance.

CAN. 983 §1. The burden of proving delegation rests on the one who claims to have been delegated.

§2. A delegate who exceeds the limits of the mandate with regard to either matters or persons does not act at all.

§3. A delegate who carries out those things for which the person was delegated in some manner other than that determined in the mandate is not considered to exceed the limits of the mandate unless the manner was prescribed for validity by the one delegating.

CAN. 984 §1. Besides the Roman Pontiff, the following are hierarchs: first of all a patriarch, a major archbishop, a metropolitan who presides over a metropolitan Church *sui iuris,* and an eparchial bishop as well as those who succeed them in interim governance in accord with the norm of law.

§2. Besides the Roman Pontiff, the following are local hierarchs: an eparchial bishop, an exarch, an apostolic administrator, as well as those who, in the absence of the aforementioned, succeed them in interim governance, and also a protosyncellus and syncellus. However, a patriarch, major archbishop, metropolitan who presides over a metropolitan Church

concessa, nisi in eius concessione aliter cautum est aut electa est industria personae, non perimitur resoluto iure Hierarchae, cui concessa est, sed transit ad quemvis Hierarcham, qui ei in regimine succedit.

CAN. 983 §1. Ei, qui delegatum se asserit, incumbit onus probandae delegationis.

§2. Delegatus, qui sive circa res sive circa personas fines sui mandati excedit, nihil agit.

§3. Fines sui mandati excedere non intellegitur delegatus, qui alio modo ac in mandato determinatur, ea peragit, ad quae delegatus est, nisi modus ab ipso delegante ad validitatem est praescriptus.

CAN. 984 §1. Hierarchae sunt praeter Romanum Pontificem imprimis Patriarcha, Archiepiscopus maior, Metropolita, qui Ecclesiae metropolitanae sui iuris praeest, atque Episcopus eparchialis necnon illi, qui eis interim in regimine ad normam iuris succedunt.

§2. Hierarchae loci, praeter Romanum Pontificem, sunt Episcopus eparchialis, Exarchus, Administrator apostolicus, ii, qui, si praedicti desunt, interim legitime succedunt in regimine, itemque Protosyncellus et Syncellus; Patriarcha vero, Archiepiscopus maior, Metropolita, qui Ecclesiae metropolitanae sui iuris praeest, necnon illi, qui eis in-

---

983 §1: Pius XII, m.p. *Sollicitudinem Nostram,* 6 ian. 1950, can. 6 §2; m.p. *Cleri sanctitati,* 2 iun. 1957, can. 141 §2.

983 §2: Pius XII, m.p. *Sollicitudinem Nostram,* 6 ian. 1950, can. 8 §1; m.p. *Cleri sanctitati,* 2 iun. 1957, can. 144 §1. - S. Leo M., litt. *Quanta fraternitati,* a. 446, "Multum stupeo." ▲ C. 2, 12 (13), 10; 7, 48.

983 §3: Pius XII, m.p. *Sollicitudinem Nostram,* 6

ian. 1950, can. 8 §2; m.p. *Cleri sanctitati,* 2 iun. 1957, can. 144 §2.

984 §1: Pius XII, m.p. *Postquam Apostolicis Litteris,* 9 feb. 1952, can. 306 §2 n. 1. - Benedictus XII, a. 1341, prop. 85, Armenorum, damn.

984 §2: Pius XII, m.p. *Postquam Apostolicis Litteris,* 9 feb. 1952, can. 306 §2 nn. 1–2.

sui iuris, as well as those who succeed them in interim governance in accord with the norm of law, are local hierarchs only with regard to the eparchy that they govern, with due regard for can. 101.

§3. Major superiors in institutes of consecrated life who have been endowed with ordinary power of governance are also hierarchs, but not local hierarchs.

CAN. 985 §1. The power of governance is distinguished as legislative, executive and judicial.

§2. Legislative power must be exercised in the manner prescribed by law; that which a legislator below the supreme authority has in the Church cannot be validly delegated unless common law provides otherwise. An inferior legislator cannot validly issue a law contrary to higher law.

§3. Judicial power, which judges or judicial colleges have, must be exercised in the manner prescribed by law and cannot be validly delegated except to perform acts preparatory to some decree or sentence.

CAN. 986 Unless common law provides otherwise or it is evident from the nature of the matter, a person can exercise executive power over his subjects even when he is outside his own territorial boundaries or they are absent; he can also exercise this power over travelers actually living in the territory if it concerns granting favors or executing either common law or particular law by which they are bound according to the norm of can. 1491, §3.

CAN. 987 Within the context of the exec-

terim in regimine ad normam iuris succedunt, sunt Hierarchae loci tantum circa eparchiam, quam regunt, firmo can. 101.

§3. Superiores maiores in institutis vitae consecratae, qui potestate regiminis ordinaria praediti sunt, etiam sunt Hierarchae, sed non loci.

CAN. 985 §1. Potestas regiminis distinguitur in legislativam, exsecutivam et iudicialem.

§2. Potestas legislativa exercenda est modo iure praescripto et ea, quam in Ecclesia habet legislator infra supremam Ecclesiae auctoritatem, delegari valide non potest, nisi aliter iure communi cavetur; a legislatore inferiore lex iuri superiori contraria valide ferri non potest.

§3. Potestas iudicialis, quam habent iudices aut collegia iudicialia, exercenda est modo iure praescripto et delegari valide non potest nisi ad actus cuivis decreto aut sententiae praeparatorios perficiendos.

CAN. 986 Potestatem exsecutivam aliquis, etsi extra fines territorii exsistens, exercere potest in subditos, etiam a territorio absentes, nisi aliter iure communi cavetur vel ex natura rei constat; in peregrinos in territorio actu degentes, si agitur de favoribus concedendis aut de exsecutioni mandando sive iure communi sive iure particulari, quo ipsi ad normam can. 1491, §3 tenentur.

CAN. 987 Quae iure communi et iure

---

984 §3: Pius XII, m.p. *Postquam Apostolicis Litteris,* 9 feb. 1952, can. 306 §2 n. 2.

985 §1: Pius XII, m.p. *Cleri sanctitati,* 2 iun. 1957, 399 §1.

986: Pius XII, m.p. *Cleri sanctitati,* 2 iun. 1957,

can. 142 §§1, 3. - Nic. I, can. 6; Constantinop. I, can. 2; Ant. can. 22; Sard. can. 3; Constantinop. IV, can. 23. * Syn. Libanen. Maronitarum, a. 1736, pars II, cap. 1, 5; pars III, cap. IV, 24. ▲ D. 1, 18, 3.

utive power of governance, those things that in common law and particular law of a Church *sui iuris* are attributed by name to the eparchial bishop are understood to belong only to an eparchial bishop and an exarch, excluding the protosyncellus and the syncelli except by special mandate.

CAN. 988 §1. Ordinary executive power can be delegated either for a single act or for all cases unless the law expressly provides otherwise.

§2. Executive power delegated by the Apostolic See or by a patriarch can be subdelegated for a single act or for all cases unless the delegate was chosen for personal qualifications or subdelegation was expressly forbidden.

§3. Executive power delegated by another authority that has ordinary power can be subdelegated only for individual cases if it was delegated for all cases. If it was delegated for a single act or for determined acts, however, it cannot be subdelegated validly except by express grant of the one delegating.

§4. No subdelegated power can be validly subdelegated again unless the one delegating has expressly granted this.

CAN. 989 Ordinary executive power as well as power delegated for all cases must be interpreted broadly; any other, however, must be interpreted strictly. Nevertheless, one who has delegated power is understood to have been granted all those things without which the delegate cannot exercise the same power.

particulari Ecclesiae sui iuris nominatim Episcopo eparchiali in ambitu potestatis regiminis exsecutivae tribuuntur, intelleguntur competere soli Episcopo eparchiali et Exarcho exclusis Protosyncello et Syncellis nisi de mandato speciali.

CAN. 988 §1. Potestas exsecutiva ordinaria delegari potest sive ad actum sive ad universitatem casuum, nisi aliter iure expresse cavetur.

§2. Potestas exsecutiva a Sede Apostolica vel a Patriarcha delegata subdelegari potest sive ad actum sive ad universitatem casuum, nisi electa est industria personae aut subdelegatio est expresse prohibita.

§3. Potestas exsecutiva delegata ab alia auctoritate potestatem ordinariam habente, si ad universitatem casuum delegata est, in singulis tantum casibus subdelegari potest; si vero ad actum aut ad actus determinatos delegata est, subdelegari valide non potest nisi de expressa concessione delegantis.

§4. Nulla potestas subdelegata iterum valide subdelegari potest, nisi id expresse a delegante concessum est.

CAN. 989 Potestas exsecutiva ordinaria necnon potestas ad universitatem casuum delegata late interpretanda est, alia vero quaelibet stricte; cui tamen potestas delegata est, ea quoque intelleguntur concessa, sine quibus eadem potestas exerceri non potest.

988 §1: Pius XII, m.p. *Sollicitudinem Nostram,* 6 ian. 1950, can. 5 §1; m.p. *Cleri sanctitati,* 2 iun. 1957, can. 140 §1.

988 §2: Pius XII, m.p. *Sollicitudinem Nostram,* 6 ian. 1950, can. 5 §2; m.p. *Cleri sanctitati,* 2 iun. 1957, can. 140 §2.

988 §3: Pius XII, m.p. *Sollicitudinem Nostram,* 6 ian. 1950, can. 5 §3; m.p. *Cleri sanctitati,* 2 iun. 1957,

can. 140 §3. ▲ D. 1, 21, 1, pr. et 5.

988 §4: Pius XII, m.p. *Sollicitudinem Nostram,* 6 ian. 1950, can. 5 §4; m.p. *Cleri sanctitati,* 2 iun. 1957, can. 140 §4.

989: Pius XII, m.p. *Sollicitudinem Nostram,* 6 ian. 1950, can. 6 §1; m.p. *Cleri sanctitati,* 2 iun. 1957, can. 141 §1. ▲ D. 2, 1, 2.

CAN. 990 §1. Executive power delegated to several persons is presumed to be delegated to them individually.

§2. When several persons have been delegated individually to transact the same affair, the one who first begins to deal with it excludes the others from doing so unless that person is subsequently impeded or does not wish to proceed further in carrying it out.

§3. When several persons have been delegated collegially to transact an affair, all must proceed according to the prescripts established for collegial acts, unless the mandate has provided otherwise.

CAN. 991 §1. Ordinary power is lost by loss of the office to which it is connected.

§2. Unless the law provides otherwise, ordinary power is suspended if an appeal is legitimately made or a recourse is lodged against privation of or removal from office.

CAN. 992 §1. Delegated power is lost: by fulfillment of the mandate; by expiration of the time or completion of the number of cases for which it was granted; by cessation of the purpose of the delegation; by revocation of the one delegating directly intimated to the delegate as well as by resignation of the one delegated made to and accepted by the one delegating. It is not lost, however, when the authority of the one delegating expires unless this appears in attached clauses.

§2. Nevertheless, an act of delegated power

CAN. 990 §1. Potestas exsecutiva pluribus delegata praesumitur eisdem delegata singillatim.

§2. Pluribus singillatim ad idem negotium agendum delegatis, qui prius negotium tractare incohavit, alios ab eodem agendo excludit, nisi postea impeditus est aut in negotio peragendo ulterius procedere noluit.

§3. Pluribus collegialiter ad negotium agendum delegatis omnes procedere debent secundum praescripta de actibus collegialibus statuta, nisi in mandato aliter cautum est.

CAN. 991 §1. Potestas ordinaria amittitur amisso officio, cui adnexa est.

§2. Nisi aliter iure cavetur, suspenditur potestas ordinaria, si contra privationem vel amotionem ab officio legitime appellatur vel recursus interponitur.

CAN. 992 §1. Potestas delegata amittitur expleto mandato; elapso tempore collationis vel exhausto numero casuum, pro quibus collata est; cessante causa finali delegationis; revocatione delegantis delegato directe intimata necnon renuntiatione delegati deleganti facta et ab eo acceptata; non autem resoluto iure delegantis, nisi ex appositis clausulis apparet.

§2. Actus vero ex potestate delegata,

990 §1: Pius XII, m.p. *Sollicitudinem Nostram,* 6 ian. 1950, can. 9 §1; m.p. *Cleri sanctitati,* 2 iun. 1957, can. 147 §1.

990 §2: Pius XII, m.p. *Sollicitudinem Nostram,* 6 ian. 1950, can. 9 §2; m.p. *Cleri sanctitati,* 2 iun. 1957, can. 147 §2.

990 §3: Pius XII, m.p. *Sollicitudinem Nostram,* 6 ian. 1950, can. 9 §3; m.p. *Cleri sanctitati,* 2 iun. 1957, can. 147 §3.

991 §1: Pius XII, m.p. *Cleri sanctitati,* 2 iun. 1957, can. 150.

991 §2: Pius XII, m.p. *Sollicitudinem Nostram,* 6 ian. 1950, can. 12 §§1–2; m.p. *Cleri sanctitati,* 2 iun. 1957, can. 151 §§1–2.

992 §1: Pius XII, m.p. *Sollicitudinem Nostram,* 6 ian. 1950, can. 11 §1; m.p. *Cleri sanctitati,* 2 iun. 1957, can. 149 §1 n. 1. ▲ D. 2, 1, 6; 5, 1, 58.

992 §2: Pius XII, m.p. *Cleri sanctitati,* 2 iun. 1957, can. 149 §1 n. 2.

that is exercised for the internal forum alone and is placed inadvertently after the expiration of time or completion of the number of cases is valid.

CAN. 993 Executive power of governance is not suspended when a recourse is lodged unless common law expressly provides otherwise.

CAN. 994 In factual or legal common error and in positive and probable doubt of law or of fact, the Church supplies executive power of governance for the external and internal forum.

CAN. 995 The prescripts of law regarding the executive power of governance are valid, unless common law provides otherwise or it is evident from the nature of the matter, also regarding the power mentioned in cann. 441, §1 and 511, §1 and for the faculties required by law for the valid celebration and administration of the sacraments.

quae exercetur pro solo foro interno, positus per inadvertentiam elapso tempore vel exhausto numero casuum validus est.

CAN. 993 Potestas regiminis exsecutiva non suspenditur interposito recursu, nisi aliter iure communi expresse cavetur.

CAN. 994 In errore communi de facto aut de iure itemque in dubio positivo et probabili sive iuris sive facti supplet Ecclesia pro foro et externo et interno potestatem regiminis exsecutivam.

CAN. 995 Praescripta iuris de potestate regiminis exsecutiva valent, nisi aliter iure communi cavetur vel ex natura rei constat, etiam de potestate, de qua in cann. 441, §1 et 511, §1 et de facultatibus, quae ad validam sacramentorum celebrationem aut ministrationem iure requiruntur.

993: Pius XII, m.p. *Sollicitudinem Nostram,* 6 ian. 1950, can. 12 §2; m.p. *Cleri sanctitati,* 2 iun. 1957, can. 151 §2.

994: Pius XII, m.p. *Sollicitudinem Nostram,* 6 ian. 1950, can. 13; m.p. *Cleri sanctitati,* 2 iun. 1957, can. 152.

TITLE XXII. RECOURSES AGAINST ADMINISTRATIVE DECREES

TITULUS XXII. DE RECURSIBUS ADVERSUS DECRETA ADMINISTRATIVA

CAN. 996 What is established in the canons of this title concerning decrees must be applied to all individual administrative acts that are placed extra-judicially by any legitimate power in the Church in the external forum, excepting those that have been issued by the Roman Pontiff or an ecumenical council.

CAN. 997 §1. A person who considers himself or herself to have been aggrieved by a decree can make recourse, in accord with the norm of law, to the higher authority of the one who issued the decree.

§2. The first recourse against decrees of the protosyncellus or syncelli is lodged with the eparchial bishop; a recourse against decrees of those who act by delegated power is lodged with the one who delegated.

CAN. 998 §1. If a person considers himself or herself aggrieved by a decree, it is particularly desirable that there be no contention between that person and the author of the decree, but that it be dealt with by seeking an equitable solution between them, possibly using the mediation and effort of serious-minded persons in such a way that the controversy is settled through voluntary emendation of the decree, just compensation, or another suitable way.

§2. The higher authority is to urge the parties concerning these things before he accepts the recourse.

CAN. 996 Quae in canonibus huius tituli de decretis statuuntur, applicanda sunt ad omnes actus administrativos singulares, qui in foro externo ex quavis legitima potestate in Ecclesia extra iudicium ponuntur, eis exceptis, qui a Romano Pontifice vel a Concilio Oecumenico feruntur.

CAN. 997 §1. Qui se decreto gravatum esse censet, potest ad auctoritatem superiorem ei, qui hoc decretum tulit, ad normam iuris recurrere.

§2. Primus recursus adversus decreta Protosyncelli vel Syncellorum ad Episcopum eparchialem interponitur, adversus vero decreta eorum, qui ex potestate delegata agunt, ad delegantem.

CAN. 998 §1. Valde optandum est, ut, si quis gravatum se decreto putat, non fiat inter ipsum et decreti auctorem contentio, sed inter eos de aequa solutione quaerenda tractetur, gravibus quoque hominibus ad mediationem vel studium forte adhibitis ita, ut per voluntariam decreti emendationem vel per iustam compensationem vel per aliam idoneam viam controversia dirimatur.

§2. De his auctoritas superior partes hortetur, antequam recursum recipit.

997 §1: Pius XII, m.p. *Cleri sanctitati,* 2 iun. 1957, can. 145.

CAN. 999 §1. Before lodging a recourse, a person must seek the revocation or emendation of the decree in writing from its author within a peremptory time limit of ten days computed from the day of intimation of the decree. When this petition is made, by the law itself suspension of the execution of the decree is also understood to be requested.

§2. The obligation of seeking the revocation or emendation of a decree does not bind if it concerns the first recourse against decrees mentioned in can. 997, §2, or if it concerns further recourses, except for those against decrees of the eparchial bishop by which any first recourse has been decided.

CAN. 1000 §1. In cases in which recourse suspends the execution of a decree, the petition mentioned in can. 999, §1 also has the same effect.

§2. In other cases, if the author of the decree does not suspend its execution within ten days computed from the receipt of the decree, an interim suspension can be sought from the higher authority, who can decree it only for a grave reason and cautiously so that the salvation of souls suffers no harm. If recourse is lodged afterwards, the authority who deals with the recourse is to decide whether suspension of the execution of the decree must be confirmed or revoked.

§3. If no recourse has been lodged against the decree within the established time or if recourse has been lodged only to seek reparation of damages, suspension of the execution of the decree ceases by the law itself.

CAN. 1001 §1. Recourse must be lodged within the peremptory time limit of fifteen days.

§2. The time limit of fifteen days runs:

1° in a case in which the petition for the revocation or emendation of the decree must be sent beforehand, from the day of the intimation

CAN. 999 §1. Antequam aliquis recursum interponit, debet revocationem vel emendationem decreti scripto ab eiusdem auctore petere intra peremptorium terminum decem dierum a die intimationis decreti computandum; qua petitione facta etiam suspensio exsecutionis ipso iure petita intellegitur.

§2. Obligatio petendi revocationem vel emendationem decreti non urget, si agitur de primo recursu adversus decreta, de quibus in can. 997, §2, vel si agitur de ulterioribus recursibus exceptis recursibus adversus decreta Episcopi eparchialis, quibus quivis primus recursus decisus est.

CAN. 1000 §1. In casibus, in quibus recursus suspendit decreti exsecutionem, idem efficit etiam petitio, de qua in can. 999, §1.

§2. In ceteris casibus, nisi intra decem dies a recepta petitione computandos auctor decreti exsecutionem eius suspendit, potest suspensio interim peti ab auctoritate superiore, quae eam decernere potest tantum gravi de causa et cauto, ne quid salus animarum detrimenti capiat; si postea recursus interponitur, auctoritas, quae de recursu videt, decernat, utrum suspensio exsecutionis decreti sit confirmanda an revocanda.

§3. Si nullus recursus intra statutum terminum adversus decretum interpositus est vel si recursus tantum ad petendam reparationem damnorum interpositus est, suspensio exsecutionis decreti ipso iure cessat.

CAN. 1001 §1. Recursus interponi debet intra peremptorium terminum quindecim dierum.

§2. Terminus quindecim dierum decurrit:

1° in casu, in quo petitio revocationis vel emendationis decreti praemittenda est, ex die intimationis decreti, quo auctor prius de-

of the decree, by which the author of the prior decree amended or rejected the petition, or if he decreed nothing, from the thirtieth day computed from the receipt of the petition.

2° in other cases, from the day on which the decree has been intimated.

CAN. 1002 The higher authority must issue a decree by which the recourse is decided within sixty days computed from receipt of the recourse, unless particular law of the proper Church *sui iuris* establishes other time limits. If this has not been done, however, and the one making recourse petitions in writing that the decree be issued, after the lapse of thirty days computed from receipt of this petition, if still nothing has been done, the recourse is considered rejected as if it were rejected on that day by a decree, in such a way that a new recourse can be lodged against that authority.

CAN. 1003 In recourses against administrative decrees, can. 1517 is to be observed, making suitable adaptations. The person making recourse always has the right to use an advocate or procurator, but useless delays are to be avoided; indeed, a legal representative is to be appointed *ex officio* if the person making recourse lacks one and the higher authority considers it necessary. Nevertheless, the higher authority always can order the person making recourse to be present in order to be questioned.

CAN. 1004 The higher authority who deals with the recourse can not only confirm the decree or declare it null but, can also rescind or revoke it; but a higher authority cannot amend it unless the particular law of his own Church *sui iuris* also grants this power to the higher authority.

CAN. 1005 Even if the higher authority has confirmed, declared null, rescinded, revoked or amended a decree, the one who issued

cretum emendavit vel petitionem reiecit, aut, si nihil decrevit, ex tricesimo die a recepta petitione computando;

2° in ceteris casibus ex die, quo decretum intimatum est.

CAN. 1002 Auctoritas superior decretum, quo recursus deciditur, intra sexaginta dies a recepto recursu computandos ferre debet, nisi ius particulare propriae Ecclesiae sui iuris alios terminos statuit; si vero hoc factum non est et recurrens scripto petit, ut hoc decretum feratur, tricesimo die ab hac petitione recepta computando, si etiam tunc nihil factum est, recursus pro reiecto habetur ac si eo die per decretum reiectus sit ita, ut novus recursus adversus eum interponi possit.

CAN. 1003 In recursibus adversus decreta administrativa servetur congrua congruis referendo can. 1517; recurrens semper ius habet procuratorem vel advocatum adhibendi vitatis inutilibus moris; immo patronus ex officio constituatur, si recurrens patrono caret et auctoritas superior eum necessarium censet; semper tamen potest auctoritas superior iubere recurrentem ipsum comparere, ut interrogetur.

CAN. 1004 Auctoritas superior, quae de recursu videt, potest decretum non solum confirmare vel nullum declarare, sed etiam rescindere et revocare, non vero emendare, nisi iure particulari propriae Ecclesiae sui iuris etiam haec potestas auctoritati superiori tribuitur.

CAN. 1005 Etsi decretum ab auctoritate superiore confirmatum, nullum declaratum, rescissum, revocatum vel emendatum

the first decree responds regarding the reparation of damages, if they are possibly due. The higher authority, however, responds only to the extent that damages occurred by reason of his decree.

CAN. 1006 Recourse against an administrative decree of a patriarch, even if it concerns a decree that regards the eparchy of the patriarch or a decree by which the patriarch decided a recourse, is made to a special group of bishops according to the norm established by particular law, unless the question is referred to the Apostolic See. There is no further appeal against the decision of this group, except by referral to the Roman Pontiff himself.

est, de reparatione damnorum, si forte debetur, respondit ille, qui primum decretum tulit; auctoritas superior vero eatenus tantum respondet, quatenus ex suo decreto damna obvenerunt.

CAN. 1006 Recursus adversus decretum administrativum Patriarchae, etsi agitur de decreto, quod eparchiam Patriarchae respicit, vel de decreto, quo Patriarcha recursum decidit, fit ad specialem coetum Episcoporum ad normam iuris particularis constituendum, nisi quaestio ad Sedem Apostolicam defertur; adversus decisionem huius coetus non datur ulterior recursus salva provocatione ad ipsum Romanum Pontificem.

1006: Pius XII, m.p. *Cleri sanctitati,* 2 iun. 1957, can. 145.

TITLE XXIII. THE TEMPORAL GOODS OF THE CHURCH

CAN. 1007 In taking care of the spiritual well-being of people, the Church needs and uses temporal goods insofar as its proper mission demands it. Therefore, the Church has the innate right to acquire, possess, administer and alienate those temporal goods which are necessary for its own purposes, especially for divine worship, works of the apostolate, charity, and also for suitable support of ministers.

CAN. 1008 §1. The Roman Pontiff is the supreme administrator and steward of all goods of the Church.

§2. Under the supreme authority of the Roman Pontiff, ownership of temporal goods of the Church belongs to that juridic person which acquired them legitimately.

CAN. 1009 §1. Any juridic person is a subject capable of acquiring, possessing, administering and alienating temporal goods according to the norm of canon law.

§2. All temporal goods which belong to juridic persons are ecclesiastical goods.

CAN. 1007 Ecclesia in procurando bono hominum spirituali bonis temporalibus eget et utitur, quatenus propria eius missio id postulat; quare ipsi ius nativum competit acquirendi, possidendi, administrandi atque alienandi ea bona temporalia, quae ad fines ei proprios praesertim ad cultum divinum, ad opera apostolatus et caritatis atque ad congruam ministrorum sustentationem necessaria sunt.

CAN. 1008 §1. Romanus Pontifex est omnium bonorum Ecclesiae temporalium supremus administrator et dispensator.

§2. Dominium bonorum Ecclesiae temporalium sub suprema auctoritate Romani Pontificis ad eam pertinet personam iuridicam, quae bona legitime acquisivit.

CAN. 1009 §1. Subiectum capax bona temporalia acquirendi, possidendi, administrandi et alienandi ad normam iuris canonici est quaevis persona iuridica.

§2. Bona temporalia omnia, quae ad personas iuridicas pertinent, sunt bona ecclesiastica.

1007: Pius XII, m.p. *Postquam Apostolicis Litteris,* 9 feb. 1952, cann. 232 §1, 235. - Ant. can. 25; Vat. II, const. *Lumen gentium,* 8 "Sicut;" const. *Gaudium et spes,* 42 "Missio," 76 "Res quidem;" decr. *Apostolicam actuositatem,* 8 "At sancta;" decr. *Presbyterorum ordinis,* 17 "Bona ecclesiastica."

1008 §1: Pius XII, m.p. *Postquam Apostolicis Litteris,* 9 feb. 1952, can. 257.

1008 §2: Pius XII, m.p. *Postquam Apostolicis Litteris,* 9 feb. 1952, can. 236 §2.

1009 §1: Pius XII, m.p. *Postquam Apostolicis Litteris,* 9 feb. 1952, cann. 235, 236 §2, 237–238.

1009 §2: Pius XII, m.p. *Postquam Apostolicis Litteris,* 9 feb. 1952, can. 234 §1.

CHAPTER I. The Acquisition of Temporal Goods

CAN. 1010 Juridic persons can acquire temporal goods by any just means permitted to others.

CAN. 1011 Competent authority has the right to require from the Christian faithful those things which are necessary for the purposes proper to the Church.

CAN. 1012 §1. Insofar as it is necessary for the good of the eparchy, the eparchial bishop has the right, with the consent of the finance council, to impose a tax on juridic persons subject to him; this tax is to be proportionate to the income of each person. No tax can be imposed, however, on the offerings received on the occasion of the celebration of the Divine Liturgy.

§2. Taxes can be imposed on physical persons only according to the norm of particular law of their own Church *sui iuris.*

CAN. 1013 §1. An eparchial bishop has the right, within the limits established by particular law of his own Church *sui iuris,* to determine the fees for the various acts of the power of governance and to determine the offerings on the occasion of the celebration of the Divine Liturgy, sacraments, sacramentals or any other liturgical celebrations, unless common law provides otherwise.

CAPUT I. De Bonis Temporalibus Acquirendis

CAN. 1010 Personae iuridicae bona temporalia acquirere possunt omnibus iustis modis, quibus aliis licet.

CAN. 1011 Auctoritati competenti ius est exigendi a christifidelibus, quae ad fines Ecclesiae proprios sunt necessaria.

CAN. 1012 §1. Ius est Episcopo eparchiali, quatenus hoc necessarium est ad bonum eparchiae, de consensu consilii a rebus oeconomicis imponendi personis iuridicis sibi subditis tributa uniuscuiusque personae reditibus proportionata; nullum vero tributum imponi potest super oblationibus receptis occasione celebrationis Divinae Liturgiae.

§2. Personis physicis tributa imponi possunt solummodo ad normam iuris particularis propriae Ecclesiae sui iuris.

CAN. 1013 §1. Episcopi eparchialis est intra limites iure particulari propriae Ecclesiae sui iuris statutos determinare taxas pro variis actibus potestatis regiminis et oblationes occasione celebrationis Divinae Liturgiae, sacramentorum, sacramentalium vel quarumvis aliarum celebrationum liturgicarum, nisi aliter iure communi cavetur.

1010: Pius XII, m.p. *Postquam Apostolicis Litteris,* 9 feb. 1952, can. 236 §1. * Syn. Sciarfen. Syrorum, a. 1888, cap. XIII, art. VI, 1; Syn. Alexandrin. Coptorum, a. 1898, sect. III, cap. VIII, art. III, 1.

1011: Pius XII, m.p. *Postquam Apostolicis Litteris,* 9 feb. 1952, cann. 233, 239. - Apost. can. 4; S.C. de Prop. Fide, (C.G.), 2 iun. 1760. * Syn. Libanen. Maronitarum, a. 1736, pars III, cap. III, 2, XI; cap. IV, 34; Syn. Ain-Trazen. Graeco-Melchitarum, a. 1835, can. 21, 7; Syn. Sciarfen. Syrorum, a. 1888, cap. IX, art. V, 2 "Denique;" cap. XII, 4; Syn. Alexandrin. Coptorum, a. 1898, sect. III, cap. III, art. I, III, 7; cap. VIII,

art. I; Syn. Armen., a. 1911, 878–883.

1012 §1: Pius XII, m.p. *Postquam Apostolicis Litteris,* 9 feb. 1952, cann. 243–244.

1013 §1: Pius XII, m.p. *Postquam Apostolicis Litteris,* 9 feb. 1952, can. 245 §1. * Syn. Zamosten. Ruthenorum, a. 1720, tit. VIII; Syn. Libanen. Maronitarum, a. 1736, pars III, cap. V, 3; Syn. Sciarfen. Syrorum, a. 1888, cap. V, art. XI, 12; art. XV, §9, 4; Syn. Alexandrin. Coptorum, a. 1898, sect. II, cap. III, art. VI, *De Coemeterio,* X; Syn. Armen., a. 1911, 221, 345, 892–896.

§2. Patriarchs and eparchial bishops of various Churches *sui iuris* exercising their power in the same territory are to take care that, after mutual consultation, the same norm is established regarding fees and offerings.

CAN. 1014 In all churches which are habitually open to the Christian faithful, the eparchial bishop can order that offerings be collected for specific projects of the Church.

CAN. 1015 Physical and juridic persons are not permitted to collect alms without the permission of the authority to which they are subject and without the written consent of the local hierarch where the alms are collected.

CAN. 1016 §1. Offerings given for a certain purpose can be applied only for that same purpose.

§2. Unless the contrary is established, offerings given to moderators or administrators of any juridic person are presumed given to the juridic person itself.

§3. These offerings cannot be refused except for a just cause and, in matters of greater importance, with the permission of the hierarch; the permission of the same hierarch is required to accept offerings burdened by a modal obligation or condition, with due regard for can. 1042.

CAN. 1017 The Church recognizes prescription also for temporal goods, according to the norm of cann. 1540–1542.

§2. Curent Patriarchae et Episcopi eparchiales diversarum Ecclesiarum sui iuris in eodem territorio potestatem suam exercentes, ut collatis consiliis eadem norma de taxis et oblationibus statuatur.

CAN. 1014 In omnibus ecclesiis, quae habitualiter christifidelibus patent, Episcopus eparchialis praecipere potest, ut colligantur oblationes pro determinatis inceptis Ecclesiae.

CAN. 1015 Eleemosynas colligere personis physicis vel iuridicis non licet nisi de licentia auctoritatis, cui subiectae sunt, et de consensu scripto dato Hierarchae loci, ubi eleemosynae colliguntur.

CAN. 1016 §1. Oblationes ad certum finem factae nonnisi ad eundem finem destinari possunt.

§2. Nisi contrarium constat, oblationes moderatoribus vel administratoribus cuiusvis personae iuridicae factae praesumuntur ipsi personae iuridicae datae.

§3. Hae oblationes repudiari non possunt nisi iusta de causa et in rebus maioris momenti de licentia Hierarchae; eiusdem Hierarchae licentia requiritur, ut acceptentur, quae onere modali vel condicione gravantur firmo can. 1042.

CAN. 1017 Praescriptionem ad normam cann. 1540–1542 Ecclesia recipit etiam pro bonis temporalibus.

1013 §2: Pius XII, m.p. *Postquam Apostolicis Litteris,* 9 feb. 1952, can. 245 §2.

1015: Pius XII, m.p. *Postquam Apostolicis Litteris,* 9 feb. 1952, can. 240 §1. - Alexander VIII, const. *Alias emanavit,* 21 oct. 1690; Clemens XII, litt. ap. *Dudum,* 26 mar. 1736, §3; S.C. de Prop. Fide, litt. encycl. 24 sep. 1882; ep. circul. 1 ian. 1912; S.C. pro Eccl. Orient., monitum, a. 1928; decr. 7 ian. 1930; instr. 26 sep. 1932, 7; monitum, 20 iul. 1937. * Syn. Libanen. Maronitarum, a. 1736, pars I, cap. II, 10; pars II, cap. VII, 7; pars III, cap. IV, 26; Syn. Ain-Trazen. Graeco-Melchitarum, a. 1835, can. 22.

1016 §2: Pius XII, m.p. *Postquam Apostolicis Litteris,* 9 feb. 1952, can. 286 §1. - S.C. de Prop. Fide, decr. 25 dec. 1779. * Syn. Alexandrin. Coptorum, a. 1898, sect. III, cap. VIII, art. VI; Syn. Armen., a. 1911, 918, n. 3.

1016 §3: Pius XII, m.p. *Postquam Apostolicis Litteris,* 9 feb. 1952, can. 286 §§2, 4. - S.C. de Prop. Fide, instr. (ad Patriarch. Armen.), 30 iul. 1867, 4.

1017: Pius XII, m.p. *Postquam Apostolicis Litteris,* 9 feb. 1952, can. 246. - Constantinop. IV, can.18. ▲ Instit. 2, 6, pr. et 1; D. 39, 3, 2; C. 2, 19 (20), 3; 7, 33, 7; 38, 2.

CAN. 1018 If sacred objects, that is, those which have been destined for divine worship by dedication or blessing, are privately owned, private persons can acquire them through prescription, but it is not permitted to employ them for profane uses unless they have lost their dedication or blessing. However, if sacred objects belong to an ecclesiastical juridic person, only another ecclesiastical juridic person can acquire them.

CAN. 1019 Immovable property, precious movable property, that is, those things which are of great importance on account of art, history or the subject matter, personal or real rights and actions, which belong to the Apostolic See, are prescribed by a period of a hundred years; if they belong to some Church *sui iuris* or eparchy, they are prescribed by a period of fifty years but, if they belong to another juridic person, they are prescribed by a period of thirty years.

CAN. 1020 §1. Each authority is bound by the grave obligation to take care that the temporal goods acquired by the Church are registered in the name of the juridic person to whom they belong, after having observed all the prescripts of civil law which protect the rights of the Church.

§2. However, if civil law does not allow temporal goods to be registered in the name of a juridic person, each authority is to take care that, after having heard experts in civil law and the competent council, the rights of the Church remain unharmed by using methods valid in civil law.

§3. These prescripts are to be observed also with respect to temporal goods legitimately pos-

CAN. 1018 Res sacrae, quae scilicet dedicatione vel benedictione ad cultum divinum destinatae sunt, si in dominio privatorum sunt, praescriptione acquiri a privatis personis possunt, sed eas adhibere ad usus profanos non licet, nisi dedicationem vel benedictionem amiserunt; si vero ad personam iuridicam ecclesiasticam pertinent, tantum ab alia persona iuridica ecclesiastica acquiri possunt.

CAN. 1019 Res immobiles, res mobiles pretiosae, quae scilicet magni sunt momenti artis vel historiae vel materiae causa, iura et actiones sive personales sive reales, quae pertinent ad Sedem Apostolicam, spatio centum annorum praescribuntur; quae ad aliquam Ecclesiam sui iuris vel eparchiam pertinent, spatio quinquaginta annorum, quae vero ad aliam personam iuridicam, spatio triginta annorum.

CAN. 1020 §1. Omnis auctoritas gravi obligatione tenetur curandi, ut bona temporalia Ecclesiae acquisita inscribantur nomine personae iuridicae, ad quam pertinent, servatis omnibus praescriptis iuris civilis, quae iura Ecclesiae in tuto ponunt.

§2. Si vero iure civili non conceditur, ut bona temporalia nomine personae iuridicae inscribantur, omnis auctoritas curet, ut auditis peritis in iure civili et consilio competenti iura Ecclesiae adhibitis modis iure civili validis illaesa maneant.

§3. Haec praescripta serventur etiam circa bona temporalia a persona iuridica legi-

1018: Pius XII, m.p. *Postquam Apostolicis Litteris,* 9 feb. 1952, can. 248.

1019: Pius XII, m.p. *Postquam Apostolicis Litteris,* 9 feb. 1952, can. 249. - Chalc. can. 17; Constantinop. IV, can. 18.

1020 §1: Pius XII, m.p. *Postquam Apostolicis Lit-*

teris, 9 feb. 1952, can. 256 §1.

1020 §2: Pius XII, m.p. *Postquam Apostolicis Litteris,* 9 feb. 1952, can. 256 §2.

1020 §3: Pius XII, m.p. *Postquam Apostolicis Litteris,* 9 feb. 1952, can. 256 §3.

sessed by a juridic person, but whose acquisition has not yet been confirmed by written records.

§4. The immediately higher authority is bound to urge the observance of these prescripts.

CAN. 1021 §1. Each eparchy is to have, according to the norm of the particular law of its own Church *sui iuris,* a special institute which is to collect goods or offerings for the purpose of providing suitably for the appropriate and fundamentally equal support of all clerics who offer service for the benefit of the eparchy, unless provision is made for them in another way.

§2. Where insurance and social security as well as health insurance for the benefit of clerics have not yet been suitably arranged, the particular law of each Church *sui iuris* is to provide for the erection of institutes which protect these benefits under the vigilance of the local hierarch.

§3. Insofar as necessary, each eparchy is to establish, in a manner determined by the particular law of its own Church *sui iuris,* a common fund through which eparchial bishops can satisfy obligations towards other persons who serve the Church and meet the various needs of the eparchy and through which the richer eparchies can also assist the poorer ones.

time possessa, quorum acquisitio documentis nondum est firmata.

§4. Auctoritas immediate superior tenetur urgere observantiam horum praescriptorum.

CAN. 1021 §1. In singulis eparchiis habeatur ad normam iuris particularis propriae Ecclesiae sui iuris speciale institutum, quod bona vel oblationes colligat eum in finem, ut congruae necnon fundamentaliter aequali sustentationi omnium clericorum, qui in favorem eparchiae servitium praestant, apte provideatur, nisi aliter eisdem provisum est.

§2. Ubi praecaventia et securitas socialis necnon assistentia sanitaria in favorem clericorum nondum apte ordinatae sunt, iure particulari uniuscuiusque Ecclesiae sui iuris provideatur, ut erigantur instituta, quae haec sub vigilantia Hierarchae loci in tuto ponunt.

§3. In singulis eparchiis, quatenus opus est, constituatur modo iure particulari propriae Ecclesiae sui iuris determinato massa communis, qua possunt Episcopi eparchiales obligationibus erga alias personas Ecclesiae deservientes satisfacere variisque necessitatibus eparchiae occurrere quaque etiam eparchiae divitiores adiuvare pauperiores possunt.

CHAPTER II. The Administration of Ecclesiastical Goods

CAPUT II. De Bonis Ecclesiasticis Administrandis

CAN. 1022 §1. It is for the eparchial bishop to exercise vigilance over the administration

CAN. 1022 §1. Episcopi eparchialis est vigilare administrationi omnium bonorum ec-

---

1020 §4: PIUS XII, m.p. *Postquam Apostolicis Litteris,* 9 feb. 1952, can. 256 §4.

1021 §1: Vat. II, decr. *Presbyterorum ordinis,* 20 "Servitio;" PAULUS VI, m.p. *Ecclesiae sanctae,* 6 aug. 1966, I, 8.

1021 §2: Vat. II, decr. *Presbyterorum ordinis,* 21 "In nationibus;" PAULUS VI, m.p. *Ecclesiae sanctae,* 6 aug. 1966, I, 8 "Curent."

1021 §3: Vat. II, decr. *Christus Dominus,* 6 "Prae oculis;" decr. *Presbyterorum ordinis,* 21 "Prae oculis;"

PAULUS VI, m.p. *Ecclesiae sanctae,* 6 aug. 1966, I, 8 "Spectabit;" III, 8 et 19.

1022 §1: PIUS XII, m.p. *Postquam Apostolicis Litteris,* 9 feb. 1952, can. 261 §1. - Apost. cann. 38, 41; Gang. cann. 7–8; Ant. cann. 24–25; Carth. can. 33; Nic. II, cann. 12, 17; THEOPHILUS ALEXANDRIN., can. 11; S. CYRILLUS ALEXANDRIN., can. 2; Constantinop. IV, cann. 15, 18; S. ISAAC M., can. 57. * Syn. Sciarfen. Syrorum, a. 1888, cap. IX, art. V, 2 "Ius etiam;" cap. XIII, art. V, 9.

of all ecclesiastical goods which are within the boundaries of the eparchy and have not been removed from his power of governance, without prejudice to legitimate titles which attribute greater rights to him.

§2. With due regard for rights, legitimate customs, and circumstances, hierarchs are to take care, by issuing opportune instructions within the limits of common law and the particular law of their own Church *sui iuris,* that the entire administration of ecclesiastical goods is suitably ordered.

CAN. 1023 The administration of ecclesiastical goods of a juridic person pertains to the one who immediately governs it, unless the law provides otherwise.

CAN. 1024 §1. An administrator cannot place validly acts which exceed the limits and manner of ordinary administration, except with the written consent of the competent authority.

§2. The statutes are to determine the acts which exceed the limits and manner of ordinary administration; if the statutes are silent in this regard, however, the authority to whom the juridic person is immediately subject is competent to determine such acts, after having consulted the competent council.

§3. Unless and to the extent that it is to its own advantage, a juridic person is not bound to answer for acts invalidly placed by its administrators.

CAN. 1025 Before an administrator begins his or her office, he or she:

1° must promise before the hierarch or his delegate to fulfill the office faithfully;

clesiasticorum, quae intra fines eparchiae sunt nec ab eius potestate regiminis sunt subducta, salvis legitimis titulis, qui eidem potiora iura tribuunt.

§2. Habita ratione iurium, legitimarum consuetudinum et circumstantiarum, Hierarchae, editis opportunis instructionibus intra limites iuris communis et iuris particularis propriae Ecclesiae sui iuris curent, ut tota administratio bonorum ecclesiasticorum apte ordinetur.

CAN. 1023 Administratio bonorum ecclesiasticorum personae iuridicae ei competit, qui immediate eam regit, nisi aliter iure cavetur.

CAN. 1024 §1. Actus, qui fines et modum ordinariae administrationis excedunt, administrator bonorum ecclesiasticorum valide ponere non potest nisi de consensu auctoritatis competentis scripto dato.

§2. In statutis determinentur actus, qui fines et modum ordinariae administrationis excedunt; si vero de hac re silent statuta, competit auctoritati, cui persona iuridica immediate subiecta est, consulto consilio competenti huiusmodi actus determinare.

§3. Nisi quando et quatenus in rem eius versum est, persona iuridica non tenetur respondere de actibus ab administratoribus invalide positis.

CAN. 1025 Antequam administrator bonorum ecclesiasticorum suum officium init, debet:

1° coram Hierarcha vel eius delegato promissionem facere se proprium officium fideliter impleturum;

1022 §2: Pius XII, m.p. *Postquam Apostolicis Litteris,* 9 feb. 1952, can. 261 §2.

1024 §1: Pius XII, m.p. *Postquam Apostolicis Litteris,* 9 feb. 1952, can. 276 §1.

1024 §3: Pius XII, m.p. *Postquam Apostolicis Litteris,* 9 feb. 1952, can. 276 §2.

1025, 1°: Pius XII, m.p. *Postquam Apostolicis Litteris,* 9 feb. 1952, can. 267 §§1–3.

2° must sign an accurate inventory, reviewed by the hierarch, of the ecclesiastical goods entrusted to his or her administration.

CAN. 1026 One copy of the inventory of the ecclesiastical goods is to be kept in the archive of the juridic person to which they belong and another in the archive of the eparchial curia; any change which the stable patrimony of the same juridic person happens to undergo is to be noted in each copy.

CAN. 1027 Authorities are to take care that administrators of ecclesiastical goods give suitable guarantees valid in civil law so that the Church suffers no loss by reason of the death or cessation from office of the same administrators.

CAN. 1028 §1. Every administrator of ecclesiastical goods is bound to fulfill his or her office with the diligence of a good householder.

§2. Consequently, he or she must especially:

1° exercise vigilance so that the ecclesiastical goods entrusted to his or her care are in no way lost or damaged, taking out insurance policies for this purpose insofar as necessary;

2° observe the norms of both canon and civil law or those imposed by a founder, a donor, or legitimate authority, and especially be on guard so that no damage comes to the Church from the non-observance of civil laws;

3° collect the return of goods and the income accurately and on time, protect what is collect-

2° accurato inventario ab Hierarcha recognito bonorum ecclesiasticorum suae administrationi commissorum subscribere.

CAN. 1026 Inventarii bonorum ecclesiasticorum alterum exemplar asservetur in archivo personae iuridicae, ad quam pertinent, alterum in archivo curiae eparchialis; in utroque exemplari quaelibet mutatio adnotetur, quam patrimonium stabile eiusdem personae iuridicae subire contingit.

CAN. 1027 Auctoritates debent curare, ut administratores bonorum ecclesiasticorum opportunas praestent cautiones iure civili validas, ne quid Ecclesia detrimenti capiat eisdem administratoribus morientibus vel ab officio cessantibus.

CAN. 1028 §1. Omnis administrator bonorum ecclesiasticorum diligentia boni patris familias suum officium implere tenetur.

§2. Exinde praecipue debet:

1° vigilare, ne bona ecclesiastica suae curae concredita quoquo modo pereant neve quid detrimenti capiant initis in hunc finem, quatenus opus est, contractibus assecurationis;

2° normas servare iuris canonici et civilis necnon ea, quae a fundatore vel donatore aut ab auctoritate competenti imposita sunt, et praesertim cavere, ne ex iuris civilis inobservantia damnum Ecclesiae obveniat;

3° reditus bonorum ac proventus accurate et iusto tempore exigere exactosque

---

1025, 2°: Ant. can. 24; Carth. can. 33. * Syn. Libanen. Maronitarum, a. 1736, pars III, cap. IV, 27, II; pars IV, cap. I, 12; cap. III, 4; Syn. Sciarfen. Syrorum, a. 1888, cap. XIII, art. VII, 5; Syn. Leopolien. Ruthenorum, a. 1891, tit. XV, 1; Syn. Alexandrin. Coptorum, a. 1898, sect. III, cap. VIII, art. VI, 5.

1026: PIUS XII, m.p. *Postquam Apostolicis Litteris,* 9 feb. 1952, can. 267 §1 n. 3 et §2 n. 2.

1027: PIUS XII, m.p. *Postquam Apostolicis Litteris,*

9 feb. 1952, can. 268 §1.

1028 §1: PIUS XII, m.p. *Postquam Apostolicis Litteris,* 9 feb. 1952, can. 269.

1028 §2, 1°: PIUS XII, m.p. *Postquam Apostolicis Litteris,* 9 feb. 1952, can. 269 n. 1.

1028 §2, 2°: PIUS XII, m.p. *Postquam Apostolicis Litteris,* 9 feb. 1952, can. 269 n. 2.

1028 §2, 3°: PIUS XII, m.p. *Postquam Apostolicis Litteris,* 9 feb. 1952, can. 269 n. 3.

ed, and use them according to the intention of the founder or legitimate norms;

4° take care that the interest due on a loan or mortgage is paid at the stated time and that the sum of the capital debt is repaid appropriately;

5° with the consent of the hierarch, invest the money which may be left over after expenses and can be usefully set aside for the purposes of the Church or the juridic person;

6° keep well organized books of receipts and expenditures;

7° draw up a report of the administration at the end of each year;

8° organize and keep in an archive the documents on which the ecclesiastical property rights are based, and deposit authentic copies of them in the archive of the eparchial curia when it can be done conveniently.

§3. It is strongly recommended that administrators prepare a budget of incomes and expenditures each year; however, particular law can require them and determine more precisely the manner in which they are to be presented.

CAN. 1029 An administrator of ecclesiastical goods is not to make donations from movable goods that do not belong to the stable patrimony, except for donations within moderation according to legitimate custom, and unless for a just cause of piety or charity.

tuto servare et secundum fundatoris mentem aut legitimas normas impendere;

4° curare, ut foenus vel mutui vel hypothecae causa solvendum statuto tempore solvatur et debiti summa capitalis opportune reddatur;

5° pecuniam, quae de expensis forte superest et utiliter collocari potest, de consensu Hierarchae in fines Ecclesiae vel personae iuridicae collocare;

6° accepti et expensi libros bene ordinatos habere;

7° rationem administrationis exeunte unoquoque anno componere;

8° documenta, quibus iura personae iuridicae in bona ecclesiastica nituntur, ordinare et in archivo asservare, authentica vero eorum exemplaria, ubi commode fieri potest, in archivo curiae eparchialis deponere.

§3. Praevisio accepti et expensi, ut ab administratoribus bonorum ecclesiasticorum quotannis componatur, enixe commendatur; ius particulare autem potest eam praecipere et pressius determinare modum, quo exhibenda est.

CAN. 1029 Administrator bonorum ecclesiasticorum de bonis mobilibus, quae ad patrimonium stabile non pertinent, donationes praeterquam moderatas secundum legitimam consuetudinem ne faciat nisi iusta de causa pietatis aut caritatis.

1028 §2, 5°: Pius XII, m.p. *Postquam Apostolicis Litteris,* 9 feb. 1952, can. 269 n. 4. - S.C. de Prop. Fide; instr. (ad Patriarch. Armen.), 30 iul. 1867.

1028 §2, 6°: Pius XII, m.p. *Postquam Apostolicis Litteris,* 9 feb. 1952, can. 269 n. 5. * Syn. Sciarfen. Syrorum, a. 1888, cap. XIII, art. V, 6.

1028 §2, 8°: Pius XII, m.p. *Postquam Apostolicis Litteris,* 9 feb. 1952, can. 269 n. 6. * Syn. Sciarfen. Syrorum, a. 1888, cap. XIII, art. V, 6; Syn. Armen., a. 1911, 320.

1029: Pius XII, m.p. *Postquam Apostolicis Litteris,* 9 feb. 1952, can. 285. - Apost. cann. 38, 41; Ant. can. 25; Constantinop. IV, can. 15. * Syn. Libanen. Maronitarum, a. 1736, pars III, cap. IV, 2.

CAN. 1030 An administrator of ecclesiastical goods:

1° in the employment of workers is to observe meticulously also the civil law concerning labor and social policy, according to the principles handed down by the Church;

2° is to pay a just remuneration to employees so that they are able to provide fittingly for their own needs and those of their dependents.

CAN. 1031 §1. Any contrary custom being reprobated, an administrator of ecclesiastical goods must make an annual report of administration to the proper hierarch.

§2. According to the manner determined by particular law, an administrator of ecclesiastical goods is to render an account publicly concerning the goods offered to the Church, unless the local hierarch establishes otherwise for a grave reason.

CAN. 1032 An administrator of ecclesiastical goods is neither to initiate nor to contest litigation in a civil forum in the name of the juridic person without the permission of his or her own hierarch.

CAN. 1033 An administrator of ecclesiastical goods who relinquishes his or her office or function on his or her own initiative is bound to restitution, if the Church is harmed from an arbitrary withdrawal.

CAN. 1030 Administrator bonorum ecclesiasticorum:

1° in operarum locatione etiam ius civile circa laborem et vitam socialem adamussim servet secundum principia ab Ecclesia tradita;

2° eis, qui operam ex condicto praestant, iustam remunerationem tribuat ita, ut suis et suorum necessitatibus convenienter providere possint.

CAN. 1031 §1. Reprobata contraria consuetudine administrator bonorum ecclesiasticorum singulis annis rationem administrationis proprio Hierarchae reddere debet.

§2. De bonis temporalibus, quae Ecclesiae offeruntur, administrator bonorum ecclesiasticorum rationem publice reddat secundum modum iure particulari statutum, nisi Hierarcha loci gravi de causa aliud statuit.

CAN. 1032 Administrator bonorum ecclesiasticorum litem nomine personae iuridicae ne incohet neve contestetur in foro civili nisi de licentia Hierarchae proprii.

CAN. 1033 Administrator bonorum ecclesiasticorum, qui officium vel munus arbitratu suo dimisit, ad restitutionem tenetur, si ex arbitraria dimissione damnum Ecclesiae obvenit.

1030: Pius XII, m.p. *Postquam Apostolicis Litteris,* 9 feb. 1952, can. 272 §1. - Leo XIII, ep. *Noi rendiamo,* 14 mar. 1890, "La religione;" litt. encycl. *Rerum novarum,* 15 maii 1891, 32–33; Pius XI, litt. encycl. *Quadragesimo anno,* 15 maii 1931, II "Ac primum" - "Officinae;" litt. encycl. *Divini Redemptoris,* 19 mar. 1937, IV "Neque;" Pius XII, nuntius radiophonicus, 24 dec. 1942, II, *Il mondo operaio;* all. 13 iun. 1943, "Certo voi;" Ioannes XXIII, litt. encycl. *Mater et Magistra,* 15 maii 1961, II "Qua de re;" Vat. II, const. *Gaudium et spes,* 67; Ioannes Paulus II, litt. encycl.

Laborem exercens, 14 sep. 1981, 10.

1031 §1: Pius XII, m.p. *Postquam Apostolicis Litteris,* 9 feb. 1952, can. 273 §1. - S.C. de Prop. Fide, decr. 13 apr. 1807, XV. * Syn. prov. Alba-Iulien. et Fagarasien. Rumenorum, a. 1882, tit. II, sect. IV, cap. II; Syn. Sciarfen. Syrorum, a. 1888, cap. XIII, art. V, 7.

1032: Pius XII, m.p. *Postquam Apostolicis Litteris,* 9 feb. 1952, can. 275. - Carth. can. 97.

1033: Pius XII, m.p. *Postquam Apostolicis Litteris,* 9 feb. 1952, can. 277.

CHAPTER III. **Contracts and Especially Alienations**

CAN. 1034 What the civil law of the territory in which a contract is entered establishes for contracts either in general or in particular and their disposition is to be observed with the same effects in canon law insofar as the matter is subject to the power of the Church.

CAN. 1035 §1. The alienation of ecclesiastical goods, which constitute by legitimate designation the stable patrimony of a juridic person, requires the following:

1° a just cause, such as urgent necessity, evident advantage, piety, charity, or a pastoral reason;

2° a written appraisal by experts of the asset to be alienated;

3° in cases prescribed by law, written consent of the competent authority, without which the alienation is invalid.

§2. Other precautions prescribed by legitimate authority are also to be observed to avoid harm to the Church.

CAN. 1036 §1. If the value of the goods whose alienation is proposed falls within the minimum and maximum amounts established by the synod of bishops of a patriarchal Church or by the Apostolic See, consent is required of:

1° the finance council and the college of eparchial consultors, if it concerns goods of the eparchy;

2° the eparchial bishop, who in such case

CAPUT III. **De Contractibus, Praesertim de Alienationibus**

CAN. 1034 Quae ius civile territorii, ubi contractus initur, statuit de contractibus tam in genere quam in specie, et de solutionibus, eadem iure canonico in re, quae potestati Ecclesiae subest, eisdem cum effectibus serventur.

CAN. 1035 §1. Ad alienanda bona ecclesiastica, quae ex legitima assignatione patrimonium stabile personae iuridicae constituunt, requiritur:

1° iusta causa veluti urgens necessitas, evidens utilitas, pietas, caritas vel ratio pastoralis;

2° aestimatio rei alienandae a peritis scripto facta;

3° in casibus iure praescriptis consensus auctoritatis competentis scripto datus, sine quo alienatio invalida est.

§2. Aliae quoque cautelae ab auctoritate competenti praescriptae serventur, ut Ecclesiae damnum vitetur.

CAN. 1036 §1. Si valor bonorum ecclesiasticorum, quorum alienatio proponitur, continetur intra summam minimam et summam maximam a Synodo Episcoporum Ecclesiae patriarchalis vel a Sede Apostolica statutam, requiritur consensus:

1° consilii a rebus oeconomicis et collegii consultorum eparchialium, si agitur de bonis eparchiae;

2° Episcopi eparchialis, qui in casu eget

1034: Pius XII, m.p. *Postquam Apostolicis Litteris,* 9 feb. 1952, can. 278.

1035 §1: Pius XII, m.p. *Postquam Apostolicis Litteris,* 9 feb. 1952, can. 279 §1. - Anc. can. 15; Carth. cann. 26, 33; Nic. II, can. 12; S. Cyrillus Alexandrin., can. 2; Constantinop. IV, can. 15; S.C. de Prop. Fide, instr. (ad Patriarch. Armen.), 30 iul. 1867, 1. * Syn. Zamosten. Ruthenorum, a. 1720, tit. XIII; Syn.

Sciarfen. Syrorum, a. 1888, cap. XIII, art. V, 9; art. VI, 5–6; Syn. Alexandrin. Coptorum, a. 1898, sect. III, cap. VIII, art. V; Syn. Armen., a. 1911, 200, n. 3, 908–910.

1035 §2: Pius XII, m.p. *Postquam Apostolicis Litteris,* 9 feb. 1952, can. 279 §2.

1036 §1: Pius XII, m.p. *Postquam Apostolicis Litteris,* 9 feb. 1952, can. 281 §1 n. 3. * Syn. Alexandrin. Coptorum, a. 1898, sect. III, cap. VIII, art. V.

needs the consent of the finance council and the college of eparchial consultors, if it concerns goods of a juridic person subject to the same eparchial bishop;

3° the authority determined in the typicon or statutes, if it concerns goods of a juridic person not subject to an eparchial bishop.

§2. In patriarchal Churches, if the value of the goods exceeds the maximum amount established by the synod of bishops of a patriarchal Church, but not twice the amount, consent is required of:

1° the patriarch with the consent of the permanent synod, if it concerns goods of an eparchy located within the territorial boundaries of a patriarchal Church, unless the particular law of the same Church determines otherwise;

2° the eparchial bishop as well as the patriarch with the consent of the permanent synod, if it concerns goods of a juridic person subject to an eparchial bishop who exercises his power within the territorial boundaries of a patriarchal Church,

3° the patriarch with the consent of the permanent synod, if it concerns goods of a juridic person not subject to an eparchial bishop, even of pontifical right, which are located within the territorial boundaries of a patriarchal Church.

§3. In patriarchal Churches, if the value of the goods exceeds twice the maximum amount established by the synod of bishops of a patriarchal Church, if it concerns precious goods or goods given to the Church by vow, §2 is to be observed, but the patriarch needs the consent of the same synod.

§4. In other cases, consent is required of the Apostolic See, if the value of the goods exceeds

consensu consilii a rebus oeconomicis et collegii consultorum eparchialium, si agitur de bonis personae iuridicae eodem Episcopo eparchiali subiectae;

3° auctoritatis in typico vel statutis determinatae, si agitur de bonis personae iuridicae Episcopo eparchiali non subiectae.

§2. In Ecclesiis patriarchalibus, si valor bonorum summam maximam a Synodo Episcoporum Ecclesiae patriarchalis statutam excedit, sed non duplo, requiritur consensus:

1° Patriarchae datus de consensu Synodi permanentis, si agitur de bonis eparchiae intra fines territorii Ecclesiae patriarchalis sitae, nisi ius particulare eiusdem Ecclesiae aliud fert;

2° Episcopi eparchialis necnon Patriarchae datus de consensu Synodi permanentis, si agitur de bonis personae iuridicae Episcopo eparchiali intra fines territorii Ecclesiae patriarchalis potestatem suam exercenti subiectae;

3° Patriarchae datus de consensu Synodi permanentis, si agitur de bonis personae iuridicae Episcopo eparchiali non subiectae, etsi iuris pontificii, quae intra fines territorii Ecclesiae patriarchalis sita sunt.

§3. In Ecclesiis patriarchalibus, si valor bonorum summam maximam a Synodo Episcoporum Ecclesiae patriarchalis statutam duplo excedit et, si de rebus pretiosis vel ex voto Ecclesiae donatis agitur, servetur §2, sed Patriarcha indiget consensu eiusdem Synodi.

§4. In ceteris casibus requiritur consensus Sedis Apostolicae, si valor bonorum ex-

1036 §2: Pius XII, m.p. *Postquam Apostolicis Litteris,* 9 feb. 1952, can. 281 §1 n. 2 . - S.C. de Prop. Fide, 24 mar. 1851, dub. 5; Pius IX, litt. ap. *Cum ecclesiastica,* 31 aug. 1869, VII. * Syn. Libanen. Maronitarum, a. 1736, pars IV, cap. I, 12, 14; Syn. Sciarfen. Syrorum, a. 1888, cap. XIII, art. VI, 5; Syn. Alexandrin. Coptorum, a. 1898, sect. III, cap. VIII, art. V, 5; Syn. Armen., a. 1911, 910.

1036 §4: Pius XII, m.p. *Postquam Apostolicis Litteris,* 9 feb. 1952, can. 281 §1 n. 1.

the amount established or approved by the Apostolic See itself and if it concerns precious goods or goods given to the Church by vow.

CAN. 1037 To alienate temporal goods of a patriarchal Church or of the patriarch's eparchy, the patriarch needs:

1° the counsel of the permanent synod, if the value of the goods falls within the minimum and maximum amounts established by the synod of bishops of the patriarchal Church and if it concerns goods of the patriarchal Church; if it concerns only goods of the patriarch's eparchy, however, can. 1036, §1, n.1 must be observed;

2° the consent of the permanent synod, if the value of the goods exceeds the maximum amount established by the synod of bishops of the patriarchal Church, but not twice the amount;

3° the consent of the synod of bishops of the patriarchal Church, if the value of the goods exceeds twice the same amount and if it concerns precious goods or goods given to the Church by vow.

CAN. 1038 §1. Those whose counsel, consent or confirmation is required by law to alienate ecclesiastical goods, are not to give counsel, consent or confirmation before they have been thoroughly informed of the economic state of the juridic person, whose temporal goods are proposed for alienation, and of previous alienations.

§2. Counsel, consent or confirmation is considered not to have been given, unless, in seeking them, previous alienations are mentioned.

CAN. 1039 For any alienation, consent is required of those concerned.

CAN. 1040 Whenever ecclesiastical goods have been alienated against the prescripts of

CAN. 1037 Ad alienanda bona temporalia Ecclesiae patriarchalis vel eparchiae Patriarchae, Patriarcha indiget:

1° consilio Synodi permanentis, si valor bonorum continetur intra summam minimam et summam maximam a Synodo Episcoporum Ecclesiae patriarchalis statutam et si de bonis Ecclesiae patriarchalis agitur; si vero nonnisi de bonis eparchiae Patriarchae agitur, servandus est can. 1036, §1, n. 1;

2° consensu Synodi permanentis, si valor bonorum summam maximam a Synodo Episcoporum Ecclesiae patriarchalis statutam excedit, sed non duplo;

3° consensu Synodi Episcoporum Ecclesiae patriarchalis, si valor bonorum eandem summam duplo excedit et si de rebus pretiosis vel ex voto Ecclesiae donatis agitur.

CAN. 1038 §1. Ii, quorum consilium, consensus vel confirmatio ad alienanda bona ecclesiastica iure requiritur, ne dent consilium, consensum vel confirmationem, antequam exacte edocti sunt de statu oeconomico personae iuridicae, cuius bona temporalia alienanda proponuntur, et de alienationibus iam peractis.

§2. Consilium, consensus aut confirmatio pro non datis habentur, nisi in eis petendis exprimuntur alienationes iam peractae.

CAN. 1039 Pro quacumque alienatione requiritur consensus eorum, quorum interest.

CAN. 1040 Si bona ecclesiastica contra praescripta iuris canonici alienata sunt, sed

1037: Pius XII, m.p. *Postquam Apostolicis Litteris,* 9 feb. 1952, cann. 281 §1 n. 2, 282.
1038 §1: Pius XII, m.p. *Postquam Apostolicis Lit-* teris, 9 feb. 1952, can. 281 §4.
1040: Pius XII, m.p. *Postquam Apostolicis Litteris,* 9 feb. 1952, can. 284.

canon law but the alienation is valid civilly, the higher authority of the one who carried out the alienation, after having considered everything thoroughly, is to decide whether and what type of action is to be taken by whom and against whom in order to vindicate the rights of the Church.

CAN. 1041 Unless an asset is of little value, ecclesiastical goods are not to be sold or leased to the administrators of these goods or to their relatives up to the fourth degree of consanguinity or affinity without the special permission of the authority mentioned in cann. 1036 and 1037.

CAN. 1042 Canons 1035–1041 must be observed not only in alienation but also in any transaction which can worsen the patrimonial condition of a juridic person.

CHAPTER IV. **Pious Wills and Pious Foundations**

CAN. 1043 §1. A person who by natural law and canon law is able freely to dispose of his or her goods can also bestow goods for pious causes either through an act *inter vivos* or through an act *mortis causa*.

§2. In last wills and testaments for the good of the Church, the prescripts of civil law are to be observed if possible; if they have not been observed, the heirs are to be admonished regarding the obligation, to which they are bound, of fulfilling the intention of the testator.

CAN. 1044 The legitimately accepted wills

alienatio iure civili valida est, auctoritas superior illius, qui talem alienationem peregit, decernat omnibus mature perpensis, an et qualis actio, a quonam et contra quemnam proponenda sit ad Ecclesiae iura vindicanda.

CAN. 1041 Nisi res est minimi momenti, bona ecclesiastica propriis administratoribus eorumque coniunctis usque ad quartum gradum consanguinitatis aut affinitatis non sunt vendenda aut locanda sine speciali auctoritatis, de qua in cann. 1036 et 1037, licentia.

CAN. 1042 Cann. 1035–1041 servari debent non solum in alienatione, sed etiam in quolibet negotio, quo condicio patrimonialis personae iuridicae peior fieri potest.

CAPUT IV. **De Piis Voluntatibus et de Piis Fundationibus**

CAN. 1043 §1. Qui ex iure naturae vel canonico libere potest de suis bonis statuere, potest etiam ad pias causas sive per actum inter vivos sive per actum mortis causa bona relinquere.

§2. In ultimis voluntatibus in bonum Ecclesiae serventur, si fieri potest, praescripta iuris civilis; si servata non sunt, heredes moneantur de obligatione, qua tenentur, implendi testatoris voluntatem.

CAN. 1044 Voluntates christifidelium

1041: PIUS XII, m.p. *Postquam Apostolicis Litteris,* 9 feb. 1952, can. 290. * Syn. Libanen. Maronitarum, a. 1736, pars IV, cap. I, 13.

1042: PIUS XII, m.p. *Postquam Apostolicis Litteris,* 9 feb. 1952, can. 283. - S.C. de Prop. Fide, instr. (ad Patriarch. Armen.), 30 iul. 1867.

1043 §1: PIUS XII, m.p. *Postquam Apostolicis Litteris,* 9 feb. 1952, can. 251 §1. - Constantinop. IV, can.

18; S. NICEPHORUS CP. can. 53. * Syn. Libanen. Maronitarum, a. 1736, pars II, cap. XIII, 13; Syn. Sciarfen. Syrorum, a. 1888, cap. XIII, art. VI; Syn. Armen., a. 1911, 884–891.

1043 §2: PIUS XII, m.p. *Postquam Apostolicis Litteris,* 9 feb. 1952, can. 251 §2.

1044: PIUS XII, m.p. *Postquam Apostolicis Litteris,* 9 feb. 1952, can. 252.

of the Christian faithful who give or leave their goods for pious causes, whether through an act *inter vivos* or through an act *mortis causa,* are to be fulfilled most diligently even regarding the manner of administration and distribution of goods, with due regard for can. 1045.

CAN. 1045 §1. The hierarch is the executor of all pious wills whether *mortis causa* or *inter vivos.*

§2. By this right, the hierarch can and must exercise vigilance, even through visitation, so that pious wills are fulfilled, and other executors must render him an account after they have performed their function.

§3. Stipulations contrary to this right of a hierarch attached to last wills and testaments are considered non-existent.

CAN. 1046 §1. A person who has accepted goods in trust for pious causes either through an act *inter vivos* or by an act *mortis causa* must notify his or her hierarch of the trust and indicate to him all such goods with the obligations attached to them. If the donor has expressly and entirely prohibited this, however, the person is not to accept the trust.

§2. The hierarch must demand that goods held in trust be safeguarded and, according to the norm of can. 1045, §2, exercise vigilance that the pious will be executed.

§3. If it is a question of goods held in trust which have been entrusted to a member of a religious institute or a society of common life according to the manner of religious and which have been designated for churches of a place or of some eparchy, for the Christian faithful who have domicile there, or for the assistance of pi-

bona sua in pias causas donantium vel relinquentium sive per actum inter vivos sive per actum mortis causa legitime acceptatae diligentissime impleantur etiam circa modum administrationis et erogationis bonorum firmo can. 1045.

CAN. 1045 §1. Hierarcha omnium piarum voluntatum tam mortis causa quam inter vivos exsecutor est.

§2. Hoc ex iure Hierarcha vigilare potest ac debet etiam per visitationem, ut piae voluntates impleantur, eique ceteri exsecutores perfuncto munere rationem reddere debent.

§3. Clausulae huic Hierarchae iuri contrariae ultimis voluntatibus adiectae pro non appositis habentur.

CAN. 1046 §1. Qui bona ad pias causas sive per actum inter vivos sive per actum mortis causa fiduciarie accepit, debet de sua fiducia Hierarcham proprium certiorem facere eique omnia talia bona cum oneribus adiunctis indicare; si vero donator id expresse et omnino prohibuit, fiduciam ne acceptet.

§2. Hierarcha debet exigere, ut bona fiduciaria in tuto collocentur, et ad normam can. 1045, §2 vigilare, ut pia voluntas ad effectum ducatur.

§3. Si agitur de bonis fiduciariis alicui sodali instituti religiosi vel societatis vitae communis ad instar religiosorum commissis, quae destinata sunt loci vel eparchiae ecclesiis, christifidelibus, qui ibidem domicilium habent, aut piis causis iuvandis, Hierarcha, de quo in §§1 et 2, est Hierarcha loci.

1045 §1: Pius XII, m.p. *Postquam Apostolicis Litteris,* 9 feb. 1952, can. 253 §1.

1045 §2: Pius XII, m.p. *Postquam Apostolicis Litteris,* 9 feb. 1952, can. 253 §2.

1045 §3: Pius XII, m.p. *Postquam Apostolicis Litteris,* 9 feb. 1952, can. 253 §3.

1046 §1: Pius XII, m.p. *Postquam Apostolicis Litteris,* 9 feb. 1952, can. 254 §1.

1046 §2: Pius XII, m.p. *Postquam Apostolicis Litteris,* 9 feb. 1952, can. 254 §2.

1046 §3: Pius XII, m.p. *Postquam Apostolicis Litteris,* 9 feb. 1952, can. 254 §3.

ous causes, the hierarch mentioned in §§1 and 2 is the local hierarch.

CAN. 1047 §1. In law, pious foundations are:

1° autonomous pious foundations, that is, aggregates of things destined for works of piety, the apostolate, or charity, whether spiritual or temporal, and erected as a juridic person by competent authority;

2° non-autonomous pious foundations, that is, temporal goods given in some way to a juridic person with a long-term obligation, to be determined by particular law, of pursuing, from the annual revenues, the purposes mentioned in n. 1.

§2. If the temporal goods of a non-autonomous foundation have been entrusted to a juridic person subject to an eparchial bishop, they must be designated for the institute mentioned in can. 1021, §1, when the time is completed, unless some other intention of the founder had been expressly manifested; otherwise, they accrue to the same juridic person.

CAN. 1048 §1. Autonomous pious foundations can be erected only by an eparchial bishop or another higher authority.

§2. For a juridic person to be able to accept validly a non-autonomous pious foundation, written consent of that person's own hierarch is required. The hierarch is not to give the consent, however, before he has legitimately determined that the juridic person can satisfy the new obligation to be undertaken and those already undertaken. The same hierarch is also to be on guard so that the revenues completely respond to the attached obligations, according to the practices of his own Church *sui iuris*.

CAN. 1047 §1. Piae fundationes in iure sunt:

1° piae fundationes autonomae, scilicet universitates rerum ad opera pietatis, apostolatus aut caritatis spiritualis vel temporalis destinatae et ab auctoritate competenti in personam iuridicam erectae;

2° piae fundationes non autonomae, scilicet bona temporalia alicui personae iuridicae quoquo modo data cum onere in diuturnum tempus, iure particulari determinandum, ex reditibus annuis fines, de quibus in n. 1, persequendi.

§2. Bona temporalia fundationis non autonomae, si concredita sunt personae iuridicae Episcopo eparchiali subiectae, elapso tempore determinato ad institutum, de quo in can. 1021, §1, destinari debent, nisi alia fuit voluntas fundatoris expresse manifestata; secus eidem personae iuridicae cedunt.

CAN. 1048 §1. Piae fundationes autonomae nonnisi ab Episcopo eparchiali aliave auctoritate superiore erigi possunt.

§2. Ut pia fundatio non autonoma a persona iuridica valide acceptari possit, requiritur consensus Hierarchae proprii scripto datus; Hierarcha vero consensum ne det, antequam legitime comperuit personam iuridicam novo oneri suscipiendo et oneribus iam susceptis satisfacere posse; caveat quoque idem Hierarcha, ut reditus omnino respondeant oneribus adiunctis secundum morem propriae Ecclesiae sui iuris.

1047 §1: Pius XII, m.p. *Postquam Apostolicis Litteris,* 9 feb. 1952, can. 294.

1048 §2: Pius XII, m.p. *Postquam Apostolicis Litteris,* 9 feb. 1952, cann. 296, 300. * Syn. prov. Alba-Iulien. et Fagarasien. Rumenorum, a. 1900, tit. III, cap. I, 13, c); Syn. Armen., a. 1911, 447.

§3. It is for particular law to determine other conditions, without which pious foundations cannot be erected or accepted.

CAN. 1049 The hierarch, who erected a pious foundation or gave his consent to accept a pious foundation, immediately is to designate a safe place in which money and movable goods assigned to an endowment are to be deposited so that the money or value of the movable goods is protected. As soon as possible, these are to be invested cautiously and usefully for the benefit of the foundation, with express and specific mention made of the obligation; this investment is to be made according to the prudent judgment of the hierarch, after he has consulted those concerned and the competent council.

CAN. 1050 One copy of the document of foundation is to be kept in the archive of the eparchial curia and another copy in the archive of juridic person.

CAN. 1051 §1. A list of the obligations incumbent upon pious foundations is to be composed and displayed in an accessible place so that the obligations to be fulfilled are not forgotten; cann. 1044–1046 and 1031 are to be observed.

§2. A book is to be held and kept by the pastor or rector of a church in which the individual obligations, their fulfillment, and the offerings are noted.

CAN. 1052 §1. A reduction of the obliga-

§3. Iuris particularis est determinare ceteras condiciones, sine quibus piae fundationes erigi vel acceptari non possunt.

CAN. 1049 Hierarcha, qui piam fundationem erexit vel consensum ad piam fundationem acceptandam dedit, statim tutum locum designet, in quo pecunia et bona mobilia dotationis nomine assignata deponantur eum in finem, ut eadem pecunia vel bonorum mobilium pretium custodiantur et quam primum caute et utiliter de prudenti eiusdem Hierarchae iudicio consultis et eis, quorum interest, et consilio competenti collocentur in favorem eiusdem fundationis cum expresse determinata mentione oneris.

CAN. 1050 Documenti fundationis exemplar alterum in archivo curiae eparchialis, alterum in archivo personae iuridicae asservetur.

CAN. 1051 §1. Servatis cann. 1044–1046 et 1031 onerum ex piis fundationibus incumbentium tabella conficiatur, quae in loco patenti exponatur, ne obligationes implendae in oblivionem cadant.

§2. Liber habeatur et apud parochum vel rectorem ecclesiae asservetur, in quo singula onera eorumque impletio et eleemosynae adnotentur.

CAN. 1052 §1. Reductio onerum Di-

1048 §3: Pius XII, m.p. *Postquam Apostolicis Litteris,* 9 feb. 1952, can. 295. * Syn. Armen., a. 1911, 447.

1049: Pius XII, m.p. *Postquam Apostolicis Litteris,* 9 feb. 1952, cann. 297, 300.

1050: Pius XII, m.p. *Postquam Apostolicis Litteris,* 9 feb. 1952, cann. 298 §2, 300. * Syn. Armen., a. 1911, 448.

1051 §1: Pius XII, m.p. *Postquam Apostolicis Litteris,* 9 feb. 1952, cann. 299 §1, 300. * Syn. Armen., a.

1911, 448.

1051 §2: Pius XII, m.p. *Postquam Apostolicis Litteris,* 9 feb. 1952, can. 299 §2.

1052 §1: Pius XII, m.p. *Postquam Apostolicis Litteris,* 9 feb. 1952, cann. 255 §2, 301 §1. -Secret. Status, notificatio, 29 nov. 1971; normae, 17 iun. 1974; Paulus VI, litt. ap. *Firma in traditione,* 13 iun. 1974. * Syn. Libanen. Maronitarum, a. 1736, pars II, cap. XIII, 13; Syn. Armen., a. 1911, 447.

tions of celebrating the Divine Liturgy is reserved to the Apostolic See.

§2. If the document of foundation expressly provides for it, a hierarch can reduce the obligations of celebrating the Divine Liturgy because of diminished revenues.

§3. An eparchial bishop has the power, because of a diminution of revenues and while this lasts, to reduce the number of the celebrations of the Divine Liturgy to the level of the offerings legitimately in force in the eparchy, provided there is no one who is bound by obligation and can effectively be forced to increase the offering.

§4. An eparchial bishop also has the power to reduce the obligations of celebrating the Divine Liturgy which burden ecclesiastical institutes, if the revenues have become insufficient to pursue those purposes which, at the time of the acceptance of the same obligations, could have been obtained.

§5. Superiors general of clerical religious institutes or societies of common life according to the manner of religious of pontifical or patriarchal right also have the powers mentioned in §§3 and 4.

§6. An eparchial bishop can delegate the powers mentioned in §§3 and 4 only to a coadjutor bishop, auxiliary bishop, protosyncellus or syncellus, excluding any subdelegation.

CAN. 1053 The same authorities mentioned in can. 1052 also have the power of transferring, for a just reason, the obligations of cel-

vinam Liturgiam celebrandi reservatur Sedi Apostolicae.

§2. Si in documento fundationis de re expresse cavetur, Hierarcha ob imminutos reditus onera Divinam Liturgiam celebrandi reducere potest.

§3. Episcopo eparchiali competit potestas reducendi ob deminutionem redituum, dum causa perdurat, ad rationem oblationum in eparchia legitime vigentium numerum celebrationum Divinae Liturgiae, dummodo nemo sit, qui obligatione tenetur et utiliter cogi potest ad oblationum augmentum faciendum.

§4. Episcopo eparchiali etiam competit potestas reducendi onera Divinam Liturgiam celebrandi, quae instituta ecclesiastica gravant, si reditus ad ea, quae ex eisdem tempore acceptationis onerum obtineri potuerunt, consequenda insufficientes evaserunt.

§5. Potestates, de quibus in §§3 et 4, habent etiam Superiores generales institutorum religiosorum vel societatum vitae communis ad instar religiosorum clericalium iuris pontificii vel patriarchalis.

§6. Potestates, de quibus in §§3 et 4, Episcopus eparchialis delegare potest tantummodo Episcopo coadiutori, Episcopo auxiliari, Protosyncello vel Syncellis omni subdelegatione exclusa.

CAN. 1053 Eisdem auctoritatibus, de quibus in can. 1052, potestas insuper competit transferendi iusta de causa onera Di-

---

1052 §2: PIUS XII, m.p. *Postquam Apostolicis Litteris,* 9 feb. 1952, cann. 255 §2, 301 §1.

1052 §3: PAULUS VI, m.p. *Pastorale munus,* 30 nov. 1963, I, 11; Pont. Comm. Decr. Vat. II Interpr., resp. 1 iul. 1971; PAULUS VI, litt. ap. *Firma in traditione,* 13 iun. 1974, II, b).

1052 §4: PAULUS VI, m.p. *Pastorale munus,* 30

nov. 1969, I, 12; Pont. Comm. Decr. Vat. II Interpr., resp. 1 iul. 1971; PAULUS VI, litt. ap. *Firma in traditione,* 13 iun. 1974, II, b).

1052 §6: PAULUS VI, m.p. *Pastorale munus,* 30 nov. 1963, I, inscriptio.

1053: PAULUS VI, litt. ap. *Firma in traditione,* 13 iun. 1974, III, c); Secret. Status, normae, 17 iun. 1974.

ebrating the Divine Liturgy to days or institutes different from those which have been established in the foundation.

CAN. 1054 §1. The hierarch, only for a just and necessary cause, can reduce, moderate, or commute the wills of the Christian faithful who give their goods for pious causes if the founder has expressly granted this power to him.

§2. If through no fault of the administrators the fulfillment of the imposed obligations has become impossible because of diminished revenues or some other cause, the hierarch can equitably lessen these obligations, after having heard those concerned and the competent council and having kept in the best way possible the will of the founder, with due regard for can. 1052.

§3. In other cases regarding this matter, the Apostolic See or the patriarch must be approached; the latter is to act with the consent of the permanent synod.

vinam Liturgiam celebrandi in dies vel instituta diversa ab illis, quae in fundatione sunt statuta.

CAN. 1054 §1. Voluntatum christifidelium bona sua in pias causas donantium vel relinquentium reductio, moderatio, commutatio, si fundator potestatem hanc Hierarchae expresse concessit, ab eodem Hierarcha iusta tantum et necessaria de causa fieri potest.

§2. Si exsecutio onerum impositorum ob imminutos reditus aliave de causa nulla administratorum culpa impossibilis evasit, Hierarcha consultis eis, quorum interest, et consilio competenti atque servata quam optime fundatoris voluntate potest eadem onera aeque imminuere firmo can. 1052.

§3. In ceteris casibus de re adiri debet Sedes Apostolica vel Patriarcha, qui de consensu Synodi permanentis agat.

1054 §1: Pius XII, m.p. *Postquam Apostolicis Litteris,* 9 feb. 1952, can. 255 §1.

1054 §2: Pius XII, m.p. *Postquam Apostolicis Litteris,* 9 feb. 1952, can. 255 §2. - Innocentius XII, const. *Nuper,* 23 dec. 1697, §15 "Ad primum."

1054 §3: Pius XII, m.p. *Postquam Apostolicis Litteris,* 9 feb. 1952, can. 255 §1.

CAN. 1055 §1. The objects of a trial are:

1° the pursuit or vindication of the rights of physical or juridic persons or the declaration of juridic facts;

2° the imposition of a penalty for delicts.

§2. Nevertheless, in controversies arising from an act of executive power of governance, the higher authority alone is competent according to the norm of cann. 996–1006.

CAN. 1056 In cases reserved to a dicastery of the Apostolic See, tribunals must follow the norms established by that dicastery.

CAN. 1057 In the causes for canonization of the servants of God, the special norms established by the Roman Pontiff are to be observed.

CHAPTER I. **The Competent Forum**

CAN. 1058 The Roman Pontiff is judged by no one.

CAN. 1055 §1. Obiectum iudicii sunt:

1° personarum physicarum vel iuridicarum iura persequenda aut vindicanda vel facta iuridica declaranda;

2° delicta, quod spectat ad poenam irrogandam.

§2. In controversiis vero ortis ex actu potestatis regiminis exsecutivae competens est solummodo auctoritas superior ad normam cann. 996–1006.

CAN. 1056 In causis, quae alicui Dicasterio Sedis Apostolicae reservantur, tribunalia normas ab eodem Dicasterio editas sequantur oportet.

CAN. 1057 In causis servorum Dei, ut inter Sanctos referantur, serventur normae speciales a Romano Pontifice statutae.

CAPUT I. **De Foro Competenti**

CAN. 1058 Romanus Pontifex a nemine iudicatur.

1055 §1: Pius XII, m.p. *Sollicitudinem Nostram,* 6 ian. 1950, can. 1 §2. ▲ D. 50, 16, 178, (2).

1055 §2: Pius XII, m.p. *Sollicitudinem Nostram,* 6 ian. 1950, can. 36; m.p. *Cleri sanctitati,* 2 iun. 1957, can. 145. - Paulus VI, const. ap. *Regimini Ecclesiae Universae,* 15 aug. 1967, 106; Ioannes Paulus II, const. ap. *Pastor Bonus,* 28 iun. 1988, art. 123.

1056: Pius XII, m.p. *Sollicitudinem Nostram,* 6 ian. 1950, can. 4. - Ordo servandus in S. Congregationibus, Tribunalibus, Officiis Romanae Curiae, 29 sep. 1908, pars altera, *Normae peculiares,* cap. VII, art. I, n. 6.

1057: Paulus VI, m.p. *Sanctitatis clarior,* 19 mar. 1969; const. ap. *Sacra Rituum Congregatio,* 8 maii 1969, 5–13; S.C. pro Causis Sanctorum, decr. 3 apr. 1970; notificatio, 16 dec. 1972; normae, 7 feb. 1983; decr. 7 feb. 1983.

1058: Pius XII, m.p. *Sollicitudinem Nostram,* 6 ian. 1950, can. 14. - Constantinop. IV, can. 21; Vat. I, sess. IV, cap. III, *De vi et ratione primatus Romani pontificis,* "Et quoniam;" S. Zosimus, litt. *Quamvis Patrum,* 21 mar. 418; S. Bonifacius I. litt, *Retro maioribus,* 11 mar. 422; S. Gelasius, litt. *Ego quoque,* a. 493, "Nobis opponunt;" S. Nicolaus I, litt. *Omnium Nos,* a. 867, "Videte ergo;" S. Leo IX, litt. *In terra pax,* a. 1053, XI; Bonifacius VIII, bulla, *Unam sanctam,* 18 nov. 1302; Leo XIII, ep. encycl. *Satis cognitum,* 29 iun. 1896, 30.

CAN. 1059 §1. By reason of the primacy of the Roman Pontiff, any member of the Christian faithful is free to defer his or her case at any stage or grade of the trial to the Roman Pontiff. Being the supreme judge for the entire Catholic world, he renders judicial decisions personally, through the tribunals of the Apostolic See, or through judges he has delegated.

§2. This referral to the Roman Pontiff, however, does not suspend the exercise of power by a judge who has already begun to adjudicate a case except in the case of an appeal. For this reason, the judge can continue with a trial up to the definitive sentence, unless it is evident that the Roman Pontiff has called the case to himself.

CAN. 1060 §1. The Roman Pontiff alone has the right to judge:

1° patriarchs;

2° bishops in penal cases;

3° heads of state;

4° other cases that he has called to himself for judgment.

§2 With the exception of bishops exercising

CAN. 1059 §1. Ob primatum Romani Pontificis integrum est cuilibet christifideli causam suam in quovis statu et gradu iudicii cognoscendam ad ipsum Romanum Pontificem deferre, qui pro toto orbe catholico iudex est supremus et qui vel ipse per se ius dicit vel per tribunalia Sedis Apostolicae vel per iudices a se delegatos.

§2. Haec provocatio tamen ad Romanum Pontificem interposita non suspendit excepto casu appellationis exercitium potestatis iniudice, qui causam iam cognoscere coepit quique idcirco potest iudicium prosequi usque ad sententiam definitivam, nisi constat Romanum Pontificem causam ad se advocavisse.

CAN. 1060 §1. Soli Romano Pontifici ius est iudicandi:

1° Patriarchas;

2° Episcopos in causis poenalibus;

3° eos, qui supremum tenent civitatis magistratum;

4° alias causas, quas ipse ad suum advocavit iudicium.

§2. Exceptis Episcopis intra fines terri-

1059 §1: Pius XII, m.p. *Sollicitudinem Nostram,* 6 ian. 1950, cann. 32 §1, 77. - Sard. cann. 3, 5; Carth. prolog.; S. Bonifacius I, litt. *Institutio universalis,* 11 mar. 422; S. Gelasius, litt. *Ego quoque,* a. 493, "Nobis opponunt;" litt. *Valde mirati,* 5 feb. 496, "Non reticemus;" S. Nicolaus I, litt. *Proposueramus quidem,* a. 865, "Sed his;" Professio fidei (in Lugd. II) a Michaele Palaeologo Gregorio X oblata, a. 1274; Iohannes XXII, ep. *Salvator noster,* 29 apr. 1319, "Nec omittimus."

1059 §2: Pius XII, m.p. *Sollicitudinem Nostram,* 6 ian. 1950, can. 32 §2. - S. Zosimus, litt. *Quamvis Patrum,* a. 418; Sign. Apost., litt. circ. 13 dec. 1977.

1060 §1, 1°: Pius XII, m.p. *Sollicitudinem Nostram,* 6 ian. 1950, can. 15 n. 2. - Benedictus XIV, litt. *Non possumus,* 20 iul. 1746. * Syn. Libanen. Maronitarum, a. 1736, pars III, cap. VI, 10.

1060 §1, 2°: Pius XII, m.p. *Sollicitudinem Nostram,* 6 ian. 1950, cann. 15 n. 3, 17 §1. - Apost. can. 74; Ant. cann. 12–15, 17, 22, 25; Constantinop. I, can. 6; Chalc. cann. 9, 17; Sard. cann. 3–5; Carth. prolog. et

cann. 12, 19, 121–123; Constantinop. a. 394; Constantinop. IV, cann. 17, 24, 26; S. Cyrillus Alexandrin., can. 1; S. Iulius, litt. *Legi litteras,* a. 341; S. Leo M., litt. *Quanta fraternitati,* a. 446, "De conciliis;" S. Nicolaus I, litt. *Quanto maiora,* a. 886, "Non autem" et "Porro si dicitis;" Iohannes VIII, litt. *Dic ergo eis,* a. 873, "Porro Alvinus;" Pius VI, litt. *Maximum Nobis,* 18 sep. 1784, n. 3, ad 5; S.C. de Prop. Fide, decr. 20 iul. 1760, ad VIII; instr. 9 aug. 1760; (C.G.), 17 feb. 1772, ad 4; (C.G.), 8 iul. 1774, 3; 8 iul. 1774, dub. 15; 22 mar. 1777; (C.G.), 15 sep. 1777, ad 1. * Syn. Libanen. Maronitarum, a. 1736, pars III, cap. IV, 33, I; cap. VI, 2, 14; Syn. Sciarfen. Syrorum, a. 1888, cap. VII, art. III, 6, 12; Syn. Armen., a. 1911, 194.

1060 §1, 3°: Pius XII, m.p. *Sollicitudinem Nostram,* 6 ian. 1950, can. 15 n. 1. - Constantinop. IV, can. 16.

1060 §2: Pius XII, m.p. *Sollicitudinem Nostram,* 6 ian. 1950, can. 16 §1 n. 1. - Sard. can. 3; Chalc. cann. 9, 17.

their power within the territorial boundaries of the patriarchal Church, other bishops are judged in contentious cases by the tribunal designated by the Roman Pontiff, without prejudice to can. 1066, §2.

§3. A judge cannot review an act or document confirmed specifically *(in forma specifica)* by the Roman Pontiff without his prior mandate.

CAN. 1061 Persons who do not have a superior authority below the Roman Pontiff, whether they are physical persons who are not constituted in the order of the episcopacy or juridic persons, must be brought before the tribunals of the Apostolic See, without prejudice to can. 1063, §4, nn. 3 and 4.

CAN. 1062 §1. The synod of bishops of the patriarchal Church, without prejudice to the competence of the Apostolic See, is the superior tribunal within the territorial boundaries of the patriarchal Church.

§2. The synod of bishops of the patriarchal Church must elect by secret ballot for a five-year term, and from among its members, a general moderator for the administration of justice, as well as two bishops who, together with him as president, constitute a tribunal. However, if one of these three bishops is a party in the case or is unable to attend, the patriarch with the consent of the permanent synod is to substitute another bishop for him. Likewise, if an objection has been raised against any of them, the patriarch is to act in a like manner with the consent of the permanent synod.

§3. It is for this tribunal to judge the contentious cases of eparchies or bishops, even titular bishops.

torii Ecclesiae patriarchalis potestatem suam exercentibus ceteri Episcopi in causis contentiosis iudicantur a tribunali a Romano Pontifice designato salvo can. 1066, §2.

§3. Iudex de actu vel documento a Romano Pontifice in forma specifica confirmato videre non potest, nisi illius praecessit mandatum.

CAN. 1061 Coram tribunalibus Sedis Apostolicae conveniri debent personae, quae auctoritatem superiorem infra Romanum pontificem non habent, sive sunt personae physicae in ordine episcopatus non constitutae sive sunt personae iuridicae salvo can. 1063, §4, nn. 3 et 4.

CAN. 1062 §1. Synodus Episcoporum Ecclesiae patriarchalis, salva competentia Sedis apostolicae, est superius tribunal intra fines territorii eiusdem Ecclesiae.

§2. Synodus Episcoporum Ecclesiae patriarchalis per secreta suffragia eligere debet ad quinquennium ex suo gremio Moderatorem generalem administrationis iustitiae necnon duos Episcopos, qui cum eo praeside constituunt tribunal; si vero unus ex his tribus Episcopis est in causa vel adesse non potest, Patriarcha de consensu Synodi permanentis ei alium Episcopum substituat; item in casu recusationis videat Patriarcha de consensu Synodi permanentis.

§3. Huius tribunalis est iudicare causas contentiosas sive eparchiarum sive Episcoporum, etiam Episcoporum titularium.

1060 §3: Pius XII, m.p. *Sollicitudinem Nostram,* 6 ian. 1950, can. 203.

1061: Pius XII, m.p. *Sollicitudinem Nostram,* 6 ian. 1950, can. 16 §1 n. 2.

1062 §1: Constantinop. I, can. 6; Chalc. cann. 9, 17; Apost. can. 74; Ant. 3, 12–15, 17, 20, 22, 25; Sard. 3, 13–14; Carth. 12, 121, 125; Constantinop. a. 394; Protodeut. can. 13; S. Cyrillus Alexandrin., can. 1 in fine.

1062 §3: Quinisext. can. 25.

§4. An appeal in these cases is made to the synod of bishops of the patriarchal Church; with any further appeal excluded, without prejudice to can. 1059.

§5. The general moderator for the administration of justice has the right of vigilance over all tribunals located within the territorial boundaries of the patriarchal Church, as well as the right of deciding if an objection is to be raised against any judge of the ordinary tribunal of the patriarchal Church.

CAN. 1063 §1. The patriarch must erect the ordinary tribunal of the patriarchal Church, distinct from the tribunal of the eparchy of the patriarch.

§2. This tribunal is to have its own president, judges, promoter of justice, defenders of the bond as well as other necessary officials, appointed by the patriarch with the consent of the permanent synod. The president, the judges, the promoter of justice and the defender of the bond cannot be removed from office except by the synod of bishops of the patriarchal Church. However, on his own, the patriarch can accept a resignation from office.

§3. This tribunal is the appellate tribunal in second and further grades, with judges serving in rotation, for cases already decided in the lower tribunals. This tribunal also has the rights of a metropolitan tribunal in those places of the patriarchal Church where provinces have not been established.

§4. This tribunal is competent to judge in first and further grades, with judges serving in rotation, the cases:

§4. Appellatio in his causis fit ad Synodum Episcoporum Ecclesiae patriarchalis ulteriore appellatione remota salvo can. 1059.

§5. Moderatori generali administrationis iustitiae est ius vigilandi omnibus tribunalibus intra fines territorii Ecclesiae patriarchalis sitis necnon ius decisionem ferendi in recusatione contra aliquem iudicem tribunalis ordinarii Ecclesiae patriarchalis.

CAN. 1063 §1. Patriarcha erigere debet tribunal ordinarium Ecclesiae patriarchalis a tribunali eparchiae Patriarchae distinctum.

§2. Hoc tribunal proprium praesidem, iudices, promotorem iustitiae, defensores vinculi aliosque necessarios administros habeat a Patriarcha de consensu Synodi permanentis nominatos; praeses, iudices, promotor iustitiae necnon defensores vinculi amoveri non possunt nisi a Synodo Episcoporum Ecclesiae patriarchalis, renuntiationem vero ab officio Patriarcha solus acceptare potest.

§3. Hoc tribunal est tribunal appellationis in secundo et in ulterioribus gradibus iudicii ope iudicum, qui sibi invicem succedunt, pro causis in tribunalibus inferioribus iam definitis; huic tribunali competunt etiam iura tribunalis metropolitani eis in locis territorii Ecclesiae patriarchalis, ubi provinciae erectae non sunt.

§4. Huic tribunali competit iudicare ope iudicum, qui sibi invicem succedunt, in primo et in ulterioribus gradibus iudicii causas:

1063 §1: Pius XII, m.p. *Sollicitudinem Nostram*, 6 ian. 1950, can. 85 §1.

1063 §2: Pius XII, m.p. *Sollicitudinem Nostram*, 6 ian. 1950, can. 85 §2.

1063 §3: Pius XII, m.p. *Sollicitudinem Nostram*, 6 ian. 1950, cann. 73 §1, 72 §1 nn. 2–3, 5. * Syn. Liba-

nen. Maronitarum, a. 1736, pars III, cap. VI, 2, 5 et 10; Syn. Sciarfen. Syrorum, a. 1888, cap. VII, art. III, 6, 13); Syn. Alexandrin. Coptorum, a. 1898, sect. III, cap. I, art. III, IV, 8).

1063 §4: Pius XII, m.p. *Sollicitudinem Nostram*, 6 ian. 1950, can. 19. - Quinisext. can. 25.

1° of exarchs and delegates of the patriarch who are not bishops;

2° of physical or juridic persons immediately subject to the patriarch;

3° of institutes of consecrated life of pontifical right;

4° of superiors of institutes of consecrated life of pontifical right who do not have a superior within the same institute who possesses judicial power;

5° reserved to this tribunal by particular law.

CAN. 1064 §1. The metropolitan tribunal that is not distinct from the tribunal of the eparchy of the metropolitan is the appellate tribunal from sentences of the eparchial tribunals.

§2. From cases tried in the first grade of the trial before the metropolitan or another eparchial bishop who has no superior authority below the Roman Pontiff, the appeal must be made to the tribunal that the metropolitan or eparchial bishop has designated in a stable manner with the approval of the Apostolic See, with due regard for cann. 139 and 175.

CAN. 1065 The tribunal of third grade is the Apostolic See, unless common law expressly provides otherwise.

CAN. 1066 §1. In each eparchy and for all cases not expressly excepted by law, the eparchial bishop is the judge in the first grade of the trial.

§2. However, if a case concerns the rights or

1° Exarchorum et delegatorum Patriarchae, qui Episcopi non sunt;

2° personarum physicarum vel iuridicarum Patriarchae immediate subiectarum;

3° institutorum vitae consecratae iuris pontificii;

4° Superioris instituti vitae consecratae iuris pontificii, qui in eodem instituto Superiorem potestate iudiciali praeditum non habet;

5° ex iuris particularis praescripto eidem tribunali reservatas.

CAN. 1064 §1. Tribunal metropolitanum, quod non est distinctum a tribunali eparchiae Metropolitae, est tribunal appellationis a sententiis tribunalium eparchialium.

§2. A causis in primo gradu iudicii pertractatis coram Metropolita aliove Episcopo eparchiali, qui auctoritatem superiorem infra Romanum Pontificem non habet, fieri debet appellatio ad tribunal ab ipso stabili modo cum approbatione Sedis Apostolicae designatum firmis cann. 139 et 175.

CAN. 1065 Tribunal tertii gradus est Sedes Apostolica, nisi aliter iure communi expresse cavetur.

CAN. 1066 §1. In unaquaque eparchia et pro omnibus causis iure expresse non exceptis iudex in primo gradu iudicii est Episcopus eparchialis.

§2. Si vero agitur de iuribus aut bonis

1064 §1: Pius XII, m.p. *Sollicitudinem Nostram,* 6 ian. 1950, can. 72 §1 n. 1 et §4. - Nic. I, can. 5; Ant. can. 12; Sard. can. 14; Constantinop. IV, can. 26. * Syn. Libanen. Maronitarum, a. 1736, pars III, cap. IV, 32 "De iis" et III; Syn. prov. Alba-Iulien. et Fagarasien. Rumenorum, a. 1882, tit. V, §59; Syn. Alexandrin. Coptorum, a. 1898, sect. III, cap. VI, tit. II, 3.

1064 §2: Pius XII, m.p. *Sollicitudinem Nostram,* 6 ian. 1950, can. 72 §1 n. 4.

1065: Pius XII, m.p. *Sollicitudinem Nostram,* 6

ian. 1950, can. 73 §1.

1066 §1:Pius XII, m.p. *Sollicitudinem Nostram,* 6 ian. 1950, can. 37 §1; Vat. II, const. *Lumen gentium,* 27. * Syn. prov. Alba-Iulien. et Fagarasien. Rumenorum, a. 1872, tit. X, cap. I, a. 1882, tit. V, §1; Syn. Alexandrin. Coptorum, a. 1898, sect. III, cap. VI, tit. II, 1–2; Syn. Armen., a. 1911, 962–963.

1066 §2: Pius XII, m.p. *Sollicitudinem Nostram,* 6 ian. 1950, can. 37 §2.

temporal goods of a juridic person represented by the eparchial bishop, the appellate tribunal judges in the first grade of the trial, with due regard for can. 1062, §3.

CAN. 1067 §1. A tribunal of first grade for several eparchies of the same Church *sui iuris* can be erected by the patriarch with the consent of the eparchial bishops concerned, if it concerns eparchies situated within the territorial boundaries of the patriarchal Church. In other cases, it can be erected by the eparchial bishops, themselves, who have consented to this and with the approval of the Apostolic See.

§2. This tribunal must be erected if the individual eparchial bishops cannot, for whatever reason, erect their own tribunal. Within the territorial boundaries of the patriarchal Church, if the case warrants, this tribunal is to be erected by the synod of bishops of the patriarchal Church.

§3. In eparchies for which such a tribunal has been erected, a collegiate eparchial tribunal cannot be validly erected.

§4. The group of eparchial bishops who consented to such a tribunal, or an eparchial bishop elected by them, has the powers that an eparchial bishop has regarding his own tribunal. However, if this tribunal was erected by the synod of bishops of the patriarchal Church or by the Apostolic See, the norms established by the synod itself or by the Apostolic See are to be observed.

§5. Within the territorial boundaries of the patriarchal Church, an appeal from this tribunal is made to the ordinary tribunal of the patriarchal Church. However, in other cases, the appeal

temporalibus personae iuridicae ab Episcopo eparchiali repraesentatae, iudicat in primo gradu iudicii tribunal appellationis firmo can. 1062, §3.

CAN. 1067 §1. Tribunal primi gradus pro pluribus eparchiis eiusdem Ecclesiae sui iuris erigi potest a Patriarcha de consensu Episcoporum eparchialium, quorum interest, si de eparchiis intra fines territorii Ecclesiae patriarchalis sitis agitur; in ceteris casibus ab ipsis Episcopis eparchialibus, qui ad hoc consenserunt approbante Sede Apostolica.

§2. Hoc tribunal erigi debet, si singuli Episcopi eparchiales tribunal proprium quacumque de causa erigere non possunt; intra fines territorii Ecclesiae patriarchalis, si casus fert, a Synodo Episcoporum Ecclesiae patriarchalis hoc tribunal erigatur.

§3. In eparchiis, pro quibus tale tribunal erectum est, tribunal eparchiale collegiale valide erigi non potest.

§4. Coetui Episcoporum eparchialium, qui ad tale tribunal consenserunt, vel Episcopo eparchiali ab eodem electo competunt potestates, quas Episcopus eparchialis habet circa suum tribunal; si vero hoc tribunal a Synodo Episcoporum Ecclesiae patriarchalis vel a Sede Apostolica erectum est, servandae sunt normae ab ipsa Synodo vel Sede Apostolica statutae.

§5. Appellatio ab hoc tribunali fit intra fines territorii Ecclesiae patriarchalis ad tribunal ordinarium Ecclesiae patriarchalis; in ceteris casibus vero ad tribunal stabili modo

---

1067 §1: Pius XII, m.p. *Sollicitudinem Nostram*, 6 ian. 1950, can. 38 §1 n. 1.

1067 §3: Pius XII, m.p. *Sollicitudinem Nostram*, 6 ian. 1950, can. 38 §1 n. 2.

1067 §5: Pius XII, m.p. *Sollicitudinem Nostram*, 6 ian. 1950, can. 72 §1 n. 5. * Syn. Sciarfen. Syrorum, a. 1888, cap. VII, art. III, 6, 13).

is made to the tribunal designated in a stable manner by the group of bishops mentioned in §4, with the approval of the Apostolic See, or to the tribunal designated by the Apostolic See.

CAN. 1068 §1. The eparchial bishops of various Churches *sui iuris* exercising their power within the same territory can agree among themselves to establish a common tribunal, which is to adjudicate either contentious or penal cases of the Christian faithful subject to any one of these eparchial bishops.

§2. If suitable judges and other tribunal officers are lacking, the eparchial bishops are to take care that a common tribunal is constituted.

§3. The eparchial bishops who consented to the common tribunal must designate from among themselves one who has the power over this tribunal that an eparchial bishop has regarding his own tribunal.

§4. Appeals from the sentences of a common tribunal of first grade are made to the tribunal designated in a stable manner by the Apostolic See.

CAN. 1069 §1. Controversies between physical or juridic persons of the same institute of consecrated life, in which superiors are endowed with the power of governance, except secular institutes, are to be decided before the judge or tribunal determined in the typicon or statutes of the institute.

§2. Except in the case of secular institutes, if the controversy arises between physical or juridic persons of different institutes of consecrated life, or even of the same institute of

a coetu Episcoporum, de quo in §4, cum approbatione Sedis Apostolicae vel ab ipsa Sede Apostolica designatum.

CAN. 1068 §1. Episcopi eparchiales diversarum Ecclesiarum sui iuris in eodem territorio potestatem suam exercentes convenire inter se possunt de constituendo tribunali communi, quod causas sive contentiosas sive poenales christifidelium alicui ex eisdem Episcopis eparchialibus subditorum cognoscat.

§2. Si idonei iudices aliique administri tribunalium desunt, Episcopi eparchiales curent, ut tribunal commune constituatur.

§3. Episcopi eparchiales, qui ad tribunal commune consenserunt, unum ex se ipsis designare debent, cui circa hoc tribunal competunt potestates, quas Episcopus eparchialis habet circa suum tribunal.

§4. A sententiis tribunalis communis primi gradus appellatio fit ad tribunal stabili modo a Sede Apostolica designatum.

CAN. 1069 §1. Controversiae inter personas physicas vel iuridicas eiusdem instituti vitae consecratae institutis saecularibus exceptis, in quo Superiores potestate regiminis praediti sunt, definiendae sunt apud iudicem vel tribunal in typico vel statutis instituti determinatum.

§2. Si controversia, institutis saecularibus exceptis, enascitur inter personas physicas vel iuridicas diversorum institutorum vitae consecratae aut etiam eiusdem in-

---

1068 §1: Pius XII, m.p. *Sollicitudinem Nostram*, 6 ian. 1950, can. 39 §1.

1068 §3: Pius XII, m.p. *Sollicitudinem Nostram*, 6 ian. 1950, can. 39 §2.

1068 §4: Pius XII, m.p. *Sollicitudinem Nostram*,

6 ian. 1950, can. 72 §1 n. 6.

1069 §1: Pius XII, m.p. *Sollicitudinem Nostram*, 6 ian. 1950, can. 51 §§1–2.

1069 §2: Pius XII, m.p. *Sollicitudinem Nostram*, 6 ian. 1950, can. 51 §3.

eparchial right or of another, in which the superiors are not endowed with the power of governance, or between a member or a juridic person of an institute of consecrated life and any other physical or juridic person, the eparchial tribunal judges in the first grade of the trial.

CAN. 1070 Any authority that erects a tribunal is to take care that the tribunal has its own statutes approved by the same authority, in which must be determined the manner of appointing judges and other officers, the duration of their function, their remuneration and all the other matters required by law.

CAN. 1071 Any tribunal has the right to call upon the assistance of another tribunal of any Church in order to carry out certain procedural acts except, however, those acts that involve the decisions of the judges.

CAN. 1072 The incompetence of lower judges is absolute in the cases mentioned in cann. 1060, 1061, 1062, §3 and 1063, §4; the incompetence of the judge is also absolute if the competence established by reason of the grade of the trial is not observed.

CAN. 1073 §1. No one can be brought to the first grade of trial except before a judge who is competent by reason of one of the titles determined by common law.

§2. The incompetence of a judge supported by none of these titles is called relative.

§3. Unless the law expressly provides otherwise, the petitioner follows the forum of the respondent. If the respondent has more than one forum, the choice of forum is granted to the petitioner.

stituti iuris eparchialis alteriusve, in quo Superiores potestate regiminis praediti non sunt, aut inter sodalem vel personam iuridicam instituti vitae consecratae et quamcumque aliam personam physicam vel iuridicam, iudicat in primo gradu iudicii tribunal eparchiale.

CAN. 1070 Auctoritas quodcumque tribunal erigens curet, ut tribunal propria statuta ab eadem auctoritate approbata habeat, in quibus iudicum aliorumque administrorum modus nominationis, muneris tempus, remuneratio necnon alia iure requisita determinari debent.

CAN. 1071 Quodlibet tribunal ius habet in auxilium vocandi aliud tribunal cuiuscumque Ecclesiae, ut quosdam actus processuales peragat exceptis tamen illis actibus, qui decisiones iudicum implicant.

CAN. 1072 In causis, de quibus in cann. 1060, 1061, 1062, §3 et 1063, §4 inferiorum iudicum incompetentia est absoluta; item absoluta est incompetentia iudicis, si competentia ratione gradus iudicii statuta non servatur.

CAN. 1073 §1. Nemo in primo gradu iudicii conveniri potest nisi coram iudice, qui competens est ob unum ex titulis, qui iure communi determinantur.

§2. Incompetentia iudicis, cui nullus ex his titulis suffragatur, dicitur relativa.

§3. Nisi aliter iure expresse cavetur, actor sequitur forum partis conventae; si vero pars conventa multiplex forum habet, optio fori actori conceditur.

1071: S.C.S. Off., instr. (ad Ep. Rituum Orient.), a. 1883, tit. III, 15.

1072: Pius XII, m.p. *Sollicitudinem Nostram,* 6 ian. 1950, can. 21. - Sign. Apost., decl. 3 iun. 1989, 5.

1073 §1: Pius XII, m.p. *Sollicitudinem Nostram,* 6 ian. 1950, can. 22 §1. ▲ C. 7, 48, 4.

1073 §2: Pius XII, m.p. *Sollicitudinem Nostram,* 6 ian. 1950, can. 22 §2. ▲ D. 2, 1, 15; 5, 1, 1–2; C. 3, 13, 3; 7, 48, 1.

1073 §3: Pius XII, m.p. *Sollicitudinem Nostram,* 6 ian. 1950, can. 22 §3. ▲ C. 3, 13, 2 et 5; 3, 12, 22; 3, 19, 3; Basilic. 7, 5, 82.

CAN. 1074 Anyone can be brought to trial before the tribunal of domicile or quasi-domicile.

CAN. 1075 §1. A transient has a forum in the place of his or her actual residence.

§2. A person whose domicile, quasi-domicile and place of residence are unknown can be brought to trial in the forum of the petitioner provided no other legitimate forum is available.

CAN. 1076 By reason of the location of an object, a party can be brought to trial before the tribunal of the place where the object in dispute is located, whenever the action is directed against the object or concerns damages.

CAN. 1077 §1. By reason of contract, a party can be brought to trial before the tribunal of the place where the contract was entered into or must be fulfilled, unless the parties have agreed to choose another tribunal.

§2. If the case concerns obligations that originate from another title, a party can be brought to trial before the tribunal of the place where the obligation originated or must be fulfilled.

CAN. 1078 In penal cases, the accused, even if absent, can be brought to trial before the tribunal of the place where the delict was committed.

CAN. 1079 A party can be brought to trial:

1° in cases that concern administration, be-

CAN. 1074 Quilibet conveniri potest coram tribunali domicilii vel quasi-domicilii.

CAN. 1075 §1. Vagus forum habet in loco, ubi actu commoratur.

§2. Is, cuius neque domicilium aut quasi-domicilium neque locus commorationis nota sunt, conveniri potest in foro actoris, dummodo aliud forum legitimum non suppetat.

CAN. 1076 Ratione rei sitae pars conveniri potest coram tribunali loci, ubi res litigiosa sita est, quoties actio in rem directa est aut de spolio agitur.

CAN. 1077 §1. Ratione contractus pars conveniri potest coram tribunali loci, ubi contractus initus est vel impleri debet, nisi partes concorditer aliud tribunal elegerunt.

§2. Si causa versatur circa obligationes, quae ex alio titulo proveniunt, pars conveniri potest coram tribunali loci, ubi obligatio orta est vel est implenda.

CAN. 1078 In causis poenalibus accusatus, etsi absens, conveniri potest coram tribunali loci, ubi delictum patratum est.

CAN. 1079 Pars conveniri potest:

1° in causis, quae circa administrationem

1074: Pius XII, m.p. *Sollicitudinem Nostram,* 6 ian. 1950, can. 24. * Syn. Libanen. Maronitarum, a. 1736, pars III, cap. V, 12. ▲ D. 5, 1, 65; 42, 5, 1–2; C. 3, 13, 2; 12, 1, 13.

1075 §1: Pius XII, m.p. *Sollicitudinem Nostram,* 6 ian. 1950, can. 26 §1.

1075 §2: Pius XII, m.p. *Sollicitudinem Nostram,* 6 ian. *1950, can. 26 §§1–2.*

1076: Pius XII, m.p. *Sollicitudinem Nostram,* 6 ian. 1950, can. 27. - Carth. can. 120. * Syn. Libanen. Maronitarum, a. 1736, pars III, cap. I, 12. ▲ C. 3, 19, 2,

(pr. et 3); 3, 20.

1077 §1: Pius XII, m.p. *Sollicitudinem Nostram,* 6 ian. 1950, can. 28 §§1–2. ▲ C. 3, 13, 2; 3, 18; D. 5, 1, 19; 5, 1, 45 et 49; 42, 5, 1 et 3; Basilic. 7, 3, 38; 9, 7, 1 et 3.

1078: Pius XII, m.p. *Sollicitudinem Nostram,* 6 ian. 1950, can. 29. * Syn. Libanen. Maronitarum, a. 1736, pars III, cap. V, 12. ▲ D. 1, 18, 3; 9, 4, 43; 48, 3, 7; C. 3, 15, 1; 9, 9, 15.

1079, 1°: Pius XII, m.p. *Sollicitudinem Nostram,* 6 ian. 1950, can. 23 n. 3. ▲ C. 3, 21, 1; D. 5, 1, 19, (1).

fore the tribunal of the place where the administration was conducted;

2° in cases that concern inheritances or pious legacies, before the tribunal of the last domicile, quasi-domicile or place of residence, with due regard for can. 1075, §2, of the one whose inheritance or pious legacy is at issue, unless it concerns the mere execution of a legacy, which must be examined according to the ordinary norms of competence.

CAN. 1080 If none of the above-mentioned titles supports the judge and yet a case is introduced before him, the judge obtains competence if the parties and the authority to whom the tribunal is immediately subject consent.

CAN. 1081 By reason of connection, interconnected cases must be adjudicated by one and the same tribunal in the same process, unless a prescript of law prevents this.

CAN. 1082 By reason of prevention, if two or more tribunals are equally competent, the right of adjudicating the case belongs to the one that legitimately cited the respondent first.

CAN. 1083 §1. A conflict between judges as to which of them is competent, is to be decided by the appellate tribunal of that judge before whom the action was first advanced by an introductory *libellus* of litigation.

§2. If, however, one of the two tribunals is the appellate tribunal of the other, the conflict is to be decided by the tribunal of third grade for the tribunal before which the action was first advanced.

§3. There is no appeal from the decisions in these conflicts.

versantur, coram tribunali loci, ubi administratio gesta est.

2° in causis, quae respiciunt hereditates vel legata pia, coram tribunali ultimi domicilii vel quasi-domicilii vel commorationis firmo can. 1075, §2 illius, de cuius hereditate vel legato pio agitur, nisi agitur de mera exsecutione legati, quae videnda est secundum ordinarias competentiae normas.

CAN. 1080 Si nullus ex superioribus titulis iudici suffragatur et tamen causa apud ipsum introducitur, ipse competentiam obtinet, si partes et auctoritas, cui tribunal immediate subiectum est, consentiunt.

CAN. 1081 Ratione conexionis ab uno eodemque tribunali et in eodem processu cognoscendae sunt causae inter se conexae, nisi iuris praescriptum obstat.

CAN. 1082 Ratione praeventionis, si duo vel plura tribunalia aeque competentia sunt, ei ius est causam cognoscendi, quod prius partem conventam legitime citavit.

CAN. 1083 §1. Conflictus inter iudices, quisnam eorum ad aliquod negotium competens sit, definiendi sunt a tribunali appellationis illius iudicis, coram quo actio primo per libellum litis introductorium promota est.

§2. Si vero alterutrum tribunal est alterius tribunal appellationis, conflictus definiendus est a tribunali tertii gradus pro tribunali, in quo actio primo promota est.

§3. A decisionibus in his conflictibus non datur locus appellationi.

1079, 2°: Pius XII, m.p. *Sollicitudinem Nostram,* 6 ian. 1950, can. 23 n. 4. ▲ D. 5, 1, 38; C. 3, 17 et 20.

1081: Pius XII, m.p. *Sollicitudinem Nostram,* 6 ian. 1950, can. 30. ▲ C. 3, 1, 10; 3, 1, 12, (2); 3, 8, 3–4.

1082: Pius XII, m.p. *Sollicitudinem Nostram,* 6 ian. 1950, can. 31. ▲ D. 5, 1, 7; C. 2, 2, 4.

1083 §1: Pius XII, m.p. *Sollicitudinem Nostram,* 6 ian. 1950, can. 127 §1.

1083 §2: Pius XII, m.p. *Sollicitudinem Nostram,* 6 ian. 1950, can. 127 §2.

CAN. 1084 §1. The following cases are reserved to a collegiate tribunal of three judges:

1° concerning the bond of sacred ordination;

2° concerning the bond of marriage, with due regard for cann. 1372–1374;

3° penal cases concerning delicts that entail the penalty of major excommunication, privation of office, reduction to a lower grade or deposition;

4° cases that are determined by the particular law of the proper Church *sui iuris.*

§2. Other cases are to be handled by a single judge, unless the eparchial bishop reserves a certain case to a college of three judges.

§3. If it happens that a collegiate tribunal cannot be established in the first grade of the trial, as long as this impossibility lasts, the patriarch, having consulted the permanent synod, can permit the eparchial bishop to entrust cases to a single clerical judge who is to employ an assessor and an auditor where possible. The same can be permitted by a metropolitan who presides over a metropolitan Church *sui iuris* as well as a metropolitan of a patriarchal Church constituted outside the territorial boundaries of the patriarchal Church, in both situations having consulted the two eparchial bishops who are senior by episcopal ordination; in other instances, the Apostolic See is to be approached.

CAN. 1085 §1. A collegiate tribunal must proceed collegially and render its decisions by majority vote; this is for validity if it concerns:

1° the rejection of a petition of a counterclaim or of an incidental case;

CAN. 1084 §1. Tribunali collegiali trium iudicum reservantur:

1° causae de vinculo sacrae ordinationis;

2° causae de vinculo matrimonii firmis cann. 1372–1374;

3° causae poenales de delictis, quae poenam excommunicationis maioris, privationis officii, reductionis ad gradum inferiorem vel depositionis secumferunt;

4° causae determinatae iure particulari propriae Ecclesiae sui iuris.

§2. Ceterae causae tractantur a iudice unico, nisi Episcopus eparchialis certam causam collegio trium iudicum reservat.

§3. In primo gradu iudicii, si collegium constitui non potest, dum huiusmodi impossibilitas perdurat, Patriarcha consulta Synodo permanenti permittere potest, ut Episcopus eparchialis causas iudici unico clerico committat, qui, si fieri potest, assessorem et auditorem sibi asciscat; idem permittere potest Metropolita, qui Ecclesiae metropolitanae sui iuris praeest, vel etiam Metropolita Ecclesiae patriarchalis extra fines territorii eiusdem Ecclesiae constitutus, uterque consultis duobus Episcopis eparchialibus ordinatione episcopali senioribus; in ceteris casibus adeatur Sedes Apostolica.

CAN. 1085 §1. Tribunal collegiale collegialiter procedere debet et ad maiorem numerum suffragiorum decisiones ferre, ad validitatem quidem, si agitur:

1° de reiectione petitionis actionis reconventionalis vel causae incidentis;

1084 §1, 4°: Pius XII, m.p. *Sollicitudinem Nostram,* 6 ian. 1950, can. 46 §1. - Carth. cann. 12, 14, 20, 107. * Syn. Libanen. Maronitarum, a. 1736, pars III, cap. IV, 32, VII.

1084 §2: Pius XII, m.p. *Sollicitudinem Nostram,* 6 ian. 1950, cann. 46 §2, 47.

1084 §3: Paulus VI, litt. ap. *Cum matrimonialium,* 8 sep. 1973, V, §2.

1085 §1: Pius XII, m.p. *Sollicitudinem Nostram,* 6 ian. 1950, can. 48 §1. ▲ D. 42, 1, 36–37 et 39.

2° the decision of a recourse against the decree of the presiding judge;

3° the sentence, even an interlocutory one, as well as decrees that have the same force as a definitive sentence.

§2. Other procedural acts are to be completed by the *ponens,* unless the college has reserved certain acts to itself. Such reservation, however, is not for validity.

§3. If a case was adjudicated collegially in the first grade of the trial, on appeal it must also be decided collegially and not by a smaller number of judges. Nevertheless, if the case was adjudicated by a single judge, on appeal it is also to be decided by a single judge, except in the case mentioned in can. 1084, §3.

CHAPTER II. **The Officers of the Tribunal**

ART. I. *The Judicial Vicar, Judges and Auditors*

CAN. 1086 §1. The eparchial bishop is bound to appoint a judicial vicar with ordinary judicial power, distinct from the protosyncellus, unless the smallness of the eparchy or the small number of cases suggests otherwise.

§2. The judicial vicar constitutes one tribunal with the eparchial bishop, but he cannot judge cases that the eparchial bishop has reserved to himself.

§3. The judicial vicar can be given assistants who are called adjutant judicial vicars.

§4. Both the judicial vicar and the adjutant

2° de definitione recursus adversus decretum praesidis;

3° de sententia, etsi interlocutoria, necnon de decretis, quae vim sententiae definitivae habent.

§2. Ceteros actus processuales ponens peragat, nisi collegium aliquos, non quidem ad validitatem, sibi reservavit.

§3. Si causa in primo gradu iudicii collegialiter cognita est, etiam in gradu appellationis collegialiter nec a minore iudicum numero definiri debet; si vero a iudice unico, etiam in gradu appellationis a iudice unico definienda est excepto casu, de quo in can. 1084, §3.

CAPUT II. **De Administris Tribunalium**

ART. I. *De Vicario Iudiciali, de Iudicibus et de Auditoribus*

CAN. 1086 §1. Episcopus eparchialis tenetur Vicarium iudicialem constituere cum potestate iudiciali ordinaria a Protosyncello distinctum, nisi parvitas eparchiae aut paucitas causarum aliud suadet.

§2. Vicarius iudicialis unum constituit tribunal cum Episcopo eparchiali, sed non potest iudicare causas, quas Episcopus eparchialis sibi reservavit.

§3. Vicario iudiciali dari possunt adiutores, quibus nomen est Vicariorum iudicialium adiunctorum.

§4. Tum Vicarius iudicialis tum Vicarii iu-

1085 §3: Pius XII, m.p. *Sollicitudinem Nostram,* 6 ian. 1950, can. 76.

1086 §1: Pius XII, m.p. *Sollicitudinem Nostram,* 6 ian. 1950, can. 40 §1. * Syn. Zamosten. Ruthenorum, a. 1720, tit. VII; Syn. Libanen. Maronitarum, a. 1736, pars III, cap. V, 1; Syn. prov. Alba-Iulien. et Fagarasien. Rumenorum, a. 1872, tit. II, cap. VI.

1086 §2: Pius XII, m.p. *Sollicitudinem Nostram,* 6 ian. 1950, can. 40 §2.

1086 §3: Pius XII, m.p. *Sollicitudinem Nostram,* 6 ian. 1950, can. 40 §3.

1086 §4: Pius XII, m.p. *Sollicitudinem Nostram,* 6 ian. 1950, can. 40 §4.

judicial vicars must be priests of unimpaired reputation, doctors or at least licensed in canon law, known for prudence and zeal for justice and not less than thirty years of age.

CAN. 1087 §1. In an eparchy, the eparchial bishop is to appoint eparchial judges, who are to be clerics.

§2. The patriarch, having consulted the permanent synod, or the metropolitan who presides over a metropolitan Church *sui iuris,* having consulted the two eparchial bishops senior by episcopal ordination, can permit that other members of the Christian faithful also be appointed judges. When it is necessary, one of them can be assumed to form a collegiate tribunal; in other cases, the Apostolic See is to be approached regarding this matter.

§3. Judges are to be of unimpaired reputation and doctors or at least licensed in canon law and be known for prudence and zeal for justice.

CAN. 1088 §1. The judicial vicar, adjutant judicial vicar, and other judges are appointed for a determined time.

§2. If the determined time has elapsed when the eparchial see is vacant, they cannot be removed, but remain in office until the new eparchial bishop has provided for the matter.

§3. If the judicial vicar is appointed by an eparchial administrator, upon arrival of the new eparchial bishop, he needs a confirmation.

CAN. 1089 In any trial, a single judge can

diciales adiuncti esse debent sacerdotes integrae famae, in iure canonico doctores vel saltem licentiati, prudentia et iustitiae zelo probati, annos nati non minus triginta.

CAN. 1087 §1. In eparchia nominentur ab Episcopo eparchiali iudices eparchiales, qui sint clerici.

§2. Patriarcha consulta Synodo permanenti vel Metropolita, qui Ecclesiae metropolitanae sui iuris praeest, consultis duobus Episcopis eparchialibus ordinatione episcopali senioribus permittere potest, ut etiam alii christifideles iudices nominentur, ex quibus suadente necessitate unus assumi potest ad collegium efformandum; in ceteris casibus hac in re adeatur Sedes Apostolica.

§3. Iudices sint integrae famae, in iure canonico doctores vel saltem licentiati, prudentia et iustitiae zelo probati.

CAN. 1088 §1. Vicarius iudicialis, Vicarius iudicialis adiunctus et ceteri iudices nominantur ad tempus determinatum.

§2. Si tempus determinatum sede eparchiali vacante elapsum est, ii amoveri non possunt, sed in officio perdurant, donec novus Episcopus eparchialis in re providerit.

§3. Si Vicarius iudicialis ab Administratore eparchiae nominatur, adveniente novo Episcopo eparchiali indiget confirmatione.

CAN. 1089 Iudex unicus in quolibet iu-

1087 §1: Pius XII, m.p. *Sollicitudinem Nostram,* 6 ian. 1950, can. 41 §1.

1087 §2: Paulus VI, litt. ap. *Cum matrimonialium,* 8 sep. 1973, V, §1.

1087 §3: Pius XII, m.p. *Sollicitudinem Nostram,* 6 ian. 1950, can. 41 §1; Paulus VI, litt. ap. *Cum matrimonialium,* 8 sep. 1973, VII.

1088 §1: Pius XII, m.p. *Sollicitudinem Nostram,* 6 ian. 1950, cann. 40 §§5–6, 43 §1.

1088 §2: Pius XII, m.p. *Sollicitudinem Nostram,*

6 ian. 1950, can. 40 §§5–6.

1088 §3: Pius XII, m.p. *Sollicitudinem Nostram,* 6 ian. 1950, can. 40 §7.

1089: Pius XII, m.p. *Sollicitudinem Nostram,* 6 ian. 1950, can. 45; Paulus VI, litt. ap. *Cum matrimonialium,* 8 sep. 1973, V, §2, VI–VII; Secret. Status, rescr. 1 oct. 1974. * Syn. prov. Alba-Iulien. et Fagarasien. Rumenorum, a. 1882, tit. II, sect. III, cap. II; tit. V, cap. I, §5. ▲ D. 1, 22; Nov. 60, 2, pr. et 1.

employ two assessors from among the Christian faithful of upright life who consult with him.

CAN. 1090 §1. The judicial vicar is to designate in order by turn two judges from among the eparchial judges who together with the presiding judge constitute the collegiate tribunal, unless the eparchial bishop in his prudence has judged otherwise opportune.

§2. The judicial vicar is not to substitute judges once they have been designated, except for a very serious reason to be expressed for validity in a decree.

CAN. 1091 §1. The judicial vicar or the adjutant judicial vicar presides over the collegiate tribunal insofar as possible.

§2. The president of the collegiate tribunal must designate one of the judges of the same tribunal as the *ponens,* unless he wishes to fulfil this function himself.

§3. The same president can substitute another for the *ponens* for a just cause.

§4. The *ponens* reports about the case at the meeting of the judges and puts the sentence into writing.

CAN. 1092 A single judge has the rights of the tribunal and the presiding judge.

CAN. 1093 §1. A judge or the president of a collegiate tribunal can designate an auditor to instruct the case. The auditor is selected either from among the judges of the tribunal or from among the Christian faithful admitted to this office by the eparchial bishop.

§2. The eparchial bishop can approve for the

dicio duos assessores ex christifidelibus probatae vitae sibi consulentes asciscere potest.

CAN. 1090 §1. Duos iudices, qui una cum praeside tribunal collegiale constituunt, inter iudices eparchiales Vicarius iudicialis designet ex ordine per turnum, nisi pro sua prudentia Episcopus eparchialis aliud opportunum existimavit.

§2. Iudices semel designatos ne subroget Vicarius iudicialis nisi gravissima de causa in decreto ad validitatem exprimenda.

CAN. 1091 §1. Tribunali collegiali praeest, si fieri potest, Vicarius iudicialis vel Vicarius iudicialis adiunctus.

§2. Tribunalis collegialis praeses debet unum de iudicibus eiusdem tribunalis ponentem designare, nisi ipse vult hoc munus implere.

§3. Idem praeses potest ponenti alium iusta de causa substituere.

§4. Ponens in conventu iudicum de causa refert et sententiam scripto redigit.

CAN. 1092 Ad iudicem unicum iura tribunalis et praesidis spectant.

CAN. 1093 §1. Iudex vel tribunalis collegialis praeses possunt auditorem designare ad causae instructionem peragendam eum seligentes aut ex tribunalis iudicibus aut ex christifidelibus ab Episcopo eparchiali ad hoc officium admissis.

§2. Episcopus eparchialis potest ad offi-

1090 §1: Pius XII, m.p. *Sollicitudinem Nostram,* 6 ian. 1950, can. 46 §3.

1091 §1: Pius XII, m.p. *Sollicitudinem Nostram,* 6 ian. 1950, can. 48 §2.

1091 §2: Pius XII, m.p. *Sollicitudinem Nostram,* 6 ian. 1950, can. 49 §1.

1091 §3: Pius XII, m.p. *Sollicitudinem Nostram,* 6 ian. 1950, can. 49 §2.

1091 §4: Pius XII, m.p. *Sollicitudinem Nostram,* 6

ian. 1950, can. 50 §2.

1092: Pius XII, m.p. *Sollicitudinem Nostram,* 6 ian. 1950, can. 453.

1093 §1: Pius XII, m.p. *Sollicitudinem Nostram,* 6 ian. 1950, cann. 52–53; Paulus VI, litt. ap. *Cum matrimonialium,* 8 sep. 1973, VI. * Syn. Armen., a. 1911, 326. ▲ Nov. 60, 2, pr.; 82, 2.

1093 §2: Paulus VI, litt. ap. *Cum matrimonialium,* 8 sep. 1973, VII; Secret. Status, rescr. 1 oct. 1974.

office of auditor members of the Christian faithful outstanding for their good character, prudence and doctrine.

§3. It is for the auditor, according to the mandate of the judge, only to collect the proofs and hand those collected over to the judge. Unless the mandate of the judge prevents it, however, the auditor can in the meantime decide what proofs are to be collected and in which manner, if a question arises about this while the auditor is exercising his or her office.

cium auditoris admittere christifideles, qui bonis moribus, prudentia et doctrina praestant.

§3. Auditoris est secundum iudicis mandatum probationes tantum colligere easque collectas iudici tradere; potest autem, nisi iudicis mandatum obstat, interim decidere, quae et quomodo probationes colligendae sint, si forte de hac re quaestio oritur, dum ipse officium suum exercet.

ART. II. *The Promoter of Justice, the Defender of the Bond and the Notary*

ART. II. *De Promotore Iustitiae, de Defensore Vinculi et de Notario*

CAN. 1094 A promoter of justice is to be appointed in an eparchy for contentious cases that can endanger the public good and for penal cases. The promoter of justice is bound by the obligation to provide for the public good.

CAN. 1095 §1. In contentious cases it is for the eparchial bishop to judge whether or not the public good can be endangered, unless the intervention of the promoter of justice is prescribed by law or it is clearly necessary from the nature of the matter.

§2. If the promoter of justice has intervened in a previous grade of the trial, such intervention is presumed necessary in a further grade.

CAN. 1096 A defender of the bond is to be appointed in an eparchy for cases concerning the nullity of sacred ordination or the nullity or dissolution of a marriage. The defender of the bond is bound by the obligation to propose and explain everything that reasonably can be brought forth against nullity or dissolution.

CAN. 1094 Ad causas contentiosas, in quibus bonum publicum in discrimen vocari potest, et ad causas poenales constituatur ineparchia promotor iustitiae, qui obligatione tenetur providendi bono publico.

CAN. 1095 §1. In causis contentiosis Episcopi eparchialis est iudicare, utrum bonum publicum in discrimen vocari possit necne, nisi interventus promotoris iustitiae iure praecipitur vel ex natura rei evidenter necessarius est.

§2. Si in praecedenti gradu iudicii intervenit promotor iustitiae, in ulteriore gradu huius interventus praesumitur necessarius.

CAN. 1096 Ad causas, in quibus agitur de nullitate sacrae ordinationis aut de nullitate vel solutione matrimonii, constituatur in eparchia defensor vinculi, qui obligatione tenetur proponendi et exponendi omnia, quae rationabiliter adduci possunt adversus nullitatem vel solutionem.

1093 §3: Pius XII, m.p. *Sollicitudinem Nostram,* 6 ian. 1950, can. 54.

1094: Pius XII, m.p. *Sollicitudinem Nostram,* 6 ian. 1950, can. 57.

1095 §1: Pius XII, m.p. *Sollicitudinem Nostram,* 6 ian. 1950, can. 59 §1.

1095 §2: Pius XII, m.p. *Sollicitudinem Nostram,*

6 ian. 1950, can. 59 §2; S.C. de Discip. Sacr., instr. 15 aug. 1936, art. 15, §2.

1096: Pius XII, m.p. *Sollicitudinem Nostram,* 6 ian. 1950, cann. 62, 476, 477. - S.C.S. Off., instr. (ad Ep. Rituum Orient.), a. 1883, tit. II, 7, 10–11; tit. III, 21 et 23; tit. V, 28.

CAN. 1097 If the promoter of justice or the defender of the bond was not cited in cases that require their presence, the acts are null unless they actually took part, even if not cited or, after they have inspected the acts, at least were able to fulfill their office before the sentence.

CAN. 1098 Unless common law expressly provides otherwise:

1° whenever the law requires the judge to hear the parties or either of them, the promoter of justice and the defender of the bond must also be heard if they take part in the trial;

2° whenever the request of a party is required for the judge to decide something, the presence of the promoter of justice or the defender of the bond, who take part in the trial, has the same force.

CAN. 1099 §1. It is for the eparchial bishop to appoint the promoter of justice and defender of the bond; in non-eparchial tribunals, they are appointed in accord with the norm of the tribunal's statutes, unless the law provides otherwise.

§2. The promoter of justice and the defender of the bond are to be Christian faithful of unimpaired reputation, doctors or at least licensed in canon law, and proven in prudence and zeal for justice.

CAN. 1100 §1. The same person can hold the office of promoter of justice and defender of the bond, but not in the same case.

§2. The promoter of justice and the defender of the bond can be appointed for all cases or

CAN. 1097 In causis, in quibus promotoris iustitiae aut defensoris vinculi praesentia requiritur, eis non citatis acta nulla sunt, nisi ipsi, etsi non citati, revera interfuerunt aut saltem ante sententiam actis inspectis officio suo fungi potuerunt.

CAN. 1098 Nisi aliter iure communi expresse cavetur:

1° quoties lex praecipit, ut iudex partes earumve alteram audiat, etiam promotor iustitiae et defensor vinculi, si iudicio intersunt, audiendi sunt;

2° quoties instantia partis requiritur, ut iudex aliquid decernere possit, instantia promotoris iustitiae vel defensoris vinculi, qui iudicio intersunt, eandem vim habet.

CAN. 1099 §1. Episcopi eparchialis est promotorem iustitiae et defensorem vinculi nominare; in tribunalibus non eparchialibus iidem nominantur ad normam statutorum tribunalis, nisi aliter iure cavetur.

§2. Promotor iustitiae et defensor vinculi sint christifideles integrae famae, in iure canonico doctores vel saltem licentiati ac prudentia et iustitiae zelo probati.

CAN. 1100 §1. Eadem persona, non autem in eadem causa, officium promotoris iustitiae et defensoris vinculi gerere potest.

§2. Promotor iustitiae et defensor vinculi constitui possunt ad universitatem causarum

---

1097: Pius XII, m.p. *Sollicitudinem Nostram,* 6 ian. 1950, can. 63 §§1–2.

1098: Pius XII, m.p. *Sollicitudinem Nostram,* 6 ian. 1950, can. 64.

1099 §1: Pius XII, m.p. *Sollicitudinem Nostram,* 6 ian. 1950, can. 66 §1; Paulus VI, rescr. 26 mar. 1976; Sign. Apost., decl. 12 nov. 1977.

1099 §2: Pius XII, m.p. *Sollicitudinem Nostram,* 6 ian. 1950, can. 66 §1.

1100 §1: Pius XII, m.p. *Sollicitudinem Nostram,* 6 ian. 1950, can. 65 §1.

1100 §2: Pius XII, m.p. *Sollicitudinem Nostram,* 6 ian. 1950, cann. 65 §2, 67 §2.

for individual cases; however, the eparchial bishop can remove them for a just cause.

CAN. 1101 §1. A notary is to take part in any process, so much so that the acts are to be considered null if the notary has not signed them.

§2. Acts that notaries prepare warrant public trust.

ART. III. *The Officers of the Tribunals Taken from Different Eparchies or Churches* Sui Iuris

CAN. 1102 §1. Judges and other officers of the tribunals can be taken from any eparchy, religious institute or society of common life in the manner of religious, of one's own or even of another Church *sui iuris,* with the written consent, however, of the proper eparchial bishop or major superior.

§2. Unless the mandate of delegation states otherwise, a delegated judge can ask for the assistance of officers living within the territory of the person mandating.

CHAPTER III. **The Obligations of Judges and Other Tribunal Officials**

CAN. 1103 §1. All the Christian faithful, but especially bishops, are to strive diligently to avoid litigation among the people of God as much as possible, without prejudice to justice, or to resolve litigation peacefully as soon as possible.

§2. Whenever the judge perceives some hope

vel ad singulas causas; possunt vero ab Episcopo eparchiali iusta de causa amoveri.

CAN. 1101 §1. Cuilibet processui intersit notarius ita, ut nulla habeantur acta, si non sunt ab eo subscripta.

§2. Acta, quae notarii conficiunt, publicam fidem faciunt.

ART. III. *De Administris Tribunalium ex Diversis Eparchiis vel Ecclesiis Sui Iuris Assumendis*

CAN. 1102 §1. Iudices aliique administri tribunalium assumi possunt ex qualibet eparchia vel instituto religioso vel societate vitae communis ad instar religiosorum propriae vel etiam alterius Ecclesiae sui iuris de consensu vero scripto dato proprii Episcopi eparchialis vel Superioris maioris.

§2. Iudex delegatus, nisi aliud fert delegationis mandatum, uti potest auxilio administrorum intra territorium mandantis degentium.

CAPUT III. **De Obligationibus Iudicum et Aliorum Administrorum Tribunalium**

CAN. 1103 §1. Christifideles omnes, in primis autem Episcopi, sedulo annitantur, ut salva iustitia lites in populo Dei, quatenus fieri potest, vitentur vel pacifice quam primum componantur.

§2. Iudex in limine litis et etiam quolibet

1101 §1: Pius XII, m.p. *Sollicitudinem Nostram,* 6 ian. 1950, can. 56 §1.

1101 §2: Pius XII, m.p. *Cleri sanctitati,* 2 iun. 1957, can. 440 §1. * Syn. Libanen. Maronitarum, a. 1736, pars III, cap. V, 2–3; Syn. Armen., a. 1911, 323.

1102 §1: Pius XII, m.p. *Sollicitudinem Nostram,* 6 ian. 1950, can. 71.

1102 §2: Pius XII, m.p. *Sollicitudinem Nostram,* 6 ian. 1950, can. 93.

1103 §1: Pius XII, m.p. *Sollicitudinem Nostram,* 6 ian. 1950, can. 94 §1. ▲ Instit. 4, 16, pr.

1103 §2: Pius XII, m.p. *Sollicitudinem Nostram,* 6 ian. 1950, can. 94 §2.

of a favorable outcome at the start of the litigation or even at any other time, the judge is not to neglect to encourage and assist the parties to collaborate in seeking an equitable solution to the controversy and to indicate to them suitable means to this end, even by using reputable persons for mediation.

§3. However, if the case concerns the private good of the parties, the judge is to discern whether the controversy can be concluded advantageously by an out-of-court settlement or arbitration.

CAN. 1104 §1. A competent judge must offer his ministry to a party legitimately requesting it.

§2. A judge cannot adjudicate any case unless the party concerned or the promoter of justice has made a petition according to the norm of the canons.

CAN. 1105 A person who has taken part in a case as a judge, promoter of justice, defender of the bond, procurator, advocate, witness or expert cannot later in another grade of the trial validly decide the same case as a judge or perform the function of assessor.

CAN. 1106 §1. A judge is not to undertake the adjudication of a case in which the judge is involved by reason of consanguinity or affinity in any degree of the direct line and up to the fourth degree inclusive of the collateral line, or by reason of guardianship, curatorship, close friendship, great animosity, the making of a profit or the avoidance of a loss.

alio momento, quoties spem boni exitus perspicit, partes hortari et adiuvare ne omittat, ut de aequa controversiae solutione quaerenda communi consilio curent, viasque ad hoc propositum assequendum idoneas ipsis indicet gravibus quoque hominibus ad mediationem adhibitis.

§3. Si vero circa bonum privatum partium causa versatur, dispiciat iudex, num transactione vel per compromissum in arbitros controversia finem habere utiliter possit.

CAN. 1104 §1. Iudex competens parti legitime requirenti suum ministerium praestare debet.

§2. Iudex nullam causam cognoscere potest, nisi petitio ad normam canonum facta est ab eo, cuius interest, vel a promotore iustitiae.

CAN. 1105 Qui causae interfuit tamquam iudex, promotor iustitiae, defensor vinculi, procurator, advocatus, testis aut peritus non potest postea valide eandem causam in alio gradu iudicii tamquam iudex definire aut in eodem munus assessoris agere.

CAN. 1106 §1. Iudex cognoscendam ne suscipiat causam, in qua ratione consanguinitatis vel affinitatis in quolibet gradu lineae rectae et usque ad quartum gradum inclusive lineae collateralis vel ratione tutelae et curatelae, intimae vitae consuetudinis, magnae simultatis vel lucri faciendi aut damni vitandi aliquid ipsius interest.

1104 §1: Pius XII, m.p. *Sollicitudinem Nostram,* 6 ian. 1950, can. 123.

1104 §2: Pius XII, m.p. *Sollicitudinem Nostram,* 6 ian. 1950, can. 226. * Syn. prov. Alba-Iulien. et Fagarasien. Rumenorum, a. 1872, tit. V, cap. II, §16.

1105: Pius XII, m.p. *Sollicitudinem Nostram,* 6 ian. 1950, can. 35.

1106 §1: Pius XII, m.p. *Sollicitudinem Nostram,* 6 ian. 1950, can. 128 §1. ▲ D. 2, 1, 10; 47, 10, 5, pr.

§2. In the same circumstances, the promoter of justice, the defender of the bond, the assessor, and the auditor must abstain from their office.

CAN. 1107 §1. If an objection is lodged against a judge of either an ordinary or delegated tribunal, even if the judge is competent, the exception is handled by the authority to which the tribunal is subject, without prejudice to can. 1062, §§2 and 5.

§2. If the eparchial bishop is the judge and the objection is lodged against him, he is to abstain from judging.

§3. If the objection is lodged against other officials of the tribunal, the president of the collegiate tribunal or the single judge deals with this exception.

CAN. 1108 If the objection is accepted, the persons must be changed but not the grade of the trial.

CAN. 1109 §1. The question of an objection must be decided most expeditiously after the parties have been heard.

§2. Acts placed by a judge before an objection is lodged are valid, but those acts placed after the objection has been lodged must be rescinded if a party requests it within ten days from the admission of the objection; after the admission of the objection, the acts are invalid.

CAN. 1110 §1. In a matter that concerns private persons only, a judge can proceed only at the request of a party. However, once a case has been legitimately introduced, a judge can

§2. In eisdem adiunctis ab officio suo abstinere debent promotor iustitiae, defensor vinculi, assessor et auditor.

CAN. 1107 §1. Si iudex sive in tribunali ordinario sive delegato, etsi competens, recusatur, auctoritas, cui tribunal immediate subiectum est, hanc exceptionem definiat salvo can. 1062, §§2 et 5.

§2. Si Episcopus eparchialis est iudex et contra eum recusatio opponitur, abstineat a iudicando.

§3. Si recusatio opponitur contra ceteros tribunalis administros, de hac exceptione videat praeses in tribunali collegiali vel iudex, si unicus est.

CAN. 1108 Recusatione admissa personae mutari debent, non vero gradus iudicii.

CAN. 1109 §1. Quaestio de recusatione expeditissime definienda est auditis partibus.

§2. Actus positi a iudice, antequam recusatur, validi sunt; qui autem positi sunt post propositam recusationem, rescindi debent, si pars petit, intra decem dies ab admissa recusatione computandos; post admissam recusationem invalidi sunt.

CAN. 1110 §1. In negotio, quod privatorum solummodo interest, iudex procedere potest dumtaxat ad instantiam partis; causa autem legitime introducta iudex procedere

1106 §2: Pius XII, m.p. *Sollicitudinem Nostram,* 6 ian. 1950, can. 128 §2.

1107 §1: Pius XII, m.p. *Sollicitudinem Nostram,* 6 ian. 1950, can. 129 §1. - Constantinop. IV, can. 26; S. Cyrillus Alexandrin., can. 1; S. Nicolaus I, litt. *Proposueramus quidem,* a. 865, "Igitur quia." * Syn. Alexandrin. Coptorum, a. 1898, sect. III, cap. VI, tit. V, art. X, 5. ▲ C. 3, 1, 16; 7, 62, 30.

1107 §2: Pius XII, m.p. *Sollicitudinem Nostram,* 6 ian. 1950, can. 129 §2.

1107 §3: Pius XII, m.p. *Sollicitudinem Nostram,* 6 ian. 1950, can. 129 §3.

1108: Pius XII, m.p. *Sollicitudinem Nostram,* 6 ian. 1950, can. 130 §2.

1109 §1: Pius XII, m.p. *Sollicitudinem Nostram,* 6 ian. 1950, can. 131. * Syn. Alexandrin. Coptorum, a. 1898, sect. III, cap. VI, tit. V, art. X, 6.

1110 §1: Pius XII, m.p. *Sollicitudinem Nostram,* 6 ian. 1950, cann. 133, 134 §2.

and must proceed, even *ex officio,* in penal and in other cases that regard the public good of the Church or the salvation of souls.

§2. Furthermore, the judge can supply for the negligence of the parties in furnishing proofs or in lodging exceptions whenever the judge considers it necessary in order to avoid a gravely unjust sentence, with due regard for can. 1283.

CAN. 1111 Judges and tribunals are to take care that, with due regard for justice, all cases are concluded as soon as possible so that in the first grade of the trial they are not prolonged beyond a year, and on the appellate level not beyond six months.

CAN. 1112 All persons who constitute a tribunal or assist it must make a promise that they will fulfill their function faithfully.

CAN. 1113 §1. Judges and tribunal personnel are always bound to observe secrecy in a penal trial as well as in a contentious trial if the revelation of some procedural act could bring disadvantage to the parties.

§2. They are also always bound, and with respect to all people, to observe secrecy concerning the discussion among the judges in a collegiate tribunal before the sentence is passed and concerning the various votes and opinions expressed there. All those to whom knowledge of this comes in any way are also bound to this secrecy.

§3. Moreover, whenever the nature of the

potest et debet, etiam ex officio, in causis poenalibus et aliis causis, quae ad bonum publicum Ecclesiae aut ad salutem animarum spectant.

§2. Potest autem praeterea iudex partium neglegentiam in probationibus afferendis vel in exceptionibus opponendis supplere, quoties id necessarium censet ad vitandam graviter iniustam sententiam firmo can. 1283.

CAN. 1111 Iudices et tribunalia curent, ut quam primum salva iustitia causae omnes terminentur ita, ut in primo gradu iudicii ultra annum ne protrahantur, in gradu appellationis vero non ultra sex menses.

CAN. 1112 Omnes, qui tribunal constituunt aut eidem opem ferunt, promissionem de munere fideliter implendo facere debent.

CAN. 1113 §1. In iudicio poenali semper, in iudicio contentioso autem, si ex revelatione alicuius actus processualis praeiudicium partibus obvenire potest, iudices et tribunalis adiutores tenentur secretum servare.

§2. Tenentur etiam semper et erga omnes ad secretum servandum de discussione, quae inter iudices in tribunali collegiali ante ferendam sententiam habetur, tum etiam de variis suffragiis et opinionibus ibidem prolatis; ad hoc secretum tenentur etiam alii omnes, ad quos notitia de re quoquo modo pervenit.

§3. Immo, quoties natura causae vel pro-

1110 §2: Pius XII, m.p. *Sollicitudinem Nostram,* 6 ian. 1950, can. 134 §1. ▲ C. 2, 10 (11); Basilic. 8, 1, 43.

1111: Pius XII, m.p. *Sollicitudinem Nostram,* 6 ian. 1950, can. 135. * Syn. Alexandrin. Coptorum, a. 1898, sect. III, cap. VI, tit. V, art. X, 1. ▲ C. 3, 1, 12, pr.; 3, 1, 13, pr., (1 et 8a); 9, 44, 3.

1112: Pius XII, m.p. *Sollicitudinem Nostram,* 6 ian. 1950, cann. 136–137. - S.C.S. Off., instr. (ad Ep. Rituum Orient.), a. 1883, tit. II, 10; tit. III, 12. ▲ D. 4,

3, 21; C. 4, 1, 12, (4b).

1113 §1: Pius XII, m.p. *Sollicitudinem Nostram,* 6 ian. 1950, can. 138 §1.

1113 §2: Pius XII, m.p. *Sollicitudinem Nostram,* 6 ian. 1950, can. 138 §2.

1113 §3: Pius XII, m.p. *Sollicitudinem Nostram,* 6 ian. 1950, can. 138 §3. - S.C.S. Off., instr. 20 feb. 1866, 14; instr. (ad Ep. Rituum Orient.), a. 1883, tit. III, 12.

case or the proofs is such that disclosure of the acts or proofs would endanger the reputation of others, provide opportunity for discord or give rise to scandal or some other disadvantage, the judge can bind the witnesses, the experts, the parties and their advocates or procurators by oath to observe secrecy.

CAN. 1114 The judge and all other officials of the tribunal are prohibited from accepting any gifts whatsoever on the occasion of their acting in a trial.

CAN. 1115 §1. The competent authority can punish with appropriate penalties, not excluding privation from office, judges who refuse to render a judgment even though they are certainly and obviously competent, who declare themselves competent with no supporting prescript of law and adjudicate and decide cases, who violate the law of secrecy, or who inflict some other damage on the parties by way of fraud or grave negligence.

§2. Other officials and personnel of a tribunal can also be punished with the same penalties if they fail in their office as described above. The judge can also punish all of them.

CAN. 1116 If the judge foresees that the petitioner will probably reject the ecclesiastical sentence, if it should be contrary to the petitioner, and therefore that the rights of the respondent would not be sufficiently protected, the judge can, at the request of the respondent or even *ex officio,* impose an appropriate security on the petitioner for the observance of the ecclesiastical sentence.

bationum talis est, ut ex actorum vel probationum evulgatione aliorum fama periclitetur vel praebeatur ansa dissidiis aut scandalum aliudve huius generis incommodum oriatur, iudex potest testes, peritos, partes earumque advocatos vel procuratores iureiurando obligare ad secretum servandum.

CAN. 1114 Iudex et omnes alii administri tribunalis occasione agendi iudicii dona quaevis acceptare prohibentur.

CAN. 1115 §1. Iudices, qui, etsi certe et evidenter competentes sunt, ius reddere recusant vel nullo suffragante iuris praescripto se competentes declarant atque causas cognoscunt ac definiunt vel secretum lege praescriptum violant vel ex dolo aut gravi neglegentia aliud partibus damnum inferunt, congruis poenis ab auctoritate competenti puniri possunt non exclusa officii privatione.

§2. Eisdem poenis puniri possunt etiam ceteri administri tribunalis et adiutores, si officio suo, ut supra, defuerunt; quos omnes etiam iudex punire potest.

CAN. 1116 Si iudex praevidet actorem probabiliter spreturum esse sententiam ecclesiasticam, cum forte haec eidem est contraria, et idcirco iuribus partis conventae non satis consultum iri, potest ad instantiam partis conventae vel etiam ex officio actori congruam cautionem imponere pro observantia sententiae ecclesiasticae.

1114: Pius XII, m.p. *Sollicitudinem Nostram,* 6 ian. 1950, can. 139. - S.C.S. Off., decr. 24 sep. 1665, prop. 26 damn. * Syn. Armen., a. 1911, 282.

1115 §1: Pius XII, m.p. *Sollicitudinem Nostram,* 6 ian. 1950, can. 140 §§1–2. * Syn. Zamosten. Ruthenorum, a. 1720, tit. VII; Syn. Libanen. Maronitarum, a.

1736, pars III, cap. IV, 32, X. ▲ C. 3, 1, 13, (8).

1115 §2: Pius XII, m.p. *Sollicitudinem Nostram,* 6 ian. 1950, can. 140 §3. * Syn. Libanen. Maronitarum, a. 1736, pars III, cap. IV, 32, X.

1116: Pius XII, m.p. *Sollicitudinem Nostram,* 6 ian. 1950, can. 141.

CHAPTER IV. The Order of Adjudication

CAN. 1117 Cases are to be adjudicated in the order in which they were presented and put on the docket, unless one of them requires speedier treatment than others. This fact must be established in a special decree that gives the substantiating reasons.

CAN. 1118 §1. Defects that can render a sentence null can be introduced as exceptions at any stage or grade of a trial; a judge can likewise declare them *ex officio.*

§2. Dilatory exceptions, especially those that regard the persons and the manner of the trial, are to be proposed before the joinder of issue unless they emerged after the issue was already joined; they must be decided as soon as possible.

CAN. 1119 §1. If an exception is proposed against the competence of the judge, that judge must deal with the matter.

§2. In the case of an exception of relative incompetence, if the judge finds for competence, the decision does not admit of appeal, but it can be attacked by way of a complaint of nullity, *restitutio in integrum,* or intervention of a third party.

§3. If the judge finds for incompetence, however, the party who feels aggrieved, can appeal to the appellate tribunal within fifteen useful days.

CAN. 1120 A judge who becomes aware of being absolutely incompetent at any stage of the trial must declare his or her incompetence.

CAPUT IV. De Ordine Cognitionum

CAN. 1117 Causae cognoscendae sunt eo ordine, quo fuerunt propositae et in albo inscriptae, nisi ex eis aliqua celerem prae ceteris expeditionem exigit, quod quidem speciali decreto rationibus suffulto statuendum est.

CAN. 1118 §1. Vitia, quibus sententiae nullitas haberi potest, in quolibet statu vel gradu iudicii excipi possunt itemque a iudice ex officio declarari.

§2. Exceptiones dilatoriae vero eae praesertim, quae respiciunt personas et modum iudicii, proponendae sunt ante litis contestationem, nisi lite iam contestata emerserunt, et quam primum definiendae.

CAN. 1119 §1. Si exceptio proponitur contra iudicis competentiam, hac de re ipse iudex videre debet.

§2. In casu exceptionis de incompetentia relativa, si iudex se competentem pronuntiat, eius decisio non admittit appellationem, sed impugnari potest per querelam nullitatis, restitutionem in integrum vel oppositionem tertii.

§3. Si vero iudex se incompetentem declarat, pars, quae se gravatam censet, potest intra quindecim dies utiles provocare ad tribunal appellationis.

CAN. 1120 Iudex in quovis statu iudicii se absolute incompetentem agnoscens suam incompetentiam declarare debet.

1117: Pius XII, m.p. *Sollicitudinem Nostram,* 6 ian. 1950, can. 142.

1118 §1: Pius XII, m.p. *Sollicitudinem Nostram,* 6 ian. 1950, can. 143 §2.

1118 §2: Pius XII, m.p. *Sollicitudinem Nostram,* 6 ian. 1950, can. 143 §1. ▲ Instit. 4, 13, 8 (7)–11 (10); D. 44, 1, 2, (4) et 3; C. 3, 1, 12, (1); 4, 19, 19; 8, 35 (36), 13.

1119 §1: Pius XII, m.p. *Sollicitudinem Nostram,* 6 ian. 1950, can. 125 §1.

1119 §2: Pius XII, m.p. *Sollicitudinem Nostram,* 6 ian. 1950, can. 125 §2.

1119 §3: Pius XII, m.p. *Sollicitudinem Nostram,* 6 ian. 1950, can. 125 §3.

1120: Pius XII, m.p. *Sollicitudinem Nostram,* 6 ian. 1950, can. 126.

CAN. 1121 §1. Exceptions of *res iudicata,* out-of-court settlement, and the other peremptory exceptions, which are called *litis finitae,* must be proposed and adjudicated before the joinder of issue. A person who raises them later must not be rejected but is liable for expenses unless the person proves that the presentation was not delayed maliciously.

§2. Other peremptory exceptions are to be proposed at the joinder of issue and must be treated at the proper time according to the norms for incidental questions.

CAN. 1122 §1. Counterclaims can be proposed validly only within thirty days from the joinder of the issue.

§2. Counterclaims are to be adjudicated, however, along with the principal action, that is, at the same grade of trial with it, unless it is necessary to adjudicate them separately or the judge considers it more opportune to do so.

CAN. 1123 Questions concerning security for judicial expenses or granting gratuitous legal assistance that has been requested from the very beginning, and other such questions as a rule must be dealt with before the joinder of the issue.

CHAPTER V. Time Limits, Delays and the Place of a Trial

CAN. 1124 §1. The time limits set by law for extinguishing rights cannot be extended

CAN. 1121 §1. Exceptiones rei iudicatae, transactionis et aliae peremptoriae, quae dicuntur litis finitae, proponi et cognosci debent ante litis contestationem; qui serius eas opposuit, non est reiciendus, sed expensas iudiciales solvere debet, nisi probat se oppositionem malitiose non distulisse.

§2. Aliae exceptiones peremptoriae proponantur in litis contestatione et suo tempore tractandae sunt secundum normas circa quaestiones incidentes.

CAN. 1122 §1. Actiones reconventionales proponi valide non possunt nisi intra triginta dies a lite contestata computandos.

§2. Actiones reconventionales autem cognoscantur simul cum actione principali, hoc est pari gradu iudicii cum ea, nisi eas separatim cognoscere necessarium est aut iudex id opportunius existimat.

CAN. 1123 Quaestiones de cautione pro expensis iudicialibus praestanda aut de concessione gratuiti patrocinii, quod statim ab initio postulatum est, et aliae huiusmodi regulariter videndae sunt ante litis contestationem.

CAPUT V. De Iudicii Terminis, Dilationibus et Loco

CAN. 1124 §1. Termini perimendis iuribus a lege constituti prorogari non pos-

---

1121 §1: Pius XII, m.p. *Sollicitudinem Nostram,* 6 ian. 1950, can. 144 §1. ▲ Instit. 4, 13, 8 (7)–11 (10); D. 44, 1, 2, (4) et 3; C. 7, 50, 2; 8, 35 (36), 8.

1121 §2: Pius XII, m.p. *Sollicitudinem Nostram,* 6 ian. 1950, can. 144 §2.

1122 §1: Pius XII, m.p. *Sollicitudinem Nostram,* 6 ian. 1950, can. 145 §1.

1122 §2: Pius XII, m.p. *Sollicitudinem Nostram,* 6 ian. 1950, can. 145 §2.

1123: Pius XII, m.p. *Sollicitudinem Nostram,* 6 ian. 1950, can. 146.

1124 §1: Pius XII, m.p. *Sollicitudinem Nostram,* 6 ian. 1950, can. 149 §1. - Carth. can. 20. ▲ C. 7, 63, 2; Nov. 115, 2; Basilic. 9, 1, 130.

nor validly shortened unless the parties request it.

§2. Before they have lapsed, though, other time limits can be extended by the judge for a just cause after having heard the parties or if they request it. However, such time limits can never be shortened validly unless the parties agree.

§3. Nevertheless, the judge is to take care that the trial does not last too long on account of such extensions.

CAN. 1125 If the law does not establish time limits for completing procedural acts, the judge must define them after having taken into consideration the nature of each act.

CAN. 1126 If the tribunal is closed on the day scheduled for a judicial act, the time limit is extended to the first day following that is not a holiday.

CAN. 1127 Insofar as possible, the tribunal is to be in a permanent location open during stated hours, while observing the norms established by particular law in this matter.

CAN. 1128 §1. A judge expelled by force from his territory or impeded from the exercise of judicial power there can exercise that power and render a sentence outside that territory. However, the judge should inform the eparchial bishop of the place regarding this fact.

§2. In addition, for a just cause and after hearing the parties, the judge can go even outside his or her territory to acquire proofs, however, with the permission of the eparchial bishop of the place where the judge goes and in the location designated by the bishop.

sunt neque valide nisi petentibus partibus coartari.

§2. Ceteri autem termini, antequam elapsi sunt, possunt iusta de causa a iudice auditis vel petentibus partibus prorogari, numquam autem nisi partibus consentientibus valide coartari.

§3. Caveat tamen iudex, ne iudicium nimis diuturnum fiat ex prorogatione.

CAN. 1125 Si lex terminos non statuit ad actus processuales peragendos, iudex illos determinare debet habita ratione naturae uniuscuiusque actus.

CAN. 1126 Si die ad actum iudicialem indicto vacavit tribunal, terminus intellegitur prorogatus ad primum sequentem diem non feriatum.

CAN. 1127 Sedes tribunalis sit, si fieri potest, stabilis quae statutis horis pateat servatis normis iure particulari de hac re statutis.

CAN. 1128 §1. Iudex ex territorio suo vi expulsus vel a potestate iudiciali ibi exercenda impeditus potest extra territorium potestatem suam exercere et sententiam ferre certiore tamen hac de re facto loci Episcopo eparchiali.

§2. Praeterea iudex iusta de causa et auditis partibus potest ad probationes acquirendas etiam extra proprium territorium se conferre de licentia tamen Episcopi eparchialis loci adeundi et in sede ab ipso designata.

1124 §2: Pius XII, m.p. *Sollicitudinem Nostram,* 6 ian. 1950, can. 149 §2. ▲ D. 2, 12, 7 et 10; C. 3, 11, 1 et 4.

1124 §3: Pius XII, m.p. *Sollicitudinem Nostram,* 6 ian. 1950, can. 149 §3.

1126: Pius XII, m.p. *Sollicitudinem Nostram,* 6

ian. 1950, can. 150. ▲ C. 3, 11, 3.

1127: Pius XII, m.p. *Sollicitudinem Nostram,* 6 ian. 1950, cann. 151, 153 §1.

1128 §1: Pius XII, m.p. *Sollicitudinem Nostram,* 6 ian. 1950, can. 152. - Quinisext. can. 37.

CHAPTER VI. **Persons to be Admitted to the Trial and the Manner of Preparing and Preserving the Acts**

CAN. 1129 §1. Unless the particular law of the Church *sui iuris* expressly provides otherwise, while cases are being heard before a tribunal, only those persons are to be present in court whom the law or the judge has established are necessary to expedite the process.

§2. A judge can punish with appropriate penalties all who are present at the trial and who are gravely lacking in the respect and obedience due the tribunal, after having given a warning in vain. In addition, the judge can even suspend advocates and procurators from exercising their function before ecclesiastical tribunals.

CAN. 1130 If a person to be questioned speaks a language that is unknown to the judge or the parties, a sworn interpreter designated by the judge is to be used. However, the statements are to be put into writing in the original language and a translation is to be added. An interpreter is also to be used if a hearing or speech impaired person must be questioned, unless the judge prefers that the person answer the questions in writing.

CAN. 1131 §1. All judicial acts, whether the acts of the case, that is, those acts that concern the merits of the question, or the acts of the process, that is, those that pertain to the manner of proceeding, must be put into writing.

§2. The individual pages of the acts are to be numbered and authenticated with a seal.

CAPUT VI. **De Personis in Aulam Admittendis et de Modo Conficiendi et Asservandi Acta**

CAN. 1129 §1. Nisi aliter iure particulari Ecclesiae sui iuris expresse cavetur, dum causae coram tribunali aguntur, ii tantummodo assint in aula, quos lex aut iudex ad processum expediendum necessarios esse statuit.

§2. Omnes iudicio assistentes, qui reverentiae et oboedientiae tribunali debitae graviter defuerunt, iudex potest monitione in cassum facta congruis poenis punire, advocatos praeterea et procuratores etiam a munere apud tribunalia ecclesiastica exercendo suspendere.

CAN. 1130 Si qua persona interroganda utitur lingua iudici vel partibus ignota, adhibeatur interpres iuratus a iudice designatus; declarationes tamen scripto redigantur lingua originaria et translatio addatur; interpres etiam adhibeatur, si surdus vel mutus interrogari debet, nisi forte mavult iudex quaestionibus a se datis scripto respondeatur.

CAN. 1131 §1. Omnia acta iudicialia sive ea, quae meritum quaestionis respiciunt, seu acta causae, sive ea, quae ad formam procedendi pertinent, seu acta processus, scripto redacta esse debent.

§2. Singula folia actorum numerentur et authenticitatis signo muniantur.

1129 §1: Pius XII, m.p. *Sollicitudinem Nostram,* 6 ian. 1950, can. 155 §1.

1129 §2: Pius XII, m.p. *Sollicitudinem Nostram,* 6 ian. 1950, can. 155 §2.

1130: Pius XII, m.p. *Sollicitudinem Nostram,* 6 ian. 1950, can. 156.

1131 §1: Pius XII, m.p. *Sollicitudinem Nostram,* 6 ian. 1950, can. 157 §1.

1131 §2: Pius XII, m.p. *Sollicitudinem Nostram,* 6 ian. 1950, can. 158 §1.

CAN. 1132 Whenever the signature of the parties or witnesses is required for judicial acts and a party or a witness is unable or unwilling to sign them, this is to be noted in the acts. The judge and the notary are also to attest that the act was read to the party or witness verbatim and that the party or witness was either unable or unwilling to sign it.

CAN. 1133 §1. At the completion of the trial, documents that are the property of private persons must be returned, but a copy of them is to be retained.

§2. The chancellor and notaries are forbidden to furnish a copy of the judicial acts and documents that have been acquired for the process without a mandate from the judge.

§3. Anonymous letters must be destroyed nor is mention to be made of them in the acts. Likewise, any other writings and signed letters that add nothing to the merits of the case, or are certainly calumnious, are to be destroyed.

CHAPTER VII. The Petitioner and the Respondent

CAN. 1134 Anyone, either baptized or non-baptized, can bring an action. However, a party who is legitimately summoned must respond.

CAN. 1135 Although a petitioner or respondent has appointed a procurator or an advocate, they themselves are nevertheless always bound to be present at the trial when the law or the judge prescribes it.

CAN. 1132 Quoties in actis iudicialibus partium aut testium subscriptio requiritur, si pars aut testis eis subscribere non potest vel non vult, id in ipsis actis adnotetur simulque iudex et notarius fidem faciant actum ipsum de verbo ad verbum parti aut testi perlectum esse et partem aut testem ei vel non potuisse vel noluisse subscribere.

CAN. 1133 §1. Iudicio expleto documenta, quae in privatorum dominio sunt, restitui debent retento tamen eorum exemplari.

§2. Cancellarius et notarii sine iudicis mandato tradere prohibentur exemplar actorum iudicialium et documentorum, quae sunt processui acquisita.

§3. Anonymae epistulae destrui debent neque de eis mentio fiat in actis; eodem modo destrui debent quaelibet alia scripta et epistulae subscriptae, quae nihil ad causae meritum conferunt vel sunt certo calumniosae.

CAPUT VII. De Actore et de Parte Conventa

CAN. 1134 Quilibet sive baptizatus sive non baptizatus potest in iudicio agere; pars autem legitime conventa respondere debet.

CAN. 1135 Etsi actor vel pars conventa procuratorem vel advocatum constituit, semper tamen tenetur in iudicio ipse adesse ad praescriptum iuris vel iudicis.

1132: Pius XII, m.p. *Sollicitudinem Nostram,* 6 ian. 1950, can. 158 §3.

1133 §1: Pius XII, m.p. *Sollicitudinem Nostram,* 6 ian. 1950, can. 160 §1.

1133 §2: Pius XII, m.p. *Sollicitudinem Nostram,* 6 ian. 1950, can. 160 §3.

1133 §3: Pius XII, m.p. *Sollicitudinem Nostram,* 6 ian. 1950, can. 160 §2.

1134: Pius XII, m.p. *Sollicitudinem Nostram,* 6 ian. 1950, can. 161; Pont. Comm. Decr. Conc. Vat. II Interpr., resp. 8 ian. 1973; Sign. Apost., decl. 31 oct. 1977. ▲ D. 3, 1, 1; 5, 1, 13.

1135: Pius XII, m.p. *Sollicitudinem Nostram,* 6 ian. 1950, can. 162.

CAN. 1136 §1. Minors and those who lack the use of reason can stand trial only through their parents or guardians or curators.

§2. If the judge decides that their rights are in conflict with the rights of the parents, guardians or curators, or that the latter cannot adequately protect the rights of the former, then they are to stand trial through a guardian or curator appointed by the judge.

§3. But in spiritual cases and in cases connected with spiritual matters, if minors have attained the use of reason, they can act and respond without the consent of their parents or guardian. If they have completed their fourteenth year of age, they can do so on their own; if not, through a guardian appointed by the judge.

§4. Those deprived of the administration of goods and those of diminished mental capacity can stand trial personally only to answer to their own delicts or at the order of the judge. In other cases, they must act and respond through their curators.

CAN. 1137 Whenever a guardian or curator appointed by civil authority is present, the ecclesiastical judge can admit the guardian or curator after having heard, if possible, the eparchial bishop of the person to whom the guardian or curator was given. However, if the guardian or curator is not present or does not seem admissible, the judge is to designate a guardian or curator for the case.

CAN. 1138 §1. Juridic persons stand trial through their legitimate representatives.

CAN. 1136 §1. Minores et ii, qui usu rationis destituti sunt, stare in iudicio tantummodo possunt per eorum parentes aut tutores vel curatores.

§2. Si iudex existimat eorum iura esse in conflictu cum iuribus parentum vel tutorum vel curatorum aut hos non satis tueri posse ipsorum iura, tunc stent in iudicio per tutorem vel curatorem a iudice constitutum.

§3. Sed in causis spiritualibus et cum spiritualibus conexis, si minores usum rationis assecuti sunt, agere et respondere possunt sine parentum vel tutoris consensu et quidem per se ipsi, si aetatem quattuordecim annorum expleverunt; secus per tutorem a iudice constitutum.

§4. Bonis interdicti et ii, qui minus firmae mentis sunt, stare in iudicio per se ipsi possunt tantummodo, ut de propriis delictis respondeant aut ad praescriptum iudicis; in ceteris agere et respondere debent per suum curatorem.

CAN. 1137 Quoties adest tutor aut curator ab auctoritate civili constitutus, idem potest a iudice ecclesiastico admitti audito, si fieri potest, Episcopo eparchiali eius, cui datus est; si vero non adest aut non videtur admittendus, ipse iudex tutorem aut curatorem pro causa designet.

CAN. 1138 §1. Personae iuridicae in iudicio stant per suos legitimos repraesentantes.

1136 §1: Pius XII, m.p. *Sollicitudinem Nostram*, 6 ian. 1950, can. 163 §1. ▲ D. 3, 1, 1–5; 22, 6, 10; 42, 1, 45, (2); C. 3, 6, 1.

1136 §2: Pius XII, m.p. *Sollicitudinem Nostram*, 6 ian. 1950, can. 163 §2. ▲ Instit. 1, 21, 3; D. 26, 1, 3, (2–4).

1136 §3: Pius XII, m.p. *Sollicitudinem Nostram*, 6 ian. 1950, can. 163 §3.

1136 §4: Pius XII, m.p. *Sollicitudinem Nostram*, 6 ian. 1950, can. 165. ▲ D. 3, 1, 1, (2–4); 27, 10, 1.

1137: Pius XII, m.p. *Sollicitudinem Nostram*, 6 ian. 1950, can. 166.

1138 §1: Pius XII, m.p. *Sollicitudinem Nostram*, 6

§2. Whenever goods are at stake, for whose alienation someone's consent or counsel or permission is required, the same consent or counsel or permission is also required to begin the trial or to contest it.

§3. However, in a case where there is no representative or the representative is negligent, the hierarch himself can, personally or through another, stand trial in the name of the juridic persons subject to his power.

CHAPTER VIII. **Procurators for the Trial and Advocates**

CAN. 1139 §1. A party can freely appoint a procurator and an advocate. However, the party can also act and respond personally, unless the judge has decided that the services of a procurator or an advocate are necessary.

§2. However, in a penal trial, the accused must always have an advocate, either appointed personally or assigned by the judge.

§3. In a contentious trial that involves minors or a case in which the public good is at risk, marriage cases excepted, the judge is to appoint *ex officio* an advocate for a party who does not have one.

CAN. 1140 §1. A party can appoint only one procurator, who cannot substitute another for himself or herself, unless permission to do so has been given in writing.

§2. However, if for some just cause, several procurators are appointed by the same party,

§2. Quoties in periculo versantur bona, ad quae alienanda alicuius consensus vel consilium vel licentia requiritur, idem consensus vel consilium vel licentia requiritur etiam ad litem incohandam vel contestandam.

§3. In casu vero defectus vel neglegentiae repraesentantis potest ipse Hierarcha per se vel per alium stare in iudicio nomine personarum iuridicarum, quae sub eius potestate sunt.

CAPUT VIII. **De Procuratoribus ad Lites et de Advocatis**

CAN. 1139 §1. Pars libere potest procuratorem et advocatum sibi constituere, sed potest etiam per se ipsa agere et respondere, nisi iudex procuratoris vel advocati ministerium necessarium existimavit.

§2. In iudicio poenali vero accusatus aut a se constitutum aut a iudice datum semper habere debet advocatum.

§3. In iudicio contentioso, si agitur de minoribus aut de causa, in qua bonum publicum in discrimen vocatur, exceptis autem causis matrimonialibus, iudex parti carenti advocatum ex officio constituat.

CAN. 1140 §1. Unum sibi pars potest constituere procuratorem, qui non potest alium sibi substituere, nisi id eidem scripto permissum est.

§2. Si vero iusta de causa plures procuratores ab eadem parte constituuntur, hi ita

---

ian. 1950, cann. 164, 168. - Carth. can. 97. ▲ D. 3, 4, 1–3; Nov. 131, 15; Basilic. 8, 2, 102.

1138 §2: Pius XII, m.p. *Sollicitudinem Nostram,* 6 ian. 1950, can. 168 §4.

1139 §1: Pius XII, m.p. *Sollicitudinem Nostram,* 6 ian. 1950, can. 170 §3. ▲ D. 49, 9, 1; C. 2, 12 (13), 26; 7, 62, 9.

1139 §2: Pius XII, m.p. *Sollicitudinem Nostram,* 6

ian. 1950, can. 170 §1. ▲ D. 3, 1, 1, (4); Basilic. 8, 1, 1.

1139 §3: Pius XII, m.p. *Sollicitudinem Nostram,* 6 ian. 1950, can. 170 §2.

1140 §1: Pius XII, m.p. *Sollicitudinem Nostram,* 6 ian. 1950, can. 171 §1. ▲ D. 49, 1, 4 (5); Nov. 71.

1140 §2: Pius XII, m.p. *Sollicitudinem Nostram,* 6 ian. 1950, can. 171 §2. ▲ D. 3, 3, 31, (1–2) et 32; Basilic. 8, 2, 31–32.

they are to be so designated that prevention is operative among them.

§3. However, several advocates can be appointed together.

CAN. 1141   The procurator and the advocate must have attained the age of majority and be of good reputation. In addition, the advocate must be a Catholic, unless the authority to which the tribunal is immediately subject permits otherwise, a doctor in canon law or otherwise truly expert and approved by the same authority.

CAN. 1142   §1. Before the procurator and the advocate undertake their function, they must present an authentic mandate to the tribunal.

§2. To prevent the extinction of a right, however, the judge can admit a procurator even if the mandate has not been presented, once a suitable security has been furnished if necessary. However, the judge's act lacks all force if the procurator does not present a mandate within the peremptory time limit established by the judge.

CAN. 1143   Without a special mandate, the procurator cannot validly renounce an action, an instance of trial or judicial acts, nor come to a settlement, make a bargain, submit to arbitration or, in general, do those things for which the law requires a special mandate.

CAN. 1144   §1. For the removal of a procurator or advocate to take effect, they must be intimated and, if the joinder of issue has already

designentur, ut detur inter ipsos locus praeventioni.

§3. Advocati autem plures simul constitui possunt.

CAN. 1141   Procurator et advocatus debent esse aetate maiores et bonae famae; advocatus debet praeterea esse catholicus, nisi auctoritas, cui tribunal immediate subiectum est, aliud permittit, et doctor in iure canonico vel alioquin vere peritus et ab eadem auctoritate approbatus.

CAN. 1142   §1. Procurator et advocatus, antequam munus suscipiunt, mandatum authenticum apud tribunal deponere debent.

§2. Ad iuris tamen exstinctionem impediendam iudex potest procuratorem admittere etiam non exhibito mandato, praestita, si res fert, idonea cautione; actus iudicis autem qualibet vi caret, si intra terminum peremptorium a iudice statuendum procurator mandatum non exhibet.

CAN. 1143   Nisi mandatum speciale habet, procurator non potest valide renuntiare actioni, litis instantiae vel actis iudicialibus nec transigere, pacisci, compromittere in arbitros et generatim ea agere, pro quibus ius requirit mandatum speciale.

CAN. 1144   §1. Ut procuratoris vel advocati amotio effectum sortiatur, necesse est ipsis intimetur et, si lis iam contestata est,

1140 §3: Pius XII, m.p. *Sollicitudinem Nostram,* 6 ian. 1950, can. 171 §3.

1141: Pius XII, m.p. *Sollicitudinem Nostram,* 6 ian. 1950, cann. 172 §§1–2, 173 §§1–2. ▲ C. 2, 12 (13), 6.

1142 §1: Pius XII, m.p. *Sollicitudinem Nostram,* 6 ian. 1950, cann. 174 §1, 176. ▲ D. 3, 3, 1 et 65; C. 2, 12 (13), 24.

1142 §2: Pius XII, m.p. *Sollicitudinem Nostram,* 6

ian. 1950, can. 177.

1143: Pius XII, m.p. *Sollicitudinem Nostram,* 6 ian. 1950, can. 179. ▲ D. 3, 3, 60; 12, 2, 17–19; C. 4, 1, 7; Basilic. 8, 2, 59.

1144 §1: Pius XII, m.p. *Sollicitudinem Nostram,* 6 ian. 1950, can. 181 §1. ▲ D. 3, 3, 16 et 17, pr.; 49, 1, 4 (5); C. 2, 12 (13), 22.

taken place, the judge and the opposing party be notified about the removal.

§2. After the definitive sentence has been rendered, the right and obligation to appeal, if the mandating party has not renounced this, remains with the procurator.

CAN. 1145 For a grave cause, the judge, either *ex officio* or at the request of the party, can remove the procurator and the advocate by decree. However, recourse can always be made to the appeal tribunal.

CAN. 1146 §1. The procurator and the advocate are forbidden to win the litigation by bribery, or bargain with the winning party for excessive profit or for a share of the object under litigation. If they do so, the agreement is null and the judge can fine them. Moreover, the authority to whom the tribunal is immediately subject can suspend the advocate from office or, in the case of a repeated offense, even remove him or her from the list of advocates.

§2. Procurators and advocates can be punished in the same way if, in deceit of the law, they withdraw cases from competent tribunals so that the cases may be decided more favorably by other tribunals.

CAN. 1147 Procurators and advocates who have betrayed their function for gifts, promises or any other reason are to be suspended from serving as legal assistants and are to be fined or punished with other suitable penalties.

CAN. 1148 As far as possible, legal representatives are to be appointed in a stable manner in each tribunal, who receive remuneration from the tribunal and who are to exercise, es-

iudex et adversa pars certiores facti sint de amotione.

§2. Lata sententia definitiva ius et obligatio appellandi, si mandans non renuit, procuratori manet.

CAN. 1145 Procurator et advocatus possunt a iudice dato decreto repelli sive ex officio sive ad instantiam partis, gravi de causa tamen et semper salvo recursu ad tribunal appellationis.

CAN. 1146 §1. Procurator et advocatus vetantur emere litem aut sibi de immodico emolumento vel rei litigiosae parte vindicata pacisci; quae si fecerunt, nulla est pactio et a iudice possunt poena pecuniaria puniri; advocatus praeterea ab officio suspendi, vel etiam, si recidivus est, ab auctoritate, cui tribunal immediate subiectum est, destitui et ex albo advocatorum expungi potest.

§2. Eodem modo puniri possunt procuratores et advocati, qui a competentibus tribunalibus causas in fraudem legis subtrahunt, ut ab aliis favorabilius definiantur.

CAN. 1147 Procuratores et advocati, qui ob dona aut pollicitationes aut quamlibet aliam rationem suum munus prodiderunt, a patrocinio exercendo suspendantur et poena pecuniaria aliisve congruis poenis puniantur.

CAN. 1148 In unoquoque tribunali, quatenus fieri potest, stabiles patroni constituantur ab ipso tribunali remunerationem recipientes, qui munus procuratoris vel advo-

1144 §2: Pius XII, m.p. *Sollicitudinem Nostram*, 6 ian. 1950, can. 181 §2. ▲ D. 49, 1, 4 (5); 49, 9, 2; C. 7, 62, 3.

1145: Pius XII, m.p. *Sollicitudinem Nostram*, 6 ian. 1950, can. 180.

1146 §1: Pius XII, m.p. *Sollicitudinem Nostram*, 6 ian. 1950, can. 182. ▲ D. 50, 13, 1, (10–12); C. 2, 6, 5 et 6, (2); 2, 12 (13), 15; Basilic. 8, 1, 14.

1147: Pius XII, m.p. *Sollicitudinem Nostram*, 6 ian. 1950, can. 183. ▲ D. 48, 19, 38, (8).

pecially in marriage cases, the function of procurator or advocate on behalf of parties who wish to select them.

cati praesertim in causis matrimonialibus pro partibus, quae eos seligere malint, exerceant.

CHAPTER IX. **Actions and Exceptions**

CAPUT IX. **De Actionibus et Exceptionibus**

CAN. 1149 Every right whatsoever is protected not only by an action, unless otherwise expressly provided, but also by an exception, which is always available and of its very nature perpetual.

CAN. 1149 Quodlibet ius non solum actione munitur, nisi aliter expresse cautum est, sed etiam exceptione, quae semper competit et est sua natura perpetua.

CAN. 1150 Every action is extinguished by prescription in accord with the norm of law, or by some other legitimate means, with the exception of actions concerning the status of persons, which are never extinguished.

CAN. 1150 Quaevis actio exstinguitur praescriptione ad normam iuris aliove legitimo modo exceptis actionibus de statu personarum, quae numquam exstinguuntur.

CAN. 1151 Unless the law expressly provides otherwise, contentious actions are extinguished by prescription five years from the day when the action could have been first proposed, without prejudice to any relevant personal statutes where they are in force.

CAN. 1151 Actiones contentiosae, nisi aliter iure expresse cavetur, praescriptione exstinguuntur quinquennio a die, a quo actio primum potuit proponi, computando firmis, ubi vigent, hac in re Statutis personalibus.

CAN. 1152 §1. Every penal action is extinguished by the death of the accused, by pardon granted by competent authority and by prescription.

CAN. 1152 §1. Omnis actio poenalis exstinguitur morte rei, condonatione auctoritatis competentis et praescriptione.

§2. A penal action is extinguished by prescription after three years, unless it is a question of:

§2. Actio poenalis praescriptione exstinguitur triennio, nisi agitur:

1° delicts reserved to the Apostolic See;

1° de delictis Sedi Apostolicae reservatis;

2° actions for those delicts mentioned in can. 1450 and 1453, which are extinguished by prescription after five years;

2° de actione ob delicta, de quibus in cann. 1450 et 1453, quae praescriptione exstinguitur quinquennio;

1149: Pius XII, m.p. *Sollicitudinem Nostram,* 6 ian. 1950, can. 184. ▲ Instit. 4, 14, pr. et 1–2; D. 44, 1, 20; 44, 4, 5 (6); 50, 16, 178, (2); 50, 17, 156, (1).

1150: Pius XII, m.p. *Sollicitudinem Nostram,* 6 ian. 1950, can. 221. - Syn. Alexandrin. Coptorum, a. 1898, sect. III, cap. VI, tit. V, art. XI, 1. ▲ C. 7, 35, 5; 7, 39, 3; 7, 40, 1; Basilic. 50, 15, 1.

1151: Pius XII, m.p. *Sollicitudinem Nostram,* 6 ian.

1950, can. 221.

1152 §1: Pius XII, m.p. *Sollicitudinem Nostram,* 6 ian. 1950, can. 222. ▲ D. 47, 1, 1; 48, 4, 11; 48, 16, 8–10; 48, 19, 20.

1152 §2: Pius XII, m.p. *Sollicitudinem Nostram,* 6 ian. 1950, can. 223. ▲ D. 48, 5, 12 (11), (4); C. 9, 22, 12; 9, 35, 5; Basilic. 60, 41, 47.

3° delicts, which are not punishable under common law, if another time limit of prescription has been established by particular law.

§3. Prescription runs from the day on which the delict was committed or, if the delict is continuous or habitual, from the day on which it ceased.

CAN. 1153 §1. Prescription extinguishes an action to execute a penalty if the guilty party was not notified of the judge's decree of execution within the time limits mentioned in can. 1152. These limits are to be computed from the day on which the condemnatory sentence became an adjudged matter *(res iudicata)*.

§2. The same is applicable, with due observance of the law, if the penalty was imposed by extra-judicial decree.

CAN. 1154 Although a penal action has been extinguished by prescription:

1° a contentious action, that might arise to recover damages on account of the delict, is not by that very fact extinguished;

2° if the public good so requires, the hierarch may apply opportune administrative remedies, not excluding suspension from the exercise of sacred ministry or removal from office.

CAN. 1155 A petitioner can bring a person to trial with several actions at once, either concerning the same or different matters, so long as the actions do not conflict among themselves and do not exceed the competence of the tribunal approached.

CAN. 1156 §1. A respondent can present a counterclaim against the petitioner before the

3° de delictis, quae non sunt iure communi punita, si iure particulari alius terminus praescriptionis statutus est.

§3. Praescriptio decurrit ex die, quo delictum patratum est, vel, si delictum est permanens vel habituale, ex die, quo cessavit.

CAN. 1153 §1. Si intra terminos, de quibus in can. 1152, ex die, quo sententia condemnatoria in rem iudicatam transiit, computandos non est reo intimatum exsecutorium iudicis decretum, actio ad poenam exsequendam praescriptione exstinguitur.

§2. Idem valet servatis servandis, si poena per decretum extra iudicium irrogata est.

CAN. 1154 Actione poenali praescriptione exstincta:

1° non est hoc ipso exstincta actio contentiosa forte ex delicto orta ad damna reparanda;

2° si bonum publicum requirit, Hierarcha remediis opportunis administrativis non exclusa suspensione ab exercitio ministerii sacri vel amotione ab officio uti potest.

CAN. 1155 Actor pluribus simul actionibus, quae tamen inter se non confligant, sive de eadem re sive de diversis, aliquem convenire potest, si aditi tribunalis competentiam non excedunt.

CAN. 1156 §1. Pars conventa potest coram eodem iudice in eodem iudicio contra

---

1152 §3: Pius XII, m.p. *Sollicitudinem Nostram*, 6 ian. 1950, can. 225.

1154: Pius XII, m.p. *Sollicitudinem Nostram*, 6 ian. 1950, can. 224. ▲ D. 47, 1, 1; 49, 13, 1; C. 4, 17; 7, 66, 3.

1154, 2°: Carth. can. 87; S. Basilius M., can. 17. * Syn. Libanen. Maronitarum, a. 1736, pars II, cap.

VI, 9.

1155: Pius XII, m.p. *Sollicitudinem Nostram*, 6 ian. 1950, can. 186 §1. ▲ D. 50, 17, 130; C. 9, 31, 1.

1156 §1: Pius XII, m.p. *Sollicitudinem Nostram*, 6 ian. 1950, can. 210 §1.

same judge in the same trial either because of the connection of the case with the principal action or to remove or lessen the petitioner's claim.

§2. A counterclaim to a counterclaim is not admissible.

CAN. 1157 The counterclaim is to be presented to the judge before whom the principal action was filed even if the judge was delegated for only one case or is otherwise relatively incompetent.

CAN. 1158 §1. A person, who through at least probable arguments has shown a right over something held by another and the threat of damage unless the thing is handed over for safekeeping, has the right to obtain its sequestration from the judge.

§2. In similar circumstances, a person can obtain an order to restrain another from the exercise of a right.

CAN. 1159 §1. Sequestration of a thing is also admitted as security for a loan provided that the right of the creditor is sufficiently evident.

§2. Sequestration can also be extended to the goods of the debtor that are discovered in the possession of others, under whatever title, and to the loans of the debtor.

CAN. 1160 Sequestration of a thing and restraint upon the exercise of a right can in no way be decreed if the harm that is feared can be repaired in another way and suitable security for its repair is offered.

CAN. 1161 A judge who grants the seques-

actorem actionem reconventionalem proponere vel propter causae nexum cum actione principali vel ad submovendam vel ad minuendam actoris petitionem.

§2. Reconventio reconventionis non admittitur.

CAN. 1157 Actio reconventionalis proponenda est iudici, coram quo actio principalis instituta est, etsi ad unam causam dumtaxat delegato vel alioquin relative incompetenti.

CAN. 1158 §1. Qui probabilibus saltem argumentis ostendit se ius habere super aliqua re ab alio detenta sibique damnum imminere, nisi res ipsa custodienda traditur, ius habet obtinendi a iudice eiusdem rei sequestrationem.

§2. In similibus rerum adiunctis obtineri potest, ut exercitium iuris alicui inhibeatur.

CAN. 1159 §1. Ad crediti quoque securitatem sequestratio rei admittitur, dummodo de creditoris iure satis constet.

§2. Sequestratio extendi potest etiam ad res debitoris, quae quolibet titulo apud alias personas reperiuntur, et ad debitoris credita.

CAN. 1160 Sequestratio rei et inhibitio exercitii iuris decerni nullatenus possunt, si damnum, quod timetur, potest aliter reparari et idonea cautio de eo reparando offertur.

CAN. 1161 Iudex potest ei, cui seques-

1156 §2: Pius XII, m.p. *Sollicitudinem Nostram,* 6 ian. 1950, can. 210 §2. ▲ D. 44, 1, 22.

1157: Pius XII, m.p. *Sollicitudinem Nostram,* 6 ian. 1950, can. 212. ▲ Nov. 96, 2, 1.

1158 §1: Pius XII, m.p. *Sollicitudinem Nostram,* 6 ian. 1950, can. 189 §1. ▲ D. 2, 8, 7, (2); C. 4, 4; 7, 65, 5.

1158 §2: Pius XII, m.p. *Sollicitudinem Nostram,* 6 ian. 1950, can. 189 §2.

1159 §1: Pius XII, m.p. *Sollicitudinem Nostram,* 6 ian. 1950, can. 190 §1.

1159 §2: Pius XII, m.p. *Sollicitudinem Nostram,* 6 ian. 1950, can. 190 §2.

1160: Pius XII, m.p. *Sollicitudinem Nostram,* 6 ian. 1950, can. 191.

1161: Pius XII, m.p. *Sollicitudinem Nostram,* 6 ian. 1950, can. 192.

tration of a thing or the restraint upon the exercise of a right can first impose an obligation upon the person to compensate for damages if that person's right is not proven.

CAN. 1162 The civil law of the place where the thing, whose possession is in question, is located is to be observed regarding the nature and force of a possessory action.

CAN. 1163 §1. Whenever a petition is introduced to obtain provision for the support of a person, the judge, having heard the parties, can determine, by a decree to be executed immediately, having stipulated any suitable guarantees if necessary, that, without prejudice to the right to be defined by the sentence, necessary maintenance be provided in the meantime.

§2. Once a petition has been presented by a party or by the promoter of justice to obtain this decree, the judge, after having heard the other party, is to decide the matter most expeditiously, though never beyond ten days. After this time has passed without result, or if the petition has been rejected, recourse is possible to the authority to whom the tribunal is immediately subject, provided that this authority is not the judge himself or, if one prefers, to the appellate judge who likewise shall decide the matter most expeditiously.

trationem rei vel inhibitionem exercitii iuris concedit, praeviam imponere cautionem de damnis reparandis, si ius suum non probavit.

CAN. 1162 Ad naturam et vim actionis possessoriae quod attinet, servetur ius civile loci, ubi sita est res, de cuius possessione agitur.

CAN. 1163 §1. Quoties introducta est petitio ad obtinendam provisionem ad hominis sustentationem, iudex auditis partibus decreto statim exsequendo statuere potest idoneis, si res fert, praescriptis cautionibus, ut interim necessaria alimenta praestentur, sine praeiudicio iuris per sententiam definiendi.

§2. Facta a parte vel a promotore iustitiae petitione ad obtinendum hoc decretum iudex audita altera parte rem expeditissime definiat, numquam autem ultra decem dies; quibus inutiliter transactis aut petitione reiecta patet recursus ad auctoritatem, cui tribunal immediate subiectum est, dummodo ipsa ne sit iudex, vel, si quis mavult, ad iudicem appellationis, qui item rem expeditissime definiat.

CHAPTER X. **Methods of Avoiding Trials**

ART. I. *Out-of-Court Settlement*

CAN. 1164 In an out-of-court settlement, the civil law of the place where the settlement is reached is to be observed.

CAN. 1165 §1. A settlement cannot validly

CAPUT X. **De Modis Evitandi Iudicia**

ART. I. *De Transactione*

CAN. 1164 In transactione servetur ius civile loci, ubi transactio initur.

CAN. 1165 §1. Transactio valide fieri

1163 §1: Pius XII, m.p. *Sollicitudinem Nostram*, 6 ian. 1950, can. 194.
1163 §2: Pius XII, m.p. *Sollicitudinem Nostram*, 6 ian. 1950, can. 195.

1164: Pius XII, m.p. *Sollicitudinem Nostram*, 6 ian. 1950, can. 95. ▲ D. 38, 17, 1, (12).
1165 §1: Pius XII, m.p. *Sollicitudinem Nostram*, 6 ian. 1950, can. 96 §1. ▲ D. 47, 2, 55 (54), (5); C. 2, 4, 18.

be made in cases concerning those things or those rights that pertain to the public good and other matters about which the parties cannot freely dispose.

§2. But a settlement can be made if it is a question of ecclesiastical temporal goods provided that, if the matter so requires, the formalities established by law for the alienation of ecclesiastical goods are observed.

CAN. 1166 Unless otherwise expressly provided, each party is to pay one half of the expenses incurred in reaching a settlement.

CAN. 1167 The judge is not to undertake, at least not regularly, the settlement negotiations personally, but is to entrust them to another person who is an expert in the law.

ART. II. *Arbitration*

CAN. 1168 §1. Those who are involved in a controversy may agree in writing to have the matter resolved by arbiters.

§2. The same may be agreed upon in writing by those who have entered, or are entering, into a contract, regarding controversies that might arise from that contract.

CAN. 1169 Controversies, concerning which an out-of-court settlement is forbidden, cannot be validly submitted to arbitration.

CAN. 1170 §1. One or more arbiters may be designated, but of uneven number.

§2. In the arbitration agreement itself, unless the arbiters are designated by name, at least

non potest in causis circa eas res vel ea iura, quae ad bonum publicum spectant, aliaque, de quibus partes libere disponere non possunt.

§2. Sed si quaestio fit de bonis temporalibus ecclesiasticis, transactio fieri potest, servatis tamen, si materia id postulat, sollemnibus iure statutis de alienatione bonorum ecclesiasticorum

CAN. 1166 Expensarum, quas transactio postulavit, nisi aliter expresse cautum est, utraque pars dimidium solvat.

CAN. 1167 Iudex negotium transactionis non ipse per se, regulariter saltem, suscipiat tractandum, sed illud alii in iure perito committat.

ART. II. *De Compromisso in Arbitros*

CAN. 1168 §1. Qui controversiam inter se habent, possunt scripto convenire, ut ea ab arbitris dirimatur.

§2. Idem scripto convenire possunt, qui contractum inter se ineunt vel inierunt, quod attinet ad controversias ex eo contractu forte orituras.

CAN. 1169 Non possunt valide in arbitros compromitti controversiae, de quibus transactio fieri vetatur.

CAN. 1170 §1. Unus vel plures arbitri constitui possunt, dispari tamen numero.

§2. In ipso compromisso, nisi nominatim designantur, debet saltem eorum numerus

---

1165 §2: Pius XII, m.p. *Sollicitudinem Nostram,* 6 ian. 1950, can. 96 §2.

1166: Pius XII, m.p. *Sollicitudinem Nostram,* 6 ian. 1950, can. 97 §2.

1167: Pius XII, m.p. *Sollicitudinem Nostram,* 6 ian. 1950, can. 94 §3.

1168 §1: Pius XII, m.p. *Sollicitudinem Nostram,* 6 ian. 1950, can. 98 §1. - Carth. cann. 120–122. ▲ D. 4, 8, 1; C. 2, 55 (56).

1168 §2: Pius XII, m.p. *Sollicitudinem Nostram,* 6 ian. 1950, can. 98 §2.

1169: Pius XII, m.p. *Sollicitudinem Nostram,* 6 ian. 1950, can. 99.

1170 §1: Pius XII, m.p. *Sollicitudinem Nostram,* 6 ian. 1950, can. 100 §1.

1170 §2: Pius XII, m.p. *Sollicitudinem Nostram,* 6 ian. 1950, can. 100 §2.

their number should be determined and the manner established by which they are to be appointed and substituted.

CAN. 1171 An arbitration agreement is null if:

1° the norms determined for the validity of contracts that exceed ordinary administration have not been observed;

2° it was not made in writing;

3° the procurator agreed to the arbitration without a special mandate, or the prescripts of cann. 1169 and 1170 were violated;

4° the controversy did not arise or does not arise from a certain contract according to the norm of can. 1168, §2.

CAN. 1172 The following may not validly undertake the function of arbiter:

1° minors;

2° those punished by the penalty of excommunication, even minor, suspension or deposition;

3° members of a religious institute or society of common life in the manner of religious without the permission of the superior.

CAN. 1173 The appointment of an arbiter has no effect unless he or she accepts the function in writing.

CAN. 1174 §1. If the arbiters are not designated in the arbitration agreement, or they are to be substituted, and the parties or others to whom the designation was entrusted disagree regarding all or some of the arbiters to be chosen, any party may refer the matter to the tribunal that is competent to decide the case in first grade, unless the parties have agreed other-

determinari et simul ratio statui, qua nominandi et substituendi sunt.

CAN. 1171 Compromissum est nullum, si:

1° servatae non sunt normae statutae ad validitatem contractuum, qui ordinariam administrationem excedunt;

2° scripto non est factum;

3° procurator sine mandato speciali in arbitros compromisit aut violata sunt praescripta cann. 1169 vel 1170;

4° controversia non est vel orta vel ex certo contractu oritura ad normam can. 1168, §2.

CAN. 1172 Munus arbitri valide gerere non possunt:

1° minores;

2° poena excommunicationis, etiam minoris, suspensionis vel depositionis puniti;

3° sodales instituti religiosi vel societatis vitae communis ad instar religiosorum sine licentia Superioris.

CAN. 1173 Arbitri nominatio vim non habet, nisi ipse scripto munus acceptat.

CAN. 1174 §1. Si arbitri non sunt in compromisso designati vel si sufficiendi sunt et partes aliive, quibus designatio demandata est, dissentiunt de omnibus vel nonnullis arbitris seligendis, quaelibet pars potest id tribunali, quod competens est ad causam in primo gradu iudicii definiendam, committere, nisi partes aliter convenerunt;

1171: Pius XII, m.p. *Sollicitudinem Nostram,* 6 ian. 1950, can. 101.

1172, 1°: Pius XII, m.p. *Sollicitudinem Nostram,* 6 ian. 1950, can. 103 §1 n. 1.

1172, 2°: Pius XII, m.p. *Sollicitudinem Nostram,* 6 ian. 1950, can. 103 §1 n. 2.

1172, 3°: Pius XII, m.p. *Sollicitudinem Nostram,* 6 ian. 1950, can. 103 §2.

1173: Pius XII, m.p. *Sollicitudinem Nostram,* 6 ian. 1950, can. 104.

1174 §1: Pius XII, m.p. *Sollicitudinem Nostram,* 6 ian. 1950, can. 102 §1.

wise. After having heard the other parties, the tribunal is to provide by decree.

§2. The same norm is to be observed if a party or another person neglects to designate an arbiter, provided that the party who goes to court will have designated its arbiters, if it had to do so, at least twenty days beforehand.

CAN. 1175 The tribunal mentioned in can. 1174, §1 shall examine any objection raised against the arbiters and, after hearing the arbiters in question and the parties, shall resolve the matter by decree. If the tribunal upholds the objection, it is to substitute other arbiters, unless the arbitration agreement has provided otherwise.

CAN. 1176 §1. The obligations of the arbiters are to be established in the arbitration agreement itself as well as those things regarding the observance of secrecy.

§2. Unless the parties have specified otherwise, the arbiters are free to select the procedure to be followed; it is however to be simple and the time limits brief, observing equity and bearing in mind the procedural laws.

§3. Arbiters have no coercive power at all; if required by necessity, they must approach the tribunal that is competent to hear the case.

CAN. 1177 §1. Incidental questions that may arise are to be resolved by decree of the arbiters themselves.

§2. If a prejudicial question arises that cannot be submitted to arbitration, the arbiters must suspend the process until the parties have obtained a sentence regarding it from the judge

tribunal auditis ceteris partibus decreto provideat.

§2. Eadem norma servanda est, si qua pars aliusve neglegit arbitrum designare, dummodo tamen pars, quae tribunal adiit, viginti saltem ante dies suos arbitros, si forte debuit, designaverit.

CAN. 1175 De recusatione autem arbitrorum videt tribunal, de quo in can. 1174, §1, quod auditis arbitris recusatis et partibus decreto quaestionem dirimat; si recusationem acceptat, alios arbitros sufficiat, nisi in compromisso aliter cautum est.

CAN. 1176 §1. Obligationes arbitrorum in ipso compromisso statuendae sunt, eae quoque, quae ad secretum servandum spectant.

§2. Nisi partes aliud statuerunt, arbitri rationem procedendi libere seligunt; haec autem simplex sit et termini sint breves aequitate servata et ratione habita legis processualis.

§3. Arbitri quavis potestate coercitiva carent; necessitate exigente adire debent tribunal competens ad causam cognoscendam.

CAN. 1177 §1. Quaestiones incidentes, quae forte exoriuntur, ipsi arbitri decreto dirimant.

§2. Si vero quaestio praeiudicialis oritur, de qua compromitti in arbitros non potest, arbitri debent suspendere processum, donec de illa quaestione partes a iudice obtinuerint

---

1174 §2: PIUS XII, m.p. *Sollicitudinem Nostram,* 6 ian. 1950, can. 102 §2.

1175: PIUS XII, m.p. *Sollicitudinem Nostram,* 6 ian. 1950, can. 106 §2.

1176 §1: PIUS XII, m.p. *Sollicitudinem Nostram,* 6 ian. 1950, can. 105 §1.

1176 §2: PIUS XII, m.p. *Sollicitudinem Nostram,* 6 ian. 1950, can. 107 §1.

1176 §3: PIUS XII, m.p. *Sollicitudinem Nostram,* 6 ian. 1950, can. 107 §2.

1177 §1: PIUS XII, m.p. *Sollicitudinem Nostram,* 6 ian. 1950, can. 108 §1.

1177 §2: PIUS XII, m.p. *Sollicitudinem Nostram,* 6 ian. 1950, can. 108 §2.

and notified the arbiters of it. The sentence then becomes a *res iudicata* or, if the question concerns the status of persons, the sentence may be mandated for execution.

CAN. 1178 Unless the parties have determined otherwise, the arbitral sentence is to be handed down within six months from the day when all the arbiters accepted the appointment. This time limit may be prorogated by the parties.

CAN. 1179 §1. The arbitral sentence is to be given by majority vote.

§2. If the matter allows it, the sentence is to written by the arbiters themselves in the form of a judicial sentence and signed by each of them. However, for its validity, it is required and suffices that the majority of the arbiters sign the sentence.

CAN. 1180 §1. Unless the arbitral sentence is null because of their own grave fault, the arbiters have the right to be reimbursed for their expenses. In this regard, they may demand appropriate security.

§2. It is recommended that the arbiters offer their services gratuitously; otherwise, provision is to be made for their remuneration in the arbitration agreement itself.

CAN. 1181 §1. The complete text of the arbitral sentence must be deposited within fifteen days at the chancery of the eparchial tribunal where the sentence was given. Within five days after it has been deposited, unless it is evident that the arbitral sentence is null, the judicial vicar, either personally or through another, is to issue a decree of confirmation that is to be communicated immediately to the parties.

et arbitris notificaverint sententiam, quae transiit in rem iudicatam, vel, si quaestio est de statu personarum, sententiam, quae exsecutioni mandari potest.

CAN. 1178 Nisi partes aliter statuerunt, sententia arbitralis ferri debet intra sex menses a die, quo omnes arbitri suum munus acceptaverunt, computandos; terminus prorogari potest a partibus.

CAN. 1179 §1. Sententia arbitralis ad maiorem numerum suffragiorum fertur.

§2. Si res patitur, sententia arbitralis ab ipsis arbitris redigatur ad modum sententiae iudicialis et a singulis arbitris subscribatur; ad eiusdem autem validitatem requiritur et sufficit, ut maior eorum numerus eidem subscribat.

CAN. 1180 §1. Nisi sententia arbitralis est nulla propter gravem arbitrorum culpam, arbitri ius habent ad suarum expensarum solutionem; qua de re possunt opportunas cautiones exigere.

§2. Suadetur, ut arbitri gratuitam operam praestent, secus de remuneratione in ipso compromisso provideatur.

CAN. 1181 §1. Integer textus sententiae arbitralis intra quindecim dies ad cancellariam tribunalis eparchiae, ubi sententia lata est, deponi debet; intra quinque dies a depositione computandos, nisi certo constat sententiam arbitralem nullitate affectam esse, Vicarius iudicialis per se vel per alium decretum confirmationis ferat partibus statim intimandum.

1178: Pius XII, m.p. *Sollicitudinem Nostram,* 6 ian. 1950, can. 109 §§1–2.

1179 §1: Pius XII, m.p. *Sollicitudinem Nostram,* 6 ian. 1950, can. 111 §1.

1179 §2: Pius XII, m.p. *Sollicitudinem Nostram,* 6 ian. 1950, can. 112 §1.

ian. 1950, can. 111 §§2–3.

1180 §1: Pius XII, m.p. *Sollicitudinem Nostram,* 6 ian. 1950, can. 105 §2.

1181 §1: Pius XII, m.p. *Sollicitudinem Nostram,* 6 ian. 1950, can. 112 §1.

§2. If the judicial vicar refuses to issue this decree, the interested party may have recourse to the appeal tribunal, which is to resolve the matter most expeditiously. If, however, the judicial vicar remains silent for one full month, the same party can insist that he fulfill his duty. If he still remains silent for a further five days, the party may have recourse to the appellate tribunal, which is also to resolve the matter most expeditiously.

§3. If it is evident that the arbitral sentence is null because matters prescribed for the validity of the arbitration agreement were neglected, the judicial vicar is to declare the nullity and to notify the parties of it as soon as possible. There is no recourse against this declaration.

§4. The arbitral sentence becomes a *res iudicata* upon the issuance of the decree of confirmation, without prejudice to can. 1182.

CAN. 1182   §1. An appeal from an arbitral sentence is allowed only if the parties had agreed in writing that it would be subject to such a remedy. In such case, the appeal is to be lodged before the judge who issued the decree of confirmation within ten days of its notification. If, however, another judge is competent to receive the appeal, the matter is to be brought before him within a month.

§2. An arbitral sentence, from which an appeal is allowed, becomes a *res iudicata* according to the norm of can. 1322.

CAN. 1183   According to the ordinary norm of law, the judge who issued the decree of confirmation handles: the complaint of nullity

§2. Si Vicarius iudicialis hoc decretum ferre recusat, pars, cuius interest, recurrere potest ad tribunal appellationis, a quo quaestio expeditissime definienda est; si vero Vicarius iudicialis continuum mensem silet, eadem pars instare potest, ut ipse munere suo fungatur; si vero nihilominus silet, elapsis quinque diebus pars potest recursum ad tribunal appellationis interponere, quod item quaestionem expeditissime definiat.

§3. Si certo constat sententiam arbitralem nullitate affectam esse ob neglecta praescripta ad validitatem compromissi statuta, Vicarius iudicialis nullitatem declaret ac partibus quam primum notificet omni recursu adversus hanc declarationem remoto.

§4. Sententia arbitralis transit in rem iudicatam statim ac decretum confirmationis latum est firmo can. 1182.

CAN. 1182   §1. Appellatio a sententia arbitrali tunc tantum admittitur, si partes scripto inter se convenerunt eam huic remedio subiectum iri; quo in casu appellatio interponenda est intra decem dies ab intimatione decreti confirmationis computandos coram ipso iudice, qui decretum tulit; si vero alius est iudex competens ad appellationem recipiendam, prosecutio coram eo intra mensem est facienda.

§2. Sententia arbitralis, a qua appellatio admittitur, transit in rem iudicatam ad normam can. 1322.

CAN. 1183   De querela nullitatis contra sententiam arbitralem, quae in rem iudicatam transiit, de restitutione in integrum, si de

1181 §2: Pius XII, m.p. *Sollicitudinem Nostram,* 6 ian. 1950, cann. 112 §2, 231 §3, 232.

1181 §4: Pius XII, m.p. *Sollicitudinem Nostram,* 6 ian. 1950, can. 121 §1.

1182 §1: Pius XII, m.p. *Sollicitudinem Nostram,* 6

ian. 1950, can. 120. - Carth. cann. 96, 122.

1182 §2: Pius XII, m.p. *Sollicitudinem Nostram,* 6 ian. 1950, can. 121 §2.

1183: Pius XII, m.p. *Sollicitudinem Nostram,* 6 ian. 1950, cann. 114 §1, 115.

against the arbitral sentence that has become a *res iudicata, restitutio in integrum,* if the injustice of the arbitral sentence is clearly established, the opposition of a third party, and the correction of any material error in the sentence.

CAN. 1184 §1. The execution of an arbitral sentence can take place in the same cases as those in which the execution of a judicial sentence is allowed.

§2. The eparchial bishop of the eparchy where the arbitral sentence was issued must mandate it for execution either personally or through someone else, unless the parties have designated another executor.

eiusdem sententiae iniustitia manifesto constat, de oppositione tertii necnon de correctione erroris materialis sententiae videt iudex, qui decretum confirmationis tulit, ad ordinariam normam iuris.

CAN. 1184 §1. Exsecutio sententiae arbitralis fieri potest in eisdem casibus, in quibus admittitur exsecutio sententiae iudicialis.

§2. Sententiam arbitralem exsecutioni mandare debet per se vel per alium Episcopus eparchialis eparchiae, ubi lata est, nisi partes alium exsecutorem designaverunt.

1184 §1: Pius XII, m.p. *Sollicitudinem Nostram,* 6 ian. 1950, can. 122 §1.

1184 §2: Pius XII, m.p. *Sollicitudinem Nostram,* 6 ian. 1950, can. 122 §2.

CHAPTER I. The Ordinary
Contentious Trial

ART. 1. *The Introductory Libellus of Litigation*

CAN. 1185 A person who wishes to bring another to trial must present to a competent judge an introductory *libellus* of litigation that sets forth the object of the controversy and requests the services of the judge.

CAN. 1186 §1. The judge can accept an oral petition whenever the petitioner is impeded from presenting a *libellus* introducing the litigation or the case is easily investigated and of lesser importance.

§2. In either case, however, the judge is to order the notary to put the act into writing, which is to be read and approved by the petitioner; this then takes the place of and has all the legal effects of an introductory *libellus* written by the petitioner.

CAN. 1187 §1. The *libellus*, which introduces litigation, must:

1° express to the judge before whom the case is being introduced, what is being sought and by whom it is being sought;

2° indicate the legal basis for the petitioner's case and, at least generally, the facts and proofs that will prove the allegations;

3° be signed by the petitioner or the peti-

CAPUT I. **De Iudicio Contentioso Ordinario**

ART. 1. *De Libello Litis Introductorio*

CAN. 1185 Qui aliquem convenire vult, debet libellum litis introductorium competenti iudici exhibere, in quo controversiae obiectum proponitur et ministerium iudicis expostulatur.

CAN. 1186 §1. Petitionem oralem iudex admittere potest, quoties vel actor impeditur, ne libellum litis introductorium exhibeat, vel causa est facilis investigationis et minoris momenti.

§2. In utroque tamen casu iudex notarium iubeat scripto actum redigere, qui coram actore legendus et ab eo approbandus est quique locum tenet libelli litis introductorii ab actore scripti ad omnes iuris effectus.

CAN. 1187 Libellus litis introductorius debet:

1° exprimere, coram quo iudice causa introducatur, quid petatur et a quo petatur;

2° indicare, quo iure innitatur actor et generatim saltem quibus factis et probationibus ad evincenda ea, quae asseruntur;

3° subscribi ab actore vel eius procura-

1185: Pius XII, m.p. *Sollicitudinem Nostram,* 6 ian. 1950, can. 228. ▲ C. 7, 40, 3; Nov. 53, 3.

1186 §1: Pius XII, m.p. *Sollicitudinem Nostram,* 6 ian. 1950, can. 229 §§1–2.

1186 §2: Pius XII, m.p. *Sollicitudinem Nostram,* 6 ian. 1950, can. 229 §3.

1187: Pius XII, m.p. *Sollicitudinem Nostram,* 6 ian. 1950, can. 230. ▲ D. 6, 1, 6; C. 2, 1, 3.

tioner's procurator, indicating the day, month and year, and the address where the petitioner or procurator lives or where they have stated to reside for the purpose of receiving the acts;

4° indicate the domicile or quasi-domicile of the respondent.

CAN. 1188 §1. After the single judge or the president of a collegiate tribunal has recognized that the matter is within his competence and the petitioner does not lack legitimate personal standing in the trial, he must accept or reject the introductory *libellus* as soon as possible by decree.

§2. A *libellus*, which introduces litigation, can be rejected only if:

1° the judge or tribunal is incompetent;

2° it is undoubtedly evident that the petitioner lacks personal standing in the trial;

3° can. 1187, nn. 1–3 have not been observed;

4° it is certainly clear from the introductory *libellus* itself that the petition lacks any basis and that there is no possibility that any such basis would appear through a process.

§3. If the introductory *libellus* has been rejected because of defects that can be corrected, the petitioner can resubmit a corrected *libellus* to the same judge.

§4. A party is always free within ten useful days to make recourse, with substantiating reasons, against the rejection of an introductory *libellus* either to the appellate tribunal or to the college if the *libellus* was rejected by the presiding judge. The question of the rejection is to be decided most expeditiously.

CAN. 1189 If within a month from the presentation of the introductory *libellus* the

tore appositis die, mense et anno necnon loco, ubi actor vel eius procurator habitant aut residere se dixerunt actorum recipiendorum gratia;

4° indicare domicilium vel quasi-domicilium partis conventae.

CAN. 1188 §1. Iudex unicus vel tribunalis collegialis praeses, postquam vidit et rem esse suae competentiae et actori legitimam personam standi in iudicio non deesse, debet suo decreto quam primum libellum litis introductorium aut admittere aut reicere.

§2. Libellus litis introductorius reici potest tantum, si:

1° iudex vel tribunal incompetens est;

2° sine dubio constat actori deesse legitimam personam standi in iudicio;

3° non servatus est can. 1187, nn. 1–3;

4° certo patet ex ipso libello litis introductorio petitionem quolibet carere fundamento neque fieri posse, ut aliquod ex processu fundamentum appareat.

§3. Si libellus litis introductorius reiectus est ob vitia, quae emendari possunt, actor libellum emendatum potest eidem iudici denuo exhibere.

§4. Adversus libelli litis introductorii reiectionem integrum semper est parti intra tempus utile decem dierum recursum rationibus suffultum interponere ad tribunal appellationis vel, si libellus reiectus est a praeside, ad collegium; quaestio autem reiectionis expeditissime definienda est.

CAN. 1189 Si iudex intra mensem ab exhibito libello litis introductorio computan-

---

1188 §1: Pius XII, m.p. *Sollicitudinem Nostram,* 6 ian. 1950, can. 231 §1.

1188 §3: Pius XII, m.p. *Sollicitudinem Nostram,* 6 ian. 1950, can. 231 §2.

1188 §4: Pius XII, m.p. *Sollicitudinem Nostram,* 6 ian. 1950, can. 231 §3. ▲ D. 49, 5, 6; Basilic. 9, 1, 40.

1189: Pius XII, m.p. *Sollicitudinem Nostram,* 6 ian. 1950, can. 232.

judge has not issued a decree by which he accepts or rejects the *libellus,* the interested party can insist that the judge fulfill his function. However, if the judge still remains silent for ten days after the petitioner's insistence, the *libellus* is considered as having been accepted.

dum decretum non edidit, quo libellum admittit vel reicit, pars, cuius interest, instare potest, ut iudex suo munere fungatur; si vero nihilominus iudex silet, inutiliter elapsis decem diebus a facta instantia computandis libellus pro admisso habeatur.

ART. 11. *The Citation and Intimation or Notification of Judicial Acts*

ART. 11. *De Citatione et de Intimatione vel Notificatione Actorum Iudicialium*

CAN. 1190 §1. In the decree by which the petitioner's introductory *libellus* is admitted, the judge or presiding judge of the tribunal must call the other parties to trial, that is, cite them for the joinder of issue, establishing whether they must respond in writing or appear before him to come to agreement about the issue. If from the written responses the judge perceives the need to convene the parties, he can determine that by a new decree.

CAN. 1190 §1. In decreto, quo actoris libellus litis introductorius admittitur, debet iudex vel praeses tribunalis ceteras partes in iudicium vocare seu citare ad litem contestandam statuens, utrum eae scripto respondere debeant an coram ipso se sistere ad dubia concordanda; si vero ex responsionibus scripto datis perspicit necessitatem partes convocandi, id potest novo decreto statuere.

§2. If the introductory *libellus* is considered as having been accepted according to the norm of can. 1189, the decree of citation to the trial must be issued within twenty days from the party's insistence on action as mentioned in this canon.

§2. Si libellus litis introductorius pro admisso habetur ad normam can. 1189, decretum citationis in iudicium fieri debet intra viginti dies a facta instantia, de qua in eo canone, computandos.

§3. If the parties *de facto* present themselves before the judge to pursue the case, however, there is no need for a citation, but the notary is to note in the acts that the parties were present for the trial.

§3. Si vero partes de facto coram iudice se sistunt ad causam agendam, non requiritur citatio, sed notarius indicet in actis partes iudicio affuisse.

CAN. 1191 §1. The decree of citation to the trial must be intimated immediately to the respondent and at the same time made known to any others who must appear.

CAN. 1191 §1. Decretum citationis in iudicium debet statim parti conventae intimari et simul ceteris, qui comparere debent, notum fieri.

§2. The introductory *libellus* is to be attached to the citation unless for grave reasons the judge

§2. Citationi libellus litis introductorius adiungatur, nisi iudex gravi de causa censet

---

1190 §1: Pius XII, m.p. *Sollicitudinem Nostram,* 6 ian. 1950, cann. 233 §1, 234 §1. ▲ D. 2, 5–7.

1190 §3: Pius XII, m.p. *Sollicitudinem Nostram,* 6 ian. 1950, can. 233 §2.

1191 §1: Pius XII, m.p. *Sollicitudinem Nostram,* 6 ian. 1950, can. 234.

1191 §2: Pius XII, m.p. *Sollicitudinem Nostram,* 6 ian. 1950, can. 234 §1.

determines that the *libellus* is not to be made known to the party before that party makes a deposition in the trial.

§3. If the action is initiated against a person who does not have the free exercise of his or her rights or the free administration of the things under dispute, the citation must be intimated to the one through whom that person must enter the trial in accord with the norm of law.

CAN. 1192 §1. The intimation or notification of citations, decrees, sentences, and other judicial acts must be made through the public postal services, with an acknowledgement of receipt card, or by some other very secure method, while observing the norms of particular law.

§2. The fact of intimation or notification and its method must be evident in the acts.

§3. A respondent who refuses to accept the citation or who prevents its delivery is considered to be legitimately cited.

CAN. 1193 If the citation is not legitimately intimated, the acts of the process are null, unless the party nevertheless appeared to pursue the case.

CAN. 1194 If the citation is legitimately intimated or the parties have appeared before the judge to pursue the case:

1° the matter ceases to be *res integra;*

2° the case becomes proper to the otherwise competent judge or tribunal before which the action was initiated;

libellum notificandum non esse parti, antequam haec deposuit in iudicio.

§3. Si actio instituitur adversus eum, qui non habet liberum exercitium suorum iurium vel liberam administrationem rerum, de quibus disceptatur, citatio intimanda est ei, per quem ille in iudicio stare debet ad normam iuris.

CAN. 1192 §1. Citationum, decretorum, sententiarum aliorumque actorum iudicialium intimatio vel notificatio facienda est per publicos tabellarios cum syngrapha receptionis vel alio modo, qui tutissimus est, servatis legibus iuris particularis.

§2. De facto intimationis vel notificationis et de eius modo constare debet in actis.

§3. Pars conventa, quae citationem recipere recusat vel quae impedit, ne citatio ad se perveniat, legitime citata habeatur.

CAN. 1193 Si citatio non est legitime intimata, nulla sunt acta processus, nisi pars nihilominus comparuit ad causam agendam.

CAN. 1194 Si citatio legitime intimata est aut partes coram iudice steterunt ad causam agendam:

1° res desinit esse integra;

2° causa fit propria illius iudicis aut tribunalis ceteroquin competentis, coram quo actio instituta est;

1191 §3: Pius XII, m.p. *Sollicitudinem Nostram,* 6 ian. 1950, can. 255.

1192 §1: Pius XII, m.p. *Sollicitudinem Nostram,* 6 ian. 1950, cann. 239–246, 401.

1192 §2: Pius XII, m.p. *Sollicitudinem Nostram,* 6 ian. 1950, can. 244.

1192 §3: Pius XII, m.p. *Sollicitudinem Nostram,* 6 ian. 1950, can. 240.

1193: Pius XII, m.p. *Sollicitudinem Nostram,* 6 ian. 1950, can. 245.

1194, 1°: Pius XII, m.p. *Sollicitudinem Nostram* , 6 ian. 1950, can. 247 n. 1.

1194, 2°: Pius XII, m.p. *Sollicitudinem Nostram,* 6 ian. 1950, can. 247 n. 2. ▲ D. 2, 1, 19, pr.; C. 3, 1, 16; Nov. 53, 3, pr. et 2; Nov. 123, 24.

3° the delegated power of a delegated judge is fixed in such a way that it is not lost when the authority of the one delegating ceases;

4° prescription is interrupted unless otherwise provided;

5° the instance of the litigation begins and, therefore, the principle *while litigation is pending, nothing is to be innovated* immediately takes effect.

ART. III. *The Joinder of the Issue*

CAN. 1195 §1. The joinder of the issue occurs when the object of the controversy, derived from the petitions and responses of the parties, is defined by a decree of the judge.

§2. The petitions and responses of the parties, besides those in the *libellus* that introduces the litigation, can be expressed either in a response to the citation or in oral declarations made before the judge; in more difficult cases, however, the judge must convene the parties to determine the question or questions that must be answered in the sentence.

§3. The decree of the judge must be intimated to the parties; unless they have already come to an agreement, the parties can make recourse to the judge within ten days so that the decree be changed; however, the matter must be resolved most expeditiously by a decree of that judge.

CAN. 1196 Once established, the object of the controversy cannot be changed validly except by a new decree, for a grave reason, at the

3° in iudice delegato firma redditur potestas delegata ita, ut non amittatur resoluto iure delegantis;

4° interrumpitur praescriptio, nisi aliter cautum est;

5° litis instantiae initium fit et ideo statim locum habet principium secundum quod lite pendente nihil innovetur.

ART. III. *De Litis Contestatione*

CAN. 1195 §1. Litis contestatio habetur, cum per iudicis decretum controversiae obiectum ex partium petitionibus et responsionibus desumptum definitur.

§2. Partium petitiones responsionesque praeterquam in libello litis introductorio possunt vel in responsione ad citationem exprimi vel in declarationibus ore coram iudice factis; in causis autem difficilioribus partes convocandae sunt a iudice ad dubium vel dubia concordanda, quibus in sententia respondendum sit.

§3. Decretum iudicis partibus intimandum est; quae nisi iam consenserunt, possunt intra decem dies ad eundem iudicem recurrere, ut decretum mutetur; res autem expeditissime decreto eiusdem iudicis definienda est.

CAN. 1196 Obiectum controversiae semel definitum mutari valide non potest nisi novo decreto, gravi de causa, ad instantiam

---

1194, 3°: Pius XII, m.p. *Sollicitudinem Nostram,* 6 ian. 1950, can. 247 n. 3.

1194, 4°: Pius XII, m.p. *Sollicitudinem Nostram,* 6 ian. 1950, can. 247 n. 4. ▲ D. 5, 3, 25, (7); C. 3, 19, 2, (1); Basilic. 42, 1, 25.

1194, 5°: Pius XII, m.p. *Sollicitudinem Nostram,* 6 ian. 1950, cann. 247 n. 5, 254. ▲ D. 44, 6, 1.

1195 §1: Pius XII, m.p. *Sollicitudinem Nostram,* 6 ian. 1950, cann. 248–251. ▲ C. 3, 9, 1.

1195 §2: Pius XII, m.p. *Sollicitudinem Nostram,* 6 ian. 1950, cann. 250, 251 §2.

1196: Pius XII, m.p. *Sollicitudinem Nostram,* 6 ian. 1950, can. 251 §4.

request of a party, and after having heard the other parties and considered their reasons.

CAN. 1197 After the issue has been joined, the possessor of another's property ceases to be in good faith. Therefore, if the possessor is sentenced to restore the property, the person must also return the profits made from the day of the joinder and repair any damages.

CAN. 1198 After the issue has been joined, the judge is to prescribe a suitable time for the parties to present and complete the proofs.

ART. IV. *Suspension, Abatement and Renunciation of the Trial*

CAN. 1199 If a party dies, changes status, or ceases from the office in virtue of which action is taken:

1° if the case has not yet been concluded, the trial is suspended until the heir of the deceased, the successor, or an interested party resumes the litigation;

2° if the case has been concluded, the judge must proceed to the additional acts, after having cited the procurator, if there is one, or otherwise the heir or the successor of the deceased.

CAN. 1200 §1. If the guardian, curator, procurator or advocate required according to the norm of can. 1139 ceases from that function, the trial is suspended in the meantime.

§2. The judge, however, is to appoint another guardian or curator as soon as possible; the judge can appoint a procurator or an advocate

partis et auditis ceteris partibus earumque rationibus perpensis.

CAN. 1197 Lite contestata possessor rei alienae desinit esse bonae fidei ideoque, si damnatur, ut rem restituat, fructus quoque a die litis contestationis reddere debet et damna reparare.

CAN. 1198 Lite contestata iudex congruum tempus partibus praestituat probationibus proponendis et explendis.

ART. IV. *De Litis Instantiae Suspensione, Peremptione et Renuntiatione*

CAN. 1199 Si pars moritur aut statum mutat aut cessat ab officio, cuius ratione agit:

1° causa nondum conclusa litis instantia suspenditur, donec heres defuncti aut successor aut is, cuius interest, litis instantiam resumpserit;

2° causa conclusa iudex procedere debet ad ulteriora citato procuratore, si adest, secus defuncti herede vel successore.

CAN. 1200 §1. Si a munere cessat aut tutor vel curator aut procurator vel advocatus, qui sunt ad normam can. 1139 necessarii, litis instantia interim suspenditur.

§2. Alium autem tutorem vel curatorem iudex quam primum constituat; procuratorem vero ad litem vel advocatum constituere

---

1197: Pius XII, m.p. *Sollicitudinem Nostram*, 6 ian. 1950, can. 253 n. 3. ▲ D. 5, 3, 25, (7); 10, 1, 4, (2); 22, 2, 1 et 3, (1) et 10 et 15; 44, 1, 13; C. 3, 32, 26.

1198: Pius XII, m.p. *Sollicitudinem Nostram*, 6 ian. 1950, can. 253 n. 2.

1199: Pius XII, m.p. *Sollicitudinem Nostram*, 6 ian. 1950, can. 255.

1200 §1: Pius XII, m.p. *Sollicitudinem Nostram*, 6 ian. 1950, can. 257.

for the litigation if the party has neglected to do so within the brief time period established by the judge.

CAN. 1201 If the parties, though not prevented by any impediment, propose no procedural act for six months, the trial is abated.

CAN. 1202 Abatement takes effect by the law itself against all persons, including minors, and must be declared *ex officio,* without prejudice to the right of seeking indemnity against guardians, curators, administrators, or procurators, who have not proved that they were not negligent.

CAN. 1203 Abatement extinguishes the acts of the process but not the acts of the case; indeed, these acts can also have force in another trial provided that the case involves the same persons and the same issue. Regarding those not party to the case, however, the acts have no force other than that of documents.

CAN. 1204 When a trial has been abated, each of the parties must bear the expenses that he or she incurred.

CAN. 1205 §1. The petitioner can renounce the trial at any stage or grade of the trial; likewise both the petitioner and the respondent can renounce either all or only some of the acts of the process.

§2. To renounce a trial, guardians and administrators of juridic persons need the counsel or consent of those whose involvement is required to place acts that exceed the limits of ordinary administration.

§3. To be valid, a renunciation must be writ-

potest, si pars neglexit intra brevem terminum ab ipso iudice statutum.

CAN. 1201 Si nullus actus processualis nullo obstante impedimento ponitur a partibus per sex menses, litis instantia perimitur.

CAN. 1202 Peremptio effectum habet ipso iure et adversus omnes, etiam minores, atque etiam ex officio declarari debet salvo iure petendi indemnitatem adversus tutores, curatores, administratores, procuratores, qui culpa se caruisse non probaverunt.

CAN. 1203 Peremptio exstinguit acta processus, non vero acta causae; immo haec vim habere possunt etiam in alio iudicio, dummodo causa inter easdem personas et super eadem re intercedat; sed ad extraneos quod attinet, non aliam vim obtinent nisi documentorum.

CAN. 1204 Perempti iudicii expensas, quas unaquaeque ex partibus fecit, ipsa solvere debet.

CAN. 1205 §1. In quolibet statu et gradu iudicii potest actor litis instantiae renuntiare; item tum actor tum pars conventa possunt actis processus renuntiare sive omnibus sive nonnullis tantum.

§2. Tutores et administratores personarum iuridicarum, ut renuntiare possint litis instantiae, egent consilio vel consensu eorum, quorum concursus requiritur ad ponendos actus, qui ordinariae administrationis fines excedunt.

§3. Renuntiatio ut valeat, peragenda est

1201: Pius XII, m.p. *Sollicitudinem Nostram,* 6 ian. 1950, can. 258. ▲ Nov. 93.

1202: Pius XII, m.p. *Sollicitudinem Nostram,* 6 ian. 1950, can. 259. ▲ C. 3, 1, 13, (11).

1203: Pius XII, m.p. *Sollicitudinem Nostram,* 6 ian. 1950, can. 260.

1204: Pius XII, m.p. *Sollicitudinem Nostram,* 6 ian. 1950, can. 261.

1205 §1: Pius XII, m.p. *Sollicitudinem Nostram,* 6 ian. 1950, can. 262 §1.

1205 §3: Pius XII, m.p. *Sollicitudinem Nostram,* 6 ian. 1950, can. 262 §2.

ten and signed by the party or by a procurator of the party who has a special mandate to do so; it must be communicated to the other party, accepted or not challenged by that party, and admitted by the judge.

CAN. 1206 A renunciation admitted by the judge has the same effects for the acts renounced as the abatement of the trial and it obliges the renouncing party to bear the expenses for the acts renounced.

ART. V. *Proofs*

CAN. 1207 §1. The burden of proof rests upon the person who makes the allegation.

§2. The following do not need proof:

1° matters presumed by the law itself;

2° facts alleged by one of the contending parties and admitted by the other, unless the law or the judge nevertheless requires proof.

CAN. 1208 §1. Proofs of any kind that seem useful for adjudicating the case and that are licit can be adduced.

§2. If a party insists that a proof rejected by a judge be admitted, the judge is to decide the matter most expeditiously.

CAN. 1209 If a party or a witness refuses to appear before the judge to testify, it is permissible to hear them through a person designated by the judge or to require of them a declaration either before a notary public or in any other legitimate manner.

CAN. 1210 The judge is not to proceed to collect the proofs before the joinder of the issue except for a grave cause.

scripto eademque a parte vel ab eius procuratore speciali tamen mandato munito debet subscribi, cum altera parte communicari, ab eaque acceptari vel non impugnari et ab iudice admitti.

CAN. 1206 Renuntiatio a iudice admissa pro actis, quibus renuntiatum est, eosdem parit effectus ac peremptio litis instantiae itemque obligat renuntiantem ad solvendas expensas actorum, quibus renuntiatum est.

ART. V. *De Probationibus*

CAN. 1207 §1. Onus probandi incumbit ei, qui asserit.

§2. Non indigent probatione:

1° quae ab ipso iure praesumuntur;

2° facta ab uno ex contendentibus asserta et ab altero admissa, nisi iure vel a iudice probatio nihilominus exigitur.

CAN. 1208 §1. Probationes cuiuslibet generis, quae ad causam cognoscendam utiles videntur et sunt licitae, adduci possunt.

§2. Si pars instat, ut probatio a iudice reiecta admittatur, ipse iudex rem expeditissime definiat.

CAN. 1209 Si pars vel testis se sistere ad respondendum coram iudice renuunt, licet eos audire per personam a iudice designatam aut requirere eorum declarationem coram publico notario vel quovis alio legitimo modo.

CAN. 1210 Iudex ad probationes colligendas ne procedat ante litis contestationem nisi gravi de causa.

1206: Pius XII, m.p. *Sollicitudinem Nostram,* 6 ian. 1950, can. 263.

1207 §1: Pius XII, m.p. *Sollicitudinem Nostram,* 6 ian. 1950, can. 270 §1. ▲ D. 22, 3, 2; C. 4, 20, 7; Basilic. 21, 1, 31.

1207 §2: Pius XII, m.p. *Sollicitudinem Nostram,* 6 ian. 1950, can. 269.

1210: Pius XII, m.p. *Sollicitudinem Nostram,* 6 ian. 1950, can. 252.

1° The Declarations of the Parties

CAN. 1211 The judge can always question the parties to elicit the truth more effectively and indeed must do so at the request of a party or to prove a fact that the public interest requires to be placed beyond doubt.

CAN. 1212 §1. A party legitimately questioned must respond and tell the whole truth, unless, by answering, a delict committed by that party would be revealed.

§2. If, however, a party refuses to respond, it is for the judge to evaluate what can be inferred from that refusal concerning the proof of the facts.

CAN. 1213 In cases where the public good is at stake, the judge is to administer an oath to the parties to tell the truth or at least to confirm the truth of what they have said, unless a grave cause suggests otherwise; the same can be done in other cases according to the judge's own discretion.

CAN. 1214 The parties, the promoter of justice, and the defender of the bond can present the judge with items about which a party is to be questioned.

CAN. 1215 The canons concerning the questioning of witnesses are to be observed, to the extent possible, in the questioning of the parties.

CAN. 1216 A judicial confession is the written or oral assertion of some fact made against oneself before a competent judge by any party concerning the matter of the trial, whether made voluntarily or while being questioned by the judge.

1° De Partium Declarationibus

CAN. 1211 Iudex ad veritatem aptius eruendam partes interrogare semper potest, immo debet ad instantiam partis vel ad probandum factum, quod publice interest extra dubium poni.

CAN. 1212 §1. Pars legitime interrogata respondere debet et veritatem integre fateri, nisi responsione revelatur delictum ab ipsa commissum.

§2. Si vero respondere recusavit, iudicis est aestimare, quid ad factorum probationem exinde erui possit.

CAN. 1213 In casibus, in quibus bonum publicum in causa est, iudex partibus interrogandis iusiurandum de veritate dicenda aut saltem de veritate dictorum deferat, nisi gravis causa aliud suadet; in aliis casibus potest pro sua prudentia.

CAN. 1214 Partes, promotor iustitiae et defensor vinculi possunt iudici exhibere articulos, super quibus pars interrogetur.

CAN. 1215 Circa partium interrogationes serventur congrua congruis referendo canones de interrogatione testium.

CAN. 1216 Assertio de aliquo facto scripto vel ore coram iudice competenti ab aliqua parte contra se peracta circa ipsam materiam iudicii sive sua sponte sive iudice interrogante est confessio iudicialis.

1211: Pius XII, m.p. *Sollicitudinem Nostram,* 6 ian. 1950, can. 264 §§1–2. ▲ D. 11, 1, 1 et 21; C. 3, 1, 9.

1212 §1: Pius XII, m.p. *Sollicitudinem Nostram,* 6 ian. 1950, can. 265 §1. ▲ D. 11, 1, 20, (1).

1212 §2: Pius XII, m.p. *Sollicitudinem Nostram,* 6 ian. 1950, can. 265 §2.

1213: Pius XII, m.p. *Sollicitudinem Nostram,* 6 ian. 1950, can. 266.

1214: Pius XII, m.p. *Sollicitudinem Nostram,* 6 ian. 1950, can. 267 §1.

1215: Pius XII, m.p. *Sollicitudinem Nostram,* 6 ian. 1950, can. 267 §2.

1216: Pius XII, m.p. *Sollicitudinem Nostram,* 6 ian. 1950, can. 272.

CAN. 1217 §1. The judicial confession of one party relieves the other parties from the burden of proof if it concerns some private matter and the public good is not at stake.

§2. In cases regarding the public good, however, a judicial confession and other declarations of the parties can have a probative force that the judge must evaluate together with the other circumstances of the case, but full probative force cannot be attributed to them unless other elements are present that thoroughly corroborate them.

CAN. 1218 After considering all the circumstances, it is for the judge to decide on the weight to be given an extra-judicial confession introduced into the trial.

CAN. 1219 A confession or any other declaration of a party lacks all force if it is shown that it was made due to an error of fact or extorted by force or grave fear.

2° Proof through Documents

CAN. 1220 In any kind of trial, proof by means of public and private documents is admitted.

CAN. 1221 §1. Public ecclesiastical documents are those that a person has drawn up by virtue of that person's function in the Church, after the solemnities prescribed by law have been observed.

§2. Public civil documents are those that are considered to be such in civil law.

§3. Other documents are private.

CAN. 1217 §1. Confessio iudicialis unius partis, si agitur de negotio aliquo privato et in causa non est bonum publicum, ceteras relevat ab onere probandi.

§2. In causis autem, quae ad bonum publicum spectant, confessio iudicialis et ceterae declarationes partium vim probandi habere possunt a iudice aestimandam una cum ceteris causae adiunctis, sed vis plenae probationis eis tribui non potest, nisi alia accedunt elementa, quae eas omnino corroborant.

CAN. 1218 Circa confessionem extraiudicialem in iudicium deductam iudicis est perpensis omnibus adiunctis aestimare, quanti facienda sit.

CAN. 1219 Confessio vel alia quaevis partis declaratio qualibet vi caret, si constat eam ex errore facti esse prolatam aut vi vel metu gravi extortam.

2° De Probationibus per Documenta

CAN. 1220 In quolibet iudicii genere admittitur probatio per documenta tum publica tum privata.

CAN. 1221 §1. Documenta publica ecclesiastica ea sunt, quae persona ratione sui muneris publici in Ecclesia confecit servatis sollemnibus iure praescriptis.

§2. Documenta publica civilia ea sunt, quae secundum ius civile talia censentur.

§3. Cetera documenta sunt privata.

1217 §1: Pius XII, m.p. *Sollicitudinem Nostram,* 6 ian. 1950, can. 273. ▲ D. 42, 2, 1 et 3–6; C. 7, 59.

1217 §2: Pius XII, m.p. *Sollicitudinem Nostram,* 6 ian. 1950, can. 558; Sign. Apost., rescr. 10 nov. 1970, 1); rescr. 2 ian. 1971, 1) "Ad."

1218: Pius XII, m.p. *Sollicitudinem Nostram,* 6 ian. 1950, can. 275. ▲ D. 48, 18, 1, (27).

1219: Pius XII, m.p. *Sollicitudinem Nostram,* 6 ian. 1950, can. 274. ▲ D. 9, 2, 23, (11) et 24–26; 42, 2, 2; Basilic. 60, 3, 23, (11) et 24–26.

1220: Pius XII, m.p. *Sollicitudinem Nostram,* 6 ian. 1950, can. 335. ▲ D. 22, 4, 1; C. 4, 19, 4 et 25; Nov. 73, 4–5.

1221 §1: Pius XII, m.p. *Sollicitudinem Nostram,* 6 ian. 1950, can. 336 §1.

1221 §2: Pius XII, m.p. *Sollicitudinem Nostram,* 6 ian. 1950, can. 336 §2.

1221 §3: Pius XII, m.p. *Sollicitudinem Nostram,* 6 ian. 1950, can. 336 §3.

CAN. 1222 Unless contrary and evident arguments prove otherwise, public documents are to be trusted concerning everything that they directly and principally affirm, with due regard for the civil law of the place that establishes otherwise regarding civil documents.

CAN. 1223 A private document, whether acknowledged by a party or approved by the judge, has the same probative force against the author or signer and those deriving a case from them as an extra-judicial confession. However, against others, its probative force is to be evaluated by the judge together with other aspects of the case, but it cannot be given full probative force unless there are other elements that fully corroborate it.

CAN. 1224 If the documents are shown to have been erased, emended, falsified, or affected by another defect, it is for the judge to assess whether and how much weight to be given them.

CAN. 1225 Documents do not have probative force in a trial unless they are originals or authentic copies and are deposited in the chancery of the tribunal so that the judge and the opposing party can examine them.

CAN. 1226 The judge can order that a document that is common to both parties be exhibited during the trial.

CAN. 1227 §1. Even if documents are common, no one is bound to exhibit those that cannot be communicated without danger of harm,

CAN. 1222 Documenta publica fidem faciunt de eis, quae directe et principaliter in eis affirmantur, nisi contrariis et evidentibus argumentis aliud evincitur, firmo iure civili loci, ad documenta civilia quod spectat, aliud statuente.

CAN. 1223 Documentum privatum sive agnitum a parte sive recognitum a iudice eandem probandi vim habet adversus auctorem documenti vel eum, qui documento subscripsit, et causam ab eis habentes ac confessio extraiudicialis; adversus autem extraneos vim probandi habere potest a iudice aestimandam una cum ceteris causae adiunctis, sed vis plenae probationis ei tribui non potest, nisi alia accedunt elementa, quae id omnino corroborant.

CAN. 1224 Si documenta abrasa, correcta, interpolata aliove vitio infecta demonstrantur, iudicis est aestimare, num et quanti huiusmodi documenta sint facienda.

CAN. 1225 Documenta vim probandi in iudicio non habent, nisi originalia sunt aut in exemplari authentico exhibita et penes cancellariam tribunalis deposita, ut a iudice et a partibus examinari possint.

CAN. 1226 Iudex praecipere potest, ut documentum utrique parti commune exhibeatur in iudicio.

CAN. 1227 §1. Nemo exhibere tenetur documenta, etsi communia, quae communicari non possunt sine periculo damni, de quo

---

1222: Pius XII, m.p. *Sollicitudinem Nostram*, 6 ian. 1950, cann. 337, 339. ▲ D. 22, 3, 10; C. 4, 20, 15, (6); 7, 52, 6.

1223: Pius XII, m.p. *Sollicitudinem Nostram*, 6 ian. 1950, can. 340. ▲ C. 4, 19, 5–7.

1224: Pius XII, m.p. *Sollicitudinem Nostram*, 6 ian. 1950, can. 341. ▲ D. 22, 3, 24; C. 4, 19, 24.

1225: Pius XII, m.p. *Sollicitudinem Nostram*, 6

ian. 1950, cann. 342–343. ▲ D. 2, 13, 11; 22, 4, 2; C. 2, 1, 7; Basilic. 7, 18, 20.

1226: Pius XII, m.p. *Sollicitudinem Nostram*, 6 ian. 1950, cann. 345, 347. ▲ D. 49, 14, 2, (1–2); C. 2, 1, 2 et 7; 4, 21, 22; Basilic. 7, 18, 20.

1227 §1: Pius XII, m.p. *Sollicitudinem Nostram*, 6 ian. 1950, can. 346 §1. ▲ D. 2, 13, 10. (2); C, 4, 21, 22.

as mentioned in can. 1229, §2, n. 2, or without danger of violating the obligation to observe secrecy.

§2. Nonetheless, if at least some part of a document can be transcribed and exhibited in copy form without the above-mentioned disadvantages, the judge can decree that it be produced.

3° Witnesses and Testimonies

CAN. 1228   Proof by means of witnesses is admitted in cases of any kind under the supervision of the judge.

CAN. 1229   §1. When the judge questions witnesses legitimately, they must tell the truth.

§2. With due regard for can. 1231, the following are exempted from the obligation to respond:

1° clerics regarding what has been made known to them by reason of sacred ministry; civil officials, physicians, midwives, advocates, notaries, and others also bound to observe secrecy by reason of having given advice, regarding those matters subject to this secrecy;

2° those who fear that from their own testimony ill fame, perilous ill treatment, or other grave evils will befall them, their spouse, or persons related to them by consanguinity or affinity.

a) Those Who Can Be Witnesses

CAN. 1230   All persons can be witnesses unless the law expressly excludes them in whole or in part.

in can. 1229, §2, n. 2, aut sine periculo violationis secreti servandi.

§2. Si vero aliqua saltem documenti pars describi potest et in exemplari exhiberi sine memoratis incommodis, iudex decernere potest, ut eadem producatur.

3° De Testibus et de Testimoniis

CAN. 1228 Probatio per testes in quibuslibet causis admittitur sub iudicis moderatione.

CAN. 1229 §1. Testes iudici legitime interroganti veritatem fateri debent.

§2. Firmo can. 1231 ab obligatione respondendi eximuntur:

1° clerici, quod attinet ad ea, quae ipsis manifestata sunt ratione sacri ministerii; civitatum magistratus, medici, obstetrices, advocati, notarii aliique, qui secretum servare etiam ratione praestiti consilii tenentur, quod attinet ad negotia secreto obnoxia;

2° qui ex testificatione sua sibi aut coniugi aut proximis consanguineis vel affinibus infamiam, periculosas vexationes aliave mala gravia obventura timent.

a) Qui Testes Esse Possunt

CAN. 1230 Omnes possunt esse testes, nisi iure expresse repelluntur vel in totum vel ex parte.

1227 §2: Pius XII, m.p. *Sollicitudinem Nostram,* 6 ian. 1950, can. 346 §2.

1228: Pius XII, m.p. *Sollicitudinem Nostram,* 6 ian. 1950, can. 276. ▲ D. 22, 5, 1–4 et 19 et 25; C. 4, 21, 15; Basilic. 22, 1, 73 (74).

1229 §1: Pius XII, m.p. *Sollicitudinem Nostram,* 6 ian. 1950, can. 277 §1. ▲ C. 4, 21, 22, (3).

1229 §2: Pius XII, m.p. *Sollicitudinem Nostram,* 6 ian. 1950, can. 277 §2. - Carth. can. 59.

1230: Pius XII, m.p. *Sollicitudinem Nostram,* 6 ian. 1950, can. 278. - S.C.S. Off. (Constantinop.), 2 apr. 1873, ad 1. ▲ D. 22, 5, 18 et 21, (1); Basilic. 21, 1, 17 et 20.

CAN. 1231 §1. Minors below the fourteenth year of age and those of limited mental capacity are not allowed to give testimony; they can, however, be heard following a decree of the judge that declares such a hearing expedient.

§2. The following are considered incapable of giving testimony:

1° the parties in the case or those who stand in for the parties at the trial, the judge and the judge's assistants, the advocate, and others who assist or have assisted the parties in the same case;

2° priests regarding all matters that they have come to know from sacramental confession even if the penitent seeks their disclosure; moreover, matters heard by anyone and in any way on the occasion of sacramental confession cannot be accepted even as an indication of the truth.

b) The Introduction and Exclusion of Witnesses

CAN. 1232 The party who has introduced a witness can forego the examination of that witness; the opposing party, however, can request that the witness be examined nevertheless.

CAN. 1233 §1. When proof through witnesses is requested, their names and domicile are to be made known to the tribunal.

§2. The items of discussion about which questioning of the witnesses is sought are to be presented within the time period set by the judge; otherwise, the request is to be considered as abandoned.

CAN. 1231 §1. Ne admittantur ad testimonium ferendum minores infra decimum quartum aetatis annum et mente debiles; audiri tamen possunt ex decreto iudicis, quo id expedire declaratur.

§2. Incapaces ad testimonium ferendum habentur:

1° qui partes sunt in causa aut partium nomine in iudicio consistunt, iudex eiusve assistentes, advocatus aliique, qui partibus in eadem causa assistunt vel astiterunt;

2° sacerdotes, quod attinet ad ea omnia, quae ipsis ex confessione sacramentali innotuerunt, etsi paenitens eorum manifestationem petiit; immo audita a quovis et quoquo modo occasione confessionis sacramentalis ne ut indicium quidem veritatis recipi possunt.

b) De Inducendis et Excludendis Testibus

CAN. 1232 Pars, quae testem induxit, potest eius interrogationi renuntiare; sed pars adversa postulare potest, ut nihilominus testis interrogetur.

CAN. 1233 §1. Si probatio per testes postulatur, eorum nomina et domicilium tribunali indicentur.

§2. Exhibeantur intra terminum a iudice praestitutum articuli argumentorum, super quibus petitur testium interrogatio; alioquin petitio censeatur deserta.

1231 §1: Pius XII, m.p. *Sollicitudinem Nostram,* 6 ian. 1950, can. 279 §1, 280. - Carth. can. 131. ▲ D. 22, 5, 3, (5) et 6 et 20.

1231 §2, 1°: Pius XII, m.p. *Sollicitudinem Nostram,* 6 ian. 1950, can. 279 §3 n. 1. ▲ D. 22, 5, 10 et 25; C. 4, 20, 11, pr.

1231 §2, 2°: Pius XII, m.p. *Sollicitudinem Nos-*

tram, 6 ian. 1950, can. 279 §3 n. 2.

1232: Pius XII, m.p. *Sollicitudinem Nostram,* 6 ian. 1950, can. 281 §4.

1233 §1: Pius XII, m.p. *Sollicitudinem Nostram,* 6 ian. 1950, can. 283 §1.

1233 §2: Pius XII, m.p. *Sollicitudinem Nostram,* 6 ian. 1950, can. 283.

CAN. 1234 It is for the judge to curb an excessive number of witnesses.

CAN. 1235 Before the witnesses are questioned, their names are to be communicated to the parties; if in the prudent judgment of the judge, however, that cannot be done without grave difficulty, it is to be done at least before the publication of the testimonies.

CAN. 1236 With due regard for can. 1231, a party can request the exclusion of a witness if a just cause for the exclusion is shown before the questioning of the witness.

CAN. 1237 The citation of a witness occurs through a decree of the judge legitimately intimated to the witness.

CAN. 1238 A witness who has been cited by the judge in accord with the norm of law is to appear or to inform the judge of the reason for the absence.

c) The Questioning of Witnesses

CAN. 1239 §1. Witnesses must be questioned at the tribunal unless the judge deems otherwise.

§2. Bishops and those who possess a similar favor by the law of their own state are to be heard in the place they select.

§3. The judge is to decide where to hear those for whom it is impossible or difficult to come to the tribunal because of distance, sickness, or other impediment, with due regard for cann. 1071 and 1128.

CAN. 1234 Iudicis est nimiam multitudinem testium refrenare.

CAN. 1235 Antequam testes interrogantur, eorum nomina cum partibus communicentur; si vero id prudenti iudicis existimatione fieri sine gravi difficultate non potest, saltem ante publicationem testimoniorum fiat.

CAN. 1236 Firmo can. 1231 pars petere potest, ut testis excludatur, si iusta causa demonstratur, antequam testis interrogatur.

CAN. 1237 Citatio testis fit decreto iudicis testi legitime intimato.

CAN. 1238 Testis ad normam iuris a iudice citatus pareat aut causam suae absentiae iudici notam faciat.

c) De Interrogatione Testium

CAN. 1239 §1. Testes interrogandi sunt in sede tribunalis, nisi aliud iudici videtur.

§2. Episcopi et ii, qui suae civitatis iure simili favore gaudent, audiantur in loco ab ipsis selecto.

§3. Iudex decernat, ubi audiendi sint ii, quibus propter distantiam, morbum aliudve impedimentum impossibile vel difficileest sedem tribunalis adire, firmis cann. 1071 et 1128.

1234: Pius XII, m.p. *Sollicitudinem Nostram,* 6 ian. 1950, can. 284. ▲ D. 22, 5, 1, (2); Nov. 90, 4.

1235: Pius XII, m.p. *Sollicitudinem Nostram,* 6 ian. 1950, can. 285.

1236: Pius XII, m.p. *Sollicitudinem Nostram,* 6 ian. 1950, can. 286 §§1–4. ▲ C. 4, 20, 17; Nov. 90, 7.

1237: Pius XII, m.p. *Sollicitudinem Nostram,* 6 ian. 1950, can. 287. - S.C.S. Off., instr. (ad Ep. Rituum Orient.), a. 1883, tit. II, 9.

1238: Pius XII, m.p. *Sollicitudinem Nostram,* 6

ian. 1950, can. 288 §1. ▲ D. 22, 5, 8; C. 4, 20, 15, (7).

1239 §1: Pius XII, m.p. *Sollicitudinem Nostram,* 6 ian. 1950, can. 292 §1.

1239 §2: Pius XII, m.p. *Sollicitudinem Nostram,* 6 ian. 1950, can. 292 §2 n. 1. ▲ C. 1, 3, 7; 4, 20, 16, (1); Nov. 123, 7.

1239 §3: Pius XII, m.p. *Sollicitudinem Nostram,* 6 ian. 1950, can. 292 §2 nn. 2–4. - S.C.S. Off., instr. (ad Ep. Rituum Orient.), a. 1883, tit. III, 15. ▲ D. 12, 2, 15; 22, 5, 3, (6); Nov. 90, 5.

CAN. 1240 The parties cannot be present at the questioning of the witnesses unless the judge has decided to admit them, especially when the matter concerns a private good. Their procurators or advocates, however, can be present unless the judge has decided that the questioning must proceed in secret due to the circumstances of the matters and persons.

CAN. 1241 §1. Each witness must be questioned separately.

§2. If witnesses disagree among themselves or with a party in a grave matter, the judge can have those who disagree meet together, forestalling discord and scandal insofar as possible.

CAN. 1242 The questioning of a witness is conducted by the judge, the judge's delegate or an auditor, who must be assisted by a notary. Consequently, if the parties, the promoter of justice, the defender of the bond, or the advocates present at the questioning have any other questions to be put to the witness, they are to propose them not to the witness but to the judge or to the one taking the judge's place, who is to ask the questions, unless particular law provides otherwise.

CAN. 1243 §1. The judge is to call to the attention of the witness the grave obligation to tell the whole truth and only the truth.

§2. The judge is to administer an oath to the witness according to can. 1213; a witness who refuses to take it, however, is to be heard without the oath.

CAN. 1240 Interrogationi testium partes assistere non possunt, nisi iudex, praesertim cum res est de bono privato, eas admittendas censuit; assistere tamen possunt earum procuratores vel advocati, nisi iudex propter rerum et personarum adiuncta censuit secreto esse procedendum.

CAN. 1241 §1. Testes seorsum singuli interrogandi sunt.

§2. Si testes inter se aut cum parte in re gravi dissentiunt, iudex discrepantes inter se conferre potest remotis, quatenus fieri potest, dissidiis et scandalo.

CAN. 1242 Interrogatio testis fit a iudice vel ab eius delegato aut auditore, cui assistat oportet notarius; quare partes vel promotor iustitiae vel defensor vinculi vel advocati, qui interrogationi intersunt, si alias interrogationes testi faciendas habent, has non testi, sed iudici vel eius locum tenenti proponant, ut eas ipse deferat, nisi aliter iure particulari cavetur.

CAN. 1243 §1. Iudex testi in mentem revocet gravem obligationem dicendi totam et solam veritatem.

§2. Iudex testi deferat iusiurandum secundum can. 1213; si vero testis renuit illud emittere, iniuratus audiatur.

1240: Pius XII, m.p. *Sollicitudinem Nostram,* 6 ian. 1950, can. 293.

1241 §1: Pius XII, m.p. *Sollicitudinem Nostram,* 6 ian. 1950, can. 294 §1. - S.C.S. Off., instr. (ad Ep. Rituum Orient.), a. 1883, tit. III, 13.

1241 §2: Pius XII, m.p. *Sollicitudinem Nostram,* 6 ian. 1950, can. 294 §§2–3.

1242: Pius XII, m.p. *Sollicitudinem Nostram,* 6

ian. 1950, can. 295; S.C.S. Off., instr., a. 1858; instr. (ad Ep. Rituum Orient.), a. 1883, tit. III, 13; instr. 20 iul. 1890.

1243 §1: Pius XII, m.p. *Sollicitudinem Nostram,* 6 ian. 1950, can. 289 §4.

1243 §2: Pius XII, m.p. *Sollicitudinem Nostram,* 6 ian. 1950, can. 289 §§1 et 3. ▲ C. 4, 20, 9 et 16, pr.

CAN. 1244 The judge is first of all to establish the identity of the witness, then ask what relationship the witness has with the parties, and, when addressing specific questions to the witness concerning the case, also inquire about the sources of his or her knowledge and the precise time when the witness learned what he or she asserts.

CAN. 1245 The questions are to be brief, accommodated to the mental capacity of the person being questioned, not comprised of several points at the same time, not captious or deceptive or suggestive of a response, free from any kind of offense, and pertinent to the case being tried.

CAN. 1246 §1. Questions must not be communicated to the witnesses beforehand.

§2. Nonetheless, if the matters about which testimony must be given are so removed from memory that they cannot be affirmed with certainty unless recalled in advance, the judge can advise the witness beforehand on some matters if the judge thinks this can be done without danger.

CAN. 1247 Witnesses are to give testimony orally and are not to read written materials unless they are computations and accounts; in this case, they can consult the notes that they brought with them.

CAN. 1248 §1. The notary is to write down the response immediately and must report the exact words of the witness, at least in what pertains to those points that touch directly upon the matter of the trial.

§2. The use of technical devices for voice re-

CAN. 1244 Iudex imprimis testis identitatem comprobet; exquirat, quaenam sit ei cum partibus necessitudo et, cum testi interrogationes specificas circa causam defert, sciscitetur quoque fontes eius scientiae et, quo determinato tempore ea, quae asserit, cognoverit.

CAN. 1245 Interrogationes breves sint, interrogandi captui accommodatae, non plura simul complectentes, non captiosae, non subdolae, non suggerentes responsionem, remotae a cuiusvis offensione et pertinentes ad causam, quae agitur.

CAN. 1246 §1. Interrogationes non sunt cum testibus antea communicandae.

§2. Si vero ea, quae testificanda sunt, ita a memoria sunt remota, ut, nisi antea recoluntur, certo affirmari non possint, potest iudex nonnulla testem praemonere, si id sine periculo fieri posse censet.

CAN. 1247 Testes ore testimonium dicant et scriptum ne legant, nisi de calculo et rationibus agitur; hoc enim in casu adnotationes, quas secum attulerunt, consulere possunt.

CAN. 1248 §1. Responsio statim redigenda est scripto a notario, qui referre debet ipsa verba testimonii saltem, quod attinet ad ea, quae obiectum iudicii directe attingunt.

§2. Admitti potest usus inventorum tech-

1244: Pius XII, m.p. *Sollicitudinem Nostram,* 6 ian. 1950, can. 296. ▲ D. 22, 5, 3, pr.

1245: Pius XII, m.p. *Sollicitudinem Nostram,* 6 ian. 1950, can. 297.

1246 §1: Pius XII, m.p. *Sollicitudinem Nostram,* 6 ian. 1950, can. 298 §1.

1246 §2: Pius XII, m.p. *Sollicitudinem Nostram,* 6 ian. 1950, can. 298 §2.

1247: Pius XII, m.p. *Sollicitudinem Nostram,* 6 ian. 1950, can. 299.

1248 §1: Pius XII, m.p. *Sollicitudinem Nostram,* 6 ian. 1950, can. 300.

production can be allowed provided that the responses are afterwards transcribed and, if possible, signed by those who made the responses.

CAN. 1249 The notary is to make mention in the acts whether the oath was taken, excused or refused, of the presence of the parties and other persons, of the questions added *ex officio*, and in general of everything worth remembering that may have occurred while the witnesses were being questioned.

CAN. 1250 §1. At the end of the questioning, the written record made by the notary of the witness' replies must be read before the witness, or what has been recorded by technical devices of the witness' replies must be played back, giving the witness the opportunity to add, suppress, correct or change it.

§2. Finally, the witness, the judge and the notary must sign the acts.

CAN. 1251 Although already questioned, witnesses can be recalled for questioning before the testimonies are published, either at the request of a party or *ex officio*, if the judge deems it necessary or useful, provided there is no danger of collusion or corruption.

CAN. 1252 Both the expenses that the witnesses incurred and the income that they lost by giving testimony must be paid to them according to the equitable assessment of the judge.

nicorum, quibus voces reproducuntur, dummodo deinde responsiones scripto consignentur et subscribantur, si fieri potest, ab iis, qui responsiones dederunt.

CAN. 1249 Notarius in actis mentionem faciat de praestito, remisso aut recusato iureiurando, de partium aliorumque praesentia, de interrogationibus ex officio additis et generatim de omnibus memoria dignis, quae forte acciderunt, dum testes interrogati sunt.

CAN. 1250 §1. In fine interrogationis coram teste legi debent, quae notarius de eius responsionibus scripto redegit, vel testi audita facere, quae ope inventi technici de eius responsionibus incisa sunt, dato eidem testi iure addendi, supprimendi, corrigendi, variandi.

§2. Denique actui subscribere debent testis, iudex et notarius.

CAN. 1251 Testes, etsi iam interrogati, possunt parte postulante aut ex officio, antequam testimonia publicantur, denuo ad interrogationem vocari, si iudex id necessarium vel utile ducit, dummodo tamen omnis collusionis vel corruptelae quodvis absit periculum.

CAN. 1252 Testibus secundum aequam iudicis taxationem solvi debent expensae, quas fecerunt, et lucrum, quod amiserunt, testimonii ferendi causa.

1249: PIUS XII, m.p. *Sollicitudinem Nostram,* 6 ian. 1950, can. 302.

1250 §1: PIUS XII, m.p. *Sollicitudinem Nostram,* 6 ian. 1950, can. 303 §1. - S.C.S. Off., instr. (ad Ep. Rituum Orient.), a. 1883, tit. III, 14.

1250 §2: PIUS XII, m.p. *Sollicitudinem Nostram,* 6

ian. 1950, can. 303 §2. - S.C.S. Off., instr. a. 1858; instr. (ad Ep. Rituum Orient.), a. 1883, tit. III, 14.

1251: PIUS XII, m.p. *Sollicitudinem Nostram,* 6 ian. 1950, can. 304.

1252: PIUS XII, m.p. *Sollicitudinem Nostram,* 6 ian. 1950, can. 310. ▲ C. 4, 20, 11 et 16; 7, 62, 6, (2).

d) The Trustworthiness of Testimonies

CAN. 1253   In evaluating the testimony, the judge, after having requested testimonial letters if necessary, is to consider the following:

1° what the condition or reputation of the person is;

2° whether the witness testifies from first-hand knowledge, especially regarding what has been seen or heard personally, or from his or her opinion, rumor or hearsay;

3° whether the witness is reliable and firmly consistent or inconsistent, uncertain or vacillating;

4° whether the witness has co-witnesses to the testimony or is confirmed or not by other items of proof.

CAN. 1254   The testimony of a single witness cannot produce full proof unless it concerns a qualified witness testifying about matters done *ex officio*, or unless the circumstances of things and persons suggest otherwise.

4° Experts

CAN. 1255   The services of experts must be used whenever a prescript of the law or the judge requires their examination and opinion, based on the precepts of art or science, in order to establish some fact or to discern the true nature of some matter.

CAN. 1256   It is for the judge, after having heard the parties or upon their suggestion, to appoint the experts or, if the case warrants, to accept reports already made by other experts.

d) De Testimoniorum Fide

CAN. 1253   In aestimandis testimoniis iudex requisitis, si opus est, testimonialibus litteris consideret:

1° quae condicio sit personae quaeve honestas;

2° utrum de scientia propria, praesertim de visu et auditu proprio testificetur, an de sua opinione, de fama aut de auditu ab aliis;

3° utrum testis constans sit et firmiter sibi cohaereat an varius, incertus vel vacillans;

4° utrum testimonii contestes habeat alisve probationis elementis confirmetur necne.

CAN. 1254   Unius testis testimonium plenam fidem facere non potest, nisi agitur de teste qualificato, qui testimonium fert de rebus ex officio gestis, aut rerum et personarum adiuncta aliud suadent.

4° De Peritis

CAN. 1255   Peritorum opera utendum est, quoties ex iuris vel iudicis praescripto eorum examen et votum praeceptis artis vel scientiae innixum requiruntur ad factum aliquod comprobandum vel ad veram alicuius rei naturam dignoscendam.

CAN. 1256   Iudicis est peritos nominare auditis vel proponentibus partibus aut, si casus fert, relationes ab aliis peritis iam factas assumere.

1253: Pius XII, m.p. *Sollicitudinem Nostram,* 6 ian. 1950, can. 312. ▲ D. 22, 5, 2 et 3, (pr. 1–3) et 13; Nov. 90, 1, pr.

1254: Pius XII, m.p. *Sollicitudinem Nostram,* 6 ian. 1950, can. 314 §1. - Apost. can. 75; Nic. I, cann. 2, 6; Carth. can. 132; Quinisext. can. 85; Sign. Apost., re-scr. 10 nov. 1970, 1); rescr. 2 ian. 1971, 1) "Ad." ▲ D. 48, 18, 20; C. 4, 20, 9.

1255: Pius XII, m.p. *Sollicitudinem Nostram,* 6 ian. 1950, can. 315.

1256: Pius XII, m.p. *Sollicitudinem Nostram,* 6 ian. 1950, can. 316.

CAN. 1257 Experts can be excluded or objected to for the same reasons as witnesses.

CAN. 1258 §1. Attentive to what the parties may bring forward, the judge is to determine by a decree the individual items upon which the services of the expert must focus.

§2. The acts of the case and other documents and aids that the expert may need to fulfill his or her function must be turned over to the expert.

§3. After having heard the expert, the judge is to determine the time within which the expert must complete the examination and submit the report.

CAN. 1259 §1. Each of the experts is to prepare a report separate from the others unless the judge orders that one report be made and signed by the experts individually; if this is done, differences of opinion, if there are any, are to be noted carefully.

§2. Experts must indicate clearly by what documents or other suitable means they gained certainty of the identity of the persons, things, or places, by what manner and method they proceeded in fulfilling the function entrusted to them, and the principal arguments on which they based their conclusions.

§3. The judge can summon the expert to supply explanations that later seem necessary.

CAN. 1260 §1. The judge is to weigh carefully not only the conclusions of the experts, even if they are in agreement, but also the other circumstances of the case.

CAN. 1257 Eisdem de causis ac testis etiam periti excluduntur aut recusari possunt.

CAN. 1258 §1. Iudex attentis eis, quae a partibus forte deducuntur, singula capita decreto suo definiat, circa quae periti opera versari debeat.

§2. Perito remittenda sunt acta causae aliaque documenta et subsidia, quibus egere potest ad suum munus exsequendum.

§3. Iudex ipso perito audito tempus determinet, intra quod examen perficiendum est et relatio danda.

CAN. 1259 §1. Periti suam quisque relationem a ceteris distinctam conficiant, nisi iudex iubet unam fieri a singulis subscribendam; quae si fit, opinionum diversitates, si quae fuerunt, diligenter adnotentur.

§2. Periti debent indicare perspicue, quibus documentis vel aliis idoneis modis certiores facti sint de personarum vel rerum vel locorum identitate, qua via et ratione processerint in explendo munere sibi demandato et quibus prae aliis argumentis suae conclusiones nitantur.

§3. Peritus vocari potest a iudice, ut explicationes, quae ulterius necessariae videntur, suppeditet.

CAN. 1260 §1. Iudex non peritorum tantum conclusiones, etsi concordes, sed cetera quoque causae adiuncta attente perpendat.

1257: Pius XII, m.p. *Sollicitudinem Nostram,* 6 ian. 1950, cann. 318 §2, 319.

1258 §1: Pius XII, m.p. *Sollicitudinem Nostram,* 6 ian. 1950, can. 322 §1.

1258 §2: S.C. de Discip. Sacr., instr. 15 aug. 1936, art. 147 §2.

1258 §3: Pius XII, m.p. *Sollicitudinem Nostram,* 6 ian. 1950, can. 322 §2.

1259 §1: Pius XII, m.p. *Sollicitudinem Nostram,* 6 ian. 1950, can. 325.

1259 §2: Pius XII, m.p. *Sollicitudinem Nostram,* 6 ian. 1950, can. 324 §3.

1259 §3: Pius XII, m.p. *Sollicitudinem Nostram,* 6 ian. 1950, can. 324 §2.

1260 §1: Pius XII, m.p. *Sollicitudinem Nostram,* 6 ian. 1950, can. 327 §1.

§2. When giving reasons for the decision, the judge must express what considerations prompted him or her to admit or reject the conclusions of the experts.

CAN. 1261 With due regard for particular law, the judge must fairly and equitably determine the expenses and remuneration to be paid to the experts.

CAN. 1262 §1. The parties can designate private experts who need to be approved by the judge.

§2. If the judge allows private experts, they can inspect the acts of the case insofar as it is necessary and attend the presentation of the expert testimony; moreover, they can always present their own report.

5° Access and Judicial Recognizance

CAN. 1263 If, in order to decide a case, the judge considers it opportune to have access to some place or to inspect something, the judge, after having heard the parties, is to order it by decree describing briefly what must be exhibited for the access or the judicial recognizance.

CAN. 1264 When the access or judicial recognizance has been completed, a document about it is to be drafted.

6° Presumptions

CAN. 1265 To come to a just sentence, the judge can formulate presumptions that are not established by the law itself as long as they are based on a certain and determined fact directly connected with the matter in dispute.

§2. Cum reddit rationes decidendi, exprimere debet, quibus argumentis motus peritorum conclusiones aut admiserit aut reiecerit.

CAN. 1261 Peritis solvendae sunt expensae et remuneratio a iudice ex bono et aequo determinandae servato iure particulari.

CAN. 1262 §1. Partes possunt peritos privatos a iudice approbandos designare.

§2. Periti privati, si iudex admittit, possunt acta causae, quatenus opus est, inspicere, exsecutioni peritiae interesse, semper autem possunt suam relationem exhibere.

5° De Accessu et de Recognitione Iudiciali

CAN. 1263 Si ad definitionem causae iudex opportunum duxit ad aliquem locum accedere vel aliquam rem inspicere, decreto id praestituat, quo ea, quae in accessu vel in recognitione iudiciali praestanda sunt, auditis partibus summatim describat.

CAN. 1264 Peracti accessus vel recognitionis iudicialis documentum conficiatur.

6° De Praesumptionibus

CAN. 1265 Praesumptiones, quae ab ipso iure non statuuntur, iudex, ut ad iustam sententiam deveniat, conicere potest, dummodo hoc fiat ex facto certo et determinato, quod cum obiecto controversiae cohaeret.

1260 §2: Pius XII, m.p. *Sollicitudinem Nostram,* 6 ian. 1950, can. 327 §2.

1261: Pius XII, m.p. *Sollicitudinem Nostram,* 6 ian. 1950, can. 328.

1263: Pius XII, m.p. *Sollicitudinem Nostram,* 6 ian. 1950, can. 329 §1.

1264: Pius XII, m.p. *Sollicitudinem Nostram,* 6 ian. 1950, can. 334.

1265: Pius XII, m.p. *Sollicitudinem Nostram,* 6 ian. 1950, can. 351.

CAN. 1266 A person who has a favorable presumption of law is freed from the burden of proof, which then falls to the other party.

CAN. 1266 Qui pro se habet ea, quae ab ipso iure praesumuntur, liberatur ab onere probandi, quod recidit in partem adversam.

ART. VI. *Incidental Cases*

ART. VI. *De Causis Incidentibus*

CAN. 1267 An incidental case arises whenever, after the trial has begun, a question is proposed that nevertheless pertains to the case in such a way that it frequently must be resolved before the principal question, even if was not expressly contained in the *libellus* that introduced the litigation.

CAN. 1267 Causa incidens habetur, quoties incepta litis instantia quaestio proponitur, quae, etsi libello litis introductorio non continetur expresse, nihilominus ita ad causam pertinet, ut solvi plerumque debeat ante quaestionem principalem.

CAN. 1268 An incidental case is proposed in writing or orally before the judge competent to decide the principal case, indicating the connection between this and the principal case.

CAN. 1268 Causa incidens proponitur scripto vel ore indicato nexu, qui intercedit inter ipsam et causam principalem, coram iudice competenti ad causam principalem definiendam.

CAN. 1269 §1. After having received the petition and heard the parties, the judge is to decide most expeditiously whether the proposed incidental question seems to have a foundation and a connection with the principal trial or rather must be rejected at the outset. If the judge admits the incidental question, the judge is to decide whether it is of such gravity that it must be resolved by an interlocutory sentence or by a decree.

CAN. 1269 §1. Iudex recepta petitione et auditis partibus expeditissime definiat, utrum proposita quaestio incidens fundamentum habere videatur et nexum cum causa principali an vero sit in limine reicienda, et, si eam admittit, num talis sit gravitatis, ut debeat solvi per sententiam interlocutoriam vel per decretum.

§2. If the judge decides not to resolve the incidental question before the definitive question, however, the judge is to decree that the question will be considered when the principal case is decided.

§2. Cum vero iudicat quaestionem incidentem non esse solvendam ante sententiam definitivam, decernat, ut eiusdem ratio habeatur, cum causa principalis definietur.

CAN. 1270 §1. If the incidental question must be resolved by sentence, the norms for the

CAN. 1270 §1. Si quaestio incidens solvi debet per sententiam, serventur

---

1266: Pius XII, m.p. *Sollicitudinem Nostram,* 6 ian. 1950, can. 350. ▲ D. 22, 3, 3 et 12; Basilic. 22, 1, 3 et 12.

1267: Pius XII, m.p. *Sollicitudinem Nostram,* 6 ian. 1950, can. 361.

1268: Pius XII, m.p. *Sollicitudinem Nostram,* 6 ian. 1950, can. 362.

1269 §1: Pius XII, m.p. *Sollicitudinem Nostram,* 6 ian. 1950, cann. 363, 364 §1.

1269 §2: S. Rom. Rotae Trib., *Normae* 29 iun. 1934, art. 109 §1.

1270 §1: Pius XII, m.p. *Sollicitudinem Nostram,* 6 ian. 1950, can. 364 §2.

summary contentious process are to be observed unless the judge decides otherwise due to the gravity of the matter.

§2. If the matter must be resolved by decree, however, the tribunal can entrust the matter to an auditor or the presiding judge.

CAN. 1271 Before the principal case is completed, the judge or the tribunal can revoke or reform the decree of interlocutory sentence for a just reason either at the request of a party or *ex officio* after hearing the parties.

1° Parties Who Do Not Appear

CAN. 1272 §1. If the respondent, after having been cited, has neither appeared nor given a suitable excuse for being absent or has not responded according to the norm of can. 1190, §1, the judge, having observed what is required, is to declare the respondent absent from the trial and decree that the case is to proceed to the definitive sentence and its execution.

§2. Before issuing this decree, the judge must be certain that a legitimately executed citation has reached the respondent within the useful time, even by issuing another citation if necessary.

CAN. 1273 §1. If the respondent appears at the trial later or responds before a decision in the case, the respondent can offer conclusions and proofs, with due regard for can. 1283; however, the judge is to take care that the trial is not prolonged intentionally through longer and unnecessary delays.

§2. Even if the respondent did not appear or

canones de iudicio contentioso summario, nisi attenta rei gravitate aliud iudici videtur.

§2. Si vero solvi debet per decretum, tribunal potest rem committere auditori vel praesidi.

CAN. 1271 Antequam finitur causa principalis, iudex vel tribunal potest decretum vel sententiam interlocutoriam iusta de causa revocare aut reformare sive ad instantiam partis sive ex officio auditis partibus.

1° De Partibus non Comparentibus

CAN. 1272 §1. Si pars conventa citata non comparuit nec idoneam absentiae excusationem attulit aut non respondit ad normam can. 1190, §1, iudex eam decreto a iudicio absentem declaret et decernat, ut causa servatis servandis usque ad sententiam definitivam eiusque exsecutionem procedat.

§2. Antequam hoc decretum fertur, debet etiam per novam citationem, si opus est, constare citationem legitime factam ad partem conventam tempore utili pervenisse.

CAN. 1273 §1. Si pars conventa deinde in iudicio se sistit aut responsum dedit ante causae definitionem, conclusiones et probationes afferre potest firmo can. 1283; caveat autem iudex, ne de industria in longiores et non necessarias moras iudicium protrahatur.

§2. Etsi pars conventa non comparuit

1271: Pius XII, m.p. *Sollicitudinem Nostram,* 6 ian. 1950, can. 365.

1272 §1: Pius XII, m.p. *Sollicitudinem Nostram,* 6 ian. 1950, cann. 366, 367 §1, 368 §1. - Apost. can. 74; Carth. cann. 19, 79, 100. ▲ D. 5, 1, 73; 22, 3, 19, (1); 42, 1, 53; C. 3, 1, 13, (4); 7, 43, 2; 7, 49, 5 et 7 et 10; Nov. 69, 2 et 3, pr.; 126, 2.

1272 §2: Pius XII, m.p. *Sollicitudinem Nostram,* 6 ian. 1950, can. 367 §1 n. 1 et §2.

1273 §1: Pius XII, m.p. *Sollicitudinem Nostram,* 6 ian. 1950, can. 370. - Carth. can. 19.

1273 §2: Pius XII, m.p. *Sollicitudinem Nostram,* 6 ian. 1950, can. 371. ▲ C. 7, 43, 3.

respond before a decision in the case, the respondent can challenge the sentence. If the respondent proves that there was a legitimate impediment for being detained and there was no personal fault in its not being made known beforehand, the respondent can lodge a complaint of nullity.

CAN. 1274 If the petitioner has not appeared on the day and at the hour prescribed for the joinder of the issue and has not offered a suitable excuse:

1° the judge is to cite the petitioner again;

2° if the petitioner does not comply with the new citation, the petitioner is presumed to have renounced the trial;

3° if the petitioner later wishes to intervene in the process, can. 1273 is to be observed.

CAN. 1275 §1. A party who is absent from the trial and has not given proof of a just impediment is obliged to pay the judicial expenses that have accrued because of the absence and to indemnify the other party if necessary.

§2. If both the petitioner and the respondent were absent from the trial, each of them is obliged to pay the entire expenses of the case.

2° Intervention of a Third Person in the Case

CAN. 1276 §1. A person who has an interest can be admitted to intervene in a case at any grade of the trial, either as a party defending his or her own right or in an accessory manner to help a party.

aut responsum non dedit ante causae definitionem, impugnationibus uti potest adversus sententiam; si vero probat se legitimo impedimento fuisse detentam, quod sine sua culpa antea demonstrare non potuit, querela nullitatis uti potest.

CAN. 1274 Si die et hora ad litis constestationem praestitutis actor neque comparuit neque idoneam excusationem attulit:

1° iudex eum citet iterum:

2° si actor novae citationi non paruit, praesumitur litis instantiae renuntiavisse;

3° si vero postea in processu intervenire vult, servetur can. 1273.

CAN. 1275 §1. Pars absens a iudicio, quae iustum impedimentum non probavit, tenetur obligatione solvendi expensas iudiciales, quae ob ipsius absentiam factae sunt, necnon, si opus est, indemnitatem alteri parti praestandi.

§2. Si et actor et pars conventa fuerunt absentes a iudicio, uterque per se ipse respondet, ut integrae expensae iudiciales solvantur.

2° De Interventu Tertii in Causa

CAN. 1276 §1. Is, cuius interest, admitti potest ad interveniendum in causa in quolibet gradu iudicii sive ut pars, quae proprium ius defendit, sive accessorie ad aliquam partem adiuvandam.

1274, 1°: Pius XII, m.p. *Sollicitudinem Nostram,* 6 ian. 1950, can. 373. - Apost. can. 74; Carth. can. 19. ▲ C. 3, 1, 13, (2–9); 7, 43, 8–9.

1274, 2°: Pius XII, m.p. *Sollicitudinem Nostram,* 6 ian. 1950, can. 374 §1. ▲ C. 3, 1, 13, (2–9); Nov. 112, 3, 1.

1275 §1: Pius XII, m.p. *Sollicitudinem Nostram,* 6 ian. 1950, can. 375 §1. ▲ C. 3, 1, 13, (2–9); Nov. 112, 3, 1.

1275 §2: Pius XII, m.p. *Sollicitudinem Nostram,* 6 ian. 1950, can. 375 §2.

1276 §1: Pius XII, m.p. *Sollicitudinem Nostram,* 6 ian. 1950, can. 376 §1.

§2. However, to be admitted, the person must present a *libellus* to the judge before the conclusion of the case; in the *libellus* the person is to demonstrate his or her right to intervene.

§3. A person who intervenes in a case must be admitted at that stage of the trial that the case has reached, with a brief and peremptory period of time assigned to the person to present proofs if the case has reached the probatory period.

CAN. 1277 After having heard the parties, the judge must summon to the trial a third person whose intervention seems necessary.

3° Attempts to Pending Litigation

CAN. 1278 An attempt is an act by which, while litigation is pending, an innovation is made by one party against the other or by the judge either against one or both of the parties. Unless the innovation is admitted by the law itself, an attempt is prejudicial to a party and made against his or her will regarding a matter of the trial or concerning procedural rights.

CAN. 1279 An attempt is null by the law itself; therefore, the judge must decree its revocation. However, the attempt is sanated by the law itself if, within a month from its being known, no question about it is proposed to the judge.

CAN. 1280 If a party made the innovation, the judge of the principal case is to decide questions regarding attempts most expeditiously; however, if the judge made the innovation, the appeal tribunal is to decide such questions.

§2. Sed ut admittatur, debet ante conclusionem in causa libellum iudici exhibere, in quo breviter suum ius interveniendi demonstret.

§3. Qui intervenit in causa, admittendus est in eo sta causa reperitur, assignato eidem brevi ac peremptorio termino ad probationes suas exhibendas, si causa ad periodum probatoriam pervenit.

CAN. 1277 Tertium, cuius interventus videtur necessarius, iudex auditis partibus debet in iudicium vocare.

3° De Attentatis Lite Pendente

CAN. 1278 Attentatum est actus, quo, lite pendente, ab una parte adversus alteram vel a iudice adversus alterutram vel utramque aliquid innovatur in praeiudicium partis et ea dissentiente sive circa materiam iudicii sive circa iura processualia, nisi ipso iure innovatio admittitur.

CAN. 1279 Attentatum est ipso iure nullum, quare iudex decernere debet eius revocationem; sanatur tamen ipso iure, si intra mensem a die habitae notitiae de attentato computandum quaestio de eo iudici non proponitur.

CAN. 1280 Quaestiones de attentatis expeditissim definiendae sunt a iudice causae principalis, si pars attentatum patravit; si vero ipse iudex attentatum patravit, a tribunali appellationis.

1276 §2: Pius XII, m.p. *Sollicitudinem Nostram,* 6 ian. 1950, can. 376 §2.

1276 §3: Pius XII, m.p. *Sollicitudinem Nostram,* 6 ian. 1950, can. 376 §3.

1277: Pius XII, m.p. *Sollicitudinem Nostram,* 6 ian. 1950, can. 377.

1278: Pius XII, m.p. *Sollicitudinem Nostram,* 6 ian. 1950, can. 378. ▲ D. 4, 7, 1; 44, 6, 3; C. 8, 36 (37), 2 et 5.

1279: Pius XII, m.p. *Sollicitudinem Nostram,* 6 ian. 1950, cann. 379 §§1 et 2 n. 1, 381.

1280: Pius XII, m.p. *Sollicitudinem Nostram,* 6 ian. 1950, cann. 379 §2 n. 2, 380 §2.

ART. VII. *Publication of the Acts, Conclusion of the Case and Discussion of the Case*

CAN. 1281 §1. After the proofs have been collected, the judge by a decree must, under penalty of nullity, permit the parties and their advocates to inspect at the tribunal chancery the acts not yet known to them; furthermore, a copy of the acts can also be given to advocates who request one. In cases pertaining to the public good, in order to avoid most grave dangers, the judge can decree that a specific act is not to be shown to anyone; the judge is to take care, however, that the right of defense always remains intact.

§2. To complete the proofs, the parties can propose additional proofs to the judge. When these have been collected, there is an occasion for repeating the decree mentioned in §1 if the judge thinks it necessary.

CAN. 1282 §1. When everything pertaining to the production of the proofs has been completed, the conclusion of the case (*conclusio in causa*) is reached.

§2. This conclusion occurs whenever the parties declare that they have nothing else to add, the useful time prescribed by the judge for proposing proofs has elapsed, or the judge declares that the case is instructed sufficiently.

§3. The judge is to issue a decree that the conclusion of the case has been completed, in whatever manner it has occurred.

ART. VII. *De Actorum Publicatione, de Conclusione in Causa et de Causae Discussione*

CAN. 1281 §1. Acquisitis probationibus iudex decreto partibus et earum advocatis permittere debet sub poena nullitatis, ut acta nondum eis nota apud tribunalis cancellariam inspiciant; quin etiam advocatis id petentibus dari potest actorum exemplar; in causis vero, quae ad bonum publicum spectant, iudex ad gravissima pericula evitanda aliquod actum nemini manifestandum esse decernere potest, cauto tamen, ut ius defensionis semper integrum maneat.

§2. Ad probationes complendas partes possunt alias iudici proponere; quibus, si iudex necessarium duxit, acquisitis iterum est locus decreto, de quo in §1.

CAN. 1282 §1. Expletis omnibus, quae ad probationes producendas pertinent, ad conclusionem in causa devenitur.

§2. Haec conclusio habetur, quoties aut partes declaraverunt se nihil aliud adducendum habere aut utile proponendis probationibus tempus a iudice praestitutum elapsum est aut iudex declaravit se causam satis instructam habere.

§3. De peracta conclusione in causa, quocumque modo ea accidit, iudex decretum ferat.

1281 §1: Pius XII, m.p. *Sollicitudinem Nostram,* 6 ian. 1950, can. 382–383; Cons. pro Publ. Eccl. Neg., rescr. 28 apr. 1970, 18.

1281 §2: S.C. de Discip. Sacr., instr. 15 aug. 1936, art. 175 §§3–4.

1282 §1: Pius XII, m.p. *Sollicitudinem Nostram,* 6 ian. 1950, can. 384 §1. - S.C.S. Off., instr. (ad Ep. Ri-tuum Orient.), a. 1883, tit. III, 22.

1282 §2: Pius XII, m.p. *Sollicitudinem Nostram,* 6 ian. 1950, can. 384 §2. - S.C.S. Off., instr. (ad Ep. Rituum Orient.), a. 1883, tit. IV, 24.

1282 §3: Pius XII, m.p. *Sollicitudinem Nostram,* 6 ian. 1950, can. 384 §3.

CAN. 1283 §1. After the conclusion of the case, the judge can still summon the same or other witnesses or arrange for other proofs that were not requested earlier, only:

1° in cases that concern only the private good of the parties, if all the parties consent;

2° in other cases, after hearing the parties and provided that there is a grave reason and any danger or fraud or subornation is eliminated;

3° in all cases, whenever it is likely that, unless the new proof is admitted, the sentence will be unjust because of the reasons mentioned in can. 1326, §2, nn. 1–3.

§2. However, the judge can order or allow that a document be exhibited that perhaps could not have been exhibited earlier, through no fault of the interested person.

§3. New proofs are to be published according to can. 1281, §1.

CAN. 1284 After the conclusion of the case, the judge is to determine a suitable period of time to present defense briefs or observations.

CAN. 1285 §1. The defense briefs and the observations are to be written unless the judge, with the consent of the parties, considers a debate before a session of the tribunal to be sufficient.

§2. If the defense briefs along with the principal documents are being printed, the previous permission of the judge is required, without prejudice to the obligation of secrecy, if such exists.

CAN. 1283 §1. Post conclusionem in causa iudex potest adhuc eosdem testes vel alios vocare aut alias probationes, quae antea non sunt petitae, disponere tantummodo:

1° in causis, in quibus agitur de solo bono privato partium, si omnes partes consentiunt;

2° in ceteris causis, auditis partibus et dummodo gravis exstet ratio itemque quodlibet fraudis vel subornationis periculum removeatur;

3° in omnibus causis, quoties veri simile est, nisi probatio nova admittitur, sententiam iniustam futuram esse propter rationes, de quibus in can. 1326, §2, nn. 1–3.

§2. Potest autem iudex iubere vel admittere, ut exhibeatur documentum, quod forte antea sine culpa eius, cuius interest, exhiberi non potuit.

§3. Novae probationes publicentur servato can. 1281, §1.

CAN. 1284 Facta conclusione in causa iudex congruum spatium temporis praestituat ad defensiones vel animadversiones exhibendas.

CAN. 1285 §1. Defensiones et animadversiones scripto dandae sunt, nisi disputationem pro tribunali sedente iudex partibus consentientibus satis esse censet.

§2. Si defensiones cum praecipuis documentis typis imprimuntur, praevia iudicis licentia requiritur salva secreti obligatione, si qua est.

1283 §1: Pius XII, m.p. *Sollicitudinem Nostram,* 6 ian. 1950, can. 385 §1. ▲ C. 8, 35 (36), 4.

1283 §2: Pius XII, m.p. *Sollicitudinem Nostram,* 6 ian. 1950, can. 385 §1.

1283 §3: Pius XII, m.p. *Sollicitudinem Nostram,* 6 ian. 1950, can. 385 §2.

1284: Pius XII, m.p. *Sollicitudinem Nostram,* 6 ian. 1950, can. 386 §1. ▲ Nov. 115, 2.

1285 §1: Pius XII, m.p. *Sollicitudinem Nostram,* 6 ian. 1950, can. 387 §1.

1285 §2: Pius XII, m.p. *Sollicitudinem Nostram,* 6 ian. 1950, can. 387 §§3–4.

§3. The statutes of the tribunal are to be observed regarding the length of the defense briefs, the number of copies, and other matters of this kind.

CAN. 1286 §1. When the defense briefs and observations have been communicated to each party, either party is permitted to present responses within the brief time period established by the judge.

§2. The parties are given this right only once unless the judge decides that it must be granted a second time for a grave reason; then, however, the grant made to one party is considered as made to the other also.

§3. The promoter of justice and the defender of the bond have the right to reply a second time to the responses of the parties.

CAN. 1287 §1. It is absolutely forbidden for information given to the judge by the parties, advocates, or even other persons to remain outside the acts of the case.

§2. If the discussion of the case has been done in writing, the judge can order a moderate oral debate to be held before a session of the tribunal in order to explain certain questions.

CAN. 1288 A notary is to be present at the oral debate mentioned in cann. 1285, §1 and 1287, §2 so that, if the judge orders it or a party requests it and the judge consents, the notary can immediately report in writing about what was discussed and concluded.

CAN. 1289 If the parties have neglected to prepare a defense brief within the time available to them or they have entrusted themselves to the knowledge and conscience of the judge, and

§3. Circa extensionem defensionum, numerum exemplarium aliaque huiusmodi adiuncta serventur statuta tribunalis.

CAN. 1286 §1. Communicatis vicissim defensionibus atque animadversionibus utrique parti responsiones exhibere licet intra breve tempus a iudice praestitutum.

§2. Hoc ius partibus semel tantum est, nisi iudici gravi de causa iterum videtur esse concedendum; tunc autem concessio uni parti facta alteri quoque data censeatur.

§3. Promotor iustitiae et defensor vinculi ius habent iterum replicandi partium responsionibus.

CAN. 1287 §1. Omnino prohibentur partium vel advocatorum vel etiam aliorum informationes iudici datae, quae maneant extra acta causae.

§2. Si causae discussio scripto facta est, iudex potest statuere, ut moderata disputatio fiat ore pro tribunali sedente ad quaestiones nonnullas illustrandas.

CAN. 1288 Disputationi orali, de qua in cann. 1285, §1 et 1287, §2, assistat notarius, ut, si iudex praecipit aut pars postulat et iudex consentit, de disceptatis et conclusis scripto statim referre possit.

CAN. 1289 Si partes parare sibi tempore utili praestituto defensionem neglexerunt aut se remittunt iudicis scientiae et conscientiae, iudex, si ex actis et probatis

1286 §1: Pius XII, m.p. *Sollicitudinem Nostram,* 6 ian. 1950, can. 389 §1.

1286 §2: Pius XII, m.p. *Sollicitudinem Nostram,* 6 ian. 1950, can. 389 §2.

1287 §1: Pius XII, m.p. *Sollicitudinem Nostram,* 6 ian. 1950, can. 390 §1.

1287 §2: Pius XII, m.p. *Sollicitudinem Nostram,* 6 ian. 1950, can. 390 §§2–3.

1288: Pius XII, m.p. *Sollicitudinem Nostram,* 6 ian. 1950, can. 390 §4.

1289: Pius XII, m.p. *Sollicitudinem Nostram,* 6 ian. 1950, can. 391. ▲ Nov. 125, 1.

if from the acts and proofs the judge considers the matter fully examined, the judge can pronounce the sentence immediately, after having requested the observations of the promoter of justice and the defender of the bond if they are involved in the trial.

rem habet plane perspectam, potest statim sententiam pronuntiare requisitis tamen animadversionibus promotoris iustitiae et defensoris vinculi, si iudicio intersunt.

ART. VIII. *The Pronouncements of the Judge*

ART. VIII. *De Iudicis Pronuntiationibus*

CAN. 1290 After the case has been tried in a judicial manner, if it is the principal case, the judge decides it by a definitive sentence; if an incidental case, by an interlocutory sentence, with due regard for can. 1269, §1.

CAN. 1290 Causa iudiciali modo pertractata, si est principalis, definitur a iudice per sententiam definitivam; si est incidens, per sententiam interlocutoriam firmo can. 1269, §1.

CAN. 1291 §1. For the pronouncement of any sentence, the judge must have moral certitude about the matter to be decided by the sentence.

CAN. 1291 §1. Ad promuntiationem cuiuslibet sententiae requiritur in iudicis animo moralis certitudo circa rem sententia definiendam.

§2. The judge must derive this certitude from the acts and the proofs.

§2. Hanc certitudinem iudex haurire debet ex actis et probatis.

§3. The judge, however, must evaluate the proofs conscientiously with due regard for the prescripts of the law concerning the efficacy of certain proofs.

§3. Probationes autem aestimare iudex debet ex sua conscientia firmis praescriptis legis de quarundam probationum efficacia.

§4. A judge who could not arrive at this certitude is to pronounce that the right of the petitioner is not established and is to dismiss the respondent as absolved, unless it concerns a case that enjoys the favor of the law, in which case the judge must pronounce for that.

§4. Iudex, qui eam certitudinem adipisci non potuit, pronuntiet non constare de iure actoris et partem conventam absolutam dimittat, nisi agitur de causa favore iuris fruente, quo in casu pro eadem pronuntiandum est.

1290: Pius XII, m.p. *Sollicitudinem Nostram,* 6 ian. 1950, can. 392 §1.

1291 §1: Pius XII, m.p. *Sollicitudinem Nostram,* 6 ian. 1950, can. 393 §1. - S. Nicephorus CP., can. 223; Pius XII, all. 3 oct. 1941; all. 1 oct. 1942; nuntius, 5 dec. 1954, "La certezza morale. . ." ; Ioannes Paulus II, all. 4 feb. 1980, 4–6. ▲ C. 1, 22, 2; 3, 1, 11; 7, 62, 39, (2ª).

1291 §2: Pius XII, m.p. *Sollicitudinem Nostram,* 6 ian. 1950, can. 393 §2. - S. Basilius M., can. 10; Pius XII, nuntius, 5 dec. 1954, "La certezza morale . . .;" Ioannes Paulus II, all. 4 feb. 1980, 5. ▲ D. 48, 16, 1, (4); Basilic, 60, 1, 10, (4).

1291 §3: Pius XII, m.p. *Sollicitudinem Nostram,* 6 ian. 1950, can. 393 §3. - S. Basilius M., can. 10; S. Nicephorus CP., can. 223; Pius XII, nuntius, 5 dec. 1954, "La certezza morale . . .;" Ioannes Paulus II, all. 4 feb. 1980, 5. ▲ D. 22, 5, 3, (2); Nov. 73, 3.

1291 §4: Pius XII, m.p. *Sollicitudinem Nostram,* 6 ian. 1950, can. 393 §4. - Neoc. can. 9; Pius XII, nuntius, 5 dec. 1954, "La certezza morale. . .;" Ioannes Paulus II, all. 4 feb. 1980, 6. ▲ D. 34, 5, 12, (13).

CAN. 1292 §1. In a collegiate tribunal, the president of the college is to establish the date and time when the judges are to convene for deliberation. Unless a special reason suggests otherwise, the meeting is to be held at the tribunal office and no one except the judges of the college can be present.

§2. On the day assigned for the meeting, the individual judges, without indicating their names, are to submit their written conclusions on the merits of the case with the reasons in law and in fact that led them to their conclusion. These conclusions are to be appended to the acts of the case with a notation of their authenticity signed by all the judges, and must be kept secret with due regard for §4.

§3. The individual judges are to present their conclusions in order of precedence, always beginning, however, with the *ponens* of the case. A discussion then follows under the leadership of the tribunal president, especially to determine what must be established in the dispositive part of the sentence.

§4. In the discussion, however, each judge is permitted to retract his or her original conclusion. A judge who is unwilling to accede to the decision of the others, however, can demand that the conclusions of all the judges, without indicating their names, be transmitted to the higher tribunal if there is an appeal.

§5. But if the judges are unwilling or unable to arrive at a sentence during the first discussion, the decision can be deferred to a new meeting, but not beyond one week, unless the instruction of the case must be completed according to the norm of can. 1283.

CAN. 1292 §1. In tribunali collegiali, quo die et hora iudices ad deliberandum conveniant, collegii praeses statuat et, nisi specialis causa aliud suadet, in ipsa sede tribunalis conventus habeatur, cui nemo praeter collegii iudices adesse potest.

§2. Assignato conventui die singuli iudices scripto, sed reticito nomine afferant conclusiones suas in merito causae et rationes tam in iure quam in facto, quibus ad conclusionem suam venerunt; quae conclusiones cum notula de earum authenticitate ab omnibus iudicibus subscripta actis causae adiungantur secreto servandae firma §4.

§3. Prolatis ex ordine singulorum iudicum conclusionibus secundum praecedentiam, ita tamen, ut semper a causae ponente initium fiat, habeatur discussio sub tribunalis praesidis ductu, praesertim ut constabiliatur, quid statuendum sit in parte dispositiva sententiae.

§4. In discussione autem unicuique licet a pristina sua conclusione recedere; iudex vero, qui ad decisionem aliorum accedere noluit, exigere potest, ut, si fit appellatio, conclusiones omnium iudicum reticitis nominibus ad tribunal superius mittantur.

§5. Si vero iudices in prima discussione ad sententiam devenire aut nolunt aut non possunt, differri potest decisio ad novum conventum non tamen ultra hebdomadam, nisi ad normam can. 1283 complenda est causae instructio.

1292 §1: Pius XII, m.p. *Sollicitudinem Nostram*, 6 ian. 1950, can. 395 §1.

1292 §2: Pius XII, m.p. *Sollicitudinem Nostram*, 6 ian. 1950, can. 395 §2.

1292 §3: Pius XII, m.p. *Sollicitudinem Nostram*, 6 ian. 1950, can. 395 §3.

1292 §4: Pius XII, m.p. *Sollicitudinem Nostram*, 6 ian. 1950, can. 395 §4.

1292 §5: Pius XII, m.p. *Sollicitudinem Nostram*, 6 ian. 1950, can. 395 §5.

CAN. 1293 §1. If there is only one judge, he will write the sentence himself.

§2. In a collegiate tribunal, the sentence is to be written selecting the reasons from those the individual judges brought forth during the discussion, unless a majority of the judges have already determined the reasons to be presented. The sentence must then be submitted for the approval of the individual judges.

§3. The sentence must be issued no more than one month from the day on which the case was decided, unless in a collegiate tribunal the judges set a longer period for a grave reason.

CAN. 1294 The sentence must:

1° decide the controversy discussed before the tribunal with an appropriate response given to the individual issues;

2° determine what obligations have arisen for the parties from the trial and how they must be fulfilled;

3° set forth the reasons or motives in law and in fact on which the dispositive part of the sentence is based;

4° determine the judicial expenses.

CAN. 1295 §1. After the invocation of the Divine Name, the sentence must express in order who is the judge or the tribunal, the petitioner, the respondent, and the procurator, with their names and domiciles correctly designated, and the promoter of justice and the defender of the bond if they took part in the trial.

§2. Next, it must briefly relate the facts together with the conclusions of the parties and the formula of the doubts.

CAN. 1293 §1. Si iudex est unicus, ipse sententiam redigit.

§2. In tribunali collegiali sententia redigenda est desumendo motiva ex eis, quae singuli iudices in discussione attulerunt, nisi a maiore numero iudicum definita sunt motiva praeferenda; sententia deinde singulorum iudicum approbationi subicienda est.

§3. Sententia edenda est non ultra mensem computandum a die, quo causa definita est, nisi in tribunali collegiali iudices gravi ex ratione longius tempus praestituerunt.

CAN. 1294 Sententia debet:

1° definire controversiam coram tribunali agitatam data singulis dubiis congrua responsione;

2° definire, quae sint partium obligationes ex iudicio ortae et quomodo implendae sint;

3° exponere rationes seu motiva tam in iure quam in facto, quibus pars dispositiva sententiae innititur;

4° statuere de expensis iudicialibus.

CAN. 1295 §1. Sententia post divini Nominis invocationem exprimat oportet ex ordine, quis sit iudex aut quid tribunal, quis sit actor, pars conventa, procurator, nominibus et domiciliis accurate designatis, promotor iustitiae, defensor vinculi, si partem in iudicio habuerunt.

§2. Referre postea debet breviter facti speciem cum partium conclusionibus et formula dubiorum.

1293 §1: Pius XII, m.p. *Sollicitudinem Nostram,* 6 ian. 1950, can. 396.

1293 §2: Pius XII, m.p. *Sollicitudinem Nostram,* 6 ian. 1950, can. 397 §2.

1293 §3: S.C. de Discip. Sacr., instr. 15 aug. 1936, art. 200 §1; Pius XII, m.p. *Sollicitudinem Nostram,* 6 ian. 1950, can. 400.

1294: Pius XII, m.p. *Sollicitudinem Nostram,* 6 ian. 1950, can. 397 §1. ▲ Instit. 4, 6, 32; C. 7, 45, 3; 7, 46, 4; Basilic. 9, 1, 80.

1295 §1: Pius XII, m.p. *Sollicitudinem Nostram,* 6 ian. 1950, can. 398 §§1–2.

1295 §2: Pius XII, m.p. *Sollicitudinem Nostram,* 6 ian. 1950, can. 398 §3.

§3. Then follows the dispositive part of the sentence preceded by the reasons on which it is based.

§4. It is to conclude with the indication of the date and the place where it was rendered, with the signature of the judge or, if it is a collegiate tribunal, of all the judges, and the notary.

CAN. 1296 The norms established for a definitive sentence also apply, making suitable adaptations, with regard to an interlocutory sentence.

CAN. 1297 The sentence is to be intimated as soon as possible, indicating the time within which an appeal of the sentence can be placed; it has no force before it is intimated even if the dispositive section was made known to the parties with the permission of the judge.

CAN. 1298 The intimation of the sentence can be done either by giving a copy of the sentence to the parties or their procurators or by sending them a copy according to the norm of can. 1192.

CAN. 1299 §1. If in the text of the sentence an error in calculation turns up, a material error occurs in transcribing the dispositive section or in relating the facts or the petitions of the parties, or the requirements of can. 1295, §4 are omitted, the tribunal that rendered the sentence must correct or complete it either at the request of a party or *ex officio,* but always after the parties have been heard and a decree appended to the bottom of the sentence.

§2. If any party objects, the incidental question is to be decided by a decree.

§3. Haec subsequatur pars dispositiva sententiae praemissis rationibus, quibus innititur.

§4. Claudatur cum indicatione loci et diei, in quibus lata est, et cum subscriptione iudicis vel, si de tribunali collegiali agitur, omnium iudicum et notarii.

CAN. 1296 Normae de sententia definitiva statutae valent congrua congruis referendo etiam de sententia interlocutoria.

CAN. 1297 Sententia quam primum intimetur indicatis terminis, intra quos appellatio a sententia interponi potest, neque ante intimationem vim ullam habet, etsi pars dispositiva sententiae iudice permittente partibus notificata est.

CAN. 1298 Intimatio sententiae fieri potest vel tradendo exemplar sententiae partibus vel earum procuratoribus aut eisdem mittendo idem exemplar ad normam can. 1192.

CAN. 1299 §1. Si in textu sententiae aut error irrepsit in calculos aut error materialis accidit in transcribenda parte dispositiva sententiae vel in factis vel partium petitionibus referendis aut omissa sunt ea, quae can. 1295, §4 requirit, sententia ab ipso tribunali, quod eam tulit, corrigi vel compleri debet sive ad instantiam partis sive ex officio, semper tamen auditis partibus et decreto ad calcem sententiae apposito.

§2. Si qua pars refragatur, quaestio incidens decreto definiatur.

1295 §3: PIUS XII, m.p. *Sollicitudinem Nostram,* 6 ian. 1950, can. 398 §4. - S.C.S. Off., instr. (ad Ep. Rituum Orient.) a. 1883, tit. IV, 24.

1295 §4: PIUS XII, m.p. *Sollicitudinem Nostram,* 6 ian. 1950, can. 398 §5.

1296: PIUS XII, m.p. *Sollicitudinem Nostram,* 6 ian. 1950, can. 399.

1297: PIUS XII, m.p. *Sollicitudinem Nostram,* 6

ian. 1950, can. 400; PAULUS VI, all. 11 ian. 1965, "Ancora;" all. 25 ian. 1966, "E mentre."

1298: PIUS XII, m.p. *Sollicitudinem Nostram,* 6 ian. 1950, can. 401. ▲ C. 7, 45, 6.

1299 §1: PIUS XII, m.p. *Sollicitudinem Nostram,* 6 ian. 1950, can. 402 §§1–2., ▲ D. 42, 1, 42 et 46; 49, 8, 1.

1299 §2: PIUS XII, m.p. *Sollicitudinem Nostram,* 6 ian. 1950, can. 402 §3.

CAN. 1300 Other pronouncements of the judge besides the sentence are decrees which, if they are nor merely procedural, have no force unless they express the reasons at least in a summary fashion or refer to reasons expressed in another act.

CAN. 1301 An interlocutory sentence or a decree has the force of a definitive sentence if it prevents a trial or puts an end to a trial or some grade of a trial with respect to at least some party in the case.

ART. IX. *Challenge of the Sentence*

1° Complaint of Nullity Against the Sentence

CAN. 1302 With due regard for cann. 1303 and 1304, if a case involves only private persons, the sentence itself sanates the nullities of acts established by law that were not declared to the judge before the sentence even though they were known to the party proposing the complaint.

CAN. 1303 §1. A sentence suffers from the defect of irremediable nullity if:

1° it was rendered by an absolutely incompetent judge;

2° it was rendered by a person who lacks the power of judging in the tribunal in which the case was decided;

3° a judge rendered a sentence coerced by force or grave fear;

4° the trial took place without the judicial petition mentioned in can. 1104, §2, or was not instituted against some respondent;

CAN. 1300 Ceterae iudicis pronuntiationes praeter sententiam sunt decreta, quae, si mere ordinatoria non sunt, vim non habent, nisi saltem summarie motiva exprimunt vel ad motiva in alio actu expressa remittunt.

CAN. 1301 Sententia interlocutoria vel decretum vim sententiae definitivae habent, si iudicium impediunt vel ipsi iudicio aut alicui ipsius gradui finem ponunt, quod attinet ad aliquam saltem partem in causa.

ART. IX. *De Impugnatione Sententiae*

1° De Querela Nullitatis contra Sententiam

CAN. 1302 Si agitur de causa, quae privatorum solummodo interest, nullitas actuum iudicialium iure statuta, quae, cum esset nota parti querelam nullitatis proponenti, non est ante sententiam iudici denuntiata, per ipsam sententiam sanatur firmis cann. 1303 et 1304.

CAN. 1303 §1. Sententia vitio insanabilis nullitatis laborat, si:

1° lata est a iudice absolute incompetenti;

2° lata est ab eo, qui caret potestate iudicandi in tribunali, in quo causa definita est;

3° iudex vi vel metu gravi coactus sententiam tulit;

4° iudicium factum est sine petitione iudiciali, de qua in can. 1104, §2, vel non institutum est adversus aliquam partem conventam;

1300: Pius XII, m.p. *Sollicitudinem Nostram,* 6 ian. 1950, can. 392 §2.

1301: S.C. de Discip. Sacr., instr. 15 aug. 1936, 214 §2.

1302: Secret. Status, *Normae speciales in Supremo Tribunali Signaturae Apostolicae ad experimentum servandae,* 23 mar. 1968, art. 103; Cons. pro Publ. Eccl. Neg., rescr. 28 apr. 1970, 22.

1303 §1: Pius XII, m.p. *Sollicitudinem Nostram,* 6 ian. 1950, can. 418.

1303 §1, 3°: Cons. pro Publ. Eccl. Neg., rescr. 28 apr. 1970, 22, 3.

5° it was rendered between the parties, at least one of whom did not have standing in the trial;

6° someone acted in the name of another without a legitimate mandate;

7° the right of defense was denied to one or the other party;

8° it did not decide the controversy even partially.

§2. In these cases, the complaint of nullity can be proposed by way of exception in perpetuity and also by way of action before the judge who rendered the sentence within ten years from the intimation of the sentence.

CAN. 1304 §1. A sentence suffers from the defect of remediable nullity only if:

1° it was rendered by an illegitimate number of judges contrary to the prescript of can. 1084;

2° it does not contain the motives or reasons for the decision;

3° it lacks the signatures prescribed by law;

4° it does not indicate the year, month, day and place in which it was rendered;

5° it is based on a null judicial act, whose nullity was not sanated according to the norm of can. 1302;

6° it was rendered against a party legitimately absent according to can. 1273, §2.

§2. In these cases, a complaint of nullity can be proposed within three months from the intimation of the sentence.

5° lata est inter partes, quarum altera saltem non habet personam standi in iudicio;

6° quis nomine alterius egit sine legitimo mandato;

7° ius defensionis alterutri parti denegatum est;

8° controversia ne ex parte quidem definita est.

§2. His in casibus querela nullitatis proponi potest per modum exceptionis in perpetuum, per modum vero actionis coram iudice, qui sententiam tulit, intra decem annos ab intimatione sententiae computandos.

CAN. 1304 §1. Sententia vitio sanabilis nullitatis dumtaxat laborat, si:

1° lata est a non legitimo numero iudicum contra praescriptum can. 1084.

2° motiva seu rationes decidendi non continet;

3° subscriptionibus caret iure praescriptis;

4° non refert indicationem loci, anni, mensis et diei, in quibus lata est;

5° actu iudiciali nullo innititur, cuius nullitas non est adnormam can. 1302 sanata;

6° lata est contra partem legitime absentem secundum can. 1273, §2.

§2. His in casibus querela nullitatis proponi potest intra tres menses ab intimatione sententiae computandos.

1303 §1, 5°: Pius XII, m.p. *Sollicitudinem Nostram,* 6 ian. 1950, can. 418 n. 2.

1303 §1, 6°: Pius XII, m.p. *Sollicitudinem Nostram,* 6 ian. 1950, can. 418 n. 3.

1303 §1, 7°: Cons. pro Publ. Eccl. Neg., rescr. 28 apr. 1970, 22, 2.

1303 §1, 8°: Cons. pro Publ. Eccl. Neg., rescr. 28 apr. 1970, 22, 4.

1303 §2: Pius XII, m.p. *Sollicitudinem Nostram,* 6 ian. 1950, can. 419.

1304 §1: Pius XII, m.p. *Sollicitudinem Nostram,* 6 ian. 1950, can. 420.

1304 §1, 1°: Pius XII, m.p. *Sollicitudinem Nostram,* 6 ian. 1950, can. 418 n. 1.

1304 §1, 2°: Pius XII, m.p. *Sollicitudinem Nostram,* 6 ian. 1950, can. 420 n. 2.

1304 §1, 3°: Pius XII, m.p. *Sollicitudinem Nostram,* 6 ian. 1950, can. 420 n. 3.

1304 §1, 4°: Pius XII, m.p. *Sollicitudinem Nostram,* 6 ian. 1950, can. 420 n. 4.

1304 §2: Pius XII, m.p. *Sollicitudinem Nostram,* 6 ian. 1950, can. 421.

CAN. 1305 The judge who rendered the sentence deals with the complaint of nullity. If the party fears that the judge is prejudiced and is therefore suspect, the party can demand that another judge be substituted according to the norm of can. 1108.

CAN. 1306 A complaint of nullity can be proposed together with an appeal within the time established for an appeal.

CAN. 1307 §1. Not only the parties who consider themselves aggrieved can introduce a complaint of nullity but also the promoter of justice and the defender of the bond whenever they have the right to intervene.

§2. The judge can retract or emend *ex officio* a null sentence, which that judge has rendered, within the time limit for acting established by cann. 1302, §2 and 1304, §2, unless an appeal together with a complaint of nullity has been introduced in the meantime.

CAN. 1308 Cases concerning a complaint of nullity can be treated according to the canons on the summary contentious trial.

2° The Appeal

CAN. 1309 The party who considers himself or herself aggrieved by any sentence, as well as the promoter of justice and the defender of the bond in cases that require their presence, have the right to appeal the sentence to a higher judge, without prejudice to can. 1310.

CAN. 1310 There is no appeal:

1° from a sentence of the Roman Pontiff himself or the Apostolic Signatura;

CAN. 1305 De querela nullitatis videt iudex, qui sententiam tulit; si vero pars veretur, ne hic iudex praeoccupatum animum habeat, ideoque eum suspectum existimat, exigere potest, ut alius iudex in eius locum subrogetur ad normam can. 1108.

CAN. 1306 Querela nullitatis proponi potest una cum appellatione intra terminum ad appellationem statutum.

CAN. 1307 §1. Querelam nullitatis proponere possunt non solum partes, quae se gravatas putant, sed etiam promotor iustitiae aut defensor vinculi, quoties ipsis ius est interveniendi.

§2. Ipse iudex potest ex officio sententiam nullam a se latam retractare vel emendare intra terminos ad agendum in cann. 1302, §2 et 1304, §2 statutos, nisi interea appellatio una cum querela nullitatis interposita est.

CAN. 1308 Causae de querela nullitatis secundum canones de iudicio contentioso summario tractari possunt.

2° De Appellatione

CAN. 1309 Pars, quae aliqua sententia se gravatam putat, itemque promotor iustitiae et defensor vinculi in causis, in quibus eorum praesentia requiritur, ius habent a sententia appellandi ad iudicem superiorem salvo can. 1310.

CAN. 1310 Non est locus appellationi:

1° a sententia ipsius Romani Pontificis vel Signaturae Apostolicae;

1305: Pius XII, m.p. *Sollicitudinem Nostram,* 6 ian. 1950, cann. 419, 421, 423.

1306: Pius XII, m.p. *Sollicitudinem Nostram,* 6 ian. 1950, can. 422.

1307 §1: Pius XII, m.p. *Sollicitudinem Nostram,* 6 ian. 1950, can. 424 §1.

1307 §2: Pius XII, m.p. *Sollicitudinem Nostram,* 6

ian. 1950, can. 424 §2.

1309: Pius XII, m.p. *Sollicitudinem Nostram,* 6 ian. 1950, can. 403. - Theophilus Alexandrin., can. 4; Carth. can. 96. ▲ D. 49, 1, 1, pr.; C. 7, 62, 19–20; Nov. 125, 1.

1310, 1°: Pius XII, m.p. *Sollicitudinem Nostram,* 6 ian. 1950, can. 404 n. 1. - S. Zosimus, litt. *Quamvis*

2° from a sentence tainted by a defect of nullity, unless the appeal is joined with a complaint of nullity according to the norm of can. 1306;

3° from a sentence that has become a *res iudicata;*

4° from a decree of a judge or from an interlocutory sentence that does not have the force of a definitive sentence, unless it is joined with an appeal from a definitive sentence;

5° from a sentence or a decree in a case where the law requires the matter to be decided most expeditiously.

CAN. 1311 §1. An appeal must be introduced before the judge who rendered the sentence within the peremptory time of fifteen useful days from the intimation of the sentence.

§2. If an appeal is made orally, the notary is to put it in writing in the presence of the appellant.

CAN. 1312 There is no appeal from the delegate to the one who delegated him, but to the immediate superior of the one who delegated him, unless the delegation has come from the Apostolic See itself.

CAN. 1313 If a question arises about the right of appeal, the appellate tribunal is to decide it most expeditiously according to the canons on the summary contentious trial.

2° a sententia vitio nullitatis infecta, nisi cumulatur cum querela nullitatis ad normam can. 1306;

3° a sententia, quae in rem iudicatam transiit;

4° a iudicis decreto vel a sententia interlocutoria, quae non habent vim sententiae definitivae, nisi cumulatur cum appellatione a sententia definitiva;

5° a sententia vel a decreto in causa, de qua ius cavet rem expeditissime esse definiendam.

CAN. 1311 §1. Appellatio interponi debet coram iudice, a quo sententia lata est, intra peremptorium terminum quindecim dierum utilium ab intimatione sententiae computandum.

§2. Si ore fit, notarius eam scripto coram ipso appellante redigat.

CAN. 1312 A delegato non datur appellatio ad delegantem, sed ad eius immediatum superiorem, nisi delegans est ipsa Sedes Apostolica.

CAN. 1313 Si quaestio oritur de iure appellandi, tribunal appellationis rem expeditissime definiat secundum canones de iudicio contentioso summario.

Patrum, a. 418; S. BONIFACIUS I, litt. *Retro maioribus,* a. 422; litt. *Manet beatum,* a. 422, "Congregatur;" S. NICOLAUS I, litt. *Proposueramus quidem,* a. 865, ". . . Siquidem;" HADRIANUS II, litt. *Nec scriptura pandere,* a. 869, "Quam ob rem;" S. LEO IX, litt. *In terra pax,* a. 1053, XXXII; PIUS II, const. *Exsecrabilis,* 18 ian. 1459; IULIUS II, const. *Suscepti regiminis,* 1 iul. 1509; Trid., sess. XXIV, *De ref.,* can. 20; Vat. I, sess. IV, cap. III, *De vi et ratione primatus Romani pontificis,* "Et quoniam." ▲ D. 49, 2, 1; Basilic. 9, 1, 28.

1310, 2°: PIUS XII, m.p. *Sollicitudinem Nostram,* 6 ian. 1950, can. 404 n. 3. ▲ D. 49, 1, 19; C. 7, 64, 4–5.

1310, 3°: PIUS XII, m.p. *Sollicitudinem Nostram,* 6 ian. 1950, can. 404, n. 4. ▲ C. 7, 70.

1310, 4°: PIUS XII, m.p. *Sollicitudinem Nostram,*

6 ian. 1950, can. 404 n. 6. ▲ D. 49, 5, 2; C. 7, 62, 36; 7, 65, 7; Basilic. 9, 1, 36.

1310, 5°: PIUS XII, m.p. *Sollicitudinem Nostram,* 6 ian. 1950, can. 404 n. 7. ▲ D. 49, 5, 7; Basilic. 9, 1, 41.

1311 §1: PIUS XII, m.p. *Sollicitudinem Nostram,* 6 ian. 1950, can. 405. ▲ D. 49, 4, 1 et 5, (3); Nov. 23, 1 et 4; Basilic. 9, 1, 33 et 37.

1311 §2: PIUS XII, m.p. *Sollicitudinem Nostram,* 6 ian. 1950, can. 407 §1. ▲ D. 49, 1, 2 et 7; Basilic. 9, 1, 2 et 7.

1312: PIUS XII, m.p. *Sollicitudinem Nostram,* 6 ian. 1950, can. 406.

1313: S.C. de Discip. Sacr., instr. 15 aug. 1936, art. 215 §2.

CAN. 1314 An appeal must be pursued before the appellate judge within a month of its introduction unless the judge who rendered the sentence has established a longer period for the party to pursue it.

CAN. 1315 §1. To pursue an appeal, it is required and suffices that a party calls upon the services of a higher judge for an emendation of the challenged sentence, attaches a copy of this sentence, and indicates the reasons for the appeal.

§2. Meanwhile, the judge who rendered the sentence must transmit a copy of the acts, duly authenticated by the notary, to the higher tribunal. If the acts are written in a language unknown to the appellate tribunal, they are to be carefully translated into a language known to the tribunal and with a guarantee of a faithful translation.

CAN. 1316 Once the time limit for appeal has passed without action either before the judge who rendered the sentence or before the appellate judge, the appeal is considered abandoned.

CAN. 1317 §1. The appellant can renounce the appeal with the effects referred to in can. 1206.

§2. If the defender of the bond or the promoter of justice have introduced the appeal, unless common law provides otherwise, the defender of the bond or the promoter of justice of the appellate tribunal can renounce it.

CAN. 1318 §1. An appeal made by the pe-

CAN. 1314 Appellatio prosequenda est coram iudice, ad quem dirigitur, intra mensem ab eius interpositione computandum, nisi iudex, a quo sententia lata est, longius tempus ad eam prosequendam parti praestituit.

CAN. 1315 §1. Ad prosequendam appellationem requiritur et sufficit, ut pars ministerium iudicis superioris invocet ad impugnatae sententiae emendationem adiuncto exemplari huius sententiae et indicatis appellationis rationibus.

§2. Interea iudex, a quo sententia lata est, debet actorum exemplar fide facta a notario de eius authenticitate ad tribunal superius mittere; si acta scripta sunt lingua tribunali appellationis ignota, vertantur in aliam eidem tribunali cognitam cautelis adhibitis, ut de fideli versione constet.

CAN. 1316 Inutiliter elapsis terminis appellatoriis sive coram iudice, a quo sententia lata est, sive coram iudice, ad quem appellatio dirigitur, haec deserta censetur.

CAN. 1317 §1. Appellans potest appellationi renuntiare cum effectibus, de quibus in can. 1206.

§2. Si appellatio interposita est a defensore vinculi vel apromotore iustitiae, renuntiatio fieri potest, nisi aliter iure communi cavetur, a defensore vinculi vel a promotore iustitiae tribunalis appellationis.

CAN. 1318 §1. Appellatio facta ab ac-

1315 §1: Pius XII, m.p. *Sollicitudinem Nostram,* 6 ian. 1950, can. 410 §1. ▲ D. 49, 1, 1, (4); 49, 6, 1; C. 7, 62, 31; Nov. 126, 3; Basilic. 9, 1, 42.

1315 §2: Pius XII, m.p. *Sollicitudinem Nostram,* 6 ian. 1950, cann. 159, 416. ▲ C. 7, 62, 6, (3) et 15 et 24; Nov. 126, 3.

1316: Pius XII, m.p. *Sollicitudinem Nostram,* 6 ian. 1950, can. 412. ▲ C. 7, 62, 18; 7, 67, 1 et 2; Nov. 126, 2.

1317 §1: Pius XII, m.p. *Sollicitudinem Nostram,* 6 ian. 1950, can. 404 n. 9. ▲ D. 49, 2, 1, (3); Basilic. 9, 1, 28.

1317 §2: Paulus VI, litt. *Cum matrimonialium,* 8 sept. 1973, IX §2.

1318 §1: Pius XII, m.p. *Sollicitudinem Nostram,* 6 ian. 1950, can. 413 §1. ▲ C. 7, 62, 39, (pr. et 1); 7, 68, 2.

titioner also benefits the respondent and vice versa.

§2. If there are several respondents or petitioners and the sentence is challenged by only one or against only one of them, the challenge is considered to be made by all of them and against all of them whenever the matter sought is indivisible or a joint obligation.

§3. If one party introduces an appeal against one ground of the sentence, the other party can appeal incidentally against other grounds within the peremptory period of fifteen days from the day on which the original appeal was made known to the latter, even if the time limit for an appeal has passed.

§4. Unless it is otherwise evident, an appeal is presumed to be made against all the grounds of a sentence.

CAN. 1319 An appeal suspends the execution of the sentence.

CAN. 1320 §1. Without prejudice to can. 1369, a new cause for petitioning cannot be admitted at the appellate grade, not even by way of useful accumulation; consequently, the joinder of the issue can only address whether the prior sentence is to be confirmed or revised either totally or partially.

§2. New proofs, however, are admitted only according to the norm of can. 1283.

CAN. 1321 The appellate grade must proceed in the same manner as the first grade with appropriate adjustments; but, unless perhaps

tore prodest etiam parti conventae et vicissim.

§2. Si plures sunt partes conventae vel actores et ab uno vel contra unum tantum ex ipsis sententia impugnatur, impugnatio censetur ab omnibus et contra omnes facta, quoties res petita est individua aut obligatio omnes singillatim tenet.

§3. Si interponitur ab una parte super aliquo sententiae capite, pars adversa, etsi terminus appellationis est transactus, potest super aliis capitibus incidenter appellare intra terminum peremptorium quindecim dierum computandum a die, quo ipsi appellatio principalis notificata est.

§4. Nisi aliud constat, appellatio praesumitur facta contra omnia sententiae capita.

CAN. 1319 Appellatio exsecutionem sententiae suspendit.

CAN. 1320 §1. Salvo can. 1369 in gradu appellationis non potest admitti nova petendi causa, ne per modum quidem utilis cumulationis; ideoque litis contestatio in eo tantum versari potest, ut prior sententia vel confirmetur vel reformetur sive ex toto sive ex parte.

§2. Novae autem probationes admittuntur tantum ad normam can. 1283.

CAN. 1321 In gradu appellationis eodem modo ac in primo gradu iudicii congrua congruis referendo procedendum est; sed,

---

1318 §2: Pius XII, m.p. *Sollicitudinem Nostram,* 6 ian. 1950, can. 414. ▲ D. 49, 1, 3 et 10 et 17; Basilic, 9, 1, 3 et 10 et 17.

1318 §3: Pius XII, m.p. *Sollicitudinem Nostram,* 6 ian. 1950, can. 413 §2.

1318 §4: Pius XII, m.p. *Sollicitudinem Nostram,* 6 ian. 1950, can. 413 §3. ▲ D. 49, 1, 13 et 17; Basilic. 9, 1, 13 et 17.

1319: Pius XII, m.p. *Sollicitudinem Nostram,* 6

ian. 1950, can. 415 §2.

1320 §1: Pius XII, m.p. *Sollicitudinem Nostram,* 6 ian. 1950, can. 417 §1. ▲ C. 7, 62, 39, (1); Basilic. 9, 1, 132.

1320 §2: Pius XII, m.p. *Sollicitudinem Nostram,* 6 ian. 1950, can. 417 §2. ▲ C. 7, 62, 6, (1); 7, 62, 39 (1ª); 7, 63, 4; Basilic. 9, 1, 132. .

1321: Pius XII, m.p. *Sollicitudinem Nostram,* 6 ian. 1950, can. 75.

the proofs must be completed, immediately after the joinder of the issue, the discussion of the case is to take place and the sentence rendered.

nisi forte complendae sunt probationes, statim post litis contestationem ad causae discussionem deveniatur et ad sententiam.

ART. X. *Res Iudicata, Restitutio in Integrum and the Opposition of a Third Party*

ART. X. De Re Iudicata, de Restitutione in Integrum *et de Oppositione Tertii*

1° Res Iudicata

1° De Re Iudicata

CAN. 1322 With due regard for can. 1324, a *res iudicata* occurs if:

1° a second concordant sentence is rendered between the same parties over the same issue and based on the same cause for petitioning;

2° an appeal against the sentence has not been introduced within the useful time;

3° at the appellate grade, the trial has been abated or renounced;

4° a definitive sentence has been rendered from which there is no appeal.

CAN. 1323 §1. A *res iudicata* is by law stable in such a way that it can only be challenged by a complaint of nullity, *restitutio in integrum* or the opposition of a third party.

§2. *Res iudicata* establishes the rights between the parties and permits an action on the judgment and an exception of *res iudicata*, which the judge can also declare *ex officio* in order to prevent a new introduction of the same case.

CAN. 1324 Cases concerning the status of persons, including cases concerning separation of spouses, never become *res iudicata*.

CAN. 1322 Firmo can. 1324 res iudicata habetur, si:

1° duplex intercessit inter easdem partes sententia conformis de eodem petito et ex eadem causa petendi;

2° appellatio a sententia non est intra tempus utile interposita;

3° in gradu appellationis litis instantia perempta est vel eidem renuntiatum est;

4° lata est sententia definitiva, a qua non datur appellatio.

CAN. 1323 §1. Res iudicata iure firma est ita, ut impugnari possit tantum per querelam nullitatis, restitutionem in integrum vel oppositionem tertii.

§2. Res iudicata facit ius inter partes et dat actionem iudicati atque exceptionem rei iudicatae, quam iudex ex officio quoque declarare potest ad impediendam novam eiusdem causae introductionem.

CAN. 1324 Numquam transeunt in rem iudicatam causae de statu personarum non exceptis causis de coniugum separatione.

1322: Pius XII, m.p. *Sollicitudinem Nostram,* 6 ian. 1950, can. 429. ▲ D. 42, 1, 1.
  1322, 1°: Pius XII, m.p. *Sollicitudinem Nostram,* 6 ian. 1950, can. 429 n. 1. ▲ C. 7, 70.
  1322, 2°: Pius XII, m.p. *Sollicitudinem Nostram,* 6 ian. 1950, can. 429 n. 2. ▲ C. 7, 43, 11; 7, 62, 8; 7, 67, 1; Nov. 49, 1.
  1323 §1: Pius XII, m.p. *Sollicitudinem Nostram,* 6

ian. 1950, can. 431 §1. ▲ D. 1, 5, 25; 44, 2, 27; 50, 17, 207; C. 7, 52, 1–2 et 5.
  1323 §2: Pius XII, m.p. *Sollicitudinem Nostram,* 6 ian. 1950, can. 431 §2. ▲ Instit. 4, 13, 5; D. 44, 1, 3; 44, 2, 3–5 et 7; C. 7, 64, 1.
  1324: Pius XII, m.p. *Sollicitudinem Nostram,* 6 ian. 1950, cann. 430, 497 §1. - S.C.S. Off. instr. (ad Ep. Rituum Orient.) a. 1883, tit. V, 30.

CAN. 1325 §1. If a second concordant sentence has been rendered in a case concerning the status of persons, recourse can be made at any time to the appellate tribunal if new and grave proofs or arguments are brought forward within the peremptory time limit of thirty days from the proposed challenge. Within a month from when the new proofs and arguments are brought forward, however, the appellate tribunal must establish by decree whether a new presentation of the case must be admitted or not.

§2. Recourse to a superior tribunal in order to obtain a new presentation of the case does not suspend the execution of the sentence unless either the law provides otherwise or the appellate tribunal orders its suspension according to the norm of can. 1337, §3.

2° Restitutio in Integrum

CAN. 1326 §1. *Restitutio in integrum* is granted against a sentence that has become *res iudicata* provided that its injustice is clearly established.

§2. Injustice, however, is not considered to be established clearly unless:

1° the sentence is based on proofs that afterwards are discovered to be false in such a way that without those proofs the dispositive part of the sentence is not sustained;

2° documents have been revealed afterwards that undoubtedly prove new facts and demand a contrary decision;

CAN. 1325 §1. Si duplex sententia conformis in causa de statu personarum lata est, potest quovis tempore ad tribunal appellationis provocari allatis novis eisque gravibus probationibus vel argumentis intra peremptorium terminum triginta dierum a proposita impugnatione computandum; tribunal appellationis autem intra mensem ab exhibitis novis probationibus et argumentis computandum debet decreto statuere, utrum nova causae propositio admitti debeat necne.

§2. Provocatio ad superius tribunal, ut nova causae propositio obtineatur, exsecutionem sententiae non suspendit, nisi aliter iure communi cavetur aut tribunal appellationis ad normam can. 1337, §3 suspensionem iubet.

2° De Restitutione in Integrum

CAN. 1326 §1. Adversus sententiam, quae transiit in rem iudicatam, dummodo de eius iniustitia manifesto constet, datur restitutio in integrum.

§2. De iniustitia autem manifesto constare non censetur, nisi:

1° sententia ita probationibus innititur, quae postea falsae edeprehensae sunt, ut sine illis probationibus pars dispositiva sententiae non sustineatur;

2° postea detecta sunt documenta, quae facta nova et contrariam decisionem exigentia indubitanter probant;

1325 §1: Pius XII, m.p. *Sollicitudinem Nostram*, 6 ian. 1950, cann. 430, 497; Paulus VI, litt. *Cum matrimonialium*, 8 sep. 1973, IX §1.

1326 §1: Pius XII, m.p. *Sollicitudinem Nostram*, 6 ian. 1950, can. 432 §1. ▲ D. 4, 4, 17; 48, 19, 27; C. 2, 43 (44); 2, 48 (50), 1; 7, 50, 2.

1326 §2: Pius XII, m.p. *Sollicitudinem Nostram*,

6 ian. 1950, can. 432 §2.

1326 §2, 1°: Pius XII, m.p. *Sollicitudinem Nostram*, 6 ian. 1950, can. 432 §2 n. 1. ▲ D. 44, 1, 11; C. 7, 58, 1–3.

1326 §2, 2°: Pius XII, m.p. *Sollicitudinem Nostram*, 6 ian. 1950, can. 432 §2 n. 2. ▲ D. 12, 2, 31.

3° the sentence was rendered due to the fraud of one party resulting in harm to the other party;

4° a prescript of the law that is not merely procedural was clearly neglected;

5° the sentence is contrary to a previous decision that has become *res iudicata*.

CAN. 1327 §1. *Restitutio in integrum* for the reasons mentioned in can. 1326, §2, nn. 1–3, must be sought from the judge who rendered the sentence within three months computed from the day the person became aware of these same reasons.

§2. *Restitutio in integrum* for the reasons mentioned in can. 1326, §2, nn. 4 and 5 must be sought from the appellate tribunal within three months of the intimation of the sentence; if in the case mentioned in can. 1326, §2, n. 5 notice of the previous decision occurs later, however, the time limit runs from this notice.

§3. The time limits mentioned above do not run as long as the injured person is a minor.

CAN. 1328 §1. The petition for *restitutio in integrum* suspends the execution of a sentence if execution has not yet begun.

§2. If from probable indications there is a suspicion that a petition has been made in order to delay the execution, however, the judge can decree execution of the sentence, though with suitable guarantees to the one seeking the *restitutio* that there will be indemnity if the *restitutio in integrum* is granted.

3° sententia ex dolo partis lata est in damnum alterius;

4° legis non mere processualis praescriptum evidenter neglectum est;

5° sententia adversatur praecedenti decisioni, quae in rem iudicatam transiit.

CAN. 1327 §1. Restitutio in integrum propter motiva, de quibus in can. 1326, §2, nn. 1–3, petenda est a iudice, qui sententiam tulit, intra tres menses a die cognitionis eorundem motivorum computandos.

§2. Restitutio in integrum propter motiva, de quibus in can. 1326, §2, nn. 4 et 5, petenda est a tribunali appellationis intra tres menses ab intimatione sententiae computandos; si vero in casu, de quo in can. 1326, §2, n. 5, notitia praecedentis decisionis serius habetur, terminus ab hac notitia decurrit.

§3. Termini, de quibus supra, non decurrunt, dum pars laesa minoris est aetatis.

CAN. 1328 §1. Petitio restitutionis in integrum sententiae exsecutionem nondum inceptam suspendit.

§2. Si tamen ex probabilibus indiciis suspicio est petitionem factam esse ad moras exsecutioni nectendas, iudex decernere potest, ut sententia exsecutioni demandetur, assignata tamen restitutionem in integrum petenti idonea cautione ut, si restituitur in integrum, indemnis fiat.

1326 §2, 3°: Pius XII, m.p. *Cleri sanctitati*, 2 iun. 1957, can. 432 §2 n. 3. ▲ D. 5, 1, 75; 42, 1, 33.

1326 §2, 4°: Pius XII, m.p. *Cleri sanctitati*, 2 iun. 1957, can. 432 §2 n. 4. ▲ D. 49, 1, 19; Basilic. 9, 1, 19.

1327 §1: Pius XII, m.p. *Sollicitudinem Nostram*, 6 ian. 1950, can. 433 §1.

1327 §2: Pius XII, m.p. *Sollicitudinem Nostram*, 6 ian. 1950, can. 433 §1.

1327 §3: Pius XII, m.p. *Sollicitudinem Nostram*, 6 ian. 1950, cann. 432 §1, 207. ▲ D. 4, 1, 6; 4, 6; C. 2, 24 (25), 2; Basilic 10, 1, 6.

1328 §1: Pius XII, m.p. *Sollicitudinem Nostram*, 6 ian. 1950, can. 434 §1.

1328 §2: Pius XII, m.p. *Sollicitudinem Nostram*, 6 ian. 1950, can. 434 §2.

CAN. 1329 If *restitutio in integrum* is granted, the judge must pronounce on the merits of the case.

CAN. 1329 Concessa restitutione in integrum iudex pronuntiare debet de merito causae.

3° Opposition of a Third Party

CAN. 1330 Those who fear harm to their rights from a definitive sentence rendered in a case between other parties, and which may be executed, can challenge the sentence itself before its execution.

CAN. 1331 §1. The opposition of the third party can be made either by requesting the revision of the sentence by the tribunal that rendered it or by making recourse to the appeal tribunal.

§2. If the petition has been admitted and the opponent acts at the appellate grade, he or she is bound by the norms on appeals; if before the tribunal that rendered the sentence, the norms established for the judicial decision of incidental cases are to be observed.

CAN. 1332 §1. In any case, the opponent must prove that his or her right has in fact been harmed or is going to be harmed.

§2. The harm, however, must derive from the sentence itself, inasmuch as it is, itself, the cause of the harm or, if executed, it is going to gravely prejudice the opponent.

CAN. 1333 If the opponent proves his or her right, the sentence rendered previously must be changed by the tribunal in accordance with the opponent's petition.

3° De Oppositione Tertii

CAN. 1330 Qui ex sententia definitiva inter alios lata, quae exsecutioni mandari potest, suorum iurium laesionem veretur, sententiam ipsam ante eius exsecutionem impugnare potest.

CAN. 1331 §1. Oppositio tertii fieri potest vel postulando revisionem sententiae a tribunali, quod eam tulit, vel provocando ad tribunal appellationis.

§2. Si petitio admissa est et oppositor agit in gradu appellationis, tenetur legibus pro appellatione statutis; si coram tribunali, quod sententiam tulit, servandae sunt normae datae pro causis incidentibus iudicialiter definiendis.

CAN. 1332 §1. Oppositor in quolibet casu probare debet ius suum revera esse laesum aut laesum iri.

§2. Laesio autem oriri debet ex ipsa sententia, quatenus aut ipsa est causa laesionis aut, si exsecutioni mandatur, oppositorem gravi praeiudicio est affectura.

CAN. 1333 Si oppositor ius suum probavit, sententia antea lata reformanda est a tribunali secundum oppositoris petitionem.

1330: Pius XII, m.p. *Sollicitudinem Nostram*, 6 ian. 1950, can. 425. ▲ D. 49, 1, 4, (2–3).

1331 §1: Pius XII, m.p. *Sollicitudinem Nostram*, 6 ian. 1950, can. 426 §1. ▲ D. 49, 1, 5; Basilic. 9, 1, 5.

1331 §2: Pius XII, m.p. *Sollicitudinem Nostram*, 6 ian. 1950, can. 426.

1332 §1: Pius XII, m.p. *Sollicitudinem Nostram*, 6 ian. 1950, can. 426 §2.

1332 §2: Pius XII, m.p. *Sollicitudinem Nostram*, 6 ian. 1950, can. 426 §3.

1333: Pius XII, m.p. *Sollicitudinem Nostram*, 6 ian. 1950, can. 428.

ART. XI. *Gratuitous Legal Assistance and Judicial Expenses*

CAN. 1334 The poor, that is, those who are totally unable to pay the court costs, have the right to gratuitous legal assistance; those who can pay only part of the court costs, to a reduction of the expenses.

CAN. 1335 The statutes of the tribunal must establish norms concerning:

1° the payment or compensation of judicial expenses by the parties;

2° the remuneration for the procurators, advocates and interpreters and the indemnity for the witnesses;

3° the granting of gratuitous legal assistance or reduction of the expenses;

4° the reparation of damages owed by a person who not only lost the trial but also entered into the litigation rashly;

5° the deposit of money or the guarantee furnished for the payment of expenses and reparation of damages.

CAN. 1336 There is no separate appeal from the determination of expenses, remunerations and reparation of damages, but the party can make recourse within fifteen days to the same judge who can adjust the assessment.

ART. XII. *The Execution of the Sentence*

CAN. 1337 §1. A sentence that has become a *res iudicata* can be executed, without prejudice to can. 1328.

§2. The judge who rendered the sentence

ART. XI. *De Gratuito Patrocinio et de Expensis Iudicialibus*

CAN. 1334 Pauperes, qui omnino impares sunt expensis iudicialibus sustinendis, ius habent ad gratuitum patrocinium, si ex parte tantum, ad expensarum deminutionem.

CAN. 1335 Statuta tribunalis debent normas dare:

1° de expensis iudicialibus a partibus solvendis vel compensandis;

2° de procuratorum, advocatorum et interpretum remuneratione deque testium indemnitate;

3° de gratuito patrocinio vel expensarum deminutione concedendis;

4° de reparatione damnorum, quae debetur ab eo, qui non solum in iudicio succubuit, sed temere litigavit;

5° de pecuniae deposito vel cautione praestanda circa expensas solvendas et damna reparanda.

CAN. 1336 A pronuntiatione circa expensas, remunerationes et damna reparanda non datur distincta appellatio, sed pars recurrere potest intra quindecim dies ad eundem iudicem, qui potest taxationem emendare.

ART. XII. *De Exsecutione Sententiae*

CAN. 1337 §1. Sententia, quae transiit in rem iudicatam, exsecutioni mandari potest salvo can. 1328.

§2. Iudex, qui sententiam tulit, et, si ap-

1334: Pius XII, m.p. *Sollicitudinem Nostram*, 6 ian. 1950, can. 441. - Carth. can. 75.

1335: Pius XII, m.p. *Sollicitudinem Nostram*, 6 ian. 1950, cann. 435–439, 442–444.

1336: Pius XII, m.p. *Sollicitudinem Nostram*, 6 ian. 1950, can. 440. ▲ C. 7, 51, 3; 7, 64, 10; Basilic. 9, 1,

141; 9, 3, 67.

1337 §1: Pius XII, m.p. *Sollicitudinem Nostram*, 6 ian. 1950, can. 445 §1. ▲ D. 42, 1, 2; C. 7, 53, 1; Nov. 125, 1.

1337 §2: Pius XII, m.p. *Sollicitudinem Nostram*, 6 ian. 1950, can. 445 §2 n. 1. ▲ C. 7, 69.

and, if an appeal has been introduced, also the appellate judge can order *ex officio,* or at the request of a party, a provisional execution of a sentence that has not yet become a *res iudicata,* after having set suitable guarantees, if the case warrants, for provisions or payments ordered for necessary support; they can also do so if some other just cause urges it.

§3. However, if the sentence, which has not yet become a *res iudicata,* is challenged, the judge who must investigate the challenge can suspend the execution or subject it to a guarantee if the judge sees that the challenge is probably well-founded and irreparable damage can arise from execution.

CAN. 1338 Execution cannot occur prior to the executory decree of the judge that declares that the sentence must be executed. This decree is to be included in the text of the sentence or issued separately according to the particular nature of the cases.

CAN. 1339 If the execution of a sentence requires a prior rendering of accounts, it is an incidental question that the same judge who rendered the sentence ordering the execution must decide.

CAN. 1340 §1. Unless the particular law of his own Church *sui iuris* establishes otherwise, the eparchial bishop of the eparchy in which the sentence was rendered in the first grade of the trial must execute the sentence personally or through another.

§2. However, if he refuses or neglects to do this, the execution of the sentence, either at the

pellatio interposita est, etiam iudex appellationis, sententiae, quae nondum transiit in rem iudicatam, provisoriam exsecutionem iubere possunt ex officio vel ad instantiam partis idoneis, si casus fert, praestitis cautiōnibus, si agitur de provisionibus ad necessariam sustentationem ordinatis vel alia iusta causa urget.

§3. Si vero sententia, quae nondum transiit in rem iudicatam, impugnatur, iudex, qui de impugnatione cognoscere debet, si videt hanc probabiliter fundatam esse et irreparabile damnum ex exsecutione oriri posse, potest vel exsecutionem ipsam suspendere vel eam cautioni subicere.

CAN. 1338 Non antea exsecutioni locus esse potest, quam exsecutorium iudicis decretum habetur, quo edicitur sententiam ipsam exsecutioni mandari debere; quod decretum pro diversa causarum natura vel ipso sententiae tenore includatur vel separatim edatur.

CAN. 1339 Si sententiae exsecutio praeviam rationum redditionem exigit, quaestio incidens habetur ab illo iudice decidenda, qui tulit sententiam exsecutioni mandandam.

CAN. 1340 §1. Nisi iure particulari propriae Ecclesiae sui iuris aliud statuitur, sententiam exsecutioni mandare debet per se vel per alium Episcopus eparchialis eparchiae, ubi sententia in primo gradu iudicii lata est.

§2. Si vero hic renuit vel neglegit, parte, cuius interest, instante vel etiam ex

---

1337 §3: Pius XII, m.p. *Sollicitudinem Nostram,* 6 ian. 1950, can. 445 §2 n. 2.

1338: Pius XII, m.p. *Sollicitudinem Nostram,* 6 ian. 1950, can. 446. ▲ C. 7, 53, 1; Basilic. 9, 3, 77.

1339: Pius XII, m.p. *Sollicitudinem Nostram,* 6

ian. 1950, can. 447.

1340 §1: Pius XII, m.p. *Sollicitudinem Nostram,* 6 ian. 1950, can. 448 §1.

1340 §2: Pius XII, m.p. *Sollicitudinem Nostram,* 6 ian. 1950, can. 448 §2.

request of an interested party or even *ex officio,* pertains to the authority to whom the appellate tribunal is subject.

§3. In the controversies referred to in can. 1069, §1, the execution of the sentence pertains to the superior determined in the typicon or statutes.

CAN. 1341 §1. The executor, unless the text of the sentence leaves it to the judgment of the executor, must execute the sentence according to the obvious sense of the words.

§2. The executor is permitted to deal with exceptions concerning the manner and force of the execution, but not concerning the merits of the case. However, if it is discovered from another source that the sentence is null or manifestly unjust according to the norm of cann. 1303, 1304, and 1326, §2, the executor is to refrain from executing it and, after having informed the parties, is to refer the matter to the tribunal that rendered the sentence.

CAN. 1342 §1. Whenever the petitioner is awarded something, it must be handed over to the petitioner as soon as there is a *res iudicata.*

§2. If the party is condemned to furnish a movable thing, to pay money, or to give or do something else, the judge in the text of the sentence or the executor, according to his or her judgment and prudence, is to establish a time limit to fulfill the obligation; this time limit, however, is not to be less than fifteen days nor more that six months.

officio exsecutio spectat ad auctoritatem, cui tribunal appellationis subiectum est.

§3. In controversiis, de quibus in can. 1069, §1, exsecutio sententiae spectat ad Superiorem in typico vel statutis determinatum.

CAN. 1341 §1. Exsecutor, nisi quid eius arbitrio in ipso tenore sententiae est permissum, debet sententiam secundum obviam verborum significationem exsecutioni mandare.

§2. Licet ei videre de exceptionibus circa modum et vim exsecutionis, non autem de merito causae; si vero habet aliunde compertum sententiam esse nullam vel manifesto iniustam ad normam cann. 1303, 1304 et 1326, §2, abstineat ab exsecutione et rem ad tribunal, a quo lata est sententia, remittat partibus certioribus factis.

CAN. 1342 §1. Quoties adiudicata actori res aliqua est, haec actori tradenda est statim ac res iudicata habetur.

§2. Si pars damnata est ad rem mobilem praestandam vel ad solvendam pecuniam vel ad aliud dandum aut faciendum, iudex in ipso tenore sententiae vel exsecutor pro suo arbitrio et prudentia terminum statuat ad implendam obligationem, qui tamen neque infra quindecim dies coartetur neque sex menses excedat.

1340 §3: Pius XII, m.p. *Sollicitudinem Nostram,* 6 ian. 1950, can. 448 §3.

1341 §1: Pius XII, m.p. *Sollicitudinem Nostram,* 6 ian. 1950, can. 449 §1. ▲ D. 49, 1, 4; C. 7, 65, 5.

1341 §2: Pius XII, m.p. *Sollicitudinem Nostram,* 6 ian. 1950, can. 449 §2. ▲ C. 7, 58, 4; Basilic. 9, 3, 105.

1342 §1: Pius XII, m.p. *Sollicitudinem Nostram,* 6 ian. 1950, can. 450 §1. ▲ D, 46, 3, 105.

1342 §2: Pius XII, m.p. *Sollicitudinem Nostram,* 6 ian. 1950, can. 450 §2.

CHAPTER II. **The Summary Contentious Trial**

CAN. 1343   §1. All cases not excluded by law can be treated in the summary contentious trial unless a party requests the ordinary contentious trial.

§2. If the summary contentious trial is used in cases excluded by law, the judicial acts are null.

CAN. 1344   §1. In addition to the things enumerated in can. 1187, the *libellus* that introduces the litigation must:

1° set forth briefly, completely, and clearly the facts on which the requests of the petitioner are based;

2° indicate the proofs by which the petitioner intends to demonstrate the facts, but that cannot be presented at once, in such a way that the judge can collect them immediately;

§2. The documents on which the petition is based must be attached to the introductory *libellus*, at least in an authentic copy.

CAN. 1345   §1. If the attempt at reconciliation according to the norm of can. 1103, §2 proved useless and the judge thinks that the *libellus* introducing the litigation has some foundation, the judge is to order within three days by a decree appended to the bottom of the *libellus* that a copy of the petition be communicated at once to the respondent, giving to the latter the right to send a written response to the tribunal chancery within fifteen days.

§2. This notification has the effect of the judicial citation mentioned in can. 1194.

CAN. 1346   If the exceptions of the re-

CAPUT II. **De Iudicio Contentioso Summario**

CAN. 1343   §1. Iudicio contentioso summario tractari possunt omnes causae iure non exclusae, nisi pars iudicium contentiosum ordinarium petit.

§2. Si iudicium contentiosum summarium adhibetur in causis iure exclusis, actus iudiciales sunt nulli.

CAN. 1344   §1. Libellus litis introductorius praeter ea, quae in can. 1187 recensentur, debet:

1° facta, quibus actoris petitiones innituntur, breviter, integre et perspicue exponere;

2° probationes, quibus actor facta demonstrare intendit quasque simul afferre non potest, ita indicare, ut statim colligia iudice possint.

§2. Libello litis introductorio adnecti debent saltem in exemplari authentico documenta, quibus petitio innititur.

CAN. 1345   §1. Si conamen conciliationis ad normam can. 1103, §2 inutile cessit, iudex, si aestimat libellum litis introductorium aliquo fundamento niti, intra tres dies decreto ad calcem libelli apposito praecipiat, ut exemplar petitionis statim notificetur parti conventae, dato huic iure mittendi intra quindecim dies ad cancellariam tribunalis responsionem scripto datam.

§2. Haec notificatio effectus habet citationis iudicialis, de quibus in can. 1194.

CAN. 1346   Si exceptiones partis con-

1344 §1: Pius XII, m.p. *Sollicitudinem Nostram*, 6 ian. 1950, can. 456 §1.

1344 §2: Pius XII, m.p. *Sollicitudinem Nostram*, 6 ian. 1950, can. 459.

1345 §1: Pius XII, m.p. *Sollicitudinem Nostram*, 6

ian. 1950, cann. 457, 459.

1345 §2: Pius XII, m.p. *Sollicitudinem Nostram*, 6 ian. 1950, can. 459.

1346: Pius XII, m.p. *Sollicitudinem Nostram*, 6 ian. 1950, can. 458.

spondent demand it, the judge is to establish a time limit for the petitioner to respond, in such a way that, from the points brought forth by both of the parties, the judge clarifies the object of the controversy.

CAN. 1347 §1. When the time limits mentioned in cann. 1345, §1 and 1346 have elapsed, the judge, after an examination of the acts, is to determine the formula of the doubt. Next, the judge is to cite all those who must take part to a hearing that must be held within thirty days; the formula of the doubt is to be attached to the citation of the parties.

§2. In the citation, the parties are to be informed that they can present a brief written statement to the tribunal to verify their claims at least three days before the hearing.

CAN. 1348 At the hearing, the questions referred to in cann. 1118, 1119, 1121 and 1122 are treated first.

CAN. 1349 §1. The proofs are collected at the hearing without prejudice to can. 1071.

§2. The party and his or her advocate can be present at the questioning of the other parties, the witnesses, and the experts.

CAN. 1350 The responses of the parties, the witnesses, and the experts and the petitions and exceptions of the advocates must be put in writing by the notary, but in a summary fashion and only in those matters pertaining to the substance of the dispute; the same persons must sign these acts.

CAN. 1351 The judge can admit proofs that are not brought forth or sought in the petition or response only according to the norm

ventae id exigunt, iudex actori determinet terminum ad respondendum ita, ut ex allatis utriusque partis elementis ipse controversiae obiectum perspectum habeat.

CAN. 1347 §1. Elapsis terminis ad respondendum, de quibus in cann. 1345, §1 et 1346, iudex perspectis actis formulam dubii determinet; deinde ad audientiam non ultra triginta dies celebrandam omnes citet, qui in ea interesse debent, addita pro partibus dubii formula.

§2. In citatione partes certiores fiant se posse tres saltem ante audientiam dies aliquod breve scriptum tribunali exhibere ad sua asserta comprobanda.

CAN. 1348 In audientia primum tractantur quaestiones, de quibus in cann. 1118, 1119, 1121 et 1122.

CAN. 1349 §1. Probationes colliguntur in audientia salvo can. 1071.

§2. Pars eiusque advocatus assistere possunt interrogationi ceterarum partium, testium et peritorum.

CAN. 1350 Responsiones partium, testium, peritorum, petitiones et exceptiones advocatorum redigendae sunt scripto a notario, sed summatim et in eis tantummodo, quae pertinent ad substantiam rei controversae, et ab eisdem subscribendae.

CAN. 1351 Probationes, quae non sunt in petitione vel responsione allatae aut petitae, potest iudex admittere tantum ad nor-

---

1347 §1: Pius XII, m.p. *Sollicitudinem Nostram,* 6 ian. 1950, can. 459.

1347 §2: Pius XII, m.p. *Sollicitudinem Nostram,* 6 ian. 1950, can. 460.

1349 §1: Pius XII, m.p. *Sollicitudinem Nostram,* 6 ian. 1950, can. 461.

1349 §2: Pius XII, m.p. *Sollicitudinem Nostram,* 6 ian. 1950, can. 454.

1351: Pius XII, m.p. *Sollicitudinem Nostram,* 6 ian. 1950, can. 464.

of can. 1110. After even one witness has been heard, however, the judge can only decide about new proofs in accord with the norm of can. 1283.

mam can. 1110; postquam autem vel unus testis auditus est, iudex potest tantummodo ad normam can. 1283 novas probationes decernere.

CAN. 1352 If all the proofs were not able to be collected during the hearing, a second hearing is to be scheduled.

CAN. 1352 Si in audientia omnes probationes colligi non potuerunt, altera statuatur audientia.

CAN. 1353 After the proofs have been collected, the oral discussion takes place at the same hearing.

CAN. 1353 Probationibus collectis fit in eadem audientia discussio oralis.

CAN. 1354 §1. Unless the discussion reveals that something must be supplied in the instruction of the case or something else turns up that prevents the sentence from being rendered in accord with the norm of law, at the completion of the hearing the judge is to decide the case immediately; the dispositive part of the sentence is to be read at once before the parties who are present.

CAN. 1354 §1. Nisi quid ex discussione supplendum in instructione causae comperitur, vel aliud exsistit, quod impedit, ne sententia ad normam iuris feratur, iudex expleta audientia statim causam decidat; pars dispositiva sententiae statim coram partibus praesentibus legatur.

§2. However, the tribunal can defer the decision up to the fifth useful day because of the difficulty of the matter or for some other just cause.

§2. Potest autem tribunal propter rei difficultatem vel alia iusta de causa usque ad quintum diem utilem decisionem differre.

§3. The complete text of the sentence with the reasons expressed is to be intimated to the parties as soon as possible, ordinarily in not more than fifteen days.

§3. Integer sententiae textus motivis expressis quam primum et ordinarie non ultra quindecim dies partibus intimetur.

CAN. 1355 If the appellate tribunal discovers that the summary contentious trial was used at a lower grade of a trial in a case excluded by law, it is to declare the nullity of the sentence and remit the case to the tribunal that rendered the sentence.

CAN. 1355 Si tribunal appellationis perspicit in inferiore gradu iudicii in causa iure exclusa iudicium contentiosum summarium adhibitum esse, nullitatem sententiae declarare et causam tribunali, quod sententiam tulit, remittere debet.

CAN. 1356 In other matters pertaining to the manner of proceeding, the canons for the

CAN. 1356 In ceteris, quae ad rationem procedendi attinent, serventur canones de

---

1352: Pius XII, m.p. *Sollicitudinem Nostram,* 6 ian. 1950, can. 464.

1353: Pius XII, m.p. *Sollicitudinem Nostram,* 6 ian. 1950, can. 462.

1354 §1: Pius XII, m.p. *Sollicitudinem Nostram,* 6 ian. 1950, cann. 463, 466.

1354 §2: Pius XII, m.p. *Sollicitudinem Nostram,* 6 ian. 1950, can. 463.

1354 §3: Pius XII, m.p. *Sollicitudinem Nostram,* 6 ian. 1950, cann. 466–467.

ordinary contentious trial are to be observed. In order to expedite matters without prejudice to justice, however, the tribunal, by a decree giving reasons, can choose not to observe the procedural norms that have not been established for validity.

iudicio contentioso ordinario; tribunal autem potest suo decreto motivis praedito normas processuales, quae non sunt ad validitatem statutae, non observare, ut celeritati salva iustitia consulat.

TITLE XXVI. CERTAIN
SPECIAL PROCESSES

CAPUT I. **De Processibus**
Matrimonialibus

CHAPTER I. **Marriage Processes**

ART. I. *Cases to Declare the Nullity
of Marriage*

ART. I. *De Causis ad Matrimonii
Nullitatem Declarandam*

1° The Competent Forum

1° De Foro Competenti

CAN. 1357 Any marriage case of a baptized person belongs to the Church by proper right.

CAN. 1357 Quaelibet causa matrimonialis baptizati iure proprio ad Ecclesiam spectat.

CAN. 1358 With due regard for personal statutes where they are in force, cases that principally concern the merely civil effects of marriage belong to the civil judge; if the cases concern the civil effects in an incidental and accessory manner, the ecclesiastical judge can also hear and decide them by proper authority.

CAN. 1358 Firmis, ubi vigent, Statutis personalibus causae de effectibus mere civilibus matrimonii, si principaliter aguntur, pertinent ad iudicem civilem, sed, si incidenter et accessorie, possunt etiam a iudice ecclesiastico ex propria auctoritate cognosci ac definiri.

CAN. 1359 In cases concerning the nullity of marriage not reserved to the Apostolic See, the following are competent:

CAN. 1359 In causis de matrimonii nullitate, quae non sunt Sedi Apostolicae reservatae, competentia sunt:

1° the tribunal of the place where the marriage was celebrated;

1° tribunal loci, ubi matrimonium celebratum est;

2° the tribunal of the place where the respondent has a domicile or quasi-domicile;

2° tribunal loci, ubi pars conventa domicilium vel quasi-domicilium habet;

1357: Pius XII, m.p. *Sollicitudinem Nostram,* 6 ian. 1950, can. 468. - Trid., sess. XXIV, *De matrimonio,* can. 12; Leo XIII, ep. encycl. *Immortale Dei,* 1 nov. 1885, 11–12; S.C.S. Off., instr. (ad Ep. Rituum Orient.), a. 1883, "Quaemadmodum;" Paulus VI, litt. *Cum matrimonialium,* 8 sep. 1973, I.

1358: Pius XII, m.p. *Sollicitudinem Nostram,* 6 ian. 1950, can. 469; Paulus VI, litt. *Cum matrimoni-*

alium, 8 sep. 1973, II.

1359: Pius XII, m.p. *Sollicitudinem Nostram,* 6 ian. 1950, cann. 470, 472. - Paulus VI, litt. *Cum matrimonialium,* 8 sep. 1973, III, IV, §§1–2; Pont. Comm. Decr. Conc. Vat. II Interpr., resp. 14 feb. 1977; Sign. Apost., resp. 12 apr. 1978. - S.C.S. Off., 11 aug. 1859; instr. (ad Ep. Rituum Orient.), a. 1883, tit. VI, art. 4, 45.

3° the tribunal of the place where the petitioner has a domicile, provided that both parties live in the territory of the same nation and the judicial vicar of the domicile of the respondent gives consent after he has heard the respondent;

4° the tribunal of the place where, in fact, most of the proofs must be collected, provided that the judicial vicar of the domicile of the respondent consents after he has heard the respondent.

2° The Right to Challenge a Marriage

CAN. 1360 The following are qualified to challenge a marriage:

1° the spouses;

2° the promoter of justice when nullity has become public and the convalidation of the marriage is not possible or expedient.

CAN. 1361 §1. A marriage that was not accused while both spouses were living cannot be accused after the death of either one or both of the spouses unless the question of validity is prejudicial to the resolution of another controversy either in the canonical forum or in the civil forum.

§2. If a spouse dies while the case is pending, however, can. 1199 is to be observed.

3° The Obligations of the Judges and Tribunal

CAN. 1362 Before accepting a case and whenever there seems to be hope of a favorable outcome, a judge is to use pastoral means to induce the spouses, if possible, to convalidate the

3° tribunal loci, ubi actor domicilium habet, dummodo utraque pars in territorio eiusdem nationis degat et Vicarius iudicialis domicilii partis conventae ea audita consentiat;

4° tribunal loci, ubi de facto colligendae sunt pleraeque probationes, dummodo Vicarius iudicialis domicilii partis conventae ea audita consentiat.

2° De Iure Impugnandi Matrimonium

CAN. 1360 Habiles sunt ad matrimonium impugnandum:

1° coniuges;

2° promotor iustitiae, si nullitas iam divulgata est et matrimonium convalidari non potest aut non expedit.

CAN. 1361 §1. Matrimonium, quod utroque coniuge vivente non est accusatum, post mortem alterutrius vel utriusque coniugis accusari non potest, nisi quaestio de validitate est praeiudicialis ad aliam controversiam sive in foro ecclesiastico sive in foro civili solvendam.

§2. Si vero coniux moritur pendente causa, servetur can. 1199.

3° De Obligationibus Iudicum et Tribunalis

CAN. 1362 Iudex, antequam causam acceptat et quoties spem boni exitus perspicit, pastoralia media adhibeat, ut coniuges, si fieri potest, ad matrimonium conva-

---

1360: Pius XII, m.p. *Sollicitudinem Nostram,* 6 ian. 1950, can. 478 §1. - S.C.S. Off., 27 ian. 1928, ad I; decr. 22 mar. 1939, ad I–II; 15 ian. 1940; Cons. pro Publ. Eccl. Neg., rescr. 28 apr. 1970, 8–9; Pont. Comm. Decr. Conc. Vat. II Interpr., resp. 8 ian. 1973.

1361 §1: Pius XII, m.p. *Sollicitudinem Nostram,* 6 ian. 1950, can. 479.
1362: Pius XII, m.p. *Sollicitudinem Nostram,* 6 ian. 1950, can. 473.

marriage and restore the partnership of conjugal life.

CAN. 1363 §1. When the *libellus* introducing the litigation has been admitted, the presiding judge or the *ponens* is to proceed to the intimation of the decree of citation according to the norm of can. 1191.

§2. When fifteen days have passed from the intimation and unless either party has requested a session for the joinder of the doubt, the presiding judge or the *ponens* is to define the formula of the doubt or doubts within ten days by *ex officio* decree and is to intimate it to the parties.

§3. The formula of the doubt is to ask not only whether the nullity of marriage is established in the case but also must determine on what ground or grounds the validity of the marriage is to be challenged.

§4. Ten days after the intimation of the decree, the presiding judge or the *ponens* is to arrange for the instruction of the case by a new decree if the parties have lodged no objection.

4° Proofs

CAN. 1364 §1. The defender of the bond, the legal representatives of the parties, and also the promoter of justice, if involved in the trial, have the right:

1° to be present at the questioning of the parties, the witnesses, and the experts, without prejudice to can. 1240;

2° to inspect the judicial acts, even though not yet published, and to review the documents presented by the parties.

§2. The parties cannot be present at the questioning referred to in §1, n.1.

lidandum et ad consortium vitae coniugalis restaurandum inducantur.

CAN. 1363 §1. Libello litis introductorio admisso praeses vel ponens procedat ad intimationem decreti citationis ad normam can. 1191.

§2. Transacto termino quindecim dierum ab intimatione computando praeses vel ponens, nisi alterutra pars sessionem ad litem contestandam petiit, intra decem dies formulam dubii vel dubiorum ex officio definiat decreto, quod partibus intimet.

§3. Formula dubii non tantum quaerat, num constet de nullitate matrimonii in casu, sed definire debet, quo capite vel quibus capitibus validitas matrimonii impugnetur.

§4. Post decem dies ab intimatione decreti computandos, si partes nihil opposuerunt, praeses vel ponens novo decreto causae instructionem decernat.

4° De Probationibus

CAN. 1364 §1. Defensori vinculi, partium patronis et, si in iudicio est, etiam promotori iustitiae ius est:

1° interrogationi partium, testium et peritorum adesse salvo can. 1240;

2° acta iudicialia, etsi nondum publicata, invisere et documenta a partibus producta recognoscere.

§2. Interrogationi, de qua in §1, n. 1, partes assistere non possunt.

1364 §1, 2 °: Pius XII, m.p. *Sollicitudinem Nostram*, 6 ian. 1950, cann. 476–477. - S.C.S. Off., instr. (ad Ep. Rituum Orient.), a. 1883, tit. II, 10–11; tit. III, 21–23; tit. V, 28.

1364 §2: S.C. de Discip. Sacr., instr. 15 aug. 1936, art. 128.

CAN. 1365 Unless there are full proofs from elsewhere, in order to evaluate the declarations of the parties mentioned in can. 1217, §2, the judge, if possible, is to use witnesses to the credibility of those parties in addition to other indications and supporting factors.

CAN. 1366 In cases of impotence or defect of consent because of mental illness, the judge is to use the services of one or more experts unless it is clear from the circumstances that it would be useless to do so; in other cases can. 1255 is to be observed.

CAN. 1367 If, during the instruction of the case, a very probable doubt emerges that consummation of the marriage did not occur, after suspending the case of nullity with the consent of the parties, the tribunal can complete the instruction to obtain a dissolution of a non-consummated sacramental marriage and then send the acts to the Apostolic See together with a petition for this dissolution from either one or both of the spouses and with the *votum* of the tribunal and the eparchial bishop.

5° The Sentence and the Appeal

CAN. 1368 §1. The sentence that first declared the nullity of the marriage is to be sent *ex officio* to the appellate tribunal within twenty days from the intimation of the sentence, together with the appeals, if there are any, and the other acts of the trial.

CAN. 1365 Nisi probationes aliunde plenae habentur, iudex ad partium declarationes, de quibus in can. 1217, §2, aestimandas testes de ipsarum partium credibilitate, si fieri potest, adhibeat praeter alia indicia et adminicula.

CAN. 1366 In causis de impotentia vel de defectu consensus propter mentis morbum iudex unius periti vel plurium opera utatur, nisi ex adiunctis inutilis evidenter apparet; in ceteris causis servetur can. 1255.

CAN. 1367 Si in instructione causae dubium valde probabile emersit de non secuta matrimonii consummatione, tribunal potest partibus consentientibus causam de nullitate matrimonii suspendere et instructionem complere ad obtinendam solutionem matrimonii sacramentalis non consummati; deinde acta ad Sedem Apostolicam mittat una cum petitione huius solutionis ab alterutro vel utroque coniuge facta et cum voto tribunalis et Episcopi eparchialis.

5° De Sententia et de Appellatione

CAN. 1368 §1. Sententia, quae matrimonii nullitatem primum declaravit, una cum appellationibus, si quae sunt, et ceteris actis iudicialibus intra viginti dies ab intimatione sententiae computandos ad tribunal appellationis ex officio mittatur.

1365: Pius XII, m.p. *Sollicitudinem Nostram*, 6 ian. 1950, can. 482. - S.C.S. Off., instr. a. 1858; instr. (ad Ep. Rituum Orient.), a. 1883, tit. VI, art. 5; S.C. pro Eccl. Orient., instr. 10 iun. 1935, II.

1366: Pius XII, m.p. *Sollicitudinem Nostram*, 6 ian. 1950, can. 483. - S.C.S. Off., instr. a. 1858; instr. (ad Ep. Rituum Orient.), a. 1883, tit. VI, art. 5; S.C. pro Eccl. Orient., instr. 10 iun. 1935, IV; S.C.S. Off., decr. 12 iun. 1942.

1367: Pius XII, m.p. *Sollicitudinem Nostram*, 6

ian. 1950, cann. 471 §3, 492. - S.C.S. Off., instr. (ad Ep. Rituum Orient.), a. 1883, tit. VI, art. 5; S.C. pro Eccl. Orient., instr. 10 iun. 1935, I, 4; instr. 13 iul. 1953, 5; S.C. de Discip. Sacr., instr. 7 mar. 1972, I, e); S. Rom. Rotae Trib., *Normae*, 16 ian. 1982, Allegato I, 2).

1368 §1: Pius XII, m.p. *Sollicitudinem Nostram*, 6 ian. 1950, can. 493. - S.C.S. Off., instr. (ad Ep. Rituum Orient.), a. 1883, tit. IV, 25; Paulus VI, litt. *Cum matrimonialium*, 8 sep. 1973, VIII, §1.

§2. If a sentence in favor of the nullity of a marriage was rendered in the first grade of a trial, the appellate tribunal is either to confirm the decision at once by decree or admit the case to an ordinary examination in a second grade, after having weighed carefully the observations of the defender of the bond and those of the parties if there are any.

CAN. 1369 If a new ground of nullity of the marriage is alleged at the appellate grade, the tribunal can admit it and judge it as if in the first grade.

CAN. 1370 §1. After the sentence that first declared the nullity of the marriage has been confirmed at the appellate grade either by a decree or by a second sentence, the persons whose marriage has been declared null can celebrate a new marriage as soon as the decree or second sentence has been intimated to them, unless a prohibition attached to the sentence or decree or established by the local hierarch forbids this.

§2. Can. 1325 must be observed even if the sentence that declared the nullity of the marriage was confirmed, not by a second sentence, but by a decree.

CAN. 1371 As soon as the sentence is executed, the judicial vicar must notify the local hierarch where the marriage was celebrated. The local hierarch must take care that the declaration of the nullity of the marriage and any possible prohibitions are noted as soon as possible in the marriage and baptismal registers.

§2. Si sententia pro matrimonii nullitate lata est in primo gradu iudicii, tribunal appellationis perpensis animadversionibus defensoris vinculi et, si quae sunt, etiam partium suo decreto vel decisionem continenter confirmet vel causam ad ordinarium examen secundi gradus iudicii admittat.

CAN. 1369 Si in gradu appellationis novum nullitatis matrimonii caput affertur, tribunal potest illud tamquam in primo gradu iudicii admittere et de illo iudicare.

CAN. 1370 §1. Postquam sententia, quae matrimonii nullitatem primum declaravit, in gradu appellationis confirmata est vel decreto vel altera sententia, ii, quorum matrimonium declaratum est nullum, possunt novum matrimonium celebrare statim ac decretum vel altera sententia ipsis intimata est, nisi id prohibetur vetito ipsi sententiae vel decreto apposito aut ab Hierarcha loci statuto.

§2. Can. 1325 servandus est, etsi sententia, quae matrimonii nullitatem declaravit, non altera sententia, sed decreto confirmata est.

CAN. 1371 Statim ac sententia facta est exsecutiva, Vicarius iudicialis debet eandem notificare Hierarchae loci, ubi matrimonium celebratum est; hic Hierarcha vero curare debet, ut quam primum de declarata nullitate matrimonii et de vetitis forte statutis in libris matrimoniorum et baptizatorum mentio fiat.

1368 §2: PAULUS VI, litt. *Cum matrimonialium,* 8 sep. 1973, VIII, §§2–3. - Pont. Comm. Decr. Conc. Vat. II interpr., resp. 31 oct. 1973; resp. 14 feb. 1974; resp. 1 iul. 1976.

1369: PIUS XII, m.p. *Sollicitudinem Nostram,* 6 ian. 1950, can. 494. - S.C. de Discip. Sacr., instr. 15 aug. 1936, art. 219, §2; S. Rom. Rotae Trib., *Normae,*

16 ian. 1982, Allegato I, 1).

1370 §1: PIUS XII, m.p. *Sollicitudinem Nostram,* 6 ian. 1950, can. 497 §1; PAULUS VI, litt. *Cum matrimonialium,* 8 sep. 1973, VIII, §3. - S.C.S. Off., instr. (ad Ep. Rituum Orient.), a 1883, tit. V, 30.

1371: PIUS XII, m.p. *Sollicitudinem Nostram,* 6 ian. 1950, can. 496.

6° The Documentary Process

CAN. 1372 §1. After admitting a petition, the judicial vicar or a judge designated by him can declare the nullity of a marriage by sentence if a document, subject to no contradiction or exception, clearly establishes the existence of a diriment impediment or a defect of form prescribed by law for the celebration of marriage, provided that it is equally certain that no dispensation was given, or establishes the lack of a valid mandate of a procurator. In these case, the formalities of the ordinary process are omitted except for the citation of the parties and the intervention of the defender of the bond.

§2. However, if it concerns a person who was obliged to observe the form prescribed by law for the celebration of marriage, but who attempted marriage before a civil official or non-Catholic minister, the pre-nuptial investigation mentioned in can. 784 suffices to prove his or her free status.

CAN. 1373 §1. If the defender of the bond prudently thinks that either the defects or the lack of a dispensation is not certain, the defender of the bond must appeal from the sentence mentioned in can. 1372, §1 to the judge of the tribunal of second grade. The acts must be sent to the appellate judge who must be advised in writing that a documentary process is involved.

§2. The party who considers himself or herself aggrieved retains the right of appeal.

CAN. 1374 The judge of the tribunal of second grade, with the intervention of the de-

6° De Processu Documentali

CAN. 1372 §1. Admissa petitione Vicarius iudicialis vel iudex ab ipso designatus potest praetermissis sollemnibus ordinarii processus, sed citatis partibus et cum interventu defensoris vinculi matrimonii nullitatem sententia declarare, si ex documento, quod nulli contradictioni vel exceptioni est obnoxium, certo constat de exsistentia impedimenti dirimentis vel de defectu formae celebrationis matrimonii iure praescriptae, dummodo pari certitudine pateat dispensationem datam non esse, aut de defectu validi mandati procuratoris.

§2. Si vero agitur de eo, qui formam celebrationis matrimonii iure praescriptam servare debuit, sed matrimonium attentavit coram officiali civili vel ministro acatholico, sufficit investigatio praematrimonialis, de qua in can. 784, ad comprobandum eius statum liberum.

CAN. 1373 §1. A sententia, de qua in can. 1372, §1, defensor vinculi, si prudenter existimat vel vitia vel dispensationis defectum non esse certa, appellare debet ad iudicem tribunalis secundi gradus, ad quem acta sunt mittenda quique scripto certior faciendus est agi de processu documentali.

§2. Integrum manet parti, quae se gravatam putet, ius appellandi.

CAN. 1374 Iudex tribunalis secundi gradus cum interventu defensoris vinculi et

---

1372 §1: Pius XII, m.p. *Sollicitudinem Nostram,* 6 ian. 1950, can. 498. - S.C.S. Off., decr. 21 iun. 1912, ad 2; 10 maii 1941, ad III; Paulus VI, litt. *Cum matrimonialium,* 8 sep. 1973, X–XI.

1372 §2: Pont. Comm. Cod. Iur. Can. Auth. Interpr., resp. 11 iul. 1984, II.

1373 §1: Pius XII, m.p. *Sollicitudinem Nostram,* 6 ian. 1950, can. 499; Paulus VI, litt. *Cum matrimonialium,* 8 sep. 1973, XII.

1374: Pius XII, m.p. *Sollicitudinem Nostram,* 6 ian. 1950, can. 500; Paulus VI, litt. *Cum matrimonialium,* 8 sep. 1973, XIII.

fender of the bond and after having heard the parties, will decide whether the sentence must be confirmed or whether the case must proceed instead according to the ordinary norm of law; in the latter event, the judge remands the case to the tribunal of first grade.

auditis partibus decernat, utrum sententia sit confirmanda an potius procedendum in causa sit ad ordinariam normam iuris; quo in casu eam remittit ad tribunal primi gradus.

7° General Norms

CAN. 1375 Cases for the declaration of a nullity of a marriage cannot be treated in a summary contentious trial.

CAN. 1376 In other procedural matters, the canons on trials in general and on the ordinary contentious trial must be applied unless the nature of the matter precludes it; the special norms for cases pertaining to the public good are to be observed.

CAN. 1377 In the sentence the parties are to be reminded of the moral and even civil obligations that may bind them both toward one another and toward their children to furnish support and education.

7° Normae Generales

CAN. 1375 Causae ad matrimonii nullitatem declarandam non possunt iudicio contentioso summario tractari.

CAN. 1376 In ceteris, quae ad rationem procedendi attinent, applicandi sunt, nisi rei natura obstat, canones de iudiciis in genere et de iudicio contentioso ordinario servatis normis specialibus de causis, quae ad bonum publicum spectant.

CAN. 1377 In sententia partes moneantur de obligationibus moralibus vel etiam civilibus, quibus forte tenentur, altera erga alteram et erga filios ad debitam sustentationem et educationem praestandas.

ART. 11. *Cases of Separation of Spouses*

CAN. 1378 §1. Unless other provision is legitimately made in particular places, a decree of the eparchial bishop or a judicial sentence can decide the personal separation of spouses.

§2. Where an ecclesiastical decision has no civil effects or if a civil sentence is not contrary to divine law, the eparchial bishop of the eparchy of the residence of the spouses, after having weighed the special circumstances, can grant permission to approach the civil forum.

§3. Also, if a case concerns the merely civil

ART. 11. *De Causis Separationis Coniugum*

CAN. 1378 §1. Separatio personalis coniugum, nisi aliter pro locis particularibus legitime provisum est, decerni potest decreto Episcopi eparchialis vel sententia iudicis.

§2. Ubi vero decisio ecclesiastica effectus civiles non sortitur vel si sententia civilis praevidetur non contraria iuri divino, Episcopus eparchialis eparchiae commorationis coniugum potest perpensis specialibus adiunctis licentiam concedere adeundi forum civile.

§3. Si causa versatur etiam circa effectus

1378 §1: PIUS XII, m.p. *Crebrae allatae sunt,* 2 feb. 1949, cann. 119–120.

effects of marriage, the judge is to try to defer the case to the civil forum from the start.

CAN. 1379 §1. Unless a party requests an ordinary contentious trial, the summary contentious trial is to be used.

§2. If the ordinary contentious trial has been used and an appeal is introduced, the tribunal of second grade, after having heard the parties, by decree is either to confirm the decision at once or admit the case to the ordinary examination of a trial of second grade.

CAN. 1380 Can. 1359, nn. 2 and 3 are to be observed in what pertains to the competence of the tribunal.

CAN. 1381 Before accepting the case and whenever there is hope of a favorable outcome, the judge is to use pastoral means to persuade the spouses to be reconciled and restore the partnership of conjugal life.

CAN. 1382 In cases concerning the separation of spouses, the promoter of justice must take part according to the norm of can. 1097.

ART. III. *Process in the Presumed Death of a Spouse*

CAN. 1383 §1. Whenever the death of a spouse cannot be proven by an authentic ecclesiastical act or civil document, the other spouse is not considered free from the bond of marriage until after the eparchial bishop has made a declaration of presumed death.

§2. The eparchial bishop is able to make this declaration only if, after carried out the appropriate investigations, he attains moral certitude of the death of the spouse from the depositions of witnesses, from rumor, or from evidence; the

mere civiles matrimonii, satagat iudex, ut de licentia Episcopi eparchialis causa inde ab initio ad forum civile deferatur.

CAN. 1379 §1. Nisi qua pars iudicium contentiosum ordinarium petit, iudicium contentiosum summarium adhibeatur.

§2. Si iudicium contentiosum ordinarium adhibitum est et appellatio interponitur, tribunal secundi gradus auditis partibus suo decreto vel decisionem continenter confirmet vel causam ad ordinarium examen secundi gradus iudicii admittat.

CAN. 1380 Quod attinet ad tribunalis competentiam, servetur can. 1359, nn. 2 et 3.

CAN. 1381 Iudex, antequam causam acceptat et quoties spem boni exitus perspicit, pastoralia media adhibeat, ut coniuges concilientur et ad consortium vitae coniugalis restaurandum inducantur.

CAN. 1382 Causis de coniugum separatione interesse debet promotor iustitiae ad normam can. 1097.

ART. III. *De Processu Praesumptae Mortis Coniugis*

CAN. 1383 §1. Quoties coniugis mors authentico documento ecclesiastico vel civili comprobari non potest, alter coniux a vinculo matrimonii solutus non habeatur nisi post declarationem de morte praesumpta ab Episcopo eparchiali factam.

§2. Hanc declarationem Episcopus eparchialis tantummodo facere potest, si peractis opportunis investigationibus ex testium depositionibus, ex fama aut ex indiciis moralem certitudinem de coniugis morte ob-

---

1383 §1: Pius XII, m.p. *Crebrae allatae sunt,* 2 feb. 1949, cann. 43, 59 §2; Pont. Comm. Cod. Iur. Can. Auth. Interpr., resp. 26 mar. 1952, I. - Quinisext. can. 93; S. Basilius M., cann. 31, 36.

absence of a spouse alone, even if for a long time, is not sufficient.

§3. In uncertain and complicated cases, an eparchial bishop exercising his power within the territorial boundaries of the patriarchal Church, is to consult the patriarch; other eparchial bishops are to consult the Apostolic See.

§4. The intervention of the promoter of justice, but not the defender of the bond, is required in the process of the presumed death of a spouse.

ART. IV. *The Process for Obtaining a Dissolution of a Non-Consummated Marriage or the Dissolution of a Marriage in Favor of the Faith*

CAN. 1384 In order to obtain the dissolution of a non-consummated marriage or the dissolution of a marriage in favor of the faith, the special norms issued by the Apostolic See are to be strictly observed.

CHAPTER II. Cases for Declaring the Nullity of Sacred Ordination

CAN. 1385 The cleric himself, the hierarch to whom the cleric is subject, or the hierarch in whose eparchy the cleric was ordained has the right to challenge the validity of sacred ordination.

tinuit; sola coniugis absentia, etsi diuturna, non sufficit.

§3. In casibus incertis et implexis Episcopus eparchialis intra fines territorii Ecclesiae patriarchalis potestatem suam exercens consulat Patriarcham; ceteri Episcopi eparchiales vero Sedem Apostolicam consulant.

§4. In processu praesumptae mortis coniugis requiritur interventus promotoris iustitiae, non vero defensoris vinculi.

ART. IV. *De Modo Procedendi ad Obtinendam Solutionem Matrimonii Non Consummati aut Solutionem Matrimonii in Favorem Fidei*

CAN. 1384 Ad obtinendam solutionem matrimonii non consummati aut solutionem matrimonii in favorem fidei adamussim serventur normae speciales a Sede Apostolica latae.

CAPUT II. **De Causis ad Sacrae Ordinationis Nullitatem Declarandam**

CAN. 1385 Validitatem sacrae ordinationis ius habent accusandi sive ipse clericus sive Hierarcha, cui clericus subest vel in cuius eparchia ordinatus est.

1384: *Quoad matrimonium non consummatum:* PIUS XII, m.p. *Crebrae allatae sunt,* 2 feb. 1949, can. 108; m.p. *Sollicitudinem Nostram,* 6 ian. 1950, cann. 470, 471. - Trid., sess. XXIV, *De matrimonio,* can. 6; S.C. de Prop. Fide, instr. (ad Ep. Graeco-Rumen.), a. 1858; S.C.S. Off., instr. a. 1858; instr. (ad Ep. Rituum Orient.), a. 1883, tit. VI, artt. 4–5; S.C. pro Eccl. Orient., instr. 10 iun. 1935; instr. 13 iul. 1953; PAULUS VI, const. ap. *Regimini Ecclesiae universae,* 15 aug. 1967, 56; S.C. de Discip. Sacr., instr. 7 mar. 1972; Secret. Status, rescr. ex audientia, 15 iul. 1973; IOANNES

PAULUS II, const. ap. *Pastor Bonus,* 28 iun. 1988, artt. 58 §2, 67.

Quoad solutionem matrimonii in favorem fidei: S.C.S. Off., instr. 1 maii 1934; notificatio, 28 maii 1956; resp. 2 ian. 1959; resp. 12 iul. 1960; S.C. pro Doctr. Fidei, resp. 14 iul. 1967; *Instructio pro solutione matrimonii in favorem fidei et normae procedurales . . . ,* 6 dec. 1973.

1385: PIUS XII, m.p. *Sollicitudinem Nostram,* 6 ian. 1950, can. 502 §1.

CAN. 1386 §1. The *libellus* challenging the validity of sacred ordination must be sent to the competent dicastery of the Roman Curia, which will decide whether the dicastery itself or a tribunal designated by it is to handle the case.

§2. If the dicastery hands the case over to a tribunal, the canons on trials in general and on the ordinary contentious trial are to be observed unless the nature of the matter precludes this; the canons on the summary contentious trial cannot, however, be used.

§3. Once the *libellus* has been sent, the cleric is forbidden to exercise sacred orders by the law itself.

CAN. 1387 After a second sentence has confirmed the nullity of sacred ordination, the cleric loses all rights proper to the clerical state and is freed from all its obligations.

CHAPTER III. The Procedure in the Removal or Transfer of Pastors

CAN. 1388 In the removal or transfer of pastors, cann. 1389–1400 must be observed, unless the particular law approved by the Apostolic See establishes otherwise.

ART. 1. *The Manner of Proceeding in Removing Pastors*

CAN. 1389 When the ministry of any pastor becomes harmful or at least ineffective for any reason, even through no grave personal

CAN. 1386 §1. Libellus de validitate sacrae ordinationis accusanda mitti debet ad competens Curiae Romanae Dicasterium, quod decernet, utrum causa ab ipso an a tribunali ab eo designato sit agenda.

§2. Si Dicasterium causam ad tribunal remisit, serventur, nisi rei natura obstat, canones de iudiciis in genere et de iudicio contentioso ordinario, non vero canones de iudicio contentioso summario.

§3. Misso libello clericus ordines sacros exercere ipso iure vetatur.

CAN. 1387 Post secundam sententiam, quae nullitatem sacrae ordinationis confirmavit, clericus omnia iura statui clericali propria amittit et ab omnibus obligationibus eiusdem status liberatur.

CAPUT III. De Procedura in Parochis Amovendis vel Transferendis

CAN. 1388 In amotione vel translatione parochorum servandi sunt cann. 1389–1400, nisi iure particulari a Sede Apostolica approbato aliud statuitur.

ART. 1. *De Modo Procedendi in Amotione Parochorum*

CAN. 1389 Si alicuius parochi ministerium aliqua de causa, etiam citra gravem ipsius culpam, noxium aut saltem inefficax

1386 §1: Pius XII, m.p. *Sollicitudinem Nostram*, 6 ian. 1950, can. 501 §1; Paulus VI, const. ap. *Regimini Ecclesiae universae*, 15 aug. 1968, artt. 45, 57; Ioannes Paulus II, const. ap. *Pastor Bonus*, 28 iun. 1988, artt. 58 §2, 68.

1386 §2: Pius XII, m.p. *Sollicitudinem Nostram*, 6 ian. 1950, cann. 501 §2, 503–504, 506 §2.

1386 §3: Pius XII, m.p. *Sollicitudinem Nostram*, 6

ian. 1950, can. 505.

1387: Pius XII, m.p. *Sollicitudinem Nostram*, 6 ian. 1950, can. 506 §1.

1389: Trid., sess. XXI, *De ref.*, can. 6; Vat. II, decr. *Christus Dominus*, 31 "Praeterea;" Paulus VI, litt. ap. *Ecclesiae sanctae*, 6 aug. 1966, I, 20, §1; Pont. Comm. Decr. Conc. Vat. II Interpr., resp. 7 iul. 1978.

negligence, the eparchial bishop can remove him from the parish.

CAN. 1390 The causes for which a pastor can be removed legitimately from his parish are especially the following:

1° a manner of acting that brings grave detriment or disturbance to ecclesiastical communion;

2° ineptitude or a permanent infirmity of mind or body that renders the pastor unable to fulfill his functions usefully;

3° loss of a good reputation among upright and responsible parishioners or an aversion to the pastor that apparently will not cease in a brief time;

4° grave neglect or violation of parochial obligations that persists after a warning;

5° poor administration of temporal affairs with grave damage to the Church whenever another remedy to this harm cannot be found.

CAN. 1391 §1. If the instruction carried out establishes the existence of a cause for removal, the eparchial bishop is to discuss the matter with two pastors selected from the group of pastors, whom the presbyteral council elects for this purpose in a stable manner at the proposal of the eparchial bishop. However, if the bishop then judges that removal must take place, he paternally is to persuade the pastor to resign within fifteen days, after having explained, for validity, the cause and arguments for the removal.

§2. A pastor who is a member of a religious institute or a society of common life in the manner of religious can be removed either at the discretion of the eparchial bishop, who has notified the major superior or by the major superior who has notified the eparchial bishop, without requiring each other's consent.

evasit, parochus ab Episcopo eparchiali a paroecia amoveri potest.

CAN. 1390 Causae, ob quas parochus a sua paroecia legitime amoveri potest, hae praesertim sunt:

1° modus agendi, qui communioni ecclesiasticae grave detrimentum vel perturbationem affert;

2° imperitia aut permanens mentis vel corporis infirmitas, quae parochum suis muneribus utiliter obeundis imparem reddunt;

3° bonae existimationis amissio penes probos et graves paroecianos vel aversio in parochum, quae praevidentur non brevi cessaturae;

4° gravis neglectus vel violatio obligationum parochi, quae post monitionem persistit;

5° mala rerum temporalium administratio cum gravi Ecclesiae damno, quoties huic malo aliud remedium afferri non potest.

CAN. 1391 §1. Si ex instructione peracta constat adesse causam amotionis, Episcopus eparchialis rem discutiat cum duobus parochis ex coetu parochorum, quos consilium presbyterale Episcopo eparchiali proponente ad hoc stabiliter elegit, selectis; si vero exinde censet ad amotionem esse deveniendum, causa et argumentis ad validitatem indicatis parocho paterne suadeat, ut intra tempus quindecim dierum renuntiet.

§2. Parochus, qui est sodalis instituti religiosi vel societatis vitae communis ad instar religiosorum amoveri potest ad nutum sive Episcopi eparchialis certiore facto Superiore maiore sive Superioris maioris certiore facto Episcopo eparchialinon requisito alterius consensu.

CAN. 1392 A pastor can submit a resignation even conditionally, provided that the eparchial bishop can accept it legitimately and actually does accept it.

CAN. 1393 §1. If the pastor has not responded within the prescribed days, the bishop is to repeat the invitation and extend the useful time to respond.

§2. If the bishop establishes that the pastor received the second invitation but did not respond even though not prevented by any impediment, or if the pastor refuses to resign without giving any reasons, the bishop is to issue a decree of removal.

CAN. 1394 If the pastor opposes the cause given and its reasons and alleges reasons that seem insufficient to the eparchial bishop, the bishop, in order to act validly, is:

1° to invite the pastor to organize his objections in a written report after he has inspected the acts, and offer any proofs he has to the contrary;

2° when any necessary instruction is completed, to consider the matter together with the two pastors mentioned in can. 1391, §1, unless others must be designated because those pastors are unavailable.

3° finally, to establish whether the pastor must be removed or not and promptly to issue a decree on the matter.

CAN. 1395 After the pastor has been removed, the eparchial bishop is to make provision for an assignment to some other office, if he is suitable for this, or for a pension as the case warrants and circumstances permit.

CAN. 1396 §1. The removed pastor must refrain from exercising the office of pastor, vacate the rectory as soon as possible, and hand over everything belonging to the parish to the

CAN. 1392 Renuntiatio a parocho fieri potest etiam sub condicione, dummodo haec ab Episcopo eparchiali legitime acceptari possit et reapse acceptetur.

CAN. 1393 §1. Si parochus intra praestitutos dies non respondit, Episcopus eparchialis iteret invitationem prorogando tempus utile ad respondendum.

§2. Si Episcopo eparchiali constat parochum alteram invitationem recepisse, non autem respondisse, etsi nullo impedimento detentum, aut si parochus renuntiationem sine motivis recusat, Episcopus eparchialis decretum amotionis ferat.

CAN. 1394 Si vero parochus causam adductam eiusque rationes oppugnat motiva allegans, quae insufficientia Episcopo eparchiali videntur, hic, ut valide agat:

1° invitet illum, ut inspectis actis suas impugnationes in relatione scripto danda colligat, immo probationes in contrarium, si quas habet, afferat;

2° deinde completa, si opus est, instructione una cum eisdem duobus parochis, de quibus in can. 1391, §1, nisi alii propter illorum impossibilitatem sunt designandi, rem perpendat;

3° tandem statuat, utrum parochus sit amovendus necne, et mox decretum de re ferat.

CAN. 1395 Amoto parocho Episcopus eparchialis consulat collatione alterius officii, si ille ad hoc idoneus est, vel pensione, prout casus fert et adiuncta permittunt.

CAN. 1396 §1. Parochus amotus debet a parochi officio exercendo abstinere, quam primum liberam relinquere domum paroecialem et omnia, quae ad paroeciam perti-

person to whom the eparchial bishop has entrusted the parish.

§2. If, however, the man is sick and cannot be transferred elsewhere from the rectory without inconvenience, the eparchial bishop is to leave him the use, even the exclusive use, of the rectory while this necessity lasts.

§3. While recourse against a decree of removal is pending, the bishop cannot appoint a new pastor, but is to provide a parochial administrator in the meantime.

ART. II. *The Manner of Proceeding in the Transfer of Pastors*

CAN. 1397 If the good of souls or the necessity or advantage of the Church demands that a pastor be transferred from a parish that he is governing usefully to another parish or another office, the eparchial bishop is to propose the transfer to him in writing and persuade him to consent to it out of love of God and souls.

CAN. 1398 If the pastor does not intend to submit to the counsel and persuasions of the eparchial bishop, he is to explain the reasons in writing.

CAN. 1399 §1. Notwithstanding the reasons alleged, if the eparchial bishop decides not to withdraw his proposal, he is to consider the reasons that favor or oppose the transfer with the two pastors selected from the group mentioned in can. 1391, §1. If the bishop then decides to implement the transfer, however, he is to repeat the paternal exhortations to the pastor.

§2. When this has been done, if the pastor still refuses and the eparchial bishop thinks that

nent, illi tradere, cui Episcopus eparchialis paroeciam commisit.

§2. Si vero de infirmo agitur, qui ex domo paroeciali sine incommodo non potest alio transferri, Episcopus eparchialis eidem relinquat domus paroecialis usum, etiam exclusivum, eadem necessitate durante.

§3. Pendente recursu adversus amotionis decretum Episcopus eparchialis non potest novum parochum nominare, sed per administratorem paroeciae interim provideat.

ART. II. *De Modo Procedendi in Translatione Parochorum*

CAN. 1397 Si salus animarum vel Ecclesiae necessitas aut utilitas postulat, ut parochus a sua, quam utiliter regit, ad aliam paroeciam aut ad aliud officium transferatur, Episcopus eparchialis eidem translationem scripto proponat ac suadeat, ut pro Dei atque animarum amore consentiat.

CAN. 1398 Si parochus consilio ac suasionibus Episcopi eparchialis obsequi non intendit, rationes scripto exponat.

CAN. 1399 §1. Episcopus eparchialis, si non obstantibus allatis rationibus iudicat a suo proposito non esse recedendum, cum duobus parochis ex coetu, de quo in can. 1391, §1, selectis rationes perpendat, quae translationi favent vel obstant; si vero exinde translationem peragendam censet, paternas exhortationes parocho iteret.

§2. His peractis, si adhuc et parochus renuit et Episcopus eparchialis putat transla-

---

1396 §3: Sign. Apost., decisio, 1 nov. 1970; Pont. Comm. Decr. Conc. Vat. II Interpr., resp. 1 iul. 1971.

1397: PAULUS VI, litt. ap. *Ecclesiae sanctae,* 6 aug. 1966, I, 20, §2.

the transfer must be made, he is to issue a decree of transfer, establishing that the parish will be vacant after a set day has passed.

§3. If this day has passed without action, the eparchial bishop is to declare the parish vacant.

CAN. 1400 In the case of a transfer, can. 1396, acquired rights and equity are to be observed.

tionem esse faciendam, hic decretum translationis ferat statuens paroeciam elapso determinato die esse vacaturam.

§3. Hoc die inutiliter elapso Episcopus eparchialis paroeciam vacantem declaret.

CAN. 1400 In casu translationis serventur can. 1396, iura quaesita et aequitas.

TITLE XXVII. PENAL SANCTIONS IN THE CHURCH

CHAPTER I. Delicts and Penalties in General

CAN. 1401 Since God employs every means to bring back the erring sheep, those who have received from Him the power to loose and to bind are to apply suitable medicine to the sickness of those who have committed delicts, reproving, imploring and rebuking them with the greatest patience and teaching. Indeed, they are even to impose penalties in order to heal the wounds caused by the delict, so that those who commit delicts are not driven to the depth of despair nor are restraints relaxed unto a dissoluteness of life and contempt of the law.

CAN. 1402 §1. Any contrary custom being reprobated, a canonical penalty must be imposed through a penal trial prescribed in cann. 1468–1482, with due regard for the coercive power of the judge in the cases expressed by law.

§2. If, however, in the judgment of the authority mentioned in §3, there are grave causes that preclude a penal trial and the proofs concerning the delict are certain, the delict can be

CAPUT I. De Delictis et Poenis in Genere

CAN. 1401 Cum omnem rationem init Deus, ut errantem ovem reducat, illi, qui ab Eo solvendi et ligandi potestatem acceperunt, morbo eorum, qui deliquerunt, convenientem medicinam afferant, eos arguant, obsecrent, increpent in omni patientia et doctrina, immo poenas imponant, ut vulneribus a delicto illatis medeatur ita, ut neque delinquentes ad desperationis praecipitia impellantur neque frena ad vitae dissolutionem et legis contemptum relaxentur.

CAN. 1402 §1. Poena canonica per iudicium poenale in cann. 1468–1482 praescriptum irrogari debet firma potestate coercitiva iudicis in casibus iure expressis et reprobata contraria consuetudine.

§2. Si vero iudicio auctoritatis, de qua in §3, graves obstant causae, ne iudicium poenale fiat, et probationes de delicto certae sunt, delictum puniri potest per decretum ex-

---

1401: 2 Tim. 4, 2; Quinisext. can. 102; Nic. I, can. 12; Chalc. can. 16; S. Basilius M., cann. 3, 54, 74, 84; S. Gregorius Nyssen., cann. 1, 8; Protodeut. can. 3; Trid., sess. XIII, *De ref.*, "Eadem;" Vat. II, const. *Lumen gentium*, 8 "Sicut;" Paulus VI, all. 4 oct. 1969, I "Certes."

1402 §1: Apost. can. 74; Constantinop. I, can. 6; Chalc. cann. 17, 21; Carth. cann. 12, 19–20, 28, 125; Constantinop., a. 394, "Nectarius;" Theophilus Alexandrin., cann. 6, 9; S. Cyrillus Alexandrin., can. 1.

punished by an extra-judicial decree according to the norm of cann. 1486 and 1487, provided it does not involve a privation of office, title, insignia or a suspension for more than one year, demotion to a lower grade, deposition or major excommunication.

§3. This decree can be issued, besides by the Apostolic See, within the limits of their competence, by the patriarch, major archbishop, eparchial bishop and the major superior of an institute of consecrated life who has ordinary power of governance, all others being excluded.

CAN. 1403 §1. Even when it is a question of delicts that carry an obligatory penalty by law, the hierarch, after having heard the promoter of justice, can abstain from a penal process and even abstain totally from imposing penalties, provided that, in the judgment of the hierarch himself, all these conditions simultaneously concur: the offender, not yet brought to trial and moved by sincere repentance, has confessed his delict to the hierarch in the external forum and has appropriately provided for the reparation of the scandal and harm.

§2. However, the hierarch cannot do this if it involves a delict that carries a penalty whose remission is reserved to a higher authority, unless he has obtained permission from that authority.

CAN. 1404 §1. In the matter of penalties, the more benign interpretation is to be made.

§2. It is not permitted to extend a penalty from one person to another or from one case to another, although an equal or even more serious reason is present.

CAN. 1405 §1. A person who has legislative power can also issue penal laws insofar as they are truly necessary to provide more suitably for ecclesiastical discipline; within the limits of his

tra iudicium ad normam cann. 1486 et 1487, dummodo non agatur de privatione officii, tituli, insignium aut de suspensione ultra annum, de reductione ad inferiorem gradum, de depositione vel de excommunicatione maiore.

§3. Hoc decretum praeter Sedem Apostolicam ferre possunt intra fines suae competentiae Patriarcha, Archiepiscopus maior, Episcopus eparchialis atque Superior maior instituti vitae consecratae, qui potestatem regiminis ordinariam habet, ceteris omnibus exclusis.

CAN. 1403 §1. Etsi de delictis agitur, quae poenam secumferunt iure obligatoriam, Hierarcha audito promotore iustitiae a procedura poenali, immo a poenis irrogandis prorsus abstinere potest, dummodo ipsius Hierarchae iudicio haec omnia simul concurrant: delinquens in iudicium nondum delatus suum delictum Hierarchae in foro externo sincera paenitentia motus confessus est necnon de reparatione scandali et damni congrue provisum est.

§2. Hoc vero Hierarcha facere non potest, si de delicto agitur, quod poenam secumfert, cuius remissio auctoritati superiori reservata est, donec licentiam ab eadem auctoritate obtinuerit.

CAN. 1404 §1. In poenis benignior est interpretatio facienda.

§2. Non licet poenam de persona ad personam vel de casu ad casum producere, etsi par adest ratio, immo gravior.

CAN. 1405 §1. Qui habet potestatem legislativam, potest, quatenus vere necessarium est ad aptius providendum disciplinae ecclesiasticae, etiam leges poenales ferre

competence by reason of territory or persons, moreover, he can by his own laws also strengthen with an appropriate penalty a divine law or an ecclesiastical law issued by a higher authority.

§2. Particular law can add other penalties to those already established by common law for some delict, but this is not to be done except for a very serious reason. However, if common law establishes an indeterminate or facultative penalty, particular law can establish a determined or obligatory one in its place.

§3. Insofar as it is possible, patriarchs and eparchial bishops are to take care that penal laws of particular law are uniform in the same territory.

CAN. 1406 §1. Insofar as one can impose precepts, one can, after a thorough consideration of the matter and with the utmost moderation, threaten determined penalties by precept, with the exception of those enumerated in can. 1402, §2. The patriarch, however, can threaten even these penalties by precept with the consent of the permanent synod.

§2. A warning containing the threat of penalties by which the hierarch presses a non-penal law in individual cases, is equivalent to a penal precept.

CAN. 1407 §1. If, in the judgment of the hierarch who can impose the penalty, the nature of the delict permits it, the penalty cannot be imposed unless the offender has been warned at least once beforehand to desist from the delict and has been given a suitable time for repentance.

§2. An offender who has sincerely repented

necnon suis legibus etiam legem divinam aut ecclesiasticam ab auctoritate superiore latam congrua poena munire servatis suae competentiae limitibus ratione territorii vel personarum.

§2. Poenis iure communi in aliquod delictum statutis aliae poenae iure particulari addi possunt; id autem ne fiat nisi gravissima de causa; si vero iure communi indeterminata vel facultativa poena statuitur, iure particulari in eius locum poena determinata vel obligatoria statui potest.

§3. Curent Patriarchae et Episcopi eparchiales, ut leges poenales iuris particularis in eodem territorio, quatenus fieri potest, uniformes sint.

CAN. 1406 §1. Quatenus aliquis potest praecepta imponere, eatenus potest re mature perpensa et maxima moderatione poenas determinatas per praeceptum comminari eis exceptis, quae in can. 1402, §2 enumerantur; Patriarcha vero de consensu Synodi permanentis etiam has poenas per praeceptum comminari potest.

§2. Monitio cum comminatione poenarum, qua Hierarcha legem non poenalem in casibus singularibus urget, praecepto poenali aequiparatur.

CAN. 1407 §1. Si iudicio Hierarchae, qui poenam irrogare potest, natura delicti id patitur, poena irrogari non potest, nisi delinquens antea semel saltem monitus est, ut a delicto desisteret, dato congruo ad resipiscentiam tempore.

§2. A delicto destitisse dicendus est is,

1406 §2: IOANNES VIII, litt. *Secundo iam,* 16 apr. 878; litt. *Miramur vos,* 16 apr. 878.

1407 §1: Apost. cann. 15, 31; Ant. can. 5; Nic. II, can. 18; IOANNES VIII, litt. *Secundo iam,* 16 apr. 878. * Syn. Alexandrin. Coptorum, a. 1898, sect. III, cap. VII, art. II, 8–9.

1407 §2: Nic. I, cann. 11–12; Chalc. can. 7; S. PETRUS ALEXANDRIN., can. 5; S. BASILIUS M., cann. 1 Ἔδο ξε" 5, 7; PIUS XII, nuntius, 5 feb. 1955, "Psicologicamente" et "Nell'applicazione;" PAULUS VI, all. 4 oct. 1969, I "Certes." * Syn. Armen., a. 1911, 959.

of the delict and has also made suitable reparation for the scandal and damage, or at least has seriously promised to do so, must be considered to have desisted from the delict.

§3. However, the penal warning mentioned in can. 1406, §2 suffices for the imposition of a penalty.

CAN. 1408 A penalty does not bind the guilty party until after it has been imposed by a sentence or decree, without prejudice to the right of the Roman Pontiff or an ecumenical council to establish otherwise.

CAN. 1409 §1. In the application of penal law, even if the law uses perceptive words, the judge can, according to his own conscience and prudence:

1° defer the imposition of the penalty to a more opportune time if it is foreseen that greater evils will result from an overly hasty punishment of the offender;

2° abstain from imposing a penalty or impose a lighter penalty if the offender has reformed and has provided for the reparation of the scandal and damage or if the offender has been or, it is foreseen, will be punished sufficiently by civil authority;

3° moderate the penalties within equitable limits if the offender has committed several delicts and the sum of the penalties appears excessive;

4° suspend the obligation of observing the penalty if it is the first offense of one who has been commended heretofore by an entirely upright life, provided the reparation of the scandal is not pressing. The suspended penalty ceases absolutely if the offender does not commit an offense again within the time determined by the judge; otherwise, the offender is to be punished

quem delicti sincere paenituit quique praeterea congruam reparationem scandali et damni dedit vel saltem serio promisit.

§3. Monitio poenalis vero, de qua in can. 1406, §2, sufficiens est, ut poena irrogari possit.

CAN. 1408 Poena reum non tenet, nisi postquam sententia vel decreto irrogata est, salvo iure Romani Pontificis vel Concilii Oecumenici aliter statuendi.

CAN. 1409 §1. In lege poenali applicanda, etsi lex utitur verbis praeceptivis, iudex pro sua conscientia et prudentia potest:

1° poenae irrogationem in tempus magis opportunum differre, si ex praepropera rei punitione maiora mala eventura praevidentur;

2° a poena irroganda abstinere vel poenam mitiorem irrogare, si reus emendatus est necnon de reparatione scandali et damni congrue provisum est aut si ipse reus satis ab auctoritate civili punitus est aut punitum iri praevidetur;

3° poenas intra aequos limites moderari, si reus plura delicta commisit et nimius videtur poenarum cumulus;

4° obligationem servandi poenam suspendere in favorem eius, qui omni probitate vitae hucusque commendatus primum deliquit, dummodo scandalum reparandum non urgeat; poena suspensa prorsus cessat, si intra tempus a iudice determinatum reus iterum non deliquit, secus tamquam utriusque delicti debitor gravius puniatur, nisi

---

1408: Sard. can. 14; Carth. cann. 11–12; Quinisext. can. 2 in fine; S. CYRILLUS ALEXANDRIN., can. 1; Pro-todeut. cann. 13–15; Constantinop. IV, can. 10.

more severely as the one guilty of both delicts unless in the interim the penal action for first delict has been extinguished.

§2. If a penalty is indeterminate and the law does not provide otherwise, the judge cannot impose the penalties enumerated in can. 1402, §2.

CAN. 1410   The imposition of penalties on a cleric must preserve for him what is necessary for his adequate support, unless it is a question of deposition. In this case, the hierarch is to take care that, if the deposed cleric is truly in need because of the punishment, he is provided for in the best possible way, always safeguarding his rights arising from insurance and social security as well as health insurance for him and his family if he is married.

CAN. 1411   No penalty can be imposed after a penal action has been extinguished.

CAN. 1412   §1. One who is bound by a law or precept is also subject to the penalty attached to it.

§2. If a law is changed after a delict has been committed, the law more favorable to the accused is to be applied.

§3. However, if a later law abolishes a law or at least the penalty, the penalty immediately ceases irrespective of the manner in which it had been imposed.

§4. Unless other provision is expressly made in common law, a penalty binds the offender everywhere, even when the authority of the one who imposed the penalty has lapsed.

CAN. 1413   §1. A person who has not completed the fourteenth year of age is not subject to a penalty.

§2. However, a person who has committed a

interim actio poenalis pro priore delicto exstincta est.

§2. Si poena est indeterminata neque aliter lex cavet, iudex poenas in can. 1402, §2 recensitas irrogare non potest.

CAN. 1410   In poenis clerico irrogandis ei salva esse debent, quae ad congruam sustentationem sunt necessaria, nisi agitur de depositione, quo in casu Hierarcha curet, ut deposito, qui propter poenam vere indiget, quo meliore fieri potest modo, provideatur salvis semper iuribus ortis circa praecaventiam et securitatem socialem necnon assistentiam sanitariam in favorem eius eiusque familiae, si coniugatus est.

CAN. 1411   Nulla poena irrogari potest, postquam actio poenalis exstincta est.

CAN. 1412   §1. Qui lege aut praecepto tenetur, adnexae eidem quoque poenae obnoxius est.

§2. Si, postquam delictum commissum est, lex mutatur, applicanda est lex reo favorabilior.

§3. Si vero lex posterior tollit legem vel saltem poenam, haec, quomodocumque irrogata erat, statim cessat.

§4. Poena reum ubique tenet etiam resoluto iure eius, qui poenam irrogavit, nisi aliter iure communi expresse cavetur.

CAN. 1413   §1. Nulli poenae est obnoxius, qui decimum quartum aetatis annum non explevit.

§2. Qui vero intra decimum quartum et

1410: Apost. can. 59; Pius XII, m.p. *Sollicitudinem Nostram,* 6 ian. 1950, can. 451; m.p. *Cleri sanctitati,* 2 iun. 1957, can. 57. ▲ D. 42, 1, 19; 50, 17, 173.

1412 §3: Apost. cann. 12, 32; Ant. can. 6; Carth. can. 9; S. Soph. can. 1.

delict between the fourteenth and eighteenth year of age can be punished only with penalties that do not include the loss of some good, unless the eparchial bishop or the judge, in special cases, thinks that the reform of that person can be better accomplished in another way.

CAN. 1414 §1. A person is only subject to penalties who has violated a penal law or penal precept, either deliberately or by seriously culpable omission of due diligence or by seriously culpable ignorance of the law or precept.

§2. When an external violation of a penal law or penal precept has occurred, it is presumed that it was deliberately done, unless the contrary is proven. Concerning other laws or precepts, the same is presumed only if the law or precept is violated again after a penal warning.

CAN. 1415 If, according to common practice and canonical doctrine, an extenuating circumstance is present, the judge must temper the penalty established by law or precept provided, however, there is still a delict. Indeed, according to his judgment, the judge can also abstain from imposing a penalty if he thinks that the reform of the offender as well as reparation of the scandal and damage can be better accomplished in another way.

CAN. 1416 If a delict has been committed by a recidivist or if, according to common practice and canonical doctrine another aggravating

duodevicesimum aetatis annum delictum commisit, puniri potest tantummodo poenis, quae privationem alicuius boni non includunt, nisi Episcopus eparchialis vel iudex in casibus specialibus aliter melius consuli posse censet eiusdem emendationi.

CAN. 1414 §1. Poenis is tantum subicitur, qui legem poenalem vel praeceptum poenale violavit aut deliberate aut ex graviter culpabili omissione debitae diligentiae aut ex graviter culpabili ignorantia legis vel praecepti.

§2. Posita externa legis poenalis vel praecepti poenalis violatione praesumitur eam deliberate factam esse, donec contrarium probetur; in ceteris legibus vel praeceptis id praesumitur tantummodo, si lex vel praeceptum iterum post monitionem poenalem violatur.

CAN. 1415 Si qua adest secundum communem praxim et doctrinam canonicam circumstantia attenuans, dummodo tamen delictum adhuc habeatur, iudex poenam lege vel praecepto statutam temperare debet; immo pro sua prudentia, si censet aliter posse melius consuli rei emendationi atque reparationi scandali et damni, potest etiam a poena irroganda abstinere.

CAN. 1416 Si delictum a recidivo commissum est vel si aliaadest secundum communem praxim et doctrinam canonicam cir-

---

1414 §1: Quinisext. cann. 1 "Si quis," 2 "Et nulli," 26, 93; S. Basilius M., cann. 8, 11, 27, 33, 46, 52, 54, 56–57; S. Gregorius Nyssen., can. 5; Pius XII, all. 3 oct. 1953, IV "Parmi les garanties;" all. 26 maii 1957, I, 1.

1415: Apost. cann. 62, 66; Nic. I, cann. 1, 11; Anc. cann. 3, 4, 6; Quinisext. can. 93; S. Gregorius Neo-caesarien., can. 1; S. Petrus Alexandrin., cann. 1–11; S. Athanasius Alexandrin., can. 1 "Ἐπειδή;"

S. Basilius M., cann. 7, 13, 52, 81–82; S. Gregorius Nyssen., cann. 2, 5; Protodeut. can. 8; Pius XII, all. 3 oct. 1953, IV "Parmi les garanties;" all. 5 dec. 1954, "In ciò;" all. 26 maii 1957, I, 1.

1416: Anc. cann. 16–17; Quinisext. can. 4; S. Basilius M., cann. 7, 36, 44, 46; S. Gregorius Nyssen., can. 4 "Πλὴν;" Constantinop. IV, can. 17 "Quisquis;" Trid., sess. XXV, *De ref.*, cap. 14; Pius V, const. *Cum primum*, 1 apr. 1566, §8.

circumstance is present, the judge can punish the offender more severely than the law or precept has established, not excluding the penalties enumerated in can. 1402, §2.

CAN. 1417   Those who conspire together to commit a delict and are not expressly named in a law or precept, can be punished with the same penalties as the principal perpetrator or, according to the prudence of the judge, with other penalties of the same or lesser gravity.

CAN. 1418   §1. A person who has done or omitted something in order to commit a delict and yet, contrary to his or her intent, did not commit the delict is not bound by the penalty established for a completed delict unless the law or precept provides otherwise.

§2. If the acts or omissions are by their nature conducive to the execution of the delict, however, the perpetrator is to be punished with an appropriate penalty, especially if scandal or some other grave damage resulted; however, the penalty is to be lighter that the one established for a completed delict.

§3. A person who voluntarily ceased from carrying out the delict that had been initiated is freed from any penalty, if no damage or scandal has arisen from the attempted offense.

CAN. 1419   §1. A person who can dispense from a penal law or exempt from a penal precept can also remit the penalty imposed by virtue of the same law or precept.

§2. Moreover, the power of remitting penalties can also be granted to others by the law or penal precept.

CAN. 1420   §1. The following can remit a penalty imposed by virtue of the common law:

cumstantia aggravans, iudex potest reum gravius punire, quam lex vel praeceptum statuit, non exclusis poenis in can. 1402, §2 recensitis.

CAN. 1417   Qui communi delinquendi consilio in delictum concurrunt neque in lege vel praecepto expresse nominantur, eisdem poenis ac auctor principalis puniri possunt vel ad prudentiam iudicis aliis poenis eiusdem vel minoris gravitatis.

CAN. 1418   §1. Qui aliquid ad delictum patrandum egit vel omisit nec tamen praeter suam voluntatem delictum consummavit, non tenetur poena in delictum consummatum statuta, nisi lex vel praeceptum aliter cavet.

§2. Si vero actus vel omissiones natura sua ad delicti exsecutionem conducunt, auctor congrua poena puniatur, praesertim si scandalum aliudve grave damnum evenit, leviore tamen quam ea, quae in delictum consummatum constituta est.

§3. Ab omni poena liberatur, qui sua sponte ab incepta delicti exsecutione destitit, si nullum ex conatu damnum aut scandalum ortum est.

CAN. 1419   §1. Qui a lege poenali dispensare potest vel a praecepto poenali eximere, potest etiam poenam vi eiusdem legis vel praecepti irrogatam remittere.

§2. Potest praeterea lege vel praecepto poenali aliis quoque potestas conferri poenas remittendi.

CAN. 1420   §1. Poenam vi iuris communis irrogatam remittere potest:

1417: Chalc. can. 27; Quinisext. can. 34; S. BASILIUS M., cann. 30, 71; Trid., sess. XXIV, *De ref. circa matrimonium,* cap. 6; sess. XXV, *De regularibus,* cap. 18; SIXTUS V, const. *Effraenatam,* 29 oct. 1588, §7.

1419 §1: Trid., sess. XIV, *De ref.,* can. 1; BENEDICTUS XIV, ep. encycl. *Demandatam,* 24 dec. 1743, §12; S.C. Ep. et Reg., decr. 16 oct. 1600, 12–13.

1420 §1: Apost. cann. 12, 32; Ant. can. 6; Carth.

1° the hierarch who initiated the penal trial or imposed the penalty by decree;

2° the local hierarch, where the offender actually resides, but after having consulted the hierarch mentioned in n. 1.

§2. These norms also apply regarding penalties imposed in virtue of particular law or a penal precept, unless the particular law of a Church *sui iuris* provides otherwise.

§3. However, only the Apostolic See can remit a penalty imposed by the Apostolic See, unless the remission of the penalty is delegated to the patriarch or others.

CAN. 1421 The remission of a penalty extorted by force, grave fear or fraud is null by the law itself.

CAN. 1422 §1. The remission of a penalty can also be given conditionally or to an unknowing offender.

§2. The remission of a penalty must be given in writing unless a grave cause suggests otherwise.

§3. Care is to be taken that the petition of remission or the remission itself is not divulged, except insofar as it is either useful to protect the reputation of the offender or necessary to repair scandal.

CAN. 1423 §1. Without prejudice to the right of the Roman Pontiff to reserve to himself or others the remission of any penalty, the synod of bishops of a patriarchal or major archiepiscopal Church can, by a law issued because of serious circumstances, reserve the remission of penalties to the patriarch or major archbishop with respect to their subjects who have a domicile or quasi-domicile within the

1° Hierarcha, qui iudicium poenale promovit vel decreto poenam irrogavit;

2° Hierarcha loci, ubi reus actu commoratur, consulto vero Hierarcha, de quo in n. 1.

§2. Hae normae valent etiam circa poenas vi iuris particularis vel praecepti poenalis irrogatis, nisi aliter iure particulari Ecclesiae sui iuris cavetur.

§3. Poenam vero a Sede Apostolica irrogatam sola Sedes Apostolica remittere potest, nisi Patriarchae vel aliis remissio poenae delegatur.

CAN. 1421 Remissio poenae vi aut metu gravi aut dolo extorta ipso iure nulla est.

CAN. 1422 §1. Remissio poenae dari potest etiam inscio reo vel sub condicione.

§2. Remissio poenae dari debet scripto, nisi gravis causa aliud suadet.

§3. Caveatur, ne petitio remissionis poenae vel ipsa remissio divulgetur, nisi quatenus id vel utile est ad rei famam tuendam vel necessarium ad scandalum reparandum.

CAN. 1423 §1. Salvo iure Romani Pontificis remissionem cuiusvis poenae sibi vel aliis reservandi, Synodus Episcoporum Ecclesiae patriarchalis vel archiepiscopalis maioris lege propter graves circumstantias lata reservare potest remissionem poenarum Patriarchae vel Archiepiscopo maiori pro subditis, qui intra fines territorii Ecclesiae, cui praeest, domicilium vel quasi-domicilium habent;

---

can. 9; S. Soph. can. 1; Trid., sess. XIV, *De ref.*, can. 1; BENEDICTUS XIV, ep. encycl. *Demandatam,* 24 dec. 1743, §12; S.C. de Prop. Fide, (C.G.), 17 feb. 1772. * Syn. Alexandrin. Coptorum, a. 1898, sect. III, cap.

VII, art. VI, III; Syn. Armen., a. 1911, 957.
1422 §1: * Syn. Armen., a. 1911, 959.
1423 §1: * Syn. Armen., a. 1911, 186.

territorial boundaries of the Church over which they preside. No one else can validly reserve to himself or to others the remission of the penalties established by common law except with the consent of the Apostolic See.

§2. Every reservation must be interpreted strictly.

CAN. 1424 §1. The remission of a penalty cannot be granted unless the offender has sincerely repented for the delict committed and has also adequately provided for reparation of the scandal and damage.

§2. However, if, in the judgment of that person who is competent to remit the penalty, these conditions have been fulfilled, the remission is not to be denied, insofar as possible considering the nature of the penalty.

CAN. 1425 If several penalties bind a person, a remission is valid only for the penalties expressed in it; a general remission, however, takes away all penalties except those that the offender in bad faith omitted in the petition.

CAN. 1426 §1. Unless another penalty is determined by law, according to the ancient traditions of the Eastern Churches, penalties can be imposed that require some serious work of religion or piety or charity to be performed, such as certain prayers, a pious pilgrimage, a special fast, alms, spiritual retreats.

§2. Other penalties are to be imposed on that person who is not disposed to accept these penalties.

CAN. 1427 §1. Without prejudice to particular law, a public rebuke is to occur before a

nemo alius potest valide sibi vel aliis reservare remissionem poenarum iure communi statutarum nisi de consensu Sedis Apostolicae.

§2. Omnis reservatio stricte est interpretanda.

CAN. 1424 §1. Remissio poenae dari non potest, nisi reum delicti patrati sincere paenituit necnon de reparatione scandali et damni congrue provisum est.

§2. Si vero iudicio illius, cui remissio poenae competit, impletae sunt hae condiciones, remissio, quatenus natura poenae spectata fieri potest, ne denegetur.

CAN. 1425 Si quis pluribus poenis detinetur, remissio valet tantummodo pro poenis in ipsa expressis; remissio generalis autem omnes aufert poenas eis exceptis, quas in petitione reus mala fide reticuit.

CAN. 1426 §1. Nisi alia poena iure determinata est, irrogari possunt secundum antiquas Ecclesiarum orientalium traditiones poenae, quibus imponitur aliquod grave opus religionis vel pietatis vel caritatis peragendum veluti preces determinatae, pia peregrinatio, speciale ieiunium, eleemosynae, recessus spirituales.

§2. Illi, qui has poenas non est dispositus acceptare, aliae poenae irrogentur.

CAN. 1427 §1. Salvo iure particulari correptio publica fit coram notario vel

---

1424 §1: Nic. I, cann. 11–12; Chalc. can. 7; S. PETRUS ALEXANDRIN., can. 5; S. BASILIUS M., can. 1 "Ἔδοξε," 5, 7; PIUS XII, nuntius, 5 feb. 1955, "Psicologicamente" et "Nell'applicazione;" PAULUS VI, all. 4 oct. 1969, I "Certes." * Syn. Armen., a. 1911, 959.

1424 §2: Apost. can. 52.
1426 §1: Nic. I, can. 12; Anc. can. 20; Neoc. can. 1; Carth. can. 102; Quinisext. cann. 3, 41, 87; S. PETRUS ALEXANDRIN., cann. 1–3, 5–7; S. BASILIUS M., can. 1 "Ἔδοξε;" Nic. II, cann. 1, 5, 16.

notary or two witnesses or by letter, but in such a way that the reception and tenor of the letter are established by some document.

§2. Care must be taken that the public rebuke itself does not result in a greater disgrace of the offender than is appropriate.

CAN. 1428 If the gravity of the case demands and especially if it concerns recidivists, a hierarch can, in addition to the penalties imposed by sentence in accord with the norm of law, place the offender under supervision in the manner determined by an administrative decree.

CAN. 1429 §1. A prohibition against residing in a certain place or territory can affect only clerics or religious or members of societies of common life in the manner of religious; however, the order to reside in a certain place or territory can affect only clerics ascribed to an eparchy, without prejudice to the law of institutes of consecrated life.

§2. To impose an order to reside in a certain place or territory requires the consent of the local hierarch, unless it is a question either of a house of an institute of consecrated life of pontifical or patriarchal right, in which case the consent of the competent superior is required, or of a house designated for the penance and rehabilitation of clerics of several eparchies.

CAN. 1430 §1. Penal privations can affect only those powers, offices, ministries, functions, rights, privileges, faculties, favors, titles, or insignia that are subject to the power of the authority that establishes them or of the hierarch who initiated the penal trial or imposed the pe-

duobus testibus aut per epistulam ita tamen, ut de receptione et tenore epistulae ex aliquo documento constet.

§2. Cavendum est, ne ipsa correptione publica locus detur maiori, quam par est, infamiae rei.

CAN. 1428 Si gravitas casus fert et praecipue si agitur de recidivis, Hierarcha etiam praeter poenas per sententiam ad normam iuris irrogatas reum submittere potest vigilantiae modo per decretum administrativum determinato.

CAN. 1429 §1. Prohibitio commorandi in certo loco vel territorio tantum clericos vel religiosos vel sodales societatis vitae communis ad instar religiosorum afficere potest, praescriptio vero commorandi in certo loco vel territorio nonnisi clericos eparchiae ascriptos salvo iure institutorum vitae consecratae.

§2. Ut praescriptio commorandi in certo loco vel territorio irrogetur, requiritur consensus Hierarchae loci, nisi agitur vel de domo instituti vitae consecratae iuris pontificii vel patriarchalis, quo in casu requiritur consensus Superioris competentis, vel de domo clericis plurium eparchiarum paenitentibus vel emendandis destinata.

CAN. 1430 §1. Privationes poenales afficere possunt tantum illas potestates, officia, ministeria, munera, iura, privilegia, facultates, gratias, titulos, insignia, quae sunt sub potestate auctoritatis poenam constituentis vel Hierarchae, qui iudicium poenale promovit vel

---

1429 §1: Chalc. can. 23; Quinisext. can. 41; Nic. II, can. 19; Protodeut. cann. 2, 5.

1430 §1: Apost. cann. 27, 29; Anc. can. 14; Sard. can. 20; Carth. cann. 25, 70, 104; Quinisext. can. 26;

Protodeut. can. 5; Constantinop. IV, can. 8. * Syn. Sciarfen. Syrorum, a. 1888, cap. XV, art. VI, 2; Syn. Armen., a. 1911, 949–950.

nal precept; the same applies regarding penal transfer to another office.

§2. Privation of the power of sacred orders is not possible, but only a prohibition against exercising all or some of its acts, in accordance with the norms of common law; likewise, privation of academic degrees is not possible.

CAN. 1431 §1. Those punished with a minor excommunication are deprived of the reception of the Divine Eucharist. In addition, they can be excluded from participation in the Divine Liturgy and even from entering a church if divine worship is being publicly celebrated there.

§2. The sentence itself or the decree by which this penalty is imposed must determine the extent of that penalty and, if the case warrants, its duration.

CAN. 1432 §1. A suspension can be either from all or some acts of the power of orders or governance, or from either all or some acts or rights connected with an office, ministry or function; however, the sentence itself or the decree that imposed the penalty is to define the extent of that suspension, unless it is already determined by law.

§2. No one can be suspended except from acts that are under the power of the authority that establishes the penalty or of the hierarch

decreto eam irrogat; idem valet pro translatione poenali ad aliud officium.

§2. Potestatis ordinis sacri privatio dari non potest, sed tantum prohibitio omnes vel aliquos eius actus exercendi ad normam iuris communis; item dari non potest privatio graduum academicorum.

CAN. 1431 §1. Excommunicatione minore puniti privantur susceptione Divinae Eucharistiae; excludi insuper possunt a participatione in Divina Liturgia, immo etiam ab ingressu in ecclesiam, si in ea cultus divinus publice celebratur.

§2. Ipsa sententia vel decreto, quo haec poena irrogatur, definiri debet eiusdem poenae extensio et, si casus fert, duratio.

CAN. 1432 §1. Suspensio potest esse vel ab omnibus vel aliquibus actibus potestatis ordinis aut regiminis, ab omnibus vel aliquibus actibus vel iuribus cum officio, ministerio vel munere conexis; eiusdem vero extensio ipsa sententia vel decreto, quo poena irrogatur, definiatur, nisi iure iam determinata est.

§2. Nemo suspendi potest nisi ab actibus, qui sunt sub potestate auctoritatis poenam constituentis vel Hierarchae, qui iu-

---

1431 §1: S. GREGORIUS Neocesarien., can. 11; Apost. cann. 5, 8–10, 12, 16, 24, 29–31, 36, 43, 45, 48, 54, 56–59, 63–67, 69–73, 76, 84; Nic. I, cann. 11–12, 16; Anc. cann. 16, 21; Neoc. can. 1; Ant. cann. 11, 17; Laod. can. 9; Gang. cann. 1–20; Eph. cann. 6–7; Chalc. cann. 2, 4, 8, 15–16, 20, 27; Carth. cann. 29, 79, 106; Quinisext. cann. 4–5, 11, 13, 27, 47, 50–51, 53–56, 58–59, 61–62, 64, 67–68, 71, 73–74, 76–77, 79–81, 86–88, 94, 96–97, 99, 101; S. GREGORIUS NEOCESARIEN., cann. 5, 7–9; S. BASILIUS M., cann. 2, 4, 7, 19, 22, 25, 34, 38, 44, 53, 56–68, 72–73, 75–83; S. GREGORIUS NYSSEN., cann. 3, 4 "Ἔστι," 5, "Ἐπὶ", 7; S. GENNADIUS CP., can. 1; Nic. II, cann. 1, 5–6; Protodeut. cann. 3–4, 8, 10, 12–13; Constantinop. IV, cann. 2, 7, 9, 14–16, 23. * *De*

interdicto: Syn. Libanen. Maronitarum, a. 1736, pars II, cap. VI, 6; Syn. Sciarfen. Syrorum, a. 1888, cap. XV, art. V, 4–6; Syn. Alexandrin. Coptorum, a. 1898, sect. III, cap. VII, art. IV; Syn. Armen., a. 1911, 940–944.

1432 §1: Nic. I, cann. 2, 18; Anc. cann. 1–2, 10; Ant. can. 3; Quinisext. cann. 3, 26; S. BASILIUS M., cann. 3, 12, 51, 70, 88; Nic. II, can. 4; Constantinop. IV, can. 14; Trid., sess. XIV, *De ref.*, can. 1; S.C. de Prop. Fide, instr. 20 oct. 1884. * Syn. Libanen. Maronitarum, a. 1736, pars II, cap. VI, 4; Syn. Sciarfen. Syrorum, a. 1888, cap. XV, art. V, 1–3; Syn. Alexandrin. Coptorum, a. 1898, sect. III, cap. VII, art. V; Syn. Armen., a. 1911, 934–938.

who initiates the penal trial or imposes the suspension by decree.

§3. A suspension never affects the validity of acts nor the right of residence that the offender may have by reason of an office, ministry or function; however, a suspension prohibiting a person from receiving benefits, remuneration, pensions, or any other such thing entails the obligation of making restitution for whatever has been received illegitimately, even if in good faith.

CAN. 1433 §1. A cleric demoted to a lower grade is prohibited from exercising those acts of the power of orders or governance that are not consonant with this grade.

§2. However, a cleric deposed from the clerical state is deprived of all offices, ministries or other functions, ecclesiastical pensions and any delegated power; he is unqualified for them. He is prohibited from exercising the power of orders and he cannot be promoted to higher sacred orders and is equivalent to lay persons in respect to canonical effects, with due regard for cann. 396 and 725.

CAN. 1434 §1. Major excommunication,

dicium poenale promovet vel decreto suspensionem irrogat.

§3. Suspensio numquam afficit validitatem actuum nec ius habitandi, si quod reus ratione officii, ministerii vel muneris habet; suspensio vero vetans fructus, remunerationes, pensiones aliudve percipere secumfert obligationem restituendi, quidquid illegitime, etsi bona fide, perceptum est.

CAN. 1433 §1. Clericus ad inferiorem gradum reductus vetatur illos actus potestatis ordinis et regiminis exercere, qui huic gradui consentanei non sunt.

§2. Clericus vero a statu clericali depositus privatur omnibus officiis, ministeriis alisve muneribus, pensionibus ecclesiasticis et qualibet potestate delegata; fit ad ea inhabilis; potestatem ordinis exercere prohibetur; promoveri non potest ad superiores ordines sacros et laicis, ad effectus canonicos quod attinet, aequiparatur firmis cann. 396 et 725.

CAN. 1434 §1. Excommunicatio maior

1433 §1: Apost. cann. 53, 55, 58–60, 62–66, 68–70, 83–84; Anc. can. 18; Neoc. can. 10; Ant. can. 11; Eph. cann. 2–6; Chalc. cann. 2, 10, 12, 18, 22, 27, 29; Quinisext. cann. 7, 20, 34, 92; S. Basilius M., cann. 3, 32; S. Gennadius CP., can. 1; Protodeut. cann. 10, 16; Constantinop. IV, cann. 2, 4–5, 7–8.

1433 §2: Apost. cann. 3, 5–7, 20, 25, 27, 29–31, 35, 47, 49–50, 50*, 51–53, 60, 63–66, 70, 81; Nic. I, cann. 2, 17–18; Neoc. can. 1; Ant. cann. 1, 3, 5, 10, 16; Chalc. can. 29; Carth. cann. 15, 80, 105; Constantinop., a. 394; Quinisext. cann. 4–6, 9–13, 15, 17, 22–24, 28, 31–33, 50–51, 55–56, 62, 67, 77, 79–81, 86, 88, 97; S. Basilius M., can. 55, 70; Timotheus Alexandrin., can. 26; Theophilus Alexandrin., can. 3; S. Gennadius CP., can. 1 "'Ιοθι;" Protodeut. cann. 2, 8, 10–14; Constantinop. IV, cann 10, 13–14, 17 "Quisquis," 19 "Quisquis," 20, 23–24, 26–27; S. Soph. can. 1. * Syn. Libanen. Maronitarum, a. 1736, pars II, cap. VI, 5; Syn. Sciarfen. Syrorum, a. 1888, cap. IV,

art. VI, 3–6; Syn. Alexandrin. Coptorum, a. 1898, sect. III, cap. VII, art. VII, 4–5; Syn. Armen., a. 1911, 951–952.

1434 §1: Apost. cann. 13, 28, 51, 62; Neoc. can. 2; Gang. cann. 1–20 (sensu *Epistolae Synodicae* praeviae, in fine); Ant. cann. 1–2, 4; Laod., cann. 29, 34–36; Sard. can. 2; Carth. cann. 11, 81, 109–116; S. Basilius M., can. 88 in fine; S. Gregorius Nyssen., can. 2; Constantinop. IV, cann. 2–3, 6, 11, 16, 17 "Quisquis," 19 "Quisquis," 21–22, 26; S. Soph. cann. 1, 3; Martinus V (in Constantien.), const. *Ad evitanda*, a. 1418; Leo X, const. *Exsurge Domine*, 15 iun. 1520, error 23, Martini Luther, damn.; Benedictus XIV, litt. encycl. *Inter praeteritos*, 3 dec. 1749, §48; Pius VI, const. *Auctorem fidei*, 28 aug. 1794, prop. 46, Synodi Pistorien., damn. * Syn. Diamper. Syro-Malabarensium, a. 1599, CXLVIII; Syn. Alexandrin. Coptorum, a. 1898, sect. III, cap. VII, art. III; Syn. Armen., a. 1911, 929–933.

in addition to all the things mentioned in can. 1431, §1, prohibits the reception of the other sacraments, the administration of the sacraments and sacramentals, the exercise of any offices, ministries or functions whatsoever, the placing of acts of governance, which, if they are nonetheless placed, are null by the law itself.

§2. A person punished with a major excommunication must be prevented from participating in the Divine Liturgy and in any other public celebrations whatsoever of divine worship.

§3. A person punished with a major excommunication is forbidden to benefit from privileges previously granted to himself or herself. The person cannot acquire validly a dignity, office, ministry or other function in the Church or pension, nor appropriate the benefits attached to them. The person also lacks active and passive voice.

CAN. 1435 §1. If a penalty prohibits the reception of the sacraments or sacramentals, the prohibition is suspended as long as the offender is in danger of death.

§2. If the penalty prohibits the administration of sacraments or sacramentals or the placing of an act of governance, the prohibition is suspended whenever it is necessary to care for the Christian faithful in danger of death.

CHAPTER II. Penalties for Individual Delicts

CAN. 1436 §1. A person who denies some truth that must be believed by divine and Catholic faith, or who calls it into doubt, or totally rejects the Catholic faith, and does not reconsider, though legitimately warned, is to be punished as a heretic or an apostate with a major

vetat praeter omnia illa, de quibus in can. 1431, §1, et alia sacramenta suscipere, sacramenta et sacramentalia ministrare, officiis, ministeriis velmuneribus quibuslibet fungi, actus regiminis ponere, qui, si tamen ponuntur, ipso iure nulli sunt.

§2. Excommunicatione maiore punitus a participatione in Divina Liturgia et in aliis quibuslibet publicis celebrationibus cultus divini arcendus est.

§3. Excommunicatione maiore punitus vetatur frui privilegiis antea sibi concessis; non potest valide consequi dignitatem, officium, ministerium aliudve munus in Ecclesia vel pensionem nec fructus his adnexos facit suos; caret etiam voce activa et passiva.

CAN. 1435 §1. Si poena vetat suscipere sacramenta vel sacramentalia, vetitum suspenditur, dum reus in periculo mortis versatur.

§2. Si poena vetat ministrare sacramenta vel sacramentalia vel ponere actum regiminis, vetitum suspenditur, quoties id necessarium est ad consulendum christifidelibus in periculo mortis constitutis.

CAPUT II. De Poenis in Singula Delicta

CAN. 1436 §1. Qui aliquam veritatem fide divina et catholica credendam denegat vel eam in dubium ponit aut fidem christianam ex toto repudiat et legitime monitus non resipiscit, ut haereticus aut apostata excommunicatione maiore puniatur, clericus

---

1435 §1: Nic. I, can. 13; Anc. can. 6; Neoc. can. 2; S. DIONYSIUS ALEXANDRIN., can. 5; S. BASILIUS M., can. 5; S. GREGORIUS NYSSEN., cann. 2, 5, (b); PIUS IX, litt. ap. *Cum catholica Ecclesia*, 26 mar. 1860, 7.
1436 §1: Apost., can. 62; Constantinop. I, can. 6;

Carth. can. 93; S. PETRUS ALEXANDRIN., cann. 1–12; S. BASILIUS M., cann. 73, 81; S. GREGORIUS NYSSEN., cann. 2–3; TIMOTHEUS ALEXANDRIN., can. 9. * Syn. Zamosten. Ruthenorum, a. 1720, tit. I "Quia vero;" Syn. Armen., a. 1911, 952, a).

excommunication; moreover, a cleric can be punished with other penalties, not excluding deposition.

§2. In addition to these cases, whoever obstinately rejects a teaching that the Roman Pontiff or the College of Bishops, exercising the authentic magisterium, have set forth to be held definitively, or who affirms what they have condemned as erroneous, and does not retract after having been legitimately warned, is to be punished with an appropriate penalty.*

CAN. 1437 A person who refuses subjection to the supreme authority of the Church or communion with the Christian faithful subject to it and, though legitimately warned, does not obey, is to be punished as a schismatic with a major excommunication.

CAN. 1438 A person who deliberately omits the commemoration of the hierarch in the Divine Liturgy and in the divine praises as prescribed by law, and does not reconsider, though legitimately warned, is to be punished with an appropriate penalty, not excluding major excommunication.

CAN. 1439 Parents or those who take the place of parents who hand their children over to be baptized or educated in a non-Catholic religion are to be punished with an appropriate penalty.

CAN. 1440 A person who violates the norms of law concerning participation in sacred rites *(communicatio in sacris)* can be punished with an appropriate penalty.

CAN. 1441 A person who employs sacred objects for profane use or for an evil purpose is

praeterea aliis poenis puniri potest non exclusa depositione.

§2. Praeter hos casus, qui sustinet doctrinam, quae a Romano Pontifice vel Collegio Episcoporum magisterium authenticum exercentibus ut erronea damnata est, nec legitime monitus resipiscit, congrua poena puniatur.*

CAN. 1437 Qui subiectionem supremae Ecclesiae auctoritati aut communionem cum christifidelibus eidem subiectis detrectat et legitime monitus oboedientiam non praestat, ut schismaticus excommunicatione maiore puniatur.

CAN. 1438 Qui consulto omittit commemorationem Hierarchae in Divina Liturgia et in laudibus divinis iure praescriptam, si legitime monitus non resipiscit, congrua poena puniatur non exclusa excommunicatione maiore.

CAN. 1439 Parentes vel parentum locum tenentes, qui filios in religione acatholica baptizandos vel educandos tradunt, congrua poena puniantur.

CAN. 1440 Qui normas iuris de communicatione in sacris violat, congrua poena puniri potest.

CAN. 1441 Qui res sacras in usum profanum vel in malum finem adhibet, sus-

---

*1436 §2: JOANNES PAULUS PP. II, Ap. litt. m.p. *Ad tuendam fidem,* 18 maii 1998, *Acta Apostolicae Sedis* 90 (1998) 460–461. — Trans.

1437: Apost. can. 31; Gang. can. 6; Ant. can. 5; Constantinop. I, can. 6; Carth. cann. 10–11, 53, 93; S. BASILIUS M., can. 1; Constantinop. IV, can. 10; Protodeut. cann. 13–15.

1438: Protodeut. cann. 13–15. * Syn. Zamosten. Ruthenorum, a. 1720, tit. I "Eadem."

1441: Apost. can. 73; Protodeut. can. 10; Nic. II, actio VII; CLEMENS XIII, const. *Gravissimum,* 6 mar. 1759, §1. * Syn. Libanen. Maronitarum, a. 1736, pars I, cap. I, 16; Syn. Armen., a. 1911, 952, h).

to be suspended or prohibited from receiving the Divine Eucharist.

CAN. 1442 A person who has thrown away the Divine Eucharist or taken or retained it for a sacrilegious purpose is to be punished with a major excommunication and, if a cleric, also with other penalties, not excluding deposition.

CAN. 1443 A person who has simulated the celebration of the Divine Liturgy or the other sacraments is to be punished with an appropriate penalty, not excluding a major excommunication.

CAN. 1444 A person who has committed perjury before an ecclesiastical authority or who, though not sworn, has knowingly lied to a judge under lawful questioning, or has concealed the truth, or who has induced others to commit these delicts, is to be punished with an appropriate penalty.

CAN. 1445 §1. A person who has used physical force against a bishop or has caused him some other serious injury is to be punished with an appropriate penalty, not excluding deposition, if he is a cleric. However, if the same delict has been committed against a metropolitan, patriarch, or indeed the Roman Pontiff, the offender is to be punished with a major excommunication, whose remission, in the last case, is reserved to the Roman Pontiff himself.

§2. A person who did the same to another cleric, religious, member of a society of com-

pendatur vel a Divina Eucharistia suscipienda prohibeatur.

CAN. 1442 Qui Divinam Eucharistiam abiecit aut in sacrilegum finem abduxit vel retinuit, excommunicatione maiore puniatur et, si clericus est, etiam aliis poenis non exclusa depositione.

CAN. 1443 Qui Divinae Liturgiae vel aliorum sacramentorum celebrationem simulavit, congrua poena puniatur non exclusa excommunicatione maiore.

CAN. 1444 Qui periurium commisit coram auctoritate ecclesiastica aut qui, etsi iniuratus, iudici legitime interroganti scienter falsum affirmavit aut verum occultavit aut qui ad haec delicta induxit, congrua poena puniatur.

CAN. 1445 §1. Qui vim physicam in Episcopum adhibuit vel aliam gravem iniuriam in ipsum iniecit, congrua poena puniatur non exclusa, si clericus est, depositione; si vero idem delictum in Metropolitam, Patriarcham vel immo Romanum Pontificem commissum est, reus puniatur excommunicatione maiore, cuius remissio in ultimo casu ipsi Romano Pontifici est reservata.

§2. Qui id egit in alium clericum, religiosum, sodalem societatis vitae communis ad

---

1442: Innocentius XI, const. *Ad nostri apostolatus,* 12 mar. 1677, §2; Alexander VIII, const. *Cum alias,* 22 dec. 1690, §3; Benedictus XIV, const. *Ab augustissimo,* 5 mar. 1744; S.C. Ep. et Reg., ep. encycl. 9 feb. 1751; Clemens XIII, const. *Gravissimum,* 6 mar. 1759, §§2–4; S.C.S. Off., decr. 21 iul. 1934, X. * Syn. Libanen. Maronitarum, a. 1736, pars I, cap. I, 16; Syn. Armen., a. 1911, 952, h).

1443: Gregorius XIII, const. *Officii Nostri,* 6 aug. 1574, §§1–2; Clemens VIII, const. *Etsi alias,* 1 dec. 1601; Urbanus VIII, const. *Apostolatus officium,* 23 mar. 1628; Benedictus XIV, const. *Sacerdos in aeternum,* 20 apr. 1744; ep. encycl. *Quam grave,* 2 aug.

1757, §§1–2; const. *Divinarum,* 2 aug. 1757; Clemens XIII, const. *Gravissimum,* 6 mar. 1759, §6. * Syn. Armen., a. 1911, 952, g).

1444: Apost. can. 25; S. Basilius M., cann. 10, 64, 82; Pius XII, m.p. *Sollicitudinem Nostram,* 6 ian. 1950, cann. 265 §3, 317. * Syn. Libanen. Maronitarum, a. 1736, pars III, cap. V, 9.

1445 §1: Apost. can. 55; S. Soph. can. 3; Leo X (in Lat. V), const. *Supernae dispositionis,* 5 maii 1514, §40; S.C.S. Off., decr. 21 iul. 1934. * Syn. Libanen. Maronitarum, a. 1736, pars III, cap. I, 18.

1445 §2: Apost. cann. 27, 56. * Syn. Libanen. Maronitarum, a. 1736, pars III, cap. I, 18.

mon life in the manner of religious, or a lay person who is actually exercising an ecclesiastical function, is to be punished with an appropriate penalty.

CAN. 1446 A person who does not obey the legitimate order or prohibition of his own hierarch and who, after a warning, persists in disobedience, is to be punished as an offender with an appropriate penalty.

CAN. 1447 §1. A person who incites sedition or hatred toward any hierarch or provokes his subjects to disobedience, is to be punished with an appropriate penalty, not excluding a major excommunication, especially if the delict was committed against a patriarch or indeed against the Roman Pontiff.

§2. A person who has obstructed the freedom of ministry or election or ecclesiastical authority or the legitimate use of the temporal goods of the Church, or a person who has intimidated an elector or one who exercises power or ministry, is to be punished with an appropriate penalty.

CAN. 1448 §1. A person who in a public show or speech, in published writing, or in other uses of the instruments of social communication utters blasphemy, seriously injures good morals, expresses insults, or excites hatred or contempt against religion or the Church is to be punished with an appropriate penalty.

instar religiosorum vel in laicum, qui actu munus ecclesiasticum exercet, congrua poena puniatur.

CAN. 1446 Qui proprio Hierarchae legitime praecipienti velprohibenti non obtemperat et post monitionem in inoboedientia persistit, ut delinquens congrua poena puniatur.

CAN. 1447 §1. Qui seditiones vel odia adversus quemcumque Hierarcham suscitat aut subditos ad inoboedientiam in eum provocat, congrua poena puniatur non exclusa excommunicatione maiore, praesertim si hoc delictum adversus Patriarcham vel immo adversus Romanum Pontificem commissum est.

§2. Qui impedivit libertatem ministerii vel electionis vel potestatis ecclesiasticae aut legitimum bonorum Ecclesiae temporalium usum aut perterrefecit electorem vel eum, qui potestatem vel ministerium exercet, congrua poena puniatur.

CAN. 1448 §1. Qui vel publico spectaculo vel contione vel in scripto publice evulgato vel aliter instrumentis communicationis socialis utens blasphemiam profert aut bonos mores graviter laedit aut in religionem vel Ecclesiam iniurias exprimit vel odium contemptumve excitat, congrua poena puniatur.

1446: S.C. Consist., decr. 20 aug. 1910, can. 1, n. 9.

1447 §1: Apost. cann. 31, 36; Anc. can. 18; Ant. cann. 1, 5; Chalc. cann. 18, 23; Quinisext. can. 34; S.C. Consist., decr. 20 aug. 1910, can. 18, §1.

1447 §2: Apost. can. 36; Anc. can. 15; Quinisext. can. 35; THEOPHILUS ALEXANDRIN., can. 11; S. CYRILLUS ALEXANDRIN., can. 1; Constantinop. IV, cann. 18–19; LEO IX, ep. *Quia Auctore Deo*, a. 1051; MARTINUS V (in Constantien.), const. *Inter cunctas*, 22 feb. 1418, art. 35 de quo errorum Wicleff et Huss suspecti interrogandi; INNOCENTIUS VIII, const. *Officii Nostri*, 25 ian. 1491, §§2–3; LEO X (in Lat. V),

const. *Supernae dispositionis*, 5 maii 1514, §3; (in Lat. V), const. *Regimini universalis*, 4 maii 1515, §11; Trid., sess. XXII, *De ref.*, can. 11; sess. XXV, *De ref.*, cann. 9, 12; IULIUS III, const. *Licet a diversis*, 18 mar. 1551; CLEMENS XIII, const. *Alias ad Apostolatus*, 30 ian. 1768, §§1, 5, 7–13. * Syn. Armen., a. 1911, 952, c).

1448 §1: Apost. can. 60; LEO X (in Lat. V), const. *Supernae dispositionis*, 5 maii 1514, §33; PIUS V, const. *Cum primum*, 1 apr. 1566, §10. * Syn. Libanen. Maronitarum, a. 1736, pars I, cap. I, 13–14; Syn. prov. Alba-Iulien. et Fagarasien. Rumenorum, a. 1872, tit. VI, cap. IX.

§2. A person who joins an association that plots against the Church is to be punished with an appropriate penalty.

CAN. 1449 A person who has alienated ecclesiastical goods without the prescribed consent or permission is to be punished with an appropriate penalty.

CAN. 1450 §1. A person who has committed a homicide, is to be punished with a major excommunication; a cleric is to be punished in addition with other penalties, not excluding deposition.

§2. A person who has procured a completed abortion is to be punished in the same manner, with due regard for can. 728, §2.

CAN. 1451 A person who has kidnapped or unjustly detains, seriously wounded or mutilated, or inflicted bodily or mental torture on a person, is to be punished with an appropriate penalty, not excluding a major excommunication.

CAN. 1452 A person who has caused serious injury to another or seriously harmed another's good reputation with a calumny, is to be compelled to offer appropriate satisfaction;

§2. Qui nomen dat consociationi, quae contra Ecclesiam machinatur, congrua poena puniatur.

CAN. 1449 Qui sine praescripto consensu vel licentia bona ecclesiastica alienavit, congrua poena puniatur.

CAN. 1450 §1. Qui homicidium patravit, puniatur excommunicatione maiore; clericus praeterea aliis poenis puniatur non exclusa depositione.

§2. Eodem modo puniatur, qui abortum procuravit effectu secuto, firmo can. 728, §2.

CAN. 1451 Qui hominem rapuit aut iniuste detinet, graviter vulneravit vel mutilavit, ei torturam physicam vel psychicam intulit, congrua poena puniatur non exclusa excommunicatione maiore.

CAN. 1452 Qui gravem iniuriam cuiquam intulit vel eius bonam famam per calumniam graviter laesit, ad congruam satisfactionem praestandam cogatur; si vero re-

1448 §2: CLEMENS XII, litt. ap. *In eminenti,* 28 apr. 1738; BENEDICTUS XIV, const. *Providas,* 18 mar. 1751; PIUS VII, const. *Ecclesiam,* 13 sep. 1821; LEO XII, const. *Quo graviora,* 13 mar. 1825, §11; S.C.S. Off., 27 iun. 1838; 5 aug. 1846; PIUS IX, ep. encycl. *Qui pluribus,* 9 nov. 1846; ep. encycl. *Quanta cura,* 8 dec. 1864; all. *Multiplices inter,* 25 sep. 1865; S.C. de Prop. Fide, litt. encycl. (ad Deleg. Ap. et Ep. Orient.), 24 sep. 1867; PIUS IX, const. *Apostolicae Sedis,* 12 oct. 1869, §II, 4; S.C.S. Off., decr. 12 ian. 1870; instr. 10 maii 1884, 3; S.C. de Prop. Fide, litt. encycl. 6 aug. 1885, 2; S.C.S. Off., instr. 19 maii 1886, ad I; 3 aug. 1898; S.C. pro Doctr. Fidei, 18 iul. 1974; 17 feb. 1981, 26 nov. 1983. * Syn. Leopolien. Ruthenorum, a. 1891, tit. I, cap. VI; Syn. Alexandrin. Coptorum, a. 1898, sect. II, cap. III, art. V, *De peccatis reservatis,* 6, III.

1449: Anc. can. 15; Ant. can. 25; Carth. cann. 26, 33; Constantinop. IV, can. 15. * Syn. Zamosten. Ruthenorum, a. 1720, tit. XIII "Bona;" Syn. Libanen. Maronitarum, a. 1736, pars IV, cap. I, 14; Syn. Alexandrin. Coptorum, a. 1898, sect. III, cap. VIII, art. V, 1.

1450 §1: Apost. can. 66; Anc. cann. 21–22; S.

BASILIUS M., cann. 7–8, 33, 43, 52, 54–56; S. GREGORIUS NYSSEN., can. 5 "Ἐπι" Trid., sess. XXV, *De ref.,* cap. 19; Vat. II, const. *Gaudium et spes,* 27 "Quaecumque." * Syn. Armen., a. 1911, 959, d).

1450 §2: Anc. can. 21; Quinisext. can. 91; S. BASILIUS M., cann. 2, 8; Vat. II, const. *Gaudium et spes,* 27 "Quaecumque," 51 "Deus;" PAULUS VI, all. 9 dec. 1972; S.C. pro Doctr. Fidei, decl. 18 nov. 1974; PAULUS VI, all. 23 apr. 1977; IOANNES PAULUS II, adh. ap. *Familiaris consortio,* 22 nov. 1981, art. 30 "Idcirco;" Sancta Sedes, *Carta dei diritti della famiglia,* 24 nov. 1983, art. 4, a); C. pro Doctr. Fidei, instr. *Donum vitae,* 22 feb. 1987, I, 1–2; Pont. Comm. Cod. Iur. Can. Auth. Interpr., interpr. 23 maii 1988, II, 1; IOANNES PAULUS II, adh. ap. *Christifideles laici,* 30 dec. 1988, 38. * Syn. Alexandrin. Coptorum, a. 1898, sect. II, cap. III, art. V, *De peccatis reservatis,* 6, V, 1).

1451: Apost. cann. 21, 67; Anc. can. 11; Chalc. can. 27; Quinisext. can. 92; S. BASILIUS M., cann. 22, 30; Protodeut. can. 8. * Syn. Diamper. Syro-Malabarensium, a. 1596, LXXXII, CCLIV.

however, if the person has refused, he or she is to be punished with a minor excommunication or suspension.

CAN. 1453 §1. A cleric who lives in concubinage or otherwise persists in an external sin against chastity causing scandal is to be punished with a suspension. If he persist in the delict, other penalties can gradually be added, including deposition.

§2. A cleric who has attempted a forbidden marriage is to be deposed.

§3. A religious who has taken a public, perpetual vow of chastity and is not in sacred orders, is to be punished with an appropriate penalty if he or she has committed these delicts.

CAN. 1454 A person who has falsely denounced someone for a delict, is to be punished with an appropriate penalty, not excluding a major excommunication, especially if the one denounced is a confessor, religious, member of a society of common life in the manner of religious, or a lay person appointed to an ecclesiastical function, with due regard for can. 731.

CAN. 1455 A person who has produced a false ecclesiastical document or asserted a falsehood in it, or has knowingly made use of any false or altered document whatsoever in an ecclesiastical matter, or has changed, destroyed or concealed an authentic document, is to be punished with an appropriate penalty.

cusavit, excommunicatione minore vel suspensione puniatur.

CAN. 1453 §1. Clericus concubinarius vel aliter in peccato externo contra castitatem cum scandalo permanens suspensione puniatur, cui persistente delicto aliae poenae gradatim addi possunt usque ad depositionem.

§2. Clericus, qui prohibitum matrimonium attentavit, deponatur.

§3. Religiosus, qui votum publicum perpetuum castitatis emisit et non est in ordine sacro constitutus, haec delicta committens congrua poena puniatur.

CAN. 1454 Qui falso de quovis delicto aliquem denuntiavit, congrua poena puniatur, non exclusa excommunicatione maiore, praesertim si denuntiatur confessarius, Hierarcha, clericus, religiosus, sodalis societatis vitae communis ad instar religiosorum aut laicus in munere ecclesiastico constitutus firmo can. 731.

CAN. 1455 Qui documentum ecclesiasticum falsum confecit aut in eo falsum asseruit aut qui quolibet falso vel mutato documento scienter usus est in re ecclesiastica aut verum documentum mutavit, destruxit vel occultavit, congrua poena puniatur.

1453 §1: Apost. can. 25; Nic. I, can. 3; Neoc. can. 1; Quinisext. cann. 3–4; S. Basilius M., cann. 3, 69–70, 88; Leo X (in Lat. V), const. *Supernae dispositionis*, 5 maii 1514, §§34–36; Trid., sess. XXI, *De ref.*, can. 6; sess. XXV, *De ref.*, cap. 14; Innocentius XIII, const. *Apostolici ministerii*, 23 mar. 1723, §8; Benedictus XIII, const. *In supremo*, 23 sep. 1724, §6; Benedictus XIV, const. *Ad militantis*, 30 mar. 1742, VI, §§12, 25. * Syn. Diamper. Syro-Malabarensium, a. 1599, CLXXIV–CLXXVI; Syn. Zamosten. Ruthenorum, a. 1720, tit. X "A suspecta;" Syn. Ain-Trazen. Graeco-Melchitarum, a. 1835, can. 12; Syn. prov. Alba-Iulien. et Fagarasien. Rumenorum, a. 1872, tit. VII, cap. 5; Syn. Armen., a. 1911, 952, e).

1453 §2: Anc. can. 10; Neoc. can. 1; Quinisext.

cann. 3, 6; Timotheus Alexandrin., can. 27; Benedictus XIV, const. *Etsi pastoralis*, 26 maii 1742, §VII, XXVII; instr. *Eo quamvis tempore*, 4 maii 1745, §§36–37.

1453 §3: Chalc. can. 16; Quinisext. can. 44; S. Basilius M., cann. 6, 18–19, 60; Timotheus Alexandrin., can. 28.

1454: Benedictus XIV, const. *Sacramentum Poenitentiae*, 1 iun. 1741, §3; const. *Etsi pastoralis*, 26 maii 1742, §IX, V; S.C. de Prop. Fide, litt. encycl. 6 aug. 1885.

1455: Innocentius X, const. *In supremo*, 8 apr. 1653. * Syn. Libanen. Maronitarum, a. 1736, pars III, cap. V, 9; Syn. Armen., a. 1911, 952, b).

CAN. 1456 §1. A confessor who has directly violated the sacramental seal is to be punished with a major excommunication, with due regard for can. 728, §1, n. 1; however, if he broke this seal in another manner, he is to be punished with an appropriate penalty.

§2. A person who has attempted in any way to gain information from confession or has given such information to others, is to be punished with a minor excommunication or a suspension.

CAN. 1457 A priest who has absolved an accomplice in a sin against chastity is to be punished with a major excommunication, with due regard for can. 728, §1, n. 2.

CAN. 1458 A priest who in the act, on the occasion, or under the pretext of confession, has solicited a penitent to sin against chastity, is to be punished with an appropriate penalty, not excluding deposition.

CAN. 1459 §1. Bishops who have conferred episcopal ordination upon someone without a mandate of the competent authority, and the one who has accepted ordination from them in this manner, are to be punished with a major excommunication.

§2. A bishop who has conferred diaconal or

CAN. 1456 §1. Confessarius, qui sacramentale sigillum directe violavit, excommunicatione maiore puniatur firmo can. 728, §1, n. 1; si vero alio modo hoc sigillum fregit, congrua poena puniatur.

§2. Qui notitias ex confessione habere quoquo modo conatus est vel illas iam habitas aliis transmisit, excommunicatione minore aut suspensione puniatur.

CAN. 1457 Sacerdos, qui complicem in peccato contra castitatem absolvit, excommunicatione maiore puniatur firmo can. 728, §1, n. 2.

CAN. 1458 Sacerdos, qui in actu vel occasione vel praetextu confessionis paenitentem ad peccatum contra castitatem sollicitavit, congrua poena puniatur non exclusa depositione.

CAN. 1459 §1. Episcopi, qui alicui sine auctoritatis competentis mandato ordinationem episcopalem ministraverunt, et is, qui ab ipsis ordinationem hoc modo suscepit, excommunicatione maiore puniantur.

§2. Episcopus, qui alicui ordinationem

1456 §1: S.C. de Prop. Fide, decr. 13 apr. 1807, XVII; S.C.S. Off., decr. 21 iul. 1934. * Syn. Zamosten. Ruthenorum, a. 1720, tit. III, §5 "Si quis;" Syn. Libanen. Maronitarum, a. 1736, pars II, cap. IV, 15; Syn. Alexandrin. Coptorum, a. 1898, sect. II, cap. III, art. V, XII; Syn. Armen., a. 1911, 470.

1456 §2: S. C. pro Doctr. Fidei, decl. 23 mar. 1973. * Syn. Armen., a. 1911, 470.

1457: BENEDICTUS XIV, const. *Sacramentum Poenitentiae,* 1 iun. 1741, §4; const. *Apostolici Muneris,* 8 feb. 1745, §§2–4; ep. encycl. *Inter praeteritos,* 3 dec. 1749, §§58–59; S.C.S. Off., 13 ian. 1892, ad 3; S.C. de Prop. Fide, litt. encycl. 6 aug. 1885; S. Paenit. Ap., 19 feb. 1896; S.C.S. Off., decr. 21 iul. 1934; decr. 16 nov. 1934. * Syn. Libanen. Maronitarum, a. 1736, pars II, cap. IV, 16; Syn. Alexandrin. Copto- rum, a. 1898, sect. II, cap. III, art. V, *De peccatis reservatis,* 6, III.

1458: GREGORIUS XV, const. *Universi,* 30 aug. 1622, §4; BENEDICTUS XIV, const. *Sacramentum poenitentiae,* 1 iun. 1741, §1; const. *Etsi pastoralis,*

26 maii 1742, §IX, V; S.C.S. Off., 28 apr. 1700; 13 iun. 1710; decr. 5 aug. 1745; 18 mar. 1863; instr. 20 feb. 1866, 12; decr. 27 iun. 1866; S.C. de Prop. Fide, litt. encycl. 6 aug. 1885, 1. * Syn Armen., a. 1911, 475–476, 952, f).

1459 §1: Apost. can. 76; Nic. II, can. 3; Constantinop. IV, can. 12; LEO XII, litt. *Apostolatus officium* (ad Patriarch. Graeco- Melkitarum), 4 iul. 1828, "Volumus."

1459 §2: Apost. can. 35; Ant. cann. 13, 22; Sard. can. 14*; Carth. cann. 54, 80; PIUS II, const. *Cum ex sacrorum,* 17 nov. 1461, §2; Trid., sess. XIV, *De ref.,* can. 2; sess. XXIII, *De ref.,* can. 8; SIXTUS V, const. *Sanctum et salutare,* 5 ian. 1589, §3; CLEMENS VIII, const. *Romanum Pontificem,* 28 feb. 1596, §2; URBANUS VIII, const. *Secretis,* 11 dec. 1624, §§2–3; BENEDICTUS XIII, const. *In supremo,* 23 sep. 1724, §4; const. *Pastoralis officii,* 27 mar. 1726, §5; BENEDICTUS XIV, const. *Etsi pastoralis,* 26 mar. 1742, §VII, IX; const. *Impositi Nobis,* 27 feb. 1747.

presbyteral ordination upon someone against the prescripts of the canons, is to be punished with an appropriate penalty.

CAN. 1460 A person who has approached the civil authority directly or indirectly to obtain by its intervention sacred ordination, an office, a ministry or another function in the Church, is to be punished with an appropriate penalty not excluding major excommunication and, in the case of a cleric, even deposition.

CAN. 1461 A person who has conferred or accepted sacred ordination through simony is to be deposed; however, a person who has administered or received other sacraments through simony shall be punished with an appropriate penalty, not excluding a major excommunication.

CAN. 1462 A person who has obtained, conferred or usurped in any manner whatsoever, illegitimately retains, or has transmitted to others or carried out an office, a ministry or another function in the Church through simony is to be punished with an appropriate penalty, not excluding a major excommunication.

CAN. 1463 A person who has given or promised something so that someone who exercised an office, a ministry or other function in the Church would do or omit something illegitimately is to be punished with an appropriate penalty; likewise, the one who has accepted such gifts or promises.

diaconalem vel presbyteralem contra praescripta canonum ministravit, congrua poena puniatur.

CAN. 1460 Qui auctoritatem civilem directe vel indirecte adiit, ut ea instante sacram ordinationem, officium, ministerium vel aliud munus in Ecclesia obtineret, congrua poena puniatur non exclusa excommunicatione maiore et, si de clerico agitur, etiam depositione.

CAN. 1461 Qui sacram ordinationem simoniace ministravit vel suscepit, deponatur; qui vero alia sacramenta simoniace ministravit vel suscepit, congrua poena puniatur non exclusa excommunicatione maiore.

CAN. 1462 Qui officium, ministerium vel aliud munus in Ecclesia simoniace obtinuit, contulit aut quomodocumque usurpavit aut illegitime retinet vel aliis transmisit vel exsequitur, congrua poena puniatur non exclusa excommunicatione maiore.

CAN. 1463 Qui quidvis donavit vel pollicitus est, ut aliquis officium, ministerium vel aliud munus in Ecclesia exercens illegitime aliquid ageret vel omitteret, congrua poena puniatur; item, qui ea dona vel pollicitationes acceptavit.

1460: Apost. can. 30; Nic. II, can. 3.

1461: Apost. can. 29; Chalc. can. 2; Quinisext. can. 22; S. BASILIUS M., can. 90; S. GENNADIUS CP., can. 1; S. TARASSIUS CP., can. 1; Nic. II, cann. 5, 19; EUGENIUS IV, const. *Cum detestabile*, 18 maii 1434, §1; Trid., sess. XXI, *de ref.*, can. 1; PIUS V, const. *Cum primum*, 1 apr. 1566, §§8–9; SIXTUS V, const. *Sanctum et salutare*, 5 ian. 1589, §6; CLEMENS VIII, const. *Romanum Pontificem*, 28 feb. 1596, §2; S.C. de Prop. Fide, decr. 13 apr. 1807, VIII. * Syn. Diamper. Syro-Malabarensium, a. 1599, CLXXIX; Syn. Zamosten. Ruthenorum, a. 1720, tit. XIV; Syn. Libanen. Maronitarum, a. 1736, pars II, cap. I, 7; cap. XIV, 51; Syn. Sciarfen. Syrorum, a. 1888,

cap. XVI, art. II, 7–8; Syn. Alexandrin. Coptorum, a. 1898, sect. III, cap. VII, art. VII, 7.

1462: Apost. can. 29; Chalc. can. 2; S. GENNADIUS CP., can. 1; Nic. II, can. 19; LEO X (in Lat. V), const. *Supernae dispositionis*, 5 maii 1514, §15; (in Lat. V) const. *Regimini universalis*, 4 maii 1515, §11; S.C. Consist., decr. 20 aug. 1910, cann. 18, §1 et 29, §1. * Syn. Zamosten. Ruthenorum, a. 1720, tit. XIV; Syn. Libanen. Maronitarum, a. 1736, pars II, cap. XIV, 51; Syn. Sciarfen. Syrorum, a. 1888, cap. XVI, art. II; Syn. Alexandrin. Coptorum, a. 1898, sect. III, cap. VII, art. VII, 7; Syn. Armen., a. 1911, 178.

CAN. 1464 §1. In addition to the cases already foreseen by law, a person who, by act or omission, has misused power, an office, a ministry or another function in the Church, is to be punished with an appropriate penalty, not excluding their privation, unless another penalty has been established by law or precept for such an abuse.

§2. However, a person who through culpable negligence has illegitimately placed or omitted an act of power, office, ministry or other function in the Church with harm to another is to be punished with an appropriate penalty.

CAN. 1465 A person who, ascribed to any Church *sui iuris,* including the Latin Church, and exercising an office, a ministry or another function in the Church, has presumed to induce any member of the Christian faithful whatsoever to transfer to another Church *sui iuris* contrary to can. 31, is to be punished with an appropriate penalty.

CAN. 1466 A cleric, religious, or member of a society of common life in the manner of religious who exercises a trade or business contrary to the prescripts of the canons is to be punished with an appropriate penalty.

CAN. 1467 A person who violates obligations imposed by a penalty can be punished with a heavier penalty.

CAN. 1464 §1. Qui praeter casus iure iam praevisos potestate, officio, ministerio vel alio munere in Ecclesia per actum vel omissionem abusus est, congrua poena puniatur non exclusa eorundem privatione, nisi in hunc abusum alia poena est lege vel praecepto statuta.

§2. Qui vero ex culpabili neglegentia actum potestatis, officii, ministerii vel alterius muneris in Ecclesia illegitime cum damno alieno posuit vel omisit, congrua poena puniatur.

CAN. 1465 Qui officium, ministerium vel aliud munus in Ecclesia exercens, cuicumque Ecclesiae sui iuris, etiam Ecclesiae latinae, ascriptus est, quemvis christifidelem contra can. 31 ad transitum ad aliam Ecclesiam sui iuris quomodocumque inducere praesumpsit, congrua poena puniatur.

CAN. 1466 Clericus, religiosus vel sodalis societatis vitae communis ad instar religiosorum negotiationem aut mercaturam contra canonum praescripta exercens congrua poena puniatur.

CAN. 1467 Qui obligationes sibi ex poena impositas violat, graviore poena puniri potest.

1464 §1: * Syn. Libanen. Maronitarum, a. 1736, pars I, cap. II, 2.

1464 §2: Apost. cann. 36, 58; Ant. can. 17; Carth. cann. 121, 123; Protodeut. cann. 3, 16.

1465: BENEDICTUS XIV, ep. encycl. *Demandatam,* 24 dec. 1743, §15; ep. encycl. *Allatae sunt,* 26 iul. 1755, §21; S.C. de Prop. Fide, 6 oct. 1863, A), c); LEO XIII, litt. ap. *Orientalium,* 30 nov. 1894, I.

1466: Apost. can. 44; Nic. I, can. 17; Laod. can. 4; Chalc. can. 3; Carth. cann. 5, 16; Quinisext. cann. 9–10; Trid., sess. XXII, *De ref.,* can. 1; URBANUS VIII,

litt. ap. *Ex debito,* 22 feb. 1633, §8; CLEMENS IX, const. *Sollicitudo,* 17 iun. 1669, §3; BENEDICTUS XIV, const. *Apostolicae servitutis,* 25 feb. 1741; CLEMENS XIII, ep. encycl. *Cum primum,* 17 sep. 1759, §4. * Syn. Diamper. Syro-Malabarensium, a. 1599, CLXXI–CLXXII; Syn. Zamosten. Ruthenorum, a. 1720, tit. X "Mercaturae;" Syn. Libanen. Maronitarum, a. 1736, pars III, cap. I, 9; Syn. Ain-Trazen. Graeco-Melchitarum, a. 1835, can. 13; Syn. Alexandrin. Coptorum, a. 1898, sect. II, cap. III, art. VII, §6, 2, IX.

1467: Ant. can. 5; Carth. can. 105.

TITLE XXVIII. THE PROCEDURE FOR IMPOSING PENALTIES

TITULUS XXVIII. DE PROCEDURA IN POENIS IRROGANDIS

CHAPTER I. The Penal Trial

CAPUT I. **De Iudicio Poenali**

ART. I. *The Preliminary Investigation*

ART. I. *De Praevia Investigatione*

CAN. 1468 §1. Whenever the hierarch has knowledge, which at least seems true, of a delict, he is carefully to inquire personally or through another suitable person about the facts, circumstances, and imputability, unless such an investigation seems entirely superfluous.

§2. Care must be taken so that the good name of anyone is not endangered from this investigation.

§3. The person who conducts the investigation has the same powers and obligations as an auditor in the process; the same person cannot act as a judge in the matter if a penal trial is initiated later.

CAN. 1469 §1. With due regard for cann. 1403 and 1411, if the investigation seems sufficiently instructed, the hierarch is to decide whether a procedure for imposing penalties is to be initiated and, if he decides affirmatively, whether it is to be dealt with by way of a penal trial or extra-judicial decree.

§2. The hierarch is to revoke or change his decision whenever it seems to him from new evidence and circumstances that another decision is necessary.

CAN. 1468 §1. Quoties Hierarcha notitiam saltem veri similem habet de delicto, caute inquirat per se vel per aliam idoneam personam circa facta et circumstantias, nisi haec investigatio omnino superflua videtur.

§2. Cavendum est, ne ex hac investigatione bonum cuiusquam nomen in discrimen vocetur.

§3. Qui investigationem agit, easdem ac auditor in processu habet potestates et obligationes; idemque non potest, si postea iudicium poenale promovetur, in eo iudicem agere.

CAN. 1469 §1. Firmis cann. 1403 et 1411, si investigatio satis instructa esse videtur, decidat Hierarcha, num procedura in poenis irrogandis promovenda sit, et, si affirmative decidit, utrum per iudicium poenale an per decretum extra iudicium agendum sit.

§2. Hierarcha decisionem suam revocet vel mutet, quoties ex novis factis et circumstantiis aliud sibi decernendum videtur.

1468 §1: Pius XII, m.p. *Sollicitudinem Nostram,* 6 ian. 1950, cann. 513–514. - Constantinop. I, can. 6; Carth. cann. 8, 20, 128; Chalc. can. 21; Theophilus Alexandrin., can. 9; S.C.S. Off., instr. 20 feb. 1866; instr. 6 aug. 1897.

1468 §2: Pius XII, m.p. *Sollicitudinem Nostram,* 6 ian. 1950, can. 517.

1468 §3: Pius XII, m.p. *Sollicitudinem Nostram,* 6 ian. 1950, can. 515 §§2–3.

1469 §1: Pius XII, m.p. *Sollicitudinem Nostram,* 6 ian. 1950, cann. 516 §1, 520 §§1–2.

§3. Before making any decision in the matter, the hierarch is to hear the accused and the promoter of justice regarding the delict as well as, if he considers it prudent, two judges or other experts of the law. The hierarch is also to examine carefully whether, in order to avoid useless trials, it is expedient for him or the investigator, with the consent of the parties, to resolve equitably the question of damages.

CAN. 1470 The acts of the investigation, the decrees of the hierarch who initiated and concluded the investigation, and everything that preceded the investigation are to be kept in the secret archive of the curia if they are not necessary for the procedure for imposing penalties.

§3. Antequam quicquam in re decernit, Hierarcha audiat de delicto accusatum et promotorem iustitiae atque, si ipse prudenter censet, duos iudices aliosve iuris peritos; consideret etiam Hierarcha, num ad vitanda inutilia iudicia expediat, ut partibus consentientibus ipse vel investigator quaestionem de damnis ex bono et aequo dirimat.

CAN. 1470 Investigationis acta et Hierarchae decreta, quibus investigatio initur vel clauditur, eaque omnia, quae investigationem praecedunt, si necessaria non sunt ad proceduram in poenis irrogandis, in archivo secreto curiae asserventur.

ART. II. *The Development of the Penal Trial*

CAN. 1471 §1. Without prejudice to the canons of this title and unless the nature of the matter precludes it, the canons on trials in general and on the ordinary contentious trial must be applied in a penal trial as well as the special norms for cases that pertain to the public good; however, the canons on the summary contentious trial are not to be applied.

§2. The accused is not bound to confess the delict nor can an oath be administered to the accused.

CAN. 1472 §1. If the hierarch has decreed that a penal trial must be initiated, he is to hand over the acts of the investigation to the promoter of justice who is to present a *libellus* of accusation to the judge according to the norm of cann. 1185-1187.

ART. II. *De Iudicii Poenalis Evolutione*

CAN. 1471 §1. Salvis canonibus huius tituli in iudicio poenali applicandi sunt, nisi rei natura obstat, canones de iudiciis in genere et de iudicio contentioso ordinario necnon normae speciales de causis, quae ad bonum publicum spectant, non vero canones de iudicio contentioso summario.

§2. Accusatus ad confitendum delictum non tenetur nec ipsi iusiurandum deferri potest.

CAN. 1472 §1. Si Hierarcha decrevit iudicium poenale esse ineundum, acta investigationis promotori iustitiae tradat, qui libellum accusationis iudici ad normam cann. 1185 et 1187 exhibeat.

1470: Pius XII, m.p. *Sollicitudinem Nostram,* 6 ian. 1950, can. 520 §2 nn. 1–2.

1471 §1: Pius XII, m.p. *Sollicitudinem Nostram,* 6 ian. 1950, can. 529.

1471 §2: Pius XII, m.p. *Sollicitudinem Nostram,* 6

ian. 1950, cann. 265 §1, 542, 558, 559 §1. - Neoc. can. 9; S. Basilius M., can. 70.

1472 §1: Pius XII, m.p. *Sollicitudinem Nostram,* 6 ian. 1950, cann. 507, 528, 530–531.

§2. The promoter of justice appointed to the higher tribunal acts as the petitioner before that tribunal.

CAN. 1473 To prevent scandals, to protect the freedom of witnesses, and to guard the course of justice, the hierarch, after having heard the promoter of justice and cited the accused, at any stage and grade of the penal trial can exclude the accused from the exercise of sacred orders, an office, a ministry, or another function, can impose or forbid residence in some place or territory, or even can prohibit public reception of the Divine Eucharist. Once the cause ceases, all these measures must be revoked and they end by the law itself when the penal trial ceases.

CAN. 1474 The judge who cites the accused must invite the accused to choose an advocate within a determined time; if it lapses without result, the same judge *ex officio* is to appoint an advocate for the accused. This advocate will remain in this function as long as the accused does not appoint an advocate personally.

CAN. 1475 §1. At any grade of the trial, the promoter of justice can renounce the trial at the order of or with the consent of the hierarch whose deliberation initiated the trial.

§2. For validity, the accused must accept the renunciation unless the accused was declared absent from the trial.

CAN. 1476 Besides the defense briefs and observations given in writing, if there have been any, the discussion of the case is to be made orally.

§2. Coram tribunali superiore partes actoris gerit promotor iustitiae apud illud tribunal constitutus.

CAN. 1473 Ad scandala praevenienda, ad testium libertatem protegendam et ad iustitiae cursum tuendum potest Hierarcha audito promotore iustitiae et citato ipso accusato in quolibet statu et gradu iudicii poenalis accusatum ab exercitio ordinis sacri, officii, ministerii vel alterius muneris arcere, ei imponere vel prohibere commorationem in aliquo loco vel territorio, vel etiam publicam Divinae Eucharistiae susceptionem prohibere; quae omnia causa cessante sunt revocanda et ipso iure finem habent cessante iudicio poenali.

CAN. 1474 Iudex accusatum citans debet eum invitare ad eligendum advocatum intra tempus determinatum; quo inutiliter elapso idem iudex ex officio advocatum accusato constituat tamdiu in munere mansurum, dum accusatus sibi advocatum non constituerit.

CAN. 1475 §1. In quolibet gradu iudicii renuntiatio litis instantiae fieri potest a promotore iustitiae mandante vel consentiente Hierarcha, ex cuius deliberatione iudicium promotum est.

§2. Renuntiatio, ut valeat, debet ab accusato acceptari, nisi hic a iudicio absens declaratus est.

CAN. 1476 Praeter defensiones et animadversiones scripto datas, si quae fuerint, discussio causae ore fieri debet.

1472 §2: Pius XII, m.p. *Sollicitudinem Nostram,* 6 ian. 1950, can. 574.

1473: Pius XII, m.p. *Sollicitudinem Nostram,* 6 ian. 1950, cann. 537–539.

1474: Pius XII, m.p. *Sollicitudinem Nostram,* 6 ian. 1950, can. 536.

1475 §1: Pius XII, m.p. *Sollicitudinem Nostram,* 6 ian. 1950, can. 535 §3.

1476: Pius XII, m.p. *Sollicitudinem Nostram,* 6 ian. 1950, cann. 567–568.

CAN. 1477 §1. The promoter of justice, the accused and his or her advocate, the injured party mentioned in can. 1483, §1 and that person's advocate are present for the discussion.

§2. It is for the tribunal to call the experts who collaborated in the case to the discussion so that they can explain their expert testimony.

CAN. 1478 In the discussion of the case, the accused, either personally or through his or her advocate, always has the right to speak last.

CAN. 1479 §1. When the discussion is completed, the tribunal is to render a sentence.

§2. If the need to gather new proofs has emerged from the discussion, the tribunal is to postpone the decision of the case and gather the new proofs.

CAN. 1480 The dispositive part of the sentence is to be published immediately unless the tribunal decides for a serious reason that the decision is to be kept secret until the formal intimation of the sentence, which can never be deferred beyond a month from the day when the penal case was decided.

CAN. 1481 §1. The accused can introduce an appeal even if the judge acquitted the accused only because the penalty was facultative or because the judge used the power mentioned in cann. 1409, §1 and 1415.

§2. The promoter of justice can appeal if he or she judges that the reparation of scandal or the restoration of justice has not been provided for sufficiently.

CAN. 1482 If at any stage or grade of the penal trial it is evidently established that the ac-

CAN. 1477 §1. Discussioni assistunt promotor iustitiae, accusatus eiusque advocatus, pars laesa, de qua in can. 1483, §1 eiusque advocatus.

§2. Tribunalis est peritos, qui operam in causa praestiterunt, ad discussionem vocare, ut peritias suas explicare possint.

CAN. 1478 In causae discussione accusatus semper ius habet, ut vel ipse vel suus advocatus postremus loquatur.

CAN. 1479 §1. Discussione peracta tribunal sententiam ferat.

§2. Si ex discussione emersit necessitas novarum probationum colligendarum, tribunal dilata definitione causae novas probationes colligat.

CAN. 1480 Pars dispositiva sententiae statim publicanda est, nisi tribunal gravi de causa decernit decisionem secreto servandam esse usque ad formalem sententiae intimationem, quae numquam ultra mensem a die, quo causa poenalis definita est, computandum differri potest.

CAN. 1481 §1. Appellationem interponere potest reus, etsi iudex eum absolutum dimisit ideo tantum, quia poena erat facultativa vel quia iudex potestate usus est, de qua in cann. 1409, §1 et 1415.

§2. Promotor iustitiae appellare potest, si censet reparationi scandali vel restitutioni iustitiae satis provisum non esse.

CAN. 1482 In quolibet statu et gradu iudicii poenalis, si evidenter constat delictum

---

1477 §1: Pius XII, m.p. *Sollicitudinem Nostram,* 6 ian. 1950, can. 569 §1.

1477 §2: Pius XII, m.p. *Sollicitudinem Nostram,* 6 ian. 1950, can. 569 §2.

1478: Pius XII, m.p. *Sollicitudinem Nostram,* 6 ian. 1950, can. 570 §§1–2.

1479 §1: Pius XII, m.p. *Sollicitudinem Nostram,* 6 ian. 1950, can. 571 §1.

1479 §2: Pius XII, m.p. *Sollicitudinem Nostram,* 6 ian. 1950, can. 571 §2.

1480: Pius XII, m.p. *Sollicitudinem Nostram,* 6 ian. 1950, can. 572.

1481 §1: Pius XII, m.p. *Sollicitudinem Nostram,* 6 ian. 1950, can. 573.

cused did not commit the delict, the judge must declare this in a sentence and absolve the accused even if it is also established that the penal action has been extinguished.

non esse ab accusato patratum, iudex debet id sententia declarare et accusatum absolvere, etsi simul constat actionem poenalem esse exstinctam.

ART. III. *Action for Reparation of Damages*

ART. III. *De Actione ad Damna Reparanda*

CAN. 1483 §1. In the penal trial itself, an injured party can bring a contentious action for the reparation of damages incurred personally from the delict, according to can. 1276.

CAN. 1483 §1. Pars laesa potest actionem contentiosam ad damna reparanda ex delicto sibi illata in ipso iudicio poenali exercere ad normam can. 1276.

§2. The intervention of the injured party is not admitted later if it was not made in the first grade of the penal trial.

§2. Interventus partis laesae non amplius admittitur, si factus non est in primo gradu iudicii poenalis.

§3. The appeal in the case for damages is made according to the norm of cann. 1309-1321 even if an appeal cannot be made in the penal trial; but if both appeals are introduced, although by different parties, there is to be a single appellate trial, without prejudice to can. 1484.

§3. Appellatio in causa de damnis fit ad normam cann. 1309–1321, etsi appellatio in iudicio poenali fieri non potest; si vero utraque appellatio, etsi a diversis partibus, interponitur, unicum fiat iudicium appellationis salvo can. 1484.

CAN. 1484 §1. To avoid excessive delays in the penal trial, the judge can defer the judgment for damages until he has rendered a definitive sentence in the penal trial.

CAN. 1484 §1. Ad nimias iudicii poenalis moras vitandas potest iudex iudicium de damnis differre, donec sententiam definitivam in iudicio poenali tulerit.

§2. After rendering the sentence in the penal trial, the judge who does this must adjudicate for damages even if the penal trial still is pending because of a proposed challenge or the accused has been absolved for a cause that does not remove the obligation of repairing the damages.

§2. Iudex, qui ita egit, debet, postquam sententiam tulit in iudicio poenali, de damnis cognoscere, etsi iudicium poenale propter interpositam impugnationem adhuc pendet vel accusatus absolutus est propter causam, quae non aufert obligationem damna reparandi.

CAN. 1485 Even if the sentence rendered in a penal trial has become a *res iudicata,* it in no way establishes the right of the injured party unless this party has intervened according to the norm of can. 1483.

CAN. 1485 Sententia lata in iudicio poenali, etsi in rem iudicatam transiit, nullo modo ius facit erga partem laesam, nisi haec intervenit ad normam can. 1483.

1483 §1: Pius XII, m.p. *Sollicitudinem Nostram,* 6 ian. 1950, cann. 547 §§1–2, 554.
1483 §3: Pius XII, m.p. *Sollicitudinem Nostram,* 6 ian. 1950, can. 553 §2.
1484 §1: Pius XII, m.p. *Sollicitudinem Nostram,* 6 ian. 1950, can. 548.

CHAPTER II. The Imposition of Penalties by Extra-judicial Decree

CAN. 1486 §1. For the validity of the decree that imposes a penalty, it is required that:

1° the accused be notified of the accusation as well as the proofs and be given the opportunity of fully exercising the right of self-defense, unless the accused neglected to appear after being cited in accord with the norm of law;

2° an oral discussion be held between the hierarch or his delegate and the accused with the promoter of justice and a notary present;

3° it be explained in the decree itself the reasons in fact and law on which the penalty is based.

§2. However, the penalties mentioned in can. 1426, §1, can be imposed without this procedure, provided their acceptance by the offender is established in writing.

CAN. 1487 §1. A recourse against a decree that imposes a penalty can be introduced before the competent higher authority within ten useful days after the decree has been intimated.

§2. This recourse suspends the force of the decree.

§3. There is no further recourse against the decision of the higher authority.

CAPUT II. **De Irrogatione Poenarum per Decretum Extra Iudicium**

CAN. 1486 §1. Ad validitatem decreti, quo poena irrogatur, requiritur, ut:

1° accusatus de accusatione atque probationibus certior fiat data sibi opportunitate ius ad sui defensionem plene exercendi, nisi ad normam iuris citatus comparere neglexit;

2° discussio oralis inter Hierarcham vel eius delegatum et accusatum habeatur praesentibus promotore iustitiae et notario;

3° in ipso decreto exponatur, quibus rationibus in facto et in iure punitio innitatur.

§2. Poenae autem, de quibus in can. 1426, §1, sine hac procedura imponi possunt, dummodo de earum acceptatione ex parte rei scripto constet.

CAN. 1487 §1. Recursus adversus decretum, quo poena irrogatur, intra decem dies utiles, postquam intimatum est, ad auctoritatem superiorem competentem interponi potest.

§2. Hic recursus vim decreti suspendit.

§3. Contra decisionem auctoritatis superioris non datur ulterior recursus.

CHAPTER I. Ecclesiastical Laws

CAN. 1488 Laws are established by promulgation.

CAN. 1489 §1. Laws issued by the Apostolic See are promulgated in the official commentary, *Acta Apostolicae Sedis*, unless another manner of promulgation has been prescribed in special circumstances. They begin to oblige after three months have elapsed from the date of that issue of the *Acta* unless they oblige immediately from the very nature of the matter or a shorter or longer suspensive period *(vacatio)* has been expressly established.

§2. Laws issued by other legislators are promulgated in the manner determined by these legislators and begin to oblige from the date determined by them.

CAN. 1490 Merely ecclesiastical laws bind those who have been baptized in the Catholic Church or received into it, have the sufficient use of reason, and, unless the law expressly provides otherwise, have completed seven years of age.

CAN. 1491 §1. Laws issued by the supreme authority of the Church bind everywhere all those for whom they were enacted, unless they were established for a particular territory; oth-

CAPUT I. **De Legibus Ecclesiasticis**

CAN. 1488 Leges instituuntur promulgatione.

CAN. 1489 §1. Leges a Sede Apostolica latae promulgantur per editionem in Actorum Sedis Apostolicae commentario officiali, nisi in casibus specialibus alius promulgandi modus est praescriptus; obligare incipiunt elapsis tribus mensibus a die, qui Actorum numero appositus est, computandis, nisi ex natura rei statim obligant aut brevior vel longior vacatio expresse est statuta.

§2. Leges ab aliis legislatoribus latae promulgantur modo ab his legislatoribus determinato et obligare incipiunt a die ab eisdem statuto.

CAN. 1490 Legibus mere ecclesiasticis tenentur baptizati in Ecclesia catholica vel in eandem recepti, quique sufficientem usum rationis habent et, nisi aliter iure expresse cavetur, septimum aetatis annum expleverunt.

CAN. 1491 §1. Legibus a suprema Ecclesiae auctoritate latis tenentur omnes, pro quibus datae sunt ubique terrarum, nisi pro determinato territorio conditae sunt; ceterae

---

1488: Chalc. can.1; Quinisext. can. 2; Nic. II, can. 1. ▲ C. 1, 14.
1490: S. Basilius M., cann. 20, 87; Trid., sess.

XIV, *De poenitentia,* cap. 2; Benedictus XIV, ep. encycl. *Inter omnigenas,* 2 feb. 1744, §16; ep. *Singulari,* 9 feb. 1749, §2.

er laws have force only in the territory where the authority that promulgated them exercises power of governance, unless the law provides otherwise or it is evident from the nature of the matter.

§2. Laws issued for a particular territory bind those for whom they were enacted as well as those who have a domicile or quasi-domicile there and who at the same time are actually residing there, with due regard for §3, n. 1.

§3. Travelers:

1° are not bound by the laws of the particular law of their territory as long as they are absent from it, unless either the transgression of those laws causes harm in their own territory or the laws are personal;

2° are not bound by the laws of the particular law of the territory in which they are present, with the exception of those laws which provide for public order, which determine the formalities of acts, or which regard immovable goods located in the territory;

3° are bound by the laws of the common law and the laws of the particular law of their own Church *sui iuris,* even if the latter are not in force in their own territory; but they are bound by the same laws if these do not bind in the place where they are present.

§4. Transients are bound by all laws which are in force in the place where they are present.

CAN. 1492 Laws issued by the supreme authority of the Church, which do not expressly indicate the passive subject, affect the Christian faithful of the Eastern Churches only insofar as they concern matters of faith or morals or declarations of divine law, explicitly decide questions regarding these Christian faithful, or

leges vim habent tantummodo in territorio, in quo auctoritas, quae leges promulgavit, potestatem regiminis exercet, nisi aliter iure cavetur vel ex natura rei constat.

§2. Legibus latis pro determinato territorio ii subiciuntur, pro quibus datae sunt quique ibidem domicilium vel quasi-domicilium habent et simul actu commorantur firma §3, n. 1.

§3. Peregrini:

1° non obligantur legibus iuris particularis sui territorii, dum ab eo absunt, nisi aut earum transgressio in proprio territorio nocet aut leges sunt personales;

2° neque obligantur legibus iuris particularis territorii, in quo versantur, eis exceptis, quae ordini publico consulunt aut actuum sollemnia determinant aut res immobiles in territorio sitas respiciunt;

3° sed obligantur legibus iuris communis et legibus iuris particularis propriae Ecclesiae sui iuris, etsi, ad leges eiusdem iuris particularis quod attinet, in suo territorio non vigent, non vero, si in loco, ubi versantur, non obligant.

§4. Vagi obligantur omnibus legibus, quae vigent in loco, ubi versantur.

CAN. 1492 Leges a suprema Ecclesiae auctoritate latae, in quibus subiectum passivum expresse non indicatur, christifideles Ecclesiarum orientalium respiciunt tantummodo, quatenus de rebus fidei vel morum aut de declaratione legis divinae agitur vel explicite de eisdem christifidelibus in his le-

1492: Lat. IV, 4; S.C. de Prop. Fide, 4 iun. 1631; 7 iun. 1639, 1; S.C.S. Off., 13 iun. 1710; BENEDICTUS XIV, const. *Etsi pastoralis,* 26 mai 1742, §IX, V; ep. encycl. *Allatae sunt,* 26 iul. 1755, §44; all. *Quadraginta,* 27 mar. 1757, "Audistis;" litt. encycl. (ad Del. Ap. pro Oriente), 8 nov. 1882; litt. encycl. 6 aug. 1885; decr. 18 aug. 1893, "Licet." * Syn. Armen., a. 1911, 146.

concern favors which contain nothing contrary to the Eastern rites.

CAN. 1493 §1. Under the name *common law* in this Code come, besides the laws and legitimate customs of the entire Church, also the laws and legitimate customs common to all the Eastern Churches.

§2. However, under the name *particular law* come all laws, legitimate customs, statutes and other norms of law, which are neither common to the entire Church nor to all the Eastern Churches.

CAN. 1494 Laws regard the future, not the past, unless they expressly provide for the past.

CAN. 1495 Only those laws must be considered invalidating or disqualifying which expressly establish that an act is null or that a person is unqualified.

CAN. 1496 Laws, even invalidating and disqualifying ones, do not oblige when there is a doubt about the law. When there is a doubt about a fact, however, hierarchs can dispense from laws provided that, if it is a reserved dispensation, the authority to whom it is reserved usually grants it.

CAN. 1497 §1. Ignorance or error about invalidating or disqualifying laws does not impede their effect unless it is expressly established otherwise.

§2. Ignorance or error about a law, a penalty, a fact concerning oneself, or a notorious fact concerning another is not presumed; it is presumed about a fact concerning another which is not notorious until the contrary is proven.

gibus disponitur aut de favorabilibus agitur, quae nihil ritibus orientalibus contrarium continent.

CAN. 1493 §1. Nomine iuris communis in hoc Codice veniunt praeter leges et legitimas consuetudines universae Ecclesiae etiam leges et legitimae consuetudines omnibus Ecclesiis orientalibus communes.

§2. Nomine vero iuris particularis veniunt omnes leges, legitimae consuetudines, statuta aliaeque iuris normae, quae nec universae Ecclesiae nec omnibus Ecclesiis orientalibus communes sunt.

CAN. 1494 Leges respiciunt futura, non praeterita, nisi expresse in eis de praeteritis cavetur.

CAN. 1495 Irritantes aut inhabilitantes eae tantum leges habendae sunt, quibus actum esse nullum aut inhabilem esse personam expresse statuitur.

CAN. 1496 Leges, etiam irritantes aut inhabilitantes, in dubio iuris non urgent; in dubio facti autem ab eis dispensare possunt Hierarchae, dummodo dispensatio, si est reservata, concedi soleat ab auctoritate, cui reservatur.

CAN. 1497 §1. Ignorantia vel error circa leges irritantes aut inhabilitantes earundem effectum non impediunt, nisi aliud iure expresse statuitur.

§2. Ignorantia vel error circa legem aut poenam aut circa factum proprium aut circa factum alienum notorium non praesumitur; circa factum alienum non notorium praesumitur, donec contrarium probetur.

1493 §2: Pius XII, m.p. *Postquam Apostolicis Litteris,* 9 feb. 1952, can. 317.

1494: ▲ C. 1, 14, 7; 10, 32, 66 (65) in fine; Nov. 19, 1 in fine; 76, 1, 1; 115, 1; 143, 1 in fine.

1495: ▲ C. 1, 2, 14 (4–5); 1, 14, 5; Basilic., 2, 6, 10.

1497 §1: Quinisext. cann. 3, 26; S. Basilius M., can. 27; Theophilus Alexandrin., can. 13; S. Tarasius CP, ep. ad Epp. Siciliae, "Dicite, eum." ▲ C. 1, 18, 12.

CAN. 1498 §1. The legislator authentically interprets laws as does the one to whom the same legislator has conferred the power of authentically interpreting.

§2. An authentic interpretation given in the form of law has the same force as the law itself and must be promulgated. If it only declares the words of the law which are certain in themselves, it is retroactive; if it restricts or extends the law, or if it explains a doubtful law, it is not retroactive.

§3. An interpretation in the form of a judicial sentence or of an administrative act in a particular given matter, however, does not have the force of law and only obliges the persons for whom and affects the matters for which it was given.

CAN. 1499 Laws must be understood according to the proper meaning of the words considered in their text and context. If the meaning remains doubtful and obscure, they must be understood according to parallel passages, if there are such, to the purpose and circumstances of the law, and to the mind of the legislator.

CAN. 1500 Laws which establish a penalty, restrict the free exercise of rights, or contain an exception from the law are subject to strict interpretation.

CAN. 1501 If an express prescript of law is lacking in a certain matter, a case, unless it is penal, must be resolved according to the canons of the synods and the holy fathers, legitimate custom, the general principles of canon law applied with equity, ecclesiastical jurisprudence, and the common and constant canonical doctrine.

CAN. 1498 §1. Leges authentice interpretatur legislator et is, cui potestas authentice interpretandi ab eodem collata est.

§2. Interpretatio authentica per modum legis data eandem vim habet ac ipsa lex et promulgari debet; si verba in se certa declarat tantum, valet retrorsum; si legem coartat vel extendit aut dubiam explicat, non retrotrahitur.

§3. Interpretatio autem per modum sententiae iudicialis aut actus administrativi in re speciali data vim legis non habet et obligat tantum personas atque afficit res, pro quibus data est.

CAN. 1499 Leges intellegendae sunt secundum propriam verborum significationem in textu et contextu consideratam, quae si dubia et obscura mansit, secundum locos parallelos, si qui sunt, legis finem ac circumstantias et mentem legislatoris.

CAN. 1500 Leges, quae poenam statuunt aut liberum iurium exercitium coartant aut exceptionem a lege continent, strictae interpretationi subsunt.

CAN. 1501 Si certa de re deest expressum praescriptum legis, causa, nisi est poenalis, dirimenda est secundum canones Synodorum et sanctorum Patrum, legitimam consuetudinem, generalia principia iuris canonici cum aequitate servata, iurisprudentiam ecclesiasticam, communem et constantem doctrinam canonicam.

1498 §1: ▲ C. 1, 14, 9 et 11–12.
1498 §2: ▲ Nov. 76, 1, 1; 143, 1 in fine.
1498 §3: ▲ C. 1, 14, 3 in fine.
1499: S. Basilius M., can. 87. ▲ D. 1, 3, 18–19 et 25; 50, 17, 192.
1500: ▲ D. 48, 19, 42; Basilic. 2, 3, 9.
1501: * Syn. Armen., a. 1911, 276. ▲ D. 1, 3, 4–6 et 12–13 et 32.

CAN. 1502 §1. A later law abrogates, or derogates from, an earlier law if it states so expressly, is directly contrary to it, or completely reorders the entire matter of the earlier law.

§2. However, a law of the common law, unless expressly provided otherwise in the law itself, does not derogate from a law of the particular law nor does a law of the particular law issued for a Church *sui iuris* derogate from the more particular law in force in that Church.

CAN. 1503 In case of doubt, the revocation of a pre-existing law is not presumed, but later laws must be related to the earlier ones and, insofar as possible, must be harmonized with them.

CAN. 1504 Civil law to which the law of the Church yields, is to be observed in canon law with the same effects, insofar as they are not contrary to divine law and unless canon law provides otherwise.

CAN. 1505 The expression of language in the masculine gender also regards the feminine gender unless the law provides otherwise or it is evident from the nature of the matter.

CHAPTER II. Custom

CAN. 1506 §1. A custom of the Christian community, insofar as it corresponds to the action of the Holy Spirit in the ecclesial body, can obtain the force of law.

§2. No custom can in any way derogate from divine law.

CAN. 1502 §1. Lex posterior abrogat priorem aut eidem derogat, si id expresse edicit aut si illi est directe contraria aut totam de integro ordinat legis prioris materiam.

§2. Lex iuris communis vero, nisi aliter in ipsa lege expresse cavetur, non derogat legi iuris particularis nec lex iuris particularis pro aliqua Ecclesia sui iuris lata derogat iuri magis particulari in eadem Ecclesia vigenti.

CAN. 1503 In dubio revocatio legis praeexsistentis non praesumitur, sed leges posteriores ad priores trahendae sunt et his, quatenus fieri potest, conciliandae.

CAN. 1504 Ius civile, ad quod ius Ecclesiae remittit, in iure canonico eisdem cum effectibus servetur, quatenus iuri divino non est contrarium et nisi aliter iure canonico cavetur.

CAN. 1505 Enuntiatio sermonis genere masculino etiam genus femininum respicit, nisi aliter iure cavetur vel ex natura rei constat.

CAPUT II. De Consuetudine

CAN. 1506 §1. Consuetudo communitatis christianae, quatenus actuositati Spiritus Sancti in corpore ecclesiali respondet, vim iuris obtinere potest.

§2. Iuri divino nulla consuetudo potest ullo modo derogare.

1502 §1: ▲ Instit. 1, 2, 11; D. 1, 4, 4; 42, 1, 14.
1503: ▲ D. 1, 3, 26–28; Basilic. 2, 1, 38.
1504: Pius XII, m.p. *Postquam Apostolicis Litteris,* 9 feb. 1952, can. 278 §1.
1505: Pius XII, m.p. *Postquam Apostolicis Litteris,* 9 febr. 1952, can. 318. ▲ D. 50, 16, 195, pr.
1506 §1: Nic. I, cann. 6–7; Constantinop. I, can. 2; Eph. can. 8; Carth. can. 70; Quinisext. can. 39; Nic.

II, cann. 14–15; S. Petrus Alexandrin., can. 15; S. Basilius M., cann. 1, 3–4, 87, 89, 91–92; S. Gregorius Nyssen., can. 8; Timotheus Alexandrin., can. 23; Theophilus Alexandrin., cann. 1, 3; S. Cyrillus Alexandrin., can. 3; S. Iulius, litt. *Legi litteras,* a. 341, "Quid enim."
1506 §2: Nic. II, can. 5; S. Gennadius CP., can. 1 " Ὅμως ἐπειδή."

CAN. 1507 §1. Only that custom can have the force of law which is reasonable, introduced by way of a continuous and uncontested practice by a community at least capable of receiving law, and which has been prescribed for the time established by law.

§2. A custom which is expressly reprobated by law is not a reasonable one.

§3. A custom contrary to the canon law now in force or one beyond a canonical law *(praeter legem canonicam)* obtains the force of law only if it has been legitimately observed for thirty continuous and complete years. Only a centenary or immemorial custom, however, can prevail against a canonical law which contains a clause prohibiting future customs.

§4. Even before that time, a competent legislator can approve a custom as legitimate by his consent, at least tacit.

CAN. 1508 Custom is the best interpreter of laws.

CAN. 1509 A custom, whether contrary to or beyond the law *(praeter legem),* is revoked by a contrary custom or law; however, a law does not revoke centenary or immemorial customs, unless it makes express mention of them. Regarding other customs, can. 1502, §2 applies.

CHAPTER III. **Administrative Acts**

CAN. 1510 §1. Administrative acts can be placed, within the limits of their competence, by those who have executive power of governance

CAN. 1507 §1. Ea tantum consuetudo vim iuris habere potest, quae est rationalis et a communitate legis saltem recipiendae capaci praxi continua et pacifica inducta necnon per tempus iure statutum praescripta.

§2. Consuetudo, quae a iure expresse reprobatur, non est rationabilis.

§3. Consuetudo vigenti iuri canonico contraria aut, quae est praeter legem canonicam, vim iuris obtinet tantum, si legitime per annos triginta continuos et completos servata est; contra legem canonicam vero, quae clausulam continet futuras consuetudines prohibentem, sola praevalere potest consuetudo centenaria vel immemorabilis.

§4. Legislator competens potest consuetudinem consensu suo saltem tacito etiam ante hoc tempus ut legitimam approbare.

CAN. 1508 Consuetudo est optima legum interpres.

CAN. 1509 Consuetudo sive contra sive praeter legem per contrariam consuetudinem aut legem revocatur; sed nisi expressam de eis mentionem facit, lex non revocat consuetudines centenarias vel immemorabiles; ad ceteras consuetudines quod attinet, valet can. 1502, §2.

CAPUT III. **De Actibus Administrativis**

CAN. 1510 §1. Actus administrativi poni possunt ab eis, qui potestatem regiminis exsecutivam habent, intra limites eorum

---

1507 §1: S. NICOLAUS I, litt. *Postquam beato,* 18 mar. 862, "De consuetudinibus. . .." ▲ D. 1, 3, 32–33; C. 1, 3, 38 (39), (2) in fine; 8, 52 (53), 2; Basilic. 2, 1, 42.

1507 §2: Nic. I, can. 15; Sard. can. 1; Nic. II, can. 5. * Syn. Libanen. Maronitarum., a. 1736, pars II, cap. XIV, 51.

1507 §3: ▲ D. 1, 3, 32–33; C. 8, 52 (53), 1; Basilic. 2, 1, 42.

1507 §4: GREGORIUS XVI, ep. encycl. *Inter gravissimas,* 3 feb. 1832, §5.

1508: ▲ D. 1, 3, 27; Basilic. 2, 1, 46.

as well as by those who have received such power explicitly or implicitly by the law itself or by legitimate delegation,

§2. Administrative acts are chiefly:

1° decrees which a give a decision or make a canonical provision for a special case;

2° singular precepts which directly and legitimately enjoin a specific person or persons to do or omit something, especially in order to urge the observance of the law;

3° rescripts which grant a privilege, dispensation, permission or another favor.

CAN. 1511 An administrative act has effect from the moment it is intimated or, in the case of rescripts, at the moment the letter is given. However, if the application of the administrative act is entrusted to an executor, it has effect at the moment of execution.

CAN. 1512 §1. An administrative act must be understood according to the proper meaning of the words and the common manner of speaking and must not be extended to other cases besides those expressed.

§2. In a case of doubt, an administrative act which refers to litigation, pertains to threatening or imposing penalties, restricts the rights of a person, injures the acquired rights of others, or is contrary to a law which benefits private persons, receives a strict interpretation; other administrative decrees, however, receive a broad interpretation.

§3. In the case of privileges, that interpretation must always be used so that the person to whom the privilege was granted actually does obtain some favor.

§4. Not only a dispensation, but also the very

competentiae necnon ab illis, quibus haec potestas explicite vel implicite competit sive ipso iure sive vi legitimae delegationis.

§2. Actus administrativi sunt praesertim:

1° decreta, quibus pro casu speciali datur decisio aut fit provisio canonica;

2° praecepta singularia, quibus personae aut personis determinatis aliquid faciendum aut omittendum directe et legitime imponitur praesertim ad legis observantiam urgendam;

3° rescripta, quibus conceditur privilegium, dispensatio, licentia aliave gratia.

CAN. 1511 Effectum habet actus administrativus a momento, quo intimatur, vel in rescriptis a momento, quo datae sunt litterae; si vero actus administrativi applicatio committitur exsecutori, effectum habet a momento exsecutionis.

CAN. 1512 §1. Actus administrativus intellegendus est secundum propriam verborum significationem et communem loquendi usum nec debet ad alios casus praeter expressos extendi.

§2. In dubio actus administrativus, qui ad lites refertur, ad poenas comminandas vel irrogandas attinet, iura personae coartat, iura aliis quaesita laedit aut adversatur legi in commodum privatorum, strictam recipit interpretationem; secus vero latam.

§3. In privilegiis ea semper adhibenda est interpretatio, ut ille, cui privilegium concessum est, aliquam revera gratiam consequatur.

§4. Non solum dispensatio, sed ipsa

1512 §3: Trid., sess. XXIV, *De ref.*, can. 11.

1512 §4: Trid., sess. VI, *Decretum de residentia*, cap. 2; sess. XXIV, *De ref. circa matrimonium*, cap. 5; sess. XXV, *De ref.*, cap. 18; BENEDICTUS XIV, ep. en-

cycl. *Inter omnigenas*, 2 feb. 1744, §§11, 25; ep. *Cum encyclicas*, 24 maii 1754, §6; S.C. de Prop. Fide, decr. 13 apr. 1807, IX; instr. 9 maii 1877; S. Paenit. Ap., 5 apr. 1902.

power to dispense granted for a particular case, is subject to a strict interpretation.

CAN. 1513 §1. No administrative act is revoked by a contrary law, unless it is provided otherwise in the law itself or the law was enacted by an authority higher than the one who issued the administrative act.

§2. An administrative act does not cease when the authority of the one who placed it expires, unless the law expressly provides otherwise.

§3. The revocation of an administrative act by another administrative act of a competent authority takes effect only from the moment at which the revocation is intimated to the person for whom it has been given.

§4. A dispensation which has successive application ceases also by the certain and total cessation of the motivating cause.

§5. A singular decree of precept ceases to have force through cessation of the law for whose execution it was given; a singular precept also ceases when the authority of the one who issued it expires, unless it was imposed by a legitimate document.

CAN. 1514 An administrative act which regards the external forum, with due regard for cann. 1520, §2 and 1527, must be put in writing. Furthermore, if it is given in commissorial form, the act of that execution must be put into writing.

CAN. 1515 An administrative act, even if it is a rescript given *motu proprio*, lacks effect insofar as it injures the acquired rights of others or is contrary to a law or legitimate custom, unless the competent authority expressly adds a derogating clause.

CAN. 1516 Conditions in administrative acts are considered added for validity only when they are expressed by the particles "if" *(si)*, "un-

potestas dispensandi ad certum casum concessa strictae interpretationi subest.

Can. 1513 §1. Per legem contrariam nullus actus administrativus revocatur, nisi aliter in ipsa lege cavetur aut lex lata est ab auctoritate superiore ei, qui actum administrativum emisit.

§2. Actus administrativus non cessat resoluto iure eius, qui eum posuit, nisi aliter expresse cavetur.

§3. Revocatio actus administrativi per alium actum administrativum auctoritatis competentis effectum tantummodo obtinet a momento, quo intimatur personae, pro qua datus est.

§4. Dispensatio, quae tractum habet successivum, cessat quoque certa ac totali cessatione causae motivae.

§5. Decretum praeceptumve singulare vim habere desinit etiam cessante lege, ad cuius exsecutionem datum est; praeceptum singulare cessat etiam resoluto iure praecipientis, nisi legitimo documento impositum est.

Can. 1514 Actus administrativus, qui forum externum respicit, firmis cann. 1520, §2 et 1527 scripto est consignandus; item, si fit in forma commissoria, illius actus exsecutionis.

Can. 1515 Actus administrativus, etiam si agitur de rescripto motu proprio dato, effectu caret, quatenus iura aliis quaesita laedit aut legi vel legitimae consuetudini contrarius est, nisi auctoritas competens expresse clausulam derogatoriam addidit.

Can. 1516 Condiciones in actibus administrativis tunc tantum ad validitatem censentur adiectae, quoties per particulas si,

less" *(nisi)*, "provided that"*(dummodo)* or by another particle having the same meaning in the vernacular.

nisi, dummodo, vel in lingua vernacula per aliam eiusdem significationis exprimuntur.

ART. 1. *Procedure for Issuing Extra-judicial Decrees*

ART. 1. *De Procedura in Decretis Extra Iudicium Ferendis*

CAN. 1517 §1. Before issuing an extra-judicial decree, an authority is to seek out the necessary information and proofs, hear or consult those who should by law be heard or consulted, and also hear those whom the decree directly touches and especially those whose rights can be injured.

Can. 1517 §1. Antequam decretum extra iudicium fert, auctoritas necessarias notitias et probationes exquirat; iure audiendos vel consulendos audiat vel consulat; eos, quos directe decretum attingit ac praesertim eos, quorum iura laedi possunt, audiat.

§2. The authority is to disclose to the petitioner and also to one who legitimately opposes the information and proofs which can be known without danger of public or private harm, and present the arguments that are perhaps contrary while giving them the possibility to respond, even through an advocate, within the time-limit established by the authority itself.

§2. Petitori et etiam legitime contradicenti auctoritas notitias et probationes patefaciat, quae sine periculo publici vel privati damni cognosci possunt, et rationes forte contrarias ostendat data eis opportunitate respondendi, etiam per patronum, intra terminum ab ipsa auctoritate determinatum.

CAN. 1518 The authority is to issue a decree within sixty days from the receipt of the petition to obtain it, unless the particular law of one's own Church *sui iuris* has established other time limits. If this was not done and the petitioner asks again in writing for the decree, on the thirtieth day from the receipt of the petition, if even by then nothing has been done, the petition is considered as rejected as if the rejection took place on that day by decree, so that a recourse can be introduced against it.

Can. 1518 Auctoritas decretum intra sexaginta dies a recepta petitione ad decretum obtinendum computandos ferat, nisi ius particulare propriae Ecclesiae sui iuris alios terminos statuit; si vero hoc factum non est et petitor decretum iterum scripto petit, tricesimo die ab hac petitione recepta computando, si etiam tunc nihil factum est, petitio pro reiecta habetur ac si eo die reiectio per decretum facta sit ita, ut recursus adversus eam interponi possit.

CAN. 1519 §1. The person who issues the decree is to keep in mind and aim at what seems to lead best to the salvation of souls and the public good, observing the laws and legitimate customs, justice and equity.

Can. 1519 §1. Qui decretum fert, id prae oculis habeat et intendat, quod saluti animarum et bono publico maxime conducere videtur, servatis quidem legibus et legitimis consuetudinibus, iustitia et aequitate.

§2. The reasons are to be expressed, at least summarily, in the decree. However, if the danger of public or private harm precludes that the

§2. In decreto exprimantur saltem summarie motiva; si vero periculum publici vel privati damni obstat, ne motiva patefiant,

reasons be disclosed, they are to be expressed in a secret book and shown to the one who handles the recourse that is possibly introduced against the decree, if that person requests it.

CAN. 1520 §1. A decree has legal force after it has been intimated to the one to whom it is destined in the way that is safest according to the laws and conditions of places.

§2. If the danger of public or private harm precludes the text of the decree being given in writing, the ecclesiastical authority can order the decree to be read to the person to whom it is destined before two witnesses or a notary. After a written record of the proceedings has been prepared, all those present must sign it. Having completed these things, the decree is considered to have been intimated.

§3. However, if the person to whom the decree is destined has refused intimation, or having been summoned according to the norm of law to receive or hear the decree, did not appear without a just cause in the estimation of the author of the decree, or refused to sign the written record of the proceedings, the decree is considered to have been intimated.

ART. II. *The Execution of Administrative Acts*

CAN. 1521 The executor of an administrative act invalidly carries out his or her function before receiving the written mandate and verifying its authenticity and integrity, unless the authority who placed that act communicated previous notice of the mandate to the executor.

CAN. 1522 §1. The executor of an admin-

haec in libro secreto exprimantur atque ei, qui de recursu forte adversus decretum interposito videt, ostendantur, si ipse petit.

Can. 1520 §1. Decretum vim iuris habet, postquam ei, ad quem destinatur, intimatum est modo, qui secundum locorum leges et condiciones tutissimus est.

§2. Si periculum publici vel privati damni obstat, ne textus decreti scripto tradi possit, potest auctoritas ecclesiastica iubere decretum ei, ad quem destinatur, coram duobus testibus vel coram notario legi, processu verbali redacto ab omnibus praesentibus subscribendo; his peractis decretum pro intimato habetur.

§3. Si vero is, ad quem decretum destinatur, intimationem recusavit vel ad normam iuris vocatus ad decretum accipiendum vel audiendum sine iusta causa a decreti auctore perpendenda non comparuit vel processui verbali subscribere recusavit, decretum pro intimato habetur.

ART. II. *De Exsecutione Actuum Administrativorum*

Can. 1521 Exsecutor actus administrativi invalide suo munere fungitur, antequam mandatum scripto datum recepit eiusque authenticitatem et integritatem recognovit, nisi auctoritas, quae eundem actum posuit, praeviam notitiam circa mandatum cum eo communicavit.

Can. 1522 §1. Exsecutor actus admi-

1521: S.C.S. Off., decr. 24 aug. 1892; S. Paenit. Ap., 15 ian. 1894, ad II.

1522 §1: BENEDICTUS XIV, const. *Ad Apostolicae,* 25 feb. 1742, §5; ep. encycl. *Magnae Nobis,* 29 iun.

1748, §§1, 6–8, 10, 12; Ordo servandus in S. Congregationibus, Tribunalibus, Officiis Romanae Curiae, 29 sep. 1908, pars II, *Normae peculiares,* cap. III, n. 4.

istrative decree, to whom is entrusted merely the execution of the same act, cannot refuse this execution unless it clearly appears that the act itself is null or cannot be upheld for another grave cause, or the conditions attached to the administrative act have not been fulfilled. Nevertheless, if the execution of the administrative act seems inopportune due to the circumstances of person or place, the executor is to suspend the execution and to inform immediately the authority who placed the act.

§2. If in a rescript the granting of a favor is entrusted to an executor, it is up to the prudent judgment and conscience of the executor to grant or deny the favor.

CAN. 1523 The executor of an administrative act must proceed according to the norm of the mandate. If the executor did not fulfill the conditions attached to the mandate for the validity of the act, or did not observe the substantial form of proceeding, the execution is null.

CAN. 1524 The executor of an administrative act can, according to his or her prudent judgment, substitute another as executor unless substitution has been forbidden, the executor has been chosen for personal qualifications, or a substitute has been determined. In these cases, however, the executor may entrust the preparatory acts to another.

CAN. 1525 The executor's successor in office can also execute an administrative act unless the executor was chosen for personal qualifications.

CAN. 1526 The executor is permitted to execute an administrative act again if the executor has erred in any way in the execution of the same act.

nistrativi, cui committitur mera eiusdem actus exsecutio, hanc exsecutionem denegare non potest, nisi manifesto constat eundem actum esse nullum aut alia gravi de causa sustineri non posse aut condiciones actui administrativo appositas non esse impletas; si vero exsecutio actus administrativi ratione adiunctorum personae aut loci videtur inopportuna, exsecutor exsecutionem intermittat et statim certiorem faciat auctoritatem, quae actum posuit.

§2. Si in rescripto concessio gratiae exsecutori committitur, eius est de suo prudenti iudicio et conscientia gratiam concedere vel denegare.

Can. 1523 Exsecutor actus administrativi procedere debet ad mandati normam; si condiciones ad validitatem actus mandato appositas non implevit vel substantialem procedendi formam non servavit, exsecutio nulla est.

Can. 1524 Exsecutor actus administrativi potest alium de suo prudenti iudicio sibi substituere, nisi substitutio prohibita est aut electa est industria personae aut substituti persona determinata est; his in casibus vero exsecutori licet alii committere actus praeparatorios.

Can. 1525 Actus administrativus exsecutioni mandari potest etiam ab exsecutoris successore in officio, nisi electa est industria personae.

Can. 1526 Exsecutori licet actum administrativum iterum exsecutioni mandare, si quoquo modo in eiusdem actus exsecutione erravit.

1522 §2: Ordo servandus in S. Congregationibus, Tribunalibus, Officiis Romanae Curiae, 29 sep. 1908, pars II, *Normae peculiares,* cap. III, n. 3.

1523: S.C. de Prop. Fide, (C.G.), 18 apr. 1757.
1524: S.C.S. Off., litt. encycl. 20 feb. 1888, 5; decr. 14 dec. 1898.

ART. III. *Rescripts*

CAN. 1527 §1. The canons established for rescripts are valid also for the oral granting of favors unless it is otherwise clearly evident.

§2. A person is bound to prove a favor granted orally, whenever someone legitimately requests it.

CAN. 1528 A rescript can be requested for another even without the person's assent and has force before the person's acceptance, unless it is otherwise evident from the attached clauses.

CAN. 1529 §1. The concealment of truth in the request does not prevent a rescript from having force, provided that those things have been expressed which must be expressed for validity according to the style of the curia of the hierarch who granted the rescript.

§2. Nor does a statement of falsehood prevent a rescript from having force, provided that at least one proposed motivating reason is true.

CAN. 1530 §1. A favor denied by a higher authority cannot be validly granted by a lower authority, unless the higher authority has expressly consented.

§2. A favor denied by one authority cannot be validly granted by another equally competent authority or a higher authority if no mention of the denial is made in the petition.

1° Privileges

CAN. 1531 §1. A privilege is a favor given through a special act to the benefit of certain

ART. III. *De Rescriptis*

Can. 1527 §1. Quae in canonibus de rescriptis statuuntur, de concessionibus gratiarum vivae vocis oraculo quoque valent, nisi aliud manifesto constat.

§2. Gratiam oretenus concessam aliquis probare tenetur, quoties id legitime ab eo petitur.

Can. 1528 Rescriptum impetrari potest pro alio, etiam praeter eius assensum, et valet ante eiusdem acceptationem, nisi aliud ex appositis clausulis apparet.

Can. 1529 §1. Reticentia veri in precibus non obstat, quin rescriptum vim habeat, dummodo expressa sint, quae ad validitatem sunt exprimenda secundum stilum curiae Hierarchae, qui rescriptum concedit.

§2. Nec obstat expositio falsi, dummodo una saltem causa motiva proposita vera sit.

Can. 1530 §1. Gratia ab auctoritate superiore denegata non potest ab auctoritate inferiore valide concedi, nisi auctoritas superior expresse consensit.

§2. Gratia ab aliqua auctoritate denegata non potest valide ab alia auctoritate aeque competenti aut auctoritate superiore concedi nulla facta in petitione denegationis mentione.

1° De Privilegiis

Can. 1531 §1. Privilegium, scilicet gratia in favorem certarum personarum physi-

---

1527 §2: INNOCENTIUS X, const. *Cum sicut,* 14 maii 1648, §4, I "Decimoquarto;" Ordo servandus in S. Congregationibus Tribunalibus, Officiis Romanae Curiae, 29 sep. 1908, pars II, *Normae peculiares,* cap.

III, n. 2.
1529 §1: Trid., sess. XIII, *De ref.,* can. 5.
1529 §2: Trid., sess. XIII, *De ref.,* can. 5.

physical or juridic persons; it can be granted by the legislator and by the one to whom the legislator has granted this power.

§2. Centenary or immemorial possession induces the presumption that a privilege has been granted.

CAN. 1532 §1. A privilege is presumed to be perpetual.

§2. A privilege ceases:

1° if it is personal, through the death of the person to whom it was granted;

2° if it is real or local, through the complete destruction of the thing or place;

3° through the lapse of the time period or through the completion of the number of cases for which it was granted;

4° if in the judgment of the competent authority circumstances are so changed in the course of time that it has become harmful or its use illicit.

§3. A local privilege revives if the place is restored within fifty years.

CAN. 1533 §1. No privilege ceases through renunciation unless the competent authority has accepted the renunciation.

§2. Any physical person can renounce a privilege granted only in that person's favor.

§3. A physical person cannot validly renounce a privilege granted to some juridic person or granted in consideration of the dignity of a place or of a thing. Nor is a juridic person free to renounce a privilege granted to it if the renunciation brings disadvantage to the Church or to others.

CAN. 1534 A privilege which is not burdensome to others does not cease through nonuse or contrary use. If it is to the disadvantage of others, however, it is lost if legitimate prescription or tacit renunciation takes place.

carum vel iuridicarum per specialem actum facta, concedi potest a legislatore et ab eo, cui legislator hanc potestatem concessit.

§2. Possessio centenaria vel immemorabilis praesumptionem inducit concessi privilegii.

Can. 1532 §1. Privilegium praesumitur perpetuum.

§2. Privilegium cessat:

1° si est personale, per exstinctionem personae, cui concessum est;

2° si est reale vel locale, per absolutum rei vel loci interitum;

3° elapso tempore vel expleto numero casuum, pro quibus concessum est;

4° si temporis progressu rerum adiuncta iudicio auctoritatis competentis mutantur ita, ut noxium evaserit aut eius usus illicitus fiat.

§3. Privilegium locale, si locus intra quinquaginta annos restituitur, reviviscit.

Can. 1533 §1. Nullum privilegium per renuntiationem cessat, nisi haec ab auctoritate competenti acceptata est.

§2. Privilegio in sui dumtaxat favorem concesso quaevis persona physica renuntiare potest.

§3. Privilegio concesso alicui personae iuridicae aut ratione dignitatis loci vel rei persona physica valide renuntiare non potest; nec ipsi personae iuridicae integrum est privilegio sibi concesso renuntiare, si renuntiatio cedit in Ecclesiae aliorumve praeiudicium.

Can. 1534 Per non usum vel per usum contrarium privilegium aliis non onerosum non cessat; si vero privilegium in aliorum gravamen cedit, amittitur, si accedit legitima praescriptio aut tacita renuntiatio.

CAN. 1535 A person who abuses the power given by a privilege is to be warned by the hierarch. If the person gravely abuses the privilege and the warning has been in vain, the hierarch is to deprive the person of the privilege which he himself has granted. If the privilege was granted by a higher authority, the hierarch is bound to notify that authority.

Can. 1535 Qui abutitur potestate sibi ex privilegio data, ab Hierarcha moneatur; graviter abutentem ac frustra monitum Hierarcha privet privilegio, quod ipse concessit; si vero privilegium concessum est ab auctoritate superiore, eandem Hierarcha certiorem facere tenetur.

2° Dispensations

2° De Dispensationibus

CAN. 1536 §1. A dispensation, that is, the relaxation of a merely ecclesiastical law in a special case, can be granted only for a just and reasonable cause, after taking into account the circumstances of the case and the gravity of the law from which dispensation is given; otherwise the dispensation is illicit and, unless it is given by the legislator himself or by a higher authority, it is also invalid.

§2. The spiritual good of the Christian faithful is a just and reasonable cause.

§3. In the case of doubt concerning the sufficiency of the cause, a dispensation is granted licitly and validly.

Can. 1536 §1. Dispensatio, scilicet legis mere ecclesiasticae in casu speciali relaxatio, concedi potest tantum iusta ac rationabili de causa habita ratione adiunctorum casus et gravitatis legis, a qua dispensatur; secus dispensatio illicita et, nisi ab ipso legislatore aut ab auctoritate superiore data est, etiam invalida est.

§2. Bonum spirituale christifidelium est iusta et rationabilis causa.

§3. In dubio de sufficientia causae dispensatio licite et valide conceditur.

CAN. 1537 Laws are not subject to dispensation to the extent that they determine those things which are essentially constitutive of juridic institutes or acts; nor are procedural and penal laws subject to dispensation.

Can. 1537 Dispensationi obnoxiae non sunt leges, quatenus determinant ea, quae institutorum aut actuum iuridicorum essentialiter sunt constitutiva, nec leges processuales et poenales.

CAN. 1538 §1. An eparchial bishop, whenever he judges that it contributes to their spiritual good, is able to dispense in special cases the Christian faithful, over whom he exercises power according to the norm of law, from laws of the common law and laws of the particular law

Can. 1538 §1. Episcopus eparchialis dispensare potest tam a legibus iuris communis quam a legibus iuris particularis propriae Ecclesiae sui iuris in casu speciali christifideles, in quos ad normam iuris potestatem suam exercet, quoties id ad eorum

---

1536 §1: Paulus VI, litt. ap. *Episcopalis potestatis,* 2 maii 1967, III.

1536 §2: Vat. II, decr. *Christus Dominus,* 8, b); Paulus VI, litt. ap. *Episcopalis potestatis,* 2 maii 1967, VII.

1537: Paulus VI, litt. ap. *Episcopalis potestatis,* 2 maii 1967, III.

1538 §1: Vat. II, decr. *Christus Dominus,* 8, b); Paulus VI, litt. ap. *Episcopalis potestatis,* 2 maii 1967, III.

of his own Church *sui iuris,* unless a reservation has been made by the authority which issued the laws.

§2. If it is difficult to approach the authority to which the dispensation has been reserved and, at the same time, there is danger of grave harm in delay, every hierarch is able to dispense in special cases the Christian faithful over whom he exercises power according to the norm of law, provided that it concerns a dispensation which that authority grants under the same circumstances, with due regard for can. 396.

CAN. 1539 Even when outside his territory, one who has the power to dispense is able to exercise it with respect to his subjects even though they are absent from the territory and, unless the contrary is expressly established, also with respect to travelers actually present in the territory, and with respect to himself as well.

bonum spirituale conferre iudicat, nisi ab auctoritate, quae leges tulit, reservatio facta est.

§2. Si difficile est adire auctoritatem, cui dispensatio reservata est, et simul in mora est periculum gravis damni, omnis Hierarcha in casu speciali dispensare potest christifideles, in quos ad normam iuris potestatem suam exercet, dummodo agatur de dispensatione, quam eadem auctoritas in eisdem adiunctis concedit, firmo can. 396.

Can. 1539 Qui habet potestatem dispensandi, eam exercere potest, etiam extra territorium exsistens, in subditos, etsi a territorio absentes, atque, nisi contrarium expresse statuitur, in peregrinos quoque in territorio actu degentes necnon erga seipsum.

1538 §2: S.C. de Prop. Fide, decr. 13 apr. 1807, VIII; S.C. pro Doctr. Fidei, decl. 26 iun. 1972, III.

1539: Pius XII, m.p. *Cleri sanctitati,* 2 iun. 1957, can. 142 §3; S.C. pro Eccl. Orient., resp. 24 iul. 1948.

TITLE XXX. PRESCRIPTION AND THE COMPUTATION OF TIME

CHAPTER I. Prescription

CAN. 1540 The Church receives prescription as it is in the civil law, unless common law establishes otherwise; prescription is a means of acquiring or losing a subjective right as well as of freeing oneself from obligations.

CAN. 1541 No prescription is valid unless it is based in good faith not only at the beginning but through the entire course of time required for prescription, without prejudice to can. 1152.

CAN. 1542 The following are not subject to prescription:

1° rights and obligations that are of the divine law;

2° rights that can be obtained from apostolic privilege alone;

3° rights and obligations that directly regard the spiritual life of the Christian faithful;

4° the certain and undoubted boundaries of ecclesiastical territories;

5° obligations and commitments concerning the celebration of the Divine Liturgy;

6° the canonical provision of an office which, in accord with the norm of law, requires the exercise of a sacred order;

7° the right of visitation and the obligation of

CAPUT I. De Praescriptione

CAN. 1540 Praescriptionem tamquam iuris subiectivi acquirendi vel amittendi necnon ab obligationibus se liberandi modum, prout est in iure civili, Ecclesia recipit, nisi aliud iure communi statuitur.

CAN. 1541 Nulla valet praescriptio, nisi bona fide nititur non solum initio, sed toto decursu temporis ad praescriptionem requisiti salvo can. 1152.

CAN. 1542 Praescriptioni obnoxia non sunt:

1° iura et obligationes, quae sunt legis divinae;

2° iura, quae obtineri possunt ex solo privilegio apostolico;

3° iura et obligationes, quae vitam spiritualem christifidelium directe respiciunt;

4° fines certi et indubii circumscriptionum ecclesiasticarum;

5° obligationes et onera celebrationem Divinae Liturgiae respicientia;

6° provisio canonica officii, quod ad normam iuris exercitium ordinis sacri requirit;

7° ius visitationis et obligatio oboedien-

1540: Pius XII, m.p. *Postquam Apostolicis Litteris,* 9 feb. 1952, can. 246. - Constantinop. IV, can. 18. ▲ Instit. 2, 6, pr. et 1; D. 39, 3, 2; C. 2, 19 (20), 3; 7, 33, 7; 38, 2.

1541: Pius XII, m.p. *Postquam Apostolicis Litteris,* 9 feb. 1952, can. 250. - Chalc. can. 17; Quinisext. can. 25. ▲ C. 3, 32, 4; 7, 33, 1 et 6.

obedience, in such a way that persons in the Church could not be visited by any ecclesiastical authority and would no longer be subject to any authority.

tiae ita, ut personae in Ecclesia a nulla auctoritate ecclesiastica visitari possint et nulli auctoritati iam subsint.

CHAPTER II. **Computation of Time**

CAPUT II. **De Temporis Supputatione**

CAN. 1543 Unless the law expressly provides otherwise, time is to be computed according to the norm of the following canons.

CAN. 1543 Nisi aliter iure expresse cavetur, tempus supputetur ad normam canonum, qui sequuntur.

CAN. 1544 §1. Continuous time is understood as that which undergoes no interruption.

CAN. 1544 §1. Tempus continuum intellegitur, quod nullam patitur interruptionem.

§2. Useful time is understood as that which a person has to exercise or to pursue a right, so that it does not run for a person who is unaware or for one who cannot act.

§2. Tempus utile intellegitur, quod ita ius suum exercenti aut persequenti competit, ut ignoranti aut illi, qui agere non potest, non currat.

CAN. 1545 §1. In law, a day is understood as a period consisting of 24 continuous hours and begins at midnight; a week is a period of 7 days; a month is a period of 30 days, and a year is a period of 365 days unless a month and a year are said to be taken as they are in the calendar.

CAN. 1545 §1. In iure dies intellegitur spatium constans ex 24 horis continuo supputandis et incipit a media nocte; hebdomada spatium 7 dierum, mensis spatium 30, annus spatium 365 dierum, nisi mensis et annus dicuntur sumendi, prout sunt in calendario.

§2. If time is continuous, a month and a year must always be taken as they are in the calendar.

§2. Si tempus est continuum, mensis et annus semper sumendi sunt, prout sunt in calendario.

CAN. 1546 §1. The day from which the calculation begins is not computed in the total unless its beginning coincides with the beginning of the day or the law expressly provides otherwise.

CAN. 1546 §1. Dies, a quo calculus incipit, non computatur in termino, nisi huius initium coincidit cum initio diei aut aliter expresse iure cavetur.

1542: Pius XII, m.p. *Postquam Apostolicis Litteris*, 9 feb. 1952, can. 247 nn. 1–5, 7. - Chalc. can. 17; Carth. cann. 5, 119; Quinisext. can. 25. ▲ C. 1, 3, 45 (46), (11–12).

1543: Pius XII, m.p. *Postquam Apostolicis Litteris*, 9 feb. 1952, can. 321.

1544 §1: Pius XII, m.p. *Postquam Apostolicis Litteris*, 9 feb. 1952, can. 325. ▲ D. 48, 5, 12 (11), (5); C. 7, 40, 2, (11); Basilic. 50, 15, 2.

1544 §2: Pius XII, m.p. *Postquam Apostolicis Lit-*

teris, 9 feb. 1952, can. 325.

1545 §1: Pius XII, m.p. *Postquam Apostolicis Litteris*, 9 feb. 1952, can. 322 §§1–2. ▲ D. 2, 12, 8; Basilic. 7, 17, 8.

1545 §2: Pius XII, m.p. *Postquam Apostolicis Litteris*, 9 feb. 1952, can. 324 §§1–2. ▲ D. 40, 7, 4, (5); 50, 16, 98 et 132 et 134.

1546 §1: Pius XII, m.p. *Postquam Apostolicis Litteris*, 9 feb. 1952, can. 324 §3 nn. 2–3. ▲ D. 4, 4, 3, (3); 28, 1, 5; 40, 1, 1; 44, 7, 6.

§2. The day to which the calculation is directed is computed in the total which, if the time consists of one or more months or years, one or more weeks, is reached at the end of the last day of the same number or, if a month lacks a day of the same number, at the end of the last day of the month.

§2. Dies, ad quem calculus dirigitur, computatur in termino, qui, si tempus constat ex uno vel pluribus mensibus autannis, ex una vel pluribus hebdomadibus, finitur elapso ultimo die eiusdem numeri aut, si mensis die eiusdem numeri caret, elapso ultimo die mensis.

1546 §2: Pius XII, m.p. *Postquam Apostolicis Litteris*, 9 feb. 1952, can. 324 §3 nn. 3–4.

INDEX

TABLES OF CORRESPONDING CANONS

APPENDICES

INDEX

References are to specific canons.

A

abatement *of a trial:* when it takes place, 1201; takes effect by the law itself against all persons and must be declared *ex officio,* 1202; effects regarding procedural acts, 1203; regarding expenses of an abated trial, 1204; renunciation of a trial has the same effects for the acts renounced as the a. of the trial, 1206; at the appellate grade, it produces *res iudicata,* 1322. 3°.

abduction as an impediment to matrimony, 806; as a delict, 1451; *see* kidnapping.

abortion *procuring a completed abortion:* punished with penalties established for homicide, 1450 §2; a sin whose absolution is reserved to the eparchial bishop, 728 §2; an impediment to receive or exercise sacred orders, 762 §1. 4°, 763. 2°, 766, 767 §1. 2°, 768 §1–2; concerning extinction of penal action, 1152 §1. 2°; *see* fetus.

abrogation of prior law, 1502 §1, 1503; *see* revocation;

which laws are abrogated by the Code, 6 §1; concerning agreements with nations, 4.

absence of the patriarch, 93, 142 §1; of the eparchial bishop, 204, 215 §1, 537 §2; of the pastor or parochial vicar, 292 §2–3, 302 §4;

of a spouse not sufficient to declare presumed death, 1383 §2; of a deacon in case of necessity for administering baptism, 677 §2; of an elector not convoked, 948 §2;

in institutes of consecrated life: from novitiate, 457 §2, 523 §1; from a monastery or house, 478, 550; of councillors, 500 §1;

in procedural law: of the promotor of justice or defender of the bond, 1097; of a notary, 1101 §1; of a witness, 1238; of a party, 1272–1275, 1304 §1. 6°; of one accused of a delict, 1078, 1475 §2;

executive power or power to dispense concerning subjects absent from territory, 986, 1539;

concerning laws, by which travellers are not bound while absent from their own territory, 1491 §3. 1°.

absolution *sacramental:* its necessity, 720 §1; when and under what conditions it can be imparted to several penitents at the same time, 720 §2, 721; in danger of death, 725, 730; its reservation, 727–729, 1450 §2, 1456 §1, 1457; of an accomplice, 730, 1457; of one who has falsely denounced a confessor, 731; its simulation constitutes a delict, 1443; *see* penance (as a sacrament)

in procedural law, 1291 §4, 1481 §1, 1482, 1484 §2.

abstinence *from certain actions in the case of:* clerics, 382; members of an elective synaxis, 445; tribunal officials, 1106, 1107 §2; the executor of a sentence, 1341 §2; a removed pastor, 1396 §1

regarding the Christian faithful who have abstained from the reception of the sacraments, 293; regarding feast days and days of penance, 881 §4, 882; when one may abstain from imposing a penalty, 1403 §1, 1409 §1. 1°–2°, 1415.

abuses in religious institutes, 417; of a judge and other tribunal officers, 1115; of power given by a privilege, 1535; of power, office, ministry or other function, as a delict, 1464 §1; of procurators in litigation and of advocates, 1146, 1147

vigilance of the eparchial bishop concerning a. in ecclesiastical discipline, 201 §2; vigilance of the competent authority concerning a. in associations, 577 §1; *see* vigilance.

academic degrees right of lay persons to pursue, 404 §2; of seminary teachers, 340 §1; in ecclesiastical universities or faculties, 648, 650; privation not possible, 1430 §2; *see* doctorate, licentiate.

acceptance *see* reception

of election: 939. 2°, 957 §2–3, 958, 959 §1, 964 §2; of the Roman Pontiff, 44 §1; of the patriarch, 74, 75; of the major archbishop, 153 §1–2; of a bishop, 184 §2, 185 §2

concerning postulation: *see* admission

of resignation of office: not required for the Roman Pontiff, 44 §2; of the patriarch, 126 §2; of the eparchial bishop, 210 §3, 211 §1; of a bishop coadjutor or auxiliary bishop, 218; of the eparchial administrator, 231 §1; of the eparchial finance officer during a vacancy in the eparchial see, 232 §2; of a pastor, 297 §2, 1392; of superiors in monasteries, 444 §3; of officers of the ordinary tribunal of the patriarchal Church, 1063 §3

of resignation of delegated power of governance, 992 §1; of certain gifts by juridic persons, 1016 §3; concerning pious wills, causes and foundations, 1044, 1046 §1, 1048 §2–3, 1049, 1052 §4; of public vows, 889 §4; of matrimonial rights and obligations, 818. 2°; of fitting penance, 718; of penalties, 1426 §2, 1486 §2; of gifts or promises in penal law, 1463; of the renunciation of a privilege, 1533 §1

rescript has force before acceptance, 1528

in procedural law: of prohibited gifts, 1114, 1463; of the function of arbiter, 1173, 1178; of the recusal of arbiters, 1175; of the renunciation of a trial or the acts of a process, 1205 §3, 1475 §2; of a matrimonial case, 1362, 1381.

access judicial, 1263–1264.

accomplice *in a sin against chastity:* cannot validly be absolved in the sacrament of penance, 730; attempted absolution constitutes a sin, whose absolution is reserved to the Apostolic See, 728 §1. 2°; attempted absolution is a delict to be punished by major excommunication, 1457, 1457

how an a. in a delict is to be punished, 1417

in the death of a spouse invalidly attempt marriage between themselves, 807 §2.

account of receipts and expenditures, regarding the finance council, 263 §5; witnesses are to give testimony orally and are not to read written materials unless they are computations and accounts, 1247; accounts to be rendered before the execution of the sentence, 1339

taking into account: the common good, 26 §1, 140; ministries and districts of the eparchy, 268; persons, associations, initiatives, 273 §2; nationality, language, ascription to a Church *sui iuris* or other clearly distinguishing factor, 280 §1; the preceding formation of seminary students, 344 §4; the order or hierarchy of the truths of Catholic doctrine, 348 §2; the special importance of the liturgy, 350 §3; the particular qualities and character of each people regarding the missions, 592 §1; the special character of the Eastern Churches regarding the catechetical directory, 621 §2; the level of communion with the Catholic Church, 670 §1; the penitent's condition and readiness for conversion, 732 §1; other Churches *sui iuris* regarding feast days and days of penance, 880 §2; rights, customs, circumstances, 1022 §2; procedural law, 1176 §2; the incidental case in settling the princi-

pal case, 1269 §2; the circumstances of the case and the seriousness of the law regarding dispensations, 1536 §1.

accumulation of offices, 942, 114 §3, 447 §2, 516 §2, 1086 §1; of actions and exceptions, 1155, 1156; of delicts and penalties, 1409 §1. 3°–4°, 1425; of cases by reason of connection, 1081; regarding causes for petitioning at the appellate grade, 1320 §1; touching cases for appeal, 1306, 1310. 2° and 4°; of headings of nullity of marriage at the appellate grade, 1369.

accusation of marriage, 1361 §1; of the validity of sacred ordination, 1385, 1386 §1

in penal trial, 1472 §1.

accused of a delict cannot validly be admitted to novitiate, 450. 3°; can be brought to trial in the place where the delict was committed, 1078; concerning the advocate of the a., 1139 §2, 1474; must be heard before a decision on penal procedure, 1469 §3; what the hierarch can do concerning the a. while a penal process is pending, 1473; is not bound to confess a delict nor can the a. be administered an oath, 1471 §2; to be present for oral discussion, 1477 §1; has the right to speak last in the discussion of the case, 1478; must accept the renunciation of a trial for validity, 1475 §2; regarding absolution, 1482, 1484 §2; right of defence in the imposition of penalties by decree, 1486 §1. 1°; concerning the oral discussion before the imposition of penalties by decree, 1486 §1. 2°; *see* respondent

regarding: the extinction of an action, 1152 §1, 1153 §1.

acknowledgement of receipt regarding the intimation of judicial acts, 1192 §1.

acquired right (also **acquired goods**) granted by the Apostolic See remain intact unless expressly revoked, 5; acts injuring an a.r. are to be strictly interpreted, 1512 §2; an act injuring an a.r. lacks effect unless a derogating clauses is added, 1515; when an a.r. arising from the election of a patriarch is admitted, 74; is not to be injured in dispensation from vows, 893 §1; regarding goods acquired by a monastery because of a departing member, 488 §4; in collegial acts, if the a.r. of individuals is affected, the consent of each one is required, 924. 2°; regarding the function of rector of a church, 309; on the disposal of the goods of a juridic person, 922 §1. 5°, 929, 930; in removal from office, 974 §1; in transfer of a pastor, 1400.

acquisition of temporal goods general canons, 1010–1021; right of the Church, 1007; capable sub-

garding goods, 468 §3; against administrators and those who alienate temporal goods, 1040; concerning the citation, 1191 §3, 1194. 2°; concerning a complaint of nullity, 1303 §3; is not given on a promise of marriage, except for a reparation of damages, 782 §2; against a sentence, 1302–1321; *see* appeal, complaint of nullity.

actuary in the synod for the election of a patriarch, 66 §2, 71 §1; in elections, 955 §5; in the case of someone unable or unwilling to sign judicial acts, 1132.

administration of justice, *see* moderator (general moderator for the administration of justice); regarding instruction of seminary students in parish a., 352 §2; of ecclesiastical universities or faculties, 650; regarding the prohibition of one elected from becoming involved in the a. of office, 959 §2; forbidden to clerics, as an impediment for receiving sacred orders, 762 §1. 7°.

administration of temporal goods general norms, 1022–1033; right of the Church, 1007; capable subjects, 1009 §1, 423, 558 §1, 567 §1, 582; how this capacity can be restricted in religious institutes, 423; regarding civil law, 1504, 1020 §2, 1027, 1030. 1°, 1034, 1040, 1042, 1540; ordinary a. and acts exceeding it, 1024 §§1–2, 1171. 1°, 1205 §2; to whom it pertains in juridic persons, 1023; of a juridic person which lacks members, 926 §§1 and 3; in pious causes, 1044

of a patriarchal Church, 122 §§1 and 3–4; subject immediately to the patriarch in certain institutes, 90, 486 §2

of an eparchy, 262 §§ 3–4; during the vacancy of the eparchial see, to whom it devolves regarding certain goods, 232 §1; its suitable ordering on the part of the hierarch, 1022 §2; forbidden to clerics regarding the impediment for receiving sacred orders, 762 §1. 7°

vigilance regarding: of the patriarch, 97; of the eparchial bishop, 1022 §1; of the hierarch, regarding pious wills, 1045 §2; of the eparchial finance officer, 262 §3; of the protopresbyter, 278 §1. 3°

care of the rector of a church regarding, 309

in institutes of consecrated life: 423–425, 447 §1; 516 §1, 558 §2, 567 §2; of a religious who becomes patriarch, bishop or exarch, 431 §3. 1°–2°; its cession by a novice before temporary profession, 525 §2, 529 §4, 465

forum in cases regarding, 1079. 1°; regarding an arbitration agreement, 1171. 1°; regarding an action against one who does not have free administration of things under dispute, 1191 §3

in associations of the Christian faithful, 582

bad a. as a cause for the removal of a pastor, 1390. 5°;

see administrator of temporal goods, temporal goods.

administrative authority highest in a Church *sui iuris: see* highest authority.

administrator of a juridic person regarding offerings made to it, 1016 §2; regarding the appointment of an a. in aggregates of things, 926 §3; what must be done in pious wills, if the fulfillment of the obligations has become impossible through no fault of the a., 1054 §2; the right of seeking indemnity against the a. in case of abatement in a trial, 1202; regarding the renunciation of a trial, 1205 §2.

administrator of a metropolitan Church *sui iuris* notion, 173 §1. 1°; his power, 173 §1. 2°.

administrator of a parish when constituted, 298, 1398 §3; who assumes the governance of the parish before his appointment, 300 §1; rights and obligations, 299.

administrator of a patriarchal Church notion, 127; rights and obligations, 128–131; regarding a synod for electing a patriarch, 128. 3°, 65 §1, 70, 130 §3; regarding the granting of dimissorial letters, 750 §1. 2° and §2.

administrator of an eparchy only one to be chosen or appointed, 225 §1; requirements, 227; conditions for validity, 227 §2; when, how and by whom a new a. is to be constituted, 231 §3; if he was eparchial finance officer, another finance officer must be chosen, 225 §2; rights and obligations, 228, 229, 230. 1°; regarding a coadjutor bishop, who obtains his office by the law itself, 222; the rights and obligations of a bishop translated to another see, 223. 1°; auxiliary bishops under his authority are to exercise the powers of protosyncelli or syncelli which they had when the see was occupied, 224 §3; the eparchial finance officer exercises office under his authority, 232 §1; when he can remove a chancellor or notaries from office, 255; when he can open the secret archives or safe, 260 §2; cannot erect a parish in the Church of a religious institute or a society of common life according to the manner of religious, 282 §1; when he can appoint pastors, 286, 286; when he can validly ascribe a cleric to the eparchy or dismiss him from it, 363. 2°; cannot erect associations of the Christian faithful, 575 §1. 1°; regarding the granting of dimissorial letters, 750 §1. 2° and §2; regarding the appointment of a

canonical visitation of the eparchy can take place through him, 205 §1; attends the eparchial assembly, 143 §1. 2°, 238 §1. 1°; to be consulted by the eparchial bishop in preference to others, 215 §3; can be delegated to reduce obligations for celebrating the Divine Liturgy, 1052 §6; regarding vacancy of the see, 221. 2°, 224 §3;

see bishop, titular bishop.

aversion against a pastor as a reason for removal, 1390. 3°.

B

bad faith blocks general dispensation from impediments to receive or exercise sacred orders, 768 §1; blocks general remission of penalties, 1425;

regarding one who maliciously raises peremptory exceptions in a trial, 1121 §1.

ballot in elections, 955 §4, 956 §1; in the election of the patriarch, 72 §1; in meetings of the synod of bishops of the patriarchal Church, 107; in the council of hierarchs, 166 §1; in drawing up the list of candidates for the episcopacy, 182 §3; in the election of bishops, 183 §§3–4, 186 §§2–3; secrecy regarding it, 71 §2, 182 §3, 186 §2; *see* vote.

baptism notion, 675 §1;

effects: incorporation into Christ and the Church, 7 §1, 675 §1; cannot be repeated, 672 §1; regarding capacity for other sacraments, 675 §2; as a sacrament of Christian initiation, 290 §2, 694, 695 §1, 696 §1, 697, 710; regarding ascription to a Church *sui iuris,* 29 §1, 30, 683; regarding subjection to ecclesiastical laws, 1490; regarding vocation to the Christian life, 20; how, by virtue of b., the Christian faithful participate in the Divine Liturgy, 699 §3; regarding absolution of sins committed after b., 718; regarding impediments to receiving or exercising sacred orders, 762 §2; regarding matrimonial impediments, 803 §§1–2, 811; regarding dissolution of the bond of marriage, 854–860; regarding ecclesiastical burial, 876 §§1–2;

celebration: 675 §1, 683; in case of necessity, 676; in another's territory, 678 §1; its place, 687;

minister: priest, pastor, 290 §2, 677 §1, 678; in case of necessity, 677 §2;

subject: capable of receiving, 679; infant, 681, 686 §1; one no longer an infant, 682; regarding an aborted fetus, 680;

regarding the recording, proof, baptismal register and certificate of baptism: 37, 296 §§1–2, 342 §2, 470, 535 §2, 689–691, 695 §2, 769 §1. 1°, 775, 784, 841 §2;

see baptized, sponsor.

baptized *see* Christian faithful.

bargain cannot be done by a procurator in litigation without a special mandate, 1143; for an excessive profit or for a share of the object under litigation forbidden to procurators and advocates under penalties, and is null, 1146 §1.

benefits of education and instruction should be extended to all, 630 §1.

betrothal *see* engagement.

bishop successor of the apostles, 42; communion with the Roman Pontiff, 45 §2; as a cooperator with the Roman Pontiff, 46 §1; member of the college of bishops, 49; authentic doctor and teacher of the faith, 596, 600, 605; minister and preacher of the word of God, 608, 610 §1; called an eparchial b. or a titular b., 178, 179; in what order of clerics he is constituted, 325, 326; delicts against, 1445 §1; burial in a church, 874 §3;

suitability of a candidate, 180; election or appointment, 85 §2, 149, 168, 181–186, 102 §2, 110 §3; canonical provision, 86 §1. 1° and §3, 187 §1; profession of faith and promise of obedience, 187 §2; ordination and enthronement, 75, 133 §1. 1°, 159. 1°, 187 §2, 188 §1, 745, 746; a religious who becomes a b., 431 §§2–3; emeritus, 211 §2, 218, 431 §2. 2°;

attends: an ecumenical council, 52 §1; the synod of bishops of the patriarchal Church, 102 §§1–2, 104, 105, 150 §1; the patriarchal assembly, 143 §1. 1°–2° and §2; the council of hierarchs, 164–166 §1; regarding the permanent synod, 115, 116 §§1–2, 121, 127;

obligations and rights: commemoration in the Divine Liturgy of the Roman Pontiff, the patriarch, the metropolitan, the eparchial bishop, 91, 135, 161, 209 §2; relationship to the patriarch, 56, 78 §1, 82 §2, 88; relationship to the metropolitan of a metropolitan Church *sui iuris,* 157 §1, 159. 1°, 161–163; if a protosyncellus or syncellus, he does not cease from office while the see is vacant, 224 §1. 1°; has the right to preach the word of God everywhere, 610 §1; has the task of answering the questions concerning the meaning of life, 601; confects holy myron, 693; regarding the Divine Eucharist, 699 §1, 700 §2, 701; can administer the sacrament of penance everywhere, 722 §2; regarding sacred ordinations, 743, 744–747, 749, 752, 770, 774; delicts with regard to sacred ordinations, 1459; regarding the consecration of a church, 871 §2; must be informed about the vacancy of the patriarchal see, 128. 1°;

with regard reception into the Catholic Church of a non-Catholic b., 898 §1, 899;

in penal cases is judged by the Roman Pontiff, 1060 §1. 2°; tribunal in contentious cases, 1060 §2, 1062 §3; to be heard as a witness in a place selected by him, 1239 §2; to strive to avoid litigation or to resolve it peacefully, 1103 §1.

bishop of the patriarchal curia election and function, 87, 114 §1, 102 §2, 110 §3; as administrator of the patriarchal Church during a vacancy of the patriarchal see, 127–131; when the bishops of the patriarchal curia take the place of the permanent synod, 100;

their counsel required: for appointment of an eparchial administrator, 220. 3°; for appointment of an eparchial finance officer during a vacancy of the see, 232 §3;

see bishop, titular bishop.

blasphemy penalty for, 1448 §1.

blessed veneration of b. in public worship, 885; norms to be followed in the causes for canonization of the servants of God, 1057.

blessing of marriage, 290 §2, 302 §2, 787, 789, 796 §2, 828–831§1, 832 §§2–3, 833, 834 §2, 840 §1, 841 §§1 and 3; of oil in the anointing of the sick, 741; of a church, 869, 871 §2; of a cemetery or a grave, 874 §2; of good books, 652 §1, 661 §3, 663 §1; of sacred things destined for worship, 1018.

body *see* cremation.

bond of profession of faith, sacraments and ecclesiastical governance regarding full communion of the baptized with the Catholic Church, 8; of charity regarding the union among clerics of any Church *sui iuris,* 379;

of marriage: the sacramental b. of a consummated marriage can be dissolved by no human power and for no reason other than death, 853; one bound by it is not suitable for the episcopate, 180. 3°; one bound by it cannot validly be chosen or appointed to the office of eparchial administrator, 227 §2; when another marriage is attempted, an impediment arises to receive or exercise sacred orders, 762 §1. 3°, 763. 2°, 767 §1. 2°; those bound by it invalidly attempt marriage, 802 §1; cases about it are reserved to a collegiate tribunal, 1084 §1. 2°; regarding the procedure for presumed death of a spouse, 1383 §1; *see* case (marriage), dissolution, separation;

of sacred ordination: cases about it are reserved to a collegiate tribunal, 1084 §1. 1°;

sacred b. of religious profession, 450. 7°, 502; sacred b. in an institute of consecrated life in which religious vows are not taken, 450. 7°, 554 §1, 555, 562 §4, 563 §1. 1°, 564, 568 §2;

defender of the bond, 243 §2, 1063 §2, 1096–1100, 1105, 1106 §2, 1214, 1242, 1286 §3, 1289, 1295 §1, 1307 §1, 1309, 1317 §2, 1364 §1, 1368 §2, 1372 §1, 1373 §1, 1374, 1383 §4, *see* defender of the bond;

clerics, religious, and members of a society of common life according to the manner of religious are forbidden to post b. without consulting the eparchial bishop or major superior, 385 §3, 427, 561.

books eparchial bishop to promote good b., 652 §1; norms concerning b. also apply to any other writings or messages intended for public distribution, 654; whose permission or approval is required to publish b., 657 §§1–3, 662; what is required for b. approved by one local hierarch to be used in another eparchy, 663 §2; regarding censors of b., 664 §1; which b. may not be displayed, sold or distributed in churches, 665 §1; protection of the law regarding b., 666;

require ecclesiastical approval: liturgical b. and their translations, 656 §1, 657 §§1–2; in catechetical instruction, catechisms and other writings and their translations, 658 §1; in catechetical instruction, b. dealing with faith and morals, 658 §2;

require ecclesiastical permission: b. of prayers or devotions, 656 §2;

liturgical books: who may approve them or their translations, 657 §§1–2; regarding new editions, 657 §3; patrimonial ritual to be preserved in them, 40 §1, 657 §4; prescripts to be observed regarding liturgical b., 3, 75, 91, 92 §2, 135, 161, 162, 200, 209, 278 §1. 3°, 309, 403 §1, 462 §2, 473 §1, 674, 683, 699 §§2–3, 701, 704, 710, 714 §1, 742, 836;

concerning pious foundations to be kept by the rector of the church, 1051 §2;

of receipts and expenditures must be kept by an administrator of temporal goods, 1028 §2. 6°;

secret book about recourse against administrative decrees in certain cases, 1519 §2.

boys regarding fostering vocations in families and schools, 329 §1. 1°; religious are subject to the power of the local hierarch in the religious and moral education of b., 415 §1.

bread *eucharistic:* in the Divine Liturgy must be of pure wheat and recently made, 706; is to be prepared according to the norm of the law of each Church *sui iuris,* 707 §1.

budget to be prepared annually by the finance council, 263 §5.

burden of each Church to respond to questions on the meaning of life and to provide for Christian solutions of problems, 601; of approaching the competent authority as soon as possible after dispensation by a confessor from an impediment to exercise a sacred order, 767 §3; no b. beyond what is necessary is to be imposed on non-Catholics who ask to be received into full communion with the Catholic Church, 896;

of proof: rests on the one who asserts, 1207 §1; in delegation it rests on the one who claims to be delegated, 983 §1; when it ceases after the judicial confession of one party, 1217 §1; a person who has a favorable presumption of law is freed from it, which then falls to the other party, 1266;

see obligations.

C

call the coadjutor and auxiliary bishop are called to share in the concerns of the eparchial bishop, 215 §4; of certain persons who are not bishops to an ecumenical council, 52 §2; to the synod of bishops of the patriarchal Church, 102 §1, 104 §1; to the council of hierarchs, 164 §1, 165 §1; of presbyters to administer the sacrament of penance in the parish, 289 §2; of a non-Catholic priest to bless a marriage entered into before witnesses alone, 832 §2;

in a trial: see summons.

calumny the delict of seriously harming another's good reputation, 1452; as false denunciation about any delict, 1454; *see* reputation.

candidate *regarding:* the list of candidates for the episcopate drawn up by the synod of bishops of the patriarchal Church, 182 §§1 and 3–4, 184 §1, 185 §1; scrutinies in the election of bishops, 183 §§3–4, 186 §3; what must be done before episcopal ordination, 187 §2; the list of candidates for the episcopacy drawn up by the council of hierarchs, 168;

for the office of pastor, 284 §3. 2°; for the novitiate, 449, 451, 453 §§2–3, 454, 517, 518, 519, 559; for monastic profession, 467 §1; for admission to a secular institute, 568;

for the diaconate or presbyterate: by what bishop he is to be ordained, 747, 748; requirements, 758–761; regarding dispensation from an impediment to receiving sacred orders, 767 §2; regarding what must precede sacred ordination, 769 §1, 770, 771 §§1 and 3, 772; *see* sacred ordination (candidacy).

canon law deans of faculties of c. l. are to be summoned to the patriarchal assembly, 143 §1. 4°; exempts minors in certain cases from the power of

parents, 910 §2; juridic persons are subjects of rights and obligations in it, 920; regarding temporal goods, 1009 §1, 1028 §2. 2°, 1034, 1040, 1043 §1; judicial vicar, adjunct judicial vicar, judge, promotor of justice and defender of the bond must hold doctorates or at least licentiates in it, 1086 §4, 1087 §3, 1099 §2; an advocate must hold a doctorate in it or be otherwise truly expert, 1141; its general principles must be taken into consideration in supplying law, 1501; how civil law, to which the law of the Church yields, is to be observed in c. l., 1504; when a custom contrary to the c. l. now in force obtains the force of law, 1507 §3.

capacity *juridical, regarding:* physical persons, 909 §§2–3, 910; juridic persons, 920; offices, 940 §1; disqualifying laws, 1495, 1496, 1497 §1; reception of sacraments, 675 §2, 381 §2; baptism, 679; the function of sponsor, 685 §1; chrismation with holy myron, 692; the celebration of the Divine Liturgy, 699; the ministration of the sacrament of penance, 722–725; the ministration of the anointing of the sick, 739 §1; the reception of the anointing of the sick, 737 §1, 740; the ministration of sacred ordination, 744; the reception of a sacred order, 754, 758–762; exercising sacred orders, 763; marriage, 778, 800–812, 818; the blessing of marriages, 828–831; challenging the validity of a marriage, 1360; vows, 889 §§2–3; penalties, 1413–1414; the right to stand trial, 1134, 1136, 1138; the *libellus* of accusation to be presented in a penal trial, 1472 §1; testimony to be given in a trial, 1230–1231; the community that can introduce a custom, 1507 §1; subjection to merely ecclesiastical laws, 1490–1492; *see* disqualification, incapacity, qualification, suitability;

to acquire, administer, alienate, or possess temporal goods: *see* acquisition, administration, alienation, possession of temporal goods.

captivity of the eparchial bishop renders the eparchial see impeded, 233 §1; of a spouse, regarding dissolution of marriage in favor of the faith, 860.

cardinals assist the Roman Pontiff in exercising his office, 46 §1.

care of the pastors of the Church for the integrity and unity of the faith in the variety of churches, 604; of the Churches for preaching the gospel to the whole world, 585 §1; of the bishops for the Christian faithful, with respect to the authentic magisterium, 600; to whom the c. for the integrity of faith and morals in associations belongs, 577 §1; of the patriarch, of the metropolitan of a metropolitan Church *sui iuris* and of the eparchial

approval in schools, 658 §1; *see* catechetical formation.

catechists   regarding the catechetical commission in a Church *sui iuris*, 622 §2; their formation and remuneration in missionary territories, 591. 2°.

catechumenate   notion, 587 §1; the rights of those who are ascribed to the c. regarding the liturgy, 587 §2; what norms of particular law determine regarding it, 587 §3; *see* catechumens.

catechumens   who they are and how they are connected with the Church, 9 §1; the Church's special care for them, 9 §2; their freedom in ascription to a Church *sui iuris*, 30, 588; deceased c. must be given ecclesiastical burial, 875; *see* catechumenate.

Catholic   when bound by ecclesiastical laws, 1490; marriage of a C. is governed by divine and canon law, 780 §1; but what norms the marriage of a C. with a baptized non-Catholic party is also governed, 780 §2; father, mother or spouse, with regard the ascription of children to a Church *sui iuris*, 29 §1, 34; regarding the function of sponsor, 685 §1. 2° and §3; regarding the function of advocate, 1141;

the name "Catholic" regarding: initiatives of the Christian faithful, 19; schools, 631–639, 907; universities, 640–645; autonomous faculties, 640 §2; university centers, 645; hospitals and similar institutions, 907; institutes subject to the visitation of the eparchial bishop, 205 §2;

see individual entries such as faith, church, christian faithful, minister, priest, marriage.

Catholic Church   notion, 7 §2; those in full communion with it, 8; regarding the baptized who come into full communion with it, 35, 896–901; regarding the baptized not yet in full communion with it, 322 §4, 671 §§3–4; its doctrine is to be made known in the ecumenical movement, 906;

regarding divine worship and the sacraments: degree of communion with it regarding the norms for *communicatio in sacris*, 670 §1; its faith with respect to the sacraments regarding *communication in sacris*, 671 §4; hope that one to be baptized will be brought up in it required for licit baptism, 681 §1. 1°; sponsor is to belong to it, 685 §1. 2°; a Catholic priest may celebrate the Divine Liturgy on the altar of any C. c., 705 §1; children to be baptized and brought up in it, 814. 1°, 1439; those baptized in it are bound to the form for the celebration of marriage, 834; regarding the unbaptized who have several wives or husbands at the same time, after baptism in it, 859 §1; regarding the marriage of one baptized in it with am un-

baptized spouse where cohabitation cannot be restored because of captivity or persecution, 860; regarding its rights to possess cemeteries, 874 §§1–2;

defection from the Catholic Church regarding: members of an association, 580; ballots in elections, 953 §1. 3°; removal from office by the law itself, 976 §1. 2°.

cause   *see* reason.

celebration   of an ecumenical council, 53;

of the sacraments: *see* individual entries regarding each sacrament; of the divine praises: *see* divine praises; of sacramentals: *see* sacramentals; of funerals: *see* ecclesiastical funerals;

of divine worship: subjection of religious to the local hierarchy, if it is a matter of public worship, 415 §1; allowing non-Catholics to use a Catholic building, cemetery or church, 670 §2; public c., regarding the penalty of minor excommunication, 1431 §1; one punished by major excommunication is prevented from participating in any public c., 1434 §2; *see* worship;

liturgical: regarding precedence of the patriarch in it, is he is of the same Church, 60 §1; a patriarch who has resigned his office retains his title and honors during liturgical celebrations, 62; regarding formation in seminaries, 352 §2; clerics to be assiduous in liturgical celebrations, 369 §1; right of lay persons, of whatever Church *sui iuris*, to participate actively, 403 §1; of admission to the catechumenate, 587 §1; which books can be used in liturgical celebrations, 656 §1; offerings on the occasion of liturgical celebrations, 1013;

of sacred functions: right of the eparchial bishop regarding the entire eparchy, 200; how c. of greater importance belong to the pastor, 290 §2; the local hierarch can order the rector of a church to celebrate sacred functions, 307;

the protopresbyter is to take care regarding the worthy celebration of the funeral of a deceased pastor, 278 §3;

of a hearing in a summary contentious trial, 1347 §1.

celibacy   *of clerics:* to be greatly esteemed, 373; means to attain the splendor of chastity to be established by particular law, 374; common life among celibate clerics to be fostered, 376; regarding pastoral formation in seminaries, 352 §1; regarding instruction in seminaries about obligations arising from c., 355; dispensation from c. granted by the Roman Pontiff alone, 395–397, 493 §1, 549 §3, 795 §1. 1° and §2, 796 §1, 1433 §2, 1538 §2; regarding the matrimonial impediment of sacred orders,

804; its violation through attempted marriage, with regard to the impediment to the reception or exercise of sacred orders, 762 §1. 3°, 763. 2°, 767 §1. 2°; its violation through attempted marriage as a cause for removal from office by the law itself, 976 §1. 3°; penalties against violators of c., 1453 §§1–2;

regarding the matrimonial impediment of a public perpetual vow of chastity, 805; regarding dismissal from a religious institute or society of common life according to the manner of religious by the law itself, 497 §1. 2°, 502, 551, 562 §3; penalties against violators of c., 1453.

cemetery is a blessed sacred place, 868, 874 §2; right of the Church to possess, 874 §1; can be held by a parish or religious institute, 874 §4; civil, 874 §2; when and by whom its use can be granted to non-Catholics, 670 §2.

censors judgement concerning books is committed to c. by the hierarch, 664 §1; requirements, 664 §2; how they must fulfill their function, 664 §§2–3; their list and commission, 664 §1; when their names may be revealed to the author of a work, 664 §3.

certified mail *see* acknowledgement of receipt.

certitude *moral:* required for the pronouncement of a sentence, 1291 §1; to declare presumed death, 1383 §2.

cessation of law: *see* abrogation, revocation; of a custom: *see* custom; of an administrative act in general, 1513 §§1–3; of a dispensation, which has successive application, 1513 §4; of a decree or a singular precept, 1513 §5; of a privilege, 1532 §2, 1533 §1, 1534;

of power of governance, 991 §1, 992 §1; *see* loss; of the ascription of a cleric to an eparchy, 364; of the faculty to administer the sacrament of penance, 726; of the obligation of secrecy in a secret marriage, 840 §2; of the cause for the separation of spouses, 864 §3; of an impediment, so that a marriage may be convalidated or a radical sanation granted, 843 §1, 850 §2, 852;

by the law itself of the suspension of the execution of a decree after the lapse of the time limit provided for taking recourse, 1000 §3; regarding the loss of good reputation or aversion to the pastor, 1390. 3°; of the cause for administrative remedies in a penal trial or of the penal trial itself with respect to those remedies, 1473;

of the presbyteral council, 270 §§2–3; of the pastoral council during a vacancy of the eparchial see, 274 §2;

from office or function: see death, loss, privation, removal from office, resignation, transfer; of the eparchial administrator, 231 §4; of a protosyncellus or syncellus during a vacancy of the eparchial see, 224 §1; of the eparchial finance officer after giving an account of administration to the new bishop, 232 §4; of a pastor, 297 §1; of teachers in ecclesiastical universities, 650; of a party with respect to the suspension of a trial, 1199; of a guardian, curator, procurator or advocate regarding the suspension of a trial, 1200 §1;

of a vow, 891;

of a suspended penalty, if the offender does not commit an offence again within the determined time, 1409 §1. 4°; of a penalty, if a subsequent law abolishes the law or at least the penalty, 1412 §3;

of a right: of the eparchial finance officer regarding the election or appointment of a new finance officer, 232 §3; of one granting dimissorial letters does not extinguish them, 753; of the authority by which an office was conferred does not carry with it the loss of office, 965 §2; of a hierarch is not reason for withdrawal of habitual faculties which were granted to him, 982 §2; of one delegating does not carry with it the loss of delegated power, 992 §1, 1194. 3°; of one who imposed a penalty is not reason for the c. of the obligation to observe that penalty everywhere, 1412 §4; of one who placed an administrative act does not carry with it the c. of that act, 1513 §2; of one issuing a singular precept is cause for the c. of that precept unless it was imposed by a legitimate document, 1513 §5; *see* dissolution.

cession of the administration of goods before temporary profession, 525 §2, 529 §4, 465.

challenge of the decision of a judge regarding competence, 1119 §2; of the renunciation of an instance of litigation, 1205 §3; of marriage, 1360, 1363 §3; of the cause and reasons for the removal of a pastor, 1394. 1°;

regarding a sentence or *res iudicata*, 1182–1183, 1273 §2, 1302–1321, 1323 §1, 1325 §1, 1330, 1337 §3, 1484 §2; *see* appeal, complaint of nullity, opposition of a third party, restitutio in integrum.

chancellor *patriarchal:* appointment, requirements and function, 123 §1; belongs to the patriarchal curia, 114 §1; is a notary for the whole patriarchal Church, 123 §2;

in an eparchy: to be constituted, 252 §1; can be helped by a vice-chancellor, 252 §2; belongs to the eparchial curia, 243 §2; function, 252 §1, 253 §1, 254; as supervisor of the archives, 252 §1, 257 §1, 258; signs the document concerning the en-

children, whose parents had intended to baptize them, but who died before they received baptism, can be given an ecclesiastical funeral, 708.

if a presbyter is married, good morals are required in his children for him to be appointed a pastor, 285 §2.

choice   free c. of a state of life, 22, 344 §1, 453 §2, 806, 825; made by a competent authority regarding the notion of a cleric, 323 §1; regarding the celibacy of clerics chosen for the kingdom of heaven, 373; of the means for education children to be made by parents, 627 §§2–3; of cremation, 876 §3;

of a forum is granted to the petitioner if the respondent has more than one forum, 1073 §3; of a tribunal in contracts, 1077 §1;

see selection.

chrismation with holy myron   notion, necessity and effect, 692; cannot be repeated, 672 §1; in doubt, to be administered conditionally, 672 §2; how and by whom holy myron is to be confected, 693; to be administered together with baptism, 695 §1; what is to be done if administered apart from baptism, 695 §2; to be administered by a presbyter, 694, 696; how its administration is reserved to the pastor, 290 §2; by whom it may be validly and licitly administered, 696 §§1 and 3; regarding valid reception from presbyters of the Latin Church, 696 §2; as a sacrament of Christian initiation, 290 §2, 695 §1, 696 §1, 697, 710; required for admission into a seminary, 342 §2; required for the licit reception of a sacred order, 758 §1. 1°, 769 §1. 1°; required to fulfil the function of sponsor validly, 685 §1; how the Christian faithful participate in the celebration of the Divine Liturgy by virtue of c., 699 §3; recording of c., 296 §2, 695 §2.

Christian (also as adjective)

various prerogatives proper to Christians, with regard to catechumens, 9 §2;

unity of all Christians to be fostered; *see* ecumenism, unity;

regarding cooperation among missionaries, 593 §2;

community: must give a testimony of charity, 289 §1; center and culmination of its life is the Divine Liturgy, 289 §2; must foster vocations, 329 §1; its custom can obtain the force of law, 1506 §1;

doctrine: care of the eparchial bishop that the whole of C. d. is handed on to all, 196 §1; as a purpose for associations, 574;

religion: books not in harmony with it are not to be displayed, sold or distributed in churches, 665 §1;

life: *see* life; education: *see* education; C. obedience of the Christian faithful, 15 §1; C. vocation in the world to be fostered, 18; care of the eparchial bishop for the spiritual renewal of the C. people, 615; obligations of C. families for the catechetical formation and education of children, 619, 627 §1; C. initiation: *see* christian initiation; C. virtues, concerning the formation of young people, 629; C. formation to be nourished by Sacred Scripture and supported by sacred tradition, 607; C. viewpoint as the aim of the Catholic university, 640 §1; liturgy as the source of the C. spirit, 350 §3; C. solution of more urgent problems, 601; C. discretion regarding shows conducted in parishes, churches and schools, 665 §2; the meaning of C. marriage to be expounded in preaching and catechesis, 783 §1. 1°;

complete rejection of the C. faith as the delict of apostasy, 1436 §1;

non-Catholic: when the use of places for celebrating divine worship can be granted to them, 670 §2; regarding sacramental sharing, 671 §§3–4; regarding the baptism of their infants, 681 §5; *see* non-catholic;

regarding non-Christians: dialogue and cooperation with them, 352 §2, 592 §2, 655 §1; editions of the Sacred Scriptures appropriate for their use, 655 §2;

see baptized, catholic, christian faithful.

Christian faithful   notion, 7 §1; *see* cleric, religious, lay person;

Roman Pontiff is their supreme pastor, 597 §1; importance of their common adherence in matters of faith, 598 §1; are built up by the example of the saints and sustained by their intercession, 884; bishops as their authentic instructors and teachers, 600; in full communion with the Church, 8; equality with regard dignity and action, 11; exercise and regulation of their obligations and rights, 26; they remain ascribed to their own Church *sui iuris,* even if entrusted to a pastor or hierarch of another Church, 38; not to be induced to transfer to another Church *sui iuris,* 31, 1465; the competent authority may require from them what is necessary for the purposes of the Church, 1011; regarding offerings to be collected in churches open to them, 1014; schism as the refusal of communion with them, 1437; when the C. f. of the Eastern Churches are affected by laws issued by the supreme authority of the Church, 1492; their spiritual good is a just and reasonable cause for a dispensation, 1536 §2; the rights and obligations which directly regard their spiritual life are not subject to prescription, 1542. 3°;

menism, 902, 904 §3, 906, 908; the proper local hierarch and pastor, 916 §§4–5; their wills in pious causes, 1044, 1054 §1; certain goods held in trust, 1046 §3; a common tribunal of different Churches *sui iuris*, 1068 §1; the suspension of certain penalties, 1435 §2; dispensations, 1538;

to strive to avoid litigation, 1103 §3;

qualification: for the office of patriarchal or eparchial finance officer, 122 §1, 262 §1; to preach in extraordinary circumstances, 610 §4; to administer baptism in case of necessity, 677 §2; to distribute the Divine Eucharist, 709 §2; to cooperate in the exercise of the power of governance, 979 §2; for the office of judge, 1087 §2; for the office of auditor, 1093 §§1–2; for the office of promotor of justice or defender of the bond, 1099 §2; *of a non-Catholic Eastern Church:* as a sponsor at baptism, 685 §3; regarding the form for the celebration of marriage, 781. 2°; regarding their reception into the Catholic Church, 897.

Christian initiation sacramental C. i. in the mystery of salvation is completed by the reception of the Divine Eucharist after baptism and chrismation with holy myron, 697; regarding requirements for the function of sponsor, 685 §1. 1°; a sponsor is to assist at the C. i. of a person who is no longer an infant, 684 §2; celebration of the sacraments of C. i. belongs to the pastor, 290 §2.

Christ his Church, 39, 177 §1, 595 §1; the Church as his Body, 11, 367, 379, 563 §1. 2°, 616 §1, 675 §1, 698; the unity of the Church desired by him, 350 §4; the bonds of union with him with respect to full communion with the Catholic Church, 8;

equality among the Christian faithful based on rebirth in him, 11;

constituted the Holy ever-Virgin Mary as Mother of all, 346 §2. 5°, 884;

his mysteries communicated by the Church in the sacraments, 667; he, Our Lord Jesus, sanctifies people by the power of the Holy Spirit, 667; incorporation in him through baptism, 7 §1, 675 §1; those chrismated with holy myron become co-builders of his Kingdom, 692; the priest celebrates the Divine Liturgy in his person, 698; what he did at the Last Supper is perpetuated in the Divine Liturgy, 698; how the Christian faithful actively participate in the Divine Liturgy, his Sacrifice, 699 §3; regarding the obligations of the Christian faithful during the Paschal season, in which the Lord C. himself handed down the eucharistic mysteries, 708; through sacred ordination, sacred ministers are endowed with the task and power entrusted by C. to the Apostles, 743;

by his institution, a valid marriage between the baptized is by that very fact a sacrament, 776 §2; his union with the Church is the image of sacramental marriage, 776 §2;

the Roman Pontiff is his vicar, 43; the eparchial bishop governs his eparchy as his vicar and legate with the power that he exercises personally in the name of C., 178; churches, patriarchs and bishops are to do all in their power that the light of C. may shine more brightly everywhere, illuminating all people, 601; the pastors of the Church represent him, 15 §1; all of the Christian faithful cooperate in the building up of his Body, 11; the Christian faithful of a parish are to grow in him, 289 §1; *clerics:* have a part in his mission as Pastor, 323 §1; build up his Body, 367, 379; are bound by a special obligation to the perfection proposed by him, 368; are to be exemplary models to the flock of C., the eternal Priest, 368; are to become faithful and attentive hearers of him, 369 §1; are ministers of reconciliation in his love, 384 §1; must be imbued with his spirit of poverty, 385 §1; *candidates for sacred orders in seminaries:* are to be his ministers, 345; are to cultivate an intimate familiarity with him and be impelled by his love, 346 §1; are to cultivate the virtues that his ministry commends, 346 §2. 8°; are to be formed in doctrine so that people may be illuminated by the light of C. the Teacher, 347; are to be introduced into his mystery, 348 §2; *lay persons:* are to be his witnesses, 401; their obligation and right regarding the doctrine revealed by him, 404 §1; their special obligation regarding circumstances in which people can come to know C. only through them, 406; *religious:* follow him, the Teacher and Example of holiness, more closely by consecration through public vows, 410; *members of secular institutes:* are to so act that all things may be imbued with the strength and growth of his Body with the spirit of the gospel, 563 §1. 2°;

his mandate to evangelize all peoples, 584 §1; missionaries are to give one witness for C. the Lord, 593 §2; his complete mystery to be preached, 616 §1; earthly affairs and human institutions are to be brought together for the building up of his Body, 616 §1; the disciple of C. is to be formed by catechesis through the knowledge of his teaching, 617; his spirit, with respect to the use of instruments of social communication, 651 §2; regarding feast days, 880 §3;

his charity, 192 §3, 197, 289 §1, 346 §1, 384 §1; *see* charity.

Church founded by Christ subsists in the Catholic Church and is governed by the successor of Peter and the bishops, 7 §2; is the Body of Christ, 367, 675 §1, 698; is Christ's, 39, 177 §1, 350 §4; a person is incorporated into it by baptism, 675 §1; freedom to embrace it, 586; its missionary character, 584 §1; *see* whole church;

its tradition: *see* tradition;

its unity: *see* unity;

supreme authority in it: *see* college of bishops, roman pontiff, supreme authority of the Church;

its pastors: *see* pastors;

its ministers, 323 §1, 340 §2, 345; *see* minister;

regarding the Christian faithful: co-responsibility of the Christian community, 329 §1; share in its mission, 7 §1, 19; are bound to maintain communion with it, 12 §1; are to fulfill their obligations to it, 12 §2; are to strive to promote its growth and sanctification, 13; relation with its pastors, 15, 16; right to receive assistance out of its spiritual goods, 16, 381 §2; rights to be vindicated or defended in it, 24 §1; to take account of its common good, 26 §1; are to support its initiatives in promoting education, 630 §2; are to collaborate with it in the use of the instruments of social communication, 651 §2; are to keep its prescripts concerning the sacraments, 667; are to be reconciled with it in the sacrament of penance, 718, 720 §2;

its teaching function and doctrine: 595–600; regarding its doctors, 340 §3; its magisterium to be followed, 10, 15 §1, 17, 402, 604, 605, 606 §1, 664 §2; regarding the approval or blessing of books, 661 §§2–3; in a variety of enunciations, 604; concerning the dignity and fundamental rights of the human person, on civil and social life, and on the meaning of justice, 616 §2; the entire doctrine of the C. to be presented in catechesis, 626; regarding associations, which set out to teach Christian doctrine in the name of the C., 574; faculties and universities to be promoted which are closely linked with the C.'s function of evangelization, 646; those who are engaged in catechesis represent the C., 626; regarding the ecumenical movement, 906;

catechumens are connected with it in a special manner, 9 §1; has a special care for catechumens, 9 §2; the manner for the admission of catechumens into the C., 587 §1;

regarding missionary activity in new churches, 590, 591 §1;

regarding power in it: by divine institution, 979 §1; legislative power below the supreme authority cannot be delegated, 985 §2; when power and certain faculties are supplied, 994–995; recourse against decrees by any legitimate power in the C.,

issued extrajudicially, 996;

regarding seminaries: minor seminary is to be erected for its good, 332 §1; students are to be educated to have the sense of the C., 346 §2. 7°; teachers are to submit humbly to the magisterium, 351;

regarding divine worship and the sacraments: bound to dispense the sacraments, 667; its prescripts to be observed in celebrating and receiving the sacraments, 667; divine worship carried on in its name is public, 668 §1; the celebration of the sacraments is its action, 673; in baptism a person is incorporated into it, 675 §1; according to the most ancient tradition of the Churches, a sponsor is to be used in baptism, 684 §1; the Divine Liturgy as its offering, 698; its custom concerning the celebration of the Divine Liturgy for the intentions of the Christian faithful, 715 §1; reconciliation with it in the sacrament of penance, 718, 720 §1; its prayer in sacred ordination, 744; marriage as an image of the union of Christ with it, 776 §2; spiritual effects of sacramentals obtained through its prayers, 867 §1; the C. prays for special assistance for the dead in ecclesiastical funerals, 875; how those who seemed to be close to the C. can be granted ecclesiastical funerals, 876 §2; the C. prefers the burial of bodies to cremation, 876 §3; a vow accepted in its name is public, 889 §4; when an oath can be made before the C., 895;

its rights and obligations toward: the formation of its own ministers, 328; schools, 320; Catholic education, 628 §1; the instruments of social communication, 651 §1; dispensation of the sacraments, 667;

juridic persons in it: *see* person;

the obligations of the protopresbyter regarding those things which belong to it, 278 §3;

regarding clerics: are to provide from its spiritual goods for the Christian faithful, 381 §2; are to recognize the role of lay persons in it, 381 §3; the judgement of the eparchial bishop or the patriarch concerning the safeguarding of its rights, in the case of clerics taking part in political parties or labor unions, 384 §2; are to refer their controversies to its forum, 389; are to have in their hearts a solicitude for all the Churches, 393; usefulness to it with respect to the transfer or move of a cleric to another eparchy, 365 §1;

regarding lay persons: participate in its mission, 381 §3, 399; are to attend to the teaching of its magisterium, 402, 404 §1; are to foster unity of action with the lay persons of other Churches *sui iuris,* 405; functions entrusted to or forbidden to

212 §2; c. recommending an eparchial assembly, 236; pastoral c. for the institution of a pastoral council, 272; more difficult c. regarding clerics to be cared for by the protopresbyter, 278 §2. 2°; to be considered in the naming of a pastor, 285 §3; for entrusting several parishes to a pastor, 287 §1; to be considered in the decision about the resignation of a pastor, 297 §2; special c. for erecting an eparchy, 311 §1; special c. for erecting a seminary for students of several Churches *sui iuris,* 333; special c. to which the norms of clerical formation in seminaries must be applied, 337 §2; in which people cannot hear the Gospel or come to know Christ except through lay persons, 406; special c. concerning the reduction of the time in novitiate in a transfer to another religious institute, 545 §1; extraordinary c. for granting a mandate for preaching to lay persons, 610 §4; regarding Catholic schools, 634 §2, 635; regarding dispensations relative to marriage in an urgent case, 796 §§1–2; to be evaluated regarding the separation of spouses, 863 §3, 864 §2; of life, which are sanctified through sacramentals, 867 §1; c. recommending the constitution of a commission on economic affairs, 904 §2; in issuing instructions for the administration of temporal goods, 1022 §2; in which a judge, promotor of justice, defender of the bond, assessor or auditor must abstain from office, 1106; regarding sequestration of a thing or restriction of the exercise of a right, 1158; in evaluating an extrajudicial confession, 1218; in evaluating the probative force of private documents against others, 1223; concerning the decision of a judge to proceed in secret, 1240; c. recommending that the testimony of one witness can produce full proof, 1254; to be examined regarding the decision of a judge about the conclusions of experts, 1260 §1; concerning what things established by the tribunal must be observed, 1285 §3; on account of which, in matrimonial procedure, experts are not to be called, if required, 1366; special c. in granting permission to approach a civil tribunal in cases of the separation of spouses, 1378 §2; in providing for the conferral of another office or pension on a pastor who has been removed, 1395; attenuating c. for a delict, 1415; aggravating c. for a delict, 1416; grave c. for the reservation of the remission of a penalty, 1423 §1; in the preliminary investigation of a penal trial, 1468 §1, 1469 §2; in interpreting laws, 1499; which render the execution of an administrative act inopportune, 1522 §1; regarding the cessation of a privilege, 1532 §2. 4°; in granting a dispensation, 1536 §1, 1538 §2.

citation *judicial:* by which parties are summoned to a trial, 1190 §1; manner, 1190 §§1–2; when it is not required, 1190 §3; intimation, 1191 §§1 and 3, 1192 §§1–2, 1193, 1194, 1345 §2, 1363 §§1–2; introductory *libellus* of litigation to be attached to it, 1191 §2; refusal, 1192 §3; effect, 1082, 1194; response, 1190 §1, 1195 §2; of the promotor of justice and defender of the bond, 1097; of the procurator, the heir or successor of the deceased, if, after the case is concluded, the party dies, changes status or ceases from office in virtue of which the action is taken, 1199. 2°; of witnesses, 1237, 1238; its reiteration with respect to uncooperative parties, 1272 §2, 1274. 1°–2°; in a summary contentious trial, 1345 §2, 1347 §2; in cases to declare the nullity of marriage, 1363 §1; in a documentary process, 1372 §1; in a penal trial, 1473, 1474.

city *principal:* from which the patriarch takes his title, 57 §3; from which the metropolitan of a metropolitan Church *sui iuris* takes his title, 158 §1;

regarding the canonical visitation to be made for a serious reason by the patriarch, 83 §2;

the earthly c., regarding the right of lay persons to that freedom that belongs to all citizens, 402.

civil law how the c. l. received by the Church has force in canon law, 1504; the Church's teaching about civil society is to be communicated in preaching, 616 §2; power of the patriarch in affairs which touch civil authorities, 98, 100; members of the finance council are to be experts in c. l., 263 §1; must acknowledge the right of parents concerning the instruments of education for their children, 627 §3; regarding representatives of juridic persons in it, 922 §2. 4°; a minor emancipated according to the norms of c. l. can acquire his or her own domicile, 915 §1; regarding areas in civil cemeteries reserved for the Christian faithful, 874 §2; regarding the admission of guardians and curators, 1137; regarding the imposition of penalties if c. l. provides for the matter, 1409 §1. 2°; regarding delicts, 1460;

to be observed: in naming guardians, 910 §2; in registering the names of the natural parents, 689 §3; regarding prescription, 1540; in the remuneration of lay persons devoted to the service of the Church, 409 §2; regarding the renunciation of goods by a religious, 467 §2, 533; in the will of a member of a congregation, 530; regarding the safeguarding of the rights of the author of an intellectual work, 666 §3; regarding civil effects of marriage, 780 §1, 1358, 1378 §§2–3; regarding a document about the death of a spouse, 1383 §1; in administration of temporal goods, 1020, 1027,

coercion see fear, force, fraud.

the right of all to be immune from c. in the choice of a state of life, 22; renders admission to a novitiate invalid, 450. 5°, 517 §1, 559 §1, 568 §1; renders religious profession invalid, 464. 3°, 527. 3°; to join the Church strictly forbidden, 586; prohibited in receiving sacred orders, 756; renders the celebration of marriage invalid, 825; renders a juridic act null or rescindable, 932; renders the provision of an office null, 946; regarding the nullity of a vote, 954. 1°; judicial confession extorted by c. lacks force, 1219; renders a sentence irremediably null, 1303 §1. 3°; remission of a penalty extorted by c. is null, 1421.

cohabitation peaceful c. and the application of the pauline privilege, 854 §2, 855 §1. 2°, 857. 3°, 860.

college regarding a collegial act or action of the College of Bishops, 50 §2, 54 §2; see college of bishops;

manner of proceeding: for collegial acts, 924, 956, 990 §3; if a superior requires the consent of or consultation with any group of persons, 934 §§1–3; in elections, 917–957, 63–66, 182–186; in postulation, 961–964; in synods, 102–113, 115–121; in the council of hierarchs, 164–171;

judicial: 985 §3; see tribunal;

directed by presbyters, regarding the rector of a church, 305 §3;

see group.

college of bishops present in the Church by divine institution, 42; constitution and power, 49; how it exercises supreme power, 50, 54 §2; its members joined in hierarchical communion, 45 §2, 49; its head is the Roman Pontiff, 43; is the subject of the authentic, solemn and ordinary magisterium, 597 §2, 598, 599, 600; when it possesses infallible teaching authority, 597 §2; its members attend an ecumenical council with deliberative vote, 52 §1; to reject obstinately a doctrine set forth by it to be definitively held or to hold a teaching condemned by it as erroneous constitutes a delict, 1436 §2; see ecumenical council.

college of eparchial consultors constitution and functions in an eparchy, 271; constitution and functions in an exarchy, 319; its members attend the eparchial assembly, 238 §1. 3°;

regarding the showing of the letter of canonical provision: of a coadjutor bishop, 214 §§2–3; of an auxiliary bishop, 214 §3; of the eparchial administrator named by the patriarch, 220. 4°;

during a vacancy of the eparchial see: who presides over it, 271 §5; when its president must inform the Apostolic see or the patriarch of the vacancy of the see, 221. 1°, 271 §5; when the governance of the eparchy passes to it, 221. 2°; regarding the election of an eparchial administrator or his resignation from office, 221. 3°, 226, 231 §1; it may provide for the administration of certain ecclesiastical goods, 232 §1; regarding the election of a finance officer, 232 §3; fulfills the function of the presbyteral council, 270 §2; regarding its consent, 255, 363. 2°;

when it may chose a priest to govern the eparchy while the eparchial see is impeded, 233 §2;

its consent is required: for the appointment of a pastor for a determined period of time in a special case, 284 §3. 3°; for the removal of the chancellor or other notaries by the eparchial administrator, 255; for ascription of a cleric to the eparchy, for granting the dismissal of a cleric from the eparchy or transfer to another eparchy, on the part of the eparchial administrator after the eparchial see has been vacant for one year, 363. 2°; for the eparchial administrator to grant dimissorial letters, 750 §1. 2°; to accomplish certain alienations, 1036 §1. 1°–2°;

its consultation is required: for the appointment or removal of the eparchial finance officer, 262 §§1–2; to name persons to the finance council, 263 §1; to suppress a juridic person erected by the eparchial bishop, 928. 2°;

if its consent is required, the patriarch only requires its consultation in matters regarding the eparchy which he himself governs, 271 §6.

collusion danger of c. to be avoided in questioning witnesses, 1251.

commemoration *prescribed in the Divine Liturgy and in the divine praises:* of the Roman Pontiff, 91, 92 §2, 161, 162, 209 §1; of the patriarch, 91; of the metropolitan, 135, 161; of the eparchial bishop, 209 §2; regarding the penalties for the omission of the prescribed commemorations, 1438;

of the sacrifice of the Cross in the Divine Liturgy, 698; regarding offerings for commemorations in the Divine Liturgy, 715 §2; regarding days of c. for one's country, 908.

commentary *Acta Apostolicae Sedis* as official c., 1489.

commerce forbidden to clerics, religious and members of societies of common life according to the manner of religious, 385 §2, 427, 561; penalties against transgressors, 1466.

commission *as a group of persons:* preparatory c. for the synod of bishops of the patriarchal Church, 113; of the patriarchal curia, 114 §1; concerning liturgical matters, 114 §1, 124; prior to the patriar-

in metropolitan Churches sui iuris regarding: the rights of the metropolitan, 159; the legislative power of the council of hierarchs, 167 §1; the power of the metropolitan regarding acts entrusted by c. l. to the superior administrative authority of the Church *sui iuris,* 167 §4; the convocation of the council of hierarchs on account of business for which c. l. requires the consent or counsel of that council, 170;

regarding Churches *sui iuris* which are not patriarchal, major archiepiscopal, or metropolitan, 174, 176;

in eparchies regarding: rights and obligations of the coadjutor or auxiliary bishop, 213 §§1 and 3; care of the patriarch to provide for a vacant eparchial see, 220. 5°; power of one who governs a vacant eparchy on an interim basis, 221. 2°; power of the protosyncellus and syncellus, 221. 2°, 245, 246, 248 §1; rights of the finance council, 263 §§4–5; rights and obligations of the parochial vicar, 302 §1; observance of the c. l. in preaching the word of God, 609; sacred places and churches, 868, 870; powers attributed by name to the eparchial bishop, 987; determination of fees, 1013 §1; the ordering of the administration of temporal goods, 1022 §2;

to be preserved and carefully explained in the program for clerical formation, 330 §§1 and 3;

in institutes of consecrated life regarding: eparchial functions entrusted to religious by the eparchial bishop, 415 §3; temporal goods, 425; obligations of clerics by which members are bound, 427, 561; power of superiors, 441 §§1 and 3, 511 §1; juridical force of monastic profession, 463; temporary profession, 465, 534. 1°;

a custom contrary to an impediment to receiving or exercising sacred orders established by c. l. is reprobated, 764;

regarding: physical and juridic persons, 910 §2, 921 §2, 922 §2, 928; reception or dismissal of members in associations, 578 §1, 581; competent authority to send preachers of the gospel, 585 §1; norms for books and other media for public distribution, 654; means for fulfilling an ecclesiastical office and remuneration, 937 §2; norms for election, 956 §1; delegation of legislative power, 985 §2; exercise of executive power, 993; prescripts for public power in the Church or faculties for the valid celebration or administration of the sacraments, 995; reception of the civil law on prescription, 1540;

in trials regarding: a tribunal of third instance, 1065; titles of competence, 1073 §1; certain rights of the promotor of justice and the defender of the

bond, 1098; prescription of delicts which are not punished by c. l., 1152 §2. 3°; renunciation of an appeal, 1317 §2; suspension of the execution of a sentence, 1325 §2;

in penal law regarding: penalties established by c. l., which particular law can increase, specify or make obligatory, 1405 §2; obligation to observe a penalty everywhere, 1412 §4; remission of a penalty imposed by c. l., 1420 §1; reservation of the remission of a penalty established by c. l., 1423 §1; prohibition of the exercise of an act of a sacred order, 1430 §2.

communicatio in sacris when the Christian faithful can take part in the divine worship of other Christians, 670 §1; granting the use of places for divine worship to non-Catholics according to the norms of particular law of a Church *sui iuris,* 670 §2; norms relating to the sacraments of penance, Eucharist and the anointing of the sick, 671; when a non-Catholic infant is licitly baptized by a Catholic minister, 681 §5; admission of a member of the Christian faithful of an Eastern non-Catholic Church as a sponsor, 685 §3; prohibition of concelebration of the Divine Liturgy with non-Catholic priests or ministers, 702; on the permission of the hierarch for a Catholic priest to celebrate the Divine Liturgy in a non-Catholic Church, 705 §2; a non-Catholic priest may be called to bless a marriage celebrated in a special case before witnesses alone, 832 §2; when a Catholic priest may bless marriages of the Christian faithful of some Eastern non-Catholic Church, 833 §1; regarding the form for the celebration of marriage between a Eastern Catholic party and an Eastern non-Catholic, 834 §2; when ecclesiastical burial may be granted to non-Catholics, 876 §1; norms to be observed concerning *c. in s.* in undertaking projects with the cooperation of non-Catholics, 908; violation of the norms of *c. in s.* is a delict, 1440.

communications *see* instruments of social communication

communion *hierarchical:* of the Roman Pontiff with the entire Church, 45 §2; of bishops with the head and members of their college, 7 §2, 45 §2, 49, 597 §, 600; ecclesiastical c., granted by the Roman Pontiff to a patriarch, 76 §2, 77 §2; to be manifested with the Roman Pontiff by a patriarch, 92 §1; the sign of full c. with the Roman Pontiff is his commemoration in the Divine Liturgy and the divine praises, 92 §2, 162, 209 §1; of a metropolitan Church *sui iuris* with the Roman Pontiff, and the pallium as the sign of that c., 156 §1; of clerics among themselves, 324;

with the Catholic Church: full, 8; primary obligation of the Christian faithful, 12 §1; regarding ascription to a Church *sui iuris* of baptized non-Catholics entering into full c., 35; general norms concerning baptized non-Catholics entering into full c., 896–901; degree of c. to be considered with regard participation of catholics in the worship of non-Catholics, 670 §1; care of the eparchial bishop concerning the witness of charity of those living in c., 192 §3; manner of acting against c. as a cause for the removal of a pastor, 1390. 1°; *defection from communion with respect to:* members of associations, 580; disqualification to vote, 953 §1. 3°; removal from office by the law itself, 976 §1. 2°; delict of schism, 1437, 762 §1. 2°, 763. 2°, 767 §1. 2;

between members of a secular institute, 563 §1. 3°; *lack of full communion with the Catholic Church: see* communicatio in sacris, ecumenism, non-catholic;

eucharistic: *see* eucharist.

community *Christian:* should foster vocations to the sacred ministries, 329 §1; is to render the witness of charity in the parish, 289 §1; the Divine Liturgy is the summit and center of its life, 289 §2; the pastor is to foster the growth of its life, 289 §3;

of the Christian faithful, with regard the notion of the parish, 279; of faith to be edified by theologians discharging their function, 606 §2; of religious to be consulted in naming spiritual fathers and confessors, 475 §1, 539 §2; scholastic c. to be animated by the evangelical spirit of freedom and charity, 634 §1;

ecclesial: should care for the catechetical formation of its members, 619; its care for schools, 631 §1;

non-Catholic ecclesial communities: their observers at patriarchal and eparchial assemblies, 143 §4, 238 §3; catechesis is to furnish a correct image of them, 625; regarding *communicatio in sacris* in certain sacraments, 671 §§4–5; regarding the law to be applied in marriages, 780 §2, 781. 1°; regarding the marriage of one who has rejected the Catholic faith but has not become a member of a non-Catholic e. c., 789. 6°; their teaching to be correctly explained, 906; regarding those who enter full communion with the Catholic Church, 35, 896.

commutation of vows, 891; of the wills of the Christian faithful for pious causes, 1054 §1.

competence *see* individual entries regarding authorities, synods, councils, gatherings, offices;

competent ecclesiastical authority in general: its consent necessary for the Christian faithful to lay claim to the name Catholic for their initiatives, 19; in choosing sacred ministers, 323 §1; regarding offices, ministries and functions entrusted to clerics, 371 §2; to grant the mandate to lay persons for teaching the sacred sciences, 404 §3; to entrust ecclesiastical functions to lay persons, 408 §2; to approve the typicon of a monastery, 433 §2; to erect an order or congregation, 504 §§1–2; to grant an indult of departure from an order or congregation, 549 §1; regarding associations, 573–575 §1, 576 §2; to send forth preachers of the gospel, 585 §1; regarding the norms of catechesis, 624 §1; regarding the supervision of a school, 634 §2; regarding the erection of universities and faculties, 648, 642, 649; regarding the approval of books, 661 §2; regarding the approval of acts of public worship, 668 §1; regarding the faculty to administer the sacrament of penance, 722 §3, 726 §2; for permission for a mixed marriage, 813; regarding a radical sanation for a marriage, 848 §1; regarding the separation of spouses, 863 §3, 864 §3; regarding the norms for a non-Catholic cleric to enter into full communion with the Catholic Church, 899; to punish a judge, 1115 §1; regarding the pardon of a penal action, 1152 §1; regarding the mandate for an episcopal ordination, 1459 §1; regarding juridic persons, 921 §§1 and 3, 922 §1, 927 §1, 1047 §1. 1°; regarding offices, 936, 939. 1°, 940 §2, 947, 948 §2, 959 §1, 960 §1, 961, 963 §§1 and 3–4, 964 §1, 965 §3, 974 §1, 975 §2, 976 §2, 977; regarding temporal goods, 1011, 1024 §1, 1028 §2. 2°, 1035 §1. 3° and §2, 1047 §1. 1°; regarding administrative acts, 1510 §1, 1513 §3, 1515, 1532 §2. 4°, 1533 §1;

what is to be done if the competent authority cannot be approached: in the reservation of absolution from sin, 729. 2°; in dispensation from matrimonial impediments, 767 §3, 797;

higher c. authority: *see* superior authority;

equally c. authority for granting a favor, 1530 §2;

tribunal or judge: 24 §1, 985 §3, 1066, 1058–1084, 1104–1107 §1, 1115 §1, 1119–1120, 1146 §2, 1155, 1157, 1174 §1, 1175, 1176 §3, 1182 §1, 1185, 1188 §1 and §2. 1°, 1194. 2°, 1216, 1268, 1303 §1. 1°, 1359, 1380;

to place a judicial act, 931 §1;

when the c. council is to be consulted, 1020 §2, 1024 §2, 1049, 1054 §2;

of a legislator to approve a custom, 1507 §4; of a legislator with regard penal laws, 1405 §1; of the dicastery of the Roman Curia in cases for declaring the nullity of sacred ordination, 1386 §1; of the authorities of a seminary to be determined in its statutes, 337 §1;

regarding the moderator of an educational institution, 731 §3;

in seminaries, 339 §2; in making judgements regarding persons it is not permitted to require his opinion, 339 §3; in monasteries, 474 §2, 475 §1; in orders and congregations, 538 §3, 539;

freedom of approaching a c., 339 §2, 473 §2. 2°, 474 §2, 538 §3;

his faculty to dispense: matrimonial impediments, 796 §2, 797; the impediment of exercising sacred orders in an occult urgent case, 767 §3; private vows, 893 §2;

regarding the reservation of absolution from sin, 729. 2°;

delicts: violation of the sacramental seal, 1456 §1; absolution of an accomplice, 1457; solicitation, 1458; false denunciation of a c. concerning the delict of solicitation, 731, 1454.

confirmation of the decrees of an ecumenical council by the Roman Pontiff, 51 §1, 54;

of an act or document by the Roman Pontiff *in forma specifica*, 1060 §3;

of an election: 958–960, 963 §1, 939. 2°, 947 §1, 948 §2, 133 §1. 6°, 138, 139, 159. 7°, 175; of a major archbishop by the Roman Pontiff, 153 §§2–4; not required by eparchial administrator, 221. 5°; of a judicial vicar named by the eparchial administrator, by the new eparchial bishop, 1088 §3; of the eparchial finance officer, by the new eparchial bishop, 232 §4; of the members of the finance council by the eparchial bishop, if they have been elected or appointed by others, 263 §1; of superiors in institutes of consecrated life, 515 §2, 557;

of a decree of dismissal from a religious institute, 499, 500 §4, 501 §§2 and 4, 553, 562 §3; of an indult of departure from a congregation of eparchial right granted to a member in temporary vows, 546 §2; of a sentence of arbitration, 1181 §§1–2 and 4, 1182 §1, 1183; of a sentence of matrimonial nullity in the grade of appeal, 1370, 1374; of the second sentence of nullity of sacred ordination, 1387; regarding decrees during recourse, 1000 §2, 1004, 1005; regarding the alienation of temporal goods, 1038;

as a sacrament (CIC): see chrismation with holy myron.

conflict of the rights of minors with the rights of parents or guardians or curators, 1136 §2; of competence between tribunals, 1083 §§1 and 3.

congregation *monastic (CIC): see* confederation (of monasteries);

religious: what it is, 504 §2; its structure, 505 §2; when it is clerical, 505 §3; the c., its provinces, and its houses are juridic persons, 423; erection or suppression of a c., its provinces or houses, 506, 507 §2, 508–510; competence of the Apostolic See, the patriarch, and the eparchial bishop regarding its statutes, certain dispensations and visitation, 414, 415 §2; which superiors of a c. are major superiors, 418 §1; regarding the quinquennial report of the superior general, 419 §1; when those major superiors designated by the statutes may visit houses subject to them, 420 §1; regarding a religious promoted to a dignity or office outside of the c., 431; superiors, synaxes, finance officers, 51–516; admission and the novitiate, 517–525; profession, 526–532, 534–535; formation of members and religious discipline, 536–543; transfer of members to another religious institute, 488 §3, 544–545; exclaustration and departure, 546–550; dismissal of members, 551–553; dispensation from the impediment of a public vow of chastity made in a c., 795 §1. 2° and §2; which vows are suspended while the one who vowed remains in a c., 894; regarding societies of common life according to the manner of religious, 554 §2, 556, 557, 558 §2, 560 §1, 562 §3; regarding secular institutes, 563 §2, 566.

conjugicide matrimonial impediment, 807; to whom dispensation from this impediment is reserved, 795 §2.

connection of catechumens with the Church, 9 §1; of bishops among themselves and with the successor of Peter in the exercise of the infallible magisterium, 579 §2; studies connected with divine revelation or sacred studies in ecclesiastical universities, 646, 648;

of remuneration with a former office in the case of transfer to another, 973 §2;

of cases: which are to be adjudicated by the same tribunal, 1081, 1268, 1269 §1; with spiritual cases regarding minors, 1136 §3; in a counterclaim, 1156 §1;

of acts or rights with an office, ministry or function, regarding the penalty of suspension, 1432 §1.

consanguinity computation, 918; matrimonial impediment, 808; when the impediment arising from c. cannot be dispensed, 795 §3;

persons related by consanguinity: regarding the notion of affinity, 919; to the patriarch, who cannot validly be patriarchal finance officers, 122 §1; to the eparchial bishop, who should not be protosyncellus, syncellus or members of the finance

council Ecumenical: *see* ecumenical council;

Particular (CIC): see patriarchal assembly, assembly of a metropolitan Church *sui iuris;*

of hierarchs: assists the metropolitan of a metropolitan Church *sui iuris,* 155 §1; its power validly exercised only within the territory of the metropolitan Church *sui iuris,* 157 §2; convocation, presidency, questions of procedure, transfer, prorogation, adjournment, dissolution, 156 §2, 159. 2°; who must be called and who may be invited, 164 §1; who has a deliberative vote, and who may have, 164 §2; regarding the obligation of attendance, 165; quorum, 166 §1; required balloting for decisions, 166 §2; power to issue laws and norms, 167 §1; prerequisites before laws and norms may be promulgated, 167 §2; regarding the composition of the list of candidates for appointment as metropolitan or bishops, 168; functions, 169; statutes, 171; what things are excluded from the power of the administrator of the metropolitan Church *sui iuris* except with its consent, 173 §1. 2°; to take care for the support of a retired bishop, 211 §2; decisions of the council of hierarchs of several Churches *sui iuris* cannot be to its prejudice, 322 §2; to issue a program for formation of clerics, 330 §1; is to have a commission for missionary activity, 585 §2; regarding care for the unity and integrity of faith and good morals, 605, 652 §2; regarding the catechetical directory and catechisms, 621 §§1 and 3; can establish prohibitions regarding instruments of social communication, 652 §2; regarding censors of books, 664 §1; judges concerning the administration of the sacraments to non-Catholics, 671 §§4–5; determines norms for the distribution of the Divine Eucharist on the part of the Christian faithful who are not priests or deacons, 709 §2; can change norms concerning the program of study for deacons, 760 §1; *consent of the council of hierarchs required for:* placing administrative acts which are committed by common law to the higher administrative authority of the Church *sui iuris,* 167 §4; erecting a common seminary for several eparchies, 334 §1; approving liturgical texts and their translations, 657 §§1–2; reserving the faculty of absolving from sins, 727; receiving a non-Catholic bishop from an Eastern Church into the Catholic Church, 898 §1;

of a superior of an institute of consecrated life: its necessity in institutes of religious, 422; must be heard for an indult of exclaustration to be granted to a member of the monastery, 489 §1; *its consultation required in monasteries:* to constitute the superior of a subsidiary monastery, 444 §2; for admission to the novitiate, 453 §1; to permit the

novitiate to be made in another monastery, 456 §2; to declare a dismissal by the law itself from the monastery, 497 §2; to reduce the time of the novitiate of one who is transferring from an order or congregation, 545 §1; *its consent required in monasteries:* to constitute the superior of a monastery *sui iuris,* 444 §2; to name the finance officer of a monastery *sui iuris,* 447 §3; for admission to profession, 464. 2°; to prescribe or change the boundaries of the cloister, 477 §3; for a member to become a hermit, 482; to impose an end on the eremitical life, 485; to ascribe a member who is transferring from another monastery, 488 §2; to request imposed exclaustration, 490; to expel from the monastery, 498 §1; to dismiss a member in temporary vows, 499; to dismiss a member in perpetual vows, 500 §1; *its opinion in monasteries:* to be sent to the Apostolic See regarding the granting of an indult of departure from the monastery to a member in perpetual vows, 492 §1; to be sent to the eparchial bishop regarding the granting of an indult of departure from the monastery to a member in temporary vows, 496 §2; *its consultation required in orders and congregations:* to exclude a member from the renewal of temporary vows or from making perpetual profession, 547 §1; to grant an indult of exclaustration, 548 §1; to declare a dismissal by the law itself from the institute, 551; *its consent required in orders and congregations:* to make decisions regarding the goods of a suppressed province in case of necessity, 508 §3; to name finance officers in certain cases, 516 §3; to erect, transfer or suppress the location of the novitiate, 521; to make a novitiate outside of its proper location, 522 §1; for admission to profession, 527. 2°; to grant permission for a member in perpetual vows to cede his or her goods, in congregations, 534. 2°; to give consent in the case of the transfer of a member to another religious institute, 544 §§1–2; to reduce the time for the novitiate of someone who is transferring from another religious institute, 545 §1; to grant an indult of departure from the institute to a member in temporary vows, 546 §1; to request imposed exclaustration, 548 §1; to expel from the institute, 551; to dismiss a member in temporary vows, 552 §1; *its opinion in orders and congregations:* to be sent to the competent authority concerning the granting of an indult of departure from the order or congregation, 549 §1; *its consent required in societies of common life according to the manner of religious:* to make decisions regarding the goods of a suppressed province, 556, 508 §3; to name finance officers, 558 §2, 516 §3; to dismiss a perpetually coopted member, 562 §3, 552 §1;

competent: for investing the goods of a pious foundation, 1049; in reducing the obligations of pious wills or causes, 1054 §2; regarding parishes, 295.

country   regarding days of commemoration for one's c., 908.

covenant   *matrimonial:* founded by the Creator and ordered by his laws, 776 §1; obligation of the pastors of souls to furnish assistance to spouses so that they may faithfully preserve and safeguard it, 783 §3; regarding the notion of matrimonial consent, 817 §1; *see* marriage.

credibility   of parties in the matrimonial process, 1365.

creditor   rights of a c. must be sufficiently evident in the sequestration of a thing as security, 1159 §1.

cremation   those who choose c. are to be granted ecclesiastical burial, with certain exceptions and as long as scandal is avoided, as long as it is clear that the Church prefers the burial of bodies, 876 §3.

crime   matrimonial impediment: *see* conjugicide.

culture   regarding the notion of rite and ascription to a Church *sui iuris*, 28 §1, 588; regarding formation of clerics, 347, 349 §1, 350 §1, 559 §2; regarding formation of religious, 471 §1, 536 §1; of each people to be preserved in the evangelization of peoples, 584 §2, 588, 589, 592 §1; regarding the manner of responding to questions about the meaning of life and of providing for Christian solutions to problems, 601; its diversity to be acknowledged in the promotion of literature and the arts, 603; regarding catechetical formation, 622 §1, 626; to be so oriented to the message of salvation in Catholic schools, 634 §1; right of Catholic schools regarding the pursuit of cultural goals, 634 §3; the promotion of higher c. in Catholic universities, 640 §1; means of presenting divine revelation with respect to contemporary human c. in ecclesiastical universities, 647. 1°; obligation of parents, according to their abilities, to care for the cultural education of their children, 783 §1. 1°.

curator   *regarding:* the acquisition of domicile and quasi-domicile, 915 §2; necessity of a c. in cases involving minors, 1136 §§1–2; cases of those deprived of the administration of goods or those of diminished mental capacity, 1136 §4; the admission of a curator constituted by the civil authority, 1137; citation, 1191 §3; suspension of a lawsuit, when the c. has ceased that function, 1200; the right to seek indemnity from a c. in case of the abatement of a lawsuit, 1202.

curatorship   regarding the acquisition of domicile and quasi-domicile, 915 §2; by reason of which a judge, promotor of justice, defender of the bond, assessor or auditor must abstain from their office, 1106.

curia   *Roman:* assist the Roman Pontiff in exercising his office, 46 §1; its dicasteries and other institutions included in the term "Apostolic See," 48; regarding the dicastery to which a *libellus* challenging the validity of sacred ordination should be sent, 1386 §§1–2;

patriarchal: notion, 114 §1; who belongs, 114 §2; its offices are not to be accumulated in the same persons with the offices of the curia of the eparchy of the patriarch, 114 §3; its archives, 123 §3; its commissions, 114 §1, 124; from what goods its expenses are to be paid, 125;

eparchial: assists the eparchial bishop in governance of the eparchy, 243 §1; who belongs, 243 §2; regarding its offices, 243 §3, 244; is to have a catechetical center, 623 §2; testimonial letters to be sent to it, 771 §3; regarding the attestation of marriage to be transmitted through it, 841 §2; its archives and documents, 256–261, 189 §2, 228 §2, 537 §2, 774 §1, 799, 840 §3, 1026, 1028 §2. 8°, 1050, 1470; *see* archives;

of an exarchy, 310 §1;

the style of the c. of the hierarch who granted a rescript, regarding those things required for validity, 1529 §1.

custody   of the faith handed down from the forefathers, 10; of their own rite to be preserved by the hierarchs, 40 §1; of the Divine Eucharist, 714 §1, 278 §1. 3°; of revealed truth, 595 §1; of the integrity and unity of the faith and of good morals, 605; of money or moveable goods in pious causes, 1049; of a thing through sequestration, 1158 §1.

custom   a Christian community, at least capable of receiving law, can introduce c., 1506 §1, 1507 §1; requirements for c. to obtain the force of law, 1507 §§1–3; cannot derogate from divine law, 1506 §2; its approval, as legitimate, on the part of the competent legislator, 1507 §4; is the best interpreter of law, 1508; its revocation, 1509; regarding a lacuna in the law, 1501; what c. is included under common or particular law, 1493; what c. is revoked by the Code, 6. 2°; the eparchial bishop is bound to urge its observance, 201 §1;

of the people, on account of which particular law may establish reasons for the separation of spouses, 864 §2;

ancient c. concerning sponsors at baptism, 684 §1; regarding celebration of the Divine Liturgy for the intentions of the Christian faithful, 715 §1; of the administration of the sacrament of the anointing of the sick by several priests, 737 §2; in pious foundations the hierarch is to take care that the revenues completely respond to the attached obligations, according to the c. of his own Church *sui iuris,* 1048 §2;

reprobated by the Code: 6. 2°; not reasonable, 1507 §2; of not observing the canons of common law in the election of the patriarch, 67; of selecting several eparchial administrators, 225 §1; of not instructing seminarians in their own rite, 343; introducing a new impediment to receiving or exercising sacred orders or contrary to an impediment established by common law, 764; introducing a new matrimonial impediment or contrary to existing impediments, 793; of burying the dead in a church, 874 §3; contrary to certain prerequisites for the validity of a vote in elections, 954 §1. 2°; exempting the administrators of temporal goods from the obligation of making an annual report of administration to the proper hierarch, 1031 §1; contrary to a prescript according to which a penalty must be imposed by a penal trial, 1402 §1;

regarding: the power of the patriarch, 78 §1; the rights and obligations of metropolitans, 137; the liturgical life in the eparchy, 199 §2; remuneration of the eparchial administrator, 230. 1°; the obligation of the parochial vicar to reside in the parish, 302 §4; exemption of clerics, religious and members of societies of common life according to the manner of religious from functions and public offices and from military service, 383. 3°, 427, 561; the notion of a clerical order or congregation, 505 §3; the divine praises in religious institutes, 473 §1, 538 §1; baptism of infants to be administered as soon as possible, 686 §1; reception of offerings for the Liturgy of the Presanctified, 715 §2; the manner of celebrating marriage, 836; the obligation of participating in the Divine Liturgy or the celebration of the divine praises on Sundays or feasts, 881 §1; the administration of temporal goods, 1022 §2, 1029; the effect of an administrative act contrary to c., 1515; issuing an extra-judicial decree, 1519 §1.

D

damage must be repaired by whomever illegitimately inflicted, 935;

reparation of damages: action arising from a promise of marriage, 782 §2; regarding the suspension of the execution of a decree, if recourse is sought only for r. of d., 1000 §3; who is to respond for r. of d. after a decision concerning recourse against an administrative decree, 1005; action for damages arising from a delict, 1154. 1°, 1483–1485; after joinder of issue, 1197; for norms of a tribunal regarding, 1335. 4°–5°, 1336; on account of irreparable d., the execution of a sentence may be suspended or the sentence may be subjected to a guarantee, 1337 §3; regarding abstention from penalties or remission of a penalty, 1403 §1, 1407 §2, 1409 §1. 2°, 1415, 1418 §3, 1424 §1; inflicted by officials of a tribunal, and how it is to be punished, 1115; threat of d., regarding sequestration of a thing, 1158 §1, 1160, 1161; arising from culpable negligence in the exercise of power, office, ministry or function, to be punished, 1464 §2; questions concerning d. may be raised in preliminary investigation of a penal trial, 1469 §3; *see* harm.

danger *of death regarding:* administration of certain sacraments to non-Catholic Christians, 671 §4; administration of baptism, 681 §4, 682 §2; administration of chrismation with holy myron to the Christian faithful of another Church *sui iuris,* 696 §2; the obligation to receive the Divine Eucharist, 708; administration of the sacrament of penance, 720 §2. 1°, 721 §2, 725, 730, 735 §2; administration of the anointing of the sick, 740; proof of baptism and of the free status of sponsors, 785 §2; dispensations for celebration of marriage, 796 §§1–2; celebration of marriage before witnesses alone, 832; reception into the Catholic Church of a baptized non-Catholic who has not yet completed fourteen years of age, 900 §2; suspension of penalties, 1435 §1;

in delay regarding: warning of an eparchial bishop by the patriarch, 95 §2; removal of the patriarchal finance officer, 122 §2; granting the loss of the clerical state by the patriarch with consent of the permanent synod, 397; dismissal by the law itself or expulsion of a religious, 551; convalidation of marriage, 797 §2; separation of spouses, 864 §1; dispensation in a special case, 1538 §2;

to be avoided: of error or indifferentism in seeking sacraments from non-Catholic ministers, 671 §2; of corruption of eucharistic bread, 706; of violation of the sacramental seal, 729. 2°; of celebrating marriage invalidly or illicitly, 785 §1; of falling away from the faith in a mixed marriage, 814. 1°; of false irenicism, indifferentism, and immoderate zeal in ecumenical work, 905; of collusion or corruption in recalling witnesses for questioning, 1251; in inspecting the acts of a process, 1281 §1; of fraud or subornation in admitting proofs after the conclusion of a case, 1283

which an absolute majority vote is required, 166 §2;

of the eparchial assembly to be signed by the eparchial bishop alone, when they begin to bind, 241; of the superior about the place of novitiate in monasteries, 456 §2; personal and responsible d. regarding formation in a minor seminary, 344 §2; in a special case as an administrative act, 1510 §2. 1°; concerning recourse against an administrative decree, 1002, 1006;

in trials: of the general moderator for the administration of justice concerning an objection raised against any judge of the ordinary tribunal of the patriarchal Church, 1062 §5; of judges, concerning assistance to be requested from other tribunals, 1071; regarding conflicts about competence, 1083 §3; when the d. of a collegiate tribunal must be rendered by majority vote, 1085 §1; of an auditor about the collection of proofs, 1093 §3; of a judge about relative incompetence, 1119 §2; reasons for a d. to be stated by experts, 1260 §2; of judges in a discussion in their meeting, 1292 §§4–5; reasons for a d., regarding the nullity of a sentence, 1304 §1. 2°; regarding facts requiring a contrary d. in seeking *restitutio in integrum,* 1326 §2. 2°, 1327 §1; previous d. which has become *res iudicata,* in seeking *restitutio in integrum,* 1326 §2. 5°, 1327 §2; of the judge who issued a sentence, about the prior rendering of accounts, in the execution of the sentence, 1339; in a summary contentious trial, 1354 §§1–2; concerning the nullity of marriage to be confirmed by the appellate tribunal, 1368 §2; concerning the separation of spouses, 1378 §2, 1379 §2;

regarding imposition of penalties, 1469 §§1–2, 1480, 1487 §3;

see decree.

declaration of divine law in the laws issued by the supreme legislative authority of the Church, 1492; of the words of a law in an authentic interpretation, 1498 §2; of the pastors of the Church as teachers of the faith, 15 §1; by the college of bishops of a teaching concerning faith or morals to be held definitively, 597 §2;

of transfer to another Church *sui iuris,* 36; of the canonicity of a synod of bishops of the patriarchal Church, 69, 183 §1; with which authority a d. made in an eparchial assembly is to be communicated, 242; of notaries about the conformity of copies with the original, 254. 3°; of clerics concerning service for another eparchy, 366 §1. 4°, 748 §1; of the invalidity of sacred ordination, 394. 1°, 396, 1385–1387; of a fact, in the dismissal by the law itself from a religious institute or a society of

common life according to the manner of religious, 497 §2, 551, 562 §3; of the local hierarch concerning dismissal by the law itself from an association, 580; of the paternity of one baptized, 689 §2; for proof of baptism, 689 §2; concerning the freedom of a candidate for the order of the diaconate or presbyterate, 761, 769 §1. 1°; of the Catholic party in a mixed marriage, 814. 1°, 815; concerning non-canonical possession of an office, 944; of removal from office, 976 §2; of the nullity of a decree in a recourse against it, 1004, 1005; of the vacancy of a parish in the transfer of a pastor, 1399 §3; of presumed death, 1383 §§1–2;

of the nullity of marriage: how it ordinarily takes place, 1357–1371, 1376; by documentary process, 1372–1374; cannot take place by the summary contentious process, 1375; cannot take place while a doubt concerning impotence remains, 801 §2; to be notified to the pastor, 842;

in trials: of a juridic fact constitutes the object of a trial, 1055 §1. 1°; of a judge regarding his own competence, 115 §1, 119 §3, 1120; of defects, on account of which the nullity of the sentence may be considered, 1118 §1; to be rendered in writing, 1130; of the nullity of a sentence of arbitration, 1181 §3; concerning the hearing of minors or those of limited mental capacity, 1231 §1; of the abatement of a case, 1202; of the absence of a party, 1272 §1; of the parties or of the judge in the conclusion of a case, 1282 §2; concerning *res iudicata,* 1323 §2; of the nullity of a sentence if the summary contentious process has been used illegitimately, 1355; of the renunciation of a penal trial, 1475 §2; by sentence that a delict has not been committed, 1482; of the parties, 1195 §2, 1209, 1217 §2, 1219, 1282 §2, 1365; of persons to be interrogated, 1130; *see* confession, defence, deposition, observations.

decree *of the Roman Pontiff:* recourse or appeal against such a d. not permitted, 45 §3, 966; on the alteration of the boundaries of the territory of the patriarchal Church, 146 §2;

of the Apostolic See regarding the recognition of the status of a pontifical right institute of consecrated life, 434, 505 §§1–2, 554 §2, 563 §2;

of an ecumenical council: must be approved, confirmed and promulgated by the Roman Pontiff, 51 §1, 54 §2; canons on recourse cannot be applied to such a d., 996;

of the college of bishops must be confirmed and promulgated by the Roman Pontiff, 54 §2;

of the patriarch: what things can be contained, 82 §1. 1°; when they must be read or displayed publicly, 82 §2; concerning the patriarchal assembly, which has been suspended during a vacancy in the see, 142 §2; on the status or patriarchal right of an institute of consecrated life, 505 §2. 2°, 506 §3, 554 §2, 563 §2; regarding recourse, 1006;

of the eparchial bishop: concerning the eparchial assembly, which has been suspended during a vacancy in the see, 237 §2; regarding recourse, 999 §2;

of the eparchial assembly, with whom it is to be communicated, 242; of the exarch, regarding recourse, 316; of the local hierarch, about separation of the spouses, 864 §1; of a hierarch, by which someone is forbidden to preach, 613; of a protosyncellus or syncellus or someone who acts with delegated power, regarding recourse, 997 §2;

administrative: 1510 §2. 1°, 1513 §5; procedure in issuing, 1517–1520; acts and documents regarding it to be signed by a notary, 254. 1°; recourse against, 996–1006, 316, 501 §§2–3, 552 §3, 553, 562 §3, 613; of the appointment of an exarch, 314 §3; by which the invalidity of sacred ordination is declared, 394. 1°; on the suppression of a subsidiary monastery, 438 §3; of dismissal of a member from an institute of consecrated life, 500 §4, 501, 552 §3, 553, 562 §3, 568 §2; on the location of the novitiate, 521; of the approval of an association, 573 §1; of the constitution of a juridic person, 921 §1; on the rights and obligations proper to an office, 936 §2; on the withdrawal of canonical provision of an office, 940 §2; of removal from office, 974, 977; by which an offender is placed under supervision, 1428;

regarding removal or transfer of pastors, 1393 §2, 1394. 3°, 1396 §3, 1399 §2;

by which a penalty is imposed: 1402 §§2–3, 1408, 1420 §1. 1°, 1430 §1, 1431 §2, 1432 §2, 1469 §1, 1486 §1, 1487 §§1–2; its text to be preserved in the curial archives, 259 §2; regarding the prescription of a penal action, 1153 §2;

in trials: notion of a judicial d., 1300; which has the force of a definitive sentence, 1301, 1085 §1. 3°; judicial power can be delegated for acts preparatory to some d., 985 §3; intimation of a d., 1191 §1, 1192 §1, 1363 §§1 and 4; regarding an appeal from a d. that does not have the force of a definitive sentence, 1310. 4°; when there is no appeal, 1310. 5°; of the substitution of a judge, 1090 §2; concerning the reason for the adjudication of a case outside of the order in which it was presented, 1117; to remove a procurator or advocate, 1145; executory d. of a judge regarding the extinction of an action to execute a penalty, 1153 §1; to obtain provision of support, 1163; for a tribunal to designate arbiters, 1174; to remove arbiters, 1175; by

which incidental questions are resolved by the arbiters, 1177 §1; of confirmation of the sentence of the arbiters, 1181 §§1–2 and 4, 1182 §1, 1183; concerning the introductory *libellus* of a lawsuit, 1188 §1, 1189, 1190 §1, 1345 §1; of citation, 1190 §2, 1191 §1, 1363 §1; by which the object of a controversy is defined, 1195 §§1 and 3, 1363 §2; concerning the hearing of minors and those of limited mental capacity, 1231 §1; by which a witness is cited, 1237; by which the individual items are determined about which the services of an expert are requested, 1258 §1; concerning access and judicial recognizance, 1263; about an incidental question, 1269, 1270 §2, 1271, 1299 §2; regarding a party who does not appear, 1272; on the publication of the acts, 1281; on the conclusion of the case, 1282 §3; concerning the correction of a material error in the sentence, 1299 §1; on admitting a new proposition of the case, 1325 §1; on the execution of the sentence, 1338, 1153 §1; derogating from procedural norms, 1356; concerning the instruction of a matrimonial case, 1363 §4; about a sentence for the nullity of a marriage, 1368 §2, 1370; about the reasons for the separation of spouses, 1379 §2; regarding a penal trial, 1470, 1472 §1.

dedication of a sacred thing to divine worship, 1018; of two years to philosophical studies in major seminary, 348 §1.

defect *defects:* of the introductory *libellus* of litigation which can be corrected, 1188 §3; in documents to be evaluated by the judge, 1224; of nullity in a sentence, 1118 §1, 1303 §1, 1304 §1, 1310. 2°; regarding marriage in the documentary process, 1373 §1;

of form: regarding the validity of marriage, 827, 1372; regarding the convalidation of marriage, 847; regarding the radical sanation of marriage, 848 §1, 852; of procedure in the execution of an administrative act, 1523;

of discretion of judgement in matrimonial consent, 818. 2°; of matrimonial consent, regarding the convalidation of marriage, 846; of matrimonial consent on account of mental illness in marriage nullity cases, 1366; of a dispensation in a documentary process, 1373 §1; of the representative of a juridic person in a trial, 1138 §3; of reform in dismissal of a member in perpetual vows, 500 §2. 1°, 553; of a religious spirit in dismissal of a member in temporary vows, 552 §2. 2°, 465; of time in the novitiate to be supplied, 457 §2, 523 §1; of suitability, with respect to the removal of the mandate for teaching in a Catholic university, 644; of the condition on which a vow depends, with respect to the cessation of the vow, 891.

roneous doctrine, 1436 §2; omission of the commemoration of a hierarch in the Divine Liturgy and in the divine praises, 1438; handing over children to be baptized or educated in a non-Catholic religion, 1439; violation of norms for *communicatio in sacris*, 1440; employing sacred things for a profane use or an evil purpose, 1441; throwing away, taking or retaining the Divine Eucharist for an evil purpose, 1442; simulation of the celebration of a sacrament, 1443, 762 §1. 6°, 763. 2°; perjury, lying, concealment of the truth, 1444; physical force or injury against a bishop, metropolitan, patriarch, the Roman Pontiff and other persons, 1445; persistent disobedience after a warning, 1446; incitement of sedition or hatred against a hierarch, provocation to disobedience against a hierarch, 1447 §1; obstruction of ecclesiastical freedom, 1447 §2; blasphemy, injury to good morals, insults, hatred or contempt against religion or the Church, 1448; joining an association which plots against the Church, 1448 §2; illegitimate alienation of temporal goods, 1449; homicide or abortion, 1450, 728 §2, 762 §1. 4°, 763. 2°, 766, 767 §1. 2°, 768 §1, 795 §1. 3°, 807; abduction, unjust detention, wounding, torture, 1451; mutilation, 1451, 762 §1. 5°, 763. 2°; grave insult or calumny, 1452; concubinage and sins against the chastity of a cleric or a religious, 1453 §§1 and 3; attempted marriage by a cleric, 1453 §2, 762 §1. 3°, 763. 2°, 767 §1. 2°, 976 §1. 2°; attempted marriage by a member of an institute of consecrated life, 1453 §3, 497 §1. 2°, 551, 562 §3, 762 §1. 3°, 763. 2°, 767 §1. 2°; false denunciation of a d., 1454; falsification of documents and their alteration, destruction or concealment, 1455; violation of the sacramental seal, 1456, 728 §1. 1°, 733; absolution of an accomplice in a sin against chastity, 1457, 728 §1. 2°, 730; solicitation of a sin against chastity during or under the pretext of confession, 1458; illegitimate sacred ordination, 1459; recourse to a civil power to obtain sacred ordination, an office, ministry or function in the Church, 1460; simony, 1461, 1462; usurpation or illegitimate retention of an office, ministry or function, 1462; inducing someone to illegitimate actions or omissions with regard to offices, ministries or functions, 1463; abuse of office, ministry or function, 1464 §1; culpable negligence in the exercise of power, office, ministry or function, 1464 §2; inducing someone to transfer to another Church *sui iuris*, 31, 1465; exercising a trade or business contrary to the canons by clerics or members of institutes of consecrated life, 1466; violation of an obligation imposed by a penalty, 1467.

delinquent *see* delict;

regarding: the medicinal purpose of penalties, 1401; requirements for a hierarch to be able to abstain from imposing obligatory penalties, 1403 §1; the prior warning of a penalty, 1407 §1; *see* warning; regarding disobedience to one's own hierarch, 1446.

denunciation false d. of an confessor, 731; how the false d. concerning any delict is to be punished, 1454; of the nullity of the judicial acts with regard to their sanation by a sentence, 1302.

departure from the synod of bishops of the patriarchal Church, 109; from the council of hierarchs, 165 §4; of a coadjutor or auxiliary bishop from the eparchy for a brief time, 217; of clerics from the eparchy, 386 §1, 452 §1; regarding the admission to a seminary of someone who has departed from another seminary or a religious institute or a society of common life according to the manner of religious, 342 §3; of a superior from that superior's monastery, 446; free d. from the novitiate, 461 §1, 525 §1; regarding the dowry of one departing from a religious institute, 454, 488 §4, 545 §4; illegitimate d. from a monastery, 495; regarding the cession or disposition of certain goods made by one who has departed from an order or congregation, 529 §4; regarding the d. of a religious from an institute, 492, 493, 494 §1, 496, 503, 529 §4, 546, 549; regarding the pauline privilege, 854, 857. 3°; regarding the separation of spouses, 864 §1; from a place, with regard to the loss of domicile and quasi domicile, 917; of an authority from the agreed opinion of persons in placing a juridic act, 934 §2. 3°;

confession of a sick person who cannot depart from the house, 729. 1°;

see absence, dismissal, expulsion, indult.

deposit of faith, 595 §1, 598 §1; divine d., to which the sacraments belong, 669;

of money, 1335. 5°.

deposition from the clerical state, 1433 §2, 394. 2°, 685 §1. 6°, 1084 §1. 3°, 1172. 2°, 1402 §2, 1410, 1436 §1, 1442, 1445 §1, 1450 §1, 1453 §1, 1458, 1460; from office, 762 §1. 7°; of witnesses, 1383 §2; of the text of a sentence of arbitration or of documents at the tribunal chancery, 1181 §1, 1225; of the ecclesiastical habit by a member expelled from a religious institute or from a society of common life according to the manner of religious, 498 §1, 551, 562 §3.

deprivation how one deprived of the administration of goods may stand trial, 1136 §4.

determination of the question   when and how it takes place, 1190 §1, 1195 §2.

devices   *technical devices for reproduction:* regarding writings or messages, governed by the norms of law for books, 654; of voices in the interrogation of witnesses, 1248 §2, 1250 §1.

dicastery   *of the Apostolic See:* included in the term "Apostolic See" in the Code, 48; in cases which are reserved to dicasteries, tribunals are to follow the norms established by the d., 1056; competent in cases to declare the nullity of sacred ordination, 1386 §§1–2.

dignity   *of the human person:* it belongs to the Church to defend, 595 §2; the obligation of preachers of the word of God to teach the Church's doctrine regarding it, 616 §2; Catholics are to cooperate with other Christians in defending it, 908;

equality of the Christian faithful regarding it, 11; of other persons to be considered in manifesting their opinions, 15 §3; of lay persons to be acknowledged and fostered by clerics, 381 §3;

error regarding the d. of the sacrament of marriage, 822;

ecclesiastical: equality of patriarchs by reason of d., 59 §1; regarding precedence of patriarchs in certain churches, 59 §4; regarding the requirements for the patriarchal d., 64; right of the patriarch to confer, 89 §3; right of the eparchial bishop to confer, 194; of the metropolitan joined to a determined eparchial see, 135 §1; exarchs, protosyncelli and syncelli hold the first d. after the episcopal d., 321, 250; clerics cannot make use of rights and insignia attached to dignities conferred on them outside of the place in which the authority who conferred the d. exercises power, except under certain conditions, 388; merely honorary titles cannot be conferred on religious, with certain exceptions, 430; outside of their own institute, with regard to religious, 431 §§1 and 2. 1°; one punished by a major excommunication cannot validly receive a d., 1434 §3;

regarding a privilege granted by reason of the d. of a place, 1522 §3.

dimissorial letters   required for diaconal or presbyteral ordination, 747; their issue, 750, 472, 537 §1, 560 §1; not to be issued unless testimonies required by law have been received, 751; to what bishop they may be sent, 752, 478, 537 §2, 560 §1; can be limited by restrictions or revoked, 753; ordaining bishop can abide by their attestation, but is not bound to, 770; regarding the authentic testimony of sacred ordination, 774 §2.

diocese (CIC)   *see* eparchy.

diocesan bishop (CIC)   *see* eparchial bishop.

directory   *of a seminary:* notion, 337 §§2–3; responsibility of the rector that the d. is observed by everyone, 338 §1;

catechetical: by whom it is to be compiled, 621 §1; what things are to be contained in it, 621 §2.

discernment   of spirits to be cultivated in the seminary, 346 §1. 8°; intellectual d. in seminary courses, by which truth and falsehood are distinguished, 349 §2; spiritual d., by which clerics employ temporal goods for their proper use, 385 §1; Christian d., regarding shows selected by pastors and rectors of churches, 665 §2; of judgement for entering into marriage, 818. 2°; prudent d. of the authority removing from office, 975 §2.

discipline   disciplinary heritage, with regard to rites, 28 §1, 405;

ecclesiastical: to be fostered by the patriarch in assemblies of bishops, 84 §1; regarding the patriarchal assembly, 140; regarding the council of hierarchs, 169; vigilance concerning d. on the part of the metropolitan, 133 §1. 4°, 138, 139, 159. 4°, 175; vigilance concerning d. and its promotion on the part of the eparchial bishop, 201 §2, 577 §2; vigilance concerning d. with regard to associations, 577; regarding the assembly of hierarchs of several Churches *sui iuris*, 322 §1;

monastic or religious, 413, 415 §3, 437 §3, 471–480, 524 §3, 536–543; regarding the imposition of penal laws, 1405 §1;

of a seminary, 337 §§1–2, 339 §2, 346 §3;

regarding the force of the disciplinary laws of the synod of bishops of the patriarchal Church, 150 §§2–3;

to be taught: in seminaries, 330 §3, 340 §§1–2, 348, 350 §§1–2 and 4, 352 §2; regarding the mandate for teaching sacred disciplines on the part of lay persons, 404 §3; in universities and faculties, 606 §3, 641, 644, 647. 2°.

discussion   in the synod of bishops of the patriarchal Church about the territory of that Church or the Christian faithful living outside of its territory, 146 §2, 148 §3;

in trials: of the case, 1285–1288; secret d. of the judges before passing sentence, 1113 §2, 1292 §§3–4, 1293 §2; in an appeal, 1321; in a summary contentious trial, 1353, 1354 §1; in a penal trial, 1476–1479;

to impose a penalty by an extrajudicial decree, 1486 §1. 2°;

prior to the removal of a pastor, 1391 §1.

dismissal from the clerical state: *see* deposition, loss; of clerics from an eparchy, 357 §2, 359, 363, 365 §2, 366 §1. 3°, 494 §2;

in institutes of consecrated life: from the novitiate, 461, 525 §1; from a monastery, 495, 497–503; from an order or congregation, 547 §3, 550, 551–553; from a society of common life according to the manner of religious, 562 §3; from a secular institute, 568 §2;

from an association, 580, 581;

regarding the admission into a seminary of someone dismissed from another seminary or from certain institutes of consecrated life, 342 §3; arbitrary d. of an administrator of temporal goods, 1033; of wives or husbands of an unbaptized party after their baptism, 859 §§1 and 3; of the absolved party by a sentence, 1291 §4.

disobedience as delict, 1446; provocation of subject to d. to be published, 1447 §1.

disparity of cult marriage impediment, 803.

dispensation notion, 1536 §1; spiritual good of the Christian faithful as a reason, 1536 §2; can be granted where there is doubt about the sufficiency of the reason, 1536 §3; what laws are not subject to d., 1537; from penal law, regarding the remission of the penalty, 1419 §1; from laws where there is doubt about a fact, 1496; extent of the power to d., 1539; regarding interpretation, 1512 §4; its cessation, 1513 §§1–4; from the obligation of clerical celibacy is reserved to the Roman Pontiff, 395–397, 493 §1, 549 §3, 795 §1. 1° and §2, 796 §1, 1433 §2, 1538 §2; dispensations reserved to the Apostolic See, 414 §1. 2° and §2, 767 §2, 795 §2, 835;

the dispensation power: of the patriarch, 414 §1. 2° and §2, 767 § 2, 795 § 2, 835, 852; of an eparchial bishop, 1538 § 1, 414 § 1. 2°, 767 § 1, 852; of a local hierarch, 795 §1, 796 §1, 855 §2, 893 §1. 2°; of a hierarch, 1538 §2, 893 §1. 1°, 1496; of a hierarch of an institute of consecrated life, 767 §1; of superiors in institutes of consecrated life, 414 §1. 2°, 767 §1, 893 §1. 1° and 3°; of a pastor, 796 §2, 797 §1, 893 §1. 1°–2°; of a confessor, 767 §3, 796 §2, 797 §1, 893 §2; of the priest who can bless a marriage, 796 §2, 797 §1, 832 §2;

by the law itself from vows and obligations arising from profession in an indult of departure from a religious institute, 493 §1, 549 §3; from the required age for sacred ordination, 759 §2; from impediments to receive or exercise sacred orders, 767, 768; from marriage impediments, 795, 796 §§1–2, 797 §1, 798, 799, 803 §3, 841 §1, 843 §1, 848 §1, 1372 §1, 1373 §1; from the form for the celebra-

tion of marriage, 796 §§1–2, 798, 835, 841 §1, 848 §1, 1372 §1, 1373 §1; from interpellations in a case of the pauline privilege, 855 §2; from a vow, 891; from private vows, 893; from a canonical impediment in the case of postulation, 961, 963 §1.

disqualification of lay persons for functions which require sacred orders, 408 §2; to exercise sacred orders, 762 §1. 1°, 763. 3°; for marriage on account of an impediment, 790 §1, 800–812; to cast a vote in an election, 953 §1; of a deposed cleric for those things of which he has been deprived by a penalty, 1433 §2;

disqualifying law: which laws are considered disqualifying, 1495; regarding a doubt of law or fact, 1496; in case of ignorance or error regarding a disqualifying law, 1497 §1; *see* capacity, inability, incapacity, qualification, suitability.

dissolution of an ecumenical council, 51 §1, 53; of the synod of bishops of the patriarchal Church, 108 §1; of the metropolitan synod, 133 §1. 2°, 138; of the patriarchal assembly, 142 §1; of the council of hierarchs, 159. 2°; of the eparchial assembly, 237 §1, 319 §1; of the presbyteral council, 270 §3;

of the bond of marriage: of a sacramental bond after the marriage has been consummated can be given by no human power, 853; regarding a non-consummated marriage, 862, 1367, 1384; in favor of the faith, 1384; by the pauline privilege, 854–858; regarding a party who, before receiving baptism in the Catholic Church, had several husbands or wives at the same time, 859 §1; regarding a non-baptized person who, after receiving baptism in the Catholic Church, cannot restore cohabitation because of captivity or persecution, 860; its notification and recording, 842; regarding the ascription of a woman to a Church *sui iuris*, 33; when a new marriage can be celebrated after a d., 802 §2; takes place after the declaration of the presumed death of a spouse, 1383; regarding the constitution of the defender of the bond, 1096 §1.

district composed of several parishes, 276 §1; its erection, modification, suppression, 276 §2; a protopresbyter is placed in charge, 276 §1; function of the protopresbyter in it, 278 §2; care of the eparchial bishop for the apostolate in it, 203 §1; one pastor to be chosen to be sent to the eparchial assembly from each d., 238 §1. 6°; regarding the election of members of the presbyteral council, 268; regarding the appointment of the protopresbyter, 277 §1.

disturbance grave d. of conjugal life, caused by deceit, 821; of ecclesiastical communion as a reason for the removal of a pastor, 1390. 1°.

Christian faithful concerning Sundays and feast days, 881 §1;

commemorations in them: of the Roman Pontiff, 91, 92 §2, 161, 162, 209 §1; of the patriarch, 91; of the metropolitan, 135, 161; of the eparchial bishop, 209 §2; the delict of omitting a commemoration prescribed by law, 1438.

doctorate *in the sacred sciences as a requirement for:* candidates for the episcopate, 180. 6°; protosyncelli and syncelli, 247 §2; *see* academic degrees, licentiate;

in canon law as a requirement for: judicial vicar and adjunct judicial vicar, 1086 §4; judges, 1087 §3; the promotor of justice and defender of the bond, 1099 §2; advocates, 1141; *see* academic degrees, licentiate.

doctrine revealed by Christ regarding the rights and obligations of lay persons, 404 §1; of Christ regarding catechetical instruction, 617;

concerning faith and morals: of the infallible magisterium, 597; to be believed with divine and Catholic faith, 598 §1, 1436 §1; to be held definitively, 598 §2, 1436 §2; of the authentic magisterium of the Roman Pontiff or the college of bishops, 599; mandate for teaching it in Catholic universities, 644;

Catholic: in ecclesiastical universities, 647. 2°; regarding the instruments of social communication, 653; regarding censors of books, 664 §2; regarding the hierarchy of truths in it, 348 §2; drawn from divine revelation, 350 §1;

of the Church: the right of the Christian faithful to a form of the spiritual life in accord with it, 17; concerning the dignity and fundamental rights of the human person, on family life, on civil and social life, as well as on the meaning of justice, in preaching, 616 §2; regarding catechetical instruction, 626; authentic d., with respect to approved, praised or blessed texts, 661 §§2–3;

proposed by the Church's magisterium: to be taken into account by lay persons, 402, 404 §1; things contrary to it are to be avoided by all the Christian faithful, 598; regarding the censors of books, 664 §2;

Christian: obligations of the eparchial bishop regarding, 196 §1; regarding associations to foster it, 574;

ecclesiastical: regarding an association whose action causes serious harm to it, 577 §2;

canonical: on the circumstances of a delict, 1415, 1416; regarding the interpretation of laws, 1501;

care of the pastors of the Church for the integrity and unity of the faith amidst varieties of doctrinal enunciations, 604; regarding the care of theologians for doctrinal progress, 606 §1; sound d. in the instructions of the patriarch, 82 §1. 2°; sacred d. with respect to religious instruction, 471 §1, 536 §1; evangelical d. in the vocation of the Christian faithful to lead lives in harmony with it, 20; doctrinal preparation in the reception of a non-Catholic into the Catholic Church, 897;

regarding instruction: in seminaries, 330 §2, 340 §3, 347, 348 §2, 350 §§1 and 3, 351; in Catholic universities, 641, 644;

required: in an eparchial administrator, 227 §1; in a protosyncellus and syncellus, 247 §2; in a protopresbyter, 277 §1; in a pastor, 285 §1; in teachers in Catholic schools, 639; in censors of books, 664 §4; in an auditor, 1093 §2;

regarding means to be used prior to a penalty, 1401; delicts against a doctrine that must be held, 1436.

document *public:* notion of an ecclesiastical document, 1221 §1; notion of a civil document, 1221 §2; its force in a trial, 1222;

private: notion, 1221 §3; its force in a trial, 1223;

confirmed by the Roman Pontiff *in forma specifica* with regard to the power of a judge, 1060 §3;

the care of the eparchial bishop for those documents which are to be preserved in the territory of the eparchy, 261; the care of the protopresbyter for documents when a pastor is ill or deceased, 278 §3; the rights and obligations of notaries, 254. 1° and 3°; to be signed by the pastor or his delegate, 296 §3;

of ascription to a Church *sui iuris* or of transfer to another Church *sui iuris,* 37; about candidates for the episcopacy, 182 §1; of the enthronement of a bishop, 189 §2; about qualification for admission to a seminary, 342 §1; of legitimate dismissal from an eparchy, 366 §1. 3°; on suitability for admission to a religious institute, 453 §3, 519; of religious profession, 470, 535 §2; of the eparchial curia about certain things with respect to dimissorial letters of certain superiors of institutes of consecrated life, 537 §2, 560 §1; of the erection of a university or faculty, 642 §1, 649; about paternity, 689 §2; regarding candidacy for sacred ordination, 769; on the results of the pre-nuptial investigations, 787; of the consecration of a church, 871 §2; on which the rights of a juridic person over ecclesiastical goods are based, with respect to the administrator of goods, 1028 §2. 8°;

regarding the possession of temporal goods not confirmed by a d., 1020 §3;

regarding those documents which must be kept in the archives of the eparchial curia, 228 §2, 256,

257 §2, 258, 259 §1, 260 §3, 261 §1, 871 §2; to be preserved in the parish archives, 296 §4;

of a foundation: where copies are to be kept, 1050; regarding the required consent of the members of the finance council, 263 §4; regarding the reduction of obligations for celebrating the Divine Liturgy, 1052 §2;

in procedures: regarding proof by documents, 1220–1227; when they have probative force, 1225; regarding defects, 1224; their exhibition, 1226–1227, 1283 §2, 1344 §2; regarding experts, 1258 §2, 1259 §2; access or judicial recognizance, 1264; which are to be returned when the trial is over, 1133 §1; which cannot be handed over without a mandate from the judge, 1133 §2; the force of documents attributed to the acts of a case after abatement regarding those not party to the case, 1203; permission of the judge for documents to be printed, 1285 §2; regarding *restitutio in integrum*, 1326 §2. 2°; which may be inspected in a matrimonial process, 1364 §1. 2°; regarding the documentary process, 1372 §1, 1373 §1; regarding the process for the presumed death of a spouse, 1383 §1;

regarding the cessation of a decree or an individual precept, 1513 §5;

about public correction, 1427 §1; the delict of falsification, alteration, destruction, or hiding of a d., 1455;

see testimony.

domicile   how acquired, 912 §1, 913–915; how lost, 917; how a proper hierarch and pastor are determined through it, 916 §§1–2 and 4–5; of religious or members of a society of common life according to the manner of religious, 913; of spouses, 914; of minors, 915 §1; of those who are under care or guardianship, 915 §2; only eparchial, 916 §2; regarding travelers and transients, 911;

regarding: election of members of the presbyteral council, 276 §1. 2°; the loss of the clerical state granted by the patriarch, 397; recourse against a decree of dismissal for monks in the patriarchal Church, 501 §3; a bishop to whom dimissorial letters are to be sent by superiors in certain institutes of consecrated life, 537 §2, 560 §1; an indult of departure from an order or congregation, 549 §2. 1°–2°; the faculty to administer the sacrament of penance, 722 §4, 726 §3; the proper bishop of a candidate for sacred ordination, 748 §1; dispensation from the required age for sacred ordination granted by the patriarch, 759 §2; dispensation from certain impediments for receiving or exercising sacred orders granted by the patriarch, 767

§2; the lawful blessing of marriage, 831 §1. 1°; the convocation of electors, 948 §1; the beneficiary of certain goods held in trust, 1046 §3; forum, 1074, 1074 §2, 1079. 2°, 1359. 2°–4°; the introductory *libellus* of a lawsuit, 1187. 4°; witnesses, 1233 §1; reservation of penalties to the patriarch or major archbishop, 1423 §1; those subject to laws, 1491 §2.

donation   by what right an administrator can make a d., 1029; made to the Church by vow, with regard to alienation, 1036 §§3–4, 1037. 3°; regarding the delict of corruption, 1463; *see* offering.

donor   those things which have been imposed by the d. must be observed by the administrator of goods, 1028 §1. 2°; what things the d. of goods held in trust cannot prohibit, 1046 §1.

doubt   *in doubt:* laws do not bind, 1496; of fact, how it belongs to the hierarch to dispense from laws, 1496; positive and probable, the Church supplies certain powers and faculties, 994, 995; the validity of marriage is to be upheld, 779; what the pastor must do in d. concerning the existence of an impediment to marriage, 788; marriage is not to be impeded or declared null in case of d. concerning the impediment of impotence, 801 §2; about baptism, regarding the impediment of disparity of cult, 803 §2; about consanguinity in the direct line or in the second degree of the collateral line, marriage is never to be permitted, 808 §3; the privilege of the faith enjoys the favor of the law, 861; that consummation of a marriage did not occur in a case of matrimonial nullity, 1367; the revocation of a law is not presumed, but is to be reconciled with prior laws, 1503; regarding the interpretation of an administrative act, 1512 §2; about the sufficiency of the reason, a dispensation is lawfully and validly granted, 1536 §3;

about how a law is to be interpreted, 1499; an authentic interpretation, given in the form of law, explaining a doubtful law is not retroactive, 1498 §2;

on the conferral of the sacraments of baptism, chrismation with sacred myron or sacred ordination, 672 §2, 803 §3;

regarding the territorial boundaries of the patriarchal Church, 146 §2;

in a trial: how the formulation of the d. is to be determined, 1190 §1, 1195 §2, 1347 §1, 1363 §§2–3; the obligation of the judge to prove a fact beyond d. which is in the public interest, 1211; determined by a sentence, 1294. 1°, 1295 §2; with respect to the consummation of marriage, 1367; regarding the rejection of an introductory *libellus* of litigation, if it is undoubtedly evident that the petitioner lacks personal standing in the trial, 1188 §2. 2°; regarding facts which undoubtedly prove the necessity of *restitutio in integrum*, 1326 §2. 2°;

a declaration about the reception of baptism founded on solid arguments, 691; the certain and undoubted boundaries of ecclesiastical territories are not subject to prescription, 1542. 4°;

when someone who calls what is to be believed by divine and catholic faith into doubt must be punished as a heretic, 1436 §1.

dowry norms concerning the d. to be determined in monasteries by the typicon, 454; what is owed to the one transferring to another religious institute, 488 §4, 545 §4.

E

Easter regarding the obligation to receive the Divine Eucharist at E. time, 708.

Eastern Catholic Church the Code affects only these Churches, unless it is otherwise expressly stated, 1; their function in fostering unity among all Eastern Churches, 903; *see* Church *sui iuris,* Eastern Churches.

Eastern Churches their ancient law, with regard the Code, 2; regarding the ascription of the Christian faithful to them, 38; their rites to be preserved and fostered, 39; their patriarchs, 55, 58, 59, 76 §1, 111 §3; major archbishop, 151; their practice regarding the state of married clerics, 373; their special character to be taken into account in a catechetical directory, 621 §2; regarding chrismation with holy myron, 694, 696 §§1–2; their tradition regarding engagements, 782 §1; feast days and days of penance common to them, 880 §1; regarding unity among them, 903; their ancient traditions regarding penalties, 1426 §1; which laws issued by the supreme authority of the Church affect their Christian faithful, 1492; regarding the notion of common law or particular law, 1493 §1; *see* Church *sui iuris.*

Eastern non-Catholic Church its image to be correctly presented, 625; *communicatio in sacris* regarding the sacraments, 671 §§2–3 and 5; when a member may be admitted as a sponsor, 685 §3; regarding its marriage law, 780 §2. 1°, 781; regarding the marriage of one who rejects the Catholic faith, even without becoming a member of a non-Catholic Church, 789. 6°; when its priest may be called for the celebration of marriage in case of necessity, 832 §2; regarding the blessing of its marriages requested from a Catholic priest, 833; regarding the form for the celebration of marriage, 834 §2; regarding members coming

into full communion with the Catholic Church, 896–900; regarding the ecumenical movement, 902–908.

ecclesiastical funerals notion, 875; belong to the pastor, 290 §2; must be given to the Christian faithful and catechumens, 875; when they may be granted to baptized non-Catholics, 876 §1; regarding children and others who seemed to be close to the Church, who died before they received baptism, 876 §2; regarding cremation, 876 §3; those who are to be denied e. f., 877; all personal favoritism is to be avoided, 878 §1; regarding offerings on the occasion of e. f., 878 §2, 1013; when a grave must be blessed on the occasion of e. f., 874 §2; regarding registration of a funeral after burial, 879; *see* funerals.

economy of salvation instruction concerning it in seminaries, 348 §2, 350 §2.

ecumenical council where the college of bishops exercises its power in a solemn manner, 50 §1; is the subject of the infallible magisterium, 597 §2; competence of the Roman Pontiff regarding it, 51; who is to take part, 52; interrupted during a vacancy of the Apostolic See, 53; binding force of its decrees, 54 §1; recourse against its acts not permitted, 996; *see* college of bishops.

ecumenism general canons, 902–908; obligation of all the Christian faithful to participate in ecumenical work, 902; special function of the Eastern Catholic Churches, 903; to be fostered by special norms of particular law in each Church *sui iuris,* with the Roman Pontiff directing it for the whole Church, 904 §1; commission for it in a Church *sui iuris,* 904 §2; how it is to be fostered in eparchies, 904 §3; how ecumenical work is to be carried out, 905–908; *see* observers;

is one of the necessary dimensions of every theological discipline in seminaries, 350 §4; seminary students to be taught about its apostolate, 352 §3; regarding the ecumenical dimension of catechesis, 625.

education *Christian:* right of the Christian faithful, 20; to be fostered in missionary territories, 592 §1; judgement of the eparchial bishop regarding whether schools fulfill its requirements or not, 633 §1;

Catholic: general canons, 627–630; obligation of parents regarding children, 627; obligation of the Church, 628 §1; obligation of those to whom the care of souls has been entrusted, 628 §2; the whole human person is to be formed, 629; to be fostered by the Christian faithful everywhere, 630; regarding schools, 631 §1, 633 §1; *see* schools;

the free reception of a sacred order, 761; the obligation to reveal impediments to him, 771 §2; testimonial letters, 769 §1. 6°; investigations concerning candidates for sacred ordination, 771 §4; recording of sacred ordination and a certificate attesting to its conferral, 774, 775; norms for the recording of marriage, 841 §1; radical sanation of marriage, 852; permission to erect sacred places, 868; consent for building a church, 870; reservation of the consecration of a church, 871 §2; reduction of a church to profane use, 873;

regarding religious institutes: exempt from his governance, 412 §2, 486; immediately subject to him, 413, 505 §2. 3°; his competence over institutes of eparchial right, 414 §§1 and 3, 418 §2, 419 §1; regarding the erection of institutes of eparchial right, 434, 435 §1, 437, 506 §1; his consent for the erection of a dependent monastery of a religious house, 436 §2, 509 §1; his consent for a school, guest house, or similar buildings or for the conversion of a monastery to other uses, 437 §§2–3, 509 §2; his counsel or consent for the suppression of an institute or religious house, 438 §§1 and 3, 507 §2, 510; his counsel or consent for a monastic confederation, 439 §§1–2, 440 §§1–2; his right to preside at an elective synaxis, 443 §1; his counsel or consent for licit admission to the novitiate, 452 §1, 517 §1; to whom religious should send dimissorial letters, 472, 537 §2; must be informed about the boundaries of the cloister, 477 §3; his consent concerning a hermit outside of the monastery precincts, 483; his counsel concerning the grant of stauropegial status to a monastery, 486 §1; his consent for transfer to another institute of consecrated life, 487 §§2–3, 544 §2; can grant an induct of exclaustration for three years, 489 §2, 548; to whom the one exclaustrated is subject, 491; regarding departure or dismissal of a member from an institute during temporary profession, 496 §2, 499, 552 §1; regarding the departure of a member in perpetual vows, 549 §2. 1°–2°; regarding the dismissal of members, 500 §4, 552 §1, 553; reception by him of a religious constituted in a sacred order who has departed or been dismissed, 494, 502, 549 §3, 553; his norms concerning wearing the habit by members outside of their own houses, 540; regarding religious pastors or parochial vicars, 282, 284 §§2–3. 1°, 286. 1°, 301 §3, 303, 480, 543, 1391 §2;

with respect to societies of common life according to the manner of religious, 554 §2 [505 §2. 3°, 413, 414 §§1 and 3, 418 §2, 419 §1], 556 [506 §1, 507 §2, 509, 510], 560 §1 [537 §2], 562 §3 [500 §4, 502, 494, 552 §1];

with respect to secular institutes, 563 §2 [505 §2], 566 [414 §§1 and 3, 506 §1, 509, 510], 568 [450];

with respect to new forms of consecrated life, 571;

with respect to associations: is to promote them, 203 §3; is to be vigilant of them in his eparchy, 577; erects or approves eparchial associations, 575 §1. 1°; his consent for the erection of a branch of a non-eparchial association, 575 §2; suppresses associations erected or approved by himself, 583 §2. 2°;

with respect to the temporal goods of the Church: can impose a tax for the good of the eparchy, 1012; regarding fees, offerings and alms, 1013–1016; is to constitute a common fund for the eparchy, 1021 §3, 1047 §2; is to be vigilant of the administration of goods in his eparchy, 1022 §1; his consent or counsel required to alienate goods, 1036, 1039; erects autonomous pious foundations, 1048 §1; regarding the reduction of obligations for celebrating the Divine Liturgy, 1052 §§3–4 and 6;

with respect to judicial power: 191 §1, 1066, 1107 §2; his appeal tribunal, 1064; tribunal of first instance for several eparchies, 1067; tribunal of first instance common to eparchies of different Churches *sui iuris*, 1068; can reserve a certain case to a college of three judges, 1084 §2; when he may commit cases reserved to a college of judges to a single judge, 1084 §3; regarding the constitution or removal of a judicial vicar and adjunct judicial vicar, 1086 §§1–2, 1088 §§2–3; regarding the appointment or removal of judges, 1087 §§1–2, 1088, 1102 §1; can change the order of designation of judges, 1090 §1; admits auditors to their office, 1093 §§1–2; appoints or removes the promotor of justice and defender of the bond, 1099 §1, 1100 §2; approves the statutes of the eparchial tribunal, 1070; judges in which cases the public good can be endangered, 1095 §1; his consent is required for judges or tribunal officials subject to him to be appointed in another eparchy, 1102 §1; is to strive to avoid litigation, or to resolve it peacefully, 1103 §1; a judge who exercises his power outside of his own territory must inform the e. b. of that place, 1128 §1; his permission for a judge of another eparchy to collect proofs in the bishop's eparchy, 1128 §2; must be heard to admit a guardian or curator appointed by a civil authority, 1137; can appoint a guardian for a minor, 910 §2; his approval of a procurator or advocate, 1141; regarding the suspension of an advocate, 1146 §1; by whom a sentence is to be sent for execution, 1184 §2, 1340 §§1–2; his opinion concerning the petition of spouses to obtain the dissolution of a

of a tribunal: ordinary tribunal of the patriarchal Church, 1063 §1; metropolitan tribunal, 133 §1. 3°, 138, 139, 159. 3°, 175; of first instance for several eparchies of the same Church *sui iuris,* 1067 §§1–3; when an eparchial collegial tribunal cannot be erected, 1067 §3;

of an association: 203 §3, 573 §1, 574, 575 §1, 582, 583 §1; of a branch of an association, 575 §2;

regarding institutes of consecrated life: of a monastic confederation, 423, 439; of a monastery, 423, 434, 435, 436 §2, 437 §§1 and 3; regarding a stauropegial monastery, 486 §1; of an order, congregation or society of common life according to the manner of religious, 423, 504, 505 §§1–2, 506 §§1–2, 507, 556, 558 §1; of a province, 423, 508 §2, 556, 558 §1, 567 §1; of a house, 423, 509, 437 §§1 and 3, 556, 558 §1, 566, 567 §1, 575 §2; of a novitiate, 521; of a secular institute, 566, 506, 507 §1, 567 §1;

regarding exemption of a juridic person in the very act of e. in a patriarchal Church, 90;

of the prescribed commissions for Churches *sui iuris* in a patriarchal Church, 124; of a juridic person, 921, 922 §1, 923, 928, 929; of a finance council, 263 §1; of a seminary, 328, 332, 334, 335 §1; of a school, 630 §2, 631 §2, 632; of universities or faculties, 642 §1, 648, 649; of sacred places, 868; of an office, 937 §1; of institutes for insurance, social security and health insurance for clerics, 1021 §2; of a pious foundation, 1047 §1. 1°, 1048 §§1 and 3.

error its force with respect to laws, 1497; with respect to the execution of an administrative act, 1526; its force in a juridic act, 933; in matrimonial consent, 820–823; substantial e. renders the provision and resignation of an office null, 946, 968; its force in the confession or declaration of a party in a trial, 1219; must be corrected in the text of a sentence, 1183, 1299 §1;

in common error the Church supplies executive power of governance, the faculties which are required for the celebration or administration of sacraments, and in religious institutes, the power of superiors or synaxes determined by common law, the typicon or statutes, 994, 995, 441 §1, 511 §1;

danger of e. must be avoided in receiving sacraments from a non-Catholic minister, 671 §2;

returning the erring, with regard penal law, 1401; penalty for one who affirms a doctrine which has been condemned as erroneous, 1436 §2; permission to publish books signified that the work is free from errors regarding faith and morals, 661 §1.

eucharist *see* divine eucharist, divine liturgy.

evangelical counsels in institutes of common life according to the manner of religious, 554 §1; in secular institutes, 563 §1. 1°.

evangelization *of peoples:* obligation of the Church, 584 §1; which are missionary territories, 594; how it is to take place, 584 §2; obligation of each Church regarding the preaching of the Gospel to the whole world under the guidance of the Roman Pontiff, 585 §1; commission to promote the Church's missionary activity in certain Churches *sui iuris,* 585 §2; the promotion of initiatives for the missions in each eparchy, 585 §3; the obligation of the Christian faithful, 585 §4, 586; with respect to safeguarding religious freedom, 586; the catechumenate, 587; the freedom of catechumens to be ascribed to any Church *sui iuris,* 30, 588; care should be taken lest anything be recommended that might prevent the ascription of catechumens in a Church *sui iuris* more appropriate to their culture, 588; formation of missionaries, 589; care for young Churches, 590; care of missionaries for promoting vocations among neophytes, 591. 1°; formation and remuneration of catechists, 591. 2°; care for the apostolate of the laity in missionary territories, 592 §1; dialogue and cooperation with non-Christians, 592 §2; cooperation among presbyters in missionary territories, 593 §1; regarding collaboration with other Christian missionaries, 593 §2, 908;

regarding seminary formation for dialogue with non-believers, 352 §2; as a reason for the transfer or movement of clerics to another eparchy, 361; regarding the connection of ecclesiastical universities and faculties with the task of evangelization, 646.

evil regarding the promotion by the eparchial bishop of instruments of social communication, 652 §1; when danger of e. exempts from the obligation to respond in a trial, 1229 §2. 2°; greater e. as a reason to defer penalty, 1409 §1. 1°;

regarding penalties against one who uses sacred things for an e. purpose, 1441.

examination *in the synod of bishops of the patriarchal Church:* regarding the agenda to be followed in the e. of questions, 108 §1; of the report of administration and the budget of income and expenditures of the patriarchal finance officer, 122 §4; of the list of candidates for the episcopacy, 182 §3;

of the report of administration of the eparchial finance officer by the eparchial bishop through the finance council, 262 §4;

tion to be done by the pastor, 289 §1; of the function of catechists, 591. 2°;

of a pious will: executor is the hierarch, 1045 §1; under the vigilance of the eparchial bishop or hierarch, 201 §2, 1045 §2, 1046 §2; if it is impossible, by whom and how its obligations can be reduced, 1054 §2;

of the decree of dismissal of a religious in perpetual vows, 500 §4, 553; of a decree of dismissal of a perpetually coopted member of a society of common life according to the manner of religious or of a secular institute, 562 §3, 568 §2;

in trials: of a legacy, with regard to the forum, 1079. 2°; regarding the prescription of an action to execute a penalty, 1153 §1; of a decree to provide support, 1163 §1; of the function of experts, 1258 §2; of expert testimony, 1262 §2;

of a sentence, 1177 §2, 1184, 1272 §1, 1319, 1325 §2, 1328, 1330, 1332 §2, 1337–1342, 1371;

of a delict, 1418 §§2–3; illegitimate e. of an office, ministry or function must be punished, 1462.

exemption regarding the removal of certain persons from the care of the pastor, 283; of a seminary from parochial governance, 336 §2; of institutes of consecrated life on the part of the Roman Pontiff, 412 §2; of a religious who becomes patriarch, bishop or exarch from the power of his superiors, 431 §2. 1°; of a place or of a juridic person on the part of the patriarch, 90; regarding stauropegial monasteries, *see* stauropegium; exempt priests, with regard to the norms of the eparchial bishop concerning admission to celebration of the Divine Liturgy, 703 §3; of minors from the power of parents or guardians, 910 §2; from the obligation of responding in a trial, 1229 §2; from a penal precept, 1419 §1; regarding ignorance, which does not exempt from impediments to sacred orders, 765; regarding the licit celebration of marriage in a place exclusively of another Church *sui iuris,* 831 §1. 3°;

clerics to use any e. of civil law, 383. 3°.

expert, expertise right of those who are engaged in the sacred sciences to express their opinion on matters in which they have e., 21; when they may be invited to the synod of bishops of the patriarchal Church, 102 §3; qualification of lay persons to be heard as experts by ecclesiastical authorities, 408 §1; regarding the function of theologians and their e., 606 §1; regarding the collaboration of the Christian faithful who are e. in the production and transmission of communications, 651 §2; eparchial bishops are to provide for the instruction of experts in the instruments of social communication, 652 §1; commission of experts in finances to be established in each Church *sui iuris,* 904 §2;

work of experts required: to establish that an ill member is unsuited to lead the life of the religious institute, regarding admission to a renewal of temporary profession or making perpetual profession, 547 §2; to establish psychological incapacity to receive or exercise sacred orders, 762 §1. 1°, 763. 3°; regarding the restoration of sacred icons or images, 887 §2, 888 §3; in the registration of goods in the name of a juridic person with respect to civil law, 1020 §2; regarding the appraisal of a thing to be alienated, 1035 §1. 2°;

experts in the law: in the procedure to impose penalties, 1469 §3;

in procedures: in the ordinary contentious trial, 1105, 1113 §3, 1167, 1255–1262; in the summary contentious trial, 1349 §2, 1350; in a matrimonial process, 1364. 1°, 1366; in a penal process, 1469 §3, 1477 §2;

as a required qualification: in the patriarchal and eparchial finance officer regarding finance, 122 §1, 262 §1; in a bishop, protosyncellus and syncelli regarding some sacred science, 180. 6°, 247 §2; in members of a finance council regarding civil law, 263 §1; in seminary teachers regarding their own science, 340 §1; in an advocate regarding canon law, 1141;

its defect in a pastor as a cause for removal, 1390. 2° . . .

expression of language in the masculine gender also regards the female gender, 1505.

expulsion of a member of a religious institute or society of common life according to the manner of religious, who is the cause for very serious harm or external scandal, 498 §§1 and 3, 551, 562 §3.

F

faculties by what prescripts habitual f. are governed, 982; prescripts regarding executive power of governance are valid for f. required by law for the valid celebration of sacraments, 995; which and when the Church supplies, 995, 994; which may be affected by penal privations, 1430 §1;

which f. the protosyncellus and syncellus have, 248 §2; of the protopresbyter, 278 §1; of the parochial vicar, regarding the celebration of marriage, 302 §2; of a priest to whom the care of a parish has been entrusted during the absence of the pastor, 292 §3; of one to whom falls the interim governance of an impeded eparchy, 320 §2; for preaching, 610 §§2–3, 611; for administering the sacrament of penance, 474 §2, 475 §1, 722 §§2–3, 723–727, 729. 2°, 735 §2; *see* confessor; for blessing marriages, 302 §2, 796 §2, 828 §1, 829 §3, 830, 833 §1, 840 §1, 841 §1; of celebrating the sacraments according to the prescripts of another Church *sui iuris*, 674 §2; of presbyters of the Latin Church to administer chrismation with holy myron, 696 §2; for consecrating a church, 871 §2;

regarding a facultative penalty, 1405 §2, 1481 §1.

faculty Catholic: which are equivalent to a Catholic university, 640 §2;

regarding theological courses in a Catholic university in which there is no faculty of theology, 643;

ecclesiastical: notion, 648; to be fostered, 646; erection and approval, 649, 642; its purpose, 647; regarding statutes, 650; not equivalent to a Catholic university, 640 §2; deans of ecclesiastical faculties are to be summoned to the patriarchal assembly, 143 §1. 4°; the right of lay persons to attend and pursue ecclesiastical degrees in them, 404 §2;

regarding the cooperation of theologians with persons who excel in other fields of learning, 606 §3.

faith the deposit of f., entrusted by Christ to the Church to be guarded, investigated, and faithfully announced and explained, 595 §1; the infallible magisterium concerning it, 597; what things must be believed with divine and Catholic faith, 598 §1, 1436 §1; what things must be held definitively regarding it, 598 §2, 1436 §2; to be preserved and openly professed, 10; when and to what doctrine the assent of f. must not be given, but rather the religious submission of mind and will, 599; bishops, the pastors of the Church, as the authentic doctors and teachers of f., 15 §§1 and 3, 600, 604, 605;

joins catechumens to the Church, 9 §1;

is to be nourished in pastoral care, catechesis, preaching and education, 602, 603, 614 §1, 617, 627 §1;

rights and obligations concerning faith: of the Apostolic See, of synods, and of councils, 605, 652 §2; of the patriarch, 95 §1; of the metropolitan, 133 §1. 4°, 138, 139, 159. 4°, 175; of the council of hierarchs, 169; of the eparchial bishop, 196, 577 §2, 636 §2, 652 §2; of a pastor, 289 §1; of teachers in seminaries, 340 §2, 350 §1; of theologians, 606 §1; regarding seminary students, 346 §2. 1°, 347; of parents, 618, 627 §1; of Catholic schools, 634 §1, 636 §2; regarding a Catholic university, 641, 644;

mandate for teaching about it, 636 §2, 644;

required: in candidates for the episcopate, 180. 1,36 ; for certain sacraments to be administered to non-Catholics, 671 §4; regarding baptism, 681 §1. 1°, 682 §1; in a sponsor, 685 §2; in the Christian faithful selected for the pastoral council, 273 §4;

profession of faith required: from one elected patriarch, 76 §1; from one elected major archbishop, 153 §3; before episcopal ordination, 187 §2; by an eparchial administrator, 220. 4°;

a profession of the Catholic f. is sufficient to receive Eastern non-Catholics into the Catholic Church, 897;

its integrity in the use of the instruments of social communication, 652 §2, 658 §2, 659, 661 §1, 662 §2;

manner of living it with regard to the notion of rite, 28 §1; rite affirms the divine unity of the Catholic f., 39; education in it with regard to the ascription to a Church *sui iuris* of children of unbaptized parents, 29 §2. 3°;

lay persons are to radiate f., 401; obligation of the Christian faithful to preserve it, 8, 15 §§1 and 3, 289 §1, 598–600; to whom vigilance concerning f. in associations belongs, 577 §1;

in the evangelization of peoples, 584 §2;

danger of falling away from the f. to be avoided in mixed marriages, 814. 1°;

defection from the faith, rejection of the faith: as a delict, 1436 §1; is cause for dismissal by the law itself from a religious institute or from a society of common life according to the manner of religious, 497 §1. 1°, 551, 562 §3; regarding ascription to and dismissal from an association, 580; regarding the impediment to receive or to exercise sacred orders, 768 §1. 2°, 763. 2°, 767 §1. 2°; regarding the licit celebration of marriage, 789. 6°; is a cause for disqualification from voting, 953 §1. 3°; is a cause for removal by the law itself from office, 976 §1. 2°;

care of the pastor for those who have abandoned the f., 293;

regarding the privilege of the f., 861; *see* privilege;

regarding the favor of the f., *see* favor;

other meanings: faithfulness to one's promises, with regard the formation of seminary students, 346 §2. 8°; trustworthy persons, 771 §3; attestation, 1132, 1222; of testimonies, 1253–1254; *see* bad faith, good faith.

false when a f. statement does not prevent a rescript from having force, 1529 §2; in the denunciation of a confessor of the delict of solicitation, 731, 1454; delicts of falsehood, 1444, 1454, 1455; in the proofs on which the sentence is based, regarding *restitu-*

bunals, 1146 §2; certain witnesses with respect to the place where they are to be interrogated, 1239 §2; the suspension of a penalty against a first offender, 1409 §1. 4°; provisions for a punished cleric and for his family if he is married, 1410; laws which can affect the Christian faithful of the Eastern Churches because hey concern popular matters, 1492; privileges, 1531 §1, 1533 §2;

granted by rescript: 1510 §2. 3°; as a privilege, 1531 §1; regarding the interpretation of a privilege, 1512 §3; power of the executor regarding it, 1522 §2; when the radical sanation of a marriage takes effect, 848 §2; when a f. can be granted if it has been previously denied by another authority, 1530; its privation can be given as a penalty, 1430 §1;

granted orally: which canons are valid for it, 1527 §1; is to be proven when someone legitimately requests it, 1527 §2.

favoritism *to be avoided towards persons:* in naming pastors, 285 §3; by censors of books, 664 §2; in ecclesiastical funerals, 878 §1.

fear a juridic act placed out of grave f. is valid, unless otherwise stated, but can be rescinded, 932 §2;

regarding invalidity: entrance into an institute of consecrated life, 450. 5°, 517 §1, 559 §1, 568; making or receiving religious profession, 464. 3°, 527. 3°; of marriage, 825;

regarding nullity: of a vow, 889 §3; of provision of office, 946; of a vote in an election, 954. 1°; of a resignation, 968; of a sentence, 1303 §1. 3°; of the remission of a penalty, 1421;

in trials, a confession or other declaration of a party given under grave f. lacks all force, 1219.

feast days and days of penance what authority is competent to establish, 880 §§1–2; common to all Eastern Churches, 880 §3; which can be suppressed or transferred by the particular law of a Church *sui iuris,* 880 §3;

the obligations of the Christian faithful on Sundays and feast days, 881 §§1–2 and 4; the obligations of the Christian faithful on days of penance, 882; regarding the obligations of those who are outside the territorial boundaries of their own Church *sui iuris,* or in families in which the spouses are ascribed to different Churches *sui iuris,* 883;

regarding the celebration of the Divine Liturgy for the people, 94, 198, 294; regarding the celebration of the divine praises, 199 §§2–3; with regard to the frequency of the celebration of the Divine

Liturgy by clerics, 378; regarding the homily, 614 §2.

federation (CIC) *see* confederation.

fees to be determined by the eparchial bishop, 1013 §1; the same norms are to be established regarding them in the same territory, 1013 §2.

fetus regarding the baptism of an aborted f., 680.

fellowship young people to be formed by educators to be disposed to loving f. with others, 629.

finance council belongs to the eparchial curia, 243 §2; constitution and composition, 263 §§ 1–3; when the function of selecting the finance officer belongs to it, 225 §2; to be heard in matters of greater importance regarding economic affairs, 263 §4; its functions in general, 263 §§ 4–5; regarding the consent of its members required in certain cases, 263 §4; relations with the eparchial finance officer to be determined in greater detail, 262 §3; accounts of administration submitted by the eparchial finance officer to be examined by it, 262 §4; to prepare budgets of receipts and expenditures and to approve the account of income and expenses, 263 §5; its consultation required for the nomination or removal of the eparchial finance officer, 262 §§ 1–2; its consent required for imposing a tax on juridic persons and to alienate certain goods, 1012 §1, 1036 §1. 1°–2°;

regarding parishes, 295.

finance officer *of the patriarchal Church:* belongs to the patriarchal curia, 114 §1; must be distinct from the finance officer of the eparchy of the patriarch, 122 §1; qualifications, 122 §1; appointment, 122 §2; cannot be removed during his term of office except with the consent of the synod of bishops of the patriarchal Church or, if there is danger in delay, the permanent synod, 122 §2; function, 122 §§1 and 3; what things the synod of bishops may request and subject to its own examination, 122 §4;

eparchial: belongs to the eparchial curia, 243 §2; is a member of the finance council by the law itself, 263 §2; is to be summoned to the eparchial assembly, 238 §1. 2°; by whom and how appointed, 262 §§1–2, 80. 4°, 133 §1. 6°, 138, 139, 159. 7°, 175; qualifications, 262 §1; how the f. o. may be removed for a grave cause, 262 §2; functions, 262 §§2–3; election or appointment while the eparchial see is vacant, 232 §3; if he becomes eparchial administrator, the finance council is to select someone else in the interim, 225 §2; how the office is to be fulfilled during a vacancy of the eparchial see, 232 §1, 262 §5; regarding resignation or removal during a vacancy of the eparchial see, 232 §2, 231 §§1–2; regarding the submission of a report of administration, 232 §4, 262 §4;

of a seminary, 338 §1;

in monasteries: by whom and how appointed, 447 §3; exercises office under the direction of the superior, 447 §1; the superior of a monastery *sui iuris* is not to carry out this office, 447 §2; in dependent monasteries the superior may carry out this office if necessity requires, 447 §2;

in orders and congregations: types of f. o., 516 §1; their designation or appointment, 516 §3; whose office the major superior may not fulfill, 516 §2; office of local f. o. may be fulfilled by the superior if necessity requires, 516 §2;

in societies of common life according to the manner of religious, 558 §2, 516.

fine   *see* penalty (pecuniary).

five years   term for members of the permanent synod, 115 §1; regarding the visit to Rome, 163, 208; regarding the canonical visitation of the eparchy, 205 §1; regarding the report on the state of the eparchy or exarchy, 206, 318; regarding the renewal of the presbyteral council, 270 §1; term for the constitution of the college of eparchial consultors, 271 §§2–3; minimum length of presbyteral ordination as required for the episcopacy, 180. 5°; when, after f. y. have elapsed following a move to another eparchy, a cleric is ascribed to that eparchy, 360 §2; regarding the reception by the eparchial bishop of a religious constituted in sacred orders who has left his own institute, 494 §2, 549 §3; regarding residence required to acquire a domicile, 912 §1; term for the general moderator for the administrator of justice in patriarchal Churches, 1062 §2; regarding the extinction of a contentious action, 1151; regarding the extinction of certain penal actions, 1152 §2. 2°.

force   *physical or moral force regarding:* the invalidity of entrance into an institute of consecrated life, 450. 5°, 517 §1, 559 §1, 568 §1; the invalidity of making or receiving religious profession, 464. 3°, 527. 3°; the invalidity of marriage, 825; the nullity or rescinding of a juridic act, 932; the nullity of a sentence, 1303 §1. 3°; the nullity of the remission of a penalty, 1421;

how physical f. against a bishop, metropolitan, patriarch or the Roman Pontiff is to be punished, 1445 §1; physical f. against a cleric, religious, member of a society of common life according to the manner of religious or lay person exercising an ecclesiastical function is to be punished, 1445 §2;

of law regarding: the Code, 6; transfer to another

Church *sui iuris,* 36; decrees of an ecumenical council or the college of bishops, 54; laws and decision of the synod of bishops of the patriarchal Church, 107 §2, 110 §1, 150 §§2–3; the decisions of an assembly of hierarchs of several Churches *sui iuris,* 322 §§2–3; the cession of the administration of goods and disposition of the goods of a religious, 529 §4; reservation of the absolution from sin, 729; collegial acts, 924. 1°; elections, 956 §1; postulation, 962; resignation from office, 970 §1; decrees which have the f. of a definitive sentence, 1085 §1. 3°; the act of a judge in the admission of a procurator in certain cases, 1142 §2; a possessory action, 1162; the appointment of an arbiter, 1173; the acts of a case extinguished by abatement, 1203; recourse against a decree by which a penalty is imposed, 1487 §2; the authentic interpretation of a law, 1498 §2; custom, 1506 §1, 1507 §§1 and 3; an extrajudicial decree, 1520 §1;

probative force of: a judicial confession, 1217 §2; documents, 1223, 1225;

regarding a judge expelled from his territory, 1128 §1;

proper f. of profession in congregations, 504 §2;

what takes place by force of: the office of the Roman Pontiff, 43, 45 §1, 597 §1; sacramental ordination and hierarchical communion with regard to the college of bishops, 49; a concession by the Apostolic See, 565; a vow or sacred bond of obedience, 412 §1, 545 §1, 555, 564; legitimate custom, 505 §3; office, 722 §4; the granting of faculties, 722 §4; a function, 735 §1; common or particular law, 1420 §§1–2.

foresight, foreseen   social: *see* social security;

regarding anticipated income and expenditures in the budget of the finance council, 263 §5; of death of an infant to be baptized, 681 §4; of the continuation of conditions for at least a month for the celebration of marriage before witnesses alone, 832 §1. 2°; regarding serious inconvenience for reception into the Catholic Church of a non-Catholic who has not yet completed fourteen years of age, 900 §2; of sufficient means to achieve the purposes of a juridic person, 921 §3; of a judge in imposing guarantees on a petitioner for the observance of an ecclesiastical sentence, 1116; of the eparchial bishop in granting permission to approach the civil forum in cases for the separation of spouses, 1376 §2; regarding certain cases of the removal of a pastor, 1390. 3°; of greater evils resulting from an overly hasty punishment of the offender or if it is f. that the offender will be punished sufficiently by civil authority, 1409 §1. 1°–2°.

form for the celebration of marriage: *see* marriage; of the gospel in the formation of seminary students, 346 §2. 1°; proper f. of the spiritual life as a right of the Christian faithful, 17; of the apostolate, 140, 203 §1, 592 §1; clerics to be an exemplary f. to the flock, 368; new forms of consecrated life can only be approved by the Apostolic See, 571; of insanity as an impediment to receive or to exercise sacred orders, 762 §1. 1°, 763. 3°; confirmation of an act or document *in forma specifica* on the part of the Roman Pontiff, 1060 §3; of procedure, 1131 §1, 1523; commissorial f. in the case of administrative acts, 1514.

formalities *required with regard to:* the validity of a juridic act, 931 §1, 1491 §3. 2°; erection or conversion to another use of a monastery, 437 §3; alienation of goods, 1165 §2; public documents, 1221 §1; the documentary process, 1372;

regarding the obligation of laws which determine the f. of acts, 1491 §3. 2°;

regarding: the solemn manner for the exercise of power over the whole Church in an ecumenical council, 50 §1; the solemn magisterium of the Church, 598 §1; the right of the eparchial bishop to perform functions in a solemn fashion, 200.

formation regarding the program for the formation of clerics, 330 §3;

in a minor seminary, 331 §1; in a major seminary, 340 §2, 343–356, 344 §4, 345, 346 §1, 349 §1, 352 §§1 and 3, 353, 356 §1; regarding formative courses for clerics, 372 §1; of lay persons to fulfill a function in the Church, 409 §1; of novices in a monastery, 459 §1; of the disciple of Christ in catechetical instruction, 617; of children in faith and Christian living, 618; religious f. in Christian associations, movements and groups, 620; of catechists, 622 §2; of the Christian faithful in giving catechesis, 624 §3; of the whole human person to be a concern of all educators, 629; cultural, human and social f. in Catholic schools, 634 §3; Catholic f. to be supplied in certain schools, 637; of persons outstanding in doctrine in Catholic universities, 641; continuing f. to be promoted in ecclesiastical universities and faculties, 647. 2°; of experts in the use of the instruments of social communications, 652 §1;

see education, instruction.

formula regarding the intimation of the election of the patriarch, 73; regarding the profession of faith and promise to fulfill his office faithfully to be made by the new patriarch, 76 §1; for the quinquennial report regarding monasteries, 419 §1; for the anointing of the sick, 742; of the doubt in trials, 1295 §2, 1347 §1, 1363 §§2–3.

forum *competent:* 1058–1084; right of the Christian faithful to approach it, 24 §1; the Roman Pontiff is judged by no one, 45 §3, 1058, 1060 §3; referral of cases to the Roman Pontiff, 1059; who is judged by the Roman Pontiff alone, 1060 §1, 1072; tribunals of the Apostolic See, 1060 §2, 1061, 1065, 1072; regarding the synod of bishops of the patriarchal Church, 110 §2, 1062, 1072; the ordinary tribunal of the patriarchal Church, 114 §1, 1063, 1072; the metropolitan tribunal, 133 §1. 3°, 138, 139, 159. 3°, 175, 1064; the eparchial tribunal, 1066; the tribunal of first instance for several eparchies of the same Church *sui iuris,* 1067; the common tribunal for eparchial bishops of different Churches *sui iuris,* 1068; regarding institutes of consecrated life, 1069; regarding absolute and relative incompetence, 1072, 1073 §2; of the respondent, 1073; of the petitioner, 1075 §2, 1359. 3°; choice regarding the competent f., 1073 §3; of domicile or quasi-domicile, 1074; of transients, 1075 §1; by reason of the location of a thing, 1076; by reason of contract, 1077; of the place where the delict was committed, 1078; in cases regarding administration, inheritance or pious legacies, 1079; if the parties and the authority to which the tribunal is subject consent, 1080; by reason of connection of cases, 1081; by reason of prevention, 1082; in a conflict of competence, 1083; regarding cases reserved to a collegiate tribunal, 1084 §1; in marriage cases, 1359, 1380; in cases to declare the nullity of sacred ordination, 1386 §1; of the Church regarding cases between clerics;

external: an administrative act having to do with the external f. must be reduced to writing, 1514; regarding a favor granted orally, 1527 §2; regarding the power of governance, 980, 511 §2, 441 §2; with respect to a supplied power or faculty, 994, 995, 511 §1, 441 §1; a matrimonial impediment is public if it can be proven in the external f., 791; regarding the recording of a dispensation from a marriage impediment or of a convalidation, declaration of nullity, or dissolution of marriage, 798, 799, 842; concerning how the declarations and promises required in mixed marriages and the interpellation made in the dissolution of a marriage through the pauline privilege is to be established in the external f., 815, 856 §3; norms for recourses against administrative decrees are applied to individual administrative acts by any legitimate power in the Church that are placed extrajudicially in the external f., 996; when a hierarch can abstain from imposing penalties, if the offender has confessed his delict to him in the external f., 1403;

internal forum regarding: power of governance, 980, 992 §2, 511 §2, 441 §2; supplied power or fac-

garding a citation, 1191 §3; from the burden of proof of one who has the favorable presumption of law, 1266; from the obligations of the clerical state after the confirmation of the sentence for the nullity of sacred ordination, 1387; regarding the penalty on the part of one who ceased from carrying out a delict, 1418 §3; of witnesses is to be protected, 1473; from obligations in the notion of prescription, 1540;

seminary students are to learn to use f. wisely, 346 §3;

the rectory is to be freed by a removed pastor, 1396 §1;

regarding penalties against those who impede f. of ministry, election, or ecclesiastical power, 1447 §2;

see coercion, fear, force.

friendship close f., on account of which a judge, promotor of justice, defender of the bond, assessor and auditor must abstain from their office, 1106.

fruit Christian faithful are to make the faith bear f. in good works, 10.

function *(munus)* *of Christ:* sacred ministers share in the task entrusted by Christ to his apostles, 743; all of the Christian faithful are sharers in it, 7 §1;

of the Church: to evangelize, 646; to announce the gospel everywhere, 651 §1;

of the Roman Pontiff: see office (of the roman pontiff);

of the College of Bishops: manner of its collegial exercise is to be determined by the Roman Pontiff, 50 §3;

of teaching: to whom the teaching f. in the name of the Church pertains and who takes part in it, 596; cooperation of theologians regarding it, 606 §2;

of the ministry of the word of God: who has this in the first place and how it is to be exercised, 608;

special f. of the Eastern Catholic Churches regarding ecumenism, 903;

in the patriarchal Church: when the patriarch is to visit Rome during his tenure of office, 92 §3; the patriarch can entrust the f. of conducting affairs that regard the entire patriarchal Church to any cleric, 89 §2; regarding the power of the patriarch in places or juridic persons exempted from the power of the eparchial bishop or in stauropegial monasteries, 90, 486 §2; regarding the removal of the patriarchal finance officer during the term of office, 122 §2; what a visitator sent by the patriarch should do before he begins his function, 148 §2;

of the eparchial bishop: pastor, 192 §1; care of the patriarch that he fulfills it, 95 §2;

of an exarch with regard to privileges or insignia during and after his f., 321;

of a titular bishop, 179, 181 §1, 187 §1; fulfilling some f. as a reason for the absence of a coadjutor bishop or auxiliary bishop, 217; of protosyncelli and syncelli regarding their privileges and insignia during office, 250; regarding the removal of the eparchial finance officer during the term of office, 262 §2; how a f. proper to an eparchy may be entrusted to religious, 415 §3; to foster ecumenism entrusted to a member of the Christian faithful in an eparchy, 904 §3; of the finance council, 263 §5; of priests exercised for the good of the eparchy regarding active and passive voice in the presbyteral council, 267 §1. 2°; of the presbyteral council, 270 §§2–3; of the college of eparchial consultors, 271 §§1–2; of the protopresbyter, 276 §1;

regarding a pastor: of teaching, 289 §1; of sanctifying, 289 §2; of governing, 289 §3; impeded f. with regard to the appointment of a parish administrator or with regard to one who assumes the interim care of the parish, 298, 300 §1; regarding reasons for removal, 1390. 2°;

pastoral f. in parishes, 289 §3, 291, 298, 300 §1, 302 §3; regarding the parochial vicar, 302 §3; of a parish administrator, 299 §3; of sacred ministers in missionary territories, 591. 2°;everyone to whom the care of souls is entrusted is bound, in virtue of this f., by the obligation to provide for the administration of the sacrament of penance to the Christian faithful committed to them, 735 §1;

regarding clerics: right to it and the obligation to undertake it, 371 §§1–2; obligation to use exemptions regarding public civil functions, 383. 3°; use of goods which they acquire on the exercise of a f., 385 §1; right to remuneration for it, 390 §1; its privation in the loss of the clerical state, 395;

committed to a religious outside of the religious' own institute, 415 §3, 431 §1 and §2. 2°; of the visitator of religious, 420 §1;

of an actuary in an election, 955 §5; relinquished by an administrator of temporal goods at his or her own initiative, 1033;

of an executor of a pious will regarding the rendering of an account after the f. has been performed, 1045 §2;

regarding the executor of an administrative act, 1521;

in procedural law: duration of f. of officials in a tribunal to be determined by statutes, 1070; of a judge, 1189; of a *ponens,* 1091 §2; of an assessor, 1105; promise to fulfill a f. faithfully, 1112; of an advocate or procurator, 1129 §2, 1142 §1, 1147, 1148, 1200 §1, 1474; of arbiters, 1172, 1173, 1178; of the judicial vicar in the confirmation of a sentence of arbitration, 1181 §2; of a guardian or curator, 1200 §1; regarding the force of documents drawn up by virtue of a public f., 1221 §1; of experts, 1258 §2, 1259 §2; prohibition against the exercise of a f. on the part of one accused in a penal trial, 1473;

of parents to educate their children, 627 §2; of sponsors, 684 §2, 685, 686 §2; proper f. of the Christian faithful, according to which they are to cooperate in the building up of the body of Christ. 11; formation of the Christian faithful who have frequent dealings with the Christian faithful of another Church *sui iuris* by reason of their f., 41; qualification of lay persons for ecclesiastical functions, 408 §2; lay persons are fully subject to ecclesiastical authority in the exercise of an ecclesiastical f., 408 §3; obligation of lay persons to acquire a suitable formation to fulfill their f., 409 §1;

in penal law regarding: penal privation, 1430 §1; suspension, 1432 §§1 and 3; deposition from the clerical state, 1433 §§2; major excommunication, 1434 §1; individual delicts, 1445 §2, 1454, 1460, 1462–1465;

regarding removal from office, 939 §1.

functions   the right of the eparchial bishop regarding those f. which must be conducted solemnly by him vested in all pontifical insignia, 200; when those f. which are proper to the eparchial bishop may be carried out by a coadjutor or auxiliary bishop, 216; of greater importance in a parish belong to the pastor, 290 §2; parochial f. cannot be performed by the rector of a church without the consent of the pastor, 306 §1; ordered for the rector of a church by the local hierarch, 307; which f. cannot be performed by anyone without the required permission in a church which is entrusted to a rector, 308; of the sacred liturgy, regarding minor clerics, 327; which f. of sacred ministers can be committed to lay persons, if sacred ministers are absent, 403 §2.

fund   *parish:* offerings received by parish clergy are to be put into the parish f., 291;
in each eparchy for the needs of the eparchy, 1021 §3.

funeral   the care of the protopresbyter for the f. of a deceased pastor, 278 §3; *see* ecclesiastical funerals.

furnishings   *sacred:* care of the protopresbyter for them, 278 §1. 3° and §3; care of the rector of a church for them, 309.

G

generosity   clerics are to be an example to all in g. and works of charity, 381 §1.

gift   *of the Holy Spirit:* in sacred ordination, 323 §1; to be discerned in new forms of consecrated life, 571; in chrismation with sacred myron, 692;
sacred gifts in the Divine Liturgy are bread and wine, 706;
those aspiring to the sacred ministry are to become solicitous to gain all people for the kingdom of God by the g. of their very lives, 346 §1;
which gifts a judge and tribunal officials are forbidden to accept on the occasion of a trial, 1114; regarding the delict of corruption, 1147, 1463; regarding ecclesiastical funerals, 875, 876 §2.

good   object of a vow, 889 §1; of the cleric as a cause for transfer or move to another eparchy, 365 §1; of the spouses as an end of marriage, 776 §1; of the family in granting forgiveness to an adulterous partner, 863 §1;
of religious life to be encouraged: by the patriarch, 84 §1; by bishops, 202; in the assembly of hierarchs of several Churches *sui iuris,* 322 §1;
of the eparchy: to be cared for in the presbyteral council, 264, 270 §3; regarding the election of members of the presbyteral council, 267 §1. 2°; regarding taxes, 1012 §1;
nothing is to be done by a parochial administrator which can harm the parish's goods, 299 §2;
spiritual: of the Christian faithful to be fostered, 82 §1. 2°; regarding the means for the protection and enhancement of the spiritual g. of the Christian faithful of the patriarchal Church everywhere in the world to be proposed to the Apostolic See, 148 §3; of persons with regard to the right of the Church to temporal goods, 1007; of the Christian faithful as a cause for dispensation from a law, 1536 §2, 1538 §1; *spiritual goods of the Church:* rights of the Christian faithful to them, 16; obligation of clerics to provide assistance to the Christian faithful from them, 381 §2;
private g., in trials, 1103 §3, 1240, 1283 §1. 1°, 1302;
of institutes of consecrated life regarding exemption, 412 §2;

privation of goods in penal law, 1413 §2;

regarding: g. name to be safeguarded, 1468 §2; g. initiatives to be promoted, 652 §1; clerics are witnesses to the heavenly goods, 385 §1; those deprived of goods, 1136 §4.

good faith   regarding the dispensation from the impediments for receiving or exercising sacred orders, 768 §1; possessor of another's property ceases to be in g.f. after the joinder of issue, 1197; regarding the obligation of making restitution in certain penalties of suspension, 1432 §3; regarding prescription, 1541.

good morals   care of bishops, synods, councils and the Apostolic See for, 605;

required: in a candidate for the episcopate, 180. 1°; in a candidate for the office of pastor and, if he is married, in his wife and children, 285 §§1–2; in the Christian faithful designated to the pastoral council, 273 §4; regarding a candidate for the novitiate, 453 §3, 519; in a candidate for sacred ordination, 758 §1. 2°; in the Christian faithful admitted to the office of auditor, 1093 §2;

nothing to be written in newspapers, periodicals or magazines that are wont to attack g.m., 660; penalties against one who seriously offends g.m., 1448 §1.

good reputation   *see* reputation.

governance   bond of ecclesiastical governance regarding full communion of the Christian faithful with the Catholic Church, 8;

of the whole Church, 47, *see* ecumenical council, roman pontiff;

of the patriarchal Church or eparchy when the see is impeded, 132, 984 §§1–2; regarding the exercise of episcopal power, 178; regarding the notion of a hierarch, 984 §§1–2; regarding the habitual faculties of a hierarch, 982 §1;

of an eparchy: of the eparchial bishop, 178, 95 §2, 269 §2, 271 §6, 984 §2; the eparchial bishop may not involve himself in the g. of the eparchy in virtue of any title before his enthronement, 189 §3; regarding a vacant see, 286, 221. 2°, 228 §2, 537 §2, 984 §§1–2; when the see is impeded, 233, 984 §§1–2; regarding the apostolic administrator, 234 §1; the eparchial curia assists the eparchial bishop in it, 243 §1; regarding the protosyncellus and syncelli, 245, 246, 248 §1; budget for it, 263 §5; regarding the notion of a titular bishop, 179; regarding the exemption of an institute of consecrated life, 412 §2;

of an exarchy: in whose name it is done, 312, 316, 317; of a vacant or impeded exarchy, 314 §3, 320, 984 §2;

of a parish, 300 §2, 1397; of a college directed by presbyters, 305 §3; how a seminary is exempt from parochial g., 336 §2; internal g. in religious institutes, 413, 432, 437 §3, 509 §2; of a province directed by a major superior, 508 §1; in a society of common life according to the manner of religious, 554 §1, 557; of an association, 576 §1; of an ecclesiastical university, 650; knowledge of sins received from confession can in no way be used for external g., 734 §2; immediate g. of a juridic person regarding the administration of temporal goods, 1023; regarding those punished by major excommunication, 1434 §1; regarding suspension of a penalty which forbids the placement of an act of governance, 1435 §2;

regarding power of governance, 248 §1, 441 §2, 511 §2, 662 §1, 724 §2, 893 §1. 1° and 3°, 899, 979–995, 1013 §1, 1022 §1, 1055 §2, 1069, 1401 §3, 1432 §1, 1433 §1, 1491 §1, 1510 §1; *see* power;

regarding the norms by which a juridic institute is governed, 46 §2, 124, 327, 424, 558 §2, 567 §2, 572, 573 §2, 780, 782 §1.

grace   *divine:* eparchial bishop is to strive that the Christian faithful grow in it, 197; clerics are to implore the g. of conforming themselves to Christ, 369 §1; the Church, moved by the Holy Spirit, recognizes itself to be completely missionary, 584 §1; when absolution of several penitents at the same time is admitted, lest they be forced to go without sacramental grace for a long time, 720 §2. 2°; received in the anointing of the sick, 737 §1; by which spouses are consecrated and strengthened in marriage, 776 §2; of the Holy Spirit in the ecumenical movement, 902.

grade   of judgement, 1059 §1, 1063 §§3–4, 1064 §2, 1066, 1069 §2, 1072, 1073 §1, 1084 §3, 1085 §3, 1095 §2, 1105, 1108, 1111, 1118 §1, 1122 §2, 1174 §1, 1205 §1, 1276 §1, 1301, 1321, 1340 §1, 1355, 1368 §2, 1369, 1379 §2, 1473, 1475 §1, 1482, 1483 §2; of tribunal, 1065, 1067 §1, 1068 §4, 1083 §2, 1373 §1, 1374, 1379 §2; of appeal, 1085 §3, 1320 §1, 1321. 3°, 1331 §2, 1369, 1370 §1; *see* degree, level;

"gradually," 346 §3, 634 §1, 1453 §1.

grave fear   *see* fear.

grounds   *of matrimonial nullity:* to be determined in the formulation of the doubt, 1363 §3; what is to be done if a new g. is alleged at the appellate grade, 1369.

of a sentence, against which an appeal is introduced, 1318 §3.

group   *manner of proceeding:* if a superior requires its counsel or consent, 934 §1; in elections, 917–957, 63–67, 182–186; in postulation, 961–964;

regarding collegial acts, *see* college;

of eparchies with regard to the supreme power of the Roman Pontiff, 45 §1;

of bishops: legitimately constituted regarding the approval of liturgical texts, 657 §1; special g. for determination of recourse against decrees of the patriarch, 1006; of eparchial bishops who consent to the erection of a tribunal of first grade for several eparchies, 1067 §§4–5;

of the Christian faithful as a Church *sui iuris*, 27;

certain group of persons: for whom a syncellus is constituted in an eparchy, 246; not to be withdrawn from the care of the pastor, 283;

patriarchal assembly is a consultative g., 140; of presbyters representing the presbyterate is the presbyteral council, 264; the pastoral council is only a consultative g., 273 §1; constituted of the more prudent presbyters to substitute for the college of eparchial consultors, 319 §2; of novices can sometimes stay outside of the novitiate, 522 §2; various groups of the Christian faithful, regarding catechisms adapted to them, 621 §3; of pastors, from whom two must be selected to discuss the removal or transfer of pastors with the eparchial bishop, 1391 §1, 1399 §1;

coming into full communion with the Catholic Church, 35, 896; *see* community.

guarantees valid in civil law to be given by administrators of temporal goods, 1027; imposed on a petitioner for the observance of an ecclesiastical sentence, 1116; to be furnished by a procurator who has not exhibited a mandate, 1142 §2; to avoid sequestration, 1160; prior to sequestration, 1161; to fulfill a decree regarding the support of a person, 1163 §1; for the expenses of arbiters, 1180 §1; for judicial expenses, 1123, 1335. 5°; for the execution of a sentence for *restitutio in integrum,* 1328 §2; in provisional execution of a sentence, 1337 §§2–3.

guardian how constituted for minors, 910 §2, 1136 §2, 1137, 1200 §2; regarding the domicile or quasi-domicile of a minor, 915; regarding the subjection of a minor to the power of a g., 910 §2; regarding the necessity of a g. in the trial of minors, 1136 §§1–3; in what cases minors may act and respond without the consent of a g., 1136 §3; regarding the admission of a g. constituted by the civil authority into a trial, 1137; regarding the suspension of a trial when the g. ceases from his function, 1200; regarding seeking indemnity against a g. in the case of the abatement of a trial, 1202; when a g. may renounce a trial, 1205 §2; can designate a sponsor, 685 §1. 4°.

guardianship regarding the acquisition of domicile and quasi-domicile, 915 §2; a judge, promotor of justice, defender of the bond, assessor and auditor must abstain from their office on account of g., 1106.

guilt, guilty party *see* accused, offender.

H

habit of monks, 476; of members of orders and congregations, 540; novitiate begins in monasteries with the reception of the monastic h., 455.

hagiography its importance in catechesis, 621 §2.

harm to parish property to be avoided by the parochial administrator, 299 §2; imminent and grave h. as a reason for the expulsion of a member from a religious institute or a society of common life according to the manner of religious, 498 §1, 551, 562 §3; grave h. to doctrine or ecclesiastical discipline in associations, 577 §2; it is the care of the pastors of the Church that the integrity and unity of the faith not suffer harm, 604; spiritual h. to be avoided by the Christian faithful in the use of certain instruments of social communication, 665 §3; arising from the false denunciation of a confessor to be repaired, 731; imminent h., regarding the power of dispensation granted to a confessor from the impediment of exercising sacred orders, 767 §3; danger of h. to be avoided in exhibiting documents, 1227 §1; when *restitutio in integrum* may be permitted, 1326 §1. 3°; public or private h. in the case of issuing an extra judicial decree, 1517 §2, 1519 §2, 1520 §2; to avoid the danger of grave h. in delay, when the hierarch can grant a dispensation reserved to another authority, 1538 §2;

to the Church: from the non-observance of civil laws by the administrator of temporal goods, to be avoided, 1028 §2. 2°; from the arbitrary dismissal from an office or a function by the administrator of temporal goods, to be repaired, 1033; on account of the poor administration of temporal things, as a cause for the removal of a pastor, 1390. 5°;

to the penitent to be completely avoided by the confessor, with regard to the use of knowledge acquired in confession, 734 §1; to others regarding the loss of a privilege, 1534;

see damage.

harmony the unity of Christians is to be fostered harmoniously, 84 §1; of a pastor and parochial vicar in the care of a parish, 302 §3; of moderators and teachers in a seminary, 340 §2; based on justice among all people to be fostered by clerics, 384 §1; meetings of religious superiors to be promoted to foster h. in apostolic works, 416.

hatred penalties against one who arouses h. against any hierarch, 1447 §1; penalties against one who arouses h. against religion or the Church, 1448 §1.

head of the college of bishops is the Roman Pontiff, 43, 49, 600, 899;

patriarch presides over the patriarchal Church as a father and h., 55.

health *regarding health care:* clerics, 192 §5, 390 §2, 1021 §2, 1410; lay employees of the Church, 409 §2; in employing workers, 1030. 1°.

hearing in a summary contentious trial, 1347, 1348, 1349 §1, 1352, 1353, 1354 §1.

on the part of the patriarch: of the synod with regard more serious business, 82 §3; of bishops to prepare for the synod of bishops, 108 §2;

on the part of the eparchial bishop: of presbyters, 192 §4; of the finance council, 263 §4; of the presbyteral council, 269 §2; of pastors and parochial vicars for the appointment of a protopresbyter, 277 §1; of the protopresbyter and other Christian faithful on the naming of a pastor, 285 §3; of a pastor on the naming of a parochial vicar, 301 §3;

on the part of a hierarch: of the promotor of justice to refrain from a penal process or from imposing penalties, 1403 §1; of others regarding decisions concerning the use of a penal process, 1469 §3; of the promotor of justice and of the accused in decisions about administrative remedies during the penal trial, 1473;

on the part of a local hierarch, of the religious superior in the designation of spiritual fathers, confessors and priests for the celebration of the Divine Liturgy and the preaching of the word of God, 475, 539 §2;

of the metropolitan and of eparchial bishops in extraordinary matters or in matters entailing special difficulty, 160; of a bishop of the permanent synod, if it is a matter regarding his eparchy or office, 116 §3; of the superior administrative authority of the Church *sui iuris* concerned, if it is a matter regarding the boundaries of the patriarchal Church, 146 §2; of the Christian faithful, about the suitability of candidates for the episcopacy on the part of members of the synod of bishops of the patriarchal Church, 182 §1; regarding the qualification of lay persons to be heard as consultors, 408 §1; of the religious superior together with the council in the granting of an indult of exclaustration, 489 §1, 548 §1; of others,

particularly of those whose rights can be injured, before issuing a decree, 1520 §2;

in procedural law: of the parties, of the promotor of justice, of the defender of the bond, of witnesses, 1098. 1°, 1109 §1, 1124 §2, 1128 §2, 1163 §1, 1174 §1, 1196, 1209, 1231 §1, 1239 §§2–3, 1243 §2, 1256, 1263, 1269 §1, 1271, 1277, 1283 §1. 2°, 1299 §1, 1359. 3°–4°, 1374, 1379 §2; of the eparchial bishop for the admission of a guardian constituted by civil authority, 1137; of arbiters against whom an objection has been lodged, 1175; of an expert, 1258 §3; in penal procedure, 1469 §3, 1473.

heresy as a delict of the denial of a truth which must be believed with divine and Catholic faith or of a doubt concerning it, 1436 §1; with what penalties it is punished, 1436 §1;

effect of disqualification regarding: reception into associations, 580; reception or exercise of a sacred order, 762 §1. 2°, 763. 2°, 767 §1. 2°; casting a vote, 953 §1. 3°; *see* major excommunication;

is a cause by the law itself: for removal from office, 976 §1. 2°; of dismissal from a religious institute or from a society of common life according to the manner of religious, 497 §1. 1°, 551, 562 §3; of dismissal from an association, 580;

regarding marriage, 789. 6°.

hermit who, 481; requirements for legitimately undertaking the eremitical life, 482; regarding the place where the h. lives, 483; dependence on the superior of the monastery, 484; the right of the superior to impose an end on the eremitical life, 485; regarding ascetics who imitate the eremitical life, 570.

hierarch notion, 984 §1; regarding the Christian faithful of another Church *sui iuris* committed to him, 38; are to care for the faithful and accurate observance of the rite, 40 §1; if he presides over a Church *sui iuris,* how he may participate in the synod of bishops of the whole Church, 46 §2; with regard to meetings encouraged by the patriarch, 84 §2; can be warned by the patriarch concerning the imposition of penalties on a cleric, 89 §1; his participation in the synod of bishops of the patriarchal Church, if he is not a bishop, 102 §3; the Christian faithful can propose topics to him for the patriarchal assembly, 144 §1; regarding the one who governs a Church *sui iuris* that is not patriarchal, nor major archiepiscopal, nor metropolitan, 174–176; their letters are to be preserved in the parochial archives, 296 §4; regarding the promotion of vocations, 329 §1. 3°; to which h. a seminary common to several eparchies is subject, 336 §1; institutes clergy conferences to promote the sacred sciences and pastoral matters, 372 §2; can grant permission for his clerics to volunteer for military service, 383. 2°; regarding the prohibition from preaching, 613; his obligations regarding universities, 645, 646; regarding the publication of books, 664 §3; letters of recommendation for his clerics, 703 §1; his judgement about sufficient probation for a neophyte to receive sacred orders, 762 §1. 8°; regarding permission given by him for one who is afflicted with a psychic illness to exercise sacred orders, 763. 3°; the h. of an institute of consecrated life can dispense from the impediments to receive or exercise sacred orders, with certain exceptions, 767 §1; his consent for the translation, alienation or restoration of icons or sacred images, 887; can dispense his subjects from private vows, 893 §1. 1°; regarding habitual faculties granted to him, 982 §2; with respect to the repudiation or acceptance of offerings which are burdened with a modal obligation or condition, 1016 §3; their care regarding the administration of ecclesiastical goods, 1022 §2; receives the promise of administrators of ecclesiastical goods to faithfully fulfill their office, 1025. 1°; reviews the inventory of ecclesiastical goods, 1025. 2°; his consent for the investment of money which may be left over after expenses, 1028 §2. 5°; the administrator of ecclesiastical goods must make a report of administration to him, 1031 §1; regarding pious wills, 1045, 1046 §§2–3, 1048; regarding goods held in trust, 1046 §2; regarding mobile goods assigned to an endowment, 1049; when he may reduce the obligations of celebrating the Divine Liturgy, 1052 §2; regarding pious causes, 1054 §§1–2; regarding the imposition of penalties, 1403; 1428, 1430 §1, 1432 §2, 1468–1470, 1472 §1, 1473, 1475 §1, 1486 §1. 2°; regarding the warning containing the threat of penalties, 1406 §2; judges the possibility of a prior warning of a penalty, if the nature of the delict permits, 1407 §1; must provide for a deposed cleric who is truly in need because of his punishment, 1410; regarding the remission of penalties, 1420 §§1–2; delicts against him, 1438, 1447 §1, 1454; can stand trial in case of the lack or negligence of the one representing a juridic person, 1138 §3; can accuse the validity of sacred ordination, 1385; his power to dispense from laws, 1496, 1538 §2; the style of his curia must be followed in rescripts, 1529 §1; regarding the abuse of power given as a privilege, 1535;

see local hierarch, personal hierarch, proper hierarch.

history circumstances of h., regarding the notion of rite, 28 §1; courses on it in seminary, 349 §2; mis-

sionaries are to be instructed in the h. of the peoples to be evangelized, 589; regarding the translation, prescription or alienation of objects of historical value and their care, 1019, 872 §2, 887, 1036 §§2–3, 1037. 3°.

Holy See notion, 48; agreements entered into by it with nations and other political societies are not abrogated by the Code, 4; *see* apostolic see.

Holy Spirit moves catechumens, 9 §1; in whom the people of God who constitute an eparchy are gathered, 177 §1; acts in raising up vocations to the sacred ministry, 329 §1. 1°; in whom seminary students are to cultivate an intimate familiarity with Christ, 346 §1; under whose guidance the Christian faithful in religious institutes follow Christ more closely, 410; patriarchs and eparchial bishops are to strive to discern new gifts of consecrated life entrusted by the H. S. to the Church, 571; in whom the Church recognizes itself to be totally missionary, 584 §1; assists the Church in guarding, investigating, proclaiming and expounding the deposit of faith, 595 §1; by whose strength people are sanctified through the sacraments, 667; in baptism, 675; in chrismation with holy myron, 692; in the Divine Liturgy, 698; in the sacrament of penance, 718; in sacred ordination, 323 §1, 743; in ecumenical work, 902; custom corresponds to the action of the H. S. in the ecclesial body, 1506 §1.

homicide penalties for this delict, 1450 §1; the impediment to receive or exercise sacred orders arises from this, 762 §1. 4°, 763. 2°, 766, 767 §1. 2°, 768 §§1–2; impediment to receive or exercise sacred orders regarding one who has attempted suicide, 762 §1. 5°, 763. 2°; regarding the extinction of the penal action, 1152 §1. 2°; of one's own or of another's spouse, *see* conjugicide.

homily notion, 614 §1; has the preeminent place in the ministry of the word of God, 607; is reserved to a priest or, according to the norm of particular law, a deacon, 614 §4; when it should take place, 614 §2; the care of the eparchial bishop concerning it, 196 §1; regarding the obligations of the pastor, 614 §§2–3; regarding the obligations of the rector of the Church, 614 §2; seminary students are to be instructed in homiletics, 352 §2.

honesty required in lay persons to be heard as experts or consultors by ecclesiastical authorities, 408 §1; of a person to be considered by the judge in evaluating testimony, 1253. 1°;

marriage impediment of public h., *see* propriety.

hope the life of h. regarding the connection of catechumens with the Church, 9 §1; care of the pastor

infallibility of the Roman Pontiff and of the college of bishops, 597, 600.

infamy regarding the dispensation granted by a confessor from the impediment of exercising a sacred order, 767 §3; a witness is excused from the obligation to respond in a trial on account of the fear of i., 1229 §2. 2°; to be avoided in public rebuke, 1427 §2.

infancy catechetical instruction is to be received from i., 404 §1;

after infancy: a minor can acquire his or her own quasi-domicile, 915 §1; when someone may be baptized, 682; regarding the function of sponsor, 684 §2; regarding the proof of the baptism, 691.

infant who is to be called an i., 909 §2; is considered not responsible for himself or herself, 909 §2; one who habitually lacks the use of reason is equated with an i., 909 §3; when one is licitly baptized, 681; regarding sponsors, 684 §2, 686 §2; the care of the parents that an i. be baptized as soon as possible, 686; instruction of the parents regarding baptism, 686 §2; participation of an i. in the Divine Eucharist after baptism and chrismation with holy myron, 710.

information the right and obligation of the patriarch to seek i. regarding the Christian faithful living outside the territorial boundaries of the patriarchal Church, 148 §1; about candidates for the episcopacy in the patriarchal Church, 182 §§1–2; to be given to those whose consent or counsel is required to place juridical acts, 934 §3; prohibited i., regarding a judge, 1287 §1;

the Roman Pontiff to be informed about a vacancy of the patriarchal see, 128. 1°.

inheritance the will of the testator to be fulfilled, 1043 §2; regarding the competent forum, 1079. 2°; regarding the suspension of the instance of litigation if a party dies or changes status or ceases from an office in virtue of which action is taken, 1199.

innate right *of the Church:* to preach the gospel, 595 §1; to acquire, possess, administer and alienate temporal goods, 1007.

insanity one suffering from i. is impeded from receiving or exercising sacred orders, 762 §1. 1°, 763. 3°; regarding the dismissal of a religious in temporary vows, 547 §§2–3;

see lack of use of reason.

insignia pontifical i. of a bishop, 200; of the dignity next to that of the bishop belong to presbyters who are exarchs, protosyncelli and syncelli, 250, 321 §1; attached to dignities conferred on clerics, 388; of one's own Church *sui iuris* are preferably

to be retained in concelebration with bishops and presbyters of different Churches *sui iuris,* 701; there privation as a penalty, 1402 §2, 1430 §1.

instance *of litigation:* its beginning occurs with the citation, 1194. 5°, 1267; without a special mandate, a procurator cannot renounce it, 1143; regarding its suspension, abatement, or renunciation, 1199–1206, 1274. 2°, 1322. 3°, 1465 §1.

institutes juridic: laws determining those things which are essentially constitutive of i. are not subject to dispensation, 1537;

which assist the Roman Pontiff in exercising his function, 46 §1; of the Roman Curia, 48;

of higher studies regarding: the instruction of certain religious, 471 §2, 536 §2; equivalent to Catholic universities, 640 §2; the notion of a Catholic university, 642 §1; ecumenism, 906; *see* faculty, university;

Catholic i. subject to the visitation of the eparchial bishop, 205 §2; Catholic i. with regard to ecumenism, 907;

of consecrated life, *see* congregation, institutes of consecrated life, monastery, order, religious institutes, secular institute, society of common life according to the manner of religious;

special i. for the formation for ministry of students more advanced in age, 344 §4; regarding the right obtained by certain i. to ascribe clerics, 357 §1; for the suitable support of clerics in an eparchy, 1021 §1, 1047 §2; for insurance, social security and health care for clerics, 1021 §2, 390 §2; of religious studies, 404 §2; of Christian education and cultural development to be established in mission territories, 592 §1; about instruments of social communication, 652 §1; of education, regarding the administration of the sacrament of penance by the moderator, 734 §3; which i. are juridic persons, 921 §2; regarding the power of the eparchial bishop over the reduction or transfer of obligations to celebrate the Divine Liturgy in ecclesiastical i., 1052 §4, 1053.

institutes of consecrated life *see* congregation, monastery, order, religious institutes, secular institute, society of common life according to the manner of religious;

the approval of new forms of consecrated life is reserved to the Apostolic See alone, 571;

vocations for them to be fostered, 194, 380; to be fostered in mission territories, 592 §1; obligation of members regarding their own rite, 40 §2; what things the patriarch can order to be read or displayed publicly in them, 82 §2; which members are to be summoned to the patriarchal assembly,

law, 653; regarding the collaboration of the Christian faithful, 651 §1, 652 §1; instruction in them in seminary with regard to the apostolate, 352 §2; to what authority it belongs to forbid the Christian faithful to use them or share them with others, to the extent that they are detrimental to the integrity of faith and morals, 652 §2; regarding ecumenism, 906; penalties for those who use them against good morals, religion, or the Church, 1448 §1.

insurance *regarding:* clerics, 192 §5, 390 §2, 1021 §2, 1410; lay employees of the Church, 409 §2; in employing workers, 1030. 1°;

to be taken out by the administrator of temporal goods, 1028 §2. 1°;

see health care, social security.

intact rights and privileges remain i., 5, 339 §2, 700 §2, 1281 §1;

when a thing ceases to be i. *(res integra)* in a trial, 1194. 1°.

integral *reordering of material:* in the Code, 6. 1°; through a later law, 1502 §1.

integration regarding the instruction of future ministers of the Church, 340 §2;

of formation in seminaries, 345; into a community, 619.

integrity *of faith and morals:* must be preserved when the Christian faithful inform others of their opinion about those things which pertain to the good of the Church, 15 §3; the eparchial bishop is to guard it firmly, 196 §2; to what authority belongs the vigilance over it in associations, 577; to be preserved in the evangelization of peoples, 584 §2; it belongs to the pastors of the Church in the first place to take care lest it suffer harm in the varieties of doctrinal enunciations, 604; it belongs to the Apostolic See and the bishops to promote, guard and defend it authoritatively, 605; which authority can remove the mandate to teach subjects having to do with faith and morals if the i. of doctrine is lacking, 644; to what authority it belongs to forbid the Christian faithful to use the instruments of social communication or share them with others, to the extent that they are detrimental to the i. of faith and morals, 652 §2;

of the mystery of Christ in preaching, 616 §1; of the doctrine of the Church in catechesis, 626; of confession in the sacrament of penance, 720 §1;

the eparchial administrator must be outstanding in it, 227 §1;

of good reputation: *see* reputation.

intention required i. in a candidate for a religious institute, 448. 517 §1; regarding the reception of baptism, 682 §2; of a sponsor, with regard fulfilling his or her function, 685 §1. 3°; for the celebration of the Divine Liturgy, 715 §1, 716;

regarding the goal of formation in a seminary, 340 §2; regarding the i. of the founder of an order or congregation, 505 §3;

regarding intentional delays in a trial, 1273 §1.

interdict (CIC) *see* minor excommunication.

interest the administrator is to take care that i. is paid at the stated time, 1028 §2. 4°.

interpreter in the sacrament of confession, with respect to keeping the seal, 733 §2; in a trial, 1130, 1335. 2°; *see* seal, secret;

custom is the best i. of laws, 1508.

interpretation *of laws:* by whom an authentic i. is made and what force it has, 1498; with what rules it is to be made, 1499; what matters are to be strictly interpreted, 1500; how it belongs to the patriarch to interpret the laws of the synod of bishops of the patriarchal Church, 112 §2;

of power, 989; benign i. in penalties, 1404 §1; strict i. of reservations, 1423 §2; of an administrative act, 1512 §§1–2; of a privilege, 1512 §3; of a dispensation and of the power to dispense, 1512 §4.

interrogation of one having recourse against an extrajudicial administrative decree, 1003;

in trials: when an interpreter is to be used, 1130; of the parties, 1211–1215; regarding a judicial confession, 1216; who is exempt from it, 1229 §2; of witnesses, 1229 §1, 1233 §2, 1235, 1239–1246, 1249, 1250 §1, 1251; foregoing the examination of a witness, 1232; request for the exclusion of a witness before questioning, 1236; the right of a party to be present at the i. in the summary contentious process, 1349 §2; right of the defender of the bond, the representative of a party, and the promotor of justice to be present at the i. in the matrimonial process, 1364. 1°; at which the parties in a matrimonial process may not be present, 1364 §2; in the summary contentious process, 1356; in a penal trial, 1471 §1; those who affirm what is false or conceal the truth under a judge's questioning are to be punished, 1444;

regarding the i. of a visitator, 420 §2.

intervention regarding the delict of one who approaches a civil authority to obtain certain things in the Church through its i., 1460;

of a third party in a case: who may be admitted, 1276 §1; the *libellus* by which the right to intervene in the case is demonstrated, 1276 §2; is to be admitted at the stage which the case has reached, 1276 §3; if it seems necessary, the judge may call a third party, 1277.

intimation of an administrative act, 1511; of the revocation of an administrative act, 1513 §3;

of a decree: 1520, 999 §1, 1001 §2; of removal from office, 974 §2; of a judicial decree, 1192 §§1–2, 1195 §3; of the execution of the sentence, 1153 §1; by which a penalty is imposed, 1487 §1; of the confirmation of a sentence of arbitration, 1181 §1, 1182 §1; of citation, 1191 §§1 and 3, 1192 §§1–2, 1193, 1194, 1363 §§1–2 and 4; of the citation of a witness, 1237; of the confirmation of a sentence of nullity of marriage, 1370 §1;

of a sentence, 1192 §§1–2, 1297, 1298, 1303 §2, 1304 §2, 1311 §1, 1327 §2, 1354 §3, 1368 §1, 1370 §1, 1480;

of election: 957 §§1–2; of a patriarch, 73, 74; of a major archbishop, 153 §1; of a bishop, 184 §1, 185 §2;

of the admission of a postulation, 964 §2;

of the translation of a bishop to another eparchial see, 223; of the loss of an office after the lapse of a determined period of time or when a certain age has been reached, 965 §3; of the acceptance of a resignation, 970 §§1–2; of transfer to another office, 972 §3; regarding the revocation of delegated power, 992 §1; of the removal of a procurator or an advocate, 1144 §1; *see* knowledge, notification.

invalidity *see* nullity, validity;

of a juridic act, 934 §§1–2. 1°–2°; in executing an administrative act, 1521; of a dispensation, 1536 §1; of acts regarding temporal goods, 1024 §§1 and 3; of alienation, 1035 §1. 3°; of judicial acts after the recusal of a judge has been admitted, 1109 §2;

of sacred ordination, 394. 1°, 396; of acts contrary to the vows by a perpetually professed religious, 466, 533; regarding acts contrary to the vows by a temporarily professed religious, 529 §1, 465; of the absolution of an accomplice in a sin against chastity, 730;

of marriage: 785 §1, 790 §2, 800–812, 820, 821, 824 §2, 825–827, 843 §1, 844, 846 §1, 847, 848 §1, 850; *see* consent, convalidation, impediments, marriage, nullity.

inventory of documents in the archives, 256 §2, 261 §1; of ecclesiastical goods, 1025. 2°, 1026.

investigation by the synod of bishops of the patriarchal Church about doubts or alterations concerning the territorial boundaries of that Church, 146 §2; of the pastoral council about works in the eparchy, 272; about a doubt concerning baptism, chrismation with sacred myron and sacred ordi-

nation, 672 §2; about the death of a spouse, 1383 §2;

concerning suitability: of a presbyter for the office of pastor, 285 §3; of a candidate for sacred ordination, 771 §§3–4; regarding marriage, 784, 787, 788, 1372 §2;

theological i. in the formation of seminary students, 349 §2; of theological truths regarding the function of theologians, 606 §2; scientific i. in higher education, provided by the Catholic university, 640 §1, 641; scientific i. of divine revelation in ecclesiastical universities and faculties, 647. 1°;

when a case is easily investigated, 1186 §1;

preliminary i. in the penal process, 1468, 1469 §§1 and 3, 1470, 1472 §1.

investment of money left over after expenses, 1028 §2. 5°; of goods held in trust, 1046 §2; of the endowment of a pious foundation, 1049.

invitation of catechumens to lead the evangelical life, 9 §2;

of certain persons to the synod of bishops of the patriarchal Church, 102 §3; of persons of another Church *sui iuris* to the patriarchal assembly, 143 §3; of non-Catholic observers to the patriarchal assembly, 143 §4; of bishops of another Church *sui iuris* to the council of hierarchs, 164 §1; for a bishop to resign made by the synod of bishops of the patriarchal Church, 210 §3; of certain persons, not excluding persons of another Church *sui iuris*, to the eparchial assembly, 238 §2; of non-Catholic observers to the eparchial assembly, 238 §3; of certain persons, even of another Church *sui iuris*, to the pastoral council, 273 §3; of confessors to a seminary, 339 §2; regarding the faculty of presbyters or deacons to preach where they are invited, 610 §§2–3, 611, 612 §2; for a pastor to resign, 1393, 1391 §1; to be made by the judge for the accused to select an advocate, 1474.

invocation of the Divine Name of God the Father and the Son and the Holy Spirit in the celebration of baptism, 675 §1; in taking an oath, 895; before a sentence, 1295 §1.

irregularity (CIC) *see* impediments (to receive or exercise sacred orders).

items to be defined by decree, regarding the function of an expert, 1258 §1.

J

joinder of issue when it occurs, 1195 §1; how the petitions and responses of the parties may be expressed, 1195 §2; regarding the decree by which

1300; complaints of nullity, 1302, 1303 §1. 1° and 3° and §2, 1304 §1. 1°, 1305, 1307 §2; appeals, 1310. 4°, 1311 §1, 1314–1316; *res iudicata*, 1323 §2; *restitutio in integrum*, 1327 §1, 1328 §2, 1329; execution of the sentence, 1337 §§2–3, 1338; summary contentious process, 1345 §1, 1346, 1347 §1, 1354 §1; matrimonial processes, 1358, 1362, 1366, 1372 §1, 1374; cases for the separation of spouses, 1378 §3, 1381; the imposition of penalties, 1402 §1, 1409, 1413 §2, 1415–1417; penal trials, 1474, 1481 §1, 1482, 1484;

delegated j., 1059 §1, 1102 §2;

sole judge: cases tried by a single j. not reserved to a collegiate tribunal, 1084 §2; right or obligation to employ an auditor or assessor, 1089, 1084 §3, 1093 §§1 and 3; has the rights of the tribunal and the presiding j., 1092; he writes the sentence himself, 1293 §1; to what authority it pertains to permit cases reserved to a collegiate tribunal to be tried in first instance by a single j., 1084 §3; regarding the introductory *libellus* of the lawsuit, 1188 §1;

collegiate tribunal of three judges: 1090 §1, 1091, 1093 §1; what cases are reserved to it, 1084 §1; manner of proceeding, 1085; regarding the issuing of a sentence, 1292, 1293 §2; *see* tribunal.

judgment   it belongs to the Church to make j. about any human matter whatever, 595 §2;

of the Church concerning the validity of marriage, 781;

it is not permitted to request an opinion from confessors or spiritual fathers in a j. concerning persons;

prudent: of the Apostolic See, 322 §1, 671 §3; of the patriarch, 106 §1. 2°, 119; of the synod of bishops of the patriarchal Church, 111 §3, 121, 671 §4; of the council of hierarchs, 168, 671 §4; of the eparchial bishop, 236, 238 §2, 280 §1, 301 §3, 384 §2, 414 §1. 3°, 415 §2, 633 §1, 637, 671 §4, 757, 1399 §§1–2, 1538 §1; authentic j. of the eparchial bishop, 391; of the local hierarch, 278 §2. 1°, 306 §2, 479, 876 §§1–2; of the hierarch, 372 §2, 664 §3, 762 §1. 8°, 1049, 1403 §1, 1407 §1; of a religious who becomes patriarch, bishop or exarch, 431 §2. 1°; of the competent authority, 319 §1, 371 §2, 762 §1. 1°, 769 §1. 6°, 934 §2. 3°, 975 §2, 1402 §2, 1532 §1. 4°; of the one to whom the remission of a penalty belongs, 1424 §2; of a confessor, 729. 2°; of a priest, 740; of the executor of a decree, 1522 §2, 1524; of experts, 547 §2, *see* experts; of a judge, *see* judge; concerning books, 664 §1;

on the suitability of persons, 285 §3, 461 §2;

defect of discretionary j. with regard to marriage, 818. 2°.

judicial incompetence   *absolute:* when it occurs, 1072; regarding an exception concerning it, 1119 §§1 and 3; must be declared at any stage of a trial, 1120; brings about the irremediable nullity of a sentence, 1303 §1. 1°;

relative: when it occurs, 1073 §2; regarding an exception concerning it, 1119; with respect to a counterclaim, 1157;

if the judge or tribunal is incompetent, the introductory *libellus* of the lawsuit must be rejected, 1188 §2. 1°;

if judges declare themselves competent with no supporting prescript of law, they may be punished, 1115 §1.

jurisdiction   *see* power.

jurisprudence   ecclesiastical j., with regard to places where an express precept of the law is lacking, 1501.

K

key   to the curial archives, 257 §1, 123 §3; to the secret archives or safe, 260 §1, 123 §3.

kidnapping   of a person is to be punished, 1451; impediment to marriage, 806; *see* abduction.

knowledge   regarding the right of the Christian faithful to manifest their views to the pastors of the Church, 15 §3;

required in: seminary teachers, 340 §1; lay persons who are heard by ecclesiastical authority as experts or consultors, 408 §1; novice directors, 458 §1, 524 §1; regarding the scientific suitability of those teaching disciplines having to do with faith and morals in Catholic universities, 644; censors of books, 664 §2; candidates for sacred ordination, 758 §1. 4°, 760; regarding experts, 1255;

use of k. acquired from confession forbidden, 734 §1; from confession with regard to the sacramental seal, the prohibition of its use for external governance, incapacity to give testimony, and penalties, 733 §2, 734 §2, 1231 §2. 2°, 1456 §2; of the nullity of a marriage does not necessarily exclude matrimonial consent, 823; of an impediment regarding the convalidation of marriage, 845 §2; of the adultery of the other spouse, 863 §2; of the discussion of the judges meeting before a sentence, with regard to the observance of secrecy, 1113 §2; of a witness to be evaluated by the judge, 1244, 1253. 2°; of a judge to which the parties can entrust themselves, 1289; which at least seems true of a delict in the preliminary investigation of a penal trial, 1468 §1; necessary k. to issue an extrajudicial decree, 1517; *see* notice;

"knowingly": regarding certain delicts, 1444, 1455.

944; testimonial l. required by a judge about witnesses, 1253; *see* dimissorial letters;

regarding the study or cultivation of literature: in novitiate, 459 §2, 525 §1; to be fostered, recognizing just freedom and cultural diversity, 603.

level of schools, 631 §2, 658 §1;

of sacred order, 324–326, 608, 743; of sacred order, with regard the penalty of reduction to an inferior l., 1084 §1. 3°, 1402 §2, 1433 §1;

of offerings legitimately in force in an eparchy, 1052 §3.

libellus *introductory libellus:* by whom and to whom it is submitted, 1185; regarding the oral petition, 1186; what it ought to contain, 1185, 1187, 1344; it be admitted or rejected as soon as possible, 1188 §1, 1345 §1; when it may be rejected, 1188 §2; when an emended *l.* may be proposed again, 1188 §3; recourse against its rejection, 1188 §4; when it is considered admitted, if the judge is silent, 1189; regarding the decree of its admission and the citation, 1190 §§1–2; to be attached to the citation, 1191 §2; how it may be completed on the occasion of the joinder of issue, 1195 §2; regarding an incidental case not contained in it, 1267; in the intervention of a third party in the case, 1276 §2; what it ought to contain and what ought to be attached to it in the summary contentious trial, 1344; notification of its admission in the summary contentious trial, regarding the citation, 1345; in matrimonial procedure, 1363 §1; regarding the tribunal to determine a conflict on the competence of judges, 1083 §3;

accusing the validity of sacred ordination: to whom it is to be sent, 1386 §1; after it is sent, a cleric is forbidden by the law itself to exercise sacred orders, 1386 §3;

of accusation in a penal trial to be submitted by the promotor of justice, 1472 §1.

licentiate *in sacred sciences required:* for candidates for the episcopate, 180. 6°; for protosyncellus and syncelli, 247 §2; *see* doctorate;

in canon law required: for judicial vicar and adjunct judicial vicar, 1086 §4; for judges, 1087 §3; for promotor of justice and defender of the bond, 1099 §2.

life Christ is, 616 §1; new l. to which a person is regenerated in baptism, 675 §1; new l. in the sacrament of penance, 718;

consecrated: regarding new forms, 571; regarding societies of apostolic l., 572; *see* institutes of consecrated life, society of common life according to the manner of religious;

regarding state of l., 22, 608; *see* status (of persons);

conjugal: *see* partnership (of conjugal life);

of faith, hope and charity which catechumens live, 9 §1; in harmony with the gospel teaching to which the Christian faithful are called by baptism, 20; the eparchial bishop is to furnish an example of holiness by his simplicity of l., 197; liturgical l. in the eparchy is to be moderated by the eparchial bishop, 199 §1; the celebration of the Divine Liturgy is the center and culmination of the whole l. of the Christian community, 289 §2; of Christ is to be followed by seminary students, 346 §2. 1°; the obligation of clerics to represent the love of God toward all people by their whole l., 367; the l. of faith of the Christian faithful is to be conscious and reflective, 602;

spiritual: those rights and obligations which directly regard it are not subject to prescription, 1542. 3°; regarding the right of the Christian faithful to follow their own form of it, 17; means and institutions to foster it, 192 §4; in the seminary, 346 §2, 350 §1; regarding the obligations of clerics, 376;

Christian: those who are heard regarding candidates for the episcopate must be outstanding in it, 182 §1; to be fostered in a parish by the pastor, 289 §§2–3; regarding the first educators of it, 329 §1. 1°; its source and culmination is the Divine Liturgy, 346 §2. 2°; regarding the notion of the catechumenate, 587 §1; in a homily its norms are to be expounded, 614 §1; children are to be formed in its practice, 618; one to be baptized who is no longer an infant must be sufficiently proven in it, 682 §1; regarding the function of sponsor, 684 §2; the sacrament of penance has a great role in fostering it, 289 §2, 718; regarding cremation, 876 §3;

of a seminary: regarding the directory, 337 §2; its source and culmination is the Divine Liturgy, 346 §2. 2°;

regarding the gift of one's own life that all people may be gained for the kingdom of God, in the formation of seminary students, 346 §1;

family: regarding preaching the word of God, 616 §2; lay persons are witnesses to Christ in it, 401; a holier and fuller l. of spouses is to be fostered by pastors of souls, 783 §3; married clerics are to furnish an outstanding example in leading it, 375;

religious: superiors are to take care that the members entrusted to them live their l. in accord with the typicon or statutes, 421, 426; regarding return to the monastery after departure from it, 493 §2;

regarding a member unsuited for it, 547 §2;

monastic life regarding: the notion of a monastery, 433 §1; admission into a monastery, 448; novices, 456 §1; the novice director, 458 §1; a hermit, 482;

gospel l. to be led by catechumens, 9 §2; holy l. to be led by the Christian faithful, 13; conditions of life to be considered by the eparchial bishop, 192 §1; the means and institutions to foster the intellectual l., 192 §4; regarding the destruction of the acts regarding penalties, 259 §2; suited to the clerical state to be fostered by the protopresbyter among the clerics of the district, 278 §1. 2°; the pastor must bear witness in his l., 293; regarding testimonies about the background of a person's l., 366 §1. 3°; common l. among celibate clerics to be fostered, 376; the example of l. on the part of clerics is required to foster vocations, 380; clerics are to strive to be witnesses of higher goods by their simplicity of l., 385 §1; lay persons are witnesses to Christ in private and in politico-social l., 401; of holiness in the formation of members of a monastery, 471 §1; eremitical l., 482, 484, 485, 570; secular l. with regard to departure from a religious institute, 492 §1, 493, 496, 546 §2, 549 §§1 and 3; of communion regarding the notion of a secular institute, 563 §1. 3°; fraternal l. in societies of apostolic life, 572; ecclesial l. regarding the evangelization of peoples, 584 §2; regarding people's perennial questions about the meaning of l., 601; economic l. and work regarding the preaching of the word of God, 616 §2; regarding instruction in schools, 634 §1; teachers are to be exemplary in the witness of their lives, 639; regarding the baptism of an infant in critical condition, 681 §4; suitable to the function of sponsor, 685 §2; the Christian faithful are to be disposed to amend their lives in the sacrament of the anointing of the sick, 737 §1; with respect to suicide, 762 §1. 5°, 763. 2°; regarding the investigation of the l. of candidates for sacred ordination, 771 §3; common l. with respect to the impediment of public propriety, 810 §1. 1° and 3°; common l. regarding the separation of spouses, 864 §1; its various circumstances are sanctified through sacramentals, 867 §1; ecumenism is fostered by the example of l., 903; social l. regarding the observance of civil law, 1030. 1°; regarding assessors of proven l., 1089; the close relationship of l. regarding the function of officials of a tribunal, 1106; dissoluteness of l. to be avoided, 1401; regarding the first offence of one who had been commended heretofore by an upright l., 1409 §1. 4°.

line regarding the computation of degrees of consanguinity and affinity, 918, 919.

litigation the administrative act which refers to l.

receives a strict interpretation, 1512 §2; the administrator of temporal goods is not to initiate or contest l. in the civil forum without permission, 1032; to be avoided, 1103 §1; while it is pending, nothing is to be altered, 1194. 5°; regarding attempts while l. is pending, 1278–1280; procurators and advocated are forbidden to win l. by bribery, 1146 §1; regarding the exceptions of *litis finitae*, 1121 §1; regarding consent or counsel or permission required to initiate or contest l. if ecclesiastical goods are at stake, 1138 §2; *see* case, contention, controversy, instance (of litigation), joinder of issue, libellus (introductory).

liturgy Divine: *see* Divine Liturgy;

as divine praises: *see* divine praises;

of the Presanctified: offerings for it, 715 §2;

of the word: right of catechumens to be admitted to it, 587 §2;

liturgical patrimony: in the notion of rite, 28 §1; lay persons are to study it zealously, 405;

liturgical laws issued by the synod of bishops of the patriarchal Church have the force of law everywhere in the world, 150 §2;

the eparchial bishop is the moderator, promotor and guardian of the entire liturgical life in the eparchy, 199 §1;

ceremonies or liturgical celebrations regarding: precedence of the patriarch, 60 §1; title and honors of a patriarch who has resigned his office, 62; the obligations of clerics, 369 §1; right of lay persons to participate actively in liturgical celebrations of any Church *sui iuris*, 403 §1; admission to the catechumenate, 587 §1; right of catechumens to be admitted to them, 587 §2; offerings on the occasion of liturgical ceremonies, 1013 §1;

commissions for l., 114 §1, 124;

books or liturgical texts which may be used in liturgies, 655 §3, 656 §1, 657; *see* books (liturgical);

regarding minor clerics, 327; how it is to be taught in seminaries, 350 §3, 352 §2; in the formation of deacons not destined for the priesthood, 354; religious are subject to the local hierarch in the instruction of the Christian faithful regarding l., 415 §1; the homily is a part of the l. and has an eminent place in the ministry of the word of God, 607, 614 §1; the liturgical year, 614 §1; in the formation of catechists, 591. 2°; its importance in a catechetical directory, 621 §2; which editions of sacred scripture may be used for liturgical purposes, 655 §3; regarding concelebration of the Divine Liturgy between bishops and presbyters of different Churches *sui iuris*, 701; regarding liturgical vestments, 707, 701;

§2; prescripts of liturgical books and customs to be observed, 836; what is required for licit celebration, 831; place and time of celebration, 838; what things are forbidden in its celebration, 839; regarding the persistence of matrimonial consent when the form prescribed is defective, 827;

secret celebration of marriage: when and by whom it may be permitted and what it includes, 840 §1; when the obligation of secrecy ceases, 840 §2; recording, 296 §2, 840 §3;

mixed: notion, 813; conditions for granting permission, 814; what things are to be determined by the particular law of a Church *sui iuris,* 815; regarding the form of celebration, 834; regarding the ascription of children to a Church *sui iuris,* 29 §1; in case of the pauline privilege, 858; regarding radical sanation, 852; pastoral care for it, 816;

simple convalidation of marriage: what is required, 843; what is the renewal of consent and how it is to be done, 844–846; how it is to be done in case of defect of the form of celebration, 847;

radical sanation of marriage: notion, 848 §1; at what moment it occurs, 848 §2; when it may be granted, 849, 850, 851 §1; if matrimonial consent is lacking, it cannot be granted, 851 §1; by what authority it is granted, 852;

dissolution of the bond: is not granted for a sacramental, consummated m., 853; of a non-consummated m., 862, 1384;

dissolution of the bond by the pauline privilege: what it is granted, 854 §1; regarding interpellations, 855–857; when the baptized party has the right to celebrate a new m., 857, 858; the privilege of the faith enjoys the favor of law, 861;

regarding the case of a man who before baptism had several wives at the same time, or a woman who before baptism had several husbands at the same time, 859 §1; regarding the case of one baptized in the Catholic Church who, by reason of captivity or persecution, cannot restore cohabitation, 860;

separation while the bond remains: on account of adultery, 863; on account of other causes, 864; procedure, 863 §3, 1378–1382; obligation regarding support and education of children, 865; regarding the restoration of the partnership of conjugal life, 866;

attempted: as a cause for the removal of a cleric from office by the law itself, 976 §1. 3°; as a cause for dismissal by the law itself from a religious institute or society of common life according to the manner of religious, 497, 551, 562 §3; as an impediment to receive or exercise sacred orders, 762 §1.

3°, 763. 2°, 767 §1. 2°; as the impediment of public propriety, 810 §1. 3°; as a delict, if attempted by a cleric or religious with a public perpetual vow of chastity, 1453 §§2–3;

of clerics: its dignity, 373; married presbyters cannot be bishops or eparchial administrators, 180. 3°, 227 §2; regarding the appointment of a pastor, 285 §2; regarding the obligation to shine forth with the splendor of chastity and furnishing an outstanding example in family life and educating children, 374, 375; right to suitable support for their families, insurance, social security and health benefits, 390; testimony of marriage and the consent of his wife required for sacred ordination, 769 §1. 2°;

regarding affinity, 919 §1;

declaration of the nullity of m.: *see* case;

see consent, engagement, impediments.

Mary   *Holy ever-Virgin Mary:* the Church commends her to the special and filial veneration of the Christian faithful, 884; her Dormition is a feast day of obligation, 880 §3; seminary students are to venerate her with filial piety, 346 §2. 5°; clerics to honor her, 369 §1.

Mass (CIC)   *see* Divine Liturgy

matters   who represents a juridic person in various m., 79, 133 §2, 157 §3, 190, 290 §1, 335 §2; regarding delegated executive power, 990 §§2–3; norms for m. by which the patrimonial condition of a juridic person can be worsened, 1042; in more serious m. the patriarch will not fail to hear the synod, 82 §3; regarding meetings encouraged by the patriarch, 84 §2; to whom m. which affect the entire patriarchal Church may be entrusted, 89 §2; of greater importance, in which it is expedient that patriarchs act after consulting one another, 99 §2; in synods, 102 §3, 106 §1. 1° and 3°, 111 §2, 116 §3, 119, 120; in the patriarchal assembly, 140; in extraordinary m. or in m. entailing special difficulty, eparchial bishops are not to omit hearing the metropolitan, and the metropolitan is not to omit hearing the eparchial bishops, 160; in the council of hierarchs, 166 §2, 170; of an eparchy, 215 §4, 246, 249, 253 §1, 256 §1, 269 §2, 271 §1; of an order or congregation, 529 §5; who is to abstain from business m. on Sundays and feast days of obligation, 881 §4; regarding cooperation with other Christians, 908; regarding trials, 1083 §1, 1110 §1, 1167, 1217 §1, 1229 §2. 1°.

maturity   *of the human person:* right of the Christian faithful to Christian education by which they are properly instructed how to achieve it, 20; regarding seminary formation, 346 §3;

baptism, 290 §2, 677 §1; permission to baptize in the territory of another, 678 §1; regarding the baptism of the Christian faithful of another Church *sui iuris*, 678 §2; recording the name of the m. of baptism, 689 §1; is to see regarding the witness of baptism, 688; when he must designate a sponsor, 685 §1. 4°; informs the pastor about the baptism, 690; *see* baptism;

of chrismation with holy myron: is a presbyter with holy myron confected by a bishop, 693, 694; regarding valid and licit ministration, 696; is bound to inform the pastor is he ministers chrismation with holy myron separately from baptism, 695 §2; *see* chrismation with holy myron;

of the Divine Eucharist: only bishops and presbyters have the power to celebrate the Divine Liturgy, 699 §1; a priest, or, according to the norm of particular law, a deacon, distributes the Divine Eucharist, 709 §1; regarding the authority who is to establish norms according to which other Christian faithful may distribute the Divine Eucharist, 709 §2; regarding the delict of simulation of the Divine Liturgy, 1443; *see* divine eucharist, divine liturgy;

of the sacrament of penance: is only a priest, 722 §2; is m. of divine justice and mercy, 732 §2; regarding the faculty required for presbyters, 722–726; manner of acting with penitents, 732; regarding absolution of an accomplice, 730, 1457; regarding the delict of solicitation, 731, 1458; regarding the sacramental seal, 733 §1, 734, 1456 §1; obligation of administering this sacrament, 381 §2, 735; *see* penance (as a sacrament);

of the anointing of the sick: is any priest, and only a priest, 739 §1; to whom it pertains to administer this sacrament, 739 §2; regarding the blessing of the oil, 741; *see* anointing of the sick;

of sacred ordination: is only a bishop, 744; to whom episcopal ordination is reserved, 745; delicts regarding episcopal ordination without a mandate, 1459 §1; regarding presbyteral and diaconal ordinations, 747–749, 1459 §2; regarding the Church *sui iuris*, 746 §2, 748 §2; *see* sacred ordination;

of the blessing of marriage: is the priest assisting, 828 §2, 834 §2; who is competent to give the blessing, 290 §2, 302 §2, 828 §1, 829 §§1–2; required faculties, 302 §2, 829 §3, 830; faculty in certain cases regarding non-Catholics, 833 §1; recording the minister's name, 841 §1; regarding the special case in which a competent priest cannot be present, 832, 841 §3; regarding the prohibition of the celebration of marriage together with

a non-Catholic minister, 839; obligations regarding a secret marriage, 840 §1; permission of a hierarch required in certain marriages, 789; regarding dispensation in danger of death or in an urgent case, 796 §2, 797, 798; *see* marriage;

clerics should be m. of preaching, 369 §1; clerics are to be m. of the reconciliation of all in the love of Christ, 384 §1;

pastor as minister of the parish, 289 §3;

Catholic: regarding the administration of sacraments to Catholics, 671 §1; regarding the administration of some sacraments to non-Catholics, 671 §§3–4, 681 §5; regarding the blessing of the marriage of Christian faithful of Eastern non-Catholic Churches, 833;

non-Catholic: when it is permitted to receive certain sacraments from them, 671 §2; prohibition of concelebration of the Divine Liturgy with them, 702; regarding the forbidden celebration of marriage together with them, 839; if one is lacking, when ecclesiastical funerals may be granted to non-Catholics, 876 §1; their assistance in schools, hospitals and similar institutions, 907; regarding attempted marriage before one, 810 §1. 3°, 1372 §2;

in minor orders, 327.

ministry of the whole Church: solicitude for it, 329 §1;

of priest: in the Divine Liturgy acting in the person of Christ, 698; in the sacrament of penance, 718;

of deacons in the celebration of the Divine Liturgy, 699 §2;

vocations to ministries: to be fostered, 329, 380, 591. 1°; signs of a vocation to them in minor seminary students, 331 §1;

formation for ministries: in minor seminary, 331 §1, 344 §3; in major seminary, 346 §1 and §2. 6°, 349 §2, 350 §1, 352 §2; in ecclesiastical universities and faculties, 647. 2°;

regarding clerics: their first obligation, 367; how they participate in one m., 324; cooperation in ministries, 376; they are to foster vocations to it by the witness of their m., 380; right to obtain, 371 §1; obligation to undertake and fulfill, 371 §2; disposition to exercise it missions and areas suffering from a shortage of clerics, 393; those who move or transfer to another eparchy, 361, 366 §1. 2°; how those who exercise ministries among the Christian faithful of the Eastern Churches are to be formed, 41; how they are to use goods offered on occasion of the exercise of m., 385 §1; when they are to be exempt from testifying in a trial by

sion of the synod of bishops of the patriarchal Church and of the council of hierarchs regarding the m., 585 §2; a priest is to be designated in each eparchy to promote undertakings on behalf of the m., 585 §3; regarding care for young Churches to reach maturity, 590;

mission territories: notion, 594; what is to be fostered in them in a special way, 592; cooperation of all presbyters working in them, 593 §1.

moderation, moderator of preaching the gospel to the whole world by the Roman Pontiff, 585 §1; of the ecumenical movement by the Apostolic Roman See, 904 §1; of the Church with regard to schools, 631 §2; of the Church's magisterium regarding teachers of sacred disciplines, 351;

of ecclesiastical authority regarding: exercise of rights which are proper to the Christian faithful, 26 §2; schools, 634 §2;

of the council of hierarchs regarding morals, 169;

of the eparchial bishop: as m. of the entire liturgical life of the eparchy, 199 §1; regarding coordination of the works of the apostolate, 203 §1; regarding preaching the word of God, 609; regarding catechetical formation, 623 §1;

of the local hierarch concerning reservation of the Divine Eucharist, 714 §2;

regarding a parish entrusted to several presbyters, 287 §2;

in a seminary: its general m. belongs to the rector, 338 §2; regarding other moderators, 332 §2, 337 §1, 338 §2, 340 §2; students are to learn to direct themselves by degrees, 346 §3;

clerics are not to have an active part in moderating labor unions, 384 §2;

in institutes of consecrated life: the finance officer exercises his or her office under the m. of the superior, 447 §1, 516 §1; of a member who is formed outside of his or her own house, 471 §2, 536 §2; regarding the novitiate, 522 §1, 524 §§2–3; of clerics of presbyters regarding the notion of a clerical order or congregation, 505 §3; regarding preaching, 612 §1; autonomy regarding the m. of the institute's own schools, 638 §1;

care of the moderators of Catholic schools: about avoiding the use of certain instruments of social communication, 665 §2; about ecumenism, 906, 907;

moderators of an educational institution are to administer the sacrament of penance to their students, 734 §3;

ecumenism is to be applied by moderators of the instruments of social communication, 906;

to whom the m. of a juridic person belongs, 922 §2. 3°; consultation of the moderators of a juridic person regarding its suppression, 927 §2; offerings made to the moderators of a juridic person are presumed to be given to the juridic person itself, 1016 §2;

of a judge regarding proofs, 1228;

as a reduction of the wills of the Christian faithful in pious causes, 1054 §1;

in threatening penalties by precept, 1406 §1; of penalties within equitable limits, if the offender has committed several delicts, 1409 §1. 3°;

general moderator of the administration of justice: in patriarchal Churches, 1062 §§2 and 5.

modification of patriarchal Churches, 57 §1; of the title of a patriarchal Church, 57 §2; of the territorial boundaries of a patriarchal Church, 146 §2; of a metropolitan Church *sui iuris*, 155 §2; of an eparchy, 85 §1, 177 §2; of an exarchy, 85 §3, 311 §2, 312, 319 §1; of a district, 176 §2; of a parish, 280 §2; of the program of formation of clerics, 330 §1; regarding typica of monasteries and statutes of congregations of eparchial right, 576 §2; of an ecclesiastical office, 936 §3.

monastery what it is, 433 §1; is a juridic person, 423; types, 434; its church is dedicated by consecration, 871 §1; can have its own cemetery, 874 §4; regarding the visitation of the eparchial bishop or the Apostolic See, 414 §1. 3° and §2, 415 §2; competence of the eparchial bishop and the Apostolic See regarding its statutes and certain dispensations, 414 §§1–2; regarding a member promoted to a dignity or office outside of the m., 431; profession in it, 462–470; formation of members and discipline to be observed in it, 471–480; which vows are suspended while the one who has taken the vows remains in the m., 894;

sui iuris: notion, 433 §2; erection and suppression, 435 §1, 437, 438 §§1–2 and 4; aggregation of monasteries to a confederation and separation from it, 439–440 §1; its superior is a major superior, 418 §1; their superiors are to be summoned to the assembly of the patriarchal Church and to the eparchial assembly, 143 §1. 3°, 238 §1. 9°; regarding the quinquennial report, 419 §1; superiors, synaxes, finance officers, 441 §§1–2, 442, 443, 445–447; admission to it and the novitiate, 448–461; regarding dimissorial letters, 472, 750 §1; regarding hermits, 481–485; transfer of members to another m., 487, 488 §§1–2 and 4; transfer of members from a m. to an order or congregation, 488 §3, 544–545; transfer of members of an order or congregation to a m., 544–545; exclaustration of members and departure from a m., 489–496; regarding dismissal of members, 497–503;

stauropegial: notion, 486 §2; how it can be erected, 486 §1; its erection reserved to the patriarch, 435 §2; power of the patriarch over it, 101, 486 §2; is of patriarchal right, 434; regarding the power of the administrator of the patriarchal Church, 129; regarding its suppression, 438 §§1 and 4;

dependent: what is a filial m., 436 §1; what is a subsidiary m., 436 §1; regarding its erection, 436 §2, 437; regarding its suppression, 438; visitation of the superior of the monastery *sui iuris,* 420 §1; superiors, synaxes, finance officers, 441 §1, 444 §§2–3, 445–447 §§2–3; if ascribed to another Church *sui iuris,* it must observe the rite of that Church, 432.

money invested by an administrator of temporal goods, 1028 §2. 5º; of an endowment is to be deposited in a safe place, 1049; statutes of a tribunal are to establish norms for the deposit of m. for the payment of expenses and the reparation of damages, 1335. 5º; regarding the execution of a sentence by which a party is condemned to pay m., 1342 §2;

monetary penalty (fine) for procurators or advocates, 1146 §1, 1147.

month its juridical computation, 1545, 1546 §2;

to be recorded: by a notary, 254. 2º; in the introductory *libellus* of litigation, 1187. 3º; in the text of a sentence, 1304 §1. 4º;

one month with respect to: convocation of a synod for election of a patriarch, 65 §2; absence of an eparchial bishop from his eparchy, 204 §2; absence of a coadjutor bishop and auxiliary bishop from their eparchy, 217; appointment of an eparchial administrator by the patriarch, 220. 3º; absence of a pastor from his parish, 292 §2; marriage celebrated before witnesses alone, 832 §1. 2º; a new election after one previously elected has not accepted, 957 §3; insistence that the judicial vicar perform his duty if he remains silent regarding an arbitral sentence, 1181 §2; time limit for the prosecution of an appeal, 1182 §1, 1314; silence of a judge concerning the admission or rejection of the introductory *libellus* of litigation, 1189; sanation of attempts while a lawsuit is pending, 1279; time limit for writing a sentence, 1293 §3; decision on a new presentation of the case, 1325 §1; intimation of a sentence in a penal trial, 1480;

two months: with respect to the translation of a bishop to another see, 223;

three months with respect to: a metropolitan's request for the pallium, 156 §1; reception of episcopal ordination by one elected or appointed bishop, 188 §1; absence from the novitiate, 457 §2, 523 §1; acquisition of a quasi-domicile, 912 §2, 913; lack of effect if acceptance of a resignation has not been intimated, 970 §1; complaint of nullity of a sentence on account of a remediable fault, 1304 §2; time limit for requesting *restitutio in integrum,* 1327 §§1–2; suspensive period for law after publication in the official commentary *Acta Apostolicae Sedis,* 1489 §1;

four months with respect to: canonical possession of an eparchy to be taken by the one elected or appointed eparchial bishop, 188 §2; ascription to an eparchy after the legitimate movement of a cleric, 360 §2;

six months with respect to: illegitimate absence of an eparchial bishop from his eparchy, 204 §4; reduction of the novitiate after a transfer to another religious institute, 545 §1; separation of spouses, 863 §§2–3; canonical provision, 941, 943 §2; obligation of judges that cases not be protracted in appeal, 1111; time limit for issuing an arbitral sentence, 1178; abatement of an instance of litigation, 1201; time limits established by a judge or the executor of a sentence for certain obligations, 1342 §2;

where the Divine Liturgy is celebrated at least several times in a month, the Divine Eucharist is to be reserved there, 714 §1.

morals teaching of the infallible magisterium regarding m., 597 §§1–2; teaching of the authentic magisterium regarding m., 599; regarding the binding force of laws to the extent they concern matters of m., 1492; to whom it pertains to promote, guard and defend good m., 605; the eparchial bishop is to propose to the Christian faithful the truths of the faithful to be applied to m., 196 §1; mandate to teach subjects having to do with m. in Catholic universities, 644; to whom it pertains to issue prohibitions regarding instruments of social communication if they are harmful to the integrity of m., 652 §2; what particular law must determine about the use of certain instruments of social communication which deal with m., 653; which books dealing with m. require ecclesiastical approval, 658 §2; regarding ecclesiastical permission to publish, 659, 661 §1, 662 §2; regarding the prohibition to write in newspapers, magazines and periodicals that are wont to attack openly good m., 660; books not in harmony with m. are not to be displayed, sold or distributed in churches, 665 §1;

good or sound morals required in: a bishop, 180. 1º; a pastor, 285 §1; the wife and children of a married presbyter for him to be appointed pastor, 285

§2; members of the pastoral council, 273 §4; those to be admitted to the novitiate, 453 §3, 519; a candidate for sacred ordination, 758 §1. 2°, 769 §1. 4°, 771 §3; an auditor, 1093 §2; *see* probity;

regarding the removal of teachers of Catholic religion, 636 §2;

regarding a cleric to be ascribed to an eparchy, 366 §1. 3°;

integrity of morals to be preserved: by the Christian faithful, 15 §3; in associations, 577 §1; in expressing the gospel in the culture of each individual people, 584 §2;

care of the council of hierarchs for m., 169;

regarding the destruction of procedural acts for imposing penalties in matters of m., 259 §2;

penalties against one who harms m. by using instruments of social communication, 1448 §1.

mortgage   care of the administrator that interest on it be paid at the stated time, 1028 §2. 4°.

mother   Holy Mary, M. of God, whom Christ has made M. of all people, 346 §2. 5°, 369 §1, 884;

regarding the ascription of a child to a Church *sui iuris*, 29 §1 and §2. 1°; regarding the admission of a child who must support her into an institute of religion, 452 §2, 517 §1; when a m. may administer baptism to her child, 677 §2; cannot validly undertake the function of sponsor, 685 §1. 5°; regarding the notation of her name in the baptismal register if she is not married, 689 §2.

motives   is to be expressed in an extrajudicial decree, 1519 §2;

in a sentence: if issued by a collegiate tribunal, the sentence is to select m., 1293 §2; both in law and in fact must be set forth, 1294. 3°, 1354 §3; if m. are absent, the sentence suffers from remediable nullity, 1304 §1. 2°;

regarding a petition for *restitutio in integrum,* 1327 §§1–2;

in the pronouncements of the judge besides the sentence the m. are to be set forth, 1300; in a decree concerning the non-observance of certain procedural norms in a summary contentious trial, 1356;

regarding the procedure in the removal of pastors, 1393 §2, 1394;

see cause, reason.

movement   of a cleric to another eparchy, 360–363, 365 §1.

mute   if a m. must be interrogated in a trial, an interpreter may be used unless the judge prefers that answers be given in writing, 1130.

mutilation   grave and malicious m. as an impediment to the reception or exercise of sacred orders, 762 §1. 5°, 763. 2°; grave m. of a person is to be punished, 1451.

myron   *see* chrismation with holy myron.

N

name   of God the Father, Son and Holy Spirit in the formula of baptism, 675 §1; divine N. in taking an oath, 895; divine N. to be invoked in a sentence, 1295 §1; the eparchial bishop exercises his power in the n. of Christ, 178;

in the name of the Church: to teach in the n. of the Church belongs to bishops alone, 596; associations which set out to teach Christian doctrine in the n. of the Church, 574; public divine worship is carried out in the name of the Church, 668 §1; a public vow is accepted by a legitimate ecclesiastical superior in the n. of the Church, 889 §4;

an eparchy is entrusted to an eparchial bishop to shepherd in his own n., 178; an eparchy is not entrusted to titular bishops to be governed in their own n., 179; an exarch governs an exarchy in his own n. or in the n. of the one who appointed him, 312, 316; election of the patriarch is intimated in the n. of the synod of bishops of the patriarchal Church, 73; a proxy acting in the n. of another is not admitted to the eparchial assembly, 239; a protopresbyter fulfills his function in the n. of the eparchial bishop, 239; an administrator of the ecclesiastical goods is not to initiate or contest litigation in a civil forum in the name of the juridic person without the permission of the proper hierarch, 1032; goods assigned in the n. of an endowment are to be deposited in a safe place, 1049; when a hierarch may stand trial in the n. of a juridic person subject to him, 1138 §3; those who stand trial in the n. of the parties are considered incapable of giving testimony, 1231 §2. 1°; even if a person has the right to cast a vote in his or her own n. under several titles, that person can only vote once, 950; to whom the goods registered in the name of a juridic person belong, 1020 §§1–2;

when an initiative may claim the n. "Catholic," 19; regarding institutes which are equivalent to a minor seminary, 331 §1; of an association to be determined in its statutes, 576 §1; of judges not indicated in their conclusions before a sentence, 1292 §§2 and 4;

if someone acts in the n. of another without a legitimate mandate, the sentence is vitiated by irremediable nullity, 1300 §1. 6°;

the good n. of someone must not be endangered in the preliminary investigation of a penal trial, 1468 §2;

of persons: of candidates for the episcopate in the synod of bishops of the patriarchal Church, 182 §§3–4; of candidates for sacred orders, 771 §1; in a baptismal register, 689 §2; of those ordained to be recorded in the curial archives, 774 §1; in a marriage register, 841 §1; in the text of a sentence, 1295 §1; hierarch to express approval or permission in his own n. to publish books, 664 §3; of witnesses to be indicated to the tribunal and communicated to the parties, 1233 §1, 1235;

regarding conspirators in a delict, 1417;

who is not included under the n. of religious superiors, 418 §2;

"by name," 987, 1170 §2.

nation *regarding:* agreements entered into or approved by the Holy See, 4; pastoral care of the eparchial bishop for the Christian faithful regardless of n., 192 §1; the assembly of hierarchs of several Churches *sui iuris,* 322 §1; the common program of clerical formation, 330 §2; a seminary for several Churches *sui iuris,* 332 §2; the curriculum of studies of a minor seminary, 344 §3; the forum in cases for declaring the nullity of marriage, 1359. 3°.

nativity of Our Lord Jesus Christ: its day is a feast day of obligation, 880 §3;

place of birth is to be recorded in the baptismal register, 689 §1.

natural law concerning the free disposition of goods, 1043 §1.

necessity, need *of the Church:* the Christian faithful are obliged to assist with the n. of the Church, 25 §1, 1011; manner of exercise of the office of the Roman Pontiff and the college of bishops to be determined according to it, 45 §2, 50 §3; regarding inquiries about it in the council of hierarchs, 168; regarding the fostering of vocations, 329; seminary students to be taught about the needs of the Church, 352 §3; regarding the obligations of clerics to undertake and fulfill offices, ministries or functions entrusted to them, 371 §2; if it so recommends, certain functions of sacred ministers can be entrusted to lay persons, 403 §2; regarding the transfer of a pastor, 1397;

of an eparchy regarding: the appointment of an auxiliary bishop, 212 §1; emoluments to be reserved for the n. of the eparchy while the eparchial see is vacant, 230. 2°; the eparchial assembly, 235; pastoral work and the presbyteral

council, 264; move of a cleric to another eparchy, 361; ascription of a cleric to an eparchy, 366. 1°; taxes, 1012 §1; the common fund, 1021 §3;

for canonical provision in promotion to the episcopacy, 187 §1; for pastoral action in the erection, alteration or suppression of districts, 276 §2; for ministers in the pastoral formation of seminary students, 352 §1; for the apostolate in the exemption of institutes of consecrated life, 412 §2; of religious to be provided for by superiors, 421; of an ill pastor removed from office, regarding the use of the rectory, 1396 §2;

of the Christian faithful: right to make their needs known to the pastors of the Church, 15 §2; care of the council of hierarchs for them, 169; how the needs of another Church *sui iuris* are to be cared for by the eparchial bishop, 193 §2, 207; regarding the assistance of members of orders and congregations requested by the local hierarch or the pastor, 542; attention should be given above all to the pastoral n. of the Christian faithful regarding celebration of the Divine Liturgy individually or in concelebration, 700 §1;

grave necessity: regarding the illicit admission into a religious institute of those who must support a father, mother, grandfather or grandmother who are in grave n., 452 §2, 517; requirements to absolution to be imparted to several penitents at the same time, 720 §2. 2° and §3;

in case of necessity: who can baptize besides the pastor, 677 §2; any priest must administer the anointing of the sick, 739 §2; in the anointing of the sick, a single anointing with the proper formula suffices, 742;

in case of true necessity: the archives or secret safe of the eparchial curia can be opened during a vacancy of the eparchial see, 260 §2; it is permitted to confer on one person two or more offices which cannot appropriately be fulfilled together at the same time by the same person, 942;

in case of urgent necessity: the superior general can decide about the goods of a suppressed province, 508 §3; certain sacraments can be administered to Christian non-Catholics under certain conditions, 671 §4; baptism may be administered by doing only those things necessary for validity, 676; any priest who has the faculty of administering the sacrament of penance must do so, 735 §2; ecclesiastical goods belonging to the stable patrimony of a juridic person can be alienated, 1035 §1. 1°;

in case of extreme necessity: a presbyter can be designed to govern the impeded patriarchal see, 132

§1; a bishop can be ordained by one or two bishops, 746 §1;

outside of a case of necessity: baptism should be celebrated in the parish church, 687 §1; chrismation with holy myron must be administered together with baptism, 695 §1; which prescripts are to be observed in the celebration of marriage, 836;

of place or time regarding: persons or institutes which cooperate with the Roman Pontiff, 46 §1; participation of the Christian faithful of an eparchy in the apostolate, 203 §2; formation of the members of a monastery, 471 §1; the determination of the policies of an association, 576 §1; remedies to remove any dangers of the invalid or illicit celebration of marriage, 785 §1;

if necessary, as necessary, if necessity requires, insofar as it is necessary, if the judge deems it necessary (and similar phrases): 289 §2, 366 §1. 3°, 404 §1, 524 §2, 592 §1, 910 §2, 1021 §3, 1028 §2. 1°, 1253, 1262 §2, 1272 §2, 1275 §1, 1394. 2°; a vice-chancellor of the eparchial curia may be appointed, 252 §2; parochial vicars may be associated with the pastor to fulfill pastoral care, 301 §1; the office of superior of religious can be joined to that office of finance officer, 447 §2, 516 §2; superiors in monasteries must give the people catechetical instruction, 479; Catholics can receive certain sacraments from non-Catholic ministers, 671 §1; a legal representative can be appointed in recourse against an administrative decree, 1003; taxes can be imposed, 1012 §1; one lay judge can be included in constituting a collegiate tribunal, 1087 §2; a judge can supply for the negligence of the parties, 1110 §2; the judge can adjudicate counterclaims separately from the principal action, 1122 §2; the judge may require the ministry of a procurator or advocate, 1139 §1, 1200 §1; arbiters must approach a tribunal to impose penalties, 1176 §3; the joinder of issue does not take place in writing, but the parties are to be summoned to it, 1190 §1; a witness can be interrogated again before the testimonies are published, 1251; proofs can be completed before the conclusion of the case, 1281 §2; laws can be strengthened by penalties, 1405 §1; to repair scandal a petition for the remission of a penalty or the remission itself can be divulged, 1422 §3; a prohibition against administering the sacraments or sacramentals is suspended to care for the Christian faithful in danger of death, 1435 §2;

what is necessary: to be established for an ordaining bishop regarding dimissorial letters for religious, 537 §2; for matrimonial consent, 819; to

celebrate marriage validly with regard to the presence of the parties and the manifestation of consent, 837 §1; to renew matrimonial consent if its defect can be proved, 846 §3; for the removal of a procurator or advocate to take effect, 1144 §1;

regarding: the convocation of the synod of bishops of the patriarchal Church, 106 §1. 2°; the preservation of documents in the parish archives, 296 §4; the service of clerics wheresoever n. requires, 393; remuneration by which workers and their families are provided with necessities, 409 §2, 1030. 2°; women dismissed by a baptized husband who had several wives before baptism, or men dismissed by a baptized woman who had several husbands before baptism, 859 §3; the intervention of the promotor of justice, 1095; the intervention of a third party in a case, 1277; new proofs in a penal process, 1479 §2;

about necessities regarding: the support of clerics, 25 §1, 1007, 1410; the purposes of the Church, 1011; the permanent synod, 128. 3°; statutes of the patriarchal assembly, 145; documents for candidates for the episcopacy, 182 §1; those things which can be imposed on a baptized non-Catholic who comes into full communion with the Catholic Church, 896; fulfilling and office, 937 §1; delays in a trial, 1273 §1;

regarding the n. to accept the resignation of an eparchial administrator, 231 §1; liturgy as a necessary source of doctrine and truly Christian spirit, 350 §3; ecumenism as a necessary dimension of every theological discipline, 350 §4; parents, whose work is necessary to raise and educate their children, cannot licitly be admitted to the novitiate, 452 §2, 517 §1; regarding the civil effects of a religious' renunciation of his or her own goods, 467 §2, 533; regarding the n. of certitude in cases of the dismissal of a member from temporary vows, 552 §1. 3°; necessary instruments for the education of their children to be chosen by parents, 627 §2; regarding the n. of proofs in dispensation from an occult impediment in the external forum, 799; knowledge or opinion of the nullity of a marriage does not necessarily exclude matrimonial consent, 823; regarding a necessary domicile or quasi-domicile, 915 §1; regarding necessary information for those whose consent or counsel is required to place juridic acts, 934 §3; necessary cause regarding the reduction, moderation or commutation of the wills of the Christian faithful in pious causes, 1054 §1; necessary officials of the ordinary tribunal of the patriarchal Church, 1063 §2; only those who are necessary to expedite the process are to be present in court,

1129 §1; regarding the necessary provision for a person's support, 1163 §1, 1337 §2; regarding necessary procurators and advocates, 1139 §1, 1200 §1; regarding the necessary explanations of experts, 1259 §3; regarding the acts of the preliminary investigation in a penal process, 1470; necessary information to be sought out before an extrajudicial decree is issued, 1517 §1.

neglect regarding those who are called to an election, 984 §§2–3; of prescripts established for the validity of an arbitration, 1181 §3; evident n. of a not merely procedural prescript of the law is cause for *restitutio in integrum*, 1326 §2. 4°; grave n. of the obligations of a pastor as a cause for removal, 1390. 4°.

negligence of a metropolitan to be supplied by the patriarch, 80. 2°; of an eparchial bishop in appointing an eparchial finance officer is to be supplied by the metropolitan, 133 §1. 6°, 138, 139, 159. 7°, 175; of local administrators to be supplied by the eparchial finance officer, 262 §3; to be avoided by clerics in acquiring for themselves knowledge of the profane sciences, 372 §3; of a religious superior regarding abuses in that superior's house, and the obligation of the local hierarch regarding them, 417; of a major superior regarding canonical visitation to be supplied by the local hierarch, 420 §3; of an order or congregation causing the illness of a member in temporary vows impedes the exclusion of that member from a renewal of temporary profession or from making perpetual profession, 547 §2; to be avoided regarding the reception of the blessing of a marriage celebrated before witnesses alone, 832 §3; supplied by another in the canonical provision of an office affects the juridical condition of the person upon whom the officer was conferred in no way, 945; of the parties in offering proofs can be supplied by the judge, 1110 §2; grave n. of the officers of a tribunal with damage on the parties can be punished with penalties, 1115 §1; of one representing a juridic person in a trial can be supplied by a competent hierarch, 1138 §3; how n. in designating arbiters can be supplied by a tribunal, 1174 §2; of a party in constituting a procurator or an advocate in suspension of an instance and the right of the judge to provide for it by a decree, 1200 §2; of the parties in preparing defense briefs regarding the right of the judge to pronounce the sentence, 1289; by what authority the n. of the eparchial bishop regarding a sentence to be sent for execution is to be supplied, 1340 §2; culpable n. in illegitimately placing an act or omitting an act with harm to another is to

be punished, 1464 §2; of the one cited to exercise the right of self-defence in the imposition of penalties by an extrajudicial decree, 1486 §1. 1°.

neophyte care of missionaries to foster vocations to the sacred ministry among them, 591. 1°; regarding the impediment to receive sacred orders, 762 §1. 8°.

non-Catholic not bound by merely ecclesiastical laws, 1490; concerning their reception into the Catholic Church, 35, 896–901; obligations of the eparchial bishop, 192 §2–3; obligations of the pastor, 293; how their hierarchs can participate in an assembly of hierarchs of several Churches *sui iuris*, 322 §1; can be invited to a patriarchal or eparchial assembly, 143 §4, 238 §3; in schools, 634 §2; when baptized licitly by a Catholic minister, 681 §4–5; godparent, 685 §3; minister of the sacrament of penance, Eucharist, and anointing of the sick, 671 §2; concerning sacramental sharing, 670 §2, 671 §2–5, 681 §5, 685 §3, 702, 705 §2, 832 §2, 833 §1, 834 §2, 876 §1, 908, 1440; prohibition of concelebrating Divine Eucharist with, 702; cannot be admitted to novitiate, 450. 1°, 517 §1, 559 §1, 568 §1; relative to their matrimonial law, 780 §2, 781; in a mixed marriage, 813–816; attempted marriage before non-Catholic minister, 810 §1. 3°, 1372 §2; non-Catholic priest can be called in celebrating marriage before witnesses alone, 832 §2; concerning the faculty of a Catholic priest for blessing their marriages, 833; the form for celebration of marriage entered into with Eastern non-Catholics, 834 §2; marriage with non-Catholic after granting Pauline privilege, 858; petitioner in case, 1134; cannot be advocate, unless permitted by competent authority, 1141; concerning burial, 876 §1; *see* Ecumenism, Mixed Marriage;

concerning the delict of one who hands children over to be baptized or educated in a non-Catholic religion, 1439.

norms *according to the norm of law: passim, see* law (individual entries);

according to the norm of the canons: passim;

according to the norm of the typicon: see typicon;

according to the norm of the statutes: see statutes;

special norms established by the Roman Pontiff: for persons who assist the Roman Pontiff in exercising his office, 46 §1; for the participation of hierarchs who preside over Churches *sui iuris* in the synod of bishops, 46 §2; regarding the precedence of patriarchs, 58; for the report of the patriarch regarding the Church over which he presides, 92 §3; for a vacancy in the patriarchal see, 128. 2°; in

the election or appointment of the administrator of an eparchy outside of the territorial boundaries of the patriarchal Church, 221. 5°; as soon as possible about an impeded eparchial see outside of the territorial boundaries of the patriarchal Church and about the assumption of its governance, 233 §3;

the eparchial bishop is to be notified: of an impediment to attendance at the eparchial assembly, 239; about a vacant or impeded parish and about the assumption of its governance, 300 §2; about the ascription of a cleric of his eparchy to another eparchy, 366 §2; on the boundaries of the cloister and their alteration, 477 §3; of the exercise of judicial power within his eparchy of a judge of another eparchy, 1128 §1; by the major superior of the removal of a member of his institute from the office of pastor by that same superior, 1391 §2;

the local hierarch is to be notified: of the absence of a pastor for more than a week from his parish, 292 §2; by a cleric from another eparchy of his residence in the hierarch's territory, 386 §2; of dispensation or convalidation of marriage in certain cases, 798;

is (or are) to be notified: as soon as possible the authority to whom it belongs to appoint an exarch, of the vacant or impeded exarchy, 320 §2; the pastor, with whom the baptism of a religious was recorded, of that religious' profession, 470, 535 §2; as soon as possible the authority to which an institute of consecrated life is subject about the dismissal of a member by the law itself, 497 §2, 551, 562 §3; immediately the major superior of the expulsion of a member by a local superior, 551; if the case warrants, the authority which erected or approved an association, by the eparchial bishop of the action of the association, 577 §2; the pastor of the place of the administration of baptism while he was absent, 690; the pastor of the place where baptism was administered of the administration of chrismation with holy myron separately from baptism, 695 §2; the pastor who is to celebrate a marriage of the pre-nuptial investigation done by another pastor, 787; the non-Catholic party of the required promises made by the Catholic party in a mixed marriage, 814. 2°, 815; the competent non-Catholic authority of the blessing of the marriage of Christian faithful of a non-Catholic Eastern Church in certain cases, 833 §2; the pastor of the place of the celebration of a marriage of the convalidation, nullity or dissolution of that marriage, 842; the proper hierarch about goods received in trust, 1046 §1; the opposing party of the removal of a procurator or advocate, 1144 §1; the parties about the referral of an evidently null or manifestly unjust sentence by the executor to the tribunal from which it was issued, 1341 §2; the parties about the useful time for them to prove their assertions in the summary contentious trial, 1347 §2; the judge of the tribunal of second grade to follow the documentary process if the defender of the bond appeals to him, 1373 §1; the major superior about the removal of a member of his institute as pastor, 1391 §2; the accused about the accusation and proofs in the imposition of penalties by extrajudicial decree, 1486 §1. 1°; the competent authority if the executor of an administrative act deems the execution inopportune, 1522 §1; the authority which granted a privilege about the grave abuse of that privilege, 1535;

regarding the means by which experts are notified regarding the identity of persons, things, or places, 1259 §2;

see intimation, notice.

notoriety ignorance or error are not presumed regarding a notorious fact concerning another, 1497 §2;

of concubinage regarding the impediment of public propriety, 810 §1. 2°.

novice directors necessity and qualities, 458 §1, 524 §1; rights and obligations, 458 §2, 459, 524 §3; novices are subject to their power, 524 §4, 545 §1; their assistants, 524 §2; their substitutes if the novitiate is made outside of the house in which the novitiate is located, 522 §1.

novitiate prior preparation of a candidate to assume the religious state, 449, 518; who may not validly be admitted, 450, 517 §1, 559 §1, 568; who may not licitly be admitted, 451, 452, 517 §1, 559 §1; competent superior for admission, 453 §1, 519; suitability and full freedom of the candidate to choose the religious state must be evident, 453 §2, 519; regarding the documents and testimonies concerning the suitability and good conduct of the candidate, 453 §3, 519; regarding norms concerning the dowry, 454, 517 §1; when it begins, 455, 520; in which monastery it is to be spent, 456; location of the n. in orders and congregations, 521, 522; what is required for its validity, 457 §1, 522, 523 §1; what absence from it does not affect its validity, 457 §2, 523 §1; not to be prolonged beyond three years in a monastery, 457 §3; comprises a full and continuous year in orders and congregations, 523 §1; if a longer period is required in the statutes, this is not required for the validity of profession, 523 §2; director of novices, 458, 524;

assistants to the director in orders and congregations, 524 §2; formation of novices, 459, 525 §1; a novice cannot validly renounce his or her goods or burden them with obligations, except for the renunciation of goods before perpetual profession on the condition that the profession subsequently take place, 460, 525 §1, 467 §1, 533; cession by a novice of the administration of goods and disposition of their use and usufruct before temporary profession, 525 §2, 465; a novice can freely leave the institute or be dismissed by it, 461 §1, 525 §1; what is to happen at the conclusion of the n., 461 §1, 525 §1; its prorogation, 461 §2, 525 §1; a validly completed n. is required for the validity of profession, 464. 1°, 527. 1°, 532; regarding a member of a monastery who transfers to another monastery *sui iuris*, 488 §§1–2; regarding a member who transfers to another religious institute, 545 §§1–2; a member who has left an institute, if received back into the institute, is to repeat the complete novitiate, 493 §2, 549 §3;

regarding admission into societies of common life according to the manner of religious, 559 §1, 450, 451.

null   sacred ordination never becomes null, 394; regarding acts contrary to perpetual religious profession, 466, 533;

regarding nullifying laws, 1495, 1496, 1497 §1; *see* invalidity.

nullity   acts determined by an invalidating law, 1495;

acts of the eparchial administrator, if conditions are neglected for the validity of the election or appointment of the administrator, 227 §2; acts placed by a protosyncellus or syncellus without a special mandate, if such a mandate is required by law for these acts, 248 §1; of a renunciation of goods by a candidate for perpetual profession made before the prescribed time, 467 §1, 533; of a vow on account of fear or fraud, 889 §3; regarding the canonical effect of taking an oath outside of cases established by law, 895; juridic acts placed out of force, 932 §1; juridic acts placed out of ignorance or error, 933; of the provision of an office that by law is not vacant, 943 §1; of canonical effects regarding the promise of an office, 943 §3; of the provision of an office out of fear, fraud, error or simony, 946; of an election on account of the neglect of electors, 948 §3; of an election on account of the admission to vote of someone who does not belong to the group, 951; of an election on account of freedom impeded in any way, 952; of a vote, if it is not free, secret, certain, absolute, determinate, or on account of fear or fraud, 954 §1; of acts placed by one elected before

receiving confirmation of the election, 959 §2; of postulation not sent within the prescribed time to the competent authority, 963 §2; of resignation on account of fear, fraud, error or simony, 968; of a decree, declared by the authority which deals with recourse against that decree, 1004, 1005; of the remission of a penalty extorted by force, fear or fraud, 1421; of acts of governance on account of major excommunication, 1434 §1; of an administrative act with regard to execution, 1522 §1; of the execution of an administrative act on account of the neglect of the norms of the executory mandate, 1523; of prescription which is not based on good faith, 1541;

of marriage, 801 §2, 823, 842, 1096, 1357–1377; *see* case, marriage;

of sacred ordination, 1096, 1385–1387;

in procedural matters: of acts on account of the absence of the promotor of justice or the defender of the bond because they were not cited, 1097; of acts which are not signed by a notary, 1101 §1; of an agreement concerning litigation, 1146 §1; of acts on account of the citation not having been intimated, 1193; of an attempt while litigation is pending, 1279; regarding inspection of the acts by the parties and advocates, 1281 §1; how the n. established by law of judicial acts is sanated by a sentence, 1302; of judicial acts on account of the use of the summary contentious trial in cases excluded by law, 1343 §2;

of a sentence: see complaint of nullity; defects that can render a sentence null can be introduced as exceptions in any stage and grade of judgement, 1118 §1; of arbitration, 1180 §1, 1181 §§1 and 3, 1183; irremediable, 1303 §1; remediable, 1304 §1; regarding appeal, 1310. 2°; if the n. is known by the executor, he or she is to abstain from the execution and remit the matter to the tribunal by which the sentence was issued, 1341 §2; on account of the illegitimate use of the summary contentious trial, 1355;

see invalidity.

O

oath   what it is and when it can be taken with a juridic effect, 895;

in a trial: to keep secrecy, 1113 §3; of an interpreter, 1130; of the parties, 1213; of witnesses, 1243 §3; cannot be administered to the accused, 1471 §2; notation of an o., 1249;

regarding the affirmations of the spouses in danger of death, 785 §2; regardign delicts, 1444.

obedience   the Christian faithful are bound by Christian o. to accept what the pastors of the Church, as teachers of the faith, declare, or what they determine as leaders of the Church, 15 §1; owed to the patriarch by the bishops of the patriarchal Church, 88 §1, 187 §2; of the patriarch to the Roman Pontiff, 92 §1; promise of o. to the Roman Pontiff before any episcopal ordination, 187 §2; regarding the promise of o. to the patriarch of candidates for episcopal ordination in patriarchal Churches, 187 §2; special obligation of clerics to show o. to the Roman Pontiff, the patriarch and the eparchial bishop, 370; seminary students to be educated in the virtue of o., 346 §2. 7°; vow of o. of religious, 410, 462 §1, 504, 526 §1; members of institutes of consecrated life have an obligation to obey the Roman Pontiff in virtue of the vow of o. or of the sacred bond of o., 412 §1, 555, 564; a religious who becomes patriarch, bishop or exarch remains subject to the Roman Pontiff alone in virtue of the vow of o., 431 §2. 1°; subjection of one who is exclaustrated to the eparchial bishop in virtue of the vow of obedience, 491; of a novice to the novice director and superiors, 524 §4, 545 §1; due to a tribunal, 1129 §2; regarding the delict of schism, 1437; delict of disobedience, 1446; delict of provocation to disobedience, 1447 §1; obligation of o. not subject to prescription, 1542. 7°.

oblation   of the Church in the Divine Liturgy, 698.

obligations   *see* individual words about persons;
rights and obligations: of all the Christian faithful, 10–26; of the Church, 328, 595 §1; of members of the college of bishops to attend an ecumenical council, 52 §1; of the patriarch, 78–113, 148 §1, 486 2; of the major archbishop, 152; of the administrator of the patriarchal Church, 129; of the metropolitan, 133–1339, 157 §2, 159, 175; of the eparchial bishop, 134 §2, 150 §1, 158 §2, 190–211, 415 §2, 486 §2; of the exarch, 313–319; of one who assumes the governance of a vacant or impeded eparchy, 320 §1; of the coadjutor bishop and auxiliary bishop, 213–218; of the apostolic administrator, 234 §2; of the eparchial administrator, 223. 1°, 229; of the protosyncellus regarding one who has interim governance of a vacant or impeded eparchy, 221. 2°, 233 §1; of the protopresbyter, 278; of the pastor, 281 §1, 288–297; of the administrator of a parish, 299; of the parochial vicar, 302–303; of the rector of a church, 306–310; of members of certain institutes of consecrated life who are pastors, 282 §2; regarding parishes entrusted to several presbyters, 287 §2; of moderators, officials and teachers of a seminary, 337 §1;

of clerics, 367–393; regarding a cleric who has lost the clerical state, 395–397, 1387; of lay persons, 400–409; regarding religious institutes in general, 412–432; of the novice director, 458 §2; of one transferring to another religious institute, 488, 545; of parents, 628 §2; of spouses regarding the partnership of the whole of life, 777; essential o. of marriage regarding the incapacity to enter into marriage, 818. 2°; of a juridic person, 920; proper to each office, 936 §2; of a procurator with regard to an appeal, 1144 §2; regarding prescription, 1542. 1° and 3°;

grave: that those legitimately summoned to the synod of bishops of the patriarchal Church attend, 68 §1; to observe secrecy regarding balloting in the synod to elect a patriarch, 71 §2; that those legitimately summoned to the council of hierarchs attend, 165 §1; for the eparchial bishop to provide everything for the Christian faithful of another Church *sui iuris* and entrusted to his own Church retain, cherish and observe their own rite and foster relations with the superior authority of that Church, 193 §1; of catechetical instruction, 617; of priests regarding offerings for the celebration of the Divine Liturgy, 717; of those who have the care of souls regarding the administration of the sacrament of penance, 735 §1; that temporal goods acquired for the Church be registered in the name of the juridic person to which they belong, 1020 §1; of a witness to tell the whole truth and only the truth, 1243 §1;

of the metropolitan of a metropolitan Church *sui iuris* to request the pallium, 156 §1; principal o. of the chancellor, 252 §1; regarding the eparchial finance officer during a vacancy of the eparchial see, 262 §5, 232; of clerics regarding the formation of ordinands, 355; of members of institutes of consecrated life to obey the Roman Pontiff, 412 §1, 555, 564; of the local hierarch regarding abuses in religious houses, 417; of superiors regarding novices, 456 §3; of clerics regarding religious and members of a society of common life according to the manner of religious, 427, 561; of a member in perpetual vows, 466–469, 533; of a member in temporary vows, 528–529, 465; regarding the renunciation of patrimony in congregations, 534. 3°; of a hermit, 484; of a religious pastor, 543; of an exclaustrated member, 491, 548 §2; which o. are dispensed in an indult of departure from a religious institute, 493 §1, 549 §3; which o. cease by dismissal from an institute of consecrated life, 502, 553, 562 §3; of a pastor and rector of a church regarding the homily, 614 §2; regarding the pastor's preaching, 614 §3; of parents, 618, 628 §2,

care of the rector of a seminary for o. of the seminary's statutes and directory, 338 §2; of monastic life required in a director of novices in a monastery, 458 §1; of the religious state required in a novice director in orders and congregations, 524 §1; obligatory o. of statutes for a member in temporary and perpetual vows, 528; of the obligations of profession with respect to a religious who is a pastor, 543; of the constitutes in societies of apostolic life, 572; of the interstices with regard to licit ordination, 758 §1. 6°; of the norms of particular law on premarital preparation, 784; of secrecy, and its cessation, regarding a secret marriage, 840 §2; regarding prescripts concerning feast days and days of penance in families in which the spouses are ascribed to different Churches *sui iuris*, 883 §2; regarding certain prescripts about temporal goods, 1020 §4; security for the o. of an ecclesiastical sentence, 1116; regarding procedural norms in the summary contentious trial, 1356; regarding the non-observance of civil law from which the Church may suffer damage, 1028 §2. 2°.

observations in a trial to be presented after the conclusion of the case, 1284; to be given in writing, unless an oral discussion is determined, 1285 §1; to be communicated to each other and the right of the parties to respond to them, 1286 §1; of the promotor of justice and defender of the bond before the pronouncement of the sentence, 1289; in a penal trial, 1476.

observers from non-Catholic Churches or ecclesial communities can be invited to the patriarchal assembly and eparchial assembly, 143 §4, 238 §3.

offence against the Creator gives a reason for the application of the pauline privilege, 854 §2, 855 §1. 2°.

offender *regarding:* destruction of the procedural acts for inflicting penalties, 259 §2; penal law to be applied, 1408, 1409 §1, 1412 §§2 and 4; attenuating and aggravating circumstances, 1415, 1416; obligation of a penalty everywhere, 1412 §4; remission of a penalty, 1420 §1. 2°, 1422 §§1 and 3; 1424 §1, 1425; acceptance of certain penalties, 1486 §2, 1426 §2; public rebuke, 1427 §2; submission to supervision, 1428; the penalty of suspension, 1432 §3; suspension of a prohibition to receive the sacraments or sacramentals in danger of death, 1435 §1; delict of injury, 1445 §1; appeal, 1481 §1; *see* accused, offence.

offerings made for a specific purpose cannot be applied except for that same purpose, 1016 §1; made to moderators or administrators of a juridic person are presumed to be given to that juridic person, 1016 §2; regarding their repudiation or acceptance, 1016 §3;

competent authority to determine o. regarding the Divine Liturgy, sacraments, sacramentals and any liturgical celebration, 1013 §1; patriarchs and eparchial bishops are to take care that o. are the same in the same territory, 1013 §2; received on the occasion of the performance of a function by a pastor or other clerics assigned to a parish, to be put into the parish fund, 291; to provide for the expenses of a seminary, 341 §1, 1012, 1014; the eparchial bishop can order that o. be collected for determined initiatives of the Church in churches which are habitually open to the Christian faithful, 1014; to be collected in each eparchy for the institute for the support of clerics, 1021 §1;

on the occasion of the celebration of the Divine Liturgy: priests may receive those o. which the Christian faithful offer for the celebration of the Divine Liturgy for their intentions, 715 §1; must not be placed in the parish fund; it is for the eparchial bishop to determine them, 1013 §1; it is commended that bishops introduce the practice of receiving only those o. which the Christian faithful make voluntarily, 716; priests are readily to celebrate the Divine Liturgy for the intention of the Christian faithful without any offering, 716; it is a grave obligation for priests to observe the norms of that Church *sui iuris* to which the Christian faithful from whom he has received o. are ascribed regarding o. for the celebration of the Divine Liturgy, 717; on these o. no tax may be imposed, 1012 §1; regarding reduction of the number of celebrations to the level of o. in force in the eparchy, 1052 §3;

when it is permitted to receive o. for the Liturgy of the Presanctified and for commemorations in the Divine Liturgy, 715 §2;

regarding ecclesiastical funerals it is commended that bishop introduce the practice of receiving only those o. which the Christian faithful make voluntarily, 878 §2;

the will of the donors it to be observed, 926 §1, 929, 930.

office notion, 936 §1; rights and obligations proper to individual offices, 936 §2; competent authority regarding its change, suppression and canonical provision, 936 §3; care for the means required for its fulfillment and the just remuneration for those who carry it out, 937;

provision for offices, 938–964; *see* canonical possession, conferral, election, postulation, provision;

if exercise of a sacred order is required, its provision is not subject to prescription, 1542. 6°;

loss of offices, 965–978; *see* loss, privation, removal, resignation, transfer;

ordinary power is attached to it by the law itself, 981 §1; regarding delegated power, 981 §1; when it is lost, the ordinary power attached to it is lost, 991 §1; regarding the suspension of ordinary power, 991 §2; removal from o. as an administrative remedy, 1154. 2°; cessation from o. regarding the suspension of an instance of litigation, 1199; regarding the penalty of privation of office, 1084 §1. 3°, 1402 §2, 1430 §1; penal transfer to another o., 1430 §1; regarding the penalty of suspension, 1432 §§1 and 3; a cleric deposed from the clerical state is deprived of all offices, 1433 §2; regarding the penalty of major excommunication, 1434 §§1 and 3; regarding individual delicts, 1460, 1462–1465; prohibition against the exercise of an o. on the part of an accused in a penal trial, 1473;

of the Roman Pontiff (munus): is the same as that given by the Lord uniquely to Peter, the first of the apostles, 43; what power the Roman Pontiff enjoys by virtue of his o., 43, 44 §1; in fulfilling his o., the Roman Pontiff is united to the other bishops and the whole Church, 45 §2; who may assist the Roman Pontiff in exercising his o. and fulfill the function entrusted to them in his name, 46 §1; regarding resignation, 44 §2; infallibility of the magisterium in virtue of it, 597 §1;

of persons: see individual entries;

regarding: the patriarch, 62, 76 §1, 77 §1; the major archbishop, 153 §3; bishops, 104 §1, 116 §3, 165 §1; the eparchial bishop, 189 §3, 210 §§1–2, 211 §1, 223. 3°; the coadjutor bishop and auxiliary bishop, 214 §1, 215 §4, 218, 222; bishops of the patriarchal curia, 87; bishops outside of the territorial boundaries of the patriarchal Church, 102 §2, 110 §3, 149; the local hierarch, 829 §1, 830 §1; the personal hierarch, 829 §2; the exarch, 314 §2; the eparchial administrator, 220. 4°, 224. 3°, 226, 227 §2, 231 §4; the protosyncellus and syncelli, 130 §2, 224 §§1–2, 247 §3, 248 §1, 251; the chancellor and notaries, 255; the eparchial finance officer, 232 §§1 and 4; those who govern an impeded eparchial see, 233 §§1 and 3; persons of the eparchial curia, 244; the protopresbyter, 277 §§1 and 3; the pastor, 277 §1, 284 §3, 297, 336 §2, 543, 829 §§1–2, 830 §1; the removed pastor, 1395, 1396 §1; transfer of a pastor to another o., 1397; the parochial vicar, 302 §§1–2; officials and teachers of a seminary, 337 §1; clerics, 371 §§1–2, 379, 383. 1° and 3°; 385 §1, 386 §1, 390 §1, 395; superiors in religious institutes, 418 §1, 422 §1, 430, 442, 444 §§1 and 3, 445, 513 §1, 514 §2; fi-

nance officers of religious, 447 §§1–2, 516 §§1–2; religious, 430, 431 §1, 469, 529 §6, 543; teachers in an ecclesiastical university, 650; censors of books, 664 §2; an administrator of temporal goods, 1025, 1027, 1028 §1, 1033; judges and other officials of tribunals and assistants, 1063 §2, 1088 §2, 1093, 1097, 1100 §1, 1106 §2, 1115; advocates, 1146 §1; the executor of an administrative act, 1525;

offices of either curia of the patriarch are not to be accumulated in the same persons, 114 §3; power of the metropolitan regarding one who has been proposed or elected to an o., in case of the neglect of the eparchial bishop, 133 §1. 6°, 138, 139, 159. 7°, 175; of those who are assigned to a place or juridic person exempt from the power of the eparchial bishop and subject immediately to the patriarch, or to a stauropegial monastery, 90, 486 §2; it is not permitted to confer on religious merely honorific titles of offices, with certain exceptions, 430;

ex officio: the chancellor and vice chancellor are notaries, 123 §2; when a bishop coadjutor can be appointed, 212 §2; entrusted care of the Christian faithful regarding the administration of the anointing of the sick, 739 §2; a legal representative is to be appointed in certain recourses against administrative decrees, 1003; when a judge may and must proceed in a matter that concerns private persons only, 1110 §1; a judge can impose security for the observance of an ecclesiastical sentence on the petitioner, 1116; a judge can declare defects that can render a sentence null, 1118 §1; when a judge is to appoint an advocate, 1139 §3, 1474; a procurator and advocate can be removed by a decree of the judge for a grave cause, 1145; abatement of an instance of litigation must be declared, 1202; questions added are to be recorded by the notary, 1249; witnesses can be heard again before the testimonies are published, 1251; matters done, regarding a qualified witness, 1254; when a decree or sentence of a judge may be reformed, 1271, 1299 §1; a judge can retract or emend a null sentence which that judge has rendered, observing certain conditions, 1307 §2; the judge can declare an exception of *res iudicata,* 1323 §2; provisional execution of a sentence can be ordered, 1337 §2; the authority to which an appeal tribunal is subject may carry out the execution of the sentence in certain cases, 1340 §2; the formulation of the doubt or doubts is defined in cases to declare the nullity of marriage, 1363 §2; the sentence which has declared the nullity of marriage is to be sent to the appeal tribunal, 1368 §1;

by reason of office: if frequent dealings are had

with the Christian faithful of another Church *sui iuris,* instruction in the rite of that Church is required, 41; some priests must be *ex officio* members of the presbyteral council, 266. 2°; the parochial vicar must assist the pastor in the entire parish ministry and, if the need arises, take his place, 302 §1;

in virtue of office: all to whom the care of souls has been committed have the faculty to preach, 611; who have the faculty to administer the sacrament of penance, 722 §4, 723, 726 §3; whose marriages the personal hierarch and pastor can bless, 829 §2;

clerics and public civil offices, 383. 1° and 3°; students in Catholic universities are to be formed to be ready to fill the more responsible offices in society, 641; whoever holds an o. forbidden to clerics is impeded from receiving sacred orders until he becomes free by relinquishing it, 762 §1. 7°.

officials *of a tribunal:* appointment, 1063 §2, 1070; what is to be done if they are lacking in an eparchy, 1068 §2; can be taken from other eparchies or Churches *sui iuris,* 1102 §1; of a delegated judge, 1102 §2; objection against, 1107 §3; oath to fulfill office faithfully, 1112; penalties if they fail in their office, 1115 §2;

in a seminary, 337 §1, 338 §1;

regarding an attempted marriage before civil o., 810 §1. 3°, 1372 §2.

oil regarding chrismation with holy myron, 693; used in the sacrament of the anointing of the sick, 741.

opinion from whom it is not permitted to request an opinion in evaluating persons in a seminary, 339 §3; of a religious superior and council concerning a indult of departure from a religious institute, 492 §1, 549 §1; of experts in a case, 1255; of a tribunal and of the eparchial bishop to obtain the dissolution of a sacramental non-consummated marriage, 1367;

certain persons can be invited to the synod of bishops of the patriarchal Church to give their o., 102 §3; questions open to o. are not to be proposed as the doctrine of the Church, 402; of censors of books is to be given in writing, 664 §3; of the nullity of a marriage does not necessarily exclude consent, 823; renewal of consent in a marriage which a party believes to have been invalid from the beginning, 844; given in the meeting of the judges before the sentence must always be kept secret and from everyone, 1113 §2; of a witness to be evaluated in testimonies, 1253. 2°; differences of o. in the report of experts, signed by

the experts individually, are to be noted carefully, 1259 §1;

as an expression of the intellect: one position of the college of bishops is to be held definitively regarding doctrine of faith or morals, 597 §2; the right of the Christian faithful to manifest their views to the pastors of the Church, 15 §3; about the qualities of persons, 168; one's own judgement is not to be proposed as the doctrine of the Church in matters which are open to various opinions, 402; those whose consent or counsel is required for juridic acts are obliged to offer their o. sincerely, 934 §4; regarding reprobation, 605.

as consent to place a juridic act, 934 §2. 1°.

opposition (of a third party) who and when it may be proposed, 1330, 1332; how it may occur, 1331 §1; how it is to be handled, 1331 §1; effect, if the opponent proves it, 1333; *res iudicata* can be challenged by it, 1323 §1; decision of a judge about his own competence can be challenged by it, 1119 §2.

order as an institute of consecrated life: *see* religious order;

travellers are bound by laws which provide for public o., 1491 §3. 2°;

as norms to be observed: in an ecumenical council, 51 §2; in the synod of bishops of the patriarchal Church, 108 §2, 113; in the council of hierarchs, 171; with judges in the meeting before a sentence, 1292 §3; in expressing certain things in a sentence, 1295 §1;

of precedence among the ancient patriarchal sees, 59 §2; of the erection of the major archiepiscopal Church with regard to the precedence of honor of a major archbishop, 154;

in a group of persons: in the permanent synod, regarding substitution of members, 115 §3; regarding judges, 1063 §§3–4, 1090 §1;

right of the Church to announce moral principles regarding the social o., 595 §2; of a seminary, 337 §2; or hierarchy of truths of the Catholic faith regarding formation in seminaries, 348 §2; of anointing in the anointing of the sick, 742; of presenting icons or sacred images for the veneration of the Christian faithful, 886; of adjudication, 1117; regarding instruction of a higher o. in Catholic universities, 640 §1;

see sacred order.

ordering of temporal things according to God with regard to the proper vocation of lay persons, 401; of earthly things and human institutions toward the salvation of people according to the counsel of God the Creator, 616 §1; of the whole of human culture to the message of salvation regarding instruction in Catholic schools, 634 §1; of the truths of divine revelation in an ecclesiastical university, 647. 1°; of marriage to the good of the spouses and the procreation and education of children, 776 §1, 819;

integral reordering of the matter of a law regarding the abrogation of that law, 6. 1°, 1502 §1.

ordinary (CIC) *see* hierarch.

ordinary contentious trial *see* trial (ordinary contentious)

ordination *see* sacred ordination.

orientation catechesis should be ecumenical in o., 625.

original a notary declares conformity of acts and documents with the o., 254. 3°; permission to publish some work or the approval, praise or blessing of some work is valid for the o. text, 663 §1; force of proof of o. documents, 1225;

regarding the o. language in a tribunal, 1130.

organization regarding the Church in this world, 7 §2; regarding the understanding of the doctrine of Christ through catechetical formation, 617;

what authority is competent for the o. of divine public worship, 668 §2, 657, 199 §1; of courses and examinations in the program for clerical formation, 330 §3; of the catechumenate through the norms of particular law, 587 §3; regarding insurance, social security and health benefits for clerics, 1021 §2; of the administration of temporal goods regarding the instructions of the hierarch, 1022 §2; regarding books of income and expenses and documents regarding temporal goods, 1028 §1. 6° and 8°; of provisions for necessary support in the execution of a sentence, 1337 §2.

ownership to whom the o. of goods belongs, 1008 §2; of private persons over sacred things, 1018; of private persons regarding the return of documents after a trial is completed, 1133 §1; of the goods of religious who become patriarch, bishop or exarch, 431 §3. 1°–2°; of the goods of religious in temporary profession, 529 §2; *see* possession, property.

P

pallium when the metropolitan of a metropolitan Church *sui iuris* is to request it and what it signifies, 156 §1; what the metropolitan cannot do before its imposition, 156 §2.

parents their primary right and obligations to care

for the physical, religious, moral, social and cultural education of their children, 783 §1. 1°, 627 §1, 628; the Church is to care for the Catholic education of children together with p., 628 §1; all to whom the care of souls is entrusted must assist p. to educate their children, 628 §2; their care to foster vocations through the spirit of the gospel in their families, 329 §1. 1°; have the obligation to form their children in the faith and practice of the Christian life, 618; their obligation to educate their children in the context of the Christian family illumined by faith and animated by mutual love, especially in piety toward God and love of neighbor, 627 §1; their freedom to choose instruments of education, 627 §3; are to be concerned about Catholic schools, 631 §1; are to take care that their children are sent to Catholic schools, all other things being equal, 633 §2; teachers are to collaborate with them, 639;

regarding: ascription of children to a Church *sui iuris*, 29 §1 and §2. 2°–3°, 34; consent for the baptism of children, 681 §1. 2° and §5; designation of sponsors, 685 §1. 4°; their obligation that an infant be baptized as soon as possible, 686 §1; the care of the pastor for their preparation for the baptism of their children, 686 §2; their names to be recorded in the baptismal register, 689; marriage of a minor child while the p. are unwilling or unaware, 789. 4°; the impediment of spiritual relationship, 811 §1; ecclesiastical funerals for children, 876 §2; prohibition to receive a baptized non-Catholic who has not yet completed his or her fourteenth year into the Catholic Church while the p. are opposed, 900 §1; those things in which minors are exempt from the power of p. by divine or canon law, 910 §2; right to stand trial in the name of minor children, 1136 §§1–3;

who may not licitly be admitted to a religious institute, 452 §2, 517 §1;

penalties for those p. who hand over their children to be baptized or educated in a non-Catholic religion, 1439;

regarding those who take the place of p., 29 §2. 2°, 618, 627 §1, 681 §1. 2° and §5, 1136 §§1–3, 1439;

see father, mother.

parish notion, 279; its erection, modification, suppression, 148 §3, 280 §2; regarding its erection in a church of a religious institute or society of common life according to the manner of religious, 282; not to be erected in the church of a monastery, 480; is a juridic person by the law itself, 280 §3; is represented by the pastor, 290 §1; is territorial or personal, 280 §1; are joined together into a district, 276 §1, 277 §1; function of the protopresbyter regarding them, 278 §1. 3° and §4;

is entrusted to a pastor, 281 §1, 284–294, *see* pastor; what things should not be removed from the power of the pastor, 283; regarding parochial vicars, 301–303; regarding presbyters and deacons assigned to a p., 624 §2; regarding the removal or transfer of pastors, 1389–1400; when it is vacant or the pastor is impeded, 298, 300; rights and obligations of its administrator, 299; appropriate councils are to be held in it according to the norm of particular law, 295, 408 §1;

its church: is to be dedicated by consecration, 871 §1; names of candidates for sacred orders are to be made known publicly in it, 771 §1; baptism is to be celebrated in it, 687 §1; marriage is to be celebrated in it, 838 §1;

its registers, files, archives, seal, 37, 261, 278 §1. 3°, 296, 841, 842, 879, 1051 §2;

the divine praises are to be celebrated in it, 199 §2; its functions with respect to rectors of churches, 306, 307; should ensure the catechetical instruction of its members and their integration into the same community, 619;

which offerings are to be put in its account, 291;

a seminary is exempt from its governance, 336 §2; seminary students are to be instructed in p. administration, 352 §2;

regarding the acquisition of domicile and quasi-domicile, 912.

part, portion *of votes required:* two thirds majority, 72 §1, 322 §2, 962; absolute majority, 72 §1, 166 §2, 186 §3, 221. 3°, 924. 1°, 956 §1; relative majority on the third ballot, 183 §3, 956 §1;

of members present required in meetings: two thirds, 69, 183 §1; majority, 107 §1, 166 §1, 924. 1°, 956 §1;

regarding more than a third p. of electors who have been overlooked in elections, 948 §3;

regarding the required consent of persons: at least a third, 108 §3; majority, 164 §1; absolute majority, 934 §1;

in an ecumenical council of those who are not bishops is to be determined by the supreme authority of the Church, 52 §2; in the patriarchal assembly of persons of another Church sui iuris according to the norm of the statutes, 143 §3; sizeable p. of the people on feasts and solemnities, 199 §3; of lay persons in the eparchial assembly is not to exceed one third, 238 §1. 10°; regarding the notion of clerics, who have a p. in the mission and power of Christ the Pastor, 323 §1; proper p.

of lay persons in the mission of the Church is to be recognized by clerics, 381 §3; active p. in political parties or in the direction of labor unions to be avoided by clerics, religious and members of societies of common life according to the manner of religious, 384 §2, 427, 561; all the Christian faithful for their p. are to collaborate in the apostolate of social communications, 651 §2; *see* participation;

of the divine praises are to be celebrated in the cathedral church, 199 §2; of the eparchy with regard to canonical visitation, 205 §1; no p. of power can be retained in the constitution of an eparchial administrator, 226; entrusted to a syncellus of an eparchy, 246; appropriate p. of the members of the presbyteral council are to be elected, 266. 1°; some p. of the presbyteral council is to be renewed within a five year period, 270 §1; regarding the withdrawal of certain things from the care of a pastor, 283; of a parish with regard to the constitution of a parochial vicar, 301 §2; determined by particular law for which clerics are to contribute to the common eparchial fund, 390 §2, 1021 §2; of a cloister, 477 §2; of a monastery with regard to the place set aside for a hermit, 483; of an order or congregation regarding the notion of a province, 508 §1; change of a significant p. of goods is not to be made in favor of an order or congregation in the cession of goods by a member in temporary vows, 529 §4; homily s p. of the liturgy, 614 §1; regarding a Catholic school which is attended by a majority of non-Catholic students, 634 §2; of liturgical books regarding new editions, 657 §3; of the divided territory of a juridic person, 929; of a document, which can be exhibited in a trial, 1227 §2; who can be excluded in p. by the law from giving testimony, 1230; regarding a controversy which has not been settled even in p. by a sentence, 1303 §1. 8°; regarding those who can pay only p. of the court costs, 1334;

dispositive part of a sentence: 1292 §3, 1294. 3°, 1295 §3, 1297, 1299 §1, 1326 §2. 1°, 1354 §1, 1480

on the p. of someone, 221. 5°, 552 §2. 1°, 717, 1486 §2.

participation of the Church in the bloody sacrifice of the Cross through the Divine Liturgy, 698;

of the Christian faithful in: the functions of Christ, 7 §1; the mission of the Church, 19; the Divine Eucharist and the apostolate to be fostered by the eparchial bishop, 197, 203 §2;the divine praises to be fostered by the pastor, 289 §2; the ministry of the word of God, 608; the celebration of the sacraments, 673; the sacrifice of Christ

by the Roman Pontiff or by the synod of bishops of the patriarchal Church, 78 §2, 110 §1, 182 §3;

determines: requirements for the patriarchal dignity, 64; times for the pastoral visitation of eparchies by the patriarch, 83 §1; feast days, in which the Divine Liturgy is to be celebrated for the people by the patriarch, 94; invitation of those who are not bishops to the synod of bishops of the patriarchal Church, 102 §3; a special group of bishops to consider recourses against administrative decrees of the patriarch, 1006;

to be observed regarding: time for the convocation of the synod of bishops of the patriarchal Church, 65 §2; presidency of the synod of bishops of the patriarchal Church, 70; ordination of bishops by the patriarch, 86 §1. 2°; consent of the eparchial bishop or major superior in entrusting to a cleric the function of conducting affairs that regard the entire patriarchal Church, 89 §2; times of the synod of bishops of the patriarchal Church, 106 §2; presence of members in the synod of bishops of the patriarchal Church, 107 §1; term of office for the patriarchal finance officer, 122 §2; administrator of the patriarchal Church, 127, 128. 2°, 220. 2°; information and documents concerning the suitability of candidates for the episcopate, 182 §1; designation of tellers in case of an election of bishops by mail, 186 §1; powers of an auxiliary bishop during a vacancy of the eparchial see, 224 §3; ascription of clerics to the patriarchal Church, 357 §2; reservation of the indult of departure from a monastery to the patriarch, 496 §2; confirmation of the dismissal of a member from a monastery by the patriarch, 499; reservation of the faculty to confect holy myron to the patriarch, 693; the faculty of the patriarch to celebrate sacred ordinations in another's eparchy, 749; right to receive non-Catholics into the Catholic Church, 898 §2; certain alienations of the temporal goods of an eparchy, 1036 §2. 1°;

may determine: presbyters and deacons to act as tellers or actuary in the synod for the election of a patriarch, 72 §1; restriction of the deliberative vote of titular bishops in the synod of bishops of the patriarchal Church, 102 §2; power of the patriarch regarding vacant eparchial sees, 220. 2°; the necessity of the judgement of the patriarch concerning clerics having an active role in political parties or labor unions, 384 §2; cases reserved to the ordinary tribunal of the patriarchal Church, 1063 §4. 5°;

determined by the Roman Pontiff regarding: extension of the power of the patriarch beyond the territorial boundaries of the patriarchal Church, 78

§2; choice of candidates for the episcopacy, 182 §3;

see particular law, particular law of a Church *sui iuris.*

particular law of "other" Churches *sui iuris* determined by the Roman Pontiff or by the hierarch who presides over the Church with the consent of the Apostolic See, 174, 176; *see* particular law, particular law of a Church *sui iuris.*

partnership the doctrine of the Church regarding civil and social p. to be preached, 616 §2;

of conjugal life: of the whole of life is constituted by a man and woman through an irrevocable consent in marriage, 776 §1; equal rights and obligations of spouses in marital p., 777; couple, to have matrimonial consent, must at least not be ignorant of the fact that marriage is a permanent p., 819; deception regarding a quality of a person which can disturb the matrimonial p., with respect to the validity of marriage, 821; will to persevere in the p. of married life, with respect to radical sanation of marriage, 849 §2; regarding the separation of spouses on account of adultery, 863, 864 §3, 866, 1362, 1381; the local hierarch and other pastors of souls are to assist spouses to foster the unity of p. in their conjugal and family life, 816; *see* marriage.

party, parties in a trial: *passim* in procedural law;

see petitioner, respondent;

in marriage: *passim* in marriage law; *see* husband, spouse, wife;

to an agreement: regarding a common seminary, 334 §2; regarding the movement of a cleric, 360 §1;

injured, 932 §2, 1327 §3, 1483 §§1–2, 1485.

paschal the eparchial bishop is to strive that the Christian faithful know the p. mystery in depth and live it, 197.

pastor care of a parish is committed to him as to its own shepherd, 279, 281 §1, 287 §1; how each person acquires a p., 916 §§1–4; represents the parish, 290 §1; what should not be withdrawn from his care, 283; generally is to have the care of only one parish, 287 §1; constituted for the care of the Christian faithful of another Church *sui iuris,* 193 §§2–3; in the same parish there is to be only one p., 287 §2; regarding particular law by which a parish is entrusted to several presbyters at the same time, 287 §2; cannot validly be a juridic person, 281 §2; the rector in a seminary holds the office of p., 336 §2; qualifications, 285; may not be a monk, 480; appointment, 284 §§1–2, 286;

canonical provision and taking possession of office, 288; stability in office, 284 §3; regarding his absence, 292 §§2–3; who governs a parish if there is a vacancy or the p. is impeded, 298–300; cessation from office, 297, 1389–1400; regarding resignation from office, 297 §§1–2;

parochial vicars as cooperators with the p., 301–303; is to be heard in the appointment of a protopresbyter, 277 §1; care of the protopresbyter for pastors who are ill, 278 §3; their presence in the patriarchal or eparchial assembly, 143 §. 6°, 238 §1; declaration in his presence of transfer to another Church *sui iuris*, 36; impediments to sacred orders are to be revealed to him, 771 §2; is charged with inquiring about the life and conduct of candidates for sacred orders, 771 §3; impediments to marriage are to be revealed to him, 786; regarding assistance to be furnished to him by religious, 542; to whom the government of a vacant or impeded exarchy is to pass, 320 §1;

rights: if he is a religious or a member of a society of common life according to the manner of religious, 282 §2, 543; regarding parochial functions, 290 §2, 306 §1; to vacations, 292 §2; to a just remuneration, 291, 390; regarding the administration of baptism, 677 §1; regarding the administration of the anointing of the sick, 739 §2; regarding the celebration of marriage, if he is the p. of the groom, 831 §2;

powers and faculties: to preach, 611; to administer the sacrament of penance, 723 §1; to bless marriages, 828, 829 §§1–2, 830 §1, 831 §1; regarding the form for the celebration of marriage and impediments, 796 §2, 797, 798; regarding permission to celebrate marriage in a sacred place outside of the parish church, 838 §1; to dispense from private vows, 893 §1. 1°–2°; to receive individual lay persons into the Catholic Church, 898 §2;

obligations: regarding the Christian faithful of another Church *sui iuris*, 38, 678; to put certain offerings received by him into the parish account, 291; if he is a religious or a member of a society of common life according to the manner of religious, 282 §2, 543; to reside in the parish, 292 §1; to furnish an example of ministry to everyone, 293 §1; regarding those things which should be reported on a baptismal certificate, 296 §2; regarding the teaching, sanctifying and governing functions, 289; to celebrate the Divine Liturgy for the people, 294; to foster vocations, 329 §1. 2°; to preach, 614 §§2–3; regarding catechetical instruction, 624; to prepare parents for the celebration of their infant's baptism, 686 §2; to instruct the Christian faithful about the obligation to receive

the Divine Eucharist, 708; regarding the publication of the names of candidates for sacred orders, 771 §§1 and 3; to prepare the Christian faithful for marriage, 783–785; to inform the p. to whom it belongs to bless a marriage about the prenuptial investigations, 787; to defer doubts concerning impediments to marriage to the hierarch, 788; to preserve secrecy regarding a secret marriage, 840 §1;

must record in the prescribed registers: ascription to a Church *sui iuris* or transfer to another Church *sui iuris*, 37, 296 §2; administration of baptism, 689, 690; administration of chrismation with holy myron, 296 §2, 695 §2; celebration of marriage, 296 §2, 841, 842; adoption, 296 §2; perpetual profession in a religious institute, 296 §2, 470, 532 §2; sacred ordination, 296 §2, 775; ecclesiastical burial, 879; obligations of pious foundations, 1051 §2.

pastoral council notion and functions, 272, 273 §1; in an exarchy, 319 §1; composition, 273; constitution and statutes, 274 §1; convocation and presidency, 275; its delegates are to attend the eparchial assembly, 238 §1. 7°; chooses pay persons to attend the eparchial assembly, 238 §1. 10°; ceases when the eparchial see is vacant, 274 §2;

regarding parishes, 295.

pastors Christ the Pastor, 323 §1, 346 §1;

of the Church: to be obeyed by the Christian faithful as teachers of the faith, 15 §1; right of the Christian faithful to manifest their needs, wishes and opinion to them, 15 §§2–3; right of the Christian faithful to receive from them assistance out of the spiritual goods of the Church, 16; their care for the integrity and unity of the faith, 604; their care for the restoration of Christian unity, 902; the Roman Pontiff is the pastor of the entire Church, 43, 45 §2, 92 §1, 597 §1; the eparchial bishop is the pastor of the eparchy, 177 §1;

the care of souls in a determined parish is entrusted to a pastor as to its own shepherd, 281 §1, 193;

of souls, 655 §2, 738, 783 §§1 and 3, 785 §1, 816.

patriarch notion, 56; dignity, 55, 59 §1; precedence of honor, 58–60, 62, 154; is a hierarch, 984 §1; is local hierarch for the eparchy he governs, 982 §2; has the same rights and obligations as an eparchial bishop in his own eparchy, in stauropegial monasteries, and in places where neither an eparchy nor an exarchy has been erected, 101, 486 §2; election, 63–77, 102 §1, 110 §3; enthronement, 75–77 §1; synodal letter about his election, enthronement, profession of faith and promise to

tion or recusal of a bishop of the tribunal of the synod of bishops of the patriarchal Church, 1062 §2; vacant eparchial sees, 220. 2°–4°, 221. 1° and 5°, 226, 231 §§1–2, 232 §§1–3; impeded eparchial sees, 233 §§1 and 3; reception of a bishop of a non-Catholic Church into the Catholic Church, 898 §1;

rights with respect to: notification of acts of the Roman Pontiff, 81; instructions and encyclical letters to the whole patriarchal Church, 82 §1. 2°–3° and §2; decrees about the methods to be observed in applying law or that urge the observance of laws, 82 §1.1°; vigilance over all clerics, 89 §1; commission of functions which regard the whole patriarchal Church, 89 §2; conferring dignities, 89 §3; his commemoration in the Divine Liturgy and in the divine praises, 91; prayers and pious exercises, 96; agreements with the civil authority, 98; reservation to himself of matters which have to do with several eparchies and affect the civil authorities, 100; selection of persons of the patriarchal curia, 114 §2; appointment or removal of the patriarchal finance officer, 122 §§1–2; appointment or removal of the chancellor of the patriarchal curia, the vice-chancellor, and other notaries, 123 §§1–2; the constitution of commissions prescribed by law, 124; erection of a seminary common to several eparchies, 334 §1; ascription of clerics to an eparchy, 357 §1, 363. 1°; reverence and obedience of clerics due to him, 370; judgement about clerics taking an active part in political parties or labor unions, 384 §2; loss of the clerical state, 394. 3°, 397, 398; erection or approval of universities or faculties, 642 §2, 649; approval of liturgical texts and their translations, 657 §§1–2; consent for the alienation or translation of relics, icons or images, 888 §2; the reception of non-Catholics into the Catholic Church, 898 §§1–2; the suppression of juridic persons, 928. 1°; imposition of penalties by decree, 1402 §1; threat of penalties, 1406 §1; remission of penalties, 1420 §3, 1423 §1;

power concerning sacraments with respect to: confection of holy myron, 693; sacred ordinations, 748 §2, 749; dispensation from the required age to receive sacred ordination, 759 §2; dispensations from impediments to receive or exercise sacred orders, 767 §§1–2; an invalidating clause added to a prohibition of the celebration of marriage, 794 §2; dispensation from marriage impediments, 795 §2, 799; blessing of the marriages of his subjects everywhere, 829 §3; dispensation from the form for the celebration of marriage, 835; granting the radical sanation of a marriage, 852;

obligations with respect to: the commemoration of

the Roman Pontiff in the Divine Liturgy and in the divine praises, 92 §2; election of bishops, 182 §3, 184–186; vacant eparchial sees, 220. 1° and 5°; a bishop illegitimately absent from his eparchy, 204 §4; the function of eparchial bishops regarding faith and morals, 95 §1, 196; the faithful fulfillment of the pastoral function of eparchial bishops, 95 §2; promoting unity of action in the same territory, 84 §1; the reverence and fraternal charity due to bishops, 88 §1; controversies between bishops, 88 §2; vigilance over all clerics, 89 §1; the Divine Liturgy for the people, 94; vigilance over the correct administration of goods, 97; care for personal statutes, 99; the patriarchal curia, 114 §§1 and 3; an exarchy requesting presbyters from him, 315 §1; questions on the meaning of life and answers to life's problems, 601; uniformity of norms for fees and offerings and of penal laws in the same territory, 1013 §2, 1405 §3;

when he requires the consent of the synod of bishops of the patriarchal Church, *see* synod of bishops of the patriarchal Church;

when he requires the consent or counsel of the permanent synod, *see* permanent synod;

with respect to religious institutes: immediately subject to him, 413, 414 §2, 418 §2; stauropegial monasteries, *see* stauropegium; an order or congregation of patriarchal right, 505 §§1–2. 2°, 506 §§2–3, 507; when he may erect orders or congregations, 506 §2; his consent to erect the first house of an institute of patriarchal right in another eparchy, 509 §1; his consent for a confederation of monasteries, 439 §2; his power to suppress institutes or their sole house, 438 §1, 507 §1, 510; when he may suppress a confederation of monasteries and make determinations regarding its goods, 440 §§2–3; is to foster meetings of superiors, 416; letters of religious sent to him or received from him are not subject to inspection, 429; which superiors should send him a quinquennial report, 419 §1; must be consulted by the eparchial bishop to erect a monastery *sui iuris* or a congregation, 435 §1, 506 §1; his consent for a monk to be appointed pastor, 480; his consent for transfer to another institute, 487 §§2–3, 544 §1; when he may grant an indult of exclaustration, 489 §1, 548 §1; grant of an indult of departure from a monastery can be reserved to him by particular law, 496 §2; when he may grant an indult of departure from a congregation, 549 §2. 1°; when the confirmation of a decree of dismissal from an institute is reserved to him, 499, 500 §4, 553; is to deal with recourses against a decree of dismissal from an institute, 501 §3, 553;

with respect to societies of common life according to the manner of religious, 554 §2 [505 §2. 2° and 3, 413, 414 §2, 418 §2, 419 §1], 556 [506, 507 §2, 509 §1, 510], 562 §3 [500 §4];

with respect to secular institutes, 563 §2 [505 §2. 2°], 565, 566 [414, 506, 507 §2, 509, 510];

with respect to new forms of consecrated life, 571;

with respect to associations of the Christian faithful, 575 §1. 2°, 579, 583 §2. 1°;

when patriarchs of other Churches *sui iuris* are to be consulted, 720 §3, 904 §2.

patriarchal assembly notion, 140; when it is to be convoked, 141; the rights of the patriarch, 142 §1, 144; the patriarch is not to omit to hear it in more serious matters, 82 §3; the rights of the synod of bishops of the patriarchal Church, 140, 144 §1, 145; is suspended during a vacancy in the patriarchal see, 142 §2; who must be summoned, 143 §1; the obligation to attend on the part of those who are summoned, 143 §2; who may be invited, 143 §§3–4; its statutes must be approved by the synod of bishops of the patriarchal Church, 145; regarding the qualification of lay persons to be members, 408 §1.

patriarchal Church presided over by a patriarch, 55; its erection, restoration, alteration and suppression is reserved to the supreme authority of the Church, 57 §1; is a juridic person by the law itself, 921 §2; is represented in all its juridic affairs by the patriarch, 79; its title and see, 57 §§2–3, 5 §4, 60; regarding the precedence of honor, 59. 60; its territory, 146; regarding temporal goods, 62, 122 §1, 1036 §3, 1037; its ordinary tribunal, 1063, 1067 §2; *see* metropolitan of the patriarchal Church, particular law, patriarch, patriarchal assembly, synod of bishops of the patriarchal Church, territory.

patrimony *liturgical, theological, spiritual and disciplinary:* regarding the notion of "rite," 28 §1; the rites of the Eastern Churches are to be preserved and fostered as the p. of the whole Church of Christ, 39; how lay persons are to study it zealously, 405; *see* rite;

the perennially valid philosophical p. in the instruction of seminary students, 349 §1;

stable economic patrimony of a juridic person: any change in it is to be noted in both copies of the inventory of ecclesiastical goods, 1026; the administrator of moveable goods belonging to it cannot make donations from them, 1029; what is required for the alienation of goods which constitute it, 1035;

what is to be preserved in any transaction by which the patrimonial condition of a juridic person can be worsened, 1042;

economic p. of a religious with respect to an obligatory renunciation introduced by the statutes, 534. 3°;

regarding patrimonial rights of the author of an intellectual work, 666 §1.

patrology its importance in catechesis, 621 §2.

peace among peoples to be fostered by clerics, 384 §1; on earth to be built up, with regard to the instruction of preachers of the word of God, 616 §2; to be fostered by Catholics together with other Christians, 908;

peaceful cohabitation with regard to the pauline privilege, 854 §2, 855 §1. 2°, 857. 3°; litigation to be avoided among the people of God or settled peacefully as soon as possible, 1103 §1.

penal trial *see* trial (penal).

penalties their purpose, 1401; right of the Christian faithful that they not be punished except according to the norm of law, 24 §3; to be imposed through a penal trial, 1402 §1, 1408; regarding the imposition of p. through an extrajudicial decree, 1153 §2, 1402 §§2–3, 1408, 1486–1487; when one may abstain for imposing p., 1403, 1409 §1. 2°;

ignorance or error concerning p. is not presumed, 1497 §2; laws which establish p. or administrative acts which have to do with warning or imposing p. are subject to strict interpretation, 1500, 1512 §2; penal laws are not subject to dispensation, 1537; the more benign interpretation is to be made regarding p., 1404 §1; if a law is changed, the law more favorable to the accused is to be applied, 1412 §2; if a later law removes a penalty, it ceases, no matter how it was imposed, 1412 §3; cannot be extended from one person to another or one case to another, 1404 §2; their constitution, 1405–1406; regarding the warning, 1406 §2, 1407 §§1 and 3, 1414 §2; their application by a judge, 1409; what must be preserved in the imposition of p. on a cleric, 1410; cannot be imposed after a penal action is extinguished, 1411; who is subject to them, 1412–1413; regarding attenuating or aggravating circumstances, 1415–1416; regarding those who conspire to commit a delict, 1417; regarding an attempted delict, 1418; their remission, 1419–1425; regarding the reservation of their remission, 1423, 1445 §1; regarding their suspension in danger of death, 1435;

right and obligation of the patriarch regarding clerics who seem to merit p., 89 §1; who should not be summoned to the synod of bishops of the patriarchal Church or the council of hierarchs on account of p., 102 §1, 164 §1, 1433, 1434; regarding the destruction of the acts regarding p. in the archives of the curia, 259 §2; regarding those who cannot be admitted to the novitiate, 450. 2°–3°, 1426 §1, 517 §1; which p. exclude one from the function of sponsor, 685 §1. 6°; which p. exclude one from the function of arbiter, 1172. 26,36 ; whoever places an act of orders while prohibited from the exercise of that order by some canonical penalty is impeded from receiving or exercising sacred orders, 762 §1. 6°, 763. 2°; the imposition of p. for delicts as the object of a trial, 1055 §1. 2°; regarding an action to execute p., 1153; regarding judges and other officials of a tribunal, assistant at a trial, procurators and advocates, 1115, 1129 §2, 1146, 1147; regarding the submission of a matter to supervision in addition to the imposition of p., 1428;

specific penalties: works of religion or piety or charity, 1426, 450. 2°, 517; public rebuke, 1427; prohibition or command to reside in a certain place or territory, 1429; privation of power, office, ministry, function, right, privilege, or faculty, 1430 §1, 1464 §1; privation of title, 1430 §1, 1402 §2, 1409 §2; privation of insignia, 1430 §1, 1402 §2, 1409 §2; privation of office, 1430 §1, 978, 1084 §1. 36,36 , 1115, 1402 §2, 1409 §2; privation of the right to function as sponsor, 685 §1. 66,36 ; minor excommunication, 1431, 685 §1. 6°, 1172. 2°, 1452, 1456 §2; suspension, 1432, 685 §1. 6°, 1129 §2, 1146, 1147, 1172. 2°, 1402 §2, 1409 §2, 1441, 1452, 1453 §1, 1456 §2; reduction of a cleric to a lower grade, 1433 §1, 102 §1, 164 §1, 1084 §1. 3°, 1402 §2, 1409 §2; deposition from the clerical state, 1433 §2, 102 §1, 164 §1, 394. 2°, 685 §1. 6°, 1084 §1. 3°, 1172. 2°, 1402 §2, 1409 §2, 1436 §1, 1442, 1445 §1, 1453 §§1–2, 1458, 1460; major excommunication, 1434, 102 §1, 164 §1, 1084 §1. 3°, 1172. 2°, 1402 §2, 1409 §2, 1436 §1, 1437, 1438, 1442, 1443, 1445 §1, 1450, 1451, 1454, 1456 §1, 1459 §1, 1460–1462; fines, 1146 §1, 1147; suspension or removal of an advocate, 1146 §1; appropriate penalty, 1115, 1129 §2, 1147, 1418 §2, 1436 §2, 1438–1440, 1443–1449, 1451, 1453 §3, 1454, 1455, 1456 §1, 1458–1466; other indeterminate p., 1436 §1, 1442, 1450, 1453 §1; heavier penalty can be imposed on one who violates obligations imposed by a penalty, 1467;

when a judge, under penalty of nullity, must permit the parties and their advocates to inspect acts not yet known to them, 1281 §1.

penance (as a remedy) regarding salutary p., 552 §2. 2°; when, if a p. has been in vain, there is cause for dismissal from a religious institute, 552 §2. 2°,

499; works of p. imposed by a confessor, 732 §1; regarding a member who returns after having departed a religious institute illegitimately, 495.

penance (as a sacrament) notion, 718; is administered only by a priest, 722 §1; priest is a minister of divine justice and mercy in it, 732 §2; its seal is inviolable, 733 §1; the confessor's obligation of observing secrecy, 728 §1. 1°, 733 §1, 734 §§1–2, 1231 §2. 2°, 1456 §1; obligation to observe secrecy on the part of an interpreter or others, 733 §2, 1456 §2; prohibited use of knowledge acquired from confession, 734 §§1–2; the moderator of an educational institute is not to administer it to students, 734 §3; things heard by anyone or in any way on the occasion of a confession cannot be received as an indication of truth in trials, 1231 §2. 2°;

when it is to be preceded by the celebration of the Divine Liturgy or the reception of the Divine Eucharist, 711;

faculty to administer: of bishops by the law itself and everywhere, 722 §2; of presbyters, to act validly and licitly, 722 §§3–4; those who have this faculty in virtue of office, 723; who can grant this faculty, 724; not required in danger of death, 735 §2; its limitation through the reservation of absolution, 727–729, 1450 §2, 1456 §1, 1457; its cessation by the revocation or loss of office, 726; faculty supplied, 995;

right to receive it by any priest who has the faculty, 474 §2, 538 §3;

requirements to receive it, 671 §§2–3, 721;

when it can be received by non-Catholics, 671 §§3–5;

obligation to provide it for the Christian faithful belongs to: those who have the cure of souls, 197, 289 §2, 735 §1; to priests in urgent necessity and in danger of death, 735 §2; religious superiors, 475 §1, 538 §3;

when it is to be received: as soon as possible in cases of grave sin, 719; *frequently:* by the Christian faithful, 289 §2, 719; by seminary students, 346 §2. 4°; by clerics, 369 §1; by religious, 472 §2. 2°, 474 §1, 538 §§2–3;

its celebration: individual confession is the one ordinary means, 720 §1; regarding absolution of several penitents at the same time, 720 §§2–3, 721; proper place, 736; its simulation constitutes a delict, 1443;

regarding celebration of the Divine Liturgy, if the celebrant is conscious of a grave sin and cannot confess, 711;

see absolution, confession (sacramental), confessor.

right of visitation or the obligation of obedience, 1542. 7°;

a group of persons regarding the consent or counsel required for a juridic act, 934 §1;

personal favoritism to be avoided, 285 §3, 664 §2, 878 §1; *see* favoritism;

"personal" regarding: the Roman Pontiff's manner of acting, 45 §2; the power of the patriarch, 78 §1; the power of the metropolitan of a metropolitan Church *sui iuris,* 157 §1; the power of the eparchial bishop, 178; the nature of circumstances in the constitution of a coadjutor bishop, 212 §2; parishes, pastor and hierarch, 280 §1, 829 §2; formation in seminaries, 330 §3, 344 §2; needs of religious, 421; matrimonial consent, 776 §1; instruction of spouses, 783 §1. 2°; access to the local hierarch, 796 §3; convocation to an election, 948 §1; actions, 1019; separation of spouses, 1378 §1; laws, 1491 §3. 1°;

circumstances of persons to be taken into consideration, 297 §2, 319 §1, 859 §3, 1240, 1254, 1522 §1;

regarding personal statutes, 99, 1151, 1358; *see* personal statutes;

personal considerations, 248 §2, 320 §2, 982 §2, 988 §2, 1524, 1525; *see* considerations;

regarding those goods which accrue to someone personally, 431 §3. 3°.

personal hierarch   who may bless marriages, 829 §2.

personal statutes   the patriarch is to care for their observance, 99 §1; patriarchs in the same territory are to act after consulting one another regarding them, 99 §2; to be observed in trials, 1151, 1358.

personality   *juridical:* to whom it may be granted, 921 §3; *see* person (juridic);

of an author manifested by his or her intellectual work, 666 §1.

petition, request   for transfer to another Church *sui iuris,* 32 §2; for a report of administration from a finance officer, 122 §§3–4, 262 §4; concerning the modification of the territorial boundaries of a patriarchal Church to the Roman Pontiff, 146 §2; for the pallium, 156 §1; for an auxiliary bishop by the eparchial bishop, 212 §1; for acts or documents from a notary, 254. 3°; for presbyters for an exarchy, 315 §1; for an indult of exclaustration, 489 §1, 548 §2; for imposed exclaustration, 489 §1, 548 §1; for an indult of departure from a religious institute, 492 §1, 496, 546 §2, 549 §1; for permission to cede goods in congregations, 534. 2°; of an unmarried mother regarding the recording of her own name in the baptismal register, 689 §2; for admission to receive sacred orders, 761; for re-

scinding a juridic act, 932 §2; for rescinding an election, 948 §2; for confirmation of an election, 959 §1; for the revocation or emendation of a decree before recourse, 999, 1000 §§1–2, 1001 §2. 1°; regarding recourse to request reparation of damages only, 1000 §3; for a decree by which a recourse is decided, 1002; for consultation, consent or confirmation regarding the alienation of goods, 1038 §2; for the remission of a penalty, 1422 §3, 1425; regarding extrajudicial decrees, 1517 §2, 1518, 1519 §2; for proof of a favor granted orally, 1527 §2; for a favor, 1530 §2;

to obtain a dispensation from impediments to receive or exercise sacred orders, 768 §1; concealment of the truth in a r. regarding the force of a rescript, 1529 §1;

in trials: regarding the action to request the celebration of a marriage arising from a promise to marry, 782 §2; for the ministry of a judge through an introductory *libellus* of litigation or an oral p., 1104, 1185, 1186 §1, 1187. 1°, 1188 §2. 4°, 1303 §1. 4°, 1344 §1. 1° and §2, 1345 §1, 1351, 1372 §1, *see* accusation, challenge; for the restriction or prorogation of time limits, 1124 §§1–2; for rescinding an act placed by a judge after lodging an objection for his recusal, 1109 §2; regarding counterclaims, 1085 §1. 1°, 1156 §2; to obtain provision for a person's support, 1163; regarding the joinder of issue, 1195 §§1–2; for indemnification against guardians, curators, administrators or procurators, 1202; for the questioning of witnesses, 1233 §2; for the exclusion of a witness, 1236; for an incidental case, 1085 §1. 1°, 1269 §1; for a copy of the acts, 1281 §1; for proofs after the conclusion of a case, 1283 §1; regarding an error in the text of a sentence, 1299 §1; in an indivisible matter regarding an appeal, 1318 §2; regarding the identity of the thing requested and the reason for the request in two conforming sentences, 1322. 1°; regarding a new cause for petitioning in the appellate grade, 1320 §1; for *restitutio in integrum,* 1327 §§1–2, 1328; regarding the opposition of a third party, 1331 §2, 1333; for the ordinary contentious trial, 1343 §1, 1379 §1; regarding advocates in a summary contentious trial, 1350; regarding proofs in a summary contentious trial, 1351; for a session for the joinder of the doubt in a case to declare the nullity of a marriage, 1363 §2; for the dissolution of a sacramental, non-consummated marriage, 1367.

petitioner   general norm, 1134; in matrimonial procedure, 1360, 1361; concerning minors, those who lack the use of reason, those are deprived of the administration of goods or those of diminished mental capacity, 1136, 1137; concerning juridic persons, 1138; in a case regarding the validity of sacred ordination, 1385; in a penal case, 1472.

follows the forum of the respondent, 1073 §3; when the forum of the petitioner can be chosen, 1075 §2, 1080, 1359. 3°;

concerning: the introductory *libellus* of litigation, 1185–1189; presence in a case, 1135, 1136 §3; absence in a case, 1274, 1275; renunciation of a trial or of an act of the process, 1205 §1; an appeal, 1318 §§1–2;

as a party in a case: *passim* in procedural law; *see* party.

philosophy regarding philosophical instruction in a seminary, 348, 349 §1, 353; regarding required knowledge for a candidate to the diaconate, 760 §1.

physician exempt from the obligation to respond in a trial in certain cases, 1229 §2. 1°.

piety for God in the education of children, 627 §1; filial p. for the Holy ever-Virgin Mary, 346 §2. 5°; exercises of p., 96, 346 §2. 6°, 473 §2. 1°, 538 §2; instructions of the patriarch to foster p., 82 §1. 2°;

required in candidates for: the episcopate, 180. 1°; the office of eparchial administrator, 227 §1; the function of director of novices, 458 §1, 524 §1;

as a reason: for the alienation of temporal goods, 1035 §1. 1°; for donations, 1029.

pilgrimage a large gathering of penitents on a p. is not considered a sufficient reason to impart general absolution to several penitents at the same time, 720 §2. 2°; can be imposed as a penance, 1426 §1.

pious cause right of leaving goods to it, 1043 §1; to be fulfilled, 431 §3. 3°, 438 §4, 440 §3, 507 §1, 508 §3, 922 §1. 5°, 926 §1, 929, 930, 1028 §2. 3°, 1044, 1054 §2; the hierarch as its executor, 1045; regarding goods in trust, 1046; moderation, reduction, transfer, or commutation of obligations, 1052–1054; *see* pious foundation, pious will.

pious foundation can be autonomous or non-autonomous, 1047 §1; notion of an autonomous p. f., which is a juridic person, 1047 §1. 1°; notion of a non-autonomous, 1047 §1. 2°; its erection or acceptance, 1048; on the custody and investment of money and moveable goods, 1049; regarding copies of the document of foundation, 1050; concerning the list of obligations and the book in which the fulfillment of obligations and offerings are noted, 1051; regarding obligations for the celebration of the Divine Liturgy, 1052–1053; its statutes to be kept with regard to schools, 638 §2; its statutes to be kept by the rector of the Church,

306 §2; regarding the consent of the finance council, if required by the document of foundation, 263 §4; *see* founder, pious cause, pious will.

pious will right to leave goods for them, 1043 §1; what is to be observed in last wills, 1043 §2; to be fulfilled, 431 §3. 3°, 438 §4, 440 §3, 507 §1, 508 §3, 922 §1. 5°, 926 §1, 929, 930, 1028 §2. 3°, 1044, 1047 §2, 1054 §2; vigilance of the eparchial bishop over them, 201 §2; the hierarch as executor, 1045; regarding goods held in trust, 1046; reduction, moderation, commutation of pious wills, 1054 §§1 and 3; reduction of obligations, 1054 §§2–3; regarding the competent forum, 1079. 2°; *see* pious cause, pious foundation.

place *see* sacred place, see, territory;

legitimate place for meetings and voting of: the synod of bishops of the patriarchal Church, 65 §1, 68 §2, 69, 104 §2, 183 §1; the council of hierarchs, 165 §2; elections, 948 §1, 949 §1; receiving consent or counsel regarding juridic acts to be placed, 948 §1, 934 §1;

regarding: obligation of the law, 1491 §3. 3° and §4; power of the patriarch regarding personal statutes, 99 §2; rights and obligations of the patriarch where provinces, eparchies or exarchies have not been erected, 80. 1°, 101; rights and obligations of the administrator of the patriarchal Church, where neither an eparchy nor an exarchy has been erected, 129; archives of the eparchial curia, 256 §1, 259 §1; adaptation of the laws which bind an exarch, 319 §1; use of rights and insignia which are attached to dignities conferred on clerics, 388; a hermit, 483; superior authority which can grant approval or permission to publish books, 662 §1; celebration of the Divine Liturgy, 707 §1; celebration of the sacrament of penance, 736; sacred ordination, 774 §1; cessation of the impediment of abduction, 806; celebration of marriage, 831 §1. 3°, 838 §1, 841 §1; observance of prescripts about feast days and days of penance, 883 §2; acquisition of domicile or quasi-domicile on the part of religious or members of a society of common life according to the manner of religious, 913; the proper hierarch of the Christian faithful of Eastern Churches where not even an exarchy has been erected for them, 916 §5; loss of domicile or quasi-domicile, 917; the list of obligations incumbent upon pious foundations, 1051 §1; the deposit of money and movable goods of a pious foundation, 1049; goods held in trust which have been designated for the Churches of a p., 1046 §3; the competence of the ordinary tribunal of the patriarchal Church where provinces have not been erected, 1063 §3; forum, 1075–1079. 1°,

1359; p. of a trial, 1128; interrogation of witnesses, 1239 §2; the report of experts, 1259 §2; civil law to be observed, 1162, 1164, 1222; judicial access, 1263; particular provisions for the separation of spouses, 1378 §1; prohibition against or an order to reside in a certain p., 1429, 1473; manner of the intimation of a decree, 1520 §1; privileges, 1532 §1. 2° and §3, 1533 §3;

regarding the eparchial bishop, hierarch, pastor of a p.: *see* individual entries;

exempted by the patriarch, 90;

of residence for the patriarch who has resigned his office, 62; of residence for an eparchial bishop emeritus, 211 §1; exclusive p. regarding the celebration of marriage, 831 §1. 3°;

needs, culture, customs, circumstances or conditions of a place are to be taken into consideration: in determining the rights and obligations of a metropolitan and the metropolitan synods, 137; in works of the apostolate, 203 §2; in accepting or deferring the resignation of a pastor, 297 §2; in the formation of seminary students, 347, 352 §1; in the statutes of associations, 576 §1; regarding schools, 635; in preventing the danger of an invalid or illicit celebration of marriage, 785 §1; in the execution of an administrative act, 1522 §1; regarding the dismissed wives of an unbaptized man or the dismissed husbands of an unbaptized woman after reception of baptism in the Catholic Church, 859 §3; in cases establishing the separation of spouses, 864 §2;

to be recorded: by notaries, 254. 2°; in the baptismal register, 689 §1; regarding sacred ordination, 774 §1; in the marriage register, 841 §1; in an introductory *libellus* of litigation, 1187. 3°; in a sentence, 1295 §4, 1304 §1. 4°;

other meanings: if a law remains doubtful or obscure, it is to be interpreted according to parallel places, 1499; "in the first p.," 59 §2; proxies to be sent "in his p.," 105, 143 §2, 165 §3; "in p." of another, 238 §1. 6°, 271 §5, 491, 618, 627 §1, 681 §1. 2° and §5, 723 §1, 1305; "to take p.," 119, 128. 2°, 170, 488 §2, 607, 1194. 5°; "to give p.," 933, 1083 §3, 1140 §2, 1427 §2; "to take the p. of," 1186 §2, 1242, 1439; "there is p." or "there is no p.," 1281 §1, 1310, 1338; in place of some penalty, 1405 §2.

plot   penalty against those who join an association that plots against the Church, 1448 §2.

political   clerics have civil and p. rights no different than other citizens, 383; what things are forbidden to clerics, religious and members of societies of common life according to the manner of religious regarding p. parties, 384 §2, 427, 561; lay

persons are witnesses to Christ in socio-p. life, 401;

regarding agreements with p. societies, 4.

ponens   designated by the president of a collegiate tribunal, 1091 §2; president of the tribunal can substitute another for the *p.*, 1091 §3; reports about the case at the meeting of the judges and puts the sentence into writing, 1091 §4; which procedural acts the *p.* is to complete, 1085 §2; is to initiate the discussion of the case, 1292 §3; in cases for the declaration of the nullity of a marriage, 1363 §§1–2 and 4.

pontificals   *see* insignia.

poor persons   the obligation of the Christian faithful to assist them, 25 §2; the pastor is to seek them out with paternal charity, 289 §2; regarding the fund by which richer eparchies can assist poorer eparchies, 1021 §3; their right to gratuitous legal assistance in a trial or to a reduction of legal expenses, 1334.

possession   *canonical possession regarding:* an eparchy, 188 §2, 189 §1, 223, 231 §4, 270 §2; the office of coadjutor bishop or auxiliary bishop, 214 §1, 222; an exarchy, 314 §3; the office of eparchial administrator, 220. 4°, 224 §1. 3°; the office of local hierarch, 829 §1; a parish, 288; the office of pastor, 829 §1; an office in the case of transfer to another office, 973;

when a vacant office which is possessed by another illegitimately, may be conferred after the illegitimacy of the possession has been declared, 944;

regarding temporal goods: right of the Church, 1007; subjects capable of p., 1009 §1, 423, 558 §1, 567 §1, 582; how the ability to possess temporal goods may be excluded or restricted in religious institutes, 423; regarding goods whose acquisition has not yet been confirmed by documents, 1020 §3; *see* acquisition, ownership, temporal goods;

regarding a possessory action, 1162; after the joinder of issue the possessor of a thing ceases to be in good faith, 1197;

a centenary or immemorial privilege carries the presumption of the granting of the privilege, 1531 §2;

right of the Church to possess cemeteries, 874 §1.

postulation   *for an office:* provision is made for an office by the admission of a p., 939. 3°; when it may be done, 961; when it has force, 962; regarding its transmission to the competent authority, its admission, revocation, intimation and acceptance, 963–964; effects, 963 §3, 964 §3, 939. 3°.

tor bishop, 212 §2; of an auxiliary bishop, 224 §3; of an exarch, 313, 315 §2, 987; of a local hierarch, 322 §1, 415 §1, 418 §2, 794 §2, 831 §1. 3°; of a hierarch, 887 §1, 1054 §1, 1138 §3; of the one who governs a vacant or impeded exarchy, 320 §2; of a protosyncellus, 245, 248 §1, 221. 2°, 224 §3, 251 §§2–3; of a syncellus, 246, 248 §1, 224 §3, 251 §§2–3; of an eparchial administrator, 220. 4°, 221. 5°, 229; of a protopresbyter, 278 §1; of the authority which granted dignities to clerics, 388; of the authority which reserves absolution from sins, 729. 3°; of the college of eparchial consultors during a vacancy in the eparchial see, 221. 2°, 226; of the priest who substitutes for an absent pastor, 292 §3; of the superior or synaxis in a religious institute, 441 §§1–2, 511, 557, 414 §1. 2°, 418 §1, 431 §2. 1°, 524 §4, 550; of the president of a monastic confederation, 441 §3; of a novice director, 524 §4;

regarding: dispensations regarding marriage or the convalidation of marriage, 796 §2, 797 §2; one who has p. over the matter of a vow, 892; defect of p. to dispense in the authority to which the confirmation of an election belongs in postulations, 963 §1; reduction or transfer of obligations to celebrate the Divine Liturgy, 1052 §§3–6, 1053; one who abuses p. granted by a privilege, 1535;

of dispensation: how it is to be interpreted, 1512 §4; over whom it may be exercised, 1539; of a confessor from certain impediments to exercise sacred orders in more urgent cases, 767 §3;

no p. is acquired over a person by one who confers an office while supplying for another, 945; any legitimate p. in the Church, regarding recourse against administrative decrees, 996; by what p. a decree can be emended on account of recourse, 1004;

human: the Church has the right to preach the gospel independent of any human p., 595 §1; no human p. can supply matrimonial consent, 817 §2; no human p. can dissolve the bond of a sacramental, consummated marriage, 853;

of parents or guardians to whom minors are subject, 910 §2, 915 §1.

practice   a more complete p. of their own rite is to be acquired day by day by clerics and members of institutes of consecrated life, 40 §2; care of the eparchial bishop for those who have fallen away from the p. of religion, 192 §1; of the primitive Church regarding married clerics, 373; obligation of parents to form their children in the p. of the Christian life, 618; which is commended with respect to the offerings made spontaneously on the occasion of the Divine Liturgy or of funerals, 716, 878 §2; of presenting sacred icons or images for

the veneration of the Christian faithful to remain firm, 886; common canonical p. regarding attenuating or aggravating circumstances in penal law, 1415, 1416; continuous and uninterrupted p. required in a custom, 1507 §1.

prayer   *to God:* in the novitiate, 459 §1; to be made by priests before the celebration of the Divine Liturgy, 707 §1; in preparation for participation in the Divine Eucharist, 713 §2; to obtain unity among all of the Eastern Churches, 903; prayer books required ecclesiastical approval, 656 §2; when specific prayers may be imposed as a penalty, 1426 §1;

power of the patriarch regarding prayers, 96; exercises of piety, which contribute to a spirit of p., are to be fostered in seminary, 346 §2. 6°; clerics are to be assiduous in p., 369 §1; to be performed in anointing of the sick, 737 §1; to be performed in sacred ordination, 744.

preaching   general norms, 609–616; nourished by Sacred Scripture and supported by sacred tradition, 607; the care of each of the Churches concerning the preaching of the gospel to the whole world, 585 §1; innate right and obligation of the Church, 595 §1; right and obligation of bishops, 608, 610 §1; right and obligation of the eparchial bishop, 196 §1, 201 §2, 415 §1, 609, 610 §§1 and 4, 615; obligation of the pastor, 289 §1, 614 §§2–3; those who possess the faculty to preach in virtue of office, 611; faculty of presbyters and deacons, 608, 610 §§2–3, 611, 612 §2, 614 §4; recourse *in devolutivo* against a decree by which someone is prohibited from p., 613; regarding the regulation of p. and the invitation to preach in institutes of consecrated life, 612; regarding the designation of a priest who is to preach in monasteries, 475 §2; clerics are to be true ministers of p., 369 §1; vocations are to be fostered by p., 380; about Christian marriage, 783 §1. 1°; regarding ecumenism, 906.

precaution   lest the eparchy suffer any harm from the absence of the eparchial bishop, 204 §2; lest formation program of clerics common to a whole region or nation be detrimental to the specific character of the rites, 330 §2; regarding the participation of infants in the Divine Eucharist, 710; lest the salvation of souls suffer harm with respect to the suspension of a decree during recourse, 1000 §2; in the alienation of temporal goods, 1035 §2; in loaning money, 1049; in the translation of judicial acts, 1315 §2; in the preliminary investigation in a penal process, 1468 §1.

precedence   order of precedence with regard to: patriarchs, 58, 59 §§1, 3 and 4, 60, 62; ancient patriarchal sees, 59 §2; major archbishops, 154; metropolitans, 136; the administrator of the patriarchal Church and bishops of the same Church, 130 §3; breaking a tie vote in the election of bishops, 183 §4; the judges of a collegiate tribunal, 1292 §3;

in a temporal sense: 344 §4, 515 §2, 789. 3°, 1095 §2, 1326 §2. 5°, 1327 §2, 1470.

precept of the Lord to help the poor, 25 §2;

regarding feasts of precept: *see* feast days and days of penance;

regarding the catechumenate, 587 §1; of art or science with respect to the opinion of experts, 1255;

as an administrative act: notion, 1510 §2. 2°; its cessation, 1513 §5;

regarding penal law: in threatening penalties, 1406 §1, 1420 §2, 1464 §1; a warning which is equivalent to a penal p., 1406 §2; regarding the preceptive language of a penal law and the application of penalties by a judge, 1409 §1, 1415, 1416; who is subject to penalties attached to a p., 1412 §1, 1414 §1; presumption about deliberate violation of a p., 1414 §2; punishment of conspirators in a delict who are not expressly named in the p., 1418 §1; regarding remission of a penalty, 1419, 1420 §2.

prejudice *anything prejudicial to be avoided:* to the eparchy or eparchial rights during the vacancy of the see, 228 §2; to the rights of the pastor while the parish is vacant, 299; to parochial ministry in exercising the function of rector of a church, 306 §2;

regarding: the force of decisions of an assembly of hierarchs of several Churches *sui iuris,* 322 §2; a declaration to prove baptism, 691; suspension of a vow, 892; secrecy to be observed in trials, 1113 §1; the right defined by sentence in an interim decision concerning a person's support, 1163 §1; attempts while litigation is pending, 1278; the opposition of a third party, 1332 §2; renunciation of a privilege, 1533 §3;

regarding prejudicial questions in a trial, 1177 §2, 1361 §1.

presbyter *see* priest; belong to one presbyterate (*presbyterium*), 177 §1, 264, 268, 593 §1; *see* presbyterate;

is constituted by sacred ordination, 325–327, 743; *see* sacred order, sacred ordination;

special solicitude of the eparchial bishop for them, 192 §4; regarding the function of the ministry of the word of God, 608; regarding the faculty to preach, 610 §2, 611–612; cooperates in catechetical formation, 624 §2; with regard to the power to celebrate the Divine Liturgy, 699 §§1–2;

regarding the concelebration of the Divine Liturgy, 700 §2, 701; administers chrismation with holy myron, 694, 696; distributes the Divine Eucharist, 709 §1; regarding the faculty to administer the sacrament of penance, 722–726, 475 §1;

regarding information about candidates for sacred orders, 182 §1, 769 §1. 4°, 771 §3;

regarding offices and functions: of protosyncellus and syncellus, 247 §2, 250; of eparchial administrator, 227 §2; of patriarchal chancellor, 123 §1; of chancellor of the eparchial curia, 252 §1; of protopresbyter, 276 §1, 277 §2; of pastor, 281 §1, 284 §2, 285 §§1–2, 286, 287; of parochial vicar, 301 §1; of rector of a church, 304, 305 §§1 and 3; in the college of eparchial consultors, 271 §§4–5, 319; of teller or actuary in the synod of bishops of the patriarchal Church, 71 §1; of eparchial visitator, 205 §1; of one who assumes governance while the see is impeded, 132 §1, 173 §3, 233; of spiritual director in a seminary, 339 §1;

with respect to the care of the Christian faithful of another Church *sui iuris,* 193 §§2–3, 678 §2;

regarding his presence: at the patriarchal assembly, 143 §1. 3°; at the eparchial assembly, 238 §1. 6°–7°; at the presbyteral council, 267;

regarding the notion of a clerical institute of consecrated life, 505 §3, 554 §2;

a p. sent to an exarchy outside of the territorial boundaries of the patriarchal Church is subject to the power of the exarch, 315 §2;

regarding loss of the clerical state, 394. 3°.

presbyteral council notion, 264; functions in the eparchy, 264, 269 §§2–3; statutes, 265; constitution or dissolution, 266–268, 270; in an exarchy, 319 §1; relation to the eparchial bishop, 269.

presbyterate, presbyterium an eparchy is entrusted to a bishop to shepherd with its cooperation, 177 §1; regarding the notion and constitution of the presbyteral council, 264, 268; regarding the presbyters in mission territories as forming one p., 593 §1.

prescription received by the Church as in civil law unless otherwise determined by common law, 1540; is not valid unless based on good faith, 1541; what is not subject to p., 1542; is interrupted by the citation, 1194. 4°;

in temporal goods: 1017, 1540–1542; regarding sacred things, 1018; time required, 1019;

of an action: general norm, 1150; does not take place concerning the status of persons, 1150; of a contentious action, 1151; of a penal action, 1152, 1154; to execute a penalty, 1153 §1;

of a privilege, 1534;

regarding custom, 1507 §1.

prescripts of the liturgical books: *see* books (liturgical), liturgy;

of the Code regarding agreements of the Holy See with nations, 4; of law or of an instruction of the Roman Pontiff about a vacancy of the patriarchal see, 128. 2°; contained in the acts of the Roman Pontiff regarding the obligations of a metropolitan, 159. 8°; of the supreme authority of the Church regarding catechetical instruction, 621 §1; of the Church regarding the sacraments, 667; of the Church regarding the valid administration of sacred ordination, 744;

of law, 24 §2, 196 §1, 758 §1. 3°, 921 §1, 941, 972 §2, 975, 985 §§2–3, 995, 1040, 1081, 1115 §1, 1135, 1221 §1, 1255, 1304 §1. 3°, 1438; of common law, 427, 465, 561, 759 §2; of a Church *sui iuris*, 17, 198, 199 §1, 294, 759 §1, 881 §1, 883 §2; of particular law, 230. 2°, 369 §2, 758 §1. 6°, 1063 §4. 5°; of civil law, 409 §2, 666 §3, 910 §2, 1020 §§1–2, 1043 §2, 1540; of the canons or law, 64, 138, 231 §3, 404 §3, 525 §1, 538 §2, 551, 797 §1, 828 §1, 856 §2, 858, 937 §2, 963 §2, 982 §1, 990 §3, 1020 §3, 1171. 3°, 1181 §3, 1291 §3, 1304 §1. 1°, 1326 §2. 4°, 1402 §1, 1449, 1459 §2, 1466, 1501; of the typicon, 432, 444 §2, 450, 453 §3, 455, 476, 477 §§1 and 3, 488 §2; of the statutes, 274 §1, 432, 520, 523 §2, 535 §1, 540, 545 §2, 550, 552 §2, 927 §2; of the competent authority, 973 §1, 1035 §2; of the one delegating, 983 §3; of the judge, 1135, 1136 §4, 1255;

regarding the form for the celebration of marriage: *see* marriage;

regarding: commissions in the patriarchal Church, 124; the parochial fund, 291; the obligation of the parochial vicar to reside in the parish, 302 §4; the formation of novices, 456 §3; boundaries of the cloister, 477 §3; the writings of members of institutes of consecrated life, 659; conditions for the protection of law of the texts of laws and official acts, 666 §2; certain sacraments administered by non-Catholic ministers, 720 §3; secrecy, 1115 §1; the manner of recording marriage, 841 §1; guarantees in a trial, 1163 §1; a command to reside in a certain place or territory, 1429; the manner for promulgating laws, 1489 §1; cases prescribed by law, 422 §1, 852, 965 §1, 1035. 3°.

presence of the universal Christian viewpoint to be fostered by a Catholic university, 640 §1;

of members in: the synod of bishops of the patriarchal Church, 68 §2, 69, 70, 104 §2, 107 §1, 183 §§1 and 3; the council of hierarchs, 165 §2, 166; a group with regard to a collegial or juridic act to

be validly placed, 924. 1°, 934 §1; an elective assembly, 949, 956 §1;

regarding baptism administered when the pastor is not present, 690; of the parties for the valid celebration of marriage, 837 §1; of the promotor of justice or defender of the bond in cases, 1097, 1309; of the promotor of justice or defender of the bond is governed by the norms established for the p. of the parties, 1098. 2°; of the parties and of others in a trial to be recorded by a notary, 1249; regarding the dispositive part of the sentence to be read to the parties in a summary contentious trial, 1354 §1; of the promotor of justice and a notary at the oral discussion before the imposition of a penalty by extrajudicial decree, 1486 §1. 2°; regarding a decree issued extrajudicially before two witnesses or a notary, 1520 §2.

presentation of an infant for baptism on the part of the sponsor, 684 §2.

president, presiding officer of an ecumenical council is the Roman Pontiff, 51 §1;

of the patriarchal Church, 56, 60 §1, 78 §1, 82, 84, 86 §2, 92 §§2–3, 94, 96, 114 §2, 123 §2, 132 §1, 140, 146 §1, 148 §§1 and 3, 233 §1, 357 §1, 414 §2, 438 §1, 480, 507 §2, 549 §2. 1°, 767 §2, 829 §3, 1423 §1; of the major archiepiscopal Church, 151, 1423 §1; of the metropolitan Church *sui iuris*, 155 §1, 157 §1, 158 §1, 159, 162, 163, 167 §4, 583 §2. 1°, 984 §§1–2, 1084 §3, 1087 §2; of a Church *sui iuris* which is neither patriarchal, major archiepiscopal, nor metropolitan, 174, 176;

of the synod to elect a patriarch, 70, 73; of the synod of bishops of the patriarchal Church, 103; of the permanent synod, 116 §§1–2, 117; of the patriarchal assembly, 142 §1; of the patriarchal chancery and the archives of the patriarchal curia, 123 §1; of a province within the territorial boundaries of the patriarchal Church, 133 §1, 136;

of the metropolitan synod, 133 §1. 2°; of the council of hierarchs, 159. 2°, 165 §4;

of the eparchial consultors, 221. 1°, 271 §5; of the eparchial assembly, 237 §1; of the presbyteral council, 269 §1; of the finance council, 263 §1; of the pastoral council, 275; regarding the eparchial bishop in an elective synaxis, 443 §1;

the protopresbyter in the election of a pastor to be sent to the eparchial assembly, 238 §1. 6°;

of a monastic confederation: *see* confederation (of monasteries);

of a group: can vote to break a tie, 924. 1°; in elections, 948 §1. 955 §§2 and 5, 956 §2, 957 §2;

presiding judge of a tribunal: of a collegiate tribunal is the judicial vicar or adjunct judicial vicar, 1091 §1; of the synod of bishops of the patriarchal Church, 1062 §2; of the ordinary tribunal of the patriarchal Church, 1063 §2; regarding recourse against his decree, 1085 §1. 2°; manner for designating two judges who constitute a collegiate tribunal along with him, 1090 §1; designates the *ponens* and can substitute another for him or her, 1091 §§2–3; his rights belong to a single judge, 1092; designates an auditor, 1093 §1; provides for the recusal of an official of the tribunal, 1107 §3; regarding the rejection of the introductory *libellus* of litigation, 1188 §§1 and 4; regarding the citation, 1190 §1; regarding incidental cases, 1270 §2; regarding the meeting of judges before the sentence, 1292 §§1 and 3; in matrimonial cases, 1363 §§1–2 and 4;

regarding: the divine praises, over which the eparchial bishop is to preside frequently, 199 §3; concelebration, 700 §2.

presumption   what is presumed by the law itself does not need proof, 1207 §2. 1°; which a judge may formulate, 1265; regarding the burden of proof, if a person has a favorable p. of law, 1266;

of consent: of the Apostolic See in certain cases of transfer to another Church *sui iuris,* 32 §2; regarding sacred functions with all pontifical insignia outside of the territory of a bishop's own eparchy, 200;

of permission: of a pastor for a parochial vicar to perform sacred functions of greater importance, 290 §2; of the rector of a church or a higher authority to perform sacred functions in a church entrusted to a rector, 308; of the local hierarch, for a cleric to leave his eparchy for a notable period of time, 386 §1; of the pastor or local hierarch to administer baptism, 677 §1; of the rector of a church or superior for the licit use of the faculty to administer the sacrament of penance, 722 §4; regarding the administration of the anointing of the sick, 739 §2, 740;

regarding: goods acquired by a member in temporary vows, 529 §3; validation of marriage, 779, 803 §2; matrimonial consent, 824 §1, 827; privilege of the faith, 861; tacit condonation of adultery by the other spouse, 863 §2; the use of reason by one no longer an infant, 909 §2; validity of a juridic act, 931 §2; delegation of executive power, 990 §1; offerings made to moderators or administrators of juridic persons, 1016 §2; the intervention of the promotor of justice, 1095 §2; renunciation of a trial by the petitioner, 1274. 2°; an appeal against the grounds of a sentence, 1318 §4;

death of a spouse, 1383; deliberate violation of a law, 1414 §2; ignorance or error regarding a law, penalty or fact, 1497 §2; revocation of a law, 1503; granting of a privilege, 1531 §2; perpetuity of a privilege, 1532 §1;

regarding one who presumes to induce a member of the Christian faithful to transfer to another Church *sui iuris,* 31, 1465.

pretext   it is not permitted to interfere with the office of novice director under any p., 524 §3; regarding the delict of solicitation under p. of confession, 1458.

prevention   between several equally competent tribunals, 1082; between several procurators, 1140 §2; regarding several persons delegated to transact the same matter, 990 §2;

of scandal, 1473.

price   regarding the faith guarded and handed down by forefathers at a great p., 10;

of moveable goods to be protected, 1049.

priest   *see* bishop, presbyter;

Christ is the eternal p., 368; the Christian faithful share in the priestly function of Christ through baptism, 7 §1;

celibacy is highly suited to the priesthood, 373;

priestly vocation is to be fostered, 195, 329;

ordinarily administers baptism, 677 §1; permission to administer baptism cannot be denied by the pastor of a different Church *sui iuris* to a priest of the Church *sui iuris* to which the one to be baptized is to be ascribed, 678 §1;

regarding the Divine Liturgy: acts in the person of Christ, 698; the unity of the priesthood is appropriately manifested in concelebration, 700 §2; functions, obligations, rights and prohibitions, 699–705, 707 §1, 715–717; regarding the celebration of the Divine Liturgy in certain monasteries, 475 §2; the homily is reserved to him, 614 §4;

distributes the Divine Eucharist, 709 §1;

regarding the sacrament of penance: is the minister of divine justice and mercy, 718, 722 §1, 732 §2; in danger of death, 720 §2. 1°, 725, 735 §2; in an urgent case, 735 §2; absolution of several penitents at the same time on account of a lack of priests, 720 §2. 1°–2°; in religious institutes, 474 §2, 538 §3; is to be called by the pastor if necessary, 289 §2;

is minister of the anointing of the sick, 737, 739–741;

in the sacrament of matrimony: regarding dispensations from impediments, 796 §2, 797 §1, 798;

549 §3; record of p. and notation of it in the baptismal register, 296 §2, 470, 535 §2; *see* vows (perpetual);

temporary religious profession: duration and renewal, 526; requirements for validity, 527; required in orders for the validity of perpetual profession, 532; effects, 529; what norms should be observed for it in monasteries, 465; regarding admission to novitiate, 450. 4°; regarding the time of novitiate in monasteries, 457 §1; regarding cession of the administration of goods and disposition of their use and revenue, 525 §2; illness as a reason for the exclusion of a member from the renewal of temporary p., 547 §2; regarding transfer to another institute, 545 §2; regarding departure from the institute, 493, 496 §1, 546; regarding dismissal from the institute, 499, 547 §3; *see* vows (temporary);

regarding societies of common life according to the manner of religious, 554 §1, 559 §1, 560, 562 §§2–4;

in a secular institute, 563 §1. 1°;

public p. of chastity by virgins or widows, 570;

a civil p. in the case of clerics, 371 §3;

regarding professional schools, 635.

profit procurators and advocates are forbidden to bargain for excessive p., 1146 §1;

regarding the obligation of tribunal officials to abstain from office, 1106.

program *(ratio) for the formation of clerics:* notion, 330 §1; competent authority, 330 §§1–2; what it is to include, 330 §3; regarding the directory of the seminary, 337 §2; regarding the seminary's curriculum of studies, 344 §3; in monasteries, 471 §2; in orders and congregations, 536 §2; in societies of common life according to the manner of religious, 559 §2;

of studies in ecclesiastical universities and faculties, 650.

prohibition of those who care for the interim governance of an eparchy from withdrawing, destroying or changing documents of the eparchial curia, 228 §2; from receiving sacraments, 381 §2; of clerics, religious, and members of societies of common life according to the manner of religious from exercising commerce or business affairs and from posting bond, 385 §§2–3, 427, 561; of a cleric who has lost the clerical state from exercising power of orders, 395; of a member expelled from a religious institute or from a society of common life according to the manner of religious from exercising a sacred order, 498 §3, 551,

562 §3; strictly forbidden to coerce, induce through improper practices or allure anyone to embrace the Church, 586; from preaching, 611, 612 §2, 613; who is competent to prohibit the Christian faithful from attending a particular school, 633 §1; who is competent to prohibit the Christian faithful from using instruments of social communication, 652 §2; of the use of knowledge acquired in confession, 734 §1; of a bishop from celebrating sacred ordination in the eparchy of another, 749; of a deacon from ascending to the presbyterate, 755; one who refuses to receive a higher order cannot be prohibited from exercising a sacred order, with certain exceptions, 757; regarding impediments to receive or exercise sacred orders, 762 §1. 6°, 763. 2°; regarding entering marriage, 778, 794, 813, 1370 §1, 1453 §2; sterility does not prohibit marriage, 801 §3; from making a vow, 889 §2; of a pastor from receiving a non-Catholic into the Catholic Church, 898 §3; of subdelegation of executive power delegated by the Apostolic See or by the patriarch, 988 §2; of the donor regarding the acceptance of a trust, 1046 §1; from accepting gifts on the occasion of a trial, 1114; from handing over copies of judicial acts and documents, 1133 §2; of information which remains outside of the acts of the case, 1287 §1; from residing in a certain place or territory, 1429 §1, 1473; from exercising all or some acts of a sacred order regarding penal law, 1430 §2, 1433 §2; from receiving the Divine Eucharist, 1441, 1473; with regard to the delict of disobedience, 1446; of a future custom, 1507 §3; from substituting the executor of an administrative act, 1524.

promise made to God, 889 §1, 891; *see* vow;

of obedience to the Roman Pontiff and, in certain cases, to the patriarch, before episcopal ordination, 187 §2;

faithfully to fulfill an office or function: of the one elected patriarch, 76 §1; of the major archbishop after the confirmation of his election, 153 §3; of administrators of the eparchial curia, 244 §2. 1°; of an administrator of ecclesiastical goods, 1025. 1°; of those who constitute a tribunal, 1112;

of marriage, 782 §2; in a mixed marriage, 814. 1°–2°, 815; of an office has no canonical effect, 943 §3;

seminary students to cultivate fidelity to promises, 346 §2. 8°.

regarding the delict of corruption, 1147, 1463.

promotor of the whole liturgical life of an eparchy is the eparchial bishop, 199 §1; regarding promotors of new forms of consecrated life, 571.

appear, 1273, 1275 §1; of a third party who intervenes in a case, 1276 §3; publication of the acts regarding proofs, 1281 §1, 1283 §3; how they may be completed after the publication of the acts, 1281 §2; regarding the conclusion of the case, 1282 §§1–2; when proofs may be proposed after the conclusion of the case, 1283 §§1–2; regarding the pronouncement of the sentence, 1289, 1291 §§2–3; regarding new proofs or the completion of proofs in an appeal, 1320 §2, 1321; new and serious proofs in bringing forward to an appeals tribunal a case regarding the status of persons after two conforming sentences, 1325 §1; regarding *restitutio in integrum*, 1326 §2. 1°–2°; in the opposition of a third party, 1332 §1, 1333; in the summary contentious trial, 1344 §1. 2°, 1347 §2, 1349 §1, 1351–1353; in matrimonial procedures, 1359. 4°, 1364–1366, 1372 §2; new proofs to be collected in a penal trial after the discussion of the case, 1479 §2;

regarding: formulas for the profession of faith and the promise to fulfill an office faithfully, 76 §1; vocation in a seminary, 331 §2; pastoral formation of seminary students, 353; charisms of lay persons to be recognized by clerics, 381 §3; the member who has the care of a candidate for novitiate, 518; the novice director, 449, 522 §1; the moderator for the formation of religious outside of their own houses, 471 §1, 536 §2; the Christian life of one to be baptized after infancy, 682 §1; the custom of the Church about offerings on the occasion of the Divine Liturgy, 715 §1; a neophyte to be admitted to sacred orders, 762 §1. 8°; prudence and zeal for justice in a judicial vicar, adjunct judicial vicar, promotor of justice and defender of the bond, 1086 §4, 1087 §3, 1099 §2; assessors of proven life, 1089.

proper hierarch how members of the Christian faithful acquire a p. h., 916 §§1, 3 and 5; approves formative courses for clerics, 372 §1; his permission for clerics to volunteer for military service, 383. 2°; report of the administration of good to be given to him, 1031 §1; his permission for a lawsuit in the civil forum regarding the temporal goods of the Church, 1032; with respect to pious causes, 1046 §1; his consent for a non-autonomous pious foundation to be accepted validly by a juridic person, 1048 §2.

proper law p. marriage l. of a non-Catholic Church or ecclesial community, 780 §2, 781. 1°.

proper right *of the Church:* to take any marriage case of a baptized person, 1357; to form clerics and other ministers, 328;

of persons, 26 §2, 82 §1, 628 §2, 1276 §1.

property for whom p. is acquired regarding goods which come to a religious in perpetual vows who becomes patriarch, bishop or exarch, 431 §3. 1°; *see* ownership, possession;

essential properties of marriage, 776 §3, 814. 3°, 824 §2.

propriety marriage impediment of public p., 810.

prorogation of the synod of bishops of the patriarchal Church, 108 §1; of the metropolitan synod, 133 §1. 2°, 138; of the patriarchal assembly, 142 §1; of the council of hierarchs, 159. 2°; of the eparchial assembly, 237 §1; of a novitiate, 461 §2, 525 §1; of time limits in a trial, 1124, 1126; of time limits for an arbitral sentence, 1178; of useful time to respond in the procedure for the removal of pastors, 1393 §1.

protopresbyter placed over a district composed of several parishes, 276 §1; his appointment, 277 §§1–2; his removal, 277 §3; his rights and obligations, 278; his convocation to the eparchial assembly, 238 §1. 5°; presides at the election of a presbyter of his district to be sent to the eparchial assembly, 238 §1. 6°; is to be heard by the eparchial bishop in the appointment of pastors, 285 §3.

protosyncellus who is, 245; must be constituted in each eparchy, 245; is a local hierarch, 984 §2; belongs to the eparchial curia, 243 §2; which powers and faculties he has, 191 §2, 221. 2°, 224 §§2–3, 245, 248, 251 §§2–3, 987; regarding delegated power for the reduction of obligations to celebrate the Divine Liturgy, 1052 §6; syncelli have his power in their own area of authority, 246; is appointed freely and can be removed by the eparchial bishop, 247 §1; his function must be conferred on a coadjutor bishop, 215 §1; his function is to be conferred on an auxiliary bishop, 215 §2; suspension of his power, 251 §3; cessation from office, 251 §§1–2, 224 §§1–2; requirements, 247 §§2–4; his dealings with the eparchial bishop, 249; regarding privileges and insignia, 250; regarding visitation of the eparchy, 205 §1; attends the eparchial assembly, 238 §1. 2°; regarding permission together with that of the chancellor to have access to the archives of the eparchial curia, 257 §1, 258; is ordinarily not to be named judicial vicar, 1186 §1; first recourse against his decree is made to the eparchial bishop, 997 §2; during a vacancy of the eparchial see, 221. 2°, 224, 251 §2; when the eparchial see is impeded, 233 §1; when the exarchy is vacant or impeded, 320.

province a metropolitan presides over it, 133 §1; is a juridic person by the law itself, 921 §2; rights of the metropolitan in the eparchies of the province, 133 §1, 138, 139, 159. 1° and 3°–7°; the metropolitan represents it, 133 §2; the metropolitan who presides over a p. precedes a titular metropolitan everywhere, 136; regarding a bishop who belongs to no p., 139; when a p. may be erected, united, divided, have its boundaries modified or suppressed by the patriarch, 85 §1; right of the patriarch to erect them regarding the determination of the territorial boundaries of the patriarchal Church, 146 §1; in places where provinces have not been erected or during a vacancy of the metropolitan see, it is for the patriarch to exercise the rights of the metropolitan and fulfill his obligations, 80. 1° and 3°; regarding gatherings of hierarchs and of the Christian faithful to be fostered in it by the patriarch, 84 §2; in places where provinces have not been erected the rights of the metropolitan tribunal belong to the ordinary tribunal of the patriarchal Church, 1063 §3;

of institutes of consecrated life: notion, 508 §1; its constitution, circumscription, division, suppression, 508 §1, 556; is a juridic person by the law itself, 423, 558 §1, 567 §1; ascribed to another Church *sui iuris*, 432, 517 §2; to whom it belongs to make decisions regarding the goods of a suppressed p., 508 §3, 556; provincial superior is a major superior, 418 §1; regarding sending desires to the general synaxis, 512 §2, 557; its finance officer, 516 §§1–2, 558 §2.

provision *canonical provision of office:* general norms, 936–964; *see* conferral, election, office, postulation; an office cannot validly be obtained without it, 938; if it requires the exercise of a sacred order, it is not subject to prescription, 1542. 6°; competent authority, 936 §3; ways of p., 939; decree about p., 1510 §2. 1°; when it is null or can be rescinded, if the one provided lacks the required qualifications, 940 §2; regarding time limits, 941, 943 §2; of an office which is not vacant by law is null by the law itself, 943 §1; regarding the juridic condition of one on whom an office has been conferred by one supplying for another, 945; is null is done out of grave fear unjustly inflicted, fraud, substantial error or simony, 946; regarding notification of removal from office to all those who have some right over the canonical p. of that office, 966; resignation from office must be made to the authority to whom it pertains to make canonical p. of that office, 969; the patriarch is competent to send letter of canonical p. to a metropolitan or bishop, 86 §1. 1°; of a bishop, 187 §1; letter of canonical p. to be read publicly at the enthronement of an eparchial bishop, 189 §1;

the rights and obligations of a coadjutor bishop are to be determined in the letter of canonical p., 213 §1; regarding canonical p. of office taken by a coadjutor or auxiliary bishop, 214; by it a pastor obtains the care of souls, 288; regarding transfer to another office, 972 §1;

regarding: provisions of the Roman Pontiff about a vacant eparchial see in a patriarchal Church, 220. 2°; the salvation of souls, 727; particular law, 220. 2°, 263 §1, 329 §2, 591. 2°, 837 §2, 937 §2, 1021 §§1–2; support, housing, subsistence, necessities, 62, 87, 211 §2, 297 §2, 385 §1, 390 §1, 859 §3, 977, 1021 §1, 1163 §1, 1337 §2, 1410; remuneration, 291, 409 §2, 591. 2°, 1030. 2°, 1180 §2, 390 §1; the action of the Apostolic See in certain cases, 81, 148 §3, 159. 8°; statutes, 113, 171, 267 §2, 514 §3, 922 §2; needs of the Christian faithful, 169, 193 §§1–2; insurance, social security, health benefits, 192 §5, 390 §2, 409 §2, 1021 §2; temporal goods, 262 §3; obligations of the protopresbyter, 278 §1. 3° and §3; a parish, 292 §3, 302 §3, 1396 §3; maintenance and adornment of a church, 309; a vacant or impeded exarchy, 320 §2; seminaries, 332 §2, 341 §1; exemption of institutes of consecrated life, 412 §2; young Churches in the missions, 590; catechisms, 621 §3; religious education, 628 §2; Catholic university centers, 645; instruments of social communication, 652 §1; the administration of the sacrament of penance, 735 §1; marriage by proxy, 837 §2; a juridic person which lacks members, 926 §1; the office of judicial vicar or adjunct judicial vicar after a vacancy in the eparchial see, 1088 §2; the public good and the promotor of justice, 1094; designation of arbiters by the tribunal, 1174 §1; ecclesiastical discipline and penalties, 1405 §1; reparation of scandal and harm, 1403 §1, 1409 §1. 2°, 1424 §1; reparation of scandal or restitution of justice, 1481 §2;

"unless otherwise provided," 211 §1, 220. 2°, 221. 2°, 230, 232 §1, 233 §1, 263 §1, 452 §2, 1378 §1.

provocation of subjects to disobedience is to be punished as a delict, 1447 §1.

proxy no one can send a p. in his place to the synod of bishops of the patriarchal Church or the council of hierarchs, 105, 165 §3; eparchial bishops can send a p. to the patriarchal assembly, 143 §2; not admitted in the eparchial assembly, 239; regarding copies of documents received by p., 257 §2; marriage by p. cannot validly be celebrated, unless the particular law of a Church *sui iuris* establishes otherwise, 837 §2; in elections votes cannot be cast by p. unless the law provides otherwise, 949 §1; in recourses against administrative decrees, 1003.

members of a society of common life according to the manner of religious, 913; of spouses, 914; of minors, 915 §1; of those who are under guardianship or curatorship, 915 §2; only eparchial, 916 §2; with respect to travellers and transients, 911;

regarding: election of members of the presbyteral council, 297 §1. 2°; grants of the loss of clerical status by the patriarch, 397; dispensation from the required age for sacred ordination granted by the patriarch, 759 §2; dispensation from certain impediments to receive or exercise sacred orders granted by the patriarch, 767 §2; licit blessing of marriage, 831 §1. 1°; convocation of electors, 948 §1; forum, 1074, 1075 §2, 1079. °, 1187. 4°, 1359. 2°; the introductory *libellus* of litigation, 1187. 4°; penalties reserved to the patriarch or major archbishop, 1423 §1; subjection to laws, 1491 §2.

questions   concerning the meaning of life are to be answered in the first place by patriarchs and bishops, 601; lay persons are not to propose their own judgement as the doctrine of the Church in q. which are open to various opinions, 402;

to be dealt with in: an ecumenical council, 51 §2; encyclical letters of the patriarch, 82 §1. 3°; the synod of bishops of the patriarchal Church, 108 §§2–3; the metropolitan synod, 133 §1. 2°; the patriarchal assembly, 144; the council of hierarchs, 159. 2°; the eparchial assembly, 240 §§1 and 4; the presbyteral council, 269 §1; *see* arguments;

regarding: new q. and the obligations of theologians, 606 §1; new q. of the contemporary age in universities and faculties, 641, 647. 1°; faith and morals in writings published by religious, 662 §2; recourse against an administrative decree of the patriarch, 1006;

in trials: principal, 1267; regarding the notion of an incidental case, 1267; how incidental q. are to be settled, 1269, 1270, 1299 §2, 1339; regarding proofs to be decided by the auditor, 1093 §3; about recusal, 1109 §1, 1175; regarding peremptory exceptions, 1121 §2; regarding judicial expenses or gratuitous legal representation, 1123; regarding responses of the deaf or mute to q., 1130; on the merits in the acts of the case, 1131 §1; on temporal goods in a transaction, 1165 §2; incidental, prejudicial, or q. about the status of persons in arbitration, 1177; to be settled most expeditiously in arbitration, 1181 §2; on the rejection of the introductory *libellus* of litigation, 1188 §4; on attempts while litigation is pending, 1279, 1280; some q. to be explained in the oral discussion, 1287 §2; on the correction of the text of the sentence, 1299 §2; on the right to appeal to be settled most expeditiously, 1313; on rendering accounts before the ex-

ecution of the sentence, 1339; which q. are to be dealt with first at the hearing in a summary contentious trial, 1348, 1118, 1119, 1121, 1122; prejudicial q. about the validity of marriage, 1361 §1; of damages in the preliminary investigation of a penal trial, 1469 §3.

quinquennial   *see* five years.

R

reason   faith and r. converge in the one truth, 641;

as the intellectual faculty: a minor is presumed to have its use after completing the seventh year of age, 909 §2; use of r. regarding a minor in spiritual cases and in case connected with spiritual things, 1136 §3; use of r. sufficient for subjection to laws, 1490; regarding those who lack the use of r., 681 §4, 740, 818. 1°, 889 §2, 909 §3, 1136 §§1–3; *see* lack of the use of reason;

for absence from the synod of bishops of the patriarchal Church or council of hierarchs to be presented in writing, 68 §2, 104 §2, 165 §2; of apostolate, 140; special r. obliges clerics to perfection, 368; special r. for canonical visitation, 414 §1. 3°; special r. of time and place requiring schools, 635; for the denial of permission or approval regarding books, 664 §3; large gathering of penitents not a sufficient r. for absolution of several people at the same time, 720 §2. 2°; reasons opposed to Christian life regarding cremation, 876 §3; overriding r. regarding the agreement of a counsel of persons required for some act, 934 §2. 3°; reasons opposed to transfer to another office, 972 §2; pastoral r. regarding alienations, 1035 §1. 1°; regarding the competent forum, 1072, 1076, 1077 §1, 1081, 1082; to be expressed in a recourse, decree, decision, the conclusions of the judges, or a sentence, 1117, 1188 §4, 1260 §2, 1229 §2, 1294. 3°, 1295 §3, 1304 §1. 2°, 1486 §1. 3°; for appeal to be indicated, 1315 §1; for the betrayal of their function by procurators or advocates, 1147; of the parties to be considered, 1196; of an unjust sentence, 1283 §1. 3°; for the removal of a pastor, 1394; for the transfer of a pastor, 1398, 1399 §1; equal or more serious r. regarding analogy in applying penalties, 1404 §2; regarding the issue of an extrajudicial decree, 1517 §2.

canonical r. required for the absence of a patriarch from his see, 93;

most grave reason required: for the translation of the see of the patriarchal Church, 57 §3; for a rescript for the loss of the clerical state for a presbyter to be granted, 394. 3°; for a petition for an indult of departure from a religious institute, 492

non-Catholic Church as a sponsor, 685 §3; for the concelebration of bishops and presbyters of different Churches *sui iuris*, 701; for the administration of the Divine Eucharist outside of a celebration of the Divine Liturgy, 713 §1; for the sacrament of penance to be administered outside of its proper place, 736 §2; for sacred ordination to be celebrated outside of its proper time and place, 773; to grant permission for a mixed marriage to take place, 814; for certain exceptions in the requirements for the licit celebration of marriage, 831 §1. 2° and §2; for departure, in a pauline privilege case, 854 §2, 857. 3°; for a non-consummated marriage to be dissolved by the Roman Pontiff, 862; for a dispensation from private vows, 893 §1; for either spouse to have his or her own domicile or quasi-domicile, 914; for resignation from office, 967; a just and proportionate r. required to accept a resignation from office, 970 §3; for removal from an office which is conferred at the prudent discretion of the competent authority, 975 §2; for refusing certain offerings, 1016 §3; of piety or charity, to make certain donations, 1029; for alienating temporal goods, such as urgent necessity, evident utility, piety, charity or a pastoral reason, 1035 §1. 1°; for transferring obligations to celebrate the Divine Liturgy, 1053; just and necessary r. required for the reduction, moderation or commutation of the wills of the Christian faithful, 1054 §1; for the substitution of the *ponens* on a collegiate tribunal, 1091 §3; for the removal of the promotor of justice or the defender of the bond, 1100 §2; to extend certain time limits in a trial, 1124 §2; for a judge to leave his own territory to gather proofs, 1128 §2; for several procurators to be constituted by the same party, 1140 §2; to exclude a witness or an expert, 1236, 1257; for the provisional execution of a sentence, 1337 §2; to defer a decision in the summary contentious process, 1354 §2; a just and reasonable r. required to grant a dispensation, 1536; regarding the notification of the intimation of a decree, if the one for whom the decree is intended is absent or refuses to sign the written record of the proceedings, 1520 §3;

no reason exists: for violating the sacramental seal, 733 §1; for permitting coercion regarding the exercise or reception of sacred orders, 756; for the dissolution of the bond of a sacramental marriage, once the marriage has been consummated, 853;

purpose: of a vow, regarding the cessation of the vow, 891; of delegation, regarding the cessation of delegation, 1513 §4;

motive: if the r. for a dispensation ceases, the dispensation ceases, 1513 §4; for the validity of a rescript at least one must be true, 1529 §2;

of evangelization, regarding the transfer or move of a cleric to another eparchy, 361;

determined by the statutes required for removing superiors in orders and congregations, 514 §2; of dismissal or departure from a religious institute or from a society of common life according to the manner of religious, regarding admission to a seminary, 342 §2;

of impediments, regarding their multiplication, 766; it is necessary to legitimately establish the r. a prior marriage was invalid or dissolved before proceeding to the licit celebration of a new marriage, 802 §2; regarding error about a quality of a person, which gives a r. for the marriage, 820 §2; of a psychic nature, regarding incapacity to assume the obligations of marriage, 818. 3°; right to a new marriage in a pauline privilege case, if the non-baptized party departs without a just r., 857. 3°;

regarding the separation of spouses: the spouse who provided a r. for the adulterous partner does not have the right to separate, 863 §1; legitimate reasons, 864 §§1–2;

of the diminution of revenues for the obligations of celebrating the Divine Liturgy, 1052 §3; which renders the execution of the obligations impossible, regarding the reduction of obligations, 1054 §2;

any reason or whatever reason, regarding: the impeded patriarchal see, 132 §1; the disagreement of patriarchs in certain provisions for the Christian faithful residing outside the territory of the patriarchal Church, 193 §3; fewer than the minimum number of members of the college of eparchial consultors, 271 §3; the impeded parish, 298; departure from a monastery and the return of the dowry, 454; the impossibility of erecting a tribunal in the constitution of a tribunal of first instance for several eparchies, 1067 §2;

regarding the removal of pastors, 1389, 1390, 1391 §1, 1394 §1;

when the r. ceases, what things are to be revoked, relating to administrative remedies in a penal trial, 1473; for absolution in a penal trial, 1484 §2, 1481 §1; for the absence of a witness, 1238; new r. for petitioning regarding the nullity of marriage in an appeal, 1320 §1; same r. for petitioning, regarding *res iudicata*, 1322. 1°;

regarding the expulsion of a member, who is the r. for scandal or damage, 498 §1, 551; of physical or psychological infirmity regarding the exclusion of a member from the renewal of temporary profession or admission to perpetual profession, 547 §2; of celebrating marriage, regarding the cessation of the reservation of absolution from sin, if a spouse confesses, 729. 1°; of vacation, regarding the absence from the eparchy of a coadjutor bishop or auxiliary bishop, 217; of studies or illness in the absence of a member from a monastery for more than a year, 478; of art, history, or material, regarding precious objects, 1019; of a loan or mortgage, regarding the payment of interest, 1028 §1. 4°; regarding acts *mortis causa*, 1043, 1044, 1045 §1, 1046 §1; of giving testimony, regarding expenses to be paid for witnesses, 1252;

of experiment: regarding the transfer of a member of a monastery to another monastery, 488 §2; regarding the reception in an eparchy for five years of a religious constitute in a sacred order, who has departed from a religious institute, 494 §2, 549 §3;

by reason: of incorporation into Christ, 7 §1; catechumens are joined to the Church by special r., 9 §1; of the primacy of the Roman Pontiff, 412 §2; of office, 41, 266. 2°, 302 §§1–2, 1199, 1432 §3; of function, 41, 217, 1221 §1; of ministry, 41; of organic progress, 40 §1; of dignity, 59 §1; of marriage, adoption, sacred order or religious profession regarding canonical status, 296 §2; by another r. than that of territory, regarding the circumscription of an exarchy, 311 §1; of place or persons, 319 §1; of sacred ordination, 323 §2, 325; of membership regarding goods acquired, 488 §4; of culture, 647. 1°; of the sacrament regarding the firmness of marriage, 776 §3; of an impediment or defect of form of the celebration regarding the invalidity of marriage, 827; a vow obliges what person by r. of its very nature, 890; by another reason than minority regarding domicile or quasi-domicile, 915 §2; of consanguinity. affinity, guardianship, curatorship, close friendship, animosity or profit, 1106 §1; of the nature of the act, 1125; of sacred ministry or of having given advice, 1229 §2. 1°; of territory or of persons, 1405 §1; of circumstances of person or place, 1522 §1; of the dignity of a person or a thing, 1533 §3.

rebuke how the penalty of a public r. is to be carried out, 1427 §1; what is to be guarded against, 1427 §2;

of the restless in religious institutes to be fostered by superiors, 421.

recall of a cleric from a move, 362 §1; "r. to mind," 1243 §1.

reception of the gift of the Holy Spirit in sacred ordination, 323 §1;

on the part of the Roman Pontiff: of the united action of bishops dispersed throughout the world, 50 §2; of the collegial manner of action of the college of bishops, 54 §2;

of non-Catholics into the Catholic Church, 834 §1, 897–901, 1490; into a seminary, 342 §2; into an institute of consecrated life, 450. 5°, 517 §1, 559 §1, 568 §1; of one who has departed from a religious institute, back into the same institute, 493 §2, 549 §3; regarding members of associations, 578 §1, 580;

of religious profession, 464. 2°–3°, 470, 527. 2°–3°, 535 §2;

of the ancient law of the Eastern Churches in the Code, 2; of prescription as it is in civil law, 1017, 1540;

of offerings: by clerics assigned to a parish, 291; on the occasion of the celebration of the Divine Liturgy, 715, 716, 1012 §1; on the occasion of funerals, 878 §2;

regarding: the formula and manner for the intimation of the election of a patriarch, 73; dignity in the patriarchal Church, 89 §3; apostolic letters about the appointment of a bishop, 188 §1; acts, 167 §2, 1187. 3°; votes, 183 §3; an authentic copy of documents, 257 §2; the mandate to teach, 404 §3, 596; the letters of religious which are not subject to inspection, 429; notice about the recording of a marriage, 841 §2; the intimation of an election, 957 §2; recourse against administrative decrees, 998 §2, 1000 §2, 1001 §2. 1°, 1002; remuneration, 1148; appeal, 1182 §2; citation, 1192 §3; those things that cannot be received even as an indication of the truth in a trial, 1231 §2. 2°; the petition in an incidental case, 1269 ; the invitation to resign from the office of pastor, 1393 §2; a letter of public rebuke, 1427 §1; a community capable of receiving law in customary law, 1507 §1; the strict interpretation of laws, 1512 §2; the petition for a decree, 1518; r. of the written mandate for the execution of a decree, 1521;

regarding the r. of a religious constituted in a sacred order who has departed from his own institute by a benevolent eparchial bishop, 494 §1, 549 §3; acknowledgement of receipt, 1192 §1.

recognition of the sacred bond of profession in secular institutes, 563 §1. 1°; in the external forum of the effects of the exercise of power of governance only for the internal forum, 980 §2; of a private document in a trial, 1223.

higher, 1119 §3, 1325, 1331 §1;

pronouncements referring to reasons expressed in another act, 1300.

refugees clerics are to be examples in works of charity and hospitality especially toward r., 383 §1.

refusal to receive a higher sacred order, 757; of a decree of confirmation of an arbitral sentence, 1181 §2; of citation, 1192 §3; to swear an oath, 1249; of resignation in the procedure for the removal of pastors, 1393 §2.

region *regarding:* the right to approach the Apostolic See in special cases in questions about retaining one's own rite, 35; gatherings about matters affecting the r. to be fostered by the patriarch, 84 §2; the patriarch is to see that in regions where personal statutes are in force they are observed, 99 §1; the territory of the patriarchal Church, 146 §1; the assembly of hierarchs of several Churches *sui iuris,* 322 §1; works to foster vocations, 329 §2; a common program for the formation of clerics, 330 §2; a common major seminary, 332 §2; ministries in regions which suffer from a lack of clergy, 393; the catechetical commission, 622 §1; a civil act of adoption, 689 §3.

registers *special registers in the archives of the eparchial curia:* for recording sacred ordinations, 774; for recording secret marriages, 840 §3; *parish:* which r. are to be kept, 296 §1; care of the pastor for them, 296 §1; how they are to be kept, 296 §§4–5; care of the protopresbyter for them, 278 §1. 3°and §3; baptismal r. and what is to be recorded in them, 37, 296 §2, 689, 841 §§2–3, 842, 1371; marriage r. and what is to be recorded in them, 798, 841 §§1 and 3, 842, 1371; of the dead and what is to be recorded in them, 879; of pious foundations and what is to be recorded in them, 1051 §2.

rejection of an indult of departure from a monastery in the act of intimation, 493 §1, 549 §3; of a candidate for sacred ordination regarding dimissorial letters, 750 §2; regarding recourse against administrative decrees, 1001 §2. 1°, 1002; of a petition for a counterclaim to be dealt with by a collegiate tribunal, 1085 §1. 1°; regarding recourse in a petition to obtain provision of support for a person, 1163 §2; of an introductory *libellus* of litigation, 1188, 1189; of proof by a judge if a party insists that it be admitted, 1208 §2; is not permitted regarding one who introduces peremptory exceptions after the joinder of issue, 1121 §1; of the conclusions of experts by the judge, 1260 §2; of an incidental case at the outset of litigation, 1269 §1; of

a petitioner to obtain administrative recourse, 1518.

relationship spiritual: impediment to marriage, 811 §1; what it is, among whom and how it arises, 811 §§1–2;

legal r. arising from adoption as a matrimonial impediment, 812; *see* adoption;

of a witness to the parties is to be asked by the judge, 1244;

with someone, to someone or between some things: with the Latin Church, 1; with the Christian faithful of another Church *sui iuris,* 41; with a higher authority of a Church *sui iuris* regarding the Christian faithful residing outside of the territorial boundaries of their own Church *sui iuris,* 193 §1; of the eparchial finance officer to the finance council, 262 §3; between all the disciplines to be dealt with in a seminary, 348 §2; of a novice director to the synaxis, 458 §2.

release from sins: *see* absolution;

from the bond of marriage: *see* dissolution;

from a right: *see* loss;

from the obligation to a former monastery in transfer to another, 488 §1; from a sacred bond in certain institutes of consecrated life, 562 §4, 568 §2; from the partnership of conjugal life in the separation of spouses, 863 §§1 and 3; regarding temporal goods regarding civil law, 1034;

regarding the power to bind and loose in penal law, 1401.

relics forbidden to sell, 888 §1; regarding alienation and restoration, 888 §§2–3, 887 §2.

religion the good of r. to be fostered, 84 §1, 202, 322 §1; care of the pastor for those who have fallen away from the practice of r., 192 §1;

regarding: religious freedom, 586; religious submission, 599, 600; religious formation and education, 620, 628 §2, 783 §1. 1°; teachers of Catholic r., 636 §2; books, newspapers or magazines that are wont to attack or are not in harmony with Catholic r., 660, 665 §1; works of r. in penal law, 1426 §1; delicts against, 1448 §1;

regarding those things which must be religiously preserved or defended, 39, 456 §3, 605, 913; regarding sacraments to be celebrated and received religiously, 667, 839;

a vow is to be fulfilled by the virtue of r., 889 §1;

those who hand over children to be baptized or educated in a non-Catholic r. are to be punished, 1439.

the religious state, 410; of goods regarding the novitiate, 460, 525 §1; of goods regarding a candidate for perpetual profession, 467 §1, 533; obligatory r. of patrimony can be introduced in the statutes of a congregation regarding members in perpetual vows, 534. 3°; of the right to separation by a spouse, 866; of delegated power, 992 §1; of an action, litigation, judicial acts or an appeal, 1143, 1205, 1206, 1232, 1274. 2°, 1317, 1322. 3°, 1475; of a privilege, 1533, 1534.

reparation of damages, 731, 782 §2, 935, 1000 §3, 1005, 1154. 1°, 1160, 1161, 1197, 1335. 4°–5°, 1336, 1403 §1, 1407 §2, 1409 §1. 2°, 1415, 1424 §1, 1483 §1, 1484 §2; *see* damage;

regarding irreparable harm in the execution of a sentence, 1337 §3;

of scandal: 1403 §1, 1407 §2, 1409 §1. 2° and 4°, 1415, 1422 §3, 1424 §1, 1481 §2; *see* scandal.

repayment of a debt, 1028 §2. 4°.

report *of administration regarding:* the finance officer of the patriarchal Church, 122 §§3–4; the administrator of the patriarchal Church, 131; the eparchial administrator, 231 §4; the eparchial finance officer, 232 §4, 262 §4; the administrator of a parish, 299 §3; associations, 582; impediments to receive sacred orders, 762 §1. 7°; the administrator of temporal goods, 1028 §1. 7°, 1031; the executor of a pious will, 1045 §2;

written: on the state of the patriarchal Church made by the patriarch to the Roman Pontiff, 92 §3; of a visitator sent by the patriarch beyond the territorial boundaries of the patriarchal Church, 148 §3; of tellers in the election of bishops, 186 §2; the quinquennial r. of a diocesan bishop, 206–207; quinquennial r. of an exarch, 318; of the rector of a seminary each year about the progress of formation and the state of the seminary, 356 §1; quinquennial r. of the president of a monastic confederation, the superior of a non-confederated monastery *sui iuris*, and a superior general on the state of the institute, 419, 554 §2; on the approval of translations of liturgical books intended for liturgical use in patriarchal or metropolitan Churches *sui iuris*, 657 §2; by experts in a trial, 1256, 1258 §3, 1259 §1, 1262 §2; by a pastor regarding his removal, 1394. 1°.

represent representation of Christ on the part of the Church's pastors, 15 §1; representation of the kingdom of God and the love of God on the part of clerics, 367; representation of the presbyterate in the presbyteral council, 264, 268; representation of different kinds of persons, associations and other initiatives in the pastoral council, 273

§2; representation of the whole order or congregation in the synaxis, 512 §1; all engaged in catechesis r. the Church, 626;

representation of juridic persons: the patriarch and the patriarchal Church, 79; the metropolitan and his province, 133 §2; the metropolitan of a metropolitan Church *sui iuris* and the Church over which he presides, 157 §3; the eparchial bishop and his eparchy, 190; the pastor and his parish, 290 §1; the rector and the seminary, 335 §2; regarding clerics who r. an authority who conferred on them a dignity, 388; in the ecclesiastical and civil forum, 922 §2. 4°, 1066 §2, 1138 §§1 and 3.

reproach "above all r.," 123 §1, 691.

reprobation of opinions which are contrary to the integrity and unity of the faith and good morals, 605;

of a custom, 1507 §2, 6. 2°, 67, 225 §1, 343, 764, 793, 874 §3, 954 §1. 2°, 1031 §1, 1402 §1; *see* custom.

reputation right to a good r. and the prohibition of illegitimate harm to it, 23;

good reputation required in: a candidate for the episcopate, 180. 2°; a procurator for a lawsuit and an advocate, 1141;

unblemished reputation required in: a notary, 253 §2; a judicial vicar and adjunct judicial vicar, 1086 §4; judges, 1087 §3; the promotor of justice and defender of the bond, 1099 §2;

to be safeguarded: by an oath in trials, 1113 §3; in the prior investigation in a penal trial, 1468 §2; in the remission of a penalty, 1422 §3; regarding cases which deal with clerics, 253 §2;

its loss as a reason for the removal of a pastor, 1390. 3°; witnesses concerning it, 1253. 2°; about the death of a spouse, 1383 §2; regarding the delict of calumny, 1452; regarding the false denunciation of any delict, 1454;

see infamy.

request *of a party regarding:* the right of a judge to proceed, 1110 §1; the imposition of a security on the petitioner for the execution of the sentence, 1116; the removal of a procurator or advocate, 1145; the rejection of the introductory *libellus* of a lawsuit, 1189, 1190 §2; the change of the object of controversy, 1196; the interrogation of the parties, 1211; the revocation or reformulation of a decree or interlocutory sentence, 1271; the correction of an error in the text of a sentence, 1299 §1; the execution of a sentence, 1337 §2, 1340 §2;

of a third of the members of the synod of bishops of the patriarchal Church concerning the convocation of the synod, 106 §1. 3°; for a case of the dismissal of a religious member to be handled judicially, 501 §2; for gratuitous legal representation, 1123; regarding witnesses, 1232, 1233 §1, 1251; regarding the discussion of a case, 1288; for the revision of a sentence in the opposition of a third party, 1331 §1;

regarding requests: for ecclesiastical communion made by the patriarch, 76 §2; for confirmation of his election made by the major archbishop, 153 §2; for the ministry of a judge, 1185.

require *if, whenever something requires:* circumstances, 170; the good of the Church, 332 §1; necessity, 671 §; the mission of the Church, 1007; the matter, 1165 §2; the transaction, 1166; the salvation of souls, the needs of the Church or usefulness, 1397.

res iudicata when it takes place, 1322; effects, 1323, 1310. 3°; cases regarding the status of persons never become *r.i.*, 1324; regarding *restitutio in integrum.* 1326 §1 and §2. 5°; with respect to the execution of a sentence, 1337, 1342 §1; in a condemnatory sentence regarding the prescription of an action to execute a penalty, 1153 §1; in a sentence issued in a penal trial regarding the injured party, 1485; its exceptions, 1121 §1; in a sentence on a prejudicial question regarding arbitration, 1177 §2; in an arbitral sentence, 1181 §4, 1182 §2, 1183.

rescinding a juridic act, 932 §2, 933; the canonical provision of an office, 940 §2; an election, 948 §2; an administrative decree, 1004, 1005; acts placed by a judge after an objection for his recusal is lodged, 1109 §2.

rescript notion, 1510 §2. 3°; at what point it takes effect, 1511; when it lacks effect, 1515; regarding the granting of a favor, 1522 §2, 1527 §1; can be requested on behalf of another, 1528; regarding the concealment of truth or statement of falsehood, 1529;

of the Apostolic See on transfer to another Church *sui iuris*, 36; of the Apostolic See or the patriarch regarding its execution in an eparchy, 248 §2; of the Apostolic See or the patriarch on the loss of the clerical state, 394. 3°, 398; of the Apostolic See, the patriarch, or a local hierarch on a dispensation granted in the internal forum, 799.

reservation *to the Roman Pontiff:* of episcopal ordination, 745; regarding dispensation from the obligation of celibacy, 395–397, 795 §1. 1° and §2, 796 §1, 1433 §2, 1538 §2;

to the supreme authority of the Church of the erection, restoration, modification and suppression of a patriarchal Church, 57 §1;

to the Apostolic See: of the removal of an eparchial

administrator, 231 §2; regarding the suppression of a monastic confederation, 440 §§2–3; regarding the goods of a suppressed monastery *sui iuris* or a suppressed monastic confederation, 438 §4, 440 §3; of an indult of departure from a religious institute, 492 §2, 549 §2; of the suppression of an order, 507 §1; of the suppression of the sole house of an order, 510; of the approval of new forms of consecrated life, 571; of the approval of liturgical texts, 657 §1; of absolution from a sin, 728 §1; of dispensation from the required age for sacred ordination by more than a year, 759 §2; of dispensation from certain impediments in matrimonial matters, 795 §2; of dispensation from the form for the celebration of marriage, 835; of the reduction of obligations to celebrate the Divine Liturgy, 1052 §1; of delicts with regard to the prescription of a penal action, 1152 §2. 1°;

to the patriarch: of the removal of an eparchial administrator, 231 §2; of the erection of a stauropegial monastery, 435 §2; of the suppression of a monastery *sui iuris* or a filial monastery, 438 §1; of the approval of the statutes of a monastic confederation, 440 §§2–3; regarding an indult of departure from a monastery, 496 §2; regarding the suppression of the sole house of a congregation, 510; of the approval of liturgical texts, 657 §1; regarding the confection of holy myron, 693; of episcopal ordination, 745; of dispensation from the required age for sacred ordination by more than one year, 759 §2; of dispensation from impediments to receive or exercise sacred orders, 767 §2; of dispensation from the form for the celebration of marriage, 835;

to the metropolitan of a metropolitan Church *sui iuris* of the approval of liturgical texts, 657 §1;

to a metropolitan of episcopal ordination, 745;

to an eparchial bishop: regarding the power of the protosyncellus or syncelli, 248 §1; regarding the dismissal of a religious from temporary vows, 552 §1; of absolution from the sin of abortion, 728 §2; of the consecration of a church, 871 §2;

to the competent authority: of the aggregation of a monastery to a confederation or its separation from one, 440 §1; of the dismissal of a religious from temporary vows, 552 §1;

of absolution from sin: when and with whose consent it may take place, 727; to the Apostolic See regarding the violation of the sacramental seal and the absolution of an accomplice, 728 §1, 1456 §1, 1457; to the eparchial bishop regarding a procured abortion, 728 §2, 1450 §2; when it lacks force, 729;

of the remission of a penalty: regarding the Roman

Pontiff, 1423 §1, 1445 §1; when, how, and by what legislators it may take place, 1423 §1; is to be interpreted strictly, 1423 §2; regarding abstinence from imposing a penalty, 1403 §2;

of dispensation from a law, 1496, 1538 §2; to the administrator of the patriarchal Church of presiding in the interim over the synod of bishops for the election of a patriarch, 70; to the synod of bishops of the patriarchal Church of acts determined by common law, 110 §4; to the permanent synod of the decision about certain matters, 119; to the council of hierarchs, of matters determined by common law, 170; of the homily to a priest or deacon, 614 §4;

of emoluments for the needs of the eparchy, 230. 2°; of a seminary to the students of one Church *sui iuris*, 333; regarding the erection of associations, 574, 575 §1. 1°; of liturgical celebrations to the Christian faithful, 587 §2; regarding an act of orders and impediments to receive or exercise sacred orders, 762 §1. 6°, 763. 2°;

of cases or judicial acts: to the Apostolic See regarding the nullity of marriage, 1359; to some dicastery of the Apostolic See regarding norms to be observed, 1056; to the ordinary tribunal of the patriarchal Church, 1063 §4. 5°; to a collegiate tribunal, 1084 §§1–2, 1085 §2; to the eparchial bishop, 1086 §2.

residence   to acquire domicile or quasi-domicile, 912, 913; determining the proper local hierarch and pastor, 916 §§2–3; regarding subjection to laws, 1491 §1; regarding the power of the local hierarch concerning the prohibition of marriage, 794 §1; regarding dispensations of a local hierarch from matrimonial impediments, 795 §1, 796 §1; of the Christian faithful outside of the territory of the patriarchal Church, 148 §1; of a pastor elsewhere than near the parish church, 292 §1; of a cleric outside of his own eparchy, regarding subjection to the eparchial bishop, 386 §2; of an exclaustrated member, regarding the obligations of the vow of obedience, 491, 548 §2; of a group of novices outside of the novitiate, 522 §2; of a candidate for sacred ordination, regarding testimonial letters, 769 §1. 6°; month long r., or in the case of a transient, actual r., relative to the lawful celebration of marriage, 831 §1. 1°; regarding convocation for an election, 948 §1; actual r. of a transient, regarding the competent forum, 1075 §1; unknown r. with respect to the forum of the petitioner, 1075 §2; determining the forum in cases concerning inheritance or a pious legacy, 1079. 2°; of spouses, regarding deferral to the civil forum in cases of separation, 1378 §2; regarding the hierarch who can remit penalties, 1420 §1. 2°;

prohibition of r. as a penalty, 1429 §1; prescribed r. as a penalty, 1429 §§1–2; imposed or prohibited r. as an administrative remedy while a penal case is pending, 1473;

regarding the see of the patriarch, 57 §3, 65 §1, 93; of bishops of the patriarchal curia at that curia, 87;

obligation of residence: of the patriarch in his see, 93; of bishops in the eparchy, 95 §2, 204 §1, 217; of a pastor in the rectory, 292 §1; of a parochial vicar in the parish, 302 §4; of clerics in the eparchy, 386 §1; of a superior in that superior's monastery, 446;

of the patriarch who has resigned his office, 62, 431 §2. 2°; of an eparchial bishop emeritus, 211 §1, 431 §2. 2°; of a resigned pastor, 297 §2; of the petitioner or petitioner's procurator to be indicated in the introductory *libellus* of litigation, 1187. 3°; right to r. not affected by suspension, 1432 §3.

resignation   *from office:* way an office can be lost, 965 §1; regarding the title "emeritus," 965 §4; ability to resign, 967; when a r. is null by the law itself, 968; what is required for a r. to be valid, 969; when it takes effect, 969, 970 §1; when it may be revoked, 970 §2; its acceptance, 969, 970; the one resigning can obtain the same office by some other title, 971;

from office regarding: the Roman Pontiff, 44 §2; the patriarch, 62, 126; a bishop, 104 §1, 165 §1; an eparchial bishop, 210, 211 §1, 219; a coadjutor or auxiliary bishop, 218; an eparchial administrator, 231 §§1 and 3; an eparchial finance officer, 232 §2; a protosyncellus or syncellus, 251 §1; a pastor, 297, 1391 §1, 1392, 1393 §2; superiors in monasteries, 444 §3; the president, judges, promotor of justice and defenders of the bond of the ordinary tribunal of the patriarchal Church, 1063 §2.

resources   regarding the obligation to support the poor, 25 §2; *see* income.

respondent   general norm, 1134; petitioner follows forum of r., 1073 §3; regarding multiple forums, 1073 §3; regarding the forum in cases to declare the nullity of marriage, 1359. 2°–4°; to be dismissed as absolved if the right of the petitioner is not established, 1291 §4;

regarding: introductory *libellus* of litigation, 1187. 4°, 1345 §1; citation, 1082, 1190–1194; safeguarding the rights of the r., 1116; presence or absence in a trial, 1135, 1136 §3, 1272, 1273, 1275; renunciation of the acts of a process, 1205 §1; institution of a counterclaim, 1156 §1; text of the sentence, 1295 §1; nullity of the sentence, 1303 §1. 4°; appeal, 1318 §§1–2; exceptions of the r. in the summary contentious trial, 1346;

the sanctifying function: of the pastor, 289 §2; of sacred ministers, 743.

satisfaction in the sacrament of penance, 718; appropriate s. for injury or calumny, 1452;

regarding: pastoral functions, 95 §2; obligations, 278 §1. 2°, 1021 §3, 1048 §2; a petition, 315 §1.

scandal *as a reason:* for the expulsion of a religious or member of a society of common life according to the manner of religious, 498 §1, 551, 562 §3; for the dismissal of a member in temporary vows, 552 §2. 2°; for remedies imposed by the eparchial bishop regarding associations, 577 §2; for the cessation of the obligation to preserve secrecy about a secret marriage, 840 §2; for the denial of an ecclesiastical funeral, 877;

to be avoided in: cremation, 876 §3; the notification of acts or proofs, 1113 §3; witnesses meeting together, 1241 §2;

to be repaired after a delict, 1403 §1, 1407 §2, 1409 §1. 2° and 4°, 1415, 1422 §3, 1424 §1, 1481 §2; regarding an attempted delict, 1418 §§2–3; in a delict of a cleric against chastity, 1453 §1; how it may be prevented in a penal trial, 1473.

schism as a delict to be punished, 1437;

disqualifications regarding: reception into associations, 580; reception or exercise of a sacred order, 762 §1. 2°, 763. 2°, 767 §1. 2° and §§2–3; casting a vote, 953 §1. 3°; *see* major excommunication;

is a reason by the law itself for: removal from office, 976 §1. 2°; dismissal from an association, 580.

school right of the Church to erect and moderate them, 631 §2; the Christian faithful should support the initiatives of the Church in erecting, directing and supporting them, 630 §2; when a s. is juridically considered "Catholic," 632; the Catholic s. is to be fostered with special care, 631 §1; obligations of the eparchial bishop for them, 633 §1, 635, 636, 637, 638; parents should send their children to Catholic schools, 633 §2; purposes of Catholic schools, 634; regarding catechetical formation, 636 §1, 658 §1; regarding the appointment, approval or removal of teachers of the Catholic religion, 636 §2; in which schools Catholic formation is to be provided, 637; to whom the right of canonical visitation over them belongs, 638; what is required in s. teachers, 639; regarding shows sponsored by schools, 665 §2; regarding ecumenism, 906, 907; the pastor is to visit them, 289 §3; to be animated with the spirit of the gospel, 329 §1. 1°; permission required to open a s. in a religious house, 437 §2, 509 §2; schools are to be constituted in missionary territories, 592 §1.

sciences connected with divine revelation regarding the purposes of ecclesiastical universities and faculties, 646, 647. 1°, 648;

sacred sciences, regarding: the purposes of ecclesiastical universities and faculties, 648; the just freedom of those engaged in them, 21; meetings of clerics to foster them, 278 §2. 1°, 372 §2; seminary teachers, 340 §3, 351; the obligation of clerics to engage in them, 372 §1; the rights of lay persons, 404 §§2–3; their principles to be recognized and applied in pastoral care, 602; theologians, 606 §1;

sacred science required in: a candidate for the episcopacy, 180. 6°, the protosyncellus and syncellus, 247 §2; *see* doctorate, licentiate;

human s. in the formation of seminary students, 349 §1; profane s. not to be neglected by clerics, 372 §3; regarding institutes of religious studies, 404 §2; novices are not to devote time to their study, 459 §2, 525 §1; cooperation of those engaged in theological disciplines with people who excel in other s., 606 §3; their principles to be recognized and applied in pastoral care, 602;

regarding the freedom of scientific investigation in Catholic universities, 641.

scrutineer *see* teller.

scrutiny *see* ballot.

seal of the gift of the Holy Spirit in chrismation with holy myron, 692;

sacramental: inviolability, 733 §1; danger of violation to be avoided, 729. 2°; penalties against violators, 1456 §1; absolution from the sin of its direct violation is reserved to the Apostolic See, 728 §1. 1°;

regarding the delict of one who has attempted to gain information from a confession or has given such information to others, 1456 §1;

parish, 296 §3.

secrecy *regarding:* ballots, 71 §2, 182 §3, 186 §2; the nullity of a ballot, 954 §1. 2°; the outcome of an election, 73, 149, 185 §1; the list of candidates for the episcopacy, 168, 182 §3; intimation of the election, 184 §1, 185 §2; election of bishops by letter, 186 §2; acts and business transacted in the synod of bishops of the patriarchal Church, 111 §2; votes in the permanent synod, 118; information or testimonies regarding persons, 182 §1, 366 §1. 3°; those who exercise offices in the eparchial curia, 244 §2. 2°; voting on the dismissal of a religious, 500 §1; the interpreter and all others to whom knowledge comes from the confession of sins, 733 §2; renewal of matrimonial consent, 845 §2, 846

Christian community for vocations, 329 §1; to gain all people for the kingdom of God, 346 §1;

of the eparchial bishop: toward the Christian faithful entrusted to his care, 192 §1; toward presbyters, 192 §4; regarding the share in it which the coadjutor and auxiliary bishops have, 215 §4; for catechetical formation, 623 §1;

daily s. of the pastor, 293; of superiors for members who are illegitimately absent from their own house, 495, 550; of theologians to build up the community of faith, 606 §2; of parents, teachers and the ecclesial community for schools, 631 §1; of experts in using the instruments of social communication regarding collaboration with bishops, 651 §2; of a spouse for the good of the family in not refusing to pardon an adulterous partner, 863 §1;

of clerics: for the whole Church, 361; for vocations, 380; regarding all Churches, 393;

regarding: the inventory of the documents of the archives of the eparchial curia, 256 §2.

son *Christ:* of the Holy ever-Virgin Mary, 369 §1; invocation in the formula of baptism, 675 §1.

souls regarding zeal for s. in a candidate for the episcopacy, 180. 1°; seminary students are to be formed to respond in the service of s. everywhere in the world, 352 §3; regarding harm to s. resulting from the departure of a cleric from an eparchy, 452 §1;

regarding: pastors of s., 655 §2, 738, 783 §1, 785 §1, 816; care of s., 238 §1. 6°, 281 §1, 288, 611, 628 §2, 735 §1; *see* care of souls; salvation of s., 595 §2, 727, 873 §2, 1000 §2, 1110 §1, 1397, 1519 §1; *see* salvation (of souls);

Sacred Scripture is to be, as it were, the soul of all theology, 350 §2.

spirit *of the gospel:* with which the actions of lay persons should be imbued, 402; regarding the notion of a secular institute, 563 §1. 2°; of a Catholic school, 634 §1;

of prayer, poverty, universal, truly Christian in the formation of seminary students, 346 §2. 6° and 8°, 350 §3, 352 §3; of the poverty of Christ with which clerics must be imbued, 385 §1; lacking in religious s. as a reason for the dismissal of a member in temporary vows, 552 §2. 2°; of Christ with which the use of the instruments of social communication must be imbued, 651 §2; regarding exhortation about the life of the s., 346 §2. 6°; regarding discernment of spirits in the formation of seminary students, 346 §2. 8°.

spiritual needs of the Christian faithful, 15 §2, 193 §2; goods of the Church, 16, 381 §2; life, 17, 192 §4,

346 §2, 350 §1, 376, 1542. 3°; ritual patrimony, 28 §1, 405; good of the Christian faithful, 82 §1. 2°, 148 §3, 1536 §2, 1538 §1; good of people, 1007; purpose, 203 §3, 936 §1; resources, 278 §2. 2°; assistance, 278 §3, 816; nourishment, 289 §2; state of the exarchy, 318 §1; formation, 330 §3, 345; discretion, 385 §1; renewal of the Christian people, 615; help to be given to young people in universities, 645; harm to be avoided, 665 §3; usefulness, 671 §2; effects of sacramentals, 867 §1; assistance for the departed prayed for in funerals, 875; preparation for reception into the Catholic Church, 897; assistance for non-Catholic Christians, 907; works of charity, 1047 §1. 1°; cases of minors, 1136 §3; *see* father (spiritual), relationship (spiritual), retreat (spiritual), spiritual direction.

spiritual direction in a seminary, 339 §1, 344 §2, 346 §2. 4°; clerics are to attach great importance to it, 369 §2.

spiritual exercises (CIC) *see* retreat.

spirituality missionary, by which missionaries must be formed, 589.

sponsor there must be at least one, 684 §1; function, 618, 684 §2; qualifications, 685 §§1–2; appointment, 686 §2; what is to be done in the absence of a s., 688; recording of the s. in the baptismal register, 689 §1; regarding the impediment of spiritual relationship, 811; a non-Catholic can be admitted together with a Catholic s., 685 §3.

sponsorship regarding shows conducted under the s. of a pastor, rector of a church or moderator of a Catholic school, 665 §2.

spouse united by God after the pattern of Christ's indefectible union with the Church, 776 §2; matrimony ordered to the good of the s., 776 §; 1; equal rights and obligations of s. concerning the partnership of conjugal life, 777; their obligations between themselves and towards their children, 783 §1. 1°, 618, 627 §1, 633 §2; *see* parents; obligation to work for the building up of the people of God through marriage and the family, 407; preparation for marriage, 783 §§1–2; obligation of the local hierarch and other pastors of souls to furnish assistance in the partnership of conjugal and family life, 783 §3, 816; obligation of keeping the secret in a secret marriage, 840 §1; regarding the recording of the names of s. in marriage and baptismal registers, 841;

rights regarding the accusation of marriage, 1360. 1°, 1381; obligation of the judge regarding the restoration of the partnership of conjugal life, 1362, 1381; cases for separation, 863–866, 1324, 1378–1382; petition for the dissolution of a sacramental non-consummated marriage, 1367, 1384;

regarding the dissolution of the matrimonial bond, 856 §1, 860; presumed death of a s., 1383 §§1–2 and 3; when exempted from testifying in a trial, 1229 §2. 2°;

regarding: domicile or quasi-domicile, 914; transfer to another Church *sui iuris*, 33, 34; impediment of crime, 807, 795 §1. 3° and §2; prescripts concerning feast days and days of penance, if ascribed to different Churches *sui iuris*, 883 §2; affinity, 919; admission to sacred orders, 758 §3, 769 §1. 2°;

clerical: care of the eparchial bishop for his family, 192 §5; care of the protopresbyter for his spiritual and material necessities, 278 §3; regarding the office of pastor, 285 §2; regarding formation in a seminary, 352 §1; his state is to be held in honor, 373; must shine forth with the splendor of chastity, 374; must furnish an outstanding example of family life and of raising children, 375; right to support, pension, social security and health insurance for his family, 390, 1410;

during the marriage, cannot validly be admitted to a novitiate, 450. 6°; regarding the function of sponsor, 685 §1. 5°.

state (**nation**)   heads of s. have the right to be judged by the Roman Pontiff alone, 1060 §1. 3°; when s. officials are exempt from the obligation to respond in a trial, 1229 §2. 1°; regarding those who enjoy the favor of law in their s. to be questioned by a judge in a place selected by themselves, 1239 §2.

status, state   *of persons:* with respect to apostolic initiatives to be fostered, 19; right to freedom from any coercion in choosing a state of life, 22; whatever diminishes its free choice is to be avoided, 344 §1; right to a copy of a document from the eparchial curia about it, 257 §2; canonical s. regarding notation in parish registers and testimonies regarding it, 296 §§2–3; regarding the marriage register, 784, 1372 §2; of life regarding the ministry of the word of God, 608; matrimonial s. in preparation for marriage, 783 §1; actions concerning it are never extinguished, 1150; its change regarding the suspension of a trial, 1199; cases regarding it never become *res iudicata*, 1177 §2, 1324, 1325 §1;

clerical: *see* clerical state;

of married clerics is to be held in honor, 373;

economic s. of a juridic person, 1038 §1;

religious: notion, 410; to be fostered and promoted by all, 411; monastic s. regarding full freedom to choose, 453 §2; the religious or monastic s. is definitively assumed by perpetual profession, 462

§1, 531; care of superiors about attaining its purpose, 421; obligation of religious to strive for its perfection, 426; its observance required in a novice director, 524 §1; societies of common life according to the manner of religious imitate its manner of life, 554 §1;

of a stauropegial monastery, 486 §1;

of clerics or lay persons in secular institutes, 563 §1. 4°;

of the patriarchal Church in the report made by the patriarch to the Roman Pontiff, 92 §3; of the eparchy and of the Christian faithful ascribed to another Church *sui iuris* in the quinquennial report of the eparchial bishop, 206 §1, 207; spiritual and temporal s. of the exarchy in the quinquennial report of the exarch, 318; of a seminary in the report of the seminary rector, 356 §1; of the institutes over which they preside in the quinquennial report of the president of a monastic confederation, the superior of a non-confederated monastery *sui iuris* and a superior general, 419 §1, 554 §2;

of a trial, 1059 §1, 1118 §1, 1120, 1205 §1, 1276 §3, 1473, 1482.

statutes   included in the term "particular law," 1493 §2;

personal: *see* personal statutes;

of a juridic person, 922, 925, 927 §2, 929, 930, 1024 §2, 1036 §1. 3°; of the synod of bishops of the patriarchal Church, 113; of the patriarchal assembly, 143 §1. 6°, 145; of the council of hierarchs, 171; of the presbyteral council, 265, 266. 2°, 267 §2, 268, 270 §1; of the pastoral council, 274 §1; of the assembly of hierarchs of several Church *sui iuris*, 322 §§1 and 4; of an institute which is equivalent to a minor seminary, 331 §1; of a seminary, 335 §2, 337, 338 §2, 342 §1; of religious institutes, 410; of a monastic confederation, 439 §§1–2, 441 §3, 500 §1; of an order or congregation, 414 §1. 1°–2° and §3, 420 §1, 421, 422 §1, 423, 424, 426, 430, 431 §2. 2°, 432, 500 §§1–3, 508 §§2–3, 511, 512, 513 §1, 514, 515 §§1–2, 516 §3, 518–520, 523 §2, 524 §§1 and 3, 526, 527. 2° and 4°, 528, 534. 3°, 535 §1, 536, 537 §1, 538 §§1–2, 539 §2, 540, 541, 543, 545 §2, 550, 552 §§1–2, 578 §3, 662 §2, 724 §2, 1036 §1. 3°, 1069 §1; of a society of common life according to the manner of religious, 554 §1, 557, 558 §3, 559, 560 §1, 561, 562 §2, 1036 §1. 3°, 1069 §1; of a secular institute, 563 §1. 1° and 3°, 566, 568, 1036 §1. 3°; regarding new forms of consecrated life, 571; of an association, 573 §2, 576 §1, 578 §1, 581, 582; of an ecclesiastical university, 650; of a foundation, 306 §2, 309, 638 §2, 1053; of a tribunal, 1070, 1099 §1, 1285 §3, 1335.

1487 §§1 and 3; revocation of an administrative act by a contrary law, 1513 §1; granting a favor which had been denied, 1530; abuse of a power given by a privilege, 1535; the liceity of a dispensation, 1536 §1;

forum regarding those who have no s. a. below the Roman Pontiff, 1061, 1064 §2.

superior of an institute of consecrated life   the Roman Pontiff is the supreme, 412 §1, 431 §2. 1°, 555, 564;

the local hierarch or patriarch is not included under this term, 418 §2;

major: who are, 418 §1; if possesses ordinary power of governance the s. is a hierarch, but not a local hierarch, 984 §3; requirements in orders and congregations, 513 §1; when consultation is required, 89 §2, 114 §2, 385 §3; when consent is required, 89 §§2–3, 282 §1; regarding the agreement to erect a parish in a church of the institute, 282 §2; report of the rector of a seminary to him, 356 §1; is to visit the seminary frequently to look after the formation of his students, 356 §2; regarding the canonical visitation of houses, 420 §§1 and 3; regarding merely honorary titles, 430; regarding the moderation of preaching, 612 §1; grants members permission to publish writings about the Catholic faith or morals, 662 §2; when he may forbid a deacon advancement to the presbyterate, 755; regarding the prohibition to exercise a sacred order by one who refuses to receive a higher sacred order, 757; it to be given the declaration required for ordination to the diaconate or presbyterate, 761; the testimony of the reception of the order is to be shown to him, 774 §2; to what pastor he is to send notice of ordination to the diaconate, 775; regarding dispensation from private vows, 893 §1. 3°; regarding trials, 1069, 1102 §1, 1340 §3; who may issue a decree by which a penalty is imposed, 1402 §3; in monasteries *sui iuris*, orders or congregations: *see below;*

the president of a monastic confederation is a major superior, 418 §1; *see* confederation of monasteries;

regarding: the notion of the religious state, 410; power, 414 §1. 2°, 431 §2. 1°; 441 §§1–2, 511, 995, 996; consent to the convocation of members to the patriarchal assembly, 143 §1. 6°; the convocation of superiors to the eparchial assembly, 238 §1. 9°; testimony regarding the admission of certain people to seminary, 342 §3; exhortation to ministries in missions or areas suffering from a shortage of clergy, 393; consent for the eparchial bishop to entrust works or functions proper to

the eparchy to religious, 415 §3; neglect about members who have committed a delict outside of the house, 415 §4; their assembly, 416; failure to take care of abuses, 417; care for members, 421; their permanent council, 422; the obligation of striving for perfection, 426; letters of religious, 429; consent for a religious to be promoted to a dignity or office outside of the institute, 431 §1; consent for members to join an association, 578 §3; preaching, 612 §2; the administration of the sacrament of penance, 722 §4, 723 §2, 724 §2; testimonial letters about candidates for sacred ordination, 769 §1. 4° and 6°; dispensation from private vows, 893 §1. 1° and 3°; forum, 1063 §4. 4°, 1069; permission for members validly to exercise the function of arbiter, 1172. 3°; execution of a sentence, 1340 §2; command to reside in a certain place or territory, 1429 §2;

of a monastery regarding: the constitution of the s., 444 §2, 445; power, 441 §1; resignation from office, 444 §3; obligation to reside in the monastery, 446; office of finance officer, 447 §§1–2; debts and obligations of a member, 468 §2; the divine praises, Divine Liturgy, spiritual fathers and confessors, spiritual retreats, 473 §2, 475 §1; cloister, 477 §1; absence of members from the monastery, 478; catechetical formation to be given to the people, 479; hermits, 483, 484; members who have abandoned the monastery, 495;

of a monastery sui iuris: is a major s., 418 §1; power, 441 §§1–2; requirements, 442; election, 443; constituted for what term, 444 §1; is to be convoked to the patriarchal and eparchial assembly, 143 §1. 3°, 238 §1. 9°; regarding the quinquennial report, 419; to be consulted regarding the suppression of a monastery by the patriarch, 438 §1; regarding the suppression of a subsidiary monastery, 438 §3; appoints the finance officer, 447 §3; regarding the novitiate, 450. 5°, 453 §§1–2, 456 §§2–3, 458 §2, 461 §1; regarding the profession of members, 464. 2°, 470; can give dimissorial letters for his members, 472; regarding the designation of confessors by the local hierarch, 475 §1; how the boundaries of the cloister may be determined or changed, 477 §3; regarding hermits, 482, 485; regarding transfer of members to another institute of consecrated life, 487 §§3 and 5, 488 §2, 544 §§1–2, 545 §1; with regard to an indult of exclaustration, departure from the monastery, expulsion or dismissal of members, 489 §1, 490, 491, 492 §1, 496, 497 §2, 498 §§1–2, 499, 500 §1, 501 §4;

in orders and congregations: requirements, 513 §1; their constitution, 513 §1, 514, 515 §2; regarding finance officers, 516 §§1–2; regarding the novice di-

outside of the territorial boundaries of the patriarchal Church, 149; statutes, 113; decisions of an assembly of hierarchs of several Churches *sui iuris* cannot be prejudicial to it, 322 §2; with respect to administrative power, 110 §4, 150 §2; is assisted by the patriarchal assembly, 140; decides controversies regarding the translation of a metropolitan or bishop to another see, 85 §2. 2°; determines the order of substitution for members of the permanent synod who are impeded, 115 §3; while it is in session the competence of the permanent synod does not cease, 119; regarding the election of two bishops who take the place of the permanent synod along with the patriarch in certain cases, 121; regarding the goods of the patriarchal Church, 122 §4; regarding the expenses of the patriarchal curia, 125; can accept the resignation of the patriarch, 126 §2; determines times for the convocation of the metropolitan synod, 133 §1. 2°; issues petitions to the Roman Pontiff about the territorial boundaries of the patriarchal Church, 146 §2; discusses the care of the Christian faithful outside of the territorial boundaries of the patriarchal Church, 148 §3; determines topics to be discussed in the patriarchal assembly and approves its statutes, 144 §1, 145; takes care for the support of a bishop emeritus, 211 §2; establishes and changes the program for the formation of clerics, 330 §1; can elect religious to certain offices, 431 §1; the commission for missionary activity assists it, 585 §2; regarding care for the unity and integrity of the faith and for good morals, 605, 652 §2; regarding the catechetical directory and catechisms, 621 §§1 and 3; can establish prohibitions regarding the instruments of social communication, 652 §2; regarding censors of books, 664 §1; judges regarding the grave necessity for the administration of certain sacraments to non-Catholics, 671 §§4–5; establishes norms for the distribution of the Divine Eucharist by those who are not priests or deacons, 709 §2; can change the norms for the curriculum of studies for deacons, 760 §1; regarding the minimum and maximum sum determined by it for the alienations of goods, 1036 §§1 and 3, 1037; its competence as the supreme tribunal of the patriarchal Church, 110 §2, 1062; removes the president, judges, promotor of justice and defenders of the bond of the ordinary tribunal of the patriarchal Church, 1063 §2; can erect a tribunal of the first grade for several eparchies, 1067 §2; can reserve the remission of penalties to the patriarch, 1423 §1;

its consent required for: the transfer of the see for the residence of the patriarch, 57 §3; the erection,

alteration, and suppression of provinces or eparchies, 85 §1; the constitution of a coadjutor or auxiliary bishop, 85 §2. 1°; the translation of a metropolitan or bishop, 85 §2. 2°; entering into agreements with the civil authority, 98; its own translation, prorogation, suspension or dissolution, 108 §1; the erection of a seminary common to several eparchies, 334 §1; granting the loss of the clerical state, 397; the suppression of a confederation of monasteries *sui iuris*, 440 §2; the erection of a Catholic or ecclesiastical university, 642 §2, 649; the approval of liturgical texts and their translations, 657 §§1–2; the reservation of sins, 727; the reception into the Catholic Church of a bishop of an Eastern non-Catholic Church, 898 §1; the suppression of a juridic person not erected by the patriarch, with certain exceptions, 928. 1°; certain alienations of temporal goods, 1036 §3, 1037. 3°;

its consent regarding the convocation of the patriarchal assembly other than at the prescribed time, 141;

when it should be heard by the patriarch, 82 §3, 148 §3.

T

talents *of young people:* of students in seminary to be fostered, 344 §2, 352 §1; in the formation of religious to be developed, 471 §1, 536 §1.

tax *for the seminary:* 341 §1, 1012; which houses of religious are not subject to it, 341 §2, 471 §2, 536 §2;

for the good of the eparchy: right of the eparchial bishop to impose it, 1012 §1; no t. can be imposed on offerings received on the occasion of the celebration of the Divine Liturgy, 1012 §1; can be imposed on physical persons only according to the norm of particular law of the Church *sui iuris*, 1012 §2.

teachers seminary students are to be instructed in the light of Christ the Teacher, 347; religious follow Christ the teacher of holiness, 410;

of faith: bishops, 600; to be obeyed, 15 §1;

in the Church's magisterium: the Roman Pontiff is the supreme teacher of all of the Christian faithful, 597 §1; bishops are t. of faith and morals, 597 §2, 600;

in seminaries: necessity and qualities, 332 §2, 340 §1; obligations, 340 §§2–3, 351; remuneration, 337 §1; are to follow the footsteps of the holy fathers and doctors highly praised by the Church, especially of the East, to illustrate doctrine from the treasure handed down by them, 340 §3;

proof, with certain exceptions, 1254; regarding expenses incurred by witnesses, 1252.

thanksgiving in the Divine Liturgy, 698.

theologians their function, 606 §§1–2; are to strive to cooperate with persons who excel in other sciences, 606 §3.

theology Sacred Scripture is, as it were, the soul of t., 350 §2; how the theological disciplines are to be treated in a seminary, 350 §1; ecumenism is one of the necessary dimensions of every theological discipline, 350 §4; courses in t. in a seminary, 348, 349 §2, 353; regarding faculties of t., 143 §1. 4°, 643, *see* faculty; regarding the curriculum of studies required for the diaconate, 760; regarding ritual patrimony, 28 §1, 405, *see* rite.

threat of dismissal to be given in warnings for the dismissal of a member in perpetual vows, 500 §2. 2°; 553;
of penalties: by precept, 1406 §1; by warning, by which a law is pressed, 1406 §2; an administrative act concerning a t. receives a strict interpretation, 1512 §2.

three years of studies in the formation of deacons not destined for the priesthood, 354; novitiate in monasteries, 457 §§1 and 3; regarding the indult of exclaustration, 489 §2; minimum time for temporary profession, 526 §2, 545 §2; regarding the extinction of a penal action in general, 1152 §2.

tie vote regarding voting in the third and fourth ballot in the election of bishops, 183 §4; regarding collegial acts to be broken by the vote of the one presiding, 924. 1°.

time continuous, 1544 §1; useful, 1544 §2; how a month and year are to be computed if continuous, 1545 §2; regarding the computation of the day to which a calculation is directed, 1546 §2; regarding the obligation of laws, *see* suspensive period; required for a custom to obtain the force of law, 1507 §§1 and 3–4; time limits, *see* time limits; regarding the cessation of a privilege, 1532 §2. 3°; required for prescription regarding good faith throughout the entire course, 1541;
regarding: acquired rights and privileges granted by the Apostolic See, 5; the divine message of salvation, 14; the equality of patriarchs by reason of patriarchal dignity, 59 §1; canonical visitation by the patriarch for a serious reason, 83 §2; urgent matters, 100, 551, 720 §2. 1°–2°, 797 §2; designation of bishops who substitute for impeded members of the permanent synod, 115 §3; courses in a seminary, 348 §1; formation of novices, 459;

celebration of the Divine Liturgy or reception of the Divine Eucharist, 700 §2, 707 §1, 708; fast and penance, 719; absolution of several penitents at the same time, 720 §2. 1°–2°, 721 §1; administration of the anointing of the sick, 738, 740; testimonial letters about a candidate for sacred ordination, 769 §1. 6°; the celebration of marriage, 781. 2°, 803 §2, 838 §2; prohibition of marriage in a special case, 794 §1; provision for the support of one removed from an office, 977; collection of the return of goods and income, 1028 §1. 3°; payment of a loan, 1028 §1. 4°; treatment of certain exceptions, 1121 §2; resignation from office by a pastor in the process for removal, 1391 §1, 1393 §1;

vacation, 292 §2, 302 §4, 392; brief absence of a coadjutor or auxiliary bishop from the eparchy, 217; prohibited use of knowledge of sins acquired from confession at any t., 734 §2; regarding the cessation of a vow, 891; regarding the acceptance of obligations to celebrate the Divine Liturgy, 1052 §4; suitable t. for repentance to be given to an offender in the warning before a penalty, 1407 §1; more opportune t. regarding a delay in the imposition of a penalty, 1409 §1. 1°; its necessities, circumstances, culture, conditions, signs, progress, 46 §1, 137, 203 §2, 347, 352 §1, 471 §1, 576 §1, 601, 635, 785 §1, 1532 §1. 4°; present t., 345; regarding the service to be furnished to the people of their own time, 347; suitable t., 144 §2, 182 §2, 233 §1, 240 §§2–3, 296 §4, 615, 738; absence of a cleric for a notable t. from the eparchy, 386 §1; residence of a cleric in another eparchy for more than a brief t., 386 §2;

time established for: convocation of the synod of bishops of the patriarchal Church, 65 §2, 106 §2; the pastoral visitation of the patriarch, 83 §1; promulgation of the laws of the synod of bishops of the patriarchal Church, 111 §1; convocation of the permanent synod, 120; convocation of the metropolitan synod, 133 §1. 2°, 138; a new election for major archbishop after confirmation of election has been refused by the Roman Pontiff, 153 §4; convocation of the council of hierarchs, 159. 2°, 170; appointment of the eparchial finance officer, 133 §1. 6°, 138, 139, 159. 7°; appointment or election of the eparchial administrator, 226; appointment of members of the college of eparchial consultors, 271 §4; convocation of an assembly of hierarchs of several Churches *sui iuris*, 322 §1; meetings to be promoted with religious superiors, 416; convocation of a group for elections, 948 §1; postulation, 963 §2; loss of delegated power, 992; the function of tribunal officials, 1070;

determined time for: provision of an office, 943 §2;

property of a debtor, 1159 §2;

of the Code indicated in the canons, 400, 996, 1471 §1;

regarding: a titular metropolitan, 85 §2. 2°, 136; titular bishops, 85 §2. 2°, 102 §2, 143 §1. 2°, 179, 1062 §3, *see* titular bishop.

titular bishop   notion, 179; regarding his translation to another see by the patriarch, 85 §2. 2°; his deliberative vote in the synod of bishops of the patriarchal Church can be restricted, 102 §2; attends the patriarchal assembly, 143 §1. 2°; by whom he is to be judged, 1062 §3; *see* bishop.

topics   *to be treated in:* the patriarchal assembly, 144 §1; in the eparchial assembly, 240 §§1–3; *see* questions;

abstruse t. to be laid aside in preaching, 616 §1; of discussion about which witnesses are to be questioned, 1233 §2.

regarding the t. of the economy of salvation to be taught in a seminary, 350 §2; the more important t. of seminary discipline, 337 §2.

torture   of a person is to be punished, 1451.

trade   forbidden to clerics, religious and members of societies of common life according to the manner of religious, 385 §2, 427, 554 §3; penalties for violation of these canons, 1466.

tradition   sacred t., by which the ministry of the word of God must be nourished, 607; which comes down from the Apostles through the Fathers shines forth in the rites of the Eastern Churches, 39; the rites dealt with in this Code arose from the Alexandrian, Antiochene, Armenian, Chaldean and Constantinopolitan traditions, 28 §2;

of the whole Church: most ancient t. regarding the patriarchal institution, 55; about the celibacy of clerics, 373;

of the Eastern Churches: on chrismation with holy myron, 694; on engagement, 782 §1; faithfulness towards them in the ecumenical movement, 903; about penalties, among which some work of religion, piety or charity may be imposed, 1426 §1;

of the proper Church sui iuris to be observed: in determining solemnities on which an eparchial bishop is not to be absent from his eparchy, 204 §3; in the formation of clerics, 330 §3, 346 §2. 6°, 354; in the catechetical directory, 621 §2; regarding the obligation to receive the Divine Eucharist, 708;

of monastic life to be observed in monasteries, 433 §1.

transient (*vagus*)   who is, 911; is obliged to all laws in force in the place where he or she is, 1491 §4; who is the proper local hierarch and pastor, 916 §3; regarding the licit celebration of marriage, 789. 1°, 831 §1. 1°; has a forum in the place where he or she actually resides, 1075 §1.

transfer   *to another Church sui iuris:* inducement to t. forbidden, 31, 1465; cannot validly take place without the consent of the Apostolic See, 32 §1; when the consent of the Apostolic See may be presumed, 32 §2; regarding the right of the woman at the time of the celebration of marriage or during the marriage, 33; regarding parents and their children, 34; from what moment it takes effect, 34; recording it, 37;

of a cleric to another eparchy: requirements for its validity, 359; when it is not to be denied, 361; requirements for its liceity, 365;

of a member of an institute of consecrated life to another institute: regarding admission into the novitiate, 450. 7°; to another monastery, 487; from a monastery *sui iuris* to an order or congregation, 488 §3, 544, 545 §§1–2; to another order or congregation or from them to a monastery *sui iuris,* 544–545; from a society of common life according to the manner of religious to another society of that kind or to a religious institute, 562 §§1–2; regarding the consent of the competent authority, 487 §§1–4, 544 §§1–3, 562 §1; if it takes place to an institute of another Church *sui iuris* the consent of the Apostolic See is required for validity, 487 §4, 544 §4, 562 §1; when it takes effect, 487 §5, 545 §2, 562; regarding the rights, obligations, novitiate or profession of the one transferring, 488 §§1–2 and 4, 545, 562 §2;

of the ordinary power of the patriarch or of the metropolitan of a metropolitan Church *sui iuris* to the administrator of the patriarchal Church or of the metropolitan Church *sui iuris,* 130 §1, 173 §1. 2°; of the ordinary power of the eparchial bishop to the patriarch during a vacancy of the eparchial see, 220. 2°; of the governance of the eparchy while the eparchial see is vacant, 221. 2°; of the governance of the exarchy while it is vacant, 320 §1; forbidden t. to a new marriage, 789. 5°; to a non-Catholic Church of ecclesial community, 789. 6°; of the habitual faculty of a hierarch to one who succeeds him in governance, 982 §2; of a sentence to *res iudicata,* 1153 §1, 1177 §2, 1181 §4, 1182 §2, 1183, 1310. 3°, 1326 §§1 and 2. 5°, 1337, 1485, *see* res iudicata;

of an ecumenical council, 51 §1; of the synod of bishops of the patriarchal Church, 108 §1; of the

triarchal Church and its competence, 1062 §§1–3, 1066 §2; regarding the right of the general moderator of for the administration of justice to exercise vigilance over tribunals, 1062 §5; the ordinary t. of the patriarchal Church, 114 §1, 1063, 1067 §5; the metropolitan t., 133 §1. 3°, 138, 139, 159. 3°, 175, 1064; the eparchial t., 1066 §1, 1069 §2, 1086 §2; for several eparchies of the same Church *sui iuris,* 1067; a common t. constituted by the eparchial bishops of different Churches *sui iuris,* 1068; regarding physical or juridical persons of institutes of consecrated life, with the exception of secular institutes, 1069; designated for appeals by certain tribunals, 1067 §5; of appeal or higher, 1062 §4, 1063 §3, 1064 §2, 1065, 1066 §2, 1067 §5, 1068 §4, 1083 §§1–2, 1119 §3, 1145, 1181 §2, 1188 §4, 1280, 1313, 1315 §2, 1317 §2, 1325, 1327 §2, 1331 §1, 1340 §2, 1355, 1368, *see* appeal;

regarding: competence, 1058, 1060, 1062 §§1 and 3, 1063 §§3–4, 1064, 1066, 1067 §§1 and 4, 1068 §1, 1069, 1072–1083, 1155, 1188 §2. 1°, 1194. 2°, 1359; statutes, 1070, 1099 §1, 1285 §3, 1335; location, 1127, 1239 §1; chancery, 1181 §1, 1225, 1281 §1, 1345 §1; right to call on assistance from another t., 1071; rights of the authority to which it is immediately subject, 1141, 1146 §1, 1163 §2; appointment of the promotor of justice or defender of the bond, 1099 §1; taking or recusal of officials, 1102, 1107 §§1 and 3; obligations of officials, 1111, 1112, 1113 §§1–2, 1114, 1115 §2; prorogation of time limits, 1126; those to be admitted to court, 1129 §1; reverence and obedience due to it, 1129 §2; obligations of the advocate or procurator, 1141, 1142 §1, 1146 §2; legal representatives, 1148; arbitration, 1174, 1175, 1176 §3, 1181 §§1–2; witnesses, 1233 §1, 1239 §§1 and 3; incidental cases, 1270 §2, 1271; defence briefs and observations, 1285 §§1 and 3; oral discussion, 1287 §2; correction of an error in the text of the sentence, 1299 §1; defects of irremediable nullity in a sentence, 1303 §1. 2°; opposition of a third party, 1331, 1333; the execution of the sentence, 1340 §2; the summary contentious trial, 1345 §1, 1347 §2, 1355, 1356; cases for the declaration of the nullity of marriage, 1359, 1367, 1368, 1369, 1373 §1, 1374; cases for the separation of spouses, 1379 §2, 1380; cases for the declaration of the nullity of sacred ordination, 1386 §§1–2; the promotor of justice or experts in a penal trial, 1472 §2, 1477 §2; the sentence in a penal trial, 1479, 1480.

truth Christ is, 616 §1; the Divine Name is invoked as a witness to the t. in an oath, 895;

revealed t. regarding the teaching function of the Church, 595 §1; of the faith to be proposed by the eparchial bishop in preaching, 196 §1; theological t. regarding the function of theologians, 606 §2;

of divine revelation is systematically to be structures and analyzed in ecclesiastical universities, 647. 1°; instruction in the truths of the faith required for the baptism of one no longer and infant, 682 §1; those things to be believed with divine and Catholic faith regarding the delict of heresy or apostasy, 1436 §1;

the pastor must bear witness to the truth to all, 293; regarding formation in seminaries, 347, 348 §2; a religious must respond to the visiting superior according to it, 420 §2;

in a trial: how it is to be elicited by the judge, 1211; a party must tell the whole t., 1212 ; the oath to tell the t. or regarding the t. of things said, 1213, 1243 §2; the obligation of witnesses to tell the t., 1229 §1; things heard on the occasion of sacramental confession cannot be received even as indications of the t., 1231 §2. 2°.

two years to be dedicated to philosophical studies in the formation of clerics, 348 §1.

typicon of a monastery *sui iuris,* 433 §2, 436 §1; by whom it is approved, 414 §1. 1° and §2, 433 §2, 486 §2; regarding dispensations, 414 §1. 2° and §2, 486 §2; life in the monastery to be organized according to it, 421, 426, 430, 431 §2. 2°, 432, 437 §1, 473 §1, 474, 476, 477 §1, 578 §3; regarding the designation, power and obligations of superiors, 422 §1, 438 §3, 441 §1, 442, 443 §1, 444 §§1–2, 446, 447 §3, 472, 473 §2, 478, 662 §2, 724 §2; regarding the constitution of the superior's council, 422 §1; regarding its norms for the novitiate, 449, 450, 453 §3, 454, 455, 458, 459 §1, 461; regarding its norms for monastic profession, 462 §2, 463, 464. 4°, 465; how the manner of the formation of monks should be determined in it, 471 §1; hermits are obligated by it, 484; regarding transfer to another monastery, 488 §2; with regard to the dismissal of a member in perpetual vows, 500 §§1–2; regarding temporal goods, 423, 424, 1036 §1. 3°; regarding trials, 1069 §1, 1340 §3.

U

union spouses are united by God after the pattern of Christ's indefectible u. with the Church, 776 §2; between churches is to be manifested in concelebration between bishops and presbyters of different Churches *sui iuris,* 701;

of provinces and eparchies in patriarchal Churches, 85 §1; of a part of the territory of a juridic person to another juridic person, 929;

regarding the permission of a hierarch to bless the marriage of one who is bound by natural obligations toward a third party and children from a previous u., 789. 3°;

eparchial bishops of several Churches *sui iuris* in the same territory are foster united action, 84 §1, 202.

unity *of the faith:* it belongs to bishops, but in a unique way to the Apostolic See, to promote it authoritatively, 605; of the Catholic faith is affirmed in the variety of rites, 39; to be safeguarded firmly by the eparchial bishop, 196 §2; seminary teachers are to aim at the u. of faith among the varieties of disciplines, 340 §2; care of the Church's pastors lest it suffer harm, 604;

of the whole Church to be safeguarded by the eparchial bishop, 201 §1;

of Christians: solicitude for it belongs to the whole Church, 902; regarding the special function of the Eastern Churches, 903; to be kept in mind by hierarchs in the observance of rites, 40 §1; to be fostered by eparchial bishops gathered in councils, 84 §1; the eparchial bishop is to care for it in a special manner that it may be fostered by the Christian faithful entrusted to his care, 192 §2; regarding theological disciplines, 350 §4;

of the charity of Christ, in which the Christian faithful form one body, 197; of the people of god is signified and perfected in the Divine Liturgy, 698; of the priesthood and of the sacrifice is properly manifested in concelebration, 700 §2;

of the seminary is to be fostered by the rector, 338 §2; to be fostered by clerics among all people, 384 §1; the synaxis must be the sign of the u. of the whole order or congregation, 512 §1; of the partnership of conjugal and family life to be cared for by local hierarchs and other pastors of souls regarding mixed marriages, 816;

as an essential property of marriage, 776 §3, 822;

of action: of the college of bishops dispersed throughout the world, 50 §2; to be fostered by patriarchs, metropolitans, eparchial bishops, and local hierarchs gathered in councils, 84 §1, 202, 322 §1; among lay persons of different Churches *sui iuris* to be fostered in the variety of rites, 405.

universal Church *see* Church.

university *Catholic:* its notion and erection, 642; purpose, 640 §1; what institutes of study are equivalent to it, 640 §2; method of dealing with each discipline, 641; regarding theological courses if there is no faculty of theology, 643; mandate to teach in disciplines having to do with faith and morals, 644, 642; regarding residences and university centers, 645; their rectors are to be summoned to the patriarchal assembly, 143 §1. 4°; re-

garding the cooperation of theologians with persons who excel in other sciences, 606 §3;

ecclesiastical: notion, 648; to be promoted, 646; erection or approval, 649, 642; purpose, 647; regarding statutes, 650; their rectors are to be summoned to the patriarchal assembly, 143 §1. 4°; the right of lay persons to attend them and receive academic degrees, 404 §2; regarding the cooperation of theologians with persons who excel in other sciences, 606 §3.

use *of reason:* sufficient, so that one is bound by merely ecclesiastical law, 1490; regarding those capable of making a vow, 889 §2;

one lacking the use of reason: equivalent to infants, 909 §3; cannot validly celebrate marriage, 818. 1°; regarding baptism, 681 §§3–4; one gravely ill is presumed to wish to receive the sacrament of the anointing of the sick, 740; is incapable of making a vow, 889 §2; how such a person may stand trial, 1136 §§1–3;

regarding acquired rights and privileges granted by the Apostolic See, 5;

of the sacred sciences to be acquired by clerics, 372 §1; how the u. of a Catholic building or cemetery or church can be granted to non-Catholics by the eparchial bishop, 670 §2; prohibited u. of knowledge acquired from confession, 734 §1; when a church may be reduced to profane but not sordid u., 873; profane u. of sacred things is prohibited unless they have lost their dedication or blessing, 1018, 1441; of technical devices for voice reproduction can be admitted in a trial, 1248 §2; of the rectory regarding a pastor who has been removed and is ill, 1396 §2; common u. of language, according to which an administrative act is to be understood, 1512 §1; regarding the cessation of a privilege, 1532 §2. 4°; 1534;

of the instruments of social communication: to be imbued with the spirit of Christ, 651 §2; how the Christian faithful are to be educated about it, 652; what things are to be determined about it in particular law, 653; regarding copies of the Sacred Scriptures with notes appropriate for the u. of non-Christians, 655 §2; regarding editions or translations of the Sacred Scriptures intended for liturgical or catechetical u., 655 §3; regarding books of prayers or devotions intended for private u., 656 §2; regarding translations or new editions of liturgical books intended for liturgical u., 657 §§2–3; regarding delicts, 1448 §1;

of goods: regarding the right of the Church, 1007; clerics are to put their goods to correct u., 385 §1; in the typicon or statutes norms are to be established concerning the u. of goods to foster, express and protect the poverty of religious, 424; regarding a religious who becomes patriarch, bishop or exarch, 431 §3. 1°–2°; to be freely ceded by a religious before temporary profession, 525 §2, 465; regarding the penalty if legitimate u. is impeded, 1447 §2;

regarding the conversion of a monastery or religious house to other uses, 437 §3, 509 §2;

of exemptions from exercising public functions or military service with regard to clerics, 383. 3°; of the assistance of a superior's council, 422 §1; of freedom, 402, 606 §1; of the pauline privilege, 858; of a language unknown to the judge or the parties, 1130; of the assistance of experts, 1255, 1366; of preceptive language in penal law, 1409 §1; of a false or altered document regarding penalties, 1455; regarding the power of a judge in a penal trial, 1481 §1.

usurpation of an office, ministry or function is to be punished, 1462.

V

vacancy of the Roman or Apostolic See, 47, 53; of a particular see, 65 §2, 126–131, 142 §2; of a metropolitan see within the territorial boundaries of the patriarchal Church, 80. 3°; of the metropolitan see in metropolitan Churches *sui iuris*, 173 §§1 and 3; of the eparchial see, 129, 173 §3, 181 §1, 219–232, 234 §1, 237 §2, 251 §2, 260 §2, 262 §5, 270 §2, 271 §5, 274 §2, 286, 363. 2°, 537 §2, 1088 §2; of an exarchy, 320; of a parish, 285 §3, 298–300, 1399 §§2–3; of an office, 529 §6, 941, 943 §§1–2, 944, 947, 973 §1; of a tribunal, 1126.

vacation regarding the absence of a coadjutor or auxiliary bishop from the eparchy, 217;

right to a time for vacation: of clerics, 392; of a pastor, 292 §2; of a parochial vicar, 302 §4.

validity *see* invalidity, individual entries;

regarding the sacraments: in general, 669, 995; baptism, 672 §2, 676, 901; chrismation with holy myron, 672 §2, 696 §§1–2; of the Eucharist, 671 §2; of penance, 671 §2, 722 §§3–4, 725; of the anointing of the sick, 671 §2, 739 ; of sacred ordination, 394, 672 §2, 744, 754, 1385, 1386 §1; of marriage, 762 §1. 3°, 776 §2, 779, 781, 785 §1, 789, 790 §1, 800–812, 826, 828 §1, 829 §§1–2, 830 §3, 832 §§1–2, 833 §1, 834 §2, 837, 847, 852, 855 §1, 919 §1, 1361 §1, 1363 §3; of the radical sanation of a marriage, 849 §1, 850 §2, 851 §1; of the convalidation of a marriage, 843 §2, *see* convalidation of marriage;

regarding: resignation from office by the Roman Pontiff, 44 §2; transfer to another Church *sui iuris*, 32 §1; the enthronement of a patriarch or major archbishop, 75, 153 §3; the exercise of power by the patriarch, 77 §1, 78 §2; the canonicity of the synod of bishops of the patriarchal Church or the council of hierarchs, 107 §1, 166 §1; the office of patriarchal finance officer, 122 §1; the exercise of power by the metropolitan or council of hierarchs, 157 §2; the promulgation of the laws of the council of hierarchs, 167 §2; the assent of the Roman Pontiff to candidates for the episcopacy, 182 §4; the election or appointment of the eparchial administrator, 227 §2; the resignation of the eparchial administrator, 231 21; the college of eparchial consultors restored by no new member, 271 §3; the incompatibility of the office of pastor with a juridic person, 281 §2; the statutes of an assembly of hierarchs of several Churches *sui iuris*, 322 §4; the erection of a seminary if the seminary is to be held in common, 334 §2; ascription of a cleric to an eparchy or transfer to another, 359, 363, 364; change in the statutes of a congregation, 414 §3; erection of a dependent monastery, 436 §2; admission into the novitiate, 450, 517 §1; the novitiate, 456 §2, 457 §§1–2, 464. 1°, 522 §1, 523 §1, 527. 1°; the goods of a novice, 460; religious profession, 464, 466, 523 §2, 527, 529 §1, 532, 533; transfer to a religious institute of another Church *sui iuris*, 487 §4, 544 §4; the consent of the eparchial bishop for the erection or an association in a house of a religious institute, 575 §2; an indult of departure from an order or congregation, 546 §2; the dismissal of a religious, 500 §§1–2, 553; the erection or suppression of a house of an order or congregation, 509 §1, 510; the office of superior in an order or congregation, 513; reception into associations, 580; permission to publish books, approval, praise or blessing of a work, 663 §1; the function of sponsor, 685 §1; the alienation or translation of relics, icons or images, 888 §2; voting and ballots, 107, 166 §1, 186 §1, 949 §1, 1085 §1; elections, 221. 3°–4°, 227 §2, 948 §2, 953 §2; dispensations from impediments, 768, 797 §2; interpellations, 856 §2; the power of governance of a non-Catholic bishop received into the Catholic Church, 899; delegation or subdelegation of power, 985 §§2–3, 988 §§3–4; the acts of a juridic person, 931–933, 934 §§1–2, 1432 §3; convocation of electors, 948 §1; resignation, 969, 1205 §3; an act placed with delegated power after the time period has expired or the number of cases has been exhausted, 992 §2; acts which exceed the limits or manner of ordinary administration,

1024 §1; acceptance of a non-autonomous foundation, 1048 §2; offices, 938, 940 §2; the erection of a collegial eparchial tribunal where a common tribunal has been erected, 1067 §3; decisions of a collegiate tribunal, 1085 §§1–2; substitution of judges, 1090 §2; a case to be adjudicated by those who have already taken part in it, 1105; the act of a recused judge, 1109 §2; counterclaims, 1122 §1; restriction of time periods in a trial, 1124 §§1–2; those things which a procurator cannot do without a special mandate, 1143; the procurator's mandate, 1372 §1; an out of court settlement, 1165 §1; arbitration, 1169, 1171. 1°, 1172, 1179 §2, 1181 §3; removal of pastors, 1391 §1, 1394; reservation of the remission of a penalty, 1423 §1; remission of a penalty, 1425; continuation of a dignity, office, ministry, function or pension by someone punished with a major excommunication, 1434 §3; the decree by which a penalty is imposed, 1486 §1; conditions attached to administrative acts, 1516, 1523; rescripts, 1528, 1529 §1; granting a favor previously denied by some authority, 1530; resignation of a privilege, 1533 §3; dispensations, 1536 §§1 and 3; prescription, 1541;

in civil law regarding: the testament of a religious, 530; ways to safeguard the goods of the Church, 1020 §2; guarantees for the goods of the Church, 1027; alienations, 1040;

the norms of the Code regarding: the major archbishop and the major archiepiscopal Church, 152; exarchs and exarchies, 313; ascription of clerics to other institutes than an eparchy, 357 §2; orders and congregations, 509 §2, 525 §1, 533, 549 §3, 551; societies of common life according to the manner of religious, 556; writings and messages intended for public distribution, 654; the administration of sacraments to non-Catholics, 671 §3; a woman who before receiving baptism in the Catholic Church had several husbands at the same time, 859 ; removal from office, 975 §1; the power of religious and the faculties which are required for the valid celebration or administration of sacraments, 995; the interlocutory sentence, 1296; penalties imposed by particular law or a penal precept, 1420 §2; custom, 1509; favors granted orally, 1527 §1; *see* norms, statutes;

regarding: the perennially valid philosophical patrimony, 349 §1; catechists as valid cooperators with the sacred ministers, 591. 2°.

various churches care for the same sense of faith to be preserved in them, 604; *see* Church *sui iuris,* eparchy.

verification of the authenticity and integrity of the mandate of the executor of an administrative act, 1521.

vicar the Roman Pontiff is the v. of Christ, 43; the eparchial bishop governs the eparchy as the v. of Christ, 178;

judicial vicar: function, 191 §2, 1086 §§1–2, 1090, 1091 §1; belongs to the eparchial curia, 243 §2; requirements, 1086 §4; appointment, 1086 §1, 1088 §§1 and 3; term of office, 1088 §1; remains in office during a vacancy of the eparchial see, 1088 §2; attends the eparchial assembly, 238 §1. 2°; regarding arbitration, 1181 §§1–3; regarding matrimonial cases, 1359. 3°–4°, 1371, 1372 §1;

adjunct judicial vicar: function, 1086 §3, 1091 §1; requirements, 1086 §4; appointment, 1086 §3, 1088 §1; term of office, 1088 §1; remains in office during a vacancy of the eparchial see, 1088 §2;

parochial vicar: is a presbyter assigned to the pastor for the pastoral care of a parish, 301 §1; appointment, 301 §3, 284 §2; cessation from office, 303, 1391 §2; rights and obligations, 290 §2, 301 §2, 302, 739 §2; while the parish is vacant or the pastor is impeded, 300; is to be heard in the appointment of the protopresbyter, 277 §1;

cannot be instituted for the entire patriarchal or metropolitan Church *sui iuris,* 78 §1, 157 §1;

of the superior of religious, 418 §1.

vicar forane (CIC) *see* protopresbyter.

vicar general (CIC) *see* protosyncellus.

vicarious power of the protosyncellus, 245; ordinary v. p. of governance, 981 §2; *see* power.

vice-chancellor can be given as an assistant to the chancellor of the eparchial curia, 252 §2; is a notary of the eparchial curia by the law itself, 252 §3;

regarding substitutes for the chancellor in the patriarchal curia, 123 §2; *see* substitute.

vice president in the patriarchal assembly, 142 §1.

vices exercises in the novitiate to root out v., 459 §1.

vigil of solemnities regarding the celebration of the divine praises in parishes, 199 §2; of Sunday or feast days regarding the obligation to participate in the Divine Liturgy or the divine praises, 881 §2.

vigilance *of the patriarch:* over clerics, 89 §1; in the administration of goods, 97;

of the metropolitan, that faith and ecclesiastical discipline be carefully observed, 133 §1. 4°, 138, 139, 159. 4°, 175;

of the eparchial bishop: in the liturgical life of the eparchy, 199 §1; lest abuses creep into ecclesiastical discipline, 201 §2; over all associations exercising activity in his territory, 577 §2; over catechetical formation, 636 §1; over the administration of all goods within the territory of the eparchy, 1022 §1;

of the local hierarch: special v. over dowries, 454; over the reservation of the Divine Eucharist, 714 §2; over institutes for insurance, social security and health benefits for clerics, 1021 §2;

of the eparchial finance officer over the administration of goods in the whole eparchy, 262 §3; of the ecclesiastical authority that erected or approved an association over that association, 577 §1, 582; of an administrator that the goods entrusted to his or her care not be lost or damaged, 1028 §2. 1°; of a hierarch that pious wills be carried out, 1045 §2, 1046 §2; of the general moderator for the administration of justice over all tribunals within the territorial boundaries of the patriarchal Church, 1062 §5;

as a canonical penalty, 1428.

vindication of the rights of physical of juridic persons as the object of a trial, 1055 §1. 1°; legitimate v. of rights in the ecclesiastical forum belongs to all the Christian faithful, 24 §1; of the right to religious freedom to be preserved by all, 586; of the right of the Church to publish writings everywhere, 651 §1; of rights regarding the reduction of a church to profane use, 873 §2; of the rights of the Church over temporal goods, 1040;

of the proper, ordinary and immediate power of eparchial bishops through the power of the Roman Pontiff over all eparchies, 45 §1;

of the name "Catholic" by no initiative without the consent of the competent authority, 19;

regarding forbidden agreements about a share of the object under litigation, 1146 §1.

violation of the right to safeguard one's privacy, 23; of secrecy, 1115 §1, 1227 §1; of certain prescripts regarding arbitration, 1171. 3°; of the obligations of the pastor, 1390. 4°; of a penal law or a penal precept, 1414; of the norms of law about *communicatio in sacris*, 1440; regarding the sacramental seal, 728 §1. 1°, 729. 2°, 733 §1, 1456 §1; of obligations imposed by a penalty, 1267.

virgins consecrated v. living apart in the world and professing chastity by a public vow can be constituted by particular law, 570.

virtue by v. of baptism and chrismation with holy myron the Christian faithful participate in the sacrifice of Christ, 699 §3;

of religion, by which a vow must be fulfilled, 889 §1;

virtues: required in a pastor, 285 §1; to be cultivated in seminary students, 346 §2. 7°–8°; to be acquired by novices, 459 §1, 525 §1; Christian virtues in the education of young men, 629.

visit, visitation the right of v. is not subject to prescription, 1542. 7°;

to Rome: of the patriarch, 92 §3; of the metropolitan of a metropolitan Church *sui iuris*, 163; quinquennial v. of an eparchial bishop, 163, 208; quinquennial v. of an exarch, 317;

pastoral v. of an eparchy by the patriarch, 83 §1;

canonical visitation: of a church, city, or eparchy done by the patriarch for a grave reason, 83 §2; of the eparchy, 83, 133 §1. 5°, 138, 139, 159. 5°, 175, 205, 296 §4, 414 §1. 3°, 415 §2; of the patriarch regarding religious institutes or societies of common life according to the manner of religious, 414 §1. 3° and §2, 554 §2; of the eparchial bishop regarding religious institutes or societies of common life according to the manner of religious, 205 §3, 414 §1. 3°, 415 §2, 420 §3, 554 §2; of schools by the eparchial bishop, 638; of religious houses by superiors, 420, 524 §3;

of the Christian faithful outside of the territorial boundaries of the patriarchal Church by a visitator sent by the patriarch, 148 §3; of schools by the pastor, 289; of a seminary by the eparchial bishop or superior regarding his students, 356 §2; of members who are ill by the superior, 421; regarding pious wills, 1045 §2.

visitator sent by the patriarch to the Christian faithful beyond the territorial boundaries of the patriarchal Church, 148; regarding religious institutes, 420 §1; how religious are to act with the v., 420 §2; regarding the function of novice director, 524 §3.

vocation of the Christian faithful to fulfill the mission of the Church in the world, 7 §1; Christian v. in the world to be fostered by associations, 18; of the Christian faithful to a life in keeping with the teaching of the gospel, 20; priestly, diaconal, monastic, missionary vocations and vocations to institutes of consecrated life to be fostered by the eparchial bishop, 195; of each one to holiness, 197; of minor clerics, 327; vocations to be fostered, particularly to the sacred ministry, by the whole Christian community, by parents, teachers, educators of Christian life, clerics, pastors, eparchial bishops, 329 §1; works to foster vocations to be provided for by particular law, 329 §2; regarding formation in a seminary, 331, 346 §2. 6° and 8°; obligation of clerics with respect to vocations to the sacred ministry and to life in institutes of consecrated life, 380; proper v. of lay persons, 401, 407; missionary vocations to be inspired and supported by the Christian faithful, 585 §4; vocations to the sacred ministry to be fostered among neophytes by missionaries, 591. 1°; of the penitent to holiness to be cared for by the confessor, 732 §2.

voice *active:* whoever lacks it is unqualified to vote, 953 §1. 2°; in the election of the Patriarch, 66 §1;

active and passive: in a presbyteral council, 267; relative to religious who become Patriarch, bishop or exarch, 431 §2; exclaustrated member lacks it, 491, 548 §2; member in temporary vows lacks it, unless it is otherwise provided in the statutes, 528, 465; one punished by major excommunication lacks it, 1434 §3;

concerning the use of technical devices for voice reproduction, 1248 §2;

the granting of favors done orally are governed by the canons on rescripts, 1527 §1.

voluntary military service, 383. 2°; homicide as an impediment to receive or exercise sacred orders, 762 §1. 4°, 763. 2°, 766, 767 §1. 2°, 768 §§1–2; emendation of a decree, 998 §1.

vote, voting of the presiding officer to break a tie, 924. 1°;

in elections: to whom the right of casting a v. belongs, 949 §1; of the sick in the house where an election takes place, 949 §2; no one can cast more than one, 950; no one who does not belong to the group can be admitted to the v., 951; those disqualified from casting a v., 953 §1; when an election is null, if someone disqualified from casting a v. is permitted to, 953 §2; when it is null, 954 §1; conditions placed on a v. before an election are considered not to have been placed, 954 §2; regarding the function of tellers, 955 §2; if their number is not equal to the number of electors, the voting is without effect, 955 §3; how a tie v. after the third ballot is to be resolved, 956 §1;

in postulation, 961, 962;

in the synod of bishops of the patriarchal Church: regarding the election of the patriarch, 72 §1; in other matters, 102 §2, 105, 107 §2; regarding the election of bishops, 183 §§3–4; regarding the constitution of the tribunal of the synod, 1062 §2;

by letter in the election of bishops in the patriarchal Church, 186; in the permanent synod when it should be kept secret, 118; in the council of hierarchs, 164 §2, 165 §§2–3, 166 §2; of the college of eparchial consultors in the election of the eparchial administrator, 221. 3°; in the eparchial

assembly, 238 §2, 241; in the assembly of hierarchs of several Churches *sui iuris,* 322 §§2–3; in the elective synaxis, 445; secrecy regarding the dismissal of members from perpetual vows, 500 §1;

of judges in a collegiate tribunal: regarding the validity of decisions, 1085 §1; regarding secrecy regarding it, 1113 §2;

regarding an arbitral sentence, 1179 §1;

deliberative: of bishops in an ecumenical council, 52 §1; of titular bishops in certain matters can be restricted in the synod of bishops of the patriarchal Church, 102 §2; in the council of hierarchs, 164 §2, 165 §2, 166 §2; in the assembly of hierarchs of several Churches *sui iuris,* 322 §2;

consultative: of the eparchial assembly, 241; of the finance council, 263 §4.

vow *as a promise to God:* concept, 889 §1; who can make a v., 889 §2; for what reasons it is null, 889 §3; public or private, 889 §4; whom it binds, 890; regarding the dispensation of a private v., 893; suspension of, 892, 894; when a v. ceases, 891;

religious: see profession (religious); public vows of obedience, chastity and poverty, 410, 462 §1, 504, 526 §1; instruction for vows, 459 §1; to be kept faithfully, 426; regarding subjection to the Roman Pontiff, 412 §1, 431 §2. 1°; public perpetual v. of chastity as an impediment to marriage, 795 §1. 2° and §2, 805; regarding the impediment to receive or exercise sacred orders, 762 §1. 3°, 763. 2°, 767 §1. 2°; regarding delicts against chastity, 1453 §3;

religious vows remain: in someone who becomes patriarch, bishop, exarch or pastor, 431 §2. 1°, 543; during the novitiate after transfer to another institute, 545 §1, 488 §2; in an exclaustrated member, 491, 548 §2;

perpetual religious vows: see profession (perpetual religious); acts contrary to these are invalid, 466; indult of departure from an institute includes dispensation from them, 493 §1, 549 §3; regarding a member in perpetual vows, 428, 472, 489 §1, 492 §1, 494 §1, 500 §1, 528, 534. 2°, 537 §1, 545 §2, 549 §1, 553; *see* member;

temporary religious vows: see profession (temporary religious); acts contrary to these are illicit, but not invalid, 529 §1; indult of departure from an institute includes dispensation from these, 546 §2, 465; regarding a member in temporary vows, 528, 529 §§3–5, 545 §2, 488 §3, 546 §1, 547, 552 §1; *see* member;

institutes of consecrated life without vows, 554 §1, 563 §1. 1° and 3°, 572;

relative to alienation of property given to the Church by v., 1036 §§3–4, 1037. 3°.

W

warning to whom it pertains to issue a w. about those things which can endanger the integrity and unity of the faith and good morals, 605;

of the patriarch to: a metropolitan who has not appointed an eparchial finance officer, 80. 4°; a hierarch who has not punished an offending cleric, 89 §1; an eparchial bishop who has gravely offended in some matter, 95 §2;

to an eparchial bishop who has not named a finance officer, 133 §1. 6°, 138, 139, 159. 7°, 175, 175;to a negligent superior regarding a religious who has committed a delict outside of the house, abuses which have crept into the houses of the institute, or failure to make a canonical visitation, 415 §4, 417, 420 §3; to a religious before dismissal from an institute, 500 §2. 2°–4°, 552 §2. 2°, 553; on the part of a judge to those who have been lacking in due reverence and obedience to the tribunal, 1129 §2; to a pastor regarding causes for removal, 1390. 4°; to one abusing a privilege, 1535;

regarding: time limits to respond to the interpellations in a pauline privilege case, 856 §1; one who is to be baptized who is no longer an infant, that he or she is to have sorrow for personal sins, 682 §1; the obligations of heirs to fulfill the will of a testator, 1043 §2; certain obligations of parties in a sentence concerning the nullity of marriage, 1377;

obligatory w. before imposing a penalty, if the nature of the delict permits, 1407 §1; penal w., with a threat of penalties, 1406 §2, 1407 §3, 1414 §2;

regarding delicts: of heresy and apostasy, 1436 §1; of affirming erroneous doctrine, 1436 §2; of schism, 1437; of omission of the commemoration of a hierarch in the Divine Liturgy and in the divine praises, 1438; of disobedience, 1446.

water in baptism, 675 §1.

week its juridical computation, 1545 §1, 1546 §2;

regarding the absence of a pastor from his parish, 292 §2; judged are not to defer a decision more than a w. if they have not arrived at a sentence in the first discussion, 1292 §5.

whole Church 12 §2, 39, 43, 45 §§1–2, 46 §2, 47, 49, 50 §§1 and 3, 92 §§1 and 3, 208 §1, 329, 352 §3, 373, 412 §2; *see church.*

widows consecrated w. living apart in the world and professing chastity by a public vow can be constituted by particular law, 570.

wife good morals are required in the w. of a married presbyter who is a candidate for the office of pastor, 285 §2; her consent is required for her husband to be admitted to sacred ordination, 769 §1. 2°; regarding a man who before the reception of baptism in the Catholic Church had several unbaptized wives at the same time, 859 §1; *see* spouse, woman.

will pious, of donors, of founders, of benefactors: *see* pious will;

submission of w. to be given to doctrine regarding faith and morals, 599;

explicit w. of catechumens to be incorporated into the Church, 9 §1; joint w. of parents regarding the ascription of a child to a Church *sui iuris*, 29 §1; regarding the obligation of a protosyncellus and syncelli not to act against the w. of the eparchial bishop, 249; joint w. of a pastor and parochial vicar regarding care of the parish, 302 §3; of a cleric about ascription to a new eparchy after a move, 360 §2; to receive baptism required to baptize one who is no longer an infant, 682 §1; regarding matrimonial consent, 817 §1, 822, 824 §2, 844; of non-Catholics with regard to ecclesiastical funerals, 876 §1.

wine natural uncorrupt w. from the fruit of the grape in the Divine Liturgy, 706.

withdrawal of a habitual faculty granted to a hierarch does not take place when the authority of the one to whom it was granted expires, with certain exceptions, 982 §2.

witness invocation of the Divine Name as a w. of the truth in an oath, 895;

clerics are witnesses of higher goods, 385 ; lay persons are witnesses to Christ, 401; persons are to be formed in a Catholic university to bear w. to their faith in the world, 641; the baptized become more apt witnesses to the reign of Christ by chrismation with holy myron, 692;

regarding: the declaration of transfer to another Church *sui iuris*, 36; the enthronement of a bishop, 189 §2; the celebration of baptism, 688, 689 §1; the recording of the names of the parents of a child born to an unwed mother in the baptismal register, 689 §2; the proof of the reception of baptism, 691; the celebration of marriage, 828 §1, 832 §§1 and 3, 840 §1, 841 §§1 and 3; resignation from office, 969; public rebuke, 1427 §1; the intimation of a decree, 1520 §2;

in trials: who participated in a case cannot adjudicate as a judge or act as assessor in the same case in another grade, 1105; when a w. may be obliged to observe secrecy, 1113 §3; regarding signing the acts, 1132; how a w. is to be heard if the w. refuses to appear before the judge to testify, 1209; canons on the questioning of witnesses to be observed also concerning the interrogation of the parties, 1215; proof by witnesses is always admitted, 1228; regarding the obligation to tell the truth, 1229 §1, 1243 §1; regarding those who fear serious evils will befall them from their testimony, 1229 §2. 2°; who may be witnesses, 1230, 1231; their introduction, exclusion, citation, obligation to be present, 1232–1238, 1257; their interrogation, 1239–1242, 1244–1251, 1349 §2, 1350, 1351, 1364 §1. 1° and §2; regarding oaths, 1243, 1249; their indemnification, 1252, 1335. 2°; regarding the evaluation and credibility of testimony, 1253, 1254; when a w. may be admitted after the conclusion of a case, 1283 §1; in a summary contentious trial, 1349 §2, 1350, 1351; in cases to declare the nullity of marriage, 1364 §1. 1°, 1365; in the procedure regarding the presumed death of a spouse, 1383 §2; their freedom to be protected in a penal trial, 1473.

woman   her right with respect to the ascription to the Church *sui iuris* of her husband at the celebration of marriage or during the marriage, 33; one who attempts marriage with a w. joined in a valid union or bound by a public perpetual vow of chastity is impeded from receiving or exercising sacred orders, 762 §1. 3°, 763. 2°, 767 §1. 2°; regarding the notion of marriage, 776 §1; cannot celebrate marriage validly before the completion of her fourteenth year, 800 §1; regarding the impediment of impotence, 801 §1; regarding the impediment of public propriety, 810 §2; regarding matrimonial consent, 817 §1, 819; unbaptized w. who has several husbands at the same time, after she has received baptism in the Catholic Church, can keep one of them, 859 §1.

word   *what is meant by the word:* Apostolic See or Holy See, 48; vice-chancellor, 252 §2; adjunct judicial vicar, 1086 §3; lay persons, 399; common law, 1493 §1; particular law, 1493 §2.

work   in employment of workers the civil law is to be meticulously observed concerning labor and social policy, 1030. 1°; preachers of the word of God are to teach the doctrine of the Church regarding the meaning of justice to be pursued in economic life and w., 616 §2; strength for apostolic w. is to be drawn from the word of God and the sacraments, 346 §2; regarding illness contract-

ed on account of w. in a religious institute, 547 §2.

workers   care of the pastor for them, 289 §3.

works   *of the apostolate:* obligation of the Christian faithful regarding them, 25 §1, 289 §3; to be coordinated and fostered under the direction of the eparchial bishop, 203 §1; regarding formation in a minor seminary, 331 §1; clerics are to devote their goods to them, 385 §1; regarding religious, 415 §§1 and 3, 416; and of ministry and teaching regarding formation in ecclesiastical universities, 647. 2°; as a purpose for the temporal goods of the Church, 1007; pious foundations can be destined for them, 1047 §1. 1°;

of piety as a destination for a pious foundation, 1047; pastoral w. with respect to the presbyteral and pastoral councils, 264, 272; of social justice regarding cooperation with non-Catholics, 908; common w. in the same territory to be assisted with combined resources by patriarchs, eparchial bishops and local hierarchs, 84 §1, 202, 322 §1; of evangelization regarding young Churches, 590;

of charity: obligation of the Christian faithful regarding them, 10, 25 §1; clerics are to devote their goods to them, 385 §1; as a purpose for associations, movements and groups of the Christian faithful, 620; cooperation with non-Catholics in them, 908; as a purpose for the temporal goods of the Church, 1007; pious foundations can be destined for them, 1047 §1;

ecumenical, 902, 905; *see* ecumenism;

to foster vocations: to be encouraged by the whole Christian community, 329 §1; to be instituted by particular law in all Churches, 329 §2;

about preparatory w. for participation in the Divine Eucharist, the norms of the proper Church *sui iuris* are to be observed, 713 §2; of penance imposed by a confessor, 732 §1;

pious w. proper to a religious institute, regarding the right to carry them out in monasteries and houses, 437 §1, 509 §2; novices are not to be assigned to w. outside of the monastery during the time of the novitiate, 459 §2, 525 §1; which w. are legitimately assumed by a monastery, regarding the formation of members, 471 §1; a member who leaves a religious institute legitimately can request nothing from it for any w. done in it, 503 §1, 553;

regarding the licit admission into the novitiate of parents whose w. are necessary to raise and educate their children, 452 §2, 517 §1;

from what w. the Christian faithful are to abstain

on Sundays and feasts of obligation, 881 §4;

intellectual works of an author: under the protection of the law, 666 §1; significance of ecclesiastical permission or approval regarding it, 661 §§1–2; what it means if it is blessed or praised by the eparchial bishop or a higher authority, 661 §3; the permission to publish it or its approval, praise, or blessing is valid for the original text, but not for new editions or translations, 663 §1; regarding reasons which the hierarch must communicate with the author in case permission to publish them is denied, 664 §3;

grave work of religion or piety or charity imposed as a penance, 1426 §1;

regarding the employment of workers, 1030. 1°.

world lay persons living in the w. have a special mission, 399; renunciation of the w. in the religious state, 410; the place where the hermit lives is to be separated in a special manner from the w., 483; regarding virgins and widows in the w. publicly professing chastity, 570.

worship of God and the Saints, 201 §2; of the Holy ever-Virgin Mary and of the other Saints, 884–885; regarding the veneration of sacred icons, images and relics, 886–888; the eparchial bishop's function regarding w., 199 §1, 201 §2, 415 §1, 554 §2; the right of the Christian faithful to celebrate according to the prescripts of their own Church *sui iuris*, 17; abstinence from those things which impede w. on feast days of obligation, 881 §4; a church is the building exclusively dedicated to w., 869; regarding a church, which can no longer be used for w., 873; sacred places destined for w. cannot be erected except with the permission of the eparchial bishop, 868; the eparchial bishop can grant the use of sacred places to non-Catholics for the worthy celebration of w., 670 §2; regarding the acquisition of sacred things destined for w., 1018; one of the purposes for ecclesiastical temporal goods, 1007; the obligation of the Christian faithful to assist the Church, so that it has those things necessary for w., 25 §1; associations fostering w. are to be erected by ecclesiastical authority alone, 574;

public: notion, 668 §1; competent authority for its ordering, 199 §1, 657 §§1–3, 668 §2; veneration of Saints and Blesseds permitted, 885;

private: notion, 668 §1;

regarding exercises of piety: *see* piety;

prohibited participation in worship: punished by minor excommunication, 1431 §1; by major excommunication, 1434 §1, 1435 §2;

regarding formation in the practice of the rite, 41.

wounding serious wounding to be punished, 1451.

writings the right of the Church freely to publish them is to be vindicated everywhere, 651 §1; intended to catechetical formation in schools require ecclesiastical approval, 658 §1; regarding ecclesiastical permission for those w. which illustrate faith and morals, 659, 662 §2;

written materials: which ones should be destroyed in a trial, 1133 §3; witnesses are not to read them, with certain exceptions, 1247;

written statement which can be presented to the tribunal in a summary contentious trial, 1347 §2.

Y

year its juridical computation, 1545, 1546 §2; to be noted, 254. 2°, 1187. 3°, 1304 §1. 4°;

liturgical, 614 §1; academic, 760 §§1–2; novitiate, 457 §2, 523 §1; higher, regarding the impediment of age, 800 §2; coming, 263 §5; one, 286. 2°, 457 §1, 478; not beyond one y., 461 §2, 488 §2, 1111; beyond one y., 759 §2, 1402 §2; within a y., 92 §3, 270 §§2–3; once a y., 170, 292 §2; twice a y., 120; annually, each y., every y., 106 §2, 122 §3, 204 §2, 205 §1, 259 §2, 262 §4, 263 §5, 292 §2, 356 §1, 392, 473 §2. 3°, 582, 1028 §2. 7° and §3, 1031 §1; of the previous y., 122 §3; after a y., 363. 2°; three, 760 §2; four, 760 §1; five, 141, 172, 318 §1, 419 §1, 420 §3; six, 482; seventh, 1490; ten, 442, 458 §1, 524 §1, 1303 §2; fourteenth, 29, 30, 34, 800 §1, 900 §1, 1136 §3, 1231 §1, 1413 §§1–2; sixteenth, 800 §1; seventeenth, seventeen, 450. 4°, 517 §1; eighteenth, 450. 4°, 909 §1, 1413 §2; twenty third, 759 §1; twenty fourth, 759 §1; thirty, 247 §2, 1019, 1086 §4, 1507 §3; thirty five, 180. 4°, 227 §2, 513 §2; forty, 442; fifty, 1019, 1532 §3; seventy fifth, 210 §1, 218, 297 §2, 444 §3; one hundred, 927 §1, 1019; annual revenues, 1047 §1. 2°; *see* two years, three years, four years, five years, six years, seven years, ten years.

yield civil law, to which the law of the Church yields, 1504.

young persons pastor is to be eager to provide for their needs, 289 §3; religious education of y. p. is to be provided for by those to whom the care of souls has been entrusted, 628 §2; educators are to see to the formation of the whole human person in the case of y. p., 629; regarding their cultural, human and social formation in Catholic schools, 634 §3; care for y. p. of university age, 645; obligation of the pastors of souls for catechesis regarding marriage suited to y. p., 783 §1;

young men: families and schools are to be so animated by the spirit of the gospel that young men may freely hear and willingly respond to the

TABLES OF CORRESPONDING CANONS

Code of Canon Law (CIC)
Code of Canons of the Eastern Churches (CCEO)

At times there is a literal correspondence among the canons of the 1983 Code of Canon Law (CIC) and the 1990 Code of Canons of the Eastern Churches (CCEO). At other times there is substantial correspondence among them even though there are notable differences terminologically. At still other times there is only a partial correspondence among the canons of the two codes. Finally, at times there is no correspondence among the canons of the CIC and the CCEO, and this is indicated by an "X" in the appropriate columns.*

CIC	CCEO	CIC	CCEO	CIC	CCEO	CIC	CCEO
1	1	18	1500	35	1510, §1	53	X
2	3	19	1501	36	1512, §§1–2	54	1511; 1520, §1
3	4	20	1502	37	1514	55	1520, §2
4	5	21	1503	38	1515	56	1520, §3
5	6, 2°	22	1504	39	1516	57	1518
6	2; 6, 1°	23	1506, §1	40	1521	58	1513, §5
7	1488	24	1506, §2; 1507,	41	1522, §1	59	1510, §2, 3°;
8	1489		§§1–2	42	1523		1527, §1
9	1494	25	1507, §1	43	1524	60	X
10	1495	26	1507, §§3–4	44	1525	61	1528
11	1490	27	1508	45	1526	62	1511
12	1491, §§1, 2, 3°	28	1509	46	1513, §2	63	1529
13	1491, §3, 1°–2°,	29	X	47	1513, §3	64	X
	§4	30	X	48	1510, §2, 1°	65	1530
14	1496	31	X	49	1510, §2, 2°	66	X
15	1497	32	X	50	1517, §1	67	X
16	1498	33	X	51	1514; 1519, §2	68	X
17	1499	34	X	52	X	69	X

*This table substantially reproduces Appendix 7, pages 873–897 from *Eastern Catholic Church Law, Revised and Augmented Edition* by Victor J. Pospishil (New York, New York, Saint Maron Publications, 1996), with minor corrections and editing by Francis J. Marini. A corresponding canon may agree identically, partially or substantially. "X" indicates that there is no corresponding canon. Reprinted with permission.

CIC	CCEO	CIC	CCEO	CIC	CCEO	CIC	CCEO
70	1522, §2	115	920; 923	160	x	205	8
71	x	116	x	161	x	206	9
72	x	117	922, §1	162	x	207	323, §2
73	x	118	x	163	x	208	11
74	1527, §2	119	924, 1° –2°;	164	x	209	12
75	x		956, §1	165	947, §1	210	13
76	1531	120	925; 927, §1	166	948	211	14
77	1512, §3	121	x	167	949	212	15
78	1532, §1; 1532,	122	929	168	950	213	16
	§2, 1°–2°, §3	123	930	169	951	214	17
79	x	124	931	170	952	215	18
80	1533	125	932	171	953; 1434, §3	216	19
81	x	126	933	172	954	217	20
82	1534	127	934	173	955, §1–§3, §5	218	21
83	1532, §2, 3°–4°	128	935	174	x	219	22
84	1535	129	979	175	x	220	23
85	1536, §1	130	980, §2	176	956	221	24
86	1537	131	981; 983, §1	177	957	222	25
87	1537; 1538	132	982	178	958	223	26
88	x	133	983, §2, §3	179	959; 960	224	400
89	x	134	984; 987	180	961	225	401; 406
90	1536, §1, §3	135	985	181	962	226	407; 627, §1
91	1539	136	986	182	963	227	402
92	1512, §4	137	988	183	964	228	408, §1, §2
93	1513, §4	138	989	184	965, §1, §2;	229	404
94	x	139	x		966	230	403, §2; 709,
95	x	140	990	185	965, §4		§2
96	x	141	x	186	965, §3	231	409
97	909, §1, §2	142	992	187	967	232	328
98	910	143	991	188	968	233	329
99	909, §3	144	994; 995	189	969; 970; 971	234	331, §1; 332, §1;
100	911	145	936, §1–§2	190	972		334, §3
101	x	146	938	191	973	235	331, §2
102	912	147	939	192	974, §1	236	354
103	913	148	936, §3	193	974, §2; 975	237	332, §2; 334, §1
104	914	149	940; 946	194	976	238	335
105	915	150	x	195	977	239	338, §1; 339, §1;
106	917	151	x	196	978		340, §1; 471,
107	916, §1–§3	152	942	197	1540		§2
108	918	153	943	198	1541	240	339, §2–§3
109	919	154	944	199	1542	241	342
110	x	155	945	200	1543	242	330, §1, §2;
111	29, §1; 30; 588	156	x	201	1544		536, §2
112	32, §1; 33; 34	157	x	202	1545	243	337, §2, §3
113	920	158	x	203	1546	244	346, §1
114	921, §1, §3	159	x	204	7	245	346, §2, 7°–8°

CIC	CCEO	CIC	CCEO	CIC	CCEO	CIC	CCEO
246	346, §2, 2°–6°	288	X	333	45	379	188, §1
247	355	289	383, 2°, 3°	334	46, §1	380	187, §1
248	347	290	394	335	47	381	178
249	X	291	396	336	49	382	188, §2; 189
250	348, §1	292	395	337	50	383	192, §1–§3;
251	349, §1	293	398	338	51		193, §2; 678,
252	350, §1–§2	294	X	339	52		§2
253	340, §1; 471, §2	295	X	340	53	384	192, §4–§5
254	X	296	X	341	54	385	195
255	352, §1	297	X	342	X	386	196
256	352, §2–§3	298	X	343	X	387	197
257	352, §3	299	573, §2	344	X	388	198
258	353	300	X	345	X	389	199, §3
259	336, §1; 356, §2	301	573, §1; 574	346	346, §2	390	200
260	338, §2	302	X	347	X	391	191
261	X	303	X	348	X	392	201
262	336, §2	304	576, §1	349	X	393	190
263	341, §1	305	577	350	X	394	203
264	341	306	X	351	X	395	204
265	357, §1	307	578	352	X	396	205, §1
266	358; 428	308	581	353	X	397	205, §2–§3
267	359; 364	309	X	354	X	398	X
268	360, §2; 428	310	X	355	X	399	206, §2
269	366, §1, 1°,	311	X	356	X	400	208, §2
	3°–4°	312	575, §1, 1°, 3°,	357	X	401	210, §1, §2
270	365, §1		§2	358	X	402	62; 211
271	360, §1; 361;	313	X	359	X	403	212
	362	314	576, §2	360	X	404	214
272	363, 2°	315	X	361	48	405	213, §1, §3; 215,
273	370	316	580	362	X		§1
274	371, §2	317	X	363	X	406	215, §1–§2
275	379; 381, §3	318	X	364	X	407	215, §3–§4
276	368; 369; 377;	319	582	365	X	408	216
	378	320	583, §1, §2, 2°	366	X	409	222; 224, §1, 1°,
277	373; 374	321	X	367	X		§3
278	391	322	X	368	X	410	217
279	372	323	X	369	177, §1	411	218
280	376	324	X	370	311, §1; 312	412	233, §1
281	390	325	X	371	311, §1; 312	413	233
282	385, §1	326	X	372	X	414	X
283	386, §1; 392	327	X	373	177, §2	415	X
284	387	328	X	374	X	416	219
285	382; 383, 1°;	329	X	375	X	417	224, §2
	385, §3	330	42	376	178; 179	418	223, 1°, 3°; 224,
286	385, §2	331	43	377	181, §2		§1, 1°
287	384	332	44	378	180	419	220, 2°; 221, 2°

CIC	CCEO	CIC	CCEO	CIC	CCEO	CIC	CCEO
420	x	460	235	503	x	546	301, §1
421	220, 3°; 221, 3°, 4°	461	236	504	x	547	301, §3
		462	237, §1	505	x	548	302, §1, §3
422	220, 1°; 221, 1°, 5°	463	238, §1, 1°–2°, 4°–7°, 9°–10°; §2, §3	506	x	549	x
				507	x	550	302, §4
423	225			508	x	551	x
424	x	464	239	509	x	552	303
425	227	465	240, §4	510	x	553	276, §1; 277, §1
426	x	466	241	511	272	554	277
427	220, 4°; 221, 5°; 229	467	242	512	273, §1, §2, §4	555	278
		468	237	513	274	556	304
428	228	469	243, §1	514	273, §1; 275	557	305
429	x	470	244, §1	515	279; 280, §2, §3	558	306, §1
430	231	471	244, §2			559	306, §2
431	x	472	x	516	x	560	307
432	x	473	x	517	287, §2	561	308
433	x	474	x	518	280, §1	562	309
434	x	475	245	519	281, §1	563	310
435	80, 1°, 3°; 133, §1; 134, §1	476	246	520	281, §2; 282	564	x
		477	247, §1	521	281, §1; 285, §1	565	x
436	133, §1, 4°, 5°; 137; 221, 4°	478	247, §2–§3	522	284, §3, 4°	566	x
		479	248	523	284, §1	567	x
437	x	480	249	524	285, §3	568	x
438	x	481	224, §1; 251	525	286	569	x
439	x	482	252	526	287	570	x
440	x	483	253	527	288	571	x
441	x	484	254	528	289, §1, §2	572	x
442	133, §1, 2°	485	255	529	289, §3	573	410
443	x	486	256	530	290, §2; 677, §1; 739, §2	574	410; 411
444	x	487	257			575	x
445	x	488	258	531	291	576	x
446	x	489	259	532	290, §1	577	x
447	x	490	260	533	292	578	426
448	x	491	261	534	294	579	435; 506, §1; 566
449	x	492	263, §1	535	296		
450	x	493	263, §5	536	295	580	x
451	x	494	262, §1–§4	537	295	581	508, §2
452	x	495	264	538	297; 1391, §2	582	439; 440, §1, §2
453	x	496	265	539	298		
454	x	497	266	540	299	583	x
455	x	498	267	541	300	584	438, §1, §2, §4; 507; 556
456	x	499	268	542	x		
457	x	500	269	543	x	585	438, §3; 508, §2
458	x	501	270	544	x		
459	x	502	271, §1–§5	545	301, §1, §2	586	x

CIC	CCEO	CIC	CCEO	CIC	CCEO	CIC	CCEO
587	x	618	421	650	458; 459, §1; 524, §3; 525, §1	683	415, §2, §4; 554, §2; 638
588	505, §3; 554, §2	619	421				
589	434; 505, §1, §2, 1°, 3°; 554, §2; 563, §2	620	418, §1; 441, §3			684	487, §1, §2; 488, §1–§3; 544, §1–§3; 545, §1–§3
		621	508, §1; 566	651	458, §1; 524, §1, §2		
		622	x	652	459; 525, §1		
		623	442; 513; 557	653	461; 525, §1	685	488, 545, §1–§2
590	412, §1; 555; 564	624	444, §1, §2; 514; 557	654	462, §1; 469; 531	686	490; 491; 548
591	412, §2	625	443; 515, §1, §2; 557	655	526	687	491; 548, §2
592	419; 554, §2			656	464, 1°–3°; 527, 1°–3°	688	496; 546
593	413; 554, §2	626	445; 515, §3; 557			689	547
594	413; 554, §2			657	x	690	493, §2; 546, §1
595	414, §1, 1°, 2°, §3; 554, §2; 566	627	422, §1; 557	658	464, 4° 532		
		628	414, §1, 3°; 420, §2, §3; 554, §2; 566	659	471; 536	691	492; 549, §1, §2, 2°
596	441, §1, §2; 511; 557; 995			660	x	692	493, §1; 549, §3
		629	446	661	x	693	494; 549, §3
597	448; 449; 450, 1°; 518; 559, §1; 568, §1	630	473, §2, 2°; 475; 539	662	x	694	497; 551; 562, §3
		631	512; 557	663	473, §2, 1°, 3°; 538, §2	695	x
598	426	632	x			696	500, §2, 1°; 551; 552, §2, 1°; 553; 562, §3
599	x	633	x	664	473, §2, 2°; 474, §1; 538, §3		
600	x	634	423; 558, §1; 567, §1				
601	x			665	478; 495; 550	697	500, §2, 2°–4°; §3; 551; 553; 562, §3
602	x	635	424; 425; 558, §2; 567, §2	666	x		
603	481; 570			667	477, §1; 541		
604	570	636	447; 516; 558, §3	668	460; 467; 468, §1; 529, §3; 533; 540	698	x
605	571					699	500, §1; 553; 562, §3
606	1505	637	x				
607	x	638	x	669	476; 540	700	500, §4; 501, §2, §3; 552, §3; 553; 562, §3
608	x	639	468, §2, §3; 529, §5; 533	670	x		
609	436, §2; 509, §1; 556; 566			671	431, §1		
		640	x	672	427	701	502; 553; 562, §3
610	x	641	453, §1; 519	673	x		
611	437, §1; 509, §2; 556; 566; 556; 566	642	448; 453, §2	674	x	703	503; 553; 562, §3
		643	450, 4°–7°; 517, §1; 559, §1	675	x		
				676	x	704	x
612	437, §3; 509, §2; 556; 566	644	452	677	x	705	431, §2, 1°
		645	453, §3; 519	678	415, §1; 554, §2	706	431, §3
613	418, §1; 433, §1	646	459, §1; 525, §1	679	x	707	62; 211; 431, §2, 2°
614	x	647	456, §2, §3; 522	680	x		
615	x			681	282, §2; 543	708	x
616	438; 510; 556; 566	648	457, §1, §3; 459, §2; 523	682	284, §2; 303; 431, §1; 1391, §2	709	x
617	x	649	457, §2; 523, §1			710	563, §1

CIC	CCEO	CIC	CCEO	CIC	CCEO	CIC	CCEO
711	563, §1, 4°	756	x	800	631, §2	842	675, §2; 697
712	563, §1, 1°	757	x	801	x	843	381, §2
713	563, §1, 2°	758	x	802	635	844	671
714	563, §1, 3°	759	x	803	632; 639	845	672
715	x	760	x	804	636, §1; 639	846	668, §2; 674
716	x	761	x	805	636, §2	847	693
717	566	762	x	806	634, §3; 638, §1	848	x
718	576, §2	763	610, §1	807	640, §1	849	675, §1
719	x	764	610, §2–§3	808	642, §1	850	676
720	568, §1	765	612	809	x	851	686, §2
721	x	766	610, §4	810	x	852	681, §3
722	x	767	614, §1–§2, §4	811	643	853	x
723	x	768	616	812	644	854	x
724	x	769	626	813	645	855	x
725	x	770	615	814	640, §2	856	x
726	x	771	192, §1, §3	815	646	857	687, §1
727	x	772	609; 653	816	649; 650	858	x
728	x	773	617	817	648	859	x
729	568, §2	774	618	818	x	860	687, §2
730	x	775	621, §3; 622,	819	x	861	677
731	572		§2; 623, §1	820	x	862	x
732	x	776	624	821	x	863	x
733	x	777	x	822	651	864	679
734	x	778	x	823	652, §2	865	682
735	x	779	x	824	654; 662, §1	866	x
736	x	780	x	825	655, §1, §3	867	686, §1
737	x	781	584, §1	826	655, §1; 656,	868	681, §1; §4
738	x	782	x		§1; 657, §3	869	x
739	x	783	x	827	658; 659; 665,	870	681, §2
740	x	784	x		§1	871	680
741	x	785	x	828	666, §2	872	684
742	x	786	590	829	663, §1	873	x
743	x	787	x	830	664	874	685
744	562	788	587, §1, §3	831	660	875	688
745	x	789	x	832	662, §2	876	691
746	x	790	x	833	187, §2	877	689
747	595	791	585, §3	834	668, §1	878	690
748	586	792	x	835	x	879	692
749	597	793	627, §1–§2	836	x	880	693
750	598	794	628	837	673	881	x
751	x	795	629	838	657, §1, §2;	882	694
752	599	796	631, §1		668, §2	883	x
753	600	797	627, §3;	839	x	884	x
754	10	798	633, §3	840	667	885	x
755	902; 904, §1	799	x	841	669	886	696, §3

CIC	CCEO	CIC	CCEO	CIC	CCEO	CIC	CCEO
887	696, §3	932	705, §1; 707, §1	975	726, §3	1020	751
888	x	933	705, §2	976	725	1021	472; 537, §2;
889	x	934	714, §1	977	730		560; 752
890	695, §1	935	x	978	732, §2	1022	x
891	695, §1	936	714, §1	979	x	1023	753
892	x	937	x	980	x	1024	754
893	x	938	x	981	732, §1	1025	758, §2
894	x	939	x	982	731	1026	756
895	x	940	x	983	733	1027	758, §1, 4°
896	x	941	x	984	734, §1–§2	1028	x
897	698	942	x	985	734, §3	1029	758, §1, 2°
898	699, §3	943	x	986	735	1030	755
899	x	944	x	987	x	1031	758, §1, 6°; 759
900	699, §1	945	715; 716	988	x	1032	760
901	x	946	x	989	719	1033	758, §1, 1°
902	700	947	x	990	x	1034	x
903	703, §1	948	x	991	x	1035	x
904	378	949	x	992	x	1036	761
905	x	950	x	993	x	1037	x
906	x	951	x	994	x	1038	757
907	x	952	x	995	x	1039	772
908	702	953	x	996	x	1040	764
909	707, §1	954	x	997	x	1041	762, §1, 1°–6°
910	709	955	x	998	737, §1	1042	762, §1, 7°–8°
911	x	956	x	999	741	1043	771, §2
912	x	957	x	1000	742	1044	763
913	710	958	x	1001	738	1045	765
914	x	959	718	1002	x	1046	766
915	712	960	720, §1	1003	739	1047	767, §1–§2
916	711	961	720, §2, §3	1004	x	1048	767, §3
917	x	962	721	1005	x	1049	768
918	713, §1	963	x	1006	740	1050	769, §1, 1°–3°
919	713, §2	964	736, §1	1007	x	1051	769, §1, 4°–6°;
920	708; 881, §3	965	722, §1	1008	323, §1; 743		771, §3, §4
921	708	966	722, §3	1009	325; 744	1052	770
922	x	967	722, §2; §4;	1010	773	1053	774
923	x		723, §2; 724,	1011	773	1054	775
924	706		§2	1012	744	1055	776, §1–§2
925	x	968	723	1013	745	1056	776, §3
926	707, §1	969	724	1014	746, §1	1057	817
927	x	970	x	1015	747; 748, §2	1058	778
928	x	971	x	1016	748, §1	1059	780, §1
929	707, §1	972	x	1017	749	1060	779
930	x	973	x	1018	750	1061	x
931	707, §1	974	726, §1, §2	1019	472; 537, §1	1062	782

CIC	CCEO	CIC	CCEO	CIC	CCEO	CIC	CCEO
1063	783, §1, §3	1107	827	1152	863	1197	x
1064	x	1108	828	1153	864, §1, §3	1198	894
1065	783, §2	1109	829, §1	1154	865	1199	895
1066	785	1110	829, §2	1155	866	1200	x
1067	784	1111	830	1156	843	1201	x
1068	785, §2	1112	x	1157	844	1202	x
1069	786	1113	x	1158	845	1203	x
1070	787	1114	x	1159	846	1204	x
1071	789, 1°–3°,	1115	831, §1, 1°, 2°	1160	847	1205	x
	4°–6°	1116	832, §1, §2	1161	848; 849, §2	1206	x
1072	x	1117	834, §1	1162	851	1207	871, §2
1073	790, §1	1118	838, §1	1163	850	1208	871, §2
1074	791	1119	836	1164	849	1209	x
1075	792	1120	x	1165	852	1210	872, §1
1076	793	1121	841, §1, §3	1166	867, §1	1211	x
1077	794	1122	841, §2	1167	867, §2	1211	x
1078	795	1123	842	1168	x	1212	x
1079	796	1124	813	1169	x	1213	x
1080	797	1125	814	1170	x	1214	869
1081	798	1126	815	1171	x	1215	870
1082	799	1127	834; 839	1172	x	1216	x
1083	800	1128	816	1173	x	1217	871, §1
1084	801	1129	x	1174	377	1218	x
1085	802	1130	840, §1	1175	x	1219	x
1086	803	1131	840, §1	1176	875; 876, §3	1220	872
1087	804	1132	840, §2	1177	x	1221	x
1088	805	1133	840, §3	1178	x	1222	873
1089	806	1134	776, §2	1179	x	1223	x
1090	807	1135	777	1180	x	1224	x
1091	808	1136	627, §1	1181	878	1225	x
1092	809, §1	1137	x	1182	879	1226	x
1093	810	1138	x	1183	875; 876, §1, §2	1227	x
1094	812	1139	x	1184	877	1228	x
1095	818	1140	x	1185	x	1229	x
1096	819	1141	853	1186	884	1230	x
1097	820	1142	862	1187	885	1231	x
1098	821	1143	854	1188	886	1232	x
1099	822	1144	855	1189	887, §2	1233	x
1100	823	1145	856	1190	887, §1 888	1234	x
1101	824	1146	857	1191	889, §1–§3	1235	x
1102	826	1147	858	1192	889, §4	1236	x
1103	825	1148	859	1193	890	1237	x
1104	837, §1	1149	860	1194	891	1238	x
1105	837, §2	1150	861	1195	892	1239	x
1106	x	1151	x	1196	893, §3	1240	874, §2

CIC	CCEO	CIC	CCEO	CIC	CCEO	CIC	CCEO
1241	874, §4	1285	1029	1330	x	1373	1447, §1
1242	874, §3	1286	1030	1331	1434	1374	1448, §2
1243	x	1287	1031	1332	1431, §1	1375	1447, §2
1244	880, §1	1288	1032	1333	1432	1376	1441
1245	x	1289	1033	1334	1432, §1	1377	1449
1246	880, §3	1290	1034	1335	1435, §2	1378	1443; 1457
1247	881, §1, §4	1291	1035, §1, 3°	1336	1432, §2, §3	1379	1443
1248	881, §2	1292	1036, §1; 1038	1337	1429	1380	1461
1249	x	1293	1035, 1°, 2°, §2	1338	1430	1381	1462
1250	x	1294	x	1339	1427, §1	1382	1459, §1
1251	882	1295	1042	1340	x	1383	1459, §2
1252	x	1296	1040	1341	x	1384	1462
1253	x	1297	x	1342	1402, §2	1385	x
1254	1007	1298	1041	1343	x	1386	1463
1255	1009, §1	1299	1043	1344	1409, §1, 1°, 2°,	1387	1458
1256	1008, §2	1300	1044		4°	1388	1456
1257	1009, §2	1301	1045	1345	x	1389	1464
1258	x	1302	1046	1346	1409, §1, 3°	1390	1452; 1454
1259	1010	1303	1047	1347	1407, §1, §2	1391	1455
1260	1011	1304	1048, §2, §3	1348	x	1392	1466
1261	x	1305	1049	1349	1409, §2	1393	1467
1262	x	1306	1050	1350	1410	1394	1453, §2–§3
1263	1012	1307	1051	1351	1412, §4	1395	1453, §1
1264	1013, §1	1308	1052, §1–§5	1352	1435, §1	1396	x
1265	1015	1309	1053	1353	1319; 1471, §1;	1397	1450, §1; 1451
1266	1014	1310	1054		1487, §2	1398	1450, §2
1267	1016	1311	x	1354	1419; 1423, §2	1399	x
1268	1017	1312	x	1355	1420, §1, §3	1400	1055
1269	1018	1313	1412, §2–§3	1356	1420, §2, §3	1401	x
1270	1019	1314	1408	1357	x	1402	1056
1271	x	1315	1405, §1-§2	1358	1424	1403	1057
1272	x	1316	1405, §3	1359	1425	1404	1058
1273	1008, §1	1317	1405, §1	1360	1421	1405	1060, §1, 2°–
1274	1021	1318	x	1361	1422		4°, §2, §3;
1275	x	1319	1406, §1	1362	1152, §2–§3		1061
1276	1022	1320	415, §4	1363	1153	1406	1072
1277	263, §4	1321	1414	1364	1436, §1; 1437	1407	1073
1278	x	1322	x	1365	1440	1408	1074
1279	1023	1323	1413, §1	1366	1439	1409	1075
1280	x	1324	1413, §2; 1415	1367	1442	1410	1076
1281	1024	1325	x	1368	1444	1411	1077
1282	x	1326	1416	1369	1448, §1	1412	1078
1283	1025–1026	1327	x	1370	1445	1413	1079
1284	1020, §1, §2;	1328	1418	1371	1436, §2; 1446	1414	1081
	1028	1329	1417	1372	x	1415	1082

CIC	CCEO	CIC	CCEO	CIC	CCEO	CIC	CCEO
1416	1083, §1–§2	1460	1119	1505	1188	1550	1231
1417	1059	1461	1120	1506	1189	1551	1232
1418	1071	1462	1121	1507	1190	1552	1233
1419	1066	1463	1122	1508	1191	1553	1234
1420	1086; 1088, §2,	1464	1123	1509	1192, §1–§2	1554	1235
	§3	1465	1124	1510	1192, §3	1555	1236
1421	1087	1466	1125	1511	1193	1556	1237
1422	1088, §1	1467	1126	1512	1194	1557	1238
1423	1067, §1, §4	1468	1127	1513	1195	1558	1239
1424	1089	1469	1128	1514	1196	1559	1240
1425	1984; 1090, §2	1470	1129	1515	1197	1560	1241
1426	1185; 1090, §1	1471	1130	1516	1198	1561	1242
1427	1069	1472	1131	1517	x	1562	1243
1428	1093	1473	1132	1518	1199	1563	1244
1429	1091, §2–§4	1474	1315, §2	1519	1200	1564	1245
1430	1094	1475	1133	1520	1201	1565	1246
1431	1095	1476	1134	1521	1202	1566	1247
1432	1096	1477	1135	1522	1203	1567	1248
1433	1097	1478	1136	1523	1204	1568	1249
1434	1098	1479	1137	1524	1205	1569	1250
1435	1099	1480	1138, §1, §3	1525	1206	1570	1251
1436	1100	1481	1139	1526	1207	1571	1252
1437	1101	1482	1140	1527	1208	1572	1253
1438	1063, §3; 1064	1483	1141	1528	1209	1573	1254
1439	1067, §5	1484	1142	1529	1210	1574	1255
1440	1072	1485	1143	1530	1211	1575	1256
1441	1085, §3	1486	1144	1531	1212	1576	1257
1442	1059, §1	1487	1145	1532	1213	1577	1258
1443	1065	1488	1146	1533	1214	1578	1259
1444	x	1489	1147	1534	1215	1579	1260
1445	x	1490	1148	1535	1216	1580	1261
1446	1103	1491	1149	1536	1217	1581	1262
1447	1105	1492	1149; 1150	1537	1218	1582	1263
1448	1106	1493	1155	1538	1219	1583	1264
1449	1107	1494	1156	1539	1220	1584	x
1450	1108	1495	1157	1540	1221	1585	1266
1451	1109	1496	1158	1541	1222	1586	1265
1452	1110	1497	1159	1542	1223	1587	1267
1453	1111	1498	1160	1543	1224	1588	1268
1454	1112	1499	1161	1544	1225	1589	1269
1455	1113	1500	1162	1545	1226	1590	1270
1456	1114	1501	1104, §2	1546	1227	1591	1271
1457	1115	1502	1185	1547	1228	1592	1272
1458	1117	1503	1186	1548	1229	1593	1273
1459	1118	1504	1187	1549	1230	1594	1274

CIC	CCEO	CIC	CCEO	CIC	CCEO	CIC	CCEO
1595	1275	1635	1316	1675	1361	1715	1165; 1169
1596	1276	1636	1317	1676	1362	1716	1181, §1; 1182,
1597	1277	1637	1318	1677	1363		§1; 1183
1598	1281	1638	1319	1678	1364	1717	1468
1599	1282	1639	1320	1679	1365	1718	1469
1600	1283	1640	1321	1680	1366	1719	1470
1601	1284	1641	1322	1681	1367	1720	1486
1602	1285	1642	1323	1682	1368	1721	1472
1603	1286	1643	1324	1683	1369	1722	1473
1604	1287	1644	1325	1684	1370	1723	1474
1605	1288	1645	1326	1685	1371	1724	1475
1606	1289	1646	1327	1686	1372, §1	1725	1478
1607	1290	1647	1328	1687	1373	1726	1482
1608	1291	1648	1329	1688	1374	1727	1481
1609	1292	1649	1335; 1336	1689	1377	1728	1471
1610	1293	1650	1337	1690	1375	1729	1483
1611	1294	1651	1338	1691	1376	1730	1484
1612	1295	1652	1339	1692	1378	1731	1485
1613	1296	1653	1340	1693	1379	1732	996
1614	1297	1654	1341	1694	1380	1733	998
1615	1298	1655	1342	1695	1381	1734	999
1616	1299	1656	1343	1696	1382	1735	x
1617	1300	1657	x	1697	x	1736	1000
1618	1301	1658	1344	1698	x	1737	997, §1; 1001
1619	1302	1659	1345	1699	x	1738	1003
1620	1303, §1	1660	1346	1700	x	1739	1004
1621	1303, §2	1661	1347	1701	x	1740	1389
1622	1304, §1	1662	1348	1702	x	1741	1390
1623	1304, §2	1663	1349	1703	x	1742	1391
1624	1305	1664	1350	1704	x	1743	1392
1625	1306	1665	1351	1705	x	1744	1393
1626	1307	1666	1352	1706	x	1745	1394
1627	1308	1667	1353	1707	1383	1746	1395
1628	1309	1668	1354	1708	1385	1747	1396
1629	45, §3; 1310	1669	1355	1709	1386, §1, §3	1748	1397
1630	1311	1670	1356	1710	1386, §2	1749	1398
1631	1313	1671	1357	1711	x	1750	1399, §1
1632	x	1672	1358	1712	1387	1751	1399, §2, §3
1633	1314	1673	1359	1713	x	1752	1400
1634	1315	1674	1360	1714	1164		

Code of Canons of the Eastern Churches (CCEO)
Code of Canon Law (CIC)

At times there is a literal correspondence among the canons of the 1990 Code of Canons of the Eastern Churches (CCEO) and the 1983 Code of Canon Law (CIC). At other times there is substantial correspondence among them even though there are notable differences terminologically. At still other times there is only a partial correspondence among the canons of the two codes. Finally, at times there is no correspondence among the canons of the CIC and the CCEO, and this is indicated by an "X" in the appropriate columns.*

CCEO	CIC	CCEO	CIC	CCEO	CIC	CCEO	CIC
1	1	24	221	48	361	72	X
2	6, §2	25	222	49	336	73	X
3	2	26	223	50	337	74	X
4	3	27	X	51	338	75	X
5	4	28	X	52	339	76	X
6	5, §1; 6, §1, 2°,	29	111, §1	53	340	77	X
	4°	30	111, §2	54	341	78	X
7	204	31	X	55	X	79	X
8	205	32	112, §1, 1°	56	X	80	435
9	206	33	112, §1, 2°	57	X	81	X
10	754	34	112, §1, 3°	58	X	82	X
11	208	35	X	59	X	83	X
12	209	36	X	60	X	84	X
13	210	37	X	61	X	85	X
14	211	38	112, §2	62	X	86	X
15	212	39	X	63	X	87	X
16	213	40	X	64	X	88	X
17	214	41	X	65	X	89	X
18	215	42	330	66	X	90	X
19	216	43	331	67	X	91	X
20	217	44	332	68	X	92	X
21	218	45	333; 1629, 1°	69	X	93	X
22	219	46	334; 346	70	X	94	X
23	220	47	335	71	X	95	X

*This table substantially reproduces Appendix 7, pages 852–872 from *Eastern Catholic Church Law, Revised and Augmented Edition* by Victor J. Pospishil (New York, New York, Saint Maron Publications, 1996), with minor corrections and editing by Francis J. Marini. A corresponding canon may agree identically, partially or substantially. "X" indicates that there is no corresponding canon. Reprinted with permission.

CCEO	CIC	CCEO	CIC	CCEO	CIC	CCEO	CIC
96	X	141	X	187	380; 833, 3°	226	X
97	X	142	X	188	379; 382, §2	227	425
98	X	143	X	189	382, §1, §3	228	428
99	X	144	X	190	393	229	427, §1
100	X	145	X	191	391	230	X
101	X	146	X	192	383, §1, §3, §4;	231	430
102	X	147	X		384; 771	232	X
103	X	148	X	193	383, §2	233	412; 413
104	X	149	X	194	X	234	X
105	X	150	X	195	385	235	460
106	X	151	X	196	386	236	461, §1
107	X	152	X	197	387	237	462; 468
108	X	153	X	198	388, §1	238	463
109	X	154	X	199	389	239	464
110	X	155	X	200	390	240	465
111	X	156	X	201	392	241	466
112	X	157	X	202	X	242	467
113	X	158	X	203	394	243	469
114	X	159	X	204	395	244	470; 471
115	X	160	X	205	396, §1; 397	245	475, §1
116	X	161	X	206	399, §1	246	476
117	X	162	X	207	X	247	477, §1; 478
118	X	163	X	208	400, §1	248	479
119	X	164	X	209	X	249	480
120	X	165	X	210	401	250	X
121	X	166	X	211	402	251	481
122	X	167	X	212	403, §1, §3	252	482
123	X	168	X	213	405, §1	253	483
124	X	169	X	214	404	254	484
125	X	170	X	215	405, §2; 406;	255	485
126	X	171	X		407, §2–§3	256	486, §2, §3
127	X	172	X	216	408	257	487
128	X	173	X	217	410	258	488
129	X	174	X	218	411	259	489
130	X	175	X	219	416	260	490
131	X	176	X	220	419; 421; 422;	261	491, §1, §3
132	X	177	369; 373		427, §2; 833	262	494
133	435; 436, §1;	178	376; 381, §1	221	419; 421; 422;	263	492, §1, §3;
	442, §1	179	376		427, §2; 436,		493; 1277
134	435	180	378, §1		§1, 3°	264	495, §1
135	X	181	377, §1	222	409, §1	265	496
136	X	182	X	223	418	266	497
137	436, §2	183	X	224	409, §2; 417;	267	498
138	436, §1	184	X		418, §2, 1°;	268	499
139	X	185	X		481, §1	269	500
140	X	186	X	225	423	270	501

CCEO	CIC	CCEO	CIC	CCEO	CIC	CCEO	CIC
271	502, §1, §2	314	x	358	266, §1	398	293
272	511	315	x	359	267, §1	399	x
273	512; 514, §1	316	x	360	268, §1; 271,	400	224
274	513	317	x		§1, §2	401	225, §2
275	514, §1	318	x	361	271, §1	402	227
276	553, §1	319	x	362	271, §2, §3	403	230, §3
277	553, §2; 554	320	x	363	272	404	229
278	555	321	x	364	267, §2	405	x
279	515, §1	322	x	365	270	406	225, §1
280	515, §2, §3; 518	323	207, §1;	366	269	407	226, §1
281	519; 520, §1;		1008	367	x	408	228, §1, §2
	521, §1	324	x	368	276, §1	409	231
282	520; 681, §2	325	1009, §1	369	276, §2, 2°, 4°,	410	573; 574, §2
283	x	326	x		5°	411	574, §1
284	522; 523; 682,	327	x	370	273	412	590, §2; 591
	§1	328	232	371	274, §2	413	593; 594
285	521, §2; 524	329	233	372	279	414	595; 628, §2
286	525	330	242, §1	373	277, §1	415	678, §1; 683;
287	517, §1; 526	331	234, §1; 235, §1	374	277, §3		1320
288	527, §1	332	234, §1; 237, §1	375	x	416	x
289	528; 529, §1	333	x	376	280	417	x
290	530, 1°–2°,	334	237, §2	377	276, §2, 3°;	418	620
	4°–5°; 532	335	238		1174, §1	419	592, §1
291	531	336	259, §1; 262	378	276, §2, 2°;	420	628
292	533	337	239, §3; 243		904	421	618; 619
293	x	338	239, §1; 260	379	275, §1	422	627
294	534, §1	339	239, §2; 240	380	x	423	634, §1
295	536, §1; 537	340	239, §1; 253, §1	381	275, §2; 843,	424	635, §2
296	535	341	263; 264		§1	425	635, §1
297	538, §1, §3	342	241	382	285, §1–§2	426	578; 598, §2
298	539	343	x	383	285, §3; 289	427	x
299	540	344	234	384	287	428	266, §2; 268,
300	541	345	x	385	282; 285, §4;		§2
301	545; 546; 547	346	244; 245; 246		286	429	x
302	548; 550, §1, §3	347	248	386	283, §1	430	x
303	552	348	250	387	284	431	671; 682, §1;
304	556	349	251	388	x		705; 706
305	557	350	252, §1, §2	389	x	432	x
306	558; 559	351	x	390	281	433	613, §1
307	560	352	255; 256; 257,	391	278	434	589
308	561		§1	392	283, §2	435	579
309	562	353	258	393	x	436	609, §1
310	563	354	236	394	290	437	611, 2° 3°; 612
311	370; 371, §2	355	247, §2	395	292	438	584; 616, §1,
312	370; 371, §2	356	259, §2	396	291		§3
313	x	357	265	397	x	439	582

CCEO	CIC	CCEO	CIC	CCEO	CIC	CCEO	CIC
440	582	476	669, §1	519	641; 642; 645, §1, §2	554	x
441	596, §1, §2; 620	477	667, §1	520	646	555	590, §2
442	623	478	665, §1	521	647, §1	556	x
443	625, §2	479	x	522	647, §2, §3	557	x
444	624, §1; 625, §3	480	x	523	648; 649, §1	558	634, §1; 635, §1
445	626	481	603	524	648, §3; 650, §2; 651, §1, §2	559	x
446	629	482	x			560	x
447	636, §1	483	x	525	650, §1; 652, §2, §5; 653; 668	561	x
448	597, §1; 642	484	x			562	x
449	597, §2	485	x			563	710; 711; 712; 713, §1; 714
450	643, §1, 1°–4°	486	x	526	655	564	590, §2
451	x	487	684, §3	527	656, 2°–5°	565	266, §3
452	644	488	684, §3, §4	528	x	566	717, §1
453	641; 642; 645, §1, §3	489	686, §1	529	639, §2, §3; 668, §2, §3	567	634, §1
454	x	490	686, §3	530	668, §1	568	720; 729
455	x	491	687	531	654	569	x
456	647, §2	492	691	532	658, 2°	570	603, §1; 604, §1
457	648, §1, §3; 649, §1	493	690, §1; 692	533	x	571	605
458	650, §2; 651, §1	494	693	534	x	572	731, §1
459	646; 648, §2; 650, §1; 652, §5	495	665, §2	535	x	573	299, §2, §3; 301, §3
		496	668, §2	536	659	574	301, §1
460	x	497	694	537	1019; 1021	575	312, §1, 1°, 3°; 312, §2
461	648, §3; 653	498	703	538	630, §1; 663; 664	576	304, §1; 314
462	654	499	x	539	630, §2–§3	577	305
463	x	500	696, §1; 697, 2°–3°; 699, §1	540	669, §1	578	307
464	656, 2°–5°			541	667, §1	579	x
465	x	501	700	542	x	580	316
466	x	502	701	543	681, §1	581	308
467	668, §4	503	702	544	684, §1	582	319, §1
468	639, §2–§4; 668, §3, §5	504	x	545	684, §2, §4; 685	583	320, §1, §2
469	654	505	588, §2; 589	546	688; 690, §1547; 689	584	781
470	x	506	579			585	791, 2°
471	659	507	584	548	686, §1, §3	586	748, §2
472	1019; 1021	508	581; 585; 621	549	690, §1; 691; 692; 693	587	788
473	630, §2; 663, §1–§3, §5; 664	509	609, §1	550	665, §2	588	111, §2
		510	616, §1–§2	551	694; 696, §1; 697; 703	589	x
474	630, §1; 664	511	596, §1–§2	552	696, §1; 700	590	786
475	630, §2, §3	512	631, §1–§3	553	699, §1	591	x
		513	623			592	x
		514	624			593	x
		515	625, §1, §3; 626			594	x
		516	636, §1			595	747
		517	643, §1, 1°				
		518	597, §2				

CCEO	CIC		CCEO	CIC		CCEO	CIC		CCEO	CIC
596	x		639	803, §2; 804,		681	852, §2; 868;		722	965–967
597	749			§2			870		723	967, §3; 968
598	750		640	807; 814		682	865		724	967, §3; 969
599	752		641	x		683	x		725	976
600	753		642	808		684	872		726	974, §1, §2, §4;
601	x		643	811, §1		685	874			975
602	x		644	812		686	851, 2°; 867, §1		727	x
603	x		645	813		687	857, §2; 860,		728	x
604	x		646	815			§1		729	x
605	x		647	x		688	875		730	977
606	x		648	817		689	877		731	982
607	x		649	816, §1		690	878		732	978, §1; 981
608	x		650	816, §2		691	876		733	983
609	772, §1		651	822, §1, §3		692	879		734	984–985
610	763; 764; 766		652	823		693	847, §1; 880,		735	986
611	x		653	772, §2			§2		736	964, §1
612	765		654	824, §2		694	882		737	998
613	x		655	825		695	890; 891		738	1001
614	767, §1, §2, §4		656	826, §1, §3		696	886, §1; 887		739	530, 3°; 1003,
615	770		657	826, §2, §3;		697	842, §2			§1-§2
616	768			838, §2, §3		698	897		740	1006
617	773		658	827, §1–§2		699	898; 900, §1		741	999
618	774, §2		659	827, §3		700	902		742	1001, §1
619	x		660	831, §1		701	x		743	1008
620	x		661	x		702	908		744	1009, §2;
621	775, §2		662	824, §1; 832		703	903			1012
622	775, §3		663	829		704	x		745	1013
623	775, §1		664	830		705	932, §2; 933		746	1014
624	776		665	827, §4		706	924		747	1015, §1
625	x		666	828		707	909; 924; 926;		748	1015, §2; 1016
626	769		667	840			929; 932, §1		749	1017
627	226, §2; 793;		668	834, §2; 838,		708	920; 921, §1		750	1018
	797; 1136			§1; 846, §1		709	230, §3; 910		751	1020
628	794		669	841		710	913, §1		752	1021
629	795		670	x		711	916		753	1023
630	x		671	844		712	915		754	1024
631	796, §1; 800,		672	845		713	918; 919, §1		755	1030
	§1		673	837, §2		714	934; 936		756	1026
632	803, §1		674	846		715	945, §1		757	1038
633	798		675	842, §1; 849		716	945, §2		758	1025, §1; 1027;
634	806, §2		676	850		717	x			1029; 1031,
635	802		677	530, 1°; 861		718	959			§1; 1033
636	804, §1; 805		678	383, §2		719	989		759	1031
637	x		679	864		720	960; 961		760	1032, §1, §3
638	683; 806, §1		680	871		721	962		761	1036

CCEO	CIC	CCEO	CIC	CCEO	CIC	CCEO	CIC
762	1041; 1042, 2°, 3°	801	1084	844	1157	887	1189; 1190, §3
763	1044	802	1085	845	1158	888	1190
764	1040	803	1086	846	1159	889	1191; 1192, §1
765	1045	804	1087	847	1160	890	1193
766	1046	805	1088	848	1161, §1, §2	891	1194
767	1047, §1, §2, 1°, 2°; §3, §4; 1048	806	1089	849	1161, §3; 1164	892	1195
		807	1090	850	1163	893	1196, 1°, 2°
		808	1091	851	1162	894	1198
768	1049	809	1092	852	1165	895	1199, §1
769	1050; 1051	810	1093	853	1141	896	x
770	1052, §2–§3	811	x	854	1143	897	x
771	1043; 1051, 2°	812	1094	855	1144	898	x
772	1039	813	1124	856	1145	899	x
773	1010; 1011	814	1125	857	1146	900	x
774	1053	815	1126	858	1147	901	x
775	1054	816	1128	859	1148	902	755, §1
776	1055; 1056; 1134	817	1057	860	1149	903	x
		818	1095	861	1150	904	755, §2
777	1135	819	1096, §1	862	1142	905	x
778	1058	820	1097	863	1152	906	x
779	1060	821	1098	864	1153	907	x
780	1059	822	1099	865	1154	908	x
781	x	823	1100	866	1155	909	97; 99
782	1062	824	1101	867	1166; 1167	910	98
783	1063, 1°, 2°, 4°; 1065, §2; 1136	825	1103	868	x	911	100
		826	1102, §1	869	1214	912	102, §1, §2
		827	1107	870	1215, §1	913	103
784	1067	828	1108	871	1207; 1208; 1217, §2	914	104
785	1066; 1068	829	1109			915	105
786	1069	830	1111	872	1210; 1220	916	107
787	1070	831	1115	873	1222	917	106
788	x	832	1116	874	1240; 1241, §1; 1242	918	108
789	1071, §1, 1°–4°, 6°; §2	833	x			919	109
		834	1117; 1127, §1	875	1176, §1, §2; 1183	920	113, §2; 115, §2
790	1073	835	x			921	114, §1, §3; 117
791	1074	836	1119	877	1184, §1	922	117
792	1075, §2	837	1104, §1; 1105, §1	878	1181	923	115, §2
793	1076			879	1182	924	119, 2°, 3°
794	1077	838	1118, §1, §2	880	1244, §1; 1246	925	120, §2
795	1078	839	1127, §3	881	920, §1; 1247; 1248, §1	926	x
796	1079	840	1130; 1131; 1132; 1133			927	120, §1
797	1080			882	1251	928	x
798	1081	841	1121, §1, §3; 1122	883	x	929	122
799	1082			884	1186	930	123
800	1083	842	1123	885	1187	931	124
		843	1156	886	1188	932	125

CCEO	CIC	CCEO	CIC	CCEO	CIC	CCEO	CIC
933	126	976	194	1020	1284, §2, 2°	1062	x
934	127	977	195	1021	1274, §1, §2,	1063	1438, 1°
935	128	978	196, §1		§3	1064	1438, 1°, 2°
936	145; 148	979	129	1022	1276	1065	1443
937	x	980	130	1023	1279, §1	1066	1419
938	146	981	131, §1, §2	1024	1281	1067	1423, §1; 1439,
939	147	982	132	1025	1283, 1°, 2°		§1
940	149, §1, §2	983	131, §3; 133	1026	1283, 3°	1068	x
941	x	984	134, §1, §2	1027	x	1069	1427, §1, §3
942	152	985	135, §1, §2, §3	1028	1284	1070	x
943	153	986	136	1029	1285	1071	1418
944	154	987	134, §3	1030	1286	1072	1406, §2; 1440
945	155	988	137	1031	1287	1073	1407
946	149, §3	989	138	1032	1288	1074	1408
947	165	990	140	1033	1289	1075	1409
948	166	991	143	1034	1290	1076	1410
949	167	992	142	1035	1291; 1293, §1	1077	1411
950	168	993	x	1036	1292	1078	1412
951	169	994	144, §1	1037	x	1079	1413
952	170	995	144, §2; 596,	1038	1292, §3, §4	1080	x
953	171, §1, 1°, 2°,		§3	1039	x	1081	1414
	4°	996	1732	1040	1296	1082	1415
954	172	997	1737, §1	1041	1298	1083	1416
955	173	998	1733, §1, §3	1042	1295	1084	1425, §1, §2,
956	119, 1°; 176	999	1734	1043	1299		§4
957	177	1000	1736	1044	1300	1085	1426, §1; 1441
958	178	1001	1737, §2, §4	1045	1301	1086	1420, §1–§4
959	179, §1, §4	1002	x	1046	1302	1087	1421
960	179, §2; §5	1003	1738	1047	1303	1088	1420, §5; 1422
961	180, §1	1004	1739	1048	1304	1089	1424
962	181, §1	1005	x	1049	1305	1090	1425, §3, §5
963	182	1006	x	1050	1306, §2	1091	1426, §2; 1429
964	183	1007	1254	1051	1307	1092	x
965	184, §1, §2;	1008	1256; 1273	1052	1308	1093	1428
	185; 186	1009	1255; 1257, §1	1053	1309	1094	1430
966	184, §3	1010	1259	1054	1310	1095	1431
967	187	1011	1260	1055	1400	1096	1432
968	188	1012	1263	1056	1402	1097	1433
969	189, §1	1013	1264	1057	1403, §1	1098	1434
970	189, §2, §3, §4	1014	1266	1058	1404	1099	1435
971	189, §4	1015	1265, §1	1059	1417; 1442	1100	1436
972	190	1016	1267	1060	1405, §1, 1°, 3°,	1101	1437
973	191	1017	1268		4°, §2, §3, 1°,	1102	x
974	192, 193, §4	1018	1269		3°	1103	1446
975	193, §1, §2, §3	1019	1270	1061	1405, §3, 3°	1104	1501

CCEO	CIC	CCEO	CIC	CCEO	CIC	CCEO	CIC
1105	1447	1149	1491; 1492, §2	1194	1512	1239	1558
1106	1448	1150	1492, §1	1195	1513	1240	1559
1107	1449, §2, §3, §4; 1450	1151	x	1196	1514	1241	1560
		1152	1362	1197	1515	1242	1561
1108	1450	1153	1363	1198	1516	1243	1562
1109	1451	1154	x	1199	1518	1244	1563
1110	1452	1155	1493	1200	1519	1245	1564
1111	1453	1156	1494	1201	1520	1246	1565
1112	1454	1157	1495	1202	1521	1247	1566
1113	1455	1158	1496	1203	1522	1248	1567
1114	1456	1159	1497	1204	1523	1249	1568
1115	1457	1160	1498	1205	1524	1250	1569
1116	x	1161	1499	1206	1525	1251	1570
1117	1458	1162	1500	1207	1526	1252	1571
1118	1459	1163	x	1208	1527	1253	1572
1119	1460	1164	1714	1209	1528	1254	1573
1120	1461	1165	1715	1210	1529	1255	1574
1121	1462	1166	x	1211	1530	1256	1575
1122	1463	1167	x	1212	1531	1257	1576
1123	1464	1168	x	1213	1532	1258	1577
1124	1465	1169	1715, §1	1214	1533	1259	1578
1125	1466	1170	x	1215	1534	1260	1579
1126	1467	1171	x	1216	1535	1261	1580
1127	1468	1172	x	1217	1536	1262	1581
1128	1469	1173	x	1218	1537	1263	1582
1129	1470	1174	x	1219	1538	1264	1583
1130	1471	1175	x	1220	1539	1265	1586
1131	1472	1176	x	1221	1540	1266	1585
1132	1473	1177	x	1222	1541	1267	1587
1133	1475	1178	x	1223	1542	1268	1588
1134	1476	1179	x	1224	1543	1269	1589
1135	1477	1180	x	1225	1544	1270	1590
1136	1478	1181	1716, §1	1226	1545	1271	1591
1137	1479	1182	1716, §2	1227	1546	1272	1592
1138	1480	1183	1716, §2	1228	1547	1273	1593
1139	1481	1184	x	1229	1548	1274	1594
1140	1482	1185	1502	1230	1549	1275	1595
1141	1483	1186	1503	1231	1550	1276	1596
1142	1484	1187	1504	1232	1551	1277	1597
1143	1485	1188	1505	1233	1552	1278	x
1144	1486	1189	1506	1234	1553	1279	x
1145	1487	1190	1507	1235	1554	1280	x
1146	1488	1191	1508	1236	1555	1281	1598
1147	1489	1192	1509; 1510	1237	1556	1282	1599
1148	1490	1193	1511	1238	1557	1283	1600

CCEO	CIC	CCEO	CIC	CCEO	CIC	CCEO	CIC
1284	1601	1328	1647	1373	1687	1415	1324, §1, §2;
1285	1602	1329	1648	1374	1688		1345
1286	1603	1330	x	1375	1690	1416	1326, §1
1287	1604	1331	x	1376	1691	1417	1329, §1
1288	1605	1332	x	1377	1689	1418	1328
1289	1606	1333	x	1378	1692	1419	1354, §1, §2
1290	1607	1334	x	1379	1693	1420	1355, §1; 1356
1291	1608	1335	1649, §1	1380	1694	1421	1360
1292	1609	1336	1649, §2	1381	1695	1422	1361
1293	1610	1337	1650	1382	1696	1423	1354, §3
1294	1611	1338	1651	1383	1707	1424	1358, §1
1295	1612	1339	1652	1384	x	1425	1359
1296	1613	1340	1653	1385	1708	1426	x
1297	1614	1341	1654	1386	1709–1710	1427	1339, §3
1298	1615	1342	1655	1387	1712	1428	x
1299	1616	1343	1656	1388	x	1429	1337
1300	1617	1344	1658	1389	1740	1430	1338
1301	1618	1345	1659	1390	1741	1431	1332
1302	1619	1346	1660	1391	538, §2; 682,	1432	1333, §1, §3,
1303	1620–1621	1347	1661		§2; 1742		1°, 2°, §4;
1304	1622–1623	1348	1662	1392	1743		1334, §1;
1305	1624	1349	1663	1393	1744		1336, §1, 3°
1306	1625	1350	1664	1394	1745	1433	1336, §1, 5°
1307	1626	1351	1665	1395	1746	1434	171, §1, 3°; 1331
1308	1627	1352	1666	1396	1747	1435	1352, §1; 1335
1309	1628	1353	1667	1397	1748	1436	1364; 1371, 1°
1310	1629	1354	1668	1398	1749	1437	1364
1311	1630	1355	1669	1399	1750; 1751	1438	x
1312	x	1356	1670	1400	1752	1439	1366
1313	1631	1357	1671	1401	x	1440	1365
1314	1633	1358	1672	1402	1342, §1, §2	1441	1376
1315	1634, §1, §3;	1359	1673	1403	x	1442	1367
	1474	1360	1674	1404	x	1443	1378, §2 §3;
1316	1635	1361	1675	1405	1315, §1, §3;		1379
1317	1636	1362	1676		1316; 1317	1444	1368
1318	1637	1363	1677	1406	1319	1445	1370
1319	1353; 1638	1364	1678	1407	1347	1446	1371, 2°
1320	1639	1365	1679	1408	1314	1447	1373; 1375
1321	1640	1366	1680	1409	1344; 1346	1448	1369; 1374
1322	1641	1367	1681	1410	1350	1449	1377
1323	1642	1368	1682	1411	x	1450	1397; 1398
1324	1643	1369	1683	1412	1313; 1351	1451	1397
1325	1644	1370	1684	1413	1323, 1°; 1324,	1452	1390, §3
1326	1645	1371	1685		§1, 4°	1453	1394; 1395, §1
1327	1646	1372	1686	1414	1321	1454	1390

CCEO	CIC	CCEO	CIC	CCEO	CIC	CCEO	CIC
1455	1391	1478	1725	1501	19	1524	43
1456	1388	1479	x	1502	20	1525	44
1457	1378, §1	1480	x	1503	21	1526	45
1458	1387	1481	1727	1504	22	1527	59, §2; 74
1459	1382; 1383	1482	1726	1505	x	1528	61
1460	x	1483	1729	1506	23; 24, §1	1529	63, §1, §2
1461	1380	1484	1730	1507	24, §2; 25; 26	1530	65
1462	1381; 1384	1485	1731	1508	27	1531	76
1463	1386	1486	1720	1509	28	1532	78; 83
1464	1389	1487	1353	1510	35; 48; 59, §1	1533	80
1465	x	1488	7	1511	54, §1; 62	1534	82
1466	1392	1489	8	1512	36, §1; 77; 92	1535	84
1467	1393	1490	11	1513	46; 47; 58; 93	1536	85; 90
1468	1717	1491	12, §1, §3; 13	1514	37; 51	1537	86; 87, §1
1469	1718	1492	x	1515	38	1538	87
1470	1719	1493	x	1516	39	1539	91
1471	1728	1494	9	1517	50	1540	197
1472	1721	1495	10	1518	57, §1, §2	1541	198
1473	1722	1496	14	1519	51	1542	199
1474	1723	1497	15	1520	55; 56	1543	200
1475	1724	1498	16	1521	40	1544	201
1476	x	1499	17	1522	41; 70	1545	202
1477	x	1500	18	1523	42	1546	203

APPENDIX 1

NEW LAWS FOR THE CAUSES OF SAINTS

JOHN PAUL BISHOP
Divinus perfectionis Magister
Promulgated January 25, 1983

CONGREGATION FOR THE CAUSES OF SAINTS
Norms to be Observed in Inquiries
Made by Bishops in the Causes of the
Saints
Promulgated February 7, 1983

CONGREGATION FOR THE CAUSES OF SAINTS
General Decree on the Causes of the
Servants of God Whose Judgement is
Presently Pending at the Sacred
Congregation
Promulgated February 7, 1983

JOHN PAUL
BISHOP

IOANNES PAULUS
EPISCOPUS

Divinus perfectionis Magister

Divinus perfectionis Magister

Divinus perfectionis Magister

Servant of the Servants of God For Posterity

Servus Servorum Dei Ad Perpetuam Rei Memoriam

THE DIVINE TEACHER AND MODEL OF PERFEC-TION, Christ Jesus, who together with the Father and the Holy Spirit is proclaimed as "alone holy," loved the Church as His bride and delivered Himself up for her so that He might sanctify her and make her glorious in His sight. Thus He gave the commandment to all His disciples to imitate the perfection of the Father and He sends upon all the Holy Spirit, who might inspire them from within to love God with their whole heart and to love one another as He Himself loved them. As the Second Vatican Council teaches, the followers of Christ, called and justified in the Lord Jesus not according to their works but according to His own purpose and grace, through baptism sought in faith truly become sons of God and sharers in the divine nature, and thus truly holy.[1]

In all times, God chooses from these many who, following more closely the example of Christ, give outstanding testimony to the Kingdom of heaven by shedding their blood or by the heroic practice of virtues.

The Church, in turn, from the earliest beginnings of Christianity has always believed that the Apostles and Martyrs are more closely joined to us in Christ and has venerated them, together with the Blessed Virgin Mary and the holy Angels, with special devotion, devoutly imploring the aid of their intercession. To these were soon added others

DIVINUS PERFECTIONIS MAGISTER et exemplar, Christus Iesus, qui una cum Patre et Spiritu Sancto "unus sanctus" celebratur, Ecclesiam tamquam sponsam dilexit atque seipsum pro ea tradidit, ut illam sanctificaret sibique ipse gloriosam exhiberet. Praecepto igitur dato omnibus discipulis suis, ut perfectionem Patris imitarentur, in omnes Spiritum Sanctum mittit, qui eos intus moveat, ut Deum diligant ex toto corde, utque invicem sese diligant, quemadmodum ille eos dilexit. Christi asseclae—uti per Concilium Vaticanum II monemur—non secundum opera sua, sed secundum propositum et gratiam Eius vocati atque in Iesu Domino iustificati, in fidei baptismate vere filii Dei et consortes divinae naturae, ideoque reapse sancti effecti sunt.[1]

Inter hos quovis tempore plures Deus eligit, qui Christi exemplum proximius secuti, sanguinis effusione aut heroico virtutum exercitio praeclarum Regni caelorum praebeant testimonium.

Ecclesia autem, quae inde a primaevis christianae religionis temporibus Apostolos et Martyres in Christo arctius nobis coniunctos esse semper credidit, eos simul cum beata Virgine Maria et sanctis Angelis peculiari veneratione prosecuta est, eorumque inter-

---

English translation prepared by the Congregation for the Causes of Saints, Vatican City. All rights reserved.

1. Dog. Const. *Lumen Gentium*, no. 40.

also who had imitated more closely the virginity and poverty of Christ and, finally, others whose outstanding practice of the Christian virtues and whose divine charisms commended them to the pious devotion of, and imitation by, the faithful.

When we consider the life of those who have faithfully followed Christ, we are inspired with a new reason to seek the City that is to come and we are most safely taught the path by which, amid the changing things of this world and in keeping with the state in life and condition proper to each of us, we can arrive at that perfect union with Christ, which is holiness. Surrounded as we are by such an array of witnesses, through whom God is present to us and speaks to us, we are powerfully drawn to reach His Kingdom in heaven.[2]

From time immemorial, the Apostolic See has accepted these signs and has listened to the voice of her Lord with the greatest reverence and docility. Faithful to the serious duty entrusted to her of teaching, sanctifying and governing the People of God, she proposes to the faithful for their imitation, veneration and invocation, men and women who are outstanding in the splendor of charity and other evangelical virtues and, after due investigations, she declares them, in the solemn act of canonization, to be Saints.

The instruction of causes of canonization, which Our Predecessor Sixtus V entrusted to the Congregation of Sacred Rites, which he himself had established,[3] was, with the passage of time, always improved by new norms. Worthy of special mention are those of Urban VIII,[4] which Prosper Lambertini (later Benedict XIV), drawing upon the experiences of time past, handed down to later generations in a work entitled *De Servorum Dei beatificatione et de Beatorum canonizatione.* This work served as the rule of the Sacred Congregation of Rites for almost two centuries. Finally, these norms were substantially incorporated into the *Code of Canon Law* promulgated in 1917.

cessionis auxilium pie imploravit. Quibus mox adnumerati sunt alii quoque qui Christi virginitatem et paupertatem pressius erant imitati, et tandem ceteri quos praeclarum virtutum christianarum exercitium ac divina charismata piae fidelium devotioni et imitationi commendabant.

Dum illorum vitam conspicimus, qui Christum fideliter sunt secuti, nova quadam ratione ad futuram Civitatem inquirendam incitamur et tutissime viam edocemur qua, inter mundanas varietates, secundum statum condicionemque unicuique propriam, ad perfectam cum Christo coniunctionem seu sanctitatem pervenire possumus. Nimirum tantam habentes impositam nubem testium, per quos Deus nobis fit praesens nosque alloquitur, ad Regnum suum in coelis adipiscendum magna virtute attrahimur.[2]

Quae signa et vocem Domini sui maxima cum reverentia et docilitate suscipiens, Sedes Apostolica, ab immemorabilibus temporibus, pro gravi munere sibi concredito docendi, sanctificandi atque regendi Populum Dei, fidelium imitationi, venerationi et invocationi proponit viros et mulieres caritatis aliarumque evangelicarum virtutum fulgore praestantes, eosque, post debitas pervestigationes peractas, in sollemni canonizationis actu Sanctos vel Sanctas esse declarat.

Causarum canonizationis instructio, quam Praedecessor Noster Xystus V Congregationi Sacrorum Rituum ab ipso conditae concredidit,[3] decursu temporum novis semper aucta fuit normis, praesertim Urbani VIII opera,[4] quas Prosper Lambertini (postea Benedictus XIV), experientias quoque transacti temporis colligens, posteris tradidit in opere quod *De Servorum Dei beatificatione et de Beatorum canonizatione* inscribitur, quodque regula exstitit per duo fere saecula apud Sacram Rituum Congregationem. Huiusmodi normae tandem substantialiter receptae fuerunt in *Codicem Iuris Canonici,* anno 1917 publici iuris factum.

---

2. Cf. *ibid.,* no. 50.

3. Apost. Const. *Immensa Aeterni Dei* of January 22, 1588. Cf. *Bullarium Romanum,* ed Taurinensis, t. VIII, pp. 985–999.

4. Apost. Letter *Caelestis Hierusalem cives* of July 5, 1634; *Urban VIII P.O.M. Decreta servanda in canonizatione et beatificatione Sanctorum* of March 12, 1642.

Since recent progress in the field of historical studies has shown the necessity of providing the competent Congregation with an apparatus better suited for its task so as to respond more adequately to the dictates of historical criticism, Our Predecessor of happy memory, Pius XI, in the Apostolic Letter *Già da qualche tempo*, issued *motu proprio* on February 6, 1930, established the "Historical Section" within the Sacred Congregation of Rites and entrusted it with the study of "historical" causes.[5] On January 4, 1939, the same Pontiff also ordered the publication of *Normae servandae in construendis processibus ordinariis super causis historicis*,[6] which made the "apostolic" process no longer necessary so that a single process would then be conducted with ordinary authority in "historical" causes.

In the Apostolic Letter *Sanctitas clarior*, given *motu proprio* on March 19, 1969,[7] Paul VI established that even in recent causes there would be only one cognitional process for gathering proofs, which the Bishop conducts with previous permission, nevertheless, from the Holy See.[8] The same Pontiff, in the Apostolic Constitution *Sacra Rituum Congregatio*[9] of May 8, 1969, established two new Dicasteries in place of the Sacred Congregation of Rites. To one he gave the responsibility of regulating divine Worship and to the other, that of dealing with the causes of saints; on that same occasion, he changed, somewhat, the procedure to be followed in these causes.

Most recent experience, finally, has shown us the appropriateness of revising further the manner of instructing causes and of so structuring the Congregation for the Causes of Saints that we might meet the needs of experts and the desires of Our Brother Bishops, who have often called for a simpler process while maintaining the soundness of the investigation in matter of such great import. In light of the doctrine of the Second Vatican Council on collegiality, We also think that the Bishops themselves should be more closely associated with the Holy See in dealing with the causes of saints.

Therefore, having abrogated all laws of any kind which

Cum vero maxime auctus historicarum disciplinarum progressus nostris temporibus necessitatem ostendisset aptiore laboris instrumento competentem Congregationem ditandi, ut postulatis artis criticae melius responderet, Decessor Noster f.r. Pius XI Apostolicis Litteris *Già da qualche tempo* motu proprio die 6 mensis februarii anno 1930 editis, "Sectionem historicam" apud Sacram Rituum Congregationem instituit, eique studium causarum "historicarum" concredidit.[5] Die autem 4 ianuarii anno 1939 idem Pontifex *Normas servandas in construendis processibus ordinariis super causis historicis*[6] edi iussit, quibus processum "apostolicum" reapse supervacaneum reddidit, ita ut in causis "historicis" exinde unicus processus auctoritate ordinaria factus sit.

Paulus VI autem, Litteris Apostolicis *Sanctitas clarior* motu proprio die 19 martii anno 1969 editis,[7] statuit, ut etiam in causis recentioribus unicus fieret processus cognitionalis seu ad colligendas probationes, quem Episcopus instruit praevia tamen venia Sanciae Sedis.[8] Idem Pontifex, Constitutione Apostolica *Sacra Rituum Congregatio*[9] diei 8 maii 1969, loco Sacrae Rituum Congregationis duo nova constituit Dicasteria, quorum uni munus concredidit Cultum divinum ordinandi, alteri vero causas sanctorum tractandi; eadem data occasione ordinem in iisdem procedendi aliquantum immutavit.

Post novissimas experientias, denique, Nobis peropportunum visum est instructionis causarum viam ac rationem ulterius recognoscere ipsamque Congregationem pro Causis Sanctorum ita ordinare, ut et doctorum exigentiis obviam fieremus, et desideriis Fratrum Nostrorum in episcopatu, qui pluries flagitaverunt ipsius rationis agilitatem, servata tamen soliditate investigationum in negotio tantae gravitatis. Putamus etiam, praelucente doctrina de collegialitate a Concilio Vaticano II proposita, valde convenire ut ipsi Episcopi magis Apostolicae Sedi socientur in causis sanctorum pertractandis.

In posterum, igitur, abrogatis ad rem quod

---

5. AAS 22 (1930), pp. 87–88.
6. AAS 31 (1939), pp. 174–175.
7. AAS 61 (1969), pp. 149–153.

8. *Ibid.*, nos. 3–4.
9. AAS 61 (1969), pp. 297–305.

pertain to this matter, we establish that these following norms are henceforth to be observed.

attinet omnibus legibus cuiusvis generis, has quae sequuntur statuimus normas servandas.

I. Inquiries to be Made By Bishops

1) It is the right of diocesan Bishops or Bishops of the Eastern Rite and others who have the same powers in law, within the limits of their own jurisdiction, either *ex officio* or upon the request of individual members of the faithful or of legitimate groups and their representatives, to inquire about the life, virtues or martyrdom and reputation of sanctity or martyrdom, alleged miracles, as well as, if it be the case, ancient cult of the Servant of God, whose canonization is sought.

2) In inquiries of this kind, the Bishop is to proceed according to the particular *Norms* to be published by the Sacred Congregation for the Causes of Saints. This is the order to be followed:

1. From the postulator of the cause, legitimately appointed by the petitioner, the Bishop is to seek out accurate information about the life of the Servant of God and likewise be thoroughly informed by the postulator of the reasons which seem to support promoting the cause of canonization.

2. If the Servant of God has published any writings, the Bishop is to see to it that they are examined by theological censors.

3. If the writings have been found to contain nothing contrary to faith and good morals, then the Bishop should order persons qualified for this task to collect other unpublished writings (letters, diaries, etc.) as well as all documents, which in any way pertain to the cause. After they have faithfully completed their task, they are to write a report on their investigations.

4. If the Bishop has prudently judged that, on the basis of all that has been done so far, the cause can proceed, he is to see to it that those witnesses proposed by the postulator and others to be called *ex officio* are duly examined.

If, indeed, it is urgent that witnesses be examined lest any proofs be lost, they are to be questioned even though the gathering of the documents has not yet been completed.

5. The inquiry into alleged miracles is to be conducted separately from the inquiry into virtues or martyrdom.

6. When the inquiries are complete, a transcript of all

I. De Inquisitionibus Ab Episcopis Faciends

1) Episcopis dioecesanis vel Hierarchis ceterisque in iure aequiparatis, intra fines suae iurisdictionis, sive ex officio, sive ad instantiam singulorum fidelium vel legitimorum coetuum eorumque procuratorum, ius competit inquirendi circa vitam, virtutes vel martyrium ac famam sanctitatis vel martyrii, asserta miracula, necnon, si casus ferat, antiquum cultum Servi Dei, cuius canonizatio petitur.

2) In huiusmodi inquisitionibus Episcopus iuxta peculiares Normas a Sacra Congregatione pro Causis Sanctorum edendas procedat, hoc quidem ordine:

1° A postulatore causae, legitime ab actore nominato, accuratam informationem de Servi Dei vita exquirat, simulque ab eo edoceatur de rationibus quae causae canonizationis promovendae favere videantur.

2° Si Servus Dei scripta a se exarata publice edidit, Episcopus curet ut eadem a censoribus theologis examinentur.

3° Si nihil contra fidem bonosque mores in iisdem scriptis repertum fuerit, tunc Episcopus alia scripta inedita (epistulas, diaria etc.) necnon omnia documenta, quoquo modo causam respicientia, perquiri iubeat a personis ad hoc idoneis, quae, postquam munus suum fideliter expleverint, relationem de perquisitionibus factis componant.

4° Si ex hucusque factis Episcopus prudenter iudicaverit ad ulteriora procedi posse, curet ut testes a postulatore inducti aliique ex officio vocandi rite examinentur.

Si vero urgeat examen testium ne pereant probationes, ipsi interrogandi sunt etiam nondum completa perquisitione documentorum.

5° Inquisitio de assertis miraculis ab inquisitione de virtutibus vel de martyrio separatim fiat.

6° Inquisitionibus peractis, transumptum

the acts is to be sent in duplicate to the Sacred Congregation, together with a copy of the books of the Servant of God which were examined by the theological censors and their judgment as well.

Furthermore, the Bishop is to attach a declaration on the observance of the decrees of Urban VIII regarding the absence of cult.

omnium actorum in duplici exemplari ad Sacram Congregationem mittatur, una cum exemplari librorum Servi Dei a censoribus theologis examinatorum eorumque iudicio.

Episcopus praeterea adiungat declarationem de observantia decretorum Urbani VIII super non cultu.

II. The Sacred Congregation for the Causes of Saints

3) The Sacred Congregation for the Causes of Saints is presided over by a Cardinal Prefect, assisted by a Secretary. Its duty is to deal with those matters which pertain to the canonization of Servants of God by providing advice and guidelines to Bishops in the instruction of the causes, by studying the causes thoroughly and, finally, by casting its vote.

It is also the duty of the Congregation to decide those things which pertain to the authenticity and preservation of relics.

4) The duty of the Secretary is:

1. to handle business with those outside the Congregation, especially with Bishops who are instructing causes;

2. to take part in the discussions about the merit of a cause and to cast a vote in the meeting of the Cardinal and Bishop Members of the Congregation;

3. to draw up the report that is to be given to the Supreme Pontiff on how the Cardinals and Bishops voted.

5) The Secretary is assisted in fulfilling his duty by an Undersecretary, whose task is primarily to ascertain whether the rules of law have been followed in the instruction of the causes. The Secretary is also assisted by an appropriate number of minor Officials.

6) For the purpose of studying the causes there exists in the Sacred Congregation a College of Relators, presided over by a Relator General.

7) The individual Relators are:

1. to study the causes entrusted to them, together with collaborators from outside the Congregation, and to prepare the *Positions* on virtues or on martyrdom;

2. to prepare written explanations of an historical nature which may have been requested by the Consultors;

3. to be present as experts at the meeting of the theologians, although without the right to vote.

8) One of the Relators shall be especially selected to prepare the *Positions* on miracles. He will take part in the meetings of the physicians and of the theologians.

II. De Sacra Congregatione Pro Causis Sanctorum

3) Sacrae Congregationis pro Causis Sanctorum, cui praeest Cardinalis Praefectus, adiuvante Secretario, munus est, ut ea agat quae ad canonizationem Servorum Dei pertinent, et quidem tum Episcopis in causis instruendis consilio atque instructionibus assistendo, tum causis funditus studendo, tum denique vota ferendo.

Ad eamdem Congregationem spectat decernere de iis omnibus quae ad authenticitatem et conservationem reliquiarum referuntur.

4) Secretarii officium est:

1° relationes cum externis, praesertim cum Episcopis qui causas instruunt, curare;

2° discussiones de merito causae participare, votum ferendo in congregatione Patrum Cardinalium et Episcoporum;

3° relationem, Summo Pontifici tradendam, de votis Cardinalium et Episcoporum conficere.

5) In munere suo adimplendo Secretarius adiuvatur a Subsecretario, cui competit praesertim videre si legis praescripta in causarum instructione adimpleta fuerint, necnon a congruo numero Officialium minorum.

6) Pro studio causarum apud Sacram Congregationem adest Collegium Relatorum, cui praeest Relator generalis.

7) Singulorum Relatorum est:

1° una cum externis cooperatoribus causis sibi commissis studere atque Positiones super virtutibus vel super martyrio parare;

2° enodationes historicas, si quae a Consultoribus requisitae fuerint, scriptis exarare;

3° Congressui theologorum tamquam expertos adesse, sine tamen voto.

8) Inter Relatores unus aderit specialiter deputatus pro elucubratione Positionum super miraculis, qui intererit Coetui medicorum et Congressui theologorum.

9) The Relator General, who presides over the meeting of the historical Consultors, is to be aided in his study by some Assistants.

10) The Sacred Congregation is to have one Promotor of the Faith or Prelate Theologian. His responsibility is:

1. to preside over the meeting of the theologians, with the right to vote;

2. to prepare the report on the meeting itself;

3. to be present as an expert at the meeting of the Cardinals and Bishops, although without the right to vote.

If necessary for one or another cause, a Promotor of the Faith for that particular case can be nominated by the Cardinal Prefect.

11) Consultors are to be drawn from various parts of the world to deal with the causes of Saints. Some are to be experts in historical matters and others in theology, particularly in spiritual theology.

12) There is to be a board of medical experts in the Sacred Congregation whose responsibility is to examine healings which are proposed as miracles.

III. Procedure in the Sacred Congregation

13) When the Bishop has sent to Rome all the acts and documents pertaining to a cause, the procedure in the Sacred Congregation for the Causes of Saints is as follows:

1. First of all, the Undersecretary is to verify whether all the rules of law have been followed in the inquiries conducted by the Bishop. He is to report the result of his examination in the ordinary meeting of the Congregation.

2. If the meeting judges that the cause was conducted according to the norms of law, it decides to which Relator the cause is to be assigned; the Relator, then, together with a collaborator from outside the Congregation, will prepare the *Position* on virtues or on martyrdom according to the rules of critical hagiography.

3. In ancient causes and in those recent causes whose particular nature, in the judgment of the Relator General, should demand it, the published *Position* is to be examined by Consultors who are specially expert in that field so that they can cast their vote on its scientific value and whether it contains sufficient elements required for the scope for which the *Position* has been prepared.

9) Relator generalis, qui praesidet Coetui Consultorum historicorum, adiuvatur a nonnullis Adiutoribus a studiis.

10) Apud Sacram Congregationem unus adest Promotor fidei seu Praelatus theologus, cuius est:

1° Congressui theologorum praeesse, in quo votum fert;

2° relationem de ipso Congressu parare;

3° congregationi Patrum Cardinalium et Episcoporum tamquam expertum adesse, sine tamen voto.

Pro una aliave causa, si opus fuerit, a Cardinali Praefecto nominari poterit Promotor fidei ad casum.

11) Causis sanctorum tractandis praesto sunt Consultores ex diversis regionibus acciti, alii in re historica alii in theologia praesertim spirituali periti.

12) Pro examine sanationum, quae tamquam miracula proponuntur, habetur apud Sacram Congregationem coetus in arte medica peritorum.

III. De Modo Procedendi In Sacra Congregatione

13) Cum omnia acta et documenta causam respicientia Episcopus Romam miserit, in Sacra Congregatione pro Causis Sanctorum hoc modo procedatur:

1° Ante omnia Subsecretarius scrutatur utrum in inquisitionibus ab Episcopo factis omnia legis statuta servata sint, et de exitu examinis in Congressu ordinario referet.

2° Si Congressus iudicaverit causam instructam fuisse ad legis normas, statuet cuinam ex Relatoribus committenda sit; Relator vero una cum cooperatore externo Positionem super virtutibus vel super martyrio conficiet iuxta regulas artis criticae in hagiographia servandas.

3° In causis antiquis et in iis recentioribus, quarum peculiaris indoles de iudicio Relatoris generalis id postulaverit, edita Positio examini subicienda erit Consultorum in re speciatim peritorum, ut de eius valore scientifico necnon sufficientia ad effectum de quo agitur votum ferant.

In particular cases, the Sacred Congregation can also give the *Position* to other scholars, who are not part of the group of Consultors, for their examination.

4. The *Position* (together with the votes of the historical Consultors as well as any new explanations by the Relator, should they be necessary) is handed over to the theological Consultors, who are to cast their vote on the merit of the cause; their responsibility, together wth the Promotor of the Faith, is to study the cause in such a way that, before the *Position* is submitted for discussion in their special meeting, controversial theological questions, if there be any, may be examined thoroughly.

5. The definitive votes of the theological Consultors, together with the written conclusions of the Promotor of the Faith, are submitted to the judgment of the Cardinals and Bishops.

14) The Congregation examines cases of alleged miracles in the following way:

1. The Relator assigned to this task is to prepare a *Position* on alleged miracles. They are discussed in a meeting of experts (in the case of healings, in a meeting of physicians), whose votes and conclusions are set forth in an accurate report.

2. Then the miracles are to be discussed in the special meeting of the theologians and, finally, in that of the Cardinals and Bishops.

15) The results of the discussions of the Cardinals and Bishops are reported to the Supreme Pontiff, who alone has the right to declare that public cult may be given by the Church to Servants of God.

16) By a special decree, the Sacred Congregation itself will establish the procedure to be followed henceforth in the individual causes of canonization whose judgment is presently pending at the Sacred Congregation, in accordance, however, with the spirit of this new law.

17) All that which we have established in this Our Constitution is to take effect from this very day.

Moreover, we wish that these Our statutes and rules should be, now and hereafter, binding and effective and, insofar as is necessary, we abrogate the Apostolic Constitutions and Regulations published by Our Predecessors and all other rules, including those which are worthy of special mention and derogation.

Given in Rome, at Saint Peter's, on the 25th day of the month of January in the year 1983, the 5th of Our Pontificate.

John Paul II

In singulis casibus Sacra Congregatio potest Positionem etiam aliis viris doctis, in Consultorum numerum non relatis, examinandam tradere.

4° Positio (una cum votis scriptis Consultorum historicorum necnon novis enodationibus Relatoris, si quae necessariae sint) tradetur Consultoribus theologis, qui de merito causae votum ferent; quorum est, una cum Promotore fidei, causae ita studere, ut, antequam ad discussionem in Congressu peculiari deveniatur, quaestiones theologicae controversae, si quae sint, funditus examinentur.

5° Vota definitiva Consultorum theologorum, una cum conclusionibus a Promotore fidei exaratis, Cardinalibus atque Episcopis iudicaturis tradentur.

14) De assertis miraculis Congregatio cognoscit sequenti ratione:

1° Asserta miracula, super quibus a Relatore ad hoc deputato paratur Positio, expenduntur in coetu peritorum (si de sanationibus agitur, in coetu medicorum), quorum vota et conclusiones in accurata relatione exponuntur.

2° Deinde miracula discutienda sunt in peculiari Congressu theologorum, ac denique in congregatione Patrum Cardinalium et Episcoporum.

15) Sententiae Patrum Cardinalium et Episcoporum referuntur ad Summum Pontificem, cui uni competit ius decernendi cultum publicum ecelesiasticum Servis Dei praestandum.

16) In singulis canonizationis causis, quarum iudicium in praesens apud Sacram Congregationem pendeat, Sacra ipsa Congregatio peculiari decreto statuet modum ad ulteriora procedendi, servata tamen mente huius novae legis.

17) Quae Constitutione hac Nostra praescripsimus ab hoc ipso die vigere incipiunt.

Nostra haec autem statuta et praescripta nunc et in posterum firma et efficacia esse et fore volumus, non obstantibus, quatenus opus est, Constitutionibus et Ordinationibus Apostolicis a Decessoribus Nostris editis, ceterisque praescriptionibus etiam peculiari mentione et derogatione dignis.

Datum Romae, apud Sanctum Petrum, die xxv mensis Ianuarii anno MCMLXXXIII, Pontificatus Nostri quinto.

Ioannes Paulus PP. II

CONGREGATION

FOR THE CAUSES OF SAINTS

Norms to be Observed in Inquiries Made by Bishops in the Causes of Saints

CONGREGATIO

PRO CAUSIS SANCTORUM

Normae servandae in inquisitionibus ab episcopis faciendis in causis sanctorum

THE APOSTOLIC CONSTITUTION *Divinus perfectionis Magister* of January 25, 1983 set forth the procedure for the inquiries which henceforth are to be made by Bishops in the causes of saints and likewise entrusted to this Sacred Congregation the duty of publishing particular Norms for this purpose. The Sacred Congregation has developed the following norms, which the Supreme Pontiff directed to be examined by a Plenary Meeting of the Fathers who are Members of this Congregation, which was held on June 22nd and 23rd of 1981. After consulting all the heads of the Offices of the Roman Curia, the same Pontiff approved these norms and ordered them to be published.

1. *a)* The petitioner advances the cause of canonization. Any member of the People of God or any group of the faithful recognized by ecclesiastical authority can exercise this function.

b) The petitioner handles the cause through a legitimately appointed postulator.

2. a) The postulator is appointed by the petitioner by means of a mandate written according to the norm of law, with the approval of the Bishop.

b) While the cause is being handled at the Sacred Congregation, the postulator, provided that he be approved by the Congregation itself, must reside in Rome.

3. *a)* Priests, members of Institutes of consecrated life

CUM IN CONSTITUTIONE APOSTOLICA *Divinus perfectionis Magister* diei 25 ianuarii anni 1983 statutus sit ordo procedendi in inquisitionibus quae in posterum ab Episcopis faciendae sunt in causis sanctorum, itemque Sacrae huic Congregationi munus concreditum sit peculiares ad hoc Normas edendi, eadem Sacra Congregatio sequentes confecit normas, quas Summus Pontifex a Plenario Coetu Patrum praefatae Congregationi praepositorum, diebus 22 et 23 mensis iunii anno 1981 habito, examinari voluit et, auditis quoque omnibus Patribus Dicasteriis Romanae Curiae praepositis, ratas habuit et promulgari iussit.

1. *a)* Causam canonizationis actor promovet; quo munere quilibet e populo Dei aut christifidelium coetus ab ecclesiastica auctoritate admissus, fungi potest.

b) Actor causam agit per postulatorem legitime constitutum.

2. *a)* Postulator constituitur ab actore per procurationis mandatum ad normam iuris redactum, probante Episcopo.

b) Dum causa apud Sacram Congregationem tractatur, postulator, dummodo ab ipsa Congregatione sit approbatus, in Urbe fixam sedem habere debet.

3. *a)* Munere postulatoris fungi possunt sac-

and lay persons can exercise the function of postulator; all must be experts in theological, canonical and historical matters, as well as versed in the practice of the Sacred Congregation.

b) The first duty of the postulator is to conduct thorough investigations into the life of the Servant of God in question, in order to establish his reputation of sanctity and the importance of the cause for the Church, and then to report his findings to the Bishop.

c) The postulator is also entrusted with the duty of administrating those funds offered for the cause according to the norms issued by the Sacred Congregation.

4. Through a legitimate mandate and with the consent of the petitioners, the postulator has the right to appoint others in his place who are called vice-postulators.

5. *a)* The Bishop competent to instruct causes of canonization is the one in whose territory the Servant of God died, unless particular circumstances, recognized as such by the Sacred Congregation, suggest otherwise.

b) In the case of an alleged miracle, the competent Bishop is the one in whose territory the event took place.

6. *a)* The Bishop can instruct the cause either personally or through his delegate, who is to be a priest truly expert in theological and canonical matters, as well as in historical matters, in the case of ancient causes.

b) The priest who is chosen as the promotor of justice must have the same qualities.

c) All officials, who take part in the cause, must take an oath to fulfil faithfully their duty, and are bound to maintain secrecy.

7. A cause can be recent or ancient: it is called recent if the martyrdom or virtues of the Servant of God can be proved through the oral depositions of eye witnesses; it is ancient, however, when the proofs for martyrdom or virtues can be brought to light only from written sources.

8. Whoever intends to initiate a cause of canonization is to present to the competent Bishop, through the postulator, a written petition, requesting the instruction of the cause.

9. *a)* In recent causes, the petition must be presented no sooner than five years after the death of the Servant of God.

b) If, however, it is presented after thirty years, the Bishop may not proceed further unless, upon investigation, he is convinced that there was no fraud in the case or deceit on the part of the petitioners in delaying the initiation of the cause.

erdotes, membra Institutorum vitae consecratae et laici, qui omnes oportet sint periti in re theologica, canonica et historica, necnon in praxi Sacrae Congregationis versati.

b) Postulatoris imprimis est peragere investigationes circa vitam Servi Dei de quo agitur, ad eius famam sanctitatis et causae momentum ecclesiale dignoscenda, de eisque Episcopo referre.

c) Postulatori committitur etiam munus bona pro causa oblata administrandi iuxta normas a Sacra Congregatione traditas.

4. Postulatori ius competit substituendi sibi, per legitimum mandatum ac de consensu actorum, alios qui vice-postulatores dicuntur.

5. *a)* In causis canonizationis instruendis Episcopus competens ille est in cuius territorio Servus Dei supremum diem obiit, nisi peculiaria adiuncta, a Sacra Congregatione probata, aliud suadeant.

b) Si de asserto miraculo agitur, competens est Episcopus in cuius territorio factum evenit.

6. *a)* Episcopus causam instruere valet sive per se sive per suum delegatum, qui sit sacerdos in re teologica, canonica et historica quoque, si de causis antiquis agatur, vere peritus.

b) Iisdem qualitatibus pollere debet sacerdos qui in promotorem iustitiae eligitur.

c) Omnes officiales partem in causa habentes debent iuramentum de munere fideliter adimplendo praestare, et secreto tenentur.

7. Causa potest esse recentior aut antiqua; *recentior* dicitur, si martyrium vel virtutes Servi Dei per orales depositiones testium de visu probari possunt; *antiqua* vero, cum probationes de martyrio vel virtutibus dumtaxat ex fontibus scriptis erui possunt.

8. Quicumque causam canonizationis inchoare intendit, per postulatorem Episcopo competenti supplicem libellum exhibeat, quo causae instructio petatur.

9. *a)* In causis recentioribus, libellus exhiberi debet non ante quintum annum a morte Servi Dei.

b) Si vero exhibetur post annum tricesimum, Episcopus ad ulteriora procedere nequit nisi, inquisitione peracta, sibi persuasum habuerit nullam in casu adfuisse fraudem vel dolum ex parte actorum in protracta inchoatione causae.

10. The postulator must present together with the written petition:

1. in both recent and ancient causes, a biography of any historical import of the Servant of God, should such exist, or otherwise an accurate, chronologically arranged report on the life and deeds of the Servant of God, on his virtues or martyrdom, on his reputation of sanctity and of signs. Nor should anything be omitted which seems to be contrary or less favorable to the cause;[1]

2. an authentic copy of all the published writings of the Servant of God;

3. in recent causes only, a list of persons who can help bring to light the truth about the virtues or the martyrdom of the Servant of God, and about his reputation of sanctity or of signs. Those with contrary opinions must also be included.

11. *a)* Once the petition has been accepted, the Bishop is to consult with the Conference of Bishops, at least of the region, about the appropriateness of initiating the cause.

b) Furthermore, the Bishop is to publicize the petition of the postulator in his own diocese and, if he has judged it opportune, in other dioceses, with the permission of their respective Bishops, and to invite all the faithful to bring to his attention any useful information, which they might have to offer regarding the cause.

12. *a)* If a significant obstacle to the cause emerges from the information he has received, the Bishop is to notify the postulator about it so that he can remove that obstacle.

b) If the obstacle has not been removed and the Bishop has therefore judged that the cause should not be admitted, he is to advise the postulator, giving the reasons for his decision.

13. If the Bishop intends to initiate the cause, he is to seek the vote of two theological censors on the published writings of the Servant of God. These censors are to report whether anything is found in these same writings, contrary to faith and good morals.[2]

14. *a)* If the votes of the theological censors are favorable, the Bishop is to order that all the writings of the Servant of God, those not yet published as well as each and every historical document, either handwritten or printed, which in any way pertain to the cause, are to be gathered.[3]

b) When such a search is to be made, especially in the

10. Postulator una cum supplici libello exhibere debet:

1° in causis tam recentioribus quam antiquis, biographiam alicuius historici momenti de Servo Dei, si extat, vel, ea deficiente, accuratam relationem chronologice digestam de vita et gestis ipsius Servi Dei, de eius virtutibus vel martyrio, de sanctitatis et signorum fama, non omissis iis quae ipsi causae contraria vel minus favorabilia videntur;[1]

2° omnia scripta edita Servi Dei in authentico exemplari;

3° in causis recentioribus tantum, elenchum personarum quae ad eruendam veritatem circa virtutes vel martyrium Servi Dei, necnon circa sanctitatis vel signorum famam conferre possunt vel adversari.

11. *a)* Accepto libello, Episcopus coetum Episcoporum saltem regionis de opportunitate causae inchoandae consulat.

b) Insuper in sua et, si id opportunum duxerit, in aliis dioecesibus, de consensu eorundem Episcoporum, petitionem postulatoris publici iuris faciat, omnes christifideles invitando ut utiles notitias causam respicientes, si quas suppeditandas habeant, sibi deferant.

12. *a)* Si ex informationibus receptis obstaculum alicuius momenti contra causam emerserit, de eo Episcopus postulatorem certiorem faciat, ut illud removere possit.

b) Si obstaculum remotum non fuerit et Episcopus ideo iudicaverit causam non esse admittendam, postulatorem moneat, allatis de decisione rationibus.

13. Si Episcopus causam inchoare intendit, votum super scriptis editis Servi Dei a duobus censoribus theologis exquirat, qui referant num in iisdem scriptis aliquid habeatur, quod fidei ac bonis moribus adversetur.[2]

14. *a)* Si vota censorum theologorum favorabilia sunt, Episcopus mandat ut universa scripta Servi Dei nondum edita necnon omnia et singula historica documenta sive manuscripta sive typis edita, quoquo modo causam respicientia, colligantur.[3]

b) In huiusmodi requisitione facienda, prae-

---

1. Cfr. Apost. Const. *Divinus perfectionis Magister*, no. 2, 1.

2. Cfr. *ibid.*, no. 2, 2.
3. Cfr. *ibid.*, no. 2, 3.

case of ancient causes, experts in historical matters and in matters that pertain to archives, are to be employed.

c) After the task has been completed, the experts are to hand over to the Bishop an accurate and precise report together with the collected writings. In this report, they are to indicate and testify that they fulfilled their duty properly; to include a list of the writings and documents; to give a judgment on their authenticity and their value as well as on the personality of the Servant of God, as it appears from the same writings and documents.

15. a) Once the report has been accepted, the Bishop is to hand over to the promõtor of justice or to another expert everything gathered up to that point so that he might formulate the interrogatories most effective in searching out and discovering the truth about the life of the Servant of God, his virtues or martyrdom, his reputation of holiness or of martyrdom.

b) In ancient causes, however, the interrogatories are only to consider the reputation of sanctity or martyrdom existing until the present as well as, if it be the case, the cult given to the Servant of God in more recent times.

c) In the meantime, the Bishop is to send to the Sacred Congregation for the Causes of Saints a brief report on the life of the Servant of God and the relevance of the cause, in order to ascertain whether there is any obstacle on the part of the Holy See to the cause.

16. *a)* Then the Bishop or his delegate is to examine the witnesses proposed by the postulator and others to be questioned *ex officio.* A Notary is to be employed to transcribe the deposition of the witness, which is to be confirmed by the witness himself at the end of his testimony.

If, indeed, it is urgent that witnesses be examined lest any proofs be lost, they are to be questioned even though the gathering of the documents has not yet been completed.[4]

b) The promotor of justice is to be present at the examination of the witnesses. If, however, he was not present, the acts are to be submitted afterwards for his examination so that he can make his observations and propose anything which he judges to be necessary and opportune.

c) First of all, the witnesses are to be examined according to the interrogatories; the Bishop or his delegate, however, should not fail to propose to the witnesses other necessary or useful questions so that their statements may be put in a clearer light or any difficulties which may have emerged may be plainly resolved and explained.

sertim cum de causis antiquis agatur, periti in re historica et archivistica adhibeantur.

c) Munere expleto, periti una cum scriptis collectis diligentem et distinctam relationem Episcopo tradant, in qua referant et fidem faciant de officio bene adimpleto, elenchum scriptorum et documentorum includant, iudicium de eorum authenticitate et valore promant necnon de personalitate Servi Dei, uti ex ipsis scriptis et documentis eruitur.

15. a) Relatione accepta, Episcopus omnia usque ad illud tempus acquisita promotori iustitiae vel alii viro perito tradat, ut interrogatoria conficiat quae apta sint ad verum indagandum et inveniendum de Servi Dei vita, virtutibus vel martyrio, fama sanctitatis vel martyrii.

b) In causis antiquis vero interrogatoria dumtaxat famam sanctitatis vel martyrii adhuc vigentem necnon, si casus ferat, cultum recentioribus temporibus Servo Dei praestitum respiciant.

c) Interim Episcopus brevem de Servi Dei vita ac de causae pondere notitiam ad Sacram Congregationem pro Causis Sanctorum transmittat, ad videndum utrum ex parte Sanctae Sedis aliquid causae obsit.

16. a) Deinde Episcopus vel delegatus testes a postulatore inductos et alios ex officio interrogandos examinet, adhibito notario qui verba deponentis transcribat, in fine ab eodem confirmanda.

Si vero urgeat examen testium ne pereant probationes, ipsi interrogandi sunt etiam nondum completa perquisitione documentorum.[4]

b) Examini testium adsit promotor iustitiae; quodsi idem non interfuerit, acta postea eius examini subiciantur, ut ipsemet animadvertere ac proponere possit quae necessaria et opportuna iudicaverit.

c) Testes imprimis iuxta interrogatoria examinentur; Episcopus autem vel delegatus ne omittat alias necessarias vel utiles interrogationes testibus proponere, ut quae ab ipsis dicta sint in clariore luce ponantur vel difficultates, quae emerserint, plane solvantur et explanentur.

---

4. Cfr. *ibid.,* no. 2, 4.

17. The witnesses must be eye witnesses; if the case warrants it, second-hand witnesses may be added. All, however, must be trustworthy.

18. Blood relatives and relatives through marriage of the Servant of God are the first witnesses to be proposed as well as other friends and acquaintances.

19. In order to prove the martyrdom or the practice of virtues and the reputation of signs of the Servant of God who belonged to any Institute of consecrated life, a significant number of the proposed witnesses must be from outside the Institute unless, on account of the particular life of the Servant of God, this should prove impossible.

20. Those who are not to be allowed to testify are:

1. a priest, with regard to all those things which were made known to him through the sacrament of Penance.

2. regular confessors of the Servant of God or spiritual directors, with regard also to all those things which they learned from the Servant of God in the forum of conscience outside the sacrament of Penance;

3. the postulator of the cause, during his term as postulator.

21. *a)* The Bishop or his delegate is to call some witnesses *ex officio*, who can contribute to completing the inquiry, if it be the case, particularly if they are opposed to the cause;

b) The Bishop or his delegate is also to call as *ex officio* witnesses those experts who conducted the investigations of the documents and wrote the relative report. They must declare under oath: 1.- that they conducted all the investigations and that they gathered all those things which pertain to the cause; 2.- that they neither changed nor destroyed any document or text.

22. *a)* In the case of miraculous healings, the physicians who treated the patient are to be called as witnesses.

b) If they refuse to appear before the Bishop or his delegate, the aforementioned is to see to it that they write a report, sworn if possible, about the disease and its progress, which is to be inserted into the acts, or at least their opinion is to be heard by a third party, who is then to be examined.

23. In their testimony, which is to be sworn to under oath, the witnesses must indicate the source of their knowledge of the things they assert; otherwise, their testimony is to be considered of no value.

24. If any witness prefers to give to the Bishop or his delegate a previously prepared written statement, either together with his deposition or in addition to it, such a writ-

17. Testes debent esse de visu, quibus addi possunt, si casus ferat, nonnulli testes de auditu a videntibus; omnes autem sint fide digni.

18. Tamquam testes imprimis inducantur consanguinei et affines Servi Dei aliique, qui cum eodem familiaritatem aut consuetudinem habuerint.

19. Ad probandum martyrium aut virtutum exercitium et signorum famam Servi Dei qui pertinuerit ad aliquod Institutum vitae consecratae, notabilis pars testium inductorum debent esse extranei, nisi, ob peculiarem Servi Dei vitam, id impossibile evadat.

20. Ne admittantur ad testificandum:

1° sacerdos, quod attinet ad ea omnia quae ei ex confessione sacramentali innotuerunt;

2° habituales Servi Dei confessarii vel spiritus directores, quod attinet etiam ad ea omnia quae a Servo Dei in foro conscientiae extrasacramentali acceperint;

3° postulator in causa, durante munere.

21. *a)* Episcopus vel delegatus aliquos testes ex officio vocet, qui ad inquisitionem perficiendam, si casus ferat, contribuere valeant, praesertim si ipsi causae contrarii sunt.

b) Vocandi sunt tamquam testes ex officio viri periti qui pervestigationes documentorum fecerunt et relationem de ipsis exararunt, iidemque sub iuramento declarare debent: 1° se omnes investigationes peregisse ac omnia collegisse quae causam respiciant; 2° nullum documentum aut textum se adulterasse vel mutilasse.

22. *a)* Medici a curatione, cum de miris sanationibus agitur, tamquam testes sunt inducendi.

b) Quod si renuerint se Episcopo vel delegato sistere, is curet ut scriptam sub iuramento, si fieri potest, relationem de morbo eiusque progressione conficiant actis inserendam, vel saltem eorum sententia per interpositam personam excipiatur, deinde examini subiciendam.

23. Testes in sua testificatione, iuramento firmanda, propriae scientiae fontem indicare debent circa ea quae asserunt; secus eorum testimonium nihili faciendum est.

24. Si quis testis maluerit scriptum aliquod a seipso antea exaratum Episcopo vel delegato tradere sive una cum depositione sive praeter

ten statement is to be accepted, provided the witness himself shall have proved by an oath that he himself wrote it
and that its contents are true. It is also to be made part of
the acts of the cause.

25. *a)* In whatever way the witnesses provide their information, the Bishop or his delegate is carefully to see to
it that he always authenticates it with his signature and his
seal.

b) The documents and written testimony, whether
gathered by the experts or handed over by others, are to be
authenticated by the signature and seal of any notary or
public official, who attests to its authenticity.

26. *a)* If inquiries regarding documents or witnesses
must be made in another diocese, the Bishop or his delegate is to send a letter to the competent Bishop, who is to
act according to the norm of these statutes.

b) The acts of this type of inquiry are to be kept in the
archive of the Chancery, while a copy, made according to
the norm of nos. 29 and 30, is to be sent to the Bishop, who
requested the inquiry.

27. *a)* The Bishop or his delegate is to take the greatest
care that in gathering the proofs nothing is omitted which
in any way pertains to the cause, recognizing for sure that
the positive outcome of a cause depends to a great extent
on its good instruction.

b) Once all the proofs have been gathered, the promotor of justice is to inspect all the acts and documents so
that, should he deem it necessary, he may request further
inquiries.

c) The postulator is also entitled to inspect the acts so
that, if it be the case, the proofs may be completed through
new witnesses or documents.

28. *a)* Before the inquiry is concluded, the Bishop or his
delegate is to inspect carefully the tomb of the Servant of
God, the room in which he lived or died and, if there be
any, other places where someone can display signs of cult
in his honor. He is also to make a declaration on the observance of the decrees of Urban VIII regarding the absence
of cult.[5]

b) A report is to be drawn up about everything which
has been done and it is to be inserted into the acts.

29. *a)* Once the instruction has been completed, the
Bishop or his delegate is to order that a transcript be made

eam, huiusmodi scriptum recipiatur, dummodo
ipse testis iuramento probaverit se illud scrip-
sisse et vera in eo esse contenta, idemque ad
acta causae accenseatur.

25. *a)* Quocumque modo testes suas notitias tradiderint, curet diligenter Episcopus vel
delegatus ut illas authenticas reddat semper sua
subsignatione et proprio sigillo.

b) Documenta et testimonia scripta, sive a
peritis collecta sive ab aliis tradita, authentica
declarentur per appositionem nominis et sigilli
alicuius notarii vel publici officialis fidem facien-
tis.

26. *a)* Si inquisitiones circa documenta vel
testes in alia dioecesi fieri debent, Episcopus vel
delegatus litteras ad Episcopum competentem
mittat, qui ad normam horum statutorum agat.

b) Acta huiusmodi inquisitionis in archivo
Curiae serventur, sed exemplar ad normam nn.
29–30 confectum ad Episcopum rogantem mittatur.

27. *a)* Episcopus vel delegatus summa diligentia et industria curet ut in probationibus col-
ligendis nihil omittatur, quod quoquo modo ad
causam pertineat, pro certo habens felicem exitum causae ex bona eius instructione magna ex
parte dependere.

b) Collectis igitur omnibus probationibus,
promotor iustitiae omnia acta et documenta inspiciat ut, si ipsi necessarium videatur, ulteriores
inquisitiones petere possit.

c) Postulatori quoque facultas danda est
acta inspiciendi ut, si casus ferat, per novos
testes aut documenta probationes compleri
possint.

28. *a)* Antequam absolvatur inquisitio, Episcopus vel delegatus diligenter inspiciat sepul-
crum Servi Dei, cubiculum in quo habitavit vel
obiit et, si quae sint, alia loca ubi cultus signa in
eius honorem quis exhibere possit, et declarationem faciat de observantia decretorum Urbani
VIII super non cultu.[5]

b) De omnibus peractis relatio conficiatur
actis inserenda.

29. *a)* Instructoriis actis absolutis, Episcopus vel delegatus statuat ut transumptum confi-

---

5. Cfr. *ibid.*, no. 2, 6.

unless, in light of proven circumstances, he has already permitted this to be done during the instruction itself.

b) The transcript is to be transcribed from the original acts and made in duplicate.

30. *a)* Once the transcript has been finished, a comparison is to be made with the original and the notary is at least to initial each page and stamp them with his seal.

b) The original, closed and secured with seals, is to be kept in the archive of the Chancery.

31. *a)* The transcript of the inquiry and attached documents in duplicate, duly wrapped and secured with seals, are to be sent by a secure means to the Sacred Congregation, together with a copy of the books of the Servant of God which were examined by the theological censors and their judgment.[6]

b) If a translation of the acts and documents into a language accepted at the Sacred Congregation is necessary, two copies of the translation are to be prepared and declared authentic. These are then to be sent to Rome.

c) Furthermore, the Bishop or his delegate is to send to the Cardinal Prefect a letter testifying to the trustworthiness of the witnesses and the legitimacy of the acts.

32. The inquiry on miracles is to be instructed separately from the inquiry on virtues or martyrdom and is to be conducted according to the norms which follow.[7]

33. *a)* Once the Bishop competent according to norm no. 5b has accepted the petition of the postulator together with a brief but accurate report on the alleged miracle as well as those documents which pertain to the case, he is to ask for the judgment of one or two experts.

b) If he has then decided to instruct a judicial inquiry, he is to examine all the witnesses either personally or through his delegate, according to the norms established above in nos. 15 a, 16–18 and 21–24.

34. *a)* In the case of a cure from some disease, the Bishop or his delegate is to seek help from a physician, who is to propose questions to the witnesses in order to clarify matters according to necessity and circumstances.

b) If the person healed is still alive, he is to be examined by experts so that the duration of the healing can be ascertained.

35. A transcript of the inquiry together with attached documents is to be sent to the Sacred Congregation according to what is laid down in nos. 29–31.

ciatur, nisi, attentis probatis circumstantiis, durante ipsa instructione iam fieri permiserit.

b) Transumptum ex actis originalibus transcribatur atque duplici exemplari fiat.

30. *a)* Absoluta transumpti confectione, collatio cum archetypo fiat, et notarius singulas paginas siglis saltem subscribat et suo sigillo muniat.

b) Archetypum clausum sigillisque munitum in archivo Curiae asservetur.

31. *a)* Transumptum inquisitionis et adnexa documenta in duplici exemplari ad Sacram Congregationem rite clausa, et sigillis munita tute mittantur, una cum exemplari librorum Servi Dei a censoribus theologis examinatorum eorumque iudicio.[6]

b) Si versio actorum atque documentorum in linguam apud Sacram Congregationem admissam necessaria sit, duo exemplaria versionis exarentur et authentica declarentur, Romam una cum transumpto mittenda.

c) Episcopus vel delegatus insuper litteras de fide testibus adhibenda et de legitimate actorum ad Cardinalem Praefectum mittat.

32. Inquisitio super miraculis separatim instruenda est ab inquisitione super virtutibus vel martyrio et fiat iuxta normas quae sequuntur.[7]

33. *a)* Episcopus competens ad normam n. 5 b, accepto postulatoris libello una cum brevi sed accurata relatione de asserto miraculo necnon documentis illud respicientibus, iudicium exquirat ab uno vel duobus peritis.

b) Deinde si inquisitionem iuridicam instruere statuerit, per se vel per suum delegatum omnes testes examinet, iuxta normas supra nn. 15 a, 16–18 et 21–24 statutas.

34. *a)* Si de sanatione alicuius morbi agatur, Episcopus vel delegatus auxilium quaerat a medico, qui interrogationes testibus proponat ad res clarius illustrandas iuxta necessitatem et circumstantias.

b) Si sanatus adhuc vivat, eius inspectio a peritis fiat, ut constare possit de duratione sanationis.

35. Inquisitionis transumptum una cum adnexis documentis ad Sacram Congregationem mittatur, iuxta statuta in nn. 29–31.

---

6. *Ibid.*

7. *Ibid.*, no. 2, 5.

36. Any solemn celebrations or panegyric speeches about Servants of God whose sanctity of life is still being legitimately examined are prohibited in Churches.

Furthermore, one must also refrain, even outside of Church, from any acts which could mislead the faithful into thinking that the inquiry conducted by the Bishop into the life of the Servant of God and his virtues or martyrdom carries with it the certitude that the Servant of God will be one day canonized.

His Holiness Pope John Paul II, in an Audience granted to the undersigned Cardinal Prefect of the Congregation on the 7th day of February in the year 1983, approved and ratified these norms, ordering that they be published and take effect from this very day, and are to be duly and conscientiously observed by all Bishops who instruct causes of canonization and by all others whom they concern, notwithstanding anything to the contrary, even those things worthy of special mention.

Given in Rome, from the Offices of the Sacred Congregation for the Causes of Saints, on the 7th day of the month of February in the year 1983.

> PIETRO Cardinal PALAZZINI, *Prefect*
> +Traian Crisan,
> Titular Archbishop of Drivasto,
> *Secretary*

36. De Servis Dei, quorum sanctitas vitae adhuc legitimo examini subiecta est, quaelibet sollemnia vel panegyricae orationes in ecclesiis prohibentur.

Sed etiam extra ecclesiam abstinendum est ab iis actis quibus fideles induci possint ad falso putandum inquisitionem ab Episcopo factam de Servi Dei vita et virtutibus vel martyrio certitudinem secum ferre futurae eiusdem Servi Dei canonizationis.

Quas normas SS.mus D. N. Ioannes Paulus divina Providentia Papa II, in Audientia die 7 februarii a. l983 infrascripto Congregationis Cardinali Praefecto concessa, approbare et ratas habere dignatus est, mandans ut eae publici iuris fiant et ab hoc ipso die vigere incipiant, ab omnibus Episcopis qui causas canonizationis instruunt, et a ceteris ad quos spectat, rite et religiose servandae, contrariis quibuscumque, etiam speciali mentione dignis, minime obstantibus.

Datum Romae, ex Aedibus Sacrae Congregationis pro Causis Sanctorum, die 7 mensis februarii a. 1983.

> PETRUS Card. PALAZZINI, *Praefectus*
> +Traianus Crisan,
> Archiep. tit. Drivastensis,
> *a Secretis*

General Decree on the Causes of the Servants of God Whose Judgment is Presently Pending at the Sacred Congregation

Decretum Generale de servorum Dei causis, quarum iudicium in praesens apud Sacram Congregationem pendet

THE APOSTOLIC CONSTITUTION *Divinus perfectionis Magister* of January 25, 1983, n. 16, established that the causes of the Servants of God, whose judgment is presently pending at the Sacred Congregation for the Causes of Saints, are henceforth to proceed according to the spirit of this new law. Furthermore, it gives to this same Congregation the responsibility of establishing by a special decree the rules for handling these causes from this moment on.

In the desire to fulfill its responsibility, the Sacred Congregation has divided these causes into four categories and has established the following rules:

1) As regards "recent" causes, in which the *Position* on virtues or on martyrdom has already been published, the *Position* is to be passed on to the theological Consultors for their vote in accordance with the norm of the new law.

2) As regards those causes, in which the Observations of the Promotor of the Faith or the Response of the Patron

CIRCA SERVORUM DEI CAUSAS, quarum iudicium in praesens apud Sacram Congregationem pro Causis Sanctorum pendet, in Constitutione Apostolica *Divinus perfectionis Magister* diei 25 ianuarii a. 1983, n. 16, statutum est, ne ad ulteriora procedatur nisi servata mente huius novae legis, atque insuper ipsi Sacrae Congregationi munus demandatur peculiari decreto ordinem statuendi, quo in huiusmodi causis in posterum sit procedendum.

Cui quidem muneri satisfacere sibi proponens, Sacra Congregatio huiusmodi causas in quattuor genera dividens, statuit quae sequuntur:

1) Quoad causas "recentiores", in quibus Positio super virtutibus vel super martyrio iam typis edita est, eadem Consultoribus theologis pro voto tradatur, ad normam novae legis discutienda.

2) Ad eas vero causas quod attinet, in quibus Animadversiones Promotoris fidei vel Re-

are being prepared, every care is to be taken that all the documents **that pertain to** the cause are critically examined and, if the case require it, be added to the Response.

3) In other "recent" causes, once the writings of the Servant of God have been examined, one may not proceed further unless, under the guidance of the Relator of the Cause, the *Position* on virtues or on martyrdom has first been prepared according to the critical method, after those documents **which** in any way pertain to the cause have been gathered and studied.

4) As regards "historical" causes, in which the *Position* on virtues or on martyrdom, compiled by the Historical-hagiographical Office, has already been published, that *Position,* together with the votes of the Consultors of the same Office, is to be passed to the theological Consultors for their vote according to the norm of the new law, together with any explanations, which the Relator General may judge to be necessary.

The Supreme Pontiff, John Paul II, in an Audience granted to the undersigned Cardinal Prefect of the Congregation on the 7th day of February in the year 1983, approved all the above and ordered them to be observed from this day forward.

Given in Rome, from the Offices of the Sacred Congregation for the Causes of Saints, on the 7th day of February in the year 1983.

PIETRO Cardinal PALAZZINI, *Prefect*
+Traian Crisan,
Titular Archbishop of Drivasto,
Secretary

sponsio Patroni sint in statu confectionis, omnino curetur, ut omnia documenta causam respicientia critice examinentur et, quatenus casus ferat, Responsioni addantur.

3) In ceteris causis "recentioribus", examinatis scriptis Servi Dei, ad ulteriora ne procedatur, nisi Positio super virtutibus vel super martyrio methodo critica, sub ductu Relatoris causae, parata fuerit, praevia inquisitione documentorum quae quoquo modo causam respiciant.

4) Quoad causas "historicas", de quibus adest iam typis edita Positio super virtutibus vel super martyrio ab Officio historico-hagiographico concinnata, eadem, una cum votis Consultorum huius Officii, Consultoribus theologis pro voto tradatur ad normam novae legis, additis tamen explanationibus, si quae de iudicio Relatoris generalis necessariae sint.

Quae omnia Summus Pontifex Ioannes Paulus II, in Audientia infrascripto Congregationis Cardinali Praefecto die 7 februarii a. 1983 concessa, rata habuit et ab hoc ipso die servari mandavit.

Datum Romae, ex Aedibus Sacrae Congregationis pro Causis Sanctorum, die 7 februarii a. l983.

PETRUS Card. PALAZZINI, *Praefectus*
+Traianus Crisan,
Archiep. tit. Drivastensis,
a Secretis

APPENDIX 2

PASTOR BONUS

JOHN PAUL II

Apostolic Constitution on the Roman Curia

Promulgated June 28, 1988

The publication of the English-language translation has been authorized by the Secretariat of State (letter by Archbishop Giovanni Battista Re, substitute for general affairs, to Michel Thériault dated 1 January 1998, prot. no. 414.138.), on the condition that the Canadian Conference of Catholic Bishops gives its *recognitio* to the translation, certifying that it is faithful to the Latin original. This *recognitio* was communicated to the Holy See through a letter by Rev. Émilius Goulet, P.S.S., general secretary of the CCCB, to Archbishop Re dated 12 August 1998. In turn, Archbishop Re wrote the following to Rev. Goulet on 15 October 1998: "This Office notes that the Canadian Conference of Catholic Bishops recognizes the fidelity of this translation to the official Latin text" (prot. no. 441.133). Of course, only the original Latin text is official.

1. Translation from the Latin by Francis C. C. F. Kelly, James H. Provost and Michel Thériault. In this translation, dated 31 July 1998, the English-language version of the names of the dicasteries and other agencies of the Roman Curia has been taken from a list issued by the Secretariat of State for the internal use of the Curia (letter from Most Rev. Giovanni Battista Re, Substitute for General Affairs, to Michel Thériault, 17-12-1992, prot. no. 317–300).

© Copyright Typis Polyglottis Vaticanis 1988 for the Latin text.

© Copyright 1998 for the English-language translation of the Apostolic Constitution *Pastor bonus,* by Francis C. C. F. Kelly, James H. Provost, and Michel Thériault. Reprinted with permission by Roch Page.

The English-language translations of Vatican II documents are taken from Austin Flannery (gen. ed.), *Vatican Council II: The Conciliar and Post Conciliar Documents,* new revised edition 1992, Northport, NY, Costello Pub. Co., 1992, with minor corrections.

The style manual followed in this translation is *The Chicago Manual of Style,* 14th ed., Chicago, London, The University of Chicago Press, 1993.

TABLE OF CONTENTS

Introduction

JOHN PAUL, BISHOP

IOANNES PAULUS EPISCOPUS

SERVANT OF THE SERVANTS
OF GOD
FOR AN
EVERLASTING MEMORIAL

SERVUS
SERVORUM DEI
AD PERPETUAM REI
MEMORIAM

Introduction

1. THE GOOD SHEPHERD, the Lord Christ Jesus (cf. Jn 10: 11–14), conferred on the bishops, the successors of the Apostles, and in a singular way on the bishop of Rome, the successor of Peter, the mission of making disciples in all nations and of preaching the Gospel to every creature. And so the Church was established, the people of God, and the task of its shepherds or pastors was indeed to be that service "which is called very expressively in Sacred Scripture a *diaconia* or ministry."[1]

The main thrust of this service or *diaconia* is for *more and more communion or fellowship to be generated* in the whole body of the Church, and for this communion to thrive and produce good results. As the insight of the Second Vatican Council has taught us, we come, with the gentle prompting of the Holy Spirit, to see the meaning of the mystery of the Church in the manifold patterns within this communion: for the Spirit will guide "the Church in the way of all truth (cf. Jn 16:13) and [unify] her in communion and in the work of ministry, he bestows upon her varied hierarchic and charismatic gifts [. . .]. Constantly he renews her and leads her to perfect union with her Spouse."[2] Wherefore, as the same Council affirms, "fully incorporated into the Church are those who, possessing the Spirit of Christ, accept all the means of salvation given to the Church together with her entire organization, and who— by the bonds constituted by the profession of faith, the

1. PASTOR BONUS Dominus Christus Iesus (cf. *Io* 10, 11.14) missionem discipulos faciendi in omnibus gentibus atque praedicandi Evangelium omni creaturae Apostolorum successoribus Episcopis, et singulari ratione Romano Episcopo, Petri successori, ita contulit, ut Ecclesia, Dei Populus, constitueretur atque eiusmodi Populi sui Pastorum munus esset revera servitium, quod «in Sacris Litteris "diaconia" seu ministerium significanter nuncupatur».[1]

Hoc servitium seu *diaconia* eo praesertim tendit, ut in universo ecclesiali corpore *communio magis magisque instauretur*, vigeat atque perpulchros fructus edere pergat. Etenim, sicut Concilium Vaticanum II luculenter docuit, Ecclesiae mysterium per multiplices huiusmodi communionis rationes significatur, Spiritus Sancti suavissimo instinctu: etenim Spiritus «Ecclesiam, quam in omnem veritatem inducit (cf. *Io* 16,13) et in communione et ministratione unificat, diversis donis hierarchicis et charismaticis instruit ac dirigit ... eamque perpetuo renovat et ad consummatam cum Sponso suo unionem perducit».[2] Quam ob rem, ut idem Concilium asseverat, «illi plene Ecclesiae societati incorporantur, qui Spiritum Christi habentes, integram eius ordinationem omniaque media salutis in ea instituta

---

1. *LG* 24.

2. Ibid., 4.

sacraments, ecclesiastical government, and communion—are joined in the visible structure of the Church of Christ, who rules her through the Supreme Pontiff and the bishops."[3]

Not only has this notion of communion been explained in the documents of the Second Vatican Council in general, especially in the Dogmatic Constitution on the Church, but it also received attention from the Fathers attending the 1985 and 1987 General Assemblies of the Synod of Bishops. Into this definition of the Church comes a convergence of the actual mystery of the Church,[4] the orders or constituent elements of the messianic people of God,[5] and the hierarchical constitution of the Church itself.[6] To describe it all in one broad expression, we take the words of the Dogmatic Constitution *Lumen gentium* just mentioned and say that "the Church, in Christ, is in the nature of sacrament—a sign and instrument, that is, of communion with God and of unity among the whole of humankind."[7] That is why this sacred communion thrives in the whole Church of Christ, as our predecessor Paul VI so well described it, "which lives and acts in the various Christian communities, namely, in the particular Churches dispersed throughout the whole world."[8]

2. When one thinks about this communion, which is the force, as it were, that glues the whole Church together, then the hierarchical constitution of the Church unfolds and comes into effect. It was endowed by the Lord himself with *a primatial and collegial nature at the same time* when he constituted the apostles "in the form of a college or permanent assembly, at the head of which he placed Peter, chosen from amongst them."[9] Here we are looking at that special concept whereby the pastors of the Church share in the threefold task of Christ—to teach, to sanctify, and to govern: and just as the apostles acted with Peter, so do the bishops together with the bishop of Rome. To use the words of the Second Vatican Council once more: "In that way, then, with priests and deacons as helpers, the bishops received the charge of the community, presiding in God's stead over the flock of which they are the shepherds in that they are teachers of doctrine, ministers of sacred worship and holders of office in government. Moreover, just as the

accipiunt, et in eiusdem compage visibili cum Christo, eam per Summum Pontificem atque Episcopos regente, iunguntur, vinculis nempe professionis fidei, sacramentorum et ecclesiastici regiminis ac communionis».[3]

Cuiusmodi communionis notionem non modo Concilii Vaticani II documenta in universum edisseruerunt, ac praesertim Constitutio dogmatica de Ecclesia, sed ad illam animum intenderunt etiam Synodi Patres, qui anno MCMLXXXV, itemque duos post annos Generales Synodi Episcoporum Coetus celebraverunt: quam in Ecclesiae definitionem coeunt sive ipsum Ecclesiae Mysterium,[4] sive messianici Populi Dei ordines,[5] sive hierarchica ipsius Ecclesiae constitutio.[6] Quae omnia ut una comprehensione describamus, verba sumentes ex eadem memorata Constitutione, Ecclesia est «in Christo veluti sacramentum seu signum et instrumentum intimae cum Deo unionis totiusque generis humani unitatis».[7] Quam ob rem, huiusmodi sacra communio in tota Christi Ecclesia viget, «quae—ut perbelle scripsit Paulus VI, Decessor noster—vivit et agit in variis communitatibus christianis, Ecclesiis scilicet particularibus, per omnem terrarum orbem dispersis».[8]

2. Habita igitur ratione huius communionis, universam Ecclesiam veluti conglutinantis, etiam hierarchica eiusdem Ecclesiae constitutio explicatur atque ad effectum deducitur: quae *collegiali simul ac primatiali* natura ab ipso Domino praedita est, cum «Apostolos ad modum collegii seu coetus stabilis instituit, cui ex iisdem electum Petrum praefecit».[9] Hic praesertim agitur de speciali illa ratione, qua Ecclesiae Pastores triplex Christi munus participant, docendi scilicet, sanctificandi atque gubernandi: et sicut Apostoli id una cum Petro egerunt, ita haud dissimili modo id Episcopi agunt simul cum Romano Episcopo. Ut Concilii Vaticani II verbis denuo utamur, «Episcopi igitur communitatis ministerium cum adiutoribus presbyteris et diaconis susceperunt, loco Dei praesidentes gregi, cuius sunt Pastores, ut doctrinae magistri, sacri cultus sacerdotes, gu-

---

3. Ibid., 14.
4. Ibid., ch. 1.
5. Ibid., ch. 2.
6. Ibid., ch. 3.

7. Ibid., 1.
8. Ap. Const. *Vicariae potestatis*, 6 January 1977, *AAS* 69 (1977) 6; *CLD* 8 (1973–1977) 255; cf. *LG* 15.
9. *LG* 19.

office which the Lord confided to Peter alone, as first of the apostles, destined to be transmitted to his successors, is a permanent one, so also endures the office, which the apostles received, of shepherding the Church, a charge destined to be exercised without interruption by the sacred order of bishops."[10] And so it comes about that "this college"—the college of bishops joined together with the bishop of Rome—"in so far as it is composed of many members, is the expression of the multifariousness and universality of the people of God; and of the unity of the flock of Christ, in so far as it is assembled under one head."[11]

The power and authority of the bishops bears the mark of *diaconia or stewardship,* fitting the example of Jesus Christ himself who "came not to be served, but to serve and to give his life as a ransom for many" (Mk 10:45). Therefore the power that is found in the Church is to be understood as the power of being a servant and is to be exercised in that way; before anything else it is the authority of a shepherd.

This applies to each and every bishop in his own particular Church; but all the more does it apply to the bishop of Rome, whose Petrine ministry works for the good and benefit of the universal Church. The Roman Church has charge over the "whole body of charity"[12] and so it is the servant of love. It is largely from this principle that those great words of old have come—"The servant of the servants of God"—, by which Peter's successor is known and defined.

That is why the Roman Pontiff has also taken pains to deal carefully with the business of particular Churches, referred to him by the bishops or in some other way come to his attention, in order to encourage his brothers in the faith (cf. Lk 22:32), by means of this wider experience and by virtue of his office as Vicar of Christ and pastor of the whole Church. For he was convinced that the reciprocal communion between the bishop of Rome and the bishops throughout the world, bonded in unity, charity, and peace, brought the greatest advantage in promoting and defending the unity of faith and discipline in the whole Church.[13]

3. In the light of the foregoing, it is understood that the *diaconia* peculiar to Peter and his successors is necessarily

bernationis ministri. Sicut autem permanet munus a Domino singulariter Petro, primo Apostolorum, concessum et successoribus eius transmittendum, ita permanet munus Apostolorum pascendi Ecclesiam, ab ordine sacrato Episcoporum iugiter exercendum».[10] Itaque fit ut «Collegium hoc»—Episcoporum dicimus cum Romano Pontifice coniunctorum—«quatenus ex multis compositum, varietatem et universalitatem Populi Dei, quatenus vero sub uno capite collectum, unitatem gregis Christi» exprimat.[11]

Episcoporum autem potestas atque auctoritas *diaconiae* notam prae se fert, ad ipsius Iesu Christi exemplum accommodatam, qui «non venit, ut ministraretur ei, sed ut ministraret et daret animam suam redemptionem pro multis» (*Mc* 10, 45). Potestas ergo, quae in Ecclesia datur, potissimum secundum serviendi normam et intellegenda et exercenda est, ita ut huiusmodi auctoritas pastorali nota in primis polleat.

Id vero ad singulos Episcopos in propria cuiusque particulari Ecclesia spectat; attamen tanto magis ad Romanum Episcopum pertinet, cuius ministerium Petrianum in universalis Ecclesiae bonum utilitatemque procurandam incumbit: Romana enim Ecclesia praesidet «universo caritatis coetui»,[12] ideoque caritati inservit. Ex hoc potissimum principio processerunt vetusta illa verba «Servus Servorum Dei», quibus Petri Successor denominatur atque definitur.

Quam ob causam, Romanus Pontifex Ecclesiarum etiam particularium negotia, ab Episcopis ad se delata aut utcumque cognita, diligenter perpendere curavit, ut, pleniore rerum experientia exinde adepta, vi muneris sui, Vicarii scilicet Christi totiusque Ecclesiae Pastoris, fratres suos in fide confirmaret (cf. *Lc* 22, 32). Id enim persuasum sibi habebat mutuam inter Episcopos in universo orbe constitutos et Romanum Episcopum communionem, in vinculo unitatis, caritatis et pacis, maximum afferre emolumentum unitati fidei necnon disciplinae in cuncta Ecclesia promovendae atque tuendae.[13]

3. Quibus praemissis, sic intellegitur *diaconia,* quae Petri eiusque successorum propria est,

---

10. Ibid., 20.
11. Ibid., 22.
12. St. Ignatius of Antioch, *To the Romans,* introd., Pa-

tres apostolici, ed. F. X. Funk, vol. I, ed. 2ᵃ adaucta et emendata, Tubingae, H. Laupp, 1901, p. 252.
13. Cf. *LG* 22–23, 25.

related to the *diaconia* of the other apostles and their successors, whose sole purpose is to build up the Church in this world.

From ancient times, this essential and interdependent relation of the Petrine ministry with the task and ministry of the other apostles has demanded something of a visible sign, not just by way of a symbol but something existing in reality, and it must still demand it. Deeply conscious of the burden of apostolic toil, our predecessors have given clear and thoughtful expression to this need, as we see, for example, in the words of Innocent III who wrote to the bishops and prelates of France in 1198 when he was sending a legate to them: "Although the Lord has given us the fullness of power in the Church, a power that makes us owe something to all Christians, still we cannot stretch the limits of human nature. Since we cannot deal personally with every single concern—the law of human condition does not suffer it—we are sometimes constrained to use certain brothers of ours as extensions of our own body, to take care of things we would rather deal with in person if the convenience of the Church allowed it."[14]

This gives some insight into the nature of that institution that Peter's successor has used in exercising his mission for the good of the universal Church, and some understanding of the procedures by which the institution itself has had to carry out its task: we mean the Roman Curia, which from ancient times has been labouring to lend its help in the Petrine ministry.

For the Roman Curia came into existence for this purpose, that the fruitful communion we mentioned might be strengthened and make ever more bountiful progress, rendering more effective the task of pastor of the Church which Christ entrusted to Peter and his successors, a task that has been growing and expanding from day to day. Our predecessor Sixtus V, in the Apostolic Constitution *Immensa aeterni Dei*, admitted as much: "The Roman Pontiff, whom Christ the Lord constituted as visible head of his body, the Church, and appointed for the care of all the Churches, calls and rallies unto himself many collaborators for this immense responsibility [. . .]; so that he, the hold-

ut necessario referatur ad aliorum apostolorum, eorumque successorum, diaconiam, quae ad aedificandam Ecclesiam in hoc mundo unice intendit.

Haec necessaria ministerii Petriani ratio ac necessitudo cum ceterorum apostolorum munere ac ministerio quoddam signum iam antiquitus postulavit, atque postulare debet, quod non modo ad instar symboli, sed etiam in rerum veritate exstaret. Hanc quidem necessitatem Decessores Nostri, apostolici laboris gravitate perculsi, dilucide impenseque senserunt, sicuti, exempli gratia, Innocentii III verba testantur, qui anno MCXCVIII ad Galliae Episcopos praelatosque haec scripsit, cum ad ipsos suum quendam Legatum mitteret: «Licet commissa nobis a Domino potestatis ecclesiastice plenitudo universis Christi fidelibus nos constituerit debitores, statum tamen et ordinem conditionis humanae non possumus ampliare . . . Quia vero lex humane conditionis non patitur nec possumus in persona propria gerere sollicitudines universas, interdum per fratres nostros, qui sunt membra corporis nostri, ea cogimur exercere, que, si commoditas ecclesie sustineret, personaliter libentius impleremus».[14]

Inde quidem perspiciuntur atque intelleguntur sive natura illius instituti, quo Petri successor usus est in sua exercenda missione in universalis Ecclesiae bonum, sive agendi ratio, qua ipsum institutum commissa munera ad effectum deduceret oportuit: Romanam Curiam dicimus, quae in ministerii Petriani adiutorium ab antiquis temporibus adlaborat praestandum.

Nam ut illa, quam diximus, frugifera communio firmior exstaret atque uberius usque proficeret, Romana Curia ad id exorta est, ut scilicet efficacius redderetur muneris exercitium Pastoris Ecclesiae, quod Petro eiusque successoribus ab ipso Christo traditum est, quodque in dies crevit ac dilatatum est. Enimvero Decessor Noster Xystus V in Constitutione apostolica «Immensa aeterni Dei» fatebatur: «Romanus Pontifex, quem Christus Dominus Corporis sui, quod est Ecclesia, visibile caput constituit omniumque Ecclesiarum sollicitudinem gerere voluit,

14. *Die Register Innocenz' III.*, 1, *Pontifikatsjahr 1198/99*, bearb. von. O. Hageneder und A. Haidacher, Graz, Köln, H. Böhlaus, 1964, pp. 515–516.

er of the key of all this power, may share the huge mass of business and responsibilities among them—i.e., the cardinals—and the other authorities of the Roman Curia, and by God's helping grace avoid breaking under the strain."[15]

4. Right from the most ancient times, as a matter of fact, if we may sketch out a few lines of history, the Roman Pontiffs, in the course of their service directed to the welfare of the whole Church, have engaged the help of institutions or individual men selected from that *Church of Rome* which our predecessor Gregory the Great has called the *Church of the Blessed Apostle Peter.*[16]

At first they used the services of priests or deacons belonging to the Church of Rome to function as legates, to be sent on various missions, or to represent the bishops of Rome at ecumenical councils.

When matters of particular importance were to be dealt with, the bishops of Rome called on the help of Roman synods or councils to which they summoned bishops working in the ecclesiastical province of Rome. These councils not only dealt with questions pertaining to doctrine and the magisterium, but also functioned like tribunals, judging cases of bishops referred to the Roman Pontiff.

From the time when the cardinals began to take on a special importance in the Roman Church, especially in the election of the Pope—a function reserved to them from 1059—, the Roman Pontiffs made more and more use of their services, with the result that the Roman synods and councils gradually lost their importance until they ceased entirely.

So it came about that, especially after the thirteenth century, the Supreme Pontiff was carrying out all the business of the Church together with the cardinals gathered in consistory. Thus temporary instruments, the councils or synods of Rome, were replaced by another instrument, a permanent one, always available to the Pope.

It was our predecessor Sixtus V who gave the Roman Curia its formal organization through the above-quoted

multos sibi tam immensi oneris adiutores advocat atque adsciscit ... ut partita inter eos (sc. Cardinales) aliosque Romanae Curiae magistratus ingenti curarum negotiorumque mole, ipse tantae potestatis clavum tenens, divina gratia adiutrice, non succumbat».[15]

4. Revera, ut iam quaedam historiae lineamenta proponamus, Romani Pontifices, iam inde a remotissimis temporibus, in suo ministerio ad universae Ecclesiae bonum procurandum sive singulos viros sive instituta adhibuerunt, qui ex *Romana Ecclesia* deligebantur, siquidem eadem *Ecclesia Beati Petri apostoli* a Decessore Nostro Gregorio Magno nuncupata est.[16]

Primum enim presbyterorum diaconorumve, ad eandem Ecclesiam pertinentium, opera usi sunt, qui vel legati munere fungerentur, vel pluribus missionibus interessent, vel Romanorum Pontificum partes in Oecumenicis Conciliis agerent.

Cum autem peculiaris momenti res tractandae erant, Romani Pontifices in auxilium vocaverunt Synodos vel Concilia Romana, ad quae Episcopi, in ecclesiastica provincia Romana suo munere fungentes, arcessebantur; haec vero non modo quaestiones ad doctrinam et magisterium spectantes agebant, sed etiam ad tribunalium instar procedebant, in quibus Episcoporum causae, ad Romanum Pontificem delatae, iudicabantur.

Ex quo autem tempore Cardinales speciale momentum in Romana Ecclesia adsumere coeperunt, praesertim in Papae electione, quae inde ab anno MLIX ipsis reservata est, iidem Romani Pontifices Patrum Cardinalium collata opera magis magisque usi sunt, ita ut Romanae Synodi vel Concilii munus gradatim deminueretur, donec reapse cessaret.

Quare evenit ut, praesertim post saeculum XIII, Summus Pontifex omnia Ecclesiae negotia una cum Cardinalibus, in Consistorium coadunatis, ageret. Ita factum est, ut instrumentis non stabilibus, videlicet Conciliis seu Romanis Synodis, stabile aliud succederet, quod Romano Pontifici semper praesto esset.

Decessor Noster Xystus V, per iam commemoratam Constitutionem Apostolicam «Im-

---

15. *Prooemium*, par. 1.

16. *Reg.* XIII, 42, II, p. 405, 12.

Apostolic Constitution *Immensa aeterni Dei*, on 22 January 1588, the 1587th year from the Incarnation of Our Lord Jesus Christ. He set up fifteen dicasteries, so that the single College of Cardinals would be replaced by several colleges consisting of certain cardinals whose authority would be confined to a clearly defined field and to a definite subject matter. In this way, the Supreme Pontiffs could enjoy maximum benefit from these collegial counsels. Consequently, the consistory's own original role and importance were greatly diminished.

As the centuries passed and historical outlooks and world conditions were transformed, certain changes and refinements were brought in, especially when the commissions of cardinals were set up in the nineteenth century to give the Pope assistance beyond that of the other dicasteries of the Roman Curia. Then on 29 June 1908, our predecessor Saint Pius X promulgated the Apostolic Constitution *Sapienti consilio*, in which, referring to the plan of collecting the laws of the Church into a Code of Canon Law, he wrote: "It has seemed most fitting to start from the Roman Curia so that, structured in a suitable way that everyone can understand, the Curia may more easily and effectively lend its help to the Roman Pontiff and the Church."[17] Here are the principal effects of that reform: the Sacred Roman Rota, which had ceased to function in 1870, was reestablished to deal with judicial cases, while the Congregations lost their judicial competence and became purely administrative organs. The principle was also established whereby the Congregations would enjoy their own rights, deferring to nobody else, so that each individual matter was to be dealt with by its own dicastery, and not by several ones at the same time.

This reform by Pius X, later confirmed and completed in the Code of Canon Law promulgated in 1917 by our predecessor Benedict XV, remained fairly unchanged until 1967, not long after the Second Vatican Council in which the Church delved more deeply into the mystery of its own being and gained a more lively vision of its mission.

mensa aeterni Dei», die XXII mensis Ianuarii anno MDLXXXVIII—qui fuit MDLXXXVII ab Incarnatione D.N.I.C.—Romanae Curiae compagem eius formalem dedit seriem XV Dicasteriorum instituendo, eo consilio ut uni Cardinalium Collegio plura subrogarentur collegia, e quibusdam Cardinalibus exstantia, quorum tamen auctoritas ad definitum quendam campum certamque materiam restringeretur; quam ob rem Summi Pontifices huiusmodi collegialium consiliorum viribus maxime frui poterant. Consistorii ideo nativum munus propriumque momentum valde deminuta sunt.

Volventibus tamen saeculis ac rationibus historicis rerumque condicionibus mutantibus, temperamenta quaedam atque immutationes accesserunt, praesertim cum saeculo XIX Cardinalium Commissiones institutae sunt, quarum esset Summo Pontifici adiutricem operam praeter alia Romanae Curiae Dicasteria conferre. Denique, opera et iussu S. Pii X, Decessoris Nostri, edita est Constitutio apostolica *Sapienti consilio*, die XXIX mensis Iunii anno MCMVIII, in qua, respectu etiam propositi ecclesiasticas leges in Codicem Iuris Canonici colligendi, haec Ipse scripsit: «Maxime opportunum visum est a Romana Curia ducere initium, ut ipsa, modo apto et omnibus perspicuo ordinata, Romano Pontifici Ecclesiaeque operam suam praestare facilius valeat et suppetias ferre perfectius».[17] Cuius reformationis hi praecipui fuerunt effectus: Sacra Romana Rota, quae anno MDCCCLXX munere cessaverat, ea ratione restituta est, ut iudicialia negotia ageret, dum Congregationes, amissa iudiciorum competentia, administrationis instrumenta unice fierent. Praeterea, principium instauratum est, quo Congregationes suo proprio iure, nemini alii attribuendo, gauderent, scilicet ut singulae res a suo quaeque Dicasterio, non vero simul a pluribus, tractari deberent.

Quae quidem Pii X reformatio, postea in Codice Iuris Canonici anno MCMXVII a Benedicto XV, Decessore Nostro, promulgato, sancita et completa, fere immutata permansit usque ad annum MCMLXVII, non multo post Concilium Oecumenicum Vaticanum II peractum, in quo Ecclesia altius sui ipsius mysterium exploravit suumque vividius prospectavit officium.

17. *AAS* 1 (1909) 8.

5. This growing self-awareness of the Church was bound of itself, and in keeping with our times, to produce a certain updating of the Roman Curia. While the Fathers of the Council acknowledged that the Curia had hitherto rendered outstanding assistance to the Roman Pontiff and the pastors of the Church, at the same time they expressed the desire that the dicasteries of the Curia should undergo a reorganization better suited to the needs of the times and of different regions and rites.[18] Our predecessor Paul VI quickly complied with the wishes of the Council and put into effect the reorganization of the Curia with the promulgation of the Apostolic Constitution *Regimini Ecclesiae universae* on 15 August 1967.

Through this Constitution, Paul VI laid down more detailed specifications for the structure, competence, and procedures of the already existing dicasteries, and established new ones to support specific pastoral initiatives, while the other dicasteries would carry on their work of jurisdiction or governance. The composition of the Curia came to reflect more clearly the multiform image of the universal Church. Among other things, the Curia coopted diocesan bishops as members and at the same time saw to the internal coordination of the dicasteries by periodic meetings of the cardinals who presided over them, to pool ideas and consider common problems. To provide better protection of the principal rights of the faithful, the Second Section was created in the Tribunal of the Apostolic Signatura.

Fully aware that the reform of such ancient institutions needed more careful study, Paul VI ordered the new system to be reexamined more deeply five years after the promulgation of the Constitution, and for a new look to be taken at the question whether it really conformed to the demands of the Second Vatican Council and answered the needs of the Christian people and civil society. As far as necessary, it should be recast in an even more suitable form. To carry out this task, a special group of prelates was set up, chaired by a cardinal, and this Commission worked hard at the project, up to the death of that Pontiff.

18. Cf. *CD* 9.

5. Huiusmodi itaque Ecclesiae de seipsa aucta cognitio sponte novam quandam Romanae Curiae aptationem, nostrae aetati congruentem, secum ferre debuit. Siquidem Sacrosanti Concilii Patres ipsam Romano Pontifici atque Ecclesiae Pastoribus eximium hucusque praebuisse auxilium agnoverunt, simulque ut eiusdem Romanae Curiae Dicasteria novae ordinationi, temporum, regionum rituumque necessitatibus magis aptatae, subicerentur optaverunt.[18] Hisce igitur Concilii optatis satisfaciens, Paulus VI, Decessor Noster, novam Curiae ordinationem ad effectum alacriter adduxit, data Constitutione apostolica «Regimini Ecclesiae universae», die XV mensis Augusti anno MCMLXVII.

Equidem per hanc Constitutionem Summus ille Pontifex Romanae Curiae structuram, competentiam ac procedendi rationem Dicasteriorum iam exsistentium accuratius determinavit, novaque constituit, quorum esset particularia in Ecclesia pastoralia incepta promovere, dum cetera in iurisdictionis vel gubernationis officia incumbere pergerent; quam ob rem factum est, ut compositio Curiae multiformem universalis Ecclesiae imaginem clarius referret. Inter alia, dioecesanos Episcopos in ipsam arcessivit, simulque internae coordinationi Dicasteriorum prospexit per periodicos conventus eorundem Cardinalium moderatorum ad communia problemata collatis consiliis perpendenda. Sectionem Alteram apud Tribunal Signaturae Apostolicae induxit, ad summa eaque principalia fidelium iura aptius tuenda.

Verumtamen, cum antiquorum institutorum reformationem maturiore studio egere plane novisset, idem Summus Pontifex iussit ut, quinque exactis annis a Constitutionis promulgatione, innovatus rerum ordo altius expenderetur, pariterque inspiceretur utrum Concilii Vaticani II postulatis reapse congrueret et christiani populi civilisque societatis necessitatibus responderet, atque, quantum res postularet, in aptiorem reduceretur formam. Cui muneri adimplendo Commissio, seu peculiare Praelatorum corpus, Cardinali praeside, destinata est, ipsaque usque ad eiusdem Pontificis obitum operam actuose navavit.

6. When by the inscrutable design of Providence we were called to the task of being the shepherd of the universal Church, from the very beginning of our pontificate we took steps not only to seek advice from the dicasteries on this grave matter, but also to ask the opinion of the whole College of Cardinals. These cardinals, twice gathered in general consistory, addressed the question and gave their advice on the ways and means to be followed in the organization of the Roman Curia. It was necessary to consult the cardinals first in this important matter, for they are joined to the ministry of the bishop of Rome by a close and most special bond and they "are also available to [him], either acting collegially, when they are summoned together to deal with questions of major importance, or acting individually, that is, in the offices which they hold in assisting [him] especially in the daily care of the universal Church."[19]

A very broad consultation, as we mentioned above, was again carried out, as was only fitting, among the dicasteries of the Roman Curia. The result of this general consultation was the "Draft of a special law concerning the Roman Curia," worked out over close to two years by a commission of prelates under the chairmanship of a cardinal. This draft was examined by the individual cardinals, the patriarchs of the Oriental Churches, the conferences of bishops through their presidents, the dicasteries of the Roman Curia, and was discussed at the plenary meeting of cardinals in 1985. As to the conferences of bishops, it was essential that we be thoroughly briefed about their true general feeling on the needs of the particular Churches and what they wanted and expected in this regard from the Roman Curia. In gaining a clear awareness of all this, we had strong and most timely help from the 1985 extraordinary Synod of Bishops, as we have mentioned above.

Then, taking into account the observations and suggestions that had been gathered in the course of these extensive consultations, and bearing in mind the considered judgement of certain private individuals, a commission of cardinals, which had been set up for this express purpose, prepared a particular law for the Roman Curia in harmony with the new Code of Canon Law.

6. Cum inscrutabili Providentiae consilio ad universalis Ecclesiae pascendae munus vocati simus, iam a Pontificatus primordiis sategimus non solum de re tam gravi Dicasteriorum mentem exquirere, verum etiam ab universo Cardinalium Collegio iudicium postulare. Qui Patres Cardinales, in generali Consistorio bis congregati, rei incubuerunt atque consilia praebuerunt de itinere rationibusque persequendis in Romanae Curiae ordinatione. Cardinales enim cum Romani Episcopi ministerio arctissimo ac singulari vinculo coniunguntur, eidemque «adsunt sive collegialiter agendo, cum ad quaestiones maioris momenti tractandas in unum convocantur, sive ut singuli, scilicet variis officiis, quibus funguntur, eidem ... operam praestando in cura praesertim cotidiana universae Ecclesiae»:[19] ii igitur in primis sciscitandi erant in tanti momenti causa.

Perampla sententiarum rogatio, quam supra memoravimus, apud Romanae Curiae Dicasteria, ut aequum erat, iterum facta est. Generalis consultationis fructus illud exstitit «Schema Legis peculiaris de Curia Romana», cui apparando incubuit Praelatorum Commissio, Patre Cardinali praeside, duos fere annos adlaborans, quodque singulorum Cardinalium, Ecclesiarum Orientalium Patriarcharum, Episcoporum Conferentiarum per earum Praesides, et Romanae Curiae Dicasteriorum examini subiectum est, atque in plenario Cardinalium Coetu anno MCMLXXXV excussum. Quod attinet ad Episcoporum Conferentias, oportebat ut de Ecclesiarum particularium necessitatibus atque de earum hac in materie exspectationibus optatisque ad Romanam Curiam pertinentibus per vere universalem sententiam certiores fieremus; quae omnia ut plane nosceremus, occasionem potissimum praebuit peropportunam extraordinaria Synodus pariter anno MCMLXXXV celebrata, sicut iam mentionem fecimus.

Denique Commissio Patrum Cardinalium ad hunc finem specialiter condita, ratione habita animadversionum et consiliorum ex multiplicibus consultationibus acceptorum, atque sententia etiam privatorum quorundam virorum cognita, Legem peculiarem pro Curia Romana apparavit, novo *Codici Iuris Canonici* congruenter aptatam.

19. C. 349.

It is this particular law that we wish to promulgate by means of this Apostolic Constitution, at the end of the fourth centenary of the afore-mentioned Apostolic Constitution *Immensa aeterni Dei* of Sixtus V, eighty years after the Apostolic Constitution *Sapienti consilio* of Saint Pius X, and scarcely twenty years after the coming into force of the Apostolic Constitution of Paul VI *Regimini Ecclesiae universae,* with which our own is closely linked, since both in some way derive from the Second Vatican Council and both originate from the same inspiration and intent.

7. In harmony with the Second Vatican Council, this inspiration and intent establish and express the steadfast activity of the renewed Curia, as in these words of the Council: "In exercising his supreme, full and immediate authority over the universal Church, the Roman Pontiff employs the various departments of the Roman Curia, which act in his name and by his authority for the good of the Churches and in service of the sacred pastors."[20]

Consequently, it is evident that the function of the Roman Curia, though not belonging to the essential constitution of the Church willed by God, has nevertheless *a truly ecclesial character* because it draws its existence and competence from the pastor of the universal Church. For the Curia exists and operates only insofar as it has a relation to the Petrine ministry and is based on it. But just as the ministry of Peter as the "servant of the servants of God" is exercised in relationship with both the whole Church and the bishops of the entire Church, similarly the Roman Curia, as the servant of Peter's successor, looks only to help the whole Church and its bishops.

This clearly shows that the principal *characteristic* of each and every dicastery of the Roman Curia is that of being *ministerial,* as the already-quoted words of the Decree *Christus Dominus* declare and especially these: "The Roman Pontiff *employs the various departments of the Roman Curia."*[21] These words clearly show the Curia's instrumental nature, described as a kind of agent in the hands of the Pontiff, with the result that it is endowed with no force and no power apart from what it receives from the same Supreme Pastor. Paul VI himself, in 1963, two years before he promulgated the Decree *Christus Dominus,* defined the Roman Curia "as an instrument of immediate adhesion and

Quam quidem peculiarem Legem hac praesenti Constitutione apostolica promulgare volumus, dum quartum nuper exspiravit saeculum a commemorata Constitutione apostolica «Immensa aeterni Dei» Xysti V, atque octogesimus recurrit annus a S. Pii X Constitutione apostolica «Sapienti consilio», viginti denique vix expletis annis ex quo Constitutio apostolica Pauli VI «Regimini Ecclesiae universae» vim suam exserere coepit, quacum haec Nostra arcte coniungitur, quippe quod utraque a Concilio Vaticano II, eadem ducente cogitatione et mente, originem quodammodo ducat.

7. Hae mens atque cogitatio, Concilio Vaticano II congruentes, renovatae Romanae Curiae actuositatem firmant et exprimunt. Quae quidem hisce Concilii enuntiatur verbis: «In exercenda suprema, plena et immediata potestate in universam Ecclesiam, Romanus Pontifex utitur Romanae Curiae Dicasteriis, quae proinde nomine et auctoritate illius munus suum explent in bonum Ecclesiarum et in servitium Sacrorum Pastorum».[20]

Patet igitur Romanae Curiae munus, etsi ad propriam Ecclesiae constitutionem, iure divino conditam, non pertinet, *indolem* tamen *vere ecclesialem* habere, quatenus ab universalis Ecclesiae Pastore suam et existentiam et competentiam trahat. Ea enim in tantum exstat atque adlaborat, in quantum ad ministerium Petrianum refertur in eoque fundatur. Quoniam autem Petri ministerium, utpote «servi servorum Dei», sive erga universam Ecclesiam sive erga totius Ecclesiae Episcopos exercetur, Romana etiam Curia, Petri successori inserviens, ad universam Ecclesiam atque ad Episcopos iuvandos pariter spectat.

Plane inde elucet praecipuam notam omnium singulorumque Romanae Curiae Dicasteriorum esse eius *indolem ministerialem,* sicut iam prolata verba e Decreto «Christus Dominus» declarant, et haec praesertim: «Romanus Pontifex *utitur Romanae Curiae Dicasteriis».*[21] Perspicue enim indoles instrumentalis Curiae his indicatur, et ipsa veluti instrumentum in manibus Pontificis quodammodo describitur, ita ut nulla vi nullaque potestate polleat praeter eas quas ab eodem Summo Pastore recipit. Ipse enim Paulus VI, iam duobus annis antequam Decretum *Christus*

---

20. *CD* 9.   21. Ibid.

perfect obedience," an instrument the Pope uses to fulfill his universal mission. This notion is taken up throughout the Apostolic Constitution *Regimini Ecclesiae universae.*

This instrumental and ministerial characteristic seems indeed to define most appropriately the nature and role of this worthy and venerable institution. Its nature and role consist entirely in that the more exactly and loyally the institution strives to dedicate itself to the will of the Supreme Pontiff, the more valuable and effective is the help it gives him.

8. Beyond this ministerial character, the Second Vatican Council further highlighted what we may call the *vicarious character* of the Roman Curia, because, as we have already said, it does not operate by its own right or on its own initiative. It receives its power from the Roman Pontiff and exercises it within its own essential and innate dependence on the Pontiff. It is of the nature of this power that it always joins its own action to the will of the one from whom the power springs. It must display a faithful and harmonious interpretation of his will and manifest, as it were, an identity with that will, for the good of the Churches and service to the bishops. From this character the Roman Curia draws its energy and strength, and in it too finds the boundaries of its duties and its code of behaviour.

The fullness of this power resides in the head, in the very person of the Vicar of Christ, who imparts it to the dicasteries of the Curia according to the competence and scope of each one. Since, as we said earlier, the Petrine function of the Roman Pontiff by its very nature relates to the office of the college of his brother bishops and aims at building up and making firm and expanding the whole Church as well as each and every particular Church, this same *diaconia* of the Curia, which he uses in carrying out his own personal office, necessarily relates in the same way to the personal office of the bishops, whether as members of the college of bishops or as pastors of the particular Churches.

For this reason, not only is the Roman Curia far from being a *barrier or screen* blocking personal communications and dealings between bishops and the Roman Pontiff, or restricting them with conditions, but, on the contrary, it is itself the facilitator for communion and the sharing of concerns, and must be ever more so.

Dominus promulgaretur, scilicet anno MCMLXIII, Romanam Curiam definivit instrumentum immediatae adhaesionis et absolutae oboedientiae, quo Summus Pontifex ad suam universalem missionem explendam utitur. Quae notio in Constitutione apostolica «Regimini Ecclesiae universae» passim usurpata est.

Haec indoles ministerialis vel instrumentalis aptissime revera videtur huius valde benemeriti venerandique instituti naturam definire eiusque actionem significare, quae totae in eo consistunt ut auxilium Summo Pontifici eo validius et efficacius praestet, quo magis conformiter ac fidelius eius voluntati sese praebere nitatur.

8. Praeter hanc indolem ministerialem, a Concilio Vaticano II *character*, ut ita dicamus, *vicarius* Romanae Curiae in luce ulterius ponitur, quandoquidem ipsa, ut iam diximus, non proprio iure neque proprio marte operatur: potestatem enim a Romano Pontifice acceptam exercet essentiali quadam et nativa cum Ipso necessitudine, quia huiusmodi potestatis proprium est ut agendi studium cum voluntate illius, a quo oritur, semper coniungat, ea quidem ratione ut eiusdem voluntatis fidelem interpretationem, consonantiam, immo quasi aequalitatem prae se ferat atque manifestet, in Ecclesiarum bonum atque in Episcoporum servitium. Ex huiusmodi indole Romana Curia vim roburque haurit, pariterque officiorum suorum limites ac normarum codicem invenit.

Huius autem potestatis plenitudo in capite seu in ipsa Christi Vicarii persona insidet, qui propterea Curiae Dicasteriis eam committit pro singulorum competentia atque ambitu. Quoniam autem Romani Pontificis munus Petrianum, sicut diximus, ad fratrum Episcoporum Collegii munus suapte natura refertur, ad id simul spectans ut universa Ecclesia singulaeque particulares Ecclesiae aedificentur, constabiliantur atque dilatentur, eadem Curiae *diaconia*, qua Ipse in suo personali munere exercendo utitur, necessario pariter refertur ad personale Episcoporum munus, sive utpote Episcopalis Collegii membrorum, sive utpote particularium Ecclesiarum Pastorum.

Quam ob causam non modo longe abest ut Romana Curia personales rationes ac necessitudines inter Episcopos atque Summum Pontificem quoddam veluti *diaphragma* impediat vel condicionibus obstringat, sed contra ipsa est,

9. By reason of its *diaconia* connected with the Petrine ministry, one concludes, on one hand, that the Roman Curia is closely bound to the bishops of the whole world, and, on the other, that those pastors and their Churches are the first and principal beneficiaries of the work of the dicasteries. This is proved even by the composition of the Curia.

For the Roman Curia is composed of nearly all the cardinals who, by definition, belong to the Roman Church,[22] and they closely assist the Supreme Pontiff in governing the universal Church. When important matters are to be dealt with, they are all called together into regular or special consistories.[23] So they come to have a strong awareness of the needs of all of God's people, and they labour for the good of the whole Church.

In addition to this, most of the heads of the individual dicasteries have the character and grace of the episcopate, pertaining to the one College of Bishops, and so are inspired by the same solicitude for the whole Church as are all bishops in hierarchical communion with their head, the bishop of Rome.

Furthermore, as some diocesan bishops are coopted onto the dicasteries as members and are "better able to inform the Supreme Pontiff on the thinking, the hopes and the needs of all the Churches,"[24] so the collegial spirit between the bishops and their head works through the Roman Curia and finds *concrete* application, and this is extended to the whole Mystical Body which "is a corporate body of Churches."[25]

This collegial spirit is also fostered between the various dicasteries. All the cardinals in charge of dicasteries, or their representatives, when specific questions are to be addressed, meet periodically in order to brief one another on the more important matters and provide mutual assistance in finding solutions, thus providing unity of thought and action in the Roman Curia.

Apart from these bishops, the business of the dicaster-

atque magis magisque sit oportet, communionis atque sollicitudinum participationis administra.

9. Ratione igitur suae diaconiae, cum ministerio Petriano coniunctae, eruendum est tum Romanam Curiam cum totius orbis Episcopis arctissime coniungi, tum eosdem Pastores eorumque Ecclesias primos principalioresque esse veluti beneficiarios operis Dicasteriorum. Quod eiusdem Curiae etiam compositione probatur.

Etenim Romanam Curiam omnes fere componunt Patres Cardinales, ad Romanam Ecclesiam proprio nomine pertinentes,[22] qui proxime Summum Pontificem in universali Ecclesia gubernanda adiuvant, quique insuper cuncti sive in ordinaria sive in extraordinaria Consistoria convocantur, cum graviora negotia tractanda id suadeant;[23] quo igitur fit ut, necessitates totius Populi Dei plenius cognoscentes, Ecclesiae universae bono prospicere pergant.

Huc etiam accedit quod singulis Dicasteriis praepositi episcopali charactere et gratia plerumque pollent, ad unumque Episcoporum Collegium pertinent, itemque eadem etiam erga universam Ecclesiam sollicitudine urgentur, qua omnes Episcopi, in communione hierarchica cum Romano Episcopo suo Capite, devinciuntur.

Cum insuper inter Dicasteriorum membra aliqui cooptentur dioecesani Episcopi, «qui mentem, optata ac necessitates omnium Ecclesiarum Summo Pontifici plenius referre valeant»,[24] per Romanam Curiam collegialis affectus, qui inter Episcopos eorumque Caput intercedit, ad *concretam* applicationem perducitur, idemque ad totum mysticum Corpus extenditur, «quod est etiam corpus Ecclesiarum»[25].

Qui quidem collegialis affectus inter varia quoque Dicasteria colitur. Omnes enim Cardinales Dicasteriis praepositi certis temporibus inter se conveniunt, vel ipsorum partes agentes cum peculiares quaestiones tractandae sint, ut collatis consiliis de potioribus quaestionibus certiores fiant ad illasque solvendas mutuum adiutorium conferant atque ideo agendi cogitandique unitatem in Romana Curia provideant.

Praeter hos episcopali potestate praeditos

---

22. Cf. Ap. Const. *Vicariae potestatis*, 6 January 1977, *AAS* 69 (1977) 6; *CLD* 8 (1973–1977) 255.
23. Cf. *C.I.C.* 353.

24. *CD* 10.
25. *LG* 23.

ies employs a number of collaborators who are of value and service to the Petrine ministry by work that is neither light nor easy and is often obscure.

The Roman Curia calls into its service diocesan priests from all over the world, who by their sharing in the ministerial priesthood are closely united with the bishops, male religious, most of whom are priests, and female religious, all of whom in their various ways lead their lives according to the evangelical counsels, furthering the good of the Church, and bearing special witness for Christ before the world, and lay men and women who by virtue of baptism and confirmation are fulfilling their own apostolic role. By this coalition of many forces, all ranks within the Church join in the ministry of the Supreme Pontiff and more effectively help him by carrying out the pastoral work of the Roman Curia. This kind of service by all ranks in the Church clearly has no equal in civil society and their labour is given with the intent of truly serving and of following and imitating the *diaconia* of Christ himself.

10. From this comes to light that the ministry of the Roman Curia is strongly imbued with a certain note of *collegiality*, even if the Curia itself is not to be compared to any kind of college. This is true whether the Curia be considered in itself or in its relations with the bishops of the whole Church, or because of its purposes and the corresponding spirit of charity in which that ministry has to be conducted. This collegiality enables it to work for the college of bishops and equips it with suitable means for doing so. Even more, it expresses the solicitude that the bishops have for the whole Church, inasmuch as bishops share this kind of care and zeal "with Peter and under Peter."

This comes out most strikingly and takes on a symbolic force when, as we have already said above, the bishops are called to collaborate in the individual dicasteries. Moreover, each and every bishop still has the inviolable right and duty to approach the successor of Saint Peter, especially by means of the visits *ad limina Apostolorum*.

These visits have a special meaning all of their own, in keeping with the ecclesiological and pastoral principles explained above. Indeed, they are first of all an opportunity of the greatest importance, and they constitute, as it were, the centre of the highest ministry committed to the Su-

viros ad Dicasteriorum navitatem plurimi requiruntur operis adiutores, qui suo labore, haud raro abscondito neque levi vel facili, ministerio Petriano inserviant ac prosint.

Etenim in Romanam Curiam advocantur sive dioecesani ex universo terrarum orbe presbyteri, qui sacerdotii ministerialis participes, cum Episcopis arcte coniunguntur; sive Religiosi, e quibus maxima pars sunt presbyteri, atque Religiosae Sodales, qui vitam suam ad Evangelii consilia diversimode componunt, ad Ecclesiae bonum augendum atque ad singulare Christi testimonium coram mundo praestandum; sive laici viri atque mulieres, qui ob Baptismi atque Confirmationis virtutem proprio apostolico munere funguntur. Quae plurium virium conspiratio efficit ut omnes Ecclesiae ordines in pastoralem Romanae Curiae operam continuandam efficacius usque adiuvent Summum Pontificem, cum Ipsius ministerio coniuncti. Exinde etiam patet, huiusmodi omnium Ecclesiae ordinum servitium nihil simile in civili societate invenire, atque ipsorum laborem cum animo vere serviendi praestandum esse, ad ipsius Christi diaconiam sequendam atque imitandam.

10. Clare inde elucet Romanae Curiae ministerium, sive in semet ipso consideretur, sive ob ipsius rationes cum universae Ecclesiae Episcopis, sive ob fines, ad quos contendit atque ob concordem caritatis affectum, quo ducatur oportet, quadam *collegialitatis* nota pollere, etiamsi ipsa Curia nulli sit comparanda cuiuslibet naturae collegio; quae nota eam ad inserviendum Episcoporum Collegio informat mediisque ad id idoneis instruit. Quin immo, ipsorum etiam Episcoporum sollicitudinem pro universa Ecclesia exprimit, siquidem Episcopi huiusmodi curam atque sedulitatem «cum Petro et sub Petro» participant.

Quod sane maxime excellit et symbolicam vim prae se fert, cum Episcopi—ut iam supra diximus—vocantur ut singulis Dicasteriis sociam operam praebeant. Praeterea omnibus et singulis Episcopis integrum ius manet et officium ipsum Beati Petri Successorem adeundi, potissimum per visitationes «ad Apostolorum limina».

Hae visitationes, ob supra exposita ecclesiologica et pastoralia principia, propriam peculiaremque significationem accipiunt. Sunt enim in primis maximi momenti opportunitas, et veluti centrum constituunt supremi illius ministerii,

preme Pontiff. For then the pastor of the universal Church talks and communicates with the pastors of the particular Churches, who have come to him in order to see Cephas (cf. Gal 1:18), to deal with him concerning the problems of their dioceses, face to face and in private, and so to share with him the solicitude for all the Churches (cf. 2 Cor 11:28). For these reasons, communion and unity in the innermost life of the Church is fostered to the highest degree through the *ad limina* visits.

These visits also allow the bishops a frequent and convenient way to contact the appropriate dicasteries of the Roman Curia, pondering and exploring plans concerning doctrine and pastoral action, apostolic initiatives, and any difficulties obstructing their mission to work for the eternal salvation of the people committed to them.

11. Thus since the zealous activity of the Roman Curia, united to the Petrine ministry and based on it, is dedicated to the good both the whole Church and the particular Churches, the Curia is in the first place being called on to fulfill that *ministry of unity* which has been entrusted in a singular way to the Roman Pontiff insofar as he has been set up by God's will as the permanent and visible foundation of the Church. Hence unity in the Church is a precious treasure to be preserved, defended, protected, and promoted, to be for ever exalted with the devoted cooperation of all, and most indeed by those who each in their turn *are the visible source and foundation of unity in their own particular Churches.*[26]

Therefore the cooperation which the Roman Curia brings to the Supreme Pontiff is rooted in this ministry of unity. This unity is in the first place the *unity of faith,* governed and constituted by the sacred deposit of which Peter's successor is the chief guardian and protector and through which indeed he receives his highest responsibility, that of strengthening his brothers. The unity is likewise the *unity of discipline,* the general discipline of the Church, which constitutes a system of norms and patterns of behaviour, gives shapes to the fundamental structure of the Church, safeguards the means of salvation and their correct administration, together with the ordered structure of the people of God.

Church government safeguards this unity and cares for it at all times. So far from suffering harm from the differ-

Summo Pontifici commissi: nam Ecclesiae universalis Pastor tunc communicat atque colloquitur cum particularium Ecclesiarum Pastoribus, qui ad ipsum se conferunt ut in eo Cepham videant (cf. *Gal* 1, 18), suarum dioecesium quaestiones coram atque privatim cum Ipso pertractent cum eoque ideo omnium Ecclesiarum sollicitudinem participent (cf. *2 Cor* 11, 28). Quam ob rem, per visitationes ad limina communio atque unitas in intima Ecclesiae vita maximopere foventur.

Eaedem praeterea Episcopis copiam commoditatemque praebent, ut cum competentibus Romanae Curiae Dicasteriis considerent atque explorent tum studia ad doctrinam actionemque pastoralem attinentia, tum apostolatus incepta, tum difficultates, quae aeternae salutis procurandae missioni, ipsis concreditae, se interponant.

11. Cum igitur Romanae Curiae navitas cum munere Petriano iuncta in eoque fundata, in bonum simul universae Ecclesiae sive Ecclesiarum particularium cedat, ea praeprimis ad explendum *unitatis ministerium* vocatur, quod Romano Pontifici singulariter commissum est, quatenus Ipse divino placito perpetuum atque visibile fundamentum Ecclesiae constitutus est. Quapropter unitas in Ecclesia pretiosus est thesaurus servandus, defendendus, tutandus promovendus perpetuo erigendus, omnibus studiose cooperantibus, iis potissimum qui vicissim *visibile principium et fundamentum in suis Ecclesiis particularibus sunt.*[26]

Igitur cooperatio, quam Romana Curia Summo Pontifici praestat, hoc unitatis ministerio fulcitur: haec autem in primis *unitas* est *Fidei,* quae sacro deposito, cuius Petri Successor primus est custos et tutor et a quo munus supremum confirmandi fratres suscipit, regitur et struitur. Est pariter *unitas disciplinae,* quoniam agitur de generali disciplina Ecclesiae, quae in normarum morumque complexu consistit, fundamentalem Ecclesiae constitutionem conformat, atque media salutis eorumque rectam administrationem tuetur, una cum Populi Dei ordinata compagine.

Eadem unitas, quam nullo non tempore regimen Ecclesiae universae tuendam curat a diver-

26. Cf. ibid., 23.

ences of life and behaviour among various persons and cultures, what with the immense variety of gifts poured out by the Holy Spirit, this same unity actually grows richer year by year, so long as there are no isolationist or centripetal attempts and so long as everything is brought together into the higher structure of the one Church. Our predecessor John Paul I brought this principle to mind quite admirably when he addressed the cardinals about the agencies of the Roman Curia: "[They] provide the Vicar of Christ with the concrete means of giving the apostolic service that he owes the entire Church. Consequently, they guarantee an organic articulation of legitimate autonomies, while maintaining an indispensable respect for that unity of discipline and faith for which Christ prayed on the very eve of his passion."[27]

And so it is that the highest ministry of unity in the universal Church has much respect for lawful customs, for the mores of peoples and for that authority which belongs by divine right to the pastors of the particular Churches. Clearly however, whenever serious reasons demand it, the Roman Pontiff cannot fail to intervene in order to protect unity in faith, in charity, or in discipline.

12. Consequently, since the mission of the Roman Curia is ecclesial, it claims the cooperation of the whole Church to which it is directed. For no one in the Church is cut off from others and each one indeed makes up the one and the same body with all others.

This kind of cooperation is carried out through that communion we spoke of at the beginning, namely of life, charity, and truth, for which the messianic people is set up by Christ Our Lord, taken up by Christ as an instrument of redemption, and sent out to the whole world as the light of the world and the salt of the earth.[28] Therefore, just as it is the duty of the Roman Curia to communicate with all the Churches, so the pastors of the particular Churches, governing these Churches "as vicars and legates of Christ,"[29] must take steps to communicate with the Roman Curia, so that, dealing thus with each other in all trust, they and the successor of Peter may come to be bound together ever so strongly.

This mutual communication between the centre of the

sis exsistendi et agendi modis pro varietate personarum et culturarum nedum detrimentum patiatur per donorum immensam varietatem, quae Spiritus Sanctus profundit, perenniter ditescit, dummodo ne exinde nisus sese separandi insularum ad instar vel fugae a centro exoriantur, sed omnia in altiorem unius Ecclesiae structuram componantur. Quod principium Decessor Noster Ioannes Paulus I optime commemoravit, cum Patres Cardinales allocutus haec de Romanae Curiae institutis asseveravit: eadem «Christi Vicario id praestant ut apostolico ministerio, cuius Ipse universae Ecclesiae debitor est, certe ac definite fungi possit, atque hac ratione provident ut legitim agendi libertates sese organico modo explicent, servato tamen necessario obsequio erga illam disciplinae immo etiam fidei unitatem, ad Ecclesiae naturam pertinentem, pro qua Christus antequam pateretur oravit».[27]

Quo fit ut supremum unitatis ministerium universalis Ecclesiae legitimas consuetudines, populorum mores atque potestatem, quae iure divino ad Ecclesiarum particularium Pastores pertinet, vereatur. Ipse tamen Romanus Pontifex, uti patet, praetermittere non valet quin manus apponat quotiescumque graves rationes pro tuenda unitate in fide, in caritate vel in disciplina id postulent.

12. Munus itaque Romanae Curiae ecclesiale cum sit, cooperationem totius Ecclesiae, ad quam dirigitur, requirit. Nemo enim in Ecclesia ab aliis est seiunctus, immo quisque cum ceteris omnibus unum idemque efficit corpus.

Cuiusmodi cooperatio per illam communionem agitur, e qua exordium sumpsimus, scilicet vitae, caritatis et veritatis, in quam Populus messianicus a Christo Domino est constitutus, ab Eoque ut redemptionis instrumentum assumitur et tamquam lux mundi et sal terrae ad universum mundum mittitur.[28] Sicut ergo Romanae Curiae est cum omnibus Ecclesiis communicare, ita Pastores Ecclesiarum particularium, quas ipsi «ut vicarii et legati Christi regunt»,[29] cum Romana Curia communicare satagant oportet, ut per haec fidentia commercia, firmiore vinculo cum Petri Successore obstringantur.

Quae inter Ecclesiae centrum eiusque, ut ita

---

27. Allocution to the college of cardinals, 30 August 1978, *AAS* 70 (1978) 703; *The Pope Speaks* 23 (1978) 318–319.

28. Cf. *LG* 9.

29. Ibid., 27.

Church and the periphery does not enlarge the scope of anyone's authority but promotes *communion* in the highest degree, in the manner of a living body that is constituted and activated precisely by the interplay of all its members. This was well expressed by our predecessor Paul VI: "It is obvious, in fact, that along with the movement toward the centre and heart of the Church, there must be another corresponding movement, spreading from the centre to the periphery and carrying, so to speak, to each and all of the local Churches, to each and all of the pastors and the faithful, the presence and testimony of that treasure of truth and grace of which Christ has made Us the partaker, depository and dispenser."[30]

All of this means that the ministry of salvation offers more effectively to this one and same people of God, a ministry, we repeat, which before anything else demands mutual help between the pastors of the particular Churches and the pastor of the whole Church, so that all may bring their efforts together and strive to fulfill that supreme law which is the salvation of souls.

History shows that when the Roman Pontiffs established the Roman Curia and adapted it to new conditions in the Church and in the world, they intended nothing other than to work all the better for this salvation of souls. With full justification did Paul VI visualise the Roman Curia as another cenacle or upper room of Jerusalem totally dedicated to the Church.[31] We ourselves have proclaimed to all who work there that the only possible code of action is to set the norm for the Church and to deliver eager service to the Church.[32] Indeed, in this new legislation on the Roman Curia it has been our will to insist that the dicasteries should approach all questions "by a pastoral route and with a pastoral sense of judgement, aiming at justice and the good of the Church and above all at the salvation of souls."[33]

13. Now as we are about to promulgate this Apostolic Constitution, laying down the new physionomy of the Roman Curia, we wish to bring together the ideas and intentions that have guided us.

dicamus, peripheriam mutua communicatio, dum nullius extollit auctoritatis fastigium, *communionem* inter omnes maximopere promovet, ad instar viventis cuiusdam corporis, quod ex mutuis omnium membrorum rationibus constat atque operatur. Quod feliciter expressit Paulus VI Decessor Noster: «Liquet enim motui ad centrum ac veluti ad cor Ecclesiae respondere opus esse alium motum, qui a medio ad extrema feratur atque quadam ratione omnes et singulas Ecclesias, cunctos et singulos Pastores ac fideles attingat, ita ut ille significetur et ostendatur thesaurus veritatis, gratiae et unitatis, cuius Christus Dominus ac Redemptor Nos effecit participes, custodes ac dispensatores».[30]

Quae omnia eo pertinent, ut uni eidemque Populo Dei efficacius praebeatur ministerium salutis; ministerium dicimus, quod praeprimis postulat mutuum inter particularium Ecclesiarum Pastores et universae Ecclesiae Pastorem adiutorium, ita ut omnes collatis viribus adnitantur adimplere supremam eam legem, quae est salus animarum.

Nihil omnino aliud, quam ut huic saluti animarum uberius usque consulerent, Summi Pontifices voluerunt, sive Romanam Curiam condendo, sive novis Ecclesiae mundique condicionibus ipsam aptando, sicut e rerum historia patet. Iure igitur merito Paulus VI Romanam Curiam, veluti alterum Hierosolymitanum cenaculum, et sanctae Ecclesiae prorsus debitam sibi effingebat.[31] Nosmetipsi idcirco eximus omnibus, qui in ipsa operam dant, unicam agendi rationem esse et normam Ecclesiae et erga Ecclesiam alacre praestare servitium.[32] Immo in hac nova de Romana Curia Lege statuere voluimus, ut quaestiones omnes a Dicasteriis tractentur «viis ... ac iudiciis pastoralibus, animo intento tum ad iustitiam et Ecclesiae bonum tum praesertim ad animarum salutem».[33]

13. Iam igitur promulgaturi hanc Constitutionem apostolicam, qua nova Romanae Curiae lineamenta impertiuntur, placet nunc Nobis consilia atque proposita complecti, quibus ducti sumus.

---

30. M.P. *Sollicitudo omnium Ecclesiarum*, 24 June 1969, *AAS* 61 (1969) 475; *The Pope Speaks* 14 (1969) 261.

31. Allocution to the participants in the spiritual exercises held at the Apostolic Palace, 17 March 1973, *Insegnamenti di Paolo VI* 11 (1973) 257.

32. Cf. Allocution to the Roman Curia, 28 June 1986, *Insegnamenti di Giovanni Paolo II* 9 (1986), part 1, 1954; *Origins* 16 (1986–1987) 192.

33. Art. 15.

First of all we wanted the image and features of this Curia to respond to the demands of our time, bearing in mind the changes that have been made by us or our predecessor Paul VI after the publication of the Apostolic Constitution *Regimini Ecclesiae universae.*

Then it was our duty to fulfill and complete that renewal of the laws of the Church which was brought in by the publication of the new Code of Canon Law or which is to be brought into effect by the revision of the Oriental canonical legislation.

Then we had in mind that the traditional dicasteries and organs of the Roman Curia be made more suitable for the purposes they were meant for, that is, their share in governance, jurisdiction, and administration. For this reason, their areas of competence have been distributed more aptly among them and more distinctly delineated.

Then with an eye to what experience has taught in recent years and to the never ending demands of Church society, we reexamined the juridical figure and reason of existence of those organs which are rightly called "postconciliar," changing on occasion their shape and organization. We did this in order to make the work of those institutions more and more useful and beneficial, that is, supporting special pastoral activity and research in the Church which, at an ever accelerating pace, are filling pastors with concern and which with the same urgency demand timely and well thought out answers.

Finally, new and more stable measures have been devised to promote mutual cooperation between dicasteries, so that their manner of working may intrinsically bear the stamp of unity.

In a word, our whole steadfast approach has been to make sure that the structure and working methods of the Roman Curia increasingly correspond to the ecclesiology spelled out by the Second Vatican Council, be ever more clearly suitable for achieving the pastoral purposes of its own constitution, and more and more fit to meet the needs of Church and civil society.

Voluimus in primis ut eiusdem Curiae imago et facies novis responderet nostri temporis postulatis, ratione mutationum habita, quae post editam Constitutionem apostolicam «Regimini Ecclesae universae» sive a Decessore Nostro Paulo VI sive a Nobis factae sunt.

Deinde Nostrum fuit ut Ecclesiae legum renovatio, quae per evulgatum novum Codicem Iuris Canonici inducta est, vel quae in eo est posita ut ad effectum deducatur in recognoscendo Codice Iuris Canonici Orientalis, aliquo modo expleretur atque conficeretur.

Tum in animo habuimus ut antiquitus recepta Romanae Curiae Dicasteria et Instituta magis idonea redderentur ad ipsorum fines consequendos, ad quos instituta sunt, scilicet ad participanda regiminis, iurisdictionis atque negotiorum exsecutionis munera; qua de re factum est ut horum Dicasteriorum agendi provinciae inter ipsa aptius distribuerentur ac distinctius designarentur.

Deinde, prae oculis habentes quae rerum usus hisce annis docuit quaeque semper novis ecclesialis societatis postulatis requiruntur, cogitavimus iuridicam figuram rationemque iterum considerare illorum institutorum, quae merito «post-conciliaria» appellantur, eorum forte conformationem ordinationemque mutando. Quod eo consilio fecimus, ut magis magisque utile fructuosumque ipsorum institutorum munus redderetur, scilicet in Ecclesia promovendi peculiaria pastoralia opera atque rerum studium, quae augescente in dies celeritate Pastorum sollicitudinem occupant eademque tempestivas securasque responsiones postulant.

Denique nova et etiam stabilia incepta ad mutuam operam inter Dicasteria consociandam excogitata sunt, quorum ope quaedam agendi ratio habeatur unitatis notam suapte natura prae se ferens.

Quae ut uno comprehendamus verbo, curae Nobis fuit continenter procedere ut Romanae Curiae constitutio atque agendi ratio tum ecclesiologicae illi rationi, a Concilio Vaticano II pertractatae, magis magisque responderent, tum ad ipsius constitutionis pastorales propositos fines obtinendos clariore usque modo idonea evaderent, tum ecclesialis civilisque societatis necessitatibus aptius in dies obviam irent.

It is indeed our conviction that now, at the beginning of the third millennium after the birth of Christ, the zeal of the Roman Curia in no small measure contributes to the fact that the Church might remain faithful to the mystery of her origin,[34] since the Holy Spirit keeps her ever young by the power of the Gospel.[35]

14. Having given thought to all these matters with the help of expert advisors, sustained by the wise counsel and collegial spirit of the cardinals and bishops, having diligently studied the nature and mission of the Roman Curia, we have commanded that this Apostolic Constitution be drawn up, led by the hope that this venerable institution, so necessary to the government of the Church, may respond to that new pastoral impulse by which all the faithful are moved, laity, priests and particularly bishops, especially now after the Second Vatican Council, to listen ever more deeply and follow what the Spirit is saying to the Churches (cf. Rev 2:7).

Just as all the pastors of the Church, and among them in a special way the bishop of Rome, are keenly aware that they are "Christ's servants, stewards entrusted with the mysteries of God" (1 Cor 4:1) and seek above all to be utterly loyal helpers whom the Eternal Father may easily use to carry out the work of salvation in the world, so also the Roman Curia has this strong desire, in each and every sphere of its important work, to be filled with the same spirit and the same inspiration; the Spirit, we say, of the Son of Man, of Christ the only begotten of the Father, who "has come to save what was lost" (Mt 18:11) and whose single and all-embracing wish is that all men "may have life and have it to the full" (Jn 10:10).

Therefore, with the help of God's grace and of the Most Blessed Virgin Mary, the Mother of the Church, we establish and decree the following norms for the Roman Curia.

I. GENERAL NORMS

Notion of Roman Curia

Art. 1. The Roman Curia is the complex of dicasteries and institutes which help the Roman Pontiff in the exercise

---

Siquidem persuasum Nobis est Romanae Curiae navitatem haud paulum conferre, ut Ecclesia, tertio post Christum natum adventante millennio, ortus sui mysterio fidelis perseveret,[34] cum Spiritus Sanctus virtute Evangelii eam iuvenescere faci.[35]

14. Hisce omnibus attentis, opera peritorum virorum adhibita, sapienti consilio et collegiali affectu suffulti Patrum Cardinalium et Episcoporum, diligenter perspectis Romanae Curiae natura et munere, hanc Apostolicam Constitutionem exarari iussimus, spe ducti ut veneranda haec et regimini Ecclesiae necessaria institutio, novo illi pastorali instinctui respondeat, quo praesertim post celebratum Concilium Vaticanum II fideles omnes, laici, presbyteri et praesertim Episcopi aguntur, quo penitius usque audiant atque sequantur ea quae Spiritus dicat Ecclesiis (cf. *Ap* 2, 7).

Quemadmodum enim omnes Ecclesiae Pastores, atque inter ipsos speciali modo Romanus Episcopus, persentiunt se esse «ministros Christi et dispensatores mysteriorum Dei» (*1 Cor* 4,1), atque cupiunt se praeprimis adiutores praebere fidelissimos, quibus Aeternus Pater facile utatur ad salutis opus in mundo prosequendum, ita Romana Curia, in singulis quibusque exercitatis suae magni momenti navitatis orbibus, peroptat ut ipsa quoque eodem Spiritu eodemque afflatu pervadatur: Spiritum dicimus Filii hominis, Christi Unigeniti Patris, qui «venit . . . salvare quod perierat» (*Mt* 18,11), cuiusque unicum amplissimumque optatum perpetuo eo contendit, ut omnes homines «vitam habeant et abundantius habeant» (*Io* l0,10).

Propterea, opitulante Dei gratia ac favente Beatissimae Virginis Mariae, Ecclesiae Matris, auxilio, normas de Romana Curia quae sequuntur statuimus atque decernimus.

I. NORMAE GENERALES

De Curiae Romanae Notione

Art. 1. Curia Romana complexus est Dicasteriorum et Institutorum, quae Romano Pontifici

---

34. Cf. Enc. *Dominum et vivificantem* 66, 18 May 1986, *AAS* 78 (1986) 896–897; *Origins* 16 (1986–1987) 99.

35. Cf. *LG* 4.

of his supreme pastoral office for the good and service of the whole Church and of the particular Churches. It thus strengthens the unity of the faith and the communion of the people of God and promotes the mission proper to the Church in the world.

Structure of the Dicasteries

Art. 2. §1. By the word "dicasteries" are understood the Secretariat of State, Congregations, Tribunals, Councils and Offices, namely the Apostolic Camera, the Administration of the Patrimony of the Apostolic See, and the Prefecture for the Economic Affairs of the Holy See.

§2. The dicasteries are juridically equal among themselves.

§3. Among the institutes of the Roman Curia are the Prefecture of the Papal Household and the Office for the Liturgical Celebrations of the Supreme Pontiff.

Art. 3. §1. Unless they have a different structure in virtue of their specific nature or some special law, the dicasteries are composed of the cardinal prefect or the presiding archbishop, a body of cardinals and of some bishops, assisted by a secretary, consultors, senior administrators, and a suitable number of officials.

§2. According to the specific nature of certain dicasteries, clerics and other faithful can be added to the body of cardinals and bishops.

§3. Strictly speaking, the members of a congregation are the cardinals and the bishops.

Art. 4. The prefect or president acts as moderator of the dicastery, directs it and acts in its name.

The secretary, with the help of the undersecretary, assists the prefect or president in managing the business of the dicastery as well as its human resources.

Art. 5 §1. The prefect or president, the members of the body mentioned in art. 3, §1, the secretary, and the other senior administrators, as well as the consultors, are appointed by the Supreme Pontiff for a five-year term.

§2. Once they have completed seventy-five years of age, cardinal prefects are asked to submit their resignation to the Roman Pontiff, who, after considering all factors, will make the decision. Other moderators and secretaries cease from office, having completed seventy-five years of age; members, when they have completed eighty years of age; those who are attached to any dicastery by reason of their office cease to be members when their office ceases.

De Dicasteriorum Structura

adiutricem operam navant in exercitio eius supremi pastoralis muneris ad Ecclesiae Universae Ecclesiarumque particularium bonum ac servitium, quo quidem unitas fidei et communio populi Dei roboratur atque missio Ecclesiae propria in mundo promovetur.

Art. 2. §1. Dicasteriorum nomine intelleguntur: Secretaria Status, Congregationes, Tribunalia, Consilia et Officia, scilicet Camera Apostolica, Administratio Patrimonii Sedis Apostolicae, Praefectura Rerum Oeconomicarum Sanctae Sedis.

§2. Dicasteria sunt inter se iuridice paria.

§3. Institutis autem Curiae Romanae accedunt Praefectura Pontificalis Domus et Officium de Liturgicis Celebrationibus Summi Pontificis.

Art. 3. §1. Dicasteria, nisi ob peculiarem ipsorum naturam aut specialem legem aliam habeant structuram, constant ex Cardinali Praefecto vel Archiepiscopo Praeside, coetu Patrum Cardinalium et quorundam Episcoporum, adiuvante Secretario. Iisdem adsunt Consultores et operam praestant Administri maiores atque congruus Officialium numerus.

§2. Iuxta peculiarem naturam quorundam Dicasteriorum, ipsorum coetui adscribi possunt clerici necnon alii Christifideles.

§3. Congregationis autem Membra proprie dicta sunt Cardinales et Episcopi.

Art. 4. Praefectus vel Praeses Dicasterium moderatur, id dirigit eiusdemque personam gerit.

Secretarius, cooperante Subsecretario, Praefectum vel Praesidem in Dicasterii negotiis personisque moderandis, adiuvat.

Art. 5. §1. Praefectus vel Praeses, Membra coetus, Secretarius ceterique Administri maiores necnon Consultores a Summo Pontifice ad quinquennium nominantur.

§2. Expleto septuagesimo quinto aetatis anno, Cardinales praepositi rogantur ut officii renuntiationem exhibeant Romano Pontifici, qui, omnibus perpensis, providebit. Ceteri Moderatores necnon Secretarii, expleto septuagesimo quinto aetatis anno, a munere cessant; Membra, octogesimo anno expleto; qui tamen ratione muneris alicui Dicasterio adscripti sunt, cessante munere, desinunt esse Membra.

Art. 6. On the death of the Supreme Pontiff, all moderators and members of the dicasteries cease from their office. The camerlengo of the Roman Church and the major penitentiary are excepted, who expedite ordinary business and refer to the College of Cardinals those things which would have been referred to the Supreme Pontiff.

The secretaries see to the ordinary operations of the dicasteries, taking care of ordinary business only; they need to be confirmed in office by the Supreme Pontiff within three months of his election.

Art. 7. The members of the body mentioned in art. 3, §1, are taken from among the cardinals living in Rome or outside the city, to whom are added some bishops, especially diocesan ones, insofar as they have special expertise in the matters being dealt with; also, depending on the nature of the dicastery, some clerics and other Christian faithful, with this proviso that matters requiring the exercise of power of governance be reserved to those in holy orders.

Art. 8. Consultors also are appointed from among clerics or other Christian faithful outstanding for their knowledge and prudence, taking into consideration, as much as possible, the international character of the Church.

Art. 9. Officials are taken from among the Christian faithful, clergy or laity, noted for their virtue, prudence, and experience, and for the necessary knowledge attested by suitable academic degrees, and selected as far as possible from the various regions of the world, so that the Curia may express the universal character of the Church. The suitability of the applicants should be evaluated by test or other appropriate means, according to the circumstances.

Particular Churches, moderators of institutes of consecrated life and of societies of apostolic life will not fail to render assistance to the Apostolic See by allowing their Christian faithful or their members to be available for service at the Roman Curia.

Art. 10. Each dicastery is to have its own archive where incoming documents and copies of documents sent out are kept safe and in good order in a system of "protocol" organized according to modern methods.

Procedure

Art. 11. §1. Matters of major importance are reserved to the general meeting, according to the nature of each dicastery.

§2. All members must be called in due time to the plenary sessions, held as far as possible once a year, to deal

Art. 6. Occurrente morte Summi Pontificis, omnes Dicasteriorum Moderatores et Membra a munere cessant. Excipiuntur Romanae Ecclesiae Camerarius et Paenitentiarius Maior, qui ordinaria negotia expediunt, ea Cardinalium Collegio proponentes, quae ad Summum Pontificem essent referenda.

Secretarii ordinario moderamini Dicasteriorum prospiciunt, negotia tantum ordinaria curantes; ipsi vero indigent confirmatione Summi Pontificis, intra tres ab Eius electione menses.

Art. 7. Membra coetus sumuntur ex Cardinalibus sive in Urbe sive extra Urbem commorantibus, quibus accedunt, quatenus peculiari peritia in rebus, de quibus agitur, pollent, nonnulli Episcopi, praesertim dioecesani, necnon, iuxta Dicasterii naturam, quidam clerici et alii Christifideles, hac tamen lege, ut ea, quae exercitium potestatis regiminis requirunt, reserventur iis qui ordine sacro insigniti sunt.

Art. 8. Consultores quoque nominantur ex clericis vel ceteris Christifidelibus scientia et prudentia praestantibus, ratione universalitatis, quantum fieri potest, servata.

Art. 9. Officiales assumuntur ex Christifidelibus, clericis vel laicis, commendatis virtute, prudentia, usu rerum, debita scientia, aptis studiorum titulis comprobata, ex variis orbis regionibus, quantum fieri potest, selectis, ita ut Curia indolem universalem Ecclesiae exprimat. Candidatorum idoneitas experimentis aliisve congruentibus modis pro opportunitate comprobetur.

Ecclesiae particulares, Moderatores Institutorum vitae consecratae et Societatum vitae apostolicae ne omittant adiutricem operam Apostolicae Sedi praebere, sinentes ut eorum fideles aut sodales, si opus fuerit, in Romanam Curiam arcessantur.

Art. 10. Unumquodque Dicasterium proprium habet archivum, in quo documenta recepta atque exemplaria eorum, quae missa sunt, in «protocollum» relata, ordinate, tuto et secundum hodierni temporis rationes custodiantur.

De Agendl Ratione

Art. 11. §1. Negotia maioris momenti coetui generali, iuxta cuiusque Dicasterii naturam, reservantur.

§2. Ad plenarias sessiones, semel in anno, quantum fieri potest, celebrandas, pro quaes-

with questions involving general principles, and for other questions which the prefect or president may have deemed to require treatment. For ordinary sessions it is sufficient to convoke members who reside in Rome.

§3. The secretary participates in all sessions with the right to vote.

Art. 12. Consultors and those who are equivalent to them are to make a diligent study of the matter in hand and to present their considered opinion, usually in writing.

So far as opportunity allows and depending on the nature of each dicastery, consultors can be called together to examine questions in a collegial fashion and, as the case may be, present a common position.

For individual cases, others can be called in for consultation who, although not numbered among the consultors, are qualified by their special expertise in the matter to be treated.

Art. 13. Depending on their own proper field of competence, the dicasteries deal with those matters which, because of their special importance, either by their nature or by law, are reserved to the Apostolic See and those which exceed the competence of individual bishops and their groupings, as well as those matters committed to them by the Supreme Pontiff. The dicasteries study the major problems of the present age, so that the Church's pastoral action may be more effectively promoted and suitably coordinated, with due regard to relations with the particular Churches. The dicasteries promote initiatives for the good of the universal Church. Finally, they review matters that the Christian faithful, exercising their own right, bring to the attention of the Apostolic See.

Art. 14. The competence of dicasteries is defined on the basis of subject matter, unless otherwise expressly provided for.

Art. 15. Questions are to be dealt with according to law, be it universal law or the special law of the Roman Curia, and according to the norms of each dicastery, yet with pastoral means and criteria, attentive both to justice and the good of the Church and, especially, to the salvation of souls.

Art. 16. Apart from the official Latin language, it is acceptable to approach the Roman Curia in any of the languages widely known today.

For the convenience of the dicasteries, a centre is being established for translating documents into other languages.

tionibus naturam principii generalis habentibus aliisque, quas Praefectus vel Praeses tractandas censuerit, omnia Membra tempestive convocari debent. Ad ordinarias autem sessiones sufficit ut convocentur Membra in Urbe versantia.

§3. Omnes coetus sessiones Secretarius cum iure suffragium ferendi participat.

Art. 12. Consultorum atque eorum qui ipsis assimilantur est studio rei propositae diligenter incumbere suamque sententiam, pro more scriptam, de ea exarare.

Pro opportunitate atque iuxta cuiusque Dicasterii naturam, Consultores convocari possunt ut collegialiter quaestiones propositas examinent et, si casus ferat, sententiam communem proferant.

Singulis in casibus alii ad consulendum vocari possunt, qui, etsi in Consultorum numerum non sunt relati, peculiari tamen peritia rei pertractandae commendentur.

Art. 13. Dicasteria, secundum uniuscuiusque propriam competentiam, negotia tractant, quae ob peculiare suum momentum, natura sua aut iure, Sedi Apostolicae reservantur, atque ea quae fines competentiae singulorum Episcoporum eorumve coetuum excedunt, necnon ea quae ipsis a Summo Pontifice committuntur; in studium incumbunt problematum graviorum vigentis aetatis, ut actio pastoralis Ecclesiae efficacius promoveatur apteque coordinetur, debita servata relatione cum Ecclesiis particularibus; promovent incepta pro bono Ecclesiae universalis; ea denique cognoscunt, quae Christifideles, iure proprio utentes, ad Sedem Apostolicam deferunt.

Art. 14. Dicasteriorum competentia definitur ratione materiae nisi aliter expresse cautum sit.

Art. 15. Quaestiones tractandae sunt ad tramitem iuris, sive universalis sive peculiaris Romanae Curiae, atque iuxta normas uniuscuiusque Dicasterii, viis tamen ac iudiciis pastoralibus, animo intento tum ad iustitiam et Ecclesiae bonum tum praesertim ad animarum salutem.

Art. 16. Romanam Curiam fas est adire, praeterquam officiali Latino sermone, cunctis etiam sermonibus hodie latius cognitis.

In commodum omnium Dicasteriorum «Centrum» constituitur pro documentis in alias linguas vertendis.

Art. 17. General documents prepared by one dicastery will be communicated to other interested dicasteries, so that the text may be improved with any corrections that may be suggested, and, through common consultation, it may even be proceeded in a coordinated manner to their implementation.

Art. 18. Decisions of major importance are to be submitted for the approval of the Supreme Pontiff, except decisions for which special faculties have been granted to the moderators of the dicasteries as well as the sentences of the Tribunal of the Roman Rota and the Supreme Tribunal of the Apostolic Signatura within the limits of their proper competence.

The dicasteries cannot issue laws or general decrees having the force of law or derogate from the prescriptions of current universal law, unless in individual cases and with the specific approval of the Supreme Pontiff.

It is of the utmost importance that nothing grave and extraordinary be transacted unless the Supreme Pontiff be previously informed by the moderators of the dicasteries.

Art. 19. §1. Hierarchical recourses are received by whichever dicastery has competence in that subject matter, without prejudice to art. 21, §1.

§2. Questions, however, which are to be dealt with judicially are sent to the competent tribunals, without prejudice to arts. 52–53.

Art. 20. Conflicts of competence arising between dicasteries are to be submitted to the Supreme Tribunal of the Apostolic Signatura, unless it pleases the Supreme Pontiff to deal with them otherwise.

Art. 21. §1. Matters touching the competence of more than one dicastery are to be examined together by the dicasteries concerned.

To enable them to exchange advice, a meeting will be called by the moderator of the dicastery which has begun to deal with the matter, either on his own initiative or at the request of another dicastery concerned. However, if the subject matter demands it, it may be referred to a plenary session of the dicasteries concerned.

The meeting will be chaired by the moderator of the dicastery who called the meeting or by its secretary, if only the secretaries are meeting.

§2. Where needed, permanent interdicasterial commissions will be set up to deal with matters requiring mutual and frequent consultation.

Art. 17. Quae ab uno Dicasterio praeparantur documenta generalia cum aliis communicentur Dicasteriis, quorum interest, ut textus emendationibus forte propositis perfici possit et, collatis consiliis, etiam ad eorum exsecutionem concordius procedatur.

Art. 18. Summi Pontificis approbationi subiciendae sunt decisiones maioris momenti, exceptis iis pro quibus Dicasteriorum Moderatoribus speciales facultates tributae sunt exceptisque sententiis Tribunalis Rotae Romanae et Supremi Tribunalis Signaturae Apostolicae intra limites propriae competentiae latis.

Dicasteria leges aut decreta generalia vim legis habentia ferre non possunt nec iuris universalis vigentis praescriptis derogare, nisi singulis in casibus atque de specifica approbatione Summi Pontificis.

Hoc autem sollemne sit ut nihil grave et extraordinarium agatur, nisi a Moderatoribus Dicasteriorum Summo Pontifici fuerit antea significatum.

Art. 19. §1. Recursus hierarchici a Dicasterio recipiuntur, quod competens sit ratione materiae, firmo praescripto art. 21 §1.

§2. Quaestiones vero, quae iudicialiter sunt cognoscendae, remittuntur ad competentia Tribunalia, firmo praescripto artt. 52 et 53.

Art. 20. Conflictus competentiae inter Dicasteria, si qui oriantur, Supremo Tribunali Signaturae Apostolicae subiciantur, nisi Summo Pontifici aliter prospiciendum placuerit.

Art. 21. §1. Negotia, quae plurium Dicasteriorum competentiam attingunt, a Dicasteriis, quorum interest, simul examinentur.

Ut consilia conferantur, a Moderatore Dicasterii, quod res agere coepit, conventus convocetur, sive ex officio sive rogatu alius Dicasterii, cuius interest. Si tamen subiecta materia id postulet, res deferatur ad plenariam sessionem Dicasteriorum, quorum interest.

Conventui praeest Dicasterii Moderator, qui eundem coëgit, vel eiusdem Secretarius, si soli Secretarii conveniant.

§2. Ubi opus fuerit opportune commissiones «interdicasteriales» permanentes, ad negotia tractanda, quae mutua crebraque consultatione egeant, constituantur.

Meetings of Cardinals

Art. 22. By mandate of the Supreme Pontiff, the cardinals in charge of dicasteries meet together several times a year to examine more important questions, coordinate their activities, so that they may be able to exchange information and take counsel.

Art. 23. More serious business of a general character can be usefully dealt with, if the Supreme Pontiff so decides, by the cardinals assembled in plenary consistory according to proper law.

Council of Cardinals for the Study of Organizational and Economic Questions of the Apostolic See

Art. 24. The Council of Cardinals for the Study of Organizational and Economic Questions of the Apostolic See consists of fifteen cardinals who head particular Churches from various parts of the world and are appointed by the Supreme Pontiff for a five-year term of office.

Art. 25. §1. The Council is convened by the cardinal secretary of state, usually twice a year, to consider those economic and organizational questions which relate to the administration of the Holy See, with the assistance, as needed, of experts in these affairs.

§2. The Council also considers the activities of the special institute which is erected and located within the State of Vatican City in order to safeguard and administer economic goods placed in its care with the purpose of supporting works of religion and charity. This institute is governed by a special law.

Relations with Particular Churches

Art. 26. §1. Close relations are to be fostered with particular Churches and groupings of bishops, seeking out their advice when preparing documents of major importance that have a general character.

§2. As far as possible, documents of a general character or having a special bearing on their particular Churches should be communicated to the bishops before they are made public.

§3. Questions brought before the dicasteries are to be diligently examined and, without delay, an answer or, at least, a written acknowledgement of receipt, insofar as this is necessary, should be sent.

De Cardinalium Adunationibus

Art. 22. De mandato Summi Pontificis pluries in anno Cardinales, qui Dicasteriis praesunt, in unum conveniunt, ut graviores quaestiones examinentur, labores coordinentur, utque notitiae inter eos communicari et consilia capi possint.

Art. 23. Graviora indolis generalis negotia utiliter tractari possunt, si Summo Pontifici placuerit, a Cardinalibus in Consistorio plenario iuxta legem propriam adunatis.

De Coetu Cardinalium Ad Consulendum Rebus Organicis et Oeconomicis Apostolicae Sedis

Art. 24. Coetus ex quindecim Cardinalibus constat, totidem Praesulibus Ecclesiarum particularium e variis orbis partibus, a Romano Pontifice ad quinquennium nominatis.

Art. 25. §1. Coetus ex solito bis in anno convocatur a Cardinali Secretario Status ad res oeconomicas et organicas quoad Sanctae Sedis administrationem perpendendas, auxiliantibus, quatenus opus fuerit, harum rerum peritis.

§2. Idem cognoscit etiam de navitate peculiaris Instituti, quod erectum est et collocatum intra Statum Civitatis Vaticanae, ad bona oeconomica sibi commissa custodienda atque administranda, quae ad opera religionis et caritatis sustinenda inserviunt; quod peculiari lege regitur.

De Rationibus cum Ecclesiis Particularibus

Art. 26. §1. Crebrae relationes foveantur cum Ecclesiis particularibus coetibusque Episcoporum, eorum consilium exquirendo, cum agitur de apparandis documentis maioris momenti, indolem generalem habentibus.

§2. Quantum fieri potest, antequam publici iuris fiant, communicentur cum Episcopis dioecesanis documenta generalia aut quae earundem Ecclesiarum particularium speciali modo intersint.

§3. Quaestiones Dicasteriis propositae, diligenter examinentur atque sine mora responsio aut saltem syngraphum rei acceptae, quatenus opus fuerit, mittatur.

Art. 27. Dicasteries should not omit to consult with papal legates regarding business affecting the particular Churches where the legates are serving, nor should they omit to communicate to the legates the results of their deliberations.

Ad limina Visits

Art. 28. In keeping with a venerable tradition and the prescriptions of law, bishops presiding over particular Churches visit the tombs of the Apostles at predetermined times and on that occasion present to the Roman Pontiff a report on the state of their diocese.

Art. 29. These kinds of visits have a special importance in the life of the Church, marking as they do the summit of the relationship between the pastors of each particular Church with the Roman Pontiff. For he meets his brother bishops, and deals with them about matters concerning the good of the Churches and the bishops' role as shepherds, and he confirms and supports them in faith and charity. This strengthens the bonds of hierarchical communion and openly manifests the catholicity of the Church and the unity of the episcopal college.

Art. 30. The *ad limina* visits also concern the dicasteries of the Roman Curia. For through these visits a helpful dialogue between the bishops and the Apostolic See is increased and deepened, information is shared, advice and timely suggestions are brought forward for the greater good and progress of the Churches and for the observance of the common discipline of the Church.

Art. 31. These visits are to be prepared very carefully and appropriately so that they proceed well and enjoy a successful outcome in their three principal stages—namely, the pilgrimage to the tombs of the Princes of the Apostles and their veneration, the meeting with the Supreme Pontiff, and the meetings at the dicasteries of the Roman Curia.

Art. 32. For this purpose, the report on the state of the diocese should be sent to the Holy See six months before the time set for the visit. It is to be examined with all diligence by the competent dicasteries, and their remarks are to be shared with a special committee convened for this purpose so that a brief synthesis of these may be drawn up and be readily at hand in the meetings.

Art. 27. Dicasteria consulere ne omittant Pontificios Legatos circa negotia, quae ad Ecclesias particulares, ubi munus exercent, attineant, necnon cum iisdem Legatis captas deliberationes communicare.

De Visitationibus ad Limina

Art. 28. Iuxta venerandam traditionem et iuris praescriptum, Episcopi, qui Ecclesiis particularibus praesunt, Apostolorum limina, statutis temporibus, petunt eaque occasione relationem super dioecesis statu Romano Pontifici exhibent.

Art. 29. Huiusmodi visitationes peculiare in vita Ecclesiae habent momentum, quippe quae veluti culmen efficiant relationum cuiusvis Ecclesiae particularis Pastorum cum Romano Pontifice. Ipse enim, suos in Episcopatu fratres coram admittens, cum illis de rebus agit, quae ad bonum Ecclesiarum et ad Episcoporum pascendi munus pertinent, ipsosque in fide et caritate confirmat atque sustinet; quo quidem modo vincula hierarchicae communionis roborantur et catholicitas Ecclesiae necnon Episcoporum collegii unitas veluti palam ostenditur.

Art. 30. Visitationes ad limina Dicasteria quoque Curiae Romanae respiciunt. Per has enim dialogus proficuus inter Episcopos et Apostolicam Sedem augetur ac profundior fit, mutuae informationes dantur, consilia et opportunae suggestiones ad maius bonum et profectum Ecclesiarum necnon ad disciplinam Ecclesiae communem servandam afferuntur.

Art. 31. Sedula cura apteque visitationes parentur ita ut tres principales gradus quibus constant, videlicet ad Apostolorum Principum sepulcra peregrinatio eorumque veneratio, congressio cum Summo Pontifice, atque colloquia apud Romanae Curiae Dicasteria, feliciter procedant prosperumque habeant exitum.

Art. 32. Hunc in finem, relatio super dioecesis statu Sanctae Sedi sex mensibus ante tempus pro visitatione statutum mittatur. A Dicasteriis, quibus competit, omni cum diligentia examinetur eorumque animadversiones cum peculiari coetu ad hoc constituto communicentur ut brevis synthesis de his omnibus conficiatur, quae in colloquiis prae oculis habenda sit.

Pastoral Character of the Activity of the Roman Curia

Art. 33. The activity of all who work at the Roman Curia and the other institutes of the Holy See is a true ecclesial service, marked with a pastoral character, that all must discharge with a deep sense of duty as well as in a spirit of service, as it is a sharing in the world-wide mission of the bishop of Rome.

Art. 34. Each individual dicastery pursues its own end, yet dicasteries cooperate with one another. Therefore, all who are working in the Roman Curia are to do so in such a way that their work may come together and be forged into one. Accordingly, all must always be prepared to offer their services wherever needed.

Art. 35. Although any work performed within the institutes of the Holy See is a sharing in the apostolic action, priests are to apply themselves as best they can to the care of souls, without prejudice however to their own office.

Central Labour Office

Art. 36. According to its own terms of reference, the Central Labour Office deals with working conditions within the Roman Curia and related questions.

Regulations

Art. 37. To this Apostolic Constitution is added an *Ordo servandus* or common norms setting forth the ways and means of transacting business in the Curia itself, without prejudice to the norms of this Constitution.

Art. 38. Each dicastery is to have its own *Ordo servandus* or special norms setting forth the ways and means of transacting business within it.

The *Ordo servandus* of each dicastery shall be made public in the usual manner of the Apostolic See.

II. SECRETARIAT OF STATE

Art. 39. The Secretariat of State provides close assistance to the Supreme Pontiff in the exercise of his supreme office.

Art. 40. The Secretariat is presided over by the Cardi-

De Indole Pastorali Actuositatis

Art. 33. Eorum omnium actuositas, qui apud Romanam Curiam ceteraque Sanctae Sedis instituta operantur, verum ecclesiale est servitium, indole pastorali signatum, prouti in universali Romani Pontificis missione participatio, summa cum officii conscientia atque cum animo serviendi ab omnibus praestandum.

Art. 34. Singula Dicasteria proprios fines persequuntur, ea tamen inter se conspirant; quare omnes in Romana Curia operantes id efficere debent, ut eorum operositas in unum confluat et temperetur. Omnes igitur parati semper sint ad propriam operam praestandam ubicumque necesse fuerit.

Art. 35. Etsi quaevis opera in Sanctae Sedis Institutis praestita cooperatio est in actione apostolica, sacerdotes pro viribus in curam animarum, sine praeiudicio tamen proprii officii, actuose incumbant.

De Officio Centrali Laboris

Art. 36. De laboris exercitio in Curia Romana atque de quaestionibus cum eo connexis videt, iuxta suam competentiam, *Officium Centrale Laboris.*

De Ordinibus

Art. 37. Huic Constitutioni Apostolicae accedit *Ordo servandus* seu normae communes, quibus disciplina et modus tractandi negotia in Curia ipsa praestituitur, firmis manentibus normis generalibus huius Constitutionis.

Art. 38. Unicuique Dicasterio proprius sit *Ordo servandus* seu normae speciales, quibus disciplina et negotia tractandi rationes praestituantur.

Ordo servandus uniuscuiusque Dicasterii suetis Apostolicae Sedis formis publici iuris fiat.

II. SECRETARIA STATUS

Art. 39. Secretaria Status proxime iuvat Summum Pontificem in Eius supremo munere exercendo.

Art. 40. Eidem praeest Cardinalis Secretar-

nal Secretary of State. It is composed of two sections, the First being the *Section for General Affairs,* under the direct control of the substitute, with the help of the assessor; the Second being the *Section for Relations with States,* under the direction of its own secretary, with the help of the under-secretary. Attached to this latter section is a council of cardinals and some bishops.

First Section

Art. 41. §1. It is the task of the First Section in a special way to expedite the business concerning the daily service of the Supreme Pontiff; to deal with those matters which arise outside the ordinary competence of the dicasteries of the Roman Curia and of the other institutes of the Apostolic See; to foster relations with those dicasteries and co-ordinate their work, without prejudice to their autonomy; to supervise the office and work of the legates of the Holy See, especially as concerns the particular Churches. This section deals with everything concerning the ambassadors of States to the Holy See.

§2. In consultation with other competent dicasteries, this section takes care of matters concerning the presence and activity of the Holy See in international organizations, without prejudice to art. 46. It does the same concerning Catholic international organizations.

Art. 42. It is also the task of the First Section:

1° to draw up and dispatch apostolic constitutions, decretal letters, apostolic letters, epistles, and other documents entrusted to it by the Supreme Pontiff;

2° to prepare the appropriate documents concerning appointments to be made or approved by the Supreme Pontiff in the Roman Curia and in the other institutes depending on the Holy See;

3° to guard the leaden seal and the Fisherman's ring.

Art. 43. It is likewise within the competence of this Section:

1° to prepare for publication the acts and public documents of the Holy See in the periodical entitled *Acta Apostolicae Sedis;*

2° through its special office commonly known as the *Press Office,* to publish official announcements of acts of the Supreme Pontiff or of the activities of the Holy See;

3° in consultation with the Second Section, to oversee

Sectio Prior

Art. 41. §1. Ad priorem sectionem pertinet peculiari modo operam navare expediendis negotiis, quae Summi Pontificis cotidianum servitium respiciunt; ea agere, quae extra ordinariam Dicasteriorum Romanae Curiae aliorumque Apostolicae Sedis Institutorum competentiam tractanda obveniant; rationes cum iisdem Dicasteriis fovere sine praeiudicio eorum autonomiae et labores coordinare; Legatorum Sanctae Sedis officium eorumque operam, praesertim ad Ecclesias particulares quod attinet, moderari. Ipsius est omnia explere, quae Legatos Civitatum apud Sanctam Sedem respiciunt.

§2. Collatis consiliis cum aliis competentibus Dicasteriis, eadem curat quae Sanctae Sedis praesentiam et navitatem apud Internationalia Instituta respiciunt, firmo praescripto art. 46. Idem agit quod ad Institutiones Internationales Catholicas pertinet.

Art. 42. Eiusdem etiam est:

1° componere et mittere Constitutiones Apostolicas, Litteras Decretales, Litteras Apostolicas, Epistulas aliaque documenta a Summo Pontifice ipsi commissa;

2° omnia explere acta, quae nominationes a Summo Pontifice peragendas vel probandas respiciunt in Romana Curia in aliisque Institutis, a Sancta Sede pendentibus;

3° custodire sigillum plumbeum et anulum Piscatoris.

Art. 43. Ad hanc sectionem pariter pertinet:

1° editionem curare actorum et documentorum publicorum Sanctae Sedis in commentario, quod inscribitur *Acta Apostolicae Sedis;*

2° officialia nuntia, quae sive acta Summi Pontificis sive Sanctae Sedis navitatem respiciunt, publici facere iuris per peculiare officium sibi subiectum, vulgo *Sala Stampa* appellatum;

3° invigilare, collatis consiliis cum Altera

the newspaper called *L'Osservatore Romano*, the Vatican Radio Station, and the Vatican Television Centre.

Art. 44. Through the *Central Statistical Office*, it collects, organizes, and publishes all data, set down according to statistical standards, concerning the life of the whole Church throughout the world.

Second Section

Art. 45. The Section for Relations with States has the special task of dealing with heads of government.

Art. 46. The Section for Relations with States has within its competence:

1° to foster relations, especially those of a diplomatic nature, with States and other subjects of public international law, and to deal with matters of common interest, promoting the good of the Church and of civil society by means of concordats and other agreements of this kind, if the case arises, while respecting the considered opinions of the groupings of bishops that may be affected;

2° in consultation with the competent dicasteries of the Roman Curia, to represent the Holy See at international organizations and meetings concerning questions of a public nature;

3° within the scope of its competence, to deal with what pertains to the papal legates.

Art. 47. §1. In special circumstances and by mandate of the Supreme Pontiff, and in consultation with the competent dicasteries of the Roman Curia, this Section takes action for the provision of particular Churches, and for the constitution of and changes to these Churches and their groupings.

§2. In other cases, especially where a concordat is in force, and without prejudice to art. 78, this Section has competence to transact business with civil governments.

III. CONGREGATIONS

Congregation for the Doctrine of the Faith

Art. 48. The proper duty of the Congregation for the Doctrine of the Faith is to promote and safeguard the doctrine on faith and morals in the whole Catholic world; so

---

Sectione, ephemeridi vulgo *L'Osservatore Romano* appellatae, Stationi Radiophonicae Vaticanae atque Centro Televisifico Vaticano.

Art. 44. Per Officium rationarii vulgo *Statistica* appellatum colligit, ordine componit atque palam edit omnia indicia, ad rationarii normas exarata, quae Ecclesiae universae vitam per terrarum orbem respiciunt.

Sectio Altera

Art. 45. Alterius sectionis de rationibus cum Civitatibus peculiare munus est in ea incumbere, quae cum rerum publicarum Moderatoribus agenda sunt.

Art. 46. Eidem competit:

1° rationes praesertim diplomaticas cum Civitatibus aliisque publici iuris societatibus fovere atque communia negotia tractare, ut bonum Ecclesiae civilisque societatis promoveatur, ope, si casus ferat, concordatorum aliarumque huiusmodi conventionum, et ratione habita sententiae Episcoporum coetuum, quorum intersit;

2° apud Internationalia Instituta et conventus de indolis publicae quaestionibus Sanctae Sedis partes gerere, collatis consiliis cum competentibus Romanae Curiae Dicasteriis;

3° agere, in propria laborum provincia, quae ad Legatos Pontificios attinent.

Art. 47. §1. In peculiaribus rerum adiunctis, de mandato Summi Pontificis, haec sectio, collatis consiliis cum competentibus Curiae Romanae Dicasteriis, ea explet quae ad Ecclesiarum particularium provisionem necnon ad earum earumque coetuum constitutionem aut immutationem spectant.

§2. Ceteris in casibus, praesertim ubi regimen concordatarium viget, eidem competit, firmo praescripto art. 78, ea absolvere, quae cum civilibus guberniis agenda sunt.

III. CONGREGATIONES

Congregatio de Doctrina Fidei

Art. 48. Proprium Congregationis de Doctrina Fidei munus est doctrinam de fide et moribus in universo catholico orbe promovere atque tu-

it has competence in things that touch this matter in any way.

Art. 49. Fulfilling its duty of promoting doctrine, the Congregation fosters studies so that the understanding of the faith may grow and a response in the light of the faith may be given to new questions arising from the progress of the sciences or human culture.

Art. 50. It helps the bishops, individually or in groups, in carrying out their office as authentic teachers and doctors of the faith, an office that carries with it the duty of promoting and guarding the integrity of that faith.

Art. 51. To safeguard the truth of faith and the integrity of morals, the Congregation takes care lest faith or morals suffer harm through errors that have been spread in any way whatever.

Wherefore:

1° it has the duty of requiring that books and other writings touching faith or morals, being published by the Christian faithful, be subjected to prior examination by the competent authority;

2° it examines carefully writings and opinions that seem to be contrary or dangerous to true faith, and, if it is established that they are opposed to the teaching of the Church, reproves them in due time, having given authors full opportunity to explain their minds, and having forewarned the Ordinary concerned; it brings suitable remedies to bear, if this be opportune.

3° finally, it takes good care lest errors or dangerous doctrines, which may have been spread among the Christian people, do not go without apt rebuttal.

Art. 52. The Congregation examines offences against the faith and more serious ones both in behaviour or in the celebration of the sacraments which have been reported to it and, if need be, proceeds to the declaration or imposition of canonical sanctions in accordance with the norms of common or proper law.

Art. 53. It is to examine whatever concerns the privilege of the faith, both in law and in fact.

Art. 54. Documents being published by other dicasteries of the Roman Curia, insofar as they touch on the doctrine of faith or morals, are to be subjected to its prior judgement.

Art. 55. Established within the Congregation for the Doctrine of the Faith are the Pontifical Biblical Commission and the International Theological Commission, which

tari; proinde ipsi competunt ea, quae hanc materiam quoquo modo attingunt.

Art. 49. Munus promovendae doctrinae adimplens, ipsa studia fovet ut fidei intellectus crescat ac novis quaestionibus ex scientiarum humanive cultus progressu enatis responsio sub luce fidei praeberi possit.

Art. 50. Episcopis, sive singulis sive in coetibus adunatis, auxilio est in exercitio muneris, quo ipsi authentici fidei magistri atque doctores constituuntur, quoque officio integritatem eiusdem fidei custodiendi ac promovendi tenentur.

Art. 51. Ad veritatem fidei morumque integritatem tuendam, curam impendit, ne fides aut mores per errores quomodocumque vulgatos detrimentum patiantur.

Quapropter:

1° ipsi officium est exigendi, ut libri aliaque scripta a Christifidelibus edenda, quae fidem moresque respiciant, praevio competentis auctoritatis examini subiciantur;

2° scripta atque sententias, quae rectae fidei contraria atque insidiosa videantur, excutit, atque, si constiterit ea Ecclesiae doctrinae esse opposita, eadem, data auctori facultate suam mentem plene explicandi, tempestive reprobat, praemonito Ordinario, cuius interest, atque congrua remedia, si opportunum fuerit, adhibet;

3° curat, denique, ne erroneis ac periculosis doctrinis, forte in populum christianum diffusis, apta confutatio desit.

Art. 52. Delicta contra fidem necnon graviora delicta tum contra mores tum in sacramentorum celebratione commissa, quae ipsi delata fuerint, cognoscit atque, ubi opus fuerit, ad canonicas sanctiones declarandas aut irrogandas ad normam iuris, sive communis sive proprii, procedit.

Art. 53. Eiusdem pariter est cognoscere, tum in iure tum in facto, quae privilegium fidei respiciunt.

Art. 54. Praevio eius iudicio subiciuntur documenta, ab aliis Curiae Romanae Dicasteriis edenda, quatenus doctrinam de fide vel moribus attingunt.

Art. 55. Apud Congregationem de Doctrina Fidei constitutae sunt Pontifica Commissio Biblica et Commissio Theologica Internationalis,

act according to their own approved norms and are presided over by the cardinal prefect of this Congregation.

quae iuxta proprias probatas normas agunt quibusque praeest Cardinalis eiusdem Congregationis Praefectus.

Congregation for the Oriental Churches

Art. 56. The Congregation for the Oriental Churches considers those matters, whether concerning persons or things, affecting the Catholic Oriental Churches.

Art. 57. §1. The patriarchs and major archbishops of the Oriental Churches, and the president of the Council for Promoting Christian Unity, are *ipso iure* members of this Congregation.

§2. The consultors and officials are to be selected in such a way as to reflect as far as possible the diversity of rites.

Art. 58. §1. The competence of this Congregation extends to all matters which are proper to the Oriental Churches and which are to be referred to the Apostolic See, whether concerning the structure and organization of the Churches, the exercise of the office of teaching, sanctifying and governing, or the status, rights, and obligations of persons. It also handles everything that has to be done concerning quinquennial reports and the *ad limina* visits in accordance with arts. 31–32.

§2. This however does not infringe on the proper and exclusive competence of the Congregations for the Doctrine of the Faith and for the Causes of Saints, of the Apostolic Penitentiary, the Supreme Tribunal of the Apostolic Signatura or the Tribunal of the Roman Rota, as well as of the Congregation for Divine Worship and the Discipline of the Sacraments for what pertains to dispensation from a marriage *ratum et non consummatum*.

In matters which also affect the faithful of the Latin Church, the Congregation will proceed, if the matter is sufficiently important, in consultation with the dicastery that has competence in the same matter for the faithful of the Latin Church.

Art. 59. The Congregation pays careful attention to communities of Oriental Christian faithful living within the territories of the Latin Church, and attends to their spiritual needs by providing visitors and even a hierarchy of their own, so far as possible and where numbers and circumstances demand it, in consultation with the Congregation competent for the establishment of particular Churches in that region.

Congregatio pro Ecclesiis Orientalibus

Art. 56. Congregatio ea cognoscit, quae, sive quoad personas sive quoad res, Ecclesias Orientales Catholicas respiciunt.

Art. 57. §1. Eiusdem ipso iure Membra sunt Patriarchae et Archiepiscopi Maiores Ecclesiarum Orientalium necnon Praeses Consilii ad Unitatem Christianorum fovendam.

§2. Consultores et Officiales ita seligantur, ut diversitatis rituum, quantum fieri potest, ratio habeatur.

Art. 58. §1. Huius Congregationis competentia ad omnia extenditur negotia, quae Ecclesiis Orientalibus sunt propria, quaeque ad Sedem Apostolicam deferenda sunt, sive quoad Ecclesiarum structuram et ordinationem, sive quoad munerum docendi, sanctificandi et regendi exercitium, sive quoad personas, earundem statum, iura ac obligationes. Omnia quoque explet, quae de relationibus quinquennalibus ac visitationibus ad limina ad normam artt. 31, 32 agenda sunt.

§2. Integra tamen manet propria atque exclusiva competentia Congregationum de Doctrina Fidei et de Causis Sanctorum, Paenitentiariae Apostolicae, Supremi Tribunalis Signaturae Apostolicae et Tribunalis Rotae Romanae, necnon Congregationis de Cultu Divino et Disciplina Sacramentorum ad dispensationem pro matrimonio rato et non consummato quod attinet.

In negotiis, quae Ecclesiae Latinae fideles quoque attingunt, Congregatio procedat, si rei momentum id postulet, collatis consiliis cum Dicasterio in eadem materia pro fidelibus Latinae Ecclesiae competenti.

Art. 59. Congregatio sedula cura item prosequitur communitates Christifidelium orientalium in circumscriptionibus territorialibus Ecclesiae Latinae versantium, eorumque necessitatibus spiritualibus per Visitatores, immo, ubi numerus fidelium atque adiuncta id exigant, quatenus fieri possit, etiam per propriam Hierarchiam consulit, collatis consiliis cum Congregatione pro consti-

Art. 60. In regions where Oriental rites have been preponderant from ancient times, apostolic and missionary activity depends solely on this Congregation, even if it is carried out by missionaries of the Latin Church.

Art. 61. The Congregation proceeds in collaboration with the Council for Promoting Christian Unity in matters which may concern relations with non-Catholic Oriental Churches and with the Council for Inter-Religious Dialogue in matters within the scope of this Council.

Congregation for Divine Worship and the Discipline of the Sacraments

Art. 62. The Congregation for Divine Worship and the Discipline of the Sacraments does whatever pertains to the Apostolic See concerning the regulation and promotion of the sacred liturgy, primarily of the sacraments, without prejudice to the competence of the Congregation for the Doctrine of the Faith.

Art. 63. It fosters and safeguards the regulation of the administration of the sacraments, especially regarding their valid and licit celebration. It grants favours and dispensations not contained in the faculties of diocesan bishops in this subject matter.

Art. 64. §1. By effective and suitable means, the Congregation promotes liturgical pastoral activity, especially regarding the celebration of the Eucharist; it gives support to the diocesan bishops so that the Christian faithful may share more and more actively in the sacred liturgy.

§2. It sees to the drawing up and revision of liturgical texts. It reviews particular calendars and proper texts for the Mass and the Divine Office for particular Churches and institutes which enjoy that right.

§3. It grants the *recognitio* to translations of liturgical books and their adaptations that have been lawfully prepared by conferences of bishops.

Art. 65. The Congregation fosters commissions or institutes for promoting the liturgical apostolate or sacred music, song or art, and it maintains relations with them. In accordance with the law, it erects associations which have an international character or approves or grants the *recognitio* to their statutes. Finally, it contributes to the progress

tutione Ecclesiarum particularium in eodem territorio competenti.

Art. 60. Actio apostolica et missionalis in regionibus, in quibus ritus orientales ab antiqua aetate praeponderant, ex hac Congregatione unice pendet, etiamsi a missionariis Latinae Ecclesiae peragatur.

Art. 61. Congregatio mutua ratione procedit cum Consilio ad Unitatem Christianorum Fovendam, in iis quae relationes cum Ecclesiis Orientalibus non catholicis respicere possunt necnon cum Consilio pro Dialogo inter Religiones, in materia quae ambitum eius tangit

Congregatio de Cultu Divino et Disciplina Sacramentorum

Art. 62. Congregatio ea agit quae, salva competentia Congregationis de Doctrina Fidei, ad Sedem Apostolicam pertinent quoad moderationem ac promotionem sacrae liturgiae, in primis Sacramentorum.

Art. 63. Sacramentorum disciplinam, praesertim quod attinet ad eorum validam et licitam celebrationem, fovet atque tuetur; gratias insuper atque dispensationes concedit, quae ad Episcoporum dioecesanorum facultates hac in regione non pertinent.

Art. 64. §1. Congregatio actionem pastoralem liturgicam, peculiari ratione ad Eucharisticam celebrationem quod attinet, efficacibus ac congruis mediis promovet; Episcopis dioecesanis adest, ut Christifideles sacram liturgiam magis in dies actuose participent.

§2. Textibus liturgicis conficiendis aut emendandis prospicit; recognoscit calendaria peculiaria atque Propria Missarum et Officiorum Ecclesiarum particularium necnon Institutorum, quae hoc iure fruuntur.

§3. Versiones librorum liturgicorum eorumque aptationes ab Episcoporum Conferentiis legitime paratas recognoscit.

Art. 65. Commissionibus vel Institutis ad apostolatum liturgicum vel musicam vel cantum vel artem sacram promovenda conditis favet et cum iis rationes habet; huiuscemodi consociationes, quae indolem internationalem prae se ferant, ad normam iuris erigit vel eorum statuta

of liturgical life by encouraging meetings from various regions.

Art. 66. The Congregation provides attentive supervision so that liturgical norms are accurately observed, abuses avoided, and that they be eradicated where they are found to exist.

Art. 67. This Congregation examines the fact of non-consummation in a marriage and the existence of a just cause for granting a dispensation. It receives all the acts together with the *votum* of the bishop and the remarks of the defender of the bond, weighs them according to its own special procedure, and, if the case warrants it, submits a petition to the Supreme Pontiff requesting the dispensation.

Art. 68. It is also competent to examine, in accordance with the law, cases concerning the nullity of sacred ordination.

Art. 69. This Congregation has competence concerning the cult of sacred relics, the confirmation of heavenly patrons and the granting of the title of minor basilica.

Art. 70. The Congregation gives assistance to bishops so that, in addition to liturgical worship, the prayers and pious exercises of the Christian people, in full harmony with the norms of the Church, may be fostered and held in high esteem.

Congregation for the Causes of Saints

Art. 71. The Congregation for the Causes of Saints deals with everything which, according to the established way, leads to the canonization of the servants of God.

Art. 72. §1. With special norms and timely advice, it assists diocesan bishops, who have competence to instruct the cause.

§2. It considers causes that have already been instructed, inquiring whether everything has been carried out in accordance with the law. It thoroughly examines the causes that have thus been reviewed, in order to judge whether everything required is present for a favorable recommendation to be submitted to the Supreme Pontiff, according to the previously established classification of causes.

Art. 73. The Congregation also is competent to examine what is necessary for the granting of the title of doctor to saints, after having received the recommendation of the Congregation for the Doctrine of the Faith concerning outstanding teaching.

Art. 74. Moreover, it has competence to decide every-

approbat ac recognoscit; conventus denique ex variis regionibus ad vitam liturgicam provehendam fovet.

Art. 66. Attente invigilat ut ordinationes liturgicae adamussim serventur, abusus praecaveantur iidemque, ubi deprehendantur, exstirpentur.

Art. 67. Huius Congregationis est cognoscere de facto inconsummationis matrimonii et de exsistentia iustae causae ad dispensationem concedendam. Ideoque acta omnia cum voto Episcopi et animadversionibus Defensoris Vinculi accipit et, iuxta peculiarem procedendi modum, perpendit atque, si casus ferat, Summo Pontifici petitionem ad dispensationem impetrandam subicit.

Art. 68. Ipsa competens quoque est in causis de nullitate sacrae ordinationis cognoscendis ad normam iuris.

Art. 69. Competens est quoad cultum sacrarum reliquiarum, confirmationem caelestium Patronorum et Basilicae minoris titulum concedendum.

Art. 70. Congregatio adiuvat Episcopos ut, praeter liturgicum cultum, preces necnon pia populi christiani exercitia, normis Ecclesiae plene congruentia, foveantur et in honore habeantur.

Congregatio de Causis Sanctorum

Art. 71. Congregatio ea omnia tractat, quae, secundum statutum iter, ad Servorum Dei canonizationem perducunt.

Art. 72. §1. Episcopis dioecesanis, quibus causae instructio competit, peculiaribus normis necnon opportunis consiliis adest.

§2. Causas iam instructas perpendit, inquirens utrum omnia ad normam legis peracta sint. Causas ita recognitas funditus perscrutatur ad iudicium ferendum utrum constet de omnibus quae requiruntur, ut Summo Pontifici vota favorabilia subiciantur, secundum ante constitutos gradus causarum.

Art. 73. Ad Congregationem praeterea spectat cognoscere de Doctoris titulo Sanctis decernendo, praehabito voto Congregationis de Doctrina Fidei ad eminentem doctrinam quod attinet.

Art. 74. Eius insuper est de iis omnibus de-

thing concerning the authentication of holy relics and their preservation.

Congregation for Bishops

Art. 75. The Congregation for Bishops examines what pertains to the establishment and provision of particular Churches and to the exercise of the episcopal office in the Latin Church, without prejudice to the competence of the Congregation for the Evangelization of Peoples.

Art. 76. This Congregation deals with everything concerning the constitution, division, union, suppression, and other changes of particular Churches and of their groupings. It also erects military ordinariates for the pastoral care of the armed forces.

Art. 77. It deals with everything concerning the appointment of bishops, even titular ones, and generally with the provision of particular Churches.

Art. 78. Whenever it is a matter of dealing with civil governments, either in establishing or modifying particular Churches and their groupings or in the provision of these Churches, this Congregation must procede only after consultation with the Section for Relations with States of the Secretariat of State.

Art. 79. Furthermore, the Congregation applies itself to matters relating to the correct exercise of the pastoral function of the bishops, by offering them every kind of assistance. For it is part of its duty to initiate general apostolic visitations where needed, in agreement with the dicasteries concerned and, in the same manner, to evaluate their results and to propose to the Supreme Pontiff the appropriate actions to be taken.

Art. 80. This Congregation has competence over everything involving the Holy See in the matter of personal prelatures.

Art. 81. For the particular Churches assigned to its care, the Congregation takes care of everything with respect to the *ad limina* visits; so it studies the quinquennial reports, submitted in accordance with art. 32. It is available to the bishops who come to Rome, especially to see that suitable arrangements are made for the meeting with the Supreme Pontiff and for other meetings and pilgrimages. When the visit is completed, it communicates in writing to the diocesan bishops the conclusions concerning their dioceses.

Art. 82. The Congregation deals with matters pertain-

cernere, quae ad sacras reliquias authenticas declarandas easdemque conservandas pertinent.

Congregatio pro Episcopis

Art. 75. Congregatio ea cognoscit quae Ecclesiarum particularium constitutionem et provisionem necnon episcopalis muneris exercitium respiciunt in Ecclesia Latina, salva competentia Congregationis pro Gentium Evangelizatione.

Art. 76. Huius Congregationis est ea omnia agere, quae ad Ecclesiarum particularium earumque coetuum constitutionem, divisionem, unionem, suppressionem ceterasque immutationes spectant. Eius quoque est Ordinariatus Castrenses pro pastorali cura militum erigere.

Art. 77. Omnia agit quae attinent ad Episcoporum, etiam titularium, nominationem, et generatim ad provisionem Ecclesiarum particularium.

Art. 78. Quotiescumque cum rerum publicarum Moderatoribus tractandum est sive ad Ecclesiarum particularium earumque coetuum constitutionem aut immutationem, sive ad earum provisionem quod attinet, nonnisi collatis consiliis cum Sectione de rationibus cum Civitatibus Secretariae Status procedat.

Art. 79. Congregatio in ea insuper incumbit, quae rectum muneris pastoralis Episcoporum exercitium respiciunt, eis omnimodam operam praebendo; eius enim est, si opus fuerit, communi sententia cum Dicasteriis, quorum interest, visitationes apostolicas generales indicere earumque exitus, pari procedendi modo, perpendere et, quae inde opportune decernenda sint, Summo Pontifici proponere.

Art. 80. Ad hanc Congregationem pertinent ea omnia, quae ad Sanctam Sedem spectant circa Praelaturas personales.

Art. 81. Pro Ecclesiis particularibus suae curae concreditis Congregatio omnia procurat quae visitationes ad limina respiciunt; ideoque relationes quinquennales ad normam art. 32 perpendit. Episcopis Romam adeuntibus adest, praesertim ut sive congressio cum Summo Pontifice sive alia colloquia et peregrinationes apte disponantur. Expleta visitatione, conclusiones, eorum dioeceses respicientes, cum Episcopis dioecesanis scripto communicat.

Art. 82. Congregatio ea absolvit, quae ad

ing to the celebration of particular councils as well as the erection of conferences of bishops and the *recognitio* of their statutes. It receives the acts of these bodies and, in consultation with the dicasteries concerned, it examines the decrees which require the *recognitio* of the Apostolic See.

Pontifical Commission for Latin America

Art. 83. §1. The function of the Pontifical Commission for Latin America is to be available to the particular Churches in Latin America, by counsel and by action, taking a keen interest in the questions that affect the life and progress of those Churches; and especially to help the Churches themselves in the solution of those questions, or to be helpful to those dicasteries of the Curia that are involved by reason of their competence.

§2. It is also to foster relations between the national and international ecclesiastical institutes that work for the regions of Latin America and the dicasteries of the Roman Curia.

Art. 84. §1. The president of the Commission is the prefect of the Congregation for Bishops, assisted by a bishop as vice-president.

They have as counselors some bishops either from the Roman Curia or selected from the Churches of Latin America.

§2. The members of the Commission are selected either from the dicasteries of the Roman Curia or from the *Consejo episcopal latinoamericano,* whether they be from among the bishops of Latin America or from the institutes mentioned in the preceding article.

§3. The Commission has its own staff.

Congregation for the Evangelization of Peoples

Art. 85. It pertains to the Congregation for the Evangelization of Peoples to direct and coordinate throughout the world the actual work of spreading the Gospel as well as missionary cooperation, without prejudice to the competence of the Congregation for the Oriental Churches.

Art. 86. The Congregation promotes research in mission theology, spirituality and pastoral work; it likewise proposes principles, norms, and procedures, fitting the needs of time and place, by which evangelization is carried out.

Art. 87. The Congregation strives to bring the people of

Pontificia Commissio pro America Latina

Art. 83. §1. Commissionis munus est Ecclesiis particularibus in America Latina tum consilio tum opere adesse, studio quoque incumbere quaestionibus, quae vitam ac profectum ipsarum Ecclesiarum respiciunt, praesertim ut sive Curiae Dicasteriis, quorum ratione competentiae interest, sive ipsis Ecclesiis in huiusmodi quaestionibus solvendis, auxilio sit.

§2. Ipsius quoque est fovere rationes inter ecclesiastica instituta internationalia et nationalia, quae pro Americae Latinae Regionibus adlaborant, et Curiae Romanae Dicasteria.

Art. 84. §1. Praeses Commissionis est Praefectus Congregationis pro Episcopis, qui ab Episcopo vices Praesidis agente adiuvatur.

Ipsis adsunt tamquam Consiliarii nonnulli Episcopi sive ex Curia Romana sive ex Americae Latinae Ecclesiis adlecti.

§2. Commissionis Membra sive ex Curiae Romanae Dicasteriis sive ex Consilio Episcopali Latino-Americano tum ex Episcopis Regionum Americae Latinae tum ex Institutis, de quibus in praecedenti articulo, seliguntur.

§3. Commissio proprios habet Administros.

Congregatio pro Gentium Evangelizatione

Art. 85. Ad Congregationem spectat dirigere et coordinare ubique terrarum ipsum opus gentium evangelizationis et cooperationem missionariam, salva Congregationis pro Ecclesiis Orientalibus competentia.

Art. 86. Congregatio promovet investigationes theologiae, spiritualitatis ac rei pastoralis missionariae, pariterque proponit principia, normas necnon operandi rationes, necessitatibus temporum locorumque accomodata, quibus evangelizatio peragatur.

Art. 87. Congregatio adnititur ut Populus

God, well aware of their duty and filled with missionary spirit, to cooperate effectively in the missionary task by their prayers and the witness of their lives, by their active work and contributions.

Art. 88. §1. It takes steps to awaken missionary vocations, whether clerical, religious, or lay, and advises on a suitable distribution of missionaries.

§2. In the territories subject to it, it also cares for the education of the secular clergy and of catechists, without prejudice to the competence of the Congregation of Seminaries and Educational Institutions[36] concerning the general programme of studies, as well as what pertains to the universities and other institutes of higher education.

Art. 89. Within its competence are mission territories, the evangelization of which is committed to suitable institutes and societies and to particular Churches. For these territories it deals with everything pertaining to the establishment and change of ecclesiastical circumscriptions and to the provision of these Churches, and it carries out the other functions that the Congregation for Bishops fulfills within the scope of its competence.

Art. 90. §1. With regard to members of institutes of consecrated life, whether these are erected in the mission territories or are just working there, the Congregation enjoys competence in matters touching those members as missionaries, individually and collectively, without prejudice to art. 21, §1.

§2. Those societies of apostolic life that were founded for the missions are subject to this Congregation.

Art. 91. To foster missionary cooperation, even through the effective collection and equal distribution of subsidies, the Congregation chiefly uses the Pontifical Missionary Works, namely, the Society for the Propagation of the Faith, the Society of St. Peter the Apostle, and the Holy Childhood Association, as well as the Pontifical Missionary Union of the Clergy.

Art. 92. Through a special office, the Congregation administers its own funds and other resources destined for the missions, with full accountability to the Prefecture for the Economic Affairs of the Holy See.

Dei, spiritu missionario imbutus atque sui officii conscius, precibus, testimonio vitae, actuositate et subsidiis ad opus missionale efficaciter collaboret.

Art. 88. §1. Vocationes missionarias sive clericales sive religiosas sive laicales suscitandas curat atque missionariorum aptae distributioni consulit.

§2. In territoriis sibi subiectis, ipsa pariter curat cleri saecularis atque catechistarum institutionem, salva competentia Congregationis de Seminariis atque Studiorum Institutis, ad generalem studiorum rationem necnon ad Universitates ceteraque studiorum superiorum Instituta quod attinet.

Art. 89. Eidem subsunt territoria missionum, quarum evangelizationem idoneis Institutis, Societatibus necnon Ecclesiis particularibus committit, et pro quibus ea omnia agit, quae sive ad circumscriptiones ecclesiasticas erigendas vel immutandas, sive ad Ecclesiarum provisionem pertinent ceteraque absolvit, quae Congregatio pro Episcopis intra suae competentiae ambitum exercet.

Art. 90. §1. Quod vero attinet ad sodales Institutorum vitae consecratae, in territoriis missionum erectorum aut ibi laborantium, Congregatio competentia gaudet in iis, quae ipsos qua missionarios sive singulos sive simul sumptos attingunt, firmo praescripto art. 21 §1.

§2. Huic Congregationi subiciuntur Societates vitae apostolicae pro missionibus erectae.

Art. 91. Ad cooperationem missionalem fovendam, etiam per efficacem collectionem et aequam distributionem subsidiorum, ipsa utitur praesertim Pontificiis Operibus Missionalibus, videlicet eis quae a Propagatione Fidei, a S. Petro Apostolo, a S. Infantia nomen ducunt atque Pontificia Unione Missionali Cleri.

Art. 92. Congregatio proprium aerarium aliaque bona missionibus destinata per peculiare officium administrat, firmo onere reddendi debitam rationem Praefecturae Rerum Oeconomicarum Sanctae Sedis.

36. See note * between art. 111 and art. 112.

Congregation for the Clergy

Art. 93. Without prejudice to the right of bishops and their conferences, the Congregation for the Clergy examines matters regarding priests and deacons of the secular clergy, with regard to their persons and pastoral ministry, and with regard to resources available to them for the exercise of this ministry; and in all these matters the Congregation offers timely assistance to the bishops.

Art. 94. It has the function of promoting the religious education of the Christian faithful of all ages and conditions; it issues timely norms so that catechetical instruction is correctly conducted; it gives great attention so that catechetical formation is properly given; and, with the assent of the Congregation for the Doctrine of the Faith, it grants the prescribed approval of the Holy See for catechisms and other writings pertaining to catechetical instruction. It is available to catechetical offices and international initiatives on religious education, coordinates their activities and, where necessary, lends assistance.

Art. 95. §1. The Congregation is competent concerning the life, conduct, rights, and obligations of clergy.

§2. It advises on a more suitable distribution of priests.

§3. It fosters the ongoing education of clergy, especially concerning their sanctification and the effective exercise of their pastoral ministry, most of all in the fitting preaching of the Word of God.

Art. 96. This Congregation deals with everything that has to do with the clerical state as such for all clergy, including religious, in consultation with the dicasteries involved when the matter so requires.

Art. 97. The Congregation deals with those matters that are within the competence of the Holy See:

1° both those concerning presbyteral councils, colleges of consultors, chapters of canons, pastoral councils, parishes, churches, shrines, or those concerning clerical associations, or ecclesiastical archives and records;

2° and those concerning Mass obligations as well as pious wills in general and pious foundations.

Art. 98. The Congregation carries out everything that pertains to the Holy See regarding the regulation of ecclesiastical goods, and especially their correct administration;

Congregatio pro Clericis

Art. 93. Congregatio, firmo iure Episcoporum eorumque Conferentiarum, ea cognoscit, quae presbyteros et diaconos Cleri saecularis respiciunt tum quoad personas, tum quoad pastorale ministerium, tum quoad res, quae ad hoc exercendum iis praesto sunt, atque in hisce omnibus opportuna auxilia Episcopis praebet.

Art. 94. Institutionem religiosam Christifidelium cuiuscumque aetatis et condicionis pro suo munere promovendam curat; opportunas normas praebet, ut lectiones catecheseos recta ratione tradantur; catecheticae institutioni rite impertiendae invigilat; praescriptam Sanctae Sedis approbationem pro catechismis aliisque scriptis ad institutionem catecheticam pertinentibus, de assensu Congregationis de Doctrina Fidei, concedit; officiis catecheticis atque inceptis ad religiosam institutionem spectantibus et indolem internationalem prae se ferentibus adest, eorum navitatem coordinat iisque auxilia, si opus fuerit praestat.

Art. 95. §1. Competens est ad clericorum vitam, disciplinam, iura atque obligationes quod spectat.

§2. Aptiori presbyterorum distributioni consulit.

§3. Permanentem clericorum formationem fovet, praesertim quod attinet ad ipsorum sanctificationem et ad pastorale ministerium fructuose exercendum, potissimum circa dignam verbi Dei praedicationem.

Art. 96. Huius Congregationis est tractare ea omnia, quae ad statum clericalem qua talem attinent, pro omnibus clericis, religiosis non exceptis, collatis consiliis cum Dicasteriis quorum interest, ubi res id requirat.

Art. 97. Congregatio ea agit, quae Sanctae Sedi competunt:

1° sive circa consilia presbyteralia, consultorum coetus, canonicorum capitula, consilia pastoralia, paroecias, ecclesias, sanctuaria, sive circa clericorum consociationes, sive circa ecclesiastica archiva seu tabularia;

2° circa onera Missarum necnon pias voluntates in genere et pias fundationes.

Art. 98. Congregatio ea omnia exercet, quae ad bonorum ecclesiasticorum moderamen ad Sanctam Sedem pertinent, et praesertim ad rec-

it grants the necessary approvals and *recognitiones,* and it further sees to it that serious thought is given to the support and social security of the clergy.

Pontifical Commission for Preserving the Patrimony of Art and History

Art. 99. At the Congregation for the Clergy there exists the Pontifical Commission for Preserving the Patrimony of Art and History that has the duty of acting as curator for the artistic and historical patrimony of the whole Church.

Art. 100. To this patrimony belong, in the first place, all works of every kind of art of the past, works that must be kept and preserved with the greatest care. Those works whose proper use has ceased are to be kept in a suitable manner in museums of the Church or elsewhere.

Art. 101. §1. Outstanding among valuable historical objects are all documents and materials referring and testifying to pastoral life and care, as well as to the rights and obligations of dioceses, parishes, churches, and other juridical persons in the Church.

§2. This historical patrimony is to be kept in archives or also in libraries and everywhere entrusted to competent curators lest testimonies of this kind be lost.

Art. 102. The Commission lends its assistance to particular Churches and conferences of bishops and together with them, where the case arises, sees to the setting up of museums, archives, and libraries, and ensures that the entire patrimony of art and history in the whole territory is properly collected and safeguarded and made available to all who have an interest in it.

Art. 103. In consultation with the Congregation for Seminaries and Educational Institutions and the Congregation for Divine Worship and the Discipline of the Sacraments, the Commission has the task of striving to make the people of God more and more aware of the need and importance of conserving the artistic and historical patrimony of the Church.

Art. 104. The president of the Commission is the cardinal prefect of the Congregation for the Clergy, assisted by the secretary of the Commission. Moreover, the Commission has its own staff.

tam eorundem bonorum administrationem atque necessarias approbationes vel recognitiones concedit; praeterea prospicit ut clericorum sustentationi ac sociali securitati consulatur.

Pontificia Commissio de Patrimonio Artis et Historiae Conservando

Art. 99. Apud Congregationem pro Clericis Commissio exstat, cuius officium est curae patrimonii historiae et artis totius Ecclesiae praeesse.

Art. 100. Ad hoc patrimonium pertinent imprimis omnia cuiusvis artis opera temporis praeteriti, quae summa diligentia custodiri et conservari oportet. Ea autem quorum usus proprius cessaverit, apto modo in Ecclesiae musaeis vel aliis in locis spectabilia asserventur.

Art. 101. §1. Inter bona historica eminent omnia documenta et instrumenta, quae vitam et curam pastoralem necnon iura et obligationes dioecesium, paroeciarum, ecclesiarum aliarumque personarum iuridicarum in Ecclesia conditarum respiciunt et testificantur.

§2. Hoc patrimonium historicum in tabulariis seu archivis vel etiam bibliothecis custodiatur, quae ubique competentibus curatoribus committantur, ne huiusmodi testimonia pereant.

Art. 102. Commissio Ecclesiis particularibus et Episcoporum coetibus adiutorium praebet et una cum iis, si casus ferat, agit, ut musaea, tabularia et bibliothecae constituantur atque collectio et custodia totius patrimonii artis et historiae in toto territorio apte ad effectum adducatur et omnibus, quorum interest, praesto sit.

Art. 103. Eiusdem Commissionis est, collatis consiliis cum Congregationibus de Seminariis atque Studiorum Institutis et de Cultu Divino et Disciplina Sacramentorum, adlaborare ut Populus Dei magis magisque conscius fiat momenti et necessitatis patrimonium historiae et artis Ecclesiae conservandi.

Art. 104. Eidem praeest Cardinalis Praefectus Congregationis pro Clericis, eiusdem commissionis Secretario adiuvante. Commissio praeterea proprios habet administros.

Congregation for Institutes of Consecrated Life
and for Societies of Apostolic Life

Art. 105. The principal function of the Congregation for
Institutes of Consecrated Life and for Societies of Apostolic Life is to promote and supervise in the whole Latin
Church the practice of the evangelical counsels as they are
lived in approved forms of consecrated life and, at the same
time, the work of societies of apostolic life.

Art. 106. §1. The Congregation erects and approves religious and secular institutes and societies of apostolic life,
or passes judgement on the suitability of their erection by
the diocesan bishop. It also suppresses such institutes and
societies if necessary.

§2. The Congregation is also competent to establish, or,
if need be, to rescind, the unions or federations of institutes
and societies.

Art. 107. The Congregation for its part takes care that
institutes of consecrated life and societies of apostolic life
grow and flourish according to the spirit of their founders
and healthy traditions, faithfully follow their proper purpose and truly benefit the salvific mission of the Church.

Art. 108. §1. It deals with everything which, in accordance with the law, belongs to the Holy See concerning the
life and work of the institutes and societies, especially the
approval of their constitutions, their manner of government and apostolate, the recruitment and training as well
as the rights and obligations of members, dispensation
from vows and the dismissal of members, and the administration of goods.

§2. However, the organization of philosophical and theological studies and other academic subjects comes within
the competence of the Congregation for Seminaries and Institutes of Studies.

Art. 109. It is the function of this Congregation to establish conferences of major superiors of men and women
religious, to grant approval to their statutes and to give
great attention in order that their activities are directed to
achieving their true purpose.

Art. 110. The Congregation has competence also regarding eremetical life, the order of virgins and their associations as well as other forms of consecrated life.

Art. 111. Its competence also embraces the third orders
and associations of the faithful which are erected with the
intention that, after a period of preparation, they may
eventually become institutes of consecrated life or societies
of apostolic life.

Congregatio pro Institutis Vitae
Consecratae et Societatibus Vitae
Apostolicae

Art. 105. Congregationis munus praecipuum
est praxim consiliorum evangelicorum, prout in
probatis formis vitae consecratae exercetur, et
insimul actuositatem Societatum vitae apostolicae in universa Ecclesia Latina promovere et
moderari.

Art. 106. §1. Congregatio proinde Instituta
religiosa et saecularia necnon Societates vitae
apostolicae erigit, approbat aut iudicium fert de
opportunitate eorum erectionis ab Episcopo
dioecesano faciendae. Ipsi quoque pertinet
huiusmodi Instituta et Societates, si necesse
fuerit, supprimere.

§2. Eidem etiam competit Institutorum et
Societatum uniones vel foederationes constituere aut, si oportuerit, rescindere.

Art. 107. Congregatio pro sua parte curat, ut
Instituta vitae consecratae ac Societates vitae
apostolicae secundum spiritum Fundatorum et
sanas traditiones crescant et floreant, finem proprium fideliter persequantur atque salvificae
missioni Ecclesiae reapse prosint.

Art. 108. §1. Ea omnia absolvit, quae ad
normam iuris pertinent ad Sanctam Sedem de
vita et industria Institutorum et Societatum praesertim de constitutionum approbatione, regimine
et apostolatu, sodalium cooptatione et institutione, eorum iuribus et obligationibus, votorum
dispensatione et sodalium dimissione atque etiam bonorum administratione.

§2. Ad ordinationem autem studiorum
philosophiae et theologiae necnon ad studia
academica quod attinet competens est Congregatio de Seminariis atque Studiorum Institutis.

Art. 109. Eiusdem Congregationis est Conferentias Superiorum maiorum religiosorum reli-
giosarumque erigere, earundem statuta approbare necnon invigilare ut ipsarum actio ad fines
proprios assequendos ordinetur.

Art. 110. Congregationi etiam subiciuntur
vita eremitica, ordo virginum harumque consociationes ceteraeque formae vitae consecratae.

Art. 111. Ipsius competentia amplectitur
quoque Tertios Ordines necnon consociationes
fidelium, quae eo animo eriguntur ut, praevia
praeparatione, Instituta vitae consecratae vel
Societates vitae apostolicae aliquando evadant.

Congregation of Seminaries and
Educational Institutions[37]

Art. 112. The Congregation of Seminaries and Educational Institutions gives practical expression to the concern of the Apostolic See for the training of those who are called to holy orders, and for the promotion and organization of Catholic education.

Art. 113. §1. It is available to the bishops so that in their Churches vocations to the sacred ministry may be cultivated to the highest degree, and seminaries may be established and conducted in accordance with the law, where students may be suitably trained, receiving a solid formation that is human and spiritual, doctrinal and pastoral.

§2. It gives great attention that the way of life and government of the seminaries be in full harmony with the programme of priestly education, and that the superiors and teachers, by the example of their life and sound doctrine, contribute their utmost to the formation of the personality of the sacred ministers.

§3. It is also its responsibility to erect interdiocesan seminaries and to approve their statutes.

Art. 114. The Congregation makes every effort to see that the fundamental principles of Catholic education as set out by the magisterium of the Church be ever more deeply researched, championed, and known by the people of God.

It also takes care that in this matter the Christian faithful may be able to fulfill their duties and also strive to bring civil society to recognize and protect their rights.

Art. 115. The Congregation sets the norms by which Catholic schools are governed. It is available to diocesan bishops so that, wherever possible, Catholic schools be established and fostered with the utmost care, and that in every school appropriate undertakings bring catechetical instruction and pastoral care to the Christian pupils.

Art. 116. §1. The Congregation labours to ensure that there be in the Church a sufficient number of ecclesiastical and Catholic universities as well as other educational institutions in which the sacred disciplines may be pursued in

Congregatio de Seminariis atque
Studiorum Institutis

Art. 112. Congregatio exprimit atque exercet Sedis Apostolicae sollicitudinem circa eorum formationem, qui ad sacros ordines vocantur, necnon circa promotionem et ordinationem institutionis catholicae.

Art. 113. §1. Episcopis adest, ut in eorum Ecclesiis vocationes ad sacra ministeria quam maxime colantur atque in Seminariis, ad normam iuris constituendis ac gerendis, alumni solida formatione tum humana ac spirituali, tum doctrinali et pastorali apte edoceantur.

§2. Sedulo invigilat ut seminariorum convictus regimenque rationi institutionis sacerdotalis plene respondeant atque superiores ac magistri exemplo vitae ac recta doctrina ad formandas personas sacrorum ministrorum quam maxime conferant.

§3. Eius praeterea est seminaria interdioecesana erigere eorumque statuta approbare.

Art. 114. Congregatio adnititur, ut fundamentalia principia de catholica educatione prout ab Ecclesiae Magisterio proponuntur altius usque investigentur, vindicentur atque a Populo Dei cognoscantur.

Ea pariter curat, ut in hac materia Christifideles sua officia implere possint ac dent operam et nitantur ut etiam civilis societas ipsorum iura agnoscat atque tueatur.

Art. 115. Congregatio normas statuit, quibus schola catholica regatur; Episcopis dioecesanis adest, ut scholae catholicae, ubi fieri potest, constituantur, et summa sollicitudine foveantur utque in omnibus scholis educatio catechetica et pastoralis cura alumnis Christifidelibus per opportuna incepta praebeantur.

Art. 116. §1. Congregatio vires impendit, ut Universitatum ecclesiasticarum et catholicarum ceterorumque studiorum Institutorum sufficiens copia in Ecclesia habeatur, in quibus sacrae dis-

---

37. The Congregation for Catholic Education (of Seminaries and Educational Institutions) is the name used since the coming into force of *Pastor bonus* on 1 March 1989. The name given by the Apostolic Constitution, the Congregation of Seminaries and Educational Institutions, was never officially used and was modified by a letter of the Secretariat of State of 26 February 1989 (prot. no. 236.026), which can be read in Tarcisio BERTONE, "La Congregazione per l'educazione cattolica (dei seminari e degli istituti di studio),"

in Piero Antonio BONNET and Carlo GULLO (eds.), *La Curia romana nella Cost. ap. "Pastor bonus,"* Studi giuridici, XXI, Annali di dottrina e giurisprudenza canonica, 13, Città del Vaticano, Libreria Editrice Vaticana, 1990, pp. 387–388. Since the Latin name of the Congregation was never formally amended in the official text of *Pastor bonus,* the translation of the document cannot use the current name of the dicastery.

depth, studies in the humanities and the sciences may be promoted, with due regard for Christian truth, so that the Christian faithful may be suitably trained to fulfill their own tasks.

§2. It erects or approves ecclesiastical universities and institutions, ratifies their statutes, exercises the highest supervision on them and pays great attention so that the integrity of the Catholic faith is preserved in teaching doctrine.

§3. With regard to Catholic universities, it deals with those matters that are within the competence of the Holy See.

§4. It fosters cooperation and mutual help between universities and their associations and serves as a resource for them.

IV. TRIBUNALS

Apostolic Penitentiary

Art. 117. The competence of the Apostolic Penitentiary regards the internal forum and indulgences.

Art. 118. For the internal forum, whether sacramental or non-sacramental, it grants absolutions, dispensations, commutations, validations, condonations, and other favours.

Art. 119. The Apostolic Penitentiary sees to it that in the patriarchal basilicas of Rome there be a sufficient number of penitentiaries supplied with the appropriate faculties.

Art. 120. This dicastery is charged with the granting and use of indulgences, without prejudice to the right of the Congregation for the Doctrine of the Faith to review what concerns dogmatic teaching about them.

Supreme Tribunal of the Apostolic Signatura

Art. 121. The Apostolic Signatura functions as the supreme tribunal and also ensures that justice in the Church is correctly administered.

Art. 122. This Tribunal adjudicates:

1° complaints of nullity and petitions for total reinstatement against sentences of the Roman Rota;

2° in cases concerning the status of persons, recourses when the Roman Rota has denied a new examination of the case;

ciplinae altius investigentur necnon humanitatis scientiaeque cultus, habita christianae veritatis ratione, promoveatur et Christifideles ad propria munera implenda apte formentur.

§2. Universitates et Instituta ecclesiastica erigit aut approbat, eorum statuta rata habet, supremam moderationem in eis exercet atque invigilat, ut catholicae fidei integritas in tradendis doctrinis servetur.

§3. Ad Universitates Catholicas quod attinet, ea agit quae Sanctae Sedi competunt.

§4. Cooperationem mutuumque adiutorium inter Studiorum Universitates earumque consociationes fovet iisdemque praesidio est.

IV. TRIBUNALIA

Paenitentiaria Apostolica

Art. 117. Paenitentiariae Apostolicae competentia ad ea se refert, quae forum internum necnon indulgentias respiciunt.

Art. 118. Pro foro interno, tum sacramentali tum non sacramentali, absolutiones, dispensationes, commutationes, sanationes, condonationes aliasque gratias eadem largitur.

Art. 119. Ipsa prospicit ut in Patriarchalibus Urbis Basilicis Paenitentiarii sufficienti numero habeantur, opportunis facultatibus praediti.

Art. 120. Eidem Dicasterio committuntur ea, quae spectant ad concessionem et usum indulgentiarum, salvo iure Congregationis de Doctrina Fidei ea videndi, quae doctrinam dogmaticam circa easdem respiciunt.

Supremum Tribunal Signaturae Apostolicae

Art. 121. Hoc Dicasterium, praeter munus, quod exercet, Supremi Tribunalis, consulit ut iustitia in Ecclesia recte administretur.

Art. 122. Ipsum cognoscit:

1° querelas nullitatis et petitiones restitutionis in integrum contra sententias Rotae Romanae;

2° recursus, in causis de statu personarum, adversus denegatum a Rota Romana novum causae examen;

3° exceptions of suspicion and other proceedings against judges of the Roman Rota arising from the exercise of their functions;

4° conflicts of competence between tribunals which are not subject to the same appellate tribunal.

Art. 123. §1. The Signatura adjudicates recourses lodged within the peremptory limit of thirty useful days against singular administrative acts whether issued by the dicasteries of the Roman Curia or approved by them, whenever it is contended that the impugned act violated some law either in the decision-making process or in the procedure used.

§2. In these cases, in addition to the judgement regarding illegality of the act, it can also adjudicate, at the request of the plaintiff, the reparation of damages incurred through the unlawful act.

§3. The Signatura also adjudicates other administrative controversies referred to it by the Roman Pontiff or by dicasteries of the Roman Curia, as well as conflicts of competence between these dicasteries.

Art. 124. The Signatura also has the responsibility:

1° to exercise vigilance over the correct administration of justice, and, if need be, to censure advocates and procurators;

2° to deal with petitions presented to the Apostolic See for obtaining the commission of a case to the Roman Rota or some other favour relative to the administration of justice;

3° to prorogate the competence of lower tribunals;

4° to grant its approval to tribunals for appeals reserved to the Holy See, and to promote and approve the erection of interdiocesan tribunals.

Art. 125. The Apostolic Signatura is governed by its own law.

Tribunal of the Roman Rota

Art. 126. The Roman Rota is a court of higher instance at the Apostolic See, usually at the appellate stage, with the purpose of safeguarding rights within the Church; it fosters unity of jurisprudence, and, by virtue of its own decisions, provides assistance to lower tribunals.

Art. 127. The judges of this Tribunal constitute a college.

3° exceptiones suspicionis aliasque causas contra Iudices Rotae Romanae propter acta in exercitio ipsorum muneris;

4° conflictus competentiae inter tribunalia, quae non subiciuntur eidem tribunali appellationis.

Art. 123. §1. Praeterea cognoscit de recursibus, intra terminum peremptorium triginta dierum utilium interpositis, adversus actus administrativos singulares sive a Dicasteriis Curiae Romanae latos sive ab ipsis probatos, quoties contendatur num actus impugnatus legem aliquam in decernendo vel in procedendo violaverit.

§2. In his casibus, praeter iudicium de illegitimitate, cognoscere etiam potest, si recurrens id postulet, de reparatione damnorum actu illegitimo illatorum.

§3. Cognoscit etiam de aliis controversiis administrativis, quae a Romano Pontifice vel a Romanae Curiae Dicasteriis ipsi deferantur necnon de conflictibus competentiae inter eadem Dicasteria.

Art. 124. Ipsius quoque est:

1° rectae administrationi iustitiae invigilare et in advocatos vel procuratores, si opus sit, animadvertere;

2° videre de petitionibus Sedi Apostolicae porrectis ad obtinendam causae commissionem apud Rotam Romanam, vel aliam gratiam relative ad iustitiam administrandam;

3° tribunalium inferiorum competentiam prorogare;

4° approbationem Tribunalis quoad appellationem Sanctae Sedi reservatam concedere necnon promovere et approbare erectionem tribunalium interdioecesanorum.

Art. 125. Signatura Apostolica lege propria regitur.

Tribunal Rotae Romanae

Art. 126. Hoc Tribunal instantiae superioris partes apud Apostolicam Sedem pro more in gradu appellationis agit ad iura in Ecclesia tutanda, unitati iurisprudentiae consulit et, per proprias sententias, tribunalibus inferioribus auxilio est.

Art. 127. Huius Tribunalis Iudices, probata

Persons of proven doctrine and experience, they have been selected by the Supreme Pontiff from various parts of the world. The Tribunal is presided over by a dean, likewise appointed by the Supreme Pontiff from among the judges and for a specific term of office.

Art. 128. This Tribunal adjudicates:

1° in second instance, cases that have been decided by ordinary tribunals of the first instance and are being referred to the Holy See by legitimate appeal;

2° in third or further instance, cases already decided by the same Apostolic Tribunal and by any other tribunals, unless they have become a *res iudicata*.

Art. 129. §1. The Tribunal, however, judges the following in first instance:

1° bishops in contentious matters, unless it deals with the rights or temporal goods of a juridical person represented by the bishop;

2° abbots primate or abbots superior of a monastic congregation and supreme moderators of religious institutes of pontifical right;

3° dioceses or other ecclesiastical persons, whether physical or juridical, which have no superior below the Roman Pontiff;

4° cases which the Supreme Pontiff commits to this Tribunal.

§2. It deals with the same cases even in second and further instances, unless other provisions are made.

Art. 130. The Tribunal of the Roman Rota is governed by its own law.

V. PONTIFICAL COUNCILS

Pontifical Council for the Laity

Art. 131. The Pontifical Council for the Laity is competent in those matters pertaining to the Apostolic See in promoting and coordinating the apostolate of the laity and, generally, in those matters respecting the Christian life of laypeople as such.

Art. 132. The president is assisted by an Advisory Board of cardinals and bishops. Figuring especially among the members of the Council are certain Christian faithful engaged in various fields of activity.

Art. 133. §1. The Council is to urge and support laypeo-

---

doctrina et experientia pollentes atque e variis terrarum orbis partibus a Summo Pontifice selecti, collegium constituunt; eidem Tribunali praeest Decanus ad certum tempus a Summo Pontifice ex ipsis Iudicibus pariter nominatus.

Art. 128. Hoc Tribunal iudicat:

1° in secunda instantia, causas ab ordinariis tribunalibus primae instantiae diiudicatas, quae ad Sanctam Sedem per appellationem legitimam deferuntur;

2° in tertia vel ulteriore instantia, causas ab eodem Tribunali Apostolico et ab aliis quibusvis tribunalibus iam cognitas, nisi in rem iudicatam transierint.

Art. 129. §1. Idem vero in prima instantia iudicat:

1° Episcopos in contentiosis, modo ne agatur de iuribus aut bonis temporalibus personae iuridicae ab Episcopo repraesentatae;

2° Abbates primates, vel Abbates superiores congregationis monasticae et supremos Moderatores Institutorum religiosorum iuris pontificii;

3° dioeceses ceterasve personas ecclesiasticas, sive physicas sive iuridicas, quae superiorem infra Romanum Pontificem non habent;

4° causas quas Romanus Pontifex eidem Tribunali commiserit.

§2. Easdem causas, nisi aliter cautum sit, etiam in secunda et ulteriore instantia agit.

Art. 130. Tribunal Rotae Romanae lege propria regitur.

V. PONTIFICIA CONSILIA

Pontificium Consilium Pro Laicis

Art. 131. Consilium competens est in iis, quae ad Sedem Apostolicam pertinent in laicorum apostolatu promovendo et coordinando atque, universim, in iis, quae vitam christianam laicorum qua talium respiciunt.

Art. 132. Praesidi adest Coetus praesidialis ex Cardinalibus et Episcopis constans; inter membra Consilii potissimum adnumerantur Christifideles in variis actuositatis provinciis versantes.

Art. 133. §1. Eius est incitare et sustinere

ple to participate in the life and mission of the Church in their own way, as individuals or in associations, especially so that they may carry out their special responsibility of filling the realm of temporal things with the spirit of the Gospel.

§2. It fosters joint action among laypeople in catechetical instruction, in liturgical and sacramental life as well as in works of mercy, charity, and social development.

§3. The Council attends to and organizes international conferences and other projects concerning the apostolate of the laity.

Art. 134. Within the parameters of its own competence, the Council performs all activities respecting lay associations of the Christian faithful; it erects associations of an international character and provides approval or *recognitio* for their statutes, saving the competence of the Secretariat of State. As for secular third orders, the Council deals only with those matters concerning their apostolic activities.

Pontifical Council for Promoting Christian Unity

Art. 135. It is the function of the Pontifical Council for Promoting Christian Unity to engage in ecumenical work through timely initiatives and activities, labouring to restore unity among Christians.

Art. 136. §1. It sees that the decrees of the Second Vatican Council pertaining to ecumenism are put into practice.

It deals with the correct interpretation of the principles of ecumenism and enjoins that they be carried out.

§2. It fosters, brings together, and coordinates national and international Catholic organizations promoting Christian unity, and supervises their undertakings.

§3. After prior consultation with the Supreme Pontiff, the Council maintains relations with Christians of Churches and ecclesial communities that do not yet have full communion with the Catholic Church, and especially organizes dialogue and meetings to promote unity with them, with the help of theological experts of sound doctrine. As often as may seem opportune, the Council deputes Catholic observers to Christian meetings, and it invites observers from other Churches and ecclesial communities to Catholic meetings.

laicos ut vitam et missionem Ecclesiae modo sibi proprio participent, sive singuli, sive in consociationibus, praesertim ut ipsorum peculiare officium impleant rerum temporalium ordinem spiritu evangelico imbuendi.

§2. Laicorum cooperationem fovet in cathechetica institutione, in vita liturgica et sacramentali atque in operibus misericordiae, caritatis et promotionis socialis.

§3. Idem prosequitur et moderatur conventus internationales aliaque incepta, quae ad apostolatum laicorum attinent.

Art. 134. Consilium ea omnia intra ambitum propriae competentiae agit, quae ad consociationes laicales Christifidelium spectant; eas vero, quae internationalem indolem habent, erigit earumque statuta approbat vel recognoscit, salva competentia Secretariae Status; quoad Tertios Ordines saeculares ea tantum curat, quae ad eorum apostolicam operositatem pertinent.

Pontificium Consilium ad Unitatem Christianorum Fovendam

Art. 135. Consilii munus est per opportuna incepta et navitates operi oecumenico incumbere ad unitatem inter christianos redintegrandam.

Art. 136. §1. Curat ut decreta Concilii Vaticani II, quae ad rem oecumenicam pertinent, ad usum traducantur.

Agit de recta interpretatione principiorum de oecumenismo eaque exsecutioni mandat.

§2. Coetus catholicos tum nationales tum internationales christianorum unitatem promoventes fovet, colligit atque coordinat eorumque inceptis invigilat.

§3. Rebus ad Summum Pontificem prius delatis, rationes curat cum fratribus Ecclesiarum et communitatum ecclesialium, plenam communionem cum Ecclesia catholica nondum habentium, ac praesertim dialogum et colloquia ad unitatem cum ipsis fovendam instituit, peritis doctrina theologica probe instructis opem ferentibus. Observatores catholicos deputat pro conventibus christianis atque invitat aliarum Ecclesiarum et communitatum ecclesialium observatores ad conventus catholicos, quoties id opportunum videatur.

Art. 137. §1. Since the Council often deals with matters which by their very nature touch on questions of faith, it must proceed in close connection with the Congregation for the Doctrine of the Faith, especially if declarations and public documents have to be issued.

§2. In dealing with important matters concerning the separated Oriental Churches, the Council must first hear the Congregation for the Oriental Churches.

Art. 138. Within the Council there exists a Commission to study and deal with matters concerning the Jews from a religious perspective, the Commission for Religious Relations with the Jews; the president of the Council presides over the Commission.

Pontifical Council for the Family

Art. 139. The Pontifical Council for the Family promotes the pastoral care of families, protects their rights and dignity in the Church and in civil society, so that they may ever be more able to fulfill their duties.

Art. 140. The president is assisted by an advisory board of bishops. Figuring above all among the members of the Council are laypeople, both men and women, especially married ones, from all over the world.

Art. 141. §1. The Council works for a deeper understanding of the Church's teaching on the family and for its spread through suitable catechesis. It encourages studies in the spirituality of marriage and the family.

§2. It works together with the bishops and their conferences to ensure the accurate recognition of the human and social conditions of the family institution everywhere and to ensure a strong general awareness of initiatives that help pastoral work for families.

§3. The Council strives to ensure that the rights of the family be acknowledged and defended even in the social and political realm. It also supports and coordinates initiatives to protect human life from the first moment of conception and to encourage responsible procreation.

§4. Without prejudice to art. 133, it follows the activities of institutes and associations which seek to work for the good of the family.

Art. 137. §1. Cum materia ab hoc Dicasterio tractanda suapte natura saepe quaestiones fidei tangat, ipsum oportet procedat arcta coniunctione cum Congregatione de Doctrina Fidei, praesertim cum agitur de publicis documentis aut declarationibus edendis.

§2. In gerendis autem maioris momenti negotiis, quae Ecclesias seiunctas Orientis respiciunt, prius audiat oportet Congregationem pro Ecclesiis Orientalibus.

Art. 138. Apud Consilium exstat Commissio ad res investigandas atque tractandas, quae Iudaeos sub respectu religioso attingunt; eam eiusdem Consilii Praeses moderatur.

Pontificium Consilium Pro Familia

Art. 139. Consilium pastoralem familiarum curam promovet, earumque iura dignitatemque in Ecclesia et in civili societate fovet, ut ipsae munera sibi propria aptius usque implere valeant.

Art. 140. Praesidi adest Coetus praesidialis, ex Episcopis constans; in Consilium potissimum cooptantur laici viri mulieresque, praesertim coniugio iuncti, ex variis terrarum orbis partibus.

Art. 141. §1. Consilium Ecclesiae doctrinam de familia penitius cognoscendam et apta catechesi divulgandam curat; studia praecipue de matrimonii ac familiae spiritualitate fovet.

§2. Idem satagit ut, conspirans cum Episcopis eorumque Conferentiis, humanae socialesque instituti familiaris in variis regionibus condiciones accurate cognoscantur, pariterque incepta, quae rem pastoralem familiarem adiuvant, in communem perferantur notitiam.

§3. Adnititur ut iura familiae, etiam in vita sociali et politica, agnoscantur et defendantur; incepta quoque ad humanam vitam inde a conceptione tuendam et ad procreationem responsabilem fovendam sustinet atque coordinat.

§4. Firmo praescripto art. 133, navitatem persequitur institutorum atque consociationum, quibus propositum est familiae bono inservire.

Pontifical Council for Justice and Peace

Art. 142. The goal of the Pontifical Council for Justice and Peace is to promote justice and peace in this world in accordance with the Gospel and the social teaching of the Church.

Art. 143. §1. The Council makes a thorough study of the social teaching of the Church and takes pains to see that this teaching is widely spread and put into practice among people and communities, especially regarding the relations between workers and management, relations that must come to be more and more imbued with the spirit of the Gospel.

§2. It collects information and research on justice and peace, about human development and violations of human rights; it ponders all this, and, when the occasion offers, shares its conclusions with the groupings of bishops. It cultivates relationships with Catholic international organizations and other institutions, even ones outside the Catholic Church, which sincerely strive to achieve peace and justice in the world.

§3. It works to form among peoples a mentality which fosters peace, especially on the occasion of World Peace Day.

Art. 144. The Council has a special relationship with the Secretariat Pontifical of State, especially whenever matters of peace and justice have to be dealt with in public by documents or announcements.

Pontifical Council *Cor Unum*

Art. 145. The Pontifical Council *Cor Unum* shows the solicitude of the Catholic Church for the needy, in order that human fraternity may be fostered and that the charity of Christ be made manifest.

Art. 146. It is the function of the Council:

1° to stimulate the Christian faithful as participants in the mission of the Church, to give witness to evangelical charity and to support them in this concern;

2° to foster and coordinate the initiatives of Catholic organizations that labour to help peoples in need, especially those who go to the rescue in the more urgent crises and disasters, and to facilitate their relations with public international organizations operating in the same field of assistance and good works;

Pontificium Consilium de Iustitia et Pace

Art. 142. Consilium eo spectat, ut iustitia et pax in mundo secundum Evangelium et socialem Ecclesiae doctrinam promoveantur.

Art. 143. §1. Socialem Ecclesiae doctrinam altius pervestigat, data opera ut ipsa late diffundatur et apud homines communitatesque in usum vitae deducatur, praesertim quod spectat ad rationes inter opifices et conductores operis, spiritu Evangelii magis magisque imbuendas.

§2. Notitias et inquisitiones de iustitia et pace, de populorum progressione et de hominum iurium laesionibus in unum colligit, perpendit atque exinde deductas conclusiones pro opportunitate cum Episcoporum coetibus communicat; rationes fovet cum catholicis internationalibus consociationibus aliisque institutis etiam extra Ecclesiam catholicam exstantibus, quae ad iustitiae pacisque bona in mundo consequenda sincere contendunt.

§3. Operam impendit ut inter populos sentiendi ratio de pace fovenda formetur, praesertim occasione oblata *Diei Pacis in mundo provehendae*.

Art. 144. Peculiares necessitudines cum Secretaria Status habet, praesertim quotiescumque per documenta vel per enuntiationes in rebus de iustitia et pace publice agendum est.

Pontificium Consilium «Cor Unum»

Art. 145. Consilium Ecclesiae Catholicae sollicitudinem erga egentes ostendit, ut humana fraternitas foveatur et caritas Christi manifestetur.

Art. 146. Consilii munus est:

1° Christifideles incitare ad evangelicae caritatis testimonium praebendum, utpote ipsam Ecclesiae missionem participantes, eosque in hac cura sustinere;

2° incepta catholicorum institutorum fovere et coordinare, quae egentibus populis adiuvandis incumbunt, ea praesertim quae urgentioribus angustiis et calamitatibus succurrunt, facilioresque reddere institutorum catholicorum necessitudines cum publicis internationalibus con-

3° to give serious attention and promote plans and undertakings for joint action and neighbourly help serving human progress.

Art. 147. The president of this Council is the same as the president of the Pontifical Council for Justice and Peace, who sees to it that the activities of both dicasteries are closely coordinated.

Art. 148. To ensure that the objectives of the Council are more effectively achieved, among members of the Council are also men and women representing Catholic charitable organizations.

Pontifical Council for the Pastoral Care of Migrants and Itinerant People

Art. 149. The Pontifical Council for the Pastoral Care of Migrants and Itinerant People brings the pastoral concern of the Church to bear on the special needs of those who have been forced to leave their native land or who do not have one. It also sees to it that these matters are considered with the attention they deserve.

Art. 150. §1. The Council works to see that in the particular Churches refugees and exiles, migrants, nomads, and circus workers receive effective and special spiritual care, even, if necessary, by means of suitable pastoral structures.

§2. It likewise fosters pastoral solicitude in these same Churches for sailors, at sea and in port, especially through the Apostleship of the Sea, over which it exercises ultimate direction.

§3. The Council has the same concern for those who work in airports or airplanes.

§4. It tries to ensure that the Christian people come to an awareness of the needs of these people and effectively demonstrate their own brotherly attitude towards them, especially on the occasion of World Migration Day.

Art. 151. The Council works to ensure that journeys which Christians undertake for reasons of piety, study, or recreation, contribute to their moral and religious formation, and it is available to the particular Churches in order that all who are away from home receive suitable spiritual care.

---

siliis, quae in eodem beneficentiae et progressionis campo operantur;

3° consilia atque mutuae navitatis fraternique auxilii opera studio prosequi atque promovere, quae humano profectui inserviunt.

Art. 147. Huius Consilii Praeses idem est ac Praeses Pontificii Consilii pro Iustitia et Pace, qui curat ut utriusque Instituti actuositas arcta coniunctione procedat.

Art. 148. Inter Consilii membra viri etiam et mulieres cooptantur, qui catholicorum beneficentiae institutorum veluti partes agant quo efficacius proposita Consilii ad effectum deducantur.

Pontificium Consilium de Spirituali Migrantium atque Itinerantium Cura

Art. 149. Consilium pastoralem Ecclesiae sollicitudinem convertit ad peculiares necessitates eorum, qui patrium solum relinquere coacti sint vel eo penitus careant; itemque quaestiones, ad haec attinentes, accommodato studio perpendendas curat.

Art. 150. §1. Consilium dat operam, ut in Ecclesiis particularibus efficax propriaque cura spiritualis, etiam, si res ferat, per congruas pastorales structuras, praebeatur sive profugis et exsulibus, sive migrantibus, nomadibus et circensem artem exercentibus.

§2. Fovet pariter apud easdem Ecclesias pastoralem sollicitudinem pro maritimis sive navigantibus sive in portibus, praesertim per Opus Apostolatus Maris, cuius supremam moderationem exercet.

§3. Eandem sollicitudinem adhibet iis, qui in aëroportibus vel in ipsis aëronavibus officia exercent vel opus faciunt.

§4. Adnititur, ut populus christianus, praesertim occasione oblata celebrationis *Diei universalis pro migrantibus atque exsulibus*, conscientiam eorum necessitatum sibi comparet atque proprium fraternum animum erga eos efficaciter manifestet.

Art. 151. Adlaborat ut itinera pietatis causa vel studio discendi vel ad relaxationem suscepta ad moralem religiosamque Christifidelium formationem conferant atque Ecclesiis particularibus adest ut omnes, qui exinde extra proprium domicilium versantur, apta animarum cura frui possint.

Pontifical Council for the Pastoral Assistance
to Health Care Workers

Art. 152. The Pontifical Council for the Pastoral Assistance to Health Care Workers shows the solicitude of the Church for the sick by helping those who serve the sick and suffering, so that their apostolate of mercy may ever more respond to people's needs.

Art. 153. §1. The Council is to spread the Church's teaching on the spiritual and moral aspects of illness as well as the meaning of human suffering.

§2. It lends its assistance to the particular Churches to ensure that health care workers receive spiritual help in carrying out their work according to Christian teachings, and especially that in turn the pastoral workers in this field may never lack the help they need to carry out their work.

§3. The Council fosters studies and actions which international Catholic organizations or other institutions undertake in this field.

§4. With keen interest it follows new health care developments in law and science so that these may be duly taken into account in the pastoral work of the Church.

Pontifical Council for the Interpretation of
Legislative Texts

Art. 154. The function of the Pontifical Council for the Interpretation of Legislative Texts consists mainly in interpreting the laws of the Church.

Art. 155. With regard to the universal laws of the Church, the Council is competent to publish authentic interpretations which are confirmed by pontifical authority, after having heard in questions of major importance the views of the dicasteries concerned by the subject matter.

Art. 156. This Council is at the service of the other Roman dicasteries to assist them in order to ensure that general executory decrees and instructions which they are going to publish are in conformity with the prescriptions of the law currently in force and that they are drawn up in a correct juridical form.

Art. 157. Moreover, the general decrees of the conferences of bishops are to be submitted to this Council by the dicastery which is competent to grant them the *recognitio*, in order that they be examined from a juridical perspective.

Art. 158. At the request of those interested, this Coun-

Pontificium Consilium de Apostolatu
pro Valetudinis Administris

Art. 152. Consilium sollicitudinem Ecclesiae pro infirmis ostendit adiuvando eos qui ministerium implent erga aegrotantes dolentesque, ut misericordiae apostolatus, quem exercent, novis postulationibus aptius usque respondeat.

Art. 153. §1. Consilii est Ecclesiae doctrinam diffundere circa spirituales et morales infirmitatis aspectus necnon humani doloris significationem.

§2. Ecclesiis particularibus adiutricem operam praebet, ut valetudinis administri spirituali cura iuventur in sua navitate secundum christianam doctrinam explenda, ac praeterea ne iis, qui in hoc ambitu pastoralem actionem gerunt, apta subsidia ad proprium exsequendum opus desint.

§3. Idem studii actionisque operi favet, quod sive Consociationes Internationales Catholicae sive alia instituta in hoc campo variis modis navant.

§4. Intento animo novitates in legibus et scientiis circa valetudinem prosequitur eo consilio, ut in opera pastorali Ecclesiae earum opportuna ratio habeatur.

Pontificium Consilium de Legum
Textibus Interpretandis

Art. 154. Consilii munus in legibus Ecclesiae interpretandis praesertim consistit.

Art. 155. Consilio competit Ecclesiae legum universalium interpretationem authenticam pontificia auctoritate firmatam proferre, auditis in rebus maioris momenti Dicasteriis, ad quae res ratione materiae pertinet.

Art. 156. Hoc Consilium ceteris Romanis Dicasteriis praesto est ad illa iuvanda eo proposito ut decreta generalia exsecutoria et instructiones ab iisdem edendae iuris vigentis praescriptis congruant et recta forma iuridica exarentur.

Art. 157. Eidem insuper subicienda sunt a Dicasterio competenti pro recognitione decreta generalia Episcoporum coetuum ut examinentur ratione habita iuridica.

Art. 158. Iis quorum interest postulantibus,

cil determines whether particular laws and general decrees issued by legislators below the level of the supreme authority are in agreement or not with the universal laws of the Church.

Pontifical Council for Inter-Religious Dialogue

Art. 159. The Pontifical Council for Inter-Religious Dialogue fosters and supervises relations with members and groups of non-Christian religions as well as with those who are in any way endowed with religious feeling.

Art. 160. The Council fosters suitable dialogue with adherents of other religions, as well as other forms of relations. It promotes timely studies and conferences to develop mutual information and esteem, so that human dignity and the spiritual and moral riches of people may ever grow. The Council sees to the formation of those who engage in this kind of dialogue.

Art. 161. When the subject matter so requires, the Council must proceed in the exercise of its own function in consultation with the Congregation for the Doctrine of the Faith, and, if need be, with the Congregations for the Oriental Churches and for the Evangelization of Peoples.

Art. 162. This Council has a Commission, under the direction of the president of the Council, for fostering relations with Muslims from a religious perspective.

Pontifical Council for Dialogue with Non-Believers

Art. 163. The Pontifical Council for Dialogue with Non-Believers shows the pastoral solicitude of the Church for those who do not believe in God or who profess no religion.

Art. 164. It promotes the study of atheism and of the lack of faith and religion, looking into their causes and their consequences with regard to the Christian faith, so that suitable assistance may be given to pastoral action through the work especially of Catholic educational institutions.

Art. 165. The Council sets up dialogue with atheists and unbelievers whenever they agree to sincere cooperation, and it is represented by true specialists at conferences on this matter.

Pontificium Consilium pro Dialogo inter Religiones

Art. 159. Consilium fovet et moderatur rationes cum membris coetibusque religionum, quae christiano nomine non censentur, necnon cum iis, qui sensu religioso quocumque modo potiuntur.

Art. 160. Consilium operam dat, ut dialogus cum asseclis aliarum religionum apte conseratur, aliasque rationes cum ipsis fovet; opportuna studia et conventus promovet ut mutua notitia atque aestimatio habeantur, necnon hominis dignitas eiusque spiritualia et moralia bona consociata opera provehantur; formationi eorum consulit, qui in huiusmodi dialogum incumbunt.

Art. 161. Cum subiecta materia id requirit, in proprio munere exercendo collatis consiliis procedat oportet cum Congregatione de Doctrina Fidei, et, si opus fuerit, cum Congregationibus pro Ecclesiis Orientalibus et pro Gentium Evangelizatione.

Art. 162. Apud Consilium exstat Commissio ad rationes cum Musulmanis sub religioso respectu fovendas, moderante eiusdem Consilii Praeside.

Pontificium Consilium pro Dialogo cum Non Credentibus

Art. 163. Consilium pastoralem Ecclesiae sollicitudinem manifestat erga eos qui Deo non credunt vel nullam religionem profitentur.

Art. 164. Studium promovet atheismi necnon fidei religionisque defectus, eorum causas atque consecutiones inquirendo ad christianam fidem quod attinet, eo proposito, ut apta auxilia pastorali actioni comparentur, operam potissimum ferentibus catholicis studiorum Institutis.

Art. 165. Dialogum instituit cum atheis et non credentibus, quoties hi sincerae cooperationi assentiantur; studiorum de hac materia coetibus per vere peritos interest.

Pontifical Council for Culture

Art. 166. The Pontifical Council for Culture fosters relations between the Holy See and the realm of human culture, especially by promoting communication with various contemporary institutions of learning and teaching, so that secular culture may be more and more open to the Gospel, and specialists in the sciences, literature, and the arts may feel themselves called by the Church to truth, goodness, and beauty.

Art. 167. The Council has its own special structure. The president is assisted by an advisory board and another board, composed of specialists of various disciplines from several parts of the world.

Art. 168. The Council on its own undertakes suitable projects with respect to culture. It follows through on those which are undertaken by various institutes of the Church, and, so far as necessary, lends them assistance. In consultation with the Secretariat of State, it shows interest in measures adopted by countries and international agencies in support of human culture and, as appropriate, it is present in the principal organizations in the field of culture and fosters conferences.

Pontifical Council for Social Communications

Art. 169. §1. The Pontifical Council for Social Communications is involved in questions respecting the means of social communication, so that, also by these means, human progress and the news of salvation may benefit secular culture and mores.

§2. In carrying out its functions, the Council must proceed in close connection with the Secretariat of State.

Art. 170. §1. The chief task of this Council is to arouse the Church and the Christian faithful, in a timely and suitable way, to take part in the many forms of social communication, and to sustain their action. It takes pains to see that newspapers and periodicals, as well as films and radio or television broadcasts, are more and more imbued with a human and Christian spirit.

§2. With special solicitude the Council looks to Catholic newspapers and periodicals, as well as radio and television stations, that they may truly live up to their nature and function, by transmitting especially the teaching of the

Pontificium Consilium de Cultura

Art. 166. Consilium rationes fovet inter Sanctam Sedem et humani cultus provinciam, praesertim colloquium cum variis nostri temporis Institutis scientiae et doctrinae provehendo, ut civilis cultus magis magisque Evangelio aperiatur atque scientiarum, litterarum, artiumque cultores se ad veritatem, bonitatem et pulchritudinem ab Ecclesia vocari sentiant.

Art. 167. Consilium structuram habet peculiarem, in qua, una cum Praeside, adsunt Coetus praesidialis aliusque coetus cultorum variarum disciplinarum ex pluribus orbis terrarum regionibus.

Art. 168. Consilium apta incepta ad culturam attinentia per se suscipit; ea, quae a variis Ecclesiae Institutis capiuntur, persequitur atque ipsis, quatenus opus fuerit, adiutricem operam praebet. Collatis autem consiliis cum Secretaria Status attendit ad agendi rationes, quas ad humanum cultum fovendum Civitates et internationalia Consilia susceperint, atque in culturae ambitu praecipuis coetibus pro opportunitate interest et congressiones fovet.

Pontificium Consilium de Communicationibus Socialibus

Art. 169. §1. Consilium in quaestionibus ad communicationis socialis instrumenta attinentibus versatur, eo consilio ut etiam per ea salutis nuntium et humana progressio ad civilem cultum moresque fovendos provehantur.

§2. In suis muneribus explendis arcta coniunctione cum Secretaria Status procedat oportet.

Art. 170. §1. Consilium in praecipuum munus incumbit tempestive accommodateque suscitandi ac sustinendi Ecclesiae et Christifidelium actionem in multiplicibus socialis communicationis formis; operam dandi ut sive diaria aliaque periodica scripta, sive cinematographica spectacula, sive radiophonicae ac televisificae emissiones humano et christiano spiritu magis magisque imbuantur.

§2. Peculiari sollicitudine prosequitur catholicas ephemerides, periodicas scriptiones, stationes radiophonicas atque televisificas, ut propriae indoli ac muneri reapse respondeant,

Church as it is laid out by the Church's magisterium, and by spreading religious news accurately and faithfully.

§3. It fosters relations with Catholic associations active in social communications.

§4. It takes steps to make the Christian people aware, especially on the occasion offered by World Communications Day, of the duty of each and every person to make sure that the media be of service to the Church's pastoral mission.

praesertim Ecclesiae doctrinam, prout a Magisterio proponitur, evulgando, atque religiosos nuntios recte fideliterque diffundendo.

§3. Necessitudinem fovet cum catholicis consociationibus, quae communicationibus socialibus dant operam.

§4. Curat ut populus christianus, praesertim occasione data celebrationis *Diei communicationum socialium* conscius fiat officii, quo unusquisque tenetur, adlaborandi ut huiusmodi instrumenta pastorali Ecclesiae missioni praesto sunt.

VI. ADMINISTRATIVE SERVICES

Apostolic Camera

Art. 171. §1. The Apostolic Camera, presided over by the cardinal camerlengo of the Holy Roman Church, assisted by the vice-camerlengo and the other prelates of the Camera, chiefly exercises the functions assigned to it by the special law on the vacancy of the Apostolic See.

§2. When the Apostolic See falls vacant, it is the right and the duty of the cardinal camerlengo of the Holy Roman Church, personally or through his delegate, to request, from all administrations dependent on the Holy See, reports on their patrimonial and economic status as well as information on any extraordinary business that may at that time be under way, and, from the Prefecture for the Economic Affairs of the Holy See he shall request a financial statement on income and expenditures of the previous year and the budgetary estimates for the following year. He is in duty bound to submit these reports and estimates to the College of Cardinals.

VI. OFFICIA

Camera Apostolica

Art. 171. §1. Camera Apostolica, cui praeficitur Cardinalis Sanctae Romanae Ecclesiae Camerarius, iuvante Vice-Camerario una cum ceteris Praelatis Cameralibus, munera praesertim gerit, quae ipsi peculiari lege de vacante Sede Apostolica tribuuntur.

§2. Sede Apostolica vacante, Cardinali Sanctae Romanae Ecclesiae Camerario ius est et officium, etiam per suum delegatum, ab omnibus Administrationibus, quae e Sancta Sede pendent, relationes exposcere de earum statu patrimoniali et oeconomico itemque notitias de extraordinariis negotiis, quae tunc forte aguntur, et a Praefectura Rerum Oeconomicarum Sanctae Sedis generales computationes accepti et expensi anni superioris nec non praevias aestimationes pro anno subsequente; has autem relationes et computationes Cardinalium Collegio subiciendi officio tenetur.

Administration of the Patrimony of the Apostolic See

Art. 172. It is the function of the Administration of the Patrimony of the Apostolic See to administer the properties owned by the Holy See in order to underwrite the expenses needed for the Roman Curia to function.

Art. 173. This Council is presided over by a cardinal assisted by a board of cardinals; and it is composed of two sections, the Ordinary Section and the Extraordinary, under the control of the prelate secretary.

Administratio Patrimonii Sedis Apostolicae

Art. 172. Huic officio competit bona Sanctae Sedis propria administrare, quae eo destinantur, ut sumptus ad Curiae Romanae munera explenda necessarii suppeditentur.

Art. 173. Eidem Cardinalis praeest, cui Patrum Cardinalium coetus adest, idemque duabus sectionibus, Ordinaria atque Extraordinaria, constat, sub moderamine Praelati Secretarii.

Art. 174. The Ordinary Section administers the properties entrusted to its care, calling in the advice of experts if needed; it examines matters concerning the juridical and economic status of the employees of the Holy See; it supervises institutions under its fiscal responsibility; it sees to the provision of all that is required to carry out the ordinary business and specific aims of the dicasteries; it maintains records of income and expenditures, prepares the accounts of the money received and paid out for the past year, and draws up the estimates for the year to come.

Art. 175. The Extraordinary Section administers its own moveable goods and acts as a guardian for moveable goods entrusted to it by other institutes of the Holy See.

Prefecture for the Economic Affairs of the Holy See

Art. 176. The Prefecture for the Economic Affairs of the Holy See has the function of supervising and governing the temporal goods of the administrations that are dependent on the Holy See, or of which the Holy See has charge, whatever the autonomy these administrations may happen to enjoy.

Art. 177. The Prefecture is presided over by a cardinal assisted by a board of cardinals, with the collaboration of the prelate secretary and the general accountant.

Art. 178. §1. It studies the reports on the patrimonial and economic status of the Holy See, as well as the statements of income and expenditures for the previous year and the budget estimates for the following year of the administrations mentioned in art. 176, by inspecting books and documents, if need be.

§2. The Prefecture compiles the Holy See's consolidated financial statement of the previous year's expenditures as well as the consolidated estimates of the next year's expenditures, and submits these at specific times to higher authority for approval.

Art. 179. §1. The Prefecture supervises financial undertakings of the administrations and expresses its opinion concerning projects of major importance.

§2. It inquires into damages inflicted in whatever manner on the patrimony of the Holy See, and, if need be, lodges penal or civil actions to the competent tribunals.

Art. 174. Sectio Ordinaria bona administrat, quorum cura ipsi credita est, in consilium vocatis, si opus fuerit, etiam peritis; et perpendit quae ad statum iuridicum-oeconomicum ministrorum Sanctae Sedis attinent; institutis sub ipsius administratoria moderatione exstantibus invigilat; prospicit ut omnia apparentur, quae ordinaria Dicasteriorum navitas ad proprios fines assequendos requirit; rationes accepti et expensi habet atque pecuniae dandae et recipiendae sive computationem pro anno elapso sive pro subsequenti anno aestimationem conficit.

Art. 175. Extraordinaria Sectio peculiaria bona mobilia administrat, et mobilium bonorum procurationem agit, quae a ceteris Sanctae Sedis Institutis eidem committuntur.

Praefectura Rerum Oeconomicarum Sanctae Sedis

Art. 176. Praefecturae munus competit moderandi et gubernandi bonorum administrationes, quae a Sancta Sede pendent vel quibus ipsa praeest, quaecumque est autonomia qua forte gaudeant.

Art. 177. Eidem praeest Cardinalis, cui adest coetus Cardinalium, iuvantibus Praelato Secretario et Ratiocinatore Generali.

Art. 178. §1. Perpendit sive relationes de statu patrimoniali et oeconomico sive rationes accepti atque expensi tum annualium sumptuum praeviam tum subsequentem administrationum de quibus agit art. 176, libros et documenta, si opus fuerit, inspiciendo.

§2. Generalem computationem, sive ad praeviam sumptuum aestimationem sive ad rationem expensae pecuniae Sanctae Sedis quod attinet, apparat, eandemque tempore statuto Superiori Auctoritati approbandam subicit.

Art. 179. §1. Nummariis administrationum inceptis invigilat; sententiam de operum maioris momenti adumbrationibus fert.

§2. Cognoscit de damnis patrimonio Sanctae Sedis quomodocumque illatis, ad actiones poenales vel civiles, si opus fuerit, competentibus tribunalibus proponendas.

VII. OTHER INSTITUTES OF THE ROMAN CURIA

Prefecture of the Papal Household

Art. 180. The Prefecture of the Papal Household looks after the internal organization of the papal household, and supervises everything concerning the conduct and service of all clerics and laypersons who make up the papal chapel and family.

Art. 181. §1. It is at the service of the Supreme Pontiff, both in the Apostolic Palace and when he travels in Rome or in Italy.

§2. Apart from the strictly liturgical aspect, which is handled by the Office for the Liturgical Celebrations of the Supreme Pontiff, the Prefecture sees to the planning and carrying out of papal ceremonies and determines the order of precedence.

§3. It arranges public and private audiences with the Pontiff, in consultation with the Secretariat of State whenever circumstances so demand and under whose direction it arranges the procedures to be followed when the Roman Pontiff meets in a solemn audience with heads of State, ambassadors, members of governments, public authorities, and other distinguished persons.

Office for the Liturgical Celebrations of the Supreme Pontiff

Art. 182. §1. The Office for the Liturgical Celebrations of the Supreme Pontiff is to prepare all that is necessary for the liturgical and other sacred celebrations performed by the Supreme Pontiff or in his name and supervise them according to the current prescriptions of liturgical law.

§2. The master of papal liturgical celebrations is appointed by the Supreme Pontiff to a five-year term of office; papal masters of ceremonies who assist him in sacred celebrations are likewise appointed by the secretary of state to a term of the same length.

VIII. ADVOCATES

Art. 183. Apart from the advocates of the Roman Rota and the advocates for the causes of saints, there is a roster of advocates who, at the request of interested parties, are qualified to represent them in their cases at the Supreme Tribunal of the Apostolic Signatura and to offer assistance in hierarchical recourses lodged before dicasteries of the Roman Curia.

VII. CETERA CURIAE ROMANAE INSTITUTA

Praefectura Pontificalis Domus

Art. 180. Praefectura ordinem internum ad Pontificalem Domum spectantem respicit, atque iis omnibus sive clericis sive laicis moderatur, ad disciplinam et servitium quod attinet, qui Cappellam et Familiam Pontificiam constituunt.

Art. 181. §1. Summo Pontifici adest sive in Palatio Apostolico sive cum Ipse in Urbem vel in Italiam iter facit.

§2. Ordinationi et processui studet Caeremoniarum Pontificalium, extra partem stricte liturgicam, quae ab Officio Liturgicis Celebrationibus Summi Pontificis praeposito absolvitur; praecedentiae ordinem attribuit.

§3. Admissiones publicas privatasque coram Pontifice disponit, collatis consiliis, quoties rerum natura id postulet, cum Secretaria Status, qua moderante ea ordinat, quae servanda sunt, cum ab ipso Romano Pontifice coram sollemniter admittuntur supremi populorum Moderatores, Nationum Legati, Civitatum Ministri, Publicae Auctoritates ceteraeque personae dignitate insignes.

Officium de Liturgicis Celebrationibus Summi Pontificis

Art. 182. §1. Ipsius est ea quae necessaria sunt ad liturgicas aliasque sacras celebrationes, quae a Summo Pontifice aut Eius nomine peraguntur, parare easque, iuxta vigentia iuris liturgici praescripta, moderari.

§2. Magister pontificiarum Celebrationum Liturgicarum a Summo Pontifice ad quinquennium nominatur; caeremoniarii pontificii, qui eum in sacris celebrationibus adiuvant, a Secretario Status pariter ad idem tempus nominantur.

VIII. ADVOCATI

Art. 183. Praeter Romanae Rotae Advocatos et Advocatos pro causis Sanctorum, Album adest Advocatorum, qui habiles sunt, rogatu eorum quorum interest, ut patrocinium causarum apud Supremum Signaturae Apostolicae Tribunal suscipiant necnon, in recursibus hierarchicis apud Dicasteria Curiae Romanae, operam suam praestent.

Art. 184. Candidates can be inscribed in the roster by the cardinal secretary of state, after he has consulted a commission stably constituted for this purpose. Candidates must be qualified by a suitable preparation attested by appropriate academic degrees, and at the same time be recommended by their example of a Christian life, honourable character, and expertise. Should any of this cease to be the case at a later date, the advocate shall be struck from the roster.

Art. 185. §1. The body called "Advocates of the Holy See" is composed mainly of advocates listed in the roster of advocates, and its members are able to undertake the representation of cases in civil or ecclesiastical tribunals in the name of the Holy See or the dicasteries of the Roman Curia.

§2. They are appointed by the cardinal secretary of state to a five-year term of office on the recommendation of the commission mentioned in art. 184; for serious reasons, they may be removed from office. Once they have completed seventy-five years of age, they cease their office.

IX. INSTITUTIONS CONNECTED WITH THE HOLY SEE

Art. 186. There are certain institutes, some of ancient origin and some not long established, which do not belong to the Roman Curia in a strict sense but nevertheless provide useful or necessary services to the Supreme Pontiff himself, to the Curia and the whole Church, and are in some way connected with the Apostolic See.

Art. 187. Among such institutes are the Vatican Secret Archives, where documents of the Church's governance are preserved first of all so that they may be available to the Holy See itself and to the Curia as they carry out their own work, but then also, by papal permission, so that they may be available to everyone engaged in historical research and serve as a source of information on all areas of secular history that have been closely connected with the life of the Church in centuries gone by.

Art. 188. In the Vatican Apostolic Library, established by the Supreme Pontiffs, the Church has a remarkable instrument for fostering, guarding, and spreading culture. In its various sections, it offers to scholars researching truth a treasure of every kind of art and knowledge.

Art. 184. A Cardinali Secretario Status, audita commissione stabiliter ad hoc constituta, candidati in Albo inscribi possunt, qui congrua praeparatione, aptis titulis academicis comprobata, simulque vitae christianae exemplo, morum honestate ac rerum agendarum peritia commendentur. Quibus requisitis forte postea deficientibus, ex Albo expungendi sunt.

Art. 185. §1. Ex Advocatis praesertim in Albo adscriptis Corpus Sanctae Sedis Advocatorum constituitur, qui patrocinium causarum, nomine Sanctae Sedis vel Curiae Romanae Dicasteriorum, apud ecclesiastica vel civilia tribunalia suscipere valent.

§2. A Cardinali Secretario Status, audita commissione, de qua in art. 184, ad quinquennium nominantur; graves tamen ob causas, a munere removeri possunt. Expleto septuagesimo quinto aetatis anno, a munere cessant.

IX. INSTITUTIONES SANCTAE SEDI ADHAERENTES

Art. 186. Sunt Instituta quaedam, sive antiquae originis sive novae constitutionis, quae, quamvis ad Curiam Romanam sensu proprio non pertineant, nihilominus ipsi Summo Pontifici, Curiae et Ecclesiae universae servitia necessaria aut utilia praestant et cum Apostolica Sede aliquo modo cohaerent.

Art. 187. Inter huiusmodi Instituta eminet Tabularium seu Archivum Secretum Vaticanum, in quo documenta regiminis Ecclesiae adservantur, ut imprimis ipsi Sanctae Sedi et Curiae in proprio opere perficiendo praesto sunt deinde vero, ex ipsa concessione Pontificia, omnibus historiae explorandae studiosis, atque fontes cognitionis evadere possint omnium historiae profanae quoque regionum, quae cum vita Ecclesiae saeculis praeteritis arcte cohaerent.

Art. 188. Instrumentum insuper insigne Ecclesiae ad culturam fovendam, servandam, divulgandam a Summis Pontificibus constituta est Bibliotheca Apostolica Vaticana, quae thesauros omne genus scientiae et artis in suis variis sectionibus viris doctis veritatem investigantibus praebet.

Art. 189. To seek the truth and to spread it in the various areas of divine and human sciences there have arisen within the Roman Church various academies, as they are called, outstanding among which is the Pontifical Academy of Sciences.

Art. 190. In their constitution and administration, all these institutions of the Roman Church are governed by their own laws.

Art. 191. Of more recent origin, though partly based on examples of the past, are the Vatican Polyglot Press; the Vatican Publishing House and its bookstore; the daily, weekly and monthly newspapers, among which *L'Osservatore Romano* stands out; Vatican Radio; the Vatican Television Centre. These institutes, according to their own regulations, come within the competence of the Secretariat of State or of other agencies of the Roman Curia.

Art. 192. The Fabric of Saint Peter's deals, according to its own regulations, with matters concerning the Basilica of the Prince of the Apostles, with respect to the preservation and decoration of the building and behaviour among the employees and pilgrims who come into the Church. Where necessary, the superiors of the Fabric act in harmony with the Chapter of that basilica.

Art. 193. The Office of Papal Charities carries on the work of aid of the Supreme Pontiff toward the poor and is subject directly to him.

We decree the present Apostolic Constitution to be firm, valid, and effective now and henceforth, that it shall receive its full and integral effects from the first day of the month of March of 1989, and that it must in each and everything and in any manner whatsoever be fully observed by all those to whom it applies or in any way shall apply, anything to the contrary notwithstanding, even if it is worthy of most special mention.

Given in Rome, at Saint Peter's, in the presence of the cardinals assembled in consistory, on the vigil of the solemnity of the Holy Apostles Peter and Paul, 28 June in the Marian Year 1988, the tenth of Our pontificate.

John Paul II

Art. 189. Ad veritatem inquirendam et diffundendam in variis scientiae divinae et humanae regionibus ortae sunt in sinu Ecclesiae Romanae variae, quae vocantur, Academiae, inter quas eminet Scientiarum Academia Pontificia.

Art. 190. Hae omnes Institutiones Ecclesiae Romanae reguntur propriis legibus constitutionis et administrationis.

Art. 191. Recentioris originis sunt, quamvis ex parte exemplis praeteritis inhaereant, Typographia Polyglotta Vaticana, Officina libraria editoria Vaticana, Ephemerides diurnae, hebdomadariae, menstruae, inter quas eminet *L'Osservatore Romano*, Statio Radiophonica Vaticana et Centrum Televisificum Vaticanum. Haec Instituta subiciuntur Secretariae Status aut aliis Curiae Romanae officiis iuxta proprias leges.

Art. 192. Fabrica Sancti Petri curare perget ea quae ad Basilicam Principis Apostolorum pertinent sive quoad conservationem et decorem aedificii sive quoad disciplinam internam custodum et peregrinorum, qui visendi causa templum ingrediuntur, iuxta proprias leges. In omnibus, quae id exigunt, Superiores Fabricae concorditer agant cum Capitulo eiusdem Basilicae.

Art. 193. Eleemosynaria Apostolica opus adiumenti pro Summo Pontifice exercet erga pauperes ac pendet directe ex Ipso.

Decernimus praesentem Constitutionem apostolicam firmam, validam et efficacem esse ac fore, suosque plenos et integros effectus sortiri atque obtinere a die 1 mensis Martii 1989 et ab illis ad quos spectat aut quomodolibet spectabit in omnibus et per omnia plenissime observari, contrariis quibusvis, etiam specialissima mentione dignis, non obstantibus.

Datum Romae, apud Sanctum Petrum, coram Patribus Cardinalibus in Consistorio adunatis, in pervigilio sollemnitatis Sanctorum Apostolorum Petri et Pauli, die XXVIII mensis Iunii Anno Mariali MCMLXXXVIII, Pontificatus Nostri decimo.

Ioannes Paulus PP. II

APPENDIX I

The Pastoral Significance of the Visit
ad limina Apostolorum

(cf. arts. 28–32)

That pastoral ideal which occupied the dominant place in the drafting of the Apostolic Constitution on the Roman Curia, has had the effect of attributing greater significance to visits *ad limina Apostolorum* by bishops, bringing a more adequate light to bear on the pastoral importance which the visits have gained in the present life of the Church.

1. These visits, as we know, take place when the bishops, joined as they are to the Apostolic See with the bond of communion and presiding in charity and service over the particular Churches throughout the world, set out at certain appointed times for Rome to visit the tombs of the Apostles.

On the one hand, these visits give the bishops an opportunity to sharpen their awareness of their responsibilities as successors of the Apostles and to feel more intensely their sense of hierarchical communion with the successor of Peter. On the other hand, the visits in some way constitute the highest and most central point in that universal ministry that the Holy Father is carrying out when he embraces his brother bishops, the pastors of the particular Churches, and takes up with them the business of sustaining their mission in the Church.

2. These *ad limina* visits bring into full view this movement or life-blood between the particular Churches and the Church as a whole that theologians call *perichoresis*. The process may be compared to the diastolic-systolic movements within the human body when the blood is carried to the outer limbs and from there flows back to the heart.

Some trace and example of a first *ad limina* visit is found in Paul's letter to the Galatians, in which the Apostle tells the story of his conversion and the journey he undertook among the pagans. Although he knew that he had been called and instructed personally by Christ who had conquered death, he wrote these words: "[Then] did I go up to Jerusalem to meet Cephas. I stayed fifteen days with him" (Gal 1:18). "It was not until fourteen years later that I travelled up to Jerusalem again [. . .] I expounded the whole gospel that I preach the gentiles, to make quite sure

ADNEXUM I

De pastorali momento Visitationis
«ad limina Apostolorum»,

de qua in articulis a 28 ad 32

Pastoralis illa ratio, quae in recognoscenda Apostolica Constitutione de Curia Romana primas partes habuit, id etiam effecit, ut Episcoporum Visitationi «ad limina Apostolorum» maior usque significatio attribueretur, eiusque pastorale momentum aptiore in lumine collocaretur, quod in Ecclesiae vita nostro tempore hae Visitationes consecutae sunt.

1. Sicuti cognitum est, ipsae fiunt, cum omnes Episcopi, qui, cum Apostolica Sede communionis vinculo coniuncti, per terrarum orbem Ecclesiis particularibus in caritate atque in ministerio praesunt, Romam ad Apostolorum limina visitanda statis temporibus petunt.

Ipsae enim Visitationes hinc occasionem praebent Episcopis officiorum suorum conscientiam, qua utpote Apostolorum successores premuntur, augendi et hierarchicae communionis cum Petri successore sensum alendi; hinc centrum et quodammodo caput universalis illius ministerii constituunt, quod Beatissimus Pater exercet, cum particularium Ecclesiarum Pastores, suos in episcopatu fratres, complectitur, cum iisque de rebus agit, quae ad ipsorum ecclesialem missionem sustinendam attinent.

2. Per Visitationes «ad limina» motus ille vel vitalis cursus, inter universam Ecclesiam atque particulares Ecclesias intercedens, fit aliquomodo adspectabilis, qui a theologis definitur veluti quaedam *perichoresis*, vel motibus comparatur, quibus humani corporis sanguis a corde ad extrema usque membra dilatatur atque ab istis ad cor refluit.

Primae cuiusdam Visitationis «ad limina» vestigium atque exemplar in Pauli epistola ad Galatas invenitur, in qua Apostolus suam conversionem atque iter ad paganos a se susceptum narrat, haec verba scribens, etiamsi ipse sciebat se a Christo mortis victore immediate vocatum atque edoctum esse: «Deinde . . . veni Hierosolymam videre Petrum, et mansi apud eum diebus quindecim» (1, 18); «deinde post annos quattuordecim iterum ascendi Hierosolymam . . .

that the efforts I was making and had already made should not be fruitless" (Gal 2: 1–2).

3. The natural result of this meeting with Peter's successor, first guardian of the deposit of truth passed on by the Apostles, is to strengthen unity in the same faith, hope and charity, and more and more to recognize and treasure that immense heritage of spiritual and moral wealth that the whole Church, joined with the bishop of Rome by the bond of communion, has spread throughout the world.

During the *ad limina* visit, two men stand face to face together, namely the bishop of a certain particular Church and the bishop of Rome, who is also the successor of Peter. Both carry on their shoulders the burden of office, which they cannot relieve themselves from, but they are not at all divided one from the other, for both of them in their own way represent, and must represent, the sum total of the faithful, the whole of the Church, and the sum total of the bishops, which together constitute the only "we and us" in the body of Christ. It is in their communion that the faithful under their care communicate with one another, and likewise the universal Church and particular Churches communicate with each other.

4. For all these reasons, the *ad limina* visits express *that pastoral solicitude* which thrives in the universal Church. Here we see the meeting of the pastors of the Church, joined together in a collegial unity that is based on apostolic succession. In this College, each and every one of the bishops displays that solicitude of Jesus Christ, the Good Shepherd, which all have received by way of inheritance.

This indeed is the highest ideal of the apostolate that has to be carried out in the Church and which concerns the bishops together with the successor of Peter. For each one of them stands at the centre of all the apostolate, in all its forms, that is carried out in each particular Church, joined at the same time in the universal dimension of the Church as a whole. All this apostolate, again in all its forms, demands and includes the work and help of all those who are building the Body of Christ in the Church, be it universal or particular: the priests, men and women religious consecrated to God, and the laypeople.

et contuli cum illis evangelium, quod praedico in gentibus ... ne forte in vacuum currerem aut cucurrissem» (2, 2).

3. Congressio cum Petri successore, qui veritatis depositum ab Apostolis traditum primus custodit, eo tendit, ut unitas in eadem fide, spe et caritate confirmetur, atque immensum illud spiritualium moraliumque bonorum patrimonium magis magisque cognoscatur atque existimetur, quod universa Ecclesia, cum Romano Episcopo communionis vinculo coniuncta, per terrarum orbem diffudit.

Dum Visitatio «ad limina» agitur, duo coram inter se congrediuntur viri, scilicet Ecclesiae cuiusdam particularis Episcopus atque Romae Episcopus idemque Petri successor, qui ambo suorum officiorum onus, cui derogari non licet, sustinent, sed alter ab altero minime seiunguntur: ambo enim proprio modo repraesentant, atque repraesentare debent, summam Ecclesiae, summam fidelium, summamque Episcoporum, quae quodammodo unicum «nos» in Christi corpore constituunt. In ipsorum enim communione fideles ipsis concrediti inter se communicant, atque universalis Ecclesia Ecclesiaeque particulares inter se pariter communicant.

4. Hasce omnes ob causas, Visitationes «ad limina» *pastoralem illam sollicitudinem* exprimunt, quae in universali viget Ecclesia. Agitur enim de Ecclesiae Pastorum congressione, qui collegiali unitate, in Apostolorum successione fundata, inter se uniuntur. Nam in hoc Collegio omnes et singuli Episcopi ipsius Iesu Christi, Pastoris boni, sollicitudinem manifestant, quam hereditate quadam acceperunt.

Hic sane consistit summa apostolatus ratio, qui in Ecclesia agendus est, quique ad Episcopos una cum Petri Successore maxime pertinet. Etenim unusquisque eorum centrum totius apostolatus, undequaque absoluti, constituit, qui in singulis Ecclesiis particularibus exercetur, cum universali Ecclesiae amplitudine coniunctis. Totus huiusmodi apostolatus, undequaque absolutus, omnium eorum operam atque adiumentum postulat atque complectitur, qui in Ecclesia sive universali sive particulari Christi corpus aedificant, nempe: presbyterorum, religiosorum virorum ac mulierum Deo consecratarum, atque laicorum.

5. Now if the *ad limina* visits are conceived and viewed in this way, they come to be a *specific moment of that communion* which so profoundly determines the nature and essence of the Church, as it was admirably indicated in the Dogmatic Constitution on the Church, especially in chapters II and III. Given that society nowadays is leaning towards a closer sense of communion, and the Church experiences herself as "a sign and instrument [. . .] of communion with God and of unity among the whole of humankind," (*Lumen gentium*, 1) it seems utterly necessary that a permanent communication between particular Churches and the Apostolic See should be promoted and built up, especially by sharing pastoral solicitude regarding questions, experiences, problems, projects and ideas about life and action.

When pastors converge on Rome and meet together, there comes to pass a remarkable and most beautiful sharing of gifts from among all those riches in the Church, be they universal or local and particular, in accordance with that principle of catholicity by which "each part contributes its own gifts to other parts and to the whole Church, so that the whole and each of the parts are strengthened by the common sharing of all things and by the common effort to attain to fullness in unity." (*Lumen gentium*, 13)

Furthermore and in the same way, *ad limina* visits aim not only at a direct sharing of information but also and especially to an increase and strengthening of a *collegial structure* in the body of the Church, bringing about a remarkable unity in variety.

This communication in the Church is a two-way movement. On the one hand, the bishops converge towards the centre and the visible foundation of unity. We are referring to that unity which, when it comes to full bloom, casts its benefits on their own groupings or conferences, through each pastor's responsibilities and awareness of his functions and of their fulfilment, or through the *collegial spirit* of all the pastors. On the other hand, there is the commission "which the Lord confided to Peter alone, as the first of the apostles" (*Lumen gentium*, 20) which serves the ecclesial community and the spread of her mission, in such a way that nothing is left untried that may lead to the advancement and preservation of the unity of the faith and the common discipline of the whole Church, and all become

5. Quodsi Visitationes «ad limina» singulari hac ratione considerantur, eae fiunt etiam *peculiare momentum illius communionis*, quae Ecclesiae naturam atque essentiam tam alte confingit, sicut Constitutio dogmatica de Ecclesia optime significavit, praesertim in capitibus II et III. Dum enim hodierno tempore et hominum societas ad mutuam solidioremque communionem inclinatur, et Ecclesia sentit se esse «signum et instrumentum intimae cum Deo unionis totiusque generis humani unitatis» (*Lumen gentium*, 1), prorsus necessarium videtur ut continens communicatio inter particulares Ecclesias et Apostolicam Sedem promoveatur atque augeatur, praesertim per pastoralem sollicitudinem inter se participandam quoad quaestiones, rerum usum, problemata proposita atque navitatis vitaeque consilia.

Quando Pastores Romam conveniunt et inter se congrediuntur, peculiaris ac pulcherrima donorum communicatio fit inter omnia bona quae sive particularia atque localia sive universalia in Ecclesia sunt, secundum illius catholicitatis principium, vi cuius «singulae partes propria dona ceteris partibus et toti Ecclesiae afferunt, ita ut totum et singulae partes augeantur ex omnibus invicem communicantibus et ad plenitudinem in unitate conspirantibus» (*Lumen gentium*, 13).

Eadem pariter ratione Visitationes «ad limina» eo tendunt non modo ut nuntia invicem directo tradantur atque recipiantur sed praesertim etiam ut *collegialis conformatio* in Ecclesiae corpore augescat ac solidetur, per quam peculiaris unitas in varietate efficitur.

Huius autem ecclesialis communicationis motus est duplex. Hinc Episcopi versus centrum et adspectabile unitatis fundamentum coëunt: illam dicimus unitatem, quae sive per uniuscuiusque Pastoris officia et muneris conscientiam atque exercitium, sive per *collegialem* omnium Pastorum *affectum*, in proprios coetus vel Conferentias efflorescit; hinc munus habetur «a Domino singulariter Petro, primo Apostolorum, concessum» (*Lumen gentium*, 20), quod ecclesiali communitati atque missionali propagationi inservit, ita ut nil inexpertum relinquatur quod ad fidei unitatem et communem universae Ecclesiae disciplinam provehendam atque custodien-

more and more aware that the responsibility of proclaiming the Gospel everywhere throughout the world falls chiefly on the body of the pastors.

6. From all the principles established above to describe this most important process, one may deduce in what way that apostolic custom of "seeing Peter" is to be understood and put into practice.

First of all the *ad limina* visit has a *sacred meaning* in that the bishops with religious veneration pay a visit to the tombs of Peter and Paul, the Princes of the Apostles, shepherds and pillars of the Church of Rome.

Then the *ad limina* visit has a *personal meaning* because each individual bishop meets the successor of Peter and talks to him *face to face*.

Finally, the visit has a *curial meaning,* that is, a *hallmark of community,* because the bishops enter into conversation with the moderators of the dicasteries, councils, and offices of the Roman Curia. The Curia, after all, is a certain "community" that is closely joined with the Roman Pontiff in that area of the Petrine ministry which involves solicitude for all the Churches (cf. 2 Cor 11:28).

In the course of the *ad limina* visit, the access that the bishops have to the dicasteries is of a two-fold nature:

—First, it gives them access to each individual agency of the Roman Curia, especially to questions that the agencies are dealing with directly according to their competence, questions that have been referred by law to those agencies because of their expertise and experience.

—Second, bishops coming from all over the world, where each of the particular Churches can be found, are introduced to questions of common pastoral solicitude for the universal Church.

Bearing in mind this specific point of view, the Congregation for Bishops, in consultation with the other interested Congregations, is preparing a "Directory" for publication so that the *ad limina* visits can receive long- and short-term preparation and thus proceed smoothly.

7. Each and every bishop—by the very nature of that

dam conducat, pariterque ut omnes magis magisque conscii fiant, Evangelii ubique terrarum nuntiandi curam in Pastorum corpus potissimum recidere.

6. Ex omnibus principiis, quae supra statuta sunt ad huiusmodi maximi ponderis rerum ordinem describendum, plane deducitur qua ratione apostolicus ille mos «videndi Petrum» intellegatur atque in rem deducatur oporteat.

Primum enim Visitatio «ad limina» *sacram significationem* accipit, dum Sanctorum Petri et Pauli, Apostolorum Principum, Romanae Ecclesiae pastorum atque columnarum, sepulcra ab Episcopis invisuntur ac veneratione coluntur.

Deinde Visitatio «ad limina» *significationem personalem* indicat, quoniam singuli Episcopi cum Petri successore congrediuntur atque *os ad os* cum illo loquuntur.

Denique *significatio curialis,* id est *communitatis notam* prae se ferens habetur, cum Episcopi etiam apud Romanae Curia Dicasteria, Consilia et Officia in colloquium cum eorum Moderatoribus veniunt, quandoquidem Curia quandam efficit «communitatem», quae cum Romano Pontifice arctius coniungitur in ministerii Petriani regione, quae sollicitudinem omnium Ecclesiarum (cf. 2 *Cor* 11, 28) respicit.

Aditus, quem Episcopi ad Dicasteria habent, dum Visitationem «ad limina» agunt, duplici ratione notantur:

— ipsis accessus praebetur ad singulas Romanae Curiae compages, immo ad quaestiones, quas illae directo tractant secundum singulas cuiusque rerum provincias, quae illarum iuri tributae sunt, propria adhibita peritia atque exercitatione;

— Episcopi praeterea totius terrarum orbis ambitu, in quo singulae Ecclesiae particulares exstant, in communis pastoralis sollicitudinis quaestiones introducuntur, quae universalem Ecclesiam respiciunt.

Specialem huiusmodi rerum conspectum prae oculis habens Congregatio pro Episcopis, collatis consiliis cum Congregationibus, ad quas id etiam pertinet, «Directorium» edendum curat, per quod Visitationes «ad limina» sive quoad praeteritum sive quoad proximum tempus apte accomodeque apparentur atque procedant.

7. Singuli Episcopi. ratione et vi naturae il-

"ministry" that has been entrusted to him—is called and invited to visit the "tombs of the Apostles" at certain appointed times.

However, since the bishops living within each territory, nation or region, have already gathered together and now form conferences of bishops—collegial unions with an excellent, broad theoretical basis (cf. *Lumen gentium,* 23)—it is highly appropriate that the *ad limina* visits should proceed according to this collegial principle, for that carries much significance within the Church.

The institutes of the Apostolic See, and especially the nunciatures and apostolic delegations as well as the dicasteries of the Roman Curia, are most willing to offer assistance in order to ensure that *ad limina* visits be made possible, are suitably prepared and proceed well.

To sum up: the institution of the *ad limina* visit is an instrument of the utmost value, commanding respect because it is an ancient custom and has outstanding pastoral importance. Truly, these visits express the catholicity of the Church and the unity and communion of the College of Bishops, qualities rooted in the successor of Peter and signified by those holy places where the Princes of the Apostles underwent martyrdom, qualities of a theological, pastoral, social, and religious import known to all.

This institution therefore is to be favored and promoted in every possible way, especially at this moment of the history of salvation in which the teachings and magisterium of the Second Vatican Ecumenical Council shine out with ever brighter light.

lius «ministerii» ipsis commissi. vocantur atque invitantur ut «limina Apostolorum» statis temporibus visitent.

Quoniam autem Episcopi in singulis territoriis, nationibus vel regionibus degentes iam sese simul collegerunt atque Episcopales Conferentias nunc constituunt. quae collegialis unio peramplis optimisque rationibus fundatur (cf. *Lumen gentium,* 23). maximopere congruit ut Visitationes «ad limina» secundum huiusmodi collegiale principium procedant: id enim eloquentissimam sane ecclesialem significationem praebet.

Singula quaeque Apostolicae Sedis instituta, ac praesertim Nuntiaturae ac Delegationes Apostolicae, praeter Romanae Curiae Dicasteria, parata sunt adiutricem operam libentissime navare, ut Visitationes «ad limina» facile habeantur, apte comparentur et bene procedant.

Etenim, ut omnia pressius comprehendamus, quae supra explicata sunt, Visitationis «ad limina» institutum, auctoritate sane grave ob moris antiquitatem atque ob praeclarum pastorale momentum, summae utilitatis instrumentum est, per quod sive Ecclesiae catholicitas sive Episcoporum Collegii unitas atque communio, in Petri successore fundatae, atque per illa sanctissima loca, in quibus Apostolorum Principes martyrium subierunt, significatae, re et veritate exprimuntur; quarum theologicum, pastorale, sociale religiosumquc pondus nemo est qui ignoret.

Idem propterea institutum summis viribus praedicandum atque fovendum est, praesertim hoc historiae salutis tempore, quo Concilii Oecumenici Vaticani II doctrina et magisterium maiore usque lumine splendent.

APPENDIX II

The Collaborators of the Apostolic See as a Work Community

(cf. arts. 33–36)

1. The principal feature characterizing the revision of the Apostolic Constitution *Regimini Ecclesiae universae,* so that it might be adapted to the needs that arose after its promulgation, was certainly to emphasize the pastoral nature of the Roman Curia. Viewed in this way, the true char-

ADNEXUM II

De Apostolicae Sedis adiutoribus uti Laboris Communitate

de qua in articulis a 33 ad 36

1. Praecipua nota, cuius gratia Constitutio Apostolica a verbis incipiens *Regimini Ecclesiae universae* recognita est, ut necessitatibus accommodaretur, quae post ipsam promulgatam exortae erant, haec sane fuit: scilicet ut pastoralis

acter of the functions fulfilled in the midst, as it were, of the Apostolic See shines bright and clear, so that they provide the Supreme Pontiff with suitable instruments to carry out the mission entrusted to him by Christ Our Lord.

Through that unique ministry which he offers to the Church, the Supreme Pontiff strengthens his brothers in the faith (Lk 22:32)—the pastors, namely, and the Christian faithful of the universal Church—looking only to nourish and guard that Church communion in which "there are also particular Churches that retain their own traditions, without prejudice to the Chair of Peter which presides over the whole assembly of charity (cf. S. Ignatius M., *Ad Rom.*, pref., Funk, I, p. 252), and protects their legitimate variety and at the same time keeps watch to ensure that individual differences, so far from being harmful to unity, actually serve its cause." (*Lumen gentium,* 13)

2. By constant toil, this Petrine ministry reaches out to the whole world and claims the help of persons and other means throughout the Church. Help it does receive in a direct and privileged manner from all those who are called to perform various functions in the Roman Curia and in the various institutions which compose the structure of the Holy See, be they in holy orders as bishops and priests, or men and women consecrated to God in the religious families and secular institutes, or Christian lay men and women.

Out of this diversity emerge certain quite remarkable contours and the considerable importance of these duties, which have absolutely no equivalent at any other level of civil society, with which by its very nature indeed the Roman Curia cannot be compared. On this foundation stands that leading idea of the work community constituted by all those who, being well nourished with the one and the same faith and charity and "united, heart and soul" (Acts 4:32), make up those structures of collaboration just mentioned. Therefore those who under whatever title and in any manner help in the universal mission of the Supreme Pontiff to foster the Church community, have a further call to set up a communion of purpose, of undertakings, and of rules of behaviour, that deserves the name of *community* more than does any other form of grouping.

Curiae Romanae natura aequo in lumine collocaretur, atque ex hoc rerum prospectu propria niteret indoles illorum munerum, quae in Apostolica Sede veluti in proprio centro versantur ut eadem apta instrumenta praebeant ad Summi Pontificis missionem, ipsi a Christo Domino concreditam, exercendam.

Per illud enim ministerium, quod Summus Pontifex Ecclesiae praestat, fratres in fide Ipse confirmat (cfr. *Lc* 22, 32), scilicet Pastores et Christi fideles universalis Ecclesiae, ad id unice spectans ut ecclesiastica communio alatur atque protegatur: illam dicimus communionem, in qua «legitime adsunt Ecclesiae particulares, propriis traditionibus fruentes, integro manente primatu Petri Cathedrae, quae universo caritatis coetui praesidet[36], legitimas varietates tuetur et simul invigilat ut particularia, nedum unitati noceant, ei potius inserviant» (cfr. S. Ignatii M. *Ad Rom.*, Praef.: Funk, I, p. 252), (*Lumen Gentium*, 13).

2. Huic ministerio Petriano, quod in universum terrarum orbem assiduo labore protenditur, atque hominum et instrumentorum opem in tota Ecclesia requirit, adiutricem operam directa, immo nobiliore ratione ii omnes praestant, qui, variis muneribus addicti, in Romana Curia necnon in variis institutis adlaborant, quibus Apostolicae Sedis compositio ad agendum formatur: sive in episcopali vel in sacerdotali ordine constituti, sive qua Religiosarum Familiarum atque Institutorum Saecularium Deo consecrati viri et mulieres, sive utpote fideles utriusque sexus e laicorum ordine ad haec officia exercenda vocati.

Quam ob rem huiusmodi compositione peculiaria quaedam rerum lineamenta et grave officiorum momentum exoriuntur, quae nil prorsus aequale habent in ullo alio civilis societatis ambitu, cum qua Romana Curia suapte natura omnimodo comparari nequit: hic propterea principalis innititur ratio illius laboris communitatis ab iis omnibus constitutae, qui, una eademque fide caritateque nutriti veluti «cor unum et anima una» (*Act* 4, 32), illas memoratas adiutricis operae conformationes efficiunt. Ii igitur qui cooperando Romano Pontifici ecclesialem communitatem promoventi universalem Eius missionem quovis titulo vel modo adiuvant, etiam ad consiliorum propositorumque consuetudinem atque

3. The letter of Pope John Paul II of 20 November 1982 on the meaning of work performed for the Apostolic See, took pains to elaborate on the characteristics of this work community. The letter outlined its nature, unique and yet endowed with a variety of functions. All those who share in the "single, incessant activity of the Apostolic See," (n. 1); become in some way brothers. From this consideration the letter went on to conclude that those who shared in this work should be aware "of that specific character of their positions. In any case, such a consciousness has ever been the tradition and pride of those who have chosen to dedicate themselves to that noble service." *(ib.)*. The letter adds: "This consideration applies to clerics and religious and to laity as well; both to those who occupy posts of high responsibility and to office and manual workers to whom auxiliary functions are assigned" *(ib.)*.

The same letter points out the special nature of the Apostolic See, which, to preserve the exercise of spiritual freedom and its true and visible immunity, (cfr. n. 2) constitutes a sovereign State in its own right and yet "does not possess all ordinary characteristics of a political community," *(ib.)* different from all others. The practical results of this condition are seen in the operation of its affairs, especially as regards its economic organization. In the Apostolic See there is a total absence of a taxation system that other states have by right, and it has no economic activity producing goods and income. The "prime basis of sustenance of the Apostolic See is the spontaneous offerings" *(ib.)*, by reason of a certain universal interdependence emanating from the Catholic family and elsewhere, which to a marvellous degree expresses that communion of charity over which the Apostolic See presides in the world and by which it lives.

From this basic condition flow certain consequences on the practical level and in the behaviour among the staff of the Holy See—"the spirit of thrift," "a readiness always to take account of the real but limited financial possibilities of the Holy See and their source," "a profound trust in Providence." (cfn. n. 3) And, over and beyond all these qualities, "those who work for the Holy See must therefore

vitae normarum constabiliendam communionem vocantur, cui *communitatis* appellatio melius quam ceteris omnibus consortionibus competit.

3. Epistula Summi Pontificis Ioannis Pauli II de laboris significatione, qui Apostolicae Sedi praebetur, die xx mensis Novembris MCM-LXXXII in huiusmodi laboris communitatis proprietatibus illustrandis immorata est. Eius unicam, at diversis muneribus praeditam delineavit naturam, per quam ii omnes hac ratione efficiuntur quodammodo fratres, qui «unicam et continuam participant actionem Apostolicae Sedis» (n. 1); ex hac vero consideratione illata est necessitas, ut istiusmodi laboris participes conscii sint «huius peculiaris indolis munium suorum; quae conscientia ceteroqui sollemne semper fuit et laus iis, qui nobili huic servitio se dedere voluerunt» *(ib.)*. Epistula insuper addidit: «Haec animadversio tum ecclesiasticos, tum religiosos et laicos contingit; tum qui partes magnae rationis agunt, tum officiales et operosis artibus destinatos, quibus ministeria auxiliaria delegantur»[41].

Illic pariter propria commemorata est natura Sedis Apostolicae, quae, etsi Civitatem sui iuris constituit ut spiritualis eiusdem Sanctae Sedis libertatis exercitium ipsiusque vera et visibilis immunitas (cfn. n. 2) serventur, est «Status nulli alii Civitatum formae comparandus»[43], ab iisque diversus; atque huiusmodi condicionis delineati sunt in rerum ordine exitus, praesertim ad oeconomicam rationem quod attinet: etenim Apostolicae Sedi omnino desunt sive tributa, quae ex aliorum Civitatum iuribus manant, sive nummaria navitas reditus bonaque producens. Quam ob causam fit ut «caput primarium sustentationis Sedis Apostolicae efficiatur *ex donationibus voluntariis*» *(ib.)*, ratione universalis cuiusdam necessitudinis a catholicorum hominum familia, immo aliunde etiam exhibitae, quae illam caritatis communionem mirum in modum exprimit, cui Apostolica Sedes in mundo praesidet et ex qua vivit.

Ex hac condicione quaedam consequuntur in rerum usu et in cotidiana agendi ratione eorum, qui cum Sancta Sede adiutricem operam coniungunt: nempe «spiritus parsimoniae»[45], «studium semper animadvertendi veram atque eximiam rationem nummariam eiusdem Sedis Apostolicae necnon nummariae rei originem»,

have the profound conviction that their work above all entails an ecclesial responsibility to live in a spirit of authentic faith, and that the juridical-administrative aspects of their relationship with the Apostolic See stand in a particular light" (n.5).

4. The remuneration owed to the clerical and lay staff at the Holy See, according to their personal conditions of life, is regulated by the major principles of the social teachings of the Church, which have been made quite clear by the magisterium of the Popes from the time of the publication of Leo XIII's Encyclical Letter *Rerum novarum* up to John Paul II's Encyclicals *Laborem exercens* and *Sollicitudo rei socialis.*

While labouring under a grave lack of economic means, the Holy See makes every effort to measure up to the heavy obligations to which it is held with regard to its workers—even granting them certain benefit packages—but subject to that basic situation which is peculiar to the Apostolic See and has been explained in the Pope's Letter, the fact, namely, that the Holy See cannot be compared to any other form of State, since it is deprived of the ordinary means of generating income, except the income that comes from universal charity. However the Holy See is conscious of the fact—and the same Apostolic Letter makes this clear—that the active cooperation of everybody, and especially of the lay members of the staff, is necessary so that regulations and interrelations may be protected, as well as those *rights and duties* that arise out of "social justice" when it is correctly applied to the relations between worker and employer. (cfr. n. 4). On this subject, the Apostolic Letter has pointed out the help that workers associations can give in this respect, like the "Associazione Dipendenti Laici Vaticani," recently founded through productive talks among the various administrative levels to promote the spirit of solicitude and justice. The Apostolic Letter however has cautioned us to beware lest this kind of group distort the leading ideal that must govern the work community of the See of Peter. The letter says: "However, a lapse of this type of organization into the field of extremist conflict and class struggle does not correspond to the Church's social teaching. Nor should such associations have a political character or openly or covertly serve partisan interests or other interests with quite different goals." (n. 4).

«magna Providentia fiducia» (cfr. n. 3): atque, praeter omnes hasce dotes, ii qui «Sanctae Sedi serviunt persuasissimum habere debent laborem suum exigere ecclesialem obligationem vivendi ex spiritu verae fidei, ac partes iuridiciales et ad administrationem pertinentes necessitudinis cum Sede Apostolica, in luce peculiari consistere» (n. 5).

4. Laboris remuneratio, quae Sanctae Sedis cooperatoribus sive ecclesiasticis sive laicis debetur secundum proprias eorum vitae condiciones, principalibus doctrinae socialis Ecclesiae normis regitur, a Summorum Pontificum magisterio absolutissime declaratis, iam inde ab editis Litteris Encyclicis Leonis XIII a verbis *Rerum novarum* incipientibus usque ad Ioannis Pauli II Litteras Encyclicas *Laborem exercens* et *Sollicitudo rei socialis* appellatas.

Sancta Sedes, quamquam oeconomicorum bonorum penuria laborat, gravibus oneribus omnimode respondere nititur, quibus erga suos cooperatores tenetur. illis etiam quaedam rei cotidianae beneficia praestando. ratione tamen habita illius condicionis, Apostolicae Sedi propriae et in Summi Pontificis Epistula explanatae, qua ipsa nulli alii Civitatum formae aequanda est, cum communibus facultatibus redituum comparandorum privetur, nisi eorum qui ab universali caritate manant. Attamen Sancta Sedes sibi est conscia. atque eadem Epistula de hoc perspicue agit. actuosam sociam omnium operam, peculiari autem modo laicorum administrorum, necessariam esse ut rationes et normae, *iura atque officia* protegantur, quae ex «iustitia sociali», recte ad rem deducenda, in necessitudinibus operatorem inter et conductorem oriuntur[47]. Ad quae respiciendo, Epistula operam memoravit quam, ad hunc finem spectando, operatorum Societates praestare possunt, sicut «Consociatio Laicorum Vaticanorum Administrorum», tunc temporis recens orta ad sollicitudinis et iustitiae spiritum promovendum per frugiferum inter varios officiorum ordines colloquium. Epistula vero monuit cavendum esse, ne huiusmodi instituta principale consilium detorquerent, quo communitas laboris Petri Sedi praestandi regatur oportet, hisce verbis: «Non est tamen secundum Ecclesiae socialem doctrinam eiusmodi societates ad conflictationem

5. At the same time the Supreme Pontiff declared his firm conviction that associations of this kind—like the one mentioned above—"set forward work problems and develop continuous and constructive dialogue with the competent organisms [and] will not fail to take account in every case of the particular character of the Apostolic See." (n. 4).

Now since the lay staff of Vatican City had very much at heart that there be an ever more suitable fine-tuning of working conditions and of everything touching the labour question, the Supreme Pontiff provided that "suitable executive documents" be prepared "for forthering a work community according to the principles set forth by means of suitable norms and structures" (cfr. *ib.*).

The outcome of the Pope's concern is now "The Labour Office of the Apostolic See" (L.A.A.S.), which is established by an Apostolic Letter given *motu proprio* together with the document specifying in detail the membership of the Labour Office, its authority, its functions, its regulatory and advisory organs as well as its proper norms to facilitate a fair, rapid, and efficient process; furthermore, as it has been just newly set up, this Office needs a reasonable period of time to operate *ad experimentum* so that its regulations and procedures may be confirmed and its true and objective importance reviewed. This *motu proprio* and the regulations of the new Labour Office are being published at the same time, together with the promulgation of the Apostolic Constitution on the renewal of the Roman Curia.

6. The chief purpose of the Labour Office—apart from the practical ends for which it was brought into existence—is to promote and preserve a work community among the various levels of staff of the Apostolic See, especially the laypeople. The spirit of this community should be characteristic of all who have been called to the privilege and responsibility of serving the Petrine ministry.

praeter modum vergere aut ad ordinum inter ipsos dimicationem; nec nota politica insignes esse debent aut servire, aperte vel clam, causae alicuius factionis aut aliorum entium proposita spectantium valde diversae naturae» (n. 4).

5. Eodem autem tempore Summus Pontifex suam certam declaravit fidem, eiusmodi Consociationes—cuiusmodi est illa, quae supra commemorata est—«in ineundis quaestionibus ad laborem pertinentibus et in utiliter atque continuo disserendo cum Institutis competentibus, ante oculos esse habituras quoquo modo peculiarem Sedis Apostolicae naturam» (n. 4).

Quoniam autem laicis Civitatis Vaticanae administris cordi praesertim fuit, ut operum conformatio et omnia ad laboris quaestionem attinentia aptius usque temperarentur, Summus Pontifex disposuit ut «opportuna instrumenta exsecutoria» appararentur «ut, per accommodatas normas et structuras, foveatur profectus communitatis laboris iuxta exposita principia» (cfr. ib.).

Huic Supremi Ecclesiae Pastoris sollicitudini nunc respondet institutio «Officii Laboris apud Apostolicam Sedem» (compendiariis litteris U.L.S.A. appellati), quod per Litteras Apostolicas Motu Proprio datas promulgatur una cum instrumento, quo eiusdem Officii describuntur ac singillatim exponuntur compositio, auctoritas, munera, regendi et consulendi organa cum propriis normis ad aequum, efficacem celeremque ipsius processum fovendum; idem praeterea Officium, cum nunc noviter erectum sit, accommodum navitatis tempus «ad experimentum» exigit, ut sive collata praecepta agendique modi comprobentur, sive eius momentum re et veritate recognoscatur. Quae Apostolicae Litterae Motu Proprio datae atque novi Officii Laboris disciplina simul in vulgus eduntur una cum promulgata Constitutione Apostolica de Curiae Romanae renovatione[51].

6. Laboris Officii praecipuus praevalensque finis—praeter alios, ad quorum assecutionem idem ad rem effectum est—huc potissimum spectat ut in variis adiutorum Sedis Apostolicae ordinibus, laicorum praesertim, illa promoveatur ac servetur laboris communitas, cuius nota omnes insigniri debent, qui ad honorem onusque inserviendi ministerio Petriano vocati sunt.

Again and again it is to be explained that these workers are in duty bound to foster and cultivate within themselves a special awareness of the Church, an awareness making them ever more fitted to fulfill the functions entrusted to them, no matter what these may be. These functions are not mere give and take arrangements—a certain labour given and a certain wage received—, as may happen in institutions in civil society; they constitute rather a service offered to Christ himself "who came not to be served but to serve" (Mt 20:28).

Therefore all the workers of the Holy See, clergy and laity, out of a sense of honour and sincerely conscious of their own duty before God and themselves, must resolve that their lives as priests and lay faithful shall be lived at an exemplary level, as is proposed by God's commandments, by the laws of the Church and by the pronouncements of the Second Vatican Council, especially in *Lumen gentium, Presbyterorum ordinis,* and *Apostolicam actuositatem.* However, this is a free decision, by which with full awareness certain responsibilities are taken on, the force of which is felt not only on the individuals but also on their families and even on the actual work community composed of all the collaborators of the Holy See.

"Well may we be asked 'of whose spirit we are' (cf. Lk 9:55 *Vulg.*)": thus the Pope writes at the end of the Apostolic Letter. So each and all, in searching their own sincerity as human beings and as Christians, are bound to be faithful to those promises, and to keep those bonds that they freely accepted when they were chosen to labour at the Holy See.

7. To keep in view the principles and norms indicated by the Pope in the afore-mentioned Apostolic Letter to the cardinal secretary of state, the full text is printed below. In fact, this document must be considered as the foundation and sign of the whole pattern of interdependence in order to maintain full cooperation and understanding within the work community at the service of the Apostolic See.

Iterum iterumque explicandum est, hosce adiutores ad peculiarem Ecclesiae conscientiam in se ipsis fovendam atque colendam teneri, quae eos ad munera sibi commissa adimplenda, quantacumque sint, aptiores usque reddat: munera dicimus, quae prorsus non sunt cuiusdam dati et accepti rationes, sicut illae, quae cum institutis in civili societate exstantibus intercedere possunt, sed ministerium efficiunt ipsi Christo praebitum, qui «non venit ministrari, sed ministrare» (*Mt* 20, 28).

Omnes ergo Sanctae cooperatores, sive ecclesiastici sive laici, velut ob honoris laudem comparandam, atque sincero animo proprii muneris coram Deo et hominibus conscii, sibi proponere debent ut suam sacerdotum et Christi fidelium vitam in exempli modum agant, sicut a Dei mandatis, ab ecclesiasticis legibus et ab actis Concilii Vaticani II, praesertim illis quae a verbis incipiunt *Lumen gentium, Presbyterorum ordinis* atque *Apostolicam actuositatem,* proponitur. Attamen hoc liberum est consilium, quo plena conscientia quaedam assumuntur onera, quorum momentum non modo in singulos, sed etiam in illorum familias, immo in ipsum laboris communitatis ambitum recidit, quem Sanctae Sedis cooperatores efficiunt.

«Quaerendum nobis est "cuius spiritus simus" (cfr. *Lc* 9, 55 *Vulg.*)»: ita Summus Pontifex in extrema Epistula scribit; ideo singuli atque omnes, propriam qua hominum et qua christianorum sinceritatem quaerendo, tenentur ad illa promissa vinculaque fideliter servanda, quibus libera voluntate obstricti sunt cum ad operam Sanctae Sedi praestandam sunt adlecti.

7. Quo praesentior consiliorum et normarum ratio habeatur, quae Summus Pontifex per memoratam Epistulam, ad Cardinalem a Publicis Ecclesiae negotiis missam, de laboris significatione Apostolicae Sedi praebendi significavit, ipsius integrum exemplum infra editur[52]: ea enim fundamentum et signum habenda est omnis illius necessitudinis, quae intra laboris communitatis ambitum, Apostolicae Sedi adiutricem operam navantis, ad simul agendum atque ad consensionem tuendam habeatur oportet.

LETTER OF THE
SUPREME PONTIFF JOHN PAUL II

The Meaning of Work Performed by
the Apostolic See

Addressed to the Venerable Brother
Agostino Cardinal Casaroli
Secretary of State

1. The Apostolic See, in exercising its mission, has re-course to the valid and precious work of the particular community made up of those men and women, priests, religious and laity who devote their efforts in their dicasteries and offices to the service of the universal Church.

Charges and duties are assigned to the members of this community; each of those charges and duties has its own purpose and dignity, in consideration both of the objective content and value of the work done and of the person who accomplishes it.

This concept of community, applied to those who aid the bishop of Rome in his ministry as pastor of the universal Church, permits us first of all to define the unitary character of functions which are nonetheless diverse among themselves. All persons called to perform them really participate in the single, incessant activity of the Apostolic See; that is, in that "concern for all the Churches" (cf. 2 Cor. 11:28) which enlivened the apostles' service from the earliest times and is the prerogative today in outstanding measure of the successors of St. Peter in the Roman See. It is very important that those who are associated in any way with the Apostolic See's activity should have a consciousness of that specific character of their positions. In any case, such a consciousness has ever been the tradition and pride of those who have chosen to dedicate themselves to that noble service.

This consideration applies to clerics and religious and to laity as well, both to those who hold posts of high responsibility, and to office and manual workers to whom auxiliary functions are assigned. It applies to persons attached to the service of the same Apostolic See more directly, inasmuch as they work in those organisms which are altogether known in fact under the name of "Holy See;" and it applies to those who are in the service of the Vatican City State, which is so closely linked with the Apostolic See.

In the recent Encyclical *Laborem exercens,* I recalled the principal truths of the "gospel of labour" and Catholic doc-

EPISTULA SUMMI PONTIFICIS
IOANNIS PAULI II

De laboris significatione
qui Apostolicae Sedi praebetur

Venerabili Fratri
Augustino S.R.E. Cardinali Casaroli
Status Secretario

1. APOSTOLICA SEDES, in suo munere ex-ercendo, efficaci et perutili opera utitur pecu-liaris communitatis ex iis constantis—viris et mulieribus, sacerdotibus, religiosis, laicis—qui, in eius dicasteriis et officiis, Ecclesiae universae operam navant.

Huius communitatis membris negotia man-data sunt et munia, quorum quodque suum spectat propositum suamque dignitatem habet, ratione habita tum rerum substantiae momen-tique explicati laboris, tum personae quae illum exsequitur.

Ex hac communitatis notione adhibita pro iis qui Romanum Episcopum adiuvant in suo Pastoris universalis Ecclesiae ministerio, Nobis licet ante omnia definire unicam in *diversis muneribus naturam.* Omnes enim qui ad haec ex-plenda vocantur, unicam et continuam partici-pant actionem Apostolicae Sedis, eam videlicet «sollicitudinem omnium Ecclesiarum» (cfr. 2 Cor 11, 28), quae inde a priscis temporibus servitium Apostolorum incitabat, quaeque hodie prae-cipua est praerogativa Successorum Sancti Petri in sede Romana. Multum interest quotquot Sedis Apostolicae operum quoquo modo par-ticipes sunt, huius peculiaris indolis munium suorum sibi esse conscios; quae conscientia ceteroqui sollemne semper fuit et laus iis, qui nobili huic servitio se dedere voluerunt.

Haec animadversio tum ecclesiasticos et re-ligiosos tum laicos contingit, tum qui partes magnae rationis agunt, tum officiales et operosis artibus destinatos, quibus ministeria auxiliaria delegantur. Contingit prorsus eos et qui recte proximeque Apostolicae Sedi serviunt, utpote cum suam navent operam apud ea Corpora, cui nomen est «Sancta Sedes», et qui in ministeriis sunt Vaticanae Civitatis, quae Apostolicae Sedi tam arcte coniungitur.

In recentibus Litteris Encyclicis a verbis «Laborem exercens» incipientibus praecipuas

trine on human work, a doctrine always alive in the Church's tradition. There is need for the life of that singular community which operates *sub umbra Petri*—in Peter's shadow—, in such immediate contact with the Apostolic See, to conform itself to these truths.

2. In order to apply these principles to reality, their objective significance must be borne in mind, together with the specific nature of the Apostolic See. This latter does not have the general form of true states even though, as I noted above, the entity described as the Vatican City State is closely linked with it; for true states are subjects of the political sovereignty of particular societies. On the other hand, the Vatican City State is sovereign, yet does not possess all ordinary characteristics of a political community. It is an atypical state. It exists as a fitting means of guaranteeing the exercise of the spiritual liberty of the Apostolic See; that is, as the means of assuring real and visible independence of the same in its activity of government for the sake of the universal Church, as well as of its pastoral work directed toward the whole human race. It does not possess a proper society for the service of which it was established nor does it base itself upon forms of social action which usually determine the structure and organization of every other state. Furthermore, the persons who aid the Apostolic See or even cooperate in government of the Vatican City State are with few exceptions not citizens of this state. Nor, consequently, do they have the rights and duties (those to do with taxation in particular) which ordinarily arise from belonging to a state.

The Apostolic See does not develop nor can it develop economic activity proper to a state, since it transcends the narrow confines of the Vatican City State in a much more important respect and extends its mission to the whole of the earth. Production of economic goods and enrichment by way of revenues are foreign to its institutional purposes. Besides the revenues of the Vatican City State and the limited income afforded by what remains of the funds obtained on the occasion of the Lateran Pacts as indemnity for the Papal States. and ecclesiastical goods passed to the Italian State, the prime basis of sustenance of the Apostolic See is the spontaneous offerings provided by Catholics throughout the world and by other men of good will. This corresponds to a tradition having its origin in the Gospel and the teachings of the apostles. This tradition has taken on various forms over the centuries in relation to the eco-

commemoravimus veritates de «evangelio laboris» deque doctrina catholica ad laborem humanum pertinente, semper sane in Ecclesiae traditionis valida. Ad has veritates oportet se conformet peculiaris haec communitas quae *sub umbra Petri* operatur, tam cum Sede Apostolica coniuncte.

2. Ut apte haec principia rebus ipsis inserantur, necesse est reminisci eorum veram significationem et simul *propriam* Sedis Apostolicae *naturam*. Haec—etsi, ut iam supra diximus, ei tam arcte coniungitur ens Vaticanae Civitatis Status dictum—indole caret germanorum Statuum, qui in certas societates publice dominantur. Ceterum Vaticanae Civitatis Status sui iuris est, sed non omnes habet peculiares communitatis politicae notas. Hic Status nulli alii Civitatum formae comparandus est: exsistit enim ut convenienter tueatur Sedis Apostolicae spiritualis libertatis exercitium, id est tamquam instrumentum, quo tuta reddatur eiusdem Sedis vera et visibilis libertas tum in regimine exercendo pro Ecclesia universa, tum etiam in actione pastorali explicanda pro toto genere humano; propriam non habet societatem pro cuius servitio constitutus sit, nec in formis actionis socialis consistit, quae efficiunt plerumque cuiusvis alterius Status structuram et ordinationem. Praeterea, qui Sedem Apostolicam adiuvant, vel Vaticanae Civitatis Status regimini cooperantur, ipsius cives non sunt, perpaucis exceptis, nec igitur iura et onera habent (praesertim vectigalia), quae fere ex eo oriuntur, quod quis in dicione est alicuius Status.

Sedes Apostolica—cum ob valde maioris momenti causas fines angustos transcendat Vaticanae Civitatis Statum, adeo ut in omnem orbem terrarum munus suum extendat—operositatem oeconomicam Status cuiuslibet propriam nec explet nec potest explere; ab eius institutionis propositis et fructus bonorum oeconomicorum et redituum amplificatio excluduntur. Praeter proventus Vaticanae Civitatis Status proprios et exiguos reditus—constantes ex eo quod reliquum est pecuniarum occasions Pactionum Lateranensium obtentarum uti compensationem Statuum Pontificiorum et bonorum ecclesiasticorum, quae Statui Italico obvenerant—caput primarium sustentationis Sedis Apostolicae efficitur *ex donationibus voluntariis* catholicorum totius

nomic structures prevailing in various eras. In conformity with that tradition it must be affirmed that the Apostolic See may and ought to make use of the spontaneous contributions of the faithful and other people of good will, without having recourse to other means which might appear to be less respectful of the character proper to the Apostolic See.

3. The above-mentioned material contributions are the expression of a constant and moving solidarity with the Apostolic See and the activity carried out by it. My profound gratitude goes out to such great solidarity. It ought to be with a sense of responsibility commensurate with the nature of the contributions on the part of the Apostolic See itself, its individual organs and the persons working in them. That is to say that the contributions are to be used solely and always according to the dispositions and will of those offering them: for the general intention which is maintenance of the Apostolic See and the generality of its activities or for particular purposes (missionary, charitable, etc.), when these have been expressly mentioned.

Responsibility and loyalty toward those who show their solidarity with the Apostolic See through their aid and share its pastoral concern in some way are expressed in scrupulous fidelity to all tasks and duties assigned, as well as in the zeal, hard work and professional spirit which ought to distinguish whoever participates in the same Apostolic See's activities. Right intention must likewise be always cultivated, so as to exert watchful administration—in terms of their purposes—over both material goods which are offered and over what is acquired or conserved by means of such goods. This includes safeguarding and enhancing the See of Peter's precious inheritance in the religious-cultural and artistic fields.

In making use of means allocated for these ends, the Apostolic See and those directly collaborating with it must be distinguished not only by a spirit of thrift, but also by readiness always to take account of the real but limited financial possibilities of the Holy See and their source. Obviously such interior dispositions of mind ought to be well assimilated, becoming ingrained in the minds of religious and clerics through their training. But neither should they

mundi et, forte, aliorum hominum bonae voluntatis. Hoc consentaneum est traditioni quae ab Evangelio proficiscitur (cfr. Lc 10, 7) et ab Apostolorum doctrina (cfr. 1 Cor 9, 11. 14). Secundum hanc traditionem—quae multiformis per saecula fuit ad structuras oeconomicas quod attinet diversis temporibus praevalentes—affirmandum est Sedem Apostolicam posse et debere collationibus ultroneis frui fidelium aliorumque hominum bonae voluntatis, cum non oporteat aliis fruatur opibus, quae videri possint eius singulari naturae minus convenientes.

3. *Collationes* quas supra commemoravimus constantem et animum moventem necessitudinem cum Apostolica Sede cumque eius opera significant. Tantae necessitudini, quam gratissimo animo prosequimur, ipsa Apostolica Sedes, singula eius Corpora et qui in his laborant respondere debent officii conscientia exaequata collationum naturae, quae solum et semper adhibendae sunt iuxta intentiones et voluntates largitorum: vel pro proposito generali Sedem Apostolicam eiusque operum summam sustentandi; vel pro specialibus consiliis (missionalibus, beneficis, etc.), cum haec denuntiata sint.

Officii conscientia et probitas erga eos qui, auxilio suo, Sedem Apostolicam adiuvant et quodam modo pastoralem eius sollicitudinem communicant, ostenduntur per integram fidelitatem erga officia et munera delegata, sicut et per diligentiam, sedulitatem et per habitum professionis, unde discernendi sunt quicumque eiusdem Sedis Apostolicae navitatem participant. Oportet insuper recte animatos esse, ut prudenter administrentur, ex iis ad quae spectant, et bona corporea quae offeruntur, et ea omnia quae his bonis illa Sedes comparat vel servat, additis tutela et auctu praestantis hereditatis Sedis Petri in regionibus religioso-culturalibus et artis.

In usu opum haec proposita contingentium, Sedes Apostolica et qui cum ea directe et proxime cooperantur, eminere debent non solum *spiritu parsimoniae*, verum etiam *studio semper animadvertendi* veram atque exiguam rationem nummariam eiusdem Sedis Apostolicae necnon nummariae rei originem. Eiusmodi interiores habitus, ut par est, insiti esse debebunt per eo-

be lacking from the minds of laity who through their free choice accept working for and with the Apostolic See.

Moreover, all those who have particular responsibilities in running organisms, offices and services of the Apostolic See, as well as those employed in various functions, will know how to join this spirit of thrift with constant application to making the various activities ever more effective. This can be done through organization of work based, on the one hand, on full respect for persons and the valid contribution made by each according to his proper abilities and functions and, on the other hand, upon use of appropriate structures and technical means, so that the activity engaged in corresponds more and more to the demands of service to the universal Church. Recourse shall be had to everything that experience, science and technology teach; efforts will be made in this way to use human and financial resources with greater effectiveness by avoiding waste, self-interest and pursuit of unjustified privileges, and at the same time by promoting good human relations in every sector and the true and rightful interests of the Apostolic See.

Along with such commitment should go a profound trust in Providence, which, through the offerings of good people, will not allow a lack of the means to pursue the Apostolic See's proper ends. Should a lack of means impede accomplishment of some fundamental objective, a special appeal may be made to the generosity of the people of God, informing them of needs which are not sufficiently well known. In the normal way, however, it is fitting to be content with what bishops, priests, religious institutes and faithful offer spontaneously, since they themselves can see or discern rightful needs.

4. Many of those working with the Apostolic See are clerics. Since they live in celibacy, they have no families to their charge. They deserve remuneration proportional to the tasks performed and capable of assuring them a decent manner of living and means to carry out the duties of their state, including responsibilities which they may have in certain cases toward parents or other family members dependent on them. Nor should the demands of orderly social relationships be neglected, particularly and above all their obligation to assist the needy. This obligation is more impelling for clerics and religious than for the laity, by reason of their evangelical vocation.

rum aptam formationem, in religiosorum et ecclesiasticorum animis; sed, ne laicis quidem deesse debent, qui libero assensu suo comprobaverunt se cum et pro Sede Apostolica laborare.

Insuper, ii omnes, quibus peculiaria onera iniuncta sunt in regendis Corporibus, officiis et ministeriis Sedis Apostolicae, sicut et variis muneribus addicti, hunc parsimoniae spiritum cum constante cura coniungent ut numerosa negotia efficientiora reddantur per congruam dispositionem laboris, positi hinc in plena observantia personarum et praesentis auxilii, quod quisque fert pro suis facultatibus, et muniis; hinc in usu structurarum et instrumentorum technicorum aptorum, quo opera explicata melius in dies servitii Ecclesiae universae necessitatibus respondeat. Omnia adhibentes quae experientia, scientia et technologia docent, omnes curabunt ut bona humana et nummaria maiore cum efficacia tractentur, profusionem vitando et conquisitionem utilitatum singularium, privilegiorum non excusatorum, simul bonas necessitudines humanas provehendo in omni parte et iustum Sedis Apostolicae commodum.

Ad has curas adiungenda est magna *Providentiae fiducia*, quae per bonorum donationes non sinet opes deficere, quibus Sedis Apostolicae proposita possint obtineri. Si opum penuria impediat quominus aliquod fondamentale consilium ad effectum adducatur, speciali modo compellanda erit munificentia populi Dei, eum certiorem faciendo de non satis notis necessitatibus. Plerumque tamen oportebit acquiescere in iis, quae Episcopi, sacerdotes, Instituta religiosa et fideles sponte offerunt, quoniam ipsi iustas necessitates videre vel perspicere sciunt.

4. Inter eos qui Sedi Apostolicae cooperantur multi sunt ecclesiastici, quibus in caelibatu viventibus impensa pro familiis non est praestanda. Merces ad eos spectat muneribus quae explent conveniens talisque, quae decoram sustentationem provideat et sinat eos status sui officia exsequi simulque iis satisfacere oneribus, quibus interdum gravari possunt, subveniendi videlicet parentibus suis vel aliis propinquis, qui eis sustinendi sunt. Nec neglegenda sunt ea, quae rectus eorum usus socialis postulat, praesertim et ante omnia officium succurrendi indigentibus: quod officium, ob eorum evangeli-

Remuneration of the lay employees of the Apostolic See should also correspond to the tasks performed, taking into consideration at the same time their responsibility to support their families. Study should therefore be devoted, in a spirit of lively concern and justice, to ascertaining their objective material needs and those of their families, including needs regarding education of their children and suitable provision for old age, so as to meet those needs properly. The fundamental guidelines in this sector are to be found in Catholic teaching on remuneration for work. Immediate indications for the evaluation of circumstances can be obtained from examining experiences and programs of the society—in particular, the Italian society—to which almost all lay employees of the Apostolic See belong and in which they at any rate live.

A valid collaborative function may be performed by workers' associations such as the Association of Vatican Lay Employees, which recently came into existence, in promoting that spirit of concern and justice, through representing those working within the Apostolic See. Such associations take on a specific character within the Apostolic See. They are an initiative in conformity with the Church's social teaching, for the Church sees them as one instrument for better assuring social justice in relations between worker and employer. However, a lapse of this type of organization into the field of extremist conflict and class struggle does not correspond to the Church's social teaching. Nor should such associations have a political or openly or covertly serve partisan interests or other interests with quite different goals.

I express confidence that associations such as that now existing and just mentioned will perform a useful function in the work community, operating in solid harmony with the Apostolic See, by taking inspiration from the principles of the Church's social teaching. I am likewise certain that as they set forward work problems and develop continuous and constructive dialogue with the competent organisms they will not fail to take account in every case of the particular character of the Apostolic See, as pointed out in the initial part of this letter.

In relation to what has been expounded, Your Emi-

cam vocationem, magis ecclesiasticos et religiosos impellit, quam laicos.

Merces etiam laicorum, qui Sedi Apostolicae serviunt, consentanea esse debet muniis explicatis, onere simul considerato, ab eis suscepto, sustinendi familias suas. Magnae curae et iustitiae spiritu igitur videndum est quae sint eorum verae materiales necessitates et familiarum, non exceptis iis quae ad filiorum educationem et ad oeconomicam cautionem ad senectuti cavendum pertinent, ut eisdem convenienter consuli possit. Hac in re normae fundamentales in catholica doctrina inveniuntur de *remuneratione laboris*. Normae proximae ad adiuncta iudicanda possunt ex observations experientiarum et consiliorum civilis societatis depromi, et praesertim societatis Italicae, ex qua conducuntur et in qua, quoquo modo, omnes fere vivunt laici qui Sedi Apostolicae serviunt.

Ad hunc sollicitudinis et iustitiae spiritum fovendum, vice fungentes eorum qui intra Sedem Apostolicam laborant, poterunt suum praestare officium operatorum Societates, sicut Consociatio Laicorum Vaticanorum Administrorum recenter orta, quae intra Sedem Apostolicam indole propria praeditae sunt, inceptum sunt doctrinae sociali Ecclesiae congruens, quae eas iudicat aptum subsidium esse ad tutam reddendam *iustitiam socialem* in necessitudinibus operatorem inter et conductorem. Non est tamen secundum Ecclesiae socialem doctrinam eiusmodi societates ad conflictationem praeter modum vergere aut ad ordinum inter ipsos dimicationem; nec nota politica insignes esse debent aut servire, aperte vel clam, causae alicuius factionis aut aliorum entium proposita spectantium valde diversae naturae.

Confidimus eiusmodi Consociationes, sicut ea est quam supra memoravimus—doctrinae socialis Ecclesiae principia sequentes—utile opus esse explicaturas in communitate laboris concorditer operante cum Sede Apostolica. Pro certo etiam habemus easdem, in ineundis quaestionibus ad laborem pertinentibus et in utiliter atque continuo disserendo cum Institutis competentibus, ante oculos esse habituras quoquo modo peculiarem Sedis Apostolicae naturam, sicut dictum est in prima huius Epistulae parte.

Quod ad ea attinet, quae exposuimus, Emi-

nence will wish to prepare suitable executive documents for furthering a work community according to the principles set forth by means of suitable norms and structures.

5. I emphasized in the Encyclical *Laborem exercens* that the worker's personal dignity requires expression in a particular relationship with the work entrusted to him. This relationship is objectively realizable in various ways according to the kind of work undertaken. It is realized subjectively when the worker lives it as "his own," even though he is working "for wages." Since the work in question here is performed within the Apostolic See and is therefore marked by the characteristics already mentioned, such a relationship calls for heartfelt sharing in that "concern for all the Churches" which is proper to the Chair of Peter.

Those who work for the Holy See must therefore have the profound conviction that their work above all entails an ecclesial responsibility to live in a spirit of authentic faith, and that the juridical-administrative aspects of their relationship with the Apostolic See stand in a particular light.

The Second Vatican Council provided us with copious teaching on the way in which all Christians, clerics, religious and laity can and ought to make such ecclesial concern their own.

So it seems necessary for all, especially those working with the Apostolic See, to deepen personal consciousness above all of the universal apostolic commitment of Christians and that arising from each one's specific vocation: that of the bishop, of the priest, of religious, of the laity. The answers to the present difficulties in the field of human labor are to be sought in the sphere of social justice. But they must also be sought in the area of an interior relationship with the work that each is called upon to perform. It seems evident that work—of whatever kind—carried out in the employment of the Apostolic See requires this in a quite special measure.

Besides the deepened interior relationship, this work calls for reciprocal respect, if it is to be advantageous and serene, based on human and Christian brotherhood by all and for all concerned. Only when it is allied with such brotherhood (that is, with love of man in truth), can justice manifest itself as true justice. We must try to find "of what spirit we are" (cf. Lk. 9:55, Vulg.).

nentia Tua opportuna instrumenta exsecutoria praeparabit ut, per accommodatas normas et structuras, foveatur profectus communitatis laboris iuxta exposita principia.

5. In Litteris Encyclicis a verbis «Laborem exercens» incipientibus monuimus dignitatem operatoris propriam exprimendam esse per specialem necessitudinem cum labore ei concredito. Ad hanc necessitudinem—quae ipsa per se multis modis fieri potest pro suscepti laboris genere—pervenitur subiective cum operator, quamvis operam exerceat «remuneratam», eam tamen exercet ut «propriam». Cum hic agatur de labore in ambitu Sedis Apostolicae exanclato ideoque fundamentali proprietate insignito, quae est supra memorata, haec necessitudo ardentem illam participationem postulat «sollicitudinis omnium Ecclesiarum», quae propria est Cathedrae Petri.

Qui itaque Sanctae Sedi serviunt persuasissimum habere debent laborem suum exigere ecclesialem obligationem vivendi ex spiritu verae fidei, ac partes iuridiciales et ad administrationem pertinentes necessitudinis cum Sede Apostolica, in luce peculiari consistere.

Concilium Vaticanum II multa nos docuit de ratione, qua omnes christiani, ecclesiastici, religiosi et laici, possunt—et debent—hanc ecclesialem sollicitudinem ad se revocare.

Oportere igitur videtur ut, praesertim ab iis qui Sedi Apostolicae cooperantur, *personalis* exacuatur conscientia, imprimis christianorum sedulitatis universalis simulque vocationis propriae cuiusque, sive episcopi, sive sacerdotis, sive religiosi, sive laici. Responsiones enim ad hodiernas difficultates in laboris humani provincia quaerendae sunt in finibus iustitiae socialis; sed sunt etiam quaerendae in interiore congruentia cum labore, quem quisque debet perficere. Patere videtur laborem—qualiscumque is est—sub potestate Sedis Apostolicae explicatum, id modo omnino singulari postulare.

Praeter altiorem congruentiam interiorem, hic labor, ut sit utilis et serenus, poscit mutuam observantiam, fraterna sodalitate nisam humana et christiana, ab omnibus et pro omnibus qui in illum incumbunt. Tum solum iustitia potest se aperire uti veram iustitiam, cum huic *fraternae sodalitati* coniungitur (id est amori erga

These latter questions have hardly been touched on here. They cannot be adequately formulated in administrative-juridical terms. This does not exempt us, however, from the search and effort necessary for making operative precisely within the circle of the Apostolic See that spirit of human work which comes from our Lord Jesus Christ.

As I entrust these thoughts, Most Reverend Cardinal, to your attentive consideration, I call down an abundance of the gifts of divine assistance upon the future commitment which putting them into practice requires. At the same time I impart my benediction to you from my heart and willingly extend it to all those who offer their meritorious service to the Apostolic See.

From the Vatican, 20 November 1982.

John Paul II

hominem in veritate praebito). Quaerendum nobis est «cuius spiritus simus» (cf. Lc 9, 55 Vulg.).

Hae quaestiones, quas postremo memoravimus, non possunt aeque enuntiari verbis iuridicialibus et ad administrationem pertinentibus. Hoc tamen non eximit inquisitione et nisu necessariis—et quidem in Sedis Apostolicae ambitu—ad efficientem reddendum illum humani laboris spiritum, qui a Domino nostro Iesu Christo proficiscitur.

Dum tibi, Venerabilis Frater, has cogitationes considerandas propronimus, pro futuro studio quod eaedem postulant, ut ad effectum adducantur, dona invocamus auxilii divini copiosa, tibique ex pectore Nostram impertimus Benedictionem, quam libenter etiam concedimus iis omnibus, qui bene meritam operam suam Sedi Apostolicae insumunt.

Ex Aedibus Vaticanis, die xx mensis Novembris, anno MCMLXXXII.

Ioannes Paulus PP. II

APPENDIX 3

ACCESS TO THE SOURCES

ACCESS TO THE SOURCES

MANNER OF REFERENCE TO SOURCES

Firstly, inasmuch as it is possible, reference is made to the sources closest to those from which the texts of the canon were drawn. There follow citations of more recent documents that correspond to these sources.

After the hyphen [-] are placed sources drawn from the full breadth of the history of the Church, among which the "Sacred Canons" hold first place, arranged in the order established by the second canon of the Quinisext Council. After the canons of the Council of Nicea II are listed the sources from the acts of the Roman Pontiffs, from ecumenical councils celebrated after Nicea II, and also from the dicasteries of the Roman Curia in chronological order.

After the asterisk [*] are listed sources drawn from documents of particular law of the individual Eastern Churches drawn especially from acts of the preeminent synods which were lawfully celebrated in former times. Note that in the canons on trials, reference is not made to the decrees of these synods, since the sources for the individual sections of canons can be easily found in the editions of these same decrees.

After the carat [▲] are found sources of Byzantine civil law, mentioned above in the *Presentation*.

Terms placed between quotation marks [" "] in the manner used in the parts of Eastern Catholic law promulgated before Vatican II, indicate the first word of the paragraph, a tool especially useful to identify sources drawn from longer documents whose texts lack more clear divisions.

THE DIFFERING VALUE OF THE SOURCES

Generally speaking, sources included in this edition of the *Codex Canonum Ecclesiarum Orientalium*, even if often drawn from a variety of historical and theological-juridical contexts, as is appropriate, rather directly refer to the text of the canons. The task of evaluating the real relation of a source to a given canon which could be characterized as contrary is left to scholars of canonical matters. This sometimes occurs in certain sections of the Code (e.g., in canons on the election of patriarchs, on the administration of chrismation with holy myron or on the sacrament of the Divine Eucharist, etc.). It is not easy to evaluate the level of agreement of the sources with the canons of the Code nor did it seem useful to indicate this by the placement of a sign in the sources, even though several attempts were in fact made. However sources contrary to the norms of the Code should not be lost, not only as an aid for canonical science, but also to perceive from these same sources the perennial care of the Church, holding salvation of souls most zealously before its eyes, with respect to those things which concern merely clearly ecclesiastical laws and their adaptation to modern circumstances.

EDITIONS OF SOURCES

1. With regard to the "Sacred Canons," there are many editions that can be easily consulted. Nevertheless, in this book the reader is referred solely to the edition, which in 1962–1963, was published by the Pontifical Commission for the Redaction of the Code of Eastern Canon Law, by the care of P. P.

Ioannou, in fascicle IX of the collection entitled *Fonti,* which comprise the following volumes: Tome I, Part I, *Les canons des Conciles Oecuméniques;* b) Tome I, Part II, *Les canons des Synods Particuliers;* c) Tome II, *Les canons des Pères Grecs;* d) *Index analytique.* Note that in this edition are also included canons from the eighth ecumenical council, that is, Constantinople IV (869), which are generally not found in the collections of the "Sacred Canons."

2. Sources from the acts of the Roman Pontiffs until Eugenius IV are cited from the collection entitled *Fontes Series III* which is divided into fifteen volumes. This collection was published by the Pontifical Commission for the Redaction of the Code of Eastern Canon Law and then, after 1972, by the Pontifical Commission for the Revision of the Code of Eastern Canon Law, except some acts contained in volume I of the collection which is mentioned in the following number.

3. A large number of sources taken from the acts of the Roman Pontiffs and the dicasteries of the curia are found in the collection entitled *Codicis Iuris Canonici Fontes,* edited by cardinals P. Gasparri (vol. I–VI) and J. Serédi (vol. VII–IX) and published in 1926–1939.

4. In finding sources which were taken from the acts of ecumenical councils celebrated after Constantinople IV (869), with few exceptions any edition in Latin can be used; these exceptions are specially indicated in the proper places below.

5. More recent sources after 1908 are generally taken from documents published in the official commentary *Acta Apostolicae Sedis* and may be found there easily in the usual manner. However the editions of sources, which are not found in this commentary are indicated in the individual canons below.

6. There are added indications of sources which are taken from some authors not found in the above-mentioned editions, but which are referred to in several canons of the Code, as well as from the acts of the synods of individual Eastern Churches as follows:

Individual Authors

Rabbula, F. Nau, *Les Canons et les résolutions canoniques de Rabbulas,* Paris, 1906, pp. 83–91.

S. Athanasius Athonita, Ph. Meyer, *Die Haupturkunden für die Geschichte der Athosklöster,* Leipzig, 1894: *Typicum,* pp. 102–122; *Diatyposis,* pp. 123–130; *Hypotyposis,* pp. 130–140.

S. Basilius M.

    Regulae fusius tractatae, Migne PG, 31, 889–1052.

    Regulae brevius tractatae, Migne PG, 31, 1080–1305.

S. Nerses Glaiensis, *ep. past.,* a. 1666, J. Cappelletti, *Sancti Nersetis Claiensis Armenorum Catholici Opera,* vol. I, Venetiis, 1933, pp. 92–172.

S. Nicephorus CP., *Ex eiusdem typico excerpti canones,* Pitra, II, pp. 327–348.

S. Pachomius, *Regulae,* Migne PL, 23, 61–88.

S. Saba, *Typicum,* Ed. Kurtz, in *Byzantinische Zeitschrift,* 3 (1894) 168–170.

S. Tarasius CP., *ep. ad Epp. Siciliae,* Pitra, II, pp. 309–313.

S. Theodorus Studita

    Epistolae:

        a) libri I et II, Migne PG, 99, 904–1669;

        b) ceterae in Mai A. Cozza-Luzzi, *Nova Patrum Bibliotheca,* tomus VIII, pars I, Romae, 1871, pp. 1–244.

    Testamentum, Migne PG, 99, 1813–1824.

    Orationes XI et XII, Migne PG, 99, 803–880.

    Sermones, A. Mai -Cozza Luzzi, *Nova Patrum Bibliotheca [Scriptorum veterum nova collectio e Vaticanis codicibus edita],* Romae, 1852–1905, tomus X, pars I, pp. 1–138 et pars II, pp. 1–211; tomus X, pars I, pp. 7–151.

    Iambi de variis argumentis, Migne PG, 99, 1779–1812.

    Hypotyposis Monasterii Studii, Migne PG, 99, 1703–1720.

    Poenae monasteriales, Migne PG, 99, 1733–1747.

    Quotidianae monachorum poenae, Migne PG, 99, 1747–1758.

Synods from Individual Eastern Churches

Syn. Mar Isaaci Chaldaeorum, a. 410, Mansi, III, 1165–1174.

Syn. Sahapivan. Armenorum, aa. 446–447, vide infra ad singulos canones.

Syn. Duinen. Armenorum, a. 719, vide infra ad singulos canones.

Syn. Partaven. Armenorum, a. 771, vide infra ad singulos canones.

Syn. Sisen. Armenorum, a. 1204, vide infra ad singulos canones.

Syn. Sisen. Armenorum, a. 1246, vide infra ad singulos canones.

Syn. Sisen. Armenorum, a. 1307, vide infra ad singulos canones.

Syn. Sisen. Armenorum, a. 1342, Mansi, XXV, 1185–1270.

Syn. Sergii Patriarchae Maronitarum. a. 1596, Mansi, XXXV, 1021–1026.

Syn. Iosephi Patriarchae Maronitarum. a. 1596, Mansi, XXXV, 1026–1028.

Syn. Diamper. Syro-Malabarensium, a. 1599, Mansi, XXXV, 1161–1368

Syn. Cobrin. Ruthenorum, a. 1626, De Martinis, pars I, vol. I, XLVII [Urbanus VIII, breve, *Militantis Ecclesiae*, § 2].

Syn. Zamosten. Ruthenorum, a. 1720, *Synodus provincialis Ruthenorum habita in civitate Zamoscie Anno MDCCXX*, Romae, 1724.

Syn. Libanen. Maronitarum, a. 1736, *Synodus provincialis . . . in Monte Libano celebrata. . .*, Romae, 1820.

Syn. Gusten. Maronitarum, a. 1768, vide infra ad singulos canones.

Syn. Bekorkien Maronitarum, aa. 1790 et 1856, vide infra ad singulos canones.

Syn. Monast. SS. Salvatoris, Melchitarum, a. 1811, Mansi, XLVI, 877–916.

Syn. Ain-Trazen. Graeco-Melchitarum, a. 1835, *Collectio Lacensis*, II, 579–592.

Syn. prov. Alba-Iulien. et Fagarasien. Rumenorum, a. 1872, *Concilium Primum Provinciale Alba Iuliense et Fogarasiense habitum anno MDCCCLXXII*, Blasii, 1881.

Syn. prov. Alba-Iulien. et Fagarasien. Rumenorum, a. 1882, *Concilium Secundum Provinciale Alba-Iuliense et Fogarasiense habitum anno MDCCCLXXXII*, Romae, 1885.

Syn. prov. Alba-Iulien. et Fagarasien. Rumenorum, a. 1900, *Concilium Provinciale Tertium Provinciae ecclesiaticae graeco-catholicae Alba-Iuliensis et Fogarasiensis celebratum anno 1900*, Blaj, 1906.

Syn. Sciarfen. Syrorum, a. 1888, *Synodus Sciarfensis Syrorum in Monte Libano celebrata anno MDCC-CLXXXVIII*, Romae, 1896.

Syn. Leopolien. Ruthenorum, a. 1891, *Acta et Decreta Synodi provincialis Ruthenorum Galiciae habitae Leopoli an. 1891*, Romae, 1892.

Syn. Alexandrin. Coptorum, a. 1898, *Synodus Alexandrina Coptorum habita Cairi in Aegypto anno MD-CCCXCVIII*, Romae, 1899.

Syn. Armen., a. 1911, *Acta et Decreta Concilii Nationalis Armenorum Romae habiti ad Sancti Nicolai Tolentinatis anno domini MDCCCCXI*, Romae, 1913,

7. Here follows for each canon a publication reference for those sources which are not found in the above-mentioned collections, or concerning certain sources (e.g., of the Melkites, Armenians, or Maronites), which are better identified than they were as published in the *Fonti*.

Can. 11   Synodus Episcoporum, *Elapso oecumenico*, 22 oct. 1969: Ochoa, IV, 3791.

Can. 12   Synodus Episcoporum, *Elapso oecumenico*, 22 oct. 1969: Ochoa, IV, 3791.

Can. 22   Benedictus XIV, litt. encycl. *Anno vertente, 19 iun. 1750: Magnum Bullarium Romanum*, ed. Luxemburgensis, pars XII, tomus XVIII, pp. 165–167.
S.C. de Prop. Fide, (C.P.), 29 apr. 1754: De Martinis, pars II, DXCII.

Can. 29   S.C. de Prop. Fide, instr. (pro Graeco-Melchit.), 15 feb. 1746: De Martinis, pars I, vol. III, LXXV, "Istruzione": Collectanea, I, 356, "Istruzione".

S.C. de Prop. Fide, ep. (ad Ep. auxil. Strigonien.), 27 apr. 1903: Fonti, fasc. X, 1165.

Can. 31   S.C. de Prop. Fide, 28 iul. 1626: Fonti, fasc. I, pars I, p. 515.

S.C. de Prop. Fide, 21 maii 1627: De Martinis, pars II, LI.

S.C. de Prop. Fide, instr. (pro Graeco-Melchit.), 15 feb. 1746: De Martinis, pars I, vol. III, LXXV, "Istruzione": Collectanea, I, 356, "Istruzione".

S.C. de Prop. Fide, (C.G.), 10 mar. 1760: De Martinis, pars II, DCVII.

Can. 32   Nicolaus V, const. Pervenit, 6 sep. 1448: Collectio Lacensis, vol. II, col. 601.

S.C. de Prop. Fide, 30 nov. 1629: De Martinis, pars II, LXXIV.

S.C. de Prop. Fide, 7 iun. 1639: De Martinis, pars II, CLVIII.

S.C.S. Off., 3 aug. 1639: Collectanea, I, 9; De Martinis, pars II, *Resolutiones dubiorum* (7 iun. 1639), CLVIII, pp. 83–84, responsum 7.

S.C. de Prop. Fide, (C.G.), 2 apr. 1669: De Martinis, pars II, CCC.

S.C. de Prop. Fide, instr. (pro Graeco-Melchit.), 15 feb. 1746: De Martinis, pars I, vol. III, LXXV, "Istruzione"; Collectanea, I, 356, "Istruzione".

Benedictus XIV, ep. encycl. *Allatae sunt*, 26 iul. 1755: *Magnum Bullarium Romanum*, ed. Luxemburgensis, pars XIII, tomus XIX, pp. 151–166.

Pius IX, litt. ap. *Ubi inscrutabili*, 3 iul. 1848: De Martinis, pars I, vol. VI, pars prima, XLVI.

S.C. de Prop. Fide, instr. (ad Del. Ap. Mesopotamiae), 15 iul 1876: Collectanea, II, 1458.

S.C. de Prop. Fide, ep. (ad Ep. auxil. Strigonien.), 27 apr. 1903: Fonti, fasc. X, 1165.

Can. 33   S.C.S. Off., decr. 26 nov. 1626: Fonti, fasc. I, pars I, p. 457.

S.C.S. Off., 13 feb. 1669: Fonti, fasc. I, pars I, p. 87.

Can. 35   Benedictus XIV, ep. encycl. *Allatae sunt*, 26 iul. 1755: *Magnum Bullarium Romanum*, ed. Luxemburgensis, pars. XIII, tomus XIX, pp. 151–166.

S.C. de Prop. Fide, instr. (ad Del. Ap. Mesopotamiae), 15 iul. 1876: Collectanea, II, 1458.

Can. 39   Leo X, litt. ap. *Accepimus nuper*, 18 maii 1521: M. Harasiewicz, *Annales Ecclesiae Ruthenae*, Leopoli, 1862, pp. 86–91.

Pius IV, const. *Romanus Pontifex*, 16 feb. 1564: *Bullarium Romanum novissimum*, tomus VII, p. 273.

Clemens VIII, const. *Magnus Dominus*, 23 dec. 1595: *Bullarium Romanum novissimum*, tomus X, p. 245.

Paulus V, const. *Solet circumspecta*, 10 dec. 1615: *Bullarium Romanum novissimum*, tomus XII, p. 344.

Benedictus XIV, litt. encycl. *Allatae sunt*, 26 iul. 1755: *Magnum Bullarium Romanum*, ed. Luxemburgensis, pars. XIII, tomus XIX, pp. 151–166.

Pius VI, litt. encycl. *Catholicae Communionis*, 24 maii 1787: De Martinis, pars I, vol. IV, LXVIII.

Pius IX, litt. *In suprema*, 6 ian. 1848: *Pii IX Pontificis Maximi Acta*, pars I, p. 81.

Pius IX, litt. ap. *Ecclesiam Christi*, 26 nov. 1853: De Martinis, pars I, vol. VI, pars I, CL.

Pius IX, all. *In Apostolicae Sedis*, 19 dec. 1853: *Pii IX Pontificis Maximi Acta*, pars I, p. 522.

Can. 40   Paulus V, const. *Fraternitatis tuae*, 9 mar. 1610: Collectio Lacensis, vol. II, coll. 422–424.

S.C. de Prop. Fide, decr. 2 apr. 1669: De Martinis, pars II, CCC.

S.C. de Prop. Fide, decr. 15 mar. 1729: De Martinis, pars II, DLX.

Benedictus XIII, litt. ap. *Quamquam sollicitudini*, 13 aug. 1729: Fonti, fasc. I, pars I, p. 435.

S.C. de Prop. Fide, instr. (ad Ep. Latinum Babylonen.), 23 sep. 1783: Collectanea, I, 565.

Pius VI, litt. encycl. *Catholicae Communionis*, 24 maii 1787: De Martinis, pars I, vol. IV, LXVIII.

S.C.S. Off., 14 iun. 1843: Fonti, fasc. I, pars II, pp. 5–7.

Can. 43   S.C. de Prop. Fide, litt. encycl. (ad Patriarchas Orientis), 6 iun. 1803: Collectanea, I, 671.

Pius IX, ep. encycl. *Quartus supra*, 6 ian. 1873: *Pii IX Pontificis Maximi Acta*, vol. VI. p. 101.

Can. 55   Pius VII, litt. ap. *Simul ac spectabilium*, 8 iul. 1815: De Martinis, pars I, vol. IV, L.
Syn. Bekorkien. Maronitarum, a. 1856: *Histoire des Conciles* (De Clercq), tome XI, p. 1117.
Leo XIII, m.p. *Auspicia rerum*, 19 mar. 1896: *Leonis XIII Pontificis Maximi Acta*, vol. XVI, p. 75.

Can. 57   S.C. de Prop. Fide, (C.P.), 28 ian. 1636: De Martinis, pars II, CXXX.
Benedictus XIV, litt. ap. *Quoniam, ven. Fratres*, 6 mar. 1754: De Martinis, pars I, vol. III, CLVII.
Syn. Bekorkien. Maronitarum, a. 1790: Fonti, fasc. XII, 1155.
S.C. de Prop. Fide, decr. 18 aug. 1816: De Martinis, pars I, vol. IV, p. 548, annotatio 1, decr.
"Quum relatum".
Pius VII, breve, *In communi*, 1 nov. 1816: De Martinis, pars I, vol. IV, LXIII.
S.C. de Prop. Fide, (C.G.), 15 mar. 1819: De Martinis, pars II, DCCLXXII.
Leo XII, const. ap. *Petrus Apostolorum princeps*, 15 aug. 1824: De Martinis, pars I, vol. IV, V.
Gregorius XVI, litt. ap. *Non sine*, 24 dec. 1831: De Martinis, pars I, vol. V, XXIV.
Leo XIII, litt. ap. *Christi Domini*, 26 nov. 1895: *Leonis XIII Pontificis Maximi Acta*, vol. XV, pp.
407–410.

Can. 59   S.C. de Prop. Fide, litt. 9 iul. 1894: Collectanea, II, 1875.

Can. 61   Clemens XI, litt. ap. *Singularis argumentum*, 21 maii 1712: *Clementis undecimi Pontificis Maximi epistolae, et brevia selectiora*, Romae, 1724, tomus II, pp. 176–177.

Can. 63   Clemens XIII, litt. *Succrescente zizania*, 1 aug. 1760: Mansi 46, 506:
Pius IX, ep. encycl. *Quartus supra*, 6 ian. 1873: *Pii IX Pontificis Maximi Acta*, vol. VI, p. 115.

Can. 66   S.C. de Prop. Fide, litt. (ad Patriarcham Syr.), 28 ian. 1792: Fonti, fasc. I, pars II, pp.
421–423.
Pius IX, litt. ap. *Cum ecclesiastica*, 31 aug. 1869: *Pii IX Pontificis Maximi Acta*, vol. V, p. 42.
Pius IX, ep. encycl. *Quartus supra*, 6 ian. 1873: *Pii IX Pontificis Maximi Acta*, vol. VI, p. 116.

Can. 75   S.C. de Prop. Fide, decr. 15 mar. 1729: De Martinis, pars II, DLX.
Pius IX, litt. ap. *Cum ecclesiastica*, 31 aug. 1869: *Pii IX Pontificis Maximi Acta*, vol. V, p. 42.
Pius IX, ep. encycl. *Quartus supra*, 6 ian. 1873: *Pii IX Pontificis Maximi Acta*, vol. VI, pp. 121–122.
S.C. de Prop. Fide, 30 oct. 1894: Fonti, fasc. I, pars I, p. 341.

Can. 76   Pius IV, const. ap. *Venerabilem*, 1 sep. 1562: Collectio Lacensis, vol. II, coll. 420–421.
S.C. de Prop. Fide, (C.P.), 28 ian. 1636: De Martinis, pars II, CXXX.
Clemens XI, const. ap. *Cum nos*, 21 mar. 1706: Fonti, XII, 1059 et 1134.
Clemens XI, litt. ap. *Divinae bonitatis*, 20 iun. 1715: De Martinis, pars I, vol. II, L.
Benedictus XIV, litt. ap. *Dum Nobiscum*, 29 feb. 1744: De Martinis, pars I, vol. III, XLVI.
Benedictus XIV, all. *Ecce iam*, a. 1754: De Martinis, pars I, vol. III, CLXIII.
Clemens XIII, litt. ap. *Delatis ad Nos*, 1 aug. 1760: De Martinis, pars I, vol. IV, XVI.
Pius IX, litt. ap. *Cum ecclesiastica*, 31 aug. 1869: *Pii IX Pontificis Maximi Acta*, vol, VI, pp. 121–122.

Can. 77   Pius IX, litt, ap. *Cum ecclesiastica*, 31 aug. 1869: *Pii IX Pontificis Maximi Acta*, vol. V, p. 42.
S.C. de Prop. Fide, litt. 30 oct. 1894: Fonti, fasc. I, pars I, p. 341.

Can. 78   S.C. de Prop. Fide, (C.G.), 15 sep. 1777: Collectanea, I, 523.
Ioannes Paulus II. litt. (ad Archiep. Maiorem Ucrainorum), 5 feb. 1980; *Eastern Catholic Life*, 6
apr. 1980, p. 7.
Ioannes Paulus II, decisio de qua in litt. (ad Vice-Praesidem Pont. Comm. Cod. Iur. Can. Orient.
Recogn.), 10 nov. 1988: *Nuntia* 29, p. 27.

Can. 81   S.C. de Prop. Fide, instr. (ad Patr. et Epp. Ritus Graeco-Melchit.), 29 maii 1789: Fonti, fasc.
XV, 646.

Can. 82   S. Gennadius CP., ep., ad Martyrium Ep. Antiochenum: Pitra, II, pp. 187–188

Can. 83   Benedictus XIV, const. *Apostolica praedecessorum*, 14 feb. 1742: De Martinis, pars I, vol. III, XIX.

Can. 85   S.C. de Prop. Fide, (C.P), 28 aug. 1643: Fonti, fasc. I, pars I, p. 177.
Benedictus XIV, const. *Apostolica praedecessorum*, 14 feb. 1742: De Martinis, pars I, vol. III, XIX.
S.C. de Prop. Fide, decr. 20 iul. 1760: Fonti, fasc. XV, 152 et 155.
S.C. de Prop. Fide, instr. (ad Patr. et Epp. Ritus Graeco-Melchit.), 29 maii 1789: Fonti, fasc. XV, 154.
S.C. de Prop. Fide, 18 sep. 1843: Fonti, fasc. I, pars I, p. 173.

Can. 86   Iulius III, const. ap. *Cum nos nuper*, 28 apr. 1553: S. Giamil, *Genuinae relationes inter Sedem Apostolicam et Assyriorum orientalium seu Chaldaeorum Ecclesiam*, Roma, 1902, pp. 24–27.
Benedictus XIV, const. *Apostolica praedecessorum*, 14 feb. 1742: De Martinis, pars I, vol. III, XIX.
Leo XIII, litt. ap. *Ex officio supremi*, 1 oct. 1894: *Leonis XIII Pontificis Maximi Acta*, vol. XIV, p. 333.

Can. 87   S.C. de Prop. Fide, instr. (ad Patr. et Epp. Ritus Graeco-Melchit.), 29 maii, 1789: Fonti, fasc. XV, 192.
Syn. Bekorkien. Maronitarum, 1790: Fonti, fasc. XII, 612.

Can. 88   Leo XIII, ep. *Omnibus compertum est*, 21 iul. 1900: *Leonis XIII Pontificis Maximi Acta*, vol. XX. p. 201.

Can. 89   S.C. de Prop. Fide, instr. (ad Deleg. Ap. apud Maronit.), 28 iun. 1788: Fonti, fasc. XII, 66, p. 41 in fine.
Syn. Bekorkien. Maronitarum, a. 1790: Fonti, XII, 1150.
S.C. de Prop. Fide (C.G.), 24 sep. 1816: Collectanea, I, 714.
S.C. pro Eccl. Orient., 10 ian. 1929: Fonti, XV, 150.

Can. 92   Callixtus III, const. *Reddituri de commisso*, 3 sep. 1457: *Bullarium Romanum*, ed Taurinensis, vol. V, pp. 139–140.
Gregorius XIII, const. ap. *Romani Pontificis*, 18 sep. 1579: Collectio Lacensis, vol. II, coll. 420–421.
Clemens XI, litt. ap. *Singularis argumentum*, 21 maii 1712: *Clementis undecimi Pont. Max. epistolae, et brevia selectiora*, Romae, 1724, tomus II, pp. 176–177.
Benedictus XIV, ep. encycl. *Ex quo*, 1 mar. 1756: *Magnum Bullarium Romanum*, ed. Luxemburgensis, pars XII, tomus XIX, pp. 192–211.
S.C. de Prop. Fide, litt. 4 iul. 1833: De Martinis, pars I. vol. V, LVII, annotatio 1.
S.C. de Prop. Fide, litt. 29 maii 1838: Fonti, fasc. XV. 732.
Pius IX, litt. ap. *Cum ecclesiastica*, 31 aug. 1869: *Pii IX Pontificis Maximi Acta*, pars I, vol. V, p. 43.

Can. 102   S.C. de Prop. Fide, litt. (ad Patriarcham Syr.), 28 ian. 1792: Fonti, fasc. I, pars II, pp. 421–422.

Can. 106   S.C. de Prop. Fide, instr. 9 aug. 1760: Fonti, fasc. XV, 668.

Can. 111   S.C. de Prop. Fide, decr. 27 maii 1715: De Martinis, pars II, DXLVII.
Benedictus XIII, litt. ap. *Apostolatus officium*, 19 iul. 1724: De Martinis, pars I, vol. II, I.
Benedictus XIV, litt. ap. *Singularis Romanorum*, 1 sep. 1741: De Martinis, pars I, vol. II, XV.
S.C. de Prop. Fide, (C.G.), 23 maii 1837: Fonti, fasc. XV, 826 et 829.
S.C. de Prop. Fide, litt. 29 maii 1838: Fonti, fasc. XV, 732.
S.C. de Prop. Fide, decr. 28 aug. 1841: De Martinis, pars II, DCCCLV.
Pius IX, const. ap. *Commissum humilitati*, 12 iul. 1867: *Pii IX Pontificis Maximi Acta*, pars I, vol. IV, pp. 318–322.
Leo XIII, ep. *Litteris datis*, 15 iul. 1901: *Leonis XIII Pontificis Maximi Acta*, vol XXI, pp. 117–118.

Can. 114   S.C. de Prop. Fide, 25 ian. 1830: Fonti, fasc. I. pars I, p. 355.

Can. 122   S.C. de Prop.Fide, 1 mar. 1869: Fonti, fasc. I, pars I, pp. 47–49.

Can. 126   S.C. de Prop. Fide, decl. 30 ian. 1696: De Martinis, pars II, LXXIV.
Clemens XIII, litt. ap. *Quam cara semper*, 1 aug. 1760: De Martinis, pars I, vol. IV, XVIII.

Can. 135   Benedictus XIV, ep. encycl. *Ex quo*, 1 mar. 1756: *Magnum Bullarium Romanum*, ed. Luxemburgensis, pars XIII, tomus XIX, pp. 192–211.

Can. 151   Clemens VIII, const. *Decet Romanum Pontificem*, 23 feb. 1596: *Monumenta Ucrainae Historica*, Romae, 1975, tomus IX–X, pp. 217–219.
Pius VII, litt. ap. *In universalis Ecclesiae*, 22 feb. 1807: *Analecta Ordinis Sancti Basilii, series II, Documenta Pontificum Romanorum Historiam Ucrainae Illustrantia (1075–1953)*, vol. II, pp. 313–319; De Martinis, pars I, vol. IV, XXVIII.

Can. 153   Clemens VIII, const. *Decet Romanum Pontificem*, 23 feb. 1596: *Monumenta Ucrainae Historica*, Romae, 1975, tomus IX–X, pp. 217–219.
S.C. de Prop. Fide, 9 iun. 1642: De Martinis, pars II, CLXXVIII.

Can. 162   Callixtus III, const. *Reddituri de commisso*, 3 sep. 1457: *Bullarium Romanum*, ed. Taurinensis, vol. V, pp. 139–140.
S.C. de Prop. Fide, litt. 4 iul. 1833: Fonti, fasc. I, pars II, 597.
S.C. de Prop. Fide, litt. 29 maii 1838: Fonti, fasc. XV, 732:

Can. 164   Clemens XIII, litt. ap. *In summo apostolatus*, 15 iun. 1765: De Martinis, pars I, vol. LI.
S.C. de Prop. Fide, litt. (ad Ep. Magno Varadinen. Rumen.), 23 sep. 1871: Fonti, fasc. X, 357.

Can. 169   S.C. de Prop. Fide, (C.P.), instr. (ad Poloniae Nuntium), 31 maii 1629: De Martinis, pars II, LXVIII.
S.C. de Prop. Fide, (C.P.), 7 iun. 1638: Fonti, fasc. I, pars II , pp. 147 et 159; Fonti, fasc. XI, 722.
S.C. de Prop. Fide, litt. (ad Ep. Fagarasien. et Alba-Iulien.), 12 iul. 1867: Fonti, fasc. X, 365.
Leo XIII, ep. *Litteris datis*, 15 iun. 1901: *Leonis XIII Pontificis Maximi Acta*, vol. XXI, pp. 117–118.

Can. 170   Urbanus VIII, const. *Sacrosanctum apostolatus*, 12 mar. 1625: De Martinis, pars I, vol. I, X.
S.C. de Prop. Fide, instr. 9 aug. 1760: Fonti, fasc. XV, 665.

Can. 177   Leo XII, const. ap. *Petrus Apostolorum princeps*, 15 aug. 1824: De Martinis, pars I, vol. IV, V.
Leo XIII, litt. ap. *Christi Domini*, a. 1895: *Leonis XIII Pontificis Maximi Acta*, vol. XV, pp. 407–410.

Can. 178   Leo XIII, ep. encycl. *Satis cognitum*, 29 iun. 1896, *Acta Sanctae Sedis*, 28 (1895–96) 732.

Can. 180   Syn. Sisen. Armenorum a. 1246: Fonti, fasc. VII, 260.
S.C. de Prop. Fide, decis. 22 sep. 1862: *Pii IX Pontificis Maximi Acta*, pars I, vol. IV, pp. 296–303.
Pius IX, all. *Cum ex hac vita*, 12 iul. 1867: *Pii IX Pontificis Maximi Acta*, pars I, vol. IX, pp. 296–303.

Can. 181   Iulius III, const. ap. *Cum nos nuper*, 28 apr. 1553: S. Giamil, *Genuinae relationes inter Sedem Apostolicam et Assyriorum orientalium seu Chaldaeorum Ecclesiam*, Roma, 1902, pp. 24–27.
Benedictus XIV, const. *Apostolica praedecessorum*, 14 feb. 1742: De Martinis, pars I, vol. III, XIX.
Benedictus XIV, all. *Neminem Vestrum*, 12 maii 1754: De Martinis, pars I, vol. III, CLXIII.
S.C. de Prop. Fide, decr. 20 iul. 1760: Fonti, fasc. XV, 155.
Clemens XIII, litt. ap. *Libentissime occasionem*, 1 aug. 1760: De Martinis, pars I, vol. IV, XVII.
S.C. de Prop. Fide, instr. (ad Patr. et Epp. Ritus Graeco-Melchit.) 29 maii 1789: Fonti, fasc. XV, 182 et 209.
Pius VII, litt. ap. *Ubi primum*, 3 iun. 1816: De Martinis, pars I, vol IV, LIX.

Pius VII, breve (ad Patr. et Epp. Melchit.), *Tristis quidem*, 3 iun. 1816: De Martinis, pars I, vol IV, LX.

Gregorius XVI, 24 dec. 1831: De Martinis, pars I, vol. V, XXIV.

Pius IX, all. *Cum ex hac vita*, 12 iul. 1867: *Pii IX Pontificis Maximi Acta*, pars I, vol. IV, pp. 296–303.

Pius IX, const. *Cum ecclesiastica*, 31 aug. 1869: *Pii IX Pontificis Maximi Acta*, vol. V, p. 42.

Pius IX, ep. encycl. *Quartus supra*, 6 ian. 1873: *Pii IX Pontificis Maximi Acta*, vol. VI, p. 116.

Can. 182   Pius IX, ep. encycl. *Quartus supra*, 6 ian. 1873: *Pii IX Pontificis Maximi Acta*, vol. VI, p. 115.

Can. 185   Pius IX, all. *Cum ex hac vita*, 12 iul. 1867: *Pii IX Pontificis Maximi Acta*, pars I, vol. IV, pp. 296–303:

Pius IX, const. *Cum ecclesiastica*, 31 aug. 1869, VI: *Pii IX Pontificis Maximi Acta*, pars I, vol. V, p. 38.

Can. 198   S.C. de Prop. Fide, 25 mar. 1863: Collectanea, I, 1238.

S.C. de Prop. Fide, litt. (ad Metrop. Alba-Iulien. et Fagarasien.), 30 iun. 1885: Fonti, fasc. X, 825.

Can. 199   S.C. de Prop. Fide, 4 iul. 1833: De Martinis, pars I, vol. V, LVII.

Can. 200   S.C. de Prop. Fide, ep. et instr. (ad Ep. Enonensem), a. 1784: Fonti, fasc. XV, 694.

Can. 204   Paulus V, litt. ap. *Erga Maronitarum*, 21 oct. 1619: T. Anaisi, *Bullarium Maronitarum*, Romae, 1911, pp. 127–128.

S.C. de Prop. Fide, 22 mar. 1625: Fonti, fasc. I, pars I, p. 427.

Benedictus XIV, litt. ap. *Quoniam ven. Fratres*, 6 mar. 1754: De Martinis, pars I, vol. III, CLVII.

Syn. Bekorkien Maronitarum, a. 1790: Fonti, fasc. XII, 5801.

Pius IX, all. *Cum ex hac vita*, 12 iul. 1867: *Pii IX Pontificis Maximi Acta*, pars I, vol. IV, pp. 296–303.

Can. 208   S.C. de Prop. Fide, 12 nov. 1696: Fonti, fasc. I, pars I, p. 579.

Can. 209   Callixtus III, const. *Reddituri de commisso*, 3 sep. 1457: *Bullarium Romanum*, ed. Taurinensis, vol. V, pp. 139–140.

Benedictus XIV, ep. encycl. *Ex quo*, 1 mar. 1756: *Magnum Bullarium Romanum*, ed. Luxemburgensis, pars XII, tomus XIX, pp. 192–211.

S.C. de Prop. Fide, litt. 4 iul. 1833: De Martinis, pars I, vol. V, LVII, annotatio 1.

S.C. de Prop. Fide, litt. 29 maii 1838: Fonti, fasc. XV, 732.

Can. 220   Paulus V, litt. ap. *Erga Maronitarum*, 21 oct. 1619: T. Anaisi, *Bullarium Maronitarum*, Romae, 1911, pp. 127–128.

Can. 279   S.C de Prop. Fide, instr. (ad Patr. et Epp. Ritus Graeco-Melchit.), 29 maii 1789: Fonti, fasc. XV, 617.

Can. 291   S.C. de Prop. Fide, instr. (ad Del. Ap. Aegypti), 30 apr. 1862: Collectanea, I, 1228.

Can. 294   S.C. de Prop. Fide, litt. (ad Patriarcham Chaldaeorum Timotheum Hindi), 5 apr. 1760: Fonti, fasc. I, pars I, 293.

S.C. de Prop. Fide, 16 aug. 1784: Fonti, fasc. I, pars I, p. 293.

S.C. de Prop. Fide, (C.G.), 23 mar. 1863: Collectanea, I, 1238.

Can. 296   Benedictus XIV, const. *Apostolica praedecessorum*, 14 feb. 1742: Fonti, fasc. I, pars II, p. 293

Can. 328   S.C. de Sem. et Stud. Univ., ep. 14 maii 1965: Ochoa, III, 3282.

Can. 373   Ioannes Paulus II, ep. *Novo incipiente*, 8 apr. 1979: *Acta Apostolicae Sedis* 71 (1979) 393   adnotatur quia in indice *AAS* non refertur).

S.C. de Prop. Fide, litt. 4 iul. 1833: De Martinis, pars I, vol. V, LVII, annotatio 1.

Can. 388 S.C. pro Eccl. Orient., 10 ian. 1929: Fonti, fasc. XV, 150.

Can. 394 Ioannes Paulus II, ep. *Novo incipiente,* 8 apr. 1979: *Acta Apostolicae Sedis* 71 (1979)
393 adnotatur quia in indice *AAS* non refertur).

Can. 396 Ioannes Paulus II, ep. *Novo incipiente,* 8 apr. 1979: *Acta Apostolicae Sedis* 71 (1979)
393 adnotatur quia in indice *AAS* non refertur).

Can. 412 Callixtus III, const. *Urget nos,* 20 apr. 1457: *Bullarium Romanum novissimum,* tomus I, p. 280.
Leo XIII, litt. ap. *Singulare praesidium,* 12 maii 1882: *Leonis XIII Pontificis Maximi Acta,* vol. III, pp. 58 68.

Can. 414 S.C. de Prop. Fide, decr. 15 mar. 1819: De Martinis, pars II, DCCLXXII.
S.C. de Prop. Fide, decr. 22 feb. 1877: De Martinis, pars II. MMXXX.

Can. 415 Syn. Gusten. Maronitarum, a. 1768: Fonti, fasc. XII, 1236.

Can. 431 Benedictus XIII, litt. ap. *Cum, sicut,* 16 dec. 1728: De Martinis, pars I, vol. II, XXIV.
S.C. de Prop. Fide, 5 iul. 1631: Fonti, fasc. I, pars I, pp. 179–181.

Can. 443 Clemens XIII, litt. ap. *Ex iniuncto,* 10 ian. 1759: De Martinis, pars I, vol. IV, V.

Can. 450 S.C. de Prop. Fide, litt. (ad Rectores . . .), 29 dec. 1668: Collectanea, I, 173.
S.C. de Prop. Fide, 18 iun. 1844: Fonti, fasc. I, pars I, p. 387.

Can. 475 S.C. de Prop. Fide, (C.G.) decr. 15 mar. 1819: De Martinis, pars II, DCCLXXII.

Can. 478 Secret. Status, rescr. 6 nov. 1964: Ochoa, III, 3230.

Can. 479 S.C. de Prop. Fide, instr. 8 dec. 1845: De Martinis, pars I, vol. V, supplementum, IV, annotatio 2.
S.C. de Prop. Fide, decr. 25 apr. 1850: De Martinis, pars II, DCCCXC.

Can. 522 Secret. Status, rescr. 6 nov. 1964: Ochoa, III, 3230.

Can. 526 Leo XIII, litt. ap. *Singulare praesidium,* 12 maii 1882: *Leonis XIII Pontificis Maximi Acta,* vol. III, pp. 59–69.
S.C. de Prop. Fide, decr. 3 maii 1902: Collectanea, II, 2138.

Can. 528 S.C. de Prop. Fide, 4 mar. 1895: Fonti, fasc. I, pars I, pp. 383–384.

Can. 537 Syn. Bekorkien. Maronitarum, a. 1790: Fonti, fasc. XII, 1049.
Secret. Status, rescr. 6 nov. 1964: Ochoa, III, 3230.

Can. 542 S.C. de Prop. Fide, instr. 8 dec. 1845: De Martinis, pars I, vol. V, supplementum, IV, annotatio 2.
S.C. de Prop. Fide, decr. 25 apr. 1850: De Martinis, pars II, DCCCXC.

Can. 546 Secret. Status, rescr. 6 nov. 1964: Ochoa, III, 3230.

Can. 584 Synodus Episcoporum, nuntius, 28 oct. 1977: Ochoa, V, 4535.

Can. 595 Synodus Episcoporum, decl. 25 oct. 1974: Ochoa, V, 4323.

Can. 598 Synodus Episcoporum, decl. 28 oct. 1967: Ochoa, III, 3605.

Can. 600 Synodus Episcoporum, decl. 28 oct. 1967: Ochoa, III, 3605.

Can. 619 Syn. Gusten. Maronitarum, a. 1768: Fonti, fasc. XII, 193.
Syn. Bekorkien. Maronitarum, a. 1790: Fonti, fasc. XII, 194.

Can. 648 S. C. pro Inst. Cath., *Ordinationes,* 29 apr. 1979: Ochoa, VI, 4706.

Can. 650   S. C. pro Inst. Cath., *Ordinationes,* 29 apr. 1979: Ochoa, VI, 4706.

Can. 659   S.C. pro Doctr. Fidei, resp. 25 iun. 1980: Ochoa, VI, 4782.

Can. 674   S.C. de Prop. Fide, litt. 4 iul. 1833: De Martinis, pars I, vol. V, LVII, annotatio 1.
S.C.S. Off., 14 iun. 1843: Fonti, fasc. I, pars II, pp. 5–7.

Can. 675   S.C. de Prop. Fide, (C.P.), 12 maii 1630: De Martinis, pars II, LXXVII.
S.C. de Prop. Fide, (C.P.), 13 feb. 1631: De Martinis, pars II, LXXXII.
S.C. de Prop. Fide, (C.P.), 4 iul. 1633: De Martinis, pars II, CV.
S.C.S. Off., instr. (ad Vic. Ap. Abissiniae), 2 maii 1858: Collectanea, I, 1159.

Can. 685   S.C.S. Off., 5 nov. 1676: De Martinis, pars II, CCCLXXVIII.

Can. 686   Syn. Gusten. Maronitarum, a. 1768: Fonti, fasc. XII, 134.

Can. 687   S. Macarius Hierosolymitanus: Fonti, fasc. VII, 55.
Nerses Astaraken.: Fonti, fasc. VII, 72.

Can. 693   Leo X, const. ap. *Cunctarum,* 1 aug. 1515: T. Anaisi, *Bullarium Maronitarum,* Romae, 1911, pp. 44–51.

Can. 697   S.C. de Prop. Fide, 5 apr. 1729: Fonti, fasc. XV, 116.

Can. 698   S. Ioannes Chrysostomus, *De proditione Judae,* hom. I, 6 et hom. II, 6: Migne PG, 49, 380 et 389.
S. Ioannes Chrysostomus, *De sacerdotio,* lib. 3, 4 et lib. 6, 4: Migne PG, 48, 642 et 679.

Can. 704   S.C. de Prop. Fide, (C.P.), 31 mar. 1729: Fonti, fasc. XV, 334.

Can. 705   S.C. de Prop. Fide, decr. 24 sep. 1632: De Martinis, pars II, XCVIII.
S.C. de Prop. Fide, (C.P.), 31 dec. 1745: Fonti, fasc. XV, 235.
S.C. de Prop. Fide, instr. 12 mar. 1809: Collectanea, I, 697.
S.C. de Prop. Fide, 16 aug. 1831: Fonti, fasc. I, pars I, p. 317.

Can. 706   S.C. de Prop. Fide, litt. 4 iul. 1833: De Martinis, pars I, vol. V, LVII, annotatio 1.

Can. 707   Leo X, litt. ap. *Accepimus nuper,* 18 maii 1521: M. Harasiewicz, *Annales Ecclesiae Ruthenae,* Leopoli, 1862, pp. 86–91.
Paulus III, litt. ap. *Dudum,* 23 dec. 1534: *Bullarium de Propaganda Fide,* Appendix, tomus I, pp. 21–24.
Paulus V, litt. ap. *Plane repleta,* 1 ian. 1606: T. Anaisi, *Bullarium Maronitarum.* Romae, 1911, pp. 114–115.
S.C. de Prop. Fide, 23 iun. 1633: Fonti, fasc. I, pars I, p. 195.
S. Isaac M.: Fonti, fasc. VII, 456.
Nerses Astaraken.: Fonti, fasc. VII, 332.

Can. 708   Leo X, const. ap. *Cunctarum,* 1 aug. 1515: T. Anaisi, *Bullarium Maronitarum.* Romae, 1911, pp. 44–51.
S.C. pro Eccl. Orient., decl. 14 apr. 1924: Ochoa, I, 590.
S.C. pro Eccl. Orient., resol. 26 ian. 1925: Ochoa, I, 630.

Can. 710   Leo X, litt. ap. *Accepimus nuper,* litt. ap. 18 maii 1521: M. Harasiewicz, *Annales Ecclesiae Ruthenae,* Leopoli, 1862, pp. 86–91.
Paulus III, litt. ap. *Dudum,* 23 dec. 1534: *Bullarium de Propaganda Fide,* Appendix, tomus I, pp. 21–24.
Gregorius XIII, const. ap. *Benedictus Deus,* 14 feb. 1577: Collectio Lacensis, tomus II, coll. 421–422.
S.C. de Prop. Fide, 5 apr. 1729: Fonti, fasc. XV, 116.

Can. 713   S. Isaac M.: Fonti, fasc. VII, 209.
Nerses Astaraken.: Fonti, fasc. VII, 332.

Can. 714   S.C. de Prop. Fide, litt. (ad Patr. Cyrillum Melkit.), 7 maii 1746: Fonti, fasc. XV, 118.

Can. 715   S.C.C., litt. 22 maii 1907: *Acta Sanctae Sedis*, 40 (1907) 344–346.
S.C. de Prop. Fide, 15 iul. 1908: *Acta Sanctae Sedis*, 41 (1908) 640–641.
Syn. Bekorkien. Maronitarum, a. 1790: Fonti, fasc. XII, 1433.

Can. 719   Leo X, const. ap. *Cunctarum*, 1 aug. 1515: T. Anaisi, *Bullarium Maronitarum*, Romae, 1911, pp. 44–51.

Can. 720   S. Paenit. Ap., *Facultates*, 30 aug. 1939: Ochoa, I, 1494.
S.C. pro Doctr. Fidei, resp. 20 ian. 1978: Ochoa, V, 4555.

Can. 722   S.C. de Prop. Fide, 1 iun. 1626: Fonti, fasc. I, pars I, p. 327.
S.C.S. Off., 15 maii 1766: Fonti, fasc. I, pars I, pp. 455–457.
S.C. de Prop. Fide, instr. (ad Patr. et Epp. Ritus Graeco-Melchit), 29 maii 1789: Fonti, fasc. XV, 828.
S.C. de Prop. Fide, (C.G.), 11 dec. 1838: De Martinis, pars II, DCCCXXXV.
S.C. de Prop. Fide, 31 mar. 1843: Fonti, fasc. I, pars I, p. 5.
S.C. de Prop. Fide, instr. (ad Del. Ap. Aegypti), 30 apr. 1862: Collectanea, I, 1228.
S.C. de Prop. Fide, decr. 6 oct. 1863: Collectanea, I, 1243.

Can. 724   Syn. Bekorkien. Maronitarum, a. 1790: Fonti, fasc. XII, 1259.

Can. 725   S.C.S. Off., (C.G.), 28 aug. 1669: Fonti, fasc. I, pars I, p. 213.

Can. 734   S.C.S. Off., instr. 15 iun. 1915: F. Cappello S.J., *Tractatus canonico-moralis de sacramentis*, Romae, 1939, vol. II, n. 907.

Can. 736   S.C. de Prop. Fide, decr. 22 sep. 1838: De Martinis, pars II, DCCCXXX.
S.C. de Prop. Fide, decr. 18 feb. 1851: De Martinis, pars II, DCCCCIII.

Can. 741   Syn. Duinen. Armenorum, a. 719: Fonti, fasc. VII, 561.

Can. 746   Paulus V, litt. ap. *In supremo*, 10 dec. 1615: Fonti, fasc. I, pars I, pp. 317–318.
S.C.S. Off., 13 mar. 1669: Collectanea, I, 177.
S.C. de Prop. Fide, 18 aug. 1845: Fonti, fasc. I, pars I, p. 169.

Can. 748   Leo X, litt. ap. *Accepimus nuper*, 18 maii 1521: M. Harasiewicz, *Annales Ecclesiae Ruthenae*, Leopoli, 1862, pp. 86–91.
Paulus III, litt. ap. *Dudum*, 23 dec. 1534: *Bullarium de Propaganda Fide*, Appendix, tomus I, pp. 21–24.

Can. 749   S.C.C., 17 aug. 1641: De Martinis, pars II, CLXXIII.

Can. 756   S.C. de Prop. Fide, (C.P.), 29 apr. 1754: De Martinis, pars II, DXCIII.

Can. 758   S.C. de Prop. Fide, litt. 4 iul. 1833: De Martinis, pars I, vol. V, LVII, annotatio 1.
S.C. de Prop. Fide, litt. encycl. 1 oct. 1890: Collectanea, II, 1966, annotatio 2.
S.C. de Prop. Fide, litt. 12 apr. 1894: Collectanea, II, 1866.
Pius X, litt. ap. *Ea semper*, 14 iun. 1907: *Pii X Pontificis Maximi Acta*, vol. V, pp. 60–61.

Can. 769   Syn. Bekorkien, Maronitarum, a. 1790: Fonti, fasc. XII, 644.

Can. 772   Syn. Gusten. Maronitarum, a. 1768: Fonti, fasc. XII, 663.

Can. 785   S.C. de Prop. Fide, ep. (ad Ep. Nicopolit.), 25 ian. 1817: Fonti, fasc. X, 1184.

Can. 794   S.C. de Prop. Fide, (C.P.), 22 ian. 1629: De Martinis, pars II, LXV.

Can. 801   S.C.S. Off., resp. 16 feb. 1935: Ochoa, I, 1262.
S.C.S. Off., resp. 28 sep. 1957: Ochoa, II, 2692.
S.C.S. Off., resp. 28 ian. 1964: Ochoa, III, 3169.
S.C.S. Off., resp. 25 mar. 1964: Ochoa, III, 3176,

Can. 802 S.C.S. Off., instr. (ad Ep. Orient.), 22 aug. 1890: Collectanea, II, 1740.

Can. 803 S.C.S. Off., instr. (ad omnes Ep. Ritus Orient.), 12 dec. 1888: Collectanea, II, 1696.
Syn. Partaven. Armenorum, a. 771: Fonti, fasc. VII, 410.

Can. 804 S.C. de Prop. Fide, (C.P.), 18 sep. 1629: De Martinis, pars II, LXXI.
S.C.S. Off., decr. 3 iun. 1635: De Martinis, pars II, CXXIV.
S.C.S. Off., 5 aug. 1650: De Martinis, pars II, CCV.
S.C.S. Off., 29 ian. 1660: De Martinis, pars II, CCXXX.
S.C.S. Off., mandatum, 5 maii 1660: De Martinis, pars II, CCXXXV.
S.C.S. Off., (C.G.), 28 aug. 1668: De Martinis, pars II, CCCVIII.
S.C. de Prop. Fide, litt. (ad Vic. gen. Fagarasien.), 5 feb. 1746: Fonti, fasc. X, 303, 681, 1128.
S.C. de Prop. Fide, litt. (ad Metrop. Alba-Iulien et Fagarasien.), 31 maii 1892: Fonti, fasc. X, 308.

Can. 808 Clemens VIII, breve, *Christi fidelium*, 17 aug. 1599: Collectio Lacensis, II, pp. 172–173.
Syn. Sahapivan. Armenorum, a. 446–447: Fonti, fasc. VV, 403.

Can. 809 Clemens VIII, breve, *Christi fidelium*, 17 aug. 1599: Collectio Lacensis, II, pp. 172–173.

Can. 810 Clemens VIII, breve, *Christi fidelium*, 17 aug. 1599: Collectio Lacensis, II, pp. 172–173.

Can. 811 Clemens VIII, breve, *Christi fidelium*, 17 aug. 1599: Collectio Lacensis, II, pp. 172–173.
S.C.S. Off., litt. (Leopol. Ruthen.), 29 apr. 1894: Collectanea, II, 1869.

Can. 813 S.C.S. Off., instr. (ad omnes Ep. Ritus Orient.), 12 dec. 1888: Collectanea, II, 1696.

Can. 814 S.C.S. Off., instr. (ad omnes Ep. Ritus Orient.), 12 dec. 1888: Collectanea, II, 1696.
S.C.S. Off., decr. 16 ian. 1942: Ochoa, II, 1661.

Can. 828 S.C. de Prop. Fide, litt. (ad Ep. Nicopolitan.), 11 ian. 1817: Fonti, fasc. X, 777.

Can. 836 Syn. Duinen. Armenorum, a. 719: Fonti, fasc. VII, 516.

Can. 838 Sun. Duinen. Armenorum, a. 719: Fonti, fasc. VII, 521.

Can. 839 S.C.S. Off., instr. (ad omnes Ep. Ritus Orient.), 12 dec. 1888: Collectanea, II, 1696.
S.C.S. Off., resp. 9 feb. 1965: Ochoa, III, 3257.

Can. 859 S.C.S. Off., resp. 30 iun. 1937: Ochoa, I, 1392.

Can. 880 S.C. de Prop. Fide, (C.G.), 7 feb. 1624: Collectanea, I, 8.
S.C. de Prop. Fide, 1 iun. 1626: Fonti, fasc. I, pars I, p. 139.
S.C. de Prop. Fide, 30 ian. 1635: De Martinis, pars II, CXV.
S.C. de Prop. Fide, 28 iun. 1635: Fonti, fasc. I, pars I, p. 141.
S.C.S. Off., 4 apr. 1658: De Martinis, pars II, CCXX.
S.C. de Prop. Fide, 4 feb. 1665: Fonti, fasc. I, pars I, p. 139.
S.C. de Prop. Fide, 4 feb. 1676: Fonti, fasc. I, pars I, p. 131.
S.C. de Prop. Fide, 8 aug. 1774: Fonti, fasc. I, pars. I, p. 135.
Pius VI, litt. ap. *Assueto paternae*, 8 apr. 1775: De Martinis, pars I, vol. IV, V.
S.C. de Prop. Fide, 29 sep. 1781: De Martinis, pars II, DCLXXXIII.
S.C. de Prop. Fide, 25 ian. 1830: Fonti, fasc. I, pars I, pp. 135–137.
S.C. de Prop. Fide, 13 maii 1844: Fonti, fasc. I, pars I, pp. 137–139.
S.C. de Prop. Fide, 18 iun. 1844: Fonti, fasc. I, pars I, p. 137.

Can. 881 Syn. Duinen. Armenorum, a. 719: Fonti, fasc. VII, 234.

Can. 882 S.C. de Prop. Fide, (C.P.), 31 mar. 1729: Fonti, fasc. XV, 17.
S.C. de Prop. Fide, litt. (ad Patr. Melkit. Cyrillum), 7 maii 1746: Fonti, fasc. XV, 247, 252,257.
S.C. de Prop. Fide, litt. 4 iul 1833: De Martinis, pars I, vol. V, LVII, annotatio 1.
Nerses Astaraken.: Fonti, fasc. VII, 333.
Syn. Sisen. Armenorum, a. 1204: Fonti, fasc. VII, 337.

Syn. Sisen. Armenorum, a. 1246: Fonti, fasc. VII, 338.

Syn. Sisen. Armenorum, a. 1307: Fonti, fasc. VII, 15.

Can. 883   S.C. de Prop. Fide, (C.P.), 12 mar. 1635: De Martinis, pars II, CXVII.

S.C.S. Off., 7 iun. 1673: De Martinis, pars II, CCCXLVII.

S.C.S. Off., 13 mar. 1727: Collectanea, I, 308.

S.C. de Prop. Fide, 25 ian. 1830: Fonti, fasc. I, pars I, pp. 135–137.

S.C. de Prop. Fide, (C.P.), 28 dec. 1842: De Martinis, pars I, vol. VI, annotatio 1.

Pius IX, litt. ap. *Plura sapienter*, 11 iun. 1847: De Martinis, pars I, vol. VI, XVIII.

Can. 884   Eph. antecedentia, cap. XXVI, XI: Mansi IV coll. 1082–1083.

Eph. actio I: Mansi IV, col. 1186.

Chalc. actio V, Symbolum: Mansi VII, col. 115.

Constantinop. II, collatio octava, VI: Mansi IX, col. 379.

Pius IX, bulla, *Ineffabilis Deus*, 8 dec. 1854: *Pii IX Pontificis Maximi Acta*, pars I, vol. I, pp. 597–619.

Can. 885   S.C. de Prop. Fide, (C.P.), 7 mar. 1631: De Martinis, pars II, LXXXV.

S.C. de Prop. Fide, (C.P.), 30 ian. 1635: De Martinis, pars II, CXV.

Can. 889   S.C. de Prop. Fide, (C.P.), 4 iul 1634: De Martinis, pars II, CIX.

Can. 895   Clemens XIII, litt. *Delatis ad nos*, 1 aug. 1760: De Martinis, pars I, vol. IV, XVII.

Clemens XIII, litt. *Romani Pontificis* (ad Patr. Graeco-Melkitarum), 9 iul. 1764: De Martinis, pars I, vol. IV, XLIV.

S.C. de Prop. Fide, (C.G.), 26 aug. 1793: Fonti, fasc. XV, 651.

Pius VII, litt. *Ubi primum* (ad Archiep. Alep. electum), 3 iun. 1816: De Martinis, pars I, vol. IV, LIX.

Leo XII, litt. *Apostolatus officium* (ad Patr. Graeco-Melchitarum), 4 iul. 1828: De Martinis, pars I, vol. IV, XXXVII.

Pius IX, litt. *Supremi Apostolatus*, 22 mar. 1869: De Martinis, pars I, vol. VI, CCCLI.

Can. 902   Leo XIII, m.p. *Optatissime*, 19 mar. 1895: *Leonis XIII Pontificis Maximi Acta*, vol XV, pp. 80–82.

Can. 916   Pius IV, const. *Romanus Pontifex*, 16 feb. 1564: *Bullarium Romanum novissimum*, tomus II, pp. 122–123.

S.C. de Prop. Fide, (C.G.), 29 mar. 1824: Collectanea, I, 783.

Pius IX, litt. *Ubi inscrutabili*, 3 iul. 1848: De Martinis, pars I, vol. VI, XLVI.

Pius IX, all. *Probe noscitis*, 3 iul. 1848: De Martinis, pars I, vol. VI, XLVII.

S.C. de Prop. Fide, ep. (ad Ep. Strigonien.), 1 oct. 1907: Fonti, fasc. X. 1026.

Can. 924   S.C. de Prop. Fide, instr. (ad Patr. et Epp. Graeco-Melkitas), 29 maii 1789: Fonti, fasc. XV, 828.

Can. 956   S.C. de Prop. Fide, instr. (ad Patr. et Epp. Graeco-Melkitas), 29 maii 1789: Fonti, fasc. XV, 828.

Can. 979   Secret. Status, facultas data Sign. Apost., 1 oct. 1974: Ochoa, V, 4347.

Can. 1016   S.C. de Prop. Fide, decr. 25 dec. 1779: De Martinis, pars II, DCLXXI.

S.C. de Prop. Fide, instr. (ad Patriarch. Armen.), 30 iul. 1867: Collectanea, II, 1310.

Can. 1022   S. Isaac M.: Fonti, fasc. VII, 103.

Can. 1035   S.C. de Prop. Fide, instr. (ad Patriarch. Armen.), 30 iul. 1867: Collectanea, II, 1310.

Can. 1036   S.C. de Prop. Fide, 24 mar. 1851: Fonti, fasc. I, pars I, p. 47.

Pius IX, litt. ap. *Cum ecclesiastica*, 31 aug. 1869: *Pii IX Pontificis Maximi Acta*, pars I, vol. V, pp. 38–47.

Can. 1042 S.C. de Prop. Fide, instr. (ad Patriarch. Armen.), 30 iul. 1867: Collectanea, II, 1310.

Can. 1052 Secret. Status, normae, 17 iun. 1974: Ochoa, V, 4304.

Can. 1053 Secret. Status, normae, 17 iun. 1974: Ochoa, V, 4304.

Can. 1057 S.C. pro Causis Sanctorum, notificatio, 16 dec 1972: Ochoa, IV, 4103.

Can. 1060 Benedictus XIV, litt. *Non possumus*, 20 iul. 1746: De Martinis, pars I, vol. III, LXXXI.
S.C. de Prop. Fide, decr. 20 iul 1760: Fonti, fasc. XV, 672.
S.C. de Prop. Fide, instr. 9 aug. 1760: Fonti, fasc. XV, 671.
S.C. de Prop. Fide, (C.G.), 8 iul 1774: Fonti, fasc. I, pars I, p. 359.
S.C. de Prop. Fide, 22 mar. 1777: Fonti, fasc. I, pars II, p. 215.
S.C. de Prop. Fide, (C.G.), 15 sep. 1777: Collectanea, I, 523.

Can. 1072 Sign. Apost., decl. 3 iun. 1989, *Communicationes* 21 (1989) 117–118.

Can. 1089 Secret. Status, rescr. 1 oct. 1974: Ochoa, V, 4317.

Can. 1093 Secret. Status, rescr. 1 oct. 1974: Ochoa, V, 4317.

Can. 1099 Paulus VI, rescr. 26 mar. 1976: Ochoa, V, 4440.
Sign. Apost., decl. 12 nov. 1977: Ochoa, V, 4537.

Can. 1134 Sign. Apost., decl. 31 oct. 1977: Ochoa, V, 4536.

Can. 1217 Sign. Apost., rescr. 10 nov. 1970: Ochoa, IV, 3920.
Sign. Apost., rescr. 2 ian. 1971: Ochoa, IV, 3943.

Can. 1254 Sign. Apost., rescr. 10 nov. 1970: Ochoa, IV, 3920.
Sign. Apost., rescr. 2 ian. 1971: Ochoa, IV, 3943.

Can. 1281 Cons. pro Publ. Eccl. Neg., rescr. 28 apr. 1970: Ochoa, IV, 3848.

Can. 1302 Secret. Status, *Normae spec. in Supr. Trib. Sign. Apost. ad exper. servandae*, 23 mar. 1968: Ochoa, III, 3636.
Cons. pro Publ. Eccl. Neg., rescr. 28 apr. 1970: Ochoa, IV, 3848.

Can. 1303 Cons. pro Publ. Eccl. Neg., rescr. 28 apr. 1970: Ochoa, IV, 3848.

Can. 1359 Sign. Apost., resp. 12 apr. 1978: Ochoa, V, 4561.

Can. 1360 Cons. pro Publ. Eccl. Neg., rescr. 28 apr. 1970: Ochoa, IV, 3848.

Can. 1367 S.C. pro Eccl. Orient., instr. 13 iul. 1953: Ochoa, II. 2361.

Can. 1384 S.C.S. Off., instr. 1 maii 1934: Ochoa, I, 1220.
S.C. pro Eccl. Orient., instr. 13 iul. 1953: Ochoa, II, 2361.
S.C.S. Off., notificatio, 28 maii 1956: Ochoa, II, 2503.
S.C.S. Off., resp. 2 ian. 1959: Ochoa, III, 2795.
S.C.S. Off., resp. 12 iul. 1960: Ochoa, III, 2921.
S.C. pro Doctr. Fidei, resp. 14 iul. 1967: Ochoa, III, 3579.
S.C. pro Doctr. Fidei, *Instructio pro solutine matrimonii in favorem fidei et normae procedurales* . . . , 6 dec. 1973: Ochoa, V, 4244.

Can. 1396 Sign. Apost., decisio, 1 nov. 1970: Ochoa, IV, 3915.

Can. 1450 Sancta Sedes, *Carta dei diritti della famiglia*, 24 nov. 1983: *Enchiridion Vaticanum*, 9, 538–557.

Can. 1459 Leo XII, litt. *Apostolatus officium* (ad Patriarch. Graeco-Melkitarum), 4 iul. 1828: De Martinis, pars I, vol. IV, XXXVII.

Can. 1539 S.C. pro Eccl. Orient., resp. 24 iul. 1948: Ochoa, II, 2003.